BUSINESS LAW

PETER J. SHEDD

PROFESSOR OF LEGAL STUDIES
UNIVERSITY OF GEORGIA

ROBERT N. CORLEY

DISTINGUISHED PROFESSOR OF LEGAL STUDIES EMERITUS
UNIVERSITY OF GEORGIA

PRENTICE HALL, ENGLEWOOD CLIFFS, NEW JERSEY 07632

Library of Congress Cataloging-in-Publication Data

Shedd, Peter J.
  Business law / Peter J. Shedd, Robert N. Corley.
    p.   cm.
  Includes index.
  ISBN 0-13-108127-6
  1. Commercial law—United States.   I. Corley, Robert Neil.
II. Title.
KF889.S38   1993
346.73'07—dc20
[347.3067]   92-13227
                                              CIP

Acquisitions editor: Donald Hull
Editorial/production supervision: Brian Hatch
Interior design: Suzanne Behnke
Cover design: Suzanne Behnke
Copy editor: Patricia Daly
Prepress buyer: Trudy Pisciotti
Manufacturing buyer: Patrice Fraccio
Supplements editor: Lisamarie Brassini
Editorial Assistant: Wendy Goldner

(1) ©1993, by Prentice-Hall, Inc.
A Simon & Schuster Company
Englewood Cliffs, New Jersey 07632

(2) Fundamentals of Business Law
©1990, 1986, 1982, 1978, 1974

(3) Principles of Business Law
©1989, 1986, 1983, 1979, 1975, 1971,
1967, 1962, 1957, 1952, 1948, 1940

Printed in the United States of America

10 9 8 7 6 5 4 3 2 1

ISBN 0-13-108127-6

Prentice-Hall International (UK) Limited, *London*
Prentice-Hall of Australia Pty. Limited., *Sydney*
Prentice-Hall Canada Inc., *Toronto*
Prentice-Hall Hispanoamericana, S.A., *Mexico*
Prentice-Hall of India Private Limited, *New Delhi*
Prentice-Hall of Japan, Inc., *Tokyo*
Simon & Schuster Asia Pte. Ltd., *Singapore*
Editora Prentice-Hall do Brasil, Ltda., *Rio de Janeiro*

ISBN 0-13-108127-6

90000>

9 780131 081277

BRIEF CONTENTS

CONTENTS

4   ALTERNATIVES FOR RESOLVING CONTROVERSIES AND INFLUENCING CONDUCT   56

PART TWO
■ BASIC LEGAL
CONCEPTS

5   THE LAW OF TORTS AND BUSINESS   80

PART SIX
■ BUSINESS
ORGANIZATIONS

26 FORMATION OF PARTNERSHIPS   520

27 OPERATION OF PARTNERSHIPS   536

28 DISSOLUTION OF PARTNERSHIPS   552

35   HOLDERS IN DUE COURSE AND DEFENSES   710

36   LIABILITY OF PARTIES TO COMMERCIAL PAPER   732

40   ADDITIONAL LAWS ASSISTING CREDITORS   842

41   LAWS ASSISTING DEBTORS AND CONSUMERS   866

42 BANKRUPTCY 896

PART NINE
■ PROPERTY

43 INTRODUCTION TO THE LAW OF PROPERTY 932

44   ACQUIRING TITLE TO PROPERTY   960

45   LEASES AND BAILMENTS   988

PREFACE

In cooperation with the excellent editorial staff at Prentice Hall, we are excited to introduce you to *Business Law.* This text has its roots in two books which have long histories with Prentice Hall. We believe that adopters of *Principles of Business Law* and *Fundamentals of Business Law* will recognize many features that helped make those texts so successful.

Purpose of New Text

While this text has a rich history in one sense, *Business Law* is presented at this time in realization of the forces that have shaped, and are shaping, our Legal Studies discipline. During the past decade, there has been a rapid trend to environmentalize the introductory law course taught in colleges and schools of business. As a result of this trend, the number of textbooks emphasizing the legal and regulatory environment of business has increased significantly. Indeed, many texts covering traditional Business Law topics have added a public law emphasis. The result is a blurring of the contents of many texts so that the Legal Environment and the Business Law distinction is less clear.

A primary reason why we prepared *Business Law* is to overcome this blurring of topic coverage in current textbooks. The curricula being used today in many colleges and schools of business include a Legal Environment of Business course. In addition to this Legal Environment course, one or two traditional Business Law courses are very common. We believe that this text is a superior fit for those traditional Business Law courses that are taught before or after a Legal Environment course. *Business Law* is designed for use in either one or two traditional law courses.

While some textbooks have attempted to be "all things to all people," we adopted the philosophy to provide "better coverage to less material." For example, topics concerning the public law orientation of the government's regulation of business (i.e., antitrust, labor, etc.) are not found in depth here. Rather, we have concentrated on the private law approach to commercial transactions.

Pedagogical Design

The chapters in *Business Law* are made up of three basic parts: Text, cases, and question and problem material. First, the text is written in a style designed for business students, introducing them to the legal issues they will face throughout their careers. It is not our intent to have business students search for the law's meaning and application. This text is written without much of the legalese to which law students become so familiar. Second, the chapters contain four to six edited cases. These case opinions in the judge's actual language are included to illustrate a point of law discussed in the text. Third, review questions and factual problems are included at the end of each chapter.

Several aspects of this text were designed to help enhance the "reader friendly" nature we hope is conveyed throughout the book. Of particular interest, in this pedagogical sense, are the following items:

- A Chapter Outline to provide a detailed list of the subject matter covered
- A Chapter Preview to serve as an introductory statement to help students understand how the chapter's topic fits into the overall business transaction
- A Business Management Decision to whet students' appetites for the chapter's discussion
- Marginal Definitions to reinforce the meaning of key terms and phrases
- A Case Concepts Review follows every case with questions to assist students in their comprehension of the case's major points
- A Chapter Summary to assist in the review process
- A Matching Problem at the outset of the review questions to provide students with a quick method to test their knowledge of key terms and phrases
- Several factual-oriented Review Problems to allow students to become comfortable in applying their understanding to business transactions.

In addition to these pedagogical devices, *Business Law* includes the Uniform Commercial Code and additions and revisions to it as appendices. A glossary for student referral is also provided.

Coverage of Text

The forty-five chapters in *Business Law* are divided into nine distinctive parts. These divisions permit the material to be covered in the order that professors feel best meets their students' needs. We believe this organization provides the flexibility for courses on either the semester or quarter calendar.

Part I serves as an introduction to our legal system. Topics of particular importance covered are: The structure of the courts (chapter 2), the litigation procedure (chapter 3), and alternatives to litigation (chapter 4). This part can be deleted if the students have had a Legal Environment of Business course, or it can serve as a quick review.

Part II consists of four chapters discussing some of the basic legal concepts that we feel are essential for students to understand prior to their coverage of the other topics in this text. Chapter 5 places special emphasis on the various theories that are used to impose tort liability on businesspeople and their organizations. Chapter 6 is on criminal law because of the increasing importance of white-collar crime and the problems business managers face as the result of the high crime rate. Chapter 7 introduces various forms of organizations that can be used to operate business activities. Factors that make one organization preferable to the other forms are presented. Finally, chapter 8 on international business transactions provides students with an appreciation for the growing importance of the globalization of business. As with the chapters in Part I, these four chapters can be deleted or reviewed quickly if the students have had a legal and regulatory environment course.

Part III, on contracts, is designed to give students an understanding of the basic and traditional concepts of contracts as well as of recent developments of the closely related law of sales under the Uniform Commercial Code. This Code is included as an appendix, and appropriate sections are referred to in brackets within the text. After an introductory chapter, the next four chapters (10 through 13) discuss the essential requirements for every valid contract. Chapter 14 involves issues of form and interpretation of contracts, and chapter 15 includes a discussion of contractual performance. The methods of discharging or excusing the performance of promises are the subject matter of chapter 16. Finally, issues created when third parties become involved in contracts are discussed in chapter 17.

Part IV consists of four chapters that present additional material on the sale of goods. Without repeating the details contained in the chapters on contracts, chapters 18 and 19 emphasize the provisions of Article 2 of the Uniform Commercial Code. Chapter 20 is an in-depth examination of the law of warranties. Recognizing the continuing impact of products liability to all businesses, chapter 21 is dedicated to this subject.

Part V contains four chapters on agency. Chapter 22 deals with the creation and general principles of the agency relationship. The next two chapters discuss this agency from the perspective of the law of contracts and the law of torts. Chapter 25 emphasizes how the agency relationship can be terminated without additional liability.

Part VI discusses business organizations in three stages. These stages are: (1) the methods of creating the various forms of organizations; (2) the legal aspects of operating the various forms of organizations; and (3) the law as it relates to dissolution of business organizations. This material is covered in chapters 26 through 31. Chapter 32, on accountants' liability, is designed to assist students in their understanding of the role of accountants and the growing trend of malpractice litigation as it relates to accountants' functions within business organizations.

Part VII consists of four chapters devoted to commercial paper. Chapter 33 serves as an introduction to terminology and to an understanding of the scope of Articles 3 and 4 of the Uniform Commercial Code. Chapters 34 and 35 discuss the basic elements and advantages of commercial paper. Chapter 36 concentrates on the liability of the parties involved in the commercial paper transaction. The relevant impact of the proposed revisions to Articles 3 and 4 is discussed at the end of each of these four chapters. New Article 4A, on funds transfer, also is considered in chapter 34.

Part VIII contains six chapters dealing with the law as it relates to creditors and debtors. The first two chapters (37 and 38) examine Article 9 of the Uniform Commercial Code on secured credit transactions. Chapter 39 covers the use of real estate as security for debts. Chapter 40, on additional laws assisting creditors, emphasizes the complex area of suretyship. Chapter 41 gathers in one place much of the legislation aimed at protecting debtors and consumers. Finally, chapter 42 discusses bankruptcy.

Part IX contains three chapters on the subject of property. Chapter 43 serves as an introduction to the law of property. Chapter 44 examines methods of acquiring title to both real and personal property. Transactions involving property when title is not transferred are discussed in chapter 45. Of particular note, this chapter concludes with a presentation on new Article 2A of the Uniform Commercial Code.

Acknowledgments

There are numerous individuals who have contributed their time to making *Business Law* what it is. First, we are grateful for the helpful comments and suggestions made by the following reviewers of the manuscript:

Robert B. Bennett, Jr., *Butler University*
Karl A. Boedecker, *University of San Francisco*
Pamela Giltman, *Salisbury State University*
Roger D. Staton, *Miami University of Ohio*
Gamewell Gantt, *Idaho State University*
Paul Dusseault, *Herkimer County Community College*
James Poindexter, *Duquesne University*
Nancy R. Mansfield, *Georgia State University*

We also are indebted to Professor Patricia Rogers of San Francisco State University for her preparation of chapter 8. Her insights into the important field of international business transactions have contributed greatly to this text. Pamela Giltman and Susan Cabral of Salisbury State University prepared the Test Item File that accompanies this book. We appreciate this valuable contribution to the overall package of supplements.

"Thank you" seems inadequate to describe our appreciation for two individuals at Prentice Hall. Donald Hull, our editor, provided the support, encouragement, and guidance that proved essential throughout this project. Brian Hatch oversaw the production process. His diligent efforts kept all of us on schedule.

Every major project is touched by indispensable people. At the top of our list of such persons is Mary Evans. Mary literally touched every aspect of the manuscript. Without her superior typing skills and cooperative attitude, *Business Law* would have been long delayed. We acknowledge her efforts and are grateful for her assistance.

Finally, but certainly not least, we thank you, the users of this text. Our most sincere wish is that you will find *Business Law* to be a worthwhile and enjoyable part of your education. We welcome your thoughts and suggestions. Please feel free to communicate with us through our publisher, Prentice Hall.

Good luck!

Peter J. Shedd
Robert N. Corley

ity of the owners, and the taxation of income are among the most important factors to consider when choosing an organizational form.

■ BUSINESS MANAGEMENT DECISION

You and a business associate decide to make a movie concerning the 1991 Persian Gulf war. This project will require $4,500,000 in capital, an amount that must be raised. You and your associate desire to maintain editorial and production control over this project.

What type of business organization should be created to achieve your objectives?

INTRODUCTION

1. Proprietorships

The simplest organizational form by which a business might operate is a *proprietorship*. The fundamental characteristic of this organization is that there is only one owner. Although the number of employees and the dollar volume of business may be quite large, a proprietorship has only one owner.

The creation of this organization simply involves a businessperson beginning business by obtaining the necessary local business licenses. The sole proprietor has complete control over the business decisions, but that person is 100% liable for the debts of the proprietorship. The proprietorship is not a taxable organization. Therefore, the sole proprietor incurs on a personal level the benefits and burdens of the organization's profits or losses.

Most business organizations involve two or more parties as co-owners. The proprietorship organization cannot be considered appropriate when there is more than one owner. Hence, for most businesses the organizations discussed throughout this chapter are viewed as more important when choosing an organizational form.

2. General Partnerships

Partnership A business organization consisting of two or more owners who agree to carry on a business and to share profits and losses.

A **partnership** is an association of two or more persons to carry on, as co-owners, a business for profit. It is the result of an agreement among the owners. While this agreement may be orally stated, it is always best to have it formally drafted into a document, frequently called *articles of partnership*. To facilitate the existence of co-owners, partnerships developed logically in the law. The common law of partnerships has been codified in the Uniform Partnership Act.

ADVANTAGES.   A partnership form of organization has many advantages:

1. Since it is a matter of contract between individuals, to which the state is not a party, it is easily formed.
2. Costs of formation are minimal.
3. It is not a taxable entity.
4. Each owner, as a general rule, has an equal voice in management.
5. It may operate in more than one state without being required to comply with many legal formalities.
6. Partnerships are generally subject to less regulations and less governmental supervision than corporations.

The fact that a partnership is not a taxable entity does not mean that partnership income is tax-free. A partnership files an information return allocating its income among the partners, and each partner reports for income tax purposes the portion allocated to him or her.

DISADVANTAGES.   Several aspects of partnerships may be considered disadvantageous. First, only a limited number of people may own such a business. Second, a partnership is dissolved every time a new member is added as a new partner or an old member ceases to be a partner either by withdrawal or by death. Although dissolution of partnerships is the subject of chapter 28, it should be observed here that the perpetual existence of a corporation is often perceived as a distinct advantage for corporations, compared with easily dissolved partnerships.

Third, the liability of a partner is unlimited, contrasted with the limited liability of a shareholder. The unlimited liability of a partner is applicable both to contract and tort claims. Fourth, since a partner is taxed on his or her share of the profits of a partnership, whether distributed or not, a partner may be required to pay income tax on money that is not received. This burden is an important consideration in a new business that is reinvesting its profits for expansion. A partner in such a business would have to have an independent means of paying the taxes on such income.

3. Joint Venture

A *joint venture*, or *joint adventure*, occurs when two or more persons combine their efforts in a particular business enterprise and agree to share the profits or losses jointly or in proportion to their contributions. It is distinguished from a partnership in that the joint venture is a less formal association and contemplates a single transaction or a limited activity, whereas a partnership contemplates the operation of a general business. A joint venture is a specific venture without the formation of a partnership or corporation.

A partnership in most states is a legal entity, apart from the partners; a joint venture is not. A joint venture cannot sue or be sued. A suit must be by, on behalf of, or against the joint ventures individually. Joint ventures file a partnership tax return and have many of the other legal aspects of partnerships.

The following case provides a factual setting wherein a court found a joint venture to exist. Note that the issue of whether a joint venture is present is essential in determining the extent to which the members of the joint venture are liable for a breach of contract.

Ethan Dairy Products v. Austin

448 N.W.2d 226 (S.D. 1989)

KONENKAMP, C. J.

Paul F. Austin (Austin) and American Cheesemen, Inc. (American Cheesemen) appeal from a judgment against them for breach of contract on the purchase price of 199 blocks of cheese. . . .

The president of Ethan Dairy Products (Ethan Dairy) telephoned Austin, the sole owner and president of American Cheesemen and offered to sell two hundred, 40 pound blocks of Grade A cheddar cheese. They negotiated a price of $1.315 per pound and agreed the cheese would be shipped to Oshkosh Cold Storage Company (Oshkosh Cold Storage) in Wisconsin. When the product was shipped, Ethan Dairy's invoice showed Oshkosh Cold Storage as the purchaser. Oshkosh Cold Storage rejected the cheese because its tests showed that the product did not "measure up to State brand grade." Oshkosh shipped one block back and sent a letter asking Ethan Dairy what disposition it wanted made of the remaining 199 blocks.

Austin called Ethan Dairy's president saying he would sell the cheese to someone else, but Ethan Dairy would have to take a six cent discount per pound. Ethan Dairy agreed. Using American Cheesemen's sales and shipping order form, Austin sold the cheese to Old World Creamery. Austin's letterhead and order forms made no mention of brokering, but instead referred to a "Wisconsin Facility" as the shipping point for his company, American Cheesemen. . . .

Old World Creamery made periodic payments for the cheese to Oshkosh Cold Storage. After deducting its expenses, Oshkosh Cold Storage endorsed the checks over to "P. Austin and Ethan Dairy." Austin, in turn, passed the checks on to Ethan Dairy. Old World Creamery made four payments totaling $3,864.29 before declaring bankruptcy. Austin claimed that he and his company were acting in the capacity of a broker and declined responsibility for the unpaid balance.

The trial court found Austin and Oshkosh Cold Storage jointly and severally liable for the unpaid balance because they were joint venturers on the purchase and resale of Ethan Dairy's cheese. Austin insists he was only acting as a broker between Oshkosh Cold Storage and Ethan Dairy and neither he nor his company should be held liable for the cost of the cheese. . . .

Here the trial court found that Austin negotiated the cheese purchase for himself and his company as joint ventures with Oshkosh Cold Storage. . . .

A joint venture agreement need not be express, but may be implied from the acts and conduct of the parties. The elements of a joint venture are: (1) an agreement, express or implied, among members of a group; (2) a common purpose to be carried out by the group; (3) a community of pecuniary interest in that purpose among the members; and (4) an equal right to a voice in the direction and control of the enterprise.

Applying each element to the testimony reveals ample evidentiary support for the trial court's conclusion that a joint venture existed:

1. Agreement among members of the group.

Austin testified:

> We are talking about the owner of Oshkosh Cold Storage, Walt Doemel. So at times he would ask me to find certain products for clients that he had and sometimes I would get his permission to make contacts and purchase cheese on his behalf, to later sell into the market place.

2. A common purpose.

Undoubtedly Austin and Oshkosh Cold Storage had the common purpose of purchasing and reselling cheese.

3. A community of pecuniary interest.

Concerning his financial arrangement with Oshkosh Cold Storage, Austin testified:

> Well, I believe I had something like two cents a pound over and above the costs and the freight and we just split whatever we made over and above the cost . . . less any expenses like interest and that type of thing. We split the interest, also.

4. An equal right to control the enterprise.

Through the initial negotiations and later price adjustments with Ethan Dairy, Austin never consulted with Oshkosh Cold Storage before settling on an agreed price for the cheese. At trial Austin testified that he told the Ethan Dairy's president that he was merely representing Oshkosh Cold Storage, but on cross examination:

Q: So, during all these conversations when John ordered the cheese from you [sic] and was shipped to Oshkosh and when he wanted to negotiate with you on it, he called you and you said you would take care of it. When he talked to you about payment you said we will see that you're paid, isn't that true?

A: [Austin] We, meaning Oshkosh.

Q: You didn't tell him that? All you said was we?

A: Yeah.

From these facts we are unable to conclude that the trial court erred in determining a joint venture existed between Austin and Oshkosh Cold Storage. . . .

■ *Affirmed.*

CASE CONCEPTS REVIEW

1. Who does Ethan Dairy claim are the members of the alleged joint venture?
2. What is the purported purpose of this joint venture?
3. Why is Ethan Dairy arguing that the members of the joint venture are liable for nonpayment of the cheese?
4. What factors are considered by this court in rejecting Austin's argument that he was acting as a broker between Ethan Dairy and Oshkosh Cold Storage?

LIMITED PARTNERSHIPS

4. Characteristics

Limited partnership A partnership in which one or more individuals are general partners and one or more individuals are limited partners. The limited partners contribute assets to the partnership without taking part in the conduct of the business. They are liable for the debts of the partnership only to the extent of their contributions.

A **limited partnership,** like other partnerships, comes into existence by virtue of an agreement. Like a corporation, it is authorized by statute, and the liability of one or more, but not all, of the partners is limited to the amount of capital contributed at the time of the creation of the partnership. For liability purposes, a limited partnership is, in effect, a hybrid between the partnership and the corporation.

One or more *general partners* manage the business and are personally liable for its debts. One or more *limited partners* also contribute capital and share in profits and losses, but they take no part in running the business and incur no liability with respect to partnership obligations beyond their contribution to capital. A limited partner's position is analogous to that of a corporate shareholder, whose role is that of an investor with limited liability. It is from the limited liability of the limited partners that the organization gets its name.

Limited partnerships are governed in most states by the Revised Uniform Limited Partnership Act provisions.* The purpose of this statute is to encourage trade by permitting persons to invest in a business and reap their share of the profits without becoming liable for debts or risking more than the capital contributed. This reduced risk is based on the investor's not being a general partner or participating actively in the conduct of the business.

Some limited partners have attempted to maintain their limited liability while controlling the limited partnership through a corporation acting as a general partner. When the officers and directors of this corporation are the limited partners, an issue concerning the degree of these persons' liability arises. The following case represents those states that remove the limited liability of these partners and replace it with the unlimited liability of the general partner.

---

*Because some states have not adopted the revised version of the Uniform Limited Partnership Act, the principles stated in this text may not accurately reflect the law in your state.

CASE

DeLaney v. Fidelity Lease Limited
526 S.W.2d 543 (Tex. 1975)

Fidelity Lease Unlimited is a limited partnership consisting of twenty-two limited partners and a corporate general partner. Three of the limited partners were the officers and directors of the corporate general partner. When the limited partnership breached a contract with the plaintiff, suit was brought against three of the limited partners individually. It was contended that they had become general partners by participating in the management of the limited partnership. The lower courts held that the individuals were not liable, and the plaintiff appealed.

DANIEL, J.

. . . The question here is whether limited partners in a limited partnership become liable as general partners if they "take part in the control of the business" while acting as officers of a corporation which is the sole general partner of the limited partnership. . . .

Pertinent portions of the Texas Uniform Limited Partnership Act, Article 6132a, provide:

> Sec. 8. A limited partner shall not become liable as a general partner unless, in addition to the exercise of his rights and powers as a limited partner, he takes part in the control of the business. . . .

It was alleged by plaintiffs, and there is summary judgment evidence, that the three limited partners controlled the business of the limited partnership, albeit through the corporate entity. The defendant limited partners argued that they acted only through the corporation and that the corporation actually controlled the business of the limited partnership. In response to this contention, we adopt the following statements in the dissenting opinion of Chief Justice Preslar in the court of civil appeals.

> I find it difficult to separate their acts for they were at all times in the dual capacity of limited partners and officers of the corporation. Apparently the corporation had no function except to operate the limited partnership and Appellees were obligated to their other partners to so operate the corporation as to benefit the partnership. Each act was done then, not for the corporation, but for the partnership. Indirectly, if not directly, they were exercising control

over the partnership. Truly "the corporation fiction" was in this instance a fiction.

Thus we hold that the personal liability, which attaches to a limited partner when "he takes part in the control and management of the business," cannot be evaded merely by acting through a corporation.

Crombie, Kahn, and Sanders argue that, since their only control of Fidelity's business was as officers of the alleged corporate general partner, they are insulated from personal liability arising from their activities or those of the corporation. This is a general rule of corporate law, but one of several exceptions in which the courts will disregard the corporate fiction is where it is used to circumvent a statute. That is precisely the result here, for it is undisputed that the corporation was organized to manage and control the limited partnership. Strict compliance with the statute is required if a limited partner is to avoid liability as a general partner. It is quite clear that there can be more than one general partner. Assuming that Interlease Corporation was a legal general partner . . . this would not prevent Crombie, Kahn, and Sanders from taking part in the control of the business in their individual capacities as well as their corporate capacities. In no event should they be permitted to escape the statutory liability which would have devolved upon them if there had been no attempted interposition of the corporate shield against personal liability. Otherwise, the statutory requirement of at least one general partner with general liability in a limited partnership can be circumvented or vitiated by limited partners operating the partnership through a corporation with minimum capitalization and therefore minimum liability. We hold that . . . if . . . either of these three limited partners took part in the control of the business, whether or not in his capacity as an officer of Interlease Corporation, he should be adjudged personally liable as a general partner.

■ *Reversed.*

CASE CONCEPTS REVIEW

1. Who (what) was the general partner of the limited partner, Fidelity Lease Limited?
2. What role in the corporate general partner did three of the limited partners have?
3. Why does this court conclude that these limited partners should be personally and unlimitedly liable if they engaged in the control of the limited partnership through the corporate general partner?

5. Creation

To create a limited partnership under the Revised Uniform Limited Partnership Act, the parties must sign and swear to a certificate containing, among other matters, the following information about the limited partnership agreement: the name of the partnership, the character of the business, its location, the name and place of residence of each member, those who are to be the general and those who are to be the limited partners, the term for which the partnership is to exist, the amount of cash or the agreed value of property to be contributed by each partner, and the share of profit or compensation each limited partner shall receive. Strict compliance with the statutory requirement is necessary if the limited partners are to achieve the goal of limited liability. Some states by statute require only substantial compliance, however, especially between the partners.

The certificate must be filed with the state's secretary of state office. Most states require notice by newspaper publication. In the event of any change in the facts relative to the partnership agreement contained in the certificate as filed—such as a change in the name of the partnership, the capital, or other matters—a new certificate must be filed. If such a certificate is not filed and the partnership continued, the limited partners immediately become liable as general partners.

Under the Revised Uniform Limited Partnership Act, the name of the limited partnership must contain the words *limited partnership*. The name may not contain the name of a limited partner unless his or her name is also the name of a general partner or one that had been used prior to the admission of that limited partner.

The 1980s saw the development of limited partnerships with characteristics of publicly traded corporations. These limited partnerships with thousands of limited partners are usually referred to as *master limited partnerships*. The units of the limited partners are traded like stocks and are traded on stock exchanges. They first developed in the petroleum industry as a means of passing cash flow to investors without corporate taxation. Today they are used in financing theatrical productions, health care organizations, TV stations, and professional sports teams.

Master limited partnerships distribute cash flow to partners. The distributions are a tax-free return of capital until they exceed the original investment. Losses, however, are not deductible under the 1986 tax law revision. Many master limited partnerships have been outstanding investments, but many have failed and the market has tended to be very volatile. Cash payouts are often less than the projection, and most are thinly traded. These organizations are taxed as corporations if they are publicly traded, which is defined as more than 5% of their interests changing hands during a taxable year.

6. Operation

A limited partnership under the Revised Act is required to maintain a registered office within the state and an agent to receive notices for it. The law requires that certain records, such as a list of all partners and a copy of the certificate of the limited partnership, be maintained at this office. Copies of the partnership tax returns and copies of all financial statements must be kept for three years.

The control of a limited partnership is in the hands of the general partners. Historically, limited partners who participated in the management of the partnership lost their limited liability benefits. Today, under the Revised Act a limited partner who mistakenly or intentionally engages in managerial activities becomes liable as a general partner only if the third party seeking to recover against the partnership had knowledge of the expanded participation.

While a limited partner has no right to participate in management, certain activities are within the rights of the limited partners, and their exercise does not result in that partner becoming personally liable as a general partner. These activities are listed in the following case, which illustrates that courts will narrowly construe the permissible activities of limited partners. Crossing over the line and engaging in management results in the limited partner being treated like a general partner.

CASE

Pitman v. Flanagan Lumber Co., Inc.
567 So.2d 1335 (Ala. 1990)

HOUSTON, J.

The defendant, Robert Edward Pitman, appeals from a judgment in favor of Flanagan Lumber Company, Inc. ("Flanagan"), in this action to recover a debt incurred by Ramsey Homebuilders, Ltd. ("Ramsey Homebuilders"). We affirm.

Pitman was one of two limited partners in Ramsey Homebuilders, a limited partnership that engaged in the business of residential construction. Michael C. Ramsey was the sole general partner in that partnership. Because Ramsey had a poor credit history, he was unable to borrow the money or obtain the credit that was needed to sustain the partnership's business. Pitman, who had a personal account with Flanagan, contacted Wilburn Moore, Flanagan's credit manager, and secured an account in the partnership's name. After the partnership failed to pay the account, Flanagan sued Pitman, alleging that, although Pitman was a limited partner in Ramsey Homebuilders, he was responsible for the partnership's debt under Ala. Code 1975, § 10-9A-42, which reads, in pertinent part, as follows:

(a)   Except as provided in subsection (d), a limited partner is not liable for the obligations of a limited partnership unless he is also a general partner or, in addition to the exercise of his rights and powers as a limited partner, he takes part in the control of the business. However, if the limited partner's participation in the control of the business is not substantially the same as the exercise of the powers of a general partner, he is liable only to persons who, with actual knowledge of his participation in control and in reasonable reliance thereon, transact business with the partnership.

(b)   A limited partner does not participate in the control of the business within the meaning of sub-section (a) solely by doing one or more of the following:

(1)   Being a contractor for or an agent, attorney-at-law, or employee of the limited partnership or of a general partner, or an officer, director, or shareholder of a general partner;

(2)   Consulting with and advising a general partner with respect to the business of the limited partnership or examining into the state and progress of the partnership business;

(3)   Acting as surety or guarantor for any liabilities for the limited partnership;

(4)   Approving or disapproving an amendment to the partnership agreement; or

(5)   Voting on one or more of the following matters:

(i)   The dissolution and winding up of the limited partnership;

(ii)   The sale, exchange, lease, mortgage, pledge, or other transfer of all or substantially all of the assets of the limited partnership other than in the ordinary course of its business;

(iii)   The incurrence of indebtedness by the limited partnership other than in the ordinary course of its business;

(iv)   A change in the nature of the business;

(v)   The removal of a general partner.

(c)   The enumeration in subsection (b) does not mean that the possession or exercise of any other powers by a limited partner constitutes participation by him in the business of the limited partnership.

After hearing ... evidence, the trial court found that Pitman had participated in the control of the business by interceding on the partnership's behalf to secure credit; that Flanagan had reasonably relied upon that participation in extending credit; and, therefore, that Pitman was liable to Flanagan for the debt subsequently incurred by the partnership.

Pitman argues that the evidence does not support the trial court's finding that he participated in the control of the partnership's business. He argues instead that, if anything, he was operating within the waters of the "safe harbor" provided by § 10-9A-42(b) (3) when he contacted Flanagan. . . . Flanagan contends, however, that the evidence supports the trial court's finding that Pitman participated in the control of the partnership's business. . . . We agree.

Where a trial court has heard . . . evidence, as in this case, its findings, if supported by the evidence, are presumed correct, and its judgment based upon those findings will be reversed only if, after consideration of the evidence and all reasonable inferences to be drawn therefrom, the judgment is found to be plainly and palpably wrong.

"Control" is defined in *Black's Law Dictionary* (5th ed. 1979) as the "power or authority to manage, direct, superintend, restrict, regulate, govern, administer, or oversee." In the present case, the evidence showed that Pitman interceded on behalf of the partnership in order to secure an account with Flanagan. The trial court could have found from this evidence that Pitman participated in the "control" of the partnership's business by securing one of the things that the partnership needed to survive—a source of building materials that would be provided on credit. Furthermore, the evidence supports the trial court's finding that Flanagan reasonably relied on Pitman's participation in the partnership's business by extending credit to the partnership. The trial court's judgment was not plainly and palpably wrong. . . .

■ *For the foregoing reasons, the judgment is affirmed.*

CASE CONCEPTS REVIEW

1. What was Pitman's alleged legal position in Ramsey Homebuilders?
2. Who was the general partner of Ramsey Homebuilders?
3. Why did Pitman, instead of the general partner, secure an account in the Ramsey Homebuilders' name with Flanagan Lumber?
4. Why does this court agree with the trial court's imposition of personal liability on Pitman?

The limited partnership as a tax shelter is of special value in many new businesses, especially real estate ventures such as shopping centers and apartment complexes. It gives the investor limited liability and the operators control of the venture. It allows the use of depreciation to provide a tax loss that can be deducted by the limited partner to the extent of risk in the investment. Offsetting this tax loss, usually, is a positive cash flow that gives a limited partner an income at the same time that he or she has a loss for tax purposes.

7. Dissolution

To dissolve a limited partnership voluntarily before the time for termination stated in the certificate, notice of the dissolution must be filed and published. Upon dissolution, the distribution of the assets of the firm is prescribed by statute. As a general rule, the law gives priority to limited partners over general partners after all creditors are paid.

A limited partnership is dissolved only when there is a change in the general partners. Because limited partners have no active voice in the daily management of the organization, the limited partners' interests are treated like corporate shareholders' stock. Therefore, unless there is an agreement to the contrary, limited partners are free to transfer their interests without causing a dissolution of the limited partnership.

8. Advantages and Disadvantages

Corporation A collection of individuals created by statute as a legal person, vested with powers and capacity to contract, own, control, convey property, and transact business within the limits of the powers granted.

A **corporation** is a legal entity that comes into existence when the state issues the corporate charter. Because a corporation is considered to be a legal person separate from its owners, it usually has a perpetual existence. In other words, the owners/shareholders are free to transfer their interests/shares of stocks without affecting the continuity of the business organization. Furthermore, due to the separateness of owners and organization, shareholders' liability generally is limited to their investment.

A corporation, as a general rule, is a taxable entity paying a tax on its net profits. Dividends paid to stockholders are also taxable, giving rise to the frequent observation that corporate income is subject to double taxation. The accuracy of this observation is discussed in section 10.

The advantages of the corporate form of organization may be summarized as follows:

1. It is the easiest method that will raise substantial capital from a large number of investors.
2. Tax laws have several provisions that are favorable to corporations.
3. Control can be vested in those with a minority of the investment by using techniques such as nonvoting or preferred stock.
4. Ownership may be divided into many separate and unequal shares.
5. Investors have limited liability.
6. The organization can have perpetual existence.
7. Certain laws, such as those relating to usury, are not applicable to corporations.
8. Investors, notwithstanding their status as owners, may also be employees entitled to benefits such as workers' compensation.

Among the frequently cited disadvantages of the corporate form of organization are these:

1. Cost of forming and maintaining the corporate form with its rather formal procedures
2. Expenditures such as license fees and franchise taxes that are assessed against corporations but not against partnerships
3. Double taxation of corporate income and the frequently higher rates
4. The requirement that it must be qualified to do business in all states where it is conducting intrastate business
5. Being subject to more regulations by government at all levels than are other forms
6. Being required to use an attorney in litigation, whereas an ordinary citizen can proceed on his or her own behalf

The fact that corporations are required to use an attorney in litigation is listed as a disadvantage of the corporate form of organization. As a practical matter, all forms of organization must use an attorney in any litigation of much significance, so to that extent the requirement is not a significant disadvantage. It does emphasize, however, that corporations do require the services of lawyers on an ongoing basis. The role of the lawyer and his or her relationship to a business corporation is colorfully described by Roy A. Redfield in *Factors of Growth in a Law Practice:*

When the business corporation is born, the lawyer is the midwife who brings it into existence; while it functions he is its philosopher, guide and friend; in trouble he is its champion, and when the end comes and the last sad rites must be performed, the lawyer becomes the undertaker who disincorporates it and makes final report to the Director of Internal Revenue.

The following case explains the rationale behind the rule of law that requires corporations to be represented by a licensed attorney in all litigation.

CASE

Land Management v. Department of Envir. Protec.
368 A.2d 602 (Me. 1977)

ARCHIBALD, J.

. . . The sole issue raised by this appeal is whether the presiding Justice acted properly in dismissing the plaintiff's complaint on the ground that the plaintiff was a corporation not represented by a duly admitted attorney. We conclude that the Justice below correctly dismissed the complaint, and we therefore deny the plaintiff's appeal.

The plaintiff, Land Management, Inc., is a corporation doing business in the State of Maine. On April 9, 1976, it commenced an action in the Superior Court seeking declaratory and injunctive relief against the defendants. Throughout the proceedings in the Superior Court the plaintiff was represented by its president who, admittedly, is not an attorney admitted to practice law in Maine.

All of the defendants filed motions to dismiss the plaintiff's complaint. . . . [These were granted] solely on the basis that the Plaintiff Land Management, Inc. is not entitled to proceed in this action *pro se* by and through a person who is not an attorney licensed to practice law.

In support of its position that a corporation may represent itself in Maine courts through a corporate officer who is not a duly admitted attorney, the plaintiff relies upon language found in 4 M.R.S.A. §§807 and 811.

4 M.R.S.A. §807 provides:

> Unless duly admitted to the bar of this State, no person shall practice law or any branch thereof, or hold himself out to practice law or any branch thereof, within the State or before any court therein, or demand or receive any remuneration for such services rendered in this State. Whoever, not being duly admitted to the bar of this State, shall practice law or any branch thereof, or hold himself out to practice law or any branch thereof, within the State or before any court therein, or demand or receive any remuneration for such services rendered in this

State, shall be punished by a fine of not more than $500 or by imprisonment for not more than three months, or by both. This section shall not be construed to apply to practice before any Federal Court by any person duly admitted to practice therein not to a person pleading or managing his own cause in court. . . .

4 M.R.S.A. §811 defines a "person" as "any individual, corporation, partnership or association."

On the basis of these statutory provisions, the plaintiff contends that since a corporation can only act through its agents, it may authorize a non-attorney to represent it in court. We do not agree with the plaintiff's assertion that the Legislature, in enacting §§807 and 811, intended to permit a corporation to be represented before the courts of this State by a person who is not authorized to practice law. To accept plaintiff's argument would require us to hold that a corporation may authorize a non-attorney to represent it in court, while an individual may not. We do not believe that the Legislature intended such an illogical result. The purpose of §811 for including a corporation within the definition of the word "person" was to make it clear that a corporation, as well as anyone else, is prohibited from engaging in the unauthorized practice of law. This section modified the §807 prohibition against unauthorized practice rather than expanding the right of individuals to represent themselves in either the Federal or State courts.

The rule that a corporation may appear in court only through a licensed attorney was stated succinctly in *Paradise v. Nowlin,* 86 Ca. App.2d 897, 195 P.2d 867 (1948):

> A natural person may represent himself and present his own case to the court although he is not a licensed attorney. A corporation is not a natural person. It is an artificial entity created by law and as such it can neither practice law nor appear or act in person. Out of court it must act in its affairs through its agents and representatives and in matters in court it can act only through licensed attor-

neys. A corporation cannot appear in court by an officer who is not an attorney and it cannot appear in *propria persona*.

Sound public policy reasons also require such a rule. As stated by the Ohio Supreme Court:

To allow a corporation to maintain litigation and appear in court represented by corporate officers or agents only would lay open the gates to the practice of law for entry to those corporate officers or agents who have not been qualified to practice law and who are not amenable to the general discipline of the court.

There is abundant authority, both state and federal, rejecting the argument, as advanced by the plaintiff, that a corporation has the right to appear in court without the aid of a licensed attorney.

Since the plaintiff was not represented by counsel licensed to practice law, its complaint was a nullity and was properly dismissed by the presiding Justice.

■ *Appeal denied.*

CASE CONCEPTS REVIEW

1. Who represented the Land Management, Inc. in the initial hearing before the trial court?
2. On what basis did the defendants seek to have Land Management's complaint dismissed?
3. Why does this court conclude that a corporate organization must be represented by a licensed attorney?

9. Taxation of Corporate Income

The fact that taxation is listed as both an advantage and a disadvantage of the corporate form illustrates the importance of the tax factor in choosing this particular form of organization. Corporate tax law provisions change from time to time, depending on the economy and the effect of tax policy on employment, economic growth, and so on. The current rates are as follows:

Income ($)	Tax Rate
0–50,000	15 percent
50–75,000	25 percent
Over 75,000	34 percent

Among the tax laws that favor corporations over partnerships are the following:

1. Health insurance premiums are fully deductible and are not subject to the limitations applicable to individuals.
2. Deferred compensation plans may be adopted.
3. Retained earnings are taxed at graduated rates that may be lower than the individual tax rates of the shareholders.
4. Income that is needed to be retained in the business is not taxed to persons who do not receive it, as occurs in a partnership.
5. The corporation may provide some life insurance for its employees as a deductible expense.
6. Medical expenses in excess of health insurance coverage may be paid on behalf of employees as a deductible expense.

The corporate form of organization also has some major tax disadvantages. First, corporate losses are not available as a deduction to shareholders, whereas partnership losses are immediately deductible on the individual returns of partners. Corporate losses can only be used to offset corporate profits during different taxable years.

Second, a major disadvantage to corporations occurs when a profit is made and the corporation pays a dividend to its shareholders. The dividend will have been taxed at the corporate level and then taxed again to the shareholder. The rate of the second tax depends on the personal tax rate of each shareholder receiving the dividend. This is known as the "double tax" on corporate income. (The next section explains why the "double tax" may not be as big a disadvantage as it first seems.)

Third, the corporate form is frequently at a disadvantage from a tax standpoint because the 34 percent rate over $75,000 exceeds the individual rate of the owners of the business. Finally, some states impose a higher income tax on corporate income than on individual income. In addition, many other forms of taxes are imposed on corporations that are not imposed on individuals or on partnerships.

10. Avoidance of Double Taxation

Certain techniques may be used to avoid, in part, the double taxation of corporate income. First, reasonable salaries paid to corporate employees may be deducted in computing the taxable income of the business. Thus, in a closely held corporation in which all or most shareholders are officers or employees, this technique can be used to avoid double taxation of much of the corporate income. The Internal Revenue Code disallows a deduction for excessive or unreasonable compensation, and unreasonable payments to shareholder employees are taxable as dividends. Therefore the determination of the reasonableness of corporate salaries is an ever-present tax problem in the closely held corporation that employs shareholders.

Second, the capital structure of a corporation may include both common stock and interest-bearing loans from shareholders. Envision a company that needs $200,000 to begin business. If $200,000 of stock is purchased, there will be no expense to be deducted. But suppose that $100,000 is loaned to the company at 10 percent interest. In this case, $10,000 of interest each year is deductible as an expense of the company and thus subject to only one tax as interest income to the owners. Just as in the case of salaries, the Internal Revenue Code contains a counteracting rule relating to corporations that are undercapitalized. If the corporation is undercapitalized, interest payments will be treated as dividends and disallowed as deductible expenses.

The third technique for avoiding double taxation—or to at least delay it—is simply not to pay dividends and to accumulate the earnings. Here again we have tax provisions designed to counteract the technique. There is a special income tax imposed on "excessive accumulated earnings" in addition to the normal tax rate.

Finally, a special provision in the Internal Revenue Code treats small, closely held business corporations and partnerships similarly for income tax purposes. These corporations are known as subchapter S corporations.

11. Subchapter S Corporations

The limited partnership is a hybrid between a corporation and a partnership in the area of liability. A similar hybrid known as a *tax-option* or *subchapter S corporation* exists in the tax area of the law. Such corporations have the advantages of the corporate form without the double taxation of income.

The tax-option corporation is one that elects to be taxed in a manner similar to that of partnerships—that is, to file an information return allocating income and losses among the shareholders for immediate reporting, regardless of dividend distributions, thus avoiding any tax on the corporation.

Subchapter S corporations cannot have more than thirty-five shareholders, each of whom must sign the election to be taxed in a manner similar to a partnership. There are many technical rules of law involved in subchapter S corporations. But as a rule of thumb, this method of taxation has distinct advantages for a business operating at a loss, because the loss is shared and immediately deductible on the returns of shareholders active in the business. It is also advantageous for a business capable of paying out net profits as earned, thereby avoiding the corporate tax. If net profits must be retained in the business, subchapter S tax treatment is somewhat disadvantageous because income tax is paid by the shareholders on earnings not received.

12. Professional Service Associations

Traditionally, professional services, such as those of a doctor, lawyer, or dentist, could be performed only by an individual and could not be performed by a corporation, because the relationship of doctor and patient or attorney and client was considered a highly personal one. The impersonal corporate entity could not render the personal services involved.

For many years there were significant tax advantages in corporate profit-sharing and pension plans that were not available to private persons and to partnerships to the same extent. An individual proprietor or partner was limited to a deduction of 15 percent of income or $15,000 under a *Keogh* pension plan provision. Professional persons therefore often incorporated or created professional associations to obtain the greater tax advantages of corporate pension and profit-sharing plans. To make this possible, every state enacted statutes authorizing *professional associations.* As legal entities similar to corporations, their payments to qualified pension and profit-sharing plans qualify for deductions equal to those of business corporations.

The tax laws have been changed in an attempt to equalize the tax treatment of Keogh plans and corporate pension and profit-sharing plans. While this has generally been achieved, there remain a few advantages to corporate plans. Most professional corporations that were created earlier remain in existence, and new ones are still being formed.

The law authorizing professional corporations does not authorize business corporations to practice a profession such as law or medicine. Professional corporations are special forms of business organizations that must meet strict statutory requirements. In addition, professional persons practicing a profession as a professional corporation do not obtain any limitation on their professional liability to third persons. However, as the following case illustrates, the shareholders of a professional corporation do have limited liability for corporate debts that do not directly involve the practice of the profession.

CASE

We're Assoc. v. Cohen, Stracher & Bloom
480 N.E.2d 357 (N.Y. 1985)

Plaintiffs leased office space to a professional service corporation, engaged in the practice of law. The lease was in the name of the corporation, but the landlord sought to hold the lawyers individually liable for the unpaid rent. The lower court dismissed the suit against the individuals.

WACHTLER, J.

... The issue presented on this appeal, is whether the shareholders of a professional service corporation organized under article 15 of the Business Corporation Law may be held liable in their individual capacities for rents due under a lease naming only the professional service corporation as tenant.

... [T]he Legislature, in enacting article 15 of the Business Corporation Law, did not intend to abrogate the traditional limited liability afforded corporate shareholders except as specifically provided in that article.

Plaintiff contends that the statute should be liberally construed to apply to debts incurred ancillary to the rendering of professional services; [and] that the rationale underlying the limitation of shareholder liability, i.e., the inability of shareholders to participate in the management of the corporation, does not apply to professional service corporations, which are run by their shareholders. . . .

The only specific provision relating to shareholder liability in article 15 of the Business Corporation Law . . . is section 1505(a), which states: "Each shareholder, employee or agent of a professional service corporation shall be personally and fully liable and accountable for any negligent or wrongful act or misconduct committed by him or by any person under his direct supervision and control while rendering professional services on behalf of such corporation."

The Appellate Division in this case properly interpreted this section to preclude the imposition of personal shareholder liability in instances not involving the direct rendition of professional services. . . .

The plain words of the statute, imposing personal liability only in connection with the rendition of professional services on behalf of the professional service corporation, cannot be defeated by a liberal construction which would include ordinary business debts within the definition of professional services. . . . [T]he rationale that shareholders of a professional service corporation should be held personally liable for ordinary business debts of the corporation because they are "closer" to the management of such corporation than are shareholders of an ordinary business corporation has not prevailed in our State over the general policy of allowing corporations to be formed for the express purpose of limiting liability. Even single-person businesses are allowed to incorporate, and, so long as no fraud is committed and the corporate form is respected, no individual liability will result. If shareholders of a conventional business corporation may enjoy limited liability under such circumstances, so may those of a professional service corporation except as limited by Business Corporation Law § 1505(a).

Our decision should work no injustice on those who enter into leases or any other contracts with professional service corporations, who are free to seek the personal assurances of the shareholders that the commitments of the professional service corporation will be honored. Nor do we intend to countenance any abuse of the corporate form of doing business, which, if present in a future case, could compel a different result. What we do hold is that, absent any showing of such abuse, the shareholders of a professional service corporation cannot be held personally liable for an ordinary business debt of the corporation.

■ *Affirmed.*

CASE CONCEPTS REVIEW

1. Who (what) was the named tenant in the lease of office space?
2. To what extent are shareholders in a professional service corporation personally liable?
3. Why does this court conclude that the shareholders of this professional service corporation are not personally liable for the rent arising from the office space lease?

In some ways, the total liability of a professional association may be greater than if the profession were practiced as a partnership. For example, a professional association may have liability for discriminating against owner-employees because of age, whereas a partnership would not have liability to a partner because of age discrimination. Several laws that protect shareholder employees do not protect partners.

Today, there are thousands of professional corporations in all states. They can be identified by the letters *S.C.* (Service Corporation), *P.C.* (Professional Corporation), or *Inc.* (Incorporated), or by the word *company* in the name of the professional firm.

MAKING THE DECISION

13. The Process

Earlier in this chapter, we listed advantages of incorporating a business with substantial capital. If the business is to be owned and operated by relatively few people, their choice of form of organization will be made with those factors in mind—especially taxation, liability, control, and legal capacity. *Legal capacity* is the power of the business, in its own name, to sue or be sued, own and dispose of property, and enter into contracts.

In evaluating the impact of taxation, an accountant or attorney will look at the projected profits or losses of the business, the ability to distribute earnings, and the tax brackets of the owners. An estimate of the tax burden under the various forms of organization will be made. The results will be considered along with other factors in making the decision on the form of business organization.

The generalization that partners have unlimited liability and shareholders limited liability must be qualified in the case of a closely held business. A small, closely held corporation with limited assets and capital will find it difficult to obtain credit on the strength of its own credit standing alone; and as a practical matter, the shareholders will usually be required to add their individual liability as security for the debts. If Tom, Dick, and Jane seek a loan for their corporation, they usually will be required to guarantee repayment of the loan. This is not to say that closely held corporations do not have some degree of limited liability. The investors in those types of businesses are protected with limited liability for contractlike obligations imposed as a matter of law (such as taxes) and for debts resulting from torts committed by company employees while engaged in company business. If the tax aspects dictate that a partnership and limited liability are desired by some investors, the limited partnership will be considered.

Issues of liability are not restricted to the investors in the business or to financial liability. Corporation law has developed several instances in which the directors and officers of the corporation will have liability to shareholders or the corporation for acts or omissions by those directors or officers in their official capacity. These matters are discussed more fully in chapter 30.

The significance of the law relating to control will be apparent in the discussions on formation and operation of partnerships and corporations in chapters 26–27 and 29–30. The desire of one or more individuals to control the business is often a major factor in selecting the form.

CHAPTER SUMMARY

INTRODUCTION

Proprietorships
1. A sole proprietorship is the simplest form of a business organization.
2. This form is applicable if there is only one owner of the business.
3. The sole proprietor is in full control and is liable for all the debts of the proprietorship.
4. The proprietorship is not a taxable entity. All profits or losses flow to the proprietor personality.

General Partnerships
1. The partnership is easily formed by agreement, and the costs of formation are minimal.
2. The partnership is not a taxable entity, and losses are immediately deductible.
3. Income is taxed to a partner whether received or not.
4. As a general rule, each partner has an equal voice in management.
5. The partnership can operate in any state and is subject to less government regulation.
6. A partnership may involve only a limited number of people and is easily dissolved.
7. Partners have unlimited liability.

Joint Ventures
1. A joint venture is like a partnership, but for a single transaction.
2. A joint venture is not a legal entity but is treated as a partnership for tax purposes.

LIMITED PARTNERSHIPS

Characteristics
1. A limited partnership has at least one general partner with limited liability.
2. It is not a taxable entity, and any losses are immediately deductible.
3. The general partners manage the business.

Creation
1. The steps necessary to establish a limited partnership are governed by a statute and must be followed closely.
2. A certificate containing vital information is filed in a public office, such as the secretary of state's office.
3. Limited partners do not participate in management and are thus similar to shareholders.
4. The name used gives notice of the limited liability of some owners.

Operation
1. Usually, the limited partners forgo their right to participate in management in exchange for having their liability limited to their investment.
2. Limited partners do have a number of rights, the exercise of which does not amount to participating in management.
3. Generally, today, limited partners who participate in management assume unlimited liability only to persons who know of the participation.

Dissolution
1. Statutory procedures must be followed to dissolve a limited partnership before the time stated in the certificate.
2. In general, the transfer of a limited partner's interest does not dissolve the limited partnership.

THE BUSINESS CORPORATION

Advantages
1. Investors have limited liability, and the business may have perpetual existence.
2. This is a method by which even hundreds of thousands of persons can own a business together and in varying percentages of ownership.
3. Several provisions in the tax law favor corporations.
4. As a separate entity, there are many laws covering only corporations.

Disadvantages	1. There are significant costs in forming and maintaining a corporation.
	2. Corporate income is taxed to the corporation, and dividends are taxed to the shareholders.
	3. The corporation must qualify in every state where it conducts intrastate business and is subject to greater government regulation.
	4. It must have an attorney represent it in litigation.
Taxation of Corporate Income	1. Several provisions of the Internal Revenue Code, such as those relating to health insurance, have special advantages for corporations.
Avoidance of Double Taxation	1. There are several techniques for avoiding double taxation of corporate income, such as the payment of salaries and expenses on behalf of the owners of the corporation.
Subchapter S Corporations	1. The subchapter S corporation, which is a corporation taxed in the same manner as a partnership, is of special importance in avoiding the double taxation of corporate income.
Professional Service Associations	1. Such associations were created to give professional persons some of the tax advantages of corporations.
	2. Shareholders of professional associations do not have limited malpractice liability but do have limited liability for other debts of the associations.

MAKING THE DECISION

The Process	1. Those responsible for deciding the form of organization must weigh the relative importance of a number of factors.
	2. Among the more important factors used to help determine the best form of organization for a business are taxation, liability, and control.

REVIEW QUESTIONS AND PROBLEMS

1. Match each term in column A with the appropriate statement in column B.

<table>
<tr><td align="center">A</td><td align="center">B</td></tr>
<tr><td>(1) Partnership</td><td>(a) A business owned by one person who is personally liable for all losses</td></tr>
<tr><td>(2) Proprietorship</td><td>(b) An artificial being created by a state</td></tr>
<tr><td>(3) Limited partnership</td><td>(c) Two or more persons combine their efforts for a single transaction</td></tr>
<tr><td>(4) Corporation</td><td>(d) Created when shareholders elect to be treated as partners for tax purposes</td></tr>
<tr><td>(5) Legal capacity</td><td>(e) Created by an agreement between two or more persons who agree to share profits and losses</td></tr>
<tr><td>(6) Buy-and-sell agreement</td><td>(f) Provides for compensation to a deceased or withdrawing owner of a business in return for that owner's interest</td></tr>
<tr><td>(7) Subchapter S corporation</td><td>(g) The ability of an organization to sue or to own property</td></tr>
<tr><td>(8) Joint venture</td><td>(h) Exists when some partners are treated like shareholders for liability purposes</td></tr>
</table>

2. Garrett and Lewis signed an agreement creating a limited partnership. Garrett was the general partner and Lewis was a limited partner. Neither the agreement nor the certificate required by statute were filed with the secretary of state. This limited partnership purchased merchandise on credit from Products, Ltd., which assumed that the busi-

ness was a general partnership. Should the failure to file pertinent documents related to the limited partnership make Lewis liable to Products, Ltd., as if he were a general partner? Explain.

3. The partners of a limited partnership had their signatures acknowledged by a notary, but they did not swear to the truth of the document. Is the certificate valid to the extent that the limited partners have limited liability? Explain.

4. A general partner agreed to provide a limited partner with a unilateral refund of his partnership contribution if the limited partner became dissatisfied with the conduct of the business. The other parties did not consent to the modification of the partnership agreement. Is the agreement enforceable? Why or why not?

5. Oklahoma prohibits the sale of alcoholic beverages in an "open saloon." Roby, in an attempt to circumvent this prohibition, formed a limited partnership whose capital would be used to purchase liquor. The limited partners would be individual consumers of alcoholic beverages. The partnership would enter into storage and service agreements with various private clubs to store the liquor and serve it to the partners upon proof of identification. Is the activity a legal limited partnership? Why or why not?

6. Lane and Louis were limited partners in a real estate venture. After the business was in financial difficulty, these limited partners had two meetings with the general partners to discuss the problems of the venture. In addition, Lane visited the construction site and "obnoxiously" complained about the work that was being conducted. Do these actions constitute taking part in the control of the business so that the limited partners become liable as general partners? Explain.

7. Gerald and Lionel purchased a tavern. They orally agreed that Lionel would manage the business at a stated salary and receive 50 percent of all profits for his interest as a *limited* partner. Subsequently, the Internal Revenue Service assessed a deficiency in cabaret taxes in the amount of $46,000. Lionel contended that since he was a limited partner, he was not personally liable for the taxes. Is Lionel correct? Explain.

8. Vaughan is a limited partner in the Grand Limited Partnership, a real estate syndication. He purchased his interest for $5,000 when the partnership was created. The partnership has prospered, and Vogel has offered to buy Vaughan's limited partnership interest for $6,500. The general partners are opposed to the sale because they dislike Vogel. Is Vaughan entitled to sell the interest without the consent of the general partners? Why or why not?

9. An injured worker filed an unemployment compensation claim against his corporate employer. The employer challenged the claim before the appropriate state agency. The president and sole stockholder attended the proceedings and sought to cross-examine the claimant and to argue the case. The agency refused to allow him to do so because he was not a licensed attorney. Was the agency's action correct? Explain.

10. John Thompson and Richard Allenby wish to enter the camping equipment manufacturing business. If the following facts exist, which type of business organization would be most advantageous?
    a. Thompson is an expert in the field of camping gear production and sale but has no funds. Allenby knows nothing about such production but is willing to contribute all necessary capital.
    b. Camping gear production requires large amounts of capital, much more than Thompson and Allenby can raise personally or together, yet they wish to control the business.
    c. Some phases of production and sale are rather dangerous, and a relatively large number of tort judgments may be anticipated.
    d. Sales will be nationwide.
    e. Thompson and Allenby are both sixty-five years old. No profits are expected for at least five years, and interruption of the business before that time would make it a total loss.

f. Several other persons wish to put funds into the business but are unwilling to assume personal liability.

g. The anticipated earnings over cost, at least for the first few years, will be approximately $70,000. Thompson and Allenby wish to draw salaries of $25,000 each; they also want a hospitalization and retirement plan, all to be paid from these earnings.

h. A loss is expected for the first three years, owing to the initial capital outlay and the difficulty in entering the market.

8 LEGAL ASPECTS OF INTERNATIONAL BUSINESS

CHAPTER OUTLINE

CHAPTER PREVIEW

The laws regulating international business transactions have a broad impact. As markets become increasingly globalized, businesses of all sizes become international. The transfer of goods, services, and human resources across national boundaries is no longer the exclusive domain of large multinational enterprises and transnational corporations. International business law can affect any business entity with a variety of relationships that transcend national boundaries.

For purposes of legal regulation, an *international business entity* (IBE) can be defined as any business entity with relationships that transcend national boundaries. The business entity could be a sole proprietorship, a partnership, or a corporation. A sole proprietor will need to get an export license to export certain types of goods in the same way that a large corporation would. A partnership should be aware of the restrictions of the Foreign Corrupt Practices Act even if this partnership does not meet the Department of Commerce definition of a multinational enterprise. There is a legal significance in even the simplest relationship that transcends national boundaries. Merely providing product information to a customer in another country has legal consequences.

Regulation of an IBE takes place at several levels: home country regulation, host country regulation, regional regulation, and international regulation. *Home country regulation* refers to the laws of the country where the IBE has its principal place of business or is incorporated. For purposes of this chapter, we will assume that the IBE has its principal place of business in the United States or was incorporated in one of the states of the United States. In this case, home country control includes state and federal regulation of the IBE. *Host country regulation* refers to the legal system and laws of the foreign jurisdiction. For our purposes, this would refer to the laws of any country other than the United States. *Regional regulation* refers to the laws of groups of nations that have banded together for a particular purpose. The rules governing the European Community are of particular importance. Finally, *international regulation* of IBEs includes public international law, such as the various codes of conduct for multinational enterprises, as well as private international law, including the Convention on International Sale of Goods.

■ BUSINESS MANAGEMENT DECISION

Your company, located in California, manufactures fabric that changes color when exposed to heat. You have received an order for this fabric from a clothing manufacturer in a small Asian country, and you believe this will provide a lucrative market for your product.

What type of organization would you use to conduct this international business transaction? What are some of the clauses you would need in a contract covering this transaction?

INTERNATIONAL BUSINESS TRANSACTIONS

1. Comparative Legal Systems and International Law

Comparative law is the study of different legal systems. The United States and Great Britain have common-law legal systems. This refers to the source of law—where the law is found and how it is developed. The other major legal systems are referred to as civil law. These legal systems are based on codes, such as the Napoleonic codes or Roman codes.

Some of the major differences between a common-law system and a civil-law system include the use of precedents, or previous court decisions, and the purpose of judicial proceedings. In civil-law jurisdictions, the use of previous court decisions is very limited. Previous court decisions are not extensively reported, nor are they used to control the outcome of a similar case.

Judicial proceedings are also seen as having different purposes. A common-law trial could be considered a search for justice, while a civil-law trial is a search for the truth. Judges in a civil-law trial take an active role in questioning the witnesses, and the process is not adversarial.

One of the first questions that arises when IBEs are doing business in foreign countries is, How do the IBEs find legal help? Obviously, the legal system is different, and it may be difficult to find someone who is an expert in a particular area. One place to look is in the United States, since many U.S. law firms specialize in international business. Some of these law firms are very country specific in that they have people on their staff who have worked in a foreign country, lived in that country, or come from that country; or these law firms have offices in various countries. These firms can use their expertise or can refer the matter to an office that they have in the foreign country.

Another approach to finding out about host country law is to contact a local attorney in the host country. One way to find an attorney in the foreign country is to contact the U.S. consulate or U.S. embassy in that country. They maintain lists of attorneys who speak English and who have some familiarity with U.S. law, as well as their own country's law. An IBE can also contact U.S. banks that conduct international business and can ask them to recommend a foreign attorney. Even a large accounting firm could give such referrals. If an IBE contacts a foreign attorney, it may still need to contact or retain a U.S. attorney to act as an interpreter of complex legal concepts. There is an advantage to contacting an international law firm, since its attorneys would be able to interface with the attorneys overseas.

Many people engaged in an international business view international law as being something of interest to academics, but with no practical business application. **International law** refers to the body of rules and regulations, usually in the form of treaties and conventions, regulating relationships between nations. International law is sometimes referred to as "the law of war and peace." There are, however, areas of international law that have a direct impact on IBE activities. Furthermore, this impact appears to be increasing.

International law is a law of consent. International law is only binding on those who agree to be bound, and the entities that lay down the law are the entities that are governed by it. Many would argue that international law has no power because there is no mechanism for enforcement, such as a police force or an international army. In this sense, however, international law can be compared with domestic contract law. Contract law is also the law of consent in that a person is not bound by contract law unless he or she agrees to be bound. If one party to the contract breaches the contract, the remedy is usually monetary damages, and not the possibility that the police will knock on the door with an arrest warrant for breaching the contract.

International law, however, rarely speaks clearly. It is not effective in areas where one nation is required to impair its vital interest. In other areas, such as setting standards for weights and measures, setting international standards for telecommunications, and regulating international aviation, as well as other matters dealing with health and safety, international treaties and international law have proved to be effective.

Private international law refers to the process of unification of law among nations, as well as the formation of substantive rules that affect private parties. Although treaties on private international law matters are entered into between nations, the impact is felt by individuals. For example, work is being done to de-

International law The body of rules, regulations, treaties, and conventions that govern the relationship between nations.

velop an international will as well as a treaty to deal with the issues of custody of minor children.

2. Conflict-of-Laws Principles and International Litigation

If a dispute arises during an international business transaction, there may be some confusion as to which country's laws will apply in settling the dispute. Just as the laws may vary from state to state in the United States, the laws of different countries and legal systems may be in conflict. The body of law known as conflict-of-laws or choice-of-laws helps answer the question of which country's law will apply to the dispute.

As discussed in section 4, the parties to a contract can specify in the contract that the law of a particular country will apply to a dispute arising from the contract. This is known as a choice-of-law clause. As a practical matter, however, the court of a particular country is best able to apply its own law to a case brought before it. If there is no choice-of-law clause in a contract, then the court will apply its own country's conflict-of-laws principles in deciding which law will apply. This can be a complicated process.

If a lawsuit is brought in a foreign country court, the judgment will be enforceable in that country. However, it is not always clear whether a foreign country judgment can be enforced in another country. Judgments of U.S. courts are generally not enforceable in other countries unless certain conditions are met. In the United States, foreign country judgments will generally be enforced unless there are strong public policy reasons against their enforcement.

3. Methods of Conducting International Business

International business relationships take many forms. A business does not have to be a certain size or have several offices. Any one of the following methods can be used to facilitate the movement of information, goods, services, capital, or people across national boundaries.

INFORMATION/LIAISON OFFICE.   An information or liaison office is the simplest involvement in international business. This involves setting up an office in a foreign country for the sole purpose of conveying information or answering questions. An information/liaison office does not provide any services or sell any goods. The sole purpose of the office is to distribute pamphlets, brochures, and timetables or to report any questions or concerns that a customer might have. For example, airline companies set up these types of offices in countries where they have no landing rights and conduct no business. Manufacturers also find these types of offices useful in monitoring the market for their products.

The legal significance of an information/liaison office is that the office does not, as a general rule, constitute a "presence" in the foreign country. The foreign country has no jurisdiction over the IBE using such an office. To be sued in the foreign country, another basis of jurisdiction must be found. Host country regulations as to the rental of office space and employment of persons in that office will apply.

IMPORT/EXPORT.   In the most basic import or export operation, only the goods or the product crosses national boundaries. While orders can be taken and goods shipped without any person leaving the United States, these transactions are the subject of import regulations and quotas, customs duties, and export controls, as well as the laws governing product liability in both the home and the host country. In most circumstances, a simple import/export transaction does not constitute a presence as a basis of jurisdiction in the foreign country.

DISTRIBUTORSHIPS, SALES REPRESENTATIVES, AND SALES AGENTS.   A more complex export transaction involves the use of individuals or sales organizations to sell the product in the foreign country. The three basic types of sales relationships are distributorships, sales representatives, and sale agents. Although these entities may have different designations in different countries, the basic description and legal consequences are fairly consistent.

A distributorship relationship involves the sale of goods to an individual or sales organization that, in turn, resells the product in the foreign country. The relationship between the IBE and the distributor is governed by a contract typically known as a *distributorship agreement*. Ownership of the goods or title passes to the distributor, so this relationship does not constitute a presence as a basis of jurisdiction in the foreign country. Some host countries have laws that make it difficult to terminate distributorships without just cause.

A sales representative is a person who takes orders for the product and then transmits these orders to the manufacturer. A sales representative does not take title to the goods, cannot bind the manufacturer contractually, and is not an employee of the manufacturer. The sales representative receives a commission based on the value of the goods shipped.

A sales agent is an employee of the IBE in the foreign country. A sales agent can bind the IBE contractually and be sued in the foreign country on behalf of the IBE. A sales agent does constitute a presence in the foreign country, and the foreign country can exercise jurisdiction over the IBE through the sales agent. Some countries, such as Saudi Arabia, require that all business transactions involving foreign companies be done through an appointed sales agent.

LICENSING.   A licensing relationship is based on a contract allowing a foreign individual, firm, or country to use the IBE's intellectual properties. The contract gives permission to use the IBE's patents, trademarks, and/or copyrights in that foreign country. In some instances, the contract allows the foreign firm to manufacture and sell the IBE's goods in that country for a royalty payment. Royalties are payments made in exchange for permission to use someone's intellectual properties. A licensing arrangement allows the IBE to enter a foreign market without a substantial investment, and without creating a presence and a basis for jurisdiction. Some host countries, however, do not have the same protection for patents, copyrights, or trademarks as in the United States, and some countries even restrict the amount that can be paid to the IBE as royalties.

DIRECT INVESTMENT.   There are four types of direct investment: portfolio, branch, subsidiary, and joint venture.

1. *Portfolio investment.* Portfolio investment is simply the investment of money in the securities of a foreign country. Perhaps not technically considered an international business transaction, both home country and host country laws apply to the transaction. Of particular importance are the laws of the host country governing the investment of capital by people who are not nationals of that country. These regulations may include restricting the ability to repatriate profits or transfer currency into and out of that country.

2. *Branch.* A branch is an entity in the host country whose identity is not separate from the IBE. A branch is merely an arm of the IBE, completely owned by the IBE, and does not take on any special form in the foreign country. The branch may perform the same services, manufacture similar products, or sell the same goods as the company in the home country. By merely being an extension of the IBE, the branch functions as the IBE's presence in the foreign country. The branch can bind the IBE contractually in that if the branch enters into a contract, the contract is deemed to be with the IBE. Similarly, a lawsuit brought against the branch is deemed to be a lawsuit against the IBE.

3. *Subsidiary.* A subsidiary is an entity whose identity is separate from the IBE. A subsidiary takes the form of doing business specified by the laws of the foreign country. Usually, a subsidiary is a corporation incorporated under the laws of the foreign country. Typically, the IBE will own at least 51 percent of the subsidiary's stock. Under some regulations, however, a foreign entity will be deemed to be a subsidiary if the IBE has effective control over the subsidiary. *Effective control* may mean actually controlling the day-to-day operation of the subsidiary or providing the materials needed in manufacturing the product. A subsidiary may constitute the presence of the IBE in the foreign jurisdiction. A contract entered into by the subsidiary may not, however, be binding on the IBE.

4. *Joint venture.* A joint venture is usually considered to be a partnership between two corporations or a partnership between a corporation and a governmental entity. A joint venture is normally set up for a specific purpose or function and for a limited period of time. Some countries, such as China, strongly urge IBEs to make their investment in the form of a joint venture. Because a joint venture is an entity separate and apart from either of the participants, it may not constitute a presence of the IBE in all circumstances, nor will the IBE be bound by a contract entered into by the joint venture.

4. International Contracts

International business transactions often involve a variety of contracts. As previously mentioned, these might include contracts for the leasing of office space, employment contracts, licensing contracts, distributorship contracts, sales representative contracts, or agency contracts. Furthermore, contracts may be for the purchase of raw materials as well as the sale of finished products. Contracts may also include joint venture contracts or contracts for the purchase or sale of goods between a branch, a subsidiary, and the parent company.

As a general rule, parties to an international business contract must deal with many of the same considerations that they would with a domestic contract. However, because the parties are dealing with different legal systems, customs, and languages, additional terms must be negotiated. Some contract clauses to be considered in an international contract include (1) choice of language, (2) terms of payment, (3) force majeure, (4) government approval, (5) arbitration clause, (6) choice of forum, and (7) choice of law.

A *choice of language clause* will designate the official language that will be used for the contract document itself. It will also designate the language of interpretation if a dispute arises concerning the contract. If the contract is written in more than one language, problems can arise as to the meaning of the terms used. A contract might be translated into another language for convenience, but the meaning of the terms may also change with the translation. For convenience, the official language of the contract and the language of interpretation are usually the same.

A *term of payment clause* is not uncommon in any contract. In an international contract, however, this clause is important to designate the currency to be used in payment as well as the location of payment. It is possible to limit the risk of currency fluctuations through the purchase of futures contracts, but this can only be effective if the currency payment is designated. The location of payment is also important in that some currencies are not permitted to be repatriated. This means that some types of currencies cannot leave the particular foreign country. If payment is to be made in U.S. dollars, payable in the foreign country, the IBE must be careful to ensure that the dollars can be taken out of the country. Similarly, if payment is to be made in the local currency, the IBE must ensure that the local currency can be taken back to the home country.

A *force majeure clause* is often a part of international business contracts. The term *force majeure* refers to a "superior power." Typically, this type of clause excuses nonperformance under specified circumstances. A force majeure clause may designate natural disasters such as floods, storms, earthquakes, or "acts of God" as an excuse for nonperformance. This type of clause may also designate political unrest, including war, riots, police action, or strikes, to excuse nonperformance. A force majeure clause may even include such occurrences as runaway inflation, dramatic currency devaluations, or stock market collapse as an excuse for nonperformance. In a force majeure clause, however, it is important to establish a standard such as the length of time or severity of the occurrence. It is also important to include a provision for recourse in the case of partial performance.

An international contract involves governmental regulation at several levels. As a result, it is important to include a *government approval clause*. Such a clause would specify which party is responsible for getting the necessary licenses, permits, or government permission for the transaction.

Arbitration clauses are becoming more familiar in domestic contracts, but they are regularly used in international contracts. A *mandatory* arbitration clause specifies that arbitration is required as an attempt to resolve a contractual dispute before the filing of any lawsuit. A *binding* arbitration clause specifies that the parties will be bound to follow any arbitration decision. An arbitration clause could also specify which arbitration rules would apply and where the arbitration would take place. There are several bodies that deal with international arbitration. The American Arbitration Association has rules and facilities for international arbitration, as do the International Chamber of Commerce and the Swedish Chamber of Commerce. The International Center for the Settlement of Investment Disputes has arbitration rules and facilities for certain kinds of arbitration, as does the United Nations Commission on International Trade Law, UNCITRAL. As the following case illustrates, U.S. courts will enforce these types of arbitration clauses in international contracts.

CASE

Scherk v. Alberto-Culver Co.
United States Supreme Court 417 U.S. 506 (1974)

STEWART, J.

Alberto-Culver Co., the respondent, is an American company incorporated in Delaware with its principal office in Illinois. It manufactures and distributes toiletries and hair products in this country and abroad. During the 1960's Alberto-Culver decided to expand its overseas operations, and as part of this program it approached the petitioner Fritz Scherk, a German citizen residing at the time of trial in Switzerland. Scherk was the owner of three interrelated business entities, organized under the laws of Germany and Liechtenstein, that were engaged in the manufacture of toiletries and the licensing of trademarks for such toiletries. . . . In February 1969 a contract was signed in Vienna, Austria, which provided for the transfer of the ownership of Scherk's enterprises to Alberto-Culver, along with all rights held by these enterprises to trademarks in cosmetic goods. The contract contained a number of express warranties whereby Scherk guaranteed the sole and unencumbered ownership of these trademarks. In addition, the contract contained an arbitration clause providing that "any controversy or claim |that| shall arise out of this agreement or the breach thereof" would be referred to arbitration before the International Chamber of Commerce in Paris, France, and that "|t|he laws of the State of Illinois, U. S. A. shall apply to and govern this agreement, its interpretation and performance."

The closing of the transaction took place in Geneva, Switzerland, in June 1969. Nearly one year later Alberto-Culver allegedly discovered that the trademark rights purchased under the contract were subject to substantial encumbrances that threatened to give others superior rights to the trademarks and to restrict or preclude Alberto-Culver's use of them. Alberto-Culver thereupon tendered back to Scherk the property that had been transferred to it and offered to rescind the contract. Upon Scherk's refusal, Alberto-Culver commenced this action for damages and other relief in a Federal District Court in Illinois, contending that Scherk's fraudulent representations concerning the status of the trademark rights constituted violations of § 10(b) of the Securities Exchange Act of 1934, and Rule 10b-5 promulgated thereunder.

In response, Scherk filed a motion to dismiss the action for want of personal and subject-matter jurisdiction as well as on the basis of *forum non conveniens*, or, alternatively, to stay the action pending arbitration in Paris pursuant to the agreement of the parties. . . . On December 2, 1971, the District Court denied Scherk's motion to dismiss, and, on January 14, 1972, it granted a preliminary order enjoining Scherk from proceeding with arbitration. . . . The Court of Appeals for the Seventh Circuit, with one judge dissenting, affirmed. . . .

The United States Arbitration Act, reversing centuries of judicial hostility to arbitration agreements, was designed to allow parties to avoid "the costliness and delays of litigation," and to place arbitration agreements "upon the same footing as other contracts. . . . Accordingly, the Act provides that an arbitration agreement such as is here involved "shall be valid, irrevocable, and enforceable, save upon such grounds as exist at law or in equity for the revocation of any contract." . . .

Alberto-Culver's contract to purchase the business entities belonging to Scherk was a truly international agreement. . . . |M|ost significantly, the subject matter of the contract concerned the sale of business enterprises organized under the laws of and primarily situated in European countries, whose activities were largely, if not entirely, directed to European markets. . . .

In this case . . . in the absence of the arbitration provision considerable uncertainty existed at the time of the agreement, and still exists, concerning the law applicable to the resolution of disputes arising out of the contract.

Such uncertainty will almost inevitably exist with respect to any contract touching two or more countries, each with its own substantive laws and conflict-of-laws rules. A contractual provision specifying in advance the forum in which disputes shall be litigated and the law to be applied is, therefore, an almost indispensable precondition to achievement of the orderliness and predictability essential to any international business transaction. Furthermore, such a provision obviates the danger that a dispute under the agreement might be submitted to a forum hostile to the interests of one of the parties or unfamiliar with the problem area involved. . . .

An agreement to arbitrate before a specified tribunal is, in effect, a specialized kind of forum-selection clause that posits not only the situs of suit but also the procedure to be used in resolving the dispute. The invalidation of such an agreement in the case before us would not only allow the respondent to repudiate its solemn promise but would, as well, reflect a "parochial concept that all disputes must be resolved under our laws and in our courts. . . . We cannot have trade and commerce in world markets and international waters exclusively on our terms, governed by our laws, and resolved in our courts. . . . Accordingly, the judgment of the Court of Appeals is . . .

■ *Reversed and remanded.*

CASE CONCEPTS REVIEW

1. What was the basis for the contract between Alberto-Culver and Scherk?
3. What was the purpose of including an arbitration clause in this contract?
3. What were the legal rulings of the district court and the court of appeals?
4. Why did the Supreme Court reverse the appellate court's ruling?

Parties to an international contract have some flexibility in designating where a lawsuit will be brought in the case of a contract dispute. This is known as a *choice of forum clause*. The parties may choose a country for convenience, for familiarity with the legal process, or for the efficiency of the legal system. If the choice of forum has a rational relationship to the contract or to the contracting parties, these clauses are generally enforceable.

The parties to an international contract can also designate that a particular country's laws will apply to any dispute arising out of the contract. This is known as a *choice of law clause*. The choice of forum and choice of law clauses do not have to designate the same country. A contract can specify that any dispute arising out of the contract will be tried in the United States, but the law of another country will apply. In the United States, the laws of foreign countries are considered issues of fact, and evidence is introduced as to the law of that particular country. As a practical matter, however, courts are usually better equipped to apply the law of their own country to a contract dispute.

In negotiating these various contract clauses, the IBE must be sensitive to the laws and customs of the foreign country. As with all contracts, it is the relationship and not the document that is important. Many international contracts are simple documents consisting of only a few pages. While a contract does not have to include any of the foregoing provisions, an IBE must be aware of the issues raised in these types of clauses.

5. The Multinational Enterprise

Large IBEs with production capabilities in more than one country are often called *multinational corporations* or *multinational enterprises*. The United Nations limits the use of the term *multinational corporation* to those with a parent corporation that has more than one national identity. It refers to other corporations with international production capabilities as *transnational corporations*. These business entities have been the center of controversy and frequently face criticism that they are international villains and exploiters.

Multinational enterprises face criticism in three areas. They are perceived as (1) having excessive market control, (2) having excessive political control, and (3) having a worldwide profit-maximizing point of view.

The perception that multinational enterprises exercise market control is really a restatement of the reasons why multinationals set up subsidiaries in foreign markets. Multinationals seek to take advantage of existing markets, whether for raw materials, labor, capital, or finished products. If, however, the multinational seeks to take full advantage of the markets it finds in the host country jurisdiction, then it may be faced with accusations of exploiting the foreign market.

The second area of criticism of multinationals is the political power they exercise. Much of this criticism stems from U.S. activity in Latin America during the 1970s and from disclosures linking U.S. covert actions with business organizations. It is also the case that some less developed countries' governments encourage multinational investment by offering corporate incentives. This may create a dependency between the government and the multinational to ensure that the business venture is successful and that the multinational remains in the country.

The third area of criticism is the worldwide profit-maximizing point of view of large multinationals. The common perception is that the multinational makes decisions based on a global perspective rather than on a country-by-country basis. An operation may be closed down in one country even if it is beneficial to the country if it does not fit into the multinational's overall goals. As a result, multinationals have gained a reputation for being more concerned with global profit than with local needs and benefits.

Multinational enterprises consider this criticism unfair. Multinationals provide employment and training, goods, and services to the host population and may assume investment risks that might not otherwise be undertaken. Furthermore, host countries do exercise control of multinationals in a variety of ways. The following regulations of international business do not always make it easy for them to operate.

REGULATING INTERNATIONAL BUSINESS

6. Introduction

An IBE is affected by laws and regulations from many sources, not just the laws of its home country or state. Of course, an IBE must comply with the laws of the city, county, state, and nation that is considered its home or principal place of doing business. An IBE must also comply with the laws and regulations of the host country or jurisdiction. If the host country is a member of a regional organizational structure, such as the European Community, these laws must also be observed. Finally, international regulations such as treaties or conventions may have an impact on the IBE and its business enterprise. The remainder of this chapter examines these different sources or levels of regulations.

7. International Controls

International agreements, treaties, and conventions are becoming increasingly important to IBEs. The scope of international conventions is no longer limited to relationships between governments.

Of particular interest to IBEs is the Convention on International Sale of Goods, to which the U.S. Senate gave its advice and consent in 1987. The Convention on International Sale of Goods is a type of international uniform commercial code. In fact, the Uniform Commercial Code was used as a model for the Convention. The Convention applies to sales transactions between two parties in different countries if each country has ratified it. The convention does not apply to the sale of goods to consumers. The two parties to the transaction can agree that the Convention will not apply to the transaction, but if they do not reach such an agreement, the convention is applicable. The Convention deals with issues of contract formation as well as to obligations and remedies available to parties to the transaction.

A major international institution that affects international business is the General Agreement on Tariffs and Trade (GATT). The GATT was set up in 1947 as a temporary arrangement pending the formation of an international trade organization. It has remained, however, as an important instrument for the liberalization of international trade policies. The purpose of the GATT is to reduce or eliminate trade barriers, such as tariffs, quantity restrictions, and nontariff barriers to trade. The process is one of multilateral tariff reduction negotiations. The primary principles of reciprocity and nondiscrimination are carried out through the use of most-favored-nation clauses.

Several other international bodies seek to control the activities of IBEs through the use of codes of conduct. It can be argued that these codes of conduct have no binding effect on the activities of IBEs; however, the negotiation process itself does lead to increased sensitivity of the issues involved on the part of all negotiating parties. The Tripartite Declaration of Principles Concerning Multi-National Enterprises and Social Policies was adopted by the International Labor Organization. This declaration deals with issues of labor relations, such as working conditions, training, and employment. It also deals with issues of social policy. The United Nations General assembly passed a resolution adopting the Restrictive Business Practices Code. The purpose of this code is to protect competition as well as social welfare and consumer interests. The code covers price fixing and refusals to deal, as well as mergers and trademark protection. The United Nations Conference on Trade and Development is working on an international code of conduct for the transfer of technology. One purpose of this code is to set up standards for technology transfer with respect to the interest of developing nations.

The Organization of Economic Cooperation and Development (OECD) has issued Guidelines for International Investment and Multi-National Enterprises. The member governments of the OECD have adopted guidelines regarding the disclosure of information by IBEs, competition, employment and industrial relationships, financing, and taxation. These guidelines set standards for IBEs that include refraining from restrictive business activities and respecting the rights of employees to be represented by trade unions, and they provide information regarding the IBE's activities and policies. Finally, the United National Commission on Trans-National Corporations is drafting a code of conduct. This is one of the broadest and most comprehensive codes of conduct dealing with the activities of IBEs. The code contains provisions regarding disclosing information, respecting human rights, and refraining from corrupt practices. It also sets guidelines for ownership and control, taxation, consumer protection, environmental protection, and transfer of technology.

8. Host Country Regulations

Host countries are the foreign countries in which the IBEs are doing business. Host countries have a variety of ways to regulate the conduct of IBEs. The following are types of regulations or controls an IBE may encounter in a host country. While specific regulations vary from country to country, these are the types of regulations that can affect the profitability of an international enterprise.

One of the ways of regulating the activities of business entities is by exclusionary techniques upon entry. This means that a host country can keep the international business entity out of the host country. Host countries can prohibit any business activity within their jurisdiction.

The second way of regulating is conditional entry. An IBE may be allowed to enter the foreign country but under certain conditions. These conditions might be that the IBE must do business as a joint venture, or that 50 percent of the business must be owned by a host country national, or that within a certain number of years the firm will be turned over to the host country. The host country sets the conditions at the beginning.

The third method of regulating an IBE is by control over capital movements. This refers to the type of currency that can be brought into the host country and what currency can be removed. This raises several questions that the IBE must answer. Where is the IBE going to get the funding for the project? Must the capital come from a national or from a specific government-run or -owned bank? Can the IBE bring certain currencies into the country? Can the IBE take certain currencies out of the country? Is there repatriation of profits? Can the IBE convert the currency in the host country dollars? Control over capital movements can have a big impact on the profitability of the enterprise.

A closely related type of regulation is tax legislation. Tax legislation can be very favorable (e.g., tax holidays, tax credits, and favorable tax rates). Tax legislation can start out favorably and then have an adverse impact on the business. For example, in Lebanon if you receive tax credits for five years, then you must continue to do business there for another five years. The regulation can be favorable tax terms as well as negative tax terms.

The fifth way of regulating is control through disclosure legislation. Reporting requirements to the host country might include who the IBEs hire, how much money they pay, what their future plans are, or what their secret processes might be. If an IBE has to disclose a certain amount of information, this will have an impact on how the IBE is going to conduct itself in the host country. In the United States, there are reporting requirements to the Securities and Exchange Commission and the Internal Revenue Service.

In the European Community and in Germany in particular, specific disclosure requirements take the form of mandatory worker representation and participation on boards of directors. This may not appear to be a form of disclosure. However, if there are employees on the board of directors, the employees will know about the decisions of the board of directors. Knowledge of the decisions will affect the types of decisions the board makes.

Another form of control similar to our antitrust laws is merger legislation. This type of legislation may control what businesses the foreign firm can buy, what firms the foreign firm can take over, and whether or not the foreign firm can merge with an existing firm.

One of the major ways that host countries control the activities of international businesses is through nationalization. **Nationalization** is the taking of property by the host country government. There are two types of nationalizations. One type of nationalization is called *expropriation*. The second type of nationalization is called a *confiscation*.

Expropriation is defined as a legal taking of property. An unlawful taking is known as a **confiscation**. Who defines legal taking? This is a question of international law and also a question about which the United States and other countries do not agree. A legal taking, according to the U.S. standard, is a taking for a public purpose for which just compensation has been paid. Most countries agree with this. The problem is in defining *just compensation*.

The U.S. government defines *just compensation* as "prompt, effective and adequate compensation." Other countries apply what is known as the Calvo doctrine, which holds that a foreign firm should not be treated any differently than the nationals of the host country. For example, if the host country determines that no compensation will be paid for any nationalized property, then a U.S. IBE would not be entitled to any compensation.

A U.S. firm is entitled to file a complaint with the State Department if the firm has been nationalized or property has been taken. This is a political process, not a judicial proceeding. If the State Department decides not to pursue the claim, there is no appeal. If the State Department decides to pursue the claim, it will proceed on the firm's behalf. The State Department can freeze assets held in the United States by the nationalizing host country. If any compensation is recovered from the host country, the compensation goes through the Foreign Claims Settlement Commission. The firm must present evidence to the Foreign Claims Settle-

Nationalization The taking of property or control of a private enterprise by the government.

Expropriation A nationalization or taking of property by the government that is recognized as legal.

Confiscation A nationalization or taking of property by the government that is not recognized as legal under international law.

ment Commission, and a determination will be made as to how much the firm is entitled.

The final way of controlling the activities of the international business entity is closely related to nationalization. It is known as *creeping expropriation*, and it occurs when the host country does not nationalize all of the holdings at one time. Instead, the host country makes it so difficult for the firm to operate that the host country may as well have taken it all. The host country can set up controls, laws, and restrictions so the firm must get government approval at every turn. The host country may also restrict where the IBE purchases its supplies, sells its product, or at what price. Creeping expropriation is not recognized under international law. The United States does recognize creeping expropriation and would like to establish some compensation for it, since it is the slow taking over of the assets of a firm.

The aforementioned regulations suggest what host countries can do to control the activities of international business entities. International business entities must be aware of these regulations when undertaking business ventures in foreign countries.

9. Regional Regulation—The European Community

The European Community is an example of regional regulation of IBEs. The European Community consists of three separate communities—the European Coal and Steel Community, the European Atomic Energy Community, and the European Economic Community—that were combined in 1967 into the European Communities. The Single European Act was adopted in 1986, which set the groundwork for achieving a unified internal market by 1992. The goals of the Single European Act were to achieve full economic integration of the European Community and to lay the foundation for monetary and political unity.

The laws that the European Community and the member nations pass to implement the Single European Act will have a great impact on the nations that trade with the European Community. International Business Entities must pay attention to the antitrust rules and regulations that have been enforced as Articles 85 and 86 of the Treaty of Rome. In some circumstances, the antitrust laws of the European Community are more restrictive than those of the United States. The freedom of movement of goods and workers between member states will also affect the way international business is conducted with the European Community.

10. Import Controls

As the value of the dollar fluctuates with respect to foreign currencies, the cost of foreign products imported into the United States changes. As a result, U.S. manufacturers are experiencing increased competition both in the United States and in foreign markets. In some cases, however, the cost of imports is much less than would be justified by the exchange rate. Foreign manufacturers sometimes price their U.S. products to capture a large share of the market. When foreign goods are priced extremely low with the purpose of capturing a large market share, this is known as *dumping*. United States manufacturers are unable to compete against such extremely low-priced imports and in many cases are forced to go out of business. The danger exists that once the foreign manufacturer has captured a large enough market share, it will be able to raise the price of these products to an extremely high level, injuring the U.S. consumer. Although some relief from this type of activity can be found in the U.S. antitrust laws, such relief involves an extremely long and expensive process. Title VII of the United States Tariff Act provides some relief for U.S. manufacturers from this type of activity.

The Tariff Act provides for the imposition of countervailing duties or antidumping duties to counteract the effect of foreign goods being sold at below their fair value. A U.S. manufacturer must file a complaint with the U.S. Department of Commerce's International Trade Administration, and with the International Trade Commission. The Department of Commerce makes a determination of whether or not the goods were sold at below fair value. This may mean that the goods are being sold in the United States at below cost of production or at below the price charged in the home market. The International Trade Commission then makes a determination as to whether or not this has resulted in material injury to the U.S. industry involved. If only one or two U.S. manufacturers are being injured by these import practices, relief will not be given. Industrywide injury must be found.

If the Department of Commerce and the International Trade Commission determine that the goods are sold at an unfairly low price and that industry injury has occurred as a result of foreign government subsidies, they can make a determination to impose countervailing duties. These duties are designed to counteract the government subsidies. As this is an issue between two governments and may involve highly sensitive foreign policy questions, both the procedure and the determination are taken out of the hands of the complaining U.S. manufacturer. If the unfairly low price is not a result of government subsidies, then relief takes the form of antidumping duties. A determination to impose, or not to impose, antidumping duties can be appealed by the complaining party.

The following case illustrates the method used by the International Trade Administration to calculate the fair value of products being sold in the United States.

CASE

Smith-Corona Group v. United States
713 F.2d 1568 (Fed. Cir. 1983)

SMITH, J.

This appeal presents a challenge to various price adjustments granted to the foreign manufacturers and importers of the subject merchandise by the U.S. International Trade Administration (ITA) in determining antidumping duties under 19 U.S.C. §§ 1673 *et seq....*

Appellant, Smith-Corona Group, Consumer Products Division, SCM Corporation (Smith-Corona), is the last remaining domestic manufacturer of portable electric typewriters. Brother Industries, Ltd., and Brother International Corp. (collectively Brother), are, respectively, a Japanese manufacturer and an importer of portable electric typewriters from Japan. Intervenors, Silver Seiko, Ltd., and Silver Reed America, Inc. (collectively Silver), also are, respectively, a Japanese manufacturer and an importer of the subject merchandise from Japan....

The Antidumping Act provides that if foreign merchandise is sold or is likely to be sold in the United States at less than its *fair value* to the material injury of a United States industry, then an additional antidumping duty shall be imposed. The amount of the duty shall equal the amount by which the *foreign market value* exceeds the United States price for the merchandise....

United States price, as defined in section 1677a, is computed by one of two methods: purchase price or exporter's sales price....

Where the importer is an unrelated independent party, purchase price is used. Purchase price is the actual or agreed-to price between the foreign producer and the independent importer, prior to the time of importation. Where the importer is related, an arm's length transaction does not occur until the goods are resold to a retailer or to the public. In that case, "exporter's sales price" is used. Exporter's sales price is the price at which the goods are eventually transferred in an arm's length transaction, whether from the importer to an independent retailer or directly to the public....

On the other side of the scale, foreign market value is also computed on the basis of arm's length transactions by one of three methods (1) home market sales; (2) third country sales; or (3) constructed value. The home market sales method is preferred. . . .

Thus, the ITA, using either purchase price or exporter's sales price, computes and adjusts the United States price of the merchandise. Additionally, the ITA, on the basis of either home market sales, or third country sales, or constructed value, computes and adjusts the foreign market value of the merchandise. These values, which *should* be on an equivalent basis after adjustment, are then compared and the amount by which foreign market value exceeds United States price is imposed as an additional antidumping duty. . . .

Our review of the statute reveals tremendous deference to the expertise of the Secretary of Commerce in administering the antidumping law. We find no specific limitation in the statute, nor do we find any evidence of record, that would compel reversal of the ITA's determinations in this proceeding. . . .

■ *Affirmed.*

CASE CONCEPTS REVIEW

1. What is the purpose of the antidumping duty?
2. How does the ITA determine the amount of this duty?
3. To what extent does the court review the ITA's decision?

11. Export Controls

The U.S. government has a long history of controlling what goods are exported from the United States. It would not be too gross an exaggeration to say that nothing can be sent out of the United States without government permission. In reality, the permission takes the form of an export license. There are two types of export licenses. One is called a *general license*, which the exporter essentially issues to itself. The exporter must use the proper license designation for the type of good to be exported and the country of destination, but there is no special procedure for doing this. The other type of license, known as a *validated license*, is issued by the government and does require a special procedure.

Under the Export Administration Act of 1979, amended in 1984, the President has the power to control the export of goods and commodities for one of the following four reasons: (1) national security, (2) foreign policy, (3) commodities in short supply, and (4) nuclear nonproliferation. Under this authority, several administrative agencies restrict the export of certain commodities through the use of validated licenses. Validated licenses are issued based on two criteria: (1) the type of product, and (2) the ultimate destination of the product. Certain types of products cannot be exported because of their high level of technology or their strategic or military purpose. The most extensive list of controlled or restrictive commodities is the Commodities Control List, which is maintained by the Department of Commerce, Office of Export Administration. This list was developed by the United States and sixteen allies. These countries belong to an organization called the Coordinating Committee for Multinational Export Controls (COCOM). There are some countries for which COCOM has created only a few export restrictions, but there are other countries to which virtually nothing can be exported. The countries to which goods are exported are divided into seven categories. The country with the least restrictions is Canada, to which almost anything can be exported. The most restrictive countries include Cuba, North Korea, Vietnam, and Kampuchea.

One controversial aspect of these export controls is known as *end-user's certification*. In applying for a validated license, the exporter must certify who the ultimate end user of the product will be and the country of destination. If an exporter sells a product to a customer in Canada, and the Canadian customer re-exports the product to an unauthorized end user or destination, the U.S. exporter could be charged with violating the Export Administration Act. Although the U.S. exporter may have no further control over the product, the exporter is still responsible for the ultimate destination of the product under this act. Criminal and civil penalties could apply to any violation. Although enforcement of this provision may seem difficult, it is not impossible. A violation may be reported by a disgruntled employee, a competitor, or even by the exporter.

The following case is an example of the broad impact of export controls. In this case, the unlicensed goods never left the United States, but had only been checked as luggage at the airport.

CASE

United States v. One 1980 Mercedes Benz 500 SE
772 F.2d 602 (9th Cir. 1985)

BOOCHEVER, J.

This appeal involves the forfeiture of a Mercedes Benz automobile that was used to transport unlicensed electronic testing equipment to Los Angeles International Airport where the equipment was checked as luggage to Zurich, Switzerland. The equipment was required to be licensed if exported to any country but Canada. The car's owner, Dierk Hagemann, contests the forfeiture on the grounds that his vehicle was not used in exporting or attempting to export the unlicensed equipment. . . . The district court granted summary judgment for the government. . . .

On May 28, 1982, Hagemann's wife used the automobile to drive Alfred Kessler and Kessler's two suitcases containing electronic testing equipment to Los Angeles International Airport. She left Kessler at the airport and drove the car home. Kessler then checked his luggage for a TA flight to Zurich, Switzerland at the airline's curbside check-in. The electronic equipment inside the suitcases should have been licensed, in accord with the Controlled Commodities List . . . which requires such equipment to be licensed by the Department of Commerce if exported to any country except Canada, but the equipment was not licensed. Kessler was subsequently convicted in district court of knowingly exporting equipment without a valid export license. . . .

Hagemann was convicted in district court of conspiring with Kessler and one Robert Lambert to knowingly export the equipment without a license. . . .

Hagemann claims that the district court erred in finding that the government was authorized to seize his automobile . . . when it never contained contraband. He reasons that the electronic testing equipment did not become contraband until Kessler tagged his luggage at the airport. On that basis, he claims that since the equipment was legally possessed by Kessler until that time there was no attempt or intent to export. Therefore, his car had not

been used in an illegal exportation that would justify forfeiture. . . . In short, Hagemann purports to establish that the exportation process began at the airport and not before. This is contrary to the law. . . .

First, it is clear that Kessler had the requisite culpable state of mind to export the equipment without a license in violation of the law. The machines were placed in Kessler's suitcases, the suitcases were placed in the car, Kessler and the suitcases were driven to the airport, and Kessler, without deviation proceeded directly to the curbside baggage check-in where the bags were tagged immediately for Zurich. Based on this evidence, it was undisputed that Kessler and the equipment were bound for Zurich, when they entered Hagemann's automobile to be transported to the airport. Hagemann failed to present any evidence to the contrary. Moveover, he, at the time of the forfeiture proceedings, had already been convicted of aiding, abetting, counseling, inducing, and procuring Kessler's illegal exportation of the equipment. This unrefuted evidence and inferences to be drawn from it are sufficient to establish Kessler's unlawful state of mind. . . .

Here the crime is illegal exportation. Exportation occurred as soon as the machines were delivered to a carrier for shipment abroad. . . . In this instance the machines entered the export stream at the baggage check-in at Los Angeles International Airport. It is settled that an international airport is the functional equivalent of a border, and that luggage checked at that point of embarkation is at all times thereafter in international transit. . . . Consequently, it is clear that Kessler attempted to export the machines, and used Hagemann's automobile in that effort. . . .

■ *Affirmed.*

CASE CONCEPTS REVIEW

1. How was Hagemann's car used in exporting equipment without a valid export license?
2. What is the basis of Hagemann's argument that his car never contained contraband?
3. Why does the court reject Hagemann's argument, thereby allowing the government to seize the car?

12. Antitrust Laws

The United States has an extensive system of antitrust laws. Of course, these laws apply to an IBE's activities in the United States. They also apply, however, to an IBE's activities in a foreign country. United States antitrust laws can apply to an IBE's foreign activities even if the foreign country's laws do not prohibit such conduct.

In 1979, the United States Department of Justice issued guidelines for antitrust enforcement for international business activities. Under these guidelines, the Department of Justice indicated that potential violations would be governed by the "rule of reason." This means that the Department of Justice will look at the particular conduct or activity in light of the entire business transaction, including any business justification or the availability of any less restrictive alternatives. Furthermore, the Department will investigate what impact the conduct has in the United States.

The purpose of this type of enforcement of U.S. antitrust laws is to protect two groups: (1) U.S. consumers, and (2) other U.S. exporters. If the conduct of the IBE in the foreign country has an adverse impact on foreign firms that import into the United States, U.S. consumers could be injured. United States consumers benefit from the low cost of imported goods, and if the foreign conduct causes the foreign manufacturer to raise its prices, U.S. impact could be found. Similarly, other U.S. exporters may be trying to enter the foreign country market. If the actions of one U.S. exporter, the IBE, make it difficult or impossible for another U.S. exporter to enter the market, U.S. impact could be found.

The application of U.S. antitrust laws to activities of IBEs that take place in foreign countries is controversial. The application of U.S. law to activities that take place outside of the United States is known as *extraterritoriality*. In enforcing antitrust laws, the United States bases jurisdiction on the citizenship of the IBE, as well as on the adverse impact within U.S. borders.

Affirmative responses to the following questions will result in the United States applying its antitrust laws in situations involving extraterritorial activities:

1. Does the alleged violation affect, or was it intended to affect, the foreign commerce of the United States?
2. Is the activity of the type and magnitude so as to be cognizable as a violation of the antitrust laws?
3. As a matter of international comity and fairness, should the extraterritorial jurisdiction of the United States be asserted to cover the alleged violation?

If any one of these questions is answered in the negative, the antitrust laws will not apply to activities in foreign countries.

13. Foreign Corrupt Practices Act

The Foreign Corrupt Practices Act of 1977 is an amendment to the Securities Exchange Act of 1934. There are two main sections of the Foreign Corrupt Practices Act, one dealing with bookkeeping and reporting requirements and the other dealing with conduct. Under the reporting requirements, any issuer of securities, as defined by the Securities Exchange Act of 1934, must keep its books and records in such a way that they accurately reflect the financial transactions of the issuer. Further, the issuer must establish internal accounting systems that will accurately reflect the assets of the issuer. The purpose behind the recording requirements of the

Foreign Corrupt Practices Act is to make it more difficult for firms to hide questionable payments to foreign government officials. If such payments must be recorded, they are more likely to be discovered. Even firms that are not engaged in international transaction must comply with this section of the Foreign Corrupt Practices Act. A firm could violate the Foreign Corrupt Practices Act by failing to comply with this section, and never actually make any questionable payments. This section of the foreign Corrupt Practices Act is enforced by the Securities and Exchange Commission.

The more controversial section of the Foreign Corrupt Practices Act is that addressing specific conduct. The Foreign Corrupt Practices Act prohibits giving anything of value to a foreign government official to influence a discretionary decision. The phrase *anything of value* includes money, gifts, or anything that would be deemed of value in that particular culture. The phrase *to a foreign government official* refers to individuals acting in their official capacity and to decisions they make that fall within their official functions. If, however, something is given to an individual, and there is a reasonable expectation that it will in turn to be given to a foreign official, this is a violation of the law. The term *discretionary decision* refers to the making of a decision that will assist the firm in obtaining or retaining business.

One important exception to the Foreign Corrupt Practices Act is the "grease payment exception," which means that a firm is allowed to make a payment to expedite a function that does not require a discretionary decision. If a foreign government official, such as a clerk, has the job of stamping documents or processing paperwork, it is possible to make a payment that will expedite the matter. This is particularly true if delay would cause merchandise to be destroyed or damaged as a result of the delay.

The Foreign Corrupt Practices Act is controversial in that it seeks to regulate conduct that takes place outside the boundaries of the United States. Some experts complain that this act puts U.S. businesses at a competitive disadvantage. They further argue that the United States is regulating conduct that may be perfectly legal in the host country. On the other hand, it is argued that questionable payments put other U.S. firms at a competitive disadvantage. Firms that do not make these kinds of payments may be disadvantaged when they attempt to compete in the foreign market. Or they may be disadvantaged in the United States if these questionable payments have made the competitor stronger. In either case, the result is injury to U.S. firms, and this injury occurs in the United States.

The following case illustrates one of the limitations of the Foreign Corrupt Practices Act. An employee cannot be prosecuted for violating the Foreign Corrupt Practices Act if the "employer has not and cannot be convicted of similarly violating" the act.

CASE

United States v. McLean

738 F.2d 655 (5th Cir. 1984)

DAVIS, J.

We are presented for the first time with the question of whether the Foreign Corrupt Practices Act (FCPA) permits the prosecution of an employee for a substantive offense under the Act if his employer has not and cannot be convicted of similarly violating the FCPA. We conclude that the Act prohibits such a prosecution and affirm the district court.

During the late 1970's Petroleos Mexicanos (Pemex), the national petroleum company of Mexico, purchased larger quantities of turbine compressor equipment to capture and pump to processing plants a high volume of natural gas. The Solar division of International Harvester Company (Harvester) was the dominant worldwide supplier of such equipment. George S. McLean was its vice-president and Luis A. Uriarte was its Latin American regional manager; both were Harvester employees. Crawford Enterprises, Inc., (CEI) was a broker and lessor of gas compression systems which frequently purchased equipment from Harvester for resale or lease. Harvester, as prime contractor, had supplied Pemex with equipment in the mid-seventies; during the period of accelerated development in the late 1970's, however, Harvester acted as a subcontractor for CEI, which had contracted with Pemex to build complete compression plants.

In early 1979, the United States initiated grand jury investigations into allegations that American businessmen had bribed Mexican officials in violation of the FCPA. On October 22, 1982, a forty-nine count indictment was returned in federal district court charging CEI and nine individuals, including McLean and Uriarte, with one conspiracy count to use interstate or foreign instrumentalities for the purpose of bribing Pemex officials in violation of 18 U.S.C. § 371 (1966), forty-seven substantive counts in violation of the FCPA, ... Although McLean and Uriarte's employer, Harvester, was not charged in the forty-nine count indictment, the government concedes that all acts of McLean and Uriarte were committed within the scope of their employment with Harvester. . . .

Both McLean and Uriarte filed motions to dismiss the charges pending against them on grounds that the failure of the government to convict Harvester of a violation under the FCPA barred their prosecution. . . .

The substantive violations of the Act are established in two sections. Section 78dd-1 makes it unlawful for an issuer (defined as an entity subject to the securities registration requirements of 78l and 78o of Title 15), its officers, directors, employees or agents, to use the mails or other instrumentality of interstate commerce to bribe foreign officials for various purposes including to obtain business. Section 78dd-2 provides generally the same prohibition for a domestic concern, its officers, directors, shareholders and employees. Domestic concern is broadly defined to include any United States citizen, national or resident; or any corporation (other than an issuer), partnership or other entity subject to United States jurisdiction and control. . . .

A major objective of the Eckhardt amendment is to allow the employee the benefit of the superior resources of the corporation in presenting a defense in the criminal proceeding; a closely related objective is to prevent the employer from making its employee a scapegoat. . . .

We hold that in order to convict an employee under the FCPA for acts committed for the benefit of his employer, the government must first convict the employer. Because the government failed to convict Harvester and under the plea agreement will be unable to indict Harvester and try it with McLean, the Act bars McLean's prosecution.

■ *Affirmed.*

CASE CONCEPTS REVIEW

1. For which company did McLean and Uriarte work?
2. What were the alleged violations committed by these individuals?
3. What is the statutory language relied on by the courts in concluding that employees cannot be convicted of a violation of the Foreign Corrupt Practices Act if their employer has not been convicted?

14. Antiboycott Laws

The antiboycott laws are found in provisions of the Export Administration Act of 1979 and the Internal Revenue Code. Although these provisions are not identical, they are similar enough to be discussed as a whole. Under the antiboycott laws, any "U.S. person" is prohibited from participating or cooperating in an international boycott. The exception to this rule, however, is for boycotts that have government approval. As a practical matter, these laws are applicable mainly to the Arab states' boycott of the State of Israel.

The second provision of the antiboycott laws requires the reporting of any requests to participate in the boycott or requests to furnish information regarding the nationality or religious background of employees, suppliers, or customers.

Specifically, the antiboycott laws prohibit a U.S. person from refusing to do business with anyone pursuant to a request from a boycotting country. This includes refusing to do business with the State of Israel, firms in the State of Israel, or firms that are on the "boycott black list." Further, a U.S. person may not furnish information regarding a blacklisted firm or person, or one's relationship with the boy-cotted country. If such a request to provide information is made, or a request to refrain from doing business is made, this must be reported to the Internal Revenue Service.

There are several broad exceptions to these laws that make it possible for a U.S. firm to do business with a boycotting country or firm. The law does allow a U.S. firm to comply with the laws of the boycotting country with respect to the firm's activities exclusively within that country, and the U.S. person can agree not to export goods into a boycotting country.

Some firms may fall into the trap of ignoring requests to furnish information (since that would violate the antiboycott laws), but unless these requests are reported, the law is still violated. Reporting of any violations can come from a disgruntled employee or a competitor who has reported such requests.

The penalties for violating the antiboycott laws include civil and criminal penalties, but the most significant is the potential loss of foreign tax credits on that transaction. It is no defense to the action that a controlled subsidiary participated in the boycott outside of the United States. Jurisdiction is based on the fact that the controlled subsidiary and the U.S. parent company transact business; that the activity is "in U.S. commerce." In such a case, the U.S. parent can be held to violate the antiboycott laws based on the boycott activities of its subsidiary.

CHAPTER SUMMARY

INTERNATIONAL BUSINESS TRANSACTIONS

International Business Entity	1. This is any business entity with relationships that transcend national boundaries.
	2. An IBE is subject to home country, host country, and international regulation.
Comparative Legal Systems and International Law	1. Civil law legal systems are based on codes.
	2. International law is consensual and binding only on those who agree to be bound.
	3. Private international law refers to unification of law.
	4. Conflict-of-laws rules determine which country's laws will apply to a dispute.
Methods of Conducting International Business	1. Import/export is the simplest form of business.
	2. Distributorships, sale representatives, and sales agents sell the goods in the host country.
	3. A license is the right to use another's intellectual property.
International Contracts	1. The parties to an international contract can specify contract clauses.
	2. A force majeure clause excuses performance for specified circumstances beyond the party's control.
	3. Arbitration clauses are enforced by U.S. courts.
	4. A choice-of-law and choice-of-forum clause may add certainty to where a lawsuit must be brought and which country's law will apply.
	5. The Convention on Contracts for the International Sale of goods provides certainty and rules of interpretation if there is no contract or the terms are unclear.
The Multinational Enterprise	1. The multinational enterprise faces criticism in three areas: market control, political control, and worldwide profit-maximizing perspective.
	2. Multinational enterprises respond that they provide employment, goods, and services to the host population, and assume investment risks.

International Controls	**1.** The Convention on Contracts for the International Sale of Goods is a type of international Uniform Commercial Code.
	2. The GATT seeks to reduce or eliminate trade barriers.
	3. Codes of conduct for IBEs have an impact on behavior through the process of negotiating these codes, rather than through direct enforcement.
Host Country Regulations	**1.** Host countries can influence the activities of IBEs through restricting movements of capital, tax legislation, disclosure legislation, and merger restrictions.
	2. Nationalization of IBE property can be either an expropriation, which is a legal taking, or a confiscation, for which just compensation has not been received.
Import Controls	**1.** Dumping is the practice of selling goods in the United States at unfairly low prices.
	2. A manufacturer must prove that the goods are being sold at below production cost or below home market price, and must prove injury to the industry.
	3. Countervailing duties are applied after a finding of unfair government subsidies.
Export Controls	**1.** A validated license is required for products at a certain level of technology or products that can be used for strategic or military purposes.
	2. End-user certification is required for a validated license, and the exporter must certify the country of destination.
Antitrust Laws	**1.** U.S. antitrust laws can apply to an IBE's foreign activities even if the foreign country's laws do not prohibit such conduct.
	2. Extraterritoriality is the application of U.S. law beyond its borders.
	3. There is a three-part test used by courts to determine if the antitrust laws should be enforced in any given case.
Foreign Corrupt Practices Act	**1.** The Foreign Corrupt Practices Act prohibits giving anything of value to a foreign government official to influence a discretionary decision.
	2. The Foreign Corrupt Practices Act has reporting requirements that apply to any issuer of securities, even if it is not engaged in international business.
Antiboycott Laws	**1.** Under the antiboycott laws, any "U.S. person" is prohibited from participating or cooperating in an international boycott.
	2. The antiboycott laws require the reporting of any requests to participate in the boycott or requests to furnish information regarding the nationality or religious background of employees, suppliers, or customers.

REVIEW QUESTIONS AND PROBLEMS

1. Match the words in column A with the definitions in column B.

A	B
(1) IBE	(a) Giving something of value to expedite clerical function
(2) Sales agent	(b) International UCC
(3) Force majeure	(c) Presence in the host country; employee
(4) Dumping	(d) Selling below fair value, causing industry injury
(5) Grease payment	(e) Unification of laws among countries
(6) Validated license	(f) Superior force or power
(7) Expropriation	(g) Legal taking by government of the host country

Parol evidence Legal proof based on oral statements.

sanctity of written contracts. Therefore, it is generally held that statements, promises, guarantees, and representations made by the parties prior to signing a written contract may not be considered if the written contract represents the entire agreement of the parties. This principle of law is called the **parol evidence** rule.

The parol evidence rule prevents the introduction of prior or contemporaneous oral or written agreements that might vary or contradict the final written contract. When parties to a contract embody the terms of their agreement in a writing intended to be the final and exclusive expression of their agreement, the written contract cannot be contradicted, explained, varied, or supplemented. Everything that happens prior to or contemporaneously with the execution of the written contract is assumed to be integrated into it. The written contract is deemed the only permissible evidence of the agreement. All earlier negotiations, understandings, representations, and agreements are said to have merged in the written contract. Therefore *parol* (extrinsic) evidence is not admissible to supplement, subtract from, alter, vary, or contradict the agreement as written.

The following case is an example of how the parol evidence rule typically applies to a contractual transaction.

CASE

Five Points Bank v. White
437 N.W.2d 460 (Neb. 1989)

OLBERDING, J.

. . . On February 28, 1985, Van and Bette White signed a chattel mortgage note to Five Points Bank in the principal amount of $51,000. This note consolidated past loans of approximately $38,000, plus established credit to allow Van White to continue to make payments to William Desch on a contract for the purchase of a 50-percent interest in two businesses. . . . The note was due on August 27, 1985, set up to coincide with distributions from Van White's businesses.

During the spring of 1985, Van White apparently decided he would not be able to meet his commitments and determined to get out of both businesses because of poor cash-flows. William White began to negotiate with Van White's business partner, Robert Fox, and Desch to try to work out an arrangement for William White to take Van White's place in the businesses and take over Van White's obligation to Desch.

Sometime in June 1985, William and Van White went to see Jon Luebs at the bank. William White offered to sign the promissory note to keep the bank from pressuring Van White for payment while negotiations were proceeding. At the time William White signed the note, it was not yet due and there had been no default on the note.

William White never completed the negotiations. In the fall of 1985, Van White defaulted on the bank note and returned the interest in the businesses to Desch.

The bank sued Van, Bette, and William White on the defaulted note. In his answer, William White alleged he had an oral agreement with the bank to be obligated only for amounts advanced in excess of $45,765, up to the face value of the note ($51,000). The bank filed a motion for summary judgment. The district court granted the motion and . . . William White appeals.

William White claims the trial court erred in granting the summary judgment because an issue of material fact still exists as to whether he obligated himself for the full value of the note.

William White relies upon an alleged conversation between himself and Luebs of the bank prior to William White's signing the note. During this conversation, William White claims he agreed to be obligated only for amounts advanced in excess of $45,765, the amount advanced as of the date he signed the note, up to $51,000, the face value of the note. He admits this agreement was never reduced to writing in any fashion. He also admits he did not read the note before he signed, but relied on his past relationship with the bank to seek payment only to the extent of his oral agreement. Lastly, he admits there was consideration for his signature.

The parol evidence rule renders ineffective proof of a prior or contemporaneous oral agreement which alters, varies, or contradicts the terms of a written agreement. The parol evidence rule is ordinarily applied in absence of fraud, mistake, or ambiguity. William White does not claim Five Points Bank is guilty of fraud in connection with his signing the note.

If negotiations between the parties result in an agreement which is reduced to writing, the written agreement is the only competent evidence of the contract in the absence of fraud, mistake, or ambiguity. . . . Oral testimony is not admissible under the ambiguity exception to the parol evidence rule to establish an understanding at variance with the plain terms of the written instrument.

A note in the usual commercial form is a complete contract in itself, and its terms cannot be varied or contradicted by parol evidence.

Under the unambiguous language in the note, William White obligated himself in the amount of $51,000. The conversation relating to the oral agreement on his obligation took place prior to his signing the note.

He seeks to alter the language of the note with evidence of prior oral negotiations. The parol evidence rule expressly bars such evidence. . . .

■ *Affirmed.*

CASE CONCEPTS REVIEW

1. With the signed promissory note as evidence of their agreement, what appears to be William White's liability to the bank?
2. What does William White argue was the actual agreement between these parties?
3. Why did both the trial court and this court agree with the bank's claim for payment?

18. Exceptions to the Parol Evidence Rule

Most legal rules have exceptions based on notions of equity, good conscience, and common sense. The parol evidence rule has several such exceptions. First, since the rule presumes all prior negotiations are merged into the written contract, it obviously cannot apply to agreements made after the written contract. Thus the rule does not prevent the use of oral evidence to establish modifications agreed on subsequent to the execution of the written contract. Likewise, the rule is inapplicable to evidence of a cancellation of the agreement. Other exceptions include evidence of fraudulent misrepresentations, lack of delivery of an instrument when delivery is required to give it effect, and errors in drafting or reducing the contract to writing. Moreover, oral evidence is always allowed to clarify the terms of an ambiguous contract.

Perhaps the most important exception is the *partial integration rule*. This exception requires the judge to determine if the written contract is totally or merely partially integrated. A total integration occurs when the parties intend the written contract to be the *final* and *complete* statement of their agreement. If they do, evidence of prior agreements is not permitted for any reason. A partial integration occurs when the parties intend the writing to be final on the terms as written but not necessarily complete on all terms of their agreement. Although the contract cannot be *contradicted* under the partial integration rule, it can be *supplemented* or *explained* by prior agreements between the parties.

Course of dealing A sequence of previous conduct between the same parties to a particular transaction.

Usage of trade Any practice or method of dealing so regularly followed by businesspeople in a practice or trade that parties expect to follow the same practice or method of dealing.

Course of performance The expectation of the parties who have had a history of agreements that require repeated performances.

19. Parol Evidence Rule and the Code

The Code recognizes that the parol evidence rule prevents the use of oral evidence to contradict or vary the terms of a written memorandum or of a contract that is intended to be the final expression of the parties. The impact of the rule is greatly reduced, however, by the Code's provision that a written contract may be explained or supplemented by a prior **course of dealing** between buyer and seller, by **usage of trade,** or by the **course of performance.** The Code also allows evidence of consistent additional terms to be introduced, based on the partial integration rule [2-202]. The provisions allowing such evidence are designed to ascertain the true understanding of the parties concerning the agreement and to place the agreement in its proper perspective. The assumption is that prior dealings between the parties and the usages of the trade were taken for granted when the contract was worded. Often a contract for sale involves repetitive performance by both parties over a period of time. The course of performance is indicative of the meaning that the parties, by practical construction, have given to their agreement. It is relevant to interpretation of the agreement and thus is admissible evidence.

When oral evidence of a course of dealing, trade usage, or course of performance is introduced under the Code's exceptions to the parol evidence rule, the law recognizes an order of preference in the event of inconsistencies. Express terms will prevail over an interpretation based on the course of performance, and the course of performance will prevail over an interpretation predicated on either the course of dealing or the usage of trade [2-208].

CONSTRUCTION AND INTERPRETATION OF CONTRACTS

Courts are often called on to construe or interpret contracts. Although there is a technical distinction between *construction* (courts construe a contract's legal effect) and *interpretation* (juries interpret the parties' intentions), these words are generally interchangeable. The basic purpose of construing a contract is to determine the intention of the parties. If the language is clear and unambiguous, construction is not required, and the intent expressed in the agreement will be followed. When the language of a contract is ambiguous or obscure, courts apply certain established rules of construction to ascertain the supposed intent of the parties. These rules will not be used to make a new contract for the parties or to rewrite the old one. They are applied by the court merely to resolve doubts and ambiguities within the framework of the agreement.

The general standard of interpretation is to use the meaning the contract language would convey to a reasonably intelligent person who is familiar with the circumstances in which the language was used. Thus language is judged objectively rather than subjectively and is given a reasonable meaning. What one party says he or she meant or thought he or she was saying or writing is immaterial, since words are given effect in accordance with their meaning to a reasonable person in the circumstances of the parties. In determining the intention of the parties, it is the expressed intention that controls, and this will be given effect unless it conflicts with some rule of law, moral behavior, or public policy.

The language is judged with reference to the subject matter of the contract, its nature, objects, and purposes. Language is usually given its ordinary meaning, but technical words are given their technical meaning. Words with an established legal meaning are given that legal meaning. The law of the place where the contract was made is considered a part of the contract. Isolated words or clauses are not considered; instead, the contract is considered as a whole to ascertain the intent of the parties. If one party has prepared the agreement, an ambiguity in the contract language will be construed against that party since he or she had the chance to eliminate the ambiguity.

As an aid to the court in determining the intention of the parties, special provisions prevail over general provisions, handwritten provisions prevail over typewritten ones, and typewritten provisions prevail over printed ones. Furthermore, courts may consider business custom, usage, and prior dealings between the parties.

The Uniform Commercial Code (UCC) encourages courts to supply contractual terms omitted by the parties. This gap-filling process is discussed in chapter 18.

In the interpretation of contracts, the construction the parties have themselves placed on the agreement is often the most significant source of the intention of the parties. The parties themselves know best what they meant by their words of agreement, and their action under that agreement is the best indication of what that meaning was. The following case illustrates the importance courts give to the parties' intentions.

CASE

F & F Copiers, Inc. v. Kroger Company
391 S.E.2d 711 (Ga. App. 1990)

BEASLEY, J.

. . . F & F Copiers appeals from the grant of Kroger's motion for summary judgment.

In February 1985 the parties entered into a "Service Agreement" for F & F to supply and maintain coin-operated copy machines to designated Kroger stores in certain cities in Georgia. The contract was physically prepared by Kroger but the parties mutually negotiated it, each participating by supplying clauses supplementing the standard terms and discussing each term. The agreement was for the three-year period February 18, 1985, through February 17, 1988. The consideration was 1,000 (later reduced to 750) free copies monthly to each Kroger store plus 20 percent commission to Kroger on "all paid for copies."

The final item in the contract was: "This *agreement* shall continue in effect with the right of either party hereto to cancel same by delivering to the other written notice to that effect at least thirty (30 days prior to discontinuance of service. This agreement supersedes any and all prior agreements." [Emphasis in original] . . .

Under the contract approximately 52 stores were furnished with copiers. Kroger received its last commission check in April 1986. On October 31 Kroger sent F & F 30-day notice "for cancellation and removal" of copiers from ten named stores under "Phase I of its conversion to a Kroger-owned program." F & F complied and Kroger followed with a letter dated November 4, "for cancellation and removal" as to ten other stores under "Phase II." F & F also complied with that notice but on November 18 wrote Kroger that it disagreed that Kroger could terminate the contract, contending instead that the contract was for a three-year term and the thirty-day cancellation provision only applied following expiration of that period.

F & F sued Kroger the following April, for contract breach without just cause. In July Kroger notified F & F to remove all remaining copiers, or Kroger would consider them in trespass. F & F removed the copiers.

After discovery, Kroger moved for summary judg-ment and F & F moved for partial summary judgment. The latter was denied and the former, granted.

F & F's position is that the contract encompassed a three-year period and only after expiration did the 30-day cancellation notice activate. Kroger's position is that the notice provision was effective at any time during the course of the contract and permitted unilateral termination by either party. . . .

A contract is not ambiguous even though difficult to construe, unless and until an application of the pertinent rules of interpretation leaves it uncertain as to which of two or more possible meanings represents the true intention of the parties. It is the intention of the parties at the time the contract is made which governs. This court must construe the contract, even in the presence of possible ambiguity, but no construction is permissible where the contract language is plain, unambiguous and capable of only one reasonable interpretation.

The contract is not one of adhesion because it was not prepared by one in a superior position or couched in language chosen solely by one party, but with input from two relatively evenly matched bargaining units.

The ultimate rule of contract construction is to ascertain the intention of the parties, which is accomplished by a consideration of the entire contract. . . . The language used by the parties is of primary consideration in ascertaining their intention.

This contract states unequivocally that its terms are for a specific three-year period. The ninth and last term provide for a thirty-day notice of cancellation. If the parties intended the contract to extend past the three years on a thirty-day notice contingency it could have so stated; but such is absent. Absent that, and considering the whole, the contract contains a right for either party to cancel upon notice.

There is no merit in F & F's contention that Kroger could not effect a piece-meal termination. A contract may be partially terminated and nothing inherent in this contract prevents a cancellation by stages. Moreover, the removal of copiers in the first two phases was acquiesced in by F & F, and simply constituted giving effect to the express provision for removal.

■ *Judgment affirmed.*

2. How did each of the parties (Kroger and F & F Copiers) interpret this contract term?

3. Which way does the court interpret the term? Do you agree that the court's decision represents the parties' intentions?

1. What contract term is the subject matter of this litigation?

CHAPTER SUMMARY

STATUTE OF FRAUDS

The Approach

1. Contracts within the statute of frauds are unenforceable unless evidenced by a writing.
2. The statute of frauds results in an affirmative defense that must be pleaded.

Guaranty Contracts

1. A direct primary promise to pay another's debt is not within the statute.
2. A secondary promise to pay another's debt if the debtor does not pay is within the statute and must be evidenced by a writing.
3. If the promisor's leading object or main purpose is to serve his or her own interests, the promise is not within the statute.

Contracts Involving Interests in Land

1. Any contract that creates or transfers any interest in land must be evidenced by a writing and signed by the party to be charged.
2. Sale of realty, leases for one year or more, liens, mortgages, and easements are within the statute.
3. Promises to transfer timber, minerals, oil and gas, and structures are within the statute *unless* the seller is to sever them from the realty.
4. Growing crops are goods, not interests in land, and are not within the statute regardless of who severs them.

Contracts That Cannot Be Performed within One Year

1. Any contract that, by its terms, is impossible to perform within one year is within the statute.
2. If there is *any possibility* that a contract can be performed in one year, it is not within the statute.

Contracts for the Sale of Goods

1. Contracts for the sale of goods having a *price* of $500 or more are within the statute.

Contracts for the Sale of Personal Property Other than Goods

1. Contracts for the sale of securities, for the sale of more than $5,000 of other personal property, and for the creation of a security interest generally are within the statute and must be in writing.

Writing Required by the Statute of Frauds

1. A writing satisfies the statute if it states with *reasonable* certainty the identity of the parties, the subject matter, and the essential terms and conditions and is signed by the party to be charged.
2. If there is more than one writing and one writing is signed, the unsigned writing is part of the signed writing if the writings by internal reference refer to the same subject matter or transaction.

Writing Required for Code Contracts

1. A writing satisfies the statute if it (a) indicates a sale of certain goods between the parties, (b) has a quantity term, and (c) is signed by the party to be charged.
2. Omission of any term other than quantity does not make writing insufficient. The quantity term may be supplied by any means, such as outputs and requirements.
3. The contract will not be enforced beyond the quantity stated in the writing.

Part Performance	1. If an oral contract was fully performed by both parties, the statute is not applicable.
	2. Performance must establish and point unmistakably and exclusively to the existence of an oral contract.
	3. Performance must be so substantial that it would be inequitable not to grant judicial relief.
	4. If it is reasonable to return the parties to the status quo, a court will rescind the transaction. A buyer who has only paid the price will have his or her money returned.
	5. If a buyer has paid the price and taken other actions (such as making valuable improvements to land), courts will recognize an exception to the statute.
	6. In contracts of long duration, full performance by one party makes the agreement enforceable.
Promissory Estoppel	1. If a party detrimentally relies on an oral promise, some courts will enforce the promise.
	2. The reliance must be foreseeable by the promisor, enforcement of the promise is necessary to avoid injustice, and the remedy may be as limited as justice requires.

Written Confirmation between Merchants	1. The Code has four exceptions: written confirmation between merchants, specially manufactured goods, judicial admissions, and performance.
	2. *Between merchants,* a signed confirmation of an oral contract sent within a reasonable time satisfies the statute if the merchant who actually receives it does not object by written notice within ten days.
	3. At a minimum, the confirmation must be written, signed by the sender, evidence an actual contract between the parties, and contain a quantity term.
Specially Manufactured Goods	1. Contracts involving goods specially manufactured for the buyer are enforceable even though the contracts are not evidenced by signed writings.
Judicial Admissions	1. If the party to be charged admits in his or her pleadings, testimony, or otherwise in court that a contract of sale was made, the statute is satisfied.
Part Performance	1. Part or full payment or part or complete acceptance of goods satisfies the statute. The contract is enforced only to the extent of the part performance.

The Theory	1. Evidence of prior or contemporaneous agreements (whether written or oral) is inadmissible to vary, contradict, or modify an unambiguous written contract.
	2. Parol evidence will be excluded only if the court finds that the writing was intended as a *final and complete* agreement (totally integrated).
	3. A merger or integration clause ("This is the final and complete agreement.") is generally given effect.
Exceptions to the Parol Evidence Rule	1. Parol evidence may be used to (a) show that writing was not the final and complete agreement, (b) show defects in formation, (c) show and explain ambiguity, and (d) show subsequent agreements.
Parol Evidence Rule and the Code	1. Under the Code, agreements may be explained by evidence of course of dealing, usage of trade, or course of performance.

1. Words are given their plain and ordinary meanings.
2. Ambiguities are construed against the party who drafted or used the ambiguous language.
3. Writings are to be interpreted as a whole, and language is not to be taken out of context.
4. Specific provisions control general provisions.
5. Handwritten provisions prevail over typed provisions, and typed provisions prevail over printed provisions.
6. Courts may rely on business customs, usages of trade, and the parties' prior dealings to give meaning to a contract's language.
7. The Code supplies (gap-fills) terms omitted by the parties. Code-implied terms are applicable unless the parties provide otherwise in their agreement.

REVIEW QUESTIONS AND PROBLEMS

1. Match each term in column A with the appropriate statement in column B.

A	B
(1) Guarantor of another's debt primarily wants to benefit himself or herself	(a) Party detrimentally relies on oral promise
(2) Contract that cannot be performed within one year	(b) Indicates a contract between the parties, indicates quantity, and is signed by party to be charged
(3) Promissory estoppel exception	(c) A promise to pay another's debt, grant of an interest in land, a contract that cannot be performed in one year, and sale of goods of $500 or more
(4) Equitable estoppel exception	(d) Writing that satisfies statute but is not signed by the party to be charged
(5) Sufficient writing required by the Code	(e) Written contract is final but not the complete agreement
(6) Confirmation between merchants	(f) Confirmation between merchants, specially manufactured goods, judicial admissions, performance
(7) Parol evidence rule	(g) Leading object rule
(8) Partial integration	(h) Eliminates prior or contemporaneous evidence that varies, contradicts, or modifies a written contract
(9) Contracts granting interests in land	(i) Part or full performance by one party
(10) Merger or integration clause	(j) Two-year employment contract
(11) Code exceptions to the statute of frauds	(k) "This is the parties' entire agreement."
(12) Contracts within the statute of frauds	(l) Easement, mortgage, lease for more than a year

2. A butcher sold hamburger meat on credit to the Good Eats Restaurant. When the restaurant was late in paying its bills, the butcher contacted Jim, who orally promised to pay any bill that the restaurant failed to pay. Is this oral promise enforceable in court? Why or why not? Would your answer change if Jim said, "The restaurant is on hard times. Send the bills to me, and I'll pay." Explain.

3. Livesay orally agreed to sell real estate to Drake. Before the closing, Livesay sold it to someone else and wrote Drake a letter apologizing for selling it at a higher price. The letter mentioned both prices and contained an adequate reference to the real estate. When Drake sues Livesay, will the statute of frauds be an adequate defense? Why or why not?

4. Hardin Associates, a developer of shopping centers, hired Brummet to head its development division. Brummet was hired on an oral contract of employment for an indefinite time. He was later discharged, and he sued for breach of contract. Hardin asserted the statute of frauds as a defense since the contract was to last an indefinite time. Is the defense valid? Explain.

5. On September 15, 1992, Builders orally agreed with K. Construction Company to work together on a project. Work was to begin January 1, 1993, and it was contemplated that the work would be completed by the end of 1993. Is the contract enforceable? Explain.

6. Seaman supplied fuel for ships and needed a long-term supply contract with a major oil company. In a letter dated October 11, Standard Oil offered Seaman a ten-year supply contract with three ten-year options for renewal. The letter made no mention of quantity requirements, price, particulars of performance, or other material terms. Seaman signed the letter indicating his acceptance of Standard's offer. When Standard later said it could not supply fuel, Seaman sued. Standard raised the defense of the statute of frauds. Is the October 11 letter a signed writing sufficient to satisfy the statute of frauds? Explain.

7. Chisholm had a written option to purchase 1.862 acres of land out of a 10-acre tract owned by the Cartwrights. The exact piece of property covered by the option was not specified. If Chisholm sues for specific performance of the option, will the statute of frauds be a valid defense? Explain.

8. Brown entered into an oral contract to purchase a farm from Burnside. Brown took possession of the farm, made several improvements, tore down an old farmhouse, paid taxes, and made payments on the purchase price. Burnside thereafter refused to deed the farm to Brown as orally agreed. Brown sought specific performance of the oral contract. Is the oral contract to sell real property enforceable under these circumstances? Why or why not?

9. Potter hatches turkeys in Oregon, and Hatter raises turkeys in Oklahoma. Potter and Hatter orally agreed to a buy-sell contract for young turkeys, but there was a problem in transporting the young turkeys from Oregon to Oklahoma. Hatter assured Potter that he would find a solution to the transportation problem. In reliance on this assurance, Potter turned down an offer to sell his young turkeys to a California buyer. Two months later, Hatter said he would be unable to buy the turkeys and Potter sued. Is the statute of frauds a valid defense? Why or why not?

10. Associated Lithographers made an oral contract to provide Stay Wood Products with special printed business cards, letterheads and envelopes, order forms, and an etching and rubber stamp with Stay Wood Products' name. When Stay Wood Products refused to pay, Associated Lithographers sued. Stay Wood raised the defense of the statute of frauds. Is the statute of frauds a defense? Explain.

11. Roper bought a triplewide mobile home from Flamingo Home Sales. The written installment sale contract disclaimed any warranty obligation of the seller. Roper experienced several problems with the mobile home, which Flamingo refused to repair. Roper

sued on Flamingo's oral promise that if problems did arise, Flamingo would "take care of them." Is this oral promise admissible in court? Explain why or why not.

12. Arlene sued Woodmen Insurance Company to recover medical benefits arising from her pregnancy. The policy covered medical expenses for a pregnancy that originates when the "Insured and the Insured's Spouse are both insured under the Policy." Arlene was insured under the policy when she became pregnant, but she was not married. Before she gave birth, she married for the first time. Woodmen refused to pay because her spouse was not insured under the policy when she got pregnant. Arlene claims the requirement that "insured's spouse" be insured must be fulfilled only if the "insured" is married at the time the pregnancy occurs. Is the policy language ambiguous, and should it be construed against Woodmen Insurance Company? Explain.

15

CONTRACT PERFORMANCE

CHAPTER PREVIEW

We have now encountered most of the basic issues in contract law. First, there must be an agreement consisting of offer and acceptance. Second, the agreement must be validated by bargained-for consideration. Third, the valid contract may be legally unenforceable because of defenses like incapacity, illegality, public policy, or form. Based on the assumption that a valid contract exists without any defense to its formation, the discussion here concerns performance of contracts.

This chapter focuses on the problems that may arise during the period of the performance of a contract. A major emphasis is on important provisions known as *conditions*. Questions arise as to the order of performance: Who must perform first in a bilateral contract? Usually, a default or breach of a contract will occur at or after the time when performance was due, but as noted in this chapter, a contract can be breached prior to the date for performance.

> You are the low bidder on a construction project. The proposed contract, presented to you for signing, states that "time is of the essence" in the performance of the agreement. This agreement also contains a completion date. Should you agree to this contract?

CONDITIONS

1. Definition

Condition A clause in a contract, either expressed or implied, that has the effect of investing or divesting the legal rights and duties of the parties to the contract.

A **condition** is an act or event (other than the lapse of time) that, unless excused, must occur before performance under a contract becomes due. A condition is an act or event that limits or qualifies a promise. The condition must occur before the promisor has a present duty to perform. Assume that you promise to sell me your car for $3,000 and I promise to buy your car for $3,000 if I can obtain a loan of $2,000. I have no present duty to pay you $3,000. When and if I obtain a loan of $2,000, my promise to pay you is activated. My promise to pay is a conditional promise.

There is no exclusive or conclusive test to determine whether a particular contractual provision is a promise or a condition. Although no particular words are necessary for the existence of a condition, terms such as *if, provided that, on condition that,* and others that condition a party's performance usually connote an intent for a condition rather than a promise. In the absence of a clause expressly creating a condition, whether a certain contractual provision is a condition rather than a promise must be gathered from the contract as a whole and from the intent of the parties.

Conditions determine when a party has to perform. However, many promises are unconditional and absolute. The party who makes an unconditional promise has an immediate duty to perform, regardless of the other party's duties. The failure to perform such a promise is a breach of contract unless the duty is excused. Where a promise is conditional, the duty to perform it is dormant or unactivated until the condition occurs. A duty to perform is conditional if some event must occur before the duty becomes absolute.

2. Types of Conditions

Conditions may be classified by time—*when* the conditioning event must occur in relation to the promise. Under this classification, conditions are labeled *conditions precedent, conditions concurrent,* and *conditions subsequent.*

Condition precedent
A clause in a contract providing that immediate rights and duties shall vest only on the happening of some event.

CONDITIONS PRECEDENT. A **condition precedent** is an act or event that, unless excused, must exist or occur before a duty of immediate performance of a promise arises. It usually takes the form of performance by the other party. Contracts often expressly provide that one party must perform before there is a right to performance by the other party. The first party's performance is a condition precedent to the duty of the other party to perform. Since one party must perform before the other is under a duty to do so, the failure of the first party to perform permits the other to refuse to perform and to cancel the contract. As the following case illustrates, failure to satisfy a condition precedent prevents enforcement of the contract.

CASE

Christophersen v. Blount
582 A.2d 460 (Conn. 1990)

COVELLO, J.

This is an action for the specific performance of a real estate contract. The principal issue is whether the trial court properly concluded that the plaintiff buyer's nineteen months delay in carrying out a condition precedent to the defendant sellers' obligation to perform bars his claim against them for specific performance. . . .

On April 21, 1983, the defendants agreed to sell to the plaintiff two parcels of land from a larger tract in Westport. The contract stated that the closing would take place at an unspecified date "fourteen (14) days after approval by the Westport Planning and Zoning Commission of a subdivision of the Sellers' premises." The contract further provided that "[t]he Seller hereby appoints the Purchaser as his Attorney-in-Fact to accomplish a subdivision of the Sellers' property. . . ." On November 21, 1984, nineteen months later, the plaintiff submitted an application for subdivision approval to the Westport planning and zoning commission (commission). Thereafter, the defendants' attorney wrote the commission stating that the plaintiff had no authority to seek a subdivision of the property in their behalf. The commission thereafter refused to accept the subdivision application without the defendants' personal signatures.

The plaintiff then began this action seeking specific performance of the contract. After a hearing, the trial court rendered judgment for the defendants concluding that the plaintiff had delayed an unreasonable amount of time in filing the subdivision application. . . . The plaintiff appealed to the Appellate Court. We transferred the case to this court. . . . We conclude that . . . the defendants' obligation to transfer the property terminated because of the plaintiff's failure to fulfill an express condition precedent within a reasonable time. . . .

If an express condition [in the contract] is not fulfilled, the right to enforce the contract does not come into existence. A condition precedent is a fact or event which the parties intend must exist or take place before there is a right to performance. Whether the performance of a certain act by a party to a contract is a condition precedent to the duty of the other party to act depends on the intent of the parties as expressed in the contract and read in light of the circumstances surrounding the execution of the instrument.

The contract stated that "[t]he Closing of Title shall take place . . . fourteen (14) days after approval by the [commission] of a subdivision of the Sellers' premises." The trial court correctly found that this language manifested the intent of the parties that subdivision approval be an accomplished fact before the defendants' duty to convey the property would arise. The contract further stated that "[t]he Seller hereby appoints the Purchaser as his Attorney-in-Fact to accomplish a subdivision of the Sellers' property. . . ." As between the parties, as the trial court determined, the contract imposed on the plaintiff the responsibility to procure commission approval for the subdivision and thus required the plaintiff to bear the risk of the nonoccurrence of this condition in timely fashion.

The trial court further found that the contract did not require the plaintiff to satisfy the condition by any particular date. In the absence of a specified time limit to comply with a condition precedent, the law implies a reasonable time.

What is a reasonable length of time is ordinarily a question of fact for the trier. Here, the trial court found that the plaintiff had delayed nineteen months in seeking approval for the subdivision and concluded that this was an unreasonable amount of time under the circumstances. Because this conclusion was a reasonable corollary of the predicate finding that nineteen months had elapsed, we find no legal basis for disturbing the trial court's conclusion on appeal. Since the plaintiff had failed to perform his obligations under the contract the right to enforce the contract was not in existence and the defendants were under no obligation to convey the property.

■ *The judgment is affirmed.*

1. What condition did the plaintiff have to satisfy before the defendant was obligated to transfer title to the real estate?

2. How long did it take the plaintiff to attempt to satisfy this condition? Did the sales contract specify a time for the plaintiff's action?

3. On what grounds does the court decide that the defendant is excused from performing the sales contract?

Not all the terms that impose a duty of performance on a person are of sufficient importance to constitute conditions precedent. As a general rule, if a provision is relatively insignificant, its performance is not required before recovery may be obtained from the other party. In such cases, the party who was to receive performance merely deducts the damages caused by the breach.

For example, a contractor substantially follows all the plans and specifications in building a house, but completes the work ten days late. Rescission is not justified. Such a breach is of minor importance. The purchaser would have been required to pay the contract price less any damages sustained because of the delay. It is often difficult to judge whether a breach of a particular provision is so material that it justifies rescission. If the damage caused by the breach can be readily measured in money, or if the other party receives basically what he or she was entitled to under the contract, the clause breached is not considered a condition precedent.

Conditions concurrent
Conditions concurrent are mutually dependent and must be performed at the same time by the parties to the contract. Payment of money and delivery of goods in a cash sale are conditions concurrent.

CONDITIONS CONCURRENT.   If parties are to exchange performances at the same time, their performances are **conditioned concurrently.** "I promise to sell you my stereo for $700 on April 1." Tender of $700 and tender of the stereo are concurrent conditions of exchange. Since a contract seldom states that performances are simultaneously conditioned on one another, courts will generally find concurrent conditions if both parties can perform simultaneously. Suppose, in the preceding example, no date for performance was set. In that case, neither party could demand that the other perform until he or she has performed or tendered performance. Each party's performance is conditioned on concurrent performance by the other party.

Condition subsequent
A clause in a contract providing for the happening of an event that divests legal rights and duties.

CONDITIONS SUBSEQUENT.   A **condition subsequent** stated in the contract is an event that discharges a duty of performance that has become absolute. In an insurance contract you might find the following example: "In the event of accident or loss, written notice containing all particulars shall be given by the insured to the Insurer within thirty days." The insurance company's duty to pay under the policy does not arise (become absolute) until the insured gives notice. The requirement of notice is an express condition subsequent to the insured's right to collect. Note that conditions subsequent are rare.

Conditions may also be classified according to the way they are created. This method of classification recognizes two types of conditions: *express conditions* specifically set out in the contract and *constructive conditions* that the parties did not consider but the court imposes to achieve fundamental fairness between the parties. These two types of conditions are discussed in the following sections.

3. Express Conditions

An *express condition* is included in a contract and designated as a condition that must be strictly performed before the other party's duty to perform arises. The penalty for failure to perform an express condition properly may be the loss of the right to receive payment or otherwise to obtain the return performance. The parties may stipulate that something is a condition precedent, even though it would not ordinarily be considered so. If that stipulation is made, failure to perform exactly as specified is ground for rescission unless the court construes the clause to be a penalty provision and therefore unenforceable.

A contract may provide that "time is of the essence of this agreement." This means that performance on or before the date specified is a condition precedent to the duty of the other party to pay or to perform. Note the contract's provisions in the following case, which make the time of performance very important.

CASE

Elkins Manor Assoc. v. Eleanor Concrete
396 S.E.2d 463 (W.Va. 1990)

MILLER, J.

... Elkins Manor Associates is a limited partnership which was formed to provide government subsidized housing for the elderly in Randolph County. Elkins Manor, Inc., is one of the general partners of the limited partnership. After locating a site which complied with the Federal Housing Authority (FHA) requirements, Elkins Manor secured a twelve-month construction loan for $3,099,500 from the West Virginia Housing Development Fund (WVHDF). In return, Elkins Manor agreed to comply with the guidelines of WVHDF and FHA. The controversy in this case involves Elkins Manor and one of the contractors on the housing project, Eleanor Concrete Works, Inc. (Eleanor). . . .

On July 26, 1979, Elkins Manor and Eleanor entered into a contract in which Eleanor agreed to manufacture, deliver, and install pre-cast prestressed concrete planks for use as the floors and ceilings in the housing project. Eleanor was to provide the concrete for the first floor within eighteen days after the shop drawings had been approved and a one-half floor shipment of concrete every ten days thereafter. Elkins Manor agreed to pay Eleanor a total of $159,400 for this service. . . .

The first floor of the project was installed by Eleanor in September, 1979. In October, 1979, inspectors from FHA discovered that the installed planks had not been anchored in accordance with the design specifications of the project. Upon closer examination, the inspectors observed that several of the planks were cracked and warped. Believing that the planks were unsafe, the inspectors gave Elkins Manor two alternatives: (1) to remove all of the planks which had already been installed, or (2) to test the planks to assure that they complied with the standards prescribed by the American Concrete Institute (ACI). Both FHA and WVHDF require that all subsidized projects comply with these standards and this requirement was a part of Eleanor's contract. Eleanor decided to have the concrete tested.

Meanwhile, representatives from WVHDF inspected Eleanor's plant in Putnam County and determined that the plant's manufacturing process did not comply with the standards set by ACI or by the licensor of the product, Spiroll. WVHDF refused to allow any of Eleanor's planks to be used on the Elkins Manor project until Eleanor obtained approval from both the ACI and Spiroll. Eleanor did not obtain the necessary approval until January, 1980.

During February, 1980, delivery and installation of the concrete planks proceeded relatively on time. In March, Eleanor experienced financial difficulties and did not have any trucks in which to make the deliveries to the Elkins Manor project. Because of time limitations in its construction financing, Elkins Manor was forced to hire a trucking company to load and deliver the planks. Often, when a truck was sent down to pick up the concrete planks, the truck would return empty or half full. Eleanor also failed to provide either the manpower to install the planks or the crane necessary to remove them from the truck onto the construction site, as required by its contract. Consequently, Elkins Manor had to rent its own crane and use its own personnel to install the planks. . . .

Although Elkins Manor attempted to secure another company to make the pre-cast concrete, because of the time constraints of the construction loan, the estimates provided by the other companies were very uneconomical. According to Daniel Siegel, president of Elkins Manor, a decision was made to "limp along" with Eleanor even though it was not fulfilling its contractual obligations. . . .

After the project was completed in December, 1980, Elkins Manor filed suit against Eleanor . . . for breach of the contract. . . . The trial commenced on June 21, 1988. At the close of Elkins Manor's case, Eleanor filed a motion for directed verdict. The trial court granted this motion, finding that Elkins Manor provided insufficient evidence that Eleanor had breached the contract. . . .

We have traditionally held that a verdict should not be directed against a plaintiff in a civil case unless he has failed to present a *prima facie* case. In determining whether a *prima facie* case has been established, it is incumbent upon the trial judge to weigh the evidence in the plaintiff's favor. . . .

When the evidence is viewed in the light most favorable to Elkins Manor, the directed verdict against it was error. Article II of the contract had a "time is of the essence" clause, and the detailed delivery schedule contained in the contract was not followed. The general rule is that where time is of the essence, performance beyond the period specified in the contract, unless caused by the other party or waived by such party, will constitute a breach of the contract, entitling the aggrieved party to terminate it.

Here, Elkins Manor did not terminate the contract, but rather elected to permit Eleanor to continue to perform. According to Elkins Manor, this was done because it was not possible to readily obtain another source of supply of the pre-stressed concrete planks within the time frame of the construction loan. The fact that Elkins Manor did not terminate the contract with its supplier because of the delay in performance does not mean that it has waived its right to seek damages occasioned by the delay in perform-

ance. It is generally held that an owner does not waive his right to damages occasioned by the contractor's delay in constructing a building by permitting the contractor to proceed with the work.

Other damages claimed by Elkins Manor were occasioned by Eleanor's financial inability to deliver and install its product, as required by the contract. As a consequence, Elkins Manor was required to hire a trucking company to transport the concrete planks to the construction site and pay to have them installed. This resulted in a partial failure of performance of the contract by Eleanor. . . .

Finally, the delay caused by Eleanor's failure to produce a product in conformity to the contract specifications is attributable to Eleanor. The right of the FHA to inspect was embodied in the contract. It is generally held that where a construction contract provides for inspection of the work to assure compliance with the contract specifications, the contractor is required to remedy such defects found at its own expense and is chargeable with the delay occasioned thereby. . . .

Accordingly, we reverse and remand the case for further proceedings consistent with this opinion.

■ *Reversed and remanded.*

CASE CONCEPTS REVIEW

1. What are at least three problems with the defendant's contractual performance?
2. What decision of the trial court is being appealed by Elkins Manor?
3. Why does this court decide that the trial court was incorrect in its ruling?
4. Based on this case, when should the clause "time is of the essence" be included in a contract? How can this clause work to each party's advantage and disadvantage?

Architect's certificate
A formal statement signed by an architect that a contractor has performed under his or her contract and is entitled to be paid.

Another common express condition precedent, found in many construction contracts, provides that the duty of the owner to make the final payment on completion of the building is conditioned on the builder's securing an **architect's certificate**. This is certification by the owner's architect that the construction is satisfactory and in accordance with the plans and specifications. Thus the condition is, to a large degree, outside the control of both parties and within the exclusive control of a third party, the architect.

4. Express Conditions of Personal Satisfaction

A common provision in many contracts expressly conditions a party's performance on *personal satisfaction* with the other party's performance. Suppose that Wyeth agrees to paint your portrait to your personal satisfaction for $20,000. When he is finished, you say that you are not satisfied with it and refuse to pay the $20,000. The condition precedent of your personal satisfaction, you argue, has not happened to activate your duty to pay. Would it make any difference if fifty art experts state that the portrait is a masterpiece? To answer that question and to avoid unfair forfeitures, the law has adopted rules involving two categories of satisfaction cases: situations involving personal taste, fancy, or judgment (subjective dissatisfaction) and situations involving mechanical fitness, utility, or marketability (objective dissatisfaction).

When the satisfaction condition concerns your individual taste or judgment, as in the case of Wyeth's painting, the law requires that you genuinely be dissatisfied. Your dissatisfaction must be honest and in *good faith*, which is a subjective fact question. If you are dissatisfied with the bargain (paying $20,000), however, then you are refusing to pay in bad faith. The condition in that case is excused. The testimony of the art experts can therefore be used as circumstantial evidence of bad faith. This fact issue is given to the jury to determine.

When the satisfaction condition concerns something like construction or repair that can be measured objectively, the law requires reasonable rather than personal satisfaction. If the average person would be satisfied (reasonable, objective satisfaction), then you must pay, even though you personally might be dissatisfied. Thus performance that is objectively satisfactory must be paid for, notwithstanding personal (subjective) dissatisfaction.

Many cases involving the issue of satisfaction relate to financial matters such as the extension of credit on the assignment of a lease. While most cases use a reasonableness standard, the following case illustrates that a subjective evaluation is often appropriate and that such clauses are fraught with peril.

CASE

Forman v. Benson
446 N.E.2d 535 (Ill. App. 1983)

Forman contracted to buy land from Benson for $125,000 to be paid over a ten-year period. The contract stated, "Subject to Benson's approving Forman's credit report." The credit report showed Forman had liabilities of $80,000 and liquid assets of $24,000. Forman's tax return showed a $2,000 loss for the tax year. When Benson refused to proceed with the sale of his land, Forman sued for specific performance. At the trial, a bank official testified that Forman had an excellent credit rating. The trial court found that Benson was held to a standard of reasonableness in his rejection of Forman's credit report, and found his rejection was unreasonable. Benson appealed.

HOFF, J.

. . . We have discovered no case dealing with the interpretation of the specific clause in question. However, there is some Illinois case law regarding the interpretation of "satisfaction" clauses in general. In *Reeves & Co. v. Chandler* (1903), 113 Ill. App. 167, 170, the court found that satisfaction clauses generally fall into one of two classes. In one class, the decision as to whether a party is satisfied is completely reserved to the party for whose benefit the clause is inserted, and the reasons for his decision may not be inquired into and overhauled by either the other party or the courts. Cases falling into this class generally involve matters which are dependent upon the feelings, taste, or judgment of the party making the decision. The second class of cases are those in which the party to be satisfied is to base his determination on grounds which are just and reasonable. . . . These cases generally involve matters which are capable of objective evaluation, or which involve consideration of operative fitness or mechanical utility. Matters of financial concern generally fall into this second category of cases.

In *Stribling v. Ailion* (1967), 157 S.E.2d 427, the supreme court of Georgia also interpreted a similar provision in a real estate sales contract as a matter of personal opinion and judgment. In that case, the vendor included the following stipulation in the contract:

> Seller . . . reserves the right to run a credit investigation on purchaser and if in seller's opinion purchaser's credit is not sufficient, then the terms of this contract are null and void.

The court held that the stipulation reserved the right in the seller not only to run a credit investigation, but also to determine in his sole discretion whether the buyer's credit was to his satisfaction.

Although these . . . cases seem to stand for the proposition that personal judgment is involved when the evaluation of a credit rating is at issue, a different conclusion was reached in *Weisz Trucking Co., Inc. v. Emil R. Wohl Construction* (1970), 91 Cal.Rptr. 489. In that case a contract between a contractor and a subcontractor provided that "[t]he subcontractor shall furnish, if requested a corporate surety contract bond . . . written . . . by a company acceptable to the contractor. . . ." The subcontractor thereafter submitted a surety bond in the amount of $168,000 which was written by a company with a Treasury rating of only $61,000. The contractor rejected the bond, stating that it wanted a company with a Treasury rating of $500,000. The contractor cancelled the contract and the subcontractors sued for breach. The appellate court held that the sufficiency of the performance bond should be determined by the application of an objective test of reasonableness. In reaching this conclusion, the court relied upon numerous decisions dealing with satisfaction clauses in which it was generally found that "where the contract calls for satisfaction as to commercial value or quality or sufficiency which can be evaluated objectively, the standard of a reasonable person should be used in determining whether or not satisfaction has been received." . . .

It seems clear from the foregoing cases that a reasonableness standard is favored by the law when the contract concerns matters capable of objective evaluation. However, where the circumstances are such that it is clear the provision was added as a personal concession to one of the contracting parties, the subjective, rather than the objective standard, should be applied. . . .

In the present case, it is uncontroverted that the clause in question was inserted as a concession to the defendant and as an inducement to him to sign the contract, which he subsequently did. Ken Burnell testified that the addition of the provision indeed eased defendant's mind about the plaintiff's credit worthiness. In light of the fact that the relationship between the parties was to endure over a ten-year period of time, we think it is a reasonable construction of the provision that it was intended to allow defendant the freedom of making a personal and subjective evaluation of plaintiff's credit worthiness. We, therefore, conclude that the trial court erred in applying a reasonableness standard to the instant case.

■ *Reversed.*

CASE CONCEPTS REVIEW

1. What are the two ways of analyzing personal satisfaction clauses?
2. Which of these two analyses does the court use in this case?
3. What factors does the court rely on in reaching its conclusion?

5. Constructive Conditions

A *constructive condition* is one not expressed by the parties but is read into the contract to serve justice (that is, an implied-in-law condition). In a bilateral contract, one party can perform, regardless of what the other party does. But in most cases, it would be inequitable to require one party to perform without requiring the other to perform. In the interest of fairness, courts make performances of bilateral promises constructively conditional on one another. In an employment contract, for example, one must work before getting paid. Working is a constructive condition precedent, which must occur to activate the employer's duty to pay an employee.

When parties understand that one performance must occur before the other (or such is understood by custom), the former is a constructive condition precedent to the latter. When a contractor promises to build a house for an owner who will pay $200,000, a court will construe the builder's performance as a condition that must happen to activate the owner's duty to pay.

If both performances can be performed simultaneously, the promises are constructively concurrent. To activate the other's duty to perform, a party must tender his or her performances. Most contracts for the sale of goods under the Code are examples of constructive concurrent conditions of exchange.

Note: The express contract terms or custom, usage of trade, course of dealing, and the like can change the rule. A passenger, by custom, pays for an airline ticket before the airline's duty to provide transportation is activated.

6. Tender of Performance

Tender An offer to perform a contractual promise.

A **tender** in the law of contracts is an offer to perform. When a person makes a tender, it means that he or she is ready, willing, and able to perform. The tender is especially significant in contracts requiring both parties to perform at the same time. One party can place the other party in default by making a tender of performance without having actually rendered the performance.

The concept of tender is applied not only to concurrent condition situations but also to contract performance in general. In most contracts, one party or the other is required to tender payment. Such a tender requires that there be a bona fide, unconditional offer of payment of the amount of money due, coupled with an actual production of the money or its equivalent. A tender of payment by check is not a valid tender when an objection is made to this medium of payment. When a tender is refused for other reasons, one may not later complain about the use of a check as the medium of tender. A person to whom a tender is made must specify any objection to it or waive it, so that the debtor may know and comply with the creditor's demands.

Tenders of payment are often refused for one reason or another. A party may contend that the tender was too late. The creditor may refuse to accept the offer to pay because he or she believes that the amount tendered is less than the amount of the debt. If it turns out that the tender was proper, the valid tender will have three important legal effects:

1. It stops interest from accruing after the date of the tender.
2. In case the creditor later brings legal action recovering no more than the amount tendered, he or she must pay the court costs.
3. If the debt were secured by a security interest in property belonging to the debtor, this security interest would be extinguished.

Thus a tender of payment, although it does not discharge the debt, has important advantages to the person making it.

Article 2 of the Uniform Commercial Code, which deals with the sale of goods, has two sections relating to tender. Unless the buyer and the seller have otherwise agreed, *tender of payment* by the buyer is a condition to the seller's duty to deliver the goods sold [2-511(1)]. Unless the seller demands payment in legal tender, the buyer is authorized to make payment by check [2-511(2)]. The Code also provides for the manner of a seller's *tender of delivery* of the goods involved in the contract. The Code requires that the seller make the goods available to the buyer and that the seller give the buyer reasonable notification that the goods are available [2-503(1)]. If the seller gives notice that the goods are available for the buyer and the buyer does not tender payment, then the buyer would be placed in default. Tender of delivery is a condition to the buyer's duty to accept the goods [2-507(1)].

7. Substantial Performance

Express conditions must be strictly met, or there is a material breach of contract. Constructive conditions need be only substantially performed to avoid a material breach. Because constructive conditions are imposed in the interest of good faith

Substantial performance
The performance of all the essential elements of a contract. The only permissible omissions or derivations are those that are trivial, inadvertent, and inconsequential.

and fair dealing, it naturally follows that **substantial performance** of a constructive condition satisfies the condition. Thus the other party's duty to perform is activated by substantial performance. Note that substantial performance is not complete performance, so there has been an immaterial breach and dollar damages may be awarded. Although the nonbreaching party can sue for damages for this immaterial breach, the suing party must still perform, because the constructive condition precedent has been fulfilled. Thus an immaterial breach does not excuse the nonbreaching party of the duty of performance under the contract.

The consequences of a material breach are more severe. Normally, a material breach gives the nonbreaching party an option. He or she can opt to treat the contract as rescinded or can choose to continue under the contract by treating it as only a partial breach. A partial breach, in effect, continues the contract, and all parties must continue to perform. The nonbreaching party can sue for damages that accrued from the breach, and the contract is not rescinded. If a total breach is elected, the contract is at an end, and there is an immediate right to all remedies for breach of the entire contract.

Issues of substantial performance often arise in construction contracts. Seldom is there total, complete, and perfect performance. Adjustments in the price are usually made for minor deviations. However, if a contractor fails to substantially perform as agreed, the other party may rescind the contract and the contractor is not entitled to collect anything even on the theory of quasi-contract. The following case is typical of those illustrating this very important principle.

CASE

National Chain Co. v. Campbell
487 A.2d 132 (R.I. 1985)

SHEA, J.

This is an appeal from judgments entered after a jury trial in Superior Court. The judgments awarded nominal damages of $1 to plaintiff, National Chain Company (National), and the sum of $400 on his counterclaim to the defendant, John J. Campbell (Campbell). National had sought to recover damages based on breach of contract and negligence, alleging that Campbell failed to perform in a workmanlike manner. Campbell had counterclaimed for the cost of services rendered. We reverse and remand for retrial on all issues.

National is a jewelry manufacturer with offices located in Warwick, Rhode Island. Campbell was hired to wallpaper the offices of National's president with wallcovering that had been previously purchased by National. The terms of the agreement were that Campbell would be paid on a time-spent basis. Upon completion of the job, the evidence shows that the wallpaper had ragged edges, that there were gaps at the seams, that it was curled up at the edges, and that it had glue stains, contact cement, and staples on it. National refused to pay Campbell and brought suit for recovery of the amount it had paid for the

wallpaper and for the costs incurred in removing it and repairing the wall surface damaged by Campbell. . . .

National's expert, Kenneth Normandin, an experienced wallpaper hanger, testified at trial about the quality of Campbell's work. It was his opinion that the gaps at the seams were caused by Campbell's failure to permit the material to dry and shrink to its normal shape before the seams were cut. In his words, "[I]t was just [a] terrible looking job." Normandin submitted an estimate for removing the wallpaper and preparing the walls for new wallpaper in the amount of $756, of which $300 was for stripping and preparing the walls. The balance was for installing new wallcovering for which National makes no claim.

The underlying rationale in breach-of-contract actions is to place the innocent party in the position in which he would have been if the contract had been fully performed.

A major consideration in determining the proper measure of damages is whether the contractor has substantially performed so that the purpose of the contract is accomplished. This general principle gives rise to National's second claim of error. The trial justice refused to instruct the jury that Campbell could not recover on his counterclaim unless he had substantially performed the contract in a workmanlike manner. The trial justice ruled that although the contractor could not recover on the contract, he could recover in quantum meruit or quasi-contract.

It is well settled that when a builder has substantially performed, he can recover the contract price less the amount needed by the owner to remedy the defect. The doctrine of substantial performance recognizes that it would be unreasonable to condition recovery upon strict performance where minor defects or omissions could be remedied by repair. This formula is inappropriate, however, in situations in which the contractor's performance is worthless and the work has to be redone completely. In these situations, the contractor is liable for the cost to the owner of having the job redone. To recover on an action in quantum meruit, it must be shown that the owner derived some benefit from the services and would be unjustly enriched without making compensation therefor.

We adhere to the rule . . . that "a contractor cannot recover on a building contract unless he has substantially performed and that any lesser degree of performance will not suffice." In our view, consideration of the doctrine of substantial performance is warranted by the evidence in the record before us. Whether there has been substantial performance is a question of fact for the jury to resolve relying on all the relevant evidence. It was error for the trial justice in this case to withhold that instruction from the jury. . . .

■ *Reversed and remanded.*

CASE CONCEPTS REVIEW

1. What was the trial court's ruling on the issue of whether Campbell had substantially performed his contractual duties?
2. Based on the facts presented in the case, do you believe there was substantial performance justifying the award of dollar damages to Campbell?

8. Divisibility: Installment Contracts

Whereas many contracts require a single performance by each party and are completely performed at one point of time, others require or permit performance by one or both parties in installments over a period of time. The rights and obligations of parties during the period when the contract is being performed frequently depend on whether the contract is "entire" or "divisible." A contract is said to be divisible if performance by each party is divided into two or more parts *and* performance of each part by one party is the agreed exchange for the corresponding part by the other party. It is to be noted that a contract is not divisible simply by virtue of the fact that it is to be performed in installments.

The parties may specify whether a contract is divisible or entire. Thus a contract may contain a clause stipulating that each delivery is a separate contract, or other language may be used to show the intention of the parties that their agreement is to be treated as if it were a series of contracts. Some contracts are obviously divisible. Assume Sam promises to sell and Dave promises to buy a car for $5,000 and a boat for $3,000. This contract is legally divisible into two parts, a sale of a car and a sale of a boat. If Sam tenders the car, he is entitled to $5,000 even though he has not performed the entire contract since he has not tendered the boat. Sam is liable for not tendering the boat, but he can still recover for the sale of the car.

The concept of divisibility is applicable to a variety of contracts, including insurance contracts, employment contracts, construction contracts, and sales contracts. As a general proposition, employment contracts are interpreted to be divisible, but construction contracts are usually deemed to be entire.

If a contract is divisible, the second party is under a duty to perform in part after the first party performs an installment. For example, the employer owes a duty to pay wages at the end of the pay period. A material breach of an installment justifies a rescission of the balance of the agreement. Assume that a party is to write five songs each month for a year. Only one song is written the first month. While the failure to deliver the other four would not be a substantial breach of the entire agreement, it would be a substantial breach of the installment. If the contract were treated as divisible, such a material breach would justify rescission of the contract. Likewise, if a party substantially performs an installment of a divisible contract, he or she may nevertheless recover the value of that installment, less damages, caused by any breach of the contract without rendering performance of the balance of the agreement.

There have been numerous cases involving the question of whether or not a contract is divisible. No general test can be derived from these cases. Courts are called on to determine in any given case whether the parties intended that (1) each would accept part performance of the other in return for his or her own without regard to subsequent events or (2) the divisions of the contract were made merely for the purpose of requiring periodic payments as the work progresses. In any event, the party who breaches is liable for damages resulting from his or her breach.

Under the Code, unless the parties have otherwise agreed, a sales contract is entire; all the goods called for by the contract must be tendered in a single delivery, and payment in full is due upon such tender [2-307]. If the contract permits installment deliveries, the seller can demand a proportionate share of the price for each delivery as it is made, provided the price can be apportioned, as for goods sold at a certain price per item. If there is a substantial default on an installment (the goods tendered or delivered may not conform to the contract), the buyer may reject the installment [2-612(2)]. When an installment breached indicates that the seller will not satisfactorily perform the balance of the contract or that such performance is unreliable, the buyer can rescind the entire contract [2-612(3)]. Should the buyer accept a nonconforming installment without giving notice of cancellation or demanding that the seller deliver goods that conform, that buyer may not use the breach as a basis for rescission.

9. Anticipatory Repudiation

Before the time specified for performance, there can be no actual breach, but there may be a breach by *anticipatory repudiation*. The expression means that repudiation occurs before performance is due. The repudiation may be express or implied. An express repudiation is a clear, positive, unequivocal refusal to perform. An implied repudiation results from conduct in which the promisor puts it out of his or her power to perform, making substantial performance of the promise impossible. In either case, the repudiation must be positive and unequivocal.

When a promisor repudiates the prospective duty to perform, the nonrepudiating party has an election of remedies. This latter party can treat the repudiation as an anticipatory breach and immediately seek damages for breach of contract, rather than waiting until the time set for the repudiating party's performance. Thus the doctrine excuses any express or constructive condition to the repudiating party's duty and thereby permits an immediate lawsuit. Rather than suing, the injured party can treat the repudiation as an empty threat, wait until the time for performance arrives, and exercise his or her remedies for actual breach if a breach does in fact occur. If the injured party disregards the repudiation and treats the contract as still in force, the repudiation is nullified, and the injured party is left with his or her remedies, if any, invocable at the time of performance.

The doctrine of anticipatory breach does not apply to promises to pay money on or before a specified date. If a promissory note matures on June 1, 1994, and in 1992 the maker states that he or she will not pay it when the maturity date arrives, that would not give rise to present cause of action by the holder. The following case helps to explain the logic behind anticipatory repudiation not applying to the unilateral nature of the monetary payments.

CASE

Rosenfeld v. City Paper Company
527 So.2d 704 (Ala. 1988)

Donald Rosenfeld signed a promissory note payable to the City Paper Company that contained the following provision:

> In the event that the relationship between [Rosenfeld/payor] and [CPC/payee] terminates, regardless of the reason for such termination, the outstanding balance then due on the obligation expressed herein shall be due and payable, without interest, in five [5] equal annual installments beginning one year from the date of termination of the relationship between the parties.

After the relationship terminated, Rosenfeld failed to pay the first two installments. City Paper sued for the entire amount due. The trial court granted City Paper's motion for summary judgment. Rosenfeld appeals.

Jones, J.

... City Paper Company agrees that the note contains *no* acceleration clause, and that the case law, generally speaking, supports Rosenfeld's contention that "acceleration of the maturity of unaccrued payments" is not to be read into payment contracts by implication. ... Rather, pointing to Rosenfeld's "repudiation of the entire obligation," City Paper Company seeks to have this Court join a minority of jurisdictions that apply the doctrine of anticipatory breach as an exception to the general rule of nonacceleration. ...

The parties agree that Alabama has long recognized that a party to a bilateral contract may elect to treat the contract as absolutely breached and sue at once when the other party repudiates his obligations under the contract. Likewise, the parties agree that the "application of the *anticipatory breach* doctrine" issue, in a *unilateral* or installment payment contract case, is one of first impression. ...

"Anticipatory breach" has a field of operation where the nondefaulting parties remain liable for certain obligations under a bilateral contract. To require the nonde-

faulting party to continue the discharge of his contractual duties, in face of a clear, unequivocal repudiation of the contract by the defaulting party, is a senseless requirement that unduly penalizes the nondefaulting party.

The majority of jurisdictions faced with this issue have drawn the distinction and have not allowed the "anticipatory breach" doctrine to apply to unilateral contracts, particularly for the payment of money only. The "settled" rule was succinctly expressed by Justice Cardozo in *Smyth v. United States*, 302 U.S. 329 at 356 (1937):

> [T]he doctrine of anticipatory breach has in general no application to unilateral contracts, and particularly to such contracts for the payment of money only.

Some of the cases cited above reference Professor Williston's treatise for the rationale that rejects the application of the "anticipatory breach" doctrine to installment contracts that contain no acceleration clause: "[A]llowing the promissee immediate recovery is nothing but a direct bonus to the promisee beyond what he was promised and a direct penalty to the promissor."

Indeed, the use of the "acceleration of maturity of payment" clause is in recognition of the nonapplicability of the anticipatory breach doctrine in installment payment contracts. Once the promisee has done all there is for him to do under the contract and the promissor's obligation is confined to payment by installments as specified by the contract, the doctrine of anticipatory breach has no field of operation and will not intercede to rescue the promisee from the consequences of the absence of an acceleration clause. ...

■ *Reversed and remanded.*

CASE CONCEPTS REVIEW

1. How many annual installments were to be paid by Rosenfeld? How many had not been paid when this lawsuit was filed?
2. What is the logic of anticipatory repudiation, as a doctrine of contractual performance, applying to bilateral contracts but not to unilateral contracts?

The Code provides that after a breach including anticipatory repudiation, the buyer may "cover" by making in good faith and without unreasonable delay any reasonable purchase of, or contract to purchase, goods in substitution for those due from the seller [2-712]. The difference between the cost of cover and the contract price, together with any incidental or consequential damages, may be recovered by the buyer from the seller. Failure of the buyer to effect cover does not bar him or her from recovering damages for nondelivery, but damages will be limited to those that could not have been prevented by proper cover.

A party may retract his or her repudiation, provided he or she does so prior to any material change of position by the other party in reliance on it. The retraction would simply be a notice that performance of the contract will occur after all. The Code allows a retraction of anticipatory repudiation until the repudiating party's next performance is due, unless the aggrieved party has, since the repudiation, canceled or materially changed position or otherwise indicated that he or she considers the repudiation final [2-611]. Retraction may be by any method that clearly indicates to the aggrieved party that the repudiating party intends to perform, but it must include adequate assurance that in fact performance will occur if the other party demands it [2-609]. Retraction reinstates the repudiating party's rights under the contract, with due excuse and allowance to the aggrieved party for any delay occasioned by the repudiation.

CHAPTER SUMMARY

CONDITIONS

Definition	1. A condition is an act or event that limits or qualifies a promise.
	2. A duty to perform is conditional if something other than the passage of time must occur before performance is due.
	3. Conditions set the order of performance and prevent lawsuits by establishing defenses if conditions do not occur.
	4. Failure of a promise gives rise to a remedy for breach; a failure of condition only excuses performance.
Types of Conditions	1. Conditions may be classified in terms of time (conditions precedent, concurrent, and subsequent) or manner of creation (express or constructive).
	2. A condition precedent is an act or event that, unless excused, must occur before a duty to perform is activated.
	3. Conditions concurrent require the parties to exchange performances at the same time.
	4. A condition subsequent is an act or event that discharges a duty that had previously become absolute.
Express Conditions	1. An express condition is specifically stated by the parties' agreement as activating or discharging duties.
	2. Express conditions must be strictly satisfied.
Express Conditions of Personal Satisfaction	1. If a condition involves personal taste or judgment, dissatisfaction is judged by a subjective standard. If good-faith dissatisfaction exists, the condition is not met.
	2. If a condition involves mechanical fitness, utility, or marketability, an objective standard of dissatisfaction is used to decide if the condition has been met.
Constructive Conditions	1. A court-created condition is imposed to serve justice.
	2. Substantial performance of constructive conditions will make the other party's duty to perform absolute.

Tender of Performance	**1.** Tender is an offer to perform. The party making the tender indicates that he or she is ready, willing, and able to perform.
	2. Tender of payment by the buyer is a condition to the seller's duty to deliver the goods.
	3. Tender by the seller occurs when the goods are available to the buyer. The seller must give reasonable notice that the goods are available.
Substantial Performance	**1.** Substantial performance of a constructive condition is required to make the other party's duty absolute.
	2. Substantial performance is not full performance and is an immaterial breach.
	3. Failure to perform at the proper time is not substantial performance if time was of the essence.
Divisibility: Installment Contracts	**1.** A party can recover for performance of divisible portions of a contract.
	2. Breach of one part of a divisible contract does not allow the other party to refuse to pay for the part performed.
Anticipatory Repudiation	**1.** Before the time for performance, a party may expressly or implicitly repudiate his or her duty to perform. If the party does so, it is an anticipatory repudiation.
	2. The repudiation is not favored and must be shown to be clear, positive, and unequivocal.
	3. A repudiation may be withdrawn unless it is relied on by the other party.

REVIEW QUESTIONS AND PROBLEMS

1. Match each term in column A with the appropriate statement in column B.

A	**B**
(1) Condition	(a) Condition that discharges duty
(2) Condition precedent	(b) Condition created by the court to achieve justice
(3) Condition subsequent	(c) Party clearly indicates that he or she will not perform in the future
(4) Express condition	(d) An act or event that limits or qualifies a contract duty
(5) Constructive condition	(e) An immaterial breach
(6) Substantial performance	(f) A condition created expressly by the parties' agreement
(7) Divisibility	(g) An offer to perform
(8) Anticipatory repudiation	(h) Contract can be apportioned into several contracts
(9) Tender	(i) Condition that activates a contract duty

2. Merv and Harold contract to merge their corporate holdings into a single new company provided that the merger is not to be operative unless they raise $800,000 additional capital. What happens if they cannot raise an additional $800,000? Explain.

3. Farmer Schmidt contracted to raise seed corn for the Robinson Seed Co. A provision of the contract allowed the buyer of the seed corn to release any acres of the grower's fields if they became infested with shattercane. Is this provision a condition? If so, what kind? Explain.

4. Totten hired Lampenfeld to paint his house. Totten agreed to pay in installments as the painting progressed. While Totten was on vacation, Lampenfeld started painting the house. When Totten returned, he refused to pay for the partial painting. Since he was not paid as agreed, Lampenfeld refused to complete the painting. Lampenfeld sued

Totten for the value of the painting he had done. Totten claimed that Lampenfeld had materially breached the contract by not finishing the job and thus should recover nothing. Was Totten's payment for the partial painting a condition precedent to Lampenfeld's duty to complete painting the house? Explain.

5. John contracts with Fay to install a heating system in Fay's factory for a price of $30,000 to be paid "on condition of satisfactory completion." John installs the heating system, but Fay states that she is not satisfied with it and refuses to pay the $30,000. Fay gives no reason except that she does not approve of the heating system. According to experts, the heating system as installed is entirely satisfactory. May John successfully recover $30,000 from Fay? Explain why or why not.

6. Coots contracted to sell a farm to Bell. The sale contract required Bell to pay the total purchase price in monthly installments with a thirty-day grace period for payments. It also contained provisions for Coots's immediate recovery of possession in the event of the Bell's default in making the monthly payments. Is time of the essence of this agreement? Why or why not?

7. Harte contracted with Connolly to install a new roof on Connolly's house. It was agreed that the roofing shingles were to be "russet glow," a shade of brown. The roof was installed, and many of the shingles were discolored, showing streaks of yellow. Harte replaced some of the shingles, but the new shingles did not match the others. The overall appearance of the roof is that it has been patched with nonblending colors. The roof is functional and is guaranteed to last fifteen years. Must Connolly pay? Why or why not? Would your answer change if Harte were building a house for Connolly and on the scheduled completion date had done everything required by the contract except grading and paving? Why or why not?

8. Walsh contracted with the Alaska Housing Authority to construct a gravel surface road. The road was to be constructed of 12 inches of crushed rock surfacing and a 12-inch layer of compacted wood chips to be placed below the gravel surface. Instead, the wood-chip layer after the project was completed averaged 9 inches, with a 2,000-foot section averaging only 5 inches. The insufficient layer of wood-chip insulation caused increased rutting along the road, necessitating frequent maintenance. Is Walsh entitled to be paid for the road? Why or why not? If so, how much?

9. Stacey, a pro football quarterback, signed a seven-year contract with the Professional Football League for $875,000. Stacey was to receive $50,000 upon signing and another $50,000 at the end of the first year. Although he received the $50,000 upon signing, the league could pay only $20,000 at the end of the year. At that time, the league was in financial difficulties to the tune of $1,600,000 indebtedness and an overdraft at the bank for $67,000. Should Stacey treat the contract as rescinded? Why or why not?

10. Johnson agreed to erect six signs on a highway near Clark's Place. Four small signs are to read: "4 miles to Clark's Place, 3 miles to Clark's Place," etc. One large sign is to read: "STOP! You're at Clark's Place." The sixth sign reads: "Turn around, You've just missed Clark's Place." Clark agreed to pay $300 each for the five small signs and $500 for the large sign. Johnson erected only three small signs and sues for $900. May he recover? Why or why not?

11. Rick agreed to buy two campers from McMahon and made a deposit of $1,000 as partial payment. Rick then wired McMahon not to ship the campers and explained his reasons for delaying shipment. Later, Rick decided not to buy the campers and demanded a return of his $1,000. Was Rick's instruction not to ship an anticipatory repudiation that will justify McMahon's retention of the $1,000? Explain.

12. A bank made a loan commitment for the construction of a racquetball recreational development. After the start of construction, the bank informed the developer that it would not make the loan and that the developer could sue if it didn't like it. The developer filed suit for damages, and the bank then agreed to go ahead with the loan. Will the suit be dismissed? Why or why not?

EXCUSES FOR NONPERFORMANCE AND DISCHARGE OF CONTRACTS

CHAPTER PREVIEW

Chapter 15 began our discussion of performance of contracts, emphasizing conditions and the order of performance by the parties to a contract. Two additional legal issues may arise during the performance of a contract. First, a party may be unable to perform because of circumstances beyond his or her control, or the party may contend that because of changed conditions, he or she should be excused from performing as agreed. These circumstances, known as excuses for nonperformance, begin this chapter.

Second, a contract must eventually come to an end. Most contracts end when they are fully performed, but there are other events and legal principles that may result in the discharge or termination of a contract or contract liability. The discharge of contracts is discussed in the latter portion of this chapter.

You operate a retail paint and wallpaper store. The Handy-Man Company has purchased a variety of items on credit. One account receivable, for $425, is eighteen months old. A second account receivable is for $1,800, and it is secured by Handy-Man's spraying equipment. A third account receivable is for $175, and it is only three weeks old. Today you receive a $350 check from Handy-Man with no instructions as to its application.

How should you apply this $350 against these three accounts receivable?

EXCUSES FOR NONPERFORMANCE

1. Introduction

A party to a contract may be relieved from the duty to perform or from liability for breach if he or she is legally excused from contract performance. Moreover, a duty under a conditional promise may be activated not only by performance of the condition but also if the condition is excused. Actual failure of an express or a constructive condition may be legally excused in any of the following five ways: (1) hindrance, prevention, or noncooperation; (2) waiver, estoppel, or election; (3) impossibility; (4) frustration of purpose; and (5) commercial impracticability.

2. Hindrance, Prevention, or Noncooperation

In every contract there is an implied duty of good faith and fair dealing requiring each party not to prevent or substantially hinder the other party's performance. If a party whose promise is conditional wrongfully prevents the condition from occurring, then the condition is excused. Although the cases vary, the wrongful conduct can be characterized as either hindrance, wrongful prevention, or noncooperation.

HINDRANCE.   When a party hinders another's performance of a promise, the first party makes it more difficult, but not impossible, for the second party to perform. To be an excuse for nonperformance, the hindrance must be *wrongful*, which usually means that no party reasonably contemplated or assumed the risk that occurred. For example, assume that seller agrees to sell buyer a product in short supply. Seller fails to deliver because buyer has been purchasing all of the available product from seller's only source of supply. A court held that although buyer did substantially hinder seller's performance, it was not wrongful. Seller assumed the risk of such market conditions when it unconditionally agreed to supply the product.

PREVENTION.   The wrongful prevention of performance by one party to a contract will excuse nonperformance by the other party. It is obvious that a person may not recover for nonperformance of a contract if he or she is responsible for the nonperformance. If a party creates a situation that makes it impossible for the other party to perform, the other party is excused. For example, Barrow had leased a building to Calhoun for the operation of an ice cream store. The rent was to be a percentage of the gross income. Thereafter, Calhoun established *another* ice cream store a block away and did very little business in the building rented to her by Barrow. Calhoun has prevented the normal performance of the contract by carrying on another business that detracted from the profits. Barrow may cancel the lease without liability because Calhoun has prevented the anticipated performance of the contract.

NONCOOPERATION.   As a part of the good-faith requirement, the law implies that the parties will reasonably cooperate with each other. If as the result of one party's failure to cooperate and to act in good faith the other party breaches the contract, then the noncooperating party is not entitled to the usual contract remedies. In fact, the other party may rescind the agreement because the implied condition of good faith has been breached.

A common example of noncooperation occurs in the landlord–tenant relationship. The written lease frequently contains a clause that states that the tenant may not assign or sublease rights and duties under the lease without the landlord's consent. A landlord who is unreasonable in refusing to consent to an assignment or a sublease fails to cooperate in the contract's performance. Upon such noncooperation, the tenant may be relieved of further liability.

3. Waiver

Waiver The intentional relinquishment or giving up of a known right. It may be done by express words or conduct that involves any acts inconsistent with an intention to claim the right.

Waiver has been defined as the passing by of an occasion to enforce a legal right, whereby the legal right is lost. As applied to contract law, the essence of waivers is conduct by one party that indicates an intention not to enforce certain provisions of the agreement as against the other party. Generally, waiver occurs when there is either (1) a promise to forgo the benefit of a condition or (2) an election to continue under a contract after the other party has breached.

To illustrate the first situation, assume you had promised to purchase a new car only on the condition that you could get the car within two weeks. The dealer has not promised to make the delivery within the two-week period. If the seller notifies you that delivery will take four weeks, you might waive your right to the quicker delivery and promise to buy the car anyway.

The second situation when waiver typically occurs appears to be similar but is technically distinguishable. Assume that the car dealer promises to deliver the car within two weeks, and this promise is an essential part of the time of performance. The failure to make a timely delivery is a breach of the agreement. Rather than the failure of the delivery just excusing your performance (as in a condition not being satisfied), you now have a cause of action for damages since the dealer has breached the contract. Further assume that you decide not to make a claim against the dealer and agree to buy the car at the original price whenever it is delivered. You have waived your right to complain of the dealer's breach by agreeing to continue with the revised contract.

The waiver may be retracted unless it is supported by consideration or unless the promisee has made a substantial change of position in reliance on it. One who has waived the time for performance may withdraw the waiver if he or she gives the other party a reasonable opportunity to perform the condition waived.

The Uniform Commercial Code allows a party who has waived a provision of an executory contract to retract the waiver upon giving reasonable notice that he or she will require strict performance of the original contract, "unless the retraction would be unjust in view of a material change of position in reliance of the waiver" [2-209(5)]. Under the Code, the retention or acceptance of defective goods may constitute a waiver of the defect. A buyer who fails to particularize defects in goods may in fact be waiving his or her objections based on these defects [2-605].

4. Impossibility of Performance

Actual impossibility of performance is a valid excuse for nonperformance and releases a party from the duty to perform. Impossibility is much more than mere "additional hardship." As a general rule, in the absence of an appropriate contract provision, circumstances that impose additional hardship on one party do not constitute an excuse for breach of contract. The fact that the promised performance of a contractual obligation may be more difficult than expected at the time the promise was made does not discharge the promisor from the duty to perform. Therefore, most contracts provide that manufacturers, suppliers, or builders shall be relieved from performance in case of fire, strikes, difficulty in obtaining raw materials, or other incidents imposing hardship over which they have no control. Without such a provision there would be no excuse, as they do not constitute impossibility of performance. The following case is typical of those finding no excuse in the face of significant hardship and the failure of one party to include a contractual clause relieving performance.

CASE

Kel Kim Corp. v. Central Markets, Inc.
519 N.E.2d 295 (N.Y. 1987)

PER CURIAM

. . . In early 1980, plaintiff Kel Kim Corporation leased a vacant supermarket in Clifton Park, New York, from defendants. The lease was for an initial term of 10 years with two 5-year renewal options. The understanding of both parties was that plaintiff would use the property as a roller skating rink open to the general public, although the lease did not limit use of the premises to a roller rink.

The lease required Kel Kim to procure and maintain in full force and effect a public liability insurance policy or policies in a solvent and responsible company or companies . . . of not less than Five Hundred Thousand Dollars . . . to any single person and in the aggregate of not less than One Million Dollars . . . on account of any single accident. Kel Kim obtained the required insurance coverage and for six years operated the facility without incident. In November 1985 its insurance carrier gave notice that the policy would expire on January 6, 1986 and would not be renewed due to uncertainty about the financial condition of the reinsurer, which was then under the management of a court-appointed administrator. Kel Kim transmitted this information to defendants and, it asserts, thereafter made every effort to procure the requisite insurance elsewhere but was unable to do so on account of the liability insurance crisis. Plaintiff ultimately succeeded in obtaining a policy in the aggregate amount of $500,000 effective March 1, 1986 and contends that no insurer would write a policy in excess of that amount on any roller skating rink. . . .

On January 7, 1986, when plaintiff's initial policy expired and it remained uninsured, defendants sent a notice of default, directing that it cure within 30 days or vacate the premises. Kel Kim and the individual guarantors of the lease then began this declaratory judgment action, urging that they should be excused from compliance with the insurance provision . . . because performance was impossible. . . . Special Term granted defendants' motion for summary judgment, nullified the lease, and directed Kel Kim to vacate the premises. A divided Appellate Division affirmed.

Generally, once a party to a contract has made a promise, that party must perform or respond in damages for its failure, even when unforeseen circumstances make performance burdensome. . . . Impossibility excuses a party's performance only when the destruction of the subject matter of the contract or the means of performance makes performance objectively impossible. Moreover, the impossibility must be produced by an unanticipated event that could not have been foreseen or guarded against in the contract.

Applying these principles, we conclude that plaintiff's predicament is not within the embrace of the doctrine of impossibility. Kel Kim's inability to procure and maintain requisite coverage could have been foreseen and guarded against when it specifically undertook that obligation in the lease, and therefore the obligation cannot be excused on this basis. . . .

■ *Affirmed.*

CASE CONCEPTS REVIEW

1. Why does Kel Kim argue it should be allowed to continue operating a skating rink under the long-term lease without maintaining the requisite amount of insurance?

2. The court gives two reasons why Kel Kim's argument is rejected. What are these two reasons? What is the logic underlying each reason?

As stated in the foregoing case, to have the effect of releasing a party from the duty to perform, the impossibility must render performance "physically and objectively impossible." If objective impossibility is present, the discharge is mutual; that is, the promisor is discharged, and the promisee is also discharged from his or her corresponding obligation. Many cases state that for impossibility to exist, there must be a fortuitous or unavoidable occurrence that was not reasonably foreseeable. The fact that an act of God is involved does not necessarily create an excuse. If a house under construction is destroyed by fire caused by lightning, the contractor is not excused from the obligation to complete the house. Contractors take the risk of fire unless they protect themselves by expressly contracting that they shall not be held liable for such risks.

Likewise, if the situation is caused by the promisor or by developments that the promisor could have prevented, avoided, or remedied by corrective measures, there is no excuse. For this reason, the failure of a third party, such as a supplier, to make proper delivery does not create impossibility. Impossibility will not be allowed as a defense when the obstacle was created by the promisor or was within his or her power to eliminate. It must not exist merely because of the inability or incapacity of the promisor to do it; that is, subjective impossibility is no excuse.

5. Specific Cases of Impossibility

There are four basic situations in which impossibility of performance is frequently offered as an excuse for nonperformance.

PERFORMANCE BECOMES ILLEGAL.   In the first of these, performance becomes illegal because of the enactment of some law or governmental action. A manufacturer or supplier may be prevented from making delivery of merchandise because of government restrictions. However, government action that merely makes an agreement more burdensome than was anticipated does not afford a basis for relief.

DEATH OR INCAPACITATING ILLNESS.   The second situation is the death or incapacitating illness of one of the contracting parties. This is not deemed to be a form of impossibility unless the contract demands the personal services of the disabled or deceased person. Ordinary contracts of production, processing, and sale of property are unaffected by the death or illness of one or both of the parties. In the event of death, it is assumed that the contract will be carried out by the estate of the deceased. If a contract is for personal services or it clearly implies that the continued services of the contracting party are essential to performance, death or illness will excuse nonperformance. In contracts for personal services, the death of the employer also terminates the relationship. The estate of the employer in prematurely terminating the contract is not liable for damages to the employee.

CONTINUED EXISTENCE OF CERTAIN SUBJECT MATTER.   Many agreements involve the continued existence of certain subject matter essential to completion of the contract. The third rule is that destruction of any subject matter essential to the completion of the contract will operate to relieve the parties of the obligations assumed by their agreement. A different situation arises when material that only one of the parties expected to use in his or her performance is destroyed. For example, if a factory from which the owner expected to deliver certain material is destroyed by fire, performance is not excused. Performance is still possible, even though an undue hardship may result. The material needed to fill the order can be obtained from another source. However, had the contract stipulated that the material were to be delivered from a particular factory, its destruction would have operated to excuse a failure to perform. In recent years, there has been a trend toward holding that when both parties understood that delivery was to be made from a certain source, even though it was not expressly agreed, destruction of the source of supply will relieve the obligor from performing.

LACK OF ESSENTIAL ELEMENT.   The last form of impossibility arises when there is an essential element lacking. This situation is difficult to define satisfactorily, but apparently the agreement may be rescinded when some element or property is lacking, although the parties assumed it existed or would exist. Some courts would hold that no contract, in fact, existed because of mutual mistake. This is said to be a form of impossibility at the time of making the contract, and courts have tended to act as if there had been no meeting of the minds. It must be definitely proved that performance is substantially impossible because of the missing element. For example, a builder contracts to build an office building at a certain location. Because of the nature of the soil, it is utterly impossible to build the type of building provided for in the agreement; the agreement must therefore be terminated. The missing element is the proper condition of the soil. In other words, from the very beginning, the contract terms could not possibly have been complied with, and in such cases the courts are prone to excuse the parties if nobody is at fault.

6. Commercial Frustration

Since the notion of requiring *absolute* impossibility may create harsh results in certain cases, courts may excuse performance using the *doctrine of commercial frustration*. The doctrine excuses performance when the essential purpose and value of the contract have been frustrated. Typically, something happens to prevent achievement of the object or purpose of the contract. If so, the courts may find an implied condition that the unforeseen development will excuse performance.

Commercial frustration arises whenever there is an intervening event or change of circumstances so fundamental it is entirely beyond that which was contemplated by the parties. Frustration is not impossibility, but it is more than mere hardship. It is an excuse created by law to eliminate liability when a fortuitous occurrence has defeated the reasonable expectations of the parties. It will not be used when the supervening event was foreseeable or assumed as a part of the agreement.

In the following case, the court discusses the similarities between the doctrines of impossibility and frustration as excuses for nonperformance.

CASE

Chase Precast Construction v. Paonessa Company, Inc.

566 N.E.2d 603 (Mass. 1991)

LYNCH, J.

This appeal raises the question whether the doctrine of frustration of purpose may be a defense in a breach of contract action in Massachusetts, and, if so, whether it excuses the defendant John J. Paonessa Company, Inc. (Paonessa), from performance.

The claim of the plaintiff, Chase Precast Corporation (Chase), arises from the cancellation of its contracts with Paonessa to supply median barriers in a highway reconstruction project of the Commonwealth. Chase brought an action to recover its anticipated profit on the amount of median barriers called for by its supply contracts with Paonessa but not produced.... After a jury-waived trial, a Superior Court judge ruled for Paonessa on the basis of impossibility of performance. Chase ... appealed. The Appeals Court affirmed, noting that the doctrine of frustration of purpose more accurately described the basis of the trial judge's decision than the doctrine of impossibility. We agree ... and we now affirm.

The pertinent facts are as follows. In 1982, the Commonwealth, through the Department of Public Works (department), entered into two contracts with Paonessa for resurfacing and improvements to two stretches of Route 128. Part of each contract called for replacing a grass median strip between the north and southbound lanes with concrete surfacing and precast concrete median barriers. Paonessa entered into two contracts with Chase under which Chase was to supply, in the aggregate, 25,800 linear feet of concrete median barriers according to the specifications of the department for highway construction. The quantity and type of barriers to be supplied were specified in two purchase orders prepared by Chase.

The highway reconstruction began in the spring of 1983. By late May, the department was receiving protests from angry residents who objected to use of the concrete median barriers and removal of the grass median strip. Paonessa and Chase became aware of the protest around June 1. On June 6, a group of about 100 citizens filed an

action in the Superior Court to stop installation of the concrete median barriers, and other aspects of the work. On June 7, anticipating modification by the department, Paonessa notified Chase by letter to stop producing concrete barriers for the projects. Chase did so upon receipt of the letter the following day. On June 17, the department and the citizens' group entered into a settlement which provided, in part, that no additional concrete median barriers would be installed. On June 23, the department deleted the permanent concrete median barriers item from its contracts with Paonessa.

Before stopping production on June 8, Chase had produced approximately one-half of the concrete median barriers called for by its contracts with Paonessa, and had delivered most of them to the construction sites. Paonessa paid Chase for all that it had produced, at the contract price. Chase suffered no out-of-pocket expense as a result of cancellation of the remaining portion of barriers.

This court has long recognized and applied the doctrine of impossibility as a defense to an action for breach of contract. Under that doctrine, "where from the nature of the contract it appears that the parties must from the beginning have contemplated the continued existence of some particular specified thing as the foundation of what was to be done, then, in the absence of any warranty that the thing shall exist ... the parties shall be excused ... [when] performance becomes impossible from the accidental perishing of the thing without the fault of either party."

On the other hand, although we have referred to the doctrine of frustration of purpose in a few decisions, we have never clearly defined it. Other jurisdictions have explained the doctrine as follows: when an event neither anticipated nor caused by either party, the risk of which was not allocated by the contract, destroys the object or purpose of the contract, thus destroying the value of performance, the parties are excused from further performance....

Another definition of frustration of purpose is found in the Restatement (Second) of Contracts § 265 (1981):

> Where, after a contract is made, a party's principal purpose is substantially frustrated without his fault

by the occurrence of an event the non-occurrence of which was a basic assumption on which the contract was made, his remaining duties to render performance are discharged, unless the language or the circumstances indicate the contrary.

. . . Paonessa bore no responsibility for the department's elimination of the median barriers from the projects. Therefore, whether it can rely on the defense of frustration turns on whether elimination of the barriers was a risk allocated by the contracts to Paonessa. . . .

Paonessa's contracts with the department contained a standard provision allowing the department to eliminate items or portions of work found unnecessary. The purchase order agreements between Chase and Paonessa do not contain a similar provision. This difference in the contracts does not mandate the conclusion that Paonessa assumed the risk of reduction in the quantity of the barriers. It is implicit in the judge's findings that Chase knew the barriers were for department projects. The record supports the conclusion that Chase was aware of the department's power to decrease quantities of contract items. The judge found that Chase had been a supplier of median barriers to the department in the past. The provision giving the department the power to eliminate items or portions thereof was standard in its contracts. . . . The judge found that Chase had furnished materials under and was familiar with the so-called "Unit Price Philosophy" in the construction industry, whereby contract

items are paid for at the contract unit price for the quantity of work actually accepted. Finally, the judge's finding that "[a]ll parties were well aware that lost profits were not an element of damage in either of the public works projects in issue" further supports the conclusion that Chase was aware of the department's power to decrease quantities, since the term prohibiting claims for anticipated profit is part of the same sentence in the standard provision as that allowing the engineer to eliminate items or portions of work.

. . . In this case, even if the parties were aware generally of the department's power to eliminate contract items, the judge could reasonably have concluded that they did not contemplate the cancellation for a major portion of the project of such a widely used item as concrete median barriers, and did not allocate the risk of such cancellation. . . .

■ *Judgment affirmed.*

CASE CONCEPTS REVIEW

1. What performance is required under the contract between Chase Precast and Paonessa Company?
2. On what events or decisions does Paonessa Company base its defense of frustration?
3. Why does the court accept this defense, thereby relieving Paonessa Company of damages for noncompletion of the contract?

7. Commercial Impracticability under the Code

The Code uses the term *commercial impracticability* to describe a defense similar to *commercial frustration.* The Code recognizes that without the fault of either party, unexpected developments or government action may cause the promised performance to become impracticable. In some cases, the Code authorizes substituted performance. If the loading or unloading facilities of the agreed-on carrier are unusable, a commercially reasonable substitute must be tendered and accepted if it is available [2-614].

The Code also provides that commercial impracticability is often an excuse for a seller who fails to deliver goods or is delayed in making the delivery. The excuse is limited to cases in which unforeseen supervening circumstances not within the contemplation of the parties arise [2-615(a)]. The law does not specify all the contingencies that may justify the application of the doctrine of commercial impracticability. Increased costs will not excuse the seller unless they are due to some unforeseen contingency that alters the basic nature of the contract. Currency fluctuations may significantly affect a contract, but since they are foreseeable the impracticability defense usually does not arise, as the following case illustrates.

CASE

Bernina Distributors, Inc. v. Bernina Sewing Mach.

646 F.2d 434 (Utah 1981)

A distributor of sewing machines brought an action against an importer of sewing machines for interpretation of their contract, which was for seven years commencing in 1971. The contract provided that the exchange rate between dollars and Swiss francs would be treated as an increase in invoice costs to the importer. With the precipitous decline of the dollar in relation to the Swiss francs, the importer began to surcharge the distributor 10 percent above the increased cost of purchasing Swiss francs, so it "could retain sufficient profit margin to justify sales." The trial court, however, determined that the importer could exact no profit on the additional costs incurred from the exchange rate fluctuations, and the importer now claims the contract does not have to be performed, owing to the commercial impracticability doctrine of the Uniform Commercial Code.

LOGAN, J.

. . . Importer asserts that the court's interpretation makes the contract impracticable under Utah Code Ann. §70A-2-615 (1980). That U.C.C. section excuses performance under the contract "[e]xcept so far as a seller may have assumed a greater obligation" when performance "has been made impracticable by the occurrence of a contingency the nonoccurrence of which was a basic assumption on which the contract was made. . . ." In our view the instant contract is not one made "impracticable" by the contingency of the devalued dollar. The contract, as interpreted by the trial court, always allows a gross profit margin, although the return on capital investment has been reduced considerably because of the devaluation of the dollar.

Moreover, there is considerable evidence that Importer assumed this particular risk. The contract lumps all the shipping and invoice costs in one provision which allows price increases only to the extent of the cost increases to Importer. Importer's letter to Distributor concerning a 7% devaluation of the dollar in relation to the franc, sent three weeks prior to the contract execution, shows clear foreknowledge of the possibility of currency fluctuations and, thus, supports the finding that section 2-615 is inapplicable. Uniform Commercial Code 2-615, Comment 8 states:

> [T]he exemptions of this section do not apply when the contingency in question is sufficiently foreshadowed at the time of contracting to be included among the business risks which are fairly to be regarded as part of the dickered terms, either consciously or as a matter of reasonable, commercial interpretation from the circumstances.

Finally, cost increases alone, though great in extent, do not render a contract impracticable. UCC §2-615, Comment 4. The Third Circuit held that the doctrine of impracticability was not available unless the party seeking to excuse performance could show he could perform only at a loss, and that the loss would be especially severe and unreasonable. We hold the defense of impracticability is unavailable in the instant case. . . .

■ *Affirmed.*

CASE CONCEPTS REVIEW

1. What occurred that caused the distributor of sewing machines to file suit against the importer of the machines?
2. What defense did the importer assert?
3. Why did the court conclude that the importer assumed the risk of the currency fluctuations?

Generally, a severe shortage of raw materials or of supplies due to a contingency such as war, an unforeseen shutdown of major sources of supply, or a local crop failure, which increases costs or prevents a seller from securing necessary supplies, does constitute commercial impracticability.

To use the excuse, the seller is required to notify customers seasonably of any delay or nondelivery. This notification is to allow the buyers to take prompt action to find another source of supply. The notice must include an estimate of the buyer's allocation when the seller is able to perform partially [2-615(c)] and is subject to the Code's allocation requirement [2-615(b)].

Upon receipt of a notice of a substantial or indefinite delay in delivery or of an allocation, the buyer has two alternative courses of action. The buyer may terminate the contract insofar as that delivery is concerned. He or she may also terminate and discharge the whole contract if the deficiency substantially impairs the value of the whole contract [2-616(1)]. The buyer may also modify the contract by agreeing to take his or her available quota in substitution. If the buyer fails to modify the contract within a reasonable time not exceeding thirty days, the contract lapses with respect to the deliveries covered by the seller's notice [2-616(2)].

DISCHARGE OF CONTRACTS

8. Methods

The rights and duties created by a contract continue in force until the contract is discharged. The term *discharge* is used to describe the cancellation of a contract and the acts by which the enforcement of its provisions are terminated. The usual and intended method of discharge is the complete performance by both parties of their obligations under the agreement. A valid excuse is a discharge in the sense that the excused party has no liability for failure to perform. The same may be said of grounds for rescission. A rescinded contract is in effect discharged.

Release The voluntary relinquishing of a right, lien, or any other obligation.

Although no particular form is required for an agreement to discharge a contract duty, the term **release** has traditionally been reserved for a formal written statement by one party that the other's duty is discharged. In chapter 11, the word *renunciation* was introduced; it is equivalent to a release. Either party may voluntarily renounce any right or claim arising under a contract. A renunciation is valid without consideration, provided it is in writing.

A cancellation of a written contract and the surrender of it by one party to the other will usually discharge the agreement. Such a discharge requires consideration or proof of a gift. If both parties have obligations, there is consideration on the mutual surrender of the rights to performance. If only one party has an obligation, the necessary intent to make a gift and delivery of it may be found in the delivery of the written cancelled contract. However, such evidence is not conclusive, and a jury may find that a gift was not in fact made.

The law makes a distinction between a writing that is merely the *evidence* of the obligation and one that *is* the obligation, such as a promissory note. There is no particular sanctity in the law to the physical evidence of an ordinary contract, and the destruction of this evidence does not destroy the contract. However, if the actual obligation such as a promissory note is surrendered or is intentionally destroyed by the holder of it, the obligation is discharged.

There are other methods of discharge, one of which is a novation. The term *novation* has two meanings. First, it is used to describe the situation in which the parties to a contract substitute a new debt or obligation for an existing one. The substitution of the new agreement operates to release or discharge the old one. Novation is also used to describe an agreement whereby an original party to a contract is replaced by a new party. The concept of novation is discussed further in chapter 17.

The legal concept of *accord and satisfaction* allows discharge of a contract by a performance different from that agreed on in the agreement. Section 10 of this chapter discusses this concept.

Laws sometimes have the effect of discharging obligations by prohibiting lawsuits to enforce them. For example, passage of time without litigation to enforce one's rights will operate to discharge an obligation. This is further discussed in section 11.

9. Payment

The obligation of one party to a contract is usually to pay the other for goods sold or services rendered. There are three especially significant issues about payment that affect the matter of discharge: What constitutes payment? What is good evidence that payment has been made and that the obligation has been discharged? When a debtor has several obligations to a creditor, how will a payment be applied?

WHAT CONSTITUTES PAYMENT?   Certainly, the transfer of money constitutes payment, but this is not necessarily the case when the payment is by a negotiable instrument such as a check or a promissory note. Generally, payment by delivery of a negotiable instrument drawn or indorsed by the debtor to the creditor is a conditional payment and not an absolute discharge of the obligation. If the instrument is paid at maturity, the debt is discharged; if it is not so paid, the debt then exists as it did prior to the conditional payment. In the latter situation, the creditor can either bring an action to recover on the defaulted instrument or pursue his or her rights under the original agreement.

The parties may agree that payment by a negotiable instrument is an absolute discharge, in which event, if the instrument is not paid at maturity, the only recourse of the creditor is to bring action on the instrument—the original contract is discharged. A similar situation exists when accounts receivable are transferred by a debtor to his or her creditor. A transfer of accounts is a conditional payment only. If the accounts are not collected, the debtor is still obligated to pay his or her indebtedness. If the parties intend that the receipt of negotiable instruments or accounts receivable be treated as a discharge of the obligation, they must so specify.

WHAT IS GOOD EVIDENCE OF PAYMENT AND DISCHARGE?   As to what constitutes acceptable evidence of payment and discharge, a receipt given by the creditor will usually suffice. Such receipt should clearly indicate the amount paid and specify the transaction to which it relates. However, the creditor may be able to rebut the receipt by evidence that it was in error or that it was given under mistake.

A cancelled check is also evidence of payment, but the evidence is more conclusive when the purpose for which it is given is stated on the check. The drawer of a check may specify on the instrument that the payee by endorsing or cashing it acknowledges full satisfaction of an obligation of the drawer.

Mutual debts do not extinguish each other. For one debt to constitute payment of another, in whole or in part, there must be agreement between the creditor and debtor that the one shall be applied in satisfaction of the other.

HOW IS PAYMENT APPLIED TO MULTIPLE DEBTS?   Where a debtor owes several obligations to one creditor, the debtor may direct how any payment is to be applied. The creditor who receives such payment is obligated to follow the debtor's instructions. In the absence of any instructions, the creditor may apply the payment against any one of several obligations that are due, or may credit a portion of the payment against a claim that has been discharged by the statute of limitations, but this will not cause this claim to revive as to the unpaid balance.

If the source of a payment is someone other than the debtor and this fact is known to the creditor, the payment must be applied in such a manner as to protect the third party who makes the payment. Hence, if the money for the payment is supplied by a party who has guaranteed that a particular obligation will be paid by the debtor, and the creditor knows it, the creditor is bound to apply the payment on the obligation for which the guarantor is liable.

Finally, if the creditor fails to make a particular application, the payment will be applied by the courts to the obligation oldest in point of time. However, where the creditor holds both secured and unsecured obligations, the courts of most states are inclined to apply it on an unsecured obligation. Similarly, if both principal and interest are due, the court considers the interest to be paid first, any balance being credited on the principal.

The application of these rules often has serious consequences. Debtors who are paying their own debts or whose debts are being paid by others should always direct that the payment be applied to the intended debt. Note that in the following case, the failure to direct the application of the payment resulted in a windfall to one party (the wife) and a greatly increased debt to a business.

CASE

White Const. Co., Inc. v. DuPont

478 So.2d 485 (Fla.App. 1 Dist. 1985)

Nathaniel DuPont was seriously injured, and in a lawsuit against White & Limerock Industries and Old Republic Insurance Company he was awarded $3,525,000. His wife, Janey, was awarded $1,025,000 for loss of consortium. The Old Republic Insurance Company paid $553,602.51, which represented the limits of its insurance coverage plus interest, to the registry of the trial court. The sum was paid without qualification for the benefit of the plaintiffs in partial satisfaction of the judgment. It was made without reference to any further proceedings, including appeals.

The court held a hearing and authorized the plaintiffs to withdraw the money. The withdrawal would not affect their right to collect the balance from the individual defendants. The money was disbursed by paying attorneys' fees and dividing the balance between the husband and wife, with each party receiving a check and a joint certificate of deposit.

Later, the award of damages to Janey DuPont was reversed and remanded for a retrial. The award to Nathaniel DuPont was also reversed, and eventually his award was reduced to $1,025,000.

Defendants White and Limerock contend that the payment by Old Republic should be applied against the judgment in favor of Nathaniel DuPont and that none of it should be applied to the claim of Janey DuPont. The trial judge ordered that one-half of the amount paid should be applied to the claim of Nathaniel DuPont and the other one-half applied in favor of Janey DuPont, to whatever ultimately may be determined to be due.

MILLS, J.

This appeal centers around the events of 1981 with the key question being whether there was a valid application

of the Old Republic payment and, if so, what is the impact of the application.

The Florida rule (and apparently the majority rule in the United States) as to the application of payments was first stated in *Randall v. Parramore and Smith*, 1 Fla. 409 (1847), and has been reiterated in later cases to the effect that:

> [T]he debtor who makes the payment may at the time direct its application to whatever account or item of indebtedness he wishes, and if he fails to do so the creditor may at any time make application of the payment as he desires. And if neither the debtor nor the creditor at the time of payment makes any application thereof, the law will appropriate it to the items of indebtedness according to the justice of the case, having in view the interests of third persons interested.

The debtor has the first opportunity to direct application of the payment. Neither White nor Limerock gave any direction in 1981. The trial court found that Old Republic's payment was made to Nathaniel and Janey DuPont for the benefit of the plaintiffs (plural).... If there was any indication of Old Republic's intention, it would appear to be that the payment was to go toward both Nathaniel and Janey DuPonts' judgments for compensatory damages.

In the absence of direction from the debtor as to how payment is to be credited, the creditor may apply as he desires. White and Limerock argue that the defendants had no opportunity to direct the payment, as payment was made to the registry of the court.

The rule permitting the creditor to make application of payments where the debtor fails to do so does not apply where the debtor has had no opportunity to direct the application.

The defendants failed to take advantage of opportunities to direct the payment. Both White and Limerock had the opportunity to negotiate with Old Republic and the DuPonts on this issue and could have sought direction from the court. In addition, the Old Republic payment was initially tendered to the DuPonts' counsel and only later placed in the registry of the court. If the debtor waives the right to direct application, the court will not ordinarily disturb the creditor's application.

The DuPonts contend that they made application of the Old Republic payment to their individual judgments. The closing statement, prepared by the DuPonts' law firm shows separate and equal payments to Nathaniel and Janey DuPont. From these disbursements the DuPonts received separate cashiers checks in equal amounts and a certificate of deposit in both of their names. This evidence indicates that the Old Republic payment was to the DuPonts as individuals and with the exception of the joint certificate of deposit, the monies were applied to their individual benefit. . . .

There is competent and substantial evidence that the DuPonts made a valid election in 1981 to apply the Old Republic payment to their individual judgments. The trial court correctly applied the law of payment. Old Republic wanted out of the case in 1981. White and Limerock had the opportunity to attempt to direct the Old Republic payment and did not do so. . . .

■ *Affirmed.*

CASE CONCEPTS REVIEW

1. What were the amounts of the original judgments in favor of the plaintiffs? How did these amounts change after an initial appeal?
2. Why did the insurance company pay $553,602.51 into the court for the plaintiff's benefit? How was this amount distributed?
3. What could the defendant have done to avoid the problem presented in this litigation?

10. Accord and Satisfaction

An *accord* is an agreement whereby one of the parties undertakes to give or to perform something different from what was contracted for, and the other party to accept something different from what he or she is entitled to. An accord may arise from a disputed claim in either tort or contract. The term *satisfaction* means that the substituted performance is completed.

The doctrine of accord and satisfaction requires that there be a dispute or uncertainty as to amount due and that the parties enter into an agreement that debtor will pay, and the creditor will accept, a stated amount as a compromise of their differences and in satisfaction of the debt. It must clearly appear that the parties so understood and entered into a new and substitute contract. The surrender of the legal right to litigate the dispute or the settlement agreement often serves as consideration.

The usual accord and satisfaction case involves a debtor's sending a creditor a check for less than the amount claimed by the creditor to be due. This check is usually marked "Paid in full." The courts of a few states hold that the cashing of the check constitutes an accord and satisfaction without additional proof. Most states, however, require that the party asserting the accord and satisfaction also prove (1) that the debt or claim was in fact the subject of a bona fide dispute, (2) that the creditor was aware of the dispute, and (3) that the creditor was aware that the check was tendered as full payment.

Assuming that these three elements are present, if the creditor cashes the check, the creditor cannot change the language of the check, deposit it, or cash it and still contend that there was no accord and satisfaction. If the creditor cashes the check, this act constitutes the satisfaction of the accord and completes the discharge, as the following case illustrates.

CASE

Danac, Inc. v. Gudenau & Co., Inc.
751 P.2d 947 (Alas. 1988)

RABINOWITZ, J.

. . . This appeal . . . arises from certain rulings of the superior court and a jury verdict in favor of Gudenau in connection with its claim for wrongful termination of a labor subcontract by its general contractor Danac. The issue in this appeal involves Danac's affirmative defense of accord and satisfaction. . . .

In October 1983, Gudenau, the subcontractor, entered into a subcontract with Danac, the general contractor, to shingle two buildings at the United States Coast Guard Support Center in Kodiak. The shingles were to be supplied by Danac and were subject to Coast Guard approval. A dispute arose in April 1984 concerning Danac's obligation to determine the quality of the shingles and to sort them. Gudenau informed Danac that it would have no choice but to cease operation if Danac would not supply acceptable shingles. By letter on May 4, Danac took the position that it was Gudenau's responsibility to exercise its professional judgment to determine which shingles to use for the exposed exterior or for underlayers, and which to reject altogether. Danac considered this letter notice to Gudenau of its intention to terminate the subcontract. Gudenau responded by reiterating its belief that inspection and quality control were Danac's responsibility and stating that it would not install the shingles supplied absent their approval by Danac quality control personnel. On May 9, Danac advised Gudenau orally that the subcontract would be in jeopardy and "could possibly be terminated" if crews did not return to the worksite. Gudenau did not return to work and Danac terminated the subcontract that day.

At the time of termination, Gudenau had completed 20–25% of the work required under the subcontract. According to Danac, the parties in May negotiated a final payment of $11,173.94 for all work performed, and Gudenau picked up a check for that sum on May 22. Gudenau acknowledges picking up the check but contends that no such negotiations occurred, that the parties did not agree on the amount to be paid, and that they did not agree that the $11,174 payment constituted final payment. Gerald Gudenau testified that he was surprised to find, when he picked up the check from Danac, that his company's final payment figures did not match Danac's. A notation on the check stated "Final Payment," but Gudenau crossed out the notation and cashed the check on May 24. By letter dated May 22 (but apparently not received until after the check was cashed), Gudenau informed Danac that it considered the check only partial payment for the work completed and that it did not waive any of its rights against Danac by accepting the payment.

Prior to trial Danac moved for summary judgment dismissing Gudenau's claims for damages on the ground that the parties had entered into an accord in May 1984, and "[t]hat accord having been satisfied the debt at issue in this litigation is dissolved and eliminated.". . .

In support of its summary judgment motion Danac . . . relied on the fact that Gudenau had negotiated the check on May 24, 1984.

In opposition to Danac's motion, Gudenau took the position that its letter of May 22, 1984, was a sufficient reservation of rights. . . .

On January 16, 1986, the superior court entered an order denying Danac's motion for summary judgment. Following a jury verdict and judgment in favor of Gudenau, Danac appeals. . . .

In the instant case it is undisputed that there was a bona fide dispute between the parties as to how much Danac owed Gudenau under the subcontract. It is further undisputed that Danac sent Gudenau a letter containing an offer of final payment; that Danac issued a final payment check; that Gudenau crossed out the "final payment" notation on the check and negotiated the check; and that at the same time it negotiated the final payment check, Gudenau wrote a reservation of rights letter to Danac. . . .

When Gudenau negotiated Danac's full payment check it implicitly agreed to an accord and satisfaction. Gudenau had the option to destroy the check and sue for all damages to which it believed it was entitled or to negotiate the check and consider the subcontract dispute settled. Gudenau's purported reservation of rights was ineffective in light of its acceptance of Danac's conditional tender.

Thus we conclude that the superior court erred in failing to grant Danac's motion for summary judgment dismissing Gudenau's complaint on the basis of Danac's affirmative defense of accord and satisfaction.

■ *Reversed and remanded.*

CASE CONCEPTS REVIEW

1. What is the basis for the dispute between Gudenau and Danac?
2. How did Danac attempt to resolve this dispute and settle the controversy?
3. What lesson does this case teach you when you receive a check marked "paid in full" or "final payment?"

11. Statute of Limitations

The *statute of limitations* prescribes a time limit within which the suit must be started after a cause of action arises. Failure to file suit within the time prescribed is a complete defense to the suit.

The purpose of a statute of limitations is to prevent actions from being brought long after evidence is lost or important witnesses have died or moved away. An action for breach of any contract for sale of personal property under the Code must be commenced within four years [2-725]. The Code further provides that the parties in their agreement may reduce the period of limitation to not less than one year but may not extend it. Contracts that are not controlled by the Code are covered by a variety of limitation periods. Some states distinguish between oral and written contracts, making the period longer for the latter.

Any voluntary part payment made on a money obligation by the debtor with intent to pay the balance tolls the statute, starting it to run anew. Similarly, any voluntary part payment, new promise, or clear acknowledgment of the indebtedness made after the claim has been discharged reinstates the obligation, and the statute commences to run again. A payment or part payment by a third person or a joint debtor does not operate to interrupt the running of the statute as to other debtors not participating in the payment. No new consideration is required to support the reinstatement promise. If the old obligation has been outlawed, a new promise may be either partial or conditional. Since there is no *duty* to pay the debt, the debtor may attach such conditions to the new promise as he or she sees fit or may promise to pay only part of the debt. A few states require the new promise or acknowledgment to be in writing. The Code does not alter the law on tolling of the statute of limitations [2-725(4)].

A problem exists when a party is incapacitated by minority or insanity. Most jurisdictions hold that lack of capacity stops the running of the statute and extends the period of filing suit. A minor or an insane person usually has a specified time in which to bring an action—after the minor reaches his or her majority or the insane person regains capacity—although the full period set by statute has expired earlier.

The following case illustrates how the law of payment discussed in section 9 can be combined with a statute of limitations to determine when a lawsuit may and may not be properly filed.

CASE

Regents of the University of New Mexico v. Lacey
764 P.2d 873 (N.M. 1988)

STOWERS, J.

... Plaintiff-Appellants, the Regents of the University of New Mexico (the Regents), appeal from a judgment of dismissal rendered in favor of defendant-appellee, Liberty Mutual Insurance Company (Liberty Mutual). The trial court determined that the action was time-barred under the New Mexico Hospital Lien Act.

The facts ... are as follows: On March 29, 1985, an accident occurred between Thomas R. Wadsworth, the driver of an automobile, and defendant, Vincent Lacey, the driver of a motorcycle. The automobile was insured by Liberty Mutual. As a result of this accident, Lacey was treated at the University of New Mexico Hospital, operated by the Regents, from March 29 to August 12, 1985, incurring expenses in the amount of $20,594.51....

The Regents filed their notice of a hospital lien ... and sent copies of the notices to all parties. A check in the amount of $58,265.35 was issued by Liberty Mutual on behalf of Wadsworth to Lacey and the law firm of Lamb, Metzgar, and Lines, P.A., for all the claims Lacey had against Wadsworth. The check was received by Lacey's counsel, Farrell Lines, on May 28, 1986. On November 10, 1986, Lines requested from the Regents a 50 percent reduction of the amount Lacey owed the hospital. The Regents informed Lines that the hospital is constitutionally prohibited from accepting less than full payment. Nonetheless, on January 15, 1987, Lacey, through his attorney Lines, sent to the hospital only $10,000 as full payment.

On June 19, 1987, the Regents brought this action against Lacey and Liberty Mutual for debt and money due on an open account and enforcement of their hospital lien. Liberty Mutual moved to dismiss pursuant to NMSA 1978, Section 48-8-3(B). That section provides: "Liability of the person, firm or corporation for the satisfaction of the hospital lien shall continue *for a period of one year after date of any payment of any money to the patient, his heirs or legal representatives* as damages or under a contract of compromise or settlement." (emphasis added) After hearing oral argument on the motion, the trial court determined that the Regents' suit was time-barred since the effective date for the commencement of the statutory period of limitations was May 28, 1986. On that basis the court dismissed the case against Liberty Mutual with prejudice. This appeal follows.

Arguments made by the Regents on appeal are: (1) The mere tender of a release and two-party settlement check is not "payment of any money," under Section 48-8-3(B); [and] (2) A payment to an attorney is not synonymous with payment to the legal representative under Section 48-8-3(B). . . .

The check in the amount of $58,265.35 issued by Liberty Mutual and payable to Lacey and Lamb, Metzgar and Lines was received by Lines on May 28, 1986. . . . The check was endorsed by Lacey and deposited into the law firm's trust account on November 6, 1986. The Regents had no knowledge of the check or the deposit into the trust account until November 6, 1986, when Lines informed the hospital that "we finally settled with the insurance company." The Regents contend there was no payment within the meaning of Section 48-8-3(B) until both Lacey and Lines negotiated the two-party settlement check. . . . Therefore, the Regents argue the one-year statutory time period did not begin to run before November 6, 1986.

The delivery of a check does not, ordinarily, per se, constitute payment in a legal sense. However, if when the check is delivered, the drawer has funds in the drawee bank to meet it, and the check is honored and paid upon presentment, the conditional nature of the payment becomes absolute and the date of payment will be deemed to have been made as of the date of the original delivery of the check. When a check is paid, the payment of the underlying debt becomes absolute and it is deemed paid as of the date of the giving of the check. Cases from other areas of the law also indicate that payment is made upon delivery of the check and not deposit in the bank.

Payment of any money for purposes of Section 48-8-3(B) occurred when Liberty Mutual delivered the check to Lines on May 28, 1986. Although it was not negotiated until November 6, 1986, when upon presentment the check was honored and paid, the date of payment is the date of the original delivery of the check. . . .

In addition, delivery of this check to Lines, Lacey's attorney, was "payment to the patient *** or legal representative" as prescribed in Section 48-8-3(B). Settlement checks are usually given to attorneys on behalf of their clients. A legal representative, defined in its braodest sense, is one who stands in place of another and represents the interests of another; a person who oversees the legal affairs of another. An attorney is an agent or one who is appointed and authorized to act in the place or stead of another. In considering the ordinary and usual meaning of the words used in this statute, an interpretation that an attorney may be a legal representative is not unreasonable.

. . . Payment to the patient is the act that triggers the running of the one-year limitation period. The clear language of Section 48-8-3(B) however contemplates compliance when payment is made either to "the patient . . . or legal representative." We conclude that an attorney is a legal representative for purposes of receiving payment under this statute and to commence the running of the statute of limitations therein. Where a statute grants a new remedy, and at the same time places a limitation of time within which the person complaining must act, the limitation is a limitation of the right as well as the remedy, and in the absence of qualifying provisions or saving clauses, the party seeking to avail himself of the remedy must bring himself strictly within the limitations. Upon failure to institute the action within the specified period beginning May 28, 1986, the Regents' right to do so ended. . . .

The judgment of the district court is affirmed and the parties will bear their own costs and attorney fees.

■ *Affirmed.*

CASE CONCEPTS REVIEW

1. This case involves a time period under a statute of limitations after which the hospital cannot sue to enforce its lien and collect its bills. Which is that time period?

2. What date does Liberty Mutual contend is key to the statute of limitations beginning to run? What date does the hospital contend is the key? What date was this lawsuit filed?

3. Why does the court rule in favor of the statute of limitations barring the hospital's claim?

4. What could the hospital have done to prevent this result?

CHAPTER SUMMARY

Hindrance, Prevention, or Noncooperation

1. Wrongful conduct by a party that unduly hinders or prevents the other party's performance will excuse that performance.
2. Wrongful conduct is conduct that was not reasonably contemplated or the risk of which was not assumed by the nonperforming party.

Waiver

1. Waiver is a voluntary and intentional relinquishment of an express or constructive condition.
2. A waiver may be retracted unless it is supported by consideration or the other party has relied on the waiver.
3. A waiver may be made prior to or after a party has breached the agreement.

Impossibility of Performance

1. When an unforeseen event makes performance impossible, all duties to perform are excused.
2. Occurrence of reasonably foreseeable events will not excuse duties to perform.
3. Change in market price, strikes, accidents, unavailability of materials, and governmental regulations are normally foreseeable.
4. Acts of God, supervening illegalities, war, and death of a party or destruction of the contract's subject matter are normally unforeseeable.

Specific Cases of Impossiblity

1. If the contractual performance becomes illegal, the performance is excused.
2. The death or incapacitating illness of a contracting party excuses his or her performance.
3. The destruction of the subject matter that is essential to the contract's performance excuses such performance.
4. When an essential element for contractual performance is lacking, such performance is excused.

Commercial Frustration

1. This is an intervening event or change of circumstances that was not foreseeable and that prevents achievement of the object or purpose of the contract.
2. The purpose or object frustrated must have been the *basic* purpose or object of the contract from the time the contract was made.

Commercial Impracticability under the Code

1. If the contract can be performed but performance is *unduly* burdensome, impracticability may excuse performance.
2. This is an excuse for unforeseeable events. However, events such as strikes, government regulations, increased costs, or unavailable material generally are viewed as being foreseeable.

Methods

1. The term *discharge* describes the cancellation of a contract and the acts by which enforcement of its provisions is terminated.
2. The usual method of discharge is performance.
3. A contract may also be discharged as the result of excuses for nonperformance, a mutual release of terms, rescission either by agreement of the parties or operation of law, novation, accord and satisfaction, and the expiration of the period of the statute of limitations.
4. The intentional destruction of a negotiable instrument is a form of cancellation.

Payment	1. A check constitutes only conditional payment.
	2. If a debtor owes several obligations, the debtor may specify which is being paid.
	3. If the debtor fails to specify, the creditor may apply it to any debt.
	4. If the payment is by a third party, it must be applied to the debt on which the third party is obligated.
Accord and Satisfaction	1. An accord is an agreement to change a contract, and the satisfaction is the performance of the accord.
	2. If the parties agree to settle a dispute either in contract or tort, there is an accord and satisfaction. The consideration is the agreement not to litigate the dispute.
Statute of Limitations	1. The statute of limitations prescribes a time limit beyond which a suit cannot be brought on a claim.
	2. There are various time periods for contracts and torts, and these vary from state to state.
	3. The Code period is four years.
	4. Various events may toll the running of the statute and commence the period over again. These include payment, part payment, and a new promise to pay.

REVIEW QUESTIONS AND PROBLEMS

1. Match the terms in column A with the appropriate statement in column B.

A	**B**
(1) Waiver	(a) This is not a defense to breach of contract
(2) Commercial frustration	(b) Requires reasonable cooperation
(3) Impossibility	(c) Code's version of commercial frustration
(4) Discharge by party's agreement	(d) An unforeseen event that makes performance impossible
(5) Discharge by operation of law	(e) Unforeseeable intervening event that prevents fulfillment of contract's main purpose
(6) Commercial impracticability	(f) Contract avoidance, bankruptcy, and statute of limitations
(7) Good faith	(g) Rescission, release, novation, and accord and satisfaction
(8) Hardship	(h) A voluntary, intentional relinquishment of a condition

2. Elmina contracts with Mickey to build a house for $200,000, payable on condition that Elmina present a certificate from Libby, Mickey's architect, showing that the construction work has been properly completed. Elmina properly completes the work, but Libby refuses to give the certificate because of collusion with Mickey. Is the nonoccurrence of the condition therefore excused? Explain.

3. Wells contracted with the state to erect a building according to the state's specifications and to lease it to the state. Time was made of the essence in the contract. Wells completed the building two months late. The state canceled the contract and leased space elsewhere. Wells sued and proved at trial that the delay was caused by the state's failure to indicate locations for electrical fixtures, outlets, and other details as required by the contract. Did Wells win? Why or why not?

4. Crotty contracted with A&D Construction for a new house. Crotty paid $97,000 of the purchase price but refused to pay the balance because of defects in construction. A&D offered to correct the defects, but Crotty would not allow A&D on the premises unless the company agreed to waive its lien rights. Under what legal theory would A&D be able to collect the balance due without correcting the defects? Explain.

5. A real estate broker contracted to sell a piece of land to Marilyn Curry. At her request, the contract stated, "This contract is contingent upon the buyer obtaining a rezoning for a mobile home park and campground. This contract is to be void if the rezoning is not obtained within 120 days." After sixty-five days, Curry notifies the broker that she would buy the property, irrespective of a zoning change. The zoning change was not obtained during the 120-day period. The broker now refuses to convey, and Curry sues. Who wins? Why?

6. A building leased by Newberry as a department store was destroyed by fire. When the landlord, Marcovich, refused to rebuild, Newberry sued for damages and lost profits. Marcovich defended, using impossibility as an excuse. He contended that it was not commercially feasible to rebuild due to the small amount of insurance proceeds, the blighted condition of the area, and alleged difficulty in obtaining financing. Did Marcovich prove impossibility to excuse its nonperformance in failing to rebuild? Why or why not?

7. Pate, a contractor, agreed with the city of Kiteville to construct a golf course for the amount of $230,329.88. After Pate had completed all the clearing and dirt work, a torrential rainfall of 12.47 inches occurred in a ten-hour period. It will cost $60,000 to restore the golf course to its condition prior to the rain. Is Pate relieved from the contract by the doctrine of commercial frustration? Explain why or why not.

8. A natural gas utility entered into a long-term supply contract to purchase naphtha. Due to an increase in natural gas supplies, its needs for naphtha diminished. When the price of naphtha greatly increased, the utility sought to be released from its contract because of commercial frustration. Is this a valid defense in this case? Explain.

9. John Henry Mining Company was hired to drill a coal mine. The mine failed because tunneling became too difficult. Is John Henry excused for discontinuing? Why or why not?

10. Draper agreed to sell a lot to Mohrland for $14,875. As a part of the agreement, Draper agreed to relocate a gas line that crossed the property. After signing the agreement, Draper found out that it would cost $10,050 to move the gas line. Should this fact excuse Draper's performance of the contract? Why or why not?

11. Barcomb Motor Sales agreed to purchase two bus bodies from School Lines, Inc., for the price of $46,464. School Lines required payment in full before delivery. Barcomb Motor delivered a check in the amount of the purchase price to School Lines, and Barcomb Motor's agents picked up the bus bodies. Later, Barcomb Motor's president stopped payment on the check and issued a new check in the amount of $45,064.66, the difference representing various costs incurred by Barcomb Motor in connection with the transaction. The language "Payment in full for bus bodies Serial #'s B18550 and B18551" appeared on the back of Barcomb Motor's new check. School Lines cashed the check after indorsing it with the words, "Accepted as Partial Payment." School Lines sued Barcomb Motor for the balance of the agreed-on purchase price. Barcomb Motor claimed that School Lines' acceptance and cashing of the check effected an accord and satisfaction. Was the amount owed School Lines but withheld by Barcomb Motor the subject of a bona fide dispute so the doctrine of accord and satisfaction would apply? Explain.

12. King, a tree surgeon, pruned some trees at the home of Deeb. King had estimated a cost of $480 for the work. When billed for $504, Deeb contended that he had not authorized the work. Deeb's attorney forwarded a check to King in the amount of $100, with the notation to the effect that this $100 was in full and final settlement of all claims of King against Deeb for work performed. King cashed the check and sued for the balance. Should King win? Explain.

CONTRACT RIGHTS OF THIRD PARTIES

CHAPTER PREVIEW

*T*he discussion of contracts up to this point has dealt with the law of contracts as applied to the contracting parties. However, frequently persons who are not original parties to the contracts may have rights and even duties under the contract. The rights and duties of third parties may come into play when there is (1) a *third-party beneficiary contract*—one party contracts with a second party for the purpose of conferring a benefit on a third party (beneficiary); or (2) an *assignment* of the contract—an original party to a contract (assignor) transfers to a third party (assignee) the rights or duties under the contract; or (3) a *novation*—a new third party becomes a party to an existing contract as a substitute for one of the original parties.

> You are a loan officer at a local bank. You read in the newspaper that one of your delinquent borrowers has won a $250,000 verdict in a products liability suit. Upon contacting this borrower about payment, you arrange for an assignment to your bank of the borrower's rights against the negligent defendant.
>
> What should your bank do as the assignee of this claim?

CONTRACTS FOR BENEFIT OF THIRD PARTIES

1. Nature of Such Contracts

Contracts are often made for the express purpose of benefiting some third party. Such contracts, called *third-party beneficiary contracts,* are of two types—*donee-beneficiary* and *creditor-beneficiary.* Both types of third-party beneficiaries are entitled to enforce a contract made in their behalf because the original parties provide that the benefits shall go to the beneficiary.

Donee-beneficiary A third party who receives a gift when a promisee secures a promise from a promisor for the purpose of making a gift to a third party.

DONEE-BENEFICIARY.   If the promise of the promisor was contracted for by the promisee to make a gift to the third party, such third party is a **donee-beneficiary**. The most typical example of such an agreement is a contract for life insurance in which the beneficiary is someone other than the insured. The insured has made a contract with the life insurance company for the purpose of conferring a benefit on a third party, namely the beneficiary named in the policy.

Creditor-beneficiary A third party who receives the benefits of a contract made between two contracting parties for the purpose of paying one original party's debt to the third party.

CREDITOR-BENEFICIARY.   If the promisee has contracted for a promise to pay a debt that he or she owes to a third party, such third party is a **creditor-beneficiary**. In this situation, the debtor arranges to purchase the promise of the other contracting party to satisfy the obligation owed to the third party. The promisee obtains a benefit because his or her obligation to the creditor presumably will be satisfied. For example, A operates a department store. He sells his furniture, fixtures, and inventory to B, who, as part of the bargain, agrees to pay all of A's business debts. A's purpose for making this contract was to have his debts paid, and he obtained B's promise to pay them to confer a benefit on his creditors. A's creditors are creditor-beneficiaries and can enforce their claims directly against B. Of course, to the extent that B does not pay them, the creditors still have recourse against A.

2. Legal Requirements

Incidental beneficiary
A third person who would only indirectly benefit from the performance of a contract. Such person has no right to enforce the original contract.

A third-party beneficiary is not entitled to enforce a contract unless he or she can establish that the parties actually *intended* to benefit him. This party must be something more than a mere **incidental beneficiary.** If the benefit to the third party is only incidental, the beneficiary cannot sue.

The intent to benefit the third party must clearly appear from the terms of the contract. The intent to benefit a third party is more easily inferred in creditor-beneficiary situations than in donee-beneficiary ones. The third party need not be named as an individual in the contract if he or she can show that he or she is a member of a group for whose direct benefit the contract was made. A third-party beneficiary need not have knowledge of the contract at the time it was made. The fact that the actual contracting party could also sue to enforce the agreement would not bar a suit by the beneficiary if he or she was intended to benefit directly from the contract. A third-party beneficiary need not be the exclusive beneficiary of the promise, as the following case illustrates.

CASE

Touchberry v. City of Florence
367 S.E.2d 149 (S.C. 1988)

NESS, J.

Appellant (Owner) contends the trial court erred in failing to . . . (order) the respondents to provide him with water and sewer service. We find that Owner is a third party beneficiary of a service contract between respondent City of Florence (City) and Florence County and is entitled to the writ. We reverse.

Owner lives in Florence County on property which is partially contiguous to the City. City has long had an ordinance requiring annexation of contiguous property as a condition for receiving City services and utilities.

Florence County Council (Council) created a Municipal Service Area (MSA) which included Owner's property. In 1984, Council entered a franchised agreement (agreement) with City which granted City the exclusive right to provide water and sewer services in the MSA. The agreement provides, "The City . . . agrees to provide water and wastewater facilities to any area within the [MSA] which requests such service, provided it is physically and economically feasible to provide such service."

It is uncontested that Owner's property is within the MSA, that he requested service, and that it is physically and economically feasible to provide him service. Owner's request that he receive service pursuant to the agreement was denied because he would not agree to annexation. Owner then brought this petition . . . to compel respondents to provide him service. The trial court denied the petition finding that Owner was not a third party beneficiary of the agreement and that the ordinance applied to him.

It is clear that there are two methods whereby contiguous landowners may receive services from the City. First, they may be annexed and receive services as a City resident pursuant to the ordinance. Second, if the property is within the MSA, the property owner may remain in the county and receive services pursuant to the agreement. Since it is impossible for property to be both annexed to the City and remain part of the county, the ordinance and the agreement are mutually exclusive. The lower court erred in finding Owner must be annexed in order to receive service under the agreement.

The more difficult issue is whether Owner is a third party beneficiary of the agreement. This Court has recognized that individuals may be third party beneficiaries of public contracts. The presumption that the contract is not enforceable by an individual may be overcome by showing he was intended to be the direct beneficiary of the contract. The language of the agreement here clearly shows that the contracting parties intended for the agreement to be enforceable by residents of the MSA. Owner is therefore entitled to service under the agreement.

We reverse the trial court and issue an . . . (order) to the City requiring it to provide service to Owner pursuant to the terms of the agreement. . . .

■ *Reversed.*

CASE CONCEPTS REVIEW

1. What is the basic contractual agreement with respect to water being provided by the city to county residents?

2. In what two ways does the court summarize that a landowner is entitled to water services from the city?

3. On what grounds did the owner argue that he had the right to enforce the city–county agreement, thereby being entitled to water services?

A contract made for the express purpose of benefiting a third party generally may not be rescinded without the consent of the beneficiary after its terms have been accepted by the beneficiary. The latter has a vested interest in the agreement from the moment it is made and accepted. For example, an insurance company has no right to change the named beneficiary in a life insurance policy without the consent of the beneficiary unless the contract gives the insured the right to make this change. Until the third-party beneficiary has either accepted or acted on provisions of a contract for his or her benefit, the parties to the contract may change the provisions and deny the beneficiary the benefits of the contract. Minors, however, are presumed to accept a favorable contract upon its execution, and such contract may not be changed to deprive the minor of its benefits.

ASSIGNMENTS

3. Terminology

Obligor A debtor or promisor.

Obligee A creditor or promisee.

Assignment A transfer of the rights under a contract. It may include a delegation of the duties of the assignor.

Assignor One who makes an assignment.

Assignee One to whom an assignment is made.

A bilateral contract creates *rights* for each party and imposes on each corresponding *duties*. Each party is an **obligor** (has an obligation to perform the duties), and each is an **obligee** (is entitled to receive the performance of the other). Either party may desire to transfer to another his or her rights or rights and duties. A party *assigns* rights and *delegates* duties.

The term **assignment** may mean a transfer of one's rights under a contract, or it may mean a transfer both of rights and duties. The phrase *assignment of the contract* is confusing because it does not specify whether rights or duties or both are being transferred. When the contracting parties use this ambiguous term, courts usually interpret it to mean that rights were assigned and duties were delegated. To further complicate our terminology, regardless of whether rights or duties are involved in a transfer, the person making the transfer is called the **assignor,** and the one receiving the transfer is called the **assignee.**

4. General Principles

The next seven sections discuss the legal aspects of assignments in detail. By summarizing some of these principles, this section serves as an introduction to the more detailed discussion. In essence, five points about assignments should remain at the forefront of your understanding.

First, no particular formality is essential to an assignment. Consideration, although usually present, is not required. As a general proposition, an assignment may be either oral or written, although it is, of course, desirable to have a written assignment. Some statutes require a writing in certain assignment situations. For example, an assignment of an interest in real property must be in writing in most states.

Second, consent of the nonassigning party generally is not required when the assignor transfers rights or duties to the assignee. The next two sections describe a number of exceptions to this general rule.

Third, the rights and duties arising under an original contract usually are freely assignable. Contracting parties frequently include antiassignment clauses in their agreements. The impact of the clause is discussed in section 7. The assignability of contracts involving the claims and payment of money is the subject matter of section 8.

Fourth, an assignment is a completed transaction that simply involves another contract. The main feature of an assignment is a *present transfer* of a contract right. After the assignment, the assignor has no interest in the contract right. The assignor's right belongs exclusively to the assignee. The rights of the assignee are discussed in section 9.

Fifth, a person who has duties under a contract cannot relieve himself or herself of those duties by transferring the contract or delegating the duties to another person. An obligor that delegates duties as well as assigns rights is not thereby relieved of liability for proper performance if the assignee fails to perform. In general, an assignor continues to be responsible for the ultimate performance. The continuing duty of the assignor and the obligations of the assignee, such as to give notice of the assignment, are the subject matter of sections 10 and 11.

5. Consent Required

To understand when assignments may or may not be made without the consent of the nonassigning party, you must keep in mind that contracts involve both rights and duties of the parties.

As a general rule, contract *rights* may be assigned by one party without the consent of the other party. In most contracts, it is immaterial to the party performing who receives the performance. However, there are certain exceptions to this general rule.

Of the several classes of contracts that may not be transferred without the consent of the other party, the most important are contracts involving personal rights or personal duties. A personal right or duty is one in which personal trust and confidences are involved, or one in which skill, knowledge, or experience of one of the parties is important. In such cases, the personal acts and qualities of one or both of the parties form a material and integral part of the contract. For example, a lease contract where the rent is a percentage of sales based on the ability of the lessee would be unassignable without the consent of the lessor. Likewise, a contract requiring the performance of service of a specific person would be unassignable without the consent of the other party to the original contract.

If a contract involves multiple rights and duties, those that are not personal may be assigned. It is only the personal rights and duties that may not be transferred. Frequently the duty to perform may be personal, but the right to payment is not. In these situations, the duty can be delegated only with the obligee's consent. However, the right to payment may be assigned even though the obligor objects to this transfer.

Some duties that might appear to be personal in nature are not considered so by the courts. For example, unless the contract provides to the contrary, a building contractor may delegate responsibility for certain portions of the structure to a subcontractor without consent. Since construction is usually to be done according to specifications, the duties are delegable. It is presumed that all contractors are able to follow specifications. Of course, the assignee must substantially complete the building according to the plans and specifications. The obligor will not be obligated to pay for it if it is not, and the assignor will be liable in event of default by the assignee.

Another example of a contract that is unassignable without consent is one in which an assignment would place an additional burden or risk on a party—one not contemplated at the time of the agreement. Such appears to be true of an assignment of the right to purchase on credit. Most states hold that one who has agreed to purchase property on credit, and has been given the right to do so, may not assign his or her right to purchase the property to a third party (assignee), since the latter's credit may not be as good as that of the original contracting party—the assignor. This reasoning is questionable because the seller could hold both the assignor and the assignee responsible. However, the inconvenience to the seller in connection with collecting has influenced most courts to this result. But in contracts where the seller has security for payment, such as retention of title to the property or a security interest in the property, the seller has such substantial protection that the courts have held that the right to purchase on credit is assignable.

Finally, it is important to note that the assignor is not relieved of the original liability under the contract just because the nonassigning party has consented to the delegation of duties. This general statement is equally applicable to those delegations that require the consent of the nonassigning party as to those that do not.

For example, assume that Ryder leases a truck to the Transportation Equipment Company. Later, Transportation Equipment, with the approval of Ryder, assigns the truck rental contract to Williams Transfer, which agrees to pay the rent. When Williams subsequently fails to pay the rent for the truck, Ryder could hold Transportation Equipment liable for the balance due on the truck lease. For Transportation Equipment to be relieved of liability, the subject of novations as presented in sections 12 and 13 of this chapter must be understood.

6. Consent Required under the Code

The Code contains provisions that generally approve the assignment of rights and delegation of duties by buyers and sellers of goods. The duties of either party may be delegated *unless* the parties have agreed otherwise or the nondelegating party has "... a substantial interest in having his original promisor perform or control the acts required by the contract" [2-210(1)]. Accordingly, a seller can ordinarily delegate to someone else the duty to perform the seller's obligations under the contract. This would occur when no substantial reason exists why the delegated performance would be less satisfactory than the personal performance of the assignor.

The Code does provide that rights cannot be assigned where the assignment would materially change the duty of the other party, or increase materially the burden or risk imposed on him or her by the contract, or impair materially his or her chance of obtaining return performance [2-210(2)]. These Code provisions in effect incorporate the personal rights and duties exception previously discussed.

7. Antiassignment Clauses

Some contracts contain a clause stating that the contract cannot be assigned without the consent of the other party. Older cases often held these clauses to be against public policy and unenforceable as an unlawful restraint on alienation (right to sell one's property). Recognizing freedom of contract, modern courts usually uphold the clause prohibiting assignment and find it legally operative. Nonetheless, looking to the language of the clause in non-Code cases, courts have reached different results.

VARYING INTERPRETATIONS.   Some courts hold that if the clause *prohibits* assignment, this creates a promise (*duty* in the assignor) not to assign, but the assignor still has the *power* to assign. Thus the assignment is effective, but the obligor has a legal claim against the assignor for breach of his or her *promise* (duty) not to assign. Others hold that the clause *invalidates* the contract. The assignment is still effective, but the obligor has an option to avoid the contract for breach of the condition. Still others allow the parties to prohibit an assignment. Any purported assignment is void in these states, and the assignment itself is ineffective. Rather than merely creating a *duty* (promise) not to assign, this invalidation clause deprives any party of the power to assign.

CODE INTERPRETATION.   The Code has effected significant changes regarding antiassignment clauses. First, in Article 2 it notes the progressive undermining of the original rule invalidating these clauses. The Code observes that the courts have already construed the heart out of antiassignment clauses. Second, in Article 9 it acknowledges the economic need of freedom of contract rights in modern commercial society. Thus an antiassignment clause is ineffective to prohibit the assignment of an account or contract right [9-318(4)]. In a sale of business, typically both the rights are assigned and the duties are delegated. Lacking a release, the delegating party is still liable on the duties delegated. Consequently, Article 2 of the Code provides that in a sales situation, a clause prohibiting assignment should be construed as barring only the delegation of duties [2-210(3)]. Therefore a generally phrased antiassignment clause is to be read as allowing an assignment of rights but forbidding delegation of duties. Despite the use of the term *antiassignment*, the drafters of the Code took notice that in a sales situation the parties were usually more concerned with delegation than with assignment. Moreover, they saw great commercial need for free assignability of rights and struck the compromise of allowing assignment but prohibiting delegation when confronted with an antiassignment clause.

8. Claims for Money

As a general rule, claims for money due or to become due under existing contracts may be assigned. An automobile dealer may assign to a bank the right to receive money due under contracts for the sale of automobiles on installment contracts. Although the law tends toward greatly reducing or eliminating the right of employees to assign wages, an employee may assign a portion of his or her pay to a creditor, to obtain credit or to satisfy an obligation. However, the Uniform Consumer Credit Code (adopted in several states) provides that a seller cannot take an assignment of earnings for payment of a debt arising out of a consumer credit sale. Lenders also are not allowed to take an assignment of earnings for payment of a debt arising out of a consumer loan. The Consumer Credit Code is a part of the trend toward greater consumer and debtor protection.

When a claim for money is assigned, an issue that frequently arises is the liability of the assignor in case the assignee is unable to collect from the debtor-obligor. If the assignee takes the assignment merely as *security* for a debt owed to him or her by the assignor, it is clear that if the claim is not collected the assignor still has to pay the debt to the assignee. But if someone *purchases* a claim against a third party, generally the purchaser has no recourse against the seller (assignor) if the third party (debtor-obligor) defaults. If the claim is *invalid* or sold expressly "with recourse," the assignor would be required to reimburse the assignee if the debtor-obligor did not pay.

In all cases, an assignor *warrants* that the claim he or she assigns is a valid, legal claim, that the debtor-obligor is really obligated to pay, and that there are no valid defenses to the assigned claim. If this *warranty* is breached (that is, if there are valid defenses or the claim is otherwise invalid), the assignee has recourse against the assignor.

9. Rights of the Assignee

An assignment is more than a mere authorization or request to pay or to perform for the assignee rather than the assignor. The obligor-debtor *must* pay or perform for the assignee, who now, in effect, owns the rights under the contract. If there is a valid assignment, the assignee owns the rights and is entitled to receive them. Performance for the original party will not discharge the contract. Unless the contract provides otherwise, the assignee receives the identical rights of the assignor.

Since the rights of the assignee are neither better nor worse than those of the assignor, any defense the third party (obligor) has against the assignor is available against the assignee. Part payment, fraud, duress, or incapacity can be used as a defense by the third party (obligor) if an action is brought against him or her by the assignee, just as the same defense could have been asserted against the assignor had the assignor been the plaintiff. A common expression defining the status of the assignee is that he or she "stands in the shoes" of the assignor. The following case illustrates the application of this principle.

CASE

Graves Equipment, Inc. v. M. DeMatteo Const.
489 N.E.2d 1010 (Mass. 1986)

ABRAMS, J.

At issue are the respective rights of an account debtor and an assignee in retainages withheld under a construction contract. The defendant M. DeMatteo Construction Co. (DeMatteo) appeals from a judgment in favor of the plaintiff, Graves Equipment, Inc. (Graves), in the amount of $10,692.52, plus interest and costs. That amount represents the retainages held by DeMatteo under a material supplier contract with Dirt Movers, Inc. (Dirt Movers), an assignor of Graves. DeMatteo argues that it is entitled under the terms of that contract to offset the retainages as liquidated damages for Dirt Movers' failure to perform. . . . We conclude that Graves, as assignee, is subject to the claims and defenses asserted by DeMatteo against Dirt Movers. . . .

The parties agreed to the following facts. In 1979, DeMatteo was the general contractor on a highway construction project for the Department of Public Works (DPW). On June 19, 1979, DeMatteo and Dirt Movers executed an agreement whereby Dirt Movers agreed to supply certain materials required under the DPW contract. From June through December, 1979, Dirt Movers supplied the materials as agreed and was paid a total of $209,212.61. DeMatteo withheld retainages of $10,692.52. On December 6, 1979, Dirt Movers assigned all retainages due it under the contract to Graves. Dirt Movers owes Graves $12,000.00.

The project was shut down for the winter but resumed in the spring. In April, 1980, DeMatteo directed Dirt Movers to deliver the materials, which it failed to do. As a result, DeMatteo terminated the contract and subsequently obtained the necessary materials from other suppliers at a higher cost. The excess cost, based on Dirt Movers' proportional rate of delivery prior to the winter shutdown, was $19,270.65.

The trial judge ruled that Dirt Movers' obligation under its contract with DeMatteo was for a sale of goods and was governed by Article 9 of the Uniform Commercial Code. § 9-318(1) (1984 ed.), provides: "Unless an account debtor has made an enforceable agreement not to assert defenses or claims arising out of a sale as provided in section 9-206 the rights of an assignee are subject to (a) all the terms of the contract between the account debtor and assignor and any defense or claim arising therefrom; and (b) any other defense or claim of the account debtor against the assignor which accrues before the account debtor receives notification of the assignment." The judge concluded that DeMatteo could not set off any damages incurred in 1980 against any sums due Dirt Movers as of December, 1979, on the ground that notice of the assignment was received by DeMatteo long before any breach occurred. In so ruling, the judge apparently looked to § 9-318(1)(b). That provision governs claims and defenses which arise independently of the contract that is the subject of the assignment.

However, the claims and defenses asserted by DeMatteo arise out of the terms of the material supplier contract from which the assignment was created and are therefore governed by § 9-318(1)(a). Under that provision, it is immaterial when notice of the assignment was given or when the claims and defenses accrued.

Section 9-318(1)(a) incorporates the common law rule that an assignee of contract rights stands in the shoes of the assignor and has no greater rights against the debtor than the assignor had. The judgment is reversed and the case is remanded to the Superior Court for further proceedings.

■ *So ordered.*

CASE CONCEPTS REVIEW

1. Which of the companies involved in this case were parties to the original contract?
2. Which party is the assignor, the assignee, and the nonassigning party?
3. On what basis does the court determine the rights of the assignee to collect funds retained by the nonassigning party?
4. Why did the court use subsection (a) instead of subsection (b) of §9-318(1) of the UCC?

Some contracts contain a provision to the effect that "if the seller assigns the contract to a finance company or bank, the buyer agrees that he will not assert against such assignee any defense that he has against the seller-assignor." This *waiver of defense* clause is an attempt to give the contract a quality usually described as *negotiability*, a concept discussed in chapter 33. Negotiability is a rule that cuts off defenses by giving one party a protected status. If a negotiable instrument is properly negotiated to a party, that party may have a protected status called a **holder in due course.** Thus most defenses of the original party (the buyer) cannot be asserted against the holder in due course (the finance company or bank). The purpose of the concept of negotiability is to encourage the free flow of commercial paper. Adding a provision to a contract that gives it the same effect obviously places the assignee in a favored position and makes contracts with such clauses quite marketable.

Holder in due course
One who has acquired possession of a negotiable instrument through proper negotiation for value, in good faith, and without notice of any defenses to it. Such a holder is not subject to personal defenses that would otherwise defeat the obligation embodied in the instrument.

As a part of the growing movement toward greater consumer protection, the Federal Trade Commission has ruled that such clauses cutting off defenses of consumer-debtors against delinquent sellers when a contract is assigned constitute an unfair method of competition. They are therefore illegal. The commission has also prohibited the use of the holder in due course concept against consumer-debtors. This 1976 action by the Federal Trade Commission is discussed further in chapter 35.

10. Duties of the Parties

As previously noted, an assignor is not relieved of his or her obligations by a delegation of them to the assignee. The assignor is still liable if the assignee fails to perform as agreed, in which case the assignor would have a cause of action against the assignee. If a party upon the transfer of a contract to a third person wishes to be released of liability, a legal arrangement known as a *novation* is required. The requirements for a valid novation are discussed later in this chapter.

The liability of the assignee to third persons is a much more complicated issue. The liability of the assignee is determined by a careful examination of the transactions to see whether it is an assignment of only the rights under the agreement or whether the duty has also been delegated. This is often difficult to determine when the language used refers only to an "assignment of the contract."

As a general rule, the *mere assignment* of a contract calling for the performance of affirmative duties by the assignor, with nothing more, does not impose those duties on the assignee. As a result, an assignee is not a guarantor of the products sold by the assignor, as the following case illustrates.

CASE

Cuchine v. H. O. Bell, Inc.
682 P.2d 723 (Mont. 1984)

On October 15, 1980, Timothy Cuchine purchased a pickup from H. O. Bell, Inc. (Bell) under a retail installment sales contract that was subsequently assigned to Ford Motor Credit Company. Cuchine later began experiencing some difficulties with the pickup and returned it to Bell to be repaired. When it became apparent that the truck could not be adequately repaired, Cuchine left the truck with Bell and filed a suit against Bell and the credit company for rescission of the installment contract due to breach of warranty and to recover his payments.

Cuchine contends that the credit company assumed full contract liability when the assignment was accepted. Cuchine predicates the credit company's liability under the contract on the following language, which appears in the contract in bold, capital letters:

NOTICE—ANY HOLDER OF THIS CONSUMER CREDIT CONTRACT IS SUBJECT TO ALL CLAIMS AND DEFENSES WHICH THE DEBTOR COULD ASSERT AGAINST THE SELLER OF GOODS OR SERVICES OBTAINED PURSUANT HERETO OR WITH THE PROCEEDS HEREOF. RECOVERY HEREUNDER BY THE DEBTOR SHALL NOT EXCEED AMOUNTS PAID BY THE DEBTOR HEREUNDER.

The District Court granted the credit company's motion for summary judgment and Cuchine appealed.

SHEEHY, J.

. . . The issue presented on appeal is whether the assignment of a retail installment sales contract imposes full contract liability on the assignee of certain rights under the contract.

Section 9-318 of the Uniform Commercial Code reads in pertinent part:

Unless an account debtor has made an enforceable agreement not to assert defenses or claims arising out of a sale as provided in 30-9-206, the rights of an assignee are subject to: (a) all the terms of the contract between the account debtor and assignor and any defense or claim arising therefrom; . . .

At common law, it is a well established rule that a party to a contract cannot relieve himself of the obligations which the contract imposed upon him merely by assigning the contract to a third person. Therefore, we must determine whether, under the Uniform Commercial Code, the assignment of the contract to the credit company imposed full contract liability on the credit company as assignee.

The case law as to the effect of section 9-318 of the UCC on the liabilities of an assignee of contract rights is scant, but conclusive. In *Michelin Tires v. First National Bank of Boston* (1st Cir. 1981), 666 F.2d 673, the court examined section 9-318 and determined that:

The key statutory language is ambiguous. That "the rights of an assignee are *subject* to . . . (a) all the terms of the contract" connotes only that the assignee's rights to recover are limited by the obligor's rights to assert contractual defenses as a set-off, implying that affirmative recovery against the assignee is not intended.

The court also noted that:

The words "subject to," used in their ordinary sense, mean "subordinate to," "subservient to," or "limited by." There is nothing in the use of the words "subject to," in their ordinary use, which would even hint at the creation of affirmative rights.

Such a conclusion is buttressed by the official comment to section 9-318. Official Comment I provides in pertinent part:

Subsection (1) makes no substantial change in prior law. An assignee has traditionally been subject to defenses or set-offs existing before an account debtor is notified of the assignment.

Under prior law, the assignee of a contract was generally not held liable for the assignor's breach of contract. This rule has been carried into current law as well; where it is not clearly shown that the assignee under a contract expressly or impliedly assumed the assignor's liability under the contract the assignee is not subject to the contract liability imposed by the contract on the assignor.

We believe that the intent of section 9-318 of the Uniform Commercial Code was to allow an account debtor to assert contractual defenses as a set-off; the provisions were not intended, generally, to place the assignee of a contract in the position of being held a guarantor of a product in place of the assignor. Therefore, the summary judgment of the District Court is

■ *Affirmed.*

CASE CONCEPTS REVIEW

1. Which parties entered into the original contract?
2. Which party is the assignor, the assignee, and the nonassigning party?
3. Rather than arguing that the assignee is subject to the same defenses as the assignor, what is the nonassigning party (plaintiff) arguing in this case?
4. Why does this court agree that the assignee is not liable for the nonperformance of the assignor's duties?

Notwithstanding the foregoing case, there is a decided trend that holds that an assignment of an entire contract carries an implied assumption of the liabilities. When the assignee undertakes and agrees to perform the duties as a condition precedent to enforcement of the rights, or has assumed the obligation to perform as part of a contract of assignment, he or she has liability for failure to perform. For example, if a tenant assigns a lease, the assignee is not liable for future rents if the assignee vacates the property prior to expiration of the period of the lease, unless the assignee expressly assumes the burdens of the lease at the time of the assignment. The assignee is obligated simply to pay the rent for the period of his or her actual occupancy. To the extent that an assignee accepts the benefits of a contract, he or she becomes obligated to perform the duties that are related to such benefits.

If an "entire contract" has been assigned—that is, if duties have been delegated to the assignee as well as the assignment of the rights—a failure by the assignee to render the required performance gives rise to a cause of action in favor of the third party (obligee). The obligee can sue either the assignor or the assignee or both.

Under the Code, an assignment of "the contract" or of "all my rights under the contract" or an assignment in similar general terms is an assignment of rights, and unless the language or the circumstances (as in an assignment for security) indicate the contrary, it is also a delegation of performance of the duties of the assignor and an assumption of those duties by the assignee. Its acceptance by the assignee constitutes a promise by him or her to perform those duties. This promise is enforceable by either the assignor or the other party to the original contract [2-210(4)].

When the assignor delegates his or her duties, although the assignor remains liable, the obligee may feel insecure as to the ability of the assignee to perform the delegated duties. The obligee may demand that the assignor furnish adequate assurance that the assignee will in fact render proper performance [2-210(5)].

11. Notice of Assignment

Immediately after the assignment, the assignee should notify the obligor or debtor of the assignee's newly acquired right. This notification is essential for two reasons.

First, in the absence of any notice of the assignment, the debtor is at liberty to perform (pay the debt or do whatever else the contract demands) for the original contracting party, the assignor. In fact, the debtor would not know that anyone else had the right to require performance or payment. Thus, the right of the assignee to demand performance can be defeated by his or her failure to give this notice. The assignor who receives performance under such circumstances becomes a trustee of funds or property received from the obligor and can be compelled to turn them over to the assignee. Upon receipt of notice of assignment, the third party *must perform* for the assignee, and the third party's payment or performance to the assignor would not relieve him or her of the obligation to the assignee.

Second, the notice of assignment is also for the protection of innocent third parties. The assignor has the *power*, although not the *right*, to make a second assignment of the same subject matter. If notice of the assignment has been given to the obligor, it has much the same effect as the recording of a mortgage. It furnishes protection for a party who may later consider taking an assignment of the same right. A person considering an assignment should therefore always communicate with the debtor to confirm that the right has not previously been assigned. If the debtor has not been notified of a previous assignment, and if the prospective assignee is aware of none, in many states the latter can feel free to take the assignment. That assignee should immediately give notice to the debtor. In other words, the first assignee to give notice to the debtor, provided such assignee has no knowledge of a prior assignment, will prevail over a prior assignee in most states.

In some states, it is held that the first party to receive an assignment has a prior claim, regardless of which assignee gave notice first. In these states, the courts act on the theory that the assignor has parted with all his or her interest by virtue of the original assignment and has nothing left to transfer to the second assignee. In all states, however, the party who is injured by reason of the second assignment has a cause of action against the assignor, to recover the damages that assignee has sustained. The assignor has committed a wrongful and dishonest act by making a double assignment.

Novation

12. Meaning

Novation The procedure of three parties agreeing to substitute a third party's obligation for that of one of the original contracting parties.

Novation (*novo* = new) describes an agreement whereby one of the original parties to a contract is replaced by a new party. The word *novation* originated in Roman law to refer to the *substitution* of a new contract. Thus, when a *new* person becomes a party to a *new* contract by *substitution* to the same rights and duties of an original party, a novation occurs and discharges the original contract. For example, Tommy, who is indebted to Nancy on an earlier contract, agrees with Nancy and Jesse that in consideration of Nancy's discharging Tommy, Jesse promises to do what Tommy was originally obligated to do. Jesse is thus substituted for Tommy, and a new contract exists between Nancy and Jesse.

13. Application

In this chapter, we have emphasized that an assignor generally is not relieved of the original obligation by delegating the duties to perform to an assignee. The novation in essence is an exception to this general rule. In a novation, one party is dismissed completely from the contract as a third party is substituted. In this situation, the dismissed party no longer has any liability under the original contract.

For a novation to be effective, it must be agreed to by all the parties. The remaining contracting party must agree to accept the new party and simultaneously specifically agree to release the withdrawing party. The latter must consent to withdraw and to permit the new party to take his or her place. The new party must agree to assume the burdens and duties of the retiring party. The agreement to release a former party and the agreement to assume the duties supplies bargained-for consideration to support the new or substituted contract. Note that a novation is never presumed. The burden of proving all the elements is on the party who claims a novation. The importance of satisfying this burden is illustrated in the following case.

CASE

United Fire Insurance Company v. McClelland
780 P.2d 193 (Nev. 1989)

McClelland, J.
Per Curiam

This appeal arose from an action brought against appellants United Fire Insurance Company and its parent, United Diversified Corporation, due to United Fire's refusal to pay Kenneth McClelland's claims for medical treatment. . . .

Kenneth received group accident and health insurance as a participant in the American Marketers Association Group Insurance Plan (AMA plan). United Fire issued the master policy of insurance to a trustee for the AMA plan, a Mississippi bank. Some 6,724 people were insured under this policy.

In November 1982, the California insurance commissioner issued a cease and desist order to United Fire requiring that it stop doing all business in California effective January 1, 1983. Two months later, the Nevada insurance commissioner served a similar order on United Fire.

On December 30, 1982, one of United Fire's vice presidents sent a letter to all the insureds under the AMA plan notifying them of a 23.5 percent increase in premiums and cautioning them not to "change or drop" their protection. This letter mentioned nothing about the cease and desist order or about United Fire's financial difficulties.

United Fire and California Life Insurance Company executed a reinsurance and assumption agreement (Agreement) on January 18, 1983. This Agreement provided that, as of January 1, 1983, California Life acquired all United Fire's rights and assumed all United Fire's obligations under the "policies." The "policies" included the AMA plan.

On January 24, 1983, United Fire's president wrote to all of the insureds under the AMA plan informing them that California Life had assumed United Fire's liability under the AMA policy and stating that insureds would receive an assumption certificate from California Life. California Life never sent the promised assumption certificate.

The McClellands [Kenneth and his wife, Joni] continued to receive correspondence from United Fire through May 1983. On June 30, 1983, California Life mailed a letter to the participants in the AMA plan telling them that the coverage under the group plan would be cancelled, effective October 1, 1983. Two weeks later, California Life sent a second letter, changing the cancellation date to November 1, 1983. However, the policy expressly stated that it may be terminated upon the premium due date if written notice is given the policyholder, the Mississippi bank, at least 120 days in advance of such premium date. California Life never notified the policyholder of the cancellation.

At the time of the Agreement, Kenneth was healthy and insurable. However, in March 1983, doctors diagnosed Kenneth as having an altered renal function with stones in both kidneys. Kenneth had several operations and hospitalizations to remove stones, cure infections, and implant and replace a tube from the bladder to the kidney.

Once the dispute over insurance arose, Kenneth delayed several times in receiving hospital treatment because of a lack of money. On one occasion, Kenneth refused to go to the hospital when his infection was particularly severe. When he finally did get to the hospital, it took seven days before the infection could be controlled. Kenneth's physician testified that the McClellands seemed emotionally distraught due to the amount of the medical bills which accumulated with no means of paying them.

The McClellands filed suit against appellants and California Life. Just before trial commenced, California Life agreed to pay McClellands their contract benefits under the policy. The McClellands proceeded to trial against appellants. A jury awarded Kenneth compensatory damages of $143,000, Joni compensatory damages of $73,000, and $500,000 in punitive damages.

Appellants assert that as a matter of law . . . they owed the McClellands no insurance benefits because the policy was transferred to California Life, with the McClellands' knowledge and consent, before the claims giving rise to this suit arose. Thus, they argue that the evidence of novation entitled them to judgment as a matter of law.

A novation consists of four elements: (1) there must be an existing valid contract; (2) all parties must agree to a new contract; (3) the new contract must extinguish the old contract; and (4) the new contract must be valid. If all four elements exist, a novation occurred. Additionally, the intent of all parties to cause a novation must be clear. However, consent to novation may be implied from the circumstances of the transaction and by the subsequent conduct of the parties.

Novation is a question of law only when the agreement and consent of the parties are unequivocal. Whether a novation occurred is a question of fact if the evidence is such that reasonable persons can draw more than one conclusion.

Appellants rely on the January 24, 1983 letter which United Fire sent to its insureds under the AMA plan to prove that a novation occurred. According to United Fire, the letter unmistakably indicated that United Fire would have no liability for claims incurred after the effective date, January 1, 1983. Appellants argue that the McClellands' failure to submit the disputed medical bills to United Fire confirms that the McClellands derived the same understanding from the letter.

We conclude that a novation did not occur as a matter of law due to questions regarding the McClellands' alleged consent. Therefore, the district court properly submitted the issue to the jury. Moreover, the party asserting novation has the burden of proving all the essentials of novation by clear and convincing evidence. Thus, we further conclude that substantial evidence supports the jury's determination that appellants failed to establish, by clear and convincing evidence, all the facts necessary to prove a novation.

This court will not overturn a jury verdict when substantial evidence supports it. We will look at the facts from the viewpoint of the prevailing party, assuming that the jury believed all evidence favorable to that party and that the jury drew all reasonable inferences in its favor.

In the instant case, the McClellands claim that had they known that the California insurance commissioner had prohibited United Fire from writing insurance in California and that California Life and its owner had questionable reputations, they would have sought other insurance. Thus, the jury could have found that the McClellands' acquiescence to California Life as their insurer did not constitute consent when they knew nothing of United Fire's ejection from California and Nevada or the questionable status of California Life. . . .

■ *Affirmed.*

CASE CONCEPTS REVIEW

1. Who was insured by whom under the original AMA plan?
2. Name the assignor and assignee involved in the transfer of insurance policies, including the AMA plan.
3. On what grounds does the United Fire Insurance Company argue that it is relieved of liability under the original AMA plan?
4. Why does the court conclude that a novation has not occurred?

CHAPTER SUMMARY

THIRD-PARTY BENEFICIARY CONTRACTS

Nature of Such Contracts
1. A noncontracting party may have enforceable contract rights if a party to the contract intended to confer a benefit on the third party.
2. Creditor- and donee-beneficiaries are intended beneficiaries.

	3. If performance by the promisor will satisfy a duty owed to the beneficiary by the promisee, the beneficiary is a creditor-beneficiary.
	4. If the promisee purchased a promise to make a gift to a third party, the party is a donee-beneficiary.
Legal Requirements	**1.** If a third party is not an intended beneficiary, he or she is an incidental beneficiary with no right to enforce the agreement.
	2. Original parties can modify or rescind their contract until the third party's rights vest.
	3. A third party's rights vest when he or she either relies on the contract to his or her detriment or manifests assent to the rights.
	4. A third-party beneficiary is subject to all defenses arising out of the contract.

ASSIGNMENTS

Terminology	**1.** An assignment is a transfer of rights arising from an earlier contract.
	2. A delegation is a transfer of duties arising from an earlier contract.
	3. When A assigns his or her rights against B to C, A is the assignor, B is the promisor-obligor, and C is the assignee.
	4. When A delegates his or her duties owed to B to C, A is the assignor (delegator), B is the promisee-obligee, and C is the assignee (delegatee).
	5. "Assignment of the contract" is usually held to be both an assignment and a delegation.
General Principles	**1.** There are no formal requirements for a valid assignment. Generally, neither consideration nor a writing is required.
	2. No consent of the nonassigning party usually is required. Thus, contracts are said to be freely assignable.
	3. The assignor must completely and irrevocably transfer rights to create an effective assignment.
	4. An assignor is not relieved of his or her duties by delegating them to an assignee.
Consent Required	**1.** Most rights are assignable unless the assignment would (a) materially change the other party's duty, (b) materially increase the burden or risk imposed by the contract, or (c) materially impair the other party's chance of obtaining return performance.
	2. The duties under contracts for personal services generally may not be delegated.
	3. The right to purchase on credit cannot be assigned without consent in most states.
Consent Required under the Code	**1.** The Code generally approves the assignment of rights and the delegation of duties.
	2. Unless the buyer has a substantial interest in having the seller perform, the seller may delegate the duty to deliver goods.
Antiassignment Clauses	**1.** Contractual limitations on assignments are strictly construed in most cases to prevent only a delegation of duties.
	2. A breach of such a clause may be interpreted as (a) breaching the promise not to make an assignment, (b) invalidating the contract, or (c) voiding the assignment.
Claims for Money	**1.** As a general rule, claims for money may be assigned, but there are statutory exceptions.
	2. If the assignment is as security for a debt, the assignor still owes the debt if it remains unpaid by the obligor.
	3. If the assignor sells the debt, there is no recourse against the assignor if the obligor defaults.
	4. An assignor warrants the genuineness of the money claims assigned.
Rights of the Assignee	**1.** The assignee may enforce all the rights of his or her assignor.
	2. The obligor may raise all defenses against the assignee that the obligor had against the assignor prior to the assignment.

3. Failure of the assignor to fulfill his or her duties to the obligor will be a defense against the assignee.

4. Contract provisions cutting off defenses of consumer-debtors are illegal under a Federal Trade Commission rule.

Duties of the Parties

1. An assignor is not relieved of duties by a delegation of those duties.

2. The mere assignment of rights does not include the delegation of duties.

3. Under the Code, the assignment of the contract generally includes the assignment of rights and the delegation of duties.

4. If an assignor delegates duties to an assignee, the assignee thereby becomes primarily liable to perform for the obligee.

Notice of Assignment

1. Notice of the assignment must be given by the assignee to the obligor if the assignee is to receive performance.

2. In a case of multiple assignments, the first to give notice in good faith to the obligor has priority to receive performance in most states.

NOVATION

Meaning

1. A novation means a new contract. It involves the substitution with the express consent of all parties of a third party for one of the original parties.

Application

1. In essence, a novation works as an exception to the general rule that an assignor remains liable even after an effective delegation of duties.

2. A novation requires a prior valid contract, agreement for substitution of a third party, an express release of one party, and a new valid contract.

REVIEW QUESTIONS AND PROBLEMS

1. Match each term in column A with the appropriate statement in column B.

A	B
(1) Intended third-party beneficiary	(a) Performance will satisfy a duty the promisee owes the beneficiary
(2) Incidental third-party beneficiary	(b) A present transfer of rights arising from an earlier contract
(3) Creditor-beneficiary	(c) Transfer of rights would materially change the other party's duty, increase the risk imposed by the contract, or impair return performance
(4) Donee-beneficiary	(d) Third party who has no legally enforceable rights under a contract
(5) When beneficiary's rights vest	(e) Usually both an assignment and a delegation
(6) Assignment	(f) Rights vest based on reliance or consent of third party
(7) Delegation	(g) A new contract with the substitution of a third party for an original party
(8) Nonassignable rights	(h) Third party who has legally enforceable rights under a contract
(9) Nondelegable duties	(i) Duties of personal service or duties that may materially vary the performance given to the obligee

| (10) Novation | (j) Transfer of duties arising from an earlier contract |
| (11) "Assignment of the contract" | (k) Promisee buys a promise to make a gift to a third party |

2. Boyce contracts to build a house for Anne. Pursuant to the contract, Boyce and his surety, Travelers, execute a payment bond to Anne by which they promise Anne that all of Boyce's debts for labor and materials on the house will be paid. Boyce later employs Sam as a carpenter and buys lumber from Larry's Lumber Company. Are Sam and Larry's Lumber Company intended beneficiaries of Travelers' promise to Anne? Explain.

3. Wichita State University leased an airplane to fly its football team. The lease provided that the university would provide liability insurance to cover any deaths or injuries from the operation of the plane. No such insurance was bought. The plane later crashed, killing all on board. Can the estates of the deceased football players sue the university as intended third-party beneficiaries? Explain why or why not.

4. A property settlement agreement that was part of a divorce decree required the former husband to pay child support until the child reached age twenty-two, if the child attended college and maintained at least a C average. The mother died when the child was sixteen, and the father refused to support the child after the child reached eighteen. Is the child entitled to sue the father for breach of contract? Why or why not?

5. Hunt, an employee of the Marie Reading School, was injured when the elevator he was operating fell. The school had a contract with Shaft Elevator, Inc., whereby Shaft was to inspect and service the elevator on a regular basis. Hunt contended that Shaft had not properly inspected the elevator and that its omission caused the accident. Can Hunt maintain an action against Shaft? Why or why not?

6. Gaither entered into a contract with a nonprofit corporation whereby Gaither would receive $700 per month while in medical school, provided that he would return to his small hometown, Chester, to practice medicine for ten years after becoming a licensed physician. The residents of Chester voted approval of bonds to construct a medical clinic. Gaither practiced medicine in Chester for about five weeks but then left for Mt. Clement. Do the representatives of the medical clinic and the citizens of Chester have a right to sue Gaither? Explain.

7. In violation of an injunction, the members of the defendants' unions commenced a strike, halting all mass transit in the city of New York and paralyzing its life and commerce. In contracts with the public employers, the unions had agreed not to strike. The plaintiff, a New York lawyer, brought a class-action suit against the transit unions and certain of their officers, seeking damages for the mass transit strike. The unions contended that the plaintiff was not a third-party beneficiary of the contract. Were the unions correct? Explain.

8. Green, an insured of a Prudential health policy, incurred medical expenses at Kelly Health Care. She signed an authorization that stated, "I hereby authorize payment directly to Kelly Health Care of benefits otherwise payable by me." Kelly sued Prudential, claiming to be an assignee of Green's insurance contract. Prudential contended that Kelly was not an assignee. Was Prudential correct? Explain.

9. Athens Lie Detector Company, for good consideration, gave Yarbrough an exclusive license to operate certain lie detector machines as part of the agreement. The company agreed to tell him how the manufacturing process works. Athens assigned its rights and delegated its duties under the contract to Travers. Are the rights assignable? Are the duties delegable? Explain.

10. Pizza of Gaithersburg contracted with Virginia Coffee Service to install cold-drink vending machines in its six restaurants. A year later, Macke bought the assets of Virginia Coffee Service and the contract was assigned to Macke. Pizza contends that the duties under the contract could not be delegated. What do you think? Explain.

11. Corey sold his property to Greer, who assigned the contract right to Bob. The original contract of sale provided for an extension of credit by Corey to Greer and did not require a total cash payment at the time of closing. Is a contract for the sale of real estate assignable by the buyer if it provides for credit from the seller to the buyer? Explain.

12. As part of his employment contract, an employee entered into a covenant not to compete with his corporate employer. The contract also contained a provision that stated, "This agreement is personal to each of the parties hereto, and neither party may assign or delegate any of the rights or obligations hereunder without first obtaining a written consent of the other party." Later the corporation was dissolved, and the assets were distributed to the shareholders who operated the business as a partnership. The employee filed suit to establish that the covenant not to compete was no longer enforceable. Can the partnership enforce the covenant not to compete? Explain.

13. Suppose that contract for the sale of goods contains this clause: "Under no circumstances may any rights under this contract be assigned." After the seller delivers goods to the buyer, may the seller assign the buyer's unpaid account to a third party? Explain.

14. Hudson Supply owed an open account to Eastern Brick & Tile Company (Eastern). These accounts were sold and assigned by Eastern to a finance company, the plaintiff. When plaintiff sought to collect on the assigned accounts, Hudson refused to pay on the ground that Eastern owed more money to Hudson than Hudson owed Eastern. Can a defensive setoff be asserted against the assignee of a money claim? Explain.

15. To get a construction contract, a contractor was required to put up a performance bond. The purpose of the bond was to ensure that the contractor would perform properly and pay all bills. The defendant bonding company agreed to write the bond provided that the contractor would assign (as security) payments due under the construction contract. The contractor agreed, and the assignment was executed. Thereafter, the contractor borrowed money from plaintiff bank and assigned the same right to the same payments to the bank. The bank was the first to notify the owner of its assignment. Which party has priority? Explain.

16. Martin Stern sued for his architectural services rendered to Jacobson in Jacobson's development of a hotel and casino. In April, Jacobson contracted with Stern for the architect's services and the fee. On May 1, Jacobson acquired all the stock of A.L.W., Inc., a corporation that had previously operated a casino on the site of the new development. On May 9, A.L.W. began to operate the casino, but it filed bankruptcy. Stern did not file a claim in the bankruptcy proceeding but rather brought suit directly against Jacobson. When Stern was awarded $132,590.37 by the trial court, Jacobson appealed on the ground that his obligations were adopted by A.L.W., which constituted a novation. Has a valid novation occurred that would release Jacobson from his personal liability? Explain.

CHAPTER

18

INTRODUCTION TO SALES CONTRACTS

CHAPTER PREVIEW

As we learned in Part III, the Uniform Commercial Code changes many older, classic contract rules to conform with business realities and the reasonable expectations of the contracting parties. In particular, Article 2 of the Code affects contracts involving the sale of movable objects of personal property. Because of the importance of Article 2 to businesspeople, this chapter and the next one examine in detail key provisions of this Article.

Specifically, this chapter explores the sales contract, the transfer of title to goods, and the risk of loss when goods are destroyed, damaged, or stolen. Chapter 19 covers the remedies available to the parties when there is a breach of a sales contract.

You are the general manager of a wholesale mail-order distributor. The bulk of your customers are retailers who phone in their orders.

What policy should you develop for accepting these phone orders?

ARTICLE 2 OF THE UCC

1. Summary of Common-Law Changes

Many common-law contract rules also have been changed or modified by Article 2 of the Code to achieve a more commercially desirable result, since some basic contract rules concerning employment, construction, and real property contracts are simply inappropriate in a sale-of-goods context. The important Code modifications or changes are summarized in Table 18–1. These Code rules have already been discussed in the chapters on contracts and will not be discussed further.

The rules and principles discussed in this chapter and the next are important ones contained in Article 2; they were not presented in the chapters on contracts.

2. Scope

A sales transaction can relate to real property, to goods, and to other forms of personal property. This chapter, however, is limited to sales transactions in goods under Article 2 of the Uniform Commercial Code. Article 2 of the Code does not define *transaction*. Although a few sections are limited either explicitly or implicitly to the sale of goods {2-204, 2-314, 2-402, 2-703}, courts have extended Article 2 to transactions such as leases and bailments of goods in some cases.

When you lease a car or rent a golf cart, does Article 2 apply if problems arise? Historically, the answer has been unclear. Some courts have applied the Code to all commercial leases of goods. These courts emphasize that Article 2 governs "transactions" in goods, and a lease of goods is such a transaction. On the other hand, a few courts emphasize the word *sales* in the Code and will extend Article 2 only to transactions in goods that are analogous to a sale of goods. Some leases, for example, contain an option to buy; and if exercised, it will cause the lease payments (rent) to be applied toward the purchase price. Cars, TV sets, stereo sets, and many other things are frequently leased with an option to buy. Most courts have applied Article 2 to these leases, since they have attributes (option to buy) that make the transactions analogous to a sale of goods.

This issue of the proper application of Article 2 to lease has been resolved by the addition of Article 2A to the UCC. This new Article applies specifically to the lease. In those states that have adopted Article 2A, the provisions of Article 2, dis-

TABLE 18–1 ■ Special Rules for Contracts for the Sale of Goods

UCC CODE SECTION 2	RULE
Offer and acceptance	
204	All terms need not be included in negotiations for a contract to result.
205	Firm written offers by merchants are irrevocable for a maximum of three months.
206(1)(a)	An acceptance may be made by any reasonable means of communication and is effective when deposited.
206(1)(b)	Unilateral offers may be accepted either by a promise to ship or by shipment.
206(1)(b)	Failure to reject may constitute an acceptance.
206(2)	Acceptance by performance requires notice within a reasonable time, or the offer may be treated as lapsed.
207	Variance in terms between offer and acceptance may not be a rejection and may be an acceptance.
305	The price need not be included in a contract.
311(1)	Particulars of performance may be left open.
Consideration	
203	Adding a seal is of no effect.
209(1)	Consideration is not required to support a modification of a contract for the sale of goods.
Voidable contracts	
403	A minor may not disaffirm against an innocent third party.
721	Rescission is not a bar to a suit for dollar damages.
Illegality	
302	Unconscionable bargains will not be enforced.
Form of the agreement	
201	Statute of frauds $500 price for goods Written confirmation between merchants Memorandum need not include all terms of agreement. Payment, acceptance, and receipt limited to quantity specified in writing. Specially manufactured goods Admission pleadings or court proceedings that a contract for sale was made
Rights of third parties	
210(4)	An assignment of "the contract" or of "rights under the contract" includes a delegation of duties.
Performance of contracts	
209	Claims and rights may be waived without consideration.
307, 612	Rules on divisible contracts
511	Tender of payment is a condition precedent (rather than a condition concurrent) to a tender of delivery.
610, 611	Anticipatory breach may not be withdrawn if the other party gives notice that it is final.
614	Impracticability of performance in certain cases is an excuse for nonperformance.
Discharge	
725	The statute of limitations is four years, but parties can reduce it by mutual agreement to not less than one year.

cussed herein, now are clearly governing the sales transactions. (The key provisions of Article 2A are presented in chapter 45.)

Another question that arises is the application of Article 2 when a sales transaction involves the rendering of services. Article 2 will not apply if the subject matter of the contract is service. But many contracts are "mixed" contracts in that they involve both sale of services and goods. You hire a painter to paint your house or a contractor to install a heating and air-conditioning system in an apartment complex, or a hairdresser to apply a special shampoo. In addition to providing services, these persons have also sold goods (the paint, heating and air unit, and shampoo). These contracts present borderline transactions, and courts must often make a decision regarding the applicability of Article 2. Most courts tend to apply Article 2 only if the goods aspect of the deal is predominant. Their approach, as in the following case, is to ask which part of the transaction is the predominant feature—sale of goods or sale of services?

CASE

In re Trailer and Plumbing Supplies
578 A.2d 343 (N.H. 1990)

JOHNSON, J.

This appeal in an action by the State . . . concerns the ownership of certain plumbing supplies and the applicability of the Uniform Commercial Code (UCC) to mixed contracts for goods and services. The respondent, Bay Forest Development Corporation (Bay Forest), appeals from a decision of the Superior Court, declaring Schuster Plumbing and Heating Co., Inc. (Schuster) to be the owner of certain plumbing and heating supplies. . . .

Schuster and Bay Forest formed a contract in July 1988. Schuster agreed to install plumbing for Bay Forest's condominium project and, in return, Bay Forest agreed to pay Schuster $210,000. . . . The section entitled "Payment Schedule" reads:

1. Complete project price . . . . . . $210,000.00 per 20 units.
2. All materials to be paid within 10 days of material dropped on site.
3. Progress payments to be made on labor every 30 days.

Schuster bought $26,250 worth of plumbing and heating materials (the materials at issue in this case) for the condominium project from third-party suppliers, and had them delivered to the condominium worksite. The trial court found that "the materials were delivered by a supplier to Mr. Schuster" on or about December 6, 1988 "and stored in a trailer. . . ." The trailer was leased by Bay Forest for Schuster's use at the condominium worksite. In addition to the supplies purchased for Bay Forest's condominium project, Schuster kept tools and other materials in the trailer. Schuster billed Bay Forest on December 6, 1988, for $26,250, "Progress Payment On Material Cost Only." However, Bay Forest did not pay this bill, and Schuster in turn did not install the plumbing materials in the condominiums.

On March 10, 1989, Schuster reported to the Dover police that the trailer containing the plumbing and heating materials was missing from the worksite. Once the police learned that the trailer had been moved to the property of a Bay Forest employee, the trailer, along with the materials inside it, were seized pursuant to a search warrant.

On May 23, 1989, the State filed a petition . . . in the superior court requesting the return of the plumbing and heating supplies to Schuster, who the State alleged was the rightful owner. . . . Bay Forest, claiming ownership, objected to the petition . . . The trial court found by "clear and convincing" evidence that Schuster owned the materials and denied Bay Forest's motion to reconsider. . . .

Bay Forest argues on appeal . . . that the UCC applies to the contract and confers upon Bay Forest ownership of the materials. . . .

The State, on the other hand, argues that the contract is a . . . predominantly service agreement. Therefore, the State maintains, common law, rather than the UCC, applies to the contract, and the materials belong to Schuster. We agree with the State's position. . . .

We address the question whether this contract comes within the province of the UCC. There is no dispute that the contract is in part a contract for the sale of goods and in part a services contract. Because the UCC generally applies only to the sale of goods, we must determine under what circumstances it will apply to mixed contracts for goods and services. This jurisdiction has not yet adopted a test for making such a determination.

Both Bay Forest and the State advocate the use of the "predominant factor" test. . . .

The test for inclusion or exclusion [within the UCC] is not whether they are mixed, but, granting that they are mixed, whether their predominant factor, their thrust, their purpose, reasonably stated, is the rendition of service, with goods incidentally involved (e.g., contract with artist for painting) or is a transaction of sale, with labor incidentally involved (e.g., installation of a water heater in a bathroom).

An alternative test is the "gravamen of the action" test. This test simply asks whether the underlying action is brought because of alleged defective goods or because of the quality of the service rendered. If the gravamen of the action focuses on goods, then the UCC governs. If the focus is on the quality of the services rendered, then common law applies. . . .

The case before us centers on the ownership of the plumbing and heating materials, and not the installation of those materials. There has been no allegation that the goods are defective or non-conforming, nor has there been a complaint concerning labor and installation which would suggest a gravamen of the action analysis. The issue here is simply the ownership of the goods. In this case there is no action arising out of the contract, and thus the gravamen of the action analysis is inappropriate. Hence, the "predominant factor" test should be applied, in this case, to determine if the contract should be governed by the UCC or by common law. In a future case alleging defective goods or alleging defective services, we may then consider whether the gravamen of the action analysis is appropriate.

Only two factors support classifying this contract as one for the sale of goods. First, the materials to be used are specifically itemized. Second, the contract provides for separate payment for the plumbing materials.

In contrast, several factors support a holding that the service aspect of the contract predominates. First, the language of the contract indicates an agreement for provision of services. Bay Forest's construction plan is termed a "project," and the contract states that "all plumbing [is] to be per Schuster's . . . design." Second, there is no price allocation in the contract between material and labor, and prices are not assigned to the itemized materials. Rather, the contract simply lists a "complete project price" of $210,000. Third, most of the contract price may be attributed to labor, and not to materials (the materials cost only $26,250, 12.5% of the total contract price). Fourth, Schuster was not in the business of manufacturing plumbing and heating materials or acting as a supply house. Instead, Schuster's business was the installation of plumbing and heating materials, bought from a supplier, according to its own expertise and design. Fifth, the evidence tended to show that, in the contractual parties' prior dealings, ownership of the goods did not transfer from Schuster to Bay Forest until the goods were installed in the buildings. It was thus unreasonable for Bay Forest to presume ownership of the materials while they were still in the trailer. Given the weight of these findings, we hold that this agreement is predominantly a services contract.

Because the agreement is a contract for services, the UCC does not govern this dispute. We therefore must look to the common law to determine the ownership of the materials. . . . What is affixed to the land belongs to the owner of that land. The plumbing and heating materials at issue here were never affixed to Bay Forest's realty. Therefore, the materials still belong to Schuster. . . .

Because Schuster was the rightful owner of the materials, the trial court correctly ordered them returned to Schuster.

■ *Affirmed.*

CASE CONCEPTS REVIEW

1. Bay Forest had contracted to have Schuster install plumbing in twenty units in a condominium project. Why did Schuster refuse to perform this contract?

2. What happened to the plumbing supplies after Schuster refused to install them? Why did the state get involved in this case?

3. What is the basis for the court's conclusion that Schuster is the owner of these plumbing supplies? On what law is this decision based?

Some problem areas have definite answers. Article 2 applies to specially manufactured goods [2-105(1)] and to "the serving for value of food or drink to be consumed either on the premises or elsewhere" [2-314(1)]. By statute in many states, Article 2 is inapplicable to blood transfusions, bone transfers, or organ transplants. These are considered medical services.

3. Definitions

Goods Items of tangible personal property that are movable.

GOODS. The precise meaning of the term *goods* is sometimes a problem for the courts. In general, the term **goods** encompasses things that are movable, that is, items of personal property (chattels) that are of a tangible, physical nature ⎰2-105(1)⎱. Although broadly interpreted to include even electricity, the definition of goods excludes investment securities (covered by Article 8 of the Code) and negotiable instruments (covered by Article 3 of the Code).

Being limited to goods, Article 2 necessarily excludes contracts for personal service, construction, intangible personal property, and the sale of real estate. Goods associated with real estate *may* be within Article 2 in sales of "structures," "minerals," and the "like" if severance is to be made by the seller. If severance is to be made by the buyer, the contract involves a sale of an interest in land ⎰2-107(1)⎱. Growing crops, including timber, fall within Article 2, regardless of who severs them ⎰2-107(2)⎱.

Another term used in Article 2 is *future goods*—goods that are not in existence at the time of the agreement or that have not been designated as the specific goods that will be the subject matter of the sales transaction ⎰2-105(2)⎱.

Sales transaction The transfer of title from a seller to a buyer in exchange for an agreed-upon price.

SALE. The **sales transaction** involves an exchange of title to the goods for a price ⎰2-106(a)⎱. The basic obligation of the seller is to tender the goods, while that of the buyer is to accept the goods and pay the price ⎰2-301⎱. In general, the parties to a sales contract can agree on any terms and conditions that are mutually acceptable.

Merchant A person who deals in goods of the kind involved in a transaction; or one who otherwise, by occupation, holds himself or herself out as having knowledge or skill peculiar to the practices or goods involved.

MERCHANT. Special provisions of Article 2 relate to transactions involving a **merchant,** a professional businessperson who deals in the subject matter of the sales contract or who "holds himself out as having knowledge or skill peculiar to the practices or goods involved in the transaction" ⎰2-104(1)⎱. This designation is of great importance and is recognition of a professional status for a businessperson, justifying standards of conduct different from those of "nonprofessionals." The courts of some states have held that farmers are merchants when selling grain and other items raised by them. Other courts have held that farmers are not merchants, so from state to state and case to case there is variation in whether or not Code provisions relating to merchants apply also to farmers. The issue is usually one of fact, as the court in the following case recognized.

CASE

Bauer v. Curran
360 N.W.2d 88 (Iowa 1984)

LARSON, J.

. . . In the spring of 1979, Carl Davidson, a farmer, leased approximately 100 head of pregnant stock cows from the plaintiffs. It is undisputed that Davidson did not, in this transaction, receive title to the cattle or any authority to transfer them. These cows calved in the spring of 1979, and again in the spring of 1980. In the fall of 1980, R. D. Curran, one of the defendants, purchased sixteen of these cow-calf pairs from Davidson. He later sold them through defendant Russell Sale Co., Inc., a company in which the Currans had an ownership interest. The record shows that Mr. Curran made no attempt to discover whether Davidson actually owned the cattle.

The plaintiffs argue that they retained ownership of the cattle despite Davidson's "sale" of them to Curran. The defendants, on the other hand, contend Davidson was a merchant as a matter of law and that, under Iowa Code section 554.2403(2), Davidson's buyers would have acquired title to the cattle. Section 554.2403(2) provides:

Any entrusting of possession of goods to a merchant who deals in goods of that kind gives him power to transfer all rights of the entrustor to a buyer in ordinary course of business.

The court ruled that the question of Davidson's status was one of fact and submitted the issue to the jury by a special interrogatory. The jury found Davidson was not a merchant at the time of the sale, making section 554.2403(2) inapplicable.

Merchant status is said to take three forms: The first is transactional in nature: The seller is a dealer in the type of goods involved in the questioned transaction. The second form involves the merchant who holds himself out as having some skill or knowledge focusing on the specific transaction and goods involved. The third revolves around the principal-agent relationship.

The definition of "merchant" in Iowa Code section 554.2104(1) (1983) incorporates those concepts:

"Merchant" means a person who deals in goods of the kind or otherwise by his occupation holds himself out as having knowledge or skill peculiar to the practices or goods involved in the transaction or to whom such knowledge or skill may be attributed by his employment of an agent or broker or other intermediary who by his occupation holds himself out as having such knowledge or skill.

The trial court similarly defined the term in its instructions to the jury in this case: "[M]erchant [means] a person who deals in goods of the kind involved in its [sic] transaction, in this case cattle, or otherwise by his occupation holds himself out as having knowledge or skill peculiar to the practice involved in selling or buying cattle."

This court, essentially quoting the statute, has held that a farmer, in order to be a merchant, must be:

(1) [A] dealer who deals in goods of the kind involved, or (2) he must by his occupation hold himself out as having knowledge or skill peculiar to the practices or goods involved in the transaction, or (3) he must employ an agent, broker or other intermediary who by his occupation holds himself out as having knowledge or skill peculiar to the practices or goods involved in the transaction.

The question is generally one of fact; it is only where "the facts are undisputed and reasonable minds could draw no different inferences from them" that the issue becomes one of law.

Even when the facts are not in dispute or contradicted, if reasonable minds might draw different inferences from them a jury question is engendered.

It is said that "it is the jury that is entitled to conclude whether or not one inference or another may be drawn, neither of which can be unreasonable, regarding whether the sale of goods was in fact an isolated sale or whether a party to the transaction was a merchant with respect to the goods which were the subject matter of the sale."

Most courts which have held a farmer to be a merchant have relied on evidence demonstrating that the farmer dealt in goods of the kind sold, as opposed to evidence that he held himself out as having particular skills or knowledge. The Iowa Code comments suggest that section 554.2403(2) is sufficiently broad to support a finding . . . that a farmer is a merchant. . . .

The evidence provided is sufficient basis for a decision either way on Davidson's status. Prior to the sale in question, there was evidence that Davidson had bought, sold, and leased cattle. One year, for example, Davidson leased approximately twenty head of cattle from another individual and in addition had entered into a lease-purchase agreement with a Clearview Cattle Company. Matthew Bauer, the individual who had leased the present cattle to Davidson, testified that although he had engaged in a large number of transactions in buying and selling cattle in the area, he had never seen or met Davidson prior to 1980 when they entered into the lease agreement in question.

Most other cattle sales involving Davidson were said by him to be merely attempts to cull his herd, and, while Davidson had earlier sold part of these cattle leased from plaintiff Bauer, he had done so under Bauer's name and at his direction. Davidson appears to have only occasionally bought or sold cattle.

While other factors tended to support a finding that Davidson may have been a merchant, our question is not whether there was evidence to support a finding the jury did not make but whether reasonable minds could have drawn different inferences from the facts. We conclude they could and that the issue was therefore properly submitted to the jury.

■ *Affirmed.*

CASE CONCEPTS REVIEW

1. Who was the actual owner of the cows and calves in Davidson's possession?
2. What argument does Curran make to support his having obtained title from Davidson?
3. The court lists three situations in which a person is deemed to be a merchant. What are these three?
4. Why does this reviewing court defer to the jury's finding that Davidson was not a merchant?

Good faith Honesty in fact in the conduct or transaction concerned. For a merchant, good faith also means the observance of reasonable commercial standards of fair dealing in the trade.

GOOD FAITH.   The Code provisions on the sale of goods are based on two assumptions: (1) that the parties should be given the maximum latitude in fixing their own terms and (2) that the parties will act in "good faith." **Good faith** means honesty in fact in the conduct or transaction [1-201(19)]. In the case of a merchant, good faith also includes the observance of reasonable commercial standards of fair dealing in the trade [2-103(1)(b)].

RETURNED GOODS.   The buyer and seller may agree that the buyer has the privilege of returning the goods that have been delivered. If the goods are delivered primarily for use, as in a consumer purchase, the transaction is called a *sale on approval*. If the goods are delivered primarily for resale, it is called a *sale or return* [2-326(1)]. The distinction is an important one, because goods delivered on approval are not subject to the claims of the buyer's creditors until the buyer has indicated acceptance of the goods; goods delivered on sale or return, however, are subject to the claims of the buyer's creditors while they are in the buyer's possession [2-326(2)]. Delivery of goods on consignment, such as a transaction in which a manufacturer or a wholesaler delivers goods to a retailer who has the privilege of returning any unsold goods, is a sale or return.

The distinction between sale on approval and sale or return also is important if the goods are lost, stolen, damaged, or destroyed. The issues arising in these factual situations are discussed in section 14, along with other aspects of risk of loss.

4. Abbreviations

As a matter of convenience, a number of contract terms are generally expressed as abbreviations. *F.O.B.* (free on board) is the most commonly used. *F.O.B. the place of shipment* means that the seller is obligated to place the goods in possession of a carrier, so that they may be shipped to the buyer. *F.O.B. the place of destination* means that the seller is obligated to cause the goods to be delivered to the buyer [2-319(1)(b)]. Thus, if Athens, Georgia, is the seller's place of business, "F.O.B. Athens, Georgia," is a *shipment contract.* "F.O.B. Champaign, Illinois," Champaign being the place where the buyer is to receive the goods, is a *destination contract,* and the seller must provide transportation to that place at his or her own risk and expense.

If the terms of the contract also specify *F.O.B. vessel, car, or other vehicle*, the seller must at his or her own expense and risk load the goods on board. *F.A.S.* (free alongside) *vessel* at a named port requires the seller at his or her own expense and risk to deliver the goods alongside the vessel in the manner usual in the port or on a dock designated and provided by the buyer [2-319(2)].

C.I.F. means that the price includes, in a lump sum, the cost of the goods and of the insurance and freight to the named destination [2-320]. The seller's obligation is to load the goods, to make provision for payment of the freight, and to obtain an insurance policy in favor of the buyer. Generally, C.I.F. means that the parties will deal in terms of the documents that represent the goods. (Section 6 describes this documentary transaction more specifically.) Typically, the seller performs his or her obligation by tendering to the buyer the proper documents, including a negotiable bill of lading and an invoice of the goods. The buyer is required to make payment against the tender of the required documents [2-320(4)].

The Sales Contract

The terms of a sales contract are supplied by three sources: the express agreement of the parties; course of dealing, usage of trade, and course of performance; and the Code and other applicable statutes.

5. Express Agreement

The general rule in sales law is that the parties are free to make their own contract. The parties are privileged to contract expressly regarding most basic terms— quality, quantity, price, delivery, payment, and the like. In general, their agreement is sufficient to displace any otherwise applicable Code section. But the principle of freedom of contract under the Code is not without exceptions. The parties cannot "disclaim" their Code obligations of good faith, diligence, and due care. Parties may provide a liquidated damages clause, but it cannot be a penalty [2-718(1)]. Consequential damages may be limited, but the limitations cannot be unconscionable [2-719(3)].

The buyer's duty in a sales contract is to pay for the goods. In the absence of a contrary agreement, payment is due at the time and place at which the buyer is to receive the goods [2-310(a)]. The basic obligations of the parties are concurrent conditions of exchange. Accordingly, a buyer who wants credit (to get the goods before paying in full) must specifically negotiate for it in the contract. Between merchants, most domestic sales transactions are handled on "open account" (the seller ships the goods on the buyer's simple promise to pay for them in thirty, sixty, or ninety days). The buyer is not required to sign a note evidencing obligation to pay or to grant the seller a security interest in the goods to cover the buyer's obligation.

6. Documentary Transactions

When the parties are separated by distance and the seller is unwilling to extend credit to the buyer, they may use a *documentary exchange.* As the procedure is sometimes called, the buyer is to pay "cash against documents." In this procedure, the seller uses documents of title to control the goods until he or she is paid. The document of title may be a **bill of lading** issued by a transportation company, a **warehouse receipt,** or any other document that is evidence that the person in possession of it is entitled to the goods it covers [1-201(15)]. Documents of title are multipurpose commercial instruments. They not only act as a receipt for the goods but also state the terms of the shipment or storage contract between the seller and the transit or warehouse company.

In a typical documentary exchange, the seller may ship the goods by air, rail, or truck to the buyer and receive from the airline, railroad, or trucking company a *negotiable* bill of lading made to the order of the seller. The carrier thereby obligates itself to deliver the goods to the holder of the bill of lading [7-403(4)]. At this point, the seller has shipped "under reservation." His or her procurement of the negotiable bill reserves a security interest in the goods for their price, which the buyer owes the seller [2-205]. The seller will indorse the bill of lading and send it to his or

Bill of lading A document, issued by a person engaged in the business of providing transportation, evidencing receipt of goods for shipment.

Warehouse receipt A document, issued by a person providing space, evidencing that goods have been received for storage.

her bank. The seller will attach to it a sight draft or demand for immediate payment of the purchase price by the buyer. The seller's bank will forward the documents to a bank in the city of the buyer. It is the obligation of that bank to release the bill of lading to the buyer only after the buyer has paid the draft for the purchase price [4-503(a)]. Without the bill of lading, the buyer will not be able to get the goods from the carrier. Only when the buyer is in possession under a regular chain of indorsements is he or she the holder to whom the carrier is obligated to deliver.

This is only one common type of documentary transaction. There are many variations. Similar protections can be obtained if the seller ships under a nonnegotiable bill of lading, taking care to consign the goods to himself or herself or to an agent. The carrier is now obligated to deliver to the consignee or to the person specified by the seller's written instructions [7-403(4)]. The seller will withhold any instructions to deliver to the buyer until payment is received. Under this procedure, possession of the document of title is not required to take delivery from the carrier. But note that the seller should not name the buyer as consignee in the bill of lading; if the seller does, control over the shipment is lost.

7. Course of Dealing, Usage of Trade, Course of Performance

The agreement of the parties includes in their bargain any previous course of dealing between the parties, general trade custom and usage, and any past course of performance on the present agreement. These three sources not only are relevant in interpreting express contract terms but also may constitute contract terms.

Course of dealing A sequence of previous conduct between the parties to a particular transaction.

A **course of dealing** is a sequence of prior conduct between the parties that gives a common basis of understanding for interpreting their communications and conduct between themselves [1-205(1)]. A **usage of trade** is a practice or custom in the particular trade, used so frequently that it justifies the expectation that it will be followed in the transaction in question [1-205(2)]. **Course of performance** concerns a contract that requires repeated performances. When an earlier performance has been accepted by the other party, that performance can be used to give meaning to the agreement regarding future performance [2-208(1)].

Usage of trade Any practice or method of dealing so regularly observed in a place, vocation, or trade that observance may justly be expected in the transaction in question.

When any of these sources is conflicting, the Code [2-208(2)] adopts the following initial hierarchy of presumed probative values:

Course of performance A term used to give meaning to a contract based on the parties having had a history of dealings.

1. Express terms
2. Course of performance
3. Course of dealing
4. Usage of trade

However, the last three do more than interpret the first. They may supplement, cut down, and even subtract whole terms from the express agreement of the parties. More important, course of performance, course of dealing, and usage of trade may directly override express terms, so an express contract term like "one ton of ready-to-mix concrete" is changed to "1,800 pounds of ready-to-pour concrete." This is because courts are looking for the intent of the parties, and this intent may best be found in what the parties have done rather than in what they said.

8. Gap Filling under the Code

Written contracts have gaps in them when the parties either intentionally or inadvertently leave out basic terms. Article 2 of the Code has a number of gap-filler provisions that, taken together, comprise a type of standardized statutory contract. The most important gap-filler provisions involve price, quantity, delivery, and time of performance.

PRICE.   The price term of the contract can be left open, with the price to be fixed by later agreement of the parties or by some agreed-on market standard [2-305]. It may even be agreed that the buyer or the seller shall fix the price, in which event there is an obligation to exercise good faith in doing so. If the contract is silent on price, or if for some reason the price is not set in accordance with the method agreed on, it will be determined as a reasonable price at the time of delivery. Thus, if it appears that it is their intention to do so, parties can bind themselves even though the exact price is not actually agreed on.

QUANTITY.   The Code also allows flexibility in the quantity term of a sales contract. There may be an agreement to purchase the entire output of the seller, or the quantity may be specified as all that is required by the buyer. To ensure fair dealing between the parties in "output" and "requirements" contracts, the Code provides that if parties estimate the quantity involved, no quantity that is unreasonably disproportionate to the estimate will be enforced [2-306]. If the parties have not agreed on an estimate, a quantity that is in keeping with normal or other comparable prior output or requirements is implied.

DELIVERY.   The term *delivery* signifies a transfer of possession of the goods from the seller to the buyer. A seller makes delivery when he or she physically transfers into the possession of the buyer the actual goods that conform to the requirements of the contract. A seller satisfies the requirement to "transfer and deliver" when he or she "tenders delivery" [2-507].

Tender of delivery The seller must put and hold conforming goods at the buyer's disposition and give the buyer any notification reasonably necessary to enable the buyer to take delivery.

A proper **tender of delivery** requires the seller to make available conforming goods at the buyer's disposition and to give the buyer any notification reasonably necessary to take delivery [2-503(1)]. The seller's tender must be at a reasonable hour, and he or she must keep the goods available for a reasonable time to enable the buyer to take possession.

Unless the contract provides to the contrary, the place for delivery is the seller's place of business. If the seller has no place of business, it is the seller's residence [2-308(a)]. In a contract for the sale of identified goods that are known to both parties to be at some other place, that place is the place for their delivery [2-308(a)(b)].

Goods are frequently in the possession of a bailee, such as a warehouseperson. In this event, to make delivery, the seller is obligated to (1) tender a negotiable document of title (warehouse receipt) representing the goods or (2) procure acknowledgment by the bailee (warehouseperson) that the buyer is entitled to the goods [2-503(4)(a)].

Unless otherwise agreed, the seller is required to tender the goods in a single delivery rather than in installments over a period of time. The buyer's obligation to pay is not due until such a tender is made [2-307]. In some situations, the seller may not be able to deliver all the goods at once, or the buyer may not be able to receive the entire quantity at one time, in which event more than a single delivery is allowed.

TIME OF PERFORMANCE.   The time of delivery is often left out of contracts. Such contracts may nevertheless be generally enforceable. However, if the parties intended the written agreement to be complete and an exclusive statement of the contract and the time of performance is omitted, the contract is unenforceable. In the usual case, the time may be supplied by parol evidence if it was agreed on. If it was not agreed on, a reasonable time is presumed [2-309(1)].

Determining what is a reasonable time depends on what constitutes acceptable commercial conduct under all the circumstances, including the obligation of good faith and reasonable commercial standards of fair dealing in the trade. A definite time may be implied from a usage of the trade or course of dealing or performance or from the circumstances of the contract as previously noted.

Payment is due at the time when and place where the buyer is to receive the goods [2-310]. *Receipt of goods* means taking physical possession of them. The buyer is given the opportunity to inspect the goods before paying for them [2-513(1)]. However, when the shipment is C.O.D. (cash on delivery), the buyer is not entitled to inspect the goods before payment of the price [2-513(3)(a)]. This requirement of the buyer having to pay before the inspection is not equivalent to the buyer accepting the goods [2-512(2)]. A buyer who pays for a C.O.D. shipment and then discovers that the goods are defective has all the rights and remedies discussed in the next chapter.

The parties may enter into an open-ended contract that calls for successive performances, such as delivery of 1,000 barrels of flour per week. If the contract does not state the duration, it will be valid for a reasonable time. Unless otherwise agreed, either party can terminate it at any time.

TITLE

9. In General

Title The aggregate of legal relationships concerning the ownership of property.

The concept of **title** to goods is somewhat nebulous, but it is generally equated with the bundle of rights that constitute ownership. Issues related to the passage of title are important in the field of taxation and in areas of the law such as wills, trusts, and estates. The Code has deemphasized the importance of title, and the location of title at any given time is usually not the controlling factor in determining the rights of the parties in a contract of sale. As a general rule, the rights, obligations, and remedies of the seller, the buyer, and the third parties are determined without regard to title [2-401]. However, the concept of title is still basic to the sales transaction, since by definition a sale involves the passing of title from the seller to the buyer.

The parties can, with few restrictions, determine by their contract the manner in which title to goods passes from the seller to the buyer. They can specify any conditions that must be fulfilled for title to pass. However, since the parties seldom specify when title passes from seller to buyer, the Code contains specific provisions as to when title shall pass if the location of title becomes an issue. The most important concept related to the passage of title is the identification of the goods to the sales contract. This concept is discussed in the next section, and in section 11 some Code rules on title transferring are presented.

10. Identification to the Contract

Title to goods cannot pass until the goods have been *identified* to the contract {2-401(1)}. Identification requires that the seller specify the particular goods involved in the transaction {2-501(1)}. Carson may contract with Boyd to purchase 10 mahogany desks of a certain style. Boyd may have several hundred of these desks in the warehouse. Identification takes place when Carson or Boyd specifies the particular 10 desks that will be sold to Carson. There could not, of course, be a present identification of future goods (those not yet in existence or not owned by the seller). However, there can be identification of goods that are not totally in a deliverable state. The fact that the seller must do something to the goods prior to delivery does not prevent identification and the vesting of rights in the buyer.

There are special provisions for agricultural items—crops and animals— because of their nature. When there is a sale of a crop to be grown, identification occurs when the crop is planted. If the sale is of the unborn young of animals, identification takes place when they are conceived {2-501(1)(c)}.

When goods are identified to a contract, the buyer acquires a special property interest in the goods. This special interest is an insurable one, and it may be created before the passing of title or delivery of possession of the goods.

11. Transfer of Title to Goods

In general, the Code provides that title passes to the buyer at the time and place at which the seller completes his or her performance with reference to the physical delivery of the goods {2-401(2)}. The difficulty with this general rule is that it does not specify the numerous factual circumstances under which the seller must make delivery.

For example, assume that the buyer will pick up the goods at the seller's place of business. In other words, the goods are not in storage and the seller has no duty to ship. If the goods are identified to the contract, title passes to the buyer at the time and place the contract is made {2-401(3)(b)}.

If the goods are in storage and the buyer has the responsibility to pick them up, title passes at the time when and the place where the seller delivers to the buyer the document (warehouse receipt) that entitles the buyer to get receipt of the goods {2-401(3)(a)}.

Often a sales contract involves the shipment of goods from the seller to the buyer. If a contract requires the seller to send the goods but does not require the seller to deliver them to a destination, title passes to the buyer at the time and place of shipment {2-401(2)(a)}. If the sales contract requires the seller to make delivery at a specific destination, title passes only when the goods reach that destination {2-402(2)(b)}.

If the buyer rejects the goods when tendered, title will be revested in the seller. Upon the buyer's refusal to receive or retain the goods, the title automatically returns to the seller, whether or not the buyer was justified in his or her action. The same result occurs if the buyer has accepted the goods but subsequently revokes his or her acceptance for a justifiable reason [2-401(4)].

As a means of assurance that the price will be paid before the buyer can obtain title to the goods, a seller may ship or deliver goods to the buyer and reserve title in the seller's name. Under the Code, such an attempted reservation of title does not prevent the title from passing to the buyer. It is limited to the reservation of a security interest in the goods [2-401(1)]. To give protection to the seller, the security interest must be perfected under the provisions of Article 9. (This process is discussed in chapters 37 and 38.) Accordingly, a seller who simply reserves a security interest will not have availed himself or herself of protection against the claims of third parties against the property sold unless the seller complies with the law relating to secured transactions.

12. Good-Faith Purchasers

A purchaser of goods acquires the title that his or her transferor has or had the power to transfer. If the seller has no title, the purchaser receives no title. A purchaser from a thief has no property interest in the goods because the thief had none. The original owner still has title and may recover the goods even if a certificate of title has been issued by a governmental body, as occurred in the following case.

CASE

First Nat. Bank & Trust v. Ohio Cas. Ins. Co.

244 N.W.2d 209 (Neb. 1976)

Fernandez owned a 1973 Cadillac insured by the defendant insurance company. On December 10, 1972 it was stolen, and on January 9, 1973 the company paid Fernandez $8,400 for the loss of the car. Fernandez assigned his title to the insurance company, who obtained a new certificate in its name.

In December 1972, a Nebraska certificate of title to the car was issued based on a forged Arizona certificate of title. The plaintiff bank loaned money on the car and had its lien (security interest) shown on the Nebraska certificate of title. Having obtained information from the F.B.I., the defendant on January 24, 1974, by using self-help repossession, removed the vehicle to California and sold it for $5,500. Plaintiff bank sued the defendant insurance company for the $5,500 and the trial court found for the plaintiff.

BRODKEY, J.

. . . The sole issue in this case is whether First National, having noted its lien on the Nebraska certificate of title, acquired rights superior to Ohio Casualty, in view of the fact First National's chain of title originated in a thief. The District Court answered this question in the affirmative. We disagree and reverse. . . .

[A certificate of title] does not . . . create title where none exists, nor does it give a transferee greater title than that of his transferor. . . . A thief with a certificate of title to a stolen automobile does not divest the owner of his right to take it wherever he can find it. A certificate of title is essential to convey the title of an automobile, but it is not conclusive of ownership. It is simply the exclusive method provided by statute for the transfer of title to a motor vehicle. It conveys no greater interest than the grantor actually possesses. . . .

When the property underlying the certificate of title has been obtained by illegal means, a distinction has been made between stolen property and that acquired by fraud. . . . One obtaining property by larceny cannot convey good title even to an innocent purchaser for value, but one obtaining property by fraud has a voidable title, and may convey that title to a bona fide purchaser who is then protected from claims of others. On the other hand, the right of an owner or an assignee of the owner to recover his stolen automobile remains open to him. . . .

In *Hardware Mut. Cas. Co. v. Gall*, 15 Ohio St.2d 261 (1968), the court held that a thief could not convey a valid title to a stolen motor vehicle to a bona fide purchaser for value without notice, although the certificate of title used in the purported transfer appeared valid on its face. . . . We agree with the Ohio Supreme Court. . . . That court in making its ruling stated "[W]e apparently must again dispel the erroneous notion that whoever first obtains an apparently valid Ohio certificate of title will be entitled to retain possession of the automobile regardless of whether he is the real owner or a bona fide purchaser without notice, whose title derives from a thief. . . ."

We hold that the true owner, and his lawful successors in interest, have rights paramount to those of a subsequent bona fide purchaser of a stolen automobile holding a Nebraska certificate of title on the vehicle based upon a chain of ownership originating with the thief of the car. . . .

■ *Reversed and remanded.*

CASE CONCEPTS REVIEW

1. How did the insurance company get title to this 1973 Cadillac?
2. Under what circumstances and through whom did the bank's lien arise against the same vehicle?
3. Why does this court conclude that the bank's lien on the certificate of title is inferior to the insurance company's claim of ownership?

A purchaser of a limited interest in goods has property rights only to the extent of the limited interest. If a person buys a one-half interest in a golf cart with his or her neighbor, that person's rights are limited to the one-half interest.

A purchaser of goods may acquire more rights and better title than the seller had. Such a purchaser must qualify as a good-faith purchaser for value. In addition, the seller's title must be at least voidable and not void [2-403]. The following case demonstrates the proof required for a buyer to qualify as a good-faith purchaser for value. It also illustrates that the concept of purchasers is a broad one under the Code and that the typical case involving voidable title arises when the seller is guilty of fraudulent actions.

CASE

O'Brien v. Chandler
765 P.2d 1165 (N.M. 1988)

RANSOM, J.

This action arose out of an oral agreement between Dennis McCoy, an Oklahoma cattle dealer doing business as T.C. Cattle Co., and William Chandler, a cattle broker from Texas. McCoy agreed to ship cattle to New Mexico Cattle, Inc. (feedlot) in Union County, New Mexico, for delivery to Chandler. The cattle consisted of four lots of steers and two lots of heifers with a combined total value of $119,122.30. They were delivered to the feedlot in

March 1986, after which time McCoy provided invoices to Chandler, which described the cattle and set out the sales price. Subsequently, McCoy demanded payment. Chandler refused.

Without McCoy's knowledge, Chandler obtained a loan from First National Bank in Clayton (bank) and pledged as collateral the subject cattle. A financing statement and a security agreement covering the cattle were filed of record. The bank claims that it had no knowledge of any interest McCoy may have had in the cattle when it made the loan to Chandler.

McCoy sued to recover the cattle, claiming he was to retain title until payment was made by Chandler. . . . McCoy subsequently filed a motion for partial summary judgment seeking release of the cattle from the feedlot. The bank filed a counter motion for partial summary judgment, arguing that it had perfected a security interest in the livestock superior to any claim of McCoy. The court entered judgment for the bank, relying upon the facts specifically pled in McCoy's complaint and certain provisions of the Uniform Commercial Code (U.C.C.).

The court ruled that the bank's perfected security interest in the subject cattle was superior to any interest or right of McCoy.... The district court also determined that Chandler had committed a fraud against McCoy and, after a damages hearing, awarded McCoy actual damages in the amount of $139,459.49 for the value of the cattle plus interest and $90,000 in punitive damages. [This award is subject to the bank's security interest.] ...

Because the goods were delivered to Chandler under the contract, he had the power to create a security interest in a third party. This interest attached even though Chandler was found to have committed a fraud against McCoy and thus only had voidable title to the cattle.... Section 2-403(1) provides:

> A purchaser of goods acquires all title which his transferor had or had power to transfer except that a purchaser of a limited interest acquires rights only to the extent of the interest purchased. A person with voidable title has power to transfer a good title to a good faith purchaser for value. When goods have been delivered under a transaction of purchase the purchaser has such power even though: *** (d) the delivery was procured through fraud punishable as larcenous under the criminal law.

... It is clear that the cattle had been delivered under a "transaction of purchase" and hence that Chandler was a "purchaser." ... Once McCoy delivered the cattle pursuant to his agreement with Chandler, under Section 2-403(1) Chandler had the power to transfer good title to a good faith purchaser for value.

The term "purchaser" is defined broadly under the U.C.C. to include an Article 9 secured party. Under Section 55-1-201(19), the only matter material to good faith is honesty in the conduct of the transaction at hand. Chandler had possession of the shipping invoices and represented that he had already paid for the cattle when he negotiated for the loan. McCoy has identified no fact that places into dispute the good faith status of the bank with respect to the bank's conduct in this transaction with Chandler. Therefore, the bank acquired a valid security interest in its dealings with Chandler, which the bank perfected by filing....

■ *The district court's entry of summary judgment is affirmed.*

CASE CONCEPTS REVIEW

1. Who originally owned the cattle in this case? To whom were the cattle delivered?
2. What did Chandler do, involving these cattle, prior to paying for them?
3. Because Chandler had possession of the cattle and because he refused to pay for them, how would you describe the title, if any, held by Chandler?
4. How does the court conclude that the bank's security interest is superior to McCoy's ownership interest?

The typical case in which a party has voidable title involves fraud in obtaining the title. Voidable title issues also arise when the same goods are sold to more than one buyer. For example, Franklin sells goods to Talmadge, who leaves them at Franklin's store, with the intention of picking them up later. Before Talmadge takes possession, Franklin sells them to Bell, a good-faith purchaser. Bell has title to the goods because if possession of goods is entrusted to a merchant who deals in goods of that kind, the merchant has the power to transfer all rights of the entrusting owner to a buyer in the ordinary course of business [2-403(2)(3)]. A good-faith purchaser buying from a merchant in the ordinary course of business acquires good title. This rule is applicable to any delivery of possession to a merchant with the understanding that the merchant is to have possession. Thus the rule applies to consignments and bailments as well as to cash sale, but the facts of each case must be examined to ensure that the buyer qualified as a good-faith purchaser for value.

13. In Breach-of-Contract Cases

The Code sets forth a number of rules for determining which party to a sales contract must bear the risk of loss in the event of theft, destruction, or damage to the goods during the period of the performance of the contract. The approach is contractual rather than title oriented and covers two basic situations: no breach-of-contract cases and cases in which one of the parties is in breach. Of course, the provisions are applicable only if the contract has not allocated the risk of loss [2-303].

If the contract has been breached, the loss will be borne by the party who has breached [2-510(1)]. Thus, if the seller has tendered or delivered goods that are "nonconforming," the seller bears the risk of loss. The seller remains responsible until he or she rectifies the nonconformity or the buyer accepts the goods despite their defects.

A buyer has the privilege of revoking his or her acceptance of the goods under proper circumstances (discussed in chapter 19). If the buyer rightfully revokes acceptance, the risk of loss is back on the seller to the extent that the buyer's insurance does not cover the loss. In this situation, the seller has the benefit of any insurance carried by the buyer (the party most likely to have applicable insurance), but any uninsured loss is on the breaching seller.

Loss may occur while goods are in the seller's control, before the risk of loss has passed to the buyer. If the buyer repudiates the sale (breaches the contract) at a time when the seller has identified proper goods to the contract, the seller can impose the risk of loss on the buyer for a reasonable time. The basic concept of the Code is that the burden of losses should be that of the party who has failed to perform as required by contract.

14. If No Breach Exists

Three situations may arise in no-breach risk-of-loss cases. When neither party is in breach, the contract may call for shipment of the goods, the goods may be the subject of a **bailment**, or the contract may be silent on shipment and no bailment exists.

Bailment A transfer of possession of personal property with the expectation that possession will be returned, such as in a warehouse storage contract.

SHIPMENT.   A shipment contract requires only that the seller make necessary arrangements for transport; a destination contract imposes on the seller the obligation to deliver at a destination. If a contract between buyer and seller provides for shipment by carrier under a shipment contract (F.O.B. shipping point), the risk of loss passes to the buyer when the goods are delivered to the carrier. If shipment is made under a destination contract (F.O.B. destination), risk of loss does not pass to the buyer until goods arrive at the destination and are available to the buyer for delivery [2-509(1)]. When the parties do not use symbols such as C.I.F., F.A.S., or F.O.B. or otherwise make provision for risk of loss, it is necessary to determine whether a contract does or does not require the seller to deliver to a destination. The presumption is that a contract is one of shipment, not destination, and that the buyer should bear the risk of loss until arrival, unless the seller has either specifically agreed to do so or the circumstances indicate such an obligation. The following case is typical of those involving shipment contracts.

CASE

Pestana v. Karinol Corp.
367 So.2d 1096 (Fla.App. 1979)

HUBBART, J.

. . . This is an action for damages based on a contract for sale of goods. The defendant seller . . . prevailed in this action. . . . The plaintiff buyer appeals.

The central issue presented for review is whether a contract for the sale of goods, which stipulates the place where the goods sold are to be sent by carrier but contains (a) no explicit provisions allocating the risk of loss while the goods are in the possession of the carrier and (b) no delivery terms such as F.O.B. place of destination, is a shipment contract or a destination contract under the Uniform Commercial Code. We hold that such a contract, without more, constitutes a shipment contract wherein the risk of loss passes to the buyer when the seller duly delivers the goods to the carrier under a reasonable contract of carriage for shipment to the buyer. Accordingly, we affirm.

The critical facts of this case are substantially undisputed. On March 4, 1975, the plaintiff . . . who was a resident of Mexico entered into a contract with the Karinol Corporation [the defendant herein]. . . . The terms of this contract were embodied in a one page invoice written in Spanish and prepared by the defendant Karinol. By the terms of this contract, the plaintiff . . . agreed to purchase 64 electronic watches from the defendant Karinol for $6,006. A notation was printed at the bottom of the contract which, translated into English, reads as follows: "Please send the merchandise in cardboard boxes duly strapped with metal bands via air parcel post to Chetumal. Documents to Banco de Commercio De Quintano Roo S.A.". . .

(The seller delivered the watches to an airline for shipment. When the cartons arrived the watches were missing and plaintiff buyer sued for a refund of the purchase price.)

There are two types of sales contracts under Florida's Uniform Commercial Code wherein a carrier is used to transport the goods sold: a shipment contract and a destination contract. A shipment contract is considered the normal contract in which the seller is required to send the subject goods by carrier to the buyer but is not required to guarantee delivery thereof at a particular destination. Under a shipment contract, the seller, unless otherwise agreed, must: (1) put the goods sold in the possession of a carrier and make a contract for their transportation as may be reasonable having regard for the nature of the goods and other attendant circumstances, (2) obtain and promptly deliver or tender in due form any document necessary to enable the buyer to obtain possession of the goods or otherwise required by the agreement or by usage of the trade, and (3) promptly notify the buyer of the shipment. On a shipment contract, the risk of loss passes to the buyer when the goods sold are duly delivered to the carrier for shipment to the buyer.

A destination contract, on the other hand, is considered the variant contract in which the seller specifically agrees to deliver the goods sold to the buyer at a particular destination and to bear the risk of loss of the goods until tender of delivery. This can be accomplished by express provision in the sales contract to that effect or by the use of delivery terms such as F.O.B. (place of destination). Under a destination contract, the seller is required to tender delivery of goods sold to the buyer at the place of destination. The risk of loss under such a contract passes to the buyer when the goods sold are duly tendered to the buyer at the place of destination while in the possession of the carrier so as to enable the buyer to take delivery. The parties must explicitly agree to a destination contract; otherwise the contract will be considered a shipment contract.

Where the risk of loss falls on the seller at the time the goods sold are lost or destroyed, the seller is liable in damages to the buyer for non-delivery unless the seller tenders a performance in replacement for the lost or destroyed goods. On the other hand, where the risk of loss falls on the buyer at the time the goods sold are lost or destroyed, the buyer is liable to the seller for the purchase price of the goods sold.

In the instant case, we deal with the normal shipment contract involving the sale of goods. . . . There was no specific provision in the contract between the parties which allocated the risk of loss on the goods sold while in transit. In addition, there were no delivery terms such as F.O.B. Chetumal contained in the contract.

All agree that . . . Karinol performed its obligations as a seller under the Uniform Commercial Code if this contract is considered a shipment contract. Karinol put the goods sold in the possession of a carrier and made a contract for the goods safe transportation to the plaintiff's decedent: Karinol also promptly notified the plaintiff's decedent of the shipment and tendered to said party the necessary documents to obtain possession of the goods sold.

The plaintiff . . . contends, however, that the contract herein is a destination contract in which the risk of loss on the goods sold did not pass until delivery on such goods had been tendered to him at Chetumal, Mexico—an event which never occurred. He relies for this position on the notation at the bottom of the contract between the parties which provides that the goods were to be sent to Chetumal, Mexico. We cannot agree. A "send to" or "ship to" term is a part of every contract involving the sale of goods where carriage is contemplated and has no significance in determining whether the contract is a shipment or destination contract for risk of loss purposes. As

such, the "send to" term contained in this contract cannot, without more, convert this into a destination contract.

It therefore follows that the risk of loss in this case shifted to the plaintiff . . . as buyer when the defendant Karinol as seller duly delivered the goods . . . for shipment. . . .

■ *Affirmed.*

CASE CONCEPTS REVIEW

1. What is the distinction between a shipment contract and a destination contract? How does each type of delivery term affect the risk of loss?
2. Which type of delivery term is presumed when the parties fail to designate a special type of contract?
3. Which party has the risk of loss in this case? What is the extent of that party's liability?

Bailee A party who takes possession of property with the understanding that the property must be delivered to the owner or other designated person.

BAILMENTS.   Often, the goods will be in the possession of a **bailee,** such as a warehouse, and the arrangement is for the buyer to take delivery at the warehouse. If the goods are represented by a negotiable document of title—a warehouse receipt, for instance—when the seller tenders the document to the buyer, the risk of loss passes to the buyer. Likewise, risk passes to the buyer upon acknowledgment by the bailee that the buyer is entitled to the goods [2-509(2)]. In this situation, it is proper that the buyer assume the risk, as the seller has done all that could be expected to make the goods available to the buyer. It should be noted that if a nonnegotiable document of title is tendered to the buyer, risk of loss does not pass until the buyer has had a reasonable time to present the document to the bailee [2-503(4)(b)]. A refusal by the bailee to honor the document defeats the tender, and the risk of loss remains with the seller.

OTHER CASES.   In cases other than shipment and bailments, the passage of risk of loss to the buyer depends on the status of the seller. If the seller is a merchant, risk of loss will not pass to the buyer until the goods are received [2-509(3)]. The risk of loss remains with the merchant seller even though the buyer has paid for the goods in full and has been notified that the goods are at his disposal. Continuation of the risk in this case is justified on the basis that the merchant would be likely to carry insurance on goods within his or her control, whereas a buyer would not likely do so until the goods are actually received.

A nonmerchant seller transfers the risk of loss by *tendering* the goods [2-509(3)]. A *tender of delivery* occurs when the seller makes conforming goods available to the buyer and gives reasonable notice, so that the buyer may take delivery. Both parties are in the same position insofar as the likelihood of insurance is concerned, so the risk of loss passes to the buyer in cases where it would not do so if the seller were a merchant.

Sales on approval and sales with the right to return the goods are often involved in risk-of-loss cases. A characteristic of the sale on approval is that risk of loss in the event of theft or destruction of the goods does not pass to the buyer until he or she accepts the goods [2-327(1)(a)]. The buyer's failure to give the seller notice of a decision to return the goods will be treated as an acceptance. After notification of election to return, the seller must pay the expenses of the return and bear the risk of loss. In contrast, the buyer in a sale-or-return transaction has the risk of loss in the event of theft or destruction of the goods. The risk of loss remains with the buyer in the sale-or-return situation, even during the return shipment to the seller [2-327(2)(b)].

CHAPTER SUMMARY

ARTICLE 2 OF THE UCC

Common-Law Contract Changes	**1.** See Table 18–1.
Scope	**1.** Article 2 covers the sale of goods. It does not cover the sale of real estate or service contracts.
	2. In mixed contracts, the Code is applicable if the sale of goods are the predominant part of the transaction.
Definitions	**1.** The term *goods* encompasses things that are movable, that is, items of personal property (chattels) that are of a tangible, physical nature.
	2. A *sale* consists of the passing of title to goods from the seller to the buyer for a price.
	3. A *merchant* is a professional businessperson who "holds himself out as having knowledge or skill peculiar to the practices or goods involved in the transaction."
	4. *Good faith* is honesty in fact in the transaction. In the case of a merchant, it also includes the observance of reasonable commercial standards of fair dealing in the trade.
	5. A *sale on approval* gives the buyer a reasonable time to decide if the sale shall take place. It is used in consumer purchases.
	6. A *sale or return* is a consignment of goods whereby the buyer may return the goods not sold.
Abbreviations	**1.** F.O.B.—free on board
	2. F.A.S.—free along side
	3. C.I.F.—cost, insurance, and freight
	4. These abbreviations are used to distinguish between a shipment contract and a destination contract for the purposes of passage of title and the allocation of risk of loss.

THE SALES CONTRACT

Express Agreement	**1.** The general rule in sales law is that the parties are free to make their own contract.
	2. Parties cannot disclaim their Code obligations of good faith, diligence, and care, and unconscionable provisions will not be enforced.
	3. In the absence of a contrary agreement, payment is due at the time and place at which the buyer is to receive the goods. A buyer who wants credit must specifically negotiate it in the contract.
Documentary Transactions	**1.** If a seller is unwilling to extend credit to the buyer, the seller may use a documentary exchange or cash against documents.
	2. The document of title usually involved in this transaction is either a bill of lading or a warehouse receipt.

Course of Dealing, Usage of Trade, Course of Performance	1. A *course of dealing* is a sequence of prior conduct between the parties that gives a firm basis for interpreting their communications and conduct between themselves.
	2. A *usage of trade* is a practice or custom in the particular trade used so frequently that it justifies the expectation that it will be followed in the transaction in question.
	3. *Course of performance* concerns a contract that requires repeated performances. When an earlier performance has been accepted by the other party, that performance can be used to give meaning to the agreement regarding future performance.
Gap Filling under the Code	1. The price term of the contract can be left open, with the price to be fixed by later agreement of the parties or by some agreed-on market standard.
	2. If the contract is silent on price, it will be a reasonable one.
	3. The Code also allows flexibility in the quantity term of a sales contract. There may be an agreement to purchase the entire output of the seller, or the quantity may be specified as all that is required by the buyer.
	4. If no time of delivery is stated in the contract, it may be supplied by parol evidence of the agreement. If not agreed on, a reasonable time is assumed.
	5. Unless the contract provides to the contrary, the place for delivery is the seller's place of business. If the seller has no place of business, it is his or her residence.
	6. If the time for payment has not been agreed on by the parties, the time for payment is when the buyer is to receive the delivery of the goods. However, the buyer generally may inspect the goods prior to making payment.

TITLE

In General	1. The Code has deemphasized the importance of title, and the location of title at any given time is usually not the controlling factor in determining the rights of the parties in a contract of sale.
	2. The parties can specify when title passes. If there is no provision, the Code provides a series of rules governing the passage of title.
Identification to the Contract	1. Title to goods cannot pass until the goods have been identified to the contract.
	2. Identification requires that the seller specify the particular goods involved in the transaction.
	3. Crops are identified when they are planted. Unborn animals are identified when they are conceived.
Transfer of Title to Goods	1. Identification occurs, and title passes insofar as the specific goods are concerned, when the seller completes his or her performance with respect to the physical delivery of the goods.
	2. If the seller has no responsibility for delivering goods located at the seller's place of business, title passes at the time and place of contracting if the goods are identified to the contract.
	3. If the goods are in storage and the buyer will pick them up, title transfers when the seller delivers to the buyer the necessary document that permits the buyer to receive the goods.
	4. In a shipment contract, title passes at the time and place of shipment.
	5. If the contract requires that the seller deliver at the destination, title will not pass until the seller has tendered the goods to the buyer at that location.
Good-Faith Purchasers	1. A purchaser of goods usually acquires at least as good a title as the seller possessed.
	2. A good-faith purchaser for value may acquire a better title than the seller had if the seller's title was voidable.

In Breach-of-Contract Cases

1. If the contract has been breached, the loss will be borne by the party who has breached. Thus, if the seller has tendered or delivered goods that are "nonconforming," the seller bears the risk of loss.
2. If the buyer breaches the contract at a time when the seller has identified proper goods to the contract, the risk of loss is on the buyer for a reasonable time.

If No Breach Exists

1. If a contract between buyer and seller provides for shipment by carrier under a shipment contract (F.O.B. shipping point), the risk of loss passes to the buyer when the goods are delivered to the carrier.
2. If shipment is made under a destination contract (F.O.B. destination), risk of loss does not pass to the buyer until the goods arrive at the destination and are available to the buyer for delivery.
3. It is presumed that a contract is one of shipment, not destination, and that the buyer should bear the risk of loss until arrival unless the seller has specifically agreed to do so or the circumstances indicate such an obligation.
4. If the goods are represented by a negotiable document of title, risk of loss passes to the buyer when the document is tendered.
5. In all cases other than shipment and bailment contracts, the passage of risk of loss to the buyer depends on the status of the seller. If the seller is a merchant, risk of loss will not pass to the buyer until he or she receives the goods, which means "takes physical possession of them."
6. A nonmerchant seller transfers the risk of loss by tendering the goods.

REVIEW QUESTIONS AND PROBLEMS

1. Match each term in column A with the appropriate statement in column B.

A	B
(1) Merchant	(a) Sale on consignment
(2) C.I.F.	(b) A term used in shipment by merchant vessel
(3) Bill of lading	(c) Buyer has the risk of loss if the goods are destroyed
(4) Sale of return	(d) A requirement for title to pass
(5) Shipment contract	(e) A farmer in many states
(6) F.A.S.	(f) The buyer pays the cost of insuring the goods
(7) Sale on approval	(g) Contract of shipment by a common carrier
(8) Identification	(h) May acquire a better title than his or her transferor had
(9) Good-faith purchaser	(i) Not covered by Article 2 of the Code
(10) Organ transplant	(j) Buyer's creditors have no claim on the goods in this transaction

2. Tom entered into a contract to sell Jerry twenty acres of sod for $1,000 per acre. Jerry was allowed to remove it any time during the next twelve-month period. Is the contract governed by the Uniform Commercial Code? Explain.
3. The Macon Whoopies, a newly formed hockey club, contracts to buy 150 hockey pucks from a wholesaler in Youngstown, Ohio. What are the wholesaler's delivery obligations if the agreement states

a. F.O.B. Macon?

   b. F.O.B. Youngstown?

   c. C.I.F. Macon?

   d. Ship to Macon Whoopies. Macon, Georgia?

   Explain.

4. Landrum, a collector of automobiles, was interested in buying a limited edition Chevrolet Corvette from Devenport. Devenport agreed the price would be the sticker price, $24,000 to $28,000. The car arrived with a sticker price of $24,688.21, but as a result of the demand for the car, the market price was $32,000. Is Landrum entitled to buy it for the sticker price? Why or why not?

5. Royster agreed to buy at least 31,000 tons of phosphate for three years from Columbia. When market conditions changed, Royster ordered only a fraction of the minimum and sought to renegotiate the deal. Columbia refused and sued. At trial, Royster wanted to introduce two forms of proof: (a) A usage of trade that expresses that price and quantity terms in such contracts were never considered in the trade as more than mere projections, to be adjusted according to market forces; (b) course of dealing over a six-year period, which showed repeated and substantial deviations from the stated quantities or prices in other written contracts between the parties. Is the evidence admissible? Explain.

6. Plaintiff sued an oil company to recover personal property obtained by the defendant under an alleged option contract. The purported contract gave the oil company the right to purchase the property at plaintiff's cost less depreciation to be mutually agreed on. The parties failed to agree on the amount of depreciation and plaintiff claimed that as a result, there was no valid agreement. Is the contract binding? Why?

7. On February 11, 1992, plaintiff entered into a written contract to buy three sprinkler systems from the defendant. The seller orally agreed to deliver by the middle of May 1992. The written contract contained no designated delivery date. The seller did not deliver by May 15, and plaintiff claimed a crop loss of $75,000 because of the late delivery. Is oral evidence admissible to show the agreed-on date of delivery? Explain. Is the contract enforceable without a delivery date? Why or why not?

8. The Big Knob Volunteer Fire Department agreed to purchase a fire truck from Custom Productions, Inc. The contract provided for a down payment and for title to pass upon full payment. Custom painted the buyer's name on the truck. The seller refused to deliver the truck, and the buyer filed suit for possession of the truck. Is the buyer entitled to the truck? Why or why not?

9. A package liquor store operator was in the practice of paying for large quantities of liquor in advance to take advantage of quantity discounts. He would then order the liquor as needed. A supplier was having financial difficulties, and the operator seized a large amount of undelivered liquor. The supplier went into bankruptcy, and the trustee in bankruptcy claimed the liquor. He contended that the operator did not have title to the liquor. Was the trustee in bankruptcy correct? Explain.

10. Jacobs purchased a pickup truck from Imperial Motors. Imperial had possession of the truck by virtue of a lease agreement with American Plans, which had title to the truck. Imperial went out of business, and Jacobs did not receive a title certificate to the vehicle even though he paid the purchase price. Which party is entitled to the truck? Explain.

11. Don, engaged in the business of installing underground telephone lines, ordered three reels of underground cable from Pat to be delivered at Don's place of business. Pat delivered reels of aerial rather than underground cable. When informed of the mistake, Pat told Don to return the cable, but he was unable to do so because of a trucking strike. The cable was stolen from Don's regular storage space, where it had been delivered. Pat sued for the purchase price. Who has the risk of loss? Explain.

12. A contract for the sale of goods contained no explicit provision on risk of loss while the goods were in transit, and it contained no delivery terms such as F.O.B. destination. The goods were destroyed in transit. Which party had the risk of loss? Why?

13. A seller of a mobile home sued the buyer for the price of the home. After the parties had executed the contract of sale, but before delivery to the buyer, the mobile home was stolen from the seller's lot. Who has the risk of loss? Explain.

14. Amy delivered stereo tapes, compact discs, and stereo equipment to Tex, a service station operator, for resale. The invoice provided that the equipment would be picked up if not sold in ninety days. The service station was burglarized about two weeks later, and the stereo equipment was stolen. Who must bear the loss resulting from the burglary? Why?

BREACH AND REMEDIES

CHAPTER PREVIEW

In the preceding chapter, several basic issues related to the sales contract were discussed. Throughout that discussion, we presumed that the contracting parties were willing to perform the promises made. This chapter discusses a variety of situations based on either the seller or the buyer failing to perform properly.

As a general rule, a seller is obligated to deliver or tender delivery of goods that measure up to the requirements of the contract and to do so at the proper time and at the proper place. The goods and other performance of the seller must conform to the contract. The seller is required to tender delivery as a condition to the buyer's duty to accept the goods and pay for them. Thus, the seller has performed when he or she has made the goods available to the buyer. The buyer, in turn, must render his or her performance, which means that the buyer must accept the goods and pay for them.

When one or both of these parties breach the sales contract, the Code provides for numerous remedies. These remedies are available unless, by the language in the sales contract, the buyer and seller have agreed to limit or modify the Code remedies.

■ **BUSINESS MANAGEMENT DECISION**

As the sales manager of a retail music store, you meet with a customer who has purchased a $1,500 set of drums. This customer complains that the bass drum is defective and she wants her money back.

How would you respond to this customer?

OVERVIEW OF CODE REMEDIES

1. Checklist

Two sections of the Code [2-703, 2-711] *list* the remedies of the seller and the remedies of the buyer. Each section provides both parties with four remedies, which are exact counterparts. Table 19–1 shows their significant correlation.

The four remedies are listed in the Code not only as equivalent actions but also as equivalent in order of importance. The Code assumes that, upon a breach by the buyer, the seller will resell the goods and sue the buyer for any difference between the resale price and the original contract price. When the seller breaches, the Code assumes that the buyer will cover by buying substitute goods and sue the seller for any difference between the cover price and the original contract price.

Obviously, before either party has one of the four remedies, the other party must have breached the contract. There are at least four possible situations in which either party may be in breach of contract:

1. *Anticipatory repudiation* by the buyer or by the seller
2. *Failure of performance* (buyer fails to pay or seller fails to deliver)
3. A rightful or wrongful *rejection* by the buyer
4. A rightful or wrongful *revocation of acceptance* by the buyer

Generally, the Code remedies are specified as either for the buyer's or seller's benefits. However, one remedy is available to both parties to a sales contract. This remedy, known as a request for adequate assurance of performance, is discussed in the next section.

TABLE 19-1 ■ Comparison of Code Remedies

Seller's Remedies [2-703]	Buyer's Remedies [2-711]
1. Resell the goods and recover damages [2-706].	1. Cover (buy same goods elsewhere) and recover damages [2-712].
2. Cancel the contract.	2. Reject the contract.
3. Recover damages for nonacceptance [2-708].	3. Recover damages for nondelivery [2-713].
4. Sue for the actual price of the goods [2-709].	4. Sue to get the goods (specific performance or replevy) [2-716].

2. Adequate Assurances

Under certain circumstances, either party may be concerned about the other's future performance. If a buyer is in arrears on other payments, the seller will naturally be concerned about making further deliveries. If the seller has been delivering faulty goods to other customers, the buyer will be fearful that the goods received may also be defective. The law recognizes that no one wants to buy a lawsuit and that merely having the right to sue for breach of contract is a somewhat hollow remedy. There is a need to protect the party whose reasonable expectation of due performance is jeopardized.

The Code grants this protection to seek adequate assurances by providing that the contract for sale imposes an obligation on each party that the other's expectation of receiving due performances will not be impaired [2-609]. A party who has reasonable grounds for insecurity about the other's performance can demand *in writing* that the other offer convincing proof that he or she will, in fact, perform. Having made the demand, the requesting party may then suspend performance until he or she receives assurance of the other party's commitment to perform. If no assurance is forthcoming within a reasonable time, not to exceed thirty days, the contract may be treated as repudiated [2-609(2)].

Two issues often arise: What are reasonable grounds for insecurity? What constitutes an adequate assurance of performance? The Code does not particularly answer these questions, but it does provide that between merchants commercial standards shall be applied to help provide the answers [2-609(2)]. In the event of a dispute, these are questions of fact for a jury.

Buyer's Rights and Remedies

3. Summary

If the seller breaches the sales contract, the buyer has a number of options for action. First, the buyer is authorized to determine whether a breach has occurred. This right to inspect the goods being delivered is of paramount importance to the buyer as a method of avoiding complications. If the goods delivered by the seller are not in conformity with the contract, the buyer may reject them. Even a buyer who has accepted the goods may be able to revoke the acceptance and be in the same legal position as if the goods had been rejected initially.

If the seller fails to perform, the buyer may purchase (cover) his or her needs in the marketplace. This buyer may then sue the seller for the increased costs of the goods and the expenses related to the remedy of cover.

Finally, in a limited set of circumstances, the nonbreaching buyer may be able to recover the actual goods described in the sales contract. This last remedy is an example of court-ordered specific performance.

These Code remedies available for the buyer's benefit are discussed in the next eight sections. While studying these remedies, remember that they are the exclusive basis for relief to a buyer in a commercial transaction. The following case discusses this role of the Code remedies.

CASE

Hapka v. Paquin Farms
458 N.W.2d 683 (Minn. 1990)

COYNE, J.

. . . Minnesota prohibits the planting of seed potatoes unless the seed meets minimum requirements prescribed by the commissioner of the department of agriculture. Compliance with the requirements may be evidenced by certificates of inspection which demonstrate "the varietal purity and the freedom from disease and physical injury" of the certified potatoes. . . . A certificate of inspection can be issued only if the seed potatoes have been inspected while growing in the field . . . and again after harvest at the time of shipment. Minnesota's inspection program is part of a national effort to eradicate the destructive and highly contagious disease called "bacterial ring rot" from the potato crop. . . . There is a zero tolerance for bacterial ring rot, and the discovery of a single plant in the field or a single tuber in storage infected with bacterial ring rot causes the rejection of the entire field or lot. . . .

Conrad Hapka and his son Brian are potato farmers in Marshall County, Minnesota. The Hapkas grow seed potatoes to be sold to other farmers for growing various kinds of commercial potatoes. Like the Hapkas, Richard and David Paquin, the principal owners of Paquin Farms, Inc., also enjoyed a good reputation for growing disease-free, high quality seed potatoes, which they marketed through the Paquin Potato Company. On Memorial Day, Monday, May 30, 1983, the Hapkas purchased a truckload of seed potatoes from the Paquins. This load of potatoes, like a subsequent load purchased on the following day, was grown by P & H Farms, a partnership composed of the Paquins and Gust Hangsleben, a farmer whose reputation for growing seed potatoes did not, according to the Hapkas, match that of the Paquins. Neither the Paquins nor the Hapkas arranged for the required shipping point inspection of the seed potatoes purchased on either day; instead, a random sample of seed potatoes was selected

from the lot and submitted for state inspection at a later date. . . .

The Hapkas planted the seed potatoes immediately. The planting process included cutting the potatoes into smaller pieces for propagation. The machinery used for cutting and planting those seed potatoes was later used for cutting and planting other potatoes bought from a third source and planted in another field. All of the Hapkas' fields passed the first two state inspections. On the third inspection, however, a state inspector found signs of ring rot in the fields planted with P & H Farms seed potatoes and in the fields later planted with seeds from a different source. No ring rot was found in fields planted before Memorial Day. The presence of ring rot infection was confirmed by a laboratory analysis, and all the infected fields were rejected for certification as seed potatoes.

The evidence was that the P & H seeds purchased by the Hapkas were infected with ring rot, which was spread by the Hapkas' potato cutter to the seed potatoes acquired from another source. Because of the loss of seed certification, the Hapkas were forced to sell most of their potatoes at the much lower price available for potatoes on the commercial market. One load of potatoes could not be sold and had to be destroyed. The Hapkas were also put to the expense of disinfecting and cleaning their farm machinery and warehouses.

The Hapkas sued Paquin Farms, Inc., Paquin Potato Company, P & H Farms, the Paquins individually, Gust Hangsleben, and the Minnesota Department of Agriculture. The Hapkas asserted that the state negligently failed to inspect the seed potatoes and also breached a contractual duty of inspection and then alleged that all other defendants were guilty of misrepresentation, acted negligently, breached both express and implied warranties, and were strictly liable for selling seed potatoes infected with ring rot.

At the close of the evidence, the trial court directed a verdict in favor of the state, ruled that tort theories of negligence and strict products liability were unavailable, and submitted to the jury only questions regarding misrepresentation and warranty. The jury found that no express warranties had been made and that there had been neither misrepresentation nor breach of implied warranty. The court of appeals affirmed judgment in favor of all defendants, and we granted further review. . . .

[The court then summarized that the UCC remedies were the only ones available in *commercial* transactions involving injury to *a person or property.* Such a limitation to UCC remedies does not apply to cases involving a *consumer* transaction.]

The Code itself indicates that the U.C.C. is intended to displace tort liability. . . . In its design, then, the Code not merely permits but also encourages negotiated agreements concerning all aspects of a commercial transaction including warranties, warranty disclaimers, and liability limitations. The foundational assumption of the Code as a whole is that by importing to their negotiations their experience in the marketplace, the reasonable contemplation of sophisticated parties is embodied in the transaction. It is at the time of the contract formation that experienced parties define the product, identify the risks, and negotiate a price of the goods that reflects the relative benefits and risks to each.

. . . We continue to regard the Code remedies as something less than adequate in the ordinary consumer transaction. Generally speaking, a consumer has neither the skill nor the bargaining power to negotiate either warranties or remedies. If a defective coffee pot causes a fire which destroys a consumer's home, the panoply of liability theory should be available to the consumer—strict products liability and negligence as well as breach of warranty—whether or not personal injuries accompany the property damage.

On the other hand, the law is entitled to expect the parties to commercial transactions to be knowledgeable and of relatively equal bargaining power so that warranties can be negotiated to the parties' mutual advantage. Having negotiated the warranties and any limitations of liability, that a defective product causes damage to the other property should not defeat the liability parameters the parties have set by opening the door to tort theories of recovery. While there is reason to sacrifice consistency in order to preserve tort remedies for personal injuries arising out of commercial transactions, as well as those arising out of consumer transactions, there is no similar reason in cases of property damage arising out of commercial transactions to heap tort theories of negligence and strict products liability atop those remedies already provided by the U.C.C. Accordingly, in our judgment the Uniform Commercial Code must control exclusively with respect to damages in a commercial transaction which involves property damage only. . . . If the Code is to have any efficacy, parties engaged in commercial activity must be able to depend with certainty on the exclusivity of the remedies provided by the Code in the event of a breach of their negotiated agreement.

■ *Affirmed.*

CASE CONCEPTS REVIEW

1. The Hapkas' lawsuit was based on at least four legal theories. What are these theories?
2. Which of these theories is recognized in the UCC?
3. What was the holding of the trial court? What did the court of appeals conclude?
4. What distinction does this court make with respect to remedies available to the parties wronged in a consumer transaction as opposed to a commercial transaction?
5. Why does the court create this distinction?

4. Right to Inspect

The buyer has a right before payment or acceptance to inspect the goods at any reasonable time and place and in any reasonable manner [2-513(1)]. The place for the inspection is determined by the nature of the contract. If the seller is to send the goods to the buyer, the inspection may be postponed until after arrival of the goods. The buyer must pay the expenses of inspection but can recover his or her expenses from the seller if the inspection reveals that the goods are nonconforming and the buyer therefore rejects them [2-513(2)].

If the contract provides for delivery C.O.D., the buyer must pay prior to inspection. Likewise, payment must be made prior to inspection if the contract calls for payment against documents of title [2-513(3)]. When the buyer is required to make payment prior to inspection, the payment does not impair his or her right to pursue remedies if subsequent inspection reveals defects [2-512].

The buyer's right to inspect is tied to his or her right to reject the goods if they are defective or nonconforming to the contract. The following two sections discuss the buyer's responsibility with respect to the right of rejection.

5. Right to Reject

If the goods or the tender of delivery fails to conform to the contract, the buyer has the right to reject them. Several options are available. The buyer may reject the whole, or accept either the whole or any commercial unit or units and reject the rest [2-601]. A *commercial unit* is one that is generally regarded as a single whole for purposes of sale, one that would be impaired in value if divided [2-105(6)]. When accepting nonconforming goods, the buyer does not impair his or her right of recourse against the seller. Provided that the buyer notifies the seller of the breach within a reasonable time, the buyer may still pursue his or her remedy for damages for breach of contract, even though he or she accepts the goods.

6. Notice of Rejection

Seasonably An action is taken seasonably when it is taken at, or within, the time agreed; or if no time is agreed, at or within a reasonable time.

The right to reject defective or nonconforming goods is dependent on the buyer's taking action within a reasonable time after the goods are tendered or delivered. If rejecting, the buyer must **seasonably** notify the seller of this fact. Failing to do so would render the rejection ineffective and constitute an acceptance [2-602(1)]. If the buyer continues in possession of defective goods for an unreasonable time, he or she forfeits the right to reject them. However, a buyer who fails to reject defective goods still may sue for breach of contract, as the following case illustrates.

CASE

Hislop v. Duff
502 A.2d 357 (Vt. 1985)

HAYES, J.

This case involves a dispute concerning the purchase and sale of a leaky camper-trailer. The defendant-buyer, Robert Duff, appeals from a trial court judgment for the plaintiff-seller, Ellden Hislop, for the unpaid balance of the sale price. . . .

The facts of this case are simple. In the fall of 1979, Ellden Hislop left a used 1972 camper-trailer with Bernard Brooks to sell it for him. Mr. Brooks managed a gas station and also sold trailers. Mr. Brooks showed the camper to Mr. Duff, who was interested in purchasing it. Duff inspected the trailer and became aware that the camper leaked. Both Mr. Brooks and Mr. Hislop told Duff that the leak was in the roof vent and that caulking would solve the problem. Duff, a carpenter who worked in the construction business, was familiar with the caulking process. In June 1980, Hislop and Duff entered into an agreement whereby Hislop was to sell the camper to Duff for $1,200.00. Duff gave Hislop $300.00 on June 20, and agreed to pay the balance on October 1.

The buyer caulked the vent but was unable to seal the leak. Consequently, he refused to tender the $900.00 balance owed on the camper. The seller brought suit to recover the unpaid balance. . . .

. . . Buyer asserts that the trial court erred in finding that the goods were not rejected within a reasonable time after delivery. Under 9A V.S.A. § 2-602, rejection of goods must be within a reasonable time after their tender or delivery, and rejection is ineffective unless the buyer seasonably notifies the seller. In this case, the buyer took and maintained possession of the camper-trailer for nine months before notifying seller of his rejection. This is neither a reasonable time for rejection nor a seasonable notification. Under 9A V.S.A. § 2-606(1)(c), an acceptance of goods occurs when the buyer does any act inconsistent with the seller's ownership. Duff's holding the trailer for nine months was inconsistent with Hislop's ownership. Thus, an acceptance occurred. . . .

In sum, the buyer accepted the camper-trailer in June, 1980. . . . The seller is therefore entitled to the full purchase price. A remedy for the buyer, however, may still exist. Even though the time for rejection . . . passed, a buyer may be entitled to a damage remedy. In this case, the buyer in his pleadings raised claims based on breach of express warranty, and breach of implied warranty of fitness for a particular purpose, by alleging that the camper-trailer, as delivered, did not conform to the terms of the contract. These claims, although asserted as "affirmative defenses" were, in fact, counterclaims for damages resulting from the nonconformity of the camper-trailer. The trial court should have considered them as counterclaims, but did not do so. Thus, we must remand the case for a resolution of these claims.

■ *So ordered.*

CASE CONCEPTS REVIEW

1. When did Duff agree to buy Hislop's camper-trailer?
2. How long did Duff have possession of the camper-trailer before he attempted to reject it?
3. Although the court concludes that Duff failed to reject the camper-trailer, what relief is available to Duff as a dissatisfied buyer?

The requirement of seasonable notice of rejection is very important. Without such notice, the rejection is ineffective [2-602(1)]. As a general rule, a notice of rejection may simply state that the goods are not conforming, without particular specification of the defects relied on by the buyer. If, however, the defect could have been corrected by the seller had he or she been given particularized notice, then the failure to particularize will take away from the buyer the right to rely on that defect as a breach justifying a rejection [2-605(1)(a)]. Therefore, a buyer should always give detailed information relative to the reason for the rejection.

In transactions between merchants, the merchant seller is entitled to demand a full and final written statement of all the defects. If the statement is not forthcoming after a written request for it, the buyer may not rely on these defects to justify a rejection or to establish that a breach has occurred [2-605(1)(b)].

7. Rights and Duties on Rejection

A buyer who rejects the goods after taking physical possession of them is required to hold the goods with reasonable care long enough for the seller to remove them [2-602(2)(b)]. Somewhat greater obligations are imposed on a merchant buyer who rejects goods that have been delivered [2-603]. The merchant is under a duty to follow the seller's reasonable instructions as to the disposition of the goods. If the seller does not furnish instructions as to the disposition of the rejected goods, the merchant buyer must make reasonable efforts to sell them for the seller's account if they are perishable or if they threaten to decline in value speedily. If a sale is not mandatory for the reasons just stated, the buyer has three options. The buyer may store the rejected goods for the seller's account, reship them to the seller, or resell them for the seller's account [2-604].

Code Section 2-711(3) gives a buyer a security interest in the goods in his or her possession and the right to resell them. Thus a buyer of defective goods can reject and resell the goods, deduct all expenses regarding care, custody, resale, and other matters (such as the down payment), and then remit any money left over to the seller [2-604, 2-711(3)].

8. Right to Revoke Acceptance

ACCEPTANCE.   The buyer has *accepted* goods if (1) after a reasonable opportunity to inspect them, the buyer indicates to the seller that the goods are conforming or that he or she will take or retain them in spite of their nonconformity, (2) the buyer has failed to make an effective rejection of the goods, or (3) the buyer does any act inconsistent with the seller's ownership [2-606].

REVOCATION.   The buyer may revoke his or her acceptance under certain circumstances. In many instances, the buyer will have accepted nonconforming goods because the defect was not immediately discoverable, or reasonably assumed that the seller would correct by substituting goods that did conform. In either case, the buyer has the privilege of "revoking" his or her acceptance by notifying the seller if, but only if, the nonconformity "substantially impairs the value to him" [2-608(1)]. Notice the importance of the word *him* in the following case.

CASE

Colonial Dodge, Inc. v. Miller
362 N.W.2d 704 (Mich. 1984)

KAVANAGH, J.

... This case requires the Court to decide whether the failure to include a spare tire with a new automobile can constitute a substantial impairment in the value of that automobile entitling the buyer to revoke his acceptance of the vehicle under M.C.L. § 440.2608. . . .

On April 19, 1976, defendant Clarence Miller ordered a 1976 Dodge Royal Monaco station wagon from plaintiff Colonial Dodge which included a heavy-duty trailer package with extra wide tires.

On May 28, 1976, defendant picked up the wagon, drove it a short distance where he met his wife, and exchanged it for her car. Defendant drove that car to work while his wife returned home with the new station wagon. Shortly after arriving home, Mrs. Miller noticed that their new wagon did not have a spare tire. The following morning defendant notified plaintiff that he insisted on having the tire he ordered immediately, but when told there was no spare tire then available, he informed the salesman for plaintiff that he would stop payment on the two checks that were tendered as the purchase price, and that the vehicle could be picked up from in front of his home. Defendant parked the car in front of his home where it remained until the temporary ten-day registration sticker had expired, whereupon the car was towed by the St. Clair police to a St. Clair dealership. Plaintiff had applied for license plates, registration, and title in defendant's name. Defendant refused the license plates when they were delivered to him.

According to plaintiff's witness, the spare tire was not included in the delivery of the vehicle due to a nationwide shortage caused by a labor strike. Some months later, defendant was notified his tire was available.

Plaintiff sued defendant for the purchase price of the car. On January 13, 1981, the trial court entered a judgment for plaintiff finding that defendant wrongfully revoked acceptance of the vehicle. . . .

We are satisfied defendant made a proper revocation under M.C.L. § 440.2608(1)(b). . . .

Plaintiff argues the missing spare tire did not constitute a substantial impairment in the value of the automobile, within the meaning of M.C.L. § 440.2608(1). Plaintiff claims a missing spare tire is a trivial defect, and a proper construction of this section of the UCC would not permit defendant to revoke under these circumstances. It maintains that since the spare tire is easy to replace and the cost of curing the nonconformity very small compared to the total contract price, there is no substantial impairment in value.

However, M.C.L. § 440.2608(1) says "[t]he buyer may revoke his acceptance of a lot or commercial unit whose nonconformity substantially impairs its value *to him****.*" (Emphasis added.) Number two of the Official Comment to M.C.L. § 440.2608; M.S.A. § 19.2608 attempts to clarify this area. It says that

[r]evocation of acceptance is possible only where the nonconformity substantially impairs the value of the goods to the buyer. For this purpose the test is not what the seller had reason to know at the time of contracting; the question is whether the nonconformity is such as will in fact cause a substantial im-

pairment of value to the buyer though the seller had no advance knowledge as to the buyer's particular circumstances.

We cannot accept plaintiff's interpretation of M.C.L. § 440.2608(1). In order to give effect to the statute, a buyer must show the nonconformity has a special devaluing effect on him and that the buyer's assessment of it is factually correct. In this case, the defendant's concern with safety is evidenced by the fact that he ordered the special package which included special tires. The defendant's occupation demanded that he travel extensively, sometimes in excess of 150 miles per day on Detroit freeways, and often in the early morning hours. Mr. Miller testified that he was afraid of a tire going flat on a Detroit freeway at 3 A.M. Without a spare, he testified, he would be helpless until morning business hours. The dangers attendant upon a stranded motorist are common knowledge, and Mr. Miller's fears are not unreasonable.

We hold that under the circumstances the failure to include the spare tire as ordered constituted a substantial impairment in value to Mr. Miller, and that he could properly revoke his acceptance under the UCC.

That defendant did not discover this nonconformity before he accepted the vehicle does not preclude his revocation. There was testimony that the space for the spare tire was under a fastened panel, concealed from view. This out-of-sight location satisfies the requirement . . . that the nonconformity be difficult to discover. . . .

■ *Reversed.*

CASE CONCEPTS REVIEW

1. What aspect of the station wagon being purchased was of vital importance to the Millers?
2. From whose perspective—the seller's or buyer's—is the test of "substantial impairment in value" to be evaluated?
3. Why did the court conclude that there was a hard-to-discover defect?

Revocation must take place within a reasonable time after the buyer has discovered, or should have discovered, the reason for revocation [2-608(2)]. If a buyer revokes acceptance, he or she is then placed in the same position with reference to the goods as if he or she had rejected them in the first instance [2-608(3)]. The buyer has a security interest in the goods for the payments made and is entitled to damages as if no acceptance had occurred.

The following case is typical of the factual situation that leads to a valid revocation of acceptance.

CASE

East Side Prescription v. E. P. Fournier
585 A.2d 1176 (R.I. 1991)

FAY, C. J.

. . . On July 16, 1981, Backer, as president and owner of East Side Prescription Center, Inc., purchased a 1981 Renault 18i station wagon from Fournier for $12,459.83. Backer intended to use the vehicle to deliver prescriptions, as well as for general transportation. Backer experienced problems with the car from the time he was supposed to take possession in July 1981 to the time he finally revoked his acceptance of the vehicle in December 1983. Backer initially refused to accept the vehicle because of dents on the hood and door. Fournier repaired the dents at no cost to Backer, and Backer then accepted the car. During the next twenty-seven months the car was returned to the dealership numerous times for repairs for a variety of reasons, some of which are set forth below.

In August 1981 the chrome moldings had to be refastened after a routine trip through a car wash caused them to come loose. When the mileage on the car reached the 1,000 mile mark, Backer returned to the car dealership, dropped the car off for its scheduled checkup, and informed Fournier of the various infirmities afflicting the vehicle. At that time the front end of the car was suffering from a "loud vibrating shimmying" when it traveled at fifty-five miles-per-hour, the brakes were squealing, the car was difficult to start, it was stalling intermittently, and loud sounds were emanating from the rear of the automobile. To stop the vibrating, Fournier had to replace the front axle assembly of the car. When this failed to correct the problem, a second set of axles was installed by Fournier. Prior to this time Backer had informed Fournier of several other problems he had discovered that he wished Fournier to repair. There were defects in the paint and rust on the body, and neither the heater nor the defogger was functioning properly.

Following the 1,000 mile checkup, Backer's difficulties with his Renault continued. The air-conditioning unit was malfunctioning, and numerous electrical problems existed, which Fournier failed to remedy. Fournier was able to correct a brake failure by replacing the master cylinder, but despite many efforts to eliminate the car's starting problem, the vehicle continued to start only sporadically. In 1982 the transmission malfunctioned, causing the gears to "slip" and therefore shift "serendipitously." Fournier's attempts to repair the transmission were unsuccessful. In September 1983 the transmission problem progressed and on one occasion caused the vehicle to break down, necessitating an overhaul and rebuilding of the engine.

After the engine was rebuilt, Backer continued to experience problems starting the car. Backer brought the car back to Fournier once more for repairs to the starter in November 1983. When Backer attempted to retrieve his vehicle after this set of repairs, the car failed to start. At this time Backer left the Renault at the dealership and notified Fournier of his revocation of his acceptance of the vehicle.

In the period from his initial acceptance of the vehicle in 1981 to his subsequent revocation in 1983, Backer returned the car to Fournier at least fifteen times for various repairs. Although the manufacturer's limited warranty had expired when the brakes and transmission required substantial repairs, defendant assumed the expenses because the problems pre-existed the running of the limited-warranty period.

On May 19, 1984, plaintiffs filed a . . . complaint against defendant in Superior Court, seeking damages based on plaintiffs' revocation of acceptance and defendant's breach of implied and express warranties. . . . The matter was reached for trial before a jury in Superior Court in April 1989. When plaintiffs rested their case after eight days of testimony, defendants moved for a directed verdict on all counts. The trial justice ruled in favor of defendants and granted the directed verdict. . . .

It is the opinion of this court that the issues presented in . . . this matter were not properly decided by the trial justice as a matter of law. . . . Plaintiffs' complaint concerns Backer's revocation of his acceptance of the vehicle. To revoke acceptance of the Renault, Backer had to produce evidence to the effect that the automobile did not conform to what he had agreed to purchase and that the nonconformity altered the value of the vehicle to Backer's detriment. . . .

We . . . conclude that Backer introduced sufficient evidence to enable a jury to determine whether the nonconformity substantially impaired the value of the car. . . .

When the number of problems with the vehicle becomes so large as to call into question the integrity of the automobile, the value of the vehicle to the buyer may be substantially impaired and the buyer justified in revoking his acceptance even though some of the problems have been repaired or are repairable. The record reflects Backer's perpetual problems with the car and Fournier's repeatedly unsuccessful attempts at repairing the vehicle. He was not able to utilize the vehicle for the purpose for which it was purchased because of the incessant mechanical malfunctions. It is apparent that the value of the car to Backer, the purchaser in this instance, was substantially impaired. We are of the opinion that Backer's testimony, coupled with the repair orders, constituted sufficient evidence to defeat the need for expert testimony; therefore, the trial justice erred in directing a verdict. . . .

The trial justice also considered the seasonableness of the revocation in granting the directed verdict. . . . Although the trial justice recognized that the reasonableness of the length of time that passed before Backer revoked his acceptance is generally a matter to be resolved by a jury, he determined that a jury could not reasonably find that the revocation was seasonable, relying on the facts presented. The trial justice concluded that a revocation made at the end of 1982, or perhaps even mid-1983, may have been acceptable, but in waiting until November or December of 1983, the revocation was not timely as a matter of law. We find this conclusion of the trial justice to be erroneous.

We do not agree that a revocation of acceptance of a motor vehicle thirty months after the initial acceptance after the buyer has put 38,000 miles on the car constitutes an unseasonable revocation as a matter of law. Section 2-608 permits a buyer to revoke his acceptance if, in accepting the commercial unit, he reasonably assumed that the nonconformity would be seasonably cured and if the problem is not in fact remedied in a timely manner.

In determining the timeliness of this particular revocation, we cannot discount Backer's attempts to cure the defects inherent in the vehicle. By consistently repairing the car at little or no cost to Backer, even though the warranty had expired, Fournier induced reliance by Backer and is therefore partially responsible for the lengthy period that passed before the revocation. The record reflects that the delay in revoking the acceptance of the automobile is largely attributable to Fournier's reassurances that it could and would fix the car.

After reviewing the facts and Fournier's policies in this instance, we are of the opinion that the trial justice did not consider the evidence in the light most favorable to plaintiffs and that he drew inferences contrary to Backer's position. Therefore, the decision to direct a verdict for defendants . . . was erroneous. . . .

■ *Reversed and remanded.*

1. During what time period did Mr. Backer attempt to have the defects in his automobile corrected?

2. How would you summarize the attitude and efforts of Fournier to repair Mr. Backer's car?

3. What ruling of the trial court is this court reviewing?

4. Does the outcome of this review assure that Mr. Backer will recover against the defendants and, at the same time, be free from further liability?

9. Right to Cover

Cover A good-faith, prompt, reasonable purchase of, or contract to purchase, goods in substitution for those due from the seller.

The buyer who has not received the goods bargained for may **cover**—that is, arrange to purchase the goods from some other source in substitution for those due from the seller [2-712]. This is a practical remedy, as the buyer must often proceed without delay to obtain goods needed for his or her own use or for resale. The buyer must act reasonably and in good faith in arranging for the cover [2-712(1)].

A buyer may collect from a seller the difference between what was paid for the substitute goods and the contract price [2-712(2)]. The buyer may also collect any incidental and consequential damages. *Incidental damages* are defined as those that are reasonably incurred in connection with handling rejected goods. These damages consist of "commercially reasonable charges, expenses or commissions in connection with effecting cover and any other reasonable expense incident to the delay or other breach" [2-715(1)]. *Consequential damages* include "any loss resulting from general or particular requirements and needs of which the seller at the time of contracting had reason to know and which could not reasonably be prevented by cover or otherwise" [2-715(2)]. The buyer is obligated to keep damages to a minimum by making an appropriate cover insofar as his or her right to any consequential damages is concerned.

The cover remedy provides certainty as to the amount of the buyer's damages. The difference between the contract price and the price paid by the buyer for substitute goods can be readily determined. Although the buyer must act reasonably and in good faith, the buyer need not prove that he or she obtained the goods at the cheapest price available.

10. Right to Damages for Nondelivery

The aggrieved buyer who did not receive any goods from the seller or who received nonconforming goods is not required to cover; instead, the buyer may bring an action for damages [2-712(3)]. The measure of damages for nondelivery or repudiation is the difference between the contract price and the market price when the buyer learned of the breach [2-713]. The buyer is also entitled to any incidental or consequential damages sustained. Damages to which a buyer is entitled consist of "the loss resulting in the ordinary course of events from the seller's breach as determined in any manner which is reasonable" [2-714(1)]. In a purchase for resale, it would be appropriate to measure the buyer's damage upon nondelivery as the difference between the contract price and the price at which the goods were to be resold. In other words, the damages equal the difference between the contract price and the fair market value of the goods.

Another recourse open to the buyer is the right to deduct damages from any part of the price still due under the same contract [2-717]. The buyer determines what his or her damages are and withholds this amount when paying the seller. The buyer is required to give notice to the seller of his or her intention to deduct damages. When the buyer's damages are established by the cover price, the amount is clear-cut. In other instances, the seller might question the amount of the deduction, and this dispute would have to be resolved between the parties or by a court.

Damages may be deducted only from the price due under the same contract. A buyer could not deduct damages for nondelivered goods under one contract from the price due under other contracts with the same seller.

11. Right to the Goods

Under proper circumstances, a buyer has rights in, and to, the actual goods purchased. The remedy of *specific performance* is available (1) when the goods are unique and (2) when other circumstances make it equitable that the seller render the required performance [2-716(1)]. To obtain specific performance, the buyer must have been unable to cover. The Code does not define *unique*, but it is fair to assume that it would encompass output and requirement contracts in which the goods were not readily or practically available from other sources. Even if the goods are not unique, the Code provides that the buyer may recover them under "proper circumstances." When a buyer cannot practically buy the goods elsewhere, a proper circumstance for specific performance probably exists.

Replevin A remedy by statute for the recovery of the possession of personal property.

Another remedy that enables the buyer to reach the goods in the hands of the seller is the statutory remedy of replevin. **Replevin** is an action to recover the goods that one person wrongfully withholds from another. A buyer has the right to replevin goods from the seller if the goods have been *identified* to the contract and the buyer is unable to effect cover after making a reasonable effort to do so [2-716(3)].

A related remedy that also reaches the goods in the hands of the seller is the buyer's right to recover them if the seller becomes insolvent [2-502]. The right exists only if (1) the buyer has a "special property interest" in the goods (that is, existing goods have been identified to the contract) and (2) the seller becomes insolvent within ten days after receiving the first installment payment from the buyer. Without these circumstances, the buyer is relegated to the position of a general creditor of the seller. It is apparent that if the buyer can recover the goods, he or she is in a much better position than as a general creditor, particularly if the buyer had paid a substantial amount of the purchase price. To exercise this remedy, the buyer must make and maintain a tender of any unpaid portion of the price.

SELLER'S RIGHTS AND REMEDIES

12. Summary

The Code establishes certain rights and remedies for sellers, just as it does for buyers. A seller has several alternative courses of action when a buyer breaches the contract. One of the most significant rights is to *cure* a defective performance. The seller also may cancel the contract if the buyer's breach is material. Under certain circumstances, a seller may withhold delivery or stop delivery if the goods are in transit. A seller also has the right to resell the goods and recover damages or simply to recover damages for the buyer's failure to accept the goods. Finally, the seller may, under certain circumstances, file suit to recover the price of the goods. The remedies of the seller are cumulative and not exclusive. The technical aspects of "cure" and of these remedies are discussed in the following sections.

13. Right to Cure

Cure An opportunity for the seller of defective goods to correct the defect and thereby not be held to have breached the sales contract.

Upon inspecting the goods, if the buyer finds that they do not conform to the contract, he or she may reject them, provided that he or she acts fairly in doing so. If the rejection is for a relatively minor deviation from the contract requirements, the seller must be given an opportunity to correct the defective performance. This is called **cure.** The seller may accomplish this by notifying the buyer of his or her intention to cure, then tendering proper or conforming goods if the time for performance has not expired. If the time for performance has expired, the seller—if he or she has reasonable grounds to believe that the goods will be acceptable in spite of the nonconformity—will be granted further time to substitute goods that are in accordance with the contract. The main purpose of this rule allowing cure is to protect the seller from being forced into a breach by a surprise rejection at the last moment by the buyer.

14. Right to Reclaim Goods from an Insolvent Buyer

If a seller discovers that a buyer who has been extended credit is insolvent, the seller will want to withhold delivery before it is completed. An insolvent buyer is one "who either has ceased to pay his debts in the ordinary course of business or cannot pay his debts as they become due or is insolvent within the meaning of the federal bankruptcy law" [1-201(23)].

A seller, upon discovering that a buyer is insolvent, may refuse to make any further deliveries except for cash and may demand that payment be made for all goods previously delivered under the contract [2-702(1)]. If goods are en route to the buyer, they may be stopped in transit and recovered from the carrier [2-705]. If they are in a warehouse or other place of storage awaiting delivery to the buyer, the seller may stop delivery by the bailee. Thus the seller can protect his or her interests by retaining or reclaiming the goods prior to the time they come into the possession of the insolvent buyer.

This right to reclaim the goods on the buyer's insolvency includes situations in which the goods have come into the buyer's possession. If the buyer has received goods on credit while he or she is insolvent, the seller can reclaim the goods by making a demand for them within ten days after their receipt by the buyer [2-702(2)]. By receiving the goods, the buyer has, in effect, made a representation that he or she is solvent and able to pay for them. If the buyer has made a written misrepresentation of solvency within the three-month period before the goods were delivered, and the seller has justifiably relied on the writing, the ten-day limitation period during which the seller can reclaim the goods from the insolvent buyer is not applicable to the seller's right of reclamation [2-702(2)].

The importance to a seller of the privilege of reclaiming goods or stopping them in transit should be clear. If the insolvent buyer is adjudicated a bankrupt debtor, the goods will become a part of the debtor's estate and will be sold by the trustee in bankruptcy for the benefit of *all* the creditors of the buyer. If the seller is able to reclaim the goods, his or her loss will be kept to a minimum.

15. Right to Reclaim Goods from a Solvent Buyer

The right to stop goods in transit or to withhold delivery is not restricted to the insolvency situation. If the buyer has (1) wrongfully rejected a tender of goods, (2) revoked acceptance, (3) failed to make a payment due on or before delivery, or (4) repudiated with respect to either a part of the goods or the whole contract, the seller can also reclaim the goods. This right extends to any goods directly affected by the breach.

To stop delivery by a carrier, the seller must give proper and timely notice to the carrier so there is reasonable time to follow the instructions [2-705(3)]. Once the goods have been received by the buyer, or a bailee has acknowledged that he or she holds the goods for the buyer, the right of stoppage is at an end. Only in the case of insolvency [2-704(2)] can the seller reclaim the goods after they are in the buyer's possession.

The right to stop delivery to a solvent buyer is restricted to carload, truckload, planeload, or larger shipments. This restriction is designed to ease the burden on carriers that could develop if the right to stop for reasons other than insolvency applied to all small shipments. The seller who is shipping to a buyer of doubtful credit can always send the goods C.O.D. and thus preclude the necessity for stopping the goods in transit. Of course, the seller must exercise care in availing himself or herself of this remedy, as improper stoppage is a breach by the seller and would subject him or her to an action for damages by the buyer.

16. Right to Resell Goods

The seller who is in possession of goods at the time of the buyer's breach has the right to resell the goods [2-706]. If part of the goods has been delivered, the seller can resell the undelivered portion. In this way the seller can quickly realize at least some of the amount due from the buyer. The seller also has a claim against the buyer for the difference between the resale price and the price that the buyer had agreed to pay. The resale remedy thus affords a practical method and course of action for the seller who has possession of goods that were intended for a breaching buyer. Any person in the position of a seller of goods has the right to resell the goods when a buyer defaults.

Frequently, a buyer will breach or repudiate the contract prior to the time that goods have been identified to the contract. This occurs when goods are in the process of manufacture. This does not defeat the seller's right to resell the goods. The seller may proceed to identify goods to the contract [2-704(1)(a)] and then use his or her remedy of resale. When the goods are unfinished, the seller may also use a remedy of resale if he or she can show that the unfinished goods were intended for the particular contract [2-704(1)(b)]. The seller may also resell the unfinished goods for scrap or salvage value or take any other reasonable action in connection with the goods [2-704(2)]. The only requirement is that the seller use reasonable commercial judgment in determining which course of action to take to mitigate the damages. Presumably the seller would take into consideration factors such as the extent to which the manufacture had been completed and the resalability of the goods if he or she elected to complete the manufacture. Thus, the law allows the seller to proceed in a commercially reasonable manner to protect his or her interests.

When the seller elects to use his or her remedy of resale, the resale may be either a private sale or a public (auction) sale [2-706(2)]. The resale must be identified as one relating to the broken contract. If the resale is private, the seller must give the buyer reasonable notification of his or her intention to resell [2-706(3)]. If the resale is public, the seller must give the buyer reasonable notice of the time and place so the buyer can bid or can obtain the attendance of other bidders. With goods that are perishable or threaten to decline speedily in value, the notice is not required. The seller is permitted to buy at a public sale. The prime requirement is that the sale be conducted in a commercially reasonable manner [2-706(2)]. If the resale brings a higher price than that provided for in the contract, the seller is not accountable to the buyer for any profit [2-706(6)].

17. Right to Collect Damages

In many situations, a resale would not be an appropriate or sufficient remedy. The seller may elect to bring an action for damages if the buyer refuses to accept the goods or repudiates the contract [2-708]. The measure of damages is the difference between the market price at the place for tender and the unpaid contract price, plus incidental damages [2-708]. Incidental damages include expenses reasonably incurred as a result of the buyer's breach [2-710].

Usually, this measure of damages will not put the seller in as good a position as he or she would have had if the buyer had performed and the seller had not lost the sale. Under such circumstances, the measure of damages includes the profit the seller would have made from full performance by the buyer [2-708(2)] as well as incidental damages. In computing profit, the reasonable overhead of the seller may be taken into account. The measure of damages recognizes that a seller suffers a loss, even though the seller may ultimately resell for the same amount that he or she would have received from the buyer. The seller has lost a sale and the profit on that sale.

18. Right to Collect the Purchase Price

When the buyer fails to pay the price as it becomes due, the seller may sue for the contract price of the goods if the buyer has accepted the goods, the goods were destroyed after risk of loss passed to the buyer, or the resale remedy is not practicable.

If goods are specially manufactured for a buyer and there is no market for the special goods, the seller may collect the purchase price since his or her right to resell is not available.

If the seller sues for the price, the goods are held by the seller on behalf of the buyer. In effect, the goods are to be treated as if they belong to the buyer. After the seller obtains a judgment against the buyer, the seller may still resell the goods at any time prior to collection of the judgment but must apply the proceeds toward satisfaction of the judgment. Payment of the balance due on the judgment entitles the buyer to any goods not resold [2-709(2)].

CHAPTER SUMMARY

OVERVIEW OF CODE REMEDIES

Checklist
1. See Table 19–1.

Adequate Assurances
1. This is the one remedy that is available to both buyers and sellers.
2. The Code provides that either party may demand in writing that the other give assurance that performance will be forthcoming.
3. If assurance of performance is not given, the party who requested such assurance may treat the contract as breached.

BUYER'S RIGHTS AND REMEDIES

Right to Inspect
1. A buyer has a right before payment or acceptance to inspect the goods at any reasonable time and place.
2. If the contract is C.O.D. or calls for payment against documents, a buyer must pay before he or she can inspect. Payment, however, is not acceptance, and inspection still is permitted.

Right to Reject
1. If the goods fail in any respect to conform to the contract, a buyer can reject.
2. A buyer can reject the whole or accept any commercial unit and reject the rest.

Notice of Rejection
1. Rejection must be within a reasonable time, and notice of rejection must be timely. Failure to do either will result in an acceptance.

Rights and Duties on Rejection
1. After rejection, a buyer who takes possession of the goods must protect them and follow any reasonable instructions from the seller.
2. A buyer has a security interest in the goods and can resell them to recover his or her expenses in taking possession and caring for the goods.

Right to Revoke Acceptance
1. A buyer accepts if (1) after a reasonable opportunity to inspect, he or she indicates acceptance despite any nonconformity, (2) he or she fails to make an effective rejection, or (3) he or she does any act inconsistent with the seller's ownership.
2. A buyer can revoke acceptance of nonconforming goods if the nonconformity substantially impairs the value of the goods to the buyer.
3. This right might exist even if the buyer accepted the goods while thinking the seller would cure or if the nonconformity was very difficult to discover.
4. Revocation must be within a reasonable time, and the buyer has the same rights and duties as if he or she had rejected.

Right to Cover	1. A buyer covers when he or she buys the goods elsewhere, and cover is a buyer's primary remedy.
	2. A buyer is not required to cover. If the buyer decides to cover, it must be in good faith.
Right to Damages for Nondelivery	1. After covering, a buyer can sue the seller for the difference between the cover price and the contract price, plus any incidental and consequential damages.
	2. If a buyer does not cover, he or she can sue for the difference between the contract price and the market price, plus any incidental and consequential damages.
Right to the Goods	1. When the goods are unique, or in other proper circumstances, a buyer can get specific performance. The Code remedy is more flexible than the traditional remedy of specific performance in equity.
	2. "Other proper circumstances" occur when the buyer simply cannot reasonably buy the goods elsewhere.

SELLER'S RIGHTS AND REMEDIES

Right to Cure	1. The right to cure exists for rejections that are for relatively minor deviations from the contract.
	2. If the time for performance has not expired, a seller has an absolute right to cure (correct) his or her previous nonconforming tender of goods.
	3. If the time for performance has expired, the seller can cure only if the seller had reasonable grounds to think his or her nonconforming tender would have been accepted by the buyer.
Right to Reclaim Goods from an Insolvent Buyer	1. When a seller discovers a buyer received goods while insolvent, the seller can reclaim them upon demand within ten days after receipt. If the buyer in writing three months before delivery misrepresented his or her solvency, the ten-day limitation does not apply.
	2. The seller can also refuse to make further deliveries except for cash and can stop any goods en route to the buyer.
Right to Reclaim Goods from a Solvent Buyer	1. If the buyer has improperly rejected, wrongfully revoked acceptance, failed to pay, or repudiated the contract, the seller can reclaim the goods in transit.
	2. The seller can stop goods in transit upon timely notice to the carrier. This right is limited to carload, truckload, or other large shipments.
Right to Resell Goods	1. Resale is the seller's primary remedy.
	2. A seller can resell the goods and sue for the difference between the resale price and the contract price plus any incidental and consequential damages.
Right to Collect Damages	1. If the seller does not resell, he or she can sue for the difference between the market price at the place of tender and the contract price, plus any incidental and consequential damages.
Right to Collect the Purchase Price	1. A seller can collect the contract price if the buyer accepted the goods.
	2. A seller can collect the contract price if the goods were lost or damaged within a reasonable time after the risk of loss passed to the buyer.
	3. A seller can collect the contract price if the goods were identified to the contract and the seller cannot resell them, or the facts indicate that the goods cannot be resold.

1. Match each term in column A with the appropriate statement in column B.

A	B
(1) Adequate assurance	(a) Buyer's remedy for undoing his or her acceptance
(2) Inspection	(b) Seller's primary remedy
(3) Rejection	(c) If buyer is insolvent, seller may be able to do this
(4) Acceptance	(d) Buyer's right before he or she has to pay or accept
(5) Revocation of acceptance	(e) Seller's right to correct a nonconforming tender
(6) Cover	(f) Seller's right to collect the purchase price
(7) Buyer's specific performance	(g) Buyer fails to make an effective rejection
(8) Cure	(h) Buyer's primary remedy
(9) Resale	(i) Buyer may do this if the tender of goods fails in any way to conform to the contract
(10) Seller's specific performance	(j) Buyer's remedy if goods are unique or other proper circumstances
(11) Seller can reclaim goods	(k) A remedy available to both parties

2. Amy orders three white slips from a department store. They arrive C.O.D. and Amy pays the delivery person. She opens the box and discovers that black slips were sent. If she does not want these slips, what are her rights? Explain.

3. Newman bought a mobile home from Moses. On February 9, Moses delivered the mobile home to Newman's rented lot, blocked and leveled it, and connected the sewer and water pipes. Later that day, Newman's fiancee cleaned the interior of the mobile home and moved some kitchen utensils and dishes into the mobile home. She noticed a broken window and water pipe. Newman called Moses and told him about these conditions as well as having no door keys. On February 10, a windstorm totally destroyed the mobile home. When Newman refused to pay the purchase price, Moses sued, claiming that Newman must bear the loss since Newman had accepted the mobile home. Newman contended that he had not accepted the mobile home since he had complained of specific defects. Did Newman accept the mobile home? Why or why not?

4. Casting and Made-Rite had an agreement under which Casting was to supply 1,600 barrel latches by January 27. Casting shipped 74 parts on January 21, 228 parts on February 27, 623 parts on March 9, 629 parts on April 8, and 70 parts on May 14. Made-Rite did not notify Casting of any intention to reject the barrel latches. Made-Rite inspected the latches in its possession in early April and sent back to Casting those latches found to be nonconforming, which Casting reworked and re-delivered. Has Made-Rite accepted the castings? Why or why not?

5. ODA Nursery sold 985 spreading juniper plants to Garcia Tree and Lawn. The plants were delivered on March 14. They were planted in July and August, but in October many of them started to die. In November, an inspection revealed that the plants were root-bound, and the buyer notified the seller of the defect. Is the buyer entitled to recover the costs of the plants? Why or why not?

6. Campbell bought a pump from Kee for $6,500 that Kee had advertised as a "mud pump." When the pump was delivered, Campbell discovered that the pump was not in fact a mud pump. Campbell claimed that the pump was worth $2,000 less than the mud pump advertised. He refused to pay the $6,500 purchase price but offered $4,500, which Kee refused to accept. For six months, Campbell argued with Kee over what the price should be. When a compromise could not be reached, Campbell returned the pump and refused to pay anything. When Kee sued for the $6,500 purchase price, Campbell asserted that he had rejected the pump and was not liable for anything. Did Campbell seasonably reject the pump? Explain.

7. Slacks, Inc., sells tank tops to a fashionable boutique. Upon receipt, the store inspects them, discovers defects, and seasonably rejects them. Slacks instructs the store to sell the tank tops or return them. The boutique does neither. Is it liable for anything? Explain.

8. Plaintiff, a used-car dealer, brought a car to the defendant, another dealer, for inspection in the hope that a sales agreement could be reached. Two of the defendant's employees examined the car and test-drove it. Defendant thereafter agreed to buy the car without reserving any further right to inspect. In fact, the car had several defects that were readily discernible. Can the buyer revoke in his acceptance? Why?

9. Sandra purchased a new Nissan from Rocky Mountain Nissan. During the first six months that she owned the car, it had to be towed to the dealer's shop for repairs on at least seven occasions. Sometimes the car would not start. On other occasions it would stop running and stall in traffic. Several of the dealer's mechanics told Sandra that they did not know what was wrong with the car but that it was a "lemon." She estimated that the car had been in the dealer's shop four out of the first six months that she owned it. Is she entitled to revoke her acceptance? Why or why not?

10. A country music festival promoter contracted to buy 2,000 kegs of beer at $50 per keg. When the beer that arrived was found to be flat, the promoter rejected it. He could not buy that brand from any other source in time for the festival, so he bought 2,000 kegs of another beer at $55 per keg. What are the promoter's Article 2 damages? Explain.

11. Plaintiff entered into a contract to purchase 4,000 tons of cryolite, a chemical used in the production of aluminum, from defendant. When the chemical was not delivered, plaintiff brought a suit for specific performance. He contended that cryolite was not readily available from any other source. Is plaintiff entitled to the remedy of specific performance? Why?

12. Ray ordered a color TV from a local store. When it was delivered, he noticed that the picture had a reddish tint. The man who installed the set offered to take it back to the shop to repair it, but Ray objected. "I don't want a repaired TV. I want a refund." The store maintained it would repair the set but not refund Ray's money. Later, Ray sued to recover his payments. Must Ray permit the store to correct the defect? Explain.

13. Jimmie Hart contracted to buy a certain painting through Mrs. Sims, an art dealer, for $45,000. Hart made a down payment and promised to pay the balance of the purchase price on or before November 25, 1992. Hart sent a personal check for the balance, but his check bounced due to insufficient funds in his checking account. Hart reassured Mrs. Sims that he would wire the balance to Mrs. Sims at 10:00 A.M. on November 29, 1992. On that date he called, stating he was having trouble getting the funds wired. Mrs. Sims agreed to extend the deadline to 2:00 P.M. but warned that she would sell the painting to another interested buyer if he did not meet the 2:00 P.M. deadline. Hart did wire the money, but it did not reach Mrs. Sim's bank until 3:04 P.M. At 2:30 P.M. Mrs. Sims telegraphed Hart canceling their contract. She then sold the painting to another buyer for $60,000. Hart sued, contending that Mrs. Sims did not have the right to sell the painting because he had wired the money. Did Mrs. Sims have the right to resell the painting? Why or why not?

14. Defendant ordered from the plaintiff two lead-covered steel tanks to be constructed by the plaintiff according to specifications supplied by the defendant. The tanks were designed for the special purpose of testing X-ray tubes and were required to be radiation-proof within certain federal standards. The defendant inspected the goods and accepted them notwithstanding some defects. It then attempted to revoke the acceptance but did not do so properly. The seller retained possession of the tanks, and when the buyer failed to pay for them, suit was filed for the purchase price. Is the plaintiff entitled to the purchase price? Explain.

CHAPTER

20

WARRANTIES

CHAPTER PREVIEW

*I*n the law of sales of goods, the word *warranty* describes the obligation of the seller with respect to goods that have been sold. As a general rule, a seller is responsible for transferring to the buyer a good title and goods that are of the proper quality, free from defects. A seller may also be responsible for the proper functioning of the article sold and for its suitability to the needs of the buyer. Thus a warranty may extend not only to the present condition for goods but also to the performance that is to be expected of them.

A warranty made by a seller is an integral part of the contract. If the warranty is breached and the buyer notifies the seller of the breach within a reasonable time, the buyer may bring an action for damages caused by the breach of warranty. A breach of warranty may also result in injuries to the buyer or to third persons. Suits may be brought to recover damages for these injuries as well.

The law takes the position that if the goods are defective, the seller should be held responsible. Various tort and contract theories impose liability on manufacturers, packers, producers, and sellers for injuries caused by defective products. This chapter discusses the breach of warranty theories. Other theories are discussed in chapter 21, on products liability. Keep in mind that the material in this chapter is also a part of products liability.

The Uniform Commercial Code has several provisions relating to warranties. It draws a distinction between express warranties made by a seller and those implied as a matter of law from the transaction. If the seller guarantees the product directly, it is an *express warranty*. If the warranty arises out of the transaction and its circumstances, it is called an *implied warranty*. When the seller is a merchant, special warranties often exist.

■ BUSINESS MANAGEMENT DECISION

You inherit a retail hardware store that you do not wish to operate. After being unsuccessful in selling the business, you decide to have a going-out-of-business sale. You want to sell all the merchandise on an as-is basis, but you realize that many customers rely on the expertise of your experienced sales staff and that many of your products can cause injury if used improperly.

What do you do to ensure that no express or implied warranties attach to the merchandise sold?

TYPES OF WARRANTIES

1. Express Warranties

Express warranty A positive representation concerning the nature, quality, character, use, and purpose of goods, which induces the buyer to buy and on which the seller intends the buyer to rely.

An **express warranty** is one that is made as a part of the contract for sale and becomes a part of the basis of the bargain between the buyer and the seller [2-313(1) (a)]. An express warranty, as distinguished from an implied warranty, is part of the contract because it has been included as part of the individual bargain. To create an express warranty, the seller does not have to use formal words such as *warrant* or *guarantee*, nor must he or she have the specific intention to make a warranty [2-313(3)]. For example, the following statement by a seller of a used diesel engine was held to be an express warranty and not merely sales puffery: "All you have to do is take it home, put it in your truck, and it will go right to work. This engine is in good running condition." When the engine did not perform properly, the buyer was allowed to recover based on a breach of this express warranty.

A seller may make a variety of statements about the goods. It is necessary to evaluate these to determine which statements are warranties and which do not impose legal responsibility because they are merely sales talk. An express warranty may be any positive statement by a seller of the condition of personal property made during the negotiations for its sale. A label on a bag of insecticide stated that it was developed especially to control rootworms. This was an express warranty that the insecticide was effective to control the rootworm. The word *guarantee* is often used to give an express warranty. A contract of sale of automobile tires states that the tires were guaranteed for 36,000 miles against all road hazards, including blowouts. This constituted an express warranty that the tires would not blow out during the first 36,000 miles of use.

When a statement of fact or promise about the goods is made by the seller to the buyer, an express warranty is created [2-313(1)(a)]. The express warranty is that the goods will conform to the statement of fact or promise. Any statement of fact or even of opinion, if it becomes a part of the basis of the bargain, is an express warranty. While an express warranty must become a part of the basis of the bargain, a plaintiff does not have to prove reliance on specific promises made by the seller. No particular reliance need be shown to weave an affirmation of fact into the fabric of the agreement.

Most statements of opinion, such as those concerning the value of the goods, do not give rise to an express warranty. As a general rule, a buyer is not justified in relying on mere opinions, and they are not usually a part of the basis of the bargain. However, the opinion of an expert, such as a jeweler, with regard to the value of a gem may justify the reliance of the buyer, and such an opinion becomes part of the basis of the bargain and a warranty. When a seller merely states his or her opinion or judgment on a matter of which the seller has no special knowledge, or on a matter of which the buyer may be expected to have an opinion or exercise judgment, the seller's statement does not constitute an express warranty.

An express warranty may be made in a variety of ways. The seller may specifically make a factual statement about the goods. These factual statements may be on labels or in a catalog or other sales promotion material. A direct promise may state, "This grass seed is free from weeds." Generally, words that are descriptive of the product are warranties that the goods will conform to the description [2-313(1)(b)]. Descriptions may also be in the form of diagrams, pictures, blueprints, and the like. Technical specifications of the product would constitute warranties if they were part of the basis for the bargain. An express warranty can also be based on the instructions of the seller regarding use of the product.

Just as the seller may describe the goods, he or she may also inform the buyer by showing to the buyer a model or a sample of what is being sold. Fabrics or clothing might be purchased on the basis of samples shown to the buyer, or a seller might display a working model of an engine. In either event, there would be an express warranty that the goods will conform to the sample or model if the parties have made this a part of their bargain [2-313(1)(c)].

2. Warranty of Title

A seller may expressly warrant the title to goods but usually does not do so. Therefore the law imposes a *warranty of title* to protect buyers who may overlook this aspect of the sale and those who simply assume the seller has good title to the goods. The warranty of title is treated as a separate warranty under the Code.

A seller warrants that he or she is conveying good title to the buyer and has the right to sell the goods. The seller further warrants that there are no encumbrances or liens against the property sold and that no other person can claim a security interest in them [2-312]. In effect, the seller implicitly guarantees that the buyer will be able to enjoy the use of the goods free from the claims of any third party. Of course, property may be sold to a buyer who has full knowledge of liens or encumbrances, and he or she may buy the property subject to these claims. In this event, there would not be a breach of warranty of title. The purchase price would, however, reflect that the buyer was obtaining less than complete title.

In chapter 18, it is noted that a good-faith purchaser from a seller with voidable title obtains good title. Is there a breach of the warranty of title in such a sale? While there are cases answering the question both ways, most courts would find a breach of warranty even if the buyer actually receives clear title. This results from Code language that requires that the conveyance of title be rightful and free from the difficulties of establishing clear title in such cases. The good-faith purchaser thus has a choice. He or she may claim the goods by use of the good-faith purchaser concept or may recover the purchase price or any payments made by electing to sue for breach of the implied warranty of title.

Warranty of title can be excluded or modified only by specific language or by circumstances making clear that the seller is not vouching for the title [2-312(2)]. The following case illustrates the reasoning for not allowing the warranty of title to be disclaimed without clear language.

CASE

Brokke v. Williams
766 P.2d 1311 (Mont. 1989)

TURNAGE, C. J.

. . . The issue on appeal is whether a merchant can disclaim responsibility for furnishing title to goods sold in his business by placing "sold as is" signs in his establishment. . . .

Albert D. Williams operates a pawnshop in Bozeman, Montana. Plaintiff Paul Brokke entered defendant's business on October 31, 1985, and placed a Pentax Super Program camera on layaway by paying a $20 down payment and agreeing to pay the $69.95 balance due on the purchase. The camera was stolen property.

On November 4, 1985, plaintiff paid the remaining balance on the layaway transaction and took possession of the camera, serial number 1190586. Later that same month, plaintiff was notified by the Bozeman police department that the camera was stolen property. He was directed to surrender the camera to the police department which he did on November 18, 1985.

Plaintiff promptly returned to the pawnshop and requested a refund for his purchase of the stolen merchandise. That request was denied by Williams and litigation ensued.

After justice court proceedings, hearing was held on January 21, 1988, which resulted in a District Court judgment in favor of plaintiff. Defendant appeals.

Defendant argues that he had no knowledge that the merchandise was stolen property. Williams argues further that he disclaims any warranty of title to goods sold in his business by way of large fluorescent signs posted which alert buyers that the merchandise sold on the premises is sold "as is," and by writing the same on his sales receipts. We disagree. . . .

The issue is controlled by the Montana Uniform Commercial Code (UCC). Section 30-2-312, MCA, warrants that a merchant selling goods passes clear title to the goods. Clearly, Williams breached that warranty of title required by the code when he sold stolen goods to Brokke because it had long been established that a thief cannot pass clear title to his stolen goods, nor can his successor. It is irrelevant that Williams claims he did not know the goods were stolen.

With respect to breach of warranty, Williams, as a merchant, is held to a higher standard of dealing than ordinary consumers. Further, Williams is held to the obligatory good faith required in the performance of every contract and every duty under the UCC. Good faith is defined under the UCC as "honesty in fact." . . .

The question then becomes, did Williams do anything to effectuate a disclaimer of the warranty of title in this transaction. We affirm the trial court's conclusion that he did not.

Warranty of title is not subject to the disclaimers found in § 30-2-316, MCA, pertaining to fitness and merchantability. Williams argues that his conduct of placing the signs is his notice of a specific and written disclaimer. However, that conduct does not meet the disclaimer of warranty of title found in § 30-2-312(3), MCA, which states "unless otherwise agreed" a seller who is a merchant warrants that the goods shall be delivered free of the rightful claim of any third person. Clearly, there could have been no agreement to that effect between Williams and Brokke when Brokke denies ever seeing the signs which Williams claims were up in his premises on the date of the transaction. Brokke further testified to having no conversations with Williams regarding the title of the camera. That testimony conflicts with Williams' account of having verbally informed Brokke that the title could not be guaranteed.

The trial court found that Williams had a duty to deliver clear title to the property, that he could not do so because it was stolen and that simply placing "as is" signs in his store does not defeat that duty nor relieve him of liability for defects. We agree. The trial court additionally found that it violates the public policy of this state to allow pawnbrokers to profit from the sale of stolen property. Montana law as written by our legislators and found in the UCC supports that conclusion. . . .

Brokke is entitled to a refund of the $89.95 paid to Williams plus his costs in this action as awarded by the District Court and his costs on appeal.

■ *Judgment affirmed.*

CASE CONCEPTS REVIEW

1. What event occurred that left Mr. Brokke (the plaintiff-buyer) without the camera he had purchased from Mr. Williams (defendant-seller)?

2. What is the basis for Mr. Williams's defense that he had made no warranty of title with respect to the camera?

3. What is the court's conclusion, and what are the reasons for such a conclusion concerning the existence of a warranty of title?

Judicial sales and sales by executors of estates would not imply that the seller guarantees the title. Also, a seller could directly inform the buyer that he or she is selling only the interest and that the buyer takes it subject to all encumbrances.

A seller who is a merchant, regularly dealing in goods of the kind that are the subject of the sale, makes an additional warranty. This seller warrants that the goods are free of the rightful claim of any third person by way of infringement of the third person's interests—that the goods sold do not, for example, infringe on a patent. But a buyer may furnish to the seller specifications for the construction of an article, and this may result in the infringement of a patent. Not only does the seller not warrant against such infringement, but the buyer must also protect the seller from any claims arising out of such infringement [2-312(3)].

3. Implied Warranty of Merchantability

Implied warranties come into being as a matter of law, without any bargaining. As an integral part of the normal sales transaction, implied warranties are legally present unless clearly disclaimed or negated. Implied warranties exist even if a seller is unable to discover the defect involved or unable to cure it if it can be ascertained. Liability for breach of an implied warranty is not based on fault, but on the public policy of protecting the buyer of goods.

A warranty that the goods shall be of merchantable quality is implied in a contract for sale if the seller is a merchant who deals in goods of the kind involved in the contract. It is not enough that the defendant sold the goods. The seller-defendant must have been a merchant dealing in the goods. A person making an isolated sale is not a merchant. For example, a bank selling a repossessed car is not a merchant, and there is no implied **warranty of merchantability** in such a sale.

Warranty of merchantability A promise implied in a sale of goods by merchants that the goods are reasonably fit for the general purpose for which they are sold.

The warranty extends to all sales of goods by merchants. It applies to new goods and to used goods in most states, unless the warranty is excluded.

For a consumer to prevail in an action for damages for breach of an implied warranty of merchantability, he or she must demonstrate that the commodity was not reasonably suitable for the ordinary uses for which goods of that kind and description are sold, and that such defect or breach existed at the time of sale and proximately caused the damages complained of.

For goods to be merchantable, they must at least be the kind of goods that

1. Pass without objection in the trade under the contract description
2. In the case of fungible goods, are of fair average quality within the description

3. Are fit for the ordinary purposes for which such goods are used
4. Run, within the variations permitted by the agreement, of even kind, quality, and quantity within each unit and among all units involved
5. Are adequately contained, packaged, and labeled as the agreement may require
6. Conform to the promises or affirmations of fact made on the container or label, if any [2-314]

Fungible goods Fungible goods are those of which any unit is, from its nature of mercantile usage, treated as the equivalent of any other unit. Grain, wine, and similar items are examples.

These standards provide the basic acceptable standards of merchantability. **Fungible goods** (point 2) are those usually sold by weight or measure, such as grain or flour. The term *fair average quality* generally relates to agricultural bulk commodities and means that they are within the middle range of quality under the description. Fitness for ordinary purposes (point 3) is not limited to use by the immediate buyer. If a person is buying for resale, the buyer is entitled to protection, and the goods must be honestly resalable. They must be acceptable in the ordinary market without objection. Point 5 is applicable only if the nature of the goods and of the transaction require a certain type of container, package, or label. Where there is a container or label and a representation thereon, the buyer is entitled to protection under point 6, so that he or she will not be in the position of reselling or using goods delivered under false representations appearing on the package or container. The buyer obtains this protection even though the contract did not require either the labeling or the representation.

The implied warranty of merchantability imposes a very broad responsibility on the merchant-seller to furnish goods that are at least of average quality. In any line of business, the word *merchantable* may have a meaning somewhat different from the Code definition, and the parties by their course of dealing may indicate a special meaning for the term.

One purpose of this warranty is to require sellers to provide goods that are reasonably safe for their ordinary intended use. Although the law does not require accident-proof products, it does require products that are reasonably safe for the purposes for which they were intended when they were placed in the stream of commerce. The mere fact that a product injures one person does not in and of itself establish that it is not fit for the ordinary purpose for which it was intended.

Liability for breach of the warranty of merchantability extends to direct economic loss as well as to personal injuries and to property damage. Direct economic loss includes damages based on insufficient product value. In other words, the buyer is entitled to collect the difference in value between what was received and what the product would have had if it had been of merchantable quality. Direct economic loss also includes the cost of replacements and the cost of repairs. These damages need not be established with mathematical certainty, but reasonable degrees of certainty and accuracy are required so the damages are not based on speculation.

4. Implied Warranty of Fitness for a Particular Purpose

Warranty of fitness for a particular purpose An implied promise by a seller of goods that arises when a buyer explains the special needs and relies on the seller's advice.

Under the warranty of merchantability, the goods must be fit for the *ordinary purpose* for which such goods are used. The warranty of merchantability is based on a purchaser's reasonable expectation that goods purchased from a merchant with respect to goods of that kind will be free of significant defects and will perform in the way goods of that kind should perform. It presupposes no special relationship of trust or reliance between the seller and buyer. On the other hand, the implied **warranty of fitness for a particular purpose** is narrower, more specific, and more precise. It is created if, at the time of contracting, the seller has reason to know any particular purpose for which the buyer requires the goods and is relying on the seller's skill or judgment to select or furnish suitable goods [2-315]. In these circumstances, the seller must select goods that will accomplish the purpose for which they are being purchased. It is based on a special reliance by the buyer on the seller to provide goods that will perform a specific use required and communicated by the buyer.

The implied warranty of fitness applies both to merchants and nonmerchants but normally pertains only to merchants, since a nonmerchant does not ordinarily possess the required skills or judgment on which buyers will rely. The buyer need not specifically state that he or she has a particular purpose in mind or is placing reliance on the seller's judgment if the circumstances are such that the seller has reason to realize the purpose intended or that the buyer is relying on the seller. For the warranty to apply, however, the buyer must actually rely on the seller's skill or judgment in selecting or furnishing suitable goods. If the buyer's knowledge or skill is equal to or greater than the seller's, there can be no justifiable reliance and no warranty. The existence of justifiable reliance and hence a warranty is a question of fact for a jury to answer.

The difference between the implied warranty of merchantability and the implied warranty of fitness for a particular purpose is very significant. While many cases allege a breach of both warranties, the decisions often only find a breach of one or the other, but not both. The implied warranty of fitness for a particular purpose does not exist nearly as often as the implied warranty of merchantability. Particular purpose involves a specific use by the buyer; ordinary use, as expressed in the concept of merchantability, means the customary function of the goods. Thus a household dishwasher would be of merchantable quality because it could ordinarily be used to wash dishes; but it might not be fit for a restaurant's particular purpose because it would not be suited for its dishwashing needs. Goods that are of merchantable quality may not fit for a particular purpose. Goods fit for a particular purpose will almost always be of merchantable quality. Goods that are not of merchantable quality usually will not be fit for a particular purpose.

Breach of the warranty of fitness for a particular purpose may result in disaffirmance of the contract. If the product causes an injury, including economic loss, it may also result in a suit for dollar damages. The following case is one in which both the implied warranties were breached and the buyer was able to collect damages for economic losses.

CASE

Renze Hybrids, Inc. v. Shell Oil Company
418 N.W.2d 634 (Ia. 1988)

McGIVERIN, C. J.

... This case arose out of the alleged failure of an insecticide produced by the defendant Shell Oil Company (Shell) to kill enough European corn borer larvae in the seed corn fields of plaintiff Renze Hybrids, Inc. (Renze), to avert economic loss. After the ensuing trial for breach of implied warranties, the jury found Shell 75% at fault for Renze's crop losses. . . .

I. *Background facts and proceedings.* Plaintiff Renze Hybrids, Inc., is a family owned seed corn business. . . . The corporation farmed 16 fields of seed corn in Carroll County, Iowa . . . covering approximately 1100 acres.

In early August 1983, Cyril Renze, president of the Renze corporation, became concerned with the substantial quantity of European corn borer eggs he noticed on corn plants in his daily monitoring of the Renze fields. He learned from Dr. David Foster, an extension entomologist with Iowa State University, that there were only three insecticides on the market used to kill European corn borers. Cyril Renze then approached Jerry Broiche, representative of Cal-Car Service Company, seeking help with his infestation problem. Broiche, in turn, spoke with representatives from Shell and was told that Shell's product, Pydrin, could be used to control corn borer infestation. Broiche passed on this information to Cyril Renze who then decided to spray the Renze acres with Pydrin. Broiche applied the insecticide to Renze's fields and also sprayed surrounding grasses and waterways to cover areas near the corn where European corn borer moths might breed.

Pydrin appears to have been ineffective in controlling corn borers enough to prevent economic loss in Renze's seed corn fields. Despite proper application of Pydrin while the corn borer eggs were beginning to hatch, Renze's fields sustained measurable damage from the corn borer larvae. Renze brought suit for its crop losses and other items asserting that Shell breached implied warranties of fitness for a particular purpose and merchantability. Expert witnesses for both sides testified at trial, as did Cyril Renze and Jerry Broiche.

Based upon the evidence submitted, the jury determined Renze's crop losses at $549,816.00 and his lost interest due to the crop loss to be $139,653.00, for a total of $689,469.00. On the issue of comparative fault, the jury found defendant Shell 75% at fault. Accordingly, the trial court entered a judgment in favor of plaintiff against Shell for 75% of $689,469.00 or $517,101.75 plus interest . . . from the date the petition was filed.

On appeal, Shell makes . . . assertions of error. We address them in turn, adding relevant facts from the record where necessary.

II. *Implied warranty of fitness for a particular purpose.* . . . The Uniform Commercial Code (UCC) is codified in Iowa Code chapter 554. Renze's claim of breach of warranty of fitness for a particular purpose is grounded in Iowa Code section 554.2315 which states:

> Where the seller at the time of contracting has reason to know any particular purpose for which the goods are required and that the buyer is relying on the seller's skill or judgment to select or furnish suitable goods, there is unless excluded or modified under the next section an implied warranty that the goods shall be fit for such purpose.

Recovery under this section depends upon a showing that (1) the seller had reason to know of the buyer's particular purpose; (2) the seller had reason to know the buyer was relying on the seller's skill or judgment to furnish suitable goods; and (3) the buyer in fact relied on the seller's skill or judgment to furnish suitable goods.

This is a warranty distinct from the implied warranty of merchantability. Comment 2 to UCC section 2-315 contained in Iowa Code Annotated section 554.2315 notes:

> A "particular purpose" differs from the ordinary purpose for which the goods are used in that it envisages a specific use by the buyer which is peculiar to the nature of his business whereas the ordinary purposes for which goods are used are those envisaged in the concept of merchantability and go to uses which are customarily made of the goods in question.

Shell argues that because Pydrin is one of the three commercial insecticides on the market used to kill European corn borer larvae, Renze used the insecticide for its ordinary purpose and not any particular purpose. The Pydrin label, however, lists dozens of different species of insects and the proper concentrations of Pydrin that should be mixed with water to exterminate them. Renze claims that it, through Broiche, asked Shell for the best product to deal with its specific problem of infestation by European corn borers in seed corn fields. We believe this is the type of particular purpose to which section 554.2315 was meant to apply. . . .

While Shell had no direct presale dealings with Renze, Shell had reason to know of Renze's needs through Shell's dealings with Broiche. We have stated that "the warranty of fitness under section 554.2315 is said to turn on the 'bargain-related' facts as to what the seller had reason to know about the buyer's purpose for the goods and about his reliance on the seller's skill or judgment in selecting them." Testimony by Broiche indicates that he spoke to Shell personnel and explained that he needed the best insecticide available to kill European corn borers in his client's seed corn fields. Having been approached by Broiche with this request, Shell had reason to know of Renze's particular purpose and of Renze's reliance on Shell's expertise in selecting an insecticide.

Finally, it is evident that Renze did in fact rely on Shell's skill or judgment to furnish suitable goods. We conclude there was sufficient evidence of bargain-related facts to submit this claim to the jury.

III. *Implied warranty of merchantability.* As stated above, the implied warranty of merchantability involves the fitness of goods for their ordinary purpose. . . . This theory requires the plaintiff to prove (1) a merchant sold the goods, (2) the goods were not "merchantable" at the time of sale, (3) injury or damage occurred to the plaintiff's property, (4) the defective nature of the goods caused the damage "proximately and in fact," and (5) notice was given to the seller of the damage. We conclude that substantial evidence to prove each of these elements exists in the record, and that submitting this theory to the jury was proper.

Shell's product, Pydrin, was selected as an insecticide for Renze by Broiche at Shell's suggestion after significant quantities of corn borer eggs were discovered. Broiche applied Pydrin to Renze's corn fields and surrounding grasses. Trial testimony from several witnesses indicated that the insecticide failed to kill enough corn borer larvae to prevent economic loss in Renze's fields. While no direct evidence was presented to demonstrate defects with Pydrin, there was considerable circumstantial evidence of Pydrin's failure. Testimony by several witnesses also indicated the failure of Pydrin to exterminate the corn borer larvae led to substantial damage to Renze's fields.

Substantial evidence, whether or not contradicted, is the litmus test of submissibility of an issue to the jury.

Based upon the evidence in the record, this issue was properly submitted to the jury. . . .

■ *Affirmed.*

CASE CONCEPTS REVIEW

1. Why did Cecil Renze use the insecticide Pydrin, and what were the results of this use?
2. What three things must a plaintiff prove to establish clearly the existence of an implied warranty of fitness for a particular purpose? Did Renze satisfy this evidentiary burden?
3. What five elements must be proven to have an implied warranty of merchantability arise from a factual situation? Are these elements established in this case?

LIMITATIONS

5. Express Warranties

A seller will often seek to avoid or restrict warranty liability. These attempts to limit liability may take the form of a disclaimer of warranties or a limitation of remedies. A *disclaimer of warranties* limits a seller's liability by reducing the number of circumstances in which the seller will be in breach of contract; it precludes the existence of a cause of action or greatly reduces it. A *limitation of remedies* clause restricts the remedies available to the buyer once a breach of warranty by the seller is established. The parties may also limit or alter the damages recoverable by limiting the buyer's remedy to repair or replace the nonconforming goods or parts.

The Code has provisions on exclusion or modification of warranties that are designed to protect the buyer from unexpected and unfair disclaimers of both express and implied warranties. Sometimes there are statements or conduct that create an express warranty and also statements or conduct that tend to negate or limit such warranties. To the extent that it is reasonable, the two different kinds of statements or conduct are construed as consistent with each other [2-316(1)]. However, negation of limitation of an express warranty is inoperative when such a construction is unreasonable. In other words, if the express warranty and the attempt to negate it cannot be construed as consistent, the warranty predominates. If a seller gives the buyer an express warranty and then includes in the contract a provision that purports to exclude "all warranties express or implied," that disclaimer will not be given effect. The express warranty is still enforceable.

6. Written Disclaimers of Implied Warranties

Implied warranties can be excluded if the seller makes it clear that the buyer is not to have the benefit of them. In general, to exclude or modify the implied warranty of merchantability, the word *merchantability* must be used [2-316(2)]. The warranty of merchantability may also be excluded by oral agreement or by the parties' course of performance. However, if the disclaimer is included in a written contract, it must be set forth in a conspicuous manner. The disclaimer clause of the contract should be in larger type or a different color ink or indented, so it will be brought to the buyer's attention. A disclaimer will not be effective if it is set forth in the same type and color as the rest of the contract.

To exclude or modify any implied warranty of fitness for a particular purpose, the exclusion must be conspicuously written. The statement "there are no warranties which extend beyond the description on the face hereof" is sufficient to exclude the implied warranty of fitness for a particular purpose]2-316(2)]. An exclusionary clause should be printed in type that will set it apart from the balance of the contract. The following case illustrates the type of writing required to disclaim implied warranties.

CASE

Central Mining, Inc. v. Simmons Machinery Co., Inc.

547 So.2d 529 (Ala. 1989)

ALMON, J.

Central Mining, Inc., and Marine Office of America Corporation ("MOAC") brought an action against Simmons Machinery Company, Inc., and Clark Equipment Company, alleging breach of warranty. The trial court entered summary judgment for Simmons and Clark.

On April 27, 1978, Central purchased a 1978 "Clark-Michigan 475 Loader" from Simmons, a distributor of Clark's products, and insured it with MOAC. The loader was covered by the following warranty:

Clark Equipment Company (CLARK) has warranted to the Distributor (Seller) who, pursuant to agreement with CLARK, hereby, on its own behalf, warrants to the Buyer each new CLARK product to be free from defects in material and workmanship under normal use and maintenance as herein provided.

Distributor's sole obligation under this warranty shall be limited to repairing, replacing or allowing credit for, at Distributor's option, any part which under normal and proper use and maintenance proves defective in material or workmanship within six (6) months after delivery to or one thousand (1,000) hours of use by Buyer, whichever shall occur first; provided, however, that (i) the product is placed in use not later than one year after shipment from CLARK's plant; (ii) that notice of such defect and satisfactory proof thereof is promptly given by Buyer to Distributor; and (iii) such material shall have been returned to Distributor, with transporta-

tion charges prepaid and found by Distributor to have been defective.

This warranty does not apply in respect of damage to or defects in any product caused by overloading or other misuse, neglect or accident, nor does this warranty apply to any product which has been repaired or altered in any way which, in the sole judgment of Distributor, affects the performance, stability or general purpose for which it was manufactured.

THIS WARRANTY IS IN LIEU OF ALL OTHER WARRANTIES (EXCEPT OF TITLE), EXPRESSED OR IMPLIED, AND THERE ARE NO WARRANTIES OF MERCHANTABILITY OR OF FITNESS FOR A PARTICULAR PURPOSE. IN NO EVENT SHALL DISTRIBUTOR BE LIABLE FOR CONSEQUENTIAL OR SPECIAL DAMAGES.

This warranty does not apply to parts or trade accessories not manufactured by CLARK, or attachments not manufactured or sold by CLARK. Buyer shall rely solely on the existing warranties, if any, of the respective manufacturers thereof. . . .

On August 10, 1979, the loader caught fire and was destroyed. Central and MOAC then brought this action, claiming that the loader was defective and not fit for the purpose for which it was to be used and that Clark and Simmons had breached their warranty.

Clark and Simmons moved for summary judgment, arguing that they had disclaimed any implied warranties and that the time period set forth in the express warranty had expired. The trial court granted the motion and Central and MOAC appeal.

Central and MOAC first argue that the warranty given to Central applies only to Simmons and that Clark was not a party to the warranty. The thrust of this argument is clear. If it is determined that Clark was not a party to the warranty, then it had not disclaimed its implied warranties. We hold that the trial court did not err in ruling that Clark was a party to the warranty.

The warranty, set out above, appeared as part of a document styled "Clark Equipment Company—Delivery Report and Warranty Certificate." The "Delivery Report" portion of that document contained the following statement: "NO WARRANTY REQUESTS WILL BE ACCEPTED UNTIL THIS FORM HAS BEEN COMPLETELY FILLED OUT AND RETURNED TO THE CONSTRUCTION MACHINERY DIVISION OF CLARK EQUIPMENT COMPANY." It is clear from the face of the warranty and the Delivery Report that accompanied it that Clark was a party to the warranty.

Under the terms of the warranty, Clark and Simmons were obligated to repair, replace, or allow credit for any part that proved defective within six months of delivery or 1,000 hours of use by Central, whichever came first. The fire that destroyed the loader occurred more than 15 months after delivery of the loader. Clearly, the fire occurred after the express warranty had expired. . . .

There being no reversible error shown, the judgment of the trial court is

■ *Affirmed.*

CASE CONCEPTS REVIEW

1. According to the terms of the written warranty, how long was the express warranty to last?
2. How does the written form of the warranty make it clear that all implied warranties were disclaimed?
3. Why is it an important issue to determine whether Clark was a party to the written warranty and disclaimer?

While the preceding case contains the typical clause for disclaiming implied warranties, other language has been held to create the same result. Note in the next case that the court relies on the policy that the disclaimer should not be a surprise, through hidden fine print, to the contracting parties.

CASE

Travel Craft, Inc. v. Wilhelm Mende GmbH & Co.
552 N.E.2d 443 (Ind. 1990)

SHEPARD, C. J.

. . . In 1982, Wilhelm Mende GmbH & Co., a West German Corporation, directed a sales campaign toward Travel Craft, Inc., a manufacturer of motor homes and recreational vehicles. Mende representatives traveled to Travel Craft's plant in Elkhart to persuade Travel Craft to purchase Alu-span, an aluminum-type material. The record indicates that the sales campaign was the first contact between the companies. Travel Craft did not have any prior knowledge of Alu-span.

Travel Craft decided to buy Alu-span for use in constructing its motor homes. After the initial purchase, Travel Craft and Mende negotiated a warranty. Travel Craft drafted the warranty, which stated in pertinent part:

Seller [Mende] agrees for a period of three (3) years from the date of delivery that product manufactured by it will be free under normal use from substantial defects in materials or workmanship. There are no other warranties, express or implied.

On finished motor homes, Alu-span cracked and separated from its base. As a result, Travel Craft recalled more than 100 motor homes. The cracks and separations apparently resulted from Alu-span's inherent inability to withstand the structural stress associated with its use in motor homes, rather than from any flaw in the material or manufacture.

Travel Craft sued Mende for breach of express and implied warranties. The trial court granted Mende's motions for summary judgment. The Court of Appeals affirmed. . . .

Travel Craft appeals . . . [The issue is]

Whether the trial court erred in ruling that the written warranty adequately excluded the implied warranties of merchantability and fitness for a particular purpose. . . .

Unless excluded or modified, a warranty that goods shall be merchantable is implied in a contract for their sale if the seller is a merchant with respect to goods of that kind. Travel Craft argues that the disclaimer of the implied warranty of merchantability it drafted in this case—"There are no other warranties, express or implied"—was ineffective because it did not contain the word merchantability.

The most recent Indiana authority on disclaimer of an implied warranty of merchantability holds that a disclaimer is ineffective unless it expressly and conspicuously mentions the word "merchantability." Ind. Code § 26-1-2-316(2) requires using the actual word "merchantability" in order to protect the buyer from surprise. The warranty of merchantability is so frequently implied in a sale that to exclude it one must exercise special care.

The disclaimer in this transaction would normally be inadequate because it does not mention the word merchantability. After reading Ind. Code § 26-1-2-316 and the Uniform Commercial Code's commentary, however, we conclude that this case is an exception to the rule. The commentary states that U.C.C. § 2-316(2) seeks to:

> [P]rotect a *buyer* from unexpected and unbargained language of disclaimer by denying effect to such language when inconsistent with language of express warranty and permitting the exclusion of implied warranties only by conspicuous language or other circumstances which protect the buyer from surprise.

Applying Ind. Code § 26-1-2-316(2) in favor of Travel Craft, the *buyer* and the *drafter* of the warranty, would subject the seller to the same type of surprise the provision is intended to prevent. Accepting Travel Craft's argument would turn a buyer's shield against surprise into a buyer's sword of surprise. We conclude, consequently, if the buyer drafts the disclaimer it cannot in good faith claim surprise or unexpected and unbargained for language. Our construction follows the drafter's intent that the Code be construed to promote its underlying purposes and policies, and leads us to hold in this case that the implied warranty of merchantability was effectively disclaimed, even though the word "merchantability" was not mentioned.

As for the implied warranty of fitness for a particular purpose, Ind. Code 26-1-2-316(2) provides the opportunity to disclaim simply by a conspicuous writing. We conclude that the words of this disclaimer were adequate.

The trial court properly granted Mende's motion for summary judgment aimed at implied warranties. . . .

■ *Affirmed.*

CASE CONCEPTS REVIEW

1. Which party (buyer or seller) drafted the express warranty and disclaimer of implied warranty?
2. What are the stated UCC requirements for disclaiming an implied warranty of merchantability and an implied warranty of fitness for a particular purpose?
3. Although these requirements for disclaiming implied warranties are not met, why does the court enforce the language "There are no other warranties, express or implied?"
4. Does the result of this case necessarily mean that Travel Craft has no valid claim against Mende?

Disclaimers of implied warranties are greatly limited by federal law today. As a part of the law relating to consumer protection, Congress passed the Magnuson-Moss warranty law (discussed in chapter 41). This law and the Federal Trade Commission rules adopted to carry out its purposes prohibit the disclaimer of implied warranties where an express warranty is given.

7. Other Exclusions of Implied Warranties

The Code also provides for other circumstances in which implied warranties may be wholly or partially excluded. The seller may inform the buyer that the goods are being sold "as is" or "with all faults." Other language also may call the buyer's attention to the exclusion and make it plain that the sale involves no implied warranty [2-316(3)(a)]. The Code does not guarantee every buyer a good deal. Buyers who purchase items marked "as is" (or other similar language) may acquire defective products without any rights against the seller.

The buyer's examination of the goods or a sample or a model is also significant in determining the existence of implied warranties. If, before entering into the contract, the buyer has examined the goods, sample, or model as fully as he or she desired, there is no implied warranty on defects that an examination ought to have revealed [2-316(3)(b)]. If the seller demands that the buyer examine the goods fully, but the buyer refuses to do so, there is no implied warranty on those defects that a careful examination would have revealed. By making the demand, the seller is giving notice to the buyer that the buyer is assuming the risk with regard to defects an examination ought to reveal. However, the seller will not be protected if a demand has not been made and the buyer fails to examine the goods [2-316(3)(a)].

A course of dealing between the parties, course of performance, or usage of trade can also be the basis for exclusion or modification of implied warranties. These factors can be important in determining the nature and extent of implied warranties in any given transaction [2-316(3)(c)].

8. Remedies

As noted in section 5, the Code also allows the parties to limit the remedies available in the event of a breach of warranty [2-719]. The agreement may provide for remedies in addition to, or in restriction of, those provided by the Code. The parties may also limit or alter the measure of damages. These provisions usually limit a buyer's damages to the repayment of the price on return of the goods. Contracts often allow a seller to repair defective goods or replace nonconforming parts, without further liability. These provisions in effect eliminate a seller's liability for consequential damages and allow a seller to "cure" a defect or cancel a transaction by refunding the purchase price, without further liability.

Clauses limiting the liability of a seller are subject to the Code requirement on unconscionability [2-719]. Limitations of consequential damages for personal injury related to consumer goods are prima facie unconscionable. Limitations of damages for commercial loss are presumed to be valid.

OTHER ASPECTS OF WARRANTIES

9. Notice

The Code requires a buyer to give *notice* of any alleged breach of express or implied warranties [2-607(3)(a)]. This notice must be given within a reasonable time after the facts constituting the breach are discovered or should have been discovered using reasonable care. Failure to give the required notice bars all remedies. The giving of notice within a reasonable time to a seller is a condition precedent to filing a suit for damages for breach of express or implied warranties.

POLICIES.   There are three policies behind the notice requirement. First, notice is required for the seller to exercise its right to cure. The seller should be given the opportunity to make adjustments to or replacement of defective products. Notice allows sellers to minimize their losses and the buyer's damages. For example, the purchaser of a computer with a defective part should not be allowed to wait several months and then sue for loss of use of the computer.

The second policy behind the notice requirement is to provide the seller an opportunity to arm itself for negotiation and litigation. The seller needs an opportunity to examine the product promptly so it can defend itself against possible false allegations of breach of warranty. If a delay operates to deprive the seller of a reasonable opportunity to discover facts that might provide a defense or lessen its liability, the notice probably has not been given within a reasonable time.

The third policy with respect to requiring the buyer to give notice of an alleged breach of warranty is to provide some psychological protection for sellers. They need to believe that their risk will end after a reasonable amount of time. The notice requirement is somewhat similar to a statute of limitations. Sellers know that after a time they can stop worrying about potential liability.

FORM.   The notice may be oral or in writing. Written notice is much more preferable because it serves as its own proof. The notice need not be a claim for damages or a threat to file suit. All that is required is that the buyer notify the seller of the defect in the product. As a general rule, filing a lawsuit is not notice of breach of warranty, and lawsuits without prior notice are usually dismissed for failure to give the required notice. The notice of the breach of warranty requirement does not contemplate the buyer delivering a summons and complaint to the seller as notice. The Code provides no remedy for a breach of warranty until the buyer has given notice. Therefore, filing a suit cannot constitute notice. The following case illustrates that the notice of a breach of warranty must be given, but that the notice does not have to be in any specific form or format.

CASE

AGF v. Lakes Heat Treating Co.
555 N.E.2d 634 (Ohio 1990)

RESNICK, J.

. . . Norman R. Fisher, Jr. gained experience in the field of heat treating by working with his father, who owned a heat treating company. In 1979, Fisher developed a plan to establish his own business—Great Lakes Heat Treating Company, appellant herein. He entered into negotiations with a sales representative from appellee AGF for the purchase of an automated heat treating furnace capable of processing five hundred to five hundred twenty pounds of parts per hour. By letter dated August 3, 1979, Fisher accepted a proposal on behalf of Great Lakes, purchasing a "284 Shaker Hearth Furnace." The furnace was delivered on January 31, 1980. The furnace, however, could not be assembled due to improperly fitting parts. AGF was informed of the problem, and a technician was dispatched to Great Lakes. After additional complaints by Great Lakes and several adjustments, the furnace was finally assembled.

The furnace continued to fail to operate in spite of the assembly by AGF's technician. As the court of appeals succinctly stated, "[t]his failure of operation was only the beginning of a continuous failure of the furnace to operate and/or process 500 pounds of parts per hour. Numerous complaints were lodged by appellant-G.L. [Great Lakes] with regard to the improper operation of the furnace and appellee-A.G.F. attempted to rectify the operating problems on at least six occasions. At one point, appellant-G.L.'s furnace was closed down for a period of two weeks in order to completely rebuild the furnace. Even this attempt at repair, however, failed to allow the furnace to function as originally designed at the rate of 500 pounds of parts per hour."

The . . . issue we must decide is whether appellant provided adequate notice to appellee so as to preserve its claim for breach of an express warranty. . . .

Official Comment 4 to UCC 2-607 provides: "The content of the notification need merely be sufficient to let the seller know that the transaction is troublesome and must be watched. There is no reason to require that the notification which saves the buyer's rights under this section must include a clear statement of all the objections that will be relied on by the buyer, as under the section covering statements of defects upon rejection. Nor is there reason for requiring the notification to be a claim for damages or of any threatened litigation or other resort to a remedy. This notification which saves the buyer's rights under this Article need only be such as informs the seller that the transaction is claimed to involve a breach, and thus opens the way for normal settlement through negotiation.". . .

We believe that notice may be sufficient under the statute despite the fact that the notice does not specifically allege a breach of the contract. Moreover, in our view, the statute was not meant to exclude the possibility that notice may be inferred. . . . Therefore, no specific form or words are required in the notice of breach of contract. . . .

The record in this case clearly demonstrates that appellant was in constant and continual communication with appellee regarding the ability of the furnace to perform properly. Moreover, the record contains at least eight letters sent by appellant to appellee concerning the failure of the furnace to operate properly or to operate at all. The first in this series of correspondences is dated March 20, 1980, wherein Fisher set forth a detailed list of fifteen problems appellant was experiencing with the furnace. This letter was updated and followed by letters dated March 24, 25, 26, and 31, 1980. Each of these communications either delineated a new problem with the furnace or expressed concern over a continuing problem. There came a time when Fisher indicated that Great Lakes would reject the furnace, but was asked not to do so by the AGF salesman. The president of AGF, Frank Korzeb, flew from the corporate headquarters in New Jersey to Cleveland to inspect the furnace. As a result, the contract for sale was modified so that Great Lakes would be credited with $20,000 for the problems it was experiencing with the furnace, provided Great Lakes paid $100,000 on the account. This agreement was memorialized in a letter written by Fisher and dated April 2, 1980. The furnace still continued to experience problems. In a letter dated August 11, 1980, Fisher once again informed Korzeb that the furnace was not operating properly even after various repairs performed by appellee's technicians. Subsequent letters were sent by Fisher, all relaying the same basic message that the furnace was simply not functioning properly. As a result, appellant refused to remit payment of the balance due on the sale of the furnace, this refusal being the predicate for the instant action.

Although none of the above communications contained an express recitation that appellant considered the failure of the furnace to operate properly to be a breach of contract, we believe appellant has provided appellee with ample notice. . . . A buyer need not employ any magic words or a specific statement to preserve its claim for breach of an express warranty. Under the applicable standard in this state, we conclude that the letters and oral communications provided appellee with sufficient notice. . . .

■ *Judgment accordingly.*

CASE CONCEPTS REVIEW

1. When was the furnace delivered by AGF to Great Lakes?
2. How many specific examples of communication about the furnace can you account for between January 31 and August 11, 1980? Were there other communications after this latter date?
3. Were these communications (letters and conversations) sufficient notice to AGF that Great Lakes claimed a breach of warranty?

TIME.   The requirement that notice be given within a reasonable time is interpreted flexibly. The comments to the Code encourage courts not to close the door too quickly on "retail consumers" and especially those injured by defective products. The implication is that merchant-buyers are bound by a stricter notice requirement. A "reasonable time" for notification is to be judged by different standards so in cases involving consumers it will be extended. The rule of requiring notification is not designed to deprive a good-faith consumer of his or her remedy, especially a consumer who suffered personal injury. In such cases, the notice policies collide with a countervailing policy that unsophisticated consumers who suffer real and perhaps grievous injury at the hands of the defendant-seller ought to have an easy road to recovery. The rule of requiring notification is designed to defeat commercial bad faith, not to deprive a good-faith consumer of his or her remedy.

10. Third Parties

Privity of contract The contractual connection that arises from a buyer-seller relationship.

PRIVITY OF CONTRACT.   Historically, suits for breach of warranty required **privity of contract**, a contractual connection between the parties. Lack of privity of contract was a complete defense to a suit for breach of express warranty or for breach of the implied warranties. Two aspects of privity of contract requirements are sometimes described as horizontal and vertical. The *horizontal privity* issue is, To whom does the warranty extend? Does it run only in favor of the purchaser, or does it extend to others who may use or be affected by the product? The *vertical privity* issue is, Against whom can action be brought for breach of warranty? Can the party sue only the seller, or will direct action lie against wholesalers, manufacturers, producers, and growers?

When privity of contract is required, only the buyer can collect for breach of warranty, and then can collect only from the seller. A seller who is liable may recover from the person who sold to him or her. Thus the requirement of privity of contract not only prevented many suits for breach of warranty where privity did not exist but also encouraged multiple lawsuits over the same product.

ABANDONMENT OF PRIVITY.   It is not surprising that the law has generally abandoned strict privity of contract requirements. It has done so by statute and also case by case. The abandonment has occurred in cases involving express warranties, as well as in cases involving implied warranties. Both horizontal and vertical privity have generally been eliminated or significantly reduced.

The drafters of the Code prepared three alternative provisions that states could adopt on horizontal privity]2-318[. Alternative A has been adopted by thirty jurisdictions. It provides that a warranty extends to any person in the family or household of the buyer or a guest in the home if it is reasonable to expect that such a person may consume, or be affected by, the goods and is injured by them.

Alternative B has been adopted in eight jurisdictions, and alternative C is the law in four states. The remaining states have either omitted the section entirely or have drafted their own version on the extent of the warranties. Alternatives B and C extend warranties to any natural person who may be reasonably expected to use, consume, or be affected by the goods and who is injured by them.

These Code provisions on horizontal privity do not attempt to deal with the vertical privity issue. The Code is neutral on it and leaves the development of the law to the courts, case by case. The courts of most states have abandoned the vertical privity of contract requirement, and persons injured by products are allowed to sue all businesses in the chain of distribution without regard to the presence of privity of contract. Some states have retained vertical privity in suits seeking damages for economic loss even though they have abandoned it in suits for personal injuries. The following case discusses this distinction between economic loss and personal injury recoveries.

CASE

Barré v. Gulf Shores Turf Supply, Inc.
547 So.2d 503 (Ala. 1989)

KENNEDY, J.

. . . The issue we address on appeal is whether privity of contract existed between John Barré and Gulf Shores Turf Supply, Inc., so as to allow a cause of action for breach of an express warranty involving only economic injury.

John Barré began working with Jeff Thompson under a partnership arrangement in March 1986, doing business as "T & T Yard Care," an unincorporated enterprise. Gulf Shores Turf Supply, Inc., is a dealer for the Toro Company, selling Toro brand lawn care equipment. In November 1985, before Barré and Thompson became associated in the lawn care business, Thompson had purchased a used 62-inch Toro brand side discharge mower from Gulf Shores Turf in the name of "Jeff Thompson/

T & T Lawn [sic] Care." The mower was still under the manufacturer's one-year express warranty. Gulf Shores Turf also gave Thompson and T & T Yard Care an express written warranty covering repairs for an additional 400 hours of use.

In March 1986, Barré began operating the mower in the course of business for T & T Yard Care. Barré took the mower on several occasions to Gulf Shores Turf for repair under the warranty. The mower broke down repeatedly, and Barré continued to take it to Gulf Shores Turf for further repairs under the warranty.

In May 1986, Barré purchased Thompson's interest in T & T Yard Care. The written purchase agreement listed all the equipment owned by Thompson and T & T Yard Care, including the Toro mower. The agreement failed to specify any warranties covering the mower.

Barré continued to have trouble with the mower after he purchased it from Thompson. Bob Strenstron, a representative of Gulf Shores Turf, told Barré that the repairs would be made under the warranty. A short time later, the 400-hour warranty expired, and the mower continued to have mechanical problems. Barré did not return the mower for any further repairs.

In September 1986, Barré sued Gulf Shores Turf, Inc., and the Toro Company alleging negligent repair work, breach of the original express warranty and breach of the extended warranty. Barré claimed damages for loss of business and profits due to the repeated mechanical failures of the mower and Gulf Shores Turf's failure to repair the mower. The defendants moved for summary judgment, alleging no privity of contract with Barré. The trial court entered summary judgment in favor of both defendants. Barré appealed.

On appeal, Barré argues that recovery under the warranty should be allowed because he, as owner of T & T Yard Care, was in privity of contract with Gulf Shores Turf. He argues that privity was established by his purchase of T & T Yard Care from Thompson and by his conversations and contacts with Gulf Shores Turf.

The plaintiff must prove privity of contract in an action on an express warranty where no injuries to natural persons are involved.

The appellant alleges only economic injuries through the loss of business and profits due to the numerous mechanical failures of the mower purchased from Thompson/T & T Yard Care. Therefore, the burden is on the appellant to prove that privity of contract existed between him and Gulf Shores Turf before recovery is allowed under an express warranty.

The Court's review of the transaction involving the appellant and Thompson for the sale of T & T Yard Care, and the appellant's deposition testimony concerning the conversations and contacts with Gulf Shores Turf and its agents, fails to reveal a scintilla of evidence that a contractual relationship existed between the appellant and the appellee, Gulf Shores Turf.

The benefit of a warranty does not run with the chattel on its resale, so as to give the subpurchaser any right of action thereon as against the original seller. The appellant may not maintain an action on an express warranty, where no injuries to natural persons are involved, even though Gulf Shores Turf had given the express warranty to appellant's vendor, Thompson/T & T Yard Care. The express warranty on the mower given to Thompson/T & T Yard Care did not follow with the mower on its resale automatically. There is no evidence that Gulf Shores Turf, through its agents, even knew that Barré was the owner of the mower or that he was anything other than an employee of Thompson/T & T Yard Care on the occasions when he brought the mower in for repairs. There is no evidence that Gulf Shores Turf intended to extend the express warranties to him. Therefore, we find no basis for establishing privity of contract, and Barré's breach of warranty action must fail. The summary judgment was proper.

■ *The judgment is affirmed.*

CASE CONCEPTS REVIEW

1. What product is the subject matter of this litigation?
2. To whom did Gulf Shores Turf Supply, Inc. originally sell this product?
3. How did Barré come to possess this product?
4. Would the court's decision on requiring vertical privity have been different if Barré was seeking to recover for an injury to his foot, hand, or other body part? Why?

CHAPTER SUMMARY

TYPES OF WARRANTIES

Express Warranties

1. An express warranty is a statement of fact or promise that is made as a part of the contract for sale and becomes a part of the basis of the bargain between the buyer and the seller.
2. Most statements of opinion, such as those concerning the value of the goods, do not give rise to an express warranty.
3. Express warranties may be statements about the goods in sales material, or they may arise from a sale by sample or model.

Warranty of Title

1. A seller of goods makes a warranty that he or she has title to the goods and the right to sell them.
2. The warranty of title includes a warranty that there are no encumbrances and the buyer's use of the goods will be free from the claims of others.

Implied Warranty of Merchantability	1. A warranty that the goods shall be merchantable is implied in a contract for sale if the seller is a merchant who deals in goods of the kind involved in the contract.
	2. For goods to be merchantable, they must at least be the kind of goods that are fit for the ordinary purposes for which such goods are used.
	3. Liability for breach of the warranty of merchantability extends to direct economic loss, as well as to personal injuries and property damage.
Implied Warranty of Fitness for a Particular Purpose	1. An implied warranty of fitness for a particular purpose is created if, at the time of contracting, the seller has reason to know any particular purpose for which the buyer requires the goods and is relying on the seller's skill or judgment to select or furnish suitable goods.
	2. The buyer need not specifically state that he or she has a particular purpose in mind or is placing reliance on the seller's judgment if the circumstances are such that the seller has reason to realize the purpose intended or that the buyer is relying on the seller.
	3. Breach of the warranty of fitness for a particular purpose may result in disaffirmance of the contract. If the product causes an injury including economic loss, it may also result in a suit for dollar damages.

LIMITATIONS

Express Warranties	1. If there is an express warranty and an attempt to limit warranties, both will be given effect if possible.
	2. If not, the express warranty will prevail, and the attempt to negate it will not be given effect.
Written Disclaimers of Implied Warranties	1. To exclude or modify the implied warranty of merchantability, the word *merchantability* must be used. If the disclaimer is included in a written contract, it must be set forth in a conspicuous manner.
	2. To exclude or modify any implied warranty of fitness for a particular purpose, the exclusion must be conspicuously written.
	3. Disclaimers of warranties are subject to the Magnuson-Moss warranty law.
Other Exclusions of Implied Warranties	1. The Code also provides for other circumstances in which implied warranties may be wholly or partially excluded. The seller may inform the buyer that the goods are being sold "as is," "with all faults." Other language may call the buyer's attention to the exclusion and make it plain that the sale involves no implied warranty.
	2. If, before entering into the contract, the buyer has examined the goods, sample, or model, there is no implied warranty on defects that an examination ought to have revealed to him or her.
Remedies	1. Parties may agree to limit or alter the measure of damages.
	2. Clauses limiting a seller's damages are subject to the Code rule on unconscionability.
	3. Limiting consequential damages for personal injury is prima facie unconscionable.

OTHER ASPECTS OF WARRANTIES

Notice	1. A buyer must give notice of any breach of warranty within a reasonable time.
	2. Failure to give notice prevents a suit for breach of warranty.
	3. Filing suit is not notice.
Third Parties	1. The horizontal privity issue is, To whom does the warranty extend? In most states, it extends to any person in the family or household of the buyer or a guest in the home if it is reasonable to expect that such person may consume, or be affected by, the goods and is injured by them.

2. The vertical privity issue is, Against whom can action be brought for breach of warranty? The Code leaves the development of the law to the courts, case by case. The courts of most states have abandoned the vertical privity of contract requirement, and persons injured by products are allowed to sue all businesses in the chain of distribution without regard to the presence of privity of contract.

REVIEW QUESTIONS AND PROBLEMS

1. Identify the terms in column A by matching each with the appropriate statement in column B.

A	**B**
(1) Express warranty	(a) Made only by a merchant
(2) Warranty of merchantability	(b) Arises because of special skill of the seller
(3) Fungible goods	(c) To whom does the warranty extend?
(4) Warranty of fitness for a particular purpose	(d) A guarantee
(5) Horizontal privity	(e) A condition precedent to a suit for breach of warranty
(6) Vertical privity	(f) Sold by weight or measure
(7) Notice	(g) Against whom can suit be brought

2. A seller makes the following statements about goods to the buyer. Which are puffery and which are express warranties?
  a. The jukebox is a good machine and will probably not get out of order.
  b. October is not too late to plant this grass seed.
  c. This car is supposed to last a lifetime. It's in perfect condition.
  d. This dredge pipe has expandable ends that will seal upon the spill going through.
  e. This feed additive will increase your milk production and will not harm your dairy herd.
  f. These filter tanks should be able to remove iron and manganese from the water.
  g. This used car has never been wrecked.

3. Plaintiff sued the manufacturer of a backyard driving range for personal injuries. Plaintiff was hit on the head by a golf ball following a practice swing with the golf-training device. The label on the shipping carton stated in bold type, "COMPLETELY SAFE—BALL WILL NOT HIT PLAYER." What theory did plaintiff use in this case? Explain.

4. A truck salesman told the buyer that the truck would be just right for plowing snow. In fact, the truck was incapable of pushing a snowplow. The buyer sued for breach of express warranty. Is there an express warranty? Explain.

5. Sumner, an Anchorage aircraft dealer, sold a Piper Navajo airplaine to Fel-Air, Inc., for $105,000. The title to the airplane was actually in Century Aircraft, Inc., which had leased it to Sumner with an option to purchase. Fel-Air sued Sumner for breach of the warranty of title. Sumner denied liability on the ground that Fel-Air as a good-faith purchaser for value received good title. Is Sumner liable? Why or why not?

6. In which of the following circumstances was the implied warranty of merchantability breached?
  a. In defendant's restaurant, plaintiff bought a martini with an unpitted olive. Plaintiff broke a tooth when he attempted to eat the olive.
  b. Plaintiff is bitten by a spider concealed in a pair of blue jeans sold by defendant's store.
  c. Seller sold cattle feed that contained the female hormone stilbestrol. It causes cattle to grow more rapidly than normal but also causes abortion in pregnant cows and

sterility in bulls. The plaintiff farmer raises cattle for breeding rather than for slaughter, so he sues. The label on the cattle feed package did not mention that it contained stilbestrol.

d. Plaintiff bought and used a power lawn mower. While the plaintiff was mowing, an unknown object was hurled out of the grass chute and penetrated the eye of plaintiff's five-year-old son.

e. Plaintiff's Ford Pinto's gas tank exploded on impact.

f. Plaintiff bought a cookbook from defendant retail book dealer. Four days later, while following a recipe in the book, plaintiff ate a small slice of one of the ingredients, a plant commonly known as elephant's ear, and became violently ill. Plaintiff sued for breach of the implied warranty of merchantability.

g. Plaintiff bought a product that caused her to have an allergic reaction.

7. Stewart, a practicing dentist, sold his 42-foot Trojan yacht to Smith for $52,000. Three days after delivery of the boat, Smith notified Stewart that one of the boat's fuel tanks was leaking and requested that the condition be remedied at Stewart's expense. When Stewart refused, Smith sued Stewart for breach of the warranty of merchantability. Should Smith recover? Explain.

8. Plaintiff, a hauler of scrap automobile bodies, bought a used truck from defendant. Defendant leases trucks but does not drive them. He operates a well-drilling business and does not have any particular expertise concerning diesel trucks. The engine blew up after the truck had been used for a short time, and plaintiff sued for breach of the warranty of fitness for a particular purpose. Should plaintiff recover? Explain.

9. Pat, the buyer of a tractor and backhoe, sued the seller for breach of the implied warranty of merchantability. The sales contract contained the following:

The equipment covered hereby is sold subject only to the applicable manufacturer's standard printed warranty, and no other warranties, express or implied, including the implied warranty of merchantability, shall apply.

The type size of the foregoing was slightly larger than the rest of the contract, but it was not boldface. Was the disclaimer effective to negate the implied warranty? Explain.

10. The purchase agreement for a mobile home stated **Standard Manufacturer Warranty**—OTHERWISE SOLD AS IS. The buyer subsequently discovered defects and sued for breach of the implied warranty of merchantability. He contended that the disclaimer was ineffective because it did not contain the word *merchantability* and was not conspicuous. Was the buyer correct? Why or why not?

11. Plaintiff sued the manufacturer for breach of implied warranty allegedly resulting from the use and application of a herbicide. The plaintiff did not purchase the herbicide or take possession of it. He did not see the package container of the product. He merely had defendant's distributor apply it to his farmland. The container had a disclaimer of warranty printed in bold letters on its side. The herbicide severely damaged plaintiff's corn crop. Is the disclaimer of warranty effective? Why?

12. Pam purchased a contaminated cheeseburger from a vending machine where she worked. She suffered acute food poisoning and sued the baking company that baked the bun for breach of the warranty of merchantability. The baking company moved to dismiss for lack of privity of contract. Is lack of privity of contract a defense? Explain.

13. Crew members of a fishing vessel sued manufacturers for losses allegedly caused by manufacturers' constructing and selling a vessel with a defective rudder and component parts. As a result of these defects, the vessel was placed in dry dock and the crew members were laid off. They sued for breach of express warranty. The seller moved to dismiss for lack of privity of contract. Do the crew members have a basis from which to recover their losses? Why?

PRODUCTS LIABILITY

CHAPTER PREVIEW

Products liability is a legal term that describes the liability of sellers and manufacturers of goods. One of the consequences of manufacturing or selling a product is responsibility to a consumer or user if the product is defective and causes injury to a person or to property. Injuries to property include damage to the product itself, economic losses due to the inadequate performance of the product, and injuries to the property of others.

The subject of products liability involves several legal theories. A suit for dollar damages for injuries caused by a product may be predicated on the theory of negligence; misrepresentation; breach of warranty, either express or implied; or strict liability. The legal principles relating to breach of warranty are discussed in chapter 20. Keep in mind that discussion as a major portion of the law on products liability. The other theories and the reasons for products liability are discussed in this chapter.

You are the manager responsible for the design of a proposed toy gun. To achieve a sense of realism, your design engineers envision this gun being able to fire plastic "bullets" the approximate size of real bullets.

Do you have any concerns about this proposed design?

GENERAL CONCEPTS

1. Basic Principles

The basic principle of products liability is that a manufacturer, distributor, or seller of a product is liable to compensate a person injured by a defective product. The mere occurrence of an injury due to a product does not automatically impose liability. A manufacturer or seller is not an insurer of the safety of persons using products. Manufacturers and sellers do not guarantee the safety of the consumer of their product. Products liability is not absolute liability. It is present only if there has been a violation of a legal duty to the consumer or user, and that duty is to keep a defective product out of the stream of commerce.

Products liability cases may arise out of defective design of products, defective manufacture, or the defective marketing of products. Suit may be brought against manufacturers of component parts, raw materials suppliers, anyone who provides supportive services (such as certifying, applying, or installing a product), wholesalers, and jobbers. They may be brought by the buyer, by another user of the product, or by some third party whose only connection with the product is an injury caused by it.

In most products liability cases, the injured party sues all those in the channel of distribution, including the manufacturer, the wholesaler, the distributor, and the retailer. In cases involving multiple defendants, the burden of tracing fault is on the defendant dealers and manufacturer, so a plaintiff may be compensated while leaving it to the defendants to settle the question of responsibility among themselves. Anyone who had a hand in putting the defective product in the stream of commerce, whether technically innocent or not, may have liability to the injured party.

The trend of the law on products liability is clearly in the direction of expanding liability. A manufacturer has an obligation to the public to market a safe product, free from defects. A producer is presumed to know of defects in its products and is therefore in bad faith in selling defective products. Moreover, there is a growing philosophy that the losses caused by products must be shared by business. This shift of responsibility is premised on the notion that manufacturers and sellers best understand their products and are better able to spread the loss as a cost of production and sale. When loss is written into the cost of the product, it is shared by all buyers and users of the product. The philosophy of *shared loss*—together with the increased complexity of many products and the increased chance of errors in design, manufacturing, and marketing—has dramatically enlarged the number of products liability cases in the last two decades.

The potential liability is usually covered by products liability insurance. In recent years, the cost of this insurance has skyrocketed, and it has become a significant cost item in many products with a high exposure to products liability suits. To understand products liability law and to predict its future, we turn first to its historical development.

2. History of Products Liability

Although it cannot be precisely stated when products liability law began, it seems to have evolved through these five stages:

1. Trespass (strict tort liability)
2. Negligence (tort liability)
3. Privity (*caveat emptor*)
4. Warranty (contract liability)
5. Strict liability in tort [Restatement Section 402A]

As you can see, the law has come full circle from its origins in strict liability, since it is now based on strict liability for defective products that cause harm.

TRESPASS.   Prior to 1800, there were few manufactured products and little commerce. Times were simple, and the law reflected the values of small, interdependent communities. Injuries to persons or property were compensated by law through the tort doctrine of trespass. The trespass doctrine imposed strict liability; that is, the fact that the defendant was not at fault was irrelevant.

NEGLIGENCE.   In the 1800s, small village life underwent dramatic changes. Population mushroomed, social and economic life grew complex, and the Industrial Revolution was born. As society's values changed, so did the law. Apparently premised on the notion that infant industries needed protection from widespread liability, the law replaced strict liability in trespass with negligence law. Product manufacturers were liable only if they failed to use "reasonable care" in the manufacture and sale of their products. But eliminating strict liability in tort apparently was not enough protection for these industries. The potential for products liability at that time was great, owing to the numerous sweatshops, factories with unguarded machinery tended by little children, and food products unregulated by government. Privity was born in 1842 to limit further products liability actions.

Privity The connection or relationship between a buyer and seller involved in contractual agreement.

PRIVITY.   In 1842, the English court in *Winterbottom* v. *Wright* imposed the **privity** barrier, lest the courts be faced with "an infinity of actions." The English court held that the injured driver of a defective mail coach could not maintain an action against the supplier of the coach, because no *privity of contract* existed between the driver and the supplier. Nineteenth-century American courts, with a similar reluctance to inhibit the free scope of industrial enterprise, generally followed the privity doctrine of *Winterbottom*.

The privity requirement limits the negligence action, since sellers owe the "reasonable-person" duty only to parties with whom they had actually dealt, that is, to parties with whom they had contracted. If an injured person was not the buyer of the product or had bought the product from a retailer, then the manufacturer was not liable, since no privity of contract would exist. Moreover, the retailer who was in privity could be liable only for negligence. However, the defective product was seldom the fault of the retailer who had not designed, manufactured, labeled, or packaged the product. Thus the privity rule in most cases puts the risk of harm on the injured party. The period was characterized by the rule of *caveat emptor,* "Let the buyer beware."

DEMISE OF PRIVITY.   With the advent of the twentieth century, infant industries matured, the United States became more prosperous, and the number and complexity of products expanded. The policy of protecting industry more than society became inapplicable, and the barrier of privity was soon dismantled first in tort, then in contract. The death knell of the privity doctrine in tort was sounded in the famous 1916 case of *MacPherson* v. *Buick Motor Company.* MacPherson was driving a Buick automobile when a wooden wheel collapsed, injuring him. (Note the factual similarity to *Winterbottom.*) The defendant was the manufacturer who had sold the car to the retailer who sold the car to MacPherson. In the nineteenth century, American courts had recognized exceptions to the privity rule when products—such as drugs, foods, guns, and explosives—were "inherently" or "imminently" dangerous to life or health. The New York court in *MacPherson* found that the category of inherently dangerous products "is not limited to poisons, explosives, and things which in their normal operation are implements of destruction." Rather, it held that if "the nature of a thing is such that it is reasonably certain to place life and limb in peril when negligently made, it is then a thing of danger." The privity doctrine of *Winterbottom* was effectively overruled when the court stated, "If to the element of danger there is added knowledge that the thing will be used by persons other than the purchaser, and used without new tests, then, irrespective of contract, the manufacturer of this thing of danger is under a duty to make it carefully." *MacPherson* has been universally followed.

WARRANTY.   The demise of privity in contract law was not so easily accomplished, because the claim in contract was based on a theory of breach of warranty. The problem was that since the warranty theory seemed to be more in the nature of a contract right, only parties to the contract could supposedly enforce contract rights. But over time, courts were forced to adapt legal doctrine to the realities of modern marketing. The breakthrough came in the famous 1960 case of *Henningsen* v. *Bloomfield Motors, Inc.,* which is factually similar to *Winterbottom* and *MacPherson.* Mrs. Henningsen was injured when the new family car (a 1955 Plymouth ten days old with 488 odometer miles) uncontrollably left the road owing to a defective steering wheel. The New Jersey Supreme Court said, "Where the commodities sold are such that if defectively manufactured they will be dangerous to life or limb, then society's interests can only be protected by eliminating the requirement of privity between the maker and his dealers and the reasonably expected ultimate consumer." In *Henningsen,* the injured plaintiff was not the buyer of the car and therefore was not "in the distributive chain." In addition to eliminating the necessity of establishing privity between the buyer and seller, the court also held that Mrs. Henningsen, whose husband had bought the car, could maintain an action against the remote manufacturer.

The significance of the *Henningsen* principle is recognized in the Uniform Commercial Code. As noted in chapter 20, the UCC extends the seller's warranties to parties who are not buyers of the products. But procedural problems with warranty liability, like notice of breach, caused many plaintiffs to be denied recovery. Thus one final dismantling stage remained before the law of products liability came full circle to strict tort liability.

STRICT LIABILITY IN TORT.　　The year 1963 is generally regarded as the decisive date in the evolution of products liability law. Prior to that date, actions for injuries caused by defective products were based on negligence or breach of warranty. In 1963, the California Supreme Court, in the following case, adopted a theory of strict liability in tort.

CASE

Greenman v. Yuba Power Products, Inc.
377 P.2d 897 (Cal. 1963)

TRAYNOR, J.

. . . Plaintiff brought this action for damages against the retailer and the manufacturer of a Shopsmith, a combination power tool that could be used as a saw, drill, and wood lathe. He saw a Shopsmith demonstrated by the retailer and studied a brochure prepared by the manufacturer. He decided he wanted a Shopsmith for his home workshop, and his wife bought and gave him one for Christmas in 1955. In 1957 he bought the necessary attachments to use the Shopsmith as a lathe for turning a large piece of wood he wished to make into a chalice. After he had worked on the piece of wood several times without difficulty, it suddenly flew out of the machine and struck him on the forehead, inflicting serious injuries. About ten and a half months later, he gave the retailer and the manufacturer written notice of claimed breaches of warranties and filed a complaint against them alleging such breaches and negligence.

After a trial before a jury, the court ruled that there was no evidence that the retailer was negligent or had breached any express warranty and that the manufacturer was not liable for the breach of any implied warranty. Accordingly, it submitted to the jury only the cause of action alleging breach of implied warranties against the retailer and the causes of action alleging negligence and breach of express warranties against the manufacturer. The jury returned a verdict for the retailer against plaintiff and for plaintiff against the manufacturer in the amount of $65,000. The manufacturer and plaintiff appeal. Plaintiff seeks a reversal of the part of the judgment in favor of the retailer, however, only in the event that the part of the judgment against the manufacturer is reversed.

Plaintiff introduced substantial evidence that his injuries were caused by defective design and construction of the Shopsmith. His expert witnesses testified that inade-quate set screws were used to hold parts of the machine together so that normal vibration caused the tailstock to the lathe to move away from the piece of wood being turned permitting it to fly out of the lathe. They also testified that there were other more positive ways of fastening the parts of the machine together, the use of which would have prevented the accident. The jury could therefore reasonably have concluded that the manufacturer negligently constructed the Shopsmith. The jury could also reasonably have concluded that statements in the manufacturer's brochure were untrue, that they constituted express warranties, and that the plaintiff's injuries were caused by their breach.

The manufacturer contends, however, that plaintiff did not give it notice of breach of warranty within a reasonable time and that therefore his cause of action for breach of warranty is barred by section 1769 of the Civil Code. Since it cannot be determined whether the verdict against it was based on the negligence or warranty cause of action or both, the manufacturer concludes that the error in presenting the warranty cause of action to the jury was prejudicial.

Section 1769 of the Civil Code provides: "In the absence of express or implied agreement of the parties, acceptance of the goods by the buyer shall not discharge the seller from liability in damages or other legal remedy for breach of any promise or warranty in the contract to sell or the sale. But, if, after acceptance of the goods, the buyer fails to give notice to the seller of the breach of any promise or warranty within a reasonable time after the buyer knows, or ought to know of such breach, the seller shall not be liable therefor."

Like other provisions of the uniform sales act, section 1769 deals with the rights of the parties to a contract of sale or a sale. It does not provide that notice must be given of the breach of a warranty that arises independently of a contract of sale between the parties. Such warranties are not imposed by the sales act, but are the product of common-law decisions that have recognized them in a variety of situations.

The notice requirement of section 1769, however, is not an appropriate one for the court to adopt in actions by injured consumers against manufacturers with whom they have not dealt. "As between the immediate parties to the sale [the notice requirement] is a sound commercial rule, designed to protect the seller against unduly delayed claims for damages. As applied to personal injuries, and notice to a remote seller, it becomes a boobytrap for the unwary. The injured consumer is seldom 'steeped in the business practice which justifies the rule,' and at least until he has had legal advice it will not occur to him to give notice to one with whom he has had no dealings." We conclude, therefore, that even if plaintiff did not give timely notice of breach of warranty to the manufacturer, his cause of action based on the representations contained in the brochure was not barred.

Moreover, to impose strict liability on the manufacturer under the circumstances of this case, it was not necessary for plaintiff to establish an express warranty as defined in Section 1732 of the Civil Code. A manufacturer is strictly liable in tort when an article he places on the market knowing that it is to be used without inspection for defects, proves to have a defect that causes injury to a human being. Recognized first in the case of unwholesome food products, such liability has now been extended to a variety of other products that create as great or greater hazards if defective.

Although in these cases strict liability has usually been based on the theory of an express or implied warranty running from the manufacturer to the plaintiff, the abandonment of the requirement of a contract between them, the recognition that the liability is not assumed by agreement but imposed by law . . . and the refusal to permit the manufacturer to define the scope of its own responsibility for defective products . . . make clear that the liability is not one governed by the law of contract warranties but by the law of strict liability in tort. Accordingly, rules defining and governing warranties that were developed to meet the needs of commercial transactions cannot properly be invoked to govern the manufacturer's liability to those injured by their defective products unless those rules also serve the purposes for which such liability is imposed.

The purpose of strict liability is to insure that the costs of injuries resulting from defective products are borne by the manufacturers that put such products on the market rather than by the injured persons who are powerless to protect themselves. Sales warranties serve this purpose fitfully at best. In the present case, for example, plaintiff was able to plead and prove an express warranty only because he read and relied on the representations of the Shopsmith's ruggedness contained in the manufacturer's brochure. Implicit in the machine's presence on the market, however, was a representation that it would safely do the jobs for which it was built. Under these circumstances, it should not be controlling whether plaintiff selected the machine because of the statement in the brochure, or because of the machine's own appearance of excellence that belied the defect lurking beneath the surface, or because he merely assumed that it would safely do the jobs it was built to do. It should not be controlling whether the details of the sales from manufacturer to retailer and from retailer to plaintiff's wife were such that one or more of the implied warranties of the sales act arose. "The remedies of injured consumers ought not to be made to depend upon the intricacies of the law of sales." To establish the manufacturer's liability it was sufficient that plaintiff proved that he was injured while using the Shopsmith in a way it was intended to be used as a result of a defect in design and manufacture of which plaintiff was not aware that made the Shopsmith unsafe for its intended use.

■ *Judgment affirmed.*

CASE CONCEPTS REVIEW

1. Using the legal theories on which Mr. Greenman filed this suit, what were the trial judge's rulings with respect to the retailer and the manufacturer?
2. What aspect of the Shopsmith's design caused the injury suffered by Mr. Greenman?
3. Why does this court reject the manufacturer's defense that Mr. Greenman failed to give it notice of the breach of warranty?
4. What is the impact of the court's holding that the manufacturer's liability is based on strict liability in tort instead of the breach of contractual warranties?

As a result of the *Greenman* case, tort law is now evolving with a theory of strict liability steadfastly independent of warranty. In 1965, Section 402A of the Restatement (Second) of Torts was promulgated. Section 402A, adopted by the majority of American courts, follows the strict tort liability theory of *Greenman*. This theory is covered in detail later in this chapter.

3. Theories of Liability

As noted, both tort and contract theories are used in products liability cases. A defendant may be held liable under the contract theories of breach of express or implied warranty. The implied warranty may be either the implied warranty of merchantability or the implied warranty of fitness for a particular purpose. Most cases involve the warranty of merchantability. As noted in chapter 20, an action can be maintained for breach of both express and implied warranty without privity of contract in most cases. An action based on such breach, being a contract action, does not require proof of negligence on the part of manufacturer or seller. A defendant in a products liability case may be found to have breached its warranty of merchantability without having been negligent.

As Table 21-1 explains, products liability cases may be based on conduct of the defendant, quality of the product, or performance of the product against the seller's promises or express representations. These may apply to both contract and tort actions.

A plaintiff, in bringing a products liability lawsuit, does not have to choose between these tort and contract theories, since all the theories may be joined into one lawsuit. Nonetheless, most plaintiffs prefer strict tort liability because it is usually the simplest remedy, as is explained later. At trial, a plaintiff may be forced to choose which theories are to be submitted to the jury. Damages incurred are sometimes not recoverable under strict liability, owing to either their nature or the running of the tort statute of limitations. The statute of limitations for tort actions is generally a much shorter time period than it is for contract actions. However, the rights afforded by express and implied warranties may be more difficult to assert because of the contractual rules of notice of breach and disclaimers of warranties. Thus all theories are important, and each has advantages and disadvantages in comparison with the others.

4. Negligence

Contributory negligence
In a negligence suit, failure of the plaintiff to use reasonable care.

Negligence is a tort theory used in products liability cases. To recover on a negligence theory, a plaintiff has to establish the failure of the defendant to exercise reasonable care. **Contributory negligence** on the part of the plaintiff in some states is

TABLE 21-1 ■ Theories of Products Liability

	Defendant's Conduct	Quality of Product	Seller's Representations
Tort	Negligence	Strict liability for product defects (402A Restatement of Torts)	Strict liability for misrepresentations (402B Restatement of Torts)
Contract	None	Implied warranty of merchantability (UCC 2-314) and fitness (UCC 2-315)	Express warranty (UCC 2-313)

Comparative negligence Under this doctrine, a plaintiff's negligence is compared to that of a defendant. The plaintiff's right to recover against the defendant is reduced by the percentage of the plaintiff's negligence.

a bar to recovery. In others, which follow **comparative negligence,** it will reduce the amount of recovery by the percentage of the plaintiff's fault.

The mere fact that an injury occurs from the consumption or use of a product does not ordinarily raise a presumption that the manufacturer was negligent. Negligence actions question the reasonableness of the defendant's conduct since all human activity involves an element of risk. The defendant's conduct is deemed negligent only when it is inferior to what a "reasonable" person would have done under similar circumstances. Negligence involves conduct that falls below the standard set by law for the protection of others against the unreasonably great risk of harm.

In a negligence action, privity of contract is not required, since it is not a contract action. A negligence suit can be brought not only by the person who purchased the defective product but also by any person who suffered an injury on account of a defect in the product if the defect was the proximate cause of the injury.

The Restatement of Torts (Second), Section 395, states the rules as follows:

> A manufacturer who fails to exercise reasonable care in the manufacture of a chattel which, unless carefully made, he should recognize as involving an unreasonable risk of causing physical harm to those who use it for a purpose for which the manufacturer should expect it to be used and to those whom he should expect to be endangered by its probable use, is subject to liability for physical harm caused to them by its lawful use in a manner and for a purpose for which it is supplied.

RES IPSA LOQUITUR.   The plaintiff, of course, must by appropriate evidence prove that the manufacturer was negligent—failed to exercise reasonable care. The plaintiff may be able to rely on the doctrine of *res ipsa loquitur,* "the thing speaks for itself," if (1) the instrumentality involved was within the exclusive control of the defendant at the time of the act of negligence, both as to operation and inspection; (2) the injury was not the result of any voluntary action or contribution on the part of the plaintiff; and (3) the accident ordinarily would not have occurred had the defendant used due care. If an elevator falls, killing an occupant, the manufacturer has liability, because the very happening of the accident creates a presumption of negligence.

NEGLIGENCE PER SE.   Another method of establishing negligence is to prove that the manufacturer violated some statutory regulation in the production and distribution of its product. Some industries are subject to regulation under state or federal laws on product quality, testing, advertising, and other aspects of production and distribution. Proof of a violation of a statute may be sufficient to establish negligence of a manufacturer in such industries. Negligence established by proof of violation of a statute is called *negligence per se.*

FAILURE TO WARN.   Negligence is frequently based on failure of a manufacturer to warn of a known danger related to the product. A manufacturer who knows, or should know, its product to be dangerous has a duty to exercise reasonable care and foresight in preventing it from injuring or endangering people. Reasonable care includes the duty to warn of the danger, as the following case discusses.

CASE

Woods v. Pier 51, Inc.
765 P.2d 770 (Okla. 1988)

LAVENDER, J.

Appellant Leonard Woods was employed by a transport company which delivered gasoline from refineries to retailers. Woods owned his own truck but was supplied with the tanker trailer by his employer. On the date in question in this case Woods was supplied with a tanker trailer which had been manufactured by . . . Fruehauf Trailer Corporation. This tanker trailer had been built specifically for the purpose of transporting materials such as gasoline. Woods' employer had added piping, valves and hoses so that the tanker trailer could be unloaded by gravity into underground storage tanks or could be unloaded by use of a pump into storage facilities above ground. Woods had a pump located on his truck for use in pumping the gasoline into above ground facilities.

On the date in question Woods was ordered to pick up a load of gasoline at a refinery for delivery to appellee Pier 51, Inc. Woods received a load of 8,504 gallons of gasoline at the refinery and hauled the load to Pier 51's facility on Lake Keystone near Tulsa. The gasoline storage facilities belonging to Pier 51 were above ground. The facilities consisted of three tanks, two with a capacity of four thousand gallons and one with a three thousand gallon capacity. All three tanks were interconnected at ground level by a one inch line equipped with gate valves so that the small tank could be used as a reserve and gasoline could be transferred from it to the others as their levels were pumped down. The tanks were cylindrical and placed on their sides with an upspout for loading located at the top and near the front of the tanks. The only method provided for reaching the loading ports was a fifty-five gallon barrel. The tanks were set on a bed of gravel.

When Woods arrived at the Pier 51 facilities he drove his truck and tanker rig to the tanks and positioned the equipment to unload the gasoline via the truck mounted pump into the tanks. Woods was told, however, that the man with the keys to unlock the caps on the tank upspouts was not yet at work. Woods waited for this individual to arrive. During this period of time Woods requested gauge charts for the tanks. These charts gave gallonage figures for incremental levels of gasoline in the tanks. Woods was told that these charts were in the possession of the bookkeeper and no further effort was made to provide these charts to him. When the keys to the locks on the tanks were provided to him Woods proceeded to unload the gasoline into the tanks. Since the tanks were not equipped with any method to determine level except

by manually placing a stick down into the tank and measuring in inches, Woods placed the discharge hose fitted with an aluminum down spout into the upspout of a tank and proceeded to pump gasoline into the tank until he could see gasoline begin to come out of the top of the upspout. At that point Woods would cut the engine on his truck which in turn cut the power take-off driven pump. Woods would then close the valve on his truck, and using the fifty-five gallon barrel would climb up to remove the hose and transfer it to the next tank. The small tank filled up faster than expected and more gasoline overflowed. Woods cut the engine and proceeded to remove the hose from the small tank. As he was doing so gasoline on the ground underneath him ignited and Woods was severely burned in the ensuing fire.

Woods . . . brought the present action against Pier 51, Inc. . . . under negligence theory on the allegation that Pier 51 was negligent in failing to provide Woods with a way to measure the tank levels and in failing to inform him of problems such as the tank interconnections and in failing to provide reasonably safe facilities. . . .

The matter was tried to a jury. . . . The jury . . . found Pier 51 liable but calculated that Woods' contributory negligence in the matter was thirty percent. The jury found Woods' damages as against Pier 51 to be six million dollars and further awarded four hundred thousand dollars in punitive damages. . . .

The trial court subsequently . . . granted . . . Pier 51 . . . a new trial. . . .

Woods has appealed arguing that the trial court's grant of new trial was erroneous. . . .

In order to support an actionable claim under negligence theory it is necessary for a plaintiff to establish the concurrent existence of: 1) a duty on the part of the defendant to protect the plaintiff from injury; 2) the failure of the defendant to perform that duty; and 3) injury to the plaintiff resulting from such failure. Appellee Pier 51, Inc., here argues . . . that Woods' evidence failed to establish that Pier 51 breached any duty owed to Woods. The argument here is premised on the assertion that the dangers associated with the premises were open and obvious and that there is no duty to protect a business invitee from such dangers. While the legal premise here is correct, the application to the facts is not appropriate.

In the present case Woods' evidence clearly established that the lines connecting the storage tanks together at ground level were not obvious. Further, from Woods' testimony that the third tank overflowed at a much earlier time than he had anticipated, it is possible to infer that in filling the two larger tanks gasoline had been fed down to the third tank. It is further permissible to infer that the overflow of gasoline from the third tank provided the major source for the fire which injured Woods.

Regardless of the evidence establishing Pier 51's failure to supply Woods with tank charts and its failure to supply a safe method for access to the tanks, the evidence regarding the failure to warn Woods of the tank interconnections or to insure that those interconnections were closed before Woods began filling those tanks is sufficient to support the jury verdict for Woods in negligence theory.

We next turn to the question raised by appellant Woods as to whether the trial court properly granted the motion for new trial as to Pier 51, Inc. On this point Woods states that the trial court erred as a matter of law in granting the new trial. We agree. . . .

■ *Reversed.*

CASE CONCEPTS REVIEW

1. What specific incident caused Woods' injuries?
2. What three elements must a plaintiff prove to succeed in a negligence-based cause of action?
3. This court finds one aspect of Pier 51's actions (or lack thereof) to be sufficient to find a breach of its duty to protect Woods from injury. What is that one aspect?

NEGLIGENT DESIGN.   Negligence also may be based on a design defect. In determining whether a manufacturer exercised reasonable skill and knowledge concerning the design of its product, factors include the cost of safety devices, their use by competitors, their effect or function, and the extent to which the manufacturer conducted tests and kept abreast of scientific development. A manufacturer is not an insurer, nor is it required to supply accident proof merchandise; nonetheless, the responsibilities for injuries often rest with whoever is in the best position to eliminate the danger inherent in the use of the product. For example, a manufacturer of a rotary power lawn mower may be liable for negligent design if a user is able to put his or her hands or feet in contact with the moving blades of the mower.

5. Misrepresentation

Misrepresentation
A misstatement of a material fact about a product on which a purchaser or user relies and thereby suffers an injury.

Another tort theory used in product liability cases is known as **misrepresentation.** If the seller has advertised the product through newspapers, magazines, television, or otherwise and has made misrepresentations with regard to the character or quality of the product, tort liability for personal injury may be imposed on him or her. The Restatement of Torts (Second), Section 402B, summarizes the liability of a seller for personal injuries resulting from misrepresentation:

> One engaged in the business of selling chattels who, by advertising, labels, or otherwise, makes to the public a misrepresentation of a material fact concerning the character or quality of a chattel sold by him is subject to liability for physical harm to a consumer of the chattel caused by justifiable reliance upon the misrepresentation, even though
>> (a) it is not made fraudulently or negligently, and
>> (b) the consumer has not bought the chattel from or entered into any contractual relation with the seller.

The rationale of the Restatement position is that a great deal of what the consumer knows about a product comes to him or her through the various media, and sellers should be held responsible for injuries caused by misrepresentations made to the public.

In our complex society where sellers offer apparently similar but in reality fundamentally different products, the rationale behind the rule is most persuasive. A manufacturing seller knows the capabilities of its products, for it is the one who has designed and tested them. The consumer, on the other hand, knows only the information he or she has been able to glean from the seller's marketing material. Logic dictates, then, that the seller should bear the responsibility for misrepresentation because of superior knowledge.

Liability under Section 402B does not depend on the factors giving rise to the misrepresentation, nor does it require contractual privity. It is a rule of strict liability, which, even in the absence of bad faith or negligence, makes sellers liable if a consumer of their product suffers physical harm as a result of justifiable reliance on the seller's misrepresentation.

STRICT LIABILITY

6. Theory

The latest development in products liability is the tort theory known as *strict liability*. This development imposes liability wherever damage or injury is caused by a defective product that is unreasonably dangerous to the user or consumer. It is the logical result of the elimination of the need to prove negligence and of the demise of the privity requirement in breach-of-warranty actions. The strict tort liability action is often preferable to the warranty action because disclaimers of warranty and notice of breach are not problems. As a result of the strict liability theory, the theories of negligence and breach of warranty are becoming less significant in personal injury cases.

The theory of strict tort liability was developed by legal scholars as a part of the Restatement of the Law of Torts. Section 402A of the Restatement (Second) provides the following:

402A. Special Liability of Seller of Product for Physical Harm to User or Consumer.

(1) One who sells any product in a defective condition unreasonably dangerous to the user or consumer, or to his property, is subject to liability for physical harm thereby caused to the ultimate user or consumer, or to his property if
   (a) the seller is engaged in the business of selling such a product, and
   (b) it is expected to and does reach the user or consumer without substantial change in the condition in which it is sold.

(2) The rule stated in Subsection (1) applies although
   (a) the seller has exercised all possible care in the preparation and sale of his product, and
   (b) the user or consumer has not bought the product from or entered into any contractual relation with the seller.

The courts have relied heavily on these rules in developing the law of strict tort liability. Today, a plaintiff in a strict liability lawsuit need only to prove that (1) a product was defective, (2) this defect caused the product to be unreasonably dangerous, (3) the product has not been changed or modified by the plaintiff, and (4) the plaintiff suffered damages using the product.

Strict liability is imposed on manufacturers and designers, as well as on the seller of the goods. The theory of strict liability has been applied to leases of goods as well as to sales. The potential liability extends to all commercial suppliers of goods. While in many states it is not applicable to the sale of used goods, there is a definite trend toward applying it to used goods. In almost every state, the liability extends not only to users and consumers but also to bystanders such as pedestrians.

Strict liability has been applied both to personal injuries and to damage to the property of the user or consumer. Some courts have refused to extend it to property damage, and most courts have refused to extend it to economic loss.

7. Product Defined

The question of the scope and substance of the term *product* as used in strict liability cases has received considerable discussion in recent decisions. Originally, product was confined to chattels (tangible personal property), such as food for human consumption or other products intended for intimate bodily use. Using the chattel concept, many courts have had no trouble in finding many items to be products: a can of Drano®, baseball sunglasses, a carpenter's hammer, and an automobile. But with the progress of technology and changing notions of justice and strict liability, case law has progressed so terms like *defect* and *product* remain open-ended. Recently, electricity, hot water drawn from a faucet, X-radiation, and a lot "manufactured" by considerable earthmoving have been held to be products—at least in the sense that the theory of strict liability has been applied to them. Courts now focus on the public policy reasons underlying strict liability, and they label the transaction as the sale of a product when those policies apply.

Public policy considerations advanced to support strict liability include (1) public interest in human life and health; (2) the special responsibility of one who markets a defective product that causes harm; (3) invitations and solicitations by the manufacturer to purchase the product and representations that it is safe and suitable for use; and (4) the justice of imposing the loss on the party who created the risk and reaped the benefit by placing the item in the stream of commerce.

Note that *product* also includes its container, whether or not sold with the product. A restaurant was held strictly liable for the injuries to a customer's hand when a wine glass shattered. Moreover, a gas company that furnished a gas tank incidental to the sale of gas had to assume responsibility for injuries caused by the defective tank.

8. Defect

SOURCES OF PRODUCT DEFECTS.   Product defects arise from three sources. The first and most basic is the *production defect*, arising from an error during the manufacture of the product. Production defects generally are easy to recognize. The classic example is the soft-drink bottle that explodes because of an imperfection in the glass of the bottle or inadvertent overcarbonization. A production defect, therefore, occurs when the product does not meet the manufacturer's own standards.

The second source of product defect is *design defect*. In contrast to the production defect, the product meets the standard the manufacturer intended. In a design case, the injured plaintiff will allege that the design or the manufacturer's standards were inferior and should be judged defective. The plaintiff, to prove that a particular product is defective in design, must show that there was some practical way in which the product could have been made safer.

Finally, there is the product that is made as intended according to a design that could not be improved but has some characteristic not brought to the attention of the user or consumer. There has been a failure to warn. A *failure to warn* (*marketing defect*) is the third source of product defect. The duty of the manufacturer to provide adequate warnings and directions for use is a prolific source of litigation today.

CHARACTERISTICS OF AN "ADEQUATE" WARNING.   To be "adequate," the warning must have two characteristics. First, it must be in such a *form* that it could reasonably be expected to catch the attention of a reasonable person in the context of its use. Second, the *content* of the warning must be comprehensible to the average user and must convey with a degree of *intensity* that would cause a prudent person to exercise caution commensurate with the potential danger. In sum, a warning may be inadequate in factual context, inadequate in expression of facts, or inadequate in the method by which it is conveyed. But note that a manufacturer or seller is not required to warn of dangers that are known or should be known by the user of the product.

CASE

Howard v. Poseidon Pools, Inc.,
530 N.E.2d 1280 (N.Y. 1988).

After sustaining severe injuries as the result of a diving accident, Howard sued both the manufacturer of the pool and the owner. The trial judge granted the defendants' motions for a summary judgment. The plaintiff, Howard, appeals.

MEMORANDUM

. . . Plaintiff, who was 6 feet, 3 inches tall, sustained severe and permanent injuries upon diving head first into an above-ground pool having a water depth of about four feet. Plaintiff stated that he attempted to dive through an inner tube that was floating in the water some eight feet from the deck of the pool. It is undisputed that plaintiff was an experienced swimmer familiar with diving techniques, that he had been swimming in the pool for about 45 minutes prior to the accident, and that he knew the water was shallow. At his examination before trial, plaintiff testified that he had been informed of the water depth and that when he stood in the pool, the water level was about "chest high." Additionally, plaintiff acknowledged that he was generally familiar with the danger that injury might result from diving head first into shallow water. . . .

Plaintiff argues that the defendants were under a duty to warn potential users of this type of shallow pool of the danger of injury inherent in diving into them. Even assuming such a duty existed, however, summary judgment was properly granted. . . . To carry the burden of proving a prima facie case, the plaintiff must generally show that the defendant's negligence was a substantial cause of the events which produced injury. . . . The record eliminates any legal cause other than the reckless conduct of the plaintiff who by virtue of his general knowledge of pools, his observations prior to the accident, and plain common sense must have known that, if he dove into the pool, the area into which he dove contained shallow water, and thus posed a danger of injury. Thus, plaintiff's conduct, rather than any negligence by the defendants in failing to issue warnings, was the sole proximate cause of his injuries.

■ *Affirmed.*

CASE CONCEPTS REVIEW

1. What legal argument does the plaintiff make as a basis for holding the pool manufacturer liable for his injuries?
2. Why does the court reject the plaintiff's contention and absolve the manufacturer of liability?
3. Do you think the result of this case would have been different if the plaintiff had not been in the pool and had not been informed of the water depth prior to his unfortunate dive? Why?

DEFINITION OF DEFECTIVE.   Section 402A, in part, provides, "One who sells any product in a defective condition *unreasonably dangerous* to the user or consumer or to his property is subject to liability for physical harm thereby caused to the ultimate user or consumer, or to his property." The majority of courts regard the idea of "unreasonably dangerous" as inseparable from the definition of defect.

Under the comments to Section 402A, a product is defective when "it is in a condition not contemplated by the ultimate consumer, which will be unreasonably dangerous to him." A product may be found to be unreasonably dangerous when it is "dangerous to the extent beyond that which would be contemplated by the ordinary consumer." We expect that real butter, fatty meat, and good whiskey may be dangerous, but not unreasonably so. The term *defective* as interpreted by courts is applied to an almost endless variety of product design, function, and performance contexts. The following case is one example of a potentially defective product and the importance of a proper definition of *defective*. Note the interrelationship between the concepts of design and warnings.

CASE

Robinson v. G.G.C., Inc.
808 P.2d 522 (Nev. 1991)

ROSE, J.

Appellant Jeffrey W. Robinson suffered permanent damage to his hand when he tried to remove an object from a box crushing machine. Robinson was a boxboy at Lucky's Supermarket and was operating the machine when the accident occurred. He sued the manufacturer of the machine, G.G.C., Inc., dba Enterprise Company (Enterprise) on a strict products liability theory based on defective design. The jury returned a verdict for Enterprise and Robinson asserts several errors on appeal.

On July 26, 1985, Robinson was operating a hydraulic crushing machine used to flatten cardboard boxes. As he was filling the machine, he saw something caught in the crushing device, called the ram, and reached in to pull the item out. While yanking on the object, he fell backward and lost his balance. Then he was somehow knocked forward and got his hand caught in the machine. From that position, he could not reach the stop button and had to call for someone else to shut off the machine. His hand was badly damaged.

The machine is called a crusher or a baler, and was designed by Enterprise in about 1969 and manufactured in 1979. It had a protective screen that had been broken and removed four or five months before the accident. In this model, the screen serves as a safety gate and operates in concert with the ram. The screen descends over the opening of the machine ahead of the ram, so that it closes before the ram comes all the way down. If anything falls into the path of the screen, the screen and the ram automatically retract halting the crushing process. However, on top of the machine is a limit switch which controls the safety screen. An operator can fasten the switch in an off position so that the baler will still function without operation of the safety screen. In this case, the switch had been in the off position for at least four or five months.

Robinson asserted at trial that the removable screen was a design defect that was unreasonably dangerous to the consumer. He claimed that the machine was defective because (1) it should not have been functional without the safety screen in place, and (2) the safety screen jutted out making it susceptible to damage or detachment. He proposes that the jury found against him because the court gave a misleading jury instruction. . . .

Enterprise placed warning decals on the machine which warned consumers to keep hands clear of the machine. Enterprise contends that these decals should shield it from liability. In conformance with Enterprise's theory, the court gave a jury instruction which read, "[a] product which bears suitable and adequate warnings concerning the safe manner in which the product is to be used and which is safe to use if the warning is followed is not in a defective condition."

Robinson contends that this instruction effectively directed a verdict for the defendant because it told the jury that warnings shield manufacturers from liability. This court has already held that manufacturers can still be liable for a foreseeable misuse of a product in spite of an adequate warning. . . .

The question before us now is when, in spite of an adequate warning, a manufacturer is still liable for a foreseeable misuse. When the defect in the product is the lack of a safety device, the misuse is often an accidental misuse. In these situations, a warning, although it adequately informs of the danger, is of no help to the consumer. Strict products liability law should not punish manufacturers for unanticipated injuries from reasonably safe products, but it should encourage manufacturers to take all measures to avoid accidents from product misuse. Therefore, we must require manufacturers to make their products as safe as commercial feasibility and the state of the art will allow.

Many jurisdictions have adopted the rule that a manufacturer may be liable for the failure to provide a safety device if the inclusion of the device is commercially feasible, will not affect product efficiency, and is within the state of the art at the time the product was placed in the stream of commerce. . . . These cases promote a compound goal of encouraging manufacturers to make products safe without unduly burdening them with excessive liability without fault.

If the technology is available, the cost is not prohibitive, and the product remains efficient, then a potentially dangerous product which lacks a safety device is in a defective condition.

. . . A warning is not an adequate replacement when a safety device will eliminate the need for the warning. If manufacturers have the choice between providing an effective safety screen or simply placing a decal on the product, cost will encourage the latter. Therefore, Instruction 22A, which informed the jury that an adequate warning will always shield manufacturers from liability, is not a correct statement of the law. Instead, warnings should shield manufacturers from liability *unless* the defect could have been avoided by a commercially feasible change in design that was available at the time the manufacturer placed the product in the stream of commerce.

Enterprise did include a safety screen in its product. The evidence shows that the screen was easily detachable and the machine could function without the screen in place. Still, the employer did have to alter the machine slightly to make it function without the screen. Generally, a substantial alteration will shield a manufacturer from li-

ability for injury that results from that alteration. However, if the alteration was insubstantial, foreseeable, or did not actually cause the injury, then the manufacturer of a defective product remains liable. In this case, the causal connection between the absent safety screen and the injury is clear. Therefore, the question left to the jury is whether the employer's act of overriding the limit switch was a substantial alteration of the product. . . .

For the reasons stated above, we reverse the judgment for defendant Enterprise and remand this case to the district court for a new trial.

■ *Reversed and remanded.*

CASE CONCEPTS REVIEW

1. What had happened to the protective screen prior to the plaintiff's hand injury?
2. What argument did the manufacturer make as a basis of avoiding liability?
3. How did the trial judge instruct the jury with respect to the meaning of a defective product?
4. Why does the court refuse to accept a warning in lieu of an available safety device?
5. In essence, what does this ruling say to manufacturers?

CONSUMER EXPECTATIONS TEST.   Since any attempt to define *defect* in generalized terms can be misleading, many courts adopt a *consumer expectations test.* Other courts use a *risk/utility test,* which provides that a product is unreasonably dangerous if the risk outweighs its utility.

Under the consumer expectations or contemplation test, a product that meets all demands and expectations of society but nonetheless injures someone can hardly be the fault of the manufacturer. A manufacturer is not absolutely liable. It is not an insurer. As consumers, we know and expect some products to be dangerous. Cars kill pedestrians; knives cut fingers; cigarettes cause cancer. These products are considered dangerous, but that fact does not make them defective. A product is defective when it does not meet the standards of safety consumers expect.

9. Proof Required

To establish that a defendant is strictly liable, the plaintiff must establish that the product was defective, as just discussed. In addition, the plaintiff must prove the following:

1. The defect existed at the time the product left the defendant's control.
2. The defect caused the plaintiff's injury.

Assuming the plaintiff proves the existence of a defective product, a cause of action in strict liability also requires proof that the defective product reached the plaintiff without a change of condition and that the product caused an injury to the plaintiff. For a manufacturer to have liability, the product must be defective at the time it left the manufacturer's possession. A manufacturer may introduce evidence that the product was substantially altered after leaving its possession, which evidence may rebut or overcome the plaintiff's showing that his or her injuries were the result of the product's defect. However, before a manufacturer is put to the trouble and expense of establishing that its product was altered, the plaintiff in most cases must first establish that the product was defective when it left the manufacturer's possession.

There are a few exceptions where such proof would be impossible. For example, a victim of a propane gas explosion was not required to prove the condition of the propane gas when it left the manufacturer. The court in that case held that a plaintiff's burden on the issue of defect is limited to proof that the defect that rendered the product unreasonably dangerous to the user or consumer occurred in the course of the distribution process and before the plaintiff purchased the product. In the case of a product sold in bulk, such as propane, this burden is satisfied by evidence showing that the product was defective and unreasonably dangerous when purchased or when put to use within a reasonable time after purchase.

Even if a plaintiff proves injury from a product, he or she cannot recover without proving causation between that defect and the injury. As previously noted, the defect must have existed when the product left the seller's hands. A seller is not liable if a safe product is made unsafe by subsequent changes. Furthermore, if the injury results from the plaintiff's negligence or misuse of the product, the manufacturer or seller is not liable. These principles are discussed in more detail in the next section, on defenses.

Prior to discussing defenses, we summarize the benefits to the plaintiff of the strict liability theory. In essence, under strict liability, the plaintiff's burden of proof is reduced as compared to the burden carried under a negligence or warranty theory of liability.

The crucial difference between strict liability and negligence is that the existence of due care, on the part of the seller, is irrelevant in strict liability cases. The seller is responsible for injury caused by a defective product, even if the seller has exercised all possible care in the preparation and sale of the product. The duty of a seller is not fulfilled by taking all reasonable measures to make the product safe. The strict liability issue focuses on whether the product was defective and unreasonably dangerous and not on the conduct of the seller.

In strict liability cases there are no issues on disclaimer or warranties, there is no problem of inconsistency with express warranties, and the seller's knowledge of the defect need not be proved. Of course, privity of contract is not required, and neither is reliance on a warranty by the injured party.

10. Defenses

Strict liability is not synonymous with *absolute liability*. There must be proof that some dangerous defect caused the injury, even though the product was being used in the manner reasonably anticipated by the seller or the manufacturer. In addition, there are defenses that may be asserted to avoid liability. It is often said that contributory negligence is not a defense to a suit based on the theory of strict liability. This is somewhat of an oversimplification, however, because misuse of a product is a defense. Moreover, a person who voluntarily encounters a known unreasonable danger is not entitled to recover. A seller of a product is entitled to have his or her due warnings and instructions followed; when they are disregarded and injury results, the seller is not liable. Moreover, when a user unreasonably proceeds to use a product he or she knows to be defective or dangerous, the user relinquishes the protection of the law. There is no duty on the part of manufacturers to create products that will insure against injury to the most indifferent, adventurous, or foolhardy people.

COMPARATIVE NEGLIGENCE.   In recent years, a doctrine known as *comparative negligence* has replaced contributory negligence in tort cases based on negligence. Under comparative negligence, an injured person's recovery is reduced by his or her share of fault. For example, if a plaintiff is 20 percent at fault and the defendant is 80 percent at fault, a plaintiff is entitled to recover only 80 percent of the damages sustained. Today, some courts are applying comparative negligence to suits based on strict liability.

For purposes of comparative negligence, negligence of the plaintiff is not a defense when such negligence consists merely of a failure to discover the defect in the product or to guard against the possibility of its existence. A consumer's unobservant, inattentive, ignorant, or awkward failure to discover or guard against a defect is not a damage-reducing factor. The consumer or user is entitled to believe that the product will do the job for which it was built.

When comparative negligence is used, the defenses of misuse and assumption of the risk do not bar recovery. Instead, such misconduct is compared in the apportionment of damages. Once a defendant's liability is established, and where both the defective product and plaintiff's misconduct contribute to cause the damages, the comparative fault principle operates to reduce the plaintiff's recovery by the amount that the trier of fact finds him or her at fault.

ASSUMPTION OF THE RISK.   Failure to heed a warning with regard to a product will bar a recovery. This, in effect, means that **assumption of the risk** is a defense to a strict liability action.

MISUSE AND ABNORMAL USE.   Misuse and abnormal use of a product is a defense if the manufacturer or seller could not have reasonably foreseen the misuse. However, if the misuse is foreseeable by the manufacturer, this defense to a strict liability cause of action is not available. The following case illustrates a common example of foreseeable misuse.

Assumption of the risk
Negligence doctrine that bars the recovery of damages by an injured party on the ground that such party acted with actual or constructive knowledge of the hazard causing the injury.

CASE

Andrews v. Harley Davidson, Inc.
796 P.2d 1092 (Nev. 1990)

ROSE, J.

James Andrews (Andrews) sued Harley Davidson, Inc. (Harley Davidson) alleging that it was strictly liable for injuries he incurred resulting from a design defect which caused the gas tank to separate from the frame of his Harley Davidson motorcycle. The jury returned a verdict for Harley Davidson. . . .

On March 12, 1985, Andrews accidentally drove his 1978 Harley Davidson motorcycle into the rear of a parked car. Andrews was propelled over the car and onto the sidewalk. He suffered severe injuries.

Andrews filed a suit against Harley Davidson alleging that it was strictly liable for injuries he incurred because of a design defect in his 1978 Harley Davidson motorcycle. A spring clip held the rear of the gas tank to the frame of his motorcycle. Andrews claimed that when his motorcycle hit a parked car, the spring clip broke causing the tank to rise above the motorcycle seat. As Andrews moved forward he hit the raised gas tank. Andrews contended that had the spring clip held the gas tank in place he would not have been injured or, alternatively, that his injuries would not have been as severe. He argued that a consumer would not have expected the spring clip to break.

Before trial, Andrews filed a motion . . . asking the court to exclude evidence that he was intoxicated on the night of the accident. The court held that evidence of Andrews' intoxication could be used to prove that the design of his Harley Davidson motorcycle was not the proximate cause of Andrews' injuries. Andrews' blood alcohol count, which was .146, was admitted into evidence during the trial. . . .

On January 31, 1989, the jury returned a verdict for Harley Davidson. Andrews now appeals from the jury's verdict.

The district court found that evidence of Andrews' intoxication could be used to show that the design of his Harley Davidson motorcycle was not the proximate cause of Andrews' injuries. The court appears to have reasoned that although a design defect may have caused Andrews' motorcycle to be unsafe in an accident, this defect may not have been the proximate cause of Andrews' injuries if Andrews misused the motorcycle. We disagree.

A manufacturer has a duty to design a reasonably crashworthy vehicle. In regard to the crashworthiness of a vehicle, once a court or jury determines that a design defect exists misuse precludes recovery only when the plaintiff misuses the product in a manner in which the defendant could not reasonably foresee. Negligent driving of a vehicle is a foreseeable risk against which a manufacturer is required to take precautions. Specifically, it is foreseeable that a plaintiff, who is intoxicated, will drive negligently and get in an accident since intoxication leads to a significant number of accidents yearly. Therefore, evidence of Andrews' intoxication is not relevant to whether a design defect in his motorcycle was the proximate cause of his injuries.

The trial court failed to distinguish between the proximate cause of Andrews' accident and the proximate cause of his injuries. Andrews' intoxication may have been the proximate cause of the *accident*. However, Harley Davidson's design, if it was as defective as Andrews contends, was the proximate cause of his *injuries*.

Additionally, contributory negligence is not a defense in a strict liability case where the issue is whether the design of a vehicle is crashworthy. A major policy behind holding manufacturers strictly liable for failing to produce crashworthy vehicles is to encourage them to do all they reasonably can do to design a vehicle which will protect a driver in an accident. Hence, the jury in such a case should focus on whether the manufacturer produced a defective product, not on the consumer's negligence. . . .

We conclude that the court committed prejudicial error when it allowed evidence that Andrews was intoxicated on the night of the accident to come before the jury. Evidence that a plaintiff's intoxication may have caused an accident is not relevant to the issue of whether there was a design defect or whether a design defect in his vehicle caused his injuries. The jury, however, may have concluded that Harley Davidson was not liable for Andrews' injuries, despite the existence of a design defect on his motorcycle, because Andrews was intoxicated on the night of his accident. . . .

The court erred in allowing the jury to hear evidence that Andrews was intoxicated on the night of his accident. Andrews' intoxication was not relevant as to whether the design of his Harley Davidson motorcycle was the proximate cause of his injuries. . . .

Accordingly, we reverse the jury's decision and remand this matter to district court for further proceedings consistent with this opinion.

■ *Reversed and remanded.*

CASE CONCEPTS REVIEW

1. What is the alleged design defect with the motorcycle involved in this case?
2. According to the trial court, what is the purported misuse by Andrews of the motorcycle?
3. What is meant by this court in making the distinction between "the proximate cause of the *accident*" and "the proximate cause of the *injuries*"?
4. Why does this court reject the manufacturer's defense that Andrews was contributorily negligent?

STATE OF THE ART.   A defense that is often asserted is called *state of the art*. This defense, simply stated, is that the product was manufactured according to the best and latest technology available. If a product is manufactured using the best technology but it nevertheless injures people, should the manufacturer still have liability? Most courts do not allow the state-of-the-art defense to defeat a claim based on strict liability. According to Section 402A(2)(a) of the Restatement (Second) of the Law of Torts, the rule of strict liability for a product defect can apply even when "the seller has exercised all possible care in the preparation and sale of his product." Therefore, in a strict liability claim, the sole subject of inquiry is the defective condition of the product, and not the manufacturer's knowledge, negligence, or fault.

In a negligence action, the inquiry focuses on the reasonableness of the maker's action in designing the product. However, in an action for strict liability, the focus is on the dangerous condition of the product as put into commerce. State-of-the-art evidence, or evidence of industry or federal government standards, concerns the manufacturer's standard of care, which relates to the reasonableness of the manufacturer's design choice, not the condition of the product. Therefore, this evidence is irrelevant in a strict liability case.

11. Comparison of Strict Liability and Warranty

Table 21–2 demonstrates a basic similarity between strict tort liability and the warranty of merchantability. For instance, "defective condition unreasonably dangerous" and "fit for ordinary purposes" seem to be similar tests under the notion of "defect." But plaintiffs using strict liability may have a lesser burden of proof. For example, in a breach-of-warranty case, the plaintiff may have to overcome contract defenses such as disclaimers of liability, the requirement of notice of breach, limitation of remedies, and lack of privity.

Where there is only economic loss (no physical harm to person or property), most courts will not allow a recovery in strict liability. Warranty liability for economic loss, however, is available. Moreover, the UCC provides a longer statute of limitations in which to bring the warranty action. Practical considerations such as the availability or solvency of a particular defendant may also affect the choice of theory.

CHAPTER SUMMARY

GENERAL CONCEPTS

Basic Principles	1. A manufacturer, distributor, or seller of a product is liable to compensate a person injured by a defective product.
	2. Products liability cases may arise out of defective design of products, defective manufacture, or the defective marketing of products.
	3. Losses caused by products are a cost of doing business to be shared by buyers and users.
	4. The potential liability is usually covered by products liability insurance, the cost of which has skyrocketed in recent years.
History of Products Liability	1. Prior to 1800, liability was based on tort theory of trespass.
	2. In the 1800s, negligence law and the requirement of privity of contract became law.
	3. The early 1900s saw the beginning of the demise of privity of contract.
	4. In the 1960s, the doctrine of strict liability was created.
Theories of Liability	1. There are both contract and tort theories.
	2. The theories are based on the defendant's conduct, the quality of the product, and the seller's representations. See Table 21–1.
Negligence	1. Negligence evaluates the reasonableness of the defendant's conduct. The defendant's conduct is deemed negligent only when it is inferior to what a "reasonable" person would have done under similar circumstances.
	2. A negligence suit can be brought not only by the person who purchased the defective product but also by any person who suffered an injury due to a defective product.
	3. The doctrine of *res ipsa loquitur* may be used to prove negligence.
	4. Negligence may be established by proof that the manufacturer violated some statutory regulation in the production and distribution of its product.

TABLE 21-2 ■ Comparison between Strict Liability and Warranty

	Warranty of Merchantability UCC 2-314	Strict Tort Liability Restatement (Second) Torts 402A
Condition of goods giving rise to liability	Not merchantable; that is, not fit for ordinary purpose. 2-314(1),(2)(c)	Defective condition unreasonably dangerous. 402A(1)
Character of defendant	Must be seller who is a merchant with respect to goods of that kind. 2-314(1), 2-104(1)	Must be seller who is engaged in the business of selling such a product. 402A(1)(a)
Reliance	No explicit requirement. Such warranty "taken for granted." 2-314; see, however, 2-316(3)(b)	No requirement of "any reliance on the part of the consumer upon the reputation, skill or judgment of the seller." 402A Comment m.
Disclaimer	Limitation of consequential damages for injury to the person in the case of consumer goods is prima facie unconscionable. 2-316(4), 2-719(3), 2-302.	Cause of action not affected by any disclaimer or any other agreement. 402A Comment m
Notice	Buyer must within a reasonable time after he or she discovers, or should have discovered, any breach notify seller of breach or be barred from any remedy. Reason of rule: to defeat commercial base, not to deprive a good-faith consumer of his or her remedy. 2-607(3)(a)	Consumer not required to give notice to seller of his or her injury within a reasonable time after it occurs. 402A Comment m
Causation	Buyer may recover consequential damages *resulting* from the seller's breach, including injury to person or property *proximately resulting* from any breach of warranty. 2-714, 2-715(2)(b), 2-314; see 2-316(3)(b)	Seller subject to liability for physical harm *caused.* 402A(1); see Comment n. *Contributory negligence* is not a defense.
Protected persons	The third persons protected depend on the alternative of 2-318 adopted.	Ultimate user or consumer. 402A(1), (2)b) and comment l
Protected injuries	Injuries to person or his or her property. 2-318	Physical harm to ultimate user or consumer or to his or her property. 402A(1)
Statute of limitations	Four years from tender of delivery. 2-725(1), (2)	State law varies (from one to three years from injury).

	5. Negligence is frequently based on failure of a manufacturer to warn of a known danger related to the product. A manufacturer who knows, or should know, its product to be dangerous has a duty to exercise reasonable care and foresight in preventing it from injuring or endangering people.
Misrepresentation	1. If the seller has advertised the product through newspapers, magazines, television, or otherwise and has made misrepresentations regarding the character or quality of the product, strict tort liability may be imposed on him or her.
	2. Intent to mislead is not required, and neither is privity of contract.

STRICT LIABILITY

Theory	1. In strict liability cases, the focus of attention is on the product.
	2. A manufacturer selling a defective product in a defective condition that is unreasonably dangerous to the user or his or her property is liable for physical injuries caused by the defect.
	3. The theory may apply to leases as well as sales.
Product Defined	1. Products include tangible personal property, items such as electricity, and containers for goods such as soft-drink bottles.
Defect	1. Product defects may be design defects, production defects, and marketing defects.
	2. The typical marketing defect is a failure to warn.
	3. A product is defective when it is in a condition not contemplated by the ultimate consumer, which will be unreasonably dangerous to him or her. A product is unreasonably dangerous when it is dangerous to the extent beyond that which would be contemplated by the ordinary consumer.
	4. The consumer expectations test is used to determine if a product is defective. A product is defective if it does not meet the standards of safety that consumers expect and is unreasonably dangerous.
Proof Required	1. To establish a case of strict liability, the plaintiff must prove (a) the product was defective, (b) the defect existed at the time the product left the defendant's control, and (c) the defect caused the plaintiff's injury.
	2. A plaintiff need not prove negligence of the manufacturer or seller. Disclaimers and notice of breach are not problems, and lack of privity of contract is immaterial.
	3. The defective product must be unreasonably dangerous.
Defenses	1. Contributory negligence is not a defense to a suit based on the theory of strict tort liability.
	2. Comparative negligence is often used to reduce verdicts in strict products liability cases.
	3. Assumption of the risk is a defense.
	4. Misuse and abnormal use of a product are defenses.
	5. State-of-the-art defenses normally are rejected by courts.
Comparison of Strict Liability and Warranty	1. See Table 21–2.

REVIEW QUESTIONS AND PROBLEMS

1. Match the terms in column A with the appropriate statement in column B.

A	**B**
(1) Misrepresentation	(a) The major requirement for strict liability
(2) *Caveat emptor*	(b) A test for defective products
(3) Negligence *per se*	(c) A false advertisement may constitute

    (4) *Res ipsa loquitur*
    (5) Marketing defect
    (6) Consumer expectations
    (7) Comparative negligence
    (8) Unreasonably danger-
        ous product

    (d) Violation of a statute
    (e) A partial defense
    (f) Failure to warn may constitute
    (g) Let the buyer beware
    (h) The thing speaks for itself

2. Muriel received a blood transfusion consisting of blood supplied by a blood bank. She contracted serum hepatitis as a result of the transfusion. Is the blood bank liable by reason of strict liability and breach of implied warranties? Why or why not?

3. Alan leased a mobile home, including steps, from Ben. Alan's father fell when the steps collapsed, and he sued Ben for products liability. Is there a cause of action? Why or why not?

4. Brumley purchased a radial tire. The tire had a design defect that caused it to separate, but Brumley was not warned of this defect even though the manufacturer had received several complaints. The tire blew out and Brumley was injured. Is she entitled to recover for her injuries from the manufacturer? Why or why not?

5. Automobile driver and passenger brought products liability action, alleging defective design, against automobile manufacturer for injuries sustained when the automobile was rear-ended, causing the gas tank to rupture and burn. What theories would support such a lawsuit? Explain each.

6. Pat sued the seller of a reconditioned clothes dryer. The dryer overheated, and a blanket being dried caught fire. The fire spread to the rest of the house, causing $24,000 in damages. What theory will support the plaintiff's cause of action? Explain.

7. Smith sued Ariens for injuries sustained while operating a snowmobile in a field. The snowmobile hit a rock that was partially covered by snow. On impact, the right side of Smith's face came down and hit a brake bracket on the left side of the snowmobile. The brake bracket had two sharp metal protrusions on the inside that were toward the plaintiff's face. What theory of recovery best supports the plaintiff's case? Explain. Should the plaintiff be awarded damages? Why?

8. The plaintiff bought a rotary power mower from the defendant. He had used similar mowers before and was thoroughly familiar with them. The rear of the housing of the plaintiff's mower is embossed with the warning, "Keep Hands & Feet From Under Mower." The instruction booklet twice advises the operator to mow slopes lengthwise, not up and down. While mowing up and down, the plaintiff fell and lifted the mower onto his feet. The plaintiff sues, using strict liability as his theory. Should the plaintiff recover? Explain.

9. Claude, a ski instructor, was injured while riding a chairlift at a ski area when the chair in front of him slipped back along the cable, striking his chair and knocking him thirty feet to the ground. The cause of the mishap was the failure of a cable clamp unit to secure the chain to the cable. What must Claude prove in order to recover? Explain.

10. Plaintiff was injured when a propane gas heater leaked gas and exploded. The propane did not contain ethyl mercaptan, which provides the smell of gas. Plaintiff sues on a theory of negligence. Should plaintiff win? Why?

11. Maude bought a plastic waste container, and when she got it home she found the lid did not fit properly on the top of the container. In an attempt to make it fit, she hit the corner of the lid with her hand and suffered a deep gash in her hand. Will Maude successfully recover on a theory of strict liability against the manufacturer of the plastic waste container? Explain.

12. Plaintiff is a fifteen-year-old girl employed at a fast-food restaurant. She was injured when in the midst of filling a customer's order, she made a split-second decision to remove a paper towel covering a roast without turning off the power. The meat was on a moving tray approaching a stationary blade, and her hand hit the blade. Is the manufacturer strictly liable? Why?

CHAPTER

22

THE PRINCIPAL-AGENT RELATIONSHIP

CHAPTER PREVIEW

*T*his chapter serves as an introduction to Part V on agency law. The term *agency* is used to describe the fiduciary relationship that exists when one person acts on behalf, and under the control, of another person. The principles of agency law are essential for the conduct of business transactions. A corporation, as a legal entity, can function only through agents. The law of partnership comprises, to a large degree, agency principles specially applied to that particular form of business organization. Hence, in one sense, the four chapters on agency (22 through 25) serve as an introduction to the following seven chapters on business organizations.

The person who acts for another is called an *agent*. The person for whom the agent acts, and who controls the agent, is called a *principal*. Traditionally, issues of agency law arise when the agent has attempted to enter into a contract on behalf of a principal; however, the law of agency includes several aspects of the law of torts. This chapter introduces the relationship between a principal and an agent. Chapter 23 discusses the agency relationship as it involves the agency contracting with third parties. Chapter 24 examines the legal ramifications if an agent injures a third party. In these situations, the principal usually is called a master and the agent is called a servant. Finally, chapter 25 discusses the termination of the agency relationship.

■ BUSINESS MANAGEMENT DECISION

As the sales manager of your company, you are responsible for a sales force of twenty-three people. You learn that two of your top salespeople are planning to go to work for a competitor. These salespeople have meetings scheduled with three of your recently hired salespeople. You suspect that the two might be trying to convince the three to leave with them.

What action should you take based on this information?

IN GENERAL

1. Introduction

Case law, as contrasted with statutory law, has developed most of the principles applicable to the law of agency. Agency issues are usually discussed within a framework of three parties: the principal (P), the agent (A), and the third party (T), with whom A contracts or against whom A commits a tort while in P's service. The following examples illustrate the problems and issues involved in the law of agency.

P v. A: Principal sues agent for a loss caused by A's breach of a fiduciary duty, such as to obey instructions.

P v. T: Principal sues third party for breach of a contract that A negotiated with T while A was acting on P's behalf.

A v. P: Agent sues principal for injuries suffered in the course of employment, for wrongful discharge, or for compensation owed for services rendered.

A v. T: Agent sues third party for a loss suffered by A, such as the loss of a commission due to T's interference with contractual obligations.

T v. P: Third party sues principal for breach of a contract that A negotiated with T or for damages caused by a tort committed by A.

T v. A: Third party sues agent personally for breach of a contract signed by A or for damages caused by a tort committed by A.

The contents of this chapter basically concentrate on the first and third situations in the preceding list. Issues relating to the involvement of third parties are handled in the next two chapters. The following four sections present some basic principles that are essential to understanding the relationship between a principal and an agent and their interactions with third parties.

2. Types of Principals

From the third party's perspective, an agent may act for one of three types of principals.

DISCLOSED.   An agent who reveals that he or she is working for another and who reveals the principal's identity is an agent of a *disclosed principal*. The existence of a disclosed principal will be found in most agency relationships, particularly employment situations.

UNDISCLOSED.   At the other extreme, a principal is *undisclosed* whenever a third party reasonably believes that the agent acts only on his or her own behalf. In essence, when an undisclosed principal is involved, the third party does not realize that any agency relationship exists. A well-known or wealthy principal may not want a third party to know he or she is interested in buying that third party's land, business, or merchandise. Therefore the principal hires an agent to deal with the third party. This agent would be instructed by the principal to keep that principal's existence a secret from the third party.

PARTIALLY DISCLOSED.   A third situation falls between the disclosed and undisclosed principal's circumstances. A third party may know an agent represents a principal, but that third party may not know the identity of the principal. When a third party learns of the principal's existence but not his or her identity, a *partially disclosed principal* is present. For the most part, legal issues treat undisclosed and partially disclosed principals in a similar manner.

3. Types of Agents

Agents serve a variety of functions on behalf of their principals. There are special terms used to describe these agents based on their responsibilities.

BROKERS AND FACTORS.   Some agents are known as brokers and others as factors. A **broker** is an agent with special, limited authority to procure a customer so the owner can effect a sale or exchange of property. A real estate broker has authority to find a buyer for another's real estate, but the real estate remains under the control of the owner. A **factor** is a person who has possession and control of another's personal property, such as goods, and is authorized to sell that property. A factor has a property interest and may sell the property in his or her own name, whereas a broker may not. Although the term is seldom used today, a retail merchant who has a manufacturer's goods on consignment is a factor.

GENERAL AND SPECIAL.   Agents are also classified as general or special agents. A **general agent** is one who has authority to transact all the business of the principal, of a particular kind, or in a particular case. The powers of a general agent are coextensive with the business entrusted to the agent's care, authorizing him or her to act for the principal in all matters coming within the usual and ordinary scope and character of such business. A general agent has much broader authority than a special agent. Some cases define a general agent as one authorized to conduct a series of transactions involving a continuity of service, whereas a **special agent** conducts a single transaction or a series of transactions without continuity of service. A special agent is authorized to act for the principal only in a particular transaction or in

Broker A person employed for a commission to make contracts with third persons on behalf of a principal.

Factor An agent for the sale of merchandise. A factor may hold goods in his or her own name or in the name of a principal. The factor is authorized to sell and to receive payment for the goods.

General agent An agent authorized to do all the acts connected with carrying on a particular trade, business, or profession.

Special agent An agent with a limited amount of authority. This agent usually has instructions to accomplish one specific task.

a particular way. Most agents usually are considered to be general agents of the employer as long as they stay within the scope of their employment. However, an athlete's agent assisting in contract negotiations likely would be a special agent and generally would not be authorized to make investments or purchase property.

The following case demonstrates the importance to both the principal and the agent of how an agent is classified.

CASE

Stacy v. J. C. Montgomery Insurance Corporation
367 S.E.2d 499 (Va. 1988)

Elmer Stacy owned an unoccupied dwelling house. He asked the J. C. Montgomery Insurance Corporation, an independent insurance agent, to obtain insurance coverage to protect the house. This agent experienced difficulty in obtaining the insurance because Stacy's house was unoccupied and "open to trespass." The agent did procure insurance through the Virginia Property Insurance Association. However, this insurance company gave notice of cancellation effective November 16 because the house was unoccupied. Stacy received this notice on November 8. He did not respond to the cancellation notice since he had informed an employee of the J. C. Montgomery Insurance Company on October 26 that the house had been rented as of October 22. On November 24, the house was destroyed by fire. Upon learning that he had no insurance coverage in effect on November 24, Stacy sued the agent for failing to inform the insurance company that the property had been rented. The trial court granted the agent's motion for a summary judgment. Stacy appealed.

RUSSELL, J.

. . . On appeal, the owner argues that an agent is a fiduciary, bound to act in the best interests of his principal. Citing cases relating to fiduciary relationships, he argues that the agent was under a continuing duty to keep him informed, to advise him, to follow his instructions, and to take all steps necessary to protect his interests. He also argues that once an agency relationship is established, it will be presumed to continue, in the absence of evidence to the contrary. He contends that the agency relationship here began on July 12, 1982, and lasted until the property was destroyed by fire on November 24.

The agent responds that the owner's argument ignores the distinction between general and special agencies. . . . A special agent is one who is authorized to do one

or more specific acts. In discussing the authority of a special agent, we said that his powers are strictly construed; "he possesses no implied authority beyond what is indispensable to the exercise of the power expressly conferred, and must keep within the limits of his commission."

The agent contends that it was a special agent, employed by the owner for the sole purpose of purchasing insurance. It points out that it successfully performed that function, and that the property remained continuously insured until November 16, 1982. . . .

A special agent cannot be charged with duties to his principal which cover subject matter outside the limited authority the principal has conferred upon him.

In the present case, the owner, in response to a request for admissions, admitted that he "made no explicit requests for the [agent] to perform any function other than to purchase insurance." That admission precludes the owner from reliance upon the broad allegation in his motion for judgment to the effect that he had employed the agent to "procure and maintain" fire insurance coverage. Such a narrow grant of authority as that admittedly made by the owner is the hallmark of a special agency. We conclude that the agent was merely entrusted with the authority to purchase for the owner. . . . Here, . . . the agent fully performed its contractual duty.

The owner's admission makes it unnecessary to search further for duties arising from implied authority, custom, or extrinsic requirements imposed by law. It follows that the trial court correctly determined that no material facts were genuinely in dispute and entered summary judgment in the agent's favor.

The judgment will be

■ *Affirmed.*

CASE CONCEPTS REVIEW

1. What was the basis for Stacy to claim that his agent was liable for the house not being insured?

2. What instruction from Stacy to the agent does the court rely on to conclude that a special agency existed rather than a general agency?

Independent contractor An independent contractor is one who exercises his or her independent judgment on the means used to accomplish the result.

INDEPENDENT CONTRACTORS.   Some persons who perform services for others are known a **independent contractors.** When a person contracts for the services of another in a way that gives the employing party full and complete control over the details and manner in which the work will be conducted, a principal-agent relationship is established. On the other hand, when the employing party simply contracts for a certain end result and the employed party has full control over the manner and methods to be pursued in bringing about the result, the latter party is deemed an independent contractor. The person contracting with an independent contractor and receiving the benefit of his or her service is usually called a *proprietor.* A proprietor is generally not responsible to third parties for the independent contractor's actions, either in contract or in tort.

4. Capacity of Parties

It is generally stated that anyone who may act for himself or herself may act through an agent. For example, a minor may enter into a contract, and as long as the minor does not disaffirm it, the agreement is binding. Likewise, the majority of states have held that a contract of an agent on behalf of a minor principal is voidable. Therefore such an agreement is subject to rescission or ratification by the minor, the same as if the minor personally had entered into the contract. To this general rule concerning an infant's capacity as a principal, some states recognize an exception. There is some authority to the effect that any appointment of an agent by an infant is void, not merely voidable. Under this view, any agreement entered into by an infant's agent would be ineffective, and an attempted disaffirmance by the principal would be unnecessary.

A minor may act as an agent for an adult. Any agreements the minor makes for a principal while acting within the authority of an agent are binding on the principal. Although the minor who acts as an agent has a right to terminate a contract of agency at will, so long as the minor continues employment, his or her acts within the scope of the authority conferred become those of the principal.

5. Formal Requirements

As a general rule, agency relationships are based on the consent of the parties involved. No particular formalities are required to create a principal-agent relationship. A principal may appoint an agent either in writing or orally. The agency may be either expressed or implied. The following case illustrates the essential elements of an agency relationship and acknowledges that whether one person is acting as an agent for another often is a fact-based issue.

CASE

Baker v. ICA Mortgage Corporation
588 A.2d 616 (R.I. 1991)

PER CURIAM

In this action the plaintiffs, Mr. and Mrs. Michael L. Baker (Bakers), seek to recover damages from ICA Mortgage Corporation (ICA) and Imperial Savings Association (ISA) for damages proximately caused by the criminal conduct of a member of the Rhode Island Bar, Terrence P. Traudt (Traudt), and to cancel a certain promissory note and mortgage executed by the Bakers on October 16, 1987, in connection with the refinancing of their home. . . .

This case came before the trial justice on ICA's motion for summary judgment. On February 9, 1990, the trial justice granted ICA's motion. Thereafter, in mid-February 1990 the court entered judgment on behalf of both ICA and ISA, despite the fact that ISA had not moved for summary judgment. The Bakers moved to vacate the judgment on the ground that the court erroneously disposed of the claims against ISA. In addition the Bakers moved for an injunction pending appeal. Both motions were heard and denied by the trial justice.

At all times the property owned by the Bakers was encumbered by a mortgage given by the Bakers to the Rhode Island Central Credit Union (RICCU) as security for a loan of $150,000.

The Bakers decided to refinance their mortgage with defendant ICA, and ultimately Traudt became involved in the transaction. They borrowed $175,000 from ICA, which was to be used to pay the balance of the RICCU mortgage and cover closing costs. The remainder of the funds, some $21,000, was delivered to the Bakers at the closing.

Several weeks after the closing, the Bakers began to receive notices from RICCU for payment due on the original mortgage. At this point they discovered that Traudt had failed to apply the loan proceeds to the RICCU mortgage and that the obligation had not been discharged.

The Bakers then filed a complaint in the Superior Court against ICA and ISA. ICA had assigned the mortgage to ISA shortly after the closing. In the complaint the Bakers sought to enjoin defendants from foreclosing on their property on the grounds that the note and mortgage in favor of ICA had been void and unenforceable. The Bakers base this argument upon their assertion that Traudt was acting as ICA's agent; consequently, Traudt's failure to apply the loan proceeds can be attributed to ICA. This failure, according to the Bakers, renders the $175,000 transaction null and void.

At the hearing on the motion for summary judgment, defendants argued that Traudt had been hired by the Bakers to act as their agent in the refinancing proceedings and emphasized that he was not an agent of ICA. The trial justice agreed with defendants and granted the motion for summary judgment.

On appeal the Bakers, through their attorney, consistently argue that an issue of fact exists regarding exactly whom Traudt represented. The Bakers and their attorney argue that Traudt became ICA's "settlement agent" who, according to ICA documents, "is a fiduciary agent for the Lender and the principals in the closing process." The documents sent to Traudt identify him as the closing agent.

The issue on appeal is whether a question of fact exists regarding Traudt's status as an agent for ICA.... Three elements were required to establish the existence of an agency relationship: (1) a manifestation by the principal that the agent will act for him, (2) acceptance by the agent of the undertaking, and (3) an agreement by the parties that the principal will be in control of the undertaking.

The act of sending the closing documents and the funds to Traudt with instructions on closing the loan and disbursing the funds may be interpreted as a manifestation on the part of ICA that Traudt was to act as its agent. Traudt's acceptance may be inferred from the fact that he accepted the documents and attended the closing. The final factor, that the litigants agreed that the principal would control the undertaking, may be shown by Traudt's purporting to follow ICA's instructions at the closing.

Although these facts may not by themselves necessarily prove that Traudt acted as ICA's agent in this transaction, they appear to raise a question of fact that must be resolved. Consequently the Bakers' appeal is sustained, the judgment entered is vacated, and the case is remanded to the Superior Court for further action.

■ *Reversed and remanded.*

CASE CONCEPTS REVIEW

1. What, in essence, is the argument asserted by the Bakers to prevent the enforcement of note and mortgage signed with ICA and assigned to ISA?

2. What are the three essential elements to the court finding that an agency relationship existed between ICA and Traudt?

3. What ruling of the trial court is vacated on this appeal, and how does this affect the Bakers' liability on the ICA note and mortgage?

Despite the general lack of formal requirements, some states require that the appointment of an agent be evidenced by a writing when the agent is to negotiate a contract required to be written by the statute of frauds. Recall from chapter 14 that these written contracts include those involving title to real estate, guaranty contracts, performance that cannot be completed within one year of the date of making, and sales of goods for $500 or more.

Power of attorney An instrument authorizing another to act as one's agent or attorney in fact.

Attorney in fact A person acting for another under a grant of special power created by an instrument in writing.

When a formal instrument is used for conferring authority on an agent, it is known as a **power of attorney.** Generally, this written document is signed by the principal in the presence of a notary public. The agent named in a power of attorney is called an **attorney in fact.** The term distinguishes this formally appointed agent from an attorney at law, who is a licensed lawyer.

A power of attorney may be general, which gives the agent authority to act in all respects for the principal. Sometimes an elderly person signs a power of attorney appointing a general attorney in fact to handle all the necessary matters that may arise. Under other circumstances, a power of attorney, known as a special power of attorney, may be narrowly written. For example, a seller of land may need to be out of town on the date set to close the sales transaction. This seller can sign a special power of attorney appointing a special attorney in fact to act on the seller's behalf by signing the deed and other necessary papers required to complete the closing. Furthermore, a seller or buyer of real estate typically must appoint an agent via a special power of attorney for that agent to have authority to sign a binding contract.

Powers of attorney are usually held to grant only those powers clearly given to the agent. For example, as held in the following case, the power to sell does not include the power to make a gift.

CASE

King v. Bankerd
492 A.2d 608 (Md. 1985)

COLE, J.

The single issue presented in this case is whether a power of attorney authorizing the agent to "convey, grant, bargain and/or sell" the principal's property authorizes the agent to make a gratuitous transfer of that property. . . .

Broadly defined, a power of attorney is a written document by which one party, as principal, appoints another as agent (attorney in fact) and confers upon the latter the authority to perform certain specified acts or kinds of acts on behalf of the principal. This instrument, which delineates the extent of the agent's authority, is a contract of agency that creates a principal-agent relationship.

Various rules govern the interpretation of powers of attorney. As Chief Judge Murphy observed for this Court in *Klein v. Weiss*, 284 Md. 36, 61, (1978), one "well settled" rule is that powers of attorney are "strictly construed as a general rule and [are] held to grant only those powers which are clearly delineated[.]" The rule of strict construction "cannot override the general and cardinal rule" that the court determine the intention of the parties. To ascertain this intent, . . . the language used in the instrument and the object to be accomplished must be viewed in light of the surrounding circumstances. . . .

Another accepted rule of construction is to discount or disregard, as meaningless verbiage, all-embracing expressions found in powers of attorney. Because powers of attorney are ordinarily very carefully drafted and scruti-

nized, courts give the terms used a technical rather than a popular meaning. In addition, ambiguities in an instrument are resolved against the party who made it or caused it to be made, because that party had the better opportunity to understand and explain his meaning. Finally, general words used in an instrument are restricted by the context in which they are used, and are construed accordingly.

In accordance with these principles, nearly every jurisdiction that has considered the issue in the case *sub judice* has concluded that a general power of attorney authorizing an agent to sell and convey property, although it authorizes him to sell for such price and on such terms as to him shall seem proper, implies a sale for the principal's benefit. Such a power of attorney, however, does not authorize the agent to make a gift of the property, or to convey or transfer it without a present consideration inuring to the principal.

For the reasons below, we conclude that an agent holding a broad power of attorney lacks the power to make a gift of the principal's property, unless that power (1) is expressly conferred, (2) arises as a necessary implication from the conferred powers, or (3) is clearly intended by the parties, as evidenced by the surrounding facts and circumstances.

First, the power to make a gift of the principal's property is a power that is potentially hazardous to the principal's interests. Consequently, this power will not be lightly inferred from broad, all-encompassing grants of power to the agent. Accordingly, "the agent must be circumspect with regard to the powers created—or the lack of them."

Second, the main duty of an agent is loyalty to the interest of his principal. . . . Thus, in exercising granted powers under a power of attorney, the attorney in fact is bound to act for the benefit of his principal and must avoid where possible that which is detrimental unless expressly authorized. . . . In light of the duties of loyalty that arise from the fiduciary relation, it is difficult to imagine how a gift of the principal's real property would be to the benefit of the principal when the power of attorney does not authorize such a gift or the principal does not intend to authorize such a gift. In short, the agent is under a duty to serve his principal with only his principal's purposes in mind.

Third, "[i]t would be most unusual for an owner of property to grant a power of attorney authorizing the attorney in fact to give his property away. If a person has decided to make a gift of property, he or she usually decides as to who is going to be the donee."

The general power of attorney executed by Bankerd authorized King to "convey, grant, bargain and/or sell" the subject property "on such terms as to him may seem best." A strict construction of this broad language, however, makes clear that the instrument did not expressly authorize a gratuitous transfer of property. Because an agent must act for the benefit of his principal, we decline to interpret this broad, all-encompassing language as authority for the agent to make a gift of the principal's property. . . .

■ *Affirmed.*

CASE CONCEPTS REVIEW

1. Based on the power of attorney signed by Bankerd, what was King authorized to do?
2. What is the primary purpose of the court when interpreting the meaning of a power of attorney?
3. This court discusses five rules of construction used by courts in determining the intent of the principal who signed a power of attorney. What are these five rules?

Section 14 discusses real estate listing agreements. Although these documents are used to authorize a real estate agent to find a ready, willing, and able buyer, most states do not require these agreements to be in writing. Technically the agent cannot create a binding sales contract between the buyer and seller. In other words, the real estate agent is not authorized to sign a contract on the seller's behalf. That agent's responsibility is to bring the buyer and seller together so these parties may sign a contract. Despite oral listing agreements being enforceable, agents generally insist on a written one to ease the burden of proof required to establish when a commission is owed. Furthermore, a number of states do require that listing agreements be evidenced by a writing.

DUTIES OF AGENTS

6. Introduction

Fiduciary A position of trust and confidence in relation to a person or his or her property.

The nature and extent of the duties imposed on agents and servants are governed largely by the contract of employment. In addition to the duties expressly designated, certain others are implied by the **fiduciary** nature of the relationship and by the legal effects on the principal of actions or omissions by the agent. The usual implied duties are (1) to be loyal to the principal, (2) to protect confidential information, (3) to obey all reasonable instructions, (4) to inform the principal of material facts that affect the relationship, (5) to refrain from being negligent, and (6) to account for all money or property received for the benefit of the principal. The following sections discuss how these implied duties are essential to the principal-agent relationship.

7. Duty of Loyalty

At the foundation of any fiduciary relationship is the duty of loyalty that each party owes to the other. Since an agent is in a position of trust and confidence, the agent owes an obligation of undivided loyalty to the principal. While employed, an agent should not undertake a business venture that competes or interferes in any manner with the principal's business, nor should the agent make any contract for himself or herself that should have been made for the principal. A breach of this fundamental duty can result in the principal's enjoining the agent's new business or recovering money damages, or both. The following case discusses these critical aspects of the duty of loyalty.

CASE

Augat, Inc. v. Aegis, Inc.
565 N.E.2d 415 (Mass. 1991)

WILKINS, J.

The plaintiff Isotronics, Inc. (Isotronics), a subsidiary of the plaintiff Augat, Inc. (Augat), manufactures high reliability metal microcircuit packages used to house electronic circuits. The individual defendant (Scherer) was one of three stockholders who sold Isotronics to Augat in 1975. He continued to work for Isotronics until 1980, served next as an Augat vice president, and then acted as a consultant to Augat until April, 1983. In May, 1984, one month after his agreement not to compete with Isotronics expired, Scherer formed the defendant Aegis, Inc., intending to manufacture high reliability metal and ceramic microcircuit packages.

Scherer then communicated with Jay Greenspan, who was vice president and general manager of Isotronics, offering him employment and an equity interest in Aegis. Greenspan, an able and energetic manager, held a position of trust and confidence in Isotronics and was primarily responsible for Isotronics's success in becoming the dominant force in the metal packaging industry. Greenspan was not happy at Isotronics. In 1983, he had explored the possibility of forming his own company, but had been unable to obtain financing. At that time, Greenspan had discussed his plan with four Isotronics employees who held important senior managerial positions. Greenspan told Scherer that these senior managers had been interested in Greenspan's 1983 plan. In May or June, 1984, Greenspan and Scherer approached these four men, and over the next several months had meetings with them, separately and collectively, and on occasion also with prospective investors in Aegis. Three of these four men subsequently left Isotronics and went directly to work for Aegis. One major ground for the plaintiffs' claims against the defendants is that, in secretly seeking to obtain the services of key Isotronics managers, they knowingly joined in Greenspan's breach of his duty to Isotronics. That breach, the plaintiffs assert, in time led to a disruption of Isotronics when all those managers left Isotronics within a period of approximately two months.

In the summer of 1984, Scherer devoted his efforts to obtaining financing for Aegis. Greenspan and three of the managers who had been on Greenspan's prospective list in 1983 were committed to work for Aegis, if Aegis could be funded. The existence of the prospective management team was the most important factor in the view of the venture capitalists. Scherer prepared a detailed business plan, describing Aegis's purposes; its potential competitors; the size and condition of the packaging market, including the fact that Isotronics controlled about two-thirds of that market; and, without naming the others, the experience and background of Aegis's anticipated management team. . . .

Scherer sent his business plan to potential investors late in July, 1984. Greenspan delivered a letter of resignation on August 1, 1984, not stating any specific date for his departure. He made no mention then, or at any other time, of the possible departure of those key managers with whom he and Scherer had been talking or of other Isotronics personnel with whom Greenspan had been talking about joining Aegis. The prospective management team of Aegis met early in September and agreed on their relative shares of ownership of Aegis stock. Greenspan left Isotronics on September 27. On October 9, Aegis received a commitment letter for an investment of $4,300,000. The transaction was concluded on November 6. Aegis then entered the metal packaging business, not producing its first packages until May, 1985.

Augat and Isotronics brought this action in April, 1985, advancing various claims against the defendants. . . . The matter was tried in June and July, 1988, before a judge without a jury, during twenty-four trial days. In August, 1989, the judge filed his findings of fact and rulings of law. . . .

The judge ... ruled that Greenspan violated his duty of loyalty when, while still an Isotronics employee, he secretly solicited key managerial employees to join Aegis once it was funded. We uphold this ruling. He also ruled that other former Isotronics employees had violated their duty to Isotronics, a point we reject....

We agree with the plaintiffs that the defendants are liable for Greenspan's breach of his duty of loyalty to Isotronics in not protecting Isotronics's interests against the loss of key employees to Aegis. Greenspan, as a vice president and general manager of Isotronics from 1981 to September 27, 1984, ran all aspects of Isotronics under the general supervision of the president of Augat, who was also the president of Isotronics. Greenspan was responsible for staffing and for hiring necessary replacements for any employees who might leave Isotronics. He regarded his duties to include maintaining at least one "backup" employee for each managerial position.

While Greenspan was still general manager of Isotronics he and Scherer solicited several important Isotronics employees to join Aegis if and when it were to be financed. Among those solicited, who later left Isotronics and went directly to work at Aegis, were: the vice president for marketing and sales, who left Isotronics on November 11, 1984; the new product design manager, Isotronics's most experienced engineer in the technology of making metal packages, who left on November 30, 1984; the manufacturing manager for Isotronics, who left on January 7, 1985; and Isotronics's engineering manager, who left on January 4, 1985....

It is important to define the limited basis for liability we recognize in this case. An at-will employee may properly plan to go into competition with his employer and may take active steps to do so while still employed. Such an employee has no general duty to disclose his plans to his employer, and generally he may secretly join other employees in the endeavor without violating any duty to his employer. The general policy considerations are that at-will employees should be allowed to change employers freely and competition should be encouraged. If an employer wishes to restrict the post-employment competitive activities of a key employee, it may seek that goal through a non-competition agreement. The plaintiffs did not do so in this case.

There are, however, certain limitations on the conduct of an employee who plans to compete with his employer. He may not appropriate his employer's trade secrets. He may not solicit his employer's customers while still working for his employer, and he may not carry away certain information, such as lists of customers. Of course, such a person may not act for his future interests at the expense of his employer by using the employer's funds or employees for personal gain or by a course of conduct designed to hurt the employer.

The special circumstance of this case, distinguishing it from the typical case of improper employee conduct leading to competition with a former employer, is that there is but one significant breach of duty. It is important but substantially isolated. The defendants did not knowingly participate in any breach of duty by an Isotronics's employee in any respect except in joining with Greenspan in soliciting the future employment of important employees.... The employees other than Greenspan committed no breach of duty. There is no showing that the key employees who left Isotronics for Aegis joined together to destroy Isotronics. If Scherer and Aegis had solicited the employees of Isotronics without the involvement of Greenspan prior to his departure from Isotronics, there would be no liability here.

The principle that, before he terminates his employment, a top managerial employee may not solicit the departure of employees to work for a competitor has been applied in various situations. The supervisor-manager, as a corporate pied piper, leads all his employer's employees away, thus destroying the employer's entire business. Although Greenspan's solicitation was directed only at certain key managerial personnel, his duty to maintain at least adequate managerial personnel forbade him, while still general manager of Isotronics, from seeking to draw key managers away to a competitor....

The rule we express for the purposes of this case applies only to a general manager who, while still employed, secretly solicits key managerial employees to leave their employment to join the general manager in a competitive enterprise. Greenspan admitted that he put his loyalties to the people who were to go to Aegis ahead of his obligations as an officer of Isotronics....

The case is remanded to the Superior Court for proceedings consistent with this opinion.

■ *So ordered.*

CASE CONCEPTS REVIEW

1. Who is the individual defendant in this case? What is the name of the corporate defendant?

2. The trial court and this reviewing court agree that Greenspan violated the duty of loyalty he owed to Augat, Inc. What is the basis for this conclusion?

3. Why are the individual defendant and corporate defendant also liable for Greenspan's breach of his duty of loyalty?

4. Why or how did the other top-level managers who came to work for Aegis, Inc. not breach their respective duties of loyalty owed to Augat, Inc.?

This duty of loyalty also prevents an agent from entering into an agreement on the principal's behalf if the agent is the other contracting party. To create a binding agreement with the principal, the agent first must obtain the principal's approval. Since a contract between the agent and the principal is not a deal "at arm's length," the circumstances demand the utmost good faith from the agent. Indeed, an agent must disclose fully all facts that might materially influence the principal's decision-making process.

Likewise, an agent usually cannot represent two principals in the same transactions if the principals have differing interests. To act as dual agent often leads the agent to an unavoidable breach of the duty of loyalty to one, if not both, of the principals. To prevent the breach of this basic duty in this situation, the agent should inform both principals of all the facts in the transaction, including that the agent is working for both principals. If these principals agree to continue negotiations, the agent in effect becomes a "go-between" or messenger. The agent is acting on behalf of both principals while avoiding active negotiations. Due to the nature of their business, real estate agents particularly must be aware of the hazards of dual agencies.

Transactions violating the duty of loyalty may always be rescinded by the principal, even though the agent acted for the best interests of the principal and the contract was as favorable as could be obtained elsewhere. The general rule is applied without favor, so every possible motive or incentive for unfaithfulness may be removed.

In addition to the remedy of rescission, a principal is entitled to treat any profit realized by the agent in violation of this duty as belonging to the principal. Such profits may include rebates, bonuses, commissions, or divisions of profits received by an agent for dealing with a particular third party. Here again the contracts may have been favorable to the employer, but the result is the same because the agent should not be tempted to abuse the confidence placed in him or her. The principal may also collect from the agent a sum equal to any damages sustained as the result of the breach of the duty of loyalty.

8. Duty to Protect Confidential Information

The duty of loyalty demands that information of a confidential character acquired while in the service of the principal shall not be used by the agent to advance the agent's interests in opposition to those of the principal. In other words, an agent has a duty to protect the principal's confidential information. This confidential information is usually called a *trade secret*. Trade secrets include plans, processes, tools, mechanisms, compounds, and informational data used in business operations. They are known only to the owner of the business and to a limited number of other persons in whom it may be necessary to confide. An employer seeking to prevent the disclosure or use of trade secrets or information must demonstrate that he or she pursued an active course of conduct designed to inform employees that such secrets and information were to remain confidential. An issue to be determined in all cases involving trade secrets is whether the information sought to be protected is, in fact and in law, confidential. The result in each case depends on the conduct of the parties and the nature of the information.

An employee who learns of secret processes or formulas or comes into possession of lists of customers may not use this information to the detriment of his or her employer. Former employees may not use such information in a competing business, regardless of whether the trade secrets were copied or memorized. The fact that a product is on the market does not amount to a divulgence or abandonment of the secrets connected with the product. The employer may obtain an injunction to prevent their use, as use is a form of unfair competition. The rule relating to trade secrets is applied with equal severity whether the agent acts before or after severing the connection with the principal.

Knowledge that is important but not a trade secret may be used, although its use injures the agent's former employer. Information that by experience has become a part of a former employee's general knowledge should not and cannot be enjoined from further and different uses. For this reason, there usually is nothing to hinder a person who has made the acquaintance of his or her employer's customers from later contacting those whom he or she can remember. These acquaintances are part of the employee's acquired knowledge. The employer may protect himself or herself by a clause in the employment agreement to the effect that the employee will not compete with the employer or work for a competitor for a limited period of time after employment is terminated. (See chapter 13 for a further discussion on the proper use of agreements not to compete.)

9. Duty to Obey Instructions

It is the duty of an agent to obey all instructions issued by his or her principal as long as they refer to duties contemplated by the contract of employment. Burdens not required by the agreement cannot be indiscriminately imposed by the employer, and any material change in an employee's duties may constitute a breach of the employment contract.

An instruction may not be regarded lightly merely because it departs from the usual procedure and seems fanciful and impractical to the agent. It is not the agent's business to question the procedure outlined by his or her superior. Any loss that results while the agent is pursuing any other course makes the agent absolutely liable to the principal for such resulting loss.

Furthermore, an instruction of the principal does not become improper merely because the motive is bad, unless it is illegal or immoral. The principal may be well aware of the agent's distaste for certain tasks; yet, if those tasks are called for under the employment agreement, it becomes the agent's duty to perform them. Failure to perform often results in proper grounds for discharge.

Closely allied to the duty to follow instructions is the duty to remain within the scope of the authority conferred. Because it often becomes possible for an agent to exceed his or her authority and still bind the principal, the agent has a duty not to exceed the authority granted. In case the agent does so, the employee or agent becomes responsible for any resulting loss.

Occasionally, circumstances arise that nullify instructions previously given. Because of the new conditions, the old instructions would, if followed, practically destroy the purpose of the agency. Whenever such an emergency arises, it becomes the duty of the agent, provided that the principal is not available, to exercise his or her best judgment in meeting the situation.

10. Duty to Inform

In chapter 23, we will see that knowledge acquired by an agent within the scope of his or her authority binds the principal. More succinctly, the law states that an agent's knowledge is imputed as notice to the principal. Therefore the law requires that the agent inform the principal of all facts that affect the subject matter of the agency that are obtained within the scope of the employment. The rule requiring full disclosure of all material facts that might affect the principal is equally applicable to gratuitous and to compensated agents.

This rule extends beyond the duty to inform the principal of conflicting interests of third parties or possible violations of the duty of loyalty in a particular transaction. It imposes on the agent a duty to give the principal all information that materially affects the interest of the principal. Knowledge of facts that may have greatly advanced the value of property placed with an agent for sale must be communicated before property is sold at a price previously established by the principal. Knowledge of financial problems of a buyer on credit must also be communicated to the principal.

11. Duty Not to Be Negligent

As is discussed more fully in chapter 24, the doctrine of *respondeat superior* imposes liability on a principal or master for the torts of an agent or servant acting within the scope of his or her employment. The agent or servant is primarily liable, and the principal or master is vicariously or secondarily liable.

It is an implied condition of employment contracts, if not otherwise expressed, that the employee has a duty to act in good faith and to exercise reasonable care and diligence in performing tasks. Failure to do so is a breach of the employment contract. Therefore, if the employer has liability to third persons because of the employee's acts or negligent omissions, the employer may recover his or her loss from the employee. This right may be transferred by the doctrine of subrogation to the liability insurance carrier of the employer. For example, assume that a bakery company is held liable for damages to an injured child who was struck by a company delivery truck as the result of the employee-driver's negligence. After the company's insurance company pays the total coverage to the injured party, any unpaid damages can be collected from the company. The company in turn can sue the employee for breach of the duty not to be negligent. In some states the insurance company could also collect from the employee. However, there are some reasons to keep liability from being passed ultimately to the careless employee. These reasons are discussed in chapter 24, on agency and tort responsibility.

12. Duty to Account

Money or property entrusted to the agent must be accounted for to the principal. Because of this, the agent is required to keep proper records showing receipts and expenditures so a complete accounting may be rendered. Any money collected by an agent for a principal should not be mingled with funds of the agent. If they are deposited in a bank, they should be kept in a separate account. Otherwise, any loss resulting must be borne by the agent. Also, the duty to account can arise out of the agent's breach of any other fiduciary duty.

An agent who receives money from third parties for the benefit of the principal owes no duty to account to the third parties. The only duty to account is owed to the principal. On the other hand, money paid to an agent who has no authority to collect it, and who does not turn it over to the principal, may be recovered from the agent in an action by the third party.

A different problem is presented when money is paid in error to an agent, as in the overpayment of an account. If the agent has passed the money on to the principal before the mistake is discovered, it is clear that only the principal is liable. Nevertheless, money that is still in the possession of the agent when he or she is notified of the error should be returned to the third party. The agent is not relieved of this burden by subsequently making payment to the principal.

Any payment made in error to an agent and caused by the agent's mistake or misconduct may always be recovered from him or her, even if the agent has surrendered it to the principal. Also, any overpayment may be recovered from the agent of an undisclosed principal, because the party dealing with the agent was unaware of the existence of the principal.

DUTIES OF PRINCIPALS

13. Introduction

The principal-agent relationship is a fiduciary one. Like agents, principals also have fiduciary duties. The trust and confidence of a fiduciary relationship is a two-way obligation. Thus the law requires that the principal be loyal and honest in dealing with the agents. In addition, the agent is entitled to be compensated for his or her services in accordance with the terms of the contract of employment. If no definite compensation has been agreed on, there arises a duty to pay the reasonable value of such services—the customary rate in the community. Furthermore, the principal owes duties to reimburse agents for their reasonable expenses and to hold the agents harmless for liability that may be incurred while the agent is within the scope of employment. Finally, there is a duty not to discriminate in personnel decisions.

14. Duty to Compensate: In General

Many employment contracts include provisions for paying a percentage of profits to a key employee. If the employment contract does not include a detailed enumeration of the items to be considered in determining net income, it will be computed in accordance with generally accepted accounting principles, taking into consideration past custom and practice in the operation of the employer's business. It is assumed that the methods of determining net income will be consistent and that no substantial changes will be made in the methods of accounting without the mutual agreement of the parties. The employer cannot unilaterally change the accounting methods, nor can the employee require a change to effect an increase in his or her earnings.

The right of a real estate broker or agent to a commission is frequently the subject of litigation. In the absence of an express agreement, the real estate broker earns a commission (1) if he or she finds a purchaser who is ready, willing, and able to meet the terms outlined by the seller in the listing agreement or (2) if the owner contracts with the purchaser (whether or not the price is less than the listed price), even though it later develops that the purchaser is unable to meet the terms of the contract. The contract is conclusive evidence that the broker found a ready, willing, and able purchaser. If a prospective purchaser conditions the obligation to purchase on an approval of credit or approval of a loan, that purchaser is not ready, willing, and able to buy until such approval. If it is not forthcoming, the broker is not entitled to a commission.

The duty to pay a real estate commission is dependent on which of the three types of listing has been agreed on. Under a simple *open listing*, an owner lists property with several brokers and is obligated to pay the first one who finds a satisfactory purchaser, at which time the agency of other brokers is automatically terminated. In an open listing, the owner is free to sell on his or her own behalf without a commission. The second type of listing is called an *exclusive agency listing*. For an agreed period of time, it gives the broker the exclusive right to find a buyer. In this arrangement, the seller is not free to list the property with other brokers, and a sale through other brokers would be a violation of the contract of listing, although the seller is free to find a buyer of his or her own. With the third type of listing, called an *exclusive right to sell,* even the seller is not free to find a buyer of his or her own choosing. If the seller does sell on his or her own behalf, the seller is obliged to pay a commission to the broker. The following case demonstrates the significance of exclusive right to sell listings when property is listed with more than one broker.

CASE

Clodfelter v. Plaza, Ltd.
698 P.2d 1 (N.M. 1985)

SOSA, J.

This cause of action is brought by plaintiff Clodfelter, a real estate broker, against defendant partnership, Plaza Limited (Owners), to recover the commission due on the sale of certain property in Taos. The trial court awarded Clodfelter the agreed upon commission on the property sale. We affirm the trial court.

The determinative question to be answered is whether, in an agreement between a broker and a property owner, either an "exclusive right to sell" or an "exclusive agency" clause restricts the right of a property owner to engage the services of another broker.

Clodfelter and all of the partner-Owners signed a letter of agreement on September 5, 1979. The agreement contained an "exclusive right to sell" provision and another provision allowing a sale to be made by the Owners. A second agreement, a printed form from the Multiple Listing Service (MLS) entitled "Exclusive Right to Sell," was signed September 26, 1979 by Clodfelter and one of the general partners. Clodfelter prepared brochures, advertised widely and showed the property.

In May or June 1980, the Owners signed a real estate agreement for the property with a new broker, Muchmore. The sale of the property was arranged and a "contract for sale" was entered on August 11, 1980, between the Owners and a buyer Muchmore obtained. On August 27, 1980 the Owners requested and obtained a letter from Clodfelter in which he agreed he was not entitled to a commission if the property was "sold solely through

the efforts of the owners." The Muchmore sale closed September 4, 1980 and Muchmore received a 6% commission. There is testimony disclosing that Clodfelter was never told by any of the partner-Owners that their agreement was terminated or that a new broker had been engaged to sell the property. . . .

The trial court found that on September 5, 1979 all parties entered into an agreement giving the broker the right to sell the Owners' property. This agreement included a 6% commission plus New Mexico gross receipts tax, and an "exclusive right to sell" provision, which the trial court concluded was valid and binding upon the parties. It contained no termination date and was to:

remain valid until such time as the property is sold, taken off the market or by reason that our firm has not performed the necessary functions to market the property.

Additionally, the agreement stated in the last paragraph:

If you are in agreement with the foregoing, then this letter shall serve as an agreement with this firm. Your signature below will affirm said agreement.

The agreement included a handwritten provision. "This agreement is exclusive of any sale made by owners of their property." The agreement was signed by Clodfelter, as the broker, and by all five of the partners-Owners.

Clodfelter claims he had an "exclusive right to sell" contract which precluded the Owners from selling the property through another broker. The Owners claim that the provisions for a sale by the Owners in both the September 5, 1979 agreement and the later letter of August

27, 1980, allowed them to contract with other brokers to sell the property.

The issue to be decided is whether, under the terms of the September 5, 1979 agreement, the owners could engage the services of another broker to sell their property while the contract with the first broker was still in effect. To decide this, the effect of the handwritten provision of September 5, excluding the owners from the "exclusive right to sell" provision must be determined.

There are two types of exclusive agreements commonly used in real estate contracts, the "*exclusive agency*" agreement and the "*exclusive right to sell*" agreement. . . .

The "exclusive agency" agreement prohibits an owner from selling the property *through another broker* during the listing period, but *allows the owner to sell his property through his own efforts.*

In comparison, the "exclusive right to sell" provision is more restrictive in that by contract it *precludes the sale of the property by anyone, including the owner,* thus, protecting the broker from *any* sale other than one he arranges.

In the instant case, the parties agreed to an "exclusive right to sell" provision in the contract, but by modifying the agreement to allow the Owners to sell their property, they created an "exclusive agency" contract. Virtually all jurisdictions agree with New Mexico in recognizing that an "exclusive agency" provision does not preclude the owner from selling the property *himself without the aid of any broker* . . . [but it] *precludes the owner from selling through the agency of another broker.*

Here the owners sold their property through the agency of another broker. That action constituted a breach of contract between the first broker, Clodfelter, and the Owners. . . .

In an action for breach of an exclusive agreement between a broker and a property owner, New Mexico and other jurisdictions have held that the first broker is entitled to his full commission. If an owner breaches an exclusive agreement by negotiating a sale through another broker, rendering performance by the first broker impossible, the first broker may recover his commission without showing that he could have performed by tendering a satisfactory buyer or that he was the procuring cause of the sale. . . .

Clodfelter, as a broker under an "exclusive agency" agreement that was breached, is entitled to his full commission of $50,100.00 plus New Mexico gross receipts tax in the amount of $2,004.00.

■ *The trial court is affirmed.*

CASE CONCEPTS REVIEW

1. When did the Owners enter into a listing agreement with Clodfelter? How long was this listing to last?
2. When did the Owners sign a listing agreement with Muchmore?
3. What impact did the handwritten note at the bottom of the Clodfelter agreement have on the parties' relationship?
4. While the court concludes that Clodfelter is entitled to a commission, what is the Owners' liability to Muchmore?

Multiple listing is a method of listing property with several brokers simultaneously. These brokers belong to an organization, the members of which share listings and divide the commissions. A typical commission would be split 60 percent to the selling broker, 30 percent to the listing broker, and 10 percent to the organization for operating expenses. These multiple-listing groups give homeowners the advantage of increased exposure to potential buyers. In return for this advantage, most multiple-listing agreements are of the exclusive right to sell type.

15. Duty to Compensate: Sales Representatives

Sales representatives who sell merchandise on a commission basis are confronted by problems similar to those of the broker, unless their employment contract is specific in its details. Let us assume that Low Cal Pies, Inc., appoints Albert, on a commission basis, as its exclusive sales representative in a certain territory. A grocery chain in the area involved sends a large order for pies directly to the home office of Low Cal Pies. Is Albert entitled to a commission on the sale? It is generally held that such a salesperson is entitled to a commission only on sales solicited and induced by him or her, unless the contract of employment gives the salesperson greater rights.

The sales representative usually earns a commission as soon as an order from a responsible buyer is obtained, unless the contract of employment makes payment contingent on delivery of the goods or collection of the sale's price. If payment is made dependent on performance by the purchaser, the employer cannot deny the sales representative's commission by terminating the agency prior to collection of the account. When the buyer ultimately pays for the goods, the seller is obligated to pay the commission.

An agent who receives a weekly or monthly advance against future commissions is not obligated to return the advance if commissions equal thereto are not earned. The advance, in the absence of a specific agreement, is considered by the courts as a minimum salary. For example, assume a salesperson works for six months on commission and is fired. If this person was granted a monthly draw of $1,500 and has earned only $6,000 in commissions, the general rule is that the $3,000 excess of draws over commissions does not have to be repaid.

16. Duty to Reimburse

An agent has a general right to reimbursement for money properly expended on behalf of his or her principal. It must appear that the money was reasonably spent and that its expenditure was not necessitated by the misconduct or negligence of the agent. Travel-related expenses, such as airfares, mileage, lodging, and meals, are typical examples of the items that a principal must reimburse an agent for unless those parties agree otherwise.

An agent also is entitled to be reimbursed for the costs of completing an agreement when the performance was intended to benefit the principal. This is an especially true statement when the agent has performed on behalf of an undisclosed principal. That principal must protect his or her agent by making funds available to perform the contract as agreed. Suppose that McDonald's is seeking prime locations for its franchises. Not wanting to pay an additional premium just because it is the buyer, McDonald's may hire a local real estate agent to purchase a site in its own name. McDonald's must reimburse this agent for any money that the agent may have used to complete performance of any contract signed.

17. Duty to Indemnify

Indemnify Literally, "to save harmless." Thus, one person agrees to protect another against loss.

Whereas to *reimburse* someone means to repay him or her for funds already spent, to **indemnify** means to hold a person harmless or free from liability. A servant is entitled to indemnity for certain tort losses. They are limited to factual situations in which the servant is not at fault and his or her liability results from following the instructions of the master. An agent or a servant is justified in presuming that a principal has a lawful right to give instructions and that performance resulting from the instructions will not injure third parties. When this is not the case, and the agent incurs a liability to some third party because of trespass or conversion, the principal must indemnify the agent against loss.

There will ordinarily be no indemnification for losses incurred in negligence actions because the servant's own conduct is involved. Any indemnification is usually of the master by the servant in tort situations. If the agent or servant is sued for actions within the course of employment in which he or she is not at fault, the agent or servant is entitled to be reimbursed for attorney's fees and court costs incurred if the principal or master does not furnish them in the first instance.

18. Boeing Guidelines

Of course, all of the Boeing Guidelines affect the employer-employee relationship. They outline the necessity for employees to keep their personal and company interests separate and provide guidance as to what is appropriate conduct in a variety of areas of importance to Boeing. One of the more important areas relate to "conflicts of interest," which is a term that directly relates to the duty of loyalty previously discussed.

The policy on conflict of interests states in part the following:

> It is the policy of The Boeing Company that its transactions with other business entities shall not be influenced or affected by the personal interests or activities of its employees. Employee activities or personal interests, including those of their immediate families, which could appear to influence the objective decisions required of employees in the performance of their Boeing Company responsibilities are considered to be a conflict of interest and are prohibited by this Policy unless approved in writing by The Boeing Company. Such conflicts may create a presumption of favoritism or damage the reputation of The Boeing Company or its employees in the eyes of other employees and persons with whom The Boeing Company may transact business.

> It must be emphasized that an actual conflict of interest need not be present to constitute a violation of this Policy. Activities or personal interests of employees or their immediate families which create the mere appearance of a conflict of interest must be avoided so as not to reflect negatively on the reputation of The Boeing Company or its employees.

To assist its employees in understanding the Guidelines, several examples of possible questions and answers were made available. One example follows:

> *I have been offered a job by another company which involves selling the products of that company to Boeing. Does Boeing policy allow former employees to do this?*

No. Former employees are prohibited from selling to Boeing for a period of two years. Exceptions may be granted in unusual cases only by the Directors of Materiel in the individual operating companies.

CHAPTER SUMMARY

	IN GENERAL
Types of Principals	1. A *disclosed principal* is one whose existence and identity are known by third parties.
	2. A *partially disclosed principal* is one whose existence is known but whose identity is unknown by third parties.
	3. An *undisclosed principal* is one whose identity and existence are unknown by third parties.
Types of Agents	1. A *broker* has limited authority to find a customer so a sale of property may be completed.
	2. A *factor* has possession and control of another person's property and is authorized to sell that property.
	3. A *general agent* has broad authority to conduct a series of transactions with continuity of service.
	4. A *special agent* has narrower authority and conducts a single transaction or lacks continuity of service.
	5. An *independent contractor* retains control over the details of how work is to be accomplished. The person hiring an independent contractor contracts for a certain end result.

Capacity of Parties	1. In general, a minor may act as a principal. Actions by an adult agent on behalf of a minor principal generally are voidable by the minor.
	2. In general, a minor may act as an agent. Actions by a minor agent on behalf of an adult principal generally are binding on the principal.
Formal Requirements	1. Usually, no particular requirements need to be followed to create an agency.
	2. Agency may be expressed or implied. Expressed relationships may be created orally or in writing.
	3. The appointment of an agent must be in writing when the agent is to negotiate a contract required to be in writing under the statute of frauds.
	4. A *power of attorney* is the written document used to formally appoint an agent.
	5. A power of attorney may be general or special in nature.

DUTIES OF AGENTS

Duty of Loyalty	1. This duty is the foundation of every agency relationship.
	2. This duty is breached if the agent takes for himself or herself an opportunity intended to benefit the principal.
	3. This duty is breached if the agent secretly contracts with the principal.
	4. This duty is breached if the agent attempts to represent two principals in the same transaction. This is known as the dual agency situation.
Duty to Protect Confidential Information	1. The agent must protect the principal's trade secrets and not use them for personal profit.
	2. Trade secrets might include plans, processes, tools, compounds, customer lists, and other information used in business operations.
	3. Principals often have agents sign agreements not to compete to reinforce this duty.
Duty to Obey Instructions	1. An agent must follow all reasonable instructions given by the principal.
	2. An agent must not exceed the authority granted by the principal.
	3. If an emergency prevents the agent from obeying the instructions given, that agent must seek additional directions. If the principal is not available, the agent must use his or her best judgment.
Duty to Inform	1. Agents have the duty to give their principals all the information that materially affects the principals' interest.
Duty Not to Be Negligent	1. A principal (master) may be liable for the personal injuries caused by agents (servants) within the scope of their employment.
	2. Because agents (servants) can create this liability by negligence, these parties have the legal duty to refrain from negligent acts.
Duty to Account	1. An agent always must account to the principal for any money the agent has received from or for the principal.
	2. In general, an agent's duty to account is owed only to the principal, not to third parties.
	3. However, an agent must account to third parties (a) if too much money is collected innocently and the agent still has the money, (b) if too much money is collected on purpose regardless of whether the agent has the money, and (c) if too much money is collected on behalf of an undisclosed principal.

DUTIES OF PRINCIPALS

Duty to Compensate: In General	1. Compensation of agents must be reasonable if an amount is not stated in an agreement.
	2. A percentage of profits is calculated using generally accepted accounting principles.
	3. Real estate agents are compensated in accordance with the type of listing agreement signed.

Duty to Compensate: Sales Representatives	1. Unless their agreement states otherwise, a sales representative receives a commission only on sales solicited and induced directly.
	2. The commission generally is earned as soon as an order is placed.
	3. In general, an advance against commission is considered a minimum salary, and the sales representative does not have to return the excess advance.
Duty to Reimburse	1. A principal must reimburse agents who have expended reasonable amounts on behalf of the principal.
	2. Expenses such as transportation costs, lodging, and meals are common reimbursable expenses.
Duty to Indemnify	1. To indemnify means to hold a person harmless or free from liability.
	2. An agent is entitled to be indemnified when the agent becomes liable to third parties while that agent was following the principal's instructions.

REVIEW QUESTIONS AND PROBLEMS

1. Match each term in column A with the appropriate statement in column B.

A	**B**
(1) Disclosed principal	(a) Principal whose identity and existence are unknown by third parties
(2) Undisclosed principal	(b) Agent must protect these and not use them for personal profit
(3) Broker	(c) Person who retains control over the details of how work is to be accomplished
(4) Independent contractor	(d) Type of agent who has limited authority to find a customer to complete a sale of property
(5) Power of attorney	(e) A principal whose existence and identity are known by third parties
(6) Duty of loyalty	(f) A duty generally owed only to principals but in certain situations also to third parties
(7) Trade secrets	(g) Means to hold a person harmless or free from liability—a duty owed by principals to agents
(8) Duty to account	(h) The written document used to formally appoint an agent
(9) Indemnification	(i) The foundation of every agency relationship

2. The Pedestrian Shoe Company hired Angela, age sixteen, to work during the summer. Angela was to solicit orders from shoe stores in her hometown. She was to be paid $1 for each pair of shoes ordered. Angela was so successful that she hired Beth, age twenty-five, to help, and she promised to pay Beth 50 cents for each pair of shoes ordered. Can Angela properly be an agent for Pedestrian? Can Beth properly treat as void her appointment as an agent of Angela and submit her orders to Pedestrian for the larger compensation? Explain.

3. Jon Cady hired Telfair Realty to find a buyer for his house. On July 8, an offer to purchase was presented to Jon Cady. This offer was signed "Reta May Johnson by Jared Johnson, son" as purchaser. After studying the offer, Jon Cady accepted it, and closing was scheduled for August 25. On that date, the purchaser did not appear. Reta May Johnson notified the seller and the real estate agent that she did not intend to complete the transaction. She requested that her earnest money be refunded since she was not bound to the sales contract. She argued that her son was not authorized in writing to

bind her to a real estate sales agreement. Jon Cady and Telfair Realty sued to recover their respective damages resulting from this breach of contract. Was Mrs. Johnson liable for a breach of contract? Explain.

4. New World Fashions provides guidance to persons interested in entering the retail clothing business. Anderson was hired as a sales representative of New World. After several months of working for New World, Anderson decided to start a competing business. However, prior to resigning, Anderson encouraged one of New World's prospective clients to contract with Anderson personally. He then provided to this client services typically furnished by New World. Upon discovery of these facts, New World fired Anderson and sued him to recover lost profits. Must Anderson account to New World for the financial gain he obtained in this transaction? Explain.

5. A manager of a TV station was instructed by the board of directors to fire a salesperson who had a serious drinking problem. When the manager failed to do so because of the salesperson's outstanding record, the manager was fired. He filed suit for wrongful discharge. Was the manager fired improperly? Explain.

6. The St. Paul's Insurance Company instructed its agent, Albert, to notify Thomas that his insurance policy had been canceled. Albert failed to give this notice, and three weeks later a tornado destroyed the insured property owned by Thomas. The company was forced to pay the claim. Can it recover its loss from Albert? Why or why not?

7. Amos was sales manager of Plenty, a turkey-packing company. As a member of the management group, Amos was consulted on all phases of the business. He persuaded the company to enter into a contract to purchase 20,000 turkeys but concealed for some time the fact that he was the seller of the turkeys. Plenty Company did not carry out the contract, and Amos brought suit. Was the contract enforceable? Why?

8. Levinsky had an option to purchase a parcel of land and a right of first refusal on an adjacent parcel. Solomon, acting through a real estate agent, offered to purchase both tracts. The real estate agent knew of Levinsky's rights, but he did not tell Solomon. Is Solomon charged with notice of Levinsky's rights? Explain.

9. Peterson's Florist Company hired Alex to deliver floral arrangements. One day while on a delivery, Alex fell asleep and hit a telephone pole. The delivery van was damaged to the extent of $1,600. Can Peterson's Florist Company recover this amount from Alex? Explain.

10. Perry hired the Creditor's Collection Agency to collect overdue accounts. Perry informed the agency that Terry owed $500 for merchandise received. In fact, Terry owed only $400. However, the agency did collect $500, because Terry also was mistaken about the amount owed. Later, Terry discovered the overpayment. Under what circumstances does the agency owe an accounting to Terry? Explain.

11. Patricia listed her house for sale with Rex, a real estate broker, under a listing contract that gave Rex the exclusive right to sell this house for three months. During this time, Patricia sold her house to a friend who did not know Rex. Patricia refused to pay Rex any commission because Rex was not the procuring cause of the ready, willing, and able buyer. Is Rex entitled to a commission? Why?

12. Dulcy was hired to sell merchandise in a stated territory for Paper Products, Inc. She was to receive a commission of 2 percent on all orders she submitted to the company. She received an advance of $700 a week for ten weeks, but her commissions averaged only $450 a week. If Dulcy is fired, does she owe the company the $2,500 difference? Why?

13. Bowers, a refrigeration mechanic, furnished the tools necessary to do his assigned work. The tools were very heavy and were kept in two toolboxes. Three men were needed to move one toolbox; the other could be moved only by forklift. The tools were kept inside the inner building of the employer's shop. Before the Thanksgiving weekend, Bowers locked his tools in the inner office, but they were stolen in a burglary over

that weekend. A statute required reimbursement for losses in direct discharge of an employee's duties. Must the employer reimburse the employee for the value of the tools? Why or why not?

14. Douglas, a newspaper reporter, sued his former employer, a newspaper publisher. Douglas sought to recover the attorney's fees and court costs incurred in his defense of a libel action. Douglas had been sued as the result of an article written for his employer's newspaper. Douglas had won the libel case. Is the employer obligated to indemnify Douglas for his legal expenses? Explain.

CHAPTER

23

AGENCY AND THE LAW OF CONTRACTS

CHAPTER PREVIEW

*T*he law of agency is essentially concerned with issues of contractual liability. Because corporations act only through agents, and because partners in a partnership are agents of the partnership, a substantial portion of all contracts entered into by businesses are entered into by agents on behalf of principals.

One ultimate goal of these transactions is to establish a relationship that binds the principal and third party contractually. In other words, although the agent negotiates with the third party, the principal is substituted for the agent in the contract with the third party. Despite this objective, whenever a contract is entered into by an agent, issues as to the liability of the various parties may arise. Is the agent personally liable on the contract? Is the principal bound? Can the principal enforce the agreement against the third party? This chapter discusses these issues and others that frequently arise out of contracts entered into by agents on behalf of principals.

Prior to addressing these questions, you must understand the fundamental legal concept of authority. Before an agent can create a binding contract between the principal and third party, that agent must have authority from the principal, or his or her unauthorized actions must have been ratified by the principal. As we will see, authority may be actually granted to the agent by the principal, or it may be apparent to the third party from the principal's actions or inactions.

The legal issues surrounding authority and the liability of the three parties in an agency relationship are presented in this chapter.

■ BUSINESS MANAGEMENT DECISION

You are a famous celebrity. A friend opens a restaurant using your name. You have made no investment of money, but you regularly eat at the restaurant for free. Otherwise you receive no benefits.

What risks are you taking and what should you do to minimize them?

BASIC PRINCIPLES

1. Actual Authority

Express authority A type of actual authority granted by a principal to an agent by written or spoken words.

Implied (incidental) authority A type of actual authority granted by a principal to an agent that is incidental to express authority or arises from the position held by the agent.

A principal may confer actual authority on the agent or may unintentionally, by want of ordinary care, allow the agent to believe himself or herself to possess it. Actual authority includes express authority and implied authority. The term **express authority** describes authority explicitly given to the agent through the principal's written or oral instructions. **Implied authority** is used to describe authority that is necessarily incidental to the express authority or that arises because of business custom and usage or prior practices of the parties. Implied authority is sometimes referred to as **incidental authority;** it is required or reasonably necessary to carry out the purpose for which the agency was created. Implied authority may be established by deductions or inferences from other facts and circumstances in the case, including prior habits or dealings of a similar nature between the parties.

Implied authority based on custom and usage varies from one locality to another and among different kinds of businesses. For example, Perfection Fashions, Inc., appoints Andrea as its agent to sell its casual wear to retail stores. As a part of this relationship, Andrea has express authority to enter into written contracts with the purchasers and to sign Perfection Fashions' name to such agreements. Whether

Andrea has implied or incidental authority to consign the merchandise, thereby allowing the purchaser to return items not sold, may depend on local custom and past dealings. Likewise, whether Andrea may sell on credit instead of cash may be determined by similar standards. If it is customary for other agents of fashion companies in this locality to sell on consignment or on credit, Andrea and the purchasers with whom she deals may assume she possesses such authority. Custom, in effect, creates a presumption of authority. Of course, if the agent or third party has actual knowledge that contradicts customs or past dealings, such knowledge limits the existence of implied or incidental authority.

Implied authority cannot be derived from the words or conduct of the agent. A third person dealing with a known agent may not act negligently in regard to the extent of the agent's authority or blindly trust that agent's statements. The third party must use reasonable diligence and prudence in ascertaining whether the agent is acting within the scope of his or her authority. Similarly, if persons who deal with a purported agent desire to hold the principal liable on the contract, they must ascertain not only the fact of the agency but the nature and extent of the agent's authority. Should either the existence of the agency or the nature and extent of the authority be disputed, the burden of proof regarding these matters is on the third party. However, as the following case illustrates, the existence of implied actual authority may be derived from the totality of the circumstances giving rise to the alleged contract.

CASE

Romero v. Mervyn's
784 P.2d 992 (N.M. 1989)

RANSOM, J.

This is an appeal by defendant Mervyn's from a verdict in favor of plaintiff Lucy Romero for $2,041 in compensatory and $25,000 in punitive damages on a breach of contract claim. . . .

On November 23, 1984, Romero and two of her adult daughters were shopping in Mervyn's Department Store in Albuquerque. It was the day after Thanksgiving and the store was crowded with Christmas shoppers. As Romero and her daughters were descending on an escalator, another customer either intentionally or accidentally pushed her. She fell to her hands and knees, hitting her jaw as she fell. One of her daughters testified that a commotion ensued. When Romero reached the bottom of the escalator, a salesperson at a temporary station helped her to her feet and out of the path of other shoppers. Either this employee or a security guard watching from a two-way mirror summoned the store manager to the scene.

Dennis Wolf, the acting store manager, came in response to this call. His usual job as operations manager of the store entailed responsibility for directing and training employees. It was also his duty to investigate and gather information on incidents involving customer injuries on the premises. Wolf testified that he could tell Romero was in pain and asked her whether she needed a wheelchair or ambulance. Romero replied that she did not. Wolf also testified that Romero's daughters were "very upset, a little bit hysterical," and kept asking who would pay for their mother's medical expenses. Wolf himself, according to Romero's testimony, "seemed to be kind of nervous and in a hurry since the store was busy." According to testimony by Romero and her daughters, Wolf told them that Mervyn's would pay any medical expenses. Wolf testified that, pursuant to company policy, he only told Romero that Mervyn's would submit the claim to its insurer, who would make the decision whether to pay any claims arising from the incident.

Immediately following this conversation, Romero's daughters helped their mother out of the store, brought the car around, and returned to their home in Santa Fe. The following Monday, Romero still was in pain and decided she should seek medical attention. She had another of her daughters, who lived in Albuquerque, call Mervyn's and confirm with Wolf his promise that Mervyn's would pay the expenses. She also asked him if any forms needed to be completed when her mother went to the doctor. He told her to come down to the store and pick up the necessary forms. When she did so, however, Wolf told her that he was out of the forms and then, according to her testimony, told her to go ahead and have her mother pay the expenses. Wolf testified the "forms" in question were insurance claim forms. Romero's daughter confirmed that Wolf told her the forms were for the insurance company but insisted that Wolf reiterated the promise that Mervyn's would pay the bill.

Thereafter, Romero consulted a physician and underwent physical therapy. The cost of her treatment came to $2,041. Mervyn's, however, refused to pay the bills. Romero filed suit. . . .

The jury found in favor of Romero on her contract claim, and awarded punitive damages. Mervyn's appeals, arguing the court erred . . . in submitting the question of Wolf's actual . . . authority to the jury. . . .

The jury received instructions on actual authority (express or implied). . . . In its motion for directed verdict, Mervyn's raised the issue of substantial evidence of actual authority. . . . We conclude the court did not err in instructing the jury on the issue of agency.

Authority is the power of the agent to affect the legal relations of the principal by acts done in accordance with the principal's manifestations of consent to the agent. To warrant an instruction on the issue of Wolf's actual authority to enter into a contract with Romero, substantial evidence must have been introduced that such conduct lay within the scope of Wolf's employment. . . .

We believe substantial evidence was presented on the issue of Wolf's actual authority. When Romero was hurt, Mervyn's other employees called for the "manager." Wolf was both acting manager and operations manager. When he appeared on the scene, the employees already present deferred to his handling of the situation. Mervyn's presented testimony that it was indeed part of Wolf's job to deal with customer injuries, that no one else at the store other than Wolf had such authority, and indeed that there was no one else to whom an injured customer could go. Pursuant to his duties, Wolf inquired whether Romero was hurt and gathered information concerning the accident. It was at this point, according to testimony, that the first promises were made.

Mervyn's argues there was no testimony from Wolf or another agent of Mervyn's to suggest that it lay within Wolf's actual authority to bind Mervyn's. Moreover, Mervyn's argues, the evidence supported Mervyn's allegation that store policy in fact prohibited employees from admitting responsibility for customer injuries. Neither of these points mandated a different verdict. The jury was not obliged to believe the testimony concerning store policy. In addition, an agent's actual authority need not be proved by direct testimony; it can be inferred from attending circumstances.

Mervyn's also argues that Wolf's statements at the time of the accident should not be considered as evidence of his actual authority. Mervyn's theory is that the extrajudicial statements of an agent cannot be used to prove agency, and the admissions of an agent are not binding on the principal unless made within the scope of authority. True, but here it is uncontroverted that Wolf was the acting manager of the store. After prima facie proof of managerial agency, extrajudicial declarations of the agent are admissible and may be considered in determining the scope of the agent's authority. The fact that Wolf made an offer to pay Romero's medical expenses could be considered as evidence of authority to make a contract. . . .

■ *The judgment of the trial court is affirmed.*

CASE CONCEPTS REVIEW

1. With respect to what was said about paying medical bills, what are the differing contentions of the plaintiff and the defendant?

2. On what factual basis does this court conclude that Wolf had actual authority to promise Romero that her medical bills would be paid by Mervyn's?

3. Is this court's conclusion based on the existence of an express or implied form of actual authority?

4. Do you agree with this conclusion?

All agents, even presidents of corporations, have limitations on their authority. Authority is not readily implied. Possession of goods by one not engaged in the business of selling such goods does not create the implication of authority to sell. Authority to sell does not necessarily include the authority to extend credit, although custom may create such authority. The officers of a corporation must have actual authority to enter into transactions that are not in the ordinary course of the business of the corporation. For this reason, persons purchasing real estate from a corporation usually require a resolution of the board of directors specifically authorizing the sale.

2. Apparent or Ostensible Authority

Apparent (ostensible) authority The authority that a principal leads a third party to believe exists when there is no actual authority granted by the principal to the agent.

Estoppel When one's acts, representations, or silence intentionally or through negligence induce another to believe certain facts exist, and the other person acts to his or her detriment on the belief that such facts are true, the first person is not allowed to deny the truth of the facts.

To be distinguished from implied authority is **apparent** or **ostensible authority,** terms that are synonymous. These terms describe the authority a principal, intentionally or by want of ordinary care, causes or allows a third person to believe the agent possesses. Liability of the principal for the ostensible agent's acts rests on the doctrine of **estoppel.** The estoppel is created by some conduct of the principal that leads the third party to believe that a person is the principal's agent or that an actual agent possesses the requisite authority. The third party must know about this conduct and must be injured or damaged by his or her reliance on it. The injury or damage may be a change of position, and the facts relied on must be such that a reasonably prudent person would believe that the authority of the agency existed. Thus three usual essential elements of an estoppel—conduct, reliance, and injury—are required to create apparent authority.

The theory of apparent or ostensible authority is that if a principal's words or actions lead others to believe that he or she has conferred authority on an agent, the principal cannot deny his or her words or actions to third persons who have relied on them in good faith. The acts may include words, oral or written, or may be limited to conduct that reasonably interpreted by a third person causes that person to believe that the principal consents to have the act done on his or her behalf by the purported agent. Apparent authority requires more than the mere appearance of authority. The facts must be such that a person exercising ordinary prudence, acting in good faith, and conversant with business practices would be misled.

Apparent authority may be the basis for liability when the purported agent is, in fact, not an agent. It also may be the legal basis for finding that an actual agent possesses authority beyond that actually conferred. In other words, apparent authority may exist in one not an agent or it may expand the authority of an actual agent. However, an agent's apparent authority to do an act for a principal must be based on the principal's words or conduct and cannot be based on anything the agent has said or done. An agent cannot unilaterally create his or her own apparent authority.

An agency by estoppel or additional authority by estoppel may arise from the agent's dealings being constantly ratified by the principal, or it may result from a person's acting the part of an agent without any dissent from the purported principal, as occurred in the following case.

CASE

Badger v. Paulson Investment Co., Inc.
803 P.2d 1178 (Or. 1991).

PETERSON, C. J.

This is a civil case for damages arising from the sale of securities. The defendant, Paulson Investment Company (hereinafter referred to as Paulson), is an Oregon corporation engaged in the sale of securities as both a broker-dealer and an investment adviser. Two of Paulson's "registered representatives," Zbigniew Lambo and Scott Kennedy, allegedly engaged in fraudulent securities practices and the sale of unregistered securities. The plaintiffs seek to hold Paulson liable for the acts of Lambo and Kennedy on an agency theory.

The record contains the following evidence, which we set forth as background for what follows. Before March 1982, Lambo and Kennedy were employed by T.E. Slanker, a Portland stockbroker. Slanker went out of business. Paulson took over the Slanker accounts. Lambo and Kennedy went to work for Paulson as registered representatives. Paulson informed the Slanker customers that it had taken over the Slanker accounts.

Thereafter, both Lambo and Kennedy made sales presentations to Paulson customers, including some of the plaintiffs. Solicitations and sales of the unregistered securities involved in this case were made using Paulson's letterhead. Sales presentations were made at Paulson's office.

Between August 11, 1982, and September 9, 1984, the plaintiffs purchased the unregistered securities. The securities proved to be valueless.

The plaintiffs thereafter brought claims against Paulson, Lambo and Kennedy. . . .

The trial court thereafter set aside the verdict for the plaintiffs against Paulson on the two securities claims. In addition, the trial court set aside the verdict against Paulson for punitive damages on the common-law fraud claim. The plaintiffs appealed. . . .

The plaintiffs seek to impose liability on Paulson for Kennedy's and Lambo's conduct on the following principle, as stated in the plaintiffs' brief:

> Where a principal has, by his voluntary acts, placed an agent in such a situation that a person of ordinary prudence is justified in assuming that such agent has authority to perform a particular act and deals with the agent upon that assumption, the law does not permit the principal to claim that the agent was not authorized or even was prohibited from performing the act.

This agency theory, applicable when an agent acts in excess of his or her actual authority but with the appearance of authority, is commonly referred to as "apparent authority." Apparent authority is created only by some conduct of the principal which, when reasonably interpreted, causes a third party to believe that the principal consents to have the apparent agent act for him on that matter. The third party must also rely on that belief.

Apparent authority, on the other hand, arises when the agent does not possess the actual or implied authority to act for the principal in the matter, but the principal has clothed the agent with apparent authority to act for the principal in that particular. In other words, the principal permits the agent to appear to have the authority to bind the principal. Either of these agency relationships can bind the principal creating liability for the acts of the agent. In the present case, the plaintiffs maintain that when Kennedy and Lambo sold the securities, Kennedy and Lambo were acting within their apparent authority.

In order for Paulson to be bound by Kennedy's and Lambo's conduct towards the plaintiffs on the theory of apparent authority, it must be shown that:

1. Paulson provided information to the plaintiffs that was either intended to cause the plaintiffs to believe that Kennedy and Lambo were authorized to act for Paulson, or Paulson should have realized that its conduct was likely to create such belief; and

2. From information provided by Paulson, or from the conduct of Paulson, the plaintiffs reasonably believed that Kennedy and Lambo were authorized to act for Paulson.

There is sufficient evidence to support a finding that Kennedy and Lambo were acting within the apparent authority of Paulson. Paulson is a broker-dealer and investment adviser selling securities in Oregon. Kennedy and Lambo were employed by Paulson as registered representatives. Kennedy and Lambo previously were employed by another securities firm, T.E. Slanker, which went out of business. When Kennedy went to work for Paulson, it sent its customers letters announcing Kennedy's association with Paulson. A second letter was sent a short time later to announce the assignment of Kennedy to several ongoing customer accounts. With these announcements, Paulson, who did not inform its customers of any limitations on Kennedy's authority to act for Paulson, conferred on Kennedy the authority to represent Paulson in securities sales and investment transactions.

Following the announcements, conduct evincing a grant of authority continued. Kennedy's written communications with the plaintiffs concerning the securities were on Paulson's stationery, signed by Kennedy, and mailed to Lambo. Information regarding the securities was often enclosed by Lambo in these communications, along with information on securities approved by Paulson.

Sales presentations touting the securities involved in this case were made by Kennedy and Lambo. The sales presentations occurred on Paulson's premises, and on at least one occasion, during normal business hours. Furthermore, both Kennedy and Lambo received calls regarding the securities at Paulson's place of business.

At no time were any of the plaintiffs notified that the sale of the securities had not been approved by Paulson or that Kennedy and Lambo were acting solely on their own behalf. There is evidence that Paulson provided information intended to cause third persons to believe that Kennedy and Lambo were authorized to act for it in matters pertaining to the sale of securities, including meeting with customers, making sales presentations, sending mailings and handling paperwork. Although Paulson may have forbade its sales representatives to present or sell nonapproved securities, liability based on the agency principle of apparent authority may be imposed even though the principal expressly forbade the conduct in question.

There is also evidence that from the information provided to them by Paulson, the plaintiffs reasonably believed that Kennedy and Lambo were authorized to act for Paulson concerning the securities sold by Kennedy and Lambo to the plaintiffs. The investors testified to their reliance on this apparent authority.

The evidence is sufficient to support the jury's verdict that Kennedy and Lambo conducted the illegal sales and the apparent authority of Paulson. Paulson, therefore, is liable as a principal for the plaintiffs' damages. The trial court erred in granting judgment notwithstanding the verdict to Paulson. The judgment on the claim for damages . . . must be reinstated. . . .

■ *Reversed.*

CASE CONCEPTS REVIEW

1. Were Lambo and Kennedy employed by the Paulson Investment Company?
2. Since the facts are clear that the plaintiffs purchased securities through Lambo or Kennedy or both of them, what is the basis for Paulson to argue that these agents lacked actual authority to enter into these transactions?
3. What evidence does the court rely on to find that Paulson (as principal) led the plaintiffs (as third parties) to believe that Lambo and Kennedy (as agents) had authority to enter into these transactions?

Perhaps the most common situation in which apparent authority is found to exist occurs when the actual authority is terminated but notice of this fact is not given to those entitled to receive it. Cancellation of actual authority does not automatically terminate the apparent authority created by prior transactions. The ramification of apparent authority's surviving the termination of an agency relationship requires the principal to give notice of termination to third parties. The legal aspects of this notification are discussed in chapter 25.

3. Ratification

Ratification The confirmation of an act or act of another (e.g., a principal may ratify the previous unauthorized act of his or her agent).

As previously noted, a purported principal may become bound by ratifying an unauthorized contract. Having knowledge of all material matters, the principal may express or imply adoption or confirmation of a contract entered into on his or her behalf by someone who had no authority to do so. **Ratification** is implied by conduct of the principal, which is inconsistent with the intent to repudiate the agent's action. It is similar to ratification by an adult of a contract entered while a minor. Ratification relates back to, and is the equivalent of, authority at the commencement of the act or time of the contract. It is the affirmance of a contract already made. It cures the defect of lack of authority and creates the relation of principal and agent.

CAPACITY REQUIRED.   Various conditions must exist before a ratification will be effective in bringing about a contractual relation between the principal and the third party. First, because ratification relates back to the time of the contract, ratification can be effective only when both the principal and the agent were capable of contracting at the time the contract was executed and are still capable at the time of ratification. For this reason, a corporation may not ratify contracts made by its promoters on the corporation's behalf before the corporation was formed. For the corporation to be bound by such agreements, a novation or an assumption of liability by the corporation must occur.

ACTING AS AGENT.   Second, an agent's act may be ratified only when the agent holds himself or herself out as acting for the one who is alleged to have approved the unauthorized agreement. In other words, the agent must have professed to act as an agent. A person who professes to act for himself or herself and who makes a contract in his or her own name does nothing that can be ratified, even though that person intends at the time to let another have the benefit of the agreement.

FULL KNOWLEDGE. Third, as a general rule, ratification does not bind the principal unless he or she acts with full knowledge of all the material facts attending negotiation and execution of the contract. Of course, when there is express ratification and the principal acts without any apparent desire to know or to learn the facts, the principal may not later defend himself or herself on the ground that he or she was unaware of all the material facts. However, when ratification is to be implied from the conduct of the principal, he or she must act with knowledge of all important details, as held in the following case.

CASE

Perkins v. Philbrick

443 A.2d 73 (Me. 1982)

WATHEN, J.

. . . The issue raised by this appeal is whether defendant's forged signature on settlement drafts and a release form can effectuate a settlement and bar defendant's underlying tort claim against plaintiff. . . .

In 1976 the parties were involved in an automobile accident in which defendant was injured. He hired an attorney to press his claim against plaintiff, and the attorney entered into communications with plaintiff's insurer. In late 1976, in a conversation with the attorney, the insurer's claims adjuster offered to settle defendant's claim for $26,000. The attorney replied that he would have to discuss the offer with his client. In January 1977 without prior discussion with his client the attorney told the adjuster that the settlement was acceptable. The insurer prepared drafts together with a release and inadvertently mailed them to the defendant. Two of the drafts received by the defendant were payable jointly to him and his attorney and one was payable to him and Blue Cross/Blue Shield. Defendant gave the unsigned documents to his attorney explaining that he did not want to settle for that amount. Defendant neither signed nor authorized the endorsement of any draft or the release. The two drafts payable jointly to defendant and his attorney were subsequently presented for payment bearing defendant's purported endorsement. The release form was not immediately returned to the insurer. When, after numerous calls, the claims adjuster visited the attorney's office, he was given the release purportedly signed by defendant. Sometime in February or March of 1977 the attorney gave defendant between $7,000 and $7,800 which he claimed was part of a $10,000 advance by the insurer. Throughout this period defendant took an active interest in the progress of

his claim without learning that the drafts and release had been signed and presented.

In 1979 defendant, represented by his present attorney, commenced suit against plaintiff in Superior Court, seeking damages for his injury in the 1976 accident. Plaintiff then filed this action seeking a declaratory judgment that her obligation to defendant had been discharged when the drafts issued by her insurance company were paid by the bank and the executed release form was received by the insurer. The presiding justice did not issue a declaratory judgment but instead denied plaintiff's request. He based his order on his findings that defendant had neither accepted the settlement nor authorized anyone including his attorney to do so for him by signing the release. These factual findings are undisputed, and we find no settlement has been effectuated under these circumstances. . . .

The parties' briefs focus solely upon the legal principles of authority and ratification applicable to defendant's endorsement forged by his attorney. Dealing with the issue as thus framed, we find a long established principle in Maine and many other jurisdictions that "an attorney clothed with no other authority than that arising from his employment in that capacity has no power to compromise and settle or release and discharge his client's claim." In the absence of authority, the mere fact that the release was signed with defendant's name does not constitute a bar to defendant's tort action.

Neither does the payment of the settlement draft over defendant's forged endorsement effect a settlement of the underlying claim. "Any unauthorized signature is wholly inoperative as that of the person whose name is signed, unless he ratifies it or is precluded from denying it." Thus, the forgery of defendant's name, even if accomplished by his attorney, was not an acceptance of the draft according to its terms as "a release of all claims for damages."

Plaintiff argues that even if the forgeries cannot effectuate a settlement, defendant is bound by them because he ratified the purported settlement by accepting what he thought was an advance. We conclude, as did the Superior Court, that no ratification occurred which would bar defendant's underlying tort action.

For ratification of an agent's actions to occur, it is necessary that all material facts be known by the principal. . . . The record in this case plainly shows that defendant did not have knowledge of the forgery when he accepted the advance from the attorney; therefore the court correctly concluded that ratification had not occurred.

■ *Affirmed.*

CASE CONCEPTS REVIEW

1. This case must be viewed from the perspective of Mr. Philbrick hiring an attorney to resolve a dispute with Ms. Perkins. Why does Perkins argue that Philbrick settled his claim against her?

2. Although Philbrick did not know that his attorney, without any authority to do so, had settled the original lawsuit, what did Philbrick receive from his attorney?

3. Why does this court reject Perkins's argument that Philbrick had ratified the unauthorized settlement of the original lawsuit?

CONDUCT CONSTITUTING RATIFICATION.   Ratification may be either express or implied. Any conduct that definitely indicates an intention on the part of the principal to adopt the transaction will constitute ratification. It may take the form of words of approval to the agent, a promise to perform, or actual performance, such as delivery of the product called for in the agreement. Accepting the benefits of the contract or basing a suit on the validity of an agreement clearly amounts to ratification. Knowing what the agent has done, if the principal makes no objection for an unreasonable time, ratification results by operation of law. Generally, the question of what is an unreasonable time is for the jury to decide.

The issue of whether or not ratification has occurred is also a question to be decided by the jury. Among the facts to be considered by the jury are the relationship of the parties, prior conduct, circumstances pertaining to the transaction, and the action or inaction of the alleged principal upon learning of the contract. Inaction or silence by the principal creates difficulty in determining if ratification has occurred. Failure to speak may mislead the third party, and courts frequently find that a duty to speak exists where silence will mislead. Silence and inaction by the party to be charged as a principal, or failure to dissent and speak up when ordinary human conduct and fair play would normally call for some negative assertion within a reasonable time, tends to justify the inference that the principal acquiesced in the course of events and accepted the contract as his or her own. Acceptance and retention of the fruits of the contract with full knowledge of the material facts of the transaction is probably the most certain evidence of implied ratification. As soon as a principal learns of an unauthorized act by his or her agent, the principal should promptly repudiate it to avoid liability on the theory of ratification.

An unauthorized act may not be ratified in part and rejected in part. The principal cannot accept the benefits of the contract and refuse to assume its obligations. Because of this rule, a principal, by accepting the benefits of an authorized agreement, ratifies the means used in procuring the agreement, unless within a reasonable time after learning the actual facts the principal takes steps to return, as far as possible, the benefits received. Therefore, if an unauthorized agent commits fraud in procuring a contract, acceptance of the benefits ratifies not only the contract but the fraudulent acts as well, and the principal is liable for the fraud.

4. Introduction

With respect to contractual matters, a principal may become liable to its agents and third parties. The answers to when and why such liability is created depend in part on the type of principal involved. As mentioned in the previous chapter, there are three possible choices concerning the types of principals. From the third party's perspective, a principal may be *disclosed, partially disclosed,* or *undisclosed.* When studying the rest of this chapter, keep in mind the distinctions between these categories. For the most part, the law treats the disclosed principals differently from the other types of principals. In general, the law views the liability of partially disclosed and undisclosed principals as being the same. Therefore, in the following sections, any mention of an undisclosed principal's liability includes the liability of a partially disclosed principal, unless the text states otherwise.

5. Disclosed Principal's Liability to Agents

Generally, a disclosed principal's liability to its agents is based on the fiduciary duties discussed in chapter 22. From a contractual perspective, a disclosed principal implicitly agrees to protect its agents from any liability as long as these agents act within the scope of authority granted. In other words, when a disclosed principal is involved, agency principles are applied in such a way that the third party must look to the principal for contractual performance if the agent acted within the authority given. If the third party seeks to hold the agent personally liable, that agent may insist that the disclosed principal hold him or her harmless for liability purposes. A similar result of the principal holding the agent harmless for contractual performance occurs if a disclosed principal ratifies an unauthorized agent's actions.

However, if an agent for a disclosed principal exceeds the authority granted, the principal is not liable to the agent and is not required to protect the agent from liability. In general, the agent who exceeds authority becomes personally liable to the third party and cannot rely on the principal as a substitute for liability or indemnification. The one exception to this general rule is when the disclosed principal ratifies the unauthorized actions of an agent. When ratification does occur, the liability of the parties is the same as if the agent's acts were authorized prior to their happening.

6. Disclosed Principal's Liability to Third Parties

Because of the concept of the principal holding the agent harmless, generally a disclosed principal becomes liable to third parties who negotiate and enter into contracts with authorized agents. With respect to transactions involving disclosed principals, the agent's authority may be either actual or apparent.

Furthermore, disclosed principals become liable to third parties if the unauthorized actions of an agent are ratified. With respect to such ratification, the laws of agency state that the act of ratification must occur before the third party withdraws from the contract. The reason for protecting the third party in this way is the constant legal concern with mutuality of obligations. One party should not be bound to a contract if the other party is not also bound. Therefore the law recognizes that the third party may withdraw from an unauthorized contract entered into by an agent at any time before it is ratified by the principal. If the third party were not allowed to withdraw, the unique situation in which one party is bound and the other is not would exist. Remember, though, that ratification does not require notice to the third party. As soon as conduct constituting ratification has been indulged in by the principal, the third party loses the right to withdraw.

7. Undisclosed Principal's Liability to Agents

The fact that a principal's identity or even existence is hidden from third parties does not change the principal-agent relationship. Therefore, undisclosed principals may become liable for breach of a fiduciary duty owed to agents. Furthermore, undisclosed principals are liable to agents who negotiate and enter into contracts within their actual authority. Since a third party may hold an agent of an undisclosed principal personally liable, the authorized agent may recover the amount of its liability from the undisclosed principal.

The rule of law set forth in the previous sentence limits the undisclosed principal's liability only to contracts entered pursuant to the agent's *actual* authority. When a principal is undisclosed, neither apparent authority nor ratification can occur, since these happenings arise as a result of the principal–third-party relationship. Of course, when the principal's identity or existence is unknown to the third party, there cannot be a principal–third-party relationship. In other words, an undisclosed principal has no liability to an agent who exceeds the actual authority granted by the principal.

8. Undisclosed Principal's Liability to Third Parties

The liability of undisclosed principals to third parties is limited by two important principles. First, undisclosed principals are liable to third parties only when the agent acted within the scope of actual authority. Remember, apparent authority and ratification cannot occur when the principal is undisclosed. However, an undisclosed principal who retains the benefits of a contract is liable to the third party in quasi-contract for the value of such benefits. To allow a principal to keep the benefits would be an unacceptable form of unjust enrichment at the third party's expense.

Second, the contract entered into by an actually authorized agent must be the type that can be assigned to the undisclosed principal. For example, an employment contract requiring the personal services of the agent would not bind the undisclosed principal and the third party. Suppose a group of young engineers form an architectural design firm. Wishing to be hired to design a new fifty-story building that will serve as Exxon's headquarters, these engineers decide to submit a bid. However, fearful that their lack of reputation will harm their chances of being employed, they hire Phillip Johnson, a renowned designer-architect, to present the bid. Mr. Johnson is instructed not to reveal the new firm's identity. In other words, the bid is to be submitted in Phillip Johnson's name alone. If Exxon awarded the design job to Mr. Johnson, it is very unlikely that the new firm and Exxon become contractually bound. This result would occur because of Exxon's belief that it was hiring the unique personal talents of Mr. Johnson. That is, the contract between the agent (Phillip Johnson) and the third party (Exxon) is not assignable to the undisclosed principal (young engineering firm) without the third party's consent. The vast majority of contracts negotiated by agents for undisclosed principals will not involve those agents' personal services. Thus most of these contracts will be freely assignable.

In addition to the requirements that the agent be actually authorized and that the contract be assignable, there are two further items to consider concerning the undisclosed principal's liability to third parties. These additional legal concepts are called *election* and *settlement,* and they are applicable to undisclosed principals only. The following discussions of elections and settlements do not apply to partially disclosed principals.

9. Effect of Election

Election The decision of a third party to hold either the agent or the previously undisclosed principal liable. By electing to hold one party liable, the third party has chosen not to seek a recovery against the other party.

When the existence and identity of the principal become known to the third party, the third party may look to either the agent or the principal for performance. If the third party elects to hold the principal liable, the agent is released. Similarly, if the third party elects to hold the agent liable, the previously undisclosed but now disclosed principal is released. An **election** to hold one party releases the other from liability.

It is sometimes difficult to know when an election has occurred. Clearly, conduct by the third party preceding the disclosure of the principal cannot constitute an election. Because of this rule, it has been held that an unsatisfied judgment obtained against the agent before disclosure of the principal will not bar a later action against the principal.

After disclosure, the third party may indicate an election by making an express declaration of his or her intention to hold one party and not the other liable. Most states also hold that the mere receipt, without collection, of a negotiable instrument from either the principal or agent does not constitute an election. Furthermore, it is clear that merely starting a lawsuit is not an election. However, there has been some controversy among the states about whether obtaining a judgment against the principal or agent is an election if that judgment remains uncollected. Whereas all states agree that a third party is entitled to only one satisfaction, the predominant theory is that obtaining a judgment, even if it remains uncollected, amounts to an election. This theory has been called the *judgment theory* of elections, and it was applied in the following case.

CASE

Sherrill v. Bruce Advertising, Inc.
538 S.W.2d 865 (Tex. 1976)

COULSON, J.

. . . This is an appeal from a suit on a contract for services rendered. Bruce Advertising, Inc. sued M. A. Sherrill, Trustee of the William W. Sherrill Trust and Crane-Maier and Associates, Inc. for services rendered in connection with the development of real property owned by the Sherrill Trust. The trial court entered judgment for Bruce Advertising. . . . The judgment against Crane-Maier has not been appealed and has become final. This appeal relates only to the judgment entered against M. A. Sherrill, Trustee of the William W. Sherrill Trust. We reverse.

In 1970, an agreement was entered between Crane-Maier and the Sherrill Trust whereby the Trust's real property located in Galveston County would be subdivided, developed and sold by Crane-Maier. Bruce Advertising dealt with Crane-Maier by supplying services to them on a contractual basis for development of the realty. Bruce Advertising was not aware that the Sherrill Trust owned the property which Crane-Maier was developing. Suit was brought against Crane-Maier for the services rendered by Bruce Advertising when payment was not forthcoming. After suit was instituted, Crane-Maier by way of its pleadings informed Bruce Advertising that the Sherrill Trust was owner of the property which Crane-Maier was developing. The trial court sitting without a jury entered judgment against both Crane-Maier and the Sherrill Trust holding them jointly and severally liable for the services rendered by Bruce Advertising. . . . The court stated that the association of an agreement between Crane-Maier and the Sherrill Trust constituted a joint venture for the development of the property. The Sherrill Trust has appealed the judgment claiming that as a matter of law there is no joint venture between it and Crane-Maier. We agree. . . .

However, we must consider whether the findings of fact will support the judgment against the Sherrill Trust on any other theory of law. The findings of fact show that Crane-Maier agreed with Bruce Advertising to handle the advertising requirements of the property belonging to the Sherrill Trust. They further show that an agreement was entered into between the Sherrill Trust and Crane-Maier for development and sale of the lots of the Sherrill Trust's property and that Crane-Maier was to be compensated for its services of promotion, development and sales of the project by a percentage of the sales price of each lot sold. These findings contain elements supporting the theory that Crane-Maier was the agent acting for the principal, the Sherrill Trust, in ordering advertising services from Bruce Advertising.

Whether Bruce Advertising may recover a judgment on a joint and several basis against both a principal and agent is the question presented. . . .

We may imply from the findings of fact that a principal and agent relationship existed between the Sherrill Trust and Crane-Maier, which theory is supported by Bruce Advertising's pleadings. Bruce Advertising did not know that Crane-Maier was acting for anyone other than itself. The Sherrill Trust is in the position of an undisclosed principal. An undisclosed principal is discharged from liability upon a contract if, with knowledge of the identity of the principal, the other party recovers judgment against the agent who made the contract, for the breach of the contract. While this rule has received some discredit, the Texas courts have consistently followed it. Here, the judgment against the agent Crane-Maier has become final. On the theory of principal and agent, the principal, Sherrill Trust, cannot now be held liable since there is a final judgment had against its agent for breach of the contract.

The judgment against Crane-Maier having been entered and now final, there is no theory which can support joint and several liability against the Sherrill Trust. . . .

■ *Reversed.*

CASE CONCEPTS REVIEW

1. Which parties were the principal, agent, and third party in this factual situation?

2. From the viewpoint of Bruce Advertising, Inc., how did this relationship appear? How can the position of Sherrill Trust best be described?

3. Why does the court conclude that Bruce Advertising elected to hold Crane-Maier liable, thereby relieving Sherrill Trust of any direct responsibility to Bruce Advertising?

10. Effect of Settlement

Settlement By paying (or settling with) the agent, the principal is relieved of liability to the third party. This third party will look to the agent for performance of their agreement.

Suppose that the undisclosed principal supplied the agent with money to purchase merchandise, but the agent purchased on credit and appropriated the money. In such cases the principal has been relieved of all responsibilities. The same result may occur when the undisclosed principal *settles* with the agent after the contract is made and the merchandise is received, but before disclosure is made to the third party. A majority of states have held that a bona fide **settlement** between the principal and agent before disclosure occurs releases the principal. A settlement cannot have this effect, however, when it is made after the third party has learned of the existence of the principal. This settlement rule, adopted by most states, is based on equitable principles. It is fair to the third party in that it gives him or her all the protection originally bargained for, and it is fair to the principal in that it protects him or her against a second demand for payment.

11. Introduction

Many special problems arise in the law of agency as it relates to contractual liability and authority of agents. Some of these problems are founded on the relationship of the parties. A spouse is generally liable for the contracts of the other spouse when the contracts involve family necessities. In most states this liability is statutory. Others involve special factual situations. An existing emergency that necessitates immediate action adds sufficiently to the agent's powers to enable him or her to meet the situation. If time permits and the principal is available, any proposed remedy for the difficulty must be submitted to the principal for approval. It is only when the principal is not available that the powers of the agent are extended. Furthermore, the agent receives no power greater than that sufficient to solve the difficulty.

Frequently, the liability of the principal is dependent on whether the agent is, as a matter of fact, a general agent or a special agent. If the agency is general, limitations imposed on the usual and ordinary powers of the general agent do not prevent the principal from being liable to third parties when the agent acts in violation of such limitations, unless the attention of the third parties has been drawn to them. In other words, the third party, having established that a general agency exists and having determined in a general way the limits of the authority, is not bound to explore for unexpected and unusual restrictions. The third party is justified in assuming, in the absence of contrary information, that the agent possesses the powers such agents customarily have. On the other hand, if the proof is only of a special or limited agency, any action in excess of the actual authority would not bind the principal. The authority for a special agent is strictly construed; if the agent exceeds his or her authority, the principal is not bound.

For example, a sales agent is instructed not to sell to a certain individual or not to sell to him or her on credit, although credit sales are customary. Such a limitation cannot affect the validity of a contract made with this individual, unless the latter was aware of the limitation at the time the contract was made. The principal, by appointing an agent normally possessed of certain authority, is estopped to set up the limitation as a defense unless the limitation is made known to the third party prior to the making of the contract.

12. Notice to Agents

There are other issues directly related to the authority possessed by an agent. A common problem involves whether or not notice to an agent or knowledge possessed by the agent is imputed to the principal. Some of these questions are covered by statutes. Civil practice statutes contain provisions on service of a summons on an agent. They specify who may be an agent for the service of process and, in effect, provide that notice to such agents constitutes notice to the principal.

Notice to, or knowledge acquired by, an agent while acting within the scope of his or her authority binds the principal. This rule is based on the theory that the agent is the principal's other self; therefore what the agent knows, the principal knows. While *knowledge* possessed by an agent is *notice* to the principal, the principal may not have actual knowledge of the particular fact at all. Knowledge acquired by an agent acting outside the scope of his or her authority is not effective notice unless the party relying thereon has reasonable ground to believe that the agent is acting within the scope of his or her authority (similar to apparent authority). An agent who is acquiring property for a principal may have knowledge of certain unrecorded liens against the property. The principal purchases the property subject to those liens. Equal knowledge possessed by another agent who did not represent the principal in the particular transaction, and who did not obtain the knowledge on behalf of the principal, is not imputed to the principal.

A question exists as to whether or not knowledge acquired by an agent before becoming an agent can bind the principal. The majority view is that knowledge acquired by an agent before commencement of the relationship of principal and agent is imputable to the principal if the knowledge is present and in the mind of the agent while acting for the principal in the transaction to which the information is material. There are some court decisions to the contrary that have stated that the agent must acquire the knowledge during the agency relationship before the principal is presumed to have notice of that information.

Notice or knowledge received by an agent under circumstances in which the agent would not be presumed to communicate the information to the principal does not bind the principal. This is an exception to the general rule that will be observed when the agent is acting in his or her own behalf and adversely to the principal or when the agent is under a duty to some third party not to disclose the information. Furthermore, notice to the agent, combined with collusion or fraud between the agent and the third party that would defeat the purpose of the notice, would not bind the principal.

As a general rule, an agent or person ostensibly in charge of a place of business has apparent authority to accept notices in relation to the business. An employee in charge of the receipt of mail may accept written notifications.

13. Agent's Power to Appoint Subagents

Agents are usually selected because of their personal qualifications. Owing to these elements of trust and confidence, a general rule has developed that an agent may not delegate his or her duty to someone else and clothe the latter with authority to bind the principal. An exception has arisen to this rule in cases in which the acts of the agent are purely ministerial or mechanical. An act that requires no discretion and is purely mechanical may be delegated by the agent to the third party. Such a delegation does not make the third party the agent of the principal or give the third party any action against the principal for compensation unless the agent was implicitly authorized to obtain this assistance. The acts of such a third party become in reality the acts of the agent. They bind the principal if they are within the authority given to the agent. Acts that involve the exercise of skill, discretion, or judgment may not be delegated without permission from the principal.

An agent may, under certain circumstances, have the actual or implied authority to appoint other agents for the principal, in which case they become true employees of the principal and are entitled to be compensated. This power on the part of the agent is not often implied; but if the major power conferred cannot be exercised without the aid of other agents, the agent is authorized to hire whatever help is required. Thus, a manager placed in charge of a branch store may be presumed to possess authority to hire the necessary personnel.

14. Agent's Financial Powers

An agent who delivers goods sold for cash has the implied authority to collect all payments due at the time of delivery. A salesperson taking orders calling for a down payment has implied authority to accept the down payment. By the very nature of their jobs, salespeople have no implied authority to receive payments on account, and any authority to do so must be expressly given or be implied from custom. Thus, a salesperson in a store has authority to collect payments made at the time of sale but no authority to receive payments on account. If payment to a sales agent who has no authority to collect is not delivered to the principal, it may be collected by the principal from the agent or from the party who paid the agent.

Possession of a statement of account on the billhead of the principal or in the principal's handwriting does not create implied or apparent authority to collect a debt. Payment to an agent without authority to collect does not discharge the debt.

Authority to collect gives the agent no authority to accept anything other than money in payment. Unless expressly authorized, the agent is not empowered to accept negotiable notes or property in settlement of an indebtedness. It is customary for an agent to accept checks as conditional payment. Under those circumstances, the debt is not paid unless the check is honored. If the check is not paid, the creditor principal is free to bring suit on the contract that gave rise to the indebtedness or to sue on the check, at his or her option.

A general agent placed in charge of a business has implied or incidental authority to purchase for cash or on credit. The implied authority is based on the nature of the agent's position. The public rightly concludes that a corporation or an individual acting through another person has given the agent the power and authority that naturally and properly belong to the position in which the agent is placed.

Authority to borrow money is not easily implied. It must be expressly granted or must qualify as incidental authority to the express authority, or the principal will not be bound. The authority to borrow should always be confirmed with the principal.

LIABILITY OF AGENTS AND THIRD PARTIES

15. Introduction

Sections 4 through 10 of this chapter discuss the general rules of the principal's liability. The following sections address the corresponding issues of when agents and third parties are liable. In essence, the legal principles attempt to make sure that if one party is bound to a contract, so is another party. For example, if a disclosed principal is liable to a third party, that third party must be liable to the disclosed principal. The law always attempts to find that parties are mutually obligated for contractual performances.

16. Agent's Liability to Principals

As long as the agent acts within the scope of authority actually granted, the agent has no liability to the principal. The one exception occurs when an undisclosed principal has settled with the agent prior to the principal's being disclosed to the third party. In that situation, the agent is liable to the principal to perform the contract as instructed.

If the agent of a disclosed principal exceeds the actual authority granted but binds the principal to the third party due to the existence of apparent authority, that agent is liable to the principal for the damages caused. The basis of holding the agent liable in this situation is that the agent has breached the duty to obey instructions. Of course, if the disclosed principal ratifies an agent's unauthorized actions, the agent does not become liable to the principal.

17. Agent's Liability to Third Parties

Agents generally do not become contractually bound to third parties, because the principal usually takes the agent's place for liability purposes. However, an agent of an undisclosed principal may become liable to the third party in one of two situations. First, the third party may elect to hold the agent liable instead of the principal. Second, if the principal settles with that agent before becoming disclosed, the agent and third party are contractually bound. These are the settlement and election concepts previously noted in sections 9 and 10.

With respect to contractual matters in general, an agent may become bound to the third party by the way the agent signs the agreement or due to the language of the actual contract; that is, the agent may be liable because of the contractual document. An agent can become liable to a third party if the agent exceeds actual and apparent authority and no ratification by the principal occurs. In other words, based on a breach of an implied promise that the agent is representing a principal, the agent and third party are legally bound to one another. Further details of these two methods of binding the agent to the third party follow.

BASED ON THE CONTRACT.   Three situations may arise that make the agent liable to the third party due to the contract itself. First, if the agent carelessly executes a written agreement, the agent may fail to bind the principal and may incur personal liability. For example, when an agent signs a simple contract or commercial paper, he or she should execute it in a way that clearly indicates a representative capacity. If the signature fails to indicate the actual relationship of the parties and fails to identify the party intended to be bound, the agent may be personally liable on the instrument. Many states permit the use of oral evidence to show the intention of the agent and the third party when the signature is ambiguous—the agent is allowed to offer proof that it was not intended that he or she assume personal responsibility. The Code contains express provisions on the liability of an agent who signs a commercial paper. These are discussed in chapter 36.

Second, if the agent does not disclose the agency or name the principal, the agent binds himself or herself and becomes subject to all liabilities, express and implied, created by the contract and transaction, in the same manner as if that agent were the principal. If an agent wishes to avoid personal liability, the duty is on the agent to disclose the agency. There is no duty on the third party to discover the agency.

An agent who purports to be a principal is liable as a principal. The fact that the agent is known to be a commission merchant, auctioneer, or other professional agent is immaterial. The agent must disclose not only that he or she is an agent but the identity of the principal if the agent is not to have personal liability. Any agent for an undisclosed or partially disclosed principal assumes personal liability on the contract into which he or she enters, as occurred in the following case.

CASE

Como v. Rhines

645 P.2d 948 (Mont. 1982)

This case arises out of the breach of an employment contract. Sound West, Inc., is a Montana corporation that owns a chain of stores. Jim Rhines is the president and a shareholder of Sound West. Gary Como, who has worked as an accountant and with computers, sought employment in Montana. Through an employment agency's reference, Como met with Rhines about possible employment. After a series of interviews in April 1978, Rhines agreed to hire Como and to pay his moving expenses. They agreed Como would begin working for Sound West in June. After Como moved and settled his family, he contacted Rhines about beginning his employment. Rhines was noncommittal. Following several more requests by Como for a starting date, Rhines told Como there was no job for him at Sound West. Como secured employment elsewhere and sued Rhines individually for lost wages and moving expenses. Rhines argued he was acting as an agent for Sound West, Inc.; therefore, he was not personally liable to Como. The District Court found for the plaintiff, and the defendant appealed.

DALY, J.

... Appellants raise ... [the following issue]: Did the District Court err by holding appellant Jim Rhines liable for respondent's damages? ...

The District Court concluded as a matter of law that "Jim Rhines as the president and manager of Sound West, Inc., did offer employment to Gary Como for an accounting position with express terms." ... The District Court then went on to conclude that Jim Rhines and Sound West, Inc., breached the employment contract and that both Rhines and Sound West were liable for the damages arising out of this breach.

This Court has recognized the general rule that an agent is not personally liable on a contract entered into by him on behalf of his principal if it appears, in fact, that he disclosed the identity of his principal and made the engagement for him. This Court has [also] recognized that the existence of the agency must be disclosed in appropri-

ate terms, including the name of the principal for whom the agent is acting. Moreover, merely because the agent, in making the contract for his principal, uses the trade name under which his principal transacts business is not of itself a sufficient identification of the principal to protect the agent from liability.

This general rule of agency also applies to the corporate setting:

> The rule that where an agent enters into a contract in his own name for an undisclosed principal, the other party to the contract may hold the agent personally liable, applies equally well to corporate officers or agents. It has been held that the managing officer of a corporation, even though acting for the company, becomes liable as a principal where he deals with one ignorant of the company's existence and of his relation to it, and fails to inform the latter of the facts. . . .

Here, the record does not indicate that Rhines told respondent he would be working for Sound West, Inc. In fact, this lawsuit was initiated by respondent against "Jim Rhines, d/b/a (doing business as) Sound West." While the agency was disclosed during the course of this litigation, the disclosure of the principal after the contract is executed will not relieve the agent from liability.

In the absence of a showing by appellants that respondent understood Rhines was acting as an agent for the corporation, Sound West, Inc., and not as an individual doing business as Sound West, it cannot be said the District Court erred by holding Rhines personally liable on the contract.

■ *Affirmed.*

CASE CONCEPTS REVIEW

1. What is the accurate way to describe the relationship of Sound West, Jim Rhines, and Gary Como?
2. On what basis do the trial court and this court agree that Rhines is personally liable for breaching the contract to employ Como?
3. What should Rhines have done differently as a means of avoiding this personal liability?

Third, the third party may request the agent to be bound personally on the contract. This request may be due to lack of confidence in the financial ability of the principal, because the agent's credit rating is superior to that of the principal, or some personal reason. When the agent voluntarily assumes the burden of performance in his or her personal capacity, the agent is liable in the event of nonperformance by the principal.

BASED ON BREACH OF WARRANTY. An agent's liability may be implied from the circumstances as well as being the direct result of the contract. Liability in such situations is usually said to be implied and to arise from the breach of an implied warranty. Two basic warranties are used to imply liability: the warranty of authority and the warranty that the principal is competent.

As a general rule, an agent implicitly warrants to third parties that he or she possesses power to effect the contractual relations of the principal. If in any particular transaction the agent fails to possess this power, the agent violates this implied warranty and is liable to third parties for the damages resulting from failure to bind the principal. The agent may or may not be aware of this lack of authority and may honestly believe that he or she possesses the requisite authority. Awareness of lack of authority and honesty is immaterial. If an agent exceeds his or her authority, that agent is liable to the third parties for the breach of the warranty of authority.

The agent may escape liability for damages arising from lack of authority by a full disclosure to a third party of all facts relating to the source of the agent's authority. Where all the facts are available, the third party is as capable of judging the limits of the agent's powers as is the agent.

Every agent who deals with third parties warrants that the principal is capable of being bound. Consequently, an agent who acts for a minor or a corporation not yet formed may become personally liable for the nonperformance of the principal. The same rule enables the third party to recover from the agent when the principal is an unincorporated association, such as a club, lodge, or other informal group. An unincorporated association is not a legal entity separate and apart from its members. In most states it cannot sue or be sued in the name it uses, but all members must be joined in a suit involving the unincorporated group. When an agent purports to bind such an organization, a breach of the warranty results because there is no entity capable of being bound. If the third party is fully informed that the principal is an unincorporated organization and the third party agrees to look entirely to it for performance, the agent is not liable.

The warranty that an agent has a competent principal must be qualified in one respect. An agent is not liable when, unknown to him or her, the agency has been cut short by the death of the principal. Death of the principal terminates an agency. Because death is usually accompanied by sufficient publicity to reach third parties, the facts are equally available to both parties, and no breach of warranty arises.

18. Third Party's Liability to Principals

A disclosed principal may enforce any contract made by an authorized agent for the former's benefit. This right applies to all contracts in which the principal is the real party in interest, including contracts made in the agent's name. Furthermore, if a contract is made for the benefit of a disclosed principal by an agent acting outside the scope of his or her authority, the principal is still entitled to performance, provided the contract is properly ratified before withdrawal by the third party.

An undisclosed principal is entitled to performance by third parties of all assignable contracts made for the principal's benefit by an authorized agent. It is no defense for the third party to say that he or she had not entered into a contract with the principal.

If a contract is one that involves the skill or confidence of the agent and is one that would not have been entered into without this skill or confidence, its performance may not be demanded by the undisclosed principal. This rule applies because the contract would not be assignable, since personal rights and duties are not transferable without consent of the other party.

In cases other than those involving commercial paper, the undisclosed principal takes over the contract subject to all defenses that the third party could have established against the agent. If the third party contracts to buy from such an agent and has a right of setoff against the agent, that third party has this same right to set off against the undisclosed principal. The third party may also pay the agent prior to discovery of the principal and thus discharge his liability.

19. Third Party's Liability to Agents

Normally, the agent possesses no right to bring suit on contracts made by him or her for the benefit of the principal, because the agent has no interest in the cause of action. The agent who binds himself or herself to the third party, either intentionally or ineptly by a failure to express himself or herself properly, may, however, maintain an action. An agent of an undisclosed principal is liable on the contract and may sue in his or her own name in the event of nonperformance by the third party. Thus either the agent or the undisclosed principal may bring suit, but in case of a dispute, the right of the previously undisclosed principal is superior.

Custom has long sanctioned an action by the agent based on a contract in which the agent is interested because of anticipated commissions. As a result, a factor may institute an action in his or her own name to recover for goods sold. The factor may also recover against a carrier for delay in the shipment of goods sold or to be sold.

Similarly, an agent who has been vested with title to commercial paper may sue the maker of the paper. The same is true of any claim held by the principal that is placed with the agent for collection and suit, where necessary. In all cases of this character, the agent retains the proceeds as a trust fund for the principal.

CHAPTER SUMMARY

BASIC PRINCIPLES	
Actual Authority	1. Actual authority is transmitted directly by the principal to the agent.
	2. Such authority may be expressed by the principal in either written or spoken form.
	3. In the alternative, actual authority may be implied from the actions of the principal and agent or from the nature of either party's position (such as a corporate officer).
Apparent or Ostensible Authority	1. When actual authority is missing, the doctrine of estoppel may create apparent authority.
	2. The basis of apparent authority is the indication of an agency relationship by the principal to third parties. This authority is possible only with fully disclosed principals.
	3. Apparent authority is most likely to exist when an agent is terminated and the principal fails to give notice to third parties of termination.

Ratification	1. If neither actual nor apparent authority can be found, ratification by the principal may still bind the principal and third party contractually. 2. Ratification of an unauthorized agent's acts can occur only when the principal is fully disclosed. 3. Furthermore, the principal must have full knowledge of all material facts and give a clear indication (expressed or implied) of ratification.

LIABILITY OF PRINCIPALS

Disclosed Principal's Liability to Agents	1. As long as agents act in an authorized manner, principals must indemnify agents. 2. When an agent exceeds the actual authority, the principal is not liable to the agent unless the unauthorized acts were ratified.
Disclosed Principal's Liability to Third Parties	1. If an agent negotiates a contract within either actual or apparent authority, the principal is legally bound to the third party. 2. If an agent exceeds authority, the principal is bound to the third party only if ratification occurs before the third party withdraws.
Undisclosed Principal's Liability to Agents	1. These rules apply to partially disclosed and undisclosed principals alike. 2. A principal is liable to hold an agent harmless if the agent acted within actual authority granted. (There is no apparent authority in these situations.) 3. A principal has no liability to an agent who exceeds actual authority. (Ratification is not possible.)
Undisclosed Principal's Liability to Third Parties	1. These rules apply to partially disclosed and undisclosed principals alike. 2. A principal is contractually bound to third parties if the agent acted within actual authority, and the contract can be assigned to the principal without the third parties' consent.
Election	1. These rules apply only to fully undisclosed principals. 2. Third parties must elect to hold either the agent or the previously undisclosed (now revealed) principal liable on the contract. 3. What constitutes an election is not clear. Most states follow the theory that a final judgment is an election.
Settlement	1. This applies only to fully undisclosed principals. 2. A principal is not contractually bound to a third party if that principal settles with the agent after the contract is negotiated but before the principal becomes disclosed.
Special Situations	1. Principals are liable for the knowledge possessed by the agent unless the third party has requested that the agent keep the information confidential. 2. In general, principals are liable only for the agent's actions. Agents must be given clear authority to appoint subagents. 3. Principals generally are not liable for an agent's abuse of financial powers. Such powers are very limited and must be explicitly granted by the principal to the agent.

LIABILITY OF AGENTS AND THIRD PARTIES

Agent's Liability to Principals	1. In general, an agent is not liable to the principal if that agent followed instructions and did not breach any fiduciary duties. 2. An agent of an undisclosed principal becomes liable to perform the contract if that principal has settled with the agent. 3. An agent is liable to the principal if the agent exceeded the actual authority granted unless the disclosed principal ratified the unauthorized actions.

Agent's Liability to Third Parties	1. Generally, an agent does not become contractually bound to third parties. (One purpose of the agency relationship is to substitute the principal for the agent as the party contractually liable to the third party.)
	2. An agent of an undisclosed principal does become contractually bound to the third party if that principal settles with the agent or if the third party elects to hold the agent liable.
	3. An agent becomes bound to the third party if that agent fails to indicate his or her representative capacity.
	4. An agent becomes bound to the third party when that agent breaches the implied warranty that the agent is acting within the authority granted or the warranty that there is a competent principal.
Third Party's Liability to Principals	1. A third party is contractually liable to a disclosed principal when the agent acts within the authority granted or when the principal ratifies the unauthorized acts prior to the third party's withdrawing from the contract.
	2. A third party is bound to a partially disclosed or undisclosed principal if the contract is assignable by the agent without the third party's consent.
Third Party's Liability to Agents	1. A third party is contractually liable to an agent when that agent is liable to the third party.
	2. Examples of these situations might include the application of the concepts of settlement or election when an undisclosed principal is involved, the agent failing to sign in a representative capacity, and the agent breaching the warranty of authority.

REVIEW QUESTIONS AND PROBLEMS

1. Match each term in column A with the appropriate statement in column B.

A	**B**
(1) Actual authority	(a) The required step to bind a disclosed principal and third party to a contract if the agent's actions are unauthorized
(2) Apparent authority	(b) An event that constitutes an election
(3) Ratification	(c) Because of the personal nature of the principal-agent relationship, an agent must be given clear authority to do this
(4) Election	(d) Breach of this is one example of how an agent becomes contractually liable to a third party
(5) Judgment theory	(e) Its existence is possible only when the principal is fully disclosed
(6) Settlement	(f) The process whereby a third party chooses to hold the agent or a previously undisclosed principal liable on a contract
(7) Appointment of subagents	(g) This type of authority may be conveyed by a principal to an agent by written or spoken words or by the parties' conduct
(8) Warranty of authority	(h) Method whereby an undisclosed principal is relieved of liability to a third party prior to the principal becoming disclosed

2. Pat, the owner of a grocery store chain, hires Amy to manage one store. Pat tells Amy to stock the store. Pat also tells Amy, (a) "Be sure to buy soup"; (b) "Don't buy soup"; (c) nothing about soup. Amy then proceeds to buy forty cases of soup from Tom. In which situations, if any, is Pat liable to Tom? Explain.

3. A real estate broker prepared an earnest money agreement, which included terms different from those actually agreed to by the selling owner. The owner signed the agreement, and upon discovery of the mistake, he sued the real estate dealer for causing the error. Is the agent liable to his principal? Why or why not?

4. Jim applied for health insurance coverage with Great American. The application was taken by an independent insurance agent who was not an agent of Great American. The brochure stated that a policy would be issued after investigation. At the time, Jim was told that the insurance would be effective immediately upon payment of the premium. Later Great American denied coverage and returned Jim's check. Is it liable on the contract? Why or why not?

5. Kapp authorized Schlad to have an engine repaired. Kapp specified that he would not pay more than $3,000 in repair costs. Schlad spent $6,500 on the repairs. Is Kapp or Schlad liable for the additional $3,500? Explain.

6. A buyer sued the Farm Corporation for specific performance of a contract for the sale of farmland. The contract had been signed by the president of the corporation. The board of directors had authorized the president to discuss the sale of land but had not authorized the sale. The land described in the contract was 35 percent of the corporation's assets. Is the Farm Corporation bound to perform the contract signed by its president? Explain.

7. Jerry, the managing agent of Pet Shop, Inc., borrowed $3,500 from Turner on the shop's behalf for use in the business. The company had not authorized Jerry to borrow the money, but it did repay $500 of the amount to Turner. Is Turner entitled to collect the balance due from the shop? Why or why not?

8. Oxford operates a janitorial service and cleans commercial buildings. Oxford contracted with Gresham to clean several buildings on a regular basis, not knowing that Gresham was only an agent hired to manage these buildings. Gresham failed to make several payments owed to Oxford. When Oxford sued Gresham for the money owed, Gresham argued that he was not liable, since he was merely an agent. Is Gresham correct? Why or why not?

9. Ann worked for Perry's Grocery as purchasing agent for poultry and farm produce. In all transactions with farmers, Ann acted as the principal and purchased on the strength of her own credit. Ann failed to pay for some of the produce purchased. The farmers, having ascertained that Perry's Grocery was the true principal, seek to hold it responsible. May they do so? Suppose that Perry's had previously settled with Ann. Does this fact change your response? Explain.

10. Alice was hired by Petro Chemical to be a member of the land acquisitions department. While investigating the possible purchase of a large tract of land, Alice learned that there was neither oil nor gas under the land. Trion, the owner of this land, was dismayed by Alice's findings. Trion persuaded Alice not to tell her employer of her knowledge. Indeed, if Petro Chemical purchased his land, Trion agreed to pay Alice $25,000. Trion was able to convince Petro Chemical to buy his land since it had the possibility of containing oil and gas. After this purchase, Petro Chemical discovered it had been defrauded. It sued Trion, but he claimed he could not be liable since Alice's knowledge of the barren land was imputed to Petro Chemical. Was this agent's knowledge notice to her principal? Explain.

11. An agent had authority to solicit orders for materials, but he did not have actual or apparent authority to bind his company to a contract. Proposal forms clearly stated, in average-size type, that it was not a contract until approved by an authorized official of

the company. These words appeared on the front side of the proposal, immediately preceding the space designed for signatures. The agent signed the contract form. Is the company liable? Why or why not?

12. Patricia owned a retail clothing store. As her agent, Patricia's father did business in the store's name. Indeed, a power of attorney signed by Patricia gave her father the authority "to sign and endorse all checks and drafts and to transact all business." Patricia's father borrowed money from a bank for the store's benefit. Did the power of attorney give her father the authority to approve this loan? Explain.

13. Alex, thinking he had authority to do so, signed a promissory note as an agent of Patterson's Paint Corporation. Later Alex and the payee learned that Patterson's was not bound, owing to Alex's lack of authority to borrow money. Is Alex liable if the note was signed "Patterson's Paint Corporation, by Alex Ander, as agent"? Why?

AGENCY AND THE LAW OF TORTS

CHAPTER PREVIEW

*I*n the legal sense, the word *tort* means a noncontractual, noncriminal breach of a duty. Typically, the liability that arises from a tort involves a personal injury or property damage. An automobile accident is but one, albeit a classic, example of a factual situation that creates tort liability.

The agency relationship becomes involved with tort liability whenever an agent's actions produce injury or damage to a third party or that party's property. The terms *master* and *servant* are technically more accurate than the terms *principal* and *agent* in describing the parties when tort liability is discussed. Courts, nevertheless, frequently describe the parties as *principal* and *agent*. A principal, however, is liable for torts of only those agents who are subject to the kind of control that establishes the master-servant relationship. For the purpose of tort liability, a *servant* is a person who is employed with or without pay to perform personal services for another, and who, in respect to the physical movements in the performance of such service, is subject to the master's right or power of control. A person who renders services for another but retains control over the manner of rendering such services is not a servant, but an independent contractor. Generally, the party employing an independent contractor is not liable for the latter's torts.

In addition to the tort liability that may arise from an agency relationship, this chapter also discusses other aspects of the employer-employee relationship that are related to tort liability. Among the other aspects of employment are issues relating to workers' injuries and diseases and third parties' interference with the master-servant relationship.

■ BUSINESS MANAGEMENT DECISION

You are the president of a soft-drink bottling company. Your products are delivered by drivers who own their trucks and who are paid on a commission basis. These drivers work their own hours, and they pay their assistants. You consider these drivers to be independent contractors.

What risks are present, and what should you do to minimize them?

FUNDAMENTAL PRINCIPLES

1. Introduction

The fundamental principles of tort liability in the law of agency, which are discussed in this chapter, can be summarized as follows:

1. Agents, servants, and independent contractors are personally liable for their own torts.
2. A master is liable under a doctrine known as *respondeat superior* for the torts of a servant if the servant is acting within the scope of his or her employment.
3. A principal, proprietor, employer, or contractee (each of these terms is sometimes used) is not, as a general rule, liable for the torts of an independent contractor.
4. Injured employees may have rights against their employers as well as against third parties who cause their injuries.

These four principles provide the focus for this chapter. Item 1 is discussed in the next section. Item 2 is the subject matter of sections 3 through 7. The ramifications of principle 3 are examined in sections 8 through 10. Finally, item 4 is discussed in sections 11 through 13.

2. Tort Liability of Agents, Servants, and Independent Contractors

Every person who commits a tort is personally liable to the individual whose body or property is injured or damaged by the wrongful act. An agent or officer of a corporation who commits or participates in the commission of a tort, whether or not acting on behalf of his or her corporation, is liable to third persons injured. One is not relieved of tort liability by establishing that the tortious act was committed under the direction of someone else or in the course of employment of another.

The fact that the employer or principal may be held liable does not in any way relieve the servant or agent from liability. The agent's or servant's liability is **joint and several** with the liability of the principal or master. Of course, the converse is not true. An agent, servant, or independent contractor is not liable for the torts of the principal, master, or employer.

Assume that an employer is liable as the result of a tort committed by an agent or servant. Is the employer upon paying the judgment entitled to recover from the agent or servant? The answer is technically yes, because a servant is liable for his or her own misconduct either to others or to his or her employer.

Suits by masters against servants for indemnity are not common, for several reasons. First, the servant's financial condition frequently does not warrant suit. Second, the employer knows of the risk of negligence by employees and covers this risk with insurance. If indemnity were a common occurrence, the ultimate loss would almost always fall on employees or workers. If this situation developed, it would have an adverse effect on employee morale and would make labor-management relations much more difficult. Therefore, few employers seek to enforce the right to collect losses from employees.

Just as a master may have a right to collect from the servant, under certain situations the servant may maintain a successful action for reimbursement and indemnity against the master. Such a case would occur when the servant commits a tort by following the master's instructions if that servant did not know his or her conduct was tortious. This was discussed in chapter 22.

EXAMPLE   Matthews, a retail appliance dealer, instructs Stewart to repossess a TV set from Trevor, who had purchased it on an installment contract. Matthews informs Stewart that Trevor is in arrears in his payments. Actually, Trevor is current in his payments. A bookkeeping error had been made by Matthews. Despite Trevor's protests, Stewart repossesses the TV set pursuant to Matthew's instructions. Stewart has committed the torts of trespass and wrongful conversion. Matthews must indemnify Stewart and satisfy Trevor's claim if Trevor elects to collect tort damages from Stewart.

TORT LIABILITY OF MASTERS

3. *Respondeat Superior*

A master is liable to third persons for the torts committed by servants *within the scope of their employment* and in prosecution of the master's business. This concept, frequently known as **respondeat superior** (let the master respond), imposes vicarious liability on employers as a matter of public policy. Although negligence of the servant is the usual basis of liability, the doctrine of *respondeat superior* is also applicable to intentional torts, such as trespass, assault, libel, and fraud, which are committed by a servant acting within the scope of his or her employment. It is applicable even though the master did not direct the willful act or assent to it.

This vicarious liability imposed on masters, which makes them pay for wrongs they have not actually committed, is not based on logic and reason but on business and social policy. The theory is that the master is in a better position to pay for the wrong than is the servant. This concept is sometimes referred to as the "deep pocket" theory. The business policy theory is that injuries to persons and property

---

Joint and Several Liability   Two or more persons have an obligation that binds them individually as well as jointly. This obligation can be enforced either by joint action against all persons or by separate actions against one person or against any combination of these persons.

Respondeat superior   The doctrine that places legal liability on a master for a servant's torts committed within the scope of employment.

are hazards of doing business, the cost of which the business should bear rather than have the loss borne by the innocent victim of the tort of society as a whole.

There is universal agreement that a master is vicariously liable for the actual damages caused by a servant acting within the scope of employment. However, there is disagreement about when the master is liable for punitive damages that may be awarded to punish the servant's wrong. One theory that has been widely adopted by courts in some states is called the *vicarious liability rule*. This rule states that the master is always liable for punitive damages awarded against the servant if the wrong commited occurred within the scope of the servant's employment. The logic behind this rule involves the belief that making the master liable for punitive damages will help deter reckless or intentional torts.

The more modern view of punitive damages that has been adopted by a growing number of states has been called the *complicity rule*. The advantage of this rule is that it allows for a determination of whether a master actually is blameworthy before making that master liable for punitive damages. In essence, under this second principle, to collect punitive damages from the master, an injured third party must be able to prove that either (1) the master had authorized the servant to commit the tort, (2) the master was reckless in employing or retaining the servant, (3) the servant was employed in a managerial position, or (4) the master had ratified the servant's tortious conduct.

The application of the doctrine of *respondeat superior* usually involves the issue of whether the servant was *acting within the scope of his or her employment* at the time of the commission of the tort. The law imposes liability on the master only if the tort occurs while the servant is carrying on the master's business or if the master authorizes or ratifies the servant's actions. The master's liability does not arise when the servant steps aside from his or her employment to commit the tort or when the servant does a wrongful act to accomplish a personal purpose. This is discussed further in section 5.

It is not possible to state a simple test to determine if the tort is committed within the scope of the employment. Factors to be considered include the nature of the employment, the right of control "not only as to the result to be accomplished but also as to the means to be used," the ownership of the instrumentality (such as an automobile), whether the instrumentality was furnished by the employer, whether the use was authorized, and the time of the occurrence. Most courts inquire into the intent of the servant and the extent of deviation from expected conduct involved in the tort.

As a general rule, the master cannot avoid liability by showing that the servant was instructed not to do the particular act complained of. When a servant disobeys the instructions of a master, the fact of disobedience alone does not insulate the master from liability. In addition, the master is not released by evidence that the servant was not doing the work the master had instructed him or her to do, when the servant had misunderstood the instruction. As long as the servant is attempting to further the master's business, the master is liable, because the servant is acting within the scope of his or her employment. One of the most difficult situations to resolve is going to or coming from work. Generally, traveling from home to work and vice versa is not considered to be within the servant's employment.

However, the issue of whether a servant is acting within the scope of employment usually is one of fact. Therefore, this issue typically must be resolved by a jury. Seldom will a judge be able to make a ruling involving the doctrine of *respondeat superior* as a matter of law. The peculiar facts of each case are crucial in determining whether an employer is liable for the employee's acts.

4. Expanding Vicarious Liability

In recent years, the law has been expanding the concept of vicarious liability, even to acts of persons who are not employees. A person engaged in some endeavor gratuitously may still be a "servant" within the scope of the master-servant doctrine. The two key elements for determination of whether a gratuitous undertaking is a part of the master-servant relationship are (1) whether the actor has submitted to the directions and to the control of the one for whom the service is done, and (2) whether the primary purpose of the underlying act was to serve another. If so, the "master" is liable for the torts of the unpaid "servant."

Most of the expansion of the application of *respondeat superior* and vicarious liability has been by statute. Liability for automobile accidents has been a major area of expansion. Some states have adopted what is known as the "family car doctrine." Under it, if the car is generally made available for family use, any member of the family is presumed to be an agent of the parent-owner when using the family car for his or her convenience or pleasure. The presumption may be rebutted, however. Other states have gone further and provided that anyone driving a car with the permission of the owner is the owner's agent, and the owner has vicarious liability to persons injured by the driver.

5. Exceptions: Frolics and Detours

Although it often is difficult to know with certainty whether a servant is or is not within the scope of employment, the law has recognized that the master is *not* liable when the servant is on a frolic or when the servant has detoured in a substantial manner from the master's instructions. A *frolic* exists whenever a servant pursues personal interests while neglecting the master's business. For example, a route salesman who leaves or detours from his route to accomplish a personal errand is on a frolic. If an accident occurs while this salesman is on the frolic, his master would not be liable for the third party's injuries. A very hard question to answer is this: When does a frolic or detour end so the servant is again within the scope of employment?

Not every deviation from the strict course of duty is a departure that will relieve a master of liability for the acts of the servant. The fact that a servant, while performing a duty for the master, incidentally does something for himself or herself or a third person does not automatically relieve the master from liability for negligence that causes injury to another. To sever the servant from the scope of employment, the act complained of must be such a divergence from the servant's regular duties that its very character severs the relationship of master and servant.

Another difficult situation is presented when the servant combines his or her own business with that of the master. As a general rule, this dual purpose does not relieve the master of liability. Furthermore, the doctrine of *respondeat superior* has been extended to create the master's liability for the negligence of strangers while assisting a servant in carrying out the master's business if the authority to obtain assistance is given or required, as in an emergency.

The following case illustrates the difficult factual issues presented in cases wherein it must be decided whether an employee is acting within the scope of employment.

CASE

Clover v. Snowbird Ski Resort
808 P.2d 1037 (Utah 1991)

HALL, C. J.

Plaintiff Margaret Clover sought to recover damages for injuries sustained as the result of a ski accident in which Chris Zulliger, an employee of defendant Snowbird Corporation ("Snowbird"), collided with her. From the entry of summary judgment in favor of defendants, Clover appeals.

. . . At the time of the accident, Chris Zulliger was employed by Snowbird as a chef at the Plaza Restaurant. Zulliger was supervised by his father, Hans Zulliger, who was the head chef at both the Plaza, which was located at the base of the resort, and the Mid-Gad Restaurant, which was located halfway to the top of the mountain. Zulliger was instructed by his father to make periodic trips to the Mid-Gad to monitor its operations. . . . He also had several conversations with Peter Mandler, the manager of the Plaza and Mid-Gad Restaurants, during which Mandler directed him to make periodic stops at the Mid-Gad to monitor operations.

On December 5, 1985, the date of the accident, Zulliger was scheduled to begin work at the Plaza Restaurant at 3 p.m. Prior to beginning work, he had planned to go skiing with Barney Norman, who was also employed as a chef at the Plaza. Snowbird preferred that their employees know how to ski because it made it easier for them to get to and from work. As part of the compensation for their employment, both Zulliger and Norman received season ski passes. On the morning of the accident, Mandler asked Zulliger to inspect the operation of the Mid-Gad prior to beginning work at the Plaza.

Zulliger and Norman stopped at the Mid-Gad in the middle of their first run. At the restaurant, they had a snack, inspected the kitchen, and talked to the personnel for approximately fifteen to twenty minutes. Zulliger and Norman then skied four runs before heading down the mountain to begin work. On their final run, Zulliger and Norman took a route that was often taken by Snowbird employees to travel from the top of the mountain to the Plaza. About midway down the mountain, at a point above the Mid-Gad, Zulliger decided to take a jump off a crest on the side of an intermediate run. He had taken this jump many times before. A skier moving relatively quickly is able to become airborne at that point because of the steep drop off on the downhill side of the crest. Due to this drop off, it is impossible for skiers above the crest to see skiers below the crest. The jump was well known to Snow-

bird. In fact, the Snowbird ski patrol often instructed people not to jump off the crest. There was also a sign instructing skiers to ski slowly at this point in the run. Zulliger, however, ignored the sign and skied over the crest at a significant speed. Clover, who had just entered the same ski run from a point below the crest, either had stopped or was traveling slowly below the crest. When Zulliger went over the jump, he collided with Clover, who was hit in the head and severely injured.

Clover brought claims against Zulliger and Snowbird, alleging that (1) Zulliger's reckless skiing was a proximate cause of her injuries, and (2) Snowbird is liable for Zulliger's negligence because at the time of the collision, he was acting within the scope of his employment. . . . Zulliger settled separately with Clover. Under . . . [a] motion for summary judgment, the trial judge dismissed Clover's claims against Snowbird. . . .

Under the doctrine of respondeat superior, employers are held vicariously liable for the torts their employees commit when the employees are acting within the scope of their employment. Clover's respondeat superior claim was dismissed on the ground that as a matter of law, Zulliger's actions at the time of the accident were not within the scope of his employment. . . .

Utah cases that have addressed issues of whether an employee's actions, as a matter of law, are within or without the scope of employment have focused on three criteria. First, an employee's conduct must be of the general kind the employee is employed to perform. . . . In other words, the employee must be about the employer's business and duties assigned by the employer, as opposed to being wholly involved in a personal endeavor. Second, the employee's conduct must occur substantially within the hours and ordinary spatial boundaries of the employment. Third, the employee's conduct must be motivated, at least in part, by the purpose of serving the employer's interest. . . .

In applying the . . . criteria to the facts in the instant case, it is important to note that if Zulliger had returned to the Plaza Restaurant immediately after he inspected the operations at the Mid-Gad Restaurant, there would be ample evidence to support the conclusion that on his return trip Zulliger's actions were within the scope of his employment. There is evidence that it was part of Zulliger's job to monitor the operations at the Mid-Gad and that he was directed to monitor the operations on the day of the accident. There is also evidence that Snowbird intended Zulliger to use the ski lifts and the ski runs on his trips to the Mid-Gad. It is clear, therefore, that Zulliger's actions could be considered to be of the general kind that the employee is employed to perform. It is also clear that there would be evidence that Zulliger's actions occurred within the hours and normal spatial boundaries of his employment. . . . Furthermore, throughout the trip he would have been on his employer's premises. Finally, it is clear that Zulliger's actions in monitoring the operations at the Mid-Gad, per his employer's instructions, could be considered "motivated, at least in part, by the purpose of serving the employer's interest."

The difficulty, of course, arises from the fact that Zulliger did not return to the Plaza after he finished inspecting the facilities at the Mid-Gad. Rather, he skied four more runs and rode the lift to the top of the mountain before he began his return to the base. Snowbird claims that this fact shows that Zulliger's primary purpose for skiing on the day of the accident was for his own pleasure and that therefore, as a matter of law, he was not acting within the scope of his employment. In support of this proposition, Snowbird cites . . . the dual purpose doctrine. Under this doctrine, if an employee's actions are motivated by the dual purpose of benefiting the employer and serving some personal interest, the actions will usually be considered within the scope of employment. However, if the primary motivation for the activity is personal, even though there may be some transaction of business or performance of duty merely incidental or adjunctive thereto, the person should not be deemed to be in the scope of his employment. In situations where the scope of employment issue concerns an employee's trip, a useful test in determining if the transaction of business is purely incidental to a personal motive is whether the trip is one which would have required the employer to send another employee over the same route or to perform the same function if the trip had not been made.

. . . The activity of inspecting the Mid-Gad necessitates travel to the restaurant. Furthermore, there is evidence that the manager of both the Mid-Gad and the Plaza wanted an employee to inspect the restaurant and report back by 3 p.m. If Zulliger had not inspected the restaurant, it would have been necessary to send a second employee to accomplish the same purpose. Furthermore, the second employee would have most likely used the ski lifts and ski runs in traveling to and from the restaurant.

There is ample evidence that there was a predominant business purpose for Zulliger's trip to the Mid-Gad. Therefore, this case is better analyzed under our decisions dealing with situations where an employee has taken a personal detour in the process of carrying out his duties. This court has decided several cases in which employees deviated from their duties for wholly personal reasons and then, after resuming their duties, were involved in accidents. In situations where the detour was such a substan-

tial diversion from the employee's duties that it constituted an abandonment of employment, we held that the employee, as a matter of law, was acting outside the scope of employment. However, in situations where reasonable minds could differ on whether the detour constituted a slight deviation from the employee's duties or an abandonment of employment, we have left the question for the jury.

Under the circumstances of the instant case, it is entirely possible for a jury to reasonably believe that at the time of the accident, Zulliger had resumed his employment and that Zulliger's deviation was not substantial enough to constitute a total abandonment of employment. First, a jury could reasonably believe that by beginning his return to the base of the mountain to begin his duties as a chef and to report to Mandler concerning his observations at the Mid-Gad, Zulliger had resumed his employment. . . .

Second, a jury could reasonably believe that Zulliger's actions in taking four ski runs and returning to the top of the mountain do not constitute a complete abandonment of employment. It is important to note that by taking these ski runs, Zulliger was not disregarding his employer's directions. . . . In the instant case, far from directing its employees not to ski at the resort, Snowbird issued its employees season ski passes as part of their compensation.

These two factors, along with other circumstances—such as, throughout the day Zulliger was on Snowbird's property, there was no specific time set for inspecting the restaurant, and the act of skiing was the method used by Snowbird employees to travel among the different locations of the resort—constitute sufficient evidence for a jury to conclude that Zulliger, at the time of the accident, was acting within the scope of his employment. . . .

In light of the genuine issues of material fact in regard to each of Clover's claims, summary judgment was inappropriate.

■ *Reversed and remanded for further proceedings.*

CASE CONCEPTS REVIEW

1. What is the legal ruling of the trial court that forms the basis of this review?

2. What three criteria does this court use to determine, as a matter of law, whether an employee is acting within the scope of employment?

3. What is meant by the dual purpose doctrine, and how does it apply in this case?

6. Intentional Torts

Intentional or willful torts are not as likely to occur within the scope of the servant's employment as are those predicated on a negligence theory. If the willful misconduct of the servant has nothing to do with the master's business and is based entirely on hatred or a feeling of ill will toward the third party, the master is not liable. Nor is the master liable if the employee's act has no reasonable connection with his or her employment. However, the injured third party generally does not have to prove that the master actually instructed the servant to commit the intentional tort. Once again, the key issue for determining the master's liability is whether the servant was within the scope of employment, as is illustrated in the following case.

CASE

Condict v. Condict
664 P.2d 131 (Wyom. 1983)

ROSE, J.

... Appellant Wynn Condict is the nephew of appellee Alden Condict who, with his brother, Winthrop Condict, operates a ranch in Carbon County, Wyoming. ...

Appellant's claim arises from an incident in which he was involved with Ted Jenkins, an employee of Alden Condict. There is an area on the Condict ranch where gas pumps are located close to a bridge, and, because of its weakened condition, this bridge had been designated for use by lighter-weight vehicles only. On the morning in question, Wynn Condict was at the gas pumps assigning his father's employees their various tasks for the day. At the same time, Ted Jenkins and another employee of Alden Condict were gassing two vehicles, one of which was a heavy army-surplus six-by-six truck utilized in haying operations. An altercation occurred between Jenkins and Wynn Condict when Jenkins made known his intent to drive the large army truck over the bridge, it being Wynn Condict's position that this was one of the heavy vehicles for which the bridge was not to be used. Wynn Condict became alarmed because his new pickup truck was blocking the bridge and he proceeded to back his pickup across the bridge. In the meantime, Jenkins had commandeered the army-surplus vehicle, crashed it through a gate and headed toward Wynn's vehicle. Somewhere near the end of the bridge or just off the other side, Jenkins rammed the pickup with the six-by-six truck.

As a result of this impact, appellant claims that he suffered severe injury to his back, which resulted in his bringing a personal-injury action against Alden Condict, as Jenkins' employer, in which he sought both compensatory and punitive damages.

In directing a verdict for Alden Condict, the trial judge held that plaintiff had failed to prove that Jenkins was acting in the scope of his employment at the time of the incident. ...

Appellant argues that, by holding that the evidence must show that Alden Condict specifically authorized Ted Jenkins to commit the alleged tortious act, the trial judge erroneously applied the rules announced by this court in *Sage Club v. Hunt*, Wyo. 638 P.2d 161 (1981). He also urges that the evidence introduced at trial was sufficient to make out a prima facie case under that decision. We agree with the appellant's contentions. ...

Stated succinctly, in *Sage Club v. Hunt*, we embraced a rule of law which holds an employer liable for the intentional torts of his employee committed while the employee is acting, at least in part, in furtherance of the employer's interests. We also noted in that case that an important factor in deciding the principal's liability for his agent's intentional torts is whether the "use of force is not unexpectable by the master." However, in order for a jury to assess liability, the plaintiff need not prove that the employer foresaw the precise act or exact manner of injury as long as the general type of conduct may have been reasonably expected.

Applying these rules to this litigation, we are led to the conclusion that the trial judge erroneously found that appellant Condict had failed to discharge his burden of proof. According to *Sage Club v. Hunt*, the appellant was obliged to establish that a question of fact existed as to whether Jenkins was acting within the scope of his employment at the time of the incident in question. It was not his obligation to produce evidence, either direct or circumstantial, to the effect that Alden Condict authorized Jenkins to ram the six-by-six truck into Wynn Condict's vehicle. Appellant's burden was to show that when Jenkins intentionally rammed the pickup he, Jenkins, was then engaged, at least in part, in furthering Alden Condict's interests and that Jenkins' acts were not outside the realm of foreseeability. Appellant, under *Sage Club v. Hunt*, was not required to show Alden's authorization and consent in the specific tortious activity, or that Jenkins' specific conduct was foreseeable, but only that Jenkins committed the tort while at least partially engaged in a task for which he was employed and with respect to which Alden Condict could foresee that force might be used by Jenkins. According to the record, which shows that Jenkins was on his way to perform haying operations when the incident occurred, we find that appellant established a fact issue for the jury as to scope of employment and Alden Condict's liability for the intentional acts of Jenkins. Under applicable rules, it was error for the trial court to take the case from the jury.

■ *Reversed and remanded.*

CASE CONCEPTS REVIEW

1. Who are the master, servant, and third party?
2. What is the legal ruling of the trial court that forms the basis of this appeal?
3. Why does this court reverse the trial court's ruling?

7. Tort Suits: Procedures

As previously noted, the law of torts in most states, unlike the law of contracts, allows joinder of the master and servant as defendants in one cause of action or permits them to be sued separately. Although the plaintiff is limited to one recovery, the master and servant are jointly and severally liable. The party may collect from either or both in any proportion until the judgment is paid in full. If the servant is sued first and a judgment is obtained that is not satisfied, the suit is not a bar to a subsequent suit against the master, but the amount of the judgment against the servant fixes the maximum limit of potential liability against the master.

If the servant is found to be free of liability, either in a separate suit or as a codefendant with the master, then the suit against the master on the basis of *respondeat superior* will fail. As indicated in the following case, the master's liability is predicated on the fault of the servant; if the servant is found to be free of fault, the master has no liability as a matter of law.

CASE

Roughton Pontiac Corp. v. Alston
372 S.E.2d 147 (Va. 1988)

RUSSELL, J.

This is an appeal from a judgment for the tortious conversion of personal property. The dispositive question is whether a verdict exonerating a servant of tort liability also exonerates his master.

The facts are undisputed. On March 1, 1982, Roger N. Alston (Alston) went to the business premises of Roughton Pontiac Corporation (Roughton) in Norfolk to purchase a new car. He selected a new 1981 Pontiac Phoenix which sold for $9,726.59 and tendered his own 1978 Oldsmobile as part payment. He dealt with John Tarboro (Tarboro), a Roughton employee. Alston expressed a desire to have the entire balance of the purchase price financed and filled out an application for credit with General Motors Acceptance Corporation (GMAC). Tarboro agreed to allow Alston a $1,426.59 trade-in allowance for the 1978 Oldsmobile, a sum sufficient to cover the entire down payment needed for the new car if Alston's desired financing could be obtained.

. . . Alston gave a check to Roughton for $214.25, which covered state tax, license transfer fees, title fees, and clerical fees. None of his money was applied to the purchase price. . . . Roughton gave Alston a set of keys and permitted him to drive the new car home. Alston left the old car on Roughton's lot.

Roughton submitted Alston's credit application to GMAC, which refused to accept it. GMAC indicated that it would finance the purchase only if Alston made an additional down payment of approximately $2,500. Roughton informed Alston of these developments three days after he had taken possession of the new car, but Alston refused to return it or to apply for financing elsewhere. . . .

On March 5, 1982, Tarboro took a spare key to the new Pontiac from the "warranty package," went to Alston's place of business during business hours, repossessed the Pontiac, and returned it to Roughton. There is no evidence in the record before us that Tarboro's employer directed him to take this action. Alston returned to Roughton's place of business, recovered possession of his

1978 Oldsmobile, and, several days later, accepted a refund of the $214.25 he had paid for transfer fees.

Alston brought this action against Roughton and Tarboro, jointly and severally, for conversion of the new Pontiac. At a jury trial the court ruled that title had passed to Alston as a matter of law. . . . The court submitted the case to the jury solely on the issue of damages. Alston's only proof of damages was that he had intended to drive the new car to Baltimore to give a surprise party for an uncle and that the repossession had made it necessary to call upon someone else for transportation, which had cost him "in excess of $200."

The jury returned a verdict against Roughton for $205 compensatory damages and $25,000 punitive damages. Because the verdict was silent as to Tarboro, the court instructed the jury to return to its room and deliberate upon a verdict for or against him. The jury returned and resubmitted its original verdict against Roughton to which the jury had added the words: "And the defendant, John Tarboro, not guilty." The court treated the latter statement as a verdict exonerating Tarboro and entered judgment in Alston's favor in the amount of the verdict against Roughton, and in Tarboro's favor against Alston for costs. We awarded Roughton an appeal. Alston assigned no cross-error to the judgment in Tarboro's favor, and the judgment is now final.

On appeal, Roughton contends that it was exonerated by the verdict exonerating Tarboro. . . .

Although Alston brought this action against Roughton and Tarboro jointly and severally, and alleged that both had acted with "ill-will, malevolence, grudge, spite," his proof fell far short of those allegations. In the absence of any evidence that Tarboro repossessed the Pontiac upon the orders of his employer, the proof permits the assessment of liability against Roughton only vicariously, upon *respondeat superior* principles. Thus, if we assume, without deciding, that Tarboro's act was tortious, then Roughton would be vicariously liable only because Tarboro's act was within the scope of his employ-

ment, i.e., was fairly and naturally incident to his employer's business, was done while he was engaged upon his employer's business, and was done with a view to further his employer's interests.

It is well settled in Virginia that where master and servant are sued together in tort, and the master's liability, if any, is solely dependent on the servant's conduct, a verdict for the servant necessarily exonerates the master. . . .

All our previous cases applying the foregoing principle have been *respondeat superior* claims in which the master's liability has been solely dependent upon a servant's alleged negligence. Nevertheless, the principle applies to intentional tort cases as well as to negligence cases.

Well-recognized exceptions to the rule exist where the master's liability is not derived solely from the servant's acts. His liability may be predicated upon evidence showing his own tortious acts or omissions independent of or in combination with the acts of the servant, or upon the actions of another employee. In these situations, a judgment entered against the master will be allowed to stand, notwithstanding the servant's exoneration.

Under the facts in this record, Roughton's liability, if any, was entirely dependent upon, and derivative from, Tarboro's conduct. The jury's verdict exonerating Tarboro, therefore exonerated Roughton. Accordingly, we will reverse the judgment against Roughton and enter final judgment here.

■ *Reversed.*

CASE CONCEPTS REVIEW

1. Why did John Tarboro, on behalf of Roughton, repossess the Pontiac automobile from Alston?

2. What was the trial jury's verdict with respect to Roughton's liability to Alston? With respect to Tarboro's liability?

3. Why does this court conclude that Roughton is not liable to Alston?

INDEPENDENT CONTRACTORS' TORTS

8. Control over Independent Contractors

An *independent contractor* has power to control the details of the work he or she performs for an employer. Because the performance is within his or her control, an independent contractor is not a servant, and his or her only responsibility is to accomplish the result contracted for. For example, Rush contracts to build a boat for Ski-King at a cost of $40,000, according to certain specifications. It is clear that Rush is an independent contractor; the completed boat is the result. Had Ski-King engaged Rush by the day to assist in building the boat under Ski-King's supervision and direction, the master-servant relationship would have resulted. Recall that an agent with authority to represent a principal contractually will, at the same time, be either a servant or an independent contractor for the purpose of tort liability.

The hallmark of a master-servant relationship is that the master not only controls the result of the work but also has the right to direct the manner in which the work will be accomplished. The distinguishing feature of a proprietor–independent-contractor relationship is that the person engaged to do the work has exclusive control of the manner of performing it, being responsible only to produce the desired result. Whether the relationship is master-servant or proprietor–independent-contractor is usually a question of fact for the jury or for a fact finder if the issue arises in an administrative proceeding.

Without changing the relationship from that of proprietor and independent contractor or the duties arising from that relationship, an employer of an independent contractor may retain a broad general power of supervision of the work to ensure satisfactory performance of the contract. This employer may inspect, stop the work, make suggestions or recommendations about details of the work, or prescribe alterations or deviations.

9. General Rule: No Liability

The destinction between servants and independent contractors is important because, as a general rule, the doctrine of *respondeat superior* and the concept of vicarious liability in tort are not applicable to independent contractors. There is no tort liability, as a general rule, because the theories that justify liability of the master for the servant's tort are not present when the person engaged to do the work is not a servant.

The application of the doctrine of *respondeat superior* and the tests for determining if the wrongdoer is an independent contractor are quite difficult to apply to professional and technically skilled personnel. It can be argued that a physician's profession requires such high skill and learning that others, especially laypeople, cannot as a matter of law be in control of the physician's activities. That argument, if accepted, would eliminate the liability of hospitals for acts of medical doctors.

Notwithstanding the logic of this argument, courts usually hold that *respondeat superior* may be applied to professional persons and that such persons may be servants. Of course, some professional and technical persons are independent contractors. Hospitals and others who render professional service through skilled employees have the same legal responsibilities as everyone else. If the person who commits a tort is an employee acting on the employer's behalf, the employer is liable, even though no one actually "controls" the employee in the performance of his or her skill. These concepts are applicable to doctors, chemists, airline pilots, lawyers, and other highly trained specialists.

Since it is generally understood that one is not liable for the torts of an independent contractor, contracts frequently provide that the relationship is that of proprietor–independent contractor, not master-servant. Such a provision is not binding on third parties, and the contract cannot be used to protect the contracting parties from the actual relationship as shown by the facts.

10. Exceptions: Liability Created

The rule of insulation from liability in the independent contractor situation is subject to several well-recognized exceptions. The most common of these is related to work inherently dangerous to the public, such as blasting with dynamite. The basis of this exception is that it would be contrary to public policy to allow one engaged in such an activity to avoid liability by selecting an independent contractor rather than a servant to do the work.

Another exception to insulation from vicarious liability applies to illegal work. An employer cannot insulate himself or herself from liability by hiring an independent contractor to perform a task that is illegal. Still another common exception involves employees' duties considered to be duties that cannot be delegated. In discussing the law of contracts, we noted that personal rights and personal duties could not be transferred without consent of the other party. Many statutes impose strict duties on parties such as common carriers and innkeepers. If an attempt is made to delegate these duties to an independent contractor, it is clear that the employer on whom the duty is imposed has liability for the torts of the independent contractor. In a contract to perform a service or supply a product, liability for negligence cannot be avoided by engaging an independent contractor to perform the duty. Finally, an employer is liable for the torts of an independent contractor if the tort is ratified. If an independent contractor wrongfully repossesses an automobile, and the one hiring him or her refuses to return it on demand, the tort has been ratified, and both parties have liability.

Tort liability is also imposed on the employer who is at fault, as when the employer negligently selects the employee. This is true whether the party performing the work is a servant or an independent contractor, as is illustrated in the following case.

CASE

Pontiacs v. K.M.S. Investments
331 N.W.2d 907 (Minn. 1983)

K.M.S. Investments, owners of a large apartment complex, rented an apartment to Jorge and Stephanie Pontiac in May 1978. In August, K.M.S. hired Dennis Graffice as the complex's resident manager. Graffice was hired despite having a criminal record that indicated he had been convicted of four felonies in two different states. K.M.S. made no attempt to conduct a firsthand investigation of Graffice's background. They relied solely on the completed application and a personal interview. In September 1978, while Jorge was out of town, Stephanie Pontiac was raped at knifepoint by a person she recognized as Dennis Graffice. He had entered the Pontiacs' apartment with his passkey. After Graffice was convicted of this sexual assault, the Pontiacs sued K.M.S. for damages.

KELLEY, J.

. . . At the outset, we must determine whether, in a tort action, a person may recover from an employer if the person was injured by a negligently hired employee. We have recognized that a person injured by a negligently retained employee may recover damages from the employer. The origin of the doctrine making an employer liable for negligent hiring, as well as negligent retention, arose out of the common law fellow-servant law which imposed a duty on employers to select employees who would not endanger fellow employees by their presence on the job. The concept of direct employer liability arising as a result of negligent hiring was later expanded to include a duty to "exercise reasonable care for the safety of members of the general public" so today it is recognized as the rule in the majority of the jurisdictions. . . .

Liability is predicated on the negligence of an employer in placing a person with known propensities, or propensities which should have been discovered by reasonable investigation, in an employment position in which, because of the circumstances of the employment, it should have been foreseeable that the hired individual posed a threat of injury to others.

The connection between the employment relationship and the plaintiff has been found sufficient by courts of other jurisdictions to impose upon a landlord a duty to use reasonable care in the hiring of an employee who may pose a threat of injury to tenants. The rationale employed in those cases, as well as in similar cases involving deliverymen or others who gain access to a dwelling by virtue of their employment, is that since plaintiff comes in contact with the employee as the direct result of the employment, and since the employer receives some benefit, even if only a potential or indirect benefit, by the contact between the plaintiff and the employee, there exists a duty on the employer to exercise reasonable care for the protection of the dwelling occupant to retain in such employment only those who, so far as can be reasonably ascertained, pose no threat to such occupant.

We can ascertain no substantial difference in imposing a duty on an employer to use reasonable care in the initial hiring from his duty to use that care in the retention of an employee. We therefore align ourselves with the majority of those jurisdictions which recognize a claim by an injured third party for negligent hiring . . . and hold that an employer has the duty to exercise reasonable care in view of all the circumstances in hiring individuals who, because of the employment, may pose a threat of injury to members of the public. Here, the respondent Stephanie Pontiac met Graffice as a direct result of his employment as apartment manager, and appellants received a benefit from Graffice's employment in having a caretaker for upkeep of the property and to aid tenants with complaints of property malfunction. Therefore, we hold that these appellants owed to the tenants of the Driftwood Apartments, including these respondents, the duty of exercising reasonable care in hiring a resident manager.

We next address the question of whether there was sufficient evidence to support the jury's verdict that appellants had breached their duty. . . . This is generally a jury question. Here, the jury could have found that appellants made slight effort to determine whether it was safe to hire Graffice and give him access into the living quarters of the tenants of the apartments. . . .

■ *Affirmed.*

CASE CONCEPTS REVIEW

1. In what capacity was Graffice hired by K.M.S.?
2. To what extent did K.M.S. investigate Graffice's background before he was hired?
3. What is the rational for holding a landlord liable for negligently hiring a resident manager with a criminal record?
4. In addition to being more thorough in its hiring practices, what should K.M.S. have done to help prevent the rape?

TORT LIABILITY TO EMPLOYEES

11. Common-Law Principles

Contributory negligence A defense asserted by an employer that denies recovery to an injured employee whose negligence contributed to the injury.

Fellow-servant doctrine Precludes an injured employee from recovering damages from an employer when the injury resulted from the negligent act of another employee.

Assumption of the risk Negligence doctrine that bars the recovery of damages by an injured party on the ground that such party acted with actual or constructive knowledge of the hazard causing the injury.

An employer owes certain nondelegable duties to employees. These include the duties to warn employees of the hazards of their employment, supervise their activities, furnish a reasonably safe place to work, and furnish reasonably safe instrumentalities with which to work. As part of the obligation to provide a safe place to work, the employer must instruct employees in the safe use and handling of the products and equipment used in and around the employer's plant or facilities. What is reasonable for the purposes of these rules depends on all the facts and circumstances of each case, including the age and ability of the worker as well as the condition of the premises. It might be negligent to put a minor in charge of a particular instrument without supervision, although it would not be negligent to assign an adult or experienced employee to the same equipment.

At common law, the employer who breached these duties to employees was liable in tort for injuries received by the employees. The employer was not an insurer of the employee's safety, but liability was based on negligence. In turn, the employee in tort action was confronted with overcoming three defenses available to the employer, one or more of which frequently barred recovery. The first of these defenses involved the **contributory negligence** of the employee. If the employee was even partially at fault, this defense was successful, even though the majority of the fault was the employer's. Second, if the injury was caused by some other employee, the **fellow-servant doctrine** excused the employer and limited recovery to a suit against the other employee who was at fault. Finally, in many jobs that by their very nature involved some risk of injury, the doctrine of **assumption of the risk** would allow the employer to avoid liability.

The common-law rules resulted for the most part in imposing on employees the burdens that resulted from accidental injuries, occupational diseases, and even death. Through the legislative process, society has rather uniformly determined that this result is undesirable as a matter of public policy. Statutes known as *workers' compensation* have been enacted in all the states. These laws impose liability without fault (eliminate the common-law defenses) on most employers for injuries, occupational diseases, and death of their employees.

12. Workers' Compensation

IN GENERAL.   Workers' compensation laws vary a great deal from state to state in their coverage of industries and employees, the nature of the injuries or diseases that are compensable, and the rates and source of compensation. In spite of these wide variances, certain general observations can be made.

State workers' compensation statutes provide a system of paying for death, illness, or injury that arises out of and in the course of the employment. The three defenses the employer had at common law are eliminated. The employers are strictly liable without fault. Furthermore, states have begun to hold employers liable even though an employee cannot prove the employer solely responsible for the damages done. This legal principle is applied especially when occupational diseases, as opposed to accidental injuries, are involved. For example, victims of asbestosis have been allowed to recover workers' compensation benefits even if they could not establish with certainty that the disease was contracted during this employment as opposed to a previous period of employment.

Most state statutes exclude certain types of employment from their coverage. Generally, domestic and agricultural employees are not covered. In the majority of states, the statutes are compulsory. In some states, employers may elect to be subject to lawsuits by their employees or their survivors. In such cases, the plaintiff must prove that the death or injury resulted proximately from the negligence of the employer. But the plaintiff is not subject to common-law defenses. In addition, there is no statutory limit to the amount of the damages recoverable. Thus, few employers elect to avoid coverage.

BENEFITS.   The workers' compensation acts give covered employees the right to certain cash payments for their loss of income. A weekly benefit is payable during periods of disability. In the event of an employee's death, benefits are provided for the spouse and minor children. The amount of such awards is usually subject to a stated maximum and is calculated by using a percentage of the wages of the employee. If the employee suffers permanent partial disability, most states provide compensation for injuries that are scheduled in the statute and those that are nonscheduled. As an example of the former, a worker who loses a hand might be awarded 100 weeks of compensation at $90 per week. Besides scheduling specific compensation for certain specific injuries, most acts also provide compensation for nonscheduled ones, such as back injuries, based on the earning power the employee lost owing to the injury. In addition to these payments, all statutes provide for medical benefits and funeral expenses.

In some states, employers have a choice of covering their workers' compensation risk with insurance or being self-insured (i.e., paying all claims directly) if they can demonstrate their capability to do so. In other states, employers pay into a state fund used to compensate workers entitled to benefits. In these states, the amounts of the payments are based on the size of the payroll and the experience of the employer in having claims filed.

BURDEN OF PROOF.   Although the right to workers' compensation benefits is given without regard to fault of either the employer or the employee, employers are not always liable. The tests for determining whether an employee is entitled to workers' compensation are as follows: (1) Was the injury accidental? and (2) Did the injury arise out of and in the course of the employment? Since workers' compensation laws are remedial in nature, they have been very liberally construed. In recent years, the courts have tended to expand coverage and scope of the employer's liability. It has been held that heart attacks and other common ailments are compensable as "accidental injuries," even though the employee had either a preexisting disease or a physical condition likely to lead to the disease. Likewise, the courts have been more and more liberal in upholding awards that have been challenged on the ground that the injury did not arise out of and in the course of the employment.

FEDERAL STATUTES.   Several federal statutes pertain to the liability of certain kinds of employers for injuries, diseases, and deaths arising out of the course of employment. Railroad workers are covered by the Federal Employers' Liability Act (FELA). This statute does not provide for liability without fault, as in the case of workers' compensation, but it greatly increases the chances of a worker's winning a lawsuit against an employer by eliminating or reducing the defenses the latter would have had at common law. While fault of the carrier must be proved for an employee to recover for injuries under the FELA, and a regular lawsuit must be filed in court, the Act provides the worker with a distinct advantage over many workers' compensation systems. There is no limit or ceiling to the amount an employee can recover for injuries. The Jones Act gives maritime employees the same rights against their employers as railway workers have against theirs under the FELA.

The following case discusses the employer's defenses under the FELA.

CASE

Kalanick v. Burlington Northern Railroad Company
788 P.2d 901 (Mont. 1990)

SHEEHY, J.

Burlington Northern Railroad Co. appeals from a judgment . . . awarding Richard Kalanick $431,450. . . .

The issue raised by Burlington Northern (B.N.) is:

Did the District Court err in striking the defense of contributory negligence and instructing the jury that Kalanick was not negligent as a matter of law? . . .

In April of 1986, B.N. employees on the hi-line route were informed that upper level management was soon to inspect the area. A concerted effort to clean up the right-of-way of debris became a priority job for hi-line employees. . . .

Richard Kalanick and his partner were a two-man inspection crew. They were told to pick up what debris they could manage during their inspection patrol.

Kalanick and his partner patrolled the track from a rail-mounted pickup truck known as a "high rail." Section crews were given mechanical lifting equipment to accomplish the job of lifting heavy debris such as old ties, but Kalanick and partner did not have the benefit of such a device. Consequently, if they spotted jobs requiring long periods of heavy labor, they reported them to the roadmaster for section crew assignment.

Kalanick and his partner were assigned to a 46-mile rail stretch known as the Gildford section. This section was full of debris, including approximately 1,000 ties. Kalanick understood that he and his partner were to clean up any debris which they could manage. Kalanick and partner, due to the nature of the high-rail truck and the lack of lifting equipment, necessarily had to lift and carry the ties up and down the subgrades and load them on the truck. Once loaded, they would drive to an area designated for burning, and manually unload the ties. Kalanick estimated that he and his partner loaded and unloaded some 900 ties prior to his injury.

On April 23, 1986, after several hours of lifting ties, Kalanick's back gave out.

Kalanick filed suit on August 28, 1987, alleging that B.N. negligently failed to provide him with a safe place to work, adequate instruction, reasonably safe equipment and adequate manpower to perform the job safely. B.N. filed its answer, denying the allegations and raising contributory negligence as a defense.

Jury trial commenced on December 12, 1989. At the close of evidence, the trial court struck the defense of contributory negligence, ruling it to actually be an assumption of risk defense, precluded under the Federal Employers' Liability Act. The jury returned a verdict in favor of Kalanick in the amount of $431,450. This appeal resulted.

B.N. contends that the defense of contributory negligence was improperly stricken by the trial court. Kalanick maintained at trial that B.N. was actually attempting to assert the defense of assumption of risk, which is prohibited under the FELA. . . .

While assumption of risk is prohibited, the defense of contributory negligence has not been abolished in FELA actions. The question then becomes: what constitutes contributory negligence? This has been a common problem in FELA cases. Most courts have stated that assumed risk arises out of the employment contract, while contributory negligence arises out of conduct. In *Taylor v. Burlington Northern R. Co.* (9th Cir. 1986), 787 F.2d 1309, 1316, 1317, the court stated:

> Although there is some overlap between assumption of risk and contributory negligence, generally the two defenses are not interchangeable. At common law an employee's voluntary, knowledgeable acceptance of a dangerous condition that is necessary for him to perform his duties constitutes an assumption of risk. Contributory negligence, in contrast, is a careless act or omission on the plaintiff's part tending to add new dangers to conditions that the employer negligently created or permitted to exist.

* * * * * * * * *

The employee who enters the workplace for a routine assignment in compliance with the orders and directions of his employer or its supervising agents, who by such entry incurs risks not extraordinary in scope, is not contributorily negligent, but rather is engaging in an assumption of risk.

* * * * * * * * *

Reporting to work or facing the risks inherent in one's job is the essence of assumption of risk.

Following that reasoning, Kalanick asserts that his decision to follow orders and load and unload ties rather than refuse to do the work constitutes assumption of risk. Testimony of . . . Kalanick's supervisor, reveals that Kalanick did the work expected of him, and as he was expected to do it. In addition, the testimony of three B.N. foremen was of the consensus that the assignment of heavy labor to two men with only a high-rail pickup was "unreasonable" and "unsafe," with the ultimate result that "somebody will wear out [and] get hurt."

Testimony of the B.N. employees refutes B.N.'s contentions of an absence of negligence on its part. The FELA imposes a high standard of care upon the carrier. There are duties imputed to the carrier under the Act, including: The duty to provide a safe workplace, the duty to furnish employees with suitable equipment to enable the employee to perform work safely, the duty to provide sufficient manpower to complete work in a reasonably safe manner, and the duty to assign workers to jobs for which they are qualified and to avoid placing them in jobs beyond their physical capabilities.

The record is clear that B.N. did not assign to Kalanick any lifting devices. Kalanick and his partner were expected to do substantial lifting without mechanical aid. . . . The District Court weighed that fact against assertions by B.N. that Kalanick should have availed himself of additional manpower or equipment, used "safer" lifting techniques or better discretion as to which items he lifted. B.N. contended that Kalanick, by his own failings, was contributorily negligent.

The District Court, having viewed all the evidence, determined that B.N. was attempting to interject assumption of risk, and therefore properly disallowed the defense. To impute negligence to Kalanick through instruction to the jury when no contributory negligence was shown would have been error. Because no contributory negligence was shown, the court correctly instructed the jury that Kalanick was not negligent "*as a matter of law*." (Emphasis supplied) . . .

■ *Affirmed.*

CASE CONCEPTS REVIEW

1. What is the factual basis for Burlington Northern's claim that Kalanick's negligence contributed to his back injury?
2. How did the trial court interpret this defense?
3. What distinction does this court make between assumption of risk and contributory negligence?

13. Liability of Third Parties

Irrespective of other legal relationships, any person injured by the commission of a tort has a cause of action against the wrongdoer. An employee who is injured by the wrongful conduct of the third person may recover from the third person. If the employee has been compensated for injuries by the employer under the applicable workers' compensation law, the employer is entitled to recover any workers' compensation payments from the sum that the employee recovers from the wrongful third party.

Three rather unusual tort situations have a direct relation to the employment contract. First, any third party who maliciously or wrongfully influences a principal to terminate an agent's employment thereby commits a tort. The wrongful third party must compensate the agent for any damages that result from such conduct. Second, any third person who wrongfully interferes with the prospective economic advantage of an agent has liability to the agent for the loss sustained. Third, any person who influences another to breach a contract in which the agent is interested renders himself or herself liable to that agent as well as to the principal. These three torts by third parties are discussed in detail in chapter 5.

CHAPTER SUMMARY

Introduction	1. Agents, servants, and independent contractors are personally liable for their own torts.
	2. A master is liable under the *respondeat superior* doctrine for the torts of a servant if the servant is acting within the scope of employment.
	3. A principal, proprietor, employer, or contractee (each of these terms is sometimes used) is not, as a general rule, liable for the torts of an independent contractor.
	4. Injured employees may have rights against their employer as well as against third parties who cause their injuries.
Tort Liability of Agents, Servants, and Independent Contractors	1. The person who commits a tort is liable for the harm done.
	2. A wrongdoer is not relieved of personal liability by establishing that the tort was committed in the course of employment.
	3. The servant and master are jointly and severally liable for the torts of the servant committed within the scope of employment. Thus, the fact that a master may be liable does not relieve the servant's personal liability.

TORT LIABILITY OF MASTERS

Respondeat Superior	1. Literally means "let the master respond."
	2. This legal doctrine places liability, as a matter of public policy, on employers for the torts of their employees.
	3. This doctrine allows injured persons to recover from the party with the "deeper pocket."
	4. The basic issue is whether the servant was acting within the scope of employment at the time the tort occurred.
	5. This issue is a factual one that usually must be decided by a jury.

Expanding Vicarious Liability	1. A person who is not paid may be a gratuitous "servant" and may make the "master" liable.
	2. The family car doctrine is an expansion of vicarious liability beyond the traditional master-servant relationship.
Exceptions: Frolics and Detours	1. Typically, a servant is outside the scope of employment if the servant is on a frolic of his or her own or detours from assigned tasks.
	2. A *frolic* exists when a servant pursues personal interests instead of the master's business.
	3. A *detour* may occur when a servant fails to follow the master's instructions.
Intentional Torts	1. Intentional or willful torts are less likely to occur within the servant's scope of employment than are torts caused by negligence. Thus masters generally are not liable for harm intentionally caused by servants.
Tort Suits: Procedures	1. Masters and servants generally are jointly and severally liable for the servants' torts. If the servant is not liable, neither is the master.
	2. Although legal actions may be filed against both a master and a servant, the third party is limited to only one recovery.

INDEPENDENT CONTRACTORS' TORTS

Control over Independent Contractors	1. If one has the power to control the details of the work, one is an independent contractor.
	2. In the master-servant relationship, the master has the right to direct the manner of performing the work.
General Rule: No Liability	1. The doctrine of *respondeat superior* and the concept of vicarious liability are not applicable to torts caused by independent contractors.
	2. Therefore proprietors generally are not personally liable to third parties who are injured by independent contractors.
Exceptions: Liability Created	Proprietors are liable if
	1. The work of the independent contractor is inherently dangerous.
	2. The independent contractor's work is illegal.
	3. The work to be done by the independent contractor is nondelegable.
	4. The proprietor ratifies the independent contractor's tort.
	5. The independent contractor is negligently selected by the proprietor.

TORT LIABILITY TO EMPLOYEES

Common-Law Principles	1. Employers owe duties to their employees to furnish a safe place to work, and they may be liable for breach of these duties.
	2. An employer was only liable for negligence, and the three common-law defenses were available.
Workers' Compensation	1. These are state statutes passed to ensure that injured employees do not bear the loss caused by the injury.
	2. Because employees no longer have to sue, employers are no longer protected by common-law defenses of contributory negligence, assumption of risk, and fellow-servant rule.
	3. Employees' benefits include payment of medical bills, loss of income, and rehabilitation income for disabilities suffered.
	4. Employees must prove that their injuries, illnesses, or deaths arose out of and in the course of employment.
	5. The Federal Employers' Liability Act and the Jones Act protect injured railroad and maritime employees, respectively.
Liability of Third Parties	1. Third parties who interfere with the employer-employee relationship may become liable for damages to either the employer or the employee or both.

REVIEW QUESTIONS AND PROBLEMS

1. Match the terms in column A with the appropriate statement in column B.

A	B
(1) *Respondeat superior*	(a) Example of when a proprietor becomes liable for torts of an independent contractor
(2) Family car doctrine	(b) Proof that an employee must make to recover under workers' compensation laws
(3) Frolic	(c) Type of tort for which a third party is liable for money damages
(4) Inherently dangerous work	(d) An expansion of vicarious liability that makes the owner of a vehicle liable for the torts of a family member
(5) Workers' compensation	(e) Exists when a servant pursues personal interests instead of the master's business
(6) Arising out of and in the course of employment	(f) State statutes passed to ensure that injured employees receive benefits from employers
(7) Interference with economic relationships	(g) Doctrine that allows injured persons to recover from the party with the "deeper pocket"

2. Which party, the master or the servant, has the ultimate liability for torts that are the servant's rather than the master's fault? How would your answer change if the tort by a servant was caused by the master's improper instructions?

3. While a guest at the Marshview Inn, Tom was severely beaten by Seth, a night watchman for the Inn. Tom sued the Inn and Seth, as an agent for the Inn. Because Marshview Inn was not the proper company name, Tom's suit against the Inn was dismissed. Tom's suit against Seth was dismissed since Seth was not technically an agent for the Inn. (He was an agent for the Inn's corporate owner.) Tom appealed the dismissal of his claim against Seth. What is the basis for this appeal? Should Tom be allowed to continue his claim against Seth? Why or why not?

4. Richard Welch was employed as a truck driver by Mercury Motors Express. While driving in an intoxicated condition, Welch drove off the road and hit David Faircloth. As a result of this wreck, Faircloth died. The representative of Faircloth's estate sued Mercury Motors Express under the doctrine of *respondeat superior*. The trial jury awarded the plaintiff $400,000 in compensatory damages and $250,000 in punitive damages. Since it did not dispute the fact that its driver was under the influence of alcohol at the time of the wreck, Mercury paid the compensatory damages. However, Mercury appealed and argued it is not responsible to pay the punitive damages awarded. Is a master liable in punitive damages for the willful and wanton misconduct of its employee acting within the scope of employment? Explain.

5. Steve was employed by Greta as a trainee photographer. Late one night after photographing a wedding, Steve was returning the camera equipment to the studio (he was not required to return the equipment that night) when his auto collided with Tim's auto, and Tim was killed. Tim's estate sues Greta and Steve. Is Greta liable? Explain.

6. Yancey, an offshore oil rigger, was employed by Texaco. Yancey had a schedule of seven days on and seven days off. On the seventh day of work, Yancey traveled 30 miles by boat and then drove 150 miles in his car to his home. Yancey was paid for oil-field work and for boat travel time, but his pay stopped when he disembarked. While traveling to his home, Yancey struck a car and killed Theresa. Her estate sued Texaco for her wrongful death. Is an employer liable for the torts of its employees while the employees are on their way to or from work? Why or why not?

7. Stanfield brought this action for damages arising out of an accident in which Roy's truck collided with an automobile in which Stanfield was a passenger. Roy was returning from a trip where he had performed several errands for his parents, who owned and operated sev-

eral businesses. Did the accident occur while Roy was within the scope of employment, to place liability on Roy's parents under the doctrine of *respondeat superior*? Why or why not?

8. A father allowed his son, a minor, to drive the family car. Contrary to his father's instructions, the son permitted a friend to drive the car while he (the son) rode in the front seat. The friend was negligent and collided with a car driven by Tracy. Tracy sued the father to recover for her damages. Was the father liable? Why or why not?

9. Sam was an employee of the Munchie Company. Sam's job was to drive an ice cream truck and sell ice cream from the truck. One day the truck stalled, and Sam asked Ted and his friends to push the truck. They agreed, and Sam gave each of them a can of whipped cream as compensation for their help. Ted's can exploded and injured his eye. When sued by Ted, Munchie Company argued that Sam was acting outside his scope of employment at the time he gave Ted the can of whipped cream. Is this a valid argument? Explain.

10. White, an employee of Inter-City Auto Freight, Inc., was driving a large tractor-trailer truck. In attempting to pass Mr. Kuehn, a motorist, White swerved his truck toward Kuehn. After Kuehn had moved to the next lane, he stepped on the gas, caught up with the truck, and motioned with his fist for White to pull over. White again forced Kuehn into another lane. After Kuehn regained control of his car, both parties stopped on the highway's shoulder. White got out of his cab carrying a 2-foot-long metal pipe. As he approached Kuehn, White swung the pipe. It grazed the side of Kuehn's face and knocked Kuehn's glasses to the ground. As Kuehn bent over to pick up his glasses, White hit him two more times. Prior to this incident, White's record as a driver had been very good. Kuehn sued both White and his employer, Inter-City. Should Inter-City be liable for White's assault on Kuehn? Explain.

11. Joiner employed an independent contractor to spray pesticide on his crops. During the application process, the spray damaged a nearby fishing lake owned by Boroughs. When Boroughs sued, the trial court held that Joiner was not liable as a matter of law since the injury was inflicted by an independent contractor. Boroughs contends that Joiner is liable because the work done was inherently or intrinsically dangerous. On appeal, does Borough's argument have merit? Why or why not?

12. Dr. Keldene was employed at a regular salary by the QRS shipping lines to serve aboard ship and treat passengers. Keldene treated Barry, a passenger, who died as a result of Keldene's negligence. May Barry's heirs recover from QRS? Explain.

13. A company's usual lunchtime procedures, which were known to and participated in by the employer, involved one of the employees leaving the premises and obtaining lunch for the others who remained at their work stations. In the course of such an errand, an employee was involved in an automobile accident. Is the employee entitled to workers' compensation? Why or why not?

14. Everson, a Lockheed employee, was assigned to work out of town for one week. After dinner following the third day of this job, Everson and three friends decided to "go out on the town." They drove to a bar and dance hall where they had some drinks, listened to the music, and talked about the work to be done. About 12:30 A.M., Everson left to drive back to the motel. On the way, he failed to round a curve and died as a result of the accident. Can Everson's spouse collect workers' compensation benefits? Explain.

15. Dr. Chung suffered a heart attack after office hours while jogging around the Kalani High School track. At the time of his heart attack, Chung was employed as the president of Animal Clinic. He was also the sole director and sole stockholder of the corporation. A physician testified that the heart attack was work connected. Is Chung entitled to workers' compensation? Why or why not?

16. Roberts, an engineer for Southern Railway Company, was injured when the train he was operating derailed. The track slopes downhill at that point and curves sharply. A 7-foot section of broken rail was found at the site of the accident. Whether the rail was cause or effect of the accident was an issue at trial. Southern Railway was found to be negligent by the jury, and Roberts was awarded $100,000. Will a jury's verdict in a FELA case be overturned on appeal where there is some evidence to support it? Why or why not?

TERMINATION OF THE AGENCY RELATIONSHIP

CHAPTER PREVIEW

The three preceding chapters discuss various legal issues that arise from the creation and operation of the agency relationship. This chapter concentrates on how all three parties to an agency relationship are affected by the termination of the relationship.

Two issues are basic to terminating an agency relationship. First, what acts or facts are sufficient to terminate the authority of the agent? The actual termination of the relationship between the principal and an agent can be terminated by operation of law or by the acts of either the principal or agent. These methods of termination and exceptions to them make up the bulk of this chapter.

Second, what is required to terminate the agent's authority insofar as third parties are concerned? This question recognizes that an agent may continue to have the *power* to bind the principal, but not the *right* to do so. This second issue is discussed in sections 14 and 15.

You are the personnel manager for a manufacturing firm. You developed a handbook for employees that states, "No employee will be discharged without good cause." One of the plant workers has a reputation for being late to work, slow in his performance, and a general troublemaker. However, this employee's supervisor has no documentation to support this reputation. The supervisor asks you whether he can discharge this employee.

What would you advise?

TERMINATION BY OPERATION OF LAW

1. In General

The occurrence of certain events is viewed as automatically terminating the agency. As a legal principle, any one of four happenings may end the principal-agent relationship: the death of either party, the insanity of either party, the bankruptcy of either party under specific conditions, and the destruction or illegality of the agency's subject matter.

2. Death

The death of an individual acting as a principal or agent immediately terminates the agency even if the other party is unaware of the death. Once the time of death is established, there should not be any controversy about an agency ceasing to exist. Such an event is often quite significant, as the following case illustrates.

CASE

Sturgill v. Virginia Citizens Bank
291 S.E.2d 207 (Va. 1982)

PER CURIAM

In a motion for judgment, Rose Mary McCoy Sturgill, Administratrix, attempted to recover from Virginia Citizens Bank (Bank) the $13,748.58 balance of R. V. McCoy, Jr.'s bank account which the Bank, after McCoy's death, had transferred to a third party. In a bench trial, the trial court struck the Administratrix's evidence and granted summary judgment for the Bank.

On March 28, 1975, McCoy opened an individual checking account with the Bank. Eighteen months later, McCoy telephoned Jimmy Vanover, the Bank president, stating that he had remarried and desired to change his account to a joint account. On October 11, 1976, he and "Kaye Stanley McCoy" appeared at the Bank. [Actually these persons were not legally married.] They added "Kaye McCoy's" signature to the account card and requested new checks issued bearing both their names. . . .

On the reverse side of the account card, there is this notation: "Kaye McCoy's signature added Oct. 11, 1976." Vanover admitted that in another trial he testified that the Bank's practice was to note the word "joint" on the joint account cards. This notation did not appear on McCoy's account card.

Vanover's office lies next door to the apartment complex where McCoy lived. On December 4, 1976, Vanover was working in his office when he noticed an ambulance. Upon investigation, he learned of McCoy's death: The Administratrix received McCoy's personal effects and discovered the account's existence. She testified that she called Vanover on December 6, 1976, between 9:00 and 9:05 A.M. and instructed him not to honor any checks drawn on McCoy's account. According to Vanover, the Administratrix did not call him until 10:30 A.M., after "Kaye McCoy" had cashed a check for $13,748.58. The Administratrix offered into evidence a cancelled check in the amount of $13,748.58, dated December 6, 1976, and drawn by "Kaye McCoy" on McCoy's account payable to the Bank to close the account. . . .

We first must determine what rights McCoy and Kaye Stanley had in the account. The account's signature card is a contract between a depositor and the Bank. . . . This account began as an individual account and remained unchanged. The account card, dated March 28, 1975, designates the account as an individual account in the name of R. V. McCoy, Jr., and lists only his social security number. The only change occurred 18 months later, when McCoy added "Kaye McCoy" as an authorized signature and the Bank made a notation on the card's reverse side of the transaction date. If McCoy intended to convert the individual account to a joint account, he failed. He merely added a new authorized signature, but did not create a new account or amend the existing account.

Our next inquiry is whether the Bank properly paid a check issued after McCoy's death and signed by "Kaye McCoy." McCoy added the "Kaye McCoy" signature for his personal convenience, thus establishing an agency relationship between himself and his girlfriend. Because death of a principal terminates an agent's authority, . . . "Kaye McCoy" had no authority to write checks on the account after December 4, 1976. Simply put, "a power ceases with the life of the person who gives it." Of course, a customer's death will not revoke a bank's authority to pay a check until the bank knows of the death and has had a reasonable opportunity to act on it. In this case, the Bank had immediate, actual knowledge of McCoy's death and a reasonable opportunity to act on this knowledge. It could have refused payment easily on the December 6 check.

We conclude that "Kaye McCoy" had the authority to sign checks on McCoy's account, that her authority ended at his death, and that the Bank knew of McCoy's death within a reasonable time to act on such knowledge. We reverse the judgment of the trial court and enter final judgment for the Administratrix in the amount of $13,748.58. . . .

■ *Reversed.*

CASE CONCEPTS REVIEW

1. How and when did the Bank receive notice of Mr. McCoy's death?
2. According to this court, what was the legal relationship between R. V. McCoy and Kaye S. McCoy with respect to the checking account at the Bank?
3. What should the Bank have done on December 6 when Kaye sought to cash her check in the amount of the account's balance?

3. Insanity

Like death, insanity of either the principal or agent terminates their relationship. However, unlike death, insanity of a party does not always provide a distinctive time of termination. For example, if the principal has not been adjudged insane publicly, courts often hold that an agent's contract with a third party is binding on the principal unless that third party was aware of the principal's mental illness. This ruling occurs especially when the contract is beneficial to the insane principal's estate.

4. Bankruptcy

The timing of the termination of an agency due to bankruptcy is not always clear. Bankruptcy has the effect of termination only when it affects the subject matter of the agency. Assume that a business organization files for reorganization under the bankruptcy laws. Since the court's order of relief will allow this organization to continue its business activity, its agency relationships will not be terminated. However, if the debtor's petition sought Chapter 7 liquidation, the organization's bankruptcy would terminate all its agencies. This result occurs because the organization will cease to exist as a viable principal. When a bankruptcy case will act to terminate an agency, its impact happens at the time the court grants an order of relief. At that time, a trustee typically is appointed to hold the debtor's assets. This substitution of the trustee for the debtor terminates that debtor's agency relationships. (See chapter 42 for a thorough discussion of bankruptcy.)

5. Destruction or Illegality of Subject Matter

Events other than bankruptcy may destroy the agency's subject matter. For example, if the purpose of the agency relationship becomes illegal or impossible to perform, termination occurs automatically. Whereas it may be unlikely for the purpose of most business relationships to become illegal, the purpose may become impossible to perform whenever the agency's subject matter is destroyed. Suppose that an owner of real estate hires a real estate agent to find a ready, willing, and able buyer for his four-bedroom, two-bathroom house. If that house is destroyed by fire or wind or other causes, the agent's appointment would be terminated, since the house could not now be sold in its former condition.

TERMINATION BY PARTIES' ACTIONS

6. Mutual Agreement

Termination of an agency may occur due to the terms of the principal-agent agreement. For example, an agency may be created to continue for a definite period of time. If so, it ceases, by virtue of the terms of the agreement, at the expiration of the stipulated period. If the parties consent to the continuation of the relationship beyond the period, the courts imply the formation of a new contract of employment. The new agreement contains the same terms as the old one and continues for a like period of time, except that no implied contract can run longer that one year because of the statute of frauds.

Another example is an agency created to accomplish a certain purpose, which ends automatically with the accomplishment of the purpose. Furthermore, when it is possible for one of several agents to perform the task, such as selling certain real estate, it is held that performance by the first party terminates the authority of the other agents without notice of termination being required.

An agency may always be terminated by the mutual agreement of the principal and agent. Even if their original agreement does not provide for a time period of duration, the parties may agree to cancel their relationship. Since the agency is, in essence, based on a consensual agreement, the principal and agent can agree to end their association.

7. Unilateral Action

In addition to the principal and agent's mutually agreeing to end their relationship, the law generally allows either one of these parties to act independently in terminating an agency unilaterally. As a general rule, either party to an agency agreement has full *power* to terminate the agreement whenever desired, even though he or she possesses no *right* to do so. For example, if the Paulson Company agreed to employ Alicia for one year, an agency for a definite stated period has been created. That is, these parties have agreed to be principal and agent, respectively, for a one-year period. Despite this agreement, the courts are hesitant to force either an employer or employee to remain in an unhappy situation. Therefore, these parties generally do have the power to terminate this employment contract. A premature breach of the agreement is considered to be a wrongful termination, and the breaching party becomes liable for damages suffered by the other party. Of course, if an agent is discharged for cause, such as for failing to follow instructions, he or she may not recover damages from the employer.

8. Traditional Notions of Termination at Will

Many, and perhaps most, agency contracts do not provide for the duration of the agreement. When an agency is to last for an unspecified or indefinite time period, the relationship may be terminated at the will of either the principal or the agent. There is some controversy about whether a contract for permanent employment is terminable at the employer's will. Many courts have followed the traditional view that a promise for permanent employment, not supported by any consideration other than the performance of duties and payment of wages, is a contract for an indefinite period and terminable at the will of either party at any time. However, there is an opposing view that requires the employer to prove good cause or reason to dismiss an employee who has been promised permanent employment.

As a general rule, when an agency agreement is terminable at the will of either party, both the principal and agent have the legal *right* as well as the power to terminate their relationship. When a party has the right to do so, a termination is not a breach of contract and no liability is incurred. In other words, both the principal and agent have had the ability to end an agency at any time for any reason as long as the relationship was not to last for a definite time. For a number of reasons, in recent years courts have established many exceptions to this "terminable at will" notion. The next section examines these exceptions.

9. Exceptions to Termination at Will

In England at common law, an employment contract for an indefinite period was presumed to extend for one year unless there were reasonable grounds for discharge. Early American courts followed this approach, but late in the nineteenth century, apparently influenced by the laissez-faire climate of the Industrial Revolution, the American courts rejected the English rule and developed the employment-at-will doctrine, discussed in section 8. The doctrine recognized that where an employment was for an indefinite term, an employer could discharge an employee "for good cause, for no cause, or even for cause morally wrong, without being thereby guilty of legal wrong."

By the turn of the twentieth century, the at-will doctrine was absolute. Since the 1930s, however, government regulation in the workplace has increased dramatically as legislative bodies recognize the need to curb harsh applications and abuse of the rule, especially in labor relations.

Statutory modifications of the at-will doctrine are numerous. Laws prohibiting discrimination make it unlawful for an employer to discharge an employee be-

TABLE 25-1 ■ Examples of Exceptions to Discharge at Will

ALLEGED IMPROPER GROUND FOR DISCHARGE	
Often Based on Statutes	**Usually Based on Case Law**
1. Jury service	1. Refusing to commit perjury
2. Military service	2. Refusing to lobby
3. Union activity	3. Refusing to perform an illegal act or to violate a statute
4. Discrimination	4. Complaining of sexual harassment
5. Wages garnished	5. Voting against management as an employee-shareholder
6. Refusing lie-detector test	6. Supplying information to the police
7. Responding to subpoena to testify in legal proceedings	7. Refusing to handle radioactive materials in violation of federal guidelines
8. Testifying in wage law violation cases, OSHA violation cases	8. Whistle blowing
9. Filing workers' compensation claim	9. Suing employer for unpaid commissions

Note: Not every state or every court would find liability on each of these grounds.

cause of race, color, religion, sex, age, or national origin. Labor laws prevent discharges for union activities. Other forms of discriminatory discharges have also been prohibited by various state legislatures. Table 25-1 lists typical statutory protections against the discharge-at-will rule.

Consistent with the philosophy of the statutory modifications, many state courts have recognized the need to protect workers who are wrongfully discharged under circumstances not covered by any legislation or whose job security is not safeguarded by a collective bargaining agreement or civil service regulations. The courts have accomplished this objective by requiring employers to act in good faith and by finding liability if a discharge is contrary to public policy.

GOOD-FAITH TERMINATION.   The first and more expansive of the two theories is imposing on an employer an implied duty to terminate an employee only in good faith. This contract theory often uses personnel handbooks, work rules, and oral statements to find that an express or implied contract exists requiring employers to exercise good faith in performing it. Many of these handbooks contain a statement that the employee will be terminated only if good cause is proved. The handbook's language reinforces the court's inclination to find that the employer is bound to an implied promise that makes the concept of termination at will inapplicable. The following case illustrates one court's view that handbooks and published guidelines might even create express contracts that nullify the at-will doctrine.

CASE

McGinnis v. Honeywell, Inc.
791 P.2d 452 (N.M. 1990)

MONTGOMERY, J.

This is an employee's wrongful-discharge case. The employee, Shirley McGinnis, sued her former employer, Honeywell, Inc., for breach of an implied employment contract. . . . The trial court . . . submitted the issues of breach of an employment contract and compensatory damages to a jury. The jury found in McGinnis's favor, awarding her damages of $515,161.00 for breach of her employment contract. Honeywell appeals, claiming that there was insufficient evidence of an implied employment contract. . . .

Shirley McGinnis began work in 1980 as a senior secretary at Honeywell's Albuquerque facility. At the time she applied for employment she executed an employment agreement providing:

> My employment is in accordance with any applicable written agreement and applicable personnel practices published to employees, and, *subject to such* agreements or *practices*, may be terminated by me or by Honeywell at any time. . . . [Emphasis added.]

In 1982, McGinnis was promoted to the non-supervisory position of benefits administrator in the Honeywell Human Resources Department. As benefits administrator, McGinnis became familiar with various personnel policies and manuals, including a "work force realignment guide" setting out policies as to reductions in force. . . .

Honeywell underwent two reductions in force at its Albuquerque facility. The first occurred in 1984, when approximately 100 employees (nearly 30 percent of the work force) were laid off. The second took place in late 1985 and early 1986; approximately 20 employees (nearly 10 percent of the work force) were laid off at that time. In the second reduction the Human Resources Department was ordered to reduce its staff by one person. McGinnis's position as benefits administrator was eliminated and she was laid off on January 9, 1986.

The work force realignment guide provided that in the event of a reduction in force, an exempt employee like McGinnis had the option to take a nonexempt position "if he/she formerly held that job family." At the time of the layoff, another employee, Sherri Montoya, held the position of senior human resources clerk, a nonexempt position in the same job family as the secretarial position formerly held by McGinnis. Accordingly, under the policy McGinnis had the option to assume Montoya's position, but it was not offered to her. . . .

After McGinnis's employment was terminated, she attempted to locate other work, making inquiries at "hundreds" of places, but was unemployed at the time of trial. . . .

McGinnis's complaint alleged that she had "an employment contract" with Honeywell, evidenced by various personnel manuals, oral representations and the like, and that she had been terminated in violation of the policies and procedures set forth in these documents. The case was tried on the theory that Honeywell had breached an implied employment contract, although McGinnis's position and the evidence submitted to the jury were equally consistent with breach of an express contract if one existed. . . .

On appeal, Honeywell contends that there was insufficient evidence to support a jury finding that McGinnis had an implied contract of employment which would overcome the presumption that her employment was terminable at will. . . .

At the outset of our consideration of Honeywell's contentions on the breach-of-contract issue, we are struck by the fact that the parties at trial by and large confined themselves to a dispute about whether or not an implied contract of employment existed, without addressing the point, which strikes us as fairly obvious, that there was an express contract. Honeywell acknowledges that McGinnis signed an employment agreement which, while it provided that her employment could be terminated "at any time," also provided that a termination was subject to "applicable personnel practices published to employees." Thus, if applicable personnel practices permitted her employment to be terminated only under certain conditions and in certain ways, and if such practices were published to employees, and if Honeywell terminated her in violation of these practices, then Honeywell breached an express contract of employment and is liable for the damages sustained by McGinnis as a result. . . .

The jury might very well have adopted the common-sense view that, since the parties had signed an employment agreement containing a promise by Honeywell to lay off McGinnis only in accordance with certain procedures specified in the work force realignment guide, and if that guide was "published to employees," then the parties' conduct was sufficient to manifest an intention to be bound by the agreement. At no point during the trial or before did McGinnis disavow the possibility that she might assert her claim as a breach of an express employment agreement. While the parties focused their energies on proof or disproof of the various constituent elements of an implied contract, the evidence submitted to the jury and the legal principles on which it was instructed were sufficient to embrace the theory that Honeywell had discharged McGinnis in breach of an employment contract to which it had expressly assented. . . .

Here there was evidence that it was Honeywell's policy to take uniform and consistent actions regarding termination and that supervisors were required to follow applicable policies, that Honeywell would follow its written policies to the letter, and that the realignment policy could not be ignored and had to be applied. This was evidence of the parties' norms of conduct and expectations founded upon them. It was evidence sufficient to permit the jury to find that the procedures in the realignment guide, under the parties' express agreement, limited Honeywell's ability to terminate McGinnis "at any time.". . .

It is enough in this case to recognize as adequately supporting the jury's verdict that, while McGinnis agreed that her employment could be terminated "at any time," Honeywell expressly conditioned its right to terminate her employment on certain policies and procedures communicated to its employees. Honeywell has steadfastly maintained that McGinnis was terminated in the course of an

Albuquerque facility-wide reduction in force or "layoff." If so, then McGinnis was entitled to the procedures spelled out in the realignment guide before the layoff could be implemented as to her. The jury could reasonably have found that Honeywell's failure to afford McGinnis the benefit of those procedures was a breach of its express written contract of employment for which she was entitled to damages. . . .

■ *The judgment of the district court is affirmed.*

CASE CONCEPTS REVIEW

1. What is the essence of the employment contract signed by Ms. McGinnis when she began working for Honeywell?
2. How does the "work force realignment guide" protect McGinnis?
3. Why does this court concentrate on the existence of an express contract as opposed to an implied contract? Does this distinction make any substantive difference in this case's outcome?

PUBLIC POLICY EXCEPTION. The second and more popular of the two theories is widely known as the *public policy exception*. This theory allows the discharged employee to recover if the termination violates a well-established and important public policy. Some of the examples of protected public policy preventing discharge without liability are listed in Table 25–1. Many are based on statutes prohibiting discharge for specific reasons, and others are based on the court's view of public policy as it is needed to protect employees. The court in the following case provides an analysis that is common in describing the public policy exception to the employment-at-will doctrine.

CASE

Smith v. Smithway Motor Xpress, Inc.
454 N.W.2d 682 (Ia. 1990)

ANDREASEN, J.

This case involves the discharge of an employee in retaliation for filing a workers' compensation claim. The jury found for the employee, and awarded $33,000 compensatory and $100,000 punitive damages. This appeal . . . followed.

In June of 1985 John W. Smith (Smith) began work as a truck driver for Smithway Motor Xpress, Inc. (SMX). Smith participated in SMX's orientation program and signed for a copy of the SMX safety program. Under that program, drivers were required to report any accident as soon as possible, within two hours if physically able.

On October 3, 1985, Smith injured his back while loading his truck. Smith, who was on the road at the time, contends that he called a dispatcher at SMX within fifteen minutes and was told that no other drivers were available and that he should finish his trip if possible. SMX contends that Smith did not timely report his injury to the proper company official. According to Smith, he continued with his assigned route, reporting his injury to the dispatcher on a daily basis, until he returned home seven days later. Upon returning to his home terminal, Smith filed a formal, written report of his injury with the safety director. At that time SMX made no objection to the manner in which Smith reported the injury.

Due to his injury, Smith was hospitalized and unable to work for four months. During that time he received workers' compensation benefits. SMX did not interfere with the payments of the benefits. On February 10, 1986, Smith was released to return to work by his doctor. The next day he reported to work at SMX and was fired without explanation. When Smith subsequently applied for unemployment compensation, SMX objected, stating that Smith was terminated for failing timely to report an injury as required by the SMX safety program.

Under the SMX safety program each driver was initially credited with twelve points. For each safety violation, points were deducted according to a set schedule. Loss of all twelve points resulted in termination. Prior to his back injury, Smith had all twelve points. Despite the fact that the schedule called for a six point deduction for failure timely to report an accident, SMX claimed at the unemployment compensation hearing that it assessed twelve points against Smith for failing to report his accident to the safety director within two hours. At trial, SMX raised for the first time additional alleged reasons for firing Smith, including provisions of the Federal Motor Carriers Act and a loss of trust in Smith.

The jury found that SMX had discharged Smith in retaliation for Smith's filing of a workers' compensation claim. Both parties have appealed.

SMX urges first that the district court erred in denying its motions for directed verdict and judgment notwithstanding the verdict.

Here, evidence showed that Smith was fired after filing a workers' compensation claim when SMX's own safety program would call for only a deduction of six points. While Smith, as an employee at will, was subject to termination for any reason or no reason, SMX's deviation from its established program was something the jury could consider. There was also evidence that SMX's insurance director, not its personnel director, made the decision to fire Smith. There was also evidence that the personnel director advised against the discharge, predicting litigation if Smith was fired. Moreover, the insurance director conceded that the cost of paying workers' compensation benefits entered into his decision to fire Smith. This and other evidence was sufficient to justify submitting the question to the jury.

SMX claims, however, that since it did not interfere with Smith's eligibility to receive workers' compensation benefits, our previous cases dealing with retaliatory discharge do not apply. . . .

SMX claims that since it did not interfere with Smith's workers' compensation benefits it did not clearly violate any public policy. We disagree. . . . In . . . *Frampton v. Central Ind. Gas Co.*, 297 N.E.2d 425 (1973), the seminal case in the area of retaliatory discharge for the filing of a workers' compensation claim, the Indiana Supreme Court was faced with a situation similar to the one before us. The court, construing a statute very similar to Iowa's stated:

[I]n order for the goals of the Act to be realized and for public policy to be effectuated, the employee must be able to exercise his right in an unfettered fashion without being subject to reprisal. If employers are permitted to penalize employees for filing workmen's compensation claims, a most important public policy will be undermined. The fear of being discharged would have a deleterious effect on the exercise of a statutory right. Employees will not file claims for justly deserved compensation—opting, instead, to continue their employment without incident. The end result, of course, is that the employer is effectively relieved of his obligation. . . .

We believe the threat of discharge to be a "device" within the framework of [the statute], and hence, in clear contravention of public policy.

We agree with the Indiana Supreme Court that retaliatory discharge violates public policy even if the employer does not interfere with the discharged employee's benefits. The trial court was correct in denying SMX's motions for directed verdict and judgment notwithstanding the verdict. . . .

■ *Affirmed.*

CASE CONCEPTS REVIEW

1. Did the company contest Smith's filing or receipt of workers' compensation benefits?
2. What reasons did the company give for discharging Smith?
3. What does the court conclude in deciding whether the company wrongfully discharged Smith after he received workers' compensation benefits?

The courts of various states have different attitudes about the public policy exceptions to the at-will rule. Most states will take a strict view of what public policies support an action for wrongful discharge. Employees have a cause of action for wrongful discharge when the discharge is contrary to a fundamental and well-defined public policy as evidenced by existing law. That is, a wrongful discharge is actionable when the termination clearly contravenes the public welfare and gravely violates paramount requirements of public interest. Usually the public policy must be evidenced by constitutional or statutory provisions. For example, an employee cannot be fired for refusing to engage in an unlawful action in violation of the Constitution or a statute. Employers will be held liable for those terminations that effectuate an unlawful end.

Some states have expanded this public policy exception to protect employees who report the illegal activities of others. Employees engaged in such whistle-blowing actions may not be discharged at will. However, the courts in other states have not expanded the public policy exception to the at-will doctrine in this manner. These courts have left it to the legislative bodies to broaden the public policy exception by further statutory enactment. In other situations, employers will not be liable for discharge that may have a "bad motive" in the eyes of the employee. The following case is typical of those in which the grounds for discharge were questionable but there was no liability.

Patton v. J.C. Penney Co.

719 P.2d 854 (Or. 1986)

JONES, J.

David Patton filed suit against J.C. Penney Co. and two supervisors, McKay and Chapin, alleging . . . "wrongful discharge" from employment. . . . The trial court granted defendants' motion to dismiss for failure to state a claim. . . .

Plaintiff then appealed to the Court of Appeals. That court affirmed. . . . The Court of Appeals acknowledged that there are exceptions to the general rule that an employer may discharge an employee at any time and for any reason, but the court found that plaintiff's claim did not qualify under any exception to the general rule. . . .

Defendant J.C. Penney Co. hired plaintiff in 1969. Plaintiff worked in Eugene until 1980 when he was transferred to Portland where he worked as a merchandising manager. In 1981, the store manager, defendant McKay, told plaintiff to break off a social relationship with a female co-employee. Plaintiff responded by telling McKay that he did not socialize with the co-employee at work and that he intended to continue seeing her on his own time. Apparently, the social relationship did not interfere with plaintiff's performance at work, for during this time he earned several awards for "Merchant of the Month" and one for "Merchant of the Year."

McKay later, while interrogating other employees about whether plaintiff had broken off the relationship, made statements to the effect that if plaintiff wanted to keep working he had to discontinue the relationship. Although no written or unwritten policy, rule or regulation proscribed socializing between employees, other employees told plaintiff that McKay disfavored plaintiff's fraternization with the female co-employee. Nevertheless, plaintiff continued seeing the co-employee. When McKay warned plaintiff in late 1981 that his job performance was unsatisfactory and that he would be fired if there was no improvement, plaintiff asked for a transfer to another department. McKay denied the request. In February 1982, McKay terminated plaintiff's employment for unsatisfactory job performance. The district manager, defendant Chapin, approved the termination.

Generally, an employer may discharge an employee at any time and for any reason, absent a contractual, statutory or constitutional requirement. Termination of employment ordinarily does not create a tortious cause of action. We have set forth exceptions to the general rule which are discussed in a series of cases. .

In *Nees v. Hocks*, the employer fired the employee for disregarding its wishes that the employee ask to be excused from jury duty. In fact, the employee told the court clerk that she would like to serve on jury duty. This court held that the jury system and jury duty are important American institutions and citizen obligations: "If an employer were permitted with impunity to discharge an employee for fulfilling her obligation to jury duty, the jury system would be adversely affected. The will of the community would be thwarted." Defendant could thus be held liable for discharging plaintiff for serving on the jury.

In *Delaney v. Taco Times Int'l.*, this court held that an employer could be held liable for discharging an employee who refused to sign a false and potentially defamatory statement about a former co-employee. The court found that Article I, section 10, of the Oregon Constitution, recognizes an obligation on members of society not to defame others. Therefore, the court said that the defendant could not discharge plaintiff for fulfilling a societal obligation.

A wrongful discharge claim may also exist when an employee is fired for pursuing private statutory rights directly relating to the employee's status or role as an employee. In *Holien*, the court found plaintiff's allegations that she was fired for resisting sexual harassment sufficient to state a claim because on-the-job sexual harassment by supervisors is forbidden by state and federal law. . . .

We have rejected wrongful discharge claims under a third category where the law provides other remedies than a common law remedy for wrongful discharge. For example, in *Walsh v. Consolidated Freightways*, this court found that an additional tort remedy for wrongful discharge was unnecessary when an employee was discharged for complaining about a safety violation for which there were statutory remedies.

Plaintiff does not allege that his discharge was for pursuing statutory rights related to his status as an employee. Nor does plaintiff allege interference with an interest of public importance equal or analogous to serving on a jury or avoiding false, defamatory remarks. Plaintiff claims that certain of his "fundamental, inalienable human rights were compromised, put on the auction block, and made the subject of an illicit barter in that he was forced to forego these rights or to purchase them with his job." He claims that the employer invaded his personal right of privacy and that the employer could not fire him for pursuing a private right. But these claims blur "rights" against governmental infringement with "rights" against a private employer. Plaintiff's acts were voluntary and no state or federal law mandates or prohibits discrimination on that account. It may seem harsh that an employer can fire an employee because of dislike of the employee's personal lifestyle, but because the plaintiff cannot show that the actions fit under an exception to the general rule, plaintiff is subject to the traditional doctrine of "fire at will."

■ *Affirmed.*

CASE CONCEPTS REVIEW

1. What reason was Patton given when his employment was terminated?

2. What does Patton allege was the real reason for his termination?

3. Why does this court conclude in J.C. Penney's favor?

10. Rights of Wronged Employees

The employee whose employment has been wrongfully cut short is entitled to recover compensation for work done before dismissal and an additional sum for damages. Most states permit the employee to bring an action either immediately following the breach, in which event he or she recovers prospective damages, or after the period has expired, in which event he or she recovers the damages actually sustained. In the latter case, as a general rule, the employee is compelled to deduct from the compensation called for in the agreement the amount that he or she has been able to earn during the interim.

Under such circumstances, a wrongfully discharged employee is under a duty to exercise reasonable diligence in finding other work of like character. Idleness is not encouraged by the law. Apparently, this rule does not require the discharged employee to seek employment in a new locality or to accept work of a different kind or more menial character. The duty is to find work of like kind, provided it is available in the particular locality. One way that damages for wrongful discharges may be mitigated is for the employer to rehire the employee. A discharged employee often seeks this remedy in addition to accrued back pay.

In some cases, an employer wrongfully discharges an employee but has no liability because the employee either fails to prove damage or fails to mitigate damages. The following case reached just such a result.

CASE

Dawson v. Billings Gazette

726 P.2d 826 (Mont. 1986)

GULBRANDSON, J.

Patrick Dawson appeals a jury verdict in Yellowstone County District Court which found in his favor on the issues of liability and proximate cause in his wrongful termination suit but awarded him zero damages. The District Court denied Dawson's motion for a new trial. . . .

Appellant Dawson filed suit against the Billings Gazette on September 23, 1982, alleging that he had been wrongfully terminated from his employment as a reporter with the newspaper on June 21, 1982, and that the Gazette had violated its duty of good faith and fair dealing. . . .

A jury trial was held in March, 1985, and the jury found that:

1) The Gazette had breached its duty of good faith and fair dealing to Dawson;

2) the Gazette was the proximate cause of Dawson's damages;

3) Dawson was entitled to zero damages;

4) the Gazette was not liable for punitive damages. . . .

In *Holenstein v. Andrews* (1975), 166 Mont. 60, we held that where there is substantial credible evidence in the record to support a verdict of zero damages, the verdict will be upheld.

We find substantial credible evidence in the record to support the jury's verdict.

First, Dawson had three sources of income from the time he was fired until the time of trial. He received four and one-half weeks pay for unused vacation and holiday time and two weeks severance pay from the Gazette. He received unemployment compensation and performed freelance work for several publications, including U.S.A. Today, Time Magazine, The Denver Post, The Miami Herald, The Dallas Morning News, and The Great Falls Tribune.

Second, we find that Dawson has failed to mitigate his damages. An injured party is not required to seek employment in another line of work or to move to a different locality. However, he or she must exercise ordinary diligence to procure other employment.

After he was fired Dawson applied to just four newspapers, restricted his job search to papers of equal or greater circulation than that of the Gazette, and only those located in the western United States. He totally rejected the idea of working for a smaller newspaper in fear of the resulting harm to his career. The Sacramento Bee indicated that a position might be available but Dawson rejected the inquiry because of the salary cut he would be taking.

The Gazette presented several witnesses who testified that in their positions as newspaper editors, they would be willing to hire reporters who had moved to smaller papers and even those who had been fired from other papers. Several of the witnesses themselves had taken positions with smaller papers in hopes of advancing their careers. Evidence was also presented that another reporter fired by the Gazette found comparable employment with the Bozeman Chronicle within one month of her dismissal.

It is very likely that Dawson could have obtained full-time employment with a reputable newspaper a short time after his firing if he had vigorously sought to do so. By failing to pursue comparable full-time work in the journalism field, Dawson failed to mitigate his damages.

The plaintiff has the burden of proving his own damages. In addition, the jury is not compelled to believe the plaintiff's testimony.

Dawson argues that because he was never offered a job, he has proven his damages. We reject the argument and hold that there is substantial evidence from which the jury could have concluded that Dawson suffered no damages. The jury decides what evidence to accept and what evidence to reject.

We refuse to overturn the jury verdict. . . .

■ *Affirmed.*

CASE CONCEPTS REVIEW

1. Since the jury found that Dawson had been terminated in a wrongful manner, why is he appealing?
2. What is the evidentiary basis for concluding that Dawson did not suffer any damages as the result of being wrongfully discharged?

GENERAL EXCEPTIONS TO TERMINATION

11. Introduction

In addition to the public policy reasons for not making employment relationships terminable at will, there are two other exceptions to the general rules on when and how agency relationships may be terminated. The exceptions to termination at will are usually related to employment situations and do not stop termination. They simply create liability for wrongful termination. There are also general exceptions applicable to any principal-agent relationship that actually prevent termination of the relationship. These two general exceptions are known as an agency coupled with either an interest or an obligation.

While reading the next two sections, keep in mind that agencies generally may be terminated by operation of law or by the parties' action. Also keep asking why these general exceptions are necessary. That is, look for the answers to the following questions: What is so important about the agency discussed to justify making it not subject to termination? Why is imposing liability for wrongful termination an inadequate remedy?

Agency coupled with an interest When an agent has an actual interest in the property of the principal and has a right of action against interference by third parties with that property.

12. Agency Coupled with an Interest

The first general exception to how and when an agency is terminated is the factual situation described as an **agency coupled with an interest.** This term describes the relationship that exists when the agent has an actual beneficial interest in the property that is the subject matter of the agency. A mortgage or a security agreement usually contains a provision naming the lender as the agent to sell the described property in the event of a default. Thus this lender becomes an agent with a security interest in the subject matter of the principal-agent relationship. In other words, these documents do create an agency coupled with an interest. A more modern phrase used to describe this situation is a *power given as security.* Mortgages and security agreements that give the lender the power to sell the collateral as security for repayment cannot be canceled unilaterally by the principal.

An agency coupled with an interest in property cannot be terminated unilaterally by the principal and is not terminated by events (such as death, insanity, or bankruptcy of the principal) that otherwise terminate agencies by operation of law. The net effect is that an agency coupled with an interest in property cannot be terminated without the consent of the agent.

13. Agency Coupled with an Obligation

Agency coupled with an obligation When an agent is owed money by the principal and the agency relationship is created to facilitate the agent collecting this money from a third party, an agency coupled with an obligation is created.

An agency coupled with an interest in property must be distinguished from an **agency coupled with an obligation.** This agency is created as a source of reimbursement to the agent. For example, an agent who is given the right to sell a certain automobile and to apply the proceeds on a claim against the principal is an agency coupled with an obligation. Such an agency is a hybrid between the usual agency and the agency coupled with an interest in property. The agency coupled with an obligation cannot unilaterally be terminated by the principal, but death or bankruptcy of the principal will terminate the agency by operation of law.

Under either type of agency, it should be clear that the interest in the subject matter must be greater than the mere expectation of profits to be realized or in the proceeds to be derived from the sale of the property. The interest must be in the property itself. A real estate broker is not an agent coupled with an interest, even though the broker expects a commission from the proceeds of the sale. Likewise, a principal who has appointed an agent to sell certain goods on commission has the power to terminate the agency at any time, although such conduct might constitute a breach of the agreement.

ISSUES INVOLVING THIRD PARTIES

14. Problems with Apparent Authority

As this chapter has explained, issues involving the termination of agencies concern both the principal and agent. Indeed, subject to some exceptions, termination of an agency occurs by operation of law or by the actions of the principal or agent. Whereas these parties, by the nature of the relationship, will learn of the termination, the third parties who know of the agency may not be aware that a particular relationship is terminated. Whenever a third party has been induced by the principal to believe an agency exists, there is an opportunity for the principal to become bound to the third party due to apparent authority. The existence of apparent or ostensible authority was discussed in chapter 23.

To prevent the existence of apparent authority, the law requires the principal to give notice of termination to all third parties who have learned of the agency. How and when this required notice is to be given to third parties involve whether these parties had dealt personally with the agent or had just known of the agency's existence. Also of importance is whether the notice required be personally delivered or constructively given.

15. Notice Required

Notice of an agency's termination may be delivered in one of two ways. First, the notice may be personally or privately given. Examples of this type of notice include oral communication, face to face or over the phone. Sending notice through the mail also is considered to be personally delivered when properly addressed and stamped. Second, the alternative type of notice is public or constructive notice. Such notices include an announcement in a newspaper or other periodical. Furthermore, notice can be constructively given over radio, television, or other media of communication.

The type of notice of termination required to cut off an agent's apparent authority depends on the third party's relationship to the agent. When the agency is terminated by the acts of the principal or agent, the principal has the duty to give personal notice of the termination to those third parties who have dealt with the agent. When a third party has not previously dealt with the agent, the principal satisfies the duty to give notice by providing public notice. If the principal fails to give the type of notice required, that principal is allowing the agent's apparent authority to exist, as happened in the following case.

CASE

Moore v. Puget Sound Plywood, Inc.
332 N.W.2d 212 (Neb. 1983)

In the early 1970s, the Moores purchased siding during the construction of their home. This siding, which was manufactured by Puget Sound Plywood, Inc., began to come apart during 1977. The problem became so severe in 1979 that the Moores attempted to contact their source of the siding. They discovered that company no longer existed. However, they learned that Rehcon, Inc. represented Puget Sound concerning the defective siding. Thereafter, in March, 1980, Rehcon quit in its representative capacity of Puget Sound because of a lack of cooperation. No efforts were made by Puget Sound to notify the public that Rehcon was no longer its agent. On June 24, 1980, Mr. Moore notified Rehcon of his defective siding. Subsequently, the Moores sued Puget Sound for $4,550, which was the cost of replacing the siding. The basis of this suit was a breach of warranty concerning the siding. Puget Sound defended by asserting that it had not been notified, as required, of the Moores' problem with the siding. The trial court dismissed the Moores' complaint, and they appealed.

CAPORALE, J.

. . . The Moores' . . . assignment of error relates to the lower courts' holdings that they failed to prove proper no-

tice to Puget Sound. . . . [T]he buyer must, within a reasonable time after he discovers or should have discovered any breach, notify the seller of the breach or be barred from any recovery. We have held that a purchaser must plead that he gave timely notice of the breach. The Moores did so plead. The question is, then, whether the evidence supports that allegation. The June 24, 1980, written complaint to Rehcon was given within a reasonable time of the initial discovery in 1977 and the determination in 1979 that the problem was severe enough to warrant action. It is true that by the time of that complaint Rehcon no longer had any relationship with Puget Sound. However, that fact is not in and of itself determinative.

. . . [A]pparent authority may exist beyond termination of the principal-agency relationship when notice of the termination has not been given. . . . Where a principal has, by his voluntary act, placed an agent in such a situation that a person of ordinary prudence, conversant with business usages and the nature of the particular business, is justified in presuming that such agent has authority to perform a particular act, and therefore deals with the agent, the principal is estopped as against such third person from denying the agent's authority.

Whether or not an act is within the scope of an agent's apparent authority is to be determined under the foregoing rule as a question of fact from all the circumstances of the transaction and the business. . . .

[A]pparent or ostensible authority to act as an agent may be conferred if the alleged principal affirmatively, intentionally, or by lack of ordinary care causes third persons to act upon the apparent agency. Under the facts and circumstances of this case, Mr. Moore's notice to Rehcon was notice to Puget Sound. The Moores' assignments of error are meritorious. The judgment of the District Court is reversed and the matter remanded with directions that judgment be entered in favor of the Moores in the sum of $4,550.

■ *Reversed and remanded.*

CASE CONCEPTS REVIEW

1. When did Rehcon cease to be an agent for Puget Sound Plywood?
2. When did the Moores give formal notice of the defective siding to Rehcon?
3. Prior to this notice of defect, what was the relationship between the Moores and Rehcon?
4. What should Puget Sound Plywood have done to destroy the appearance that Rehcon was its agent?

By fulfilling the duty to give notice of termination to third parties according to the factual situation and the local requirements, the principal prevents apparent authority from existing. A third party who has not dealt with the agent may not learn of the notice given publicly. If that third party relies on the continuation of the agency, it is to his or her own detriment. In other words, the principal does not become liable to the third party in such a situation. If a third party who did deal with the agent has not received direct personal notice from the principal but has learned indirectly of the agency's termination or of facts sufficient to make inquiry reasonable, the third party is no longer justified in dealing as if the agent represents the principal. In other words, a third party who has dealt with the agent cannot rely on apparent authority to bind the principal when that third party learns of the agency's termination via public, rather than personal, notice.

When the agency is terminated by action of law, such as death, insanity, or bankruptcy, no duty to notify third parties is placed on the principal. Such matters receive publicity through newspapers, official records, and otherwise, and third parties normally become aware of the termination without the necessity for additional notification. If the death of the principal occurs before an agent contracts with a third party, the third party has no cause of action against either the agent or the estate of the principal unless the agent is acting for an undisclosed principal. In the latter case, since the agent makes the contract in his or her own name, the agent is liable to the third party. Otherwise, the third party is in as good a position to know of the death of the principal as is the agent.

A special problem exists regarding notice in cases of special agents as distinguished from general agents. Ordinarily, notice is not required to revoke the authority of a special agent, since the agent possesses no continuing authority, and no one will be in the habit of dealing with him or her. Only if the principal has directly indicated that the agent has authority in a certain matter or at a certain time will notice be required, to prevent reliance on the principal's conduct by a party dealing with the agent. This is especially true if the agent is acting under a special power of attorney. Actual notice of termination is required in these cases.

CHAPTER SUMMARY

TERMINATION BY OPERATION OF LAW

1. Death of either principal or agent ends the relationship.
2. Insanity of either principal or agent ends the relationship.

3. Bankruptcy of principal or agent may end the relationship if the subject matter of the relationship is affected.

4. Destruction or illegality of the agency's subject matter ends the relationship.

TERMINATION BY PARTIES' ACTIONS

Mutual Agreement	1. Due to their contractual nature, agency relationships can be terminated by the principal's and agent's consent at any time.
	2. Such consent may be reflected in an original agreement that is to last for a stated time period.
	3. Consent to terminate also occurs if the purpose of the relationship is accomplished or if the parties agree to end the relationship prior to the stated date of termination.
Unilateral Action	1. In general, even if the agency is to last for a stated time, either the principal or agent can end the relationship at any time.
	2. The parties have the power of termination even if they lack the legal right.
	3. If a party exercises the power of termination while lacking the right, that party is liable for money damages that the premature termination causes.
Traditional Notions of Termination at Will	1. Traditionally, if there was no stated period of duration, both the principal and agent had the right and power to terminate the relationship at their desire or will.
	2. If the agency is terminable at will, the party terminating the relationship has no liability for damages.
Exceptions to Termination at Will	1. There is a growing trend to require that employers support their decisions to fire employees on a reasonable basis.
	2. Many statutes prohibit discharge for stated reasons. Case law also imposes liability contract that must be performed in good faith.
	3. Language taken from employees' handbooks has been used to create a unilateral contract that must be performed in good faith.
	4. Protected rights include those listed in Table 25–1.
Rights of Wronged Employees	1. An employee is entitled to recover actual damages sustained.
	2. Actual earnings are deducted from what would have been earned.
	3. There is a duty to mitigate damages by seeking similar work in the same community.

GENERAL EXCEPTIONS TO TERMINATION

Agency Coupled with an Interest	1. This relationship occurs when an agent has an actual beneficial interest in the property that is the subject matter of the agency.
	2. This also is described as a power given as security.
	3. This type of agency cannot be terminated by operation of law or by the unilateral acts of the principal.
Agency Coupled with an Obligation	1. This is a relationship created as a source of reimbursement to the agent.
	2. This relationship cannot be terminated by the unilateral acts of the principal. However, it can be terminated by operation of law.

ISSUES INVOLVING THIRD PARTIES

Problems with Apparent Authority	1. Although an agent's actual authority is removed when the agency is terminated, apparent authority may still exist from the third parties' perspective.
	2. The principal is required to give notice of termination to third parties to cut off the agent's apparent authority.
Notice Required	1. Notice of termination may be given personally or publicly.
	2. Personal notice includes that given face to face, over the phone, or by mail.

3. Public notice is that given constructively through newspaper, radio, television, or other means of public communication.

4. When termination occurs by the acts of the parties, personal notice must be given to the third parties who have dealt with the agent. Public notice is sufficient to cut off an agent's apparent authority when a prospective third party has not previously dealt with the agent.

5. When termination occurs by operation of law, generally no notice needs to be given by the principal to third parties.

REVIEW QUESTIONS AND PROBLEMS

1. Match each term in column A with the appropriate statement in column B.

A	B
(1) Operation of law	(a) Generally present even though the legal right of termination is lacking
(2) Power of termination	(b) One example of an employee's protected right
(3) Termination at will	(c) Often used as a basis for proving that an employer breached an implied duty or agreement
(4) Employees' handbook	(d) A relationship created as a source of reimbursement to the agent
(5) Jury service	(e) Termination by death, insanity, bankruptcy, destruction, or illegality
(6) Agency coupled with an interest	(f) Given constructively through the newspaper, radio, or television
(7) Agency coupled with an obligation	(g) Also known as a power given as security
(8) Public notice	(h) A traditional legal concept whereby the terminating party has the right and power to end a relationship

2. As a matter of law, the occurrence of any one of four events operates to terminate a principal-agent relationship. List these four events.

3. In addition to termination by operation of law, an agency may be terminated by the mutual agreement of the principal and agent. Describe three factual situations wherein the parties' agreement ends their relationship.

4. When agency relationships are terminated by the actions of the parties involved, the concepts of the *power* to terminate and *right* to terminate become important. Explain the distinction between the legal significance of these terms.

5. The Dixie Company offered Papageorge a contract of employment as a regional manager. Dixie's offer contained a proposed annual salary of $35,000. Papageorge accepted this offer, but he was not allowed to begin work. Dixie canceled the contract. When Papageorge sued, Dixie denied liability and contended that without an agreed-on duration, this employment was terminable at will. Papageorge argued that the stated annual salary implied a contract to last at least a year. Which party is correct? Why?

6. Weiner was informed that his employer's policy was not to terminate employees without just cause. His employment application stated that his employment would be subject to the provisions of the employer's "Handbook on Personnel Policies and Procedures." The handbook represented that "[t]he company will resort to dismissal for just and sufficient cause only, and only after all practical steps toward rehabilitation or salvage of the employee have been taken and failed. However, if the welfare of the company indicates that dismissal is necessary, then that decision is arrived at and is carried out forthrightly." Is this employment relationship terminable at will? Explain.

7. Palmateer was fired both for supplying information to local law enforcement authorities that an IH employee might be involved in a violation of the Criminal Code and for agreeing to assist in the investigation and the employee's trial if requested. He filed suit against IH alleging retaliatory discharge. Was Palmateer's discharge wrongful? Explain.

8. Andy was hired as a computer salesman on commission. A dispute arose over the commission, and Andy filed suit against his employer and asked the court to resolve the dispute. The employer admitted to error on the commission but discharged Andy anyway for disloyalty. The employment contract was for a definite period, which had not expired. Is Andy entitled to damages for retaliatory discharge? Why or why not?

9. Ludwick, a seamstress, worked as an at-will employee in Carolina's sewing plant. Ludwick was served with a subpoena to appear before the South Carolina Employment Security Commission. Shortly thereafter she was advised by her boss that if she obeyed the subpoena, she would be fired. Ludwick honored the subpoena and testified at the hearing. Upon returning to her job at Carolina on the following day, she was fired. Is she entitled to damages for retaliatory discharge? Explain.

10. A police officer still on probationary status with a small-town police force helped gain the release of a man who had been arrested for vagrancy under an obsolete statute. The prisoner had been jailed for twenty-one days without arraignment. The police chief, not inclined to let "big-city cops" tell him how to run his department, fired the probationary officer, who then responded with an action for wrongful discharge. Should the officer recover? Explain.

11. Vincent was hired as vice president for sales by Robert's Hawaii Tours. This employment agreement was dated July 3, 1991, and it was to last for five years. Vincent was to be paid between $1,500 to $2,200 a month by Robert's. Despite this five-year agreement and for no apparent reason, Vincent was fired on February 21, 1992. Vincent sued for the salary provided by the employment contract. Robert's argued that Vincent refused to mitigate the damages since he refused possible employment opportunities. The best offer Vincent had, to mitigate damages, was $400 per month plus a commission. He refused to accept this offer of employment. Is Vincent entitled to money damages despite his unwillingness to mitigate the damages as shown by his refusal to take the lower-paying sales job? Explain.

12. Ann, a real estate agent, was authorized by Peter to sell several lots at specified prices. Ann was to receive an 8 percent commission on each lot sold. Before any lots were sold, Peter revoked the authorization granted. Since Ann had spent her own money advertising these lots, she claimed that her authority was irrevocable as an agency coupled with either an interest or obligation. Is Ann correct? Why?

13. Dr. Thompson's malpractice insurance was obtained through the Duncan Insurance Agency. During 1989 and 1990, Thompson's insurance was with Aetna Casualty & Surety Company. In 1991, the Duncan Agency ceased being an agent for Aetna, and it became an agent for St. Paul Insurance Company. Duncan changed Thompson's coverage to St. Paul without explaining why the change occurred. In 1991, Thompson was sued for an alleged act of malpractice that occurred in July 1989. Thomspon immediately notified the Duncan Agency, which mistakenly notified St. Paul. St. Paul began defending Thompson, but it then discovered it was not the doctor's insurer in 1989. Aetna was notified, but it refused to defend the malpractice since it was not promptly and timely notified of the filed suit as the insurance policy required. Thompson sued Aetna, relying on the immediate notice given to Duncan Agency. Is Aetna liable for not defending the malpractice case against Thompson? Why?

14. Alicia, a buyer for Patterson's Department Store, was discharged. Although Turner Manufacturers knew of Alicia's position with Patterson's, it had never sold merchandise to Alicia. After Alicia was discharged, an article about her changing jobs appeared in the local newspapers, but Turner did not read it. If Alicia now purchases goods on credit from Turner and charges them to Patterson's, is Patterson's liable to Turner? Explain.

CHAPTER

26

FORMATION OF PARTNERSHIPS

CHAPTER PREVIEW

A *partnership* is defined as an association of two or more persons to carry on as co-owners of a business for profit. It is the result of an agreement between competent parties to place their money, property, or labor in a business and to divide the profits and losses. The existence of a partnership is more dependent on what the facts reveal than on what the parties state is their intent. If the parties' conduct indicates there is an agreement to carry on a business and to share profit and losses, there is a partnership even though the parties may not call themselves partners.

To overcome possible confusion about a partnership's existence, the parties should enter into a formally drafted partnership agreement. The document representing this agreement is often called the *articles of partnership*. The contents of such an agreement are of critical importance to the parties involved.

In addition to issues that arise between the partners, questions about the relationship of partners to third parties also arise. The rights and duties of third parties and of partners related to the formation of a partnership are discussed in this chapter.

You and two friends agree to practice public accounting together as partners.
Each of you agrees to pay $50,000 in capital to begin the practice.
What should be your major concerns at the outset of this relationship?

WHEN DOES A PARTNERSHIP EXIST?

1. Introduction

Between the parties, the intention to create a partnership may be expressed or implied from their conduct. The basic question is whether the parties intend a relationship that includes the essential elements of a partnership, not whether they intend to be partners. In fact, under certain circumstances, a corporation may be held to be a partnership at least between the owners of the business.

In essence, then, the parties doing business are partners if they satisfy three requirements. First, are there two or more parties involved? Second, is there a common interest to conduct business activities? Third, is there an agreement to share profits and losses?

To simplify the question of whether a partnership exists, the parties could sign a formally drafted partnership agreement. The signatures are one indication that an express partnership exists. If an expression has not been made by the parties, an implied partnership may be found from the parties' conduct.

These two types of partnerships are discussed next, followed by a section on partnerships by estoppel, which is an argument made by third parties when an express or implied partnership does not exist.

2. Express Partnerships

Any oral or written statement by the parties that they have agreed to be partners carries substantial weight in concluding that a partnership exists. Such an agreement justifies the finding that an express partnership exists. In the following case, a partnership is found to exist with respect to one activity partially because the defendants admit that they are partners with respect to a different activity.

CASE

Hofer v. St. Clair
381 S.E.2d 736 (S.C. 1989)

TOAL, J.

The plaintiff, Donald Hofer, brought this action for breach of three contracts to sell real property against defendants, James H. St. Clair and Fred U. Beam. The question on appeal is whether a partnership existed between the defendants. . . .

During the period of time the incidents which underlie this action occurred, Hofer was an engineer with the merchant marines. He alternated between four month periods of time at sea and four month periods at his home in South Carolina. During the periods Hofer was in South Carolina, he was very active in the real estate market purchasing and leasing residential property for investment. While he was at sea, his parents had a Power of Attorney to transact business for him. Hofer's mother managed Hofer's rental property.

St. Clair and Beam were partners in Rock Hill Paint and Repair. This partnership does insurance construction repair work. St. Clair and Beam were also active in the residential real estate market, buying and leasing property for investment.

In the early part of 1984, Hofer was in South Carolina. Through a local real estate agent, Hofer became aware that St. Clair and Beam were interested in selling several pieces of rental property they owned as joint tenants. When Hofer expressed an interest in the properties to the Realtor, the agent scheduled a meeting between Hofer, Hofer's mother, Beam and himself. The purpose of this meeting was to allow Hofer to inspect the various pieces of property.

As a result of this meeting, in February 1984, Hofer made offers through the real estate agent on the three pieces of property which form the basis of this action. St. Clair obtained these offers from the Realtor and discussed them with Beam. St. Clair made counteroffers on behalf of himself and Beam. The negotiating process consisted of several offers and counteroffers over the period of approximately a week, at the end of which Hofer and St. Clair met at the real estate agent's office. During this meeting, all of the changes to the original contracts were initialed and the contracts were signed by St. Clair. St. Clair also entered a management contract on the property with Hofer's mother during this meeting. Hofer left the meeting with the original contracts, and proceeded to a mortgage company, suggested by St. Clair, to make an application for financing. . . .

Shortly after this meeting, Hofer returned to sea, leaving a Power of Attorney with his parents to complete the purchases. Approximately one week later, a dispute arose. Mrs. Hofer became aware one of the properties did not have a heat pump as was represented on an MLS form Hofer had received from the real estate agent. Mrs. Hofer called St. Clair to question him about the discrepancy and demanded he either pay for the installation of a heat pump or reduce the purchase price of the property by the cost of such an installation. St. Clair told Mrs. Hofer her son could either buy the property, as it was, for the agreed upon price, or "the deal was off." Mrs. Hofer stated she could not agree to buy the property for the same price in a condition different from that represented to her son.

Several days later, Hofer's father contacted Beam to settle the misunderstanding. Beam told Hofer's father "the deal was off."

The defendants failed to convey the properties to Hofer, and sold them to a third party. Hofer brought suit for breach of contract.

The case was referred to a Referee to make findings of fact and conclusions of law and report the same to the Circuit Court. The Referee found as matters of fact that a partnership existed between the defendants. . . .

The Circuit Court adopted the Referee's findings of fact and conclusions of law as its own. This appeal by St. Clair and Beam followed.

. . . Beam and St. Clair allege the trial court erred in finding a partnership existed between St. Clair and Beam, the business of which was to conduct real estate transactions. . . .

South Carolina's Uniform Partnership Act defines a partnership as "an association of two or more persons to carry on as co-owners a business for profit." . . .

The existence of a partnership is a question of fact. The lower court found the defendants were operating a partnership, called Rock Hill Paint & Paper, the business of which was, in part, the ownership, purchase and sale of rental real estate properties. These findings are amply supported by the record.

The evidence supports the lower court's finding that a partnership existed between St. Clair and Beam. Hofer testified that during his initial meeting with Beam to view the property, Beam gave him a card for Rock Hill Paint and Repair with the names "Fred and Jim" on it. Hofer testified Beam referred on many occasions during this meeting to his "partner," Jim, and to Rock Hill Paint & Repair. Both Beam and St. Clair admitted at trial they were partners in Rock Hill Paint & Repair.

The evidence also supports the lower court's finding that the business of the partnership was, in part, to purchase, sell, lease and hold real estate for investment. The evidence showed the rental income from the properties at issue, and other jointly owned properties, was shown on the tax returns and books of Rock Hill Paint and Repair. Rental income was deposited into, and expenses were paid from, the partnership bank accounts. . . .

[The court concluded that St. Clair had acted with authority in signing contracts on behalf of the partnership and that the partnership had breached the contracts.]

■ *For the foregoing reasons, the opinion of the lower court is affirmed.*

CASE CONCEPTS REVIEW

1. At issue in this case is whether the defendants are liable as partners. Why is this a crucial issue?
2. In their dealings with Donald Hofer or his parents, did either St. Clair or Beam indicate that they were or were not partners?
3. Would Beam be liable if he were not a partner with St. Clair? Would St. Clair be liable?

While an oral agreement is binding with respect to the parties to the agreement, proof of the contents of such agreement is difficult. Often courts must accept one party's word over that of another party regarding what their agreement really stated. To avoid such conflicts, partners should reduce their agreement to the form of articles of partnership and sign the document. The typical provisions that should be included in a formal written agreement are discussed in sections 6 through 11.

3. Implied Partnerships

Even though no oral or written partnership agreement can be proven, courts still may find that a partnership exists. Such a finding is based on the conduct of the parties. When this conduct satisfies the three essential elements of a partnership, an *implied partnership* is said to exist.

If the essential elements of a partnership are present, the mere fact that the parties do not think they are becoming partners is immaterial. If the parties agree on an arrangement that is a partnership in fact, it is immaterial whether they call it something else or declare that they are not partners. On the other hand, the mere fact that the parties themselves call the relation a partnership will not make it so if they have not, by their conduct, agreed on an agreement that by the law is a partnership in fact.

The essential attributes of a partnership are a common interest in the business and management and an agreement to share in the profits and losses. This common interest may be established by a holding of property and a sharing of the profits and losses related to the property. If there is a sharing of profits, a partnership may be found to exist even though there is no sharing of losses.

The presence of a common interest in property and management is not enough to establish a partnership by implication. Nor, of itself, does an agreement to share the gross returns of a business, sometimes called gross profits, prove an intention to form a partnership. If a person receives a share of real or net profits in a business, that is prima facie but not conclusive evidence of partnership. It may be overcome by evidence that the share in the profits is received for some other purpose, such as payment of a debt by installments, wages, rent, annuity to a widow of a deceased partner, interest on a loan, or payment of goodwill by installments. Bonuses are frequently paid as a percent of profit, but they do not make the employee a partner. Likewise, many leases provide for rent based on profits.

The following case illustrates that a partnership found to involve a corporation does not necessarily mean that this partnership involves the corporation's officials by implication. The three elements of a partnership's definition do not always apply to the individuals in control of the corporate partner.

CASE

Chenault v. Jamison
578 So.2d 1059 (Ala. 1991)

INGRAM, J.

. . . This case concerns a breach of an alleged partnership agreement. The appellants, Bob Bone and Ben Chenault, claim that John W. Jamison III, individually, breached the alleged partnership agreement and breached the fiduciary duty of honesty and fair dealing between partners when he failed to include them in a project to develop real estate in Boaz.

Jamison is chairman of the board of Capital Resources Corporation, Inc., and George Bonfanti is the president. The appellants allege that Jamison represented that Bonfanti was the agent of Jamison and that Jamison, individually, was a partner to this agreement, based upon the actions of Bonfanti.

Jamison filed a motion for summary judgment, which he supported by his affidavit and by the depositions of Bone and Chenault. . . . The trial court found that no genuine issue existed as to any material fact and entered a summary judgment in favor of Jamison. Bone and Chenault appeal.

Bone and Chenault argue there was substantial evidence in this case that Jamison, in his individual capacity, was a partner with them in this real estate venture. Their contention is based upon certain actions of Bonfanti that led them to believe that Jamison had conveyed through Bonfanti his desire to become their partner. However, the record is devoid of any specific instances in which Jamison indicated that Bonfanti was acting as his agent during the negotiations that form the basis of this suit. Based on the evidence that was before the trial judge, we hold that the summary judgment in favor of Jamison was appropriate.

Bone and Chenault failed to produce sufficient evidence that Bonfanti was acting on behalf of, and at the direction of, Jamison individually. In fact, the only evidence presented in opposition to the motion for summary judgment was a letter from Jamison on Capital Resources letterhead, signed in his capacity as chairman of the board, and an affidavit from Chenault. In his affidavit, Chenault stated:

> I spoke with Mr. Jamison personally in the negotiations leading up to the partnership agreement referred to in the complaint in this case. Mr. Jamison introduced me personally to Mr. Bonfanti [the president of Capital Resources, Inc.] who Mr. Jamison said was "Okay" and Mr. Jamison clearly implied that Mr. Bonfanti would be handling the property purchase negotiations and partnership agreement for Mr. Jamison and Capital Resources Corporation. During negotiations and following the part-

nership agreement, Mr. Jamison never *denied* that Mr. Bonfanti acted as Mr. Jamison's agent. (Emphasis added.) . . .

Assuming, without deciding, that a partnership was formed, the evidence indicates that Capital Resources could have been a partner through the actions of Bonfanti and a party to the partnership agreement with Bone and Chenault; however, the evidence does not indicate that Jamison, individually, was a partner. The record supports the conclusion that Jamison dealt with this partnership agreement as the chairman of the board of Capital Resources and not in his individual capacity. Bone and Chenault were not able to point to one specific incident in which they were led to believe either that Jamison intended to be a partner or that Bonfanti was representing Jamison individually as well as representing Capital Resources.

In situations where the dispute concerning the existence of a partnership is between the alleged partners, a partnership cannot be formed by operation of law . . . , there must be an agreement, express or implied, between the partners.

In this case, the evidence fails to show any circumstances in which Bone and Chenault could have been led to reasonably believe that Jamison, individually, intended to be a partner. The appellants have not produced any evidence that Bonfanti's actions were other than those of an employee and agent of Capital Resources. Without a showing of such evidence, the factfinder could not find that Bonfanti, the president of Capital Resources, was acting as the agent of Jamison. We are satisfied that the evidence presented to the trial court made a prima facie showing that Bonfanti was acting within the scope of his employment with Capital Resources and that Bone and Chenault failed to produce substantial evidence to overcome this showing. . . .

We hold that the summary judgment in favor of Jamison, individually, was correctly entered. . . .

■ *Affirmed.*

CASE CONCEPTS REVIEW

1. This case involves an alleged partnership between at least Bob Bone, Ben Chenault, and Capital Resources Corporation, Inc. On what basis is it argued that John Jamison is a partner? What is Mr. Jamison's capacity with respect to Capital Resources?

2. What decision of the trial court is being reviewed by this court?

3. What is this court's finding with respect to evidence that indicates Mr. Jamison explicitly or implicitly agreed to be a partner?

4. Partnership by Estoppel

Estoppel To prevent a party from denying the legal consequences of that party's conduct.

Insofar as third persons are concerned, partnership liability, like the apparent authority of an agent, may be predicated on the legal theory of **estoppel.** If a person by words spoken or written or by conduct represents himself or herself or consents to another's representing him or her, as a partner in an existing partnership, that person is not a partner but is liable to any party to whom such representation has been made. If the representation is made in a public manner either personally or with consent of the apparent partner, the apparent partner is liable if credit is extended to the partnership, even if the creditor did not actually know of the representation. This is an exception to the usual estoppel requirement of actual reliance.

The courts are not in accord as to whether a person must affirmatively disclaim a reputed partnership that he or she did not consent to or claim. Some court cases hold that if a person is held out as a partner and knows it, that person should be chargeable as a partner unless he or she takes reasonable steps to give notice that he or she is not, in fact, a partner. These courts impose a duty on a person to deny that he or she is a partner, once that person knows that third persons are relying on representations that he or she is a partner. Other cases indicate that there is no duty to deny false representations of partnership if the apparent partner did not participate in making the misrepresentation.

In most states, the statutory law of partnerships recognizes partnerships by estoppel. These statutes usually incorporate the common-law elements of estoppel, as the following case illustrates.

CASE

Smith v. Norman
495 So.2d 536 (Ala. 1986)

Plaintiffs entered into contracts with Mike Norman, doing business as (dba) Norman Construction Company, for the construction of new homes. Construction on both homes was begun, but neither home was completed. Plaintiffs filed a contract action against Mike Norman and his father Max Norman, individually and as partners doing business as Norman Construction Company. Mike Norman filed for bankruptcy, so the proceedings against him were stayed. At trial, Max Norman's motion for directed verdict was granted. Plaintiffs appeal.

HOUSTON, J.

... The plaintiffs' case against Max Norman is based upon an estoppel theory. The plaintiffs contend that Norman led them to believe he was a partner with his son Mike in Norman Construction Company. They argued that during the construction work on their homes, they made payments to Mike Norman in reliance on Max Norman's representations that he was a partner in the

business. Because of this alleged reliance, they assert that Max Norman, although he was in actuality not a partner of his son, should be estopped from denying liability for the losses sustained by the plaintiffs from the alleged poor workmanship and failure to complete their homes. We disagree.

Code 1975, § 10-8-55, in pertinent part, reads as follows:

> Liability of partner by estoppel.
> (a) When a person, by words spoken or written or by conduct, represents himself, or consents to another representing him to anyone, as a partner in an existing partnership, or with one or more persons not actual partners, he is liable to any such person to whom such representation has been made who has, on the faith of such representation, given credit to the actual or apparent partnership; and if he has made such representation or consented to its being made in a public manner, he is liable to such person, whether the representation has or has not been made or communicated to such person so giving credit by or with the knowledge of the apparent partner making the representation or consenting to its being made.

(1) When a partnership liability results, he is liable as though he were an actual member of the partnership.

(2) When no partnership liability results, he is liable jointly with the other persons, if any, so consenting to the contract or representation as to incur liability, otherwise separately.

In *Mazer v. Jackson Ins. Agency*, 340 So.2d 770 (Ala. 1976), this Court discussed the doctrine of equitable estoppel:

Equitable estoppel is
... based upon the ground of public policy and good faith, and is interposed to prevent injustice and to guard against fraud by denying to a person the right to repudiate his acts, admissions, or representations, *when they have been relied on by persons to whom they were directed and whose conduct they were intended to and did influence.* The doctrine of estoppel is far reaching in its effect, extending to real as well as personal estate, and embracing almost every enterprise in which men may be engaged.

The basic elements of equitable estoppel are stated in Dobbs, Remedies § 2.3 (1973):

"An estoppel ... has three important elements. The actor, who usually must have knowledge of the true facts, communicates something in a misleading way, either by words, conduct or silence. The other relies upon that communication. And the other would be harmed materially if the actor is later permitted to assert any claim inconsistent with his earlier conduct."

A more detailed statement of the elements generally required to support an estoppel is given in 3 Pomeroy, Equity Jurisprudence § 805 (5th ed. 1941):

"... 1. There must be conduct—acts, language, or silence—amounting to a representation or a concealment of material facts. 2. These facts must be known to the party estopped at the time of his said conduct, or at least the circumstances must be such that knowledge of them is necessarily imputed to him. 3. The truth concerning these facts must be unknown to the other party claiming the benefit of the estoppel, at the time when such conduct was done, *and at the time when it was acted upon by him.* 4. The conduct must be done with the intention, or at least with the *exception*, that it will be acted upon

by the other party, or under such circumstances that it is both natural and probably that it will be so acted upon. . . . 5. The conduct must be relied upon by the other party, and thus relying, he must be led to act upon it. 6. He must in fact act upon it in such a manner as to change his position for the worse; in other words, he must so act that he would suffer a loss if he were compelled to surrender or forgo or alter what he has done by reason of the first party being permitted to repudiate his conduct and to assert rights inconsistent with it. . . ."

The undisputed facts in this case do not support a cause of action against the defendant based upon the doctrine of equitable estoppel or its statutory counterpart. The plaintiffs bore the burden of proving that they relied to their detriment on the defendant's alleged representations. They did not meet this burden.

. . . In this case, there is not a scintilla of evidence that the plaintiffs entered into their contracts with Mike Norman based upon any conduct or declaration by his father. Plaintiff Glenn Smith testified that when he entered into the contract with Mike Norman, he did not think Max Norman was a partner in Mike Norman's business. Plaintiff David Wright testified that he likewise dealt only with Mike Norman and knew of no involvement by Max Norman in the business. Although the plaintiffs allege that there was detrimental reliance in that they made payments to Mike Norman based upon Max Norman's alleged representations, their existing contracts clearly obligated them to make those payments. Had the alleged representations by Max Norman been made prior to or at the time the plaintiffs entered into their contracts with Mike Norman, the decision in this case might be different. Because the alleged representations came after the plaintiffs had obligated themselves to make the payments, however, it cannot be said that they relied upon those alleged representations to their detriment. . . .

There being no error in the record, the decision of the trial court is . . .

■ *Affirmed.*

CASE CONCEPTS REVIEW

1. What is the relationship between Mike and Max Norman?

2. What legal theory do the plaintiffs use in an attempt to hold Max Norman liable as a partner?

3. What critical fact does the court rely on to deny the plaintiffs' efforts to collect against Max Norman?

5. Introduction

The partnership agreement, usually called the *articles of partnership,* varies from business to business. Among the subjects usually contained in such agreements are the following: the names of the partners and of the partnership, its purpose and duration, the capital contributions of each partner, the method of sharing profits and losses, the effect of advances, the salaries (if any) to be paid the partners, the method of accounting and the fiscal year, the rights and liabilities of the parties upon the death or withdrawal of a partner, and the procedures to be followed upon dissolution.

The Uniform Partnership Act or other partnership statute is a part of the agreement as if it had actually been written into the contract or had been made part of its stipulations. The following sections discuss some of the more important provisions of the partnership agreement and indicate the effect of the Uniform Partnership Act on the agreement.

6. Firm Name Provision

Because a partnership is created by the agreement of the parties, they select the name to be used. This right of selection is subject to two limitations by statute in many states. First, a partnership may not use the word *company* or other language that would imply the existence of a corporation. Second, if the name is other than that of the partners, they must comply with assumed name statutes that require the giving of public notice as to the actual identity of the partners. Failure to comply with this assumed name statute may result in the partnership's being denied access to the courts to sue its debtors, or it may result in criminal actions being brought against those operating under the assumed name.

The firm name is an asset of the firm, and as such it may also be sold, assigned, or disposed of in any manner on which the parties agree. At common law, a partnership was not a legal entity that could sue and be sued in the firm name. All actions had to be brought in behalf of, or against, all the partners as individuals. Today, statutes in most states have changed the common law and allow partnerships to sue or be sued in the firm name. Most states also consider the partnership a legal entity for purposes of litigation even in the absence of a statute.

7. Capital Provision

Partnership *capital* consists of the total credits to the capital accounts of the various partners, provided the credits are for permanent investments in the business. Such capital represents the amount that the partnership is obligated to return to the partners at the time of dissolution, and it can be varied only with the consent of all the partners. Undivided profits that are permitted by some of the partners to accumulate in the business do not become part of the capital. They, like temporary advances by firm members, are subject to withdrawal at any time unless the agreement provides to the contrary.

The amount that each partner is to contribute to the firm, as well as the credit he or she is to receive for assets contributed, is entirely dependent on the partnership agreement. A person may become a partner without a capital contribution. For example, a partner may contribute services to balance the capital investment of the other partners. Such a partner, however, has no capital to be returned at the time of liquidation. Only those who receive credit for capital investments—which may include goodwill, patent rights, and so forth, if agreed on—are entitled to the return of capital when dissolution occurs. As the following case holds, business experience is not a contribution to capital.

CASE

Badran v. Bertrand
334 N.W.2d 184 (Neb. 1983)

	Amount	Percent
Virginia Bertrand	$50,000.00	50%
Sam Badran	50,000.00	50%

The parties first met in July, 1975, at Grand Island, Nebraska, where Sam was selling bedspreads and linens from his car. Shortly thereafter, the parties orally agreed to a partnership-type venture, financed by Virginia and promoted by Sam, to sell Indian jewelry and other gift items. On February 12, 1976, they opened the Holdrege Gift Shop, Holdrege, Nebraska. All funds for the purchase of merchandise and early business operations were paid from Virginia's personal funds, except money generated from sales. On June 23, 1976, the parties executed a partnership agreement, terminating in two years. The partnership never made a profit, and the shop was closed in January, 1979, when the merchandise was moved to Omaha, Nebraska, where the parties were operating Nasr's Restaurant. Some of the Indian jewelry was displayed at Nasr's, and the rest was stored in the trunk of a car owned by Virginia and possessed by Sam. There are no records of any purchases or sales in 1979. On January 7, 1980, Virginia forcibly obtained possession of all the merchandise, which she still has. This suit by Sam followed. The trial court awarded all assets to Virginia. Sam appeals, claiming his personal business expertise was a contribution of partnership capital.

COLWELL, J.

. . . Plaintiff's . . . assignment of error is that the trial court failed to find that his business expertise was a contribution of capital to the partnership. His expertise is described as a vast amount of time, experience, and knowledge as a self-employed salesman.

The partnership agreement provides in part, "(5) The initial capital of the Partnership shall be One Hundred Thousand Dollars . . . and each partner agrees to contribute *cash or property* as follows:

The record is clear that plaintiff contributed no money and that defendant knew that he could not do so; she expected him to contribute his money from future profits. Plaintiff contends that he contributed his business skills and expertise, which was "property." This claim being contrary to the agreement, and there being no competent evidence varying its terms, we look to the conduct of the parties. . . .

Sam had 35 years of experience as an itinerant, self-employed salesman dealing in bedspreads, rugs, and linens. He had no prior experience in Indian jewelry merchandising. His first purchases of jewelry were made through the assistance of his two brothers, who were dealers. An example of his claimed expertise was his ability to buy jewelry at one-third to one-fourth of its retail value, which Virginia could not do. Virginia does not deny his skill as a merchant; rather, she denies that it was more than that. During the 1976–78 period, when the shop failed to make a profit, plaintiff requested of defendant and obtained money, a car, living quarters and other family gratuities amounting to more then $80,000, a part being deemed salary by the trial court. His conduct is inconsistent with his claim.

As we view the record, plaintiff performed the services that the parties intended; those services were not unusual considering plaintiff's sales experience, skills, the attending circumstances, and bearing in mind the failure of the venture. We conclude that plaintiff made no contribution to his capital account as required and intended by the partnership agreement.

This leaves the question of the distribution of the remaining partnership assets and the settlement of its debts. . . .

It is a general rule that capital furnished by any partner, in the absence of agreement to the contrary, is a debt owing by the firm to the contributing partner, and necessarily is to be repaid him, if the firm assets are sufficient after paying the firm liabilities to outsiders.

... [U]pon dissolution, where one has contributed capital and another services, the one contributing the capital is entitled to withdraw its value. . . .

■ *Affirmed.*

CASE CONCEPTS REVIEW

1. What was the business relationship between Sam and Virginia?
2. What is the basis of their dispute over the distribution of the partnership's assets?
3. Why does the court conclude that Sam had made no capital contribution? Does this conclusion mean that Sam was not a valuable contributor to the organization's business?

8. Property Provision

In conducting its business, a partnership may use its own property, the property of the individual partners, or the property of some third person. It frequently becomes important, especially on dissolution and where claims of firm creditors are involved, to ascertain exactly what property constitutes partnership property, in order to ascertain the rights of partners and firm creditors in specific property.

As a general rule, the agreement of the parties will determine what property is properly classified as partnership property. In the absence of an express agreement, what constitutes partnership property is ascertained from the conduct of the parties and from the purpose for, and the way in which, property is used in the pursuit of the business. The following case illustrates the importance of the parties' agreement and how it can override the actual appearances of who owns property.

CASE

Bassett v. Bassett
798 P.2d 160 (N.M. 1990)

SOSA, C. J.

Plaintiff-appellee, Carl Bassett, filed suit against defendant-appellant, Elmer Bassett. Carl and Elmer are brothers. Consequently, appellee herein is designated "Carl," and appellant "Elmer." In his amended complaint, Carl alleged that he and Elmer formed a partnership about the year 1950 for the purposes of conducting a ranching and farming business. . . . Carl alleged that in 1950 the partnership purchased a section of land from L.W. Briggs and that in 1958 the partnership purchased another section of land from L.W. Briggs.

Carl alleged that although title to both parcels of land was placed in Elmer, it was agreed between the partners that Elmer held a one-half interest in the land in trust for Carl until such time as Elmer and Carl could find Carl similar land of like value. In May 1980 however, Elmer repudiated any such trust agreement, dissolved the partnership, and locked Carl out of both parcels of land. Carl alleged that Elmer held the land in trust for Carl. . . . Carl also alleged breach of contract and sought the value of his labor and expenditures on the partnership business from 1950 to 1980. . . .

In its judgment, the court awarded Carl a one-half interest in the properties, attorneys fees of $30,074, reformation of the original deeds from L.W. Briggs to Elmer to show that Carl is tenant-in-common of the properties, compensatory damages, costs and punitive damages in the amount of $176,000. . . .

Elmer maintains that there was no substantial evidence before the jury to support Carl's claim that the Briggs properties were an asset of the partnership or that a one-half interest in the properties was held in trust for Carl. We disagree. The record shows that Carl made substantial monetary contributions to the partnership and that partnership money was used to retire the debt on the Briggs properties. Further, Carl used his own resources to support the partnership business and borrowed money to make installment payments on the Briggs properties so that the partnership business could be maintained.

Carl introduced into evidence a letter to him from the National Farm Loan Association of Albuquerque in which the secretary-treasurer of the association wrote, "It is understood that this money [loaned to Carl] is to be used *** to take care of the installments now due on the indebtedness of Elmer Bassett's farm." In the context of the case, "Elmer Bassett's farm" means partnership property. Although Carl made only two payments directly to L.W. Briggs, he made several other payments to Briggs through Elmer's bank account. The fact that Elmer made the bulk of the payments does not mean that Carl did not contribute substantial income to purchase the properties. The evidence showed that partnership income usually was placed in Elmer's personal banking account, from which Elmer then wrote checks to satisfy indebtedness on the Briggs properties. . . .

Unless the contrary intention appears, property acquired with partnership funds is partnership property. There the jury was entitled to conclude that the Briggs properties were an asset of the partnership. . . .

Elmer argues that . . . no evidence has been introduced which shows that Carl owned a beneficial one-half interest in the Briggs properties. Elmer is right to assert the general rule that "where one person pays part of the purchase price and title is taken in another's name, the payor cannot secure a greater interest . . . in the property . . . than the proportion of the amount he paid bears to the total *purchase price*." This rule distinguishes between consideration paid at time of conveyance and subsequent monetary contributions to make improvements or for installments paid after title has been acquired.

While there is no direct evidence showing that Carl and Elmer paid equal portions of the down payment, there is abundant circumstantial evidence showing that from the inception of the partnership the brothers looked upon themselves as equal partners. Testimony by Carl's expert witness, an accountant who had kept the books of the partnership for many years, showed that the brothers attempted to share profits and losses equally. Testimony by Carl's wife supported Carl's position that the brothers invested equally in the land from the beginning. Over the years, Carl invested slightly *more* than fifty percent of his money in the land, a fact that circumstantially supports an original fifty-fifty contribution of the purchase price. Even if Elmer paid more to L.W. Briggs as a down payment than did Carl, it is clear that in 1950 the brothers intended to contribute equally to every partnership business investment. . . .

■ *The judgment of the trial court is affirmed.*

CASE CONCEPTS REVIEW

1. Who had the legal title to the land purchased from L.W. Briggs?
2. According to Carl, what was the purported agreement between these brothers-partners with respect to this land?
3. Why was it not clear that checks written by Elmer were drawn on Elmer's personal funds?
4. What presumption does the court rely on to award a one-half interest in the land to Carl?

The Uniform Partnership Act provides that all property specifically brought into partnership or acquired by it is partnership property. Therefore, unless a contrary intention appears, property acquired with partnership funds is partnership property. In other words, there is a presumption that property acquired with partnership funds is partnership property, but this presumption is rebuttable.

Property acquired by a partner individually is often transferred to the partnership as a part of a partner's contribution to capital. If this contribution is in a form other than money, the property no longer belongs to the contributing partner. The contributing partner has vested the firm with title and has no greater equity in the property than has any other party. At dissolution, this partner recovers only the amount allowed to him or her for the property invested. If this property is purchased by the partner on credit, the creditor has no claim against the partnership, even though the property can be traced to it. A personal loan made to a partner does not become a partnership debt unless it is expressly assumed by the partnership.

Because a partnership has the right to acquire, own, and dispose of personal property in the firm name, legal documents affecting the title to partnership personal property may be executed in the firm name by any partner. The Uniform Partnership Act also treats a partnership as a legal entity for the purposes of title to real estate that may be held in the firm name. Title so acquired can be conveyed in the partnership name. Many of the legal principles relating to partnership property are discussed in the next chapter.

9. Profit-and-Loss Provision

Unless the agreement is to the contrary, each partner has a right to share equally in the profits of the enterprise, and each partner is under a duty to contribute equally to the losses. Capital contributed to the firm is a liability owed by the firm to the contributing partners. If, on dissolution, there are not sufficient assets to repay each partner his capital, the amount is considered as a loss; and like any other loss of the partnership, it must be met.

EXAMPLE A partnership is composed of A, B, and C. A contributed $20,000, B contributed $10,000, and C contributed $4,000. The firm is dissolved, and upon the payment of debts only $10,000 of firm assets remain. Because the total contribution to capital was $34,000, the operating loss is $24,000. If these partners have not agreed otherwise, this loss must be borne equally by A, B, and C, so the loss for each is $8,000. This means that A is entitled to be reimbursed to the extent of her $20,000 contribution less $8,000, her share of the loss, or net of $12,000. B is entitled to $10,000, less $8,000, or $2,000. Because C has contributed only $4,000, he must now contribute to the firm an additional $4,000, so his loss will equal $8,000. The additional $4,000 contributed by C, plus the $10,000 remaining, will now be distributed so A will receive $12,000 and B $2,000.

Occasionally, articles of partnership specify the manner in which profits are to be divided, but they neglect to mention possible losses. In such cases the losses are borne in the same proportion that profits are to be shared. In the event that losses occur when one of the partners is insolvent and his or her share of the loss exceeds the amount owed him or her for advances and capital, the excess must be shared by the other partners. They share this unusual loss in the same ratio that they share profits. Thus, in the preceding example, if C were insolvent, A and B would each bear an additional $2,000 loss.

In addition to the right to be repaid for contributions, whether by way of capital or advances to the partnership property, the partnership must indemnify every partner for payments made and personal liabilities reasonably incurred in the ordinary and proper conduct of its business or for the preservation of its business or property.

10. Goodwill Provision

Goodwill, which is usually transferred with the name, is based on the justifiable expectation that a firm's good reputation, satisfied customers, established location, and past advertising will result in continued patronage of old customers and the probable patronage of new customers. Goodwill is usually considered in an evaluation of the assets of the business, and it is capable of being sold and transferred. Upon dissolution caused by the death of one of the partners, the surviving partner must account for the goodwill to the legal representative of the deceased partner, unless otherwise agreed on in the buy-and-sell agreement.

When goodwill and the firm name are sold, an agreement not to compete is usually part of the sales agreement. Such an agreement may be implied but should be a part of the buy-and-sell provision.

11. Buy-and-Sell Provision

Either as part of the partnership agreement or by separate contract, the partners should provide for the contingency of death or withdrawal of a partner. This contingency is covered by a *buy-and-sell agreement,* and it is imperative that the terms of the buy-and-sell provision be agreed on before either party knows whether he or she is a buyer or a seller. After the status of the parties becomes known, agreement is extremely difficult, if not impossible. If such agreement is lacking, many additional problems will arise upon the death or withdrawal of a partner, and there are many possibilities of litigation and economic loss to all concerned.

A buy-and-sell agreement avoids these types of problems by providing a method whereby the surviving partner or partners can purchase the interest of the deceased partner, or the remaining partner or partners can purchase the interest of the withdrawing partner. A method of determining the price to be paid for such interest is provided. The time and method of payment are usually stipulated. The buy-and-sell agreement should specify whether a partner has an option to purchase the interest of a dying or withdrawing partner or whether he or she has a duty to do so.

It is common for partners to provide for life insurance on each other's lives as a means of funding the buy-and-sell provision. In the event of a partner's death, proceeds of the insurance are used to purchase the deceased partner's interest. Premiums on such life insurance are not deductible for tax purposes but are usually treated as an expense for accounting purposes. There are a variety of methods for holding title to the insurance. It may be individually owned or business owned. The provisions of the policy should be carefully integrated into the partnership agreement; each partner's estate plan should also properly consider the ramifications of this insurance and of the buy-and-sell agreement.

CHAPTER SUMMARY

	WHEN DOES A PARTNERSHIP EXIST?
Express Partnerships	1. A partnership may be created by express agreement or may be implied from conduct. In either case it is a question of the intent of the parties.
Implied Partnerships	1. The essential elements of a partnership are a common interest in the business and a share in the profits and losses.
	2. The receipt of a share of the profits is prima facie evidence of a partnership, but this presumption may be overcome by evidence that the share of profits is for some other purpose.
Partnership by Estoppel	1. While parties may not be partners as between themselves, a partnership may exist insofar as third parties are concerned.
	2. A partnership by estoppel is created if a person by words or conduct represents himself or herself or consents to another's representing him or her as a partner.
	THE PARTNERSHIP AGREEMENT
Firm Name Provision	1. The partnership may not use words indicating that it is a corporation.
	2. When the partnerships' name is other than the names of the partners, it must comply with the assumed name statute.

3. The firm name is an asset and may be treated as such.

4. Partnerships can sue and be sued in their firm name.

Capital Provision

1. Partnership capital is the amount contributed by a partner and the amount that is to be returned on dissolution.

2. Undivided profits are not a part of capital.

3. A party may become a partner without a capital contribution.

Property Provision

1. All property brought into the partnership or acquired by it is partnership property.

2. Property contributed as part of a capital contribution is partnership property.

3. Partnership property may be acquired and disposed of in the partnership name.

4. Services to the partnership are not capital.

Profit-and-Loss Provision

1. Unless there is an agreement to the contrary, profits and losses are shared equally.

2. If the agreement does not cover losses, they are shared in the same manner as profits.

Goodwill Provision

1. Goodwill is an asset that may be transferred to others and that must be accounted for upon the death of a partner.

Buy-and-Sell Provision

1. The partnership agreement must provide for the contingency of the death, withdrawal, or expulsion of a partner.

2. Such agreements are usually funded with life insurance as an expense of the partnership.

REVIEW QUESTIONS AND PROBLEMS

1. Match each term in column A with the appropriate statement in column B.

A	B
(1) Partnership by estoppel	(a) An agreement that covers the rights of parties on dissolution
(2) Implied partnership	(b) The contribution of partners to the partnership
(3) Apparent partner	(c) A partnership created by conduct
(4) Articles of partnership	(d) Failure to comply may be a crime
(5) Partnership capital	(e) Partnership liability that is imposed on one who has held himself or herself out to be a partner when in fact he or she is not a partner
(6) Advance	(f) Synonymous with a partner by estoppel
(7) Assumed name statute	(g) The agreement creating a partnership
(8) Buy-and-sell agreement	(h) A loan to the partnership by a partner

2. Les and Turner entered into a written agreement whereby Turner was to farm Les's land in exchange for one-third of the crop as rental. The contract also provided that Les was to advance financing and Turner was to furnish the equipment. It was also agreed that after delivery of the one-third of the crops, all net proceeds and losses were to be shared equally. The contract specifically stated that Les and Turner were not partners, but landlord and tenant. Are Les and Turner partners? Why or why not?

3. A son sued his father, claiming a partnership interest in a business. The father had purchased all the assets of the business in his own name and was solely liable on all business debts. All the taxes were paid by the father, and no partnership tax return had been filed. The parties had equal access to the proceeds of the business. Was the son a partner? Explain.

4. David was employed by Walter to sell and service boilers. He was paid 50 percent of the net profit of each sale. Are David and Walter partners? Why or why not?

5. Charlotte and Gia, both attorneys, agreed to share office space and other overhead expense, but they did not agree to form a partnership. The sign outside their offices and their common letterhead read "Charlotte Gifford and Gia Hammond, Attorneys at Law." Using this stationery, Charlotte purchased some office equipment from Descor. Gia did not join in the contract in any way. Charlotte did not pay for the equipment. Is Gia liable to Descor? Discuss.

6. Plaintiff, a newspaper, sued Elliot to recover an account for advertising. Filip had ordered the advertising, and to obtain credit, Peoples, an employee of Filip, had represented that Elliott was a co-owner of the business. Plaintiff relied on this representation but made no effort to verify the fact. Elliott was not a co-owner and had not held himself out to be one. Is the defendant liable? Explain.

7. Defendants Marquart and Roth entered into a written agreement with plaintiff, whereby defendants were designated as the service agent for plaintiff in Missoula, Montana. Under the agreement, defendants were authorized to merchandise tires, batteries, and accessories delivered to them by plaintiff. According to the plaintiff, Marquart informed him that he and defendant Roth were going into a joint venture together to merchandise plaintiff's goods. Roth testified that the agreement was blank when Roth signed it and that Marquart was the actual operator of the business. When the goods were not paid for, plaintiff sued both parties. Did a partnership exist between Marquart and Roth, making Roth liable for the merchandise delivered? Explain.

8. A partnership known as Stein Properties brought suit in its firm name against a trustee on a deposit receipt contract. The partnership had not complied with the state's fictitious name statute. The defendant moved to dismiss the suit, contending that the partnership could not sue because of its failure to comply with the state statute. Will the suit be dismissed? Why or why not?

9. An agent for a general partnership entered into a contract in the name of the partnership to purchase certain real estate. The seller refused to close the transaction, and a suit for specific performance of the sales agreement was brought in the partnership's name without naming the partners. The defendant moved to dismiss the complaint on the ground that the plaintiff does not have legal capacity to sue. May this partnership sue in its own name? Explain.

10. Pat and Doris were equal partners in a real estate business. Doris purchased a piece of real estate in her own name; however, she reimbursed herself for the down payment from the partnership's checking account. This property was shown on the partnership's books, and all expenses connected with it were paid by the partnership. Is this real estate partnership property, each partner being entitled to one-half of the profits from its sale? Why or why not?

11. Pursuant to an oral agreement, Andy and Jeff formed a partnership to do kitchen remodeling. It was agreed that Andy was to invest $10,000 and manage the business affairs. Jeff, who would invest $1,000, was to work as job superintendent and manage the work. Profits were to be split fifty-fifty, but possible losses were not discussed. The business proved unprofitable, and Andy brought action against Jeff for one-half of the losses. To what extent is Jeff liable? Explain.

12. A partnership is to be liquidated. Smith has contributed $6,000 to capital; Charles $3,000 to capital; and Black has made no contribution to capital but has merely contributed his services. Liabilities of the partnership exceed assets by $9,000. How much must each partner contribute to pay off the liabilities? Explain.

13. Alex, Ben, and Carl formed the ABC Company, a partnership, with Alex contributing $12,000 of capital, Ben contributing $8,000, and Carl contributing $6,000. The partnership agreement provided that the partnership was to exist for twenty years, but the

partners made no provision as to the proportions in which profits and losses were to be shared. During the course of operating the partnership, Alex made a loan of $1,000 to the partnership that has not been repaid. The partnership also owes outside creditors an additional $30,000. How much will each partner be required to pay, and how much will each receive upon dissolution? Explain.

14. Why should a buy-and-sell provision be included in a partnership agreement? How can the partnership be sure of having sufficient funds to comply with a buy-and-sell provision?

27

OPERATION OF PARTNERSHIPS

CHAPTER PREVIEW

The operation of a partnership is governed by the provisions of the partnership agreement and the applicable statutory law, which in most states is the Uniform Partnership Act. Thus the rights, duties, and powers of partners are both expressed (those in the agreement) and implied (those created by law). Many of the expressed rights, duties, and powers are discussed in the preceding chapter with respect to typical provisions of the partnership agreement. Those that are implied are discussed in this chapter, along with additional observations about the partnership agreement as it affects operations. Throughout this discussion, remember that a partner is essentially an agent for the other partners and that the general principles of the law of agency are applicable.

The rights, duties, and powers of partners and the operation of the partnership are discussed in this chapter.

■ BUSINESS MANAGEMENT DECISION

> The partners in an existing partnership decide to make you a partner. You are not required to make any contribution to the firm's capital, but you are expected to work full time.
>
> To what must you get the existing partners to agree?

1. Terminology

Silent partner A partner who has no voice in the management of the partnership.

Secret partner A partner whose existence is not known to the public.

Dormant partner A partner who is both secret and silent.

Before examining the rights, duties, and powers of partners, certain terminology must be understood. A **silent partner** in a general partnership is one who does not participate in management. If the silent partner is to have limited liability, the provisions of the Uniform Limited Partnership Act must be followed. A **secret partner** is unknown to third parties and may advise management and participate in decisions, but his or her interest is not known to third parties. A **dormant partner** is both secret and silent.

These terms are used in this chapter in explaining the role of these types of partners in the operation of their partnership. Other terms defined elsewhere in this chapter are *accounting, charging order, tenancy in partnership, trading partnership,* and *nontrading partnership.*

THE RIGHTS OF PARTNERS

2. To Participate in Management

All partners have equal rights in the management and conduct of the firm's business. These rights are not necessarily determined by the capital that each partner has invested in the business. The partners may, however, agree to place the management within the control of one or more partners.

The majority of the partners decides ordinary matters arising in the conduct of the partnership business. The right to participate in management, as a partner, does not mean that partners owe each other a duty to agree. If a partner refuses to agree to a demand by another, it is usually not a breach of the fiduciary duties owed by one partner to another.

If the firm consists of only two persons who are unable to agree, and the articles of partnership make no provision for the settlement of disputes, dissolution is the only remedy. Whenever the possibility of a deadlock is present, the partnership agreement should provide for some form of arbitration of deadlocks between partners. Such provisions avoid dissolution and should always be used when there is an even number of partners.

The majority cannot, however, without the consent of the minority, change the essential nature of the business by altering the partnership agreement or by reducing or increasing the capital of the partners. It cannot embark on a new business or admit new members to the firm. In a limited partnership, the agreement cannot be modified without the unanimous consent of all partners.

Certain acts other than those enumerated previously require the unanimous consent of the partners to bind the firm, namely (1) assigning the firm property to a trustee for the benefit of creditors; (2) confessing a judgment; (3) disposing of the goodwill of the business; (4) submitting a partnership agreement to arbitration; and (5) doing any act that would make impossible the conduct of the partnership business.

3. To Be Compensated for Services

It is the duty of each partner, in the absence of an agreement to the contrary, to give his or her entire time, skill, and energy to the pursuit of the partnership affairs. No partner is entitled to payment for services rendered in the conduct of the partnership business unless an agreement to that effect has been expressed or may be implied from the conduct of the partners. Note that in the following case the unsuccessful partner-plaintiff probably expected to be compensated.

CASE

Sharp v. Laubersheimer
347 N.W.2d 268 (Minn. 1984)

In July, 1976, Sharp, Zelinsky, and Laubersheimer entered into a written agreement to form the general partnership of Maple Investments. Shortly thereafter, Salo joined as a fourth partner with the consent of the three original partners. Sharp contributed land valued at $50,000; Zelinsky, Salo, and Laubersheimer made cash contributions of $10,000, $10,000, and $5,000, respectively. The partnership agreement did not provide for compensation to the partners for services rendered to Maple.

Maple Investments began construction of commercial warehouses on the partnership property. These warehouses were sold. Laubersheimer handled the closing for the partnership. Instead of depositing the proceeds of the sale ($104,000) into the partnership's account, he placed the money in a new account that only Laubersheimer and Salo had access to. When these partners refused to release the $104,000 of partnership assets, Sharp and Zelinsky sued to recover the assets, to dissolve the partnership, and to recover compensation owed Sharp for services rendered. The trial court ruled for the plaintiffs, including the payment of $60,000 as compensation to Sharp.

PETERSON, J.

. . . We reverse the trial court's award of $60,000 compensation to Sharp for services rendered. We hold as a matter of law that the trial court erred when it awarded Sharp, a partner under an express partnership agreement, reimbursement for services rendered on a theory of quasi-contract when the partnership and joint venture agreements did not expressly provide for such compensation.

The partnership and joint venture agreements in this case did not provide for compensation to the partners of Maple. . . . According to the partnership agreement, each partner was required to contribute reasonable time and attention to the business and affairs of the partnership. Apart from the partners' sharing Maple's profits in accordance with their ratio of partnership units, no other form of remuneration is mentioned. Since the partnership agreement is silent regarding compensation, the Minnesota Uniform Partnership Act does not allow plaintiffs to be reimbursed for services rendered on behalf of the partnership. Minn.Stat. §323-17 (1982) provides in pertinent part:

> The rights and duties of the partners in relation to the partnership shall be determined, subject to any agreement between them, by the following rules: . . . (6) No partner is entitled to remuneration for acting in the partnership business, except that a surviving partner is entitled to reasonable compensation for his services in winding up the partnership affairs. . . .

Moreover, . . . [i]t is fundamental that proof of an express contract precludes recovery in *quantum meruit.*

Because there was an express contract in this case, the trial court's award of compensation under a quasi-contract or an unjust enrichment theory, which in essence amounted to an award in *quantum meruit*, was contrary to well-established Minnesota case law. . . .

We therefore reverse the trial court's award of $60,000 to Sharp for services rendered and remand with direction to order judgment consistent with this opinion.

■ *So ordered.*

CASE CONCEPTS REVIEW

1. According to the partnership agreement, what rights did the partners have to receive compensation for their services?
2. Why did this court reverse the trial court's award of $60,000 in compensation to Sharp?
3. Do you remember, from your study of contracts, why the court states that the remedy of *quantum meruit* is impermissible when an express contract exists?

An agreement to compensate may be implied from the practice of actually paying a salary. If an agreement or practice contemplates a salary to one or more partners but no amount is specified, it may be presumed that the payment of reasonable compensation is intended. This often occurs when one partner is actually engaged in the business and others are not. Often, one of the partners does not desire to participate in the management of the business. The partnership agreement in such case usually provides that the active partners receive a salary for their services in addition to their share in the profits.

4. To Interest

Contributions to capital are not entitled to draw interest unless they are not repaid when the repayment should be made. The partner's share in the profits constitutes the earnings on his or her capital investment. In the absence of an expressed provision for the payment of interest, it is presumed that interest will be paid only on advances above the amount originally contributed as capital. Advances in excess of the prescribed capital, even though credited to the capital account of the contributing partners, are entitled to draw interest from the date of the advance.

Unwithdrawn profits remaining in the firm are not entitled to draw interest. They are not considered advances or loans merely because they are left with the firm, although custom, usage, and circumstances may show an intention to treat them as loans.

5. To Information and to Inspection of Books

Every partner is entitled to full and complete information concerning the conduct of the business and to inspect the books to secure that information. The partnership agreement usually contains provisions relative to the records that the business will maintain. Each partner is under a duty to give the person responsible for keeping the records whatever information is necessary to carry on the business efficiently and effectively. It is the duty of the person keeping the records to allow each partner access to them, but no partner has a right to remove the records from the agreed-on location without the consent of the other partners. Each partner is entitled to make copies of the records, provided he or she does not make the inspection for fraudulent purposes.

Each partner has implied authority to receive notices and information for all other partners concerning matters within the pursuit of the partnership business. Knowledge held by any partner in his or her mind but not revealed to the other partners is nevertheless notice to the partnership. Knowledge of one partner is legally knowledge of all partners, provided that the facts became known or were knowledge obtained within the scope of the partnership business. A partner has a duty to communicate known facts to the other partners and to add them to the records of the partnership. Failure to do so is fraud on the partnership by the partner possessing the knowledge. This failure to inform is also a breach of the duty to assist in the maintenance of accurate records.

6. To an Accounting

Accounting The financial condition of an organization at a specific point in time.

The partners' proportionate share of the partnership assets or profits, when not determined by a voluntary settlement of the parties, may be ascertained in a suit for an **accounting.** Such suits are equitable in nature; and in states that still distinguish between suits at law and suits in equity, these actions must be filed in the court of equity.

As a general rule, a partner cannot maintain an *action at law* against other members of the firm on the partnership agreement because until there is an accounting and all partnership affairs are settled, the indebtedness among the firm members is undetermined. This general rule is subject to a few commonsense exceptions. For example, if the partnership is formed for the carrying out of a single venture or transaction, or the action involves a segregated or single unadjusted item of account, or a personal covenant or transaction entirely independent of the partnership affairs, a suit at law may be filed. Since the affairs of a partnership usually involve multiple and complicated transactions, the requirement of an accounting before a suit for damages is usually applied, as it was in the following case.

CASE

Mitchell Resort Enterprises Inc. v. C & S Builders, Inc.
570 S.W.2d 465 (Tex. 1978)

C & S Builders, Inc., sued Mitchell Resort Enterprises, Inc., for the reasonable profit of joint ventures between them. The joint ventures involved the construction and sale of townhouses. The lower court awarded the plaintiff $75,000 for lost profits, and the defendant appealed.

BROWN, J.

... Mitchell entities contend the court erred in rendering judgment for damages because C & S failed to plead, prove or request jury findings that the partnership between the parties had been dissolved and terminated which is an essential element of a cause of action for damages between partners. We agree. ...

The law is well settled that one partner may not sue another partner on a claim arising out of partnership business until an accounting and settlement of partnership affairs is made. ... Subject to certain exceptions, the general rule is that an accounting between partners is a condition precedent to an action on partnership claims and transactions. ...

... [T]his broad general rule is subject to many exceptions—such, for instance, as where the partnership was formed for the carrying out of a single venture or transaction, or the action involves a segregated or single unadjusted item of account, or a personal covenant or transaction entirely independent of the partnership affairs. These exceptions, of course, are based upon the theory that such cases do not necessarily involve an accounting, and, therefore, that resort need not be had to an equity forum. Broadly speaking, it might be said that one partner may maintain an action at law against a co-partner if the relief sought does not involve the taking of an accounting of complicated or numerous partnership transactions, but not if such accounts are involved.

C & S argues the applicability in the instant case of one of the exceptions to the general rule. We disagree.

This is not a case where the cause of action is not connected with partnership accounts and is distinct and separate from partnership dealings. Nor is the case one in which the partnership involves a single venture which is completed. Neither is the instant case one for breach of a contract to form a partnership where the partnership has never existed. This partnership was formed to build and sell townhouses. C & S seeks lost profits to that partnership.

C & S contends that it is not suing for . . . breach of contract, but on breach of a fiduciary duty and negligence. Its claim, however, either in contract or tort, involves partnership affairs and the ultimate purpose of the partnership. C & S's pleadings disclose a partnership relationship existing between it and Mitchell Enterprises; a partnership that has not been terminated; the claim sued upon is not one separate and distinct from partnership affairs, nor does the partnership involve a single completed venture bringing the claim within an exception to the general rule, but to the contrary the claim involves loss of profits to the partnership. . . .

An accounting and settlement between partners is generally a condition precedent to an action by one against another based on partnership claims and transactions. For this reason a suit for a share of property or profits or an action for contribution to losses or debts may not be maintained by a partner.

C & S having failed to plead or prove an accounting and settlement of partnership affairs, the court erred in rendering judgment for damages against Mitchell Enterprises. . . .

■ *Reversed and remanded.*

CASE CONCEPTS REVIEW

1. What was the basis of the original lawsuit filed by C & S against Mitchell Resort?
2. What is Mitchell Resort's defense to this action?
3. Why does this court hold that an accounting is a condition precedent to one partner bringing an action against another?

Because partners ordinarily have equal access to the partnership records, there is usually no need for formal accountings to determine partnership interests. A suit for an accounting is not permitted for settling incidental matters or disputes between the partners. If a dispute is of such grievous nature that the continued existence of the partnership is impossible, a suit for an accounting in equity is allowed.

In all cases, a partner is entitled to an accounting upon the dissolution of the firm. Without a dissolution of the firm, a partner has a right to a formal accounting in the following situations:

1. There is an agreement for an accounting at a definite date.
2. One partner has withheld profits arising from secret transactions.
3. There has been an execution levied against the interest of one of the partners.
4. One partner does not have access to the books.
5. The partnership is approaching insolvency, and all parties are not available.

Upon an agreement between themselves, the partners may make a complete accounting and settle their claims without resort to a court of equity.

7. To Partnership Property

A partner is a co-owner with his or her partners of partnership property. Subject to any agreement among partners, a partner has an equal right among partners to possess partnership property for partnership purposes. He or she has no right to possess partnership property for other purposes without the consent of the partners.

A partner has a right that the property will be used in the pursuit of the partnership business and to pay firm creditors. Since a partner does not own any specific item of the partnership property, he or she has no right in specific partnership property that is transferable. A partner has no right to use the firm property in satisfaction of personal debts; conversely, his or her personal creditors cannot make a levy on specific partnership property.

When a partner dies, his or her interest in specific partnership property passes to the surviving partner or partners, who have the duty of winding up the affairs of the partnership in accordance with the partnership agreement and the applicable laws. When the winding-up process is complete, the estate of the deceased partner will be paid whatever sum the estate is entitled to, according to law and the partnership agreement. The surviving partner may sell the property, real and personal, of the partnership in connection with winding up the business, to obtain the cash to pay the estate of the deceased partner.

A partner's interest *in the firm* consists of his or her rights to share in the profits that are earned and, after dissolution and liquidation, to the return of his or her capital and undistributed profits. This assumes, of course, that the partner's capital has not been absorbed or impaired by losses.

A partner may assign his or her interest, or right to share, in the profits of the partnership. Such an assignment will not of itself work a dissolution of the firm. The assignee is not entitled to participate in the management of the business. The only right of the assignee is to receive the profits to which the assignor would otherwise have been entitled and, in the event of dissolution, to receive his or her assignor's interest.

A partner's interest in the partnership cannot be levied on by his or her separate creditors and sold at public sale. A judgment creditor of a partner must proceed by obtaining a **charging order** from the court. This order charges the interest of the debtor partner with the unsatisfied amount of the judgment debt. The court will ordinarily appoint a receiver, who will recieve the partner's share of the profits and any other money due or to fall due to him or her in respect of the partnership and apply that money upon the judgment. Likewise, the court may order that the interest charged be sold. Such a sale is not a sale of the partnership assets or property. Neither the charging order nor the sale of the interest will cause a dissolution of the firm unless the partnership is one that is terminable at will. The following case illustrates these principles.

Charging order An order by a court that a creditor is entitled to receive a debtor-partner's interest in a partnership as a means of satisfying an obligation owed to the creditor.

CASE

Bohonus v. Amerco
602 P.2d 469 (Ariz. 1979)

HAYS, J.

. . . Amerco, plaintiff below, secured a judgment against Bohonus, defendant below, and sought to enforce that judgment by judicial sale of Bohonus' interest in a partnership. . . . The first issue before us is: May the trial court order the sale of partnership property to satisfy the individual debt of a partner?

The appellee, Amerco, after it secured a judgment against the appellant, Bohonus, sought a charging order from the court pursuant to . . . the Uniform Partnership Act. The court granted the request for a charging order and as a part of that order mandated the sale of appellant's interest in the assets and property of the partnership business, including a spiritous liquor license. The sheriff proceeded with the sale and filed his return.

We now look at the partnership statute. A.R.S. §29-225(b)(3) says: "A partner's right in specific partnership property is not subject to attachment or execution, except on a claim against the partnership. . . ."

A.R.S. §29-224 sets forth the extent of the property rights of the partner:

The property rights of a partner are:
1. His rights in specific partnership property.
2. His interest in the partnership.
3. His right to participate in the management.

A.R.S. §29-226 defines "a partner's interest": "A partner's interest in the partnership is his share of the profits and surplus, and the same is personal property."

A.R.S. §29-228 reads, in pertinent part, as follows:

A. On due application to a competent court by any judgment creditor of a partner, the court which entered the judgment, order, or decree, or any other court, may charge the interest of the debtor partner with payment of the unsatisfied amount of such judgment debt with interest thereon; and may then or later appoint a receiver of his share of the profits, and of any other money due or to fall due to him in respect of the partnership, and make all other orders, directions, accounts and inquiries which the debtor partner might have made, or which the circumstances of the case may require.

With the foregoing statutes in mind, we note that it is only a partner's interest in the partnership which may be charged and, in some jurisdictions, sold. It cannot be overemphasized that "interest in the partnership" has a special limited meaning in the context of the Uniform Partnership Act and hence in the Arizona statutes.

The appellee urges that somehow A.R.S. §29-228(a), supra, authorizes the sale of partnership assets and property. We note that the record reflects that pursuant to the provisions of the same statute a receiver was appointed in this case. The conclusion is that only the "interest in the partnership" may be charged and we find no provision therein for sale of assets of property of the partnership. . . .

We concur with appellee's position that the charged interest of a debtor-partner can be sold, but further enforcement of the creditor's rights must be pursuant to statute. However, this in nowise makes the sale of the partnership asset valid. . . . The Uniform Partnership Act prohibits the sale of partnership property in order to satisfy the nonpartnership debts of individual partners. . . .

■ *Reversed.*

CASE CONCEPTS REVIEW

1. Amerco successfully sued Bohonus and obtained a judgment. How did Amerco propose to collect this judgment against Bohonus?
2. This court concludes that a creditor of a partner (as opposed to a creditor of the partnership) may seek a charging order only against the partner's interest in the partnership (as opposed to a charging order against specific partnership assets). What is meant by the phrase "a partner's interest in the partnership"?
3. How can a judgment creditor of a partner collect from a partnership?

If there is more than one judgment creditor seeking a charging order, the first one to seek it is usually paid in full before others are paid anything. There is no pro rata distribution unless the partnership is dissolved.

DUTIES AND POWERS OF PARTNERS

8. Duties

A partnership is a fiduciary relationship. Each partner owes the duty of undivided loyalty to the other. Therefore every partner must account to the partnership for any benefit and hold as a trustee for the partnership's benefit any profits gained by him or her without consent of the other partners. This duty also rests on representatives of deceased partners engaged in the liquidation of the affairs of the partnership.

The partnership relation is a personal one, obligating each partner to exercise good faith and to consider the mutual welfare of all the partners in the conduct of the business. If one partner attempts to secure an advantage over the others, he or she thereby breaches the partnership relation and must account for all benefits that he or she obtains. This includes transactions with partners and with others. It also includes transactions connected with winding up the business. The duty continues, even though the partnership is dissolved, if the partnership opportunity arose prior to dissolution.

9. Power to Contract

A partner is an agent of the partnership for the purpose of its business, and the general rules of agency are applicable to all partnerships. Each partner has authority to bind the partnership with contractual liability whenever he or she is apparently carrying on the business of the partnership in the usual way. If it is apparent that a partner is not carrying on business of the partnership in the usual way, his or her act does not bind the partnership unless it is authorized by the other partners, as in the following case.

CASE

Hodge v. Garrett
614 P.2d 420 (ID. 1980)

Plaintiff Hodge sued for specific performance of a contract for the sale of a small parcel of land belonging to a partnership. The contract was signed by Rex E. Voeller, the managing partner of the partnership, which operated a drive-in theater. The parcel, adjacent to the theater, was part of the theater's driveway. The other partners contended that Voeller did not have authority to sell the parcel of land. They appealed from a trial court decision granting specific performance.

BISTLINE, J.

. . . At common law one partner could not, "without the concurrence of his copartners, convey away the real estate of the partnership, bind his partners by a deed, or transfer the title and interest of his copartners in the firm real estate." This rule was changed by the adoption of the Uniform Partnership Act. The relevant provisions are . . . as follows:

> I.C. §53-310(1): Where title to real property is in the partnership name, any partner may convey title to such property by a conveyance executed in the partnership name; but the partnership may recover such property unless the partner's act binds the partnership under the provisions of paragraph 1 of section 53-309, unless such property has been conveyed by the grantee or a person claiming through such grantee to a holder for value without knowledge that the partner, is making the conveyance, has exceeded his authority.
>
> I.C. §53-309(1): Every partner is an agent of the partnership for the purpose of its business, and the act of every partner, including the execution in the partnership name of any instrument, for apparently carrying on in the usual way the business of the partnership of which he is a member binds the part-

nership, unless the partner so acting has in fact no authority to act for the partnership in the particular matter, and the person with whom he is dealing has knowledge of the fact that he has no such authority.

The meaning of these provisions was stated in one text as follows:

> If record title is in the partnership and a partner conveys in the partnership name, legal title passes. But the partnership may recover the property (except from a bona fide purchaser from the grantee) if it can show (a) that the conveying partner was not apparently carrying on business in the usual way or (b) that he had in fact no authority and the grantee had knowledge of that fact. The burden of proof with respect to authority is thus on the partnership.

Thus this contract is enforceable if Voeller had the actual authority to sell the property, or, even if Voeller did not have such authority, the contract is still enforceable if the sale was in the usual way of carrying on the business and Hodge did not know that Voeller did not have this authority.

As to the question of actual authority, such authority must affirmatively appear, "for the authority of one partner to make and acknowledge a deed for the firm will not be presumed. . . ." Although such authority may be implied from the nature of the business, or from similar past transactions, nothing in the record in this case indicates that Voeller had express or implied authority to sell real property belonging to the partnership. There is no evidence that Voeller had sold property belonging to the partnership in the past, and obviously the partnership was not engaged in the business of buying and selling real estate.

The next question, since actual authority has not been shown, is whether Voeller was conducting the partnership business in the usual way in selling this parcel of land.

The (trial) court made no finding that it was customary for Voeller to sell real property, or even personal property, belonging to the partnership. Nor was there any evidence to this effect. Nor did the court discuss whether it was in the usual course of business for the managing partner of a theater to sell real property. . . . For a theater, "carrying on in the usual way the business of the partnership," means running the operations of the theater; it does not mean selling a parcel of property adjacent to the theater. Here the contract of sale stated that the land belonged to the partnership, and, even if Hodge believed that Voeller as exclusive manager had authority to transact all business for the firm, Voeller still could not bind the partnership through a unilateral act which was not in the usual business of the partnership. We therefore hold that the trial court erred in holding that this contract was binding on the partnership.

■ *Judgment reversed.*

CASE CONCEPTS REVIEW

1. Who entered into a real estate sales contract with Hodge?
2. What is the generally accepted legal principle concerning partners selling partnership assets?
3. Did this partner possess actual authority to sell the partnership's real estate?
4. Was this partner engaged in the usual business of the partnership when he contracted to sell this real estate?
5. What conclusion does this court reach with respect to the enforceability of the real estate sales contract?

The rules of agency relating to authority, ratification, and secret limitations on the authority of a partner are applicable to partnerships, but the extent of implied authority is generally greater for partners than for ordinary agents. Each partner has implied power to do all acts necessary for carrying on the business of the partnership. Admissions or representations pertaining to the conduct of the partnership business and made by a partner may be used as evidence against the partnership.

The nature and scope of the business and what is usual in the particular business determine the extent of the implied powers. Among the common implied powers are the following: to compromise, adjust, and settle claims or debts owed by or to the partnership; to sell goods in the regular course of business and to make warranties; to buy property within the scope of the business for cash or on credit; to buy insurance; to hire employees; to make admissions against interest; to enter into contracts within the scope of the firm; and to receive notices. In a trading partnership, a partner has the implied authority to borrow funds and to pledge the assets of the firm. Some of these implied powers are discussed more fully in the following sections.

10. Power to Impose Tort Liability

A partner has the power to impose tort liability through the doctrine of *respondeat superior.* Because a partnership is the principal of all the partners acting as agents, the law imposes tort liability on a partnership for all wrongful acts or omissions of any partner acting in the ordinary course of the partnership and for its benefit. In addition to the partnership's liability, each partner is liable for the torts of fellow partners. This result occurs because partners are jointly and severally liable for the partnership's liability and because each partner, in essence, is a principal with respect to the fellow partners acting as agents. The following case illustrates the extent to which one partner may impose tort liability on another partner.

CASE

Client's Security Fund of State v. Grandeau
526 N.E.2d 270 (N.Y. 1988)

ALEXANDER, J.

The Clients' Security Fund of the State of New York reimbursed several hundred law clients of attorney Barry J. Grandeau for losses suffered as a result of his having misappropriated their funds. As a condition of reimbursement, the clients agreed to assign and subrogate to the Clients' Security Fund their rights against Grandeau, his partner Michael T. Dahowski, and their law partnership. By statute, the Fund is authorized to recover disbursements made to clients of the attorney who engaged in the dishonest conduct. The question presented by this appeal is whether the Fund is restricted to recoupment solely from the attorney who personally engaged in the dishonest conduct, or whether it may also pursue a subrogation action against the attorney's former law partner.

The Client's Security Fund was created in 1981. . . . In providing for such a fund, the Legislature sought "to promote public confidence in the administration of justice and the integrity of the legal profession by reimbursing losses caused by the dishonest conduct of attorneys." . . .

The statute defines dishonest conduct to mean the "misappropriation or willful misapplication of clients' money, securities, or other property." . . .

The Fund has awarded approximately $589,829 to 373 claimants—all clients of the law partnership of Grandeau & Dahowski. The firm was formed by defendants Barry J. Grandeau and Michael T. Dahowski, and conducted a law practice in Poughkeepsie. By 1982, both Grandeau and Dahowski were the subject of separate disciplinary proceedings for having misappropriated the funds of the firm's clients. Upon submission of his resignation, Grandeau was disbarred for misappropriation of funds, for failing to render an accounting of funds, and for failing to keep records. Dahowski, on the other hand, was not disbarred but was censured for professional misconduct—including his failure "to oversee or review the record keeping of his law firm, thereby contributing to the conversion by [his] law partner of funds entrusted to the law firm." . . . Other than the misconduct stated, Dahowski was in no way responsible for the conversions. . . .

The Fund . . . commenced this action, seeking to recoup sums paid to the clients. Causes of action grounded in negligence, breach of trust, and breach of contract, and Dahowski's vicarious liability for Grandeau's professional misconduct are stated. Defendant Dahowski answered, but defendant Grandeau defaulted and is not a party to this appeal. Dahowski . . . moved for summary judgment . . . claiming that the action did not lie against him individually.

Supreme Court . . . awarded summary judgment to Dahowski, dismissing the complaint as to him. That court held that insofar as Dahowski never personally engaged in "dishonest conduct" as defined by the statute—but merely negligently failed to discover Grandeau's peculations—the Fund could not have reimbursed losses to the firm's clients that were attributable to his conduct. Therefore, the court concluded, there is no basis for . . . action against Dahowski. The Appellate Division modified by denying Dahowski summary judgment, concluding that the Clients' Security Fund, consistent with its purposes, is authorized to pursue its . . . claim against him. The Appellate Division thereafter certified to this court a question as to whether it had erred in so modifying. We now affirm. . . .

. . . The Fund acknowledges its authority to reimburse law clients only for losses attributable to the "dishonest conduct" of attorneys, and concedes that here Dahowski did not engage in "dishonest conduct" as that term is defined by the statute. The Fund does not seek to recoup reimbursements predicated upon claims that Dahowski engaged in negligent professional misconduct. Rather, the Fund seeks to recoup—to the extent of the reimbursements paid—those sums which each client had a right to pursue from whatever party as may be liable for the *dishonest conduct* of Grandeau.

Traditional principles of partnership law dictate that, ordinarily, one member of a partnership is liable for the tortious conduct of another, and any member of a partnership may be liable for a conversion of property committed by a member of the firm, even where the other members of the firm had no knowledge of the offending partner's action. In the circumstances of this case, each client victimized by Grandeau's misappropriation of funds acquired a viable cause of action against Dahowski as well. The aggrieved client assigned and subrogated to the Fund its right to assert such a cause of action and establish Dahowski's liability for Grandeau's tortious conduct. The Fund may therefore prosecute, standing in the shoes of the aggrieved clients, claims of negligence, breach of contract and breach of trust against Dahowski. . . .

We conclude therefore, that the Board is authorized to prosecute the instant subrogation claim not only against the attorney who engaged in the dishonest conduct—Grandeau—but against Dahowski, his former law partner, as well. . . .

■ *Affirmed.*

1. What are the names of the former law partners?
2. Which partner's actions caused the Security Fund to pay $589,829 to clients who have been wronged?

3. Against which partner is the Security Fund seeking to recover?
4. What rulings of the trial court and appellate court are being reviewed by this court?
5. What is the legal basis for allowing the Security Fund to seek a recovery against Mr. Dahowski?

If a partnership or partner has liability because of a tort of a partner, the firm has the right to collect its losses from the partner at fault. In effect, a partnership or partner that is liable in tort to a third person has a right of indemnity against the partner at fault. Likewise, if the injured third party collects directly from the partner at fault, the partner cannot seek contribution from his or her copartners. For example, in the preceding case, if the Security Fund had collected reimbursement from Grandeau, he could not have obtained contribution from Dahowski.

11. Powers over Property

Each partner has implied authority to sell to good-faith purchasers personal property that is held for the purpose of resale and to execute any documents necessary to effect a transfer of title. Of course, if the partner's authority in this connection has been limited, and that is known to the purchaser, the transfer of title will be ineffective or voidable. A partner has no power to sell the fixtures and equipment used in the business unless he or she has been duly authorized. This partner's acts are not a regular feature of the business, and a prospective purchaser should make certain that the particular partner has been given authority to sell. The power to sell, where it is present, also gives the power to make warranties that normally accompany similar sales.

The right to sell a firm's real property is to be inferred only if the firm is engaged in the real estate business. In other cases there is no right to sell and convey realty unless it has been authorized by a partnership agreement. In most states, a deed by one partner without authority is not binding on the firm, but it does convey the individual interest of the parties executing and delivering the deed. This conveyance, however, is subject to the rights of creditors of the partnership.

Under the Uniform Partnership Act, title to real property may be taken in the firm name as a *tenancy in partnership*, and any member of the firm has power to execute a deed thereto by signing the firm name. If that happens, what is the effect of a wrongful transfer of real estate that has been acquired for use in the business and not for resale? The conveyance may be set aside by the other partners, because the purchaser should have known that one partner has no power to sell real estate without the approval of the others. However, if the first purchaser has resold and conveyed the property to an innocent third party, the latter takes good title.

If the title to real estate is held in the firm name, a conveyance by the partners as individuals is not effective to convey title to the real estate. The conveyance must be in the firm name. This is true even if the conveyance is to a partner as part of a settlement agreement between the partners.

If the title to firm property is not held in the firm name but is held in the names of one or more of the partners, a conveyance by those in whose names the title is held passes good title, unless the purchaser knows or should know that title was held for the firm. There is nothing in the record title in such a situation to call the buyer's attention to the fact that the firm has an interest in the property.

12. Financial Powers

To determine the limit of a partner's financial powers, partnerships are divided into two general classes—trading and nontrading partnerships. A *trading partnership* is one that has for its primary purpose the buying and selling of merchandise. In such a trading firm, each partner has an implied power to borrow money and to extend the credit of the firm, in the usual course of business, by signing negotiable paper.

A *nontrading partnership* is one that does not buy and sell commodities but has for its primary purpose the production of commodities or is organized for the purpose of selling services: for example, professional partnerships in law, medicine, or accounting. In such partnerships, a partner's powers are more limited, and a partner does not have implied power to borrow money. However, if the partner's act is within the scope of partnership business, a member of a nontrading partnership may bind the firm by the exercise of implied authority, just as a partner in a trading partnership may.

The power to mortgage or pledge a firm's property is primarily dependent on the power to borrow money and bind the firm. A partner with authority to borrow may, as an incident to that power, give the security normally demanded for similar loans. Because no single partner without the consent of the others has the power to commit an act that will destroy or terminate the business, the power to give a mortgage on the entire stock of merchandise and fixtures of a business is usually denied. Such a mortgage would make it possible, upon default, to liquidate the firm's assets and thus destroy its business. Subject to this limitation, the power to borrow carries the power to pledge or mortgage.

CHAPTER SUMMARY

Terminology	1. A silent partner has no voice in the management of the partnership.
	2. A secret partner's existence is not known to the public.
	3. A dormant partner is both silent and secret.

RIGHTS OF PARTNERS

To Participate in Management	1. Unless the agreement provides to the contrary, each partner has an equal right to manage and to conduct the firm's business.
	2. The majority of partners can make final decisions concerning normal operations.
	3. Certain actions require unanimous consent to bind the firm.
To Be Compensated for Services	1. Partners are not generally compensated other than with a share of the profits, unless their agreement provides otherwise.
	2. Unless the agreement is to the contrary, partners have a duty to devote all of their time, skill, and energy to partnership affairs.
To Interest	1. Capital contributions do not earn interest.
	2. Interest is paid on advances above capital contributions.
	3. Interest is not paid on unwithdrawn profits.

To Information and Inspection of Books	1. Each partner is entitled to all information concerning the business and to inspect the books and records of the partnership.
	2. Partners have a duty to furnish information necessary to operate the business.
	3. Partners have a right to make copies of partnership records.
To an Accounting	1. In the event of a dispute as to the rights of the parties to assets or income, the equity action of an accounting is available to determine the rights of the partners.
	2. As a general rule, partners are not allowed to sue each other in courts of law for dollar damages.
	3. The suit for an accounting cannot be brought for minor disputes.
	4. The suit for an accounting is usually a part of the dissolution process.
To Partnership Property	1. Each partner has an equal right to possess partnership property for partnership purposes.
	2. A partner has no right in specific partnership property and no right to use partnership property for personal purposes.
	3. Upon the death of a partner, the property belongs to the surviving partners, who have a duty to wind up the affairs. These surviving partners must pay the deceased partner's estate the sum to which the deceased partner was entitled.
	4. A partner's interest cannot be levied on by his or her separate creditors. Creditors are entitled to obtain a charging order and to collect the partner's share of profits to satisfy the judgment.

DUTIES AND POWERS OF PARTNERS

Duties	1. A partnership is a fiduciary relationship, and each partner must act only on behalf of the partnership.
	2. A partner cannot take for himself or herself an opportunity of the partnership, and any gains that should have belonged to the partnership must be paid to it.
	3. All acts of partners are subject to the good-faith standard.
	4. Since knowledge of any partner is charged to all partners, there is a duty on one partner to inform all other partners of all facts affecting the partnership business.
Power to Contract	1. A partner is an agent of the partnership business, and the general rules of agency are applicable.
	2. The implied authority of a partnership is greater than that of an ordinary agent. A partner has the implied power to do all acts necessary to carry on the business.
Power to Impose Tort Liability	1. The doctrine of *respondeat superior* is applicable to the partnership relationship.
	2. If the partnership incurs liability because of the tort of a partner, it has the right to collect the loss from the partner.
Powers over Property	1. Partners have authority to sell personal property held by the partnership for resale in the ordinary course of business.
	2. A partner has no right to sell firm real estate unless it is engaged in the business of selling real estate.
	3. Real property held in the partnership name can be conveyed only with the agreement of all partners.
Financial Powers	1. In a trading partnership, each partner has the implied power to borrow money to extend the credit of the firm in the usual course of business.
	2. In a nontrading partnership, a partner does not have the implied power to borrow money.
	3. The power to mortgage property or to pledge assets is narrowly granted. However, if a partner has the power to borrow money, the power to mortgage or pledge assets is assumed.

REVIEW QUESTIONS AND PROBLEMS

1. Match each term in column A with the appropriate statement in column B.

A	B
(1) Silent partner	(a) A partnership that is engaged in the buying and selling of goods
(2) Secret partner	(b) Describes the title to property held in the partnership name
(3) Dormant partner	(c) A partner that does not participate in management
(4) Tenancy in partnership	(d) A partnership engaged in providing services
(5) Charging orders	(e) A loan to a partnership by a partner
(6) Trading partnership	(f) A partner that is unknown to third parties
(7) Nontrading partnership	(g) A court procedure for collecting an undivided debt of a partner from the partnership
(8) Advance	(h) A partner that is both secret and silent

2. The partners in a partnership composed of seven members have differing views on several partnership issues. If the partnership agreement makes no provision for the number of partners required to decide particular issues, how many votes does it take
   a. To discharge a clerk accused of stealing?
   b. To cause the dissolution of the partnership?
   c. To require the change of the partnership business from a wholesale to a retail operation?
   d. To require the submission of a partnership claim for arbitration?
   e. To submit to a confession of judgment on behalf of the partnership?

3. Peter, John, and James were partners in the ownership and operation of a fishing vessel. Peter had perfected a new type of net for catching sharks. Getting the nets ready for use took a lot of time, but their use saved the partnership time and money. Is Peter entitled to extra compensation for this contribution? Explain.

4. Albert and Maria were partners in a grocery business. The firm was in need of additional working capital, and Albert advanced $20,000. Is Albert entitled to interest on the advance? Why or why not?

5. Huffington was the managing partner of an oil and gas investment firm. He learned of an Indonesian oil deal and acquired 10 percent of it for himself. Is the partnership entitled to the investment? Explain.

6. Preston obtained a judgment against Daniel. He sought a charging order against Daniel's interest in a general partnership to collect the judgment. Jeff also obtained a judgment against Daniel. Jeff seeks to intervene in Preston's suit for a charging order, so he (Jeff) may share in it. Preston claims that he has a right to full payment before Jeff is entitled to anything. Should the charging order against Daniel's partnership interest pro rate the payment between Preston and Jeff? Explain.

7. Bedford and Eckhart formed a partnership and built a shopping center. Three years later, Bedford, the managing partner, informed Eckhart that the business was in deep financial trouble and that he had tried to sell the complex but had failed. Bedford said that the best thing to do would be for one to buy the other out, and that their equity in the business was not worth more than $3 million. Eckhart sold his half interest in the partnership to Bedford for $1.5 million. Later he discovered that their equity in the business amounted to over $10 million and that Bedford had received several offers to purchase the business. Eckhart brought suit to rescind the sale, to have the partnership dissolved, and for accounting. Should Eckhart succeed? Why or why not?

8. A partnership was in the real estate business. It was formed to buy and sell apartment buildings. Two of the three partners signed a contract to sell one of the partnership's buildings. Is the third partner bound by the contract? Why or why not?

9. Martin, Lewis, and Davis are partners in a CPA firm. Martin negligently causes an automobile accident while on his way to perform an audit. Are the firm and the other partners liable? Explain.

10. A patient sued Dr. Flynn for medical malpractice. Flynn, who is a partner in a medical partnership, sought contributions from his partners. He contended that his negligence, if any, occurred in the course of the partnership's business. Is Flynn entitled to contributions from his partners? Why or why not?

11. The Viking Partnership consisted of seven equal partners. Wells, one of the partners, purchased six shares of the Azuma Dairy Farm Corporation stock. He used partnership funds to purchase the stock. Subsequently another share was purchased, and each partner's capital account was debited for an amount equal to one-seventh of the total purchase price. Is the stock partnership property? Why or why not?

12. Wood and Simmons took title to certain land as partners and leased it to the defendant. Later, when they dissolved the partnership, Wood and his wife conveyed all their interest in the property to Simmons and his wife. Simmons and his wife then separated, and he conveyed the property to her as part of their settlement. When Mrs. Simmons filed suit for possession of the property, the defendant contended that the title to the land remained with the partnership. Was the defendant correct? Why or why not?

13. Defendants Smith and Brook were partners in the automobile business under the name of Greenwood Sales and Service. Defendant Brook borrowed $6,000 from plaintiff and gave a partnership note in return. Is Smith liable on the note? Why or why not?

14. A partner in an accounting firm borrowed $10,000 in the firm name and used the proceeds to pay an individual debt. Is the firm liable for this debt? Explain.

DISSOLUTION
OF PARTNERSHIPS

CHAPTER PREVIEW

*T*he preceding two chapters discuss the formation and operation of a partnership. In addition to the important legal topics related to those topics, you need to be familiar with the issues that arise when a partnership ceases to exist. These latter issues arise frequently because partnerships, as business organizations, are easily dissolved.

This chapter discusses how dissolutions of partnerships occur, the impact of such an event, and how the partnership assets are distributed when the business of the organization is terminated.

■ BUSINESS MANAGEMENT DECISION

You are a partner in a twenty-member accounting firm. One of your partners, Anderson, retires from the practice of accounting and leaves the partnership. Anderson's duties included purchasing equipment and library materials for the firm. You assume these duties upon Anderson's retirement.

What is the first action you need to take?

1. Terminology

Dissolution Occurs any time there is a change in the partners, either by adding a new partner or by having a preexisting partner die, retire, or otherwise leave.

Three steps are necessary to end a partnership: dissolution, winding up, and termination. **Dissolution,** the legal destruction of the partnership relation, occurs whenever any partner ceases to be a member of the firm or whenever a new partner is admitted. It is the change in the relation of the partners caused by any partner's ceasing to be associated in carrying on—as distinguished from winding up—the business. Dissolution alone does not terminate the partnership but designates the time when partners cease to carry on business together.

Winding up The process of liquidating a business organization.

Winding up involves the process of reducing the assets to cash, paying off the creditors, and distributing the balance to the partners. A winding up may be partial or complete. A partial winding up becomes necessary when a partnership lacks sufficient cash and borrowing power to pay its debts, such as those owed to one or more partners who have caused a dissolution by withdrawing from the partnership.

Termination Occurs when the winding up or liquidation is completed. This is the end of the organization and its business.

When a partnership engages in a total winding up, the completion of this process is called the **termination** of the partnership as an organization and as a viable business. Prior to the actual moment of termination, the partnership still has an existence and is able to function.

METHODS OF DISSOLUTION

2. By Acts of Partners

Dissolutions will occur without violation of the partnership agreement (1) at the end of the stipulated term or particular undertaking specified in the agreement, (2) by the express will of any partner when no definite term or particular undertaking is specified, (3) by the agreement of all the partners, or (4) by the expulsion, in good faith, of any partner from the business, in accordance with power conferred by the partnership agreement. Dissolution also may occur even though such action by a partner is a breach of the partnership agreement.

When parties agree to be partners for a specific time period or for a stated purpose, the conclusion of the period or the accomplishment of the purpose marks the dissolution of the partnership. More frequently, however, partners enter into agreement that does not have a stated duration. When a definite term of duration is not stated, a *partnership at will* exists.

In a partnership at will, any partner may, without liability, legally dissolve it at any time. Dissolution may be accomplished by giving notice to the other parties. No particular form of notice is required; it will be implied from circumstances inconsistent with the continuation of the partnership. When a partner whose services are essential leaves the organization, his or her departure is an act and notice of dissolution.

Even when the partnership agreement specifies a duration period, partners may mutually agree to dissolve their relationship. Since a partnership, in its essential form, is a contract, the partners to the contract may mutually agree to a shorter period for the life of the partnership.

Expulsion in good faith is a method of dissolution limited to the terms of the partnership agreement. Expulsion of a partner is a breach of the partnership agreement unless the agreement confers the power of the expulsion on a majority of the partners. Assume that A, B, and C are partners. A and B cannot expel C unless that power is specifically granted in the agreement. Without the power to expel, partners may seek judicial dissolution if one partner is guilty of violating the partnership agreement (see section 4). If C was not devoting his time to the business, as he was required to do in the partnership agreement, A and B could seek a dissolution on these grounds, although they could not expel C.

Dissolution may also occur in violation of the partnership agreement. Although the agreement stipulates the length of time the partnership is to last, dissolution is always possible because the relationship is a personal one that courts are hesitant to enforce. Like most agency relationships, each partner has the *power*, though not the *right*, to revoke the relationship. In the event of wrongful dissolution, the wrongdoer is liable for the damages.

However, subject to a few exceptions, a breach of a partnership agreement does not mean that the breaching partner loses his or her interest in the partnership. The law does not favor such forfeitures. Nevertheless, where the partnership agreement provides for the forfeiture of the breaching partner's interest in the firm property, such a provision will be enforced.

Breaches of the partnership agreement, whether or not committed in bad faith, do not cause a partner to lose his or her rights to share in the profits. But a partner who refuses to contribute funds essential to the operation of a partnership business may be excluded from participation in any profit. And if one of the partners abandons the business, that partner may forfeit some or all of his or her share of the profits as damages.

3. By Operation of Law

If, during the period of the partnership, events make it impossible or illegal for the partnership to continue, it will be dissolved by operation of law. Such events or conditions are the death or bankruptcy of one of the partners or a change in the law that makes the continuance of the business illegal. Of course, a partnership may also be illegal at its inception. In such a case, the courts will leave the partners where it finds them and will not grant relief to a partner in a suit against the other partner or partners.

The following case demonstrates the potential consequences of entering into a partnership with an illegal purpose.

CASE

Morelli v. Ehsan
756 P.2d 129 (Wash. 1988)

In November 1980, Tito Morelli and Dr. Mike Ehsan entered into a partnership agreement to establish and operate the Sunrise Emergency and Family Care Clinic. This clinic was to provide minor emergency treatment and health care to the general public on an out-patient basis. Morelli, who was not licensed as a doctor, and Ehsan were

to be co-general partners and were to share profits and losses equally. Morelli's title was "Director of Operations" and Ehsan's was "Medical Director."

In January 1985, after a series of disagreements, Morelli petitioned the court for a dissolution of the partnership and an accounting. Ehsan moved to dismiss Morelli's complaint contending that the partnership agreement was illegal and void. The district court granted Ehsan's motion and permanently enjoined Morelli from interfering in the operation of the clinic. Ehsan assumed all of the assets and liabilities of the business but was not required to repay Morelli any of the funds he had contributed to the partnership.

Morelli appealed, and the Court of Appeals agreed that the partnership agreement was illegal. Nevertheless, that Court remanded the case to the trial court for an accounting and distribution of the partnership assets on an equitable basis. Dr. Ehsan's petition for further review was granted.

DOLLIVER, J.

. . . Morelli contends the partnership was legal because his responsibilities and duties were limited strictly to business aspects while Ehsan's authority was limited to the clinic's medical affairs. Morelli recites facts which he claims support this view. However, the legality of a partnership to practice medicine is not a matter of fact. It is a question of law, which is addressed by both the statutory and common law of Washington.

At the time of the partnership formation, former RCW 18.71.020 provided:

> Any person who shall practice or attempt to practice or hold himself out as practicing medicine . . . without . . . a valid license . . . shall be guilty of a gross misdemeanor. . . .

Under The Professional Service Corporation Act . . . lawyers, doctors, dentists, optometrists, and other professional specialists are authorized to form a corporate entity within their respective practices. However, the corporation must be organized by "an individual or group of individuals duly licensed . . . to render the same professional services. . . ." The intent of the Legislature to bar other than similarly licensed health care professionals from involvement in professional services is amply delineated. . . .

Morelli was . . . in a general partnership with a physician as an equal partner. While Morelli asserts his only duties were as business manager, the evidence is to the contrary. The partnership agreement clearly establishes Morelli as more than a business manager of the clinic. He was a general partner entitled to equal share of the profits, to equal rights in the management, to hire nurses, and to all the rights and duties of a general partner under the laws of the state of Washington. Furthermore, the record indicates Morelli exercised those rights. . . .

Morelli also contends The Professional Service Corporation Act indicates the Legislature did not intend to prevent lay participation in a professional partnership. We disagree. The Professional Service Corporation Act is a narrow statutory exception to the common law rule that a corporation cannot engage in the practice of a learned profession through licensed employees unless legislatively authorized. As the Court of Appeals observed: "It would

be anomalous if, by simply structuring an organization as a limited partnership, rather than a corporation, lay businessmen could participate in a business that provided the same professional services.". . .

The Sunrise Emergency and Family Care Clinic partnership agreement provided Morelli a *means* and an *instrumentality* by which he shared equally in the profits and management of a medical practice. Both Morelli and Ehsan were violating statutes governing the practice of their respective professions by operating a medical clinic without both being licensed as physicians. The partnership agreement was illegal as a matter of law.

Having found the partnership agreement illegal, we next address whether the trial court properly precluded Morelli from an equitable distribution of the assets.

If the business of a partnership is illegal, we will not entertain an action for an accounting and distribution of the assets, especially when the unlawful agreement is contrary to public policy. This is consistent with the general rule that illegal agreements are void, and courts will not enforce them. The parties are left where the court finds them regardless of whether the situation is unequal as to the parties. . . .

In remanding for an accounting, the Court of Appeals fashioned a "good faith" exception, a new and unprecedented exception to the general rule that the courts will not enforce an illegal agreement where both parties are equally at fault, but will leave the parties where it found them. This exception, apparently effective when both parties believe they were acting within the law, completely undermines the purpose of the rule—deterrence. There is no deterrence from violating a law if parties may claim both were ignorant of the law. . . .

By denying Morelli an accounting, the trial court followed the law in this jurisdiction and others leaving the parties where it found them. If the court had granted Morelli affirmative relief, as ordered by the Court of Appeals on remand, the parties would be using the court to enforce their illegal partnership agreement. . . .

The trial court's judgment was correct in finding the partnership agreement illegal and denying an accounting of the partnership. . . .

■ *The judgment of the trial court is reinstated.*

CASE CONCEPTS REVIEW

1. What makes this Sunrise Emergency and Family Care Clinic partnership illegal?
2. Both the trial court and appeals court agreed that this partnership had an illegal purpose. What is the basis for the appeals court reversing the trial court?
3. Why does this court conclude that Morelli has no right to use the judiciary to recover against Ehsan?

Since a partnership is a personal relationship existing by reason of contract, when one of the partners dies, the partnership is dissolved. It is not terminated on dissolution, but it continues for the purpose of winding up the partnership's affairs. The process of winding up is, in most states, the exclusive obligation and right of the surviving partner or partners. The executor or administrator of the deceased partner has no right to participate in, or interfere with, the winding-up processes, unless, of course, the deceased was the last surviving partner. The only right of the personal representative of a deceased partner is to demand an accounting upon completion of the winding up of the partnership's affairs. As a general rule, the estate of the deceased partner is not bound on contracts entered into by the surviving partners if the contracts are unconnected with the winding up of the affairs of the partnership. This is discussed more fully later in this chapter.

The bankruptcy of a partner will dissolve the partnership because the control of that partner's property passes to the trustee in bankruptcy for the benefit of the creditors. The mere insolvency of a partner will not be sufficient to justify a dissolution. The bankruptcy of the firm itself is a cause for dissolution, as is a valid assignment of all the firm's assets for the benefit of creditors.

4. By Court Decree

When a partnership by its agreement is to be continued for a term of years, circumstances sometimes make continued existence of the firm impossible and unprofitable. Upon application of one of the partners to a court of equity, the partnership may be dissolved. Under the following circumstances and situations, a court of equity may order dissolution:

1. Total incapacity of a partner to conduct business and to perform the duties required under the contract of partnership
2. A declaration by judicial process that a partner is insane
3. Willful and persistent commitment of a breach of the partnership agreement, misappropriation of funds, or commitment of fraudulent acts
4. An innocent party's application for dissolution because the partnership was entered into as a result of fraud
5. Gross misconduct and neglect or breach of duty by a partner to such an extent that it is impossible to carry out the purposes of the partnership agreement
6. In some states, any grounds that make dissolution equitable or in the best interests of the partners

Courts will not interfere and grant a decree of dissolution for mere discourtesy, temporary inconvenience, minor differences of opinion, or errors in judgment. The misconduct must be of such gross nature that the continued operation of the business would be unprofitable. In those states that have incorporated item 6 of the preceding list into their law, courts of equity will order dissolution if there is serious disharmony among the partners.

In cases arising out of the dissolution of a partnership, a court of equity may appoint a receiver to liquidate the partnership, obtain an accounting of the proceeds, and distribute the assets. A receiver may be appointed when the evidence indicates that it is necessary to preserve the property and to protect the rights of the parties. For example, a receiver may be appointed where the remaining parties are delaying the winding-up process or are breaching any of the fiduciary duties of partners.

5. On Powers of Partners

The process of winding up, except when the agreement provides for continuation by purchase of former partners' shares, involves liquidation of the partnership assets so cash may be available to pay creditors and to make a distribution to the partners. When the agreement provides for continuation and purchase of a deceased partner's interest, the technical dissolution is followed by valuation and payment, and the new firm immediately commences business.

As a general rule, dissolution terminates the actual authority of any partner to act for the partnership except when such authority is necessary to wind up partnership affairs, to liquidate the assets of the firm in an orderly manner, or to complete transactions begun but not finished. Insofar as third persons who had dealings with the firm are concerned, apparent authority still exists until notice of termination is given.

This apparent authority means that one partner of a dissolved partnership binds the firm on contracts unconnected with winding up the firm's affairs. When a partner enters such contracts, issues arise as to whether or not the new obligations may be met with partnership funds or whether the contracting partner is entitled to contribution toward payment of the debt or obligation from the other partners.

The resolution of these issues depends on the cause of the dissolution. If the dissolution is caused by (1) the act of a partner, (2) bankruptcy of the partnership, or (3) the death of a partner, each partner is liable for his or her share of any liability incurred on behalf of the firm after dissolution, just as if there had been no dissolution, unless the partner incurring the liability had knowledge of the dissolution. Of course, such knowledge is usually present. In these situations, if knowledge of the dissolution is present, the partner incurring the liability is solely responsible and cannot require the other partners to share the burden of an unauthorized act. If the dissolution is not caused by the act, bankruptcy, or death of a partner but by some event such as a court decree, no partner has authority to act and therefore has no right to contribution from other partners for liabilities incurred after dissolution.

When dissolution results from the death of a partner, title to partnership property remains in the surviving partner or partners for purposes of winding up and liquidation. Thus, both real and personal property are, through the survivors, made available to a firm's creditors. All realty is treated as though it were personal property. It is sold, and the surviving partners finally account, usually in cash, to the personal representative of the deceased partner for the latter's share in the proceeds of liquidation.

6. On Rights of Partners

Upon dissolution, a withdrawing partner who has not breached the partnership agreement has certain options with regard to his or her interest in the dissolved partnership. This partner may require the partnership to be wound up and terminated. The partnership will be liquidated and the assets distributed among the partners. The alternative is to allow the business to continue, or accept that it has continued.

If the withdrawing partner allows the business to continue, the value of his or her interest in the partnership as of the date of dissolution is ascertained. The withdrawing partner then has the right to receive, at his or her option after an accounting, either the value of this interest in the partnership with interest or, in lieu of interest, the profits attributable to the use of his or her rights in the property of the dissolved partnership. The portion of profits to which a withdrawing partner is entitled because of the use of property will usually be less than his or her portion prior to dissolution. This is true because a portion of the profit is usually attributable to services of the continuing partners, and most courts allow for compensation to be paid to the continuing partners.

When dissolution is caused in any way other than breach of the partnership agreement, each partner has a right to insist that all the partnership assets be used first to pay firm debts. After firm obligations are paid, remaining assets are used to return capital contributions and then to provide for a distribution of profits. All the partners except those who have caused a wrongful dissolution of the firm have the right to participate in the winding up of the business. The majority selects the method and procedures to be followed in the liquidation. The assets are turned into cash unless all agree to distribute them in kind.

If a partnership that is to continue for a fixed period is dissolved by the wrongful withdrawal of one partner, the remaining members may continue as partners under the same firm name for the balance of the agreed term of the partnership. They are required to settle with the withdrawing partner for his or her interest in the partnership and to compensate that partner, but the remaining partners are allowed to subtract from the amount due in cash the damages caused by the withdrawing partner's wrongful withdrawal. In the calculation of that partner's share, the goodwill of the business is not taken into consideration. The fact that a partner breached the agreement does not take away that partner's right to an accounting and to receive his or her share of the partnership after deducting any damages caused by the breach of the agreement.

Upon dissolution, it is the duty of the remaining partner or partners to wind up the affairs. If they fail to do so and instead continue the business, they have liability to the withdrawing partner or his or her assignee or personal representative for use of partnership assets. The liability may include interest if the value of the former partner's portion of the partnership can be ascertained, or it may include liability for a share of postdissolution profits. This liability arises because the business is continuing to use the assets of all the former partners, and the continuing partners have failed to wind up the business and terminate it.

Is a partner entitled to be paid for services rendered during the winding-up process? If the dissolution is caused by the death of a partner, the answer is yes. This exception to the general rule that partners are not compensated for their services rendered to the partnership makes sense because the deceased partner obviously is unavailable to assist the surviving partners.

If the dissolution is caused by any act or occurrence other than a partner's death, the general rule of no compensation for the partners still applies. It is presumed, unless the partners agree otherwise, that all partners are contributing to the winding-up process. The partnership's income during the winding up is allocated to former and continuing partners in accordance with their shares stated in the partnership agreement.

It is often difficult to value accurately the interest of a withdrawing or deceased partner when the business continues. The buy-and-sell provisions will control the method for establishing the value of the interest as of the date of dissolution. If there are no buy-and-sell provisions and the parties cannot agree, a judicial decision on the value may be required. This decision may sometimes involve which of the parties is to continue the business, as well as the amount to be paid the withdrawing partner, but it cannot be made with mathematical certainty.

7. On New Partners

A person admitted as a new partner into an existing partnership is liable only to the extent of his or her capital contribution for all obligations incurred before admission. This new partner is not personally liable for such obligations, and the creditors of the old firm can look only to the firm's assets and to the partners of the old firm. With respect to obligations that arise after the new partner joins the partnership, the liability is personal and unlimited as though he or she has been a partner.

Prior debts sometimes become new debts (for example, upon the renewal of a note). In the following case, if the note had not been renewed, the liability of the new partner would have been limited to $100,000—his capital contribution. As a result of the renewal, the liability was over $300,000, even though the new partner was not involved in the renewal of the note. This case demonstrates the risk of unlimited liability in a partnership.

CASE

Moseley v. Commercial State Bank
457 So.2d 967 (Ala. 1984)

FAULKNER, J.

Commercial State Bank of Donaldsonville, Georgia, brought this action against Southern Distilleries, a partnership, and against the partners of Southern Distilleries for money due on several promissory notes executed by Southern Distilleries. One of the partners, Julius Moseley, appeals from a judgment against him for $303,241.52.

On September 17, 1980, five individuals formed a partnership named Southern Distilleries in order to engage in the business of producing fuel grade alcohol (gasahol). The partners signed an agreement providing that any three partners having an aggregate interest in the partnership of at least 60% were authorized to borrow money and execute promissory notes on behalf of the partnership. . . .

On December 19, 1980, three partners, Adams, Fitch and Moulthrop, executed two promissory notes on behalf of Southern Distilleries to Commercial State Bank. Both notes came due on March 19, 1981. . . . Southern Distilleries failed to satisfy either note when they came due.

On April 2, 1981, an amended partnership agreement was executed by the five original partners and by three other individuals, including the appellant, Moseley. The purpose of the amendment was to "change the percentage interests of the partners and to admit new partners." The document indicates that Moseley contributed $100,000.00 to the capital account of the partnership and acquired a "profit and loss interest in the partnership" slightly in excess of 6%. The amended agreement provides that the provisions of the prior agreement were to remain in full force and effect.

On July 21, 1981, Southern Distilleries paid the interest due on the outstanding notes and Adams, Fitch, and Moulthrop executed a new note on behalf of Southern Distilleries to the bank. . . . The bank marked the notes dated December 19 "paid" and returned them to Southern Distilleries.

Southern Distilleries failed to satisfy the July 21 note when it matured and the bank brought this action to enforce payment. In support of his contention that the trial court improperly granted the bank's motion for a summary judgment, Moseley argues: . . . that Moseley is not personally liable for the debt because it pre-existed his becoming a partner in Southern Distilleries.

Clearly, Adams, Fitch, and Moulthrop bound the partners of Southern Distilleries by executing a note on its behalf to the bank. Execution of an instrument in the partnership's name for the purpose of carrying on the usual business of the partnership binds the partners, unless the partner executing the instrument has no authority to act and the person with whom he is dealing has knowledge that he has no authority to act. A person admitted as a partner into an existing partnership is liable for partnership obligations arising before his admission into the partnership. His liability for pre-existing obligations can be satisfied only out of partnership property, however. The bank's judgment is against Moseley personally. The dispositive issue of this case, therefore, is whether the obligation sued on arose before Moseley's admission into the partnership. In support of Moseley's contention that the debt pre-existed his admission into the partnership, Moseley argues that the new note was merely a renewal of a pre-existing obligation. . . .

There is no dispute in this case as to the material facts. Moseley entered into a general partnership agreement with other individuals doing business under the name Southern Distilleries. The partners who executed the note sued on were expressly authorized to bind the other partners. Although the defendant chooses to categorize the debt created by the note sued on as the renewal of a pre-existing debt, it is clear that the obligation created by the old note terminated when the bank accepted the new note. Prior to the execution of the new note the bank could have brought an action to collect the debt. After it accepted the new note and satisfied the old one, there was no obligation which was due and payable to the bank until the new note matured. In agreeing to the forebearance of its rights to collect the money owed it by Southern Distilleries, the bank relied on the representations of the partnership agreement that the partners, including Moseley, would be bound by the new note. Since the contract sued

on was entered into by a partnership which included Moseley, and since there was valid consideration for the contract sued on, the plaintiff is entitled to enforce the contract against the defendant.

We understand that Moseley had no knowledge of the day-to-day operations of the partnership and that he did not find out about the note until the bank brought this action. While Moseley apparently considered his interest in the firm to be that of merely an investor . . . he signed an agreement granting him all the rights of a general partner in the firm and authorizing the other partners to obligate him as a general partner, which they did. . . . The parties are competent business men dealing at arm's length, who presumably have ample access to counsel. If Moseley had wished to limit his exposure to liability he should have taken steps to do so when he chose to become involved in the enterprise.

■ *Affirmed.*

CASE CONCEPTS REVIEW

1. When did Southern Distilleries originally borrow money from the Commercial State Bank?
2. When did Moseley become a partner in Southern Distilleries? What was the amount of his capital contribution?
3. When did Southern Distilleries "pay off the original loan" and obtain a new loan with Commercial State Bank?
4. What was the extent of Moseley's increased liability as a result of the new loans being obtained?

8. On Third Parties

Dissolution of a partnership terminates the authority of the partners to create liability, but it does not discharge any existing liability of any partner. An agreement between the partners themselves that one or more of the partners will assume the partnership liabilities and that a withdrawing partner will not have any liability does not bind the firm's creditors.

If a business is continued without liquidation of the partnership affairs, creditors of the first, or dissolved, partnership are also creditors of the partnership continuing the business. Likewise, if the partners assign all their interest to a former partner or a third person who continues the business without liquidation of the partnership affairs, creditors of the dissolved partnership are also creditors of the person continuing the business.

If a partner wishes to be discharged from an existing liability, he or she must get the creditor and the continuing partners to agree to this discharge. Such an arrangement in essence is a novation. This three-party agreement is discussed in detail in chapter 17.

After dissolution, two categories of parties are entitled to notice of the dissolution. First, the firm's creditors, including all former creditors, are entitled to actual notice of the dissolution. Notice of the dissolution is required, whether the dissolution is caused by an act of the parties or by operation of law, unless a partner becomes bankrupt or the continuation of the business becomes illegal. Therefore, upon death of a partner, the personal representative should give immediate notice of the death and dissolution to avoid further liability.

Transactions entered into after dissolution without such notice continue to bind withdrawing partners and the estate of deceased partners. If proper notice is given, former partners are not liable for contracts unconnected with winding up the partnership's affairs. Notice eliminates the apparent authority to bind the former firm and its partners. Failure to give notice and the continuation of apparent authority in effect creates a partnership by estoppel. As between the partners, the original partnership is dissolved, but as to third parties, a partner carrying on the business of the former partnership binds the partners if notice of dissolution is not given properly. The following case illustrates the dangers of failing to give notice of dissolution.

CASE

Royal Bank v. Weintraub, Gold & Alper
497 N.E.2d 289 (N.Y. 1986)

KAYE, J.

... On September 27, 1977, Roger Allen sought a short-term loan of $60,000 from plaintiff, the Royal Bank and Trust Company, to enable him to obtain a larger loan from another source. Allen advised plaintiff that the $60,000 would be kept in an escrow account belonging to his attorneys, the firm of Weintraub, Gold & Alper. Allen gave Royal Bank a letter dated September 27, 1977 on the law firm's stationery, addressed to him and signed by Alfred Weintraub (one of the three named partners), acknowledging that the check would be received by the firm as escrow agent, that it would be placed in the firm's trust account (identified by number) at the Madison Avenue Branch of Marine Midland Bank, and that the money would be returned to plaintiff by October 5, 1977. Plaintiff learned from its parent, the Royal Bank of Canada, that Allen was a customer with a good credit rating, and that it knew of the proposed transaction. Plaintiff also called its New York attorneys, who advised that they had not heard of the firm Weintraub, Gold & Alper, and that the three named individuals were listed separately in an attorney directory as practicing law at the address given on the firm stationery. Plaintiff's credit officer found the firm listed in the current Manhattan telephone directory, at the address and number corresponding to the letterhead.

When he dialed the number a receptionist answered "Weintraub, Gold and Alper." He then spoke to Weintraub and confirmed the escrow arrangement set forth in the September 27 letter. Plaintiff that day made the loan, giving Allen a $60,000 check payable to the law firm, which was acknowledged in writing by Weintraub. Despite demand, the check has never been returned. Plaintiff sued Allen and the firm as well as Weintraub, Gold and Alper individually, to recover the funds. Allen has confessed judgment and Weintraub has defaulted, but neither apparently can satisfy the judgment.

In support of its motion for summary judgment against the firm, and Gold and Alper individually (defendants), plaintiff produced the following additional uncontroverted evidence to establish the continued existence of the law firm in the year 1977, although none of this information was known to plaintiff at the time the loan was made. The three individuals continued to share what had been the partnership offices until at least November 1977. The receptionist answered the telephone in the firm name to give the appearance to firm clients that the firm still existed. The $60,000 check received September 27, 1977 was deposited in a special account maintained in the firm name. In July 1977, the three partners signed bank documents certifying that the partnership existed, received a loan, and opened new accounts. Liability insurance was obtained for the firm from January 9, 1977 through January 9, 1978. Firm letterhead was used for court correspondence in October 1977. The partnership filed no certificate of dissolution and made no public announcement of dissolution until the withdrawal of Alper in November 1977 when formal notices were sent out and use of the firm name ceased.

The crux of defendants' opposition to plaintiff's summary judgment motion is ... that as of January 1, 1976 the firm, which had existed since 1972 or 1973, dissolved by oral agreement between Messrs. Weintraub and Gold, that it took no new clients thereafter, that its conduct in 1977 was fully consistent with winding up, and that Weintraub therefore had no authority to bind the partnership in September 1977. Continued use of the firm name and letterhead, defendants insist, was to be only for limited duration, as an aid in the transition to individual practices. . . .

Acts of a partner in apparently carrying on the partnership business in the usual way are binding on the partnership unless that partner has no authority to act, and the person dealing with that partner knows that fact. Here, Weintraub's acts with respect to the escrow deposit were apparently for the benefit of a client and in furtherance of the partnership business. If indeed Weintraub lacked authority to act for the partnership in the particular matter, there is no evidence that plaintiff knew of this. Thus, had no issue of dissolution been raised, unquestionably defendants could have been charged with liability for Weintraub's acts.

Defendants' private agreement in late 1975 to dissolve the partnership does not alter this result. Whether or not the partnership of Weintraub, Gold & Alper continued in 1977 despite the intent of its members is an issue we need not resolve, for a partner who makes, and consents to, continued representations that a partnership in fact exists is estopped to deny that a partnership exists to defeat the claim of a creditor. Here, defendants are estopped to deny their relationship as against plaintiff. Nearly two years after alleged dissolution, the public indicia of the partnership remained undisturbed. Where the firm space, telephone number, telephone book listing and stationery continued in use by the individuals, with no discernible sign of dissolution, we conclude that the partnership continued to be liable as such to a party reasonably relying to its detriment on the impression of an ongoing entity. While partnership by estoppel should not be lightly invoked and generally presents issues of fact, here the undisputed evidence submitted on the summary judgment motion leaves no question for trial. . . .

■ *Affirmed.*

CASE CONCEPTS REVIEW

1. When did the Royal Bank and Trust Company loan money to Roger Allen and deliver the check to the law firm of Weintraub, Gold & Alper?
2. According to Gold and Alper, when did their law firm dissolve?
3. On what legal theory does this court hold that Gold and Alper are liable for the failure of Weintraub to return to the bank the money deposited with him?

The second category of parties entitled to notice of dissolution consists of persons who knew about the partnership but who were not creditors. Unlike creditors, who are entitled to actual notice of dissolution, these third parties receive sufficient notice to absolve the partners of further liability when such notice is of a public nature. Notice by publication in a newspaper in the community where the business has been transacted is sufficient public notice. Because the bankruptcy of a partner, the illegality of the partnership's activities, and court decrees are part of the public record, the requirement to give public notice to noncreditors applies only when the partnership is dissolved by the acts of the partners.

Assume a partner has not actively engaged in the conduct of the partnership business. If the third parties have not learned that he or she was a partner and have dealt with the partnership without placing their faith in this partner, there is no duty to give notice to either of the groups (creditors/noncreditors) on his or her withdrawal.

9. Solvent Partnerships

Upon dissolution of a solvent partnership and winding up of its business, an accounting is made to determine its assets and liabilities. At termination, all firm creditors other than partners are entitled to be paid before the partners are entitled to participate in any of the assets. After firm creditors are paid, the assets of the partnership are distributed among the partners as follows:

1. Each partner who has made advances to the firm or has incurred liability for, or on behalf of, the firm is entitled to be reimbursed.
2. Each partner is then entitled to the return of the capital that he or she has contributed to the firm.
3. Any balance is distributed as profits in accordance with the partnership agreement.

In many partnerships, one partner contributes capital, the other contributes labor, so the partner contributing labor has nothing to be returned in step 2. Of course, the original agreement could place a value on such labor; but unless it does, only the partner who contributes cash or other property will be repaid in step 2.

In the absence of agreement to the contrary, goodwill is a partnership asset that should be accounted for on termination of a partnership. Goodwill is usually defined as "the advantage or benefit, which is acquired by an establishment, beyond the mere value of the capital, stock, funds, or property employed therein, in consequence of the general public patronage and encouragement, which it receives from constant or habitual customers, on account of its local position, or common celebrity, or reputation for skill or affluence, or punctuality, or from other accidental circumstances or necessities, or even from ancient partialities or prejudices." A much narrower definition has been stated as the probability that the old customers will resort to the old place.

Most partnerships build goodwill as an asset. Difficult ethical questions arise, however, in professional partnerships. Traditionally, the prevailing rule relative to professional partnerships was that goodwill did not exist at dissolution, as the reputation of the business entity was dependent on the individual skills of each member.

There appears, however, to be a growing trend throughout the country that recognizes that a professional service partnership possesses goodwill. An ever-increasing number of jurisdictions have held that goodwill may lawfully exist in a professional partnership, and the actual existence of this asset in a particular partnership is a question of fact. The rationale for many of these cases is that the reputation for skill and learning in a particular profession often creates an intangible but valuable asset by gaining the confidence of clients who will speak well of the practice.

If one partner appropriates the goodwill or retains it for his or her own use, he or she must account for it to the other partner unless the other partner is in breach of the agreement. The following case discusses goodwill and the various methods that may be used to determine its value.

CASE

Swann v. Mitchell
435 So.2d 797 (Fla. 1983)

The defendants, Mitchells, own and operate an automobile dealership called Mitchell Motors. The dealership operated as a corporation from 1940 until 1954, and as a partnership thereafter. Swann served as business manager of Mitchell Motors from 1940 until 1967. In 1966, he entered into the partnership with an agreement that provided that Swann would receive 5 percent of the profits and losses of the partnership. The agreement also provided that upon Swann's death, the partnership would pay his estate any undistributed profits of the partnership. In 1967, Swann retired. On June 30, 1979, the Mitchells dissolved the partnership without notifying Swann. They transferred all the partnership's assets to a corporation and issued stock to themselves. Swann discovered the conversion to corporate form in 1980 when he received a final payment from the Mitchells intended to represent his percentage of the profits of the business to the date of dissolution. Swann sued for wrongful dissolution of the partnership and to recover a portion of the capital surplus, including the value of the goodwill of the business. The lower court held that he had no interest in the goodwill of the business.

ADKINS, J.

... The goodwill of a business may be defined as the advantage or benefit the business has beyond the mere value of its property and capital. Goodwill is usually evidenced by general public patronage and is reflected in the increase in profits beyond those that may be expected from the mere use of capital. Accordingly, goodwill should be recognized as an asset of a business, in the absence of a contract to the contrary, and taken into consideration in any sale or valuation of assets.

Courts have frequently recognized goodwill as an asset subject to consideration on an accounting between partners where its disposition is not controlled by the partnership articles and the dissolution was not caused by the wrongful act of one of the partners. . . .

Where some or all of the partners retain possession of any of the assets after dissolution of the partnership, whether their purpose is to use those assets to continue the business in another form or otherwise, they should be required to account to the partnership for the value of those assets at the time of dissolution. . . . The partnership laws of this state also forbid any number less than *all* of the partners in a partnership to dispose of the goodwill of the business. . . .

Upon dissolution of a partnership, the general rule is that it is the right of each partner to have the partnership property converted into money by sale. But, where a sale would be prejudicial to an innocent partner or where circumstances exist which would render distribution in kind, or another method of disposition, to be more favorable to the interests of the parties, such a distribution is permissible and desired. . . . [W]here an actual sale of partnership property does not occur, there are methods available to use to determine the value of the goodwill. Two methods have often been used to calculate the value of goodwill; the capitalization of earnings method and the method of subtracting the value of tangible assets of a business from the sale price of that businesss. Under the capitalization of earnings methods, the goodwill is evaluated by determining the average annual net earnings of the business, determining the value of the business and tangible assets, deducting from the total net earnings those earnings attributable to the tangible property and then capitalizing the balance. Not all aspects of goodwill as a whole are reflected by the use of these formulas. These formulas would not necessarily be reflective of the goodwill which is personal to some particular individual. Elements of goodwill attributable to the personality, skill, or business acumen of the person disposing of a business, for instance, may be evaluated by comparing the profit margin of similar businesses where no such unusual personal elements of goodwill exist to obtain a value for the portion of the goodwill attributable to such personal factors.

We do not attempt to value the goodwill of Mitchell Motors in this case. That determination is properly left to the trial court after receiving the evidence. We merely give a brief discussion of these methods to demonstrate that it is possible to value goodwill in the absence of an actual sale. . . . Accordingly, the decision of the district court is reversed . . . for further proceedings consistent with this opinion.

■ *It is so ordered.*

CASE CONCEPTS REVIEW

1. What is meant by "the goodwill of a business"?
2. How many partners are required to dispose of the partnership's goodwill in a proper manner?
3. What two methods of evaluating goodwill are discussed by this court?
4. Why is the capitalization-of-earnings method more important to the trial court upon the remand of this case?

10. Insolvent Partnerships

Marshaling of assets A principle in equity for a fair distribution of a debtor's assets among creditors.

When the firm is insolvent and a court of equity is responsible for making the distribution of the assets of the partnership, the assets are distributed in accordance with a rule known as **marshaling of assets.** Persons entering into a partnership agreement implicitly agree that the partnership assets will be used for the payment of the firm debts before the payment of any individual debts of the partners. Consequently, a court of equity, in distributing the assets, will give them to the firm's creditors before awarding them to separate creditors or individual partners. The court will give separate assets of the partners to their private creditors before awarding these assets to the firm's creditors. Neither class of creditors is permitted to use the funds belonging to the other until the claims of the other have been satisfied.

The firm's creditors have available two funds out of which to seek payment: assets of the firm and the individual assets of the partners. Individual creditors of the partners have only one fund: the personal assets of the partners. Because of this difference, equity compels the firm's creditors to exhaust the firm's assets before having recourse to the partners' individual assets. The following case provides an example of the impact of the marshaling-of-assets doctrine to the commonplace obligation of the telephone bill.

CASE

McCune & McCune v. Mountain Bell Telephone
758 P.2d 914 (Utah 1988)

ZIMMERMAN, J.

. . . George M. and James P. McCune did business as McCune & McCune, a general law partnership. Mountain Bell provided telephone service to McCune & McCune through November of 1983, when the partnership was dissolved. Upon dissolution, the partnership's telephone service was discontinued, leaving an unpaid balance due of $317.29.

In June of 1984, Mountain Bell, purportedly acting pursuant to a tariff filed with the Public Service Commission, transferred the unpaid partnership debt to . . . the individual business account of . . . partner George McCune. George McCune refused to pay the transferred debt and filed suit against Mountain Bell in district court to enjoin the disconnection of his business service account and to recover damages. Upon stipulation of the parties, that action was stayed to allow McCune to file a complaint with the Public Service Commission to determine the validity and applicability of the tariff provision giving Mountain Bell authority to cross-bill customer accounts. The Commission . . . concluded that Mountain Bell's actions were authorized by the tariff.

On petition for review, . . . George McCune argues that Mountain Bell's tariff allowing cross-billing of unpaid telephone service debts is invalid as applied to him. The tariff provision at issue purports to allow Mountain Bell to transfer unpaid bills for services rendered on any one of a customer's service accounts to any other service account of the same customer. If the bill then remains unpaid, Mountain Bell may, under other tariff provisions, suspend service on the account to which the debt was transferred. These tariffs obviously are designed to provide Mountain Bell with a simplified method of pressuring customers to pay past-due bills by ultimately permitting the company to suspend all services to one who refuses to pay any past-due account. . . . McCune contends that under the circumstances of this case, Mountain Bell's transfer of the partnership debt to his individual business account operates to enlarge Mountain Bell's rights beyond what is permitted by general partnership law; specifically, partnership law requires that partnership assets be marshalled and exhausted before a partnership creditor can reach a partner's individual assets. . . .

The applicable general law is relatively clear. Under the Utah Uniform Partnership Act, partners are jointly, rather than jointly and severally, liable for all debts and obligations of the partnership not arising from tort or breach of trust. If a debt is contractual in origin, common law requires that the partnership's assets be resorted to and exhausted before partnership creditors can reach the partners' individual assets. The Utah courts have never determined whether this common law exhaustion-of-partnership-assets requirement survives under the Utah Uniform Partnership Act. However, it appears to be generally accepted that the uniform act does not disturb this rule and may, in fact, embrace it. The salutary purpose of this common law rule is to preserve fairness among the members of a general partnership. Therefore, we conclude that partnership debts and obligations . . . must be satisfied by partnership assets to the extent any exist before a creditor can seek satisfaction from the individual assets of a partner. . . .

Mountain Bell's actions in this case, which were taken in reliance on the tariff, produced a result that is in conflict with the rule requiring that partnership assets be pursued first. Nothing in the record suggests that Mountain Bell established that the partnership's assets had been exhausted before it attempted to collect the partnership debt from one partner's individual assets. The record only shows that the partnership had been dissolved. Nothing indicates that there had been a winding up of the partnership or that its assets had been distributed to the partners. Despite the partnership's dissolution, it does not cease to exist until the winding up of partnership affairs is completed.

Before the Commission and this Court, Mountain Bell suggests that its actions do not really implicate the general partnership law. It takes the position that under the language of the tariff, any "customer" who is "indebted" to the company is subject to having the past-due debt transferred to any other service accounts with the company. Mountain Bell argues that McCune is a "customer" who is "indebted" to Mountain Bell. That logic was adopted by the Commission. The difficulty with this position is that it permits Mountain Bell to determine what "indebted" means, without regard for the general law applicable to any particular situation. As interpreted by Mountain Bell, "indebted" means only that the amount due is legally ripe for collection for someone and, therefore, that Mountain Bell can pursue any of the partners as

debtors. It is true that under general partnership law, all partnership debts are joint debts of the partners and that all partners are ultimately liable for those debts. However, a creditor's right to proceed against the individual partners is conditioned on having first proceeded against the partnership assets for satisfaction of the debt, something Mountain Bell did not do in this case. Therefore, Mountain Bell claims the right to do under the tariff precisely what it could not otherwise do legally—pursue a partner's assets first.

The tariff, as Mountain Bell and the Commission interpret it, operates so as to create a direct conflict with general partnership law. . . . Nothing in the tariff suggests that it was intended to override the well-settled general law of partnerships and give Mountain Bell the right to treat a partnership debt as an individual partner's debt. Under these circumstances, we cannot find that the Commission's contrary interpretation meets the requirement of reasonableness.

We conclude that Mountain Bell's attempt to recover the partnership debt from one of the partners without first exhausting partnership assets was in conflict with general legal principles and was not authorized by the tariff. Therefore, the Commission's decision regarding the transfer of the partnership debt to McCune's individual business account is

■ *Reversed.*

CASE CONCEPTS REVIEW

1. What action by Mountain Bell Telephone is being challenged as inappropriate?
2. How did Mountain Bell Telephone's actions violate the doctrine of marshaling of assets of the partnership and its partners?
3. Does the court's decision necessarily mean that McCune, as a partner, will never be responsible for the unpaid telephone bill? Why?

The doctrine of marshaling of assets does not apply if a partner conceals his or her existence and permits the other members of the firm to deal with the public as the owners of the business. Under these circumstances, the secret partner's conduct has led the creditors of the active partner to rely on the firm's assets as the separate property of the active partner; and by reason of his or her conduct, the secret partner is estopped from demanding an application of the equity rule that the firm's assets shall be used to pay the firm's creditors first and individual assets used to pay individual creditors. Thus the firm's assets must be shared equally with its creditors and the individual creditors of the active partner. In such a case, because the firm's assets may not be sufficient to pay all its debts when depleted by payments to individual creditors, there may be unpaid firm creditors, and secret partners will be personally liable.

Just as the individual creditors are limited to individual assets, firm creditors are limited to firm assets. Therefore, firm creditors are not entitled to payment out of the individual assets of the partners until the individual creditors have been paid. This rule applies even though the firm creditors may at the same time be individual creditors of a member of the firm. There are two main exceptions to this general rule: (1) The rule for the limit of firm creditors to firm assets applies only where there are firm assets. If no firm assets or no living solvent partner exists, the firm creditors may share equally with the individual creditors in the distribution of the individual estates of the partners. (2) If a partner has fraudulently converted the firm assets to his or her own use, the firm's creditors will be entitled to share equally with individual creditors in the guilty partner's individual assets.

The doctrine of marshaling of assets is not applicable to tort claims under the Uniform Partnership Act. Partners are individually liable in tort for the acts of the firm, its agent, and servants. The liability is joint and several. Thus the injured party may sue the partners individually or as a partnership. The firm assets need not be first used to collect a judgment, and direct action may be taken against individual assets.

CHAPTER SUMMARY

Terminology	1. Dissolution occurs whenever there is a change (deletion or addition) in the partners as members of a partnership.
	2. Winding up involves the process of reducing the assets to cash, paying creditors, returning capital contributions, and distributing the balance to the partners.
	3. Termination of a partnership occurs when the winding-up process is completed.

METHODS OF DISSOLUTION

By Acts of Partners	1. In a partnership at will, any partner may dissolve the partnership at any time without liability.
	2. Expulsion of a partner is a breach of the partnership agreement unless it provides for such expulsion.
	3. Dissolution may occur in violation of the partnership agreement, in which case there is liability for wrongful dissolution.
By Operation of Law	1. Any event that makes it impossible or illegal to continue the partnership operates as a dissolution.
	2. Death or bankruptcy of a partner or the partnership operates as a dissolution.
	3. Insolvency of a partner is not a basis for dissolution.
By Court Decree	1. A court of equity may order dissolution if a partner is incapacitated or is in willful and persistent breach of the partnership agreement.
	2. Other grounds, such as gross misconduct, may also justify a court in ordering dissolution.

THE EFFECT OF DISSOLUTION

On Powers of Partners	1. Dissolution terminates the authority of a partner to act except to wind up partnership affairs.

2. The winding-up process includes liquidating the assets, completing transactions, paying debts, and distributing the balance.

3. Partners possess apparent authority to bind the dissolved partnership unless persons dealing with the partners have actual or constructive notice of the dissolution.

4. On the death of a partner, title to partnership property remains with the surviving partners for the purpose of winding up the partnership.

On Rights of Partners

1. A withdrawing partner has the right to be paid the value of his or her interest in the partnership as of the date of dissolution.

2. A partner has the right to have partnership property used to pay firm debts.

3. If a partnership is wrongfully dissolved, the remaining partners may continue for the agreed term of the partnership. They must settle with the withdrawing partner but may deduct damages caused by the wrongful dissolution.

4. If the partnership is terminated, the former partner is entitled to a share of the net profits earned during the winding-up process.

5. If the partnership is continued, the former partner is entitled to either interest on the value of his or her share of the partnership or a share of the profits until he or she is paid off in the final accounting.

6. The winding-up parties are not entitled to be paid for services in completing unfinished business except in the case of dissolution caused by the death of a partner.

On New Partners

1. A new partner joining an existing partnership is liable for the preexisting debts of the firm only to the extent of the capital contributed.

2. This new partner is personally liable to an unlimited extent for all firm debts that arise after becoming a partner.

On Third Parties

1. An agreement between partners that a withdrawing partner will have no liability is not binding on firm creditors.

2. A withdrawing partner or the estate of a deceased partner has liability for firm debts in the event that firm assets are insufficient to discharge them.

3. Notice of dissolution must be given to third parties to abolish the partners' apparent authority to act on behalf of the firm.

4. This notice may be actual (personal) or constructive (public).

5. All creditors (past and present) must receive actual notice of dissolution if the dissolution is caused by the acts of partners or by a partner's death or incompetency.

6. All other third parties can be informed by constructive notice.

7. No notice needs to be given any third party if the dissolution was caused by bankruptcy, illegality, or court decree.

DISTRIBUTIONS ON TERMINATION

Solvent Partnerships

1. After firm creditors are paid, the assets are distributed in the following order: (1) partnership advances, (2) partnership capital, and (3) undistributed profits.

2. Goodwill is a partnership asset that must be accounted for if either partner retains it.

Insolvent Partnerships

1. If the partnership is unable to pay all of its debts, the doctrine of marshaling of assets will be followed.

2. Firm assets are paid to firm creditors. Individual assets are used to pay individual creditors. Each class must be paid in full before assets can be used to pay the other class.

3. If a firm has no assets, the firm creditors may share in the individual assets. The same is true if a partner has fraudulently converted firm assets to his or her own use.

4. The doctrine of marshaling of assets is not applicable to tort claims.

REVIEW QUESTIONS AND PROBLEMS

1. Match each term in column A with the appropriate statement in column B.

A	B
(1) Dissolution	(a) Notice in a newspaper of general circulation
(2) Winding up	(b) This partnership may be dissolved at any time for any reason
(3) Termination	(c) The process of reducing assets to cash, paying creditors, returning capital contributions, and distributing the balance to the partners
(4) Partnership at will	(d) The advantage or benefit a business has beyond its tangible assets
(5) Marshaling of assets	(e) The legal destruction of the partnership relationship that occurs whenever any partner ceases to be a member of the firm or whenever a new partner joins the firm
(6) Accounting	(f) A method for allocating property among the firm creditors and the individual creditors of the partner
(7) Notice by publication	(g) A formal determination of the partnership's financial condition
(8) Goodwill	(h) The completion of the winding-up process

2. Plaintiff and defendant were partners in a motel, restaurant, and condominium development. Plaintiff was responsible for building and selling the condominiums; defendant ran the motel and restaurant. After the condominiums were sold, plaintiff charged defendant with failure to pay taxes and with commingling partnership funds with his own money. Defendant accused plaintiff of improper accounting methods on the condominiums. Will a court order a dissolution? Why or why not?

3. Mark and Stacy, brother and sister, were partners who had irreconcilable differences. In a suit to dissolve the partnership, a referee was appointed. The referee, to dispose of the assets, asked each partner to submit a bid. The brother submitted a bid for $65,000, but the sister did not bid. She now objects to the sale to her brother. The parties had stipulated that one of them could continue the business. On dissolution, is it permissible for the court to order a sale of partnership property to one of the partners for the purpose of continuing the business? Explain.

4. Hoppen and Powell were partners. Powell breached his fiduciary duties by engaging in a similar business in competition with the partnership. Hoppen filed suit for dissolution, and the court awarded all partnership property to Hoppen because of Powell's conduct. Was the court correct? Explain.

5. Anderson, Ernst, and Sells were partners in an accounting firm. Their partnership agreement did not expressly grant the power to expel any partner. Anderson and Ernst decided that they should carry on the business without Sells, who proved to be lazy and inefficient in producing revenue. How should Anderson and Ernst proceed in removing Sells? Explain.

6. Ashley, Butler, and O'Hara operated a large canning company as a partnership. O'Hara died suddenly and unexpectedly. Scarlett, an attorney, has been appointed as executor of O'Hara's estate. Does Scarlett have a right to participate in the winding up of this partnership? Why or why not?

7. Metals Suppliers was a partnership that bought and sold precious gems and metals. Cooper, one of the partners, flew to New York City to negotiate a major contract. While Cooper was away, Golden died in an automobile accident. Before he received the news of Golden's death, Cooper signed a contract committing the partnership to buy $500,000 worth of diamonds. Is the partnership bound to this contract? Why or why not?

8. Carson, Crocket, and Kitt were partners in the importing business. They needed additional capital to expand. They located an investor named White, who agreed to purchase a one-fourth interest in the partnership by contributing $50,000 in capital. At the time White became a partner, there were several large creditors who had previously lent money to the partnership. The partnership subsequently failed, and the creditors are attempting to assert personal liability against White. Is he liable for these debts? Explain.

9. Peter and Robert Scalera operated a partnership known as Constructors I. They agreed to build a house for the Munns. The project fell into default almost immediately. The partnership ran into severe financial difficulties, and the brothers dissolved their business. Peter and Robert individually met with the Munns to inform them that the brothers were no longer doing business as partners. Each of them offered to complete the construction contract individually, and the Munns elected to have Robert do so. Robert Scalera resumed construction on plaintiff's house but was unable to finish it. The Munns had to pay another contractor to finish the job and were forced to pay for materials that Robert Scalera had charged at a supply company. The plaintiffs sued both brothers to recover damages for breach of contract. Peter Scalera defended by stating that he was discharged from his obligations under the contract because the Munns, after having been notified of the dissolution of the partnership, agreed that Robert alone would complete performance. When a partnership is dissolved, and one partner assumes the partnership's obligations with the consent of the creditors, does this free the discharged partner from liability? Explain.

10. Bush and Baker formed a partnership, but one year later mutually agreed to dissolution. The only notice of dissolution was by publication in a newspaper in the community where their business had been transacted. By agreement, Bush continued to operate the business. O'Neill Company, a previous creditor of the partnership, continued to extend credit to the business. When O'Neill Company was not paid, it brought suit against both Baker and Bush. Should Baker be held liable for the credit extended after dissolution? Why or why not?

11. I.B.M. sold machinery to a limited partnership on credit. Before this debt was paid in full, the partnership was dissolved, and the capital contributions were returned to the limited partners. Thereafter, the partnership could not pay its debts. Can I.B.M. collect from the limited partners? To what extent? Explain.

12. Patrick and Douglas operated a sawmill business as partners. The First Bank made a loan to the partnership, which was secured by a deed of trust on Patrick's home. When the partnership defaulted on this loan, the bank commenced foreclosure proceedings on the house. Patrick seeks to enjoin this foreclosure until a partnership accounting is completed. He contends that partnership assets will discharge this and all other debts. Should an injunction be issued? Why or why not?

13. A partnership consists of three partners, Monroe, Adams, and Madison, who share profits equally. The partnership agreement is silent on the sharing of losses. Monroe loaned the partnership $10,000 and made a capital contribution of $20,000; Adams made a $10,000 capital contribution; Madison made no capital contribution. The partnership now has assets of $80,000 and owes outside creditors $55,000. The partners have decided to dissolve the firm. How much is each partner entitled to receive on dissolution? Explain.

14. Bradley and Smith are the only partners in an insolvent partnership. The firm has assets of $10,000 and liabilities of $100,000. The creditors are Donaldson ($50,000), Charles ($40,000), and Williams ($10,000). The three creditors rank equally in order of priority. Bradley does not have any personal assets or liabilities. Smith has personal assets of $80,000, but he owes the Security Bank $50,000. Smith has no other personal debts. How much are Donaldson, Charles, Williams, and Security Bank each entitled to receive? Explain.

FORMATION
OF CORPORATIONS

CHAPTER PREVIEW

When owners of a business decide that a corporate organization is best suited for their purposes, issues related to how corporations are formed are among the first questions these owners face.

The law of corporations is determined for the most part by state courts and state legislative bodies. Although there is some degree of uniformity, the law of corporations does vary from state to state. Although this chapter presents some general principles about the formation of corporations, the laws of the particular states involved in the corporation's existence must be examined carefully.

The incorporation process, disregarding the creation of a corporation, and the types of ownership devices are discussed in this chapter.

You are a promoter for a corporation to be formed. Among other activities, you hire an attorney to draft the incorporation papers, you rent office space, and you contract for printing services.

What should you do to avoid becoming personally liable on these transactions?

1. Corporation Defined

A *corporation* is an artificial, intangible person or being, created by state law. Incorporating is a method by which individual persons are united into a new legal entity. For this new legal entity, they select a common name and the purposes that it is to accomplish. As a legal entity separate and apart from the persons who had it created, the corporate existence is not affected by the death, incapacity, or bankruptcy of any of the persons involved in its creation or in its operation. Its owners do not have personal liability on its contracts, and it has no liability for the obligations of its shareholders. As a legal entity, a corporation is able to own property and to sue or be sued in its own name in the same manner as a natural person. It has rights and duties separate and apart from its shareholders, and the law recognizes this separation in a variety of situations.

A corporation is also a person for purposes of both tort and criminal law. As an impersonal entity, it can act only through agents and servants, but the corporation is subject to the doctrine of *respondeat superior* and may be punished for certain criminal acts of its agents or servants.

Although a corporation is considered a person under most statutes, there are a few, such as those allowing the appointment of "suitable persons" as parole officers, in which it is not a "person." A corporation is a person for purpose of the due process clause of the Fifth and Fourteenth Amendments to the United States Constitution. For purposes of the privilege against compulsory self-incrimination, it is not a person.

Corporations may be classified in a variety of ways: public or private, for profit (business corporations) or not-for-profit. Each state classifies corporations doing business within the state as foreign or domestic, to denote the state where incorporation took place. Moreover, each state has a variety of statutes relating to specialized corporations such as cooperatives, church and religious corporations, and fraternal organizations. Although all classifications of corporations have significant importance, in this chapter and the following two we are primarily concerned with private, for-profit (business) corporations.

2. The Application for a Charter

Charter The document issued by a state that creates the corporation.

Articles of incorporation The basic governing document of a corporation.

The law prescribes the steps to be taken for the creation of the corporation. Most corporate laws provide that a specified number of adult persons, usually not less than three, may file an application for a **charter.** The application contains the names and addresses of the incorporators, the name of the proposed corporation, the object for which it is to be formed, its proposed duration, the location of its registered office, the name of its registered agent, and information about the stock of the corporation. In most states the information in the application is prepared in a format called the **articles of incorporation.**

Many of these items contained in the articles of incorporation are self-explanatory or are discussed in subsequent sections. Perhaps the least clear items are the registered office and registered agent. The *registered office* is the location where notices, such as a summons or other legal documents, may be delivered. The *registered agent* is the person designated to receive such notices for the corporation. A registered agent of a corporation need not simultaneously serve as an officer or director of such corporation, but an officer usually serves as registered agent. If a corporation fails to maintain a registered agent at its registered office, then the secretary of state becomes the agent of the corporation to receive service of process.

The information supplied about the corporate stock usually includes (1) whether there will be preferred stock or only common stock, (2) the stated or par value of the stock (if the stock has no stated value, then it is called no-par stock), (3) the number of shares of stock that will be authorized, and (4) the number of shares of stock that will actually be issued.

Some states also require the names and addresses of the subscribers to the stock and the amount subscribed and paid in by each. Most applications usually indicate whether the stock is to be paid for in cash or in property.

The application, signed by all the incorporators, is forwarded to a state official, usually the secretary of state. If the application is in order, the official then issues a charter. If the application is not in proper form or if the corporation is being formed for an illegal purpose, the secretary of state will refuse to create the corporation and deny it a charter.

Upon return of the charter properly signed by the secretary of state, it is filed by the incorporators in the proper recording office. The receipt of the charter and its filing are the operative facts that bring the corporation into existence and give it authority and power to do business. It is not necessary that stock be issued or bylaws be adopted for the corporation to exist as a legal entity.

After the charter has been received and filed, the incorporators and all others who have agreed to purchase stock meet and elect a board of directors. They may also approve the bylaws of the corporation if the applicable law so provides. In most instances, the bylaws are approved by the board, not by the shareholders. The board of directors that has been elected then meets, approves the bylaws, elects the officers, calls for the payment of the subscription price for the stock, and makes whatever decisions are necessary to commence business.

3. Corporate Name

One of the provisions in the application for a corporate charter is the proposed name of the corporation. So persons dealing with a business will know that it is a corporation and that the investors therefore have limited liability, the law requires that the corporate name include one of the following words or end with an abbreviation of them: *corporation, company, incorporated,* or *limited.* A corporate name must not be the same as, or deceptively similar to, the name of any domestic corporation or a foreign corporation authorized to do business in the state in which the application is made.

Most states have procedures for reserving a corporate name for a limited period. Inquiry is usually made concerning the availability of a name; if it is available, it is reserved while the articles of incorporation are being prepared. The name may be changed by charter amendment at any time without affecting corporate contracts or title to corporate property in any way.

4. Corporate Powers

The application for a charter includes a statement of the powers desired by the corporation. These are usually stated in quite broad language. A corporation has only such powers as are conferred on it by the state that creates it. The charter, together with the statute under which it is issued, sets forth the express powers of the corporation. All powers reasonably necessary to carry out the expressed powers are implied.

The following general powers are ordinarily granted to the corporation by statute: (1) to have perpetual existence; (2) to sue and be sued; (3) to have a corporate name and corporate seal; (4) to own, use, convey, and deal in both real and personal property; (5) to borrow and lend money other than to officers and directors; (6) to purchase, own, and dispose of securities; (7) to enter into contracts of every kind; (8) to make charitable contributions; (9) to pay pensions and establish pension plans; and (10) to have all powers necessary or convenient to effect any of the other purposes.

Ultra vires "Beyond power." The acts of a corporation are ultra vires when they are beyond the power or authority of the corporation as granted by the state in its charter.

Any acts of a corporation that are beyond the authority, express or implied, given to it by the state in the charter are said to be **ultra vires** acts—"beyond the authority." If a corporation performs acts or enters into contracts to perform acts that are *ultra vires,* the state creating such a corporation may forfeit its charter for misuse of its corporate authority. The extent of the misuse is controlling in determining whether the state will take away its franchise or merely enjoin the corporation from further *ultra vires* conduct.

Although third parties have no right to object to the *ultra vires* acts of a corporation, a stockholder may bring court action to enjoin a corporation from performing an *ultra vires* contract. If the corporation sustains losses or damages because of the *ultra vires* venture, the corporation may recover from the directors who approved the contracts. When the directors exceed corporate powers, they may become personally liable for resulting losses.

At common law, a corporation had no liability on contracts beyond its corporate powers because the corporation had capacity to do only those things expressly authorized within its charter or incidental thereto. Most modern statutes, including the Model Business Corporation Act, provide that all *ultra vires* contracts are enforceable. Neither party to such a contract may use *ultra vires* as a defense. *Ultra vires* conduct on the part of the corporation may be enjoined by the state or any shareholder; but otherwise, contracts previously made are binding, whether they be wholly executory, partially executed, or fully performed.

5. Bylaws

Bylaws Rules for government of a corporation or other organization.

A **bylaw** is a rule governing and managing the affairs of the corporation. It is binding on all shareholders but not third parties, unless the third parties have knowledge of it. The bylaws contain provisions establishing the corporate seal and the form of the stock certificate, the number of officers and directors, the method of electing them and removing them from office, as well as the enumeration of their duties. Bylaws specify the time and place of the meetings of the directors and the shareholders. Together with the articles of incorporation and the applicable statute, the bylaws provide rules for operating the corporation. The bylaws are subservient to the articles of incorporation and the statute but are of greater authority than, for instance, a single resolution of the board. Failure to follow the bylaws constitutes a breach of the fiduciary duties of a director or officer.

Bylaws are valid if they are reasonable and are consistent with the corporate charter and the applicable statutes. Bylaws may be illegal and void. For example, a bylaw of a corporation gave the president the power to manage the corporation's affairs. Such a bylaw is void because the law provides that the affairs of corporations shall be managed by a board of directors.

The power to alter, amend, or revoke the bylaws is vested in the board of directors unless reserved to the shareholders by statute or by the articles of incorporation. The board cannot, however, repeal, amend, or add to the bylaws if the change will affect the vested rights of a shareholder.

6. Domestic and Foreign Corporations

To a state or country, corporations organized under its laws are *domestic* corporations; those organized under the laws of another state or country are *foreign* corporations.

Domestic corporations become qualified to do business upon receipt and recording of their charter. Foreign corporations with significant intrastate activities must also "qualify" to do business by obtaining a certificate of authority and by paying the license fees and taxes levied on local businesses. A foreign corporation engaged wholly in *interstate* commerce through a state need not qualify in that state.

Most state statutes require foreign corporations to qualify to do business by filing a copy of their articles of incorporation with the secretary of state. They are also required to appoint an agent upon whom process may be served and to maintain an office in the state. Failure to comply results in a denial of the right of access to the courts as a plaintiff. Some states allow a plaintiff that has failed to obtain a certificate of authority a continuance in the case for a short time to obtain the certificate. In the following case, this liberal view was not enough to save the plaintiff, which only challenged the constitutionality of the requirement and lost.

CASE

Christian Services v. Northfield Villa, Inc.
385 N.W.2d 904 (Neb. 1986)

HASTINGS, J.

Plaintiff has appealed from a summary judgment in favor of the defendant, Northfield Villa, Inc., based on the incapacity of the plaintiff, a foreign corporation, to maintain a legal action in this state because of the lack of a certificate of authority. We affirm.

The original petition seeking damages in contract was filed on July 2, 1981, in which plaintiff alleged that it was a Missouri corporation. The petition contained no allegation that it possessed a certificate of authority to conduct business in Nebraska, as required by Neb. Rev. Stat. . . .

On October 18, 1984, defendant filed a motion for summary judgment, to which was attached a certain affidavit identifying certified copies of various records of the Secretaries of State of both Nebraska and Missouri. . . . Those records disclose that although a certificate of authority to transact business in Nebraska had been issued, the corporation was dissolved on August 4, 1980, for nonpayment of corporate taxes. Additionally, it appears of record that the corporate status of the plaintiff had been forfeited under the laws of the State of Missouri as of January 1, 1983, for failure to file an annual report. There is no dispute as to those facts.

On November 13, 1984, plaintiff filed a motion to continue the hearing on defendant's motion for summary judgment. . . . [The court] granted the plaintiff until December 31, 1984, to comply with the provisions of § 21-20,121 regarding a certificate of authority.

Pursuant to order of the court, further hearing was set for January 9, 1985. At that time, and pursuant to request of the plaintiff's counsel, the hearing was continued to January 21, 1985. Additional evidence was received at that time, but there was nothing offered by the plaintiff in support of any showing that it possessed a certificate of authority to do business in Nebraska. Accordingly, upon submission of the cause to the court, the motion for summary judgment was sustained.

The plaintiff claims error on the part of the trial court in . . . granting defendant's motion for summary judgment.

Section 21-20,121 provides in part as follows: "No foreign corporation transacting business in this state without a certificate of authority . . . shall be permitted to maintain any action . . . in any court of this state, until such corporation shall have obtained a certificate of authority." The interpretation of this section as it applies to the pending case is determined by *Rigid Component Systems v. Nebraska Component Systems, Inc.*, 276 N.W.2d 659 (1979).

According to *Rigid Component Systems*, . . . objection to a nonauthorized corporation's maintaining a lawsuit may be raised at any time during the pendency of such litigation, and the court may, in its discretion, limit the time that the plaintiff can have for procuring the necessary certificate of authority. Here, the plaintiff was allowed in excess of 60 days to obtain the necessary proof, and when time ran out, it did not request any extension. There was no abuse of discretion on the part of the trial court. . . .

■ *Affirmed.*

CASE CONCEPTS REVIEW

1. In what state was this lawsuit filed?
2. What was the legal status of the plaintiff in this state?
3. How much time elapsed from the filing of the lawsuit until the entry of summary judgment?
4. Do you think the outcome would have been the same if the trial court had allowed the plaintiff less than sixty days to obtain a certificate of authority?

Of course, a corporation that cannot be a plaintiff because of lack of a certificate could be sued in a state if it had sufficient minimum contacts to satisfy due process. Generally, subjecting a foreign corporation to a state's qualification statutes requires more activity within a state than for service of process or for taxation of its income and property. Qualification is essential if there are local activities that constitute transacting business.

In a real sense, this denial of access to the courts as a plaintiff prevents a corporation from conducting business, because its contracts are not enforceable by suit, and debtors would thus be able to avoid payment to the corporation. Transacting business within the state without complying with the statute also subjects the corporation and its officers to statutory penalties, such as fines.

The term *doing business* is not reducible to an exact and certain definition. The Model Business Corporation Act defines the term by saying that a foreign corporation is *doing business* when "some part of its business substantial and continuous in character and not merely casual or occasional" is transacted within a state. A corporation is not *doing business* in a state merely because it is involved in litigation or maintains a bank account or an office within a state for the transfer of its stock. The Act also states that a foreign corporation is not required to obtain a license to do business by reason of the fact that (1) it is in the mail-order business and receives orders from a state that are accepted and filled by shipment from without the state, and (2) it uses salespeople within a state to obtain orders that are accepted outside the state. If the orders are accepted or filled within the state, or if any sale, repair, or replacement is made from stock physically present within the state in which the order is obtained, a foreign corporation is required to obtain a license.

The following case involves a further discussion of the term *doing business.* This case contrasts this term with the phrase *transacting any business* and concludes that a corporation must engage in more activities within the state's boundaries to be *doing business* as opposed to *transacting business.*

CASE

Yangming Marine Transport Corporation v. Revon Products U.S.A., Inc.

536 A.2d 633 (Md. 1988)

ELDRIDGE, J.

Maryland Code of the Corporations and Associations Article states that, before doing any interstate or foreign business in Maryland, a foreign corporation shall "register" with the State Department of Assessments and Taxation (the Department). The Corporations and Associations Article provides that, before doing any intrastate business in Maryland, a foreign corporation shall "qualify" with the Department. Finally, under § 7-301 of the same Article, if a foreign corporation is doing or has done "any intrastate, interstate, or foreign business" in Maryland without registering or qualifying, then neither the corporation nor any person claiming under it may maintain a suit in any court of this State.

The principal question raised in this case is whether Yangming Marine Transport Corporation (Yangming) is doing business in Maryland, . . . and is thereby barred from maintaining this action because of its failure to register or to qualify. . . .

Yangming exists under the laws of the Republic of China and is headquartered in Taipei, Taiwan. The parties have stipulated that, at all times relevant to this case, Yangming was "engaged in the transportation of goods by sea for hire in foreign commerce." . . .

Yangming operated a weekly container shipping service between several ports on the East Coast of the United States, including Baltimore, and various ports in the Far East, including ports in Korea. Yangming's agent in Baltimore was Maher Shipping, Inc. Maher's duties included husbanding cargo for Yangming's vessels and arranging port services, facilities, and supplies for Yangming's vessels while in the Port of Baltimore. . . .

At all times relevant to this case, Yangming . . . had neither registered nor qualified to do business in Maryland.

Yangming's suit against the defendant Revon Products, U.S.A. (Revon), arose out of a dispute over freight charges. In early 1982, a Korean seller agreed to ship certain goods freight prepaid to Revon in Baltimore. The goods were to travel on one of Yangming's vessels. . . . When the goods arrived in Baltimore in the Spring of 1982, Maher informed Revon that the seller had not paid the freight charges and that Revon would not receive the goods until it discharged this $6,000 obligation. After Revon issued a check and obtained the goods, the seller claimed that it had indeed prepaid the freight and asserted that Revon could not deduct the $6,000 from the contract price. As a result, Revon stopped payment on the check.

In March 1985, Yangming filed a complaint . . . to recover the $6,000 from Revon. . . .

In December 1985, the trial court granted Revon's motion to dismiss. . . . The trial judge concluded that, because Yangming's activities in the Port of Baltimore amounted to "doing business" in Maryland, Yangming was required to register . . . or to qualify. . . . As Yangming had taken neither step, the trial judge held that § 7-301 barred Yangming from bringing an action in any court of Maryland. . . .

Yangming appealed. . . .

. . . We have held that § 7-301 . . . bars an unqualified or unregistered foreign corporation from suing in Maryland courts only if the corporation is doing such a substantial amount of localized business in this State that the corporation could be deemed "present" here. . . .

[In Maryland, when a foreign corporation is a defendant, the court may obtain personal jurisdiction over it by servicing the legal papers under the long-arm statute. To satisfy due process requirements, foreign corporations served under the long-arm statute only must be "transacting any business" in Maryland. This Court compares the "doing business" language used for plaintiffs with the phrase "transacting any business" used for defendants and concludes:]

The "transacting business" test . . . requires far fewer contacts with the State than did the "doing business" test. Consequently, under § 7-301, a foreign corporation is "doing business" in Maryland only if the corporation conducts a significantly greater amount of local activity in Maryland than would be necessary for Maryland to assert personal jurisdiction over the corporation [which is "transacting business"].

Here solicitation does not constitute "doing business." As to the conduct beyond solicitation, . . . activities merely incidental to, and directly connected with, the solicitation of interstate sales do not meet the test implicit in the statutory language in question. . . .

In sum, we have interpreted § 7-301 as allowing a foreign corporation, not engaged in significant business activity in Maryland, to maintain an action in the courts of the State despite a failure to register or qualify. We see no reason to construe § 7-301 differently in the case of a corporation that is engaged wholly in foreign commerce. Consequently, we hold that, under § 7-301, an unregistered or unqualified foreign corporation that engages in either interstate or foreign business activity in Maryland is barred from suing in the courts of this State only if the corporation also engages in localized business activity in Maryland such that it is "doing business" here.

Yangming maintains that it is engaged in transportation in international and foreign commerce, only. . . .

Revon . . . concedes that Yangming is engaged in foreign commerce. Revon maintains, however, that the trial court was correct in concluding that Yangming's activities in the port of Baltimore constituted "doing business." . . .

In the present case, there is no dispute as to the nature or extent of Yangming's activities. Yangming has an agent and, in connection with its shipping activities, enters into contracts in Maryland. There is, however, no evidence that Yangming pays taxes, maintains property, inventory, or research and development facilities, or engages in management functions in Maryland. Yangming has no office, telephone listing, bank accounts, or employees in Maryland. Moreover, as shown by the record, Yangming's attempts to solicit business were by advertising in national publications. . . .

Moreover, Yangming's activities in the Port of Baltimore are integral and necessary parts of its wholly foreign shipping business. . . . Yangming's activities in the Port of Baltimore were necessary and essential to its activities in foreign commerce; the shipowner's activities in Baltimore were not sufficiently distinct from its foreign commerce or sufficiently localized in Maryland to constitute "doing business" within the meaning of § 7-301. . . .

As Yangming was not doing business within the meaning of § 7-301, and thus was not barred from bringing this suit, Revon's motion to dismiss should not have been granted.

■ *Judgment reversed.*

CASE CONCEPTS REVIEW

1. What contacts did Yangming have with individuals or organizations in the state of Maryland?
2. What is the factual basis of Yangming's claim for $6,000 against Revon?
3. What is the distinction between the phrases *transacting business* and *doing business* in terms of the court having personal jurisdiction over the parties?
4. Why does this court conclude that Yangming was not doing business in Maryland?

7. Promoters

Blue-sky laws Popular name for state acts providing for the regulation and supervision of investment securities.

A *promoter*, as the name implies, promotes the corporation and assists in bringing it into existence. One or more promoters may be involved in making application for the charter, holding the first meeting of shareholders, entering into preincorporation subscription agreements, and engaging in other activities necessary to bring the corporation into existence. Promoters are responsible for compliance with the applicable **blue-sky laws** (statutes relating to the sale of securities), including the preparation of a prospectus if required.

LIABILITY. Many of these activities involve the incurring of contractual obligations or debts. Preparation of the application for a charter usually requires the assistance of a lawyer, and it must be accompanied by the required filing fee. Legal questions about who has liability for these obligations and debts frequently arise. Is the promoter liable? Is the corporation after formation liable? Are both liable?

Certain general principles of contract and agency law prevent simple answers to these questions. First, a promoter is not an agent prior to incorporation, because there is no principal. A party who purports to act as an agent for a nonexistent principal is generally liable as a principal. Thus, a promoter is liable on preincorporation contracts unless the other party is aware that the corporation has not been formed and agrees that the promoter is not to be bound by the contract personally. Second, the corporation technically cannot ratify the contracts of promoters because ratification requires capacity to contract both at the time of the contract and at the time of the ratification.

NO LIABILITY. To avoid the difficulties caused by these legal theories, the law has used certain fictions to create an obligation on the part of the corporation and to provide a means to eliminate liability on the part of the promoters. One fiction is that a novation occurs. This theory proceeds on the premise that when the corporation assents to the contract, the third party agrees to discharge the promoter and to look only to the corporation. Establishing a novation often fails because of a lack of proof of any agreement to release the promoter, as occurred in the following case, even though the original contract required that the promoter incorporate and transfer the contract to the new corporation.

CASE

Skandinavia, Inc. v. Cormier
514 A.2d 1250 (N.H. 1986)

Plaintiff, an underwear manufacturer, contracted to sell its business to the defendant Cormier. Plaintiff was to receive commissions on subsequent sales of underwear and other products. The agreement provided that Cormier "shall have a new corporation, 'Polypro, Inc.' formed and shall assign all of his right and obligation" under the agreement to the corporation. Pursuant to the agreement, inventory was transferred to Cormier in late June 1981. On July 22, 1981, Polypro, Inc. was formed and capitalized in the amount of $2,500. Correspondence between the parties indicates that thereafter the plaintiff conducted business with both Cormier and Polypro, Inc.

Cormier failed to pay the commission and plaintiff sued Cormier personally to collect. The trial court found for the plaintiff.

BATCHELDER, J.

. . . Cormier raises several arguments in an effort to avoid personal liability. First, he argues that Polypro, Inc., rather than himself, is liable under the agreement because he acted only as a promoter for the corporation. In support of this contention, he refers to paragraph three of the agreement: "It is understood by the parties that in order to complete this transaction, Cormier shall have a new corporation, 'Polypro, Inc.' formed and shall assign all of his right and obligation under this agreement to said Corporation."

We agree with the master that Cormier's attempt to avoid contractual liability by claiming the status of a promoter is unavailing. The contractual language quoted above does not discharge Cormier.

> As a general rule promoters are personally liable on contracts which they have entered into personally, even though they have contracted for the benefit of a projected corporation; the promoter is not discharged from liability by the subsequent adoption of the contract by the corporation when formed, unless there is a novation.

Cormier further contends that Polypro, Inc. was incorporated and acted in reliance on the agreement, thereby vesting rights in the corporation and making the corporation liable under the agreement. This argument is unpersuasive because the corporation took no action to adopt or ratify the agreement. Although the defendant contends that the corporation assumed the rights and obligations of the agreement, we find that Polypro, Inc. did not adhere to the statutory formalities required for the conduct of business affairs. No contracts were authorized by the corporation's board of directors, and no authority was granted by the corporation to any of its officers to purchase the inventory from Cormier. Accordingly, we agree with the master's finding that Polypro, Inc. did not become liable under the agreement.

Likewise, we are not persuaded that a novation occurred. "A novation is a substituted contract that includes as a party one who was neither the obligor nor the obligee of the original duty." A novation requires "(1) a previous, valid obligation; (2) the agreement of all parties to a new contract; (3) the extinguishment of the old contract; and (4) validity of the new one."

> A promoter may be discharged from liability . . . on a pre-incorporation contract by a novation if the corporation assumes the contract and the other contracting party assents to the substitution of the corporation for the promoter. . . . [But t]he doctrine of novation is highly technical, and a true novation seldom occurs in promotion cases.

Cormier could not unilaterally discharge himself from the contract he signed with the plaintiff; some affirmative action by the plaintiff was needed to release Cromier individually. The evidence indicates that the plaintiff relied on Cormier's personal wealth in entering into this unsecured agreement. We find no express intent on the plaintiff's part to release Cromier from liability. Accordingly, no express novation occurred. This court has stated, however, that "[a]ssent to the terms of a novation need not be shown by express words, but may be implied from the facts and circumstances attending the transaction and the conduct of the parties." The master ruled that this was not one of the exceptional instances in which a novation occurred after a corporate promotion contract because there was no evidence of assent to such a substitution on the plaintiff's part. He found that the evidence "demonstrated that no assignment, release, accord and satisfaction, equitable assignment, or express or implied novation occurred." . . . In this case, we agree with the master's assessment of the evidence regarding the alleged assignment and novation. . . .

■ *Affirmed.*

CASE CONCEPTS REVIEW

1. What role did Cormier play in the purchase of the underwear manufacturer?
2. Why was Polypro, Inc. formed?
3. Cormier makes three arguments why he should not be personally liable for the nonpayment of the commission. What are these arguments?
4. Why does the court reject each of these arguments?

THEORIES OF CORPORATE LIABILITY.   Another theory that is used to determine liability on preincorporation obligations may be described as the *offer and acceptance theory*. Under this theory, a contract made by a promoter for the benefit of the corporation is an offer that may be accepted by the corporation after it comes into existence. Acceptance of the benefits of the contract constitutes a formal ratification of it. If the corporation does not accept the offer, it is not liable. The promoter may or may not be liable, depending on the degree of disclosure. Corporations have also been held liable on promoters' contracts on theories that may be called the *consideration theory* and the *quasi-contract theory*. After incorporation, directors may promise to pay for expenses and services of promoters. Under the consideration theory, their promise will be binding and supported by sufficient consideration, on the theory of services previously rendered.

The quasi-contract theory holds that corporations are liable by implication for the necessary expenses and services incurred by the promoters in bringing them into existence, because such expenses and services accrue or inure to the benefit of the corporation. The corporation would be unjustly enriched if liability did not exist.

Finally, some states have abandoned trying to justify corporate liability with a legal theory and have simply provided by statute that corporations are liable for the reasonable expenses incurred by promoters.

Avoidance of Liability. The parties frequently do not intend the promoter to be liable on a preincorporation contract. A promoter may avoid personal liability by informing the other party that he or she does not intend to be liable and is acting in the name of, and solely on, the credit of a corporation to be formed. But if the promoter represents that there is an existing corporation when there is none, the promoter is liable. A promoter should make sure that contracts entered into on behalf of the proposed corporation are worded to relieve him or her of personal liability, if that is the intent.

Promoters occupy a fiduciary relationship toward the prospective corporation. Their position does not give them the right to secure any benefit or advantage over the corporation itself or over other shareholders. Promoters cannot purchase property and then sell it to the corporation at a profit; nor do they have a right to receive a commission from a third party for the sale of property to the corporation. In general, however, they may sell property acquired prior to the time they started promoting the corporation, provided that they sell it to an unbiased board of directors after full disclosure of all pertinent facts.

DISREGARDING THE CORPORATE ENTITY

8. Piercing the Corporate Veil

One of the basic advantages of the corporate form of business organization is the limitation of shareholder liability. Corporations are formed for the express purpose of limiting one's risk to the amount of one's investment in the stock. Sometimes suits are brought to hold the shareholders personally liable for an obligation of a corporation or to hold a parent corporation liable for debts of a subsidiary.

Such suits attempt to "pierce the corporate veil." They ask the court to look behind the corporate entity and take action as though no entity existed separating it from the owners. Plaintiffs in these suits may not ask that the corporate entity be disregarded simply because all the stock is owned by the members of a family or by one person or by another corporation.

The lending of money to a corporation one controls or guaranteeing its debts is not enough to justify piercing the corporate veil. It would frustrate the purposes of corporate law to expose directors, officers, and shareholders to personal liability for the debts of the corporation when they contribute funds to, or on behalf of, a corporation for the purpose of assisting the corporation to meet its financial obligations. The loan or guarantee may assist the corporate efforts to survive, thus benefiting the creditors. If such acts were grounds to eliminate the separate corporate entity, such loans and guarantees usually would not be forthcoming.

9. Alter Ego Theory

Notwithstanding the foregoing general principles, courts today frequently disregard the separate corporate entity and pierce the corporate veil. They do so to hold parent corporations liable for the debts of a subsidiary and to hold individual shareholders liable for corporate obligations. Many cases use a theory known as the *alter ego theory*.

The alter ego theory disregards the separate corporate existence when one corporation is organized, controlled, and conducted to make it a mere instrumentality of another corporation or when individual shareholders conduct themselves in disregard of the separate entity. If the corporate entity is disregarded by the shareholders themselves, so there is such a unity of ownership and interest that separateness of the corporation has ceased to exist, the alter ego doctrine will be followed.

Some of the factors considered significant in justifying a disregard of the corporate entity using the alter ego theory are (1) undercapitalization of a corporation, (2) failure to observe corporate formalities such as annual meetings, (3) nonpayment of dividends, (4) siphoning of corporate funds by the dominant stockholders, (5) nonfunctioning of other officers or directors, (6) absence of corporate records, and (7) use of the corporation as a facade for operations of the dominant stockholders.

10. Promotion of Justice Theory

In addition to the alter ego theory, courts will pierce the corporate veil if the ends of justice require it. Justice will require the disregarding of the corporate entity if the liability-causing activity did not occur only for the benefit of the corporation, if the liable corporation has been gutted and left without funds by those controlling it to avoid actual or potential liability, or if the corporation has been used to defraud or otherwise promote injustice, such as the violation of a statute.

For example, assume that A and B sold a business and agreed not to compete with the buyer for a given number of years. In violation of the contract, A and B organized a corporation in which they became the principal stockholders and managers; the buyer may enjoin the corporation from competing with him, and he may do so effectively, as he could have enjoined A and B from establishing a competing business. Similarly, assume that a state law provides that a person may not hold more than one liquor license at a time. This law cannot be circumvented by forming multiple corporations. The attempt to evade the statute would justify piercing the corporate veil. The following case distinguishes between the alter ego and promotion of justice theories and adopts the modern trend of liberally piercing the corporate veil.

CASE

Castleberry v. Branscum
721 S.W.2d 270 (Tex. 1986)

SPEARS, J.

Joe Castleberry sued Texan Transfer, Inc. and Byron Branscum and Michael Byboth, individually, on a promissory note signed by the corporation for Castleberry's shares in the closely held corporation. The jury found that Branscum and Byboth used Texan Transfer as a sham to perpetrate a fraud. Based on the jury findings, the trial court rendered judgment against Texan Transfer, disre-

garding its corporate fiction to hold both Byboth and Branscum individually liable. The court of appeals reversed. . . . We reverse the court of appeals judgment and affirm the trial court, because under the applicable law there was some evidence to support the jury's verdict, . . . and disregarding the corporate fiction is a fact question for the jury.

Disregarding the Corporate Fiction

The corporate form normally insulates shareholders, officers, and directors from liability for corporate obligations; but when these individuals abuse the corporate privilege, courts will disregard the corporate fiction and hold them individually liable. We disregard the corporate fiction, even though corporate formalities have been observed and corporate and individual property have been kept separately, when the corporate form has been used as part of a basically unfair device to achieve an inequitable result.

Specifically, we disregard the corporate fiction:

(1) when the fiction is used as a means of perpetrating fraud;

(2) where a corporation is organized and operated as a mere tool or business conduit of another corporation;

(3) where the corporate fiction is resorted to as a means of evading an existing legal obligation;

(4) where the corporate fiction is employed to achieve or perpetrate monopoly;

(5) where the corporate fiction is used to circumvent a statute; and

(6) where the corporate fiction is relied upon as a protection of crime or to justify wrong.

Many Texas cases have blurred the distinction between alter ego and the other bases for disregarding the corporate fiction and treated alter ego as a synonym for the entire doctrine of disregarding the corporate fiction. However, . . . alter ego is only one of the bases for disregarding the corporate fiction: "where a corporation is organized and operated as a mere tool or business conduit of another corporation."

Alter ego applies when there is such unity between corporation and individual that the separateness of the corporation has ceased and holding only the corporation liable would result in injustice. It is shown from the total dealings of the corporation and the individual, including the degree to which corporate formalities have been followed and corporate and individual property have been kept separately, the amount of financial interest, ownership and control the individual maintains over the corporation, and whether the corporation has been used for personal purposes. Alter ego's rationale is: "if the shareholders themselves disregard the separation of the corporate enterprise, the law will also disregard it so far as necessary to protect individual and corporate creditors."

The basis used here to disregard the corporate fiction, a sham to perpetrate a fraud, is separate from alter ego. It is sometimes confused with intentional fraud; however, "[n]either fraud nor an intent to defraud need be shown as a prerequisite to disregarding the corporate entity; it is sufficient if recognizing the separate corporate existence would bring about an inequitable result." . . . Thus, we held that note holders could disregard the corporate fiction without showing common-law fraud or deceit

when the circumstances amounted to constructive fraud. In *Tigrett v. Pointer*, the Dallas Court of Appeals disregarded the corporate fiction, stating correctly that "[w]hether [the individual] misled them or subjectively intended to defraud them is immaterial . . . [f]or the action was so grossly unfair as to amount to constructive fraud."

To prove there has been a sham to perpetrate a fraud, tort claimants and contract creditors must show only constructive fraud. We distinguished constructive from actual fraud in *Archer v. Griffith*:

> Actual fraud usually involves dishonesty of purpose or intent to deceive, whereas constructive fraud is the breach of some legal or equitable duty which, irrespective of moral guilt, the law declares fraudulent because of its tendency to deceive others, to violate confidence, or to injure public interests.

Because disregarding the corporate fiction is an equitable doctrine, Texas takes a flexible fact-specific approach focusing on equity. . . . Dean Hildebrand, a leading authority on Texas corporation law, stated well the equitable approach: "When this [disregarding the corporate fiction] should be done is a question of fact and common sense. The court must weigh the facts and consequences in each case carefully, and common sense and justice must determine [its] decision." . . . [The court then reviewed the evidence and concluded.]

. . . A jury could find that Byboth and Branscum manipulated a closely-held corporation, Texan Transfer, and formed competing businesses to ensure that Castleberry did not get paid. Castleberry had little choice but to sell his shares back to the corporation. While this evidence may be no evidence of intentional fraud, constructive fraud, not intentional fraud, is the standard for disregarding the corporate fiction on the basis of a sham to perpetrate a fraud.

In determining if there is an abuse of the corporate privilege, courts must look through the form of complex transactions to the substance. The variety of shams is infinite, but many fit this case's pattern: a closely held corporation owes unwanted obligations; it siphons off corporate revenues, sells off much of the corporate assets, or does other acts to hinder the on-going business and its ability to pay off its debts; a new business then starts up that is basically a continuation of the old business with many of the same shareholders, officers, and directors. . . .

■ *We reverse the court of appeals' judgment and affirm the trial court's judgment.*

CASE CONCEPTS REVIEW

1. Which of the six justifications for piercing the corporate veil best describes the alter ego theory?

2. What justification does this court use to pierce the corporate veil of Texan Transfer?

3. What actions of Byboth and Branscum amounted to fraud?

CORPORATE STOCK

11. Kinds of Stock

A *stock certificate* is written evidence of the ownership of a certain number of *shares of stock* of a corporation. The certificate recognizes a certain person as being a *shareholder* with rights in the corporation—primarily, the right to share in profits and to receive a portion of the assets at time of dissolution. Shareholders also have the right to elect directors, but shareholders do not take an active role in the daily management of the business.

STOCKS VERSUS BONDS.   Stock must be distinguished from a bond. A *bond* is an obligation of the corporation to pay a certain sum of money in the future at a specified rate of interest. It is comparable to a corporation's promissory note. A bondholder is a creditor of the corporation, whereas a shareholder is an owner of the corporation. A shareholder has a right to receive dividends if they are declared by the board of directors and to participate in the assets of the corporation after all creditors have been paid. A bondholder has no right to vote or to participate in the management and control of a corporation.

COMMON AND PREFERRED STOCK.   *Common stock* is the simplest type of corporate stock. It entitles the owner to share in the control, profits, and assets of the corporation in proportion to the amount of common stock held. Such a shareholder has no advantage, priority, or preference over any other class of shareholders unless otherwise specified.

Preferred stock has priority over other classes of stock in claiming dividends or assets on dissolution. The most important right given to a preferred shareholder is the right to receive a certain specified dividend, even though the earnings are not sufficient to pay like dividends to common shareholders.

Preferred stock may be cumulative or noncumulative. If *cumulative,* any dividends that are not paid because of lack of earnings accrue and are paid when earnings are available. If *noncumulative,* only the current year's preferred dividend is paid out of current earnings. If nothing is stated about the payment of the dividends, the preferred stock is cumulative, and preferred dividends and all arrears thereon must be paid before a dividend is declared on common stock.

Preferred stock also may be classified as participating or nonparticipating. Owners of *participating* preferred stock are entitled to the preferred dividend and to any dividends declared after the common shareholders have been paid an amount equal to the preferred dividend. When the only amount of dividend a preferred shareholder is entitled to receive is the preference, the preferred stock is *nonparticipating.* In this latter situation, the common shareholders receive as dividends whatever amount the company can pay after paying the preferred dividends. The common shareholders may earn an amount of dividends equal to, less than, or greater than that received by the preferred shareholders. When the preferred stock is not explicitly described in the articles of incorporation, it is presumed to be nonparticipating.

Stock warrant A certificate that gives the holder the right to subscribe for and purchase, at a stated price, a given number of shares of stock in a corporation.

STOCK WARRANT.   A **stock warrant** is a certificate that gives its holder the right to subscribe for and purchase a given number of shares of stock in a corporation at a stated price. It is usually issued in connection with the sale of other shares of stock or of bonds, although the law of some states permits the issuance of stock warrants entirely separate and apart from the sale of other securities. Warrants are transferable. The option to purchase contained in the warrant may or may not be limited as to time or otherwise conditioned. Warrants have value and can readily be sold on the market in the same fashion as other securities.

PAR VALUE STOCK.   Each share of stock traditionally is designated by the incorporators as having a stated par value. This par value notation is not necessarily related to the fair market value of the stock. In essence, the par value is the dollar amount that the corporation must receive and enter into its stated capital account for each share of stock sold.

NO-PAR STOCK.   The statutes of most states provide that a corporation may issue stock with *no par value*. The value of no-par stock is determined by its sale price in the open market or by the price set by the directors as a "stated value." Shareholders, creditors of the corporation, and the public are not misled or prejudiced by this type of stock, because there is no holding out that the stock has any particular face value. All persons dealing in no-par stock are put on notice that they should investigate the corporation's assets and its financial condition.

Watered stock Corporate stock issued by a corporation for property at an overvaluation, or stock issued for which the corporation receives nothing in payment.

WATERED STOCK.   **Watered stock** is stock that has been issued as fully paid, when in fact its full *par value* has not been paid in money, property, or services. The original owner of watered stock has liability for the unpaid portion of its stated value. If Catherine exchanges property worth $200 for 1,000 shares of $1 par value stock, she owes the corporation $800. If the corporation becomes insolvent, a creditor may require that the balance due be paid by Catherine.

The liability for watered stock arises because the stated capital account of a corporation represents the total par value of all the shares of the corporation. The public, including corporate creditors, has a right to assume that the stock issued has been paid for in full. The corporation in effect represents that assets have been received in payment equal in amount to the corporation's stated capital account. If stock is issued and the actual assets in money value received by the corporation are less than the par value, there is watered stock.

While the watering of par value stock is easy to envision, the watering of no par value is less obvious. Nevertheless, because the board of directors designates a stated value for even no-par-value stock, watering of this stock does occur when the corporation receives less than the designated value for the no-par-value shares.

The following case provides an example of the liability of shareholders who have watered a corporation's stock.

CASE

Hanewald v. Bryan's Inc.
429 N.W.2d 414 (N.D. 1988)

MESCHKE, J.

. . . On July 19, 1984, Keith and Joan Bryan incorporated Bryan's, Inc. to "engage in and operate a general retail clothing, and related items, store. . . ." The Certificate of Incorporation was issued by the Secretary of State on July 25, 1984. The first meeting of the board of directors elected Keith Bryan as president and Joan Bryan as secretary-treasurer of Bryan's, Inc. George Bryan was elected vice-president, appointed registered agent, and designated manager of the prospective business. The Articles of Incorporation authorized the corporation to issue

"100 shares of common stock with a par value of $1,000 per share" with "total authorized capitalization of $100,000.00." Bryan's, Inc. issued 50 shares of stock to Keith Bryan and 50 shares of stock to Joan Bryan. The trial court found that "Bryan's, Inc. did not receive any payment, either in labor, services, money, or property, for the stock which was issued."

On August 30, 1984, Hanewald sold his dry goods store in Hazen to Bryan's, Inc. Bryan's, Inc. bought the inventory, furniture, and fixtures of the business for $60,000 and leased the building for $600 per month for a period of five years. Bryan's, Inc. paid Hanewald $55,000 in cash and gave him a promissory note for $5,000, due August 30, 1985, for the remainder of the purchase price. The $55,000 payment to Hanewald was made from a loan by the Union State Bank of Hazen to the corporation, personally guaranteed by Keith and Joan Bryan.

Bryan's, Inc. began operating the retail clothing store on September 1, 1984. The business, however, lasted only four months with an operating loss of $4,840. In late December 1984, Keith and Joan Bryan decided to close the Hazen store. Thereafter, George Bryan, with the assistance of a brother and local employees, packed and removed the remaining inventory and delivered it for resale to other stores in Montana operated by the Bryan family. Bryan's, Inc. sent a "Notice of Rescission" to Hanewald on January 3, 1985, in an attempt to avoid the lease. The corporation was involuntarily dissolved by operation of law on August 1, 1986, for failure to file its annual report with the Secretary of State.

Bryan's, Inc. did not pay the $5,000 promissory note to Hanewald but paid off the rest of its creditors. Debts paid included the $55,000 loan from Union State Bank and a $10,000 loan from Keith and Joan Bryan. The Bryan loan had been, according to the trial court, "intended to be used for operating costs and expenses."

Hanewald sued the corporation and the Bryans for breach of the lease agreement and the promissory note, seeking to hold the Bryans personally liable. The defendants counterclaimed, alleging that Hanewald had fraudulently misrepresented the businesss's profitability in negotiating its sale. After a trial without a jury, the trial court entered judgment against Bryan's, Inc. for $38,600 plus interest on Hanewald's claims and ruled against the defendants on their counterclaim. . . .

The trial court, however, refused to hold the individual defendants personally liable for the judgment against Bryan's, Inc. . . . Hanewald appealed from the refusal to hold the individual defendants personally liable.

Insofar as the judgment fails to impose personal liability upon Keith and Joan Bryan, the corporation's sole shareholders, we agree with Hanewald that the trial court erred. We base our decision on the Bryans' statutory duty to pay for shares that were issued to them by Bryan's, Inc.

Organizing a corporation to avoid personal liability is legitimate. Indeed, it is one of the primary advantages of doing business in the corporate form. However, the limited personal liability of shareholders does not come free. . . . It is the shareholders' initial capital investments which protects their personal assets from further liability in the corporate enterprise. Thus, generally, shareholders are not liable for corporate debts beyond the capital they have contributed to the corporation. . . .

In this case, Bryan's, Inc. was authorized to issue 100 shares of stock each having a par value of $1,000. Keith Bryan and Joan Bryan, two of the original incorporators and members of the board of directors, were each issued 50 shares. The trial court determined that "Bryan's Inc. did not receive any payment, either in labor, services, money, or property, for the stock which was issued." Bryans have not challenged this finding of fact on this appeal. We hold that Bryans' failure to pay for their shares in the corporation makes them personally liable . . . for the corporation's debt to Hanewald. . . .

Our conclusion comports with the generally recognized rule, derived from common law, that a shareholder is liable to corporate creditors to the extent his stock has not been paid for. . . .

The defendants asserted, and the trial court ruled, that the $10,000 loan from Keith and Joan Bryan to the corporation was nevertheless "more than sufficient operating capital" to run the business. However, a shareholder's loan is a debt, not an asset, of the corporation. Where, as here, a loan was repaid by the corporation to the shareholders before its operations were abandoned, the loan cannot be considered a capital contribution.

We conclude that the trial court, having found that Keith and Joan Bryan had not paid for their stock, erred as a matter of law in refusing to hold them personally liable for the corporation's debt to Hanewald. The debt to Hanewald does not exceed the difference between the par value of their stock and the amount they actually paid. Therefore, we reverse in part to remand for entry of judgment holding Keith and Joan Bryan jointly and severally liable for the entire corporate debt to Hanewald.

■ *Reversed.*

CASE CONCEPTS REVIEW

1. For what amount and on what basis did Hanewald sue Bryan, Inc. and the Bryans?

2. Hanewald won a $38,600 judgment at the trial court level. Why is he appealing?

3. What is the legal basis for concluding that Keith Bryan and Jean Bryan are personally liable to Hanewald?

Treasury stock Stock of a corporation that has been issued by the corporation for value but is later returned to the corporation by way of gift or purchase.

TREASURY STOCK. **Treasury stock** has been issued by the corporation for value and returned to the corporation by gift or purchase. It may be sold at any price, including below par, and the proceeds returned to the treasury of the corporation for working capital. It differs from stock originally issued below par in that the purchaser is not liable for the difference between par and the sale price. It may be sold at any price the company sees fit to charge.

A corporation is restricted in its power to purchase treasury stock because the purchase might effect a reduction of its capital, to the detriment of creditors. In most states a corporation is permitted to purchase treasury stock only out of accumulated profits or surplus. This restriction retains stockholders' investment, equivalent to the original capital, as a protective cushion for creditors in case subsequent losses develop.

A corporation may redeem its preferred stock if there is no injury to, or objection by, creditors. Here again, many of the states require the preferred stock to be redeemed out of surplus, or they demand that authority to reduce the capital stock be obtained from the state.

12. Stock Subscriptions

A *preincorporation stock subscription* is an agreement to purchase stock in a corporation. It is a binding agreement (a subscriber cannot revoke a subscription) created among the subscribers for stock in a corporation to be formed. The subscription is usually drafted in a manner that creates a contract. Some states by statute have provided that a preincorporation subscription constitutes a binding, irrevocable offer to the corporation, by reason of the mutual promises of the parties. The offer is usually limited to a specified period of time, such as six months.

Certain conditions are inherent in the preincorporation subscription contract. The subscriber will not be liable unless the corporation is completely organized; the full amount of the capital stock is subscribed; and the purpose, articles, and bylaws of the corporation are as originally stated and relied on by the subscriber. Conditions, expressed or implied, are often waived by the subscriber if, with knowledge of the nonperformance, he or she participates in stockholders' meetings, pays part or all of his or her subscription, or acts as an officer or director of the corporation.

A subscription to stock of a corporation already in existence is a contract between the subscriber and the corporation. Such a contract may come into existence by reason of an offer either made by the corporation and accepted by the subscriber or made by the subscriber and accepted by the corporation. If the corporation opens subscription books and advertises its stock, it is seeking for an offer to be made by the subscriber. The corporation may, however, make a general offer to the public, which may be accepted by the subscriber in accordance with the terms of the general offer.

13. Right to Transfer Stock

A share of stock is personal property, and the owner has the right to transfer it just as he or she may transfer any other personal property. The right to transfer freely one's share in the corporation is one of the features of corporate life that distinguishes it from a partnership. A share of stock is generally transferred by an indorsement and the delivery of the certificate of stock and by surrender of the certificate to the stock transfer agent for reissue.

Shareholders of close corporations usually attempt to restrict the transfer of stock. Such attempts may be part of a contract, or they may be included in the bylaws. These restrictions may be a simple right of first refusal to either the corporation, the other shareholder, or both, or there may be a binding buy-and-sell agreement among the shareholders. By these restrictions there may be a sale of the stock upon the occurrence of a specified event, even if the owner or the estate of the owner does not desire to sell.

A corporate bylaw that makes shares of stock transferable only to the corporation or to those approved by the board of directors is unenforceable. It places too severe a restraint on the alienation of property. Society is best protected when property may be transferred freely, but an agreement or bylaw approved by all shareholders to the effect that no transfer of stock shall be made until it has first been offered to the other shareholders or to the corporation is generally enforced. Notice of the bylaw or agreement should be set forth in the stock certificate, because an innocent purchaser without notice of the restriction on alienation receives ownership free from the restriction.

In a closely held corporation, sometimes the buy-and-sell agreements between shareholders provide for matters such as salary continuation in the event of death or disability and the amount of dividends to be paid in the future. Some agreements even commit the shareholders to vote for certain persons in the election of directors. Such agreements are valid in closely held corporations, providing the duration of the agreement is not so long that it becomes contrary to public policy and providing the agreement does not adversely affect minority interests in the corporation. These agreements are used by the majority owners to ensure the election of the desired board of directors. Corporations are governed by the republican principle that the whole is bound by lawful acts of the majority. It is not against public policy or dishonest for shareholders to contract for the purpose of control.

The importance of shareholder buy-and-sell provisions must not be overlooked. It is just as important to have a means of getting a shareholder out of a closely held corporation as it is to have a means of getting a partner out of a partnership.

Shareholder buy-and-sell provisions should be worked out before any shareholder knows whether he or she is a buyer or a seller. Although withdrawal from active participation will not effect a dissolution, it can have the serious effect of precipitating a lawsuit, or a shareholder may continue to participate in management when he or she does not desire to do so. Frequently, a withdrawing shareholder will be forced to sell stock for less than it is worth because a buy-and-sell agreement was not worked out in advance.

14. Mechanics of Transfer

A share may be transferred or assigned by a bill of sale or by any other method that will pass title to a chose in action (a right to recover money or property from another through judicial procedure) or other intangible property. Whenever a share of stock is sold and a new stock certificate issued, the name of the new owner is entered on the stock records of the corporation. In a small corporation, the secretary of the corporation usually handles all transfers of stock and also the canceling of old certificates and issuing of new. Large corporations, in which there are hundreds and even thousands of transactions, employ transfer agents. The transfer agents transfer stock, cancel old certificates, issue new ones, keep an up-to-date list of the names of shareholders of the corporation, distribute dividends, mail out shareholders' notices, and perform many functions to assist the corporation secretary. Stock exchange rules provide that corporations listing stock for sale must maintain a transfer agency and registry, operated and maintained under exchange regulations. The registrar of stock is an agent of the corporation whose duty is to see that no stock certificates are issued in excess of the authorized capitalization of the corporation.

Article 8 of the Uniform Commercial Code deals with investment securities. The general approach of Article 8 is that securities are negotiable instruments and that bona fide purchasers have greater rights than they would have "if the things bought were chattels or simple contracts." The particular rules of Article 3 that relate to the establishment of preferred status for commercial paper are applied to securities. Defenses of the issuer are generally not effective against a purchaser for value who has received the securities without being given notice of the particular defense raised.

A bona fide purchaser is one who purchases in good faith and without notice of any adverse claim. This purchaser is the equivalent of a holder in due course of a negotiable instrument, which is discussed in chapter 35. A bona fide purchaser is not subject to "adverse claims," which include a claim that a transfer was wrongful or that some other person is the owner of, or has an interest in, the security.

CHAPTER SUMMARY

Corporation Defined	1. A corporation is an artificial, intangible entity created by state law.
	2. This organization generally is considered a person for both contract and tort law purposes.
	3. A corporation is a person under the due process clause but not under the Fifth Amendment's protection against self-incrimination.
	4. The classifications of public versus private, profit versus nonprofit, and domestic versus foreign are commonly applied to corporations.

PROCEDURE FOR INCORPORATION

The Application for a Charter	1. The incorporators prepare an application for a charter that includes basic information such as the purpose of the corporation, the location of its office and registered agent, and information about its stock.
	2. The application will indicate the amount of authorized stock and the amount to be issued.
	3. When the application is approved, it is returned as a charter, which is filed in the proper recording office.
Corporate Name	1. The name of a corporation must include words such as *corporation, company, incorporated,* or *limited,* which provides notice of the limited liability of the shareholders.
	2. A corporate name must not be deceptively similar to names of other corporations.
Corporate Powers	1. A corporation has all the powers granted in its charter and those set forth in the statutes of the state of incorporation.
	2. The usual powers include the power to sue and be sued, to own, convey, and deal in property, to enter into contracts, and to purchase and dispose of securities.
	3. The *ultra vires* act is one beyond the authority of the corporation.
	4. Neither the corporation nor parties dealing with it may avoid liability on the ground of *ultra vires.*
	5. *Ultra vires* conduct on the part of the corporation may be enjoined at the request of the shareholders or may be the basis of a revocation of the charter by the state.

Bylaws	1. After filing the charter, the incorporators meet with all stock subscribers and elect a board of directors. The board in turn meets and adopts bylaws.
	2. The bylaws provide the rules for managing the corporation. They cover such activities as the corporate seal, stock certificates, the number and manner of election of officers, and the time and place of meetings of shareholders as well as the board of directors.
Domestic and Foreign Corporations	1. A corporation organized under a state's laws is a *domestic* corporation in that state; a corporation incorporated in one state is a *foreign* corporation in all other states.
	2. Foreign corporations transacting local business in a state must qualify to do business in that state. If they fail to do so, they are denied access to the courts as well as being subject to other sanctions.
	3. If a business is only engaged in interstate commerce and is not conducting intrastate activities, it is not required to obtain a license to do business.
Promoters	1. A promoter is usually an incorporator and is active in obtaining preincorporation agreements. Promoters are responsible for compliance with all applicable laws.
	2. A promoter may be personally liable to contracts prior to incorporation, but this liability may be avoided.
	3. A corporation after it is formed may have liability on preincorporation agreements under a variety of theories.
	4. Promoters stand in a fiduciary relationship to the corporation and cannot secure benefits at the expense of other shareholders or the corporation.

DISREGARDING THE CORPORATE ENTITY

Piercing the Corporate Veil	1. Creditors may seek to look through the corporation to the shareholders and seek to impose liability as if the corporate entity did not exist.
	2. The corporate entity is not disregarded simply because all of the stock is owned by one person.
Alter Ego Theory	1. The alter ego theory is used to pierce the corporate veil where a corporation is actually nothing more than the alter ego of another corporation or of an individual.
	2. This theory is used where the business is actually operated as if the separate corporate entity did not exist.
Promotion of Justice Theory	1. Courts will pierce the corporate veil to avoid fraud, to prevent the violation of a statute, and to promote the ends of justice.

CORPORATE STOCK

Kinds of Stock	1. Some stock is preferred over others in either dividends, distributions on dissolution, or both.
	2. Unless stated otherwise, preferred stock is both cumulative and nonparticipating.
	3. A stock warrant gives a person a right to subscribe and to purchase corporate stock at a stated price. Such warrants are transferable.
	4. Stock may be issued without par value, in which case the directors provide a stated value for stated capital account purposes.
	5. Watered stock is stock that is issued as fully paid when in fact an equivalent value has not been paid to the corporation.
	6. Treasury stock is stock of the corporation that has been purchased by or returned to the corporation.
	7. Treasury stock may only be purchased out of accumulated earnings. Otherwise, the purchase could constitute a reduction of capital.
Stock Subscriptions	1. A preincorporation stock subscription is binding and irrevocable for a stated period of time after its execution.
	2. Preincorporation subscriptions are usually conditioned on such things as final organization of the corporation and subscription to all the stock.

3. Stock may also be subscribed after incorporation, and such contracts are subject to the same rules as other contracts.

Right to Transfer Stock

1. In a closely held corporation, the bylaws may grant a right of first refusal to the corporation or to other shareholders.

2. A buy-and-sell agreement may require the purchase of stock on death or withdrawal of a shareholder.

Mechanics of Transfer

1. Stock is transferred on the records of the corporation by surrender of the stock certificate and issuing a new one. Large corporations retain stock transfer agents to perform this task.

2. Article 8 of the Uniform Commercial Code deals with investment securities. If its provisions are complied with, a party purchasing stock has greater rights than the seller.

REVIEW QUESTIONS AND PROBLEMS

1. Match each term in column A with the appropriate statement in column B.

A	B
(1) Incorporator	(a) A theory used to pierce the corporate veil
(2) Bylaw	(b) Stock repurchased by the issuing corporation
(3) Foreign corporation	(c) Right to subscribe for stock
(4) Promoter	(d) One who signs an application for a corporate charter
(5) *Ultra vires*	(e) One who assists in organizing a corporation
(6) Alter ego	(f) A corporation operating in a state other than the state that issues its charter
(7) Treasury stock	(g) Stock not fully paid for
(8) Stock warrant	(h) A rule for governing a corporation
(9) Watered stock	(i) A contract defense that is unavailable to the parties to a contract today
(10) Stock dividend	(j) A transfer of earned surplus to capital stock and the issue of stock to current shareholders in the proportion of their current holdings

2. LST Company was the parent company and BAG Company was a subsidiary. LST Company extended credit to BAG Company. The latter became insolvent, and the other creditors objected to LST's sharing equally in the assets. Is LST entitled to its pro rata share of BAG's assets? Why or why not?

3. The plaintiffs entered into a series of contracts involving coal excavations with Doral Coal Company and Dean Coal Company. Robert W. William, defendant, was president of both coal companies. When royalty payments owed were not made by the corporations as agreed, plaintiffs canceled the agreements and filed suit against the defendant individually. They contended that the defendant was personally liable because he was the sole shareholder of each corporation. Is the defendant liable? Why or why not?

4. Smith attempted to file articles of incorporation on behalf of a mortgage company. The articles expressed the rates of interest the mortgage company would charge its borrowers. These rates of interest were usurious under state law. May the secretary of state lawfully reject the articles of incorporation? Why or why not?

5. The First National Bank of Lander, which was the Wyoming Bancorporation's subsidiary in Lander, Wyoming, planned to change its name to First Wyoming Bank, N.A.—Lander. First Wyoming Savings and Loan Association filed a complaint seeking permanently to enjoin the defendant from making the name change. First Wyoming

Savings alleged that it had established a trade name in the words "First Wyoming" and that the use of the name "First Wyoming Bank—Lander" would result in confusion and deception to the general public. Should the injunction be issued? Explain.

6. Through its president, a religious corporation leased liquor-dispensing equipment from the Drink-n-Drown Beverage Company. When the lessee defaulted, Drink-n-Drown filed suit for the unpaid rent. The religious corporation's board of directors asserted *ultra vires* as a defense. Is the defense justified? Explain.

7. Plaintiff, MPL Leasing, a California corporation, sold equipment to Johnson and shipped it to Alabama. When Johnson failed to pay, MPL sued Johnson in Alabama. Johnson moved to dismiss on the ground that MPL was a foreign corporation not qualified to do business in Alabama and that the state's constitution prevented unqualified corporations from enforcing their contracts in Alabama's courts. Should the case be dismissed? Explain.

8. Plaintiff does virtually all its business in Mississippi and less than 1 percent of its business in Arkansas. It is not registered to do business in the state of Arkansas as required by law. Its agents went to Arkansas and entered into a contract in Arkansas to do some work on a residence near Lake Village. It was not paid for its work and filed an action to impose a lien against the Arkansas residence. May the lien be judicially enforced? Why or why not?

9. The XYZ Corporation was to be formed by Peter, a promoter. To operate the corporation after incorporation, it was necessary for Peter to lease certain facilities. Peter executed a lease in the corporate name for office space without revealing to the lessor that the corporation had not yet been organized. The corporation subsequently came into existence, and the board declined to accept the lease of office space that Peter had executed in the corporate name.
   a. Can the corporation validly decline the lease of office space? Explain.
   b. Does Peter have any liability on any of the leases he made? Explain.

10. Plaintiff corporation, engaged in the sale of plastics, entered into a preincorporation contract that was initiated and concluded by two persons who later became officers of the corporation. It formed the basis for the subsequent sale to defendant of over $1 million in goods. Suit was brought to recover balance due on goods sold. The defendant denied liability because the plaintiff was not incorporated at the time of the contract. Should the plaintiff be allowed to recover? Explain.

11. Dearmin was president and the sole shareholder of Dearmin Brothers Excavating, Inc. The corporation experienced severe cash flow problems in 1975. To help alleviate this problem, Dearmin loaned $30,000 to the corporation and personally guaranteed several loans that were made to the corporation. Hill sold oil products to the corporation. When his bill for $6,268.46 was not paid, he instituted this suit against Dearmin personally using the alter ego doctrine. Is Dearmin personally liable? Explain.

12. David formed a corporation for tax purposes. No directors' meetings were held. David retained total control of the corporation's operations, and he took money from the corporate account for personal purchases. Creditors sought to pierce the corporate veil. Should they succeed? Explain.

13. A corporation decided to repurchase stock of a shareholder who recently died. The corporation was in existence for three years and had lost $50,000 during this period. The original shareholders had invested $25,000 in the business, of which the deceased had invested $5,000. How much may the corporation pay for the stock of the deceased? Explain.

14. Albert sold Betty some stock representing ownership of the Cobra Corporation. Albert delivered the stock certificate to Betty, but he failed to indorse it. Albert died, and the executor of his estate claims that the stock certificate should be returned, since it was not indorsed. Betty contends she is entitled to have the certificate indorsed by Albert's representative. Who is correct? Explain.

OPERATION OF CORPORATIONS

CHAPTER PREVIEW

The preceding chapter discusses the legal aspects of forming a corporation. Many of the legal principles discussed there are also applicable to the operation of a corporate entity. Many bylaw provisions, for example, are directly concerned with operations. Because some of the subjects dealt with in this chapter, such as the rights of shareholders, relate to formation problems, the preceding chapter and this one should be considered complementary.

Three distinct groups participate in the management of a corporation. *Shareholders* or *stockholders* (the words are synonymous) comprise the basic governing body. Shareholders exercise their control by electing the *board of directors,* sometimes by approving the bylaws, and by voting on matters such as merger, consolidation, or dissolution. The board of directors is the policy-making group, with responsibility for electing *officers,* who carry out the policies. The duties and powers of the shareholders, the board of directors, and the various officers are regulated by statute, by the bylaws of the corporation, and by corporate resolutions passed by the board of directors.

The powers, rights, and duties of the individuals who are corporate shareholders, directors, or officers are discussed in this chapter.

You serve as an outside director on the board of the All-at-Once Corporation. During a board meeting, the president of All-at-Once makes a fifteen-minute presentation on the benefits and detriments of merging All-at-Once with Take-Your-Time, Inc. After this presentation, the president asks for a vote of the directors approving the merger.

Should you have any concerns about casting your vote?

SHAREHOLDERS

1. Rights in General

A shareholder has the following rights, usually created by statute and reiterated in the bylaws: (1) the right to inspect the books and papers of the corporation, (2) the right to attend shareholders' meetings and to vote for directors and on certain other matters such as dissolution or merger, (3) the preemptive right, (4) the right to bring a shareholder's derivative suit, and (5) the right to share in the profits when a dividend is declared. In some states a shareholder has the additional right to cumulative voting.

The right to inspect the books and papers is limited to good-faith inspections for proper and honest purposes at the proper time and the proper place. The general rule applied by the courts reviewing inspection statutes has been that the primary purpose of the inspection must not be one that is adverse to the best interests of the corporation. A *proper purpose* is one that seeks to protect the interests of the corporation as well as the interests of the shareholder seeking the information. To protect his or her interests, a shareholder is legitimately entitled to know anything and everything that the records, books, and papers of the company would show. A shareholder must have an honest motive and not proceed for vexatious or speculative reasons. A shareholder must seek something more than satisfaction of curiosity and must not be conducting a general fishing expedition. A shareholder's desire to learn the reasons for lack of dividends or low dividends, and suspicion of mismanagement arising from such dividend policy, will constitute a proper purpose. Most courts consider an attempt to oust present management to be a proper purpose.

In general, the burden of proof rests on the corporation to prove the shareholder's purpose for inspecting corporate documents is improper. However, courts in other states have held that the burden of proving good faith and proper purpose for a shareholder's examination of corporate records rests on the shareholder. Proof of actual mismanagement or wrongdoing is not necessary, and good-faith fears of mismanagement are sufficient to justify the shareholder's inspection.

The business hours of the corporation are the reasonable and proper hours in which stockholders are entitled to inspect the books. They also have the right to the assistance of accountants and attorneys in that inspection. The assistance of qualified professionals is often required to understand the books and records and to know what to ask for.

In some states, a shareholder who is refused access to the books and records is entitled to damages as provided by statute. A typical statute provides that a shareholder who is denied the right to inspect books and records is entitled to damages equal to 10 percent of the value of the stock owned. This right to inspect includes contracts and correspondence as well as books and records. The right extends even to confidential records.

The shareholders' other rights, in addition to the right of inspection, are discussed in the following sections.

2. Meetings

Action by the shareholders normally binds the corporation only when taken in a regular or properly called special meeting after notice required by the bylaws or statute has been given. It is generally conceded, however—and most states so provide by statute—that action approved informally by *all* shareholders will bind the corporation. If there is less than unanimous approval, informal action is not possible.

NOTICE.   Notice of a special meeting must include a statement concerning matters to be acted on at the meeting; any action taken on other matters will be ineffective. If unusual action, such as a sale of corporate assets, is to be taken at the regular annual meeting, notice of the meeting must call specific attention to that fact; but otherwise, any business may be transacted at the annual meeting.

Failure to give proper notice of a meeting generally invalidates the action taken at the meeting. A stockholder who has not received notice but attends and participates in a meeting waives the lack of notice by his or her presence.

QUORUM.   A quorum of shareholders must be present to transact business. Shareholders may be present at a meeting either in person or by **proxy**. When a shareholder cannot attend the meeting, that shareholder may grant another the right to vote by signing a proxy statement. In essence, a proxy is an appointment by the shareholder of an agent to serve as a representative during the shareholder's absence. If shareholders leave during the meeting, they can no longer be counted as present.

Proxy Authority to act for another, used by absent stockholders to have their votes cast by others.

A *quorum* is usually a majority of the voting shares outstanding, unless some statute or the bylaws provide for a larger or smaller percentage. Affirmative action is approved by majority vote of the shares represented at a meeting, provided a quorum exists. Under common law, certain unusual matters such as a merger or sale of all corporate assets require a unanimous vote. Today, statutes usually provide that such actions can be taken by vote of two-thirds or three-fourths of the shareholders. Many of these statutes also provide that the dissenting shareholders have the right to surrender their shares and receive their fair value if they disapprove of the action taken.

PURPOSES.   In large, publicly held corporations, the annual meeting of shareholders serves a variety of purposes. Management has usually solicited enough proxies in advance to control any vote that is taken, so the outcome is usually a certainty. Nevertheless, many shareholders attend meetings to question management on a variety of issues and to lobby for certain policies. Management uses the annual meeting of shareholders of large corporations as a public relations opportunity, to educate the shareholders on company accomplishments as well as its problems.

3. Voting

Statutes of the states and the charters issued under their authority prescribe the matters on which shareholders are entitled to vote. Usually, they vote on the election of directors; on major policy issues such as mergers, consolidations, and dissolution; and, in some instances, on a change in the bylaws.

Some state laws allow a corporation to deny some shareholders the vote on certain issues, such as the election of directors. This denial allows a minority of shareholders to obtain control. But since public policy supports the right of an investor to vote, the status of stock as nonvoting must be communicated to the investor, or the stock purchase may be rescinded.

As a general rule, every shareholder is entitled to as many votes as he or she owns shares of stock. The shareholder whose name appears in the corporate records is usually designated by the bylaws as the person entitled to vote. Owners of preferred stock, depending on their contract with the corporation, may or may not be entitled to vote.

Cumulative voting In voting for directors, stockholders may cast as many votes as they have shares of stock multiplied by the number to be elected. Their votes may be all for one candidate or distributed among as many candidates as there are positions to be filled.

The statutes of some states provide for **cumulative voting** in the election of directors. In cumulative voting, a shareholder may cast as many votes for one board candidate as there are board members to be filled multiplied by the number of shares of stock owned. Alternatively, this shareholder may distribute the votes among the candidates as he or she sees fit. A shareholder owning 100 shares of stock has 300 votes if three directors are to be elected. He or she may cast all 300 for one candidate, or they may be spread among the candidates.

A shareholder is entitled to vote only by virtue of his or her ownership of the stock but may specifically authorize another to vote this stock. Authorization is made by power of attorney and must specifically state that the agent of the shareholder has power to vote the principal's stock. This voting by proxy is a personal relationship that the shareholder may revoke before the authority is exercised. Laws pertaining to principal and agent control this relationship.

A shareholder, unlike a director, is permitted to vote on a matter in which he or she has a personal interest. Although in certain respects shareholders represent the corporate welfare in their voting, in most respects they vote to serve their interests. But a majority of shareholders is not permitted to take action that is clearly detrimental to the corporate and minority interest.

4. Preemptive Rights

The original application for a charter specifies the amount of stock the corporation will be authorized to issue and the amount that will be issued without further notice to the state. The amount of authorized stock and the amount of issued stock are used to compute the license fees and franchise taxes due to the state of incorporation. These limitations on stocks cannot be increased or exceeded without the authority of the state.

Shareholders may authorize an increase in the authorized capital stock, but such action may not be taken by the directors. An increase in the authorized capital stock is an amendment to the corporate charter, which requires state approval.

The board of directors may sell unissued capital stock when the amount previously issued is less than that authorized. This sale does not require an amendment to the charter. All that is required is that the state be informed of the additional issue of the stock so the correct taxes may be collected.

When an increase in the capital stock has been properly authorized, the existing shareholders have a prior right over third parties to subscribe to the increased capital stock. This right is called the shareholders' *preemptive rights*. It is based on the shareholders' right to protect and maintain their proportionate control and interest in the corporation. The preemptive rights may be limited or waived by contract and by provisions in the charter or bylaws of the corporation in most states. In many states it is not applicable to treasury stock. Many publicly held corporations have eliminated it.

The preemptive rights are applicable to new authorizations of stock. They are generally not applicable to new issues of stock previously authorized. If the new issue of an original authorization takes place a long time after the original issue, many states provide that the preemptive rights exist. Most states approve the issuance of stock to employees under stock option plans without regard to the preemptive rights.

5. Derivative Suits

A shareholder cannot maintain an *action at law* for injuries to the corporation, because the corporation is a legal entity and by law has a right to bring a suit in its own name. Any cause of action based on conduct injurious to the corporation accrues in the first instance to the corporation. Nor can a shareholder bring a suit against the directors or other officers of the corporation for negligence, waste, and mismanagement in the conduct of the corporate business. The right to sue for injuries to the corporation rests strictly with the corporation itself, unless modified by statute.

A shareholder may, however, bring a suit in equity known as a shareholder's *derivative suit* to enjoin the officers of a corporation from entering into *ultra vires* contracts or from doing anything that would impair the corporate assets. Likewise, the shareholder has a right to bring suit for dollar damages on behalf of the corporation if the officers are acting outside the scope of their authority, are guilty of negligent conduct, or are engaging in fraudulent transactions that are injurious to the corporation itself. Any judgment received in such an action is paid to the corporation. The shareholder who initiates the action is permitted to recover the expenses involved in the suit.

The purpose of a derivative action is twofold: First, it is the equivalent of a suit by the shareholders to compel the corporation to sue; and second, it is a suit by the corporation, asserted by the shareholders on its behalf, against those liable to it.

As a general rule, the shareholder bringing the derivative suit must have been a shareholder at the time of the action complained of and at the time the suit was filed. Individuals are not allowed to acquire stock for the purpose of filing a derivative action or to reacquire it, as occurred in the following case.

CASE

Vista Fund v. Garis
277 N.W.2d 19 (Minn. 1979)

Plaintiffs (Vista) brought a stockholder's derivative action alleging fraud, negligence, and breach of fiduciary duties against a corporation, its officers, and directors. Plaintiff was a stockholder at the time of the transactions complained of, but later sold its stock. Just prior to filing the suit, plaintiff repurchased 100 shares of stock in the defendant corporation. Plaintiff had made a proper demand on the corporation to take action itself. The lower court found for the defendants, and the plaintiff appeals.

Scott, J.

. . . Rule 23.06, Rules of Civil Procedure, requires that a plaintiff meet certain stock ownership requirements before he may invoke the equitable remedy of a shareholder's derivative suit. The rule states, in pertinent part, as follows:

> In a derivative action brought by one or more shareholders or members to enforce a right of a corporation or of an unincorporated association, the corporation or association having failed to enforce a right which may properly be asserted by it, the complaint shall allege that the plaintiff was a shareholder or member at the time of the transaction of which he complains or that his share or membership thereafter devolved on him by operation of law.

Vista argues that a plaintiff need not be a shareholder at the time stockholder's derivative suit is commenced because Rule 23.06 requires only that "the complaint shall allege that the plaintiff was a shareholder at the time of the transaction of which he complains." This contention is without merit. The rule states that a derivative action is one "brought by one or more shareholders." The use of the term "shareholders" requires that the plaintiff own stock in the corporation at the time he brings suit. Indeed, the Federal counterpart to Rule 23.06 has been so interpreted. . . .

The trial court interpreted Rule 23.06 as requiring a plaintiff, in order to have standing to maintain a derivative action, to continuously and uninterruptedly own stock in the corporation from the time of the alleged wrongs through the time suit is commenced. Since Vista sold its stock before it commenced suit (although it purchased 100 shares of stock shortly before bringing this action), the district court ruled that it lacked standing to maintain the instant derivative action. Vista argues . . . uninterrupted ownership of the stock from the time of the alleged wrongs until commencement of suit is not required. Again, this contention is without merit.

It is consistent with the policy underlying Rule 23.06 to require continuous stock ownership. The purpose of the stockholding requirements of the rule is to prevent persons from purchasing stock solely for purposes of maintaining shareholders' derivative actions. In other words, the share ownership requirement is intended to prevent the litigating of purchased grievances or speculating in wrongs done to corporations. Once a shareholder has sold his stock he is in the same position as any other non-shareholder. Accordingly, when he reacquires stock and brings suit based on a corporate wrong occurring during his prior ownership he is in effect purchasing a grievance or speculating in corporate wrongs. Indeed, this is what occurred here. Based on the above reasoning, we conclude that continuous ownership must be required to effectuate the policy behind Rule 23.06. . . .

We find that the trial court was correct in concluding that insofar as the complaint asserts any derivative claims on behalf of Vista summary judgment was proper dismissing such claims. We agree to the extent that Rule 23.06, Rules of Civil Procedure, requires that in a derivative action the plaintiffs must be shareholders in the corporation in whose benefit it sues from the time the alleged improper acts occurred, continuously and uninterruptedly, until the time such action is commenced. . . .

■ *Affirmed.*

CASE CONCEPTS REVIEW

1. Vista Fund owned stock in the defendant corporation twice. In general, when were these two time periods?
2. Why did the trial court find that Vista lacked standing to file this derivative suit?
3. What does this court conclude about Vista's standing to bring this suit?
4. What policy is reflected in this decision?

Before shareholders may bring a derivative suit, they must show that they have done everything possible to secure action by the managing officers and directors, who have refused to act. Shareholders must first seek to persuade the officers and directors to take action. Shareholders upset at a corporate failure to bring a lawsuit may not initiate a derivative suit without first demanding it of the directors. If the directors refuse and the derivative action challenges that refusal, courts normally accept the business judgment of the directors. The directors' decision will hold unless bad faith is proved. The corporate decision not to file a lawsuit against directors or others will rarely be set aside by a court if it is made on the basis of a recommendation by outside directors or disinterested investigators. This deference to objective board decisions is based on the *business judgment rule,* which is discussed in section 12.

However, the futility of a stockholder's demand on a board of directors will excuse the demand. Futility of a stockholder's demand on a board of directors to redress an alleged wrong to the corporation is gauged by circumstances existing at the commencement of the derivative suit. For example, if the officers and directors are under an influence that sterilizes their discretion, they cannot be considered proper persons to conduct litigation on behalf of the corporation; thus, if there is a conflict of interests in the directors' decision not to sue because the directors themselves have profited from the transaction underlying the litigation, no demand need be made and the shareholders can proceed directly with the derivative suit. In such cases, the business judgment rule does not come into play. In 1991, the United States Supreme Court held that whether a demand on the corporate directors is essential or whether a demand is futile and thus excused is to be resolved by applying the appropriate state law, not federal law.

Mere dissatisfaction with the management of the corporation will not justify a derivative suit. In the law of corporations, it is fundamental that the majority shareholders control the policies and decisions of the corporation. Every shareholder implicitly agrees that he or she will be bound by the acts and decisions of a majority of the shareholders or by the agents of the corporation they choose. Courts will not undertake to control the business of a corporation, although it may be seen that better decisions might be made and the business might be more successful if other methods were pursued. If a majority of disinterested directors acting in good faith and with reasonable business judgment adopt a course of action, it will not be overturned by a derivative suit.

In essence, to be the plaintiffs in a proper derivative suit, the shareholders first must have a claim that is for the corporation's benefit and not the shareholders personally. Second, the plaintiffs must be able to represent the interests of similarly situated shareholders. The following case discusses the interesting and common issue of whether a single shareholder can bring a successful derivative suit. This issue can arise whenever there is a closely held family business.

CASE

Brandon v. Brandon Construction Company, Inc.

776 S.W.2d 349 (Ark. 1989)

PURTLE, J.

The appellant is a minority shareholder in a closely held family corporation. She filed suit in her capacity as a minority shareholder and as a representative of other shareholders similarly situated. . . .

Fred and Maxine Brandon, the parents of the appellant, and their children are the shareholders in the Brandon Construction Company. The parents own 30 shares each and the four children own 10 shares each. The parents commenced a divorce action in 1987. At the same time they also entered into an employment agreement with each other and the corporation providing that both would receive a minimum monthly salary of $12,500.00 each. The appellant and her siblings signed a consent to this contract on March 7, 1988. On May 13, 1988, the appellant notified the corporation that she was revoking her consent. She filed suit in chancery court on October 10, 1988, in both her individual and representative capacities. She sought to halt the payment of the salaries as agreed upon, alleging waste, fraud, and a breach of the fiduciary duties to the shareholders, which resulted in injuries to the corporation. Her allegations are essentially that Fred and Maxine Brandon, officers and employees of the corporation, are dismantling the corporation and distributing its assets to themselves, without regard to the minority shareholders' rights. . . .

The other minority shareholders responded that the appellant did not represent their interests as minority shareholders. They disavowed her action and stated that they were content with the salaries being paid to their parents. The other minority shareholders joined the parents in a motion for summary judgment on the basis that the appellant did not adequately represent their interests, as is necessary to maintain a shareholder's derivative action. . . . The court ruled that she did not meet the requirements . . . to "adequately represent the interests of the other shareholders." . . .

Did the appellant have standing to bring a class action on behalf of her own interests and those of the other minority shareholders? Arkansas Rules of Civil Procedure, Rule 23.1 states in part:

> The derivative action may not be maintained if it appears that the plaintiff does not fairly and adequately represent the interests of the shareholders or members similarly situated in enforcing the right of the corporation or association.

. . . The fact that the appellant is the only person willing to continue this suit does not automatically disqualify her from individually maintaining a derivative action. The first sentence of Rule 23.1 refers to "a derivative action brought by *one or more shareholders* [emphasis added] or members to enforce a right of a corporation. . . ." If the rule intended to prevent one person from maintaining such an action, it would have been simple enough to require that an action be brought by "two or more shareholders." A corporation does business through its officers and agents. However, it is the shareholders who own it. Unless individual shareholders are allowed to act to protect the corporate assets, the officers and agents could deprive the shareholders of this property by fraudulent or other illegal means. . . .

The very nature of the right created by this rule is to "enforce a right of a corporation." In the present case it appears that the appellant brought a suit on behalf of all of the shareholders of the corporation, or at least her allegations were to that effect. The actions alleged, if proven true, would destroy the corporation. On the other hand, she did not allege any particular or separate injury or loss of property to herself. The mere fact that other shareholders were willing to go along with a violation of the rights of the corporation did not foreclose the appellant from maintaining her action. Although she did not allege facts which would support an individual right of action for personal damages, she has alleged facts which would support a derivative action by a shareholder. Her allegations were that the directors and majority shareholders were committing waste, fraud, and breach of their fiduciary duties. These allegations clearly describe the kind of injury a derivative action contemplates. . . . The majority of a corporation's shareholders have no right to destroy the property rights of the minority shareholders, even if there is only one in the minority. . . .

The rule requires the appellant, in enforcing the rights of the corporation, to fairly and adequately represent the interests of the shareholders or members similarly situated. The real test is not the number of shareholders in a derivative action, but the alleged injuries and the remedies sought. The allegation in the present case is that the corporation is suffering a diminution of its assets through the overpayment of employees' salaries. Although this allegation is conclusory, there is no specific evidence that the claim is spurious. If successful, the appellant would, at least theoretically, bring a benefit to the corporation. The fact that the value of her ownership in the corporation will be enhanced if the action is successful will be her compensation for bringing the derivative action. The wrong she asserts is one committed against the corporation, not one by the corporation. Her remedy is on behalf of the corporation, not against it. The very purpose of the rule is to allow minority shareholders to proceed in the interests of the corporation in court. There would otherwise be no need for Rule 23.1.

The trial court granted a summary judgment without considering all the evidence which the appellant wanted to present on the merits of her complaint. The allegations, if proven, are sufficient to support a derivative action by the appellant on behalf of the corporation. However, the chancellor correctly held that the facts alleged would not support an individual action by the appellant. This does not mean, however, that a "class of one" action may not be maintained as a derivative action.

■ *Reversed and remanded.*

CASE CONCEPTS REVIEW

1. Why did the trial court rule that the plaintiff-appellant did not adequately represent the interests of the other shareholders?
2. What is meant by the phrase "similarly situated shareholders"?
3. Why does the court conclude that the appellant's action is appropriate?

6. Dividends

Dividend A stockholder's pro rata share in the distributed profits of a corporation.

Although a shareholder has a right to share in **dividends** when declared, whether or not a dividend is declared is within the discretion of the board of directors. Shareholders are not entitled to the payment of a dividend simply because earned surplus exists. The board of directors may see fit to continue the profits in the business for the purpose of expansion, but it must act reasonably and in good faith. Where fraud or a gross abuse of discretion is shown, and there are profits out of which dividends may be declared, the shareholders may compel the board of directors to declare dividends. Before there is a right to interfere by asking a court to order the payment of dividends, however, it must be clear that the board of directors has illegally, wantonly, and without justification refused to declare a dividend.

A *cash dividend,* when declared, becomes a debt of the corporation. Once the declaration of a dividend has been made public, it may not be rescinded. A declaration of dividends is proper as long as it does not impair the corporation's capital stock. Any dividend that reduces the net assets of the corporation below its stated capital account is illegal. Directors are personally liable to creditors for dividends improperly declared. In addition to the directors' personal liability, shareholders who receive illegal dividends generally may be compelled to return them.

The cash dividend will be paid to the person whose name appears on the corporate stock records as the owner of the share on the record date the dividend is payable. This is known as the *ex-dividend date.* The fact that it is paid to this person does not necessarily mean that the payee is entitled to keep it. If the stock has been sold prior to the dividend date but not transferred on the books of the corporation, the buyer is entitled to the dividend. On the other hand, if there is only a contract to sell the stock, the seller is entitled to any dividend paid prior to the delivery of the stock.

Stock dividend New shares of its own stock issued as a dividend by a corporation to its shareholders, to transfer retained earnings to capital stock.

A **stock dividend** involves a transfer of retained earnings to the capital account. This dividend is used when the earnings are required for growth of the business. Stock dividends of the issuing company are not taxable income to shareholders. A **stock split** differs from a stock dividend in that with the stock split there is no transfer of earnings to capital but only a reduction in par value and an increase in the number of shares.

Stock split A readjustment of the financial plan of a corporation, whereby each existing share of stock is split into new shares, usually with a lowering of par value.

7. Fiduciary Aspects

The law as it relates to shareholders' relationships in closely held corporations is somewhat different from the law as it relates to them in publicly held corporations. Publicly held corporations have many shareholders, none of whom owns a majority of the stock. As a general rule, there is no fiduciary relationship between shareholders in publicly held corporations. One owner of stock listed on the New York Stock Exchange, for example, owes no duty to other owners of the same stock unless, of course, the shareholder is also an insider subject to regulation by the Securities and Exchange Commission.

A *closely held corporation* is one in which management and ownership are substantially identical, to the extent that it is unrealistic to believe that the judgment of the directors will be independent of that of the shareholders. The shareholders in a closely held corporation owe one another substantially the same fiduciary duty that partners owe one another. They must discharge their management and shareholder responsibilities in conformity with the strict good-faith standard, and they may not act out of avarice, expediency, or self-interest in derogation of their loyalty to other shareholders and to the corporation. A shareholder in a closely held corporation may not permit his or her private interests to clash with those of the corporation and other shareholders.

Some courts have called closely held corporations "incorporated partnerships." They are corporations for liability, perpetual existence, and taxation, but the shareholders expect to act and to be treated as partners in their dealings among themselves. The practical realities dictate that the relationship be considered a fiduciary one, demanding fairness, honesty, and full disclosure of all functions.

When a minority shareholder has a complaint against a majority shareholder, the issue arises as to whether the former may sue in an individual capacity or must sue as a representative of the corporation as in a derivative suit. The following case addresses this specific issue. In this case, the minority shareholders filed a lawsuit directly against the majority shareholders, alleging wrongdoing that devalued the minority's ownership interest. The trial court dismissed the complaint since it was not filed as a derivative action to benefit the corporation. The appeals court reversed, and this appeal by the majority shareholders followed.

CASE

Crosby v. Beam
548 N.E.2d 217 (Ohio 1989)

DOUGLAS, J.

The issue before us is whether the appellees' cause of action may be maintained as an individual action or whether dismissal was proper because the suit was not instituted as a Civ.R. 23.1 shareholder's derivative suit.

A shareholder's derivative action is brought by a shareholder in the name of the corporation to enforce a corporate claim. Such a suit is an exception to the usual rule that a corporation's board of directors manages or supervises the management of a corporation. A derivative action allows a shareholder to circumvent a board's refusal to bring a suit on a claim. On the other hand, if the complaining shareholder is injured in a way that is separate and distinct from an injury to the corporation, then the complaining shareholder has a direct action.

Appellants contend that this case should have been brought as a derivative action because appellees' amended complaint alleges only that the appellants-majority shareholders misappropriated corporate funds. This misappropriation directly affected the corporation, appellants contend, and only indirectly harmed the appellees-minority shareholders. Thus, the appellants argue that the appellees could not maintain the cause as a direct action.

I. *Close Corporation*

Typically, a close corporation is a corporation with a few shareholders and whose corporate shares are not generally traded on a securities market.

Close corporations bear a striking resemblance to a partnership. In essence, the ownership of a close corporation is limited to a small number of people who are dependent on each other for the enterprise to succeed. Just like a partnership, the relationship among the shareholders must be one of trust, confidence and loyalty if the close corporation is to thrive. While a close corporation provides the same benefits as do other corporations, such as limited liability and perpetuity, the close corporation structure also gives majority or controlling shareholders opportunities to oppress minority shareholders. For example, the majority or controlling shareholders may refuse to declare dividends, may grant majority shareholders-officers exorbitant salaries and bonuses, or pay high rent for property leased from the majority shareholders.

Minority shareholders in a close corporation, denied any share of the profits by the majority shareholder's action, will either suffer a loss or try to find a buyer for their stock. This situation is contrasted with an oppressed minority shareholder in a large publicly owned corporation who can more easily sell his shares in such a corporation. Generally, there is no ready or available market for the stock of a minority shareholder in a close corporation.

This presents a plight for a minority shareholder in a close corporation who can become trapped in a disadvantageous situation from which he cannot be easily extricated.

II. *Majority Shareholders' Fiduciary Duty in a Close Corporation*

Generally, majority shareholders have a fiduciary duty to minority shareholders. Courts in sister states and Ohio appellate courts have found a heightened fiduciary duty between majority and minority shareholders in a close corporation. This duty is similar to the duty that partners owe one another in a partnership because of the fundamental resemblance between the close corporation and a partnership. . . .

Majority or controlling shareholders breach such fiduciary duty to minority shareholders when control of the close corporation is utilized to prevent the minority from having an equal opportunity in the corporation. Control of the stock in a close corporation cannot be used to give the majority benefits which are not shared by the minority. . . .

Given the foregoing, if we require a minority shareholder in a close corporation, who alleges that the majority shareholders breached their fiduciary duty to him, to institute an action pursuant to Civ.R. 23.1, then any recovery would accrue to the corporation and remain under the control of the very parties who are defendants in the litigation. Thus, a derivative remedy is not an effective remedy because the wrongdoers would be the principal beneficiaries of the recovery.

Where majority or controlling shareholders in a close corporation breach their heightened fiduciary duty to minority shareholders by utilizing their majority control of the corporation to their own advantage, without providing minority shareholders with an equal opportunity to benefit, such breach, absent a legitimate business purpose, is actionable. Where such a breach occurs, the minority shareholder is individually harmed. When such harm can be construed to be individual in nature, then a suit by a minority shareholder against the offending majority or controlling shareholders may proceed as a direct action. . . .

Accordingly, we hold that claims of a breach of fiduciary duty alleged by minority shareholders against shareholders who control a majority of shares in a close corporation, and use their control to deprive minority shareholders of the benefits of their investment, may be brought as individual or direct actions and are not subject to the provisions of Civ.R. 23.1. . . .

■ *Affirmed.*

CASE CONCEPTS REVIEW

1. How does this court describe the relationship among shareholders in a closely held corporation?
2. In what ways might the majority shareholders take advantage of the minority shareholders?
3. Who benefits the most when a derivative suit is successful?
4. Why does the court conclude that these minority shareholders should be allowed to file this action on an individual or direct basis?

Suits alleging a breach of fiduciary duty often involve the purchase of stock by a majority shareholder or director from a minority shareholder. Such purchases usually involve the use of inside information. A seller under these circumstances should be aware that the buyer has superior knowledge. In deciding such cases, there are three different views among the various states. The majority view is that a director does not stand in a fiduciary relationship to a shareholder in the acquisition of stock and therefore has no duty to disclose inside information. The minority view is that a director is under a duty to disclose all material information. The third view is that although a director ordinarily owes no fiduciary duty to shareholders when acquiring stock, under special circumstances a fiduciary relationship arises. The special facts creating the fiduciary relationship may include the familial relationship of the parties, the forthcoming sale of corporate assets, the director's initiation of the sale, and the relative ages and experience in financial affairs of the directors and the selling shareholder.

There are limits to the duties owed to minority shareholders. For example, in the absence of a valid buy-and-sell agreement, the majority shareholders or the corporation has no duty to redeem the stock upon the death of a minority shareholder. The following case provides another illustration of fiduciary duties of a limited nature.

CASE

Goode v. Ryan
489 N.E.2d 1001 (Mass. 1986)

Alice M. Marr owned 800 shares of the 11,340 shares outstanding of common stock of Gloucester Ice & Cold Storage Co., a close corporation. No provisions restricting the transfer of stock or requiring the corporation or remaining shareholders to redeem its stock on the death of a shareholder appear in the corporation's articles of organization or bylaws, or in any agreement among the shareholders.

After her death in 1977, the administrator of her estate informed the management of Gloucester of his desire to sell, or to have redeemed, the 800 shares of Gloucester stock owned by the Marr estate. By a letter dated April 4, 1978, North Shore offered to purchase the 800 shares from the Marr estate at $12.50 a share. The unaudited financial statement of Gloucester for the year ending December 31, 1977 indicated that the book value of the stock was $38.87 a share. The plaintiff did not accept the North Shore offer and, after a short time, the offer was withdrawn. At an annual meeting of stockholders in 1982, the administrator again requested redemption, but the corporation denied any obligation to do so. He then brought this action seeking a declaration that the fiduciary obligation shareholders of a close corporation owe one another requires that majority shareholders purchase, or cause the corporation to purchase, the shares of a minority shareholder on the death of the minority shareholder. The trial court entered summary judgment for the defendant. Thereafter in 1984 the corporation was dissolved and the plaintiff received the same liquidating distribution as other shareholders.

HENNESSEY, J.

... In *Donahue v. Rodd Electrotype Co. of New England*, 328 N.E.2d 505 (1975), we established the rule that shareholders in a close corporation owe one another substantially the same fiduciary duty of utmost good faith and loyalty in operation of the enterprise that partners owe one another. Applying that rule, we held in *Donahue* that a controlling shareholder selling a close corporation its own shares must cause the corporation to offer to purchase shares ratably from all other shareholders. Subsequently, we applied the rule to provide relief to a minority shareholder in a close corporation, whose employment and income from the corporation were terminated without cause by the majority shareholders. The plaintiff in the instant case asks us to apply the fiduciary principles established in those cases to hold that, on the death of a

minority shareholder, majority shareholders are obligated to purchase, or to cause the corporation to purchase, the shares owned by the minority shareholder.

As we stated in the *Donahue* case, one of the identifying characteristics of a close corporation is the absence of a ready market for corporate stock. A shareholder wishing to convert an investment in a close corporation to cash for personal financial reasons or because of unhappiness with the management of the enterprise will have only a limited number of opportunities for disposing of the asset. Similarly, the executor or administrator of the estate of a deceased shareholder in a close corporation will be confronted with an illiquid asset that may have a high value in the estate, but have little, if any, dividend value for the beneficiaries. In both situations, the only prospective purchasers for the stock may be the remaining shareholders in the corporation or the corporation itself.

Investors in other types of firms have easier mechanisms available for disposing of their interests. A shareholder in a large, public-issue corporation can sell the stock on the financial markets at no price disadvantage relative to other sellers of that stock. A member of a partnership can convert the investment to cash by exercising the right to dissolve the partnership.

The shareholder who owns less than a majority interest in a close corporation does not have any of these options. In the absence of an agreement among shareholders or between the corporation and the shareholder, or a provision in the corporation's articles of organization or bylaws, neither the corporation nor a majority of shareholders is under any obligation to purchase the shares of minority shareholders when minority shareholders wish to dispose of their interest in the corporation.

The minority shareholder in a close corporation is susceptible to oppression by the majority or controlling shareholders. In the instant case, there is no evidence of any oppressive conduct on the part of defendants directed at excluding the shares Goode represented from participation in the affairs of the corporation. In fact, the deceased shareholder, Alice Marr, never held corporate office, or served on the board of directors, or received any salary from Gloucester, and there is no indication that she or her estate was aggrieved by the absence of involvement in corporate management. The majority shareholders made no effort to curtail, or interfere with, any benefits to which Marr or her estate was entitled as a minority shareholder in Gloucester. The majority shareholders simply refused to purchase the Marr estate stock. This refusal violated no agreement or corporate governance provision and did not violate any fiduciary obligation they owed to the plaintiff. Nor are any facts present to permit us to conclude that the majority used assets of the corporation to enrich themselves at the expense of minority shareholders. The Marr estate received the same amount for each share upon the liquidation of Gloucester as the other shareholders received for their shares.

The plaintiff's argument that imposing a duty on majority shareholders or a close corporation to purchase the shares of a deceased shareholder at the request of the executor or administrator of the shareholder's estate would be consistent with the approach adopted in the Statutory Close Corporation Supplement to the Model Business Corporation Act is not correct. The provision requiring a corporation to purchase shares from the estate of a deceased shareholder applies only if the articles of incorporation of the close corporation contain the provision. Thus, the close corporation supplement leaves stock buyout arrangements to the agreement of the parties.

While the plaintiff's predicament in not being able to dispose of the Gloucester stock to facilitate prompt set-tlement of the Marr estate is unfortunate, the situation was not caused by the defendants but is merely one of the risks of ownership of stock in a close corporation. It is not the proper function of this court to reallocate the risks inherent in the ownership of corporate stock in the absence of corporate or majority shareholder misconduct. . . .

■ *Judgment affirmed.*

CASE CONCEPTS REVIEW

1. What is the legal theory used by Alice Marr's administrator in filing this lawsuit?
2. Who, according to the court, typically are potential buyers for the stock held by the administrator of a deceased shareholder of a closely held corporation?
3. What duty does the majority shareholder have to purchase these shares from the administrator?

DIRECTORS

8. Powers

Directors of a corporation are elected by the shareholders. They ordinarily attend meetings, exercise judgment on propositions brought before the board, vote, and direct management, although they need not be involved actively in the day-to-day operation of the business. A director has no power to issue orders to any officer or employee or to institute policies by himself or herself or command or veto any other action by the board.

It is not essential that directors hold stock in the corporation. Because they are to supervise the business activities, select key employees, and plan for the future development of the enterprise, they are presumably selected for their business ability.

At one time, most directors of major publicly held corporations were insiders—officials of the corporation. Today, insider-dominated corporate boards seem to be on the way out. Outside directors now constitute the majority on almost nine out of ten boards of directors. These outside directors provide greater independence, more minority representation, and greater diversification in the backgrounds of the directors. Moreover, many people feel that such boards accept more corporate social responsibility and greater accountability for their actions. They also demand higher standards of performance by corporate officers.

Directors have power to take action necessary or proper to conduct the ordinary business activities of the company. However, they may not amend the charter, approve a merger, or bring about a consolidation with another corporation without the approval of the shareholders.

9. Meetings

The bylaws usually provide for the number of directors. Historically, at least three directors were required; but in recent years, many corporate statutes have authorized two directors—and in some cases, one director. This development is especially prevalent in professional associations or corporations, which frequently have only one shareholder and thus only one director.

Since the board of directors must act as a unit, it is traditional that it assemble at board meetings. The bylaws provide for the method of calling directors' meetings and for the time and the place of the meetings. A record is usually kept of the activities of the board of directors, and the evidence of the exercise of its powers is stated in resolutions kept in the corporate minute book. A majority of the members of the board of directors is necessary to constitute a quorum, unless a bylaw provides to the contrary. Special meetings are proper only when all directors are notified or are present at the meetings. Directors may not vote by proxy, having been selected as agents because of their personal qualifications.

Modern statutes make it possible for a board to take informal action (usually by telephone), provided the action is subsequently reduced to writing and signed by all of the directors. This gives a board the flexibility and capability to make decisions without delay. Failure to have unanimous approval of such informal action or to give proper notice is fatal to actions attempted by the board of directors.

Traditionally, directors were forbidden to vote on any matter in which they had a personal interest. Even though their vote was not necessary to carry the proposition considered, many courts would regard any action voidable if it was taken as a result of that vote. Some courts went so far as to hold that if a director was present at the meeting, favorable action was not binding. Most courts held that if a director's presence was required to make a quorum, no transaction in which he or she was interested could be acted on. These rather severe rules were developed so directors would not be tempted to use their position to profit at the expense of the corporation.

Today, many states have somewhat relaxed traditional rules on directors' voting and participation. The trend of the law is to allow interested directors to be present and to be counted as a part of the quorum. Actions taken with interested directors are valid if the participating director's interest is fully and completely disclosed, provided the action is approved by a majority of disinterested directors. Even in states that have changed the earlier common-law view, a director with a personal interest in a subject is not allowed to vote on the matter. The problem of acting in good faith is discussed later in this chapter.

10. Compensation

The charter, bylaws, or a resolution by the shareholders usually stipulates payment of directors' fees. If not, service as a director is uncompensated. Directors who are appointed as officers of the corporation should have their salaries fixed at a meeting of the shareholders or in the bylaws. Because directors are not supposed to vote on any matter in which they have a personal interest, director officers of small corporations usually vote on salaries for each other but not their own, and the action to determine salaries should be ratified by the shareholders to ensure the validity of the employment contracts.

Some states by statute allow a majority of directors to fix all salaries irrespective of financial interest. In these states, courts are often called on to review the reasonableness of approved salaries.

11. In General

The officers and directors of a corporation may have personal liability both in tort and in contract. The principles of the law of agency are applicable; liability is usually to the corporation, although it may extend to shareholders and third parties as well.

The liability of corporate officers and directors for tortious conduct is predicated on basic common-law principles. Those who personally participate in a tort have personal liability to the third party on the usual common-law tort theories, as does any other agent or servant. This liability is based on the participation theory.

Several statutes impose liability on directors and officers. Officers and directors who have responsibility for federal withholding and social security taxes may be liable to the federal government for failure to collect and transfer these taxes for their employees. In the following case, notice the lengths the state government and the court went to in order to impose liability for sales taxes on an employee who had no financial interest in the corporation other than a job.

CASE

Cardellino v. Comptroller
511 A.2d 573 (Md. 1986)

The state of Maryland levied an assessment of $4,865.80 in retail sales tax against Margo Cardellino because of her status as secretary-treasurer of Prince Frederick Auto Parts, Inc. (the corporation). The corporation's articles stated that one of its purposes was to retail auto parts. Michael Finkle was the only director named, and Finkle testified that he owned, operated, and appointed himself president of the corporation. After the filing of the articles of incorporation, none of the routine corporate formalities were undertaken; no bylaws were adopted, no shares of stock were issued, and no organizational or annual meetings were held.

Margo was hired as a secretary and bookkeeper for the business, with duties that included sending out bills, keeping a record of inventory, answering the telephone, and writing checks. She was an authorized signature on the Prince Frederick Auto Parts, Inc. checking account

and had the responsibility of filing monthly sales tax returns. Finkle testified that although the accountant had recommended that appellant be made secretary and treasurer, this was never actually done.

When Margo filed the sales tax returns, she added "Secy-Treas." in the blank below her signature. She was listed as a corporate officer on personal property tax returns also. The lower courts found that the corporation was validly formed and that she was liable for the taxes as a corporate officer, and she appeals.

BISHOP, J. . . .

Incorporation

Appellant asserts that since Prince Frederick Auto Parts never undertook to accomplish any corporate formalities beyond filing articles of incorporation, a corporate entity was never actually formed. . . .

Md.Corps. & Ass'ns Code Ann., § 2-102 provides in relevant part:

§ 2-102. Formation generally.

a. *Signing, acknowledging and filing articles of incorporation.*—Except as provided elsewhere in this section, in order to form a corporation, one or more adult individuals acting as incorporators shall:

1. Sign and acknowledge articles of incorporation; and
2. File them for record with the Department.

b. *Effect of acceptance of articles of incorporation for record; . . .*

1. When the Department accepts articles of incorporation for record, the proposed corporation becomes a body corporate under the name and subject to the purposes, conditions, and provisions stated in the articles.
2. Except in a proceeding by the State for forfeiture of a corporation's charter, acceptance of the articles for record by the Department is *conclusive evidence of the formation of the corporation.*

Since the articles were filed by Prince Frederick Auto Parts, the creation of the corporate entity is conclusively established. . . . Appellant argues that since no organizational meeting was held here, the corporation never completed its organization. We hold, however, that principles of estoppel prevent appellant from asserting the alleged defect in organization.

In *Cranson v. I.B.M. Corp.,* 200 A.2d 33 (1963), the Court stated:

[W]here the corporation has obtained legal existence but has failed to comply with a condition subsequent to corporate existence, this Court has held that such nonperformance afforded the State the right to institute proceedings for the forfeiture of the charter, but that such neglect or omission could never be set up by the corporation itself, or by its members and stockholders, as a defense to an action to enforce their liabilities.

We hold that these principles are applicable here. The filing of the articles was conclusive proof of the existence of the corporation. By filing documents as a corporate officer, appellant implicitly represented to the State that the corporation was validly organized, and cannot now seek to avoid the liabilities that flow from being a corporate officer by asserting the lack of the formal steps of organization.

Appellant's Liability as a Corporate Officer

Because of Md. Ann. Code art. 81, § 328 and since appellant was found to be a corporate officer, the Tax Court and the Circuit Court affirmed the assessment against appellant for unpaid retail sales tax.

We hold that appellant was either a *de jure* or *de facto* corporate officer of Prince Frederick Auto Parts, Inc. and therefore affirm the decisions below. In *Freestate* the Court of Appeals stated:

Though ordinarily a vote of shareholders or directors is necessary to elect or appoint officers, it has been held that the appointment of an officer may be "inferred." Persons acting as officers are presumed to be such and rightfully in office in the absence of proof to the contrary.

Finkle, the sole director of the corporation, appointed appellant to undertake tasks utilizing the title of secretary-treasurer. Appellant prepared and signed the retail sales tax returns as secretary-treasurer, was specified as secretary-treasurer on personal property tax returns, and signed the personal property tax returns as an officer of the corporation. There was absolutely no testimony that appellant was misled as to the effect of the forms or was somehow prevented from reading the forms.

Even if the formal requirements of installing appellant as a corporate officer were not met, there was sufficient evidence to sustain a conclusion that appellant was the *de facto* secretary-treasurer of the corporation. As such, appellant became personally liable for the unpaid retail sales tax. To hold otherwise would allow an individual to avoid liability even though she held herself out to be a corporate officer, who under § 328 is personally obligated to pay the unpaid sales tax. Extreme caution must be exercised by a person who signs a tax return as a corporate officer under an oath which affirms the correctness of the tax information and the official status of the signer.

■ *Judgment affirmed.*

CASE CONCEPTS REVIEW

1. Was Margo Cardellino formally named as the secretary-treasurer of Prince Frederick Auto Parts, Inc.?
2. What act is essential to the creation of a corporation?
3. The phrase *de facto* means "in actuality regardless of formalities." On what basis does the court conclude that Margo Cardellino was in fact the secretary-treasurer of this corporation?

There are numerous other statutes that impose liability on officers and directors of corporations. For example, they are subject to third-party liability for aiding a corporation in such acts as patent, copyright, or trademark infringements, unfair competition, antitrust violations, violation of the laws relating to discrimination, or violations of the securities laws. They are also personally liable when they issue stock as fully paid when it is not paid in full, or when dividends are declared or treasury stock is purchased without the requisite retained earnings.

The relationship between the officers and directors and a corporation is a fiduciary one. The existence and exercise of the statutory power of directors, rather than shareholders, to manage the business and the affairs of a corporation carries with it certain fundamental fiduciary obligations to the corporation and its shareholders. These fiduciary duties of corporate directors require that they act in the best interests of the corporation's shareholders, and this duty extends to protecting the corporation and its owners from perceived harm whether a threat originates from third parties or other shareholders. Liability is often imposed for violation of these fiduciary duties owed to the corporation. When liability is sought, the usual defense is the business judgment rule discussed in the next section. The fiduciary relationship requires that directors act in good faith and with due care. It prohibits conflicts of interest and imposes a duty of undivided loyalty on officers and directors. This rule is discussed further in the following sections.

12. The Business Judgment Rule

The *business judgment rule* means that courts honoring principles of corporate self-government will not inquire into the good-faith decisions involving business judgment. Directors are not liable for breach of fiduciary duties because of mere mistakes of judgment. The rule protects directors from personal liability in damages. It applies to cases of transactional justification where an injunction is sought against board action or against its decision. It puts the focus on the decision of the board as contrasted with any possible liability of the board of directors. The rule arises from the fiduciary duties of directors. It creates a presumption that places the burden of demonstrating bad faith on the party attacking an action of a board of directors. The presumption is that the directors of corporations act on an informed basis in good faith and in the honest belief that the action taken was in the best interests of the company. Thus they are presumed not to be personally liable.

The presumption is also based on the belief that directors are better equipped than courts to make business judgments and that directors act independently, without self-dealing or personal interest, and exercise reasonable diligence. There are exceptions to the business judgment rule. The business judgment rule can only sustain corporate decision making or transactions that are within the power or authority of the board of directors. If the directors are guilty of fraud, bad faith, gross overreaching, an abuse of discretion, or gross negligence, then the business judgment rule does not prevent a court from imposing personal liability on directors or from changing a board decision. If corporate directors are not entitled to protection of the business judgment rule, the courts scrutinize directors' decisions as to their intrinsic fairness to the corporation and to its minority shareholders.

The business judgment rule is asserted in a variety of cases. As was previously indicated, many cases involve derivative suits and a board decision to sue on behalf of the corporation. In recent years corporate takeover issues have frequently been litigated. For example, boards of directors have amended corporate bylaws to change the rights of shareholders and have restructured corporations to avoid take-overs. Boards have granted officers of corporations "golden parachutes" to protect them should a takeover occur. Preferred stock has been issued to avoid proxy fights. In cases such as these, the corporation usually defends its action by using the business judgment rule. In doing so, the directors must show that they had reasonable grounds for believing that a danger to corporate policy and effectiveness existed that required the action taken. The proof in takeover cases that a defense is reasonable in relation to the defenses posed is materially enhanced where a majority of the board favoring the proposal consisted of outside independent directors who have acted on an informed basis, in good faith, and in the honest belief that the action taken was in the best interests of the company. This also applies to a decision of disinterested directors, made in good faith and in the exercise of honest judgment, not to litigate a claim of the corporation.

13. Loyalty and Good Faith

A director occupies a position of trust and confidence with respect to the corporation and cannot, by reason of his or her position, directly or indirectly derive any personal benefits that are not enjoyed by the corporation or the shareholders. This duty of loyalty or the duty to act in good faith prohibits directors from acting with a conflict of interest. The most common violation of this duty occurs when a director enters into a contract with, or personally deals with, the corporation. A conflict of interest also arises in transactions between the director's corporation and another entity in which he or she may be a director, employee, investor, or one who is otherwise interested. In all circumstances, the director or officer must fully disclose a conflict of interest to the corporation. If the director fails to do so, the contract may be rescinded.

Under common law, a contract between a corporation and one of its directors was voidable unless it was shown to be approved by a disinterested board *and* "fair" to the corporation, in that its terms were as favorable as those available from any other person. Under some modern statutes, the transaction is valid if it is approved, with knowledge of the material facts, by a vote of disinterested directors or shareholders *or* if the director can show it to be "fair."

Issues of good faith frequently arise when a corporation is in financial difficulty. For example, the good faith of a director or officer is an issue when such a person is attempting to collect a personal loan to the corporation. Directors and officers may make loans to their corporations, and they may use the same methods as other creditors to collect bona fide corporation debts owed to them, but only as long as the corporation is solvent. When a corporation is insolvent or on the verge of insolvency, its directors and officers become fiduciaries of corporate assets for the benefit of creditors. As fiduciaries, directors and officers cannot by reason of their special position give themselves preference over the other creditors in collecting bona fide business debts.

Many cases involve the *corporate opportunity doctrine.* This doctrine precludes corporate fiduciaries from diverting to themselves business opportunities in which the corporation has an expectancy, property interest, or right, or which in fairness should otherwise belong to the corporation. The doctrine follows from a corporate fiduciary's duty of undivided loyalty to the corporation. The good-faith requirement is lacking when a director or officer takes for himself or herself an opportunity that the corporation should have had.

A director must present all possible corporate opportunities to the corporation first. Only after disinterested, informed directors have determined that the corporation should not pursue such opportunities can a director pursue them for his or her own benefits. If a corporate director acquires property for himself or herself, knowing the corporation desires it, the director breaches his or her fiduciary relation to the corporation, and it may obtain the property.

Persons charged with violating the corporate opportunity doctrine sometimes seek to avoid liability by claiming that the corporation was not in a financial position to take advantage of the opportunity. In most states, if the corporation is solvent, financial inability to undertake an opportunity does not absolve a corporate fiduciary from liability for diverting what is otherwise a corporate opportunity. Financial insolvency will, however, excuse corporate fiduciaries from liability in most states. The fiduciary has the burden of proving insolvency; mere financial difficulty is not enough.

To allow a corporate fiduciary to take advantage of a business opportunity when the fiduciary determines the corporation to be unable to avail itself of it would create the worst sort of temptation for the fiduciary. He or she could rationalize an inaccurate and self-serving assessment of the corporation's financial ability and thereby compromise the duty of loyalty to the corporation. If a corporate fiduciary's duty of loyalty conflicts with personal interest, the latter must give way.

The appropriate method to determine whether or not a corporate opportunity exists is to let the corporation decide at the time the opportunity is presented. If a fiduciary is uncertain whether a given opportunity is corporate or not, or whether the corporation has the financial ability to pursue it, this fiduciary needs merely to disclose the existence of the opportunity to the directors and let them decide. Disclosure is a fundamental fiduciary duty. It cannot be burdensome, and it resolves the issue for all parties concerned and eliminates the necessity for a judicial determination after the fact.

A corporate officer or director does not become free to appropriate a business opportunity of the corporation by resigning his or her office. The duty continues after the resignation.

14. Due Care

In addition to good faith, directors must exercise due care. In its simplest terms, the duty to exercise *due care* is synonymous with a duty not to be negligent. As a general rule, directors owe that degree of care that a businessperson of ordinary prudence would exercise in the management of his or her own affairs. The nature and extent of reasonable care depend on the type of corporation, its size, and its financial resources. A bank director is held to stricter accountability than the director of an ordinary business. In large corporations many duties must be delegated, so directors' intimate knowledge of details is not possible. In corporations invested with a public interest—such as insurance companies, banks, and public utilities—rigid supervision and specific obligations are imposed on directors. If a director fails to exercise the requisite degree of care and skill, the corporation will have a right of action against him or her for any resulting losses.

As a general rule, a director should acquire at least a rudimentary understanding of the business of the corporation and should be familiar with the fundamentals of that business. Since directors are bound to exercise ordinary care, they cannot set up as a defense to a suit against them lack of knowledge needed to exercise the requisite degree of care. If one has not had sufficient business experience to perform the duties of a director, one should either acquire the knowledge by inquiry or refuse to serve.

Directors must keep informed about the activities of the corporation. Otherwise, they may not be able to participate in the overall management of corporate affairs. Directors may not shut their eyes to corporate misconduct and then claim that because they did not see the misconduct, they did not have a duty to look. They have a duty to protect the corporation. This does not require a detailed inspection of day-to-day activities but a general monitoring of corporate affairs and policies. Accordingly, a director should attend board meetings regularly. Indeed, a director who is absent from a board meeting is presumed to concur in action taken on a corporate matter, unless a dissent is filed with the secretary of the corporation within a reasonable time after learning of such action.

Although directors are not required to audit corporate books, they should be familiar with the financial affairs of the corporation through a regular review of its financial statements. In some circumstances, directors may be charged with ensuring that bookkeeping methods conform to industry custom and usage. The extent of review, as well as the nature and frequency of financial statements, depends not only on the customs of the industry but also on the nature of the corporation and the business in which it is engaged. Financial statements of some small corporations may be prepared internally and only on an annual basis; in a large, publicly held corporation, the statements may be produced monthly or at some other regular interval. Adequate financial review normally would be more informal in a private corporation than in a publicly held corporation.

Generally, directors are immune from liability if, in good faith, they rely on the opinion of counsel for the corporation or on written reports prepared by a certified public accountant or on financial statements, books of account, or reports of the corporation represented to them to be correct by the president, the officer of the corporation having charge of its books of account, or the person presiding at a meeting of the board. The review of financial statements, however, may give rise to a duty to inquire further into matters revealed by those statements. Upon discovery of an illegal course of action, a director has a duty to object, and if the corporation does not correct the conduct, to resign.

In certain circumstances, the fulfillment of the duty of a director may call for more than mere objection and resignation; sometimes a director may be required to seek the advice of legal counsel. A director may require legal advice concerning the propriety of his or her own conduct, the conduct of other officers and directors, or the conduct of the corporation. A director should consult with corporate counsel or his or her own legal adviser whenever there is doubt regarding a proposed action. Sometimes the duty of a director may require more than consulting with outside counsel. A director may have a duty to take reasonable means to prevent illegal conduct by codirectors, including the threat of suit.

A director is not an ornament, but an essential component of corporate governance. Consequently, a director cannot protect himself or herself behind a paper shield bearing the motto "dummy director." A director may incur liability by failing to do more than passively rubber-stamp the decisions of the active managers. Directors must use their best business judgment. As previously discussed, they have no liability for honest mistakes. Directors are liable to the corporation for negligence in management. As a general rule, since no duty extends to third-party creditors, there is no liability to them or to the shareholders individually.

15. Indemnification and Insurance

In recent years, dissenting shareholders, public interest groups, and government regulators have caused a dramatic increase in the number of lawsuits filed against directors and officers of publicly held corporations. Many of the lawsuits result from the failure of directors to prevent activities such as bribery of foreign officials and illegal political contributions. Most large corporations carry liability insurance for directors, and costs for this insurance are soaring because of the increased number of suits.

To reimburse directors and officers for the expenses of defending lawsuits if the insurance is nonexistent or inadequate, most states provide by statute for indemnification by the corporation. The Model Business Corporation Act provides that the standard for indemnification is that the director must have "acted in good faith and in a manner he reasonably believed to be in or not opposed to the best interests of the corporation" and, if a criminal action, "had no reasonable cause to believe his conduct was unlawful." The indemnification is automatic if the director has been successful in the defense of any action.

CHAPTER SUMMARY

SHAREHOLDERS

Rights in General	1. Shareholders have rights created by statute. These usually include the right to inspect the books and papers of the corporation, the right to attend meetings and to vote, and the right to dividends.
	2. The right to inspect the books and papers is limited to good-faith inspections for proper and honest purposes at the proper time and the proper place.
	3. An attempt to oust present management is a proper purpose for inspection.
	4. Shareholders have the right to the assistance of accountants and attorneys in that inspection.
Meetings	1. Shareholders are entitled to notice of the annual meeting and of special meetings as well. The notice must include the matters to be acted on at special meetings and all unusual matters that are on the agenda of the annual meeting.
	2. Informal action by all shareholders may be taken without an actual meeting.
	3. A quorum is usually a majority of the voting stock.
Voting	1. Shareholders usually vote to elect directors and on issues such as dissolution.
	2. Election of directors by cumulative voting is possible in some states.
	3. Shareholders may vote by proxy.
	4. Shareholders may vote on matters in which they have a personal interest.
Preemptive Rights	1. Shareholders also may have preemptive rights, which are the rights to buy a proportionate share of new stock.
	2. These rights usually are associated with newly authorized stock and not with previously authorized, but unissued, stock.
Derivative Suits	1. A shareholder has the right to bring a suit on behalf of the corporation when the directors fail to do so. Shareholders usually must demand that the directors take action before filing such a suit.
	2. The minority shareholders of a corporation agree tacitly to be bound by the acts of the majority. The majority controls the business unless acting illegally, oppressively, or fraudulently.
Dividends	1. A shareholder has a right to dividends declared but has no right to have dividends declared.

	2. It is generally up to the board of directors to declare a dividend.
	3. A stock dividend is a transfer of retained earnings to capital.
	4. A stock split is the reduction of par value and the increase in the number of shares outstanding. It in effect gives the shareholder nothing of additional value.
Fiduciary Aspects	**1.** In a publicly held corporation, the shareholders do not stand in a fiduciary relationship with each other.
	2. In a closely held corporation, the shareholders do stand in a fiduciary relationship to the enterprise and to each other.
	3. Shareholders in a closely held corporation must act in good faith. In many states, this includes the duty to disclose relevant information.

DIRECTORS

Powers	**1.** The directors determine policy in the ordinary course of business and elect the officers.
	2. Directors need not be shareholders.
Meetings	**1.** The bylaws provide the procedures for calling and conducting directors' meetings, and minutes of them are maintained.
	2. The majority of the directors constitute a quorum, and action is usually by a majority.
	3. Directors may not vote by proxy, but informal action that is unanimous is allowed in most states.
	4. Directors may not vote on matters in which they have a personal interest, although their presence may be used to constitute a quorum.
Compensation	**1.** Directors are compensated as provided in the bylaws.
	2. Directors fix the salary of officers, but generally they cannot vote on their own salary.

LIABILITY OF OFFICERS AND DIRECTORS

In General	**1.** Directors and officers may have personal liability both in tort and in contract. This liability may be to the corporation or to third parties.
	2. Directors are liable to the corporation for breach of their fiduciary duties or of duties imposed by statute.
The Business Judgment Rule	**1.** Directors are not liable for breach of fiduciary duties because of mere mistakes of judgment.
	2. The presumption is that the directors of corporations act on an informed basis in good faith and in the honest belief that the action taken was in the best interests of the company.
	3. The presumption is based on the belief that directors are better equipped than courts to make business judgments.
	4. If the directors are guilty of fraud, bad faith, gross overreaching, an abuse of discretion, or gross negligence, then the business judgment rule does not prevent a court from imposing personal liability on directors or from changing a board decision.
Loyalty and Good Faith	**1.** Directors must act in good faith. The duty of good faith creates liability if there is a conflict of interest.
	2. The *corporate opportunity doctrine* precludes corporate fiduciaries from diverting to themselves business opportunities in which the corporation has an expectancy, property interest, or right, or which in fairness should otherwise belong to the corporation.
Due Care	**1.** As a general rule, directors owe that degree of care that a businessperson of ordinary prudence would exercise in the management of his or her own affairs.
	2. Directors may rely on experts such as accountants or attorneys in exercising their responsibilities.
	3. Directors are not liable to third parties for negligence in management.
Indemnification and Insurance	**1.** Corporations usually carry liability insurance to protect directors.

REVIEW QUESTIONS AND PROBLEMS

1. Match each term in column A with the appropriate statement in column B.

	A		B
(1)	Cumulative voting	(a)	A lawsuit filed on behalf of a corporation by a shareholder as a result of the failure of the officers and directors to file the suit
(2)	Preemptive right	(b)	A majority of the shares of a corporation
(3)	Derivative suit	(c)	The record date on which a dividend is payable
(4)	Quorum	(d)	A reduction in par value and an increase in the number of shares outstanding
(5)	Proxy	(e)	Court's deference to officers and directors
(6)	Ex-dividend date	(f)	A shareholder is entitled to the number of votes in electing directors that is the product of number of shares times number of directors to be elected. All the shareholder's votes may be cast for one director.
(7)	Stock split	(g)	The right to vote someone else's stock
(8)	Business judgment rule	(h)	The right of a shareholder to purchase additional stock of subsequent stock issues so he or she may maintain the overall percentage of total stock outstanding

2. Miles, a bank shareholder, requested an unlimited inspection of the bank's books and records. He said that he wanted to ascertain whether any action had been taken contrary to the best interests of the stockholders, such as misuses of corporate funds; abuse of corporate office; diversion of corporate assets to the personal benefit of any officer, director, employee, or stockholder; misapplication of corporate assets; or favoring of certain customers of the bank because of personal connections with officers or directors of the bank. He also wanted to determine whether the directors had lived up to their fiduciary obligation to the stockholders. Must the bank honor his request? Explain.

3. All stockholders were present at the annual stockholders' meeting of a corporation whose bylaws required only a majority of shareholders to constitute a quorum. During the meeting, two stockholders who owned a majority of the stock withdrew from the meeting while it was in progress. Following their withdrawal, the remaining stockholders elected five members to the board of directors. Should the election of the directors be invalidated? Why or why not?

4. A corporation board authorized a director, Wilson, to negotiate the purchase of some land. Instead, Wilson secretly bought the land himself and sold it to the corporation at a profit. After learning of the deceit, the corporation failed to act. Do the minority shareholders have any remedy? Explain.

5. Able, Baker, and Charlie were directors of the ABC Corporation. During the early years the corporation met with moderate success and showed a small annual profit each year. There was nothing in the corporate charter or bylaws in respect to compensation for directors, and during this initial period the directors did not seek or receive any compensation. In 1992, the corporation had a banner year, several new contracts were obtained, and a new product line that the directors decided the corporation should make and sell proved highly profitable. The directors performed the usual and customary services and duties of their office in a highly competent and skillful manner, and their efforts were to a large extent responsible for the large profit obtained in 1992. After the 1992 income statement was received and examined by the directors, they met on March 15, 1993, and voted themselves retroactive bonus of $10,000 each as the reasonable value of services for the past years. Sherman, a stockholder of record, objected to this action and now brings a derivative stockholder's action against the directors and seeks to obtain a judgment against each of the directors to the extent of the bonus he received. Is this derivative suit a proper action? Why?

6. On March 1, a company declared a cash dividend of $1 per share, payable on June 1 to all stockholders of record on May 1. On April 10, Ann sold ten shares of her stock to Bob, but the transfer was not recorded on the corporation's books until May 15. To whom will the company pay the dividend? Who is entitled to the dividend? Explain.

7. There were two equal shareholders of Bonanza, Inc., a shopping center operation. Hunt, as president, managed the business. Sampson was secretary but inactive. Hunt purchased Sampson's stock for $75,000. At the time of the sale, Hunt did not inform Sampson of (1) additional leases that had been obtained, (2) a commitment for the financing of a third phase of the development, and (3) sale of part of the stock to three doctors. Is Sampson entitled to recover the difference between the selling price and the fair market value of the stock at the time of the sale? Why or why not?

8. Abner owned a majority of the stock of Lum Company, and he ran the corporation by himself. The balance of the stock was owned by Abner's brother and sister, who agreed to sell all their stock to him. At the time of the purchase, Abner was negotiating a sale of the company, but he did not reveal this fact to his brother and sister. The sale of the company resulted in a great profit to Abner. The brother and sister brought suit to recover the difference. Should the brother and sister succeed? Why?

9. Wilkes and three other individuals formed a corporation to operate a nursing home many years ago. The four corporate shareholders were also elected directors, and they served as employees of the close corporation. Plaintiff had a quarrel with one of the other directors after years of successful operation. As a result, the other board members canceled plaintiff's salary, refused to reelect him as director, and stopped paying dividends in an attempt to freeze him out. He sued for damages on the ground that the majority had breached the fiduciary duty owed to him. Is the plaintiff's argument correct? Why?

10. Alan is chairman of the board of directors of Shipping Corporation. The bylaws of the corporation provide for a seven-person board of directors, one of whom has just died. The bylaws have no provision for filling a vacancy, and Alan would like to appoint his brother. Alan attempted to telephone the other directors and inform them of what he would like to do. He contacted two directors, who agreed by telephone. A third director could not be reached. The fourth director agreed to Alan's plan on behalf of himself and the fifth director, who had given his proxy to the fourth director. The substance of the telephone calls was not reduced to writing. Can Alan legally appoint his brother as a director? Explain.

11. A Michigan statute requires all corporations to provide funds to meet any workers' compensation claim presented by an employee. Failure to so provide, by insurance or otherwise, renders the officers and directors jointly and severally liable. Plaintiff was injured during the course of his employment with the corporate defendant and was awarded 215 weeks of compensation. Shortly thereafter, the corporation went bankrupt without paying the claim. Plaintiff seeks to hold the officers and directors personally liable. Are these officers and directors liable? Explain.

12. A company was in arrears on five of its preferred dividends but paid the sixth dividend anyway because the stock subscription agreement provided that if six dividends were omitted, the preferred stockholders were entitled to assume control of the company. The dividends were paid while the capital was impaired. Are the directors personally liable for the dividends paid? Why or why not?

13. Andrews, a director of Omega Corporation, learned of a very valuable mineral discovery on certain land that could be acquired at a bargain price. Without revealing this information to Omega, Andrews, acting through his brother-in-law, acquired the mineral rights for the property and resold them to Omega at a large profit. Did Andrews incur any liability to Omega as a result of these transactions? Explain.

14. Plaintiffs sued the president, vice president, and secretary of the corporation that built them new houses. They alleged that due to faulty planning, their homes were built in an area that was often flooded by the drainage of the other areas of the development. Do the officers have personal liability? Why or why not?

DISSOLUTION
OF CORPORATIONS

CHAPTER PREVIEW

In the preceding two chapters, you have studied how the corporate organization is formed and how it operates. In this chapter, we discuss the termination or death of the corporation. Generally, a corporation is dissolved in one of three ways: (1) expiration of a stated period of duration, (2) a voluntary dissolution by management, or (3) an involuntary dissolution by other parties.

When a corporation's charter stipulates that the corporation shall exist for a definite period, the organization automatically terminates upon the expiration of the period. Only an application to continue the corporation's existence that is approved by the state granting the original charter will prevent the organization's demise.

This automatic dissolution does not occur frequently, because most charters provide for the corporation's perpetual existence. In these situations, formal action is necessary to end the corporation's life. Corporate dissolutions are often associated with the combination, through merger or consolidation, of two or more existing corporations. When such a combination of corporations occurs, the impact of antitrust law must be considered.

This chapter discusses the various methods and events of corporate dissolutions.

You are major shareholder, director, and officer of a corporation that is interested in acquiring the capability to manufacture explosives. Your corporation has the opportunity to buy the Powder Keg Company. This company has a history of manufacturing dynamite and fireworks.

If your company acquires Powder Keg, what steps should be taken to reduce your company's liability for any defective products previously manufactured by Powder Keg?

VOLUNTARY DISSOLUTIONS

1. Procedures

A corporation that has obtained its charter but has not commenced business may be dissolved by its incorporators. The incorporators file articles of dissolution with the state, and a certificate of dissolution is issued if all fees are paid and the articles are in order.

A corporation that has commenced business may be voluntarily dissolved either by the written consent of *all* its shareholders or by corporate action instituted by its board of directors and approved by the requisite percentage (usually two-thirds) of the shareholders. The board action, usually in the form of a recommendation, directs that the issue be submitted to the shareholders. A meeting of shareholders is called to consider the dissolution issue, and if the vote is in favor of it to the degree required by statute, the officers follow the statutory procedures for dissolution.

These procedures require the corporate officers to file a statement of intent to dissolve. The statement is filed with the state of incorporation, and it includes either the consent of all shareholders or the resolutions instituted by the board of directors. Upon filing the statement of intent to dissolve, the corporation must cease to carry on its business, except for winding up its affairs, even though corporate existence continues until a certificate of dissolution is issued by the state.

The filing of a statement of intent to dissolve is revocable. If the shareholders change their minds before the articles of dissolution are issued, the decision may be revoked by filing a statement of revocation of voluntary dissolution proceedings. When such a statement is filed, the corporation may resume its business.

2. Notice to Creditors

In winding up its affairs, the corporation must give notice to all known creditors of the corporation. If notice is not given, the corporation remains liable on the debts. Statutes of limitation, which eventually wipe out claims against corporations and their shareholders, do not start to run until notice of dissolution is given. In addition, directors become personally liable for any debt of which notice is not given. These debts include tort claims as well as contract claims, as the following case illustrates.

CASE

Bonsall v. Piggly Wiggly Helms, Inc.
274 S.E.2d 298 (S.C. 1981)

Bonsall was injured in a "slip and fall" accident while shopping at the defendant's grocery store. She telephoned the store and notified them of her injury. Defendant notified its insurance company, and an adjuster contacted the plaintiff and her attorney.

Thereafter, the defendant corporation was dissolved. It failed to give actual notice of intent to dissolve to the plaintiff, although it published notice of dissolution in the newspaper. The South Carolina law on corporate dissolution provides the following:

> After the filing by the Secretary of State of a statement of intent to dissolve, . . . (b) The corporation shall immediately cause notice of the filing of the statement of intent to dissolve to be mailed to each *known creditor* of the corporation. . . .

LEWIS, J.

. . . The sole question in this appeal is whether or not respondent was a "known creditor" . . . so as to require notice to her of appellant's dissolution in order to bar her claim under the two year limitation provisions of Code Section 33-21-220. We affirm the holding of the lower court that respondent was a "known creditor" to whom notice was required to be given in order to bar her tort claim.

The preponderance of the evidence supports this finding. The call by respondent to a woman at Piggly Wiggly, notifying it of her fall, resulted in an adjuster of the store contacting the respondent. This gives rise to the reasonable inference, . . . that Piggly Wiggly had notice of the respondent's fall and her resulting claim for damages.

We next consider the question of a tort claimant as a creditor. *Stewart, Admr. v. Walterboro and Western Ry. Co.*, 64 S.C. 92, considered the magnitude of the term creditor in the context of a corporate merger. The Court held that the defendant, which had since pursued a merger into a new corporation, was not dissolved as a corporation insofar as the rights of the plaintiff. Although the statute involved concerned merger and not dissolution, as pointed out by the appellant, this distinction is not of significance. Both address the viability of actions against corporate entities seeking to end their corporate existence as it existed at the time of the claim.

The respondent's tort claim made her a creditor within the meaning of Section 33-21-60, entitling her to notice of dissolution. Since notice was not given to respondent, who was a known creditor, the corporation was not dissolved insofar as the rights of the respondent. . . .

■ *Judgment affirmed.*

CASE CONCEPTS REVIEW

1. What is the factual basis of Bonsall's claim against Piggly Wiggly?
2. What type of notice, if any, did Bonsall receive upon the dissolution of Piggly Wiggly?
3. Why does the court conclude that Bonsall was a known creditor of Piggly Wiggly?
4. What type of notice is a known creditor entitled to when a corporate-debtor dissolves?

---

3. Distributions

In dissolution proceedings, corporate assets are first used to pay debts. After all debts are paid, the remainder is distributed proportionately among the shareholders. If there are insufficient assets to pay all debts, a receiver will be appointed by a court, and the proceedings will be similar to those of involuntary dissolutions, discussed later.

When all funds are distributed, the corporation will prepare duplicate articles of dissolution and forward them to the state for approval. When signed by the appropriate state official, usually the secretary of state, one copy is filed with state records and one copy is returned to the corporation to be kept with the corporate records.

If the assets of a dissolved corporation are not used to pay the organization's debts, the directors and shareholders who approved the improper distribution of assets may be personally liable to the unpaid creditors. In the following case, the timing of dissolution and the distribution of assets are discussed as the keys to whether personal liability should be placed on a director/shareholder.

CASE

W & K Farms, Inc. v. Walter
458 N.W.2d 230 (Neb. 1990)

HASTINGS, C. J.

... Appellant W & K Farms, Inc., filed a ... petition, alleging generally that Hi-Line Farms, Inc., made and delivered to plaintiff W & K Farms its promissory note in the sum of $38,595.92; that with a minor exception, no payment had been made on the note; ... that Hi-Line Farms was dissolved for nonpayment of occupation taxes on August 4, 1981; ... and that since dissolution of the corporation, defendant Walter, as the sole remaining officer and only stockholder, appropriated the corporate property as his own without regard to plaintiff's debt and had failed and refused to pay the debt.

The ... petition goes on to allege that defendant Walter holds the property of the corporation in trust for the creditors and prays for judgment against Walter in the amount of the unpaid balance of the note.

Defendant Walter ... [moved to dismiss] this ... petition. Plaintiff W & K Farms asked leave of the court to amend its ... petition by alleging that Walter was a director of the dissolved corporation. Leave was denied, ... and the ... petition was dismissed on the basis that the survival period of § 21-20,104 had expired.

Section 21-20,104 provides in part that "the dissolution of a corporation ... shall not take away or impair any remedy ... for the right or claim existing, or any liability incurred, *prior to such dissolution* if action or other proceeding thereon is commenced within two years after the date of such dissolution." (Emphasis supplied.)

It is the appellee's theory, and the holding of the trial court, that this was a suit for recovery on the note which was in fact brought more than 2 years after dissolution of the corporation. Appellant's theory of the case is that it is not suing on a liability incurred prior to dissolution.

Having been dissolved by the Secretary of State, the corporation, Hi-Line Farms, needed to be liquidated. "Liquidation," as applied to a corporation, means the winding up of the affairs of the corporation by collecting all its assets, settling with creditors and debtors, and apportioning the amount of profit and loss. Since liquidation requires that corporate debts be taken care of, any distribution of assets to shareholders without taking care of corporate debts would be illegal, and corporate creditors can assert claims against shareholders in possession of corporate assets.

Furthermore, Neb. Rev. Stat. § 21-2046 provided in part as follows: ...

A director who votes or assents to any distribution of assets of a corporation to its shareholders during the liquidation of the corporation without the payment and discharge of, or making adequate provision for, all known debts, obligations, and liabilities of the corporation shall be liable, jointly and severally with all other directors so voting or assenting, to the corporation for the value of such assets which are distributed, to the extent that such debts, obligations, and liabilities of the corporation are not thereafter paid and discharged....

Appellant sought to allege liability on the part of the appellee as a director who voted or assented to a distribution of assets of the corporation to the detriment of existing creditors.

Liquidation of Hi-Line Farms occurred *after* the corporation was dissolved. Appellant alleges that Walter, as shareholder, took control of the corporate assets after the dissolution and sought to allege that Walter, as director, assented to such distribution of the corporate assets. Appellant's claim against Walter as sole shareholder and director of Hi-Line Farms arose after dissolution and is not barred by § 21-20,104.

The trial court should have allowed W & K Farms to amend its . . . petition to allow the allegation that Walter was a director, and the court erred . . . in dismissing the petition.

The judgment of the district court is

■ *Reversed and remanded.*

CASE CONCEPTS REVIEW

1. What is the basis of W & K Farms, Inc. attempting to hold Walter personally liable for the obligations of Hi-Line Farms, Inc.?
2. How does W & K Farms purport to keep the two-year statute of limitations from preventing this lawsuit against Walter?
3. What is the distinction between the dissolution of and the liquidation of a corporation?
4. Why does this court conclude that W & K Farms should be allowed to sue Walter in his individual capacity as a director of the dissolved Hi-Line Farms, Inc.?

INVOLUNTARY DISSOLUTIONS

4. Commenced by the State

The state, having created the corporation, has the right to institute proceedings to cancel the charter. Suits by a state to cancel or forfeit a charter are known as **quo warranto** proceedings. They are filed by the attorney general, usually at the request of the secretary of state. Statutes often allow charters to be canceled by executive action also.

Quo warranto A proceeding in court by which a governmental body tests or inquires into the authority or legality of a corporation's existence.

Charters may be canceled by suit or executive action if a corporation (1) did not file its annual report, (2) neglected to pay its franchise tax and license fees, (3) procured its charter by fraud, (4) abused and misused its authority, (5) failed to appoint and maintain a registered agent for the service of notices and process or had not informed the state of the name and address of its registered agent, or (6) ceased to perform its corporate functions for a long period of time. By proper proceedings and without charter forfeiture, the attorney general may also enjoin a corporation from engaging in a business not authorized by its charter. If a corporation is dissolved for any of the foregoing reasons, it may not continue its business. Its officers and directors may wind up the business, but any other contract is null and void.

By statute in most states, the officers and directors do not have personal liability for debts incurred on behalf of the corporation when its charter is suspended for failure to comply with state laws. Such statutes only suspend the right of a corporation to transact business while the corporation is delinquent for failure to file its annual report or pay its annual fees to the state. They do not expose the corporation's officers of directors to personal liability for debts incurred during the period of delinquency.

5. Commenced by Shareholders

DEADLOCKS.   Involuntary dissolution may be ordered by a court of equity at the request of a shareholder when the directors are deadlocked in the management of corporate affairs or the shareholders are deadlocked and unable to elect a board of directors. Deadlocks require proof that irreparable injury is likely and that the deadlock cannot be broken. A mere deadlock in voting to elect directors is not sufficient in itself in most states to cause a court to order dissolution.

Since the proceedings are in a court of equity, the issue is whether dissolution will be beneficial to the shareholders and not injurious to the public. The power to order dissolution is discretionary. In exercising its discretion, the court considers the seriousness of the deadlock and whether the corporation is able to conduct business profitably despite the deadlock. It also may consider such factors as the length of time the company has been in business, the stated purpose of the business, the original incorporators, whether one shareholder has shown a clear design to take over the business and is in a financial posture to do so to the detriment of other shareholders who may be injured financially by tax consequences, what the market for sale and purchase is at the instant time, whether the shareholders are in a relatively equal bargaining position, and whether it is in the best interests of all the shareholders to leave them to find their own solutions by one party buying out the others in a fair market value situation rather than by a forced sale.

ILLEGAL, FRAUDULENT, OR OPPRESSIVE CONDUCT.   The general rule throughout the United States is that a minority shareholder or group of shareholders of a going and solvent corporation cannot, without statutory authority, maintain a suit to have the corporation dissolved. Most states have statutes that authorize courts of equity to liquidate a corporation at the request of a shareholder when it is proved that those in control of the corporation are acting illegally, fraudulently, or oppressively. It is so difficult to define oppressive conduct that each case must be decided on its own facts.

Today, conduct that is not illegal or fraudulent may be held to be oppressive. Although controlling shareholders in a closely held corporation are not fiduciaries in the strict sense of the word, the general concepts of fiduciary duties are useful in deciding if conduct is oppressive. The law imposes equitable limitations on dominant shareholders. They are under a duty to refrain from using their control to profit for themselves at the expense of the minority. Repeated violations of these duties will serve as a ground for dissolution. Even though it takes substantially less evidence to justify dissolution of a partnership than of a closely held corporation, the trend is to treat the issues as similar. *Oppressive conduct* may be summarized as conduct that is burdensome, harsh, and wrongful. It is a substantial deviation from fair dealing and a violation of fair play. It is a violation of the fiduciary duty of good faith in those states that recognize such a duty.

PROTECTION OF MINORITY SHAREHOLDERS.   Actions intended to squeeze out or freeze out minority shareholders may provide grounds for dissolution or other equitable relief. Minority shareholders have been granted relief when the majority have refused to declare dividends but have paid out all profits to themselves in the form of salaries and bonuses. Relief was also granted in a recent case where the majority shareholders of a corporation that was *not* in need of funds sold additional stock to dilute the percentage of control of the minority, who the majority knew were unable financially to exercise their preemptive right. Such conduct is a breach of the fiduciary relationship.

All states allow minority shareholders to obtain dissolution when it is established that corporate assets are being wasted or looted or the corporation is unable to carry out its purposes. Some states have by statute broadened the grounds for court-ordered dissolution. These states allow courts to order dissolution when it is reasonably necessary for the protection of the rights or interests of minority shareholders. Even in these states a corporation will not be dissolved by a court for errors of judgment or because the court confronted with a question of policy would decide it differently than would the directors. Dissolutions by decree at the request of a shareholder are rare; but as previously noted, the trend is to give greater protection to the minority shareholders.

6. Commenced by Creditors

A corporation is in the same position as a natural person insofar as its creditors are concerned. A suit may be brought against it; when a judgment is obtained, an execution may be levied against its property, which may then be sold. Corporate assets may be attached; if the corporation has no property subject to execution, its assets may be traced by order of a court of equity.

The creditors have no right, because they are creditors, to interfere with the management of the business. A creditor who has an unsatisfied judgment against a corporation may seek, as a matter of equitable relief, to set aside conveyances and transfers of corporate property that have been fraudulently transferred for the purpose of delaying and hindering creditors. Creditors may also, under the aforementioned circumstances, ask for a **receiver** to take over the assets of the corporation and to apply them to the payment of debts.

When there is an unsatisfied execution and it is established that the corporation is insolvent, a court may order a dissolution. The same is true if the corporation admits its insolvency. Dissolution in such cases proceeds in the same manner as if instituted by the state or by voluntary proceedings when insolvent. These procedures are discussed in the next section.

Receiver An officer of the court appointed on behalf of all parties to the litigation to take possession of, hold, and control the property involved in the suit, for the benefit of the party who will be determined to be entitled thereto.

7. Procedures

In liquidating a corporation, courts have the full range of judicial powers at their disposal. They may issue injunctions, appoint receivers, and take whatever steps are necessary to preserve the corporate assets for the protection of creditors and shareholders. The receiver will usually collect the assets, including any amount owed to the corporation for shares. The receiver will then sell the assets, pay the debts and expenses of liquidation, and if any funds are left, divide them proportionately among the shareholders. Courts usually require creditors to prove their claims in court in a manner similar to that in bankruptcy proceedings. When all funds in the hands of a receiver are paid out, the court issues a decree of dissolution that is filed with the secretary of state. Funds due persons who cannot be located are deposited with the state treasurer and held for a specified number of years. If not claimed by the creditor or shareholder within the declared period, the funds belong to the state.

8. Liability of Shareholders

As a general rule, shareholders are not personally liable for the debts of the firm, but a shareholder who has not fully paid the corporation for the original issue of stock is liable to the receiver or to a creditor for the unpaid balance. In addition, statutes in most states allow creditors to reach assets of the former corporation that are in the hands of shareholders. The assets of a corporation are a trust fund for the payment of creditors, and the directors must manage this fund for their benefit. The liability of shareholders to creditors of the corporation is predicated on the theory that the transfer of corporate assets on dissolution is in fraud of creditors, and a shareholder knowingly receiving such assets ought to have liability.

Claims that existed before dissolution may be enforced afterward by statute in most states. For a specified period after dissolution, remedies survive against a corporation, its directors, officers, and shareholders. Suits against the corporation may be prosecuted or defended in the corporate name even though the corporate existence has technically ended. A judgment on such a claim may be collected from the corporation if it has property or from any former insurance carrier of the corporation. A claim may also be collected from property distributed to shareholders on dissolution, or the creditor may proceed directly against the shareholder receiving property. As previously noted, failure to give notice to creditors of intent to dissolve stops the time period from running.

The time period to sue after dissolution was created to protect creditors from losses that could easily result from the "death" of the corporate debtor. However, this protection is limited to whatever period is specified by the law of the state of incorporation; liability does not continue indefinitely. In addition, there is no liability for postdissolution causes of action unless a statute imposes it. The following case discusses the common-law trust fund theory and a statutory replacement on the issue of survival of claims against a dissolved corporation.

CASE

Carson v. Davidson
808 P.2d 1377 (Kan. 1991)

MCFARLAND, J.

In this action plaintiffs William D. and Norma I. Carson are seeking to recover on a judgment they have against a dissolved corporation from defendants J.M. Davidson and Danny Martin, who were the stockholders receiving the assets of the corporation upon dissolution. Recovery is sought under the trust fund doctrine. The district court held that Kansas has not adopted the trust fund doctrine and entered summary judgment in favor of defendants. Plaintiffs appeal therefrom.

The facts may be summarized as follows. Prior to April 1983, Tuttle Creek Development, Inc. (TCD) was a valid Kansas corporation. J.M. Davidson and Danny Martin were its sole officers, directors, and stockholders, each owning 50% of the stock. The corporation's only significant asset was a facility known as Colonial Gardens Mobile Home Park.

In April of 1983, TCD and the plaintiffs entered into a contract whereby plaintiffs would purchase the facility for $650,000 the same to be paid by a combination of assumption of mortgage indebtedness, execution of promissory notes to the individual defendants herein, and actual cash outlay. The contract provided that the cash was to be paid directly to Davidson and Martin, rather than to the corporation. The closing of the sale took place in July 1983, and the defendants received the cash payment as specified.

In July 1984, the corporate charter of TCD was revoked by the Kansas Secretary of State for failure to file its 1983 annual report. The corporate existence of TCD has never been revived. In July 1983, TCD had filed for an Internal Revenue Code Sec. 337 liquidation.

On May 15, 1986, plaintiffs herein filed an action against TCD . . . alleging breach of contract. Plaintiffs claimed that the defendant had promised to secure a 30-foot easement for expansion of the mobile home park. The case was tried to a jury. . . . The verdict was returned on April 14, 1988, and no appeal was taken therefrom. In June 1988, a general execution was issued against TCD and returned unsatisfied.

On March 15, 1989, the action herein was commenced by plaintiffs to collect the TCD judgment from defendants Davidson and Martin as stockholders of TCD under the trust fund doctrine. Plaintiffs and defendants each sought summary judgment. Judgment was entered in favor of defendants on the ground the doctrine authorizing such an action had not been adopted in Kansas. Plaintiffs appeal therefrom. . . .

We conclude the trust fund doctrine is viable in Kansas. Said doctrine is summarized as follows: Under the trust fund doctrine the assets of a dissolved corporation are a trust fund against which the corporate creditors have a claim superior to that of the stockholders, and creditors have the right to follow such assets into the hands of stockholders who hold assets as though the stockholders were trustees. A stockholder of a dissolved corporation receiving assets of a dissolved corporation is liable to respond to a creditor of the corporation only to the extent of the assets so received or the value thereof if the same have been disposed of by the stockholder.

Accordingly, we hold the district court erred in entering summary judgment in favor of the defendants on the ground that the trust fund doctrine had never been adopted in Kansas. . . .

■ *Reversed and remanded.*

CASE CONCEPTS REVIEW

1. As stockholders of TCD, Davidson and Martin normally would have limited liability. Why are these plaintiffs claiming that Davidson and Martin are personally liable for the debts of TCD?
2. What is meant by the Trust Fund Doctrine?
3. Why does this court conclude that the trial court was wrong to enter summary judgment in favor of Davidson and Martin?

CONSOLIDATIONS, MERGERS, AND ACQUISITIONS

9. Definitions

Consolidation The combination of two corporations when these two entities are dissolved and a new corporation is created.

Merger The combination of two corporations when one absorbs the other. The acquiring corporation continues to exist, but the acquired corporation is dissolved.

A business may acquire other businesses in a variety of ways. It may singly purchase the assets of the other firm. Such purchases include the plant, equipment, and even the goodwill of the other business. In such cases, the selling business retains its liabilities and its corporate structure.

Businesses may also consolidate or merge. **Consolidation** is the uniting of two or more corporations. A new corporation is created and the old entities are dissolved. The new corporation takes title to all the property, rights, powers, and privileges of the old corporations, subject to the liabilities and obligations of the old corporations. In a **merger,** one of the corporations continues its existence but absorbs the other corporation, which ceases to have an independent existence. The continuing corporation may expressly or impliedly assume and agree to pay the debts and liabilities of the absorbed corporation, whose creditors become third-party creditor beneficiaries. By statute in most states, the surviving corporation is deemed to have assumed all the liabilities and obligations of the absorbed corporation.

10. Procedures

The procedures for consolidations and mergers are statutory. Usually, the board of directors gives its approval by resolution that sets forth in detail all facts of the planned merger or consolidation. The plan is submitted to the shareholders for approval. Notice of the meeting typically includes the resolution passed by the directors. If proxies are submitted for the vote, proxy material must disclose all material facts required for an intelligent decision by the shareholders. In most states, the shareholders must approve the plan by a two-thirds vote of all shares and two-thirds of each class if more than one class of stock is voting. If the consolidation or merger is approved by the shareholders of both corporations, articles of consolidation or articles of merger will be prepared and filed with the state. If the papers are in order and all fees are paid, a certificate of consolidation or a certificate of merger will be issued.

11. Rights of Dissenting Shareholders

Statutes of the appropriate state may be strictly complied with, yet the courts may block a merger or acquisition. A merger may not be effected for the purpose of freezing out or squeezing out minority shareholders. If a merger has no valid business purpose other than the elimination of minority shareholders, courts will enjoin the merger or consolidation. Even if the minority shareholders receive the investment value of their interest in the merged corporation, the policy favoring corporate flexibility is not furthered by permitting the elimination of minority interests for the benefit of the majority, when no benefit thereby accrues to the corporation. Moreover, the majority shareholders owe the minority shareholders a fiduciary obligation in dealing with corporate assets. This duty includes the protection of corporate interests and restraint from doing anything that would injure the corporation or deprive it of profits or the ability to exercise its powers. Since dissolution may cause these effects, the majority may not dissolve when the only purpose is to get rid of the minority.

A shareholder who dissents from a consolidation or merger, and who makes the dissent a matter of record prior to the decision by serving a written demand that the corporation purchase his or her stock, is entitled to be paid the fair value of the stock on the day preceding the vote on the corporate action. Procedures are established for ascertaining the fair value and for a judicial decision of that issue if necessary. Once committed to the procedure, a shareholder cannot change his or her mind and keep the stock. This stops a party from finding out the price and then accepting or rejecting it. Among the relevant factors to be considered in evaluating a dissenting shareholder's stock are the nature of the corporation, the market demand for the stock, the business of the corporation, its earnings, dividends, net assets, general economic conditions, the market prices of comparable companies, the market price and earnings ratio, management and policies, revenues for various contingencies, tax liabilities, future earnings, and the permanency of the business.

The law requires procedures to determine a fair price for the stock of the dissenting shareholders. One method for determining this fair price is known as the *weighted average method*. This method assigns a particular weight to the elements of value: assets, market price, and earnings. The results are added to determine the value per share, as illustrated by the following case.

CASE

Brown v. Hedahl's–Q B & R, Inc.
185 N.W.2d 249 (N. Dak. 1971)

The owner of shares of stock in a closely held corporation dissented to a proposed merger that was approved by the remaining shareholders. By state statute, the dissenting shareholder who filed written objections to the merger was entitled to be paid the "fair value" of his or her shares as of the day preceding the approval of the merger by the other shareholders. The shareholder contended that the stock was worth $322 per share, and the corporation contended that it was worth $100 per share. The lower court found the "fair value" to be $230 per share, and the corporation that has to purchase the stock appealed.

TEIGEN, J.

. . . It appears, as a matter of general law, that there are three primary methods used by courts in determining the fair value of shares of dissenting shareholders. These three methods are the market value method, the asset value method, and the investment or earnings value method. The market value method establishes the value of the share on the basis of the price for which a share is selling or could be sold to a willing buyer. This method is most reliable where there is an established market for the stock.

The asset value method looks to the net assets of the corporation valued as a "going concern," each share having a pro rata value of the net assets. The net assets value depends on the real worth of the assets as determined by physical appraisals, accurate inventories, and realistic allowances for depreciation and obsolescence. The investment value method relates to the earning capacity of the corporation and involves an attempt to predict its future income based primarily on its previous earnings record. Dividends paid by the corporation are considered in its investment value. Generally, all the elements involved in these methods are considered in determining the value of the dissenter's stock. . . .

In redetermining the "fair value" of a share of Q B & R stock as of March 8, 1968, we have used all three methods of valuation and have established a value under each method which we have assigned a certain percentage weight in determining the fair value of the Q B & R stock. In determining the asset value as of March 8, 1968, we have used the consolidated statement of February 29, 1968, as that is the closest statement to the date in question. We have made certain adjustments to this statement to reflect more properly the true value of the assets of Q B & R as a "going concern." . . . [After explaining the adjustments.] The book value and the adjusted value of the Q B & R assets as of February 29, 1968, are shown in the statement.

Q B & R Consolidated Statement February 29, 1968

	BOOK VALUE	ADJUSTED VALUE
Current assets:		
Cash on hand and in banks	10,583.75	10,583.75
Notes receivable	6,641.27	3,000.00
Accounts receivable	184,800.00	166,320.00
Inventories	469,932.77	469,932.77
Stocks and bonds	5,423.98	4,000.00
Cash value life insurance	10,860.00	10,860.00
Fixed assets:		
Real estate—lots	34,916.73	207,300.00
Real estate—buildings	56,150.59	(Bldgs. included above)
Furniture & fixtures	4,792.50	9,000.00
Shop equipment	13,450.98	20,250.00
Autos & trucks	14,223.92	11,385.00
Total assets:	811,776.89	912,631.52
Total liabilities:	203,228.93	203,228.93
Net asset value:	608,547.96	709,402.59

Total shares outstanding: 2,922
Asset value per share based on the adjusted statement value of Q B & R:

$$2{,}922 \overline{\smash{\big)}\,709{,}402.59} \quad 242.81$$

The asset value per share, then, based on the adjusted value of the Q B & R assets as of February 29, 1968, is $242.81 per share.

Under the investment value (or earnings value) method of valuation, the value per share of Q B & R stock as of March 8, 1968, is zero. Q B & R had sustained a series of losses for several years prior to its merger with Hedahl's, Inc. Plaintiffs' exhibit showing the comparative net profits between Q B & R and Hedahl's, Inc., from 1962 through 1967 shows that Q B & R's five-year average net earnings per share, disregarding 1967, the year prior to the merger, was a loss of 14¢ per share. Based on a six-year average, which includes 1967, the earnings per share was a loss of $4.62 per share. Based on its earnings record, Q B & R was not a good investment and its earnings value is properly fixed at zero. . . . It appears that there is no established market for the Q B & R shares and thus there is no apparent market value that can be assigned to a share of Q B & R stock. However, a reconstructed market value can be established based on the limited transactions that have occurred. . . .

Averaging all Q B & R stock transactions from June of 1963 up to December 6, 1967, the result is a reconstructed market price of $69 per share. This figure appears to be a reasonable reconstructed market price and, accordingly, will be established as the market value for a share of Q B & R stock. . . .

We hold that all three methods of valuation must be used in determining the "fair value" of a share of Q B & R stock as of March 8, 1968. We have determined the value of a share of Q B & R stock by each method. The asset value of a share of Q B & R stock is $242.81 per share; the investment or earnings value of a share of Q B & R stock is zero; and the market value of a share of Q B & R stock is $69 per share. Having determined the value of a share of Q B & R stock by each method, the problem becomes one of weighing the various factors to reach a final result that properly takes into consideration all of the elements and factors involved in determining the "fair value" of a share of Q B & R stock as a March 8, 1968. . . .

In weighing the various values involved we have considered all aspects of Q B & R as a "going concern" prior to its merger with Hedahl's, Inc. Although we have assigned weights to the several values involved, we have not used any set formula; rather, we have relied on an analysis of the particular facts of this case as being determinative of the weight given each value. We have assigned a weight of 25% to the market value of Q B & R. Normally, where there is an established market for the stock of a corporation the market price is given great weight. In other cases where there is no reliable market and none can be reconstructed, market price is not considered at all. However, as to the Q B & R stock, there has been a limited market such that we can properly reconstruct a realistic market price for a share of Q B & R stock. We have assigned a weight of 50% to the asset value of Q B & R. Normally, a higher value is assigned only in cases where the primary purpose of the corporation is to hold assets, such as real estate, for the purpose of allowing them to appreciate in value. In other words, assets are weighed more heavily when they are held for appreciation purposes rather than for commercial retail or wholesale purposes designed to generate earnings. Here the assets of Q B & R primarily consisted of inventories for sale and the necessary buildings and equipment to carry out this business purpose. The inventories held by Q B & R would depreciate in value rather than appreciate but the value of the lots and buildings is substantial in relation to the inventories and will likely appreciate in value. We have assigned a weight of 25% to the investment or earnings value of Q B & R. Normally, in a commercial business, earnings are given great weight as the primary purpose of the business is to generate earnings and not to hold assets that will appreciate in value. Q B & R was such a business, whose primary purpose was to generate earnings for its shareholders. The fact that Q B & R has failed in the past several years to generate such earnings does not mean that earnings are not an important part of the value of Q B & R stock. . . . Although earnings should ordinarily weigh heavily in determining the true value of the stock in a commercial corporation, we believe, under the circumstances, it is proper to give less weight in this case. Accordingly, we have determined that the "fair value" of a share of Q B & R stock as of March 8, 1968, is $138.65 per share.

	VALUE	× WEIGHT	= RESULT
Asset	$242.81 ×	50%	= $121.40
Market	69.00 ×	25%	= 17.25
Earnings	0.00 ×	25%	0.00
	Total value per share		$138.65

We therefore direct that the judgment be modified to conform to this opinion and as modified, it is affirmed.

■ *Affirmed.*

CASE CONCEPTS REVIEW

1. From what vote involving the Hedahl's–Q B & R, Inc. is Brown dissenting?
2. What are the respective dollar values that these parties place on the corporation's stock?
3. What are the three methods of valuing the corporation's stock discussed by this court?
4. How does the court determine the weights to be assigned to each valuation method?

There is no rule of thumb for the weight to be given any factor. Moreover, the weighted average method is not exclusive, and many courts today believe it is outmoded. Other techniques that are acceptable in the financial community, such as discounted cash flow analysis and comparisons with other tender offers, may be used. All relevant factors are considered in determining a fair price; fair value cannot be computed according to any precise mathematical formula. If the stock is regularly traded in an exchange, market value may be the dominant factor.

The laws relating to dissenting shareholders petitioning for appraisal and the right to be paid the fair values of their stock apply to a cash-for-stock merger as well as a stock-for-stock merger. Also, a shareholder who dissents from a sale or exchange of all or substantially all the assets or property of the corporation, other than in the usual course of business, has the same right to be paid for his or her stock. When the statutory procedures are followed, the dissenting shareholder ceases to be a shareholder when notice is given; he or she then becomes a creditor.

Tender offers create problems in valuing the stock of dissenting shareholders. Such offers usually include a premium, to overcome objections of many shareholders; but dissenting shareholders who refuse a tender offer and insist on a judicial determination of the fair value of shares are not entitled to receive the tender offer premium. A premerger tender offer price does not establish a floor on the amount that the court may fix as the value of shares in an appraisal proceeding, but it does have some evidentiary significance.

12. Liability of Successors

In the case of a merger or a consolidation of corporations, the changed entity ordinarily remains liable for prior debts; a business cannot shrug off personal liability to its creditors simply by merging, consolidating, switching from the partnership to the corporate form or vice versa, or changing its name. By statute in most states, the surviving corporation is deemed to have assumed all the liabilities and obligations of the absorbed corporation or of the former corporations, as the following case held. These liabilities may even include punitive damages.

CASE

Celotex Corp. v. Pickett
490 So.2d 35 (Fla. 1986)

EHRLICH, J.

The facts relevant for our review here are that the respondent husband (Pickett) was employed in a Jacksonville shipyard from 1965 through June 1968, where as part of his employment as an insulator of ships, he extensively used Philip Carey asbestos cement. Pickett developed severe lung problems, due to the devastating effects on the human body which results from exposure to asbestos. The Picketts sued, on the grounds of negligence and strict lia-

bility, several defendants including the petitioner (Celotex) in its capacity as the corporate successor to Philip Carey. Finding that Philip Carey was negligent in placing "defective" asbestos-containing insulating products on the market which caused Pickett's injuries, the jury awarded compensatory damages of $500,000 to Pickett and $15,000 to his wife. The jury also determined that Philip Carey had acted so as to warrant punitive damages in the amount of $100,000 against Celotex. Celotex's appeal of the imposition of punitive damages formed the basis for the First District's opinion below which affirmed the award.

The threshold question involved here is the legal status of Celotex as the successor to Philip Carey. The district court opinion set forth the following background:

The Philip Carey Corporation was begun in 1888 and subsequently merged with Glen Alden Corporation in 1967. Thereafter, Philip Carey merged with another Glen Alden subsidiary, Briggs Manufacturing Company, and became known as Panacon Corporation. Celotex purchased Glen Alden's controlling interest in 1972 and later purchased the remaining shares of Panacon and merged it into Celotex.

The effect of this merger . . . is controlled by section 607.231(3), Florida Statutes (1983), which reads:

(c) Such surviving or new corporation shall have all the rights, privileges, immunities and powers, and *shall be subject to all of the duties and liabilities,* of a corporation organized under this chapter. (Emphasis added.)

Celotex has admitted that it is liable, because of the merger, for the compensatory damages awarded to the Picketts. The sole and narrow issue before us here is whether punitive damages were properly assessed against petitioner, the surviving corporation in a statutory merger.

Celotex, however, maintains that the trial court and the district court below misapplied our prior decisions by holding Celotex liable for punitive damages, when Phililp Carey, not Celotex, was the "real wrongdoer." Celotex also claims that imposition of punitive damages against Celotex, simply because it is the statutory successor of Philip Carey, contravenes the purpose of such damages in Florida. We disagree with both contentions.

It is Celotex's liability for the tortious conduct of Panacon which represents the gravamen of Celotex's argument before this court. Celotex, having merged with Panacon, cannot now disclaim its lineage.

Celotex seeks here to characterize its liability as "vicarious," . . . since . . . Philip Carey/Panacon is the "real wrongdoer" and there is no evidence of fault by Celotex. We disagree with this characterization. Because of its merger agreement with Panacon, whereby "all debts, liabilities and duties" of Panacon are enforceable against Celotex, and because of the effect of section 607.231(3), the liability imposed upon Celotex is direct, not vicarious. Liability for the reckless misconduct of Philip Carey/Panacon legally continues to exist within, and under the name of, Celotex.

Where two corporations have truly merged, a corporate tortfeasor by any other name is still a tortfeasor, to paraphrase Shakespeare. [A] merger "merely directs the blood of the old corporation into the veins of the new, the old living in the new." [A] merger "is like the uniting of two or more rivers, neither stream is annihilated but all continue in existence."

Celotex's claim that the imposition of punitive damages here contravenes the purpose of such damages is unpersuasive. Punitive damages are imposed as a punishment of the defendant and as a deterrent to others. Both aspects of this purpose are present here. Celotex, as the present embodiment of Philip Carey/Panacon, is being punished for the reckless conduct giving rise to this suit. Further, allowing punitive damages in this instance may well deter other corporations from seeking to merge with other companies which have engaged in reckless conduct detrimental to the public health and thereby have the potential for the imposition of punitive damages. . . . Were we to hold that the potential for punitive damages disappears at merger, this may well encourage reckless conduct. Our holding here recognizes that since reckless wrongdoing by the predecessor can result in liability for punitive damages against the successor, acquisition candidates are deterred from such actions. Realization that their companies will sell for less, or not at all, if they engage in reckless behavior provides an incentive for acquisition candidates to conform their behavior to socially acceptable norms.

Further, corporations are in a very real sense, "molders of their own destinies" in acquisition transactions, with the full panoply of corporate transformations at their disposal. When a corporation such as Celotex here, voluntarily chooses a formal merger, it will take the "bad will" along with the "good will." We will not allow such an acquiring corporation to "jettison inchoate liabilities into a never-never land of transcorporate limbo."

We note that the weight of authority from other jurisdictions is in accord with our holding here.

We approve the decision of the First District Court of Appeal.

■ *It is so ordered.*

CASE CONCEPTS REVIEW

1. This lawsuit arises out of Pickett's extensive use of Philip Carey asbestos cement. How does Celotex Corp. become involved in this litigation?
2. What is the general liability of a successor corporation that has merged with a predecessor corporation for the products of the predecessor?
3. While Celotex acknowledges liability for Pickett's compensatory damages, on what basis does Celotex argue it is not liable for punitive damages?
4. Why does the court disagree with Celotex's argument concerning liability for punitive damages?

To avoid assuming the debts and liabilities of corporations that are being acquired, the acquiring businesses often purchase the assets of a corporation without assuming the liabilities and without any change of organization. The buyer does not become involved with the seller, and there is no merger or consolidation. As a general rule, if one corporation acquires only the assets of another corporation, the acquiring corporation is not liabile for the debts and liabilities of the transferor. An exception exists if the transfer is an attempt to defraud creditors.

This general rule is subject to attack today. Under what circumstances should an acquiring corporation have liability for the debts and the obligations of the business whose assets it acquired? This becomes a difficult question when the assets acquired include the firm name and its product line. The contract of acquisition usually provides for no assumption of liabilities, but should such a provision bind third parties when the selling corporation dissolves as soon as the sale is complete? This issue arises quite frequently in product liability cases. It is not surprising that the courts of different states have answered the liability issue differently in product liability cases. The majority view is to find no liability, but many states take the opposite view. Therefore, an examination of each state's laws and court decisions is essential prior to knowing the answer to the question posed above.

13. Antitrust Considerations

Horizontal merger Merger of corporations that were competitors prior to the merger.

Vertical merger A merger of corporations, one corporation being the supplier of the other.

Conglomerate merger Merging of companies that have neither the relationship of competitors nor that of supplier and customer.

Mergers and acquisitions are usually classified as horizontal, market extension, vertical, or conglomerate. A **horizontal merger** combines two businesses in the same field or industry, reducing the number of competitors. A *market extension merger* is an acquisition in which the acquiring company extends its markets. This market extension may be either in new products (product extension) or in new areas (geographical extension). A **vertical merger** brings together two companies, one being the customer of the other. Such a combination usually removes the customer from the market as far as other suppliers are concerned. It may remove a source of supply also if the acquiring company is a customer of the acquired one. A **conglomerate merger** is one in which the businesses involved are neither competitors nor related as customer and supplier in any given line of commerce.

STATUTES.   The law of mergers is based primarily on three statutes—the Sherman Act, the Bank Merger Act, and the Clayton Act. A horizontal merger violates the Sherman Act if it is a combination in unreasonable restraint of trade or if it results in monopolization of a line of commerce or if it is an attempt to monopolize.

A great deal of merger litigation involves banks. Their mergers are subject to the provisions of the Bank Merger Acts of 1960 and 1966, as well as the usual antitrust laws. Bank mergers are illegal unless approved by one of the agencies that regulate banks. If the merger involves a national bank, the approval of the Comptroller of the Currency is required. If the banks are state banks that are members of the Federal Reserve System, the approval of the Federal Reserve Board is necessary. Other mergers of banks insured by the Federal Deposit Insurance Corporation require approval of that agency.

CLAYTON ACT—SECTION 7.   Section 7 of the Clayton Act is the major statute in the merger and acquisition area. It was originally adopted in 1914 and later amended by the Celler-Kefauver amendment in 1950. Section 7 of the Clayton Act as amended provides essentially that no business engaged in commerce shall acquire any of the stock or assets of another such business if the effect may be substantially to lessen competition or to tend to create a monopoly in any line of commerce in any section of the country. The phrase *engaged in commerce* as used in Section 7 means engaged in the flow of interstate commerce. It was not intended to reach all businesses engaged in activities that affect commerce. Hence, the phrase does not encompass businesses engaged in intrastate activities substantially affecting interstate commerce, only those that are engaged in interstate commerce.

Violations require only a finding and conclusion that a given acquisition has a reasonable probability of lessening competition or tendency toward monopoly. Section 7 does not deal with certainties, only with probabilities. The goal of the law is to arrest incipient anticompetitive effects and trends toward undue concentration of economic power.

In determining whether or not a merger or acquisition is illegal, courts examine both the product market and the geographic market affected. The law has neither adopted nor rejected any particular tests for measuring relevant markets. Both the product market and geographic market of the companies involved are factual issues. The more narrowly the product line or geographic area is defined, the greater the impact of a merger or acquisition on competition. Thus, the relevant market frequently determines the probable anticompetitive effects of the merger. A decision that enlarges the line of commerce may be important in establishing that a merger is not anticompetitive.

For a violation of Section 7, courts must also find that within the market the effect of the merger "may be substantially to lessen competition or to tend to create a monopoly." The degree of market concentration prior to the merger and the relative position of the merged parties are important factors to be considered. If there has been a history of tendency toward concentration in an industry, increases in further concentration may be prohibited because of the policy of the law to curb such tendencies before they become harmful.

A significant concept in the merger field is the *potential entrant doctrine*. This doctrine finds that the prohibited effect may exist where an acquisition or a merger involves a potential entrant into a market. An acquisition of a competitor by a potential competitor is thus illegal where the effect may be substantially to lessen competition. The potential entrant doctrine has been used to prevent a soap company from acquiring a major bleach company. Since the soap company was a potential entrant into the bleach business, the acquisition was reviewed as anticompetitive. The same doctrine may be used also to stop geographic expansion by mergers and acquisitions. The potential entrant doctrine is applied not only because entry would bring in an additional competitor but also because the mere presence of a potential competitor at the edge of the market has positive effects on those companies actually competing.

Today those responsible for enforcing this law are primarily concerned with horizontal acquisitions. Vertical acquisitions and conglomerate mergers are likely to be challenged only if they involve a highly concentrated industry or monopoly is likely. Many large mergers and acquisitions have been consummated without legal challenge. It seems that every day there are more large mergers proposed and consummated. Although many of these involve billions of dollars, there is very little enforcement of the Clayton Act.

CHAPTER SUMMARY

VOLUNTARY DISSOLUTIONS

Procedures
1. A corporation with a charter that has not commenced business may be dissolved by its incorporators filing articles of dissolution.
2. A corporation that has commenced business may be dissolved by all of its shareholders.
3. A corporation that has commenced business may be dissolved by its board of directors with the approval of two-thirds of the shareholders.

Notice to Creditors
1. A corporation must give notice to all creditors of its intent to dissolve. The directors are personally liable to creditors to whom notice is not given.

Distributions
1. Corporate assets are first used to pay debts. Any remaining assets are distributed proportionately among the shareholders.
2. If there are insufficient assets to pay debts, a receiver will be appointed, and the dissolution will proceed as if it were involuntary.

INVOLUNTARY DISSOLUTIONS

Commenced by the State
1. The state may file a *quo warranto* proceeding to cancel a corporate charter.
2. Such proceedings are brought by failure of the corporation to comply with the law in such areas as annual reports, franchise taxes, and registered agents.

Commenced by the Shareholders
1. Shareholders may petition a court of equity to dissolve a corporation if there is a deadlock in management and irreparable injury is likely.
2. Shareholders may obtain dissolution if the directors are acting illegally, fraudulently, or oppressively.
3. Modern statutes do not allow the majority to freeze out minority shareholders, and dissolution is an appropriate remedy in such cases.
4. Shareholders in closely held corporations have duties similar to partners in a partnership.

Commenced by the Creditors
1. Creditors have no right to interfere with the management of a corporation.
2. Creditors may ask for a receiver to be appointed when they have an unsatisfied judgment. If insolvency is established, dissolution is possible.

Procedures
1. Courts of equity have the full range of procedures to protect corporate assets, the creditors, and shareholders.
2. Creditors are required to prove their claims before they share in assets.

Liability of Shareholders
1. Shareholders have no personal liability to creditors unless the stock is not paid for in full or assets have been transferred to them in default of creditors.
2. Claims against the corporation exist for a specified time after dissolution and may be enforced against shareholders receiving corporate assets.

CONSOLIDATIONS, MERGERS AND ACQUISITIONS

Definitions
1. A consolidation is the uniting of two or more corporations into a newly created one.
2. A merger occurs when one corporation absorbs another, with the latter one being dissolved.

Procedures	**1.** There are statutory procedures that must be followed. These usually require submission to the shareholders for approval.
	2. Each class of shareholders must approve the plan and usually by a two-thirds vote.
Rights of Dissenting Shareholders	**1.** Minority shareholders who dissent to a merger or consolidation are entitled to be paid the fair value of their stock immediately prior to the change in the corporation. Various methods are in use for determining fair market value.
	2. A tender offer does not establish fair market value but it is evidence of the value.
Liability of Successors	**1.** In a merger or consolidation, the new corporation is liable for the debts of the old corporation.
	2. When one corporation acquires the assets of another, there may be liability in some states, if the facts warrant it.
Antitrust Considerations	**1.** The Clayton Act provides that a merger or acquisition is illegal if the effect may be to substantially lessen competition or tend to create a monopoly.
	2. The law covers mergers between competitors that are known as horizontal mergers, mergers between buyer and seller that are known as vertical mergers, and mergers where there is no connection between the parties, which are called conglomerate mergers.
	3. In judging the legality of a merger, the court examines the product market, the geographic market, and the impact on competition.

REVIEW QUESTIONS AND PROBLEMS

1. Match each term in column A with the appropriate statement in column B.

A	B
(1) Consolidation	(a) A merger in which the acquired corporation previously competed with its acquirer
(2) Merger	(b) By what authority
(3) Horizontal merger	(c) A merger between two firms that have nothing in common
(4) Vertical merger	(d) One corporation absorbs another
(5) Conglomerate merger	(e) A technique for valuing the stock of a dissenting shareholder
(6) *Quo warranto*	(f) Uniting two corporations into a new third one
(7) Weighted average method	(g) A merger between a supplier and one of its customers
(8) Product line	(h) A theory used to extend liability for personal injuries to a successor corporation

2. What persons must approve a voluntary dissolution of a corporation if business has not been commenced? What persons must approve a voluntary dissolution if the corporation has commenced business activities?

3. Adams, the owner of all capital stock of the Gazette Corporation, a newspaper business, sold all his shares to Burr and promised to serve as adviser to the newspaper for a period of five years in return for an annual salary of $50,000. After three years, Burr petitioned for dissolution, which was obtained. Does Adams have a right to collect the balance of the salary from the corporation? Explain.

4. A corporation filed its notice of intent to dissolve with the secretary of state of the state of incorporation. It failed to give notice of dissolution to the local tax collector. Suit was filed six years later against the directors to collect the unpaid corporate property taxes. The law provided that suits against corporations survive for two years after dissolution. Which party, the corporation or its directors, is liable for the unpaid taxes? Explain.

5. Due to a deadlock in voting power, the shareholders of Cooper-George, Inc., have failed to elect new directors at two successive annual meetings. A state statute authorizes dissolution if directors are not elected for two years. The corporation has continued, however, to transact business, and the former board remains in office. If a suit is filed for dissolution, will the corporation be dissolved? Why or why not?

6. Bob and David, father and son, entered into an agreement whereby each was 50 percent stockholder of a closely held corporation operating a luncheonette. The agreement provided that the death of either party would constitute an automatic option to the survivor to purchase, at book value, the shares of stock of the deceased. Upon Bob's death, his daughter Ann (David's sister and administrator of Bob's estate) refused to sell for the value shown on the books. Having created a deadlock in management, Ann then petitioned for dissolution. Should it be granted? Explain.

7. A father and his two sons formed a corporation to conduct a general contracting business with each owning one-third of the stock. Three years later, one of the sons ceased to be employed by the corporation. There had been a dispute, and the plaintiff had been removed as an officer and director of the corporation. The corporation pays no dividends but invests its profits in real estate. Is the plaintiff entitled to have the corporation dissolved? Why or why not?

8. David was president of Music, Inc. He owned 53 percent of the common stock. David received a salary of $10,000 per year and bonuses of $7,000 per year. The corporation had a net worth of $100,000 and sales of $245,000. The net profit of the company had been under $2,000 each year, and dividends were either small or nonexistent. Minority shareholders brought suit to compel dissolution of the corporation on the ground of waste, alleging that the waste occurred in the payment of bonuses to David. Should the company be dissolved? Why or why not?

9. Plaintiff was injured in a laundromat. The laundromat was incorporated, and the defendant was its sole shareholder. The corporation was insured under a $100,000 liability policy. Plaintiff obtained a $150,000 judgment against the corporation, on which the insuror paid $100,000. Defendant liquidated the assets of the corporation and as sole shareholder retained the proceeds of the liquidation. This suit is against the defendant individually for the $50,000 of the judgment not covered by the insurance. May a judgment creditor of a dissolved corporation proceed against the sole shareholder for the value of the liquidated assets of the corporation necessary to satisfy the judgment? Why or why not?

10. Dissenting shareholders to a merger filed a suit for damages against the merging corporations and their directors. They alleged breach of fiduciary duties, fraud, and conspiracy to violate the securities laws. The defendants moved to dismiss, contending that the only remedy available to the plaintiffs was to be paid the fair value of their shares. What are the rights of these dissenting shareholders? Explain.

11. The shareholders of a corporation met to vote on a proposed merger. After the vote was taken and the meeting adjourned, a minority shareholder gave written notice of objection to the proposed merger. Are the majority shareholders entitled to obtain the fair cash value for their shares? Why or why not?

12. A corporation purchased the assets of another corporation. It did not assume the liability of the seller. If a product liability suit is brought as the result of a defect in a product sold by the selling corporation, is the buying corporation liable? Why or why not?

13. Von's Grocery, a retail grocery chain doing business in the Los Angeles area, acquired a direct competitor, Shopping Bag Food Store. As a result, Von's became the second largest grocery chain in Los Angeles, with sales of which amounted to 7.5 percent of the market. Before the merger, both companies were rapidly growing, aggressive competitors. The Los Angeles market was characterized by an increasing trend toward concentration through acquisitions and a marked decline in the number of single-store owners. Is the merger illegal under Section 7 of the Clayton Act? Explain.

ACCOUNTANTS' LEGAL LIABILITY

CHAPTER PREVIEW

*I*n cooperation with management, accountants should play important advisory roles in the creation, operation, and dissolution of every business organization. Specifically, accountants prepare tax returns and provide financial reports for managers' decision making as well as for investors and creditors. Because of the essential role between business organizations and their accountants, the topic of accountants' liability has become increasingly newsworthy.

At the end of chapter 5, there is a brief discussion of malpractice litigation against professional persons. This chapter concentrates specifically on malpractice suits filed against accountants and their firms. Throughout the 1980s, accounting firms faced increased financial exposure for claims filed against them. Indeed, each of the major firms lost major judgments or settled cases upon agreeing to pay millions of dollars.

The mounting exposure to legal liability led to merger activities in the latter part of the past decade. The combining of firms did not stop the impact of legal liability on accounting firms. Late in 1990, Laventhol & Horwath filed for bankruptcy protection, and then the partners decided to disband the firm. At the time of its bankruptcy filing, Laventhol & Horwath was named a defendant in more than 100 lawsuits. The firm was paying legal fees of approximately $1 million monthly.

The exposure to and impact of legal liability for accountants' activities is real. This chapter discusses the extent of liability for accountants acting in a negligent manner and for violating a statute. (Prior to studying this chapter, review the elements of fraud discussed in chapter 12.)

■ BUSINESS MANAGEMENT DECISION

As a partner in a CPA firm, you are primarily responsible for auditing the financial statements of a local manufacturing corporation. After the audit is completed and your firm has issued an unqualified opinion as to the accuracy of the client's financial condition, you discover a major error in the balance sheet.

In an attempt to secure a loan from the First Bank, this corporation informs you that it is presenting your opinion to the bank as evidence of its financial condition. Upon learning of this action, what should you do? What are your concerns?

1. Malpractice Theories

An accountant's liability may be based on several theories. First, liability may be based on a breach of contract. An accountant has liability for failing to perform contractual obligations as agreed. The use of this theory has several advantages to plaintiffs. For example, contributory negligence by the client is not a defense. The measure of damages is the loss of the value of the benefit to be derived from the contract, rather than any loss sustained, as in the case of a tort. Expert testimony is usually not required to prove a breach of contract. Finally, the period of the statute of limitations for a breach of a contract is usually longer than it is for a tort.

Accountants are also liable to clients for fraud and for negligence. These tort theories require proof of the elements of each tort, such as scienter, materiality, reliance, and injury in the case of fraud. Tort suits based on fraud and negligence and claims are subject to the usual tort defenses. Negligence cases require proof of the failure to exercise the necessary care and caution that the professional calling requires. Professional persons do not guarantee that they will make no mistakes; they are only required to meet the standards of their profession. Issues of negligence are submitted to a jury for decision. In many cases, juries find that liability exists even though members of the profession contend that the services performed were all that could reasonably be expected under the circumstances.

The law has also developed a hybrid theory of liability that combines contract and tort principles. It is used when an accountant performs the contract in a negligent manner. Negligent performance of a contract duty gives rise to a cause of action that some courts consider contractual and others tortious. Confusion as to the basis of the litigation (tort or contract) frequently arises as a result of this distinction. The difference is significant because (1) there are different periods of limitation for contract and tort cases, (2) each has its own theories of damages, and (3) the defenses available vary depending on the theory. As a result, plaintiffs usually include a count in their lawsuits for breach of contract, one for negligence and one for negligent breach of contract.

2. Expert Testimony

Before turning to the details of the various theories, an understanding of the role of expert testimony in malpractice cases is required. The evidence in most lawsuits against accountants includes expert testimony of CPAs other than the defendant. Accountants would like to believe the compliance with professional standards such as generally accepted accounting principles (GAAP) or generally accepted auditing standards (GAAS) should result in no liability. They argue that compliance with the standards eliminates liability because the duty imposed by such standards has been met. Accountants argue that courts cannot impose a higher standard than professional custom, because to do so would impose liability even if an accountant did everything that he or she had been taught to do.

The foregoing argument has been rejected by plaintiffs because presumably custom and professional standards could establish too low standards of care. Plaintiffs contend that professional standards and custom constitute only admissible evidence to be considered by the jury. Customary practice is only a factor to be considered in the overall decision of the jury.

The Securities and Exchange Commission imposes obligations on auditors beyond GAAP and GAAS professional standards. The SEC takes the position that auditors have a duty to communicate material information effectively. If following GAAP or GAAS does not result in such disclosure, the SEC takes the position that it has the power to promulgate additional standards and rules. Therefore, expert testimony on professional standards is not binding on the SEC.

Courts give greater weight to expert testimony in areas such as statistical sampling than they do in the communication of facts. Expert testimony on the latter is admissible and persuasive but not conclusive. Expert testimony in technical areas such as statistical sampling is treated as conclusive by most courts.

The prudent accountant should recognize that courts do not hesitate to require a higher standard than GAAP and GAAS where the facts warrant. Professional standards are not conclusive because a whole profession may lag in the adoption of new and viable concepts. A profession may not set its own test of standards. In the final analysis, courts do so because there are precautions so imperative to the public welfare that their universal disregard does not excuse their omission.

In one case, the court expressed this concept in the following language:

> Much has been said by the parties about generally accepted accounting principles and the proper way for an accountant to report real estate transactions. We think this misses the point. Our inquiry is properly focused not on whether Laventhol's report satisfies esoteric accounting norms, comprehensible only to the initiate, but whether the report fairly presents the true financial position of Firestone, as of November 30, 1969, to the untutored eye of an ordinary investor.*

*Herzfeld v. Laventhol, Krekstein, Horwath & Horwath, 378 F. SUPP. 112 (S.D.N.Y. 1974).

3. Introduction

Tort liability is predicated on the premise that people should exercise reasonable care and caution in the conduct of their affairs. For professional persons, this means that they must exercise that degree of care and caution that their professional calling requires. Failure to meet professional standards is negligence. Negligence is usually expressed in terms of a breach of a duty owed by one party which is the proximate cause of an injury to another. The issue as to whether or not there has been a breach of the duty owed is almost always a question of fact for the jury. Negligence may consist of either an act or an omission—failure to act. The act or omission must be wrongful in the sense that another's legal right has been violated. Many, if not most, cases of negligence involving accountants are based on omission as well as overt actions.

A major issue that often arises is to which parties the accountant owes the duty to exercise reasonable care. Is this duty owed only to the party who hired the accountant, or is the duty also owed to third parties who may rely on the accountant's work product to their financial detriment? The following four sections discuss a variety of aspects related to this question.

4. Liability to Clients

Negligence issues frequently arise when an auditor fails to discover fraud or embezzlement. Most courts have held that an auditor is not a fiduciary and that the auditor's duty is to act independently, objectively, and impartially and with the skills that were represented to the auditor's clients. While an auditor is not a guarantor and, at least from a personal viewpoint, has no duty to discover fraud or embezzlement, auditors have been held liable when their negligence prevents the discovery of fraud. Negligence in these cases is usually based on a failure to adhere to specific auditing procedures that, if followed, would have disclosed the fraud or embezzlement. If proper performance of the audit would have disclosed the defalcation or other wrongful conduct, failure to perform is negligence.

Failure to qualify financial statements is another example of negligence by an accountant. Since GAAS requires a clear indication of the auditor's examination, if any, and the degree of responsibility he or she is taking, failure to qualify allows a client to recover at least the cost of the audit if the financial statements are erroneous.

Negligence by accountants is often predicated on the failure to adhere to common standards of honesty and loyalty. These standards are required even where no audit is conducted.

Another common activity that may result in liability on a theory of negligence is tax return preparation. An accountant is liable for penalties and interest if he or she negligently fails to file a return on time or fails to file a correct return. Liability for negligence may also arise from erroneous tax advice.

Negligence actions often involve issues of contributory negligence or comparative negligence. Since accountants are employed to detect defalcations that the employer's negligence has made possible, contributory negligence should not prevent a recovery. Even in states that have adopted comparative negligence, it is not a defense available to accountants. Negligence of the employer is a defense only when it has contributed to the accountant's failure to perform and to report the truth.

5. Liability to Third Parties: The *Ultramares* Doctrine

As previously noted, an accountant is liable to clients for breach of contract, for fraud, and for negligence. Liability for fraud also exists in favor of third parties. Liability for breach of contract exists if the third party is one for whose *direct benefit* the contract was made. Liability for breach of contract does not exist for persons who do not qualify as third-party beneficiaries of the contract.

Liability to third parties for negligence has caused a great deal of trouble for the courts. The following case is the leading case holding that there is no liability to third parties for simple negligence.

CASE

Ultramares Corp. v. Touche
174 N.E. 441 (N.Y. 1931)

An accounting firm (Touche) examined, audited, and certified its client's financial statements to be accurate. In fact, these financial statements were erroneous, and the audit was negligently performed. Touche failed to discover that many of the accounts receivable were nonexistent. The client utilized Touche's certification of its financial statement to obtain a loan from the Ultramares Corporation. After the client filed for bankruptcy, Ultramares sued Touche to collect the unpaid loan. Although Touche admitted that it knew that in the usual course of business the certified financial statements would be exhibited to banks, creditors, stockholders, purchasers, and sellers, Touche sought to dismiss this lawsuit since there was no privity between it and Ultramares.

CARDOZO, J.

. . . We are brought to the question of duty, its origin and measure.

The defendants owed to their employer a duty imposed by law to make their certificate without fraud, and a duty growing out of contract to make it with the care and caution proper to their calling. Fraud includes the pretense of knowledge when knowledge there is none. To creditors and inventors to whom the employer exhibited the certificate, the defendants owed a like duty to make it without fraud, since there was notice in the circumstances of its making that the employer did not intend to keep it to himself. A different question develops when we ask whether they owed a duty to these to make it without negligence. If liability for negligence exists, a thoughtless slip or blunder, the failure to detect a theft or forgery beneath the cover of deceptive entries, may expose accountants to a liability in an indeterminate amount for an indeterminate time to an indeterminate class. The hazards of a business conducted on these terms are so extreme as to enkindle doubt whether a flaw may not exist in the implication of a duty that exposes to those consequences. . . . The case was submitted to the jury and the verdict was returned upon the theory that even in the absence of a misstatement of a fact there is a liability . . . for erroneous opinion. The expression of an opinion is to be subject to a warranty implied by law. What, then, is the warranty, as yet unformulated, to be? Is it merely that the opinion is honestly conceived and that the preliminary inquiry has been honestly pursued, that a halt has not been made without a genuine belief that the search has been reasonably adequate to bring disclosure of the truth? Or does it go farther and involve the assumption of a liability for any blunder or inattention that could fairly be spoken of as negligence if the controversy were one between accountant and employer for breach of a contract to render services for pay?

The assault upon the citadel of privity is proceeding in these days apace. . . . In the field of the law of torts a manufacturer who is negligent in the manufacture of a chattel in circumstances pointing to an unreasonable risk of serious bodily harm to those using it thereafter may be liable for negligence though privity is lacking between manufacturer and user. A force or instrument of harm having been launched with potentialities of danger manifest to the eye of prudence, the one who launches it is under a duty to keep it without bounds. . . . However, what is released or set in motion is a physical force. We are now asked to say that a like liability attaches to the circulation of a thought or a release of the explosive power resident in words.

. . . [C]ases in this court are said by the plaintiff to have committed us to the doctrine that words, written or oral, if negligently published with the expectation that the reader or listener will transmit them to another, will lay a basis for liability though privity be lacking. . . . [N]othing in our previous decisions commits us to a holding of liability for negligence in the circumstances of the case at hand, and that such liability, if recognized, will be an extension of the principle of those decisions to different conditions, even if more or less analogous. The question then is whether such an extension shall be made.

The extension, if made, will so expand the field of liability for negligent speech as to make it nearly, if not quite, coterminous with that of liability for fraud. Again and again, in decisions of this court, the bounds of this latter liability have been set up, with futility the fate of every endeavor to dislodge them. Scienter has been declared to be an indispensable element except where the representation has been put forward as true of one's own knowledge, or in circumstances where the expression of opinion was a dishonorable pretense. Even an opinion, especially an opinion by an expert, may be found to be fraudulent if the grounds supporting it are so flimsy as to lead to the conclusion that there was no genuine belief back of it. Further than that this court has never gone. . . . This has not meant, to be sure, that negligence may not be evidence from which a trier of the facts may draw an inference of fraud but merely that if that inference is rejected, or, in the light of all the circumstances, is found to be unreasonable, negligence alone is not a substitute for fraud. . . .

We have said that the duty to refrain from negligent representation would become coincident or nearly so with the duty to refrain from fraud if this action could be maintained. A representation even though knowingly false does not constitute ground for an action of deceit unless made with the intent to be communicated to the persons or class of persons who act upon it to their prejudice. Affirmance of this judgment would require us to hold that all or nearly all the persons so situated would suffer an impairment of an interest legally protected if the representation had been negligent. . . .

Liability for negligence if adjudged in this case will extend to many callings other than an auditor's. Lawyers who certify their opinion as to the validity of municipal or corporate bonds with knowledge that the opinion will be brought to the notice of the public, will become liable to the investors, if they have overlooked a statute or a decision, to the same extent as if the controversy were one between client and adviser. Title companies insuring titles to a tract of land, with knowledge that at an approaching auction the fact that they have insured will be stated to the bidders, will become liable to purchasers who may wish the benefit of a policy without payment of a premium. These illustrations may seem to be extreme, but they go little, if any, farther than we are invited to go now. Negligence, moreover, will have one standard when viewed in relation to the employer, and another and at times a stricter standard when viewed in relation to the public. Explanations that might seem plausible, omissions that might be reasonable, if the duty is confined to the employer, conducting a business that presumably at least is not a fraud upon his creditors, might wear another aspect if an independent duty to be suspicious even of one's principal is owing to investors. "Everyone making a promise having the quality of a contract will be under a duty to the promisee by virtue of the promise, but under another duty, apart from contract, to an indefinite number of potential beneficiaries when performance has begun. The assumption of one relation will mean the involuntary assumption of a series of new relations, inescapably hooked together." "The law does not spread its protection so far."

Our holding does not emancipate accountants from the consequences of fraud. It does not relieve them if their audit has been so negligent as to justify a finding that they had no genuine belief in its adequacy, for this again is fraud. It does no more than say that if less than this is proved, if there has been neither reckless misstatement nor insincere profession of an opinion, but only honest blunder, the ensuing liability for negligence is one that is bounded by the contract, and is to be enforced between the parties by whom the contract has been made. We doubt whether the average businessman receiving a certificate without paying for it and receiving it merely as one among a multitude of possible investors would look for anything more.

■ *The court then held that the cause of action for negligence was to be dismissed.*

CASE CONCEPTS REVIEW

1. What theory did this plaintiff assert as the basis for Touche's liability?
2. What is Touche's basic argument for having this suit dismissed?
3. Would the court reach the same conclusion if the lawsuit against Touche had been based on fraud?

In 1985, the New York Court of Appeals reaffirmed *Ultramares.* It held that accountants may not be held liable, under New York law, to third parties for professional negligence absent privity of contract or close relationship sufficiently equivalent to privity.

The court reiterated the requirement for a "contractual relationship or its equivalent." It said that before accountants may be held liable in negligence to non-contractual parties who rely to their detriment on inaccurate financial reports, certain prerequisites must be satisfied: (1) The accountants must have been aware that the financial reports were to be used for a particular purpose, (2) upon which a known party was intended to rely, and (3) some conduct of the accountants linking them to that party evinces the accountants' understanding of that party's reliance. These criteria permit some flexibility in the application of the doctrine of privity to accountants' liability but do not represent a departure from the principles in *Ultramares*.

The *Ultramares* case also recognizes that an auditor may be liable to a third party for negligence when the duties performed were for the *primary* benefit of the identified third party. This is consistent with third-party liability for breach of contract. For example, if an auditor is hired to prepare financial statements for the primary benefit of a known third party, the third party may collect its damages from a negligent accountant. The 1985 case only held that there is no liability for simple negligence to other third parties.

6. Modifications of the *Ultramares* Doctrine

Courts in Wisconsin, New Hampshire, California, New Jersey, Ohio, and other states have in recent years tended to modify and, in some cases, overrule the *Ultramares* decision. While it is still the law in many states, it is not the law in many others, and the trend of the cases is away from the reasoning of Justice Cardozo in *Ultramares*.

Some courts have expanded the liability by liberalizing the third-party beneficiary concept. These courts have not required that the accountant's services be for the primary benefit of the third party. All they have required is that the auditor know that the reports are for the benefit of a third party and that the third party be identified. Some courts have refused to extend liability to all known persons who benefit from the services and have retained the primary benefit test.

Section 552 of the *Restatement of Torts, Second,* contains provisions creating liability for negligence to third persons. These provisions provide that an accountant may be held liable to third parties who rely on financial statements, audits, etc., prepared by the accountant in cases where the latter fails to exercise ordinary care in the preparation of such statement, audits, etc., and the third party because of such reliance suffers financial loss or damage. Under §552(2), liability is limited to loss suffered "(a) By the person or one of a limited group of persons for whose benefit and guidance he [the accountant] intends to supply the information or knows the recipient intends to supply it; and (b) through reliance upon it in a transaction that he [the accountant] intends the information to influence or knows the recipient so intends or in a substantially similar transaction."

The drafters of the *Restatement (Second)* provided the following hypothetical illustrations to help clarify its provisions:

2. A is negotiating with the X Bank for a credit of $50,000. The Bank requires an audit by certified public accountants. A employs B & Company, a firm of accountants, to make the audit, telling them that it is to meet the requirements of the X

Bank. B & Company agree to make the audit, with express understanding that it is for transmission to X Bank only. The X Bank fails, and A without any further communication with B & Company submits their certification to the Y Bank, which in reliance upon it extends a credit of $50,000 to A. The audit is so carelessly made as greatly to overstate the financial resource of A, and in consequence the Y Bank suffers pecuniary loss through its extension of credit. B & Company is not liable to Y Bank.

3. The same facts as in Illustration 2, except that nothing is said about supplying the information for the guidance of X Bank only, and A merely informs B & Company that he expects to negotiate a bank loan, and has the X Bank in mind. B & Company is subject to liability to Y Bank.

4. The same facts as in Illustration 2, except that A informs B & Company he expects to negotiate a bank loan, but does not mention the name of any bank. B & Company is subject to liability to Y Bank. . . .

7. A, a certified public accountant, is employed by B Company to prepare and certify a balance sheet for the corporation. A is not informed of any intended use of the balance sheet, but A knows that such certificates are customarily used in a wide variety of financial transactions with the corporation, and that it may be relied upon by lenders, investors, shareholders, creditors, purchasers, and the like, in numerous possible kinds of transactions. In fact, B Company uses the certified balance sheet to obtain a loan from X Bank. Because of A's negligence the balance sheet presents an inaccurate picture of the finances of B Company, and through reliance upon it X Bank suffers pecuniary loss. A is not liable to X Bank.

As a result of the *Restatement,* many jurisdictions today hold accountants liable for ordinary negligence to foreseen third parties. This liability has even been extended to incomplete unaudited workpapers and adjusting entries when completed financial statements were not prepared. Since a primary function of the audit is to supply information to third parties, there are substantial numbers of foreseen third parties. There is a definite trend toward increased responsibility and liability and away from *Ultramares.*

Other courts have gone beyond §552(2) of the *Restatement of Torts* in expanding the liability of accountants to those reasonably foreseeable instead of those actually foreseen. Under §552, liability is not extended to all parties whom the accountant might reasonably foresee as using the information. Rather, its "limited group of persons" formulation extends causes of action to a limited number of third parties who are expected to gain access to the financial statement information in an expected transaction (actually foreseen).

The *Restatement*'s limitation of liability to certain third parties is too restrictive for many courts. To them, an accountant's liability to third parties should be determined under accepted principles of negligence law. According to these principles, a finding of nonliability will be made only if there is a strong public policy requiring such a finding. Liability will be imposed on accountants for the foreseeable injuries resulting from their negligent acts unless, under the facts of this particular case, as a matter of policy to be decided by the court, recovery is denied on grounds of public policy (reasonable foreseeability). The common-law liabilities are summarized in Table 32–1.

In the following case, the court discusses these various theories of holding an accountant liable to third parties before it concludes to follow the *Restatement* approach.

TABLE 32-1 ■ The Tort Liability of Accountants

THEORIES OF LIABILITY	LIABILITY TO CLIENTS	LIABILITY TO THOSE IN PRIVITY AND TO PRIMARY BENEFICIARIES	LIABILITY TO KNOWN THIRD PARTIES	LIABILITY TO UNKNOWN BUT REASONABLY FORESEEABLE THIRD PARTIES
1. Common-law fraud	Yes	Yes	Yes	Yes
2. Gross negligence—reckless statements	Yes	Yes	Yes	Yes
3. Breach of contract	Yes	Yes	No	No
4. Negligence in those states following *Ultramares*	Yes	Yes	No	No
5. Negligence in those states following §552 of the *Restatement of Torts, Second*	Yes	Yes	Yes	No
6. Negligence in some other States	Yes	Yes	Yes	Yes

CASE

First Florida Bank v. Max Mitchell & Co.
558 So.2d 9 (Fla. 1990)

GRIMES, J.

We review *First Florida Bank v. Max Mitchell & Co.*, 541 So.2d 155, 157 (Fla. 2d DCA 1989), in which the court certified the following question as one of great public importance:

> When an accountant fails to exercise reasonable and ordinary care in preparing the financial statements of his client and where that accountant personally delivers and presents the statements to a third party to induce that third party to loan to or invest in the client, knowing that the statements will be relied upon by the third party in loaning to or investing in the client, is the accountant liable to the third party in negligence for the damages the third party suffers as a result of the accountant's failure to use reasonable and ordinary care in preparing the financial statements, despite a lack of privity between the accountant and the third party?

... Max Mitchell is a certified public accountant and president of Max Mitchell and Company, P.A. In April of 1985, Mitchell went to First Florida Bank for the purpose of negotiating a loan on behalf of his client, C.M. Systems, Inc. Mitchell advised Stephen Hickman, the bank vice president, that he was a certified public accountant and delivered to Hickman audited financial statements of C.M. Systems for the fiscal years ending October 31, 1983, and October 31, 1984, which had been prepared by his firm. The October 31, 1984, audited statement indi-

cated that C.M. Systems had total assets of $3,474,336 and total liabilities of $1,296,823. It did not indicate that C.M. Systems owed money to any bank, and in a later conference with Hickman, Mitchell stated that as of April 16, 1985, C.M. Systems was not indebted to any bank. At that time, Mitchell asked Hickman to consider a $500,000 line of credit for C.M. Systems.

Over the next several weeks, Mitchell had numerous discussions with Hickman concerning various line items in Mitchell's audit of C.M. Systems. Mitchell represented that he was thoroughly familiar with the financial condition of C.M. Systems. On May 23, 1985, Hickman asked Mitchell for interim financial statements for the period which ended on April 30, 1985. Mitchell advised that they would not be available for several more weeks. Hickman asked Mitchell if there had been any material change in the company's financial condition since October 31, 1984, and Mitchell said that he was not aware of any material changes. On June 6, 1985, the bank approved the request for a $500,000 unsecured line of credit to C.M. Systems. Thereafter, C.M. Systems borrowed the entire amount of the $500,000 credit line which it was never repaid.

Subsequently, the bank discovered that the audit of C.M. Systems for the fiscal year ending October 31, 1984, had substantially overstated the assets, understated the liabilities, and overstated net income. Among other things, the audit failed to reflect that as of October 31, 1984, C.M. Systems owed at least $750,000 to several banks. In addition, several material changes had occurred in the company's balance sheet after the audit but prior to the approval of the line of credit.

The bank filed a three-count complaint against Mitchell and his firm. Because of the absence of privity between either Mitchell or his firm and the bank, the trial court granted Mitchell summary judgment on the negligence and gross negligence counts. The bank voluntarily dismissed the count based on fraud. Believing itself bound by prior decisional law of the state, the district court of appeal affirmed. Recognizing the public policy implications of the issue and the erosion of the privity doctrine in other areas of the law, the court posed the certified question for our consideration.

The seminal case on this subject is *Ultramares Corp. v. Touche*, 174 N.E.441 (1931), authored by Justice Cardozo. In that case the court held that a lender which had relied upon inaccurate financial statements to its detriment had no cause of action against the public accounting firm which had prepared them because of the lack of privity between the parties. . . .

In the more than fifty years which have elapsed since *Ultramares*, the question of an accountant's liability for negligence where no privity exists has been addressed by many courts. There are now essentially four lines of authority with respect to this issue.

(1) Except in cases of fraud, an accountant is only liable to one with whom he is in privity or near privity.

(2) An accountant is liable to third parties in the absence of privity under the circumstances described in section 552, *Restatement (Second) of Torts* which reads in pertinent part:

§ 552. Information Negligently Supplied for the Guidance of Others.

(1) One who, in the course of his business, profession or employment, or in any other transaction in which he has a pecuniary interest, supplies false information for the guidance of others in their business transactions, is subject to liability for pecuniary loss caused to them by their justifiable reliance on the information, if he fails to exercise reasonable care or competence in obtaining or communicating the information.

(2) . . . The liability stated in Subsection (1) is limited to loss suffered

(a) by the person or one of a limited group of persons for whose benefit and guidance he intends to supply the information or knows that the recipient intends to supply it; and

(b) through reliance upon it in a transaction that he intends the information to influence or knows that the recipient so intends or in a substantially similar transaction. . . .

(3) An accountant is liable to all persons who might reasonably be foreseen as relying upon his work product.

(4) An accountant's liability to third persons shall be determined by

the balancing of various factors, among which are the extent to which the transaction was intended to affect the plaintiff, the foreseeability of harm to him, the degree of certainty that the plaintiff suffered injury, the closeness of the connection between the defendant's conduct and the injury suffered, the moral blame attached to the defendant's conduct, and the policy of preventing future harm.

. . . Upon consideration, we have decided to adopt the rationale of section 552, *Restatement (Second) of Torts*, as setting forth the circumstances under which accountants may be held liable in negligence to persons who are not in contractual privity. The rule shall also apply to allegations of gross negligence, but the absence of privity shall continue to be no bar to charges of fraud. . . .

Because of the heavy reliance upon audited financial statements in the contemporary financial world, we believe permitting recovery only from those in privity or near privity is unduly restrictive. On the other hand, we are persuaded by the wisdom of the rule which limits liability to those persons or classes of persons whom an accountant "knows" will rely on his opinion rather than those he "should have known" would do so because it takes into account the fact that an accountant controls neither his client's accounting records nor the distribution of his reports. . . .

There remains the need to apply this rule to the facts at hand. At the time Mitchell prepared the audits for C.M. Systems, it was unknown that they would be used to induce the reliance of First Florida Bank to approve a line of credit for C.M. Systems. Therefore, except for the unusual facts of this case, Mitchell could not be held liable to the bank for any negligence in preparing the audit. However, Mitchell actually negotiated the loan on behalf of his client. He personally delivered the financial statements to the bank with the knowledge that it would rely upon them in considering whether or not to make the loan. Under this unique set of facts, we believe that Mitchell vouched for the integrity of the audits and that his conduct in dealing with the bank sufficed to meet the requirements of the rule which we have adopted in this opinion.

Accordingly, we answer the certified question in the affirmative. . . .

■ *It is so ordered.*

CASE CONCEPTS REVIEW

1. How is this factual situation different from the one in the *Ultramares* case?

2. What are the four choices discussed by the court

with respect to how to analyze an accountant's liability to a third party?

3. Why does this court choose to follow the *Restatement* approach?

7. Exculpatory Clauses

Section 10 of chapter 13 discussed contract clauses disclaiming tort liability even if a person is at fault. Accountants frequently include these exculpatory clauses in their audit contracts with clients. As we noted in chapter 13, these disclaimers of liability are not favored by the law and are strictly construed against the party relying on them. They are frequently declared to be illegal by courts as being contrary to public policy. Private contracts exculpating one from the consequences of one's own acts will be enforced only when there is no vast disparity in the bargaining power between the parties and the intention to do so is expressed in clear and unequivocal language. Thus, an exculpatory clause for an accountant engaged in the audit function will generally be found to contravene the public's interest because the profession is of the type generally thought suitable for public regulation and the party seeking exculpation is engaged in performing a service of great importance to the public. The client often must have an audit to comply with the law or the legitimate needs of the business community. If all accountants sought to contract upon the same terms, the client would be forced to agree to them. This inequality of bargaining power, when coupled with the public interest aspect of the service, eliminates freedom of contract and requires the court to set aside such provisions. This reasoning would certainly be applicable if the audit were required by the SEC.

It may be argued that individual accountants who are self-employed and smaller accounting firms should be able to include exculpatory clauses in contracts for their services. Such an assertion is based on the fact that equality of bargaining power does exist. An analogous situation occurred when a federal district court upheld the validity of a clause that exempted a credit agency from liability for loss or injury caused by its negligence in procuring, compiling, collecting, interpreting, communicating, or delivering information. The court found that neither a special legal relationship existed nor was there any overriding public interest present, and the contract had been entered into voluntarily by competent parties.

Should an exculpatory clause between a client and an accountant prevent a suit by a third party? Whether or not the effects of the exculpatory clause extend to the third persons is contingent on the theory used by the court for finding the accountant liable to the third party. If a third-party beneficiary to a contract approach is taken, then the beneficiary is subject to all the equities and defenses that would be available against the promisee. On the other hand, if the duty to the third person arose independently of the contract, the exculpatory clause should have no application with regard to the third party, since, as a general rule, a person who is not named in a contract has not executed it, is not a party to the contract, and is therefore not bound by its terms. The effect of a disclaimer is often a question of fact for a jury to decide.

Courts have held as a matter of law that disclaimers under certain circumstances will not avoid liability. For example, one court held that the fact that a public accounting firm issued only a qualified opinion as to the completeness and accuracy of its audit did not permit the firm to escape liability to a bank that had relied on these negligently prepared audit reports in loaning money to the firm's client. When the accountants transmitted the financial statements to their client, they wrote a covering letter expressing certain reservations about the "fairness of the accompanying statements." They further stated that "our examination included a general review of accounting procedures and such tests of accounting records as we were permitted to make." After it was established that this particular firm knew that the plaintiff would be relying on its report, the court stated that the qualifications to the audit report failed to indicate the true extent of knowledge and investigation by the accountants. Hence this attempted qualification could not be utilized to insulate the accountants from liability.

This case does not mean that qualifications are inadequate insulation against liability, but rather that qualifications can preclude liability only if certain criteria are met. If the accountants had conformed with the procedures enumerated in the AICPA Statement on Auditing Procedures regarding the proper content of qualifications, they would probably have escaped liability.

The Supreme Court of another state took a harsher approach when it held that an accounting firm's arguments lacked merit. The firm had argued that no liability to third parties should attach, since the issued financial statement was not certified and since they affirmatively stated that "they expressed no opinion." The court concluded that liability must be dependent on the accountants' undertaking, not their rejection of dependability. The court further held that the accountants could not escape liability for negligence by a general statement that they disclaimed liability.

From the foregoing we must conclude that there is no hard and fast rule controlling the validity of exculpatory clauses, disclaimers, and qualifications. In the absence of statutory provisions governing the result in a particular situation, courts will balance policy considerations. Generally, exculpatory clauses are not favored, especially when the party seeking to exclude liability maintains a superior bargaining position. Qualifications and disclaimers, if properly formulated, stand a chance of withstanding a plaintiff's challenge, since they will sufficiently alert the relying party of particular deficiencies. On the other hand, the underlying purpose of the audit report or financial statement will be defeated if a person is told that he or she cannot reasonably rely on these materials. In those situations where accountants attempt to negate liability, important policy considerations must be weighed in determining the legality of such exculpatory clauses.

STATUTORY LIABILITY

8. Introduction

Congress has increasingly placed responsibility on accountants to serve as watchdogs for improper business activities. Beginning in 1977 with the passage of the Foreign Corrupt Practices Act, Congress has required that accountants auditing businesses develop methods for their review that ensure the discovery of bribes paid to foreign officials. The details of this Act and liability for failing to comply are presented in chapter 8.

Accountants also face liability for failing to meet the disclosure requirements of the securities laws. The 1933 Securities Act requires any business that initially offers to sell its securities to the public to prepare a *registration statement* to be filed with the SEC and a *prospectus* to be given to prospective purchasers. These documents are heavily laden with financial information about the issuer-business and its principal shareholders, directors, and officers. Accountants usually are very involved in preparing the financial statements that become a part of these disclosure documents.

The 1934 Securities Exchange Act was enacted to regulate all transfers of securities after the first sale, which is governed by the 1933 Act. Thus, the 1934 Act specifies requirements for parties engaged in the exchange of securities. The parties being regulated include security brokers and the exchanges. Similar to the 1933 Act, the 1934 Act contains several provisions wherein accountants might become liable. Section 18 of the 1934 Act addresses the requirements of documents filed with the SEC by brokers, exchanges, and other businesses. Perhaps more significant is Section 10(b), and its accompanying Rule 10b-5, which prohibits fraudulent activities in the manipulation of securities' prices.

Violations of the federal securities laws can result in civil damages and criminal sanctions. These levels of liability and several other aspects of the securities law are presented in the next four sections.

9. The 1933 Securities Act

The 1933 Act makes accountants liable for errors and omissions in registration statements, prospectuses, and certain other communications. Thus, if the work product of an accountant that is used in connection with a new offering of securities contains untrue statements of material facts or omits material facts required by law, or that if not given makes the stated facts misleading, an accountant may have liability. This liability for losses sustained is to clients and to third-party investors, and it exists without proof of fraud or negligence. An accountant may also have liability for aiding and abetting a client who violates the law.

Accountants often assert a due diligence defense when sued under the 1933 Act. This defense is that the defendant accountant has, after reasonable investigation, reasonable ground to believe and did believe, at the time such part of the registration statement became effective, that the statements therein were true and that there was no omission to state a material fact required to be stated therein or necessary to make the statements therein not misleading. The burden of proof is on the accountant to prove this defense to the satisfaction of the jury. In determining whether or not an accountant has made a reasonable investigation, the law provides that the standard of reasonableness is that required of a prudent person in the management of his or her own property.

The 1933 Securities Act recognizes several additional defenses that may be used in an attempt to avoid liability. Lack of materiality is a common defense. Determining whether or not a particular fact is material depends on the facts and the parties involved. For the average investor, minor inaccuracies do not create liability. A material fact is one that would either deter or encourage a purchase because it had an important bearing on the nature or condition of the issuing corporation.

A plaintiff-purchaser can recover for a violation of the 1933 Act without proving that reliance was placed on the false or deceptive registration statement or prospectus. All this plaintiff must prove is that the documents did not comply with the SEC's disclosure requirements. However, an accountant-defendant may be able to establish an effective defense by proving that the plaintiff knew of the inaccuracy in the document prior to the purchase of securities.

10. The 1934 Securities Exchange Act

To comply with the provisions of the 1934 Act, businesses must use the services of CPAs. The responsibility of public accountants in certifying financial statements used to comply with the law is not only to the client who pays the fees but also to investors, creditors, and all others who may rely on the statements. As a result, accountants must report fairly on the fact as found, whether favorable or unfavorable to the client. The accountant's duty is to safeguard the public interest and not that of the client. Under this statute, the accountant has a duty to certify only those financial statements that are accurate.

Two major statutory provisions impose civil liability under the 1934 Act. These are Section 18 and Section 10b. Section 18 of the act imposes liability for false and misleading statements of material fact in any application, report, or document filed under the act. It is a codification of common-law fraud. Liability under Section 18 for fraud extends to both purchasers and sellers. Plaintiffs under this section must prove scienter, reliance on the false or misleading statement, and damage. It is a defense that the person sued acted in good faith and without knowledge that the statement was false and misleading. There is no liability under this section for simple negligence. Gross negligence can supply the element of intent, however.

11. Liability under Section 10b and Rule 10b-5

Most lawsuits against accountants are brought under Section 10b and Rule 10b-5 of the SEC. These provisions are concerned with manipulative and deceptive devices and contrivances. Section 10b and the rules promulgated under it provide a private civil remedy for defrauded investors, including purchasers and sellers of securities. This remedy may be invoked against "any person" who indulges in fraudulent practices in connection with the purchase or sale of securities. Rule 10b-5 declares that it is unlawful to use the mails or any instrumentality of interstate commerce or any national securities exchange to defraud any person in connection with the purchase or sale of any security.

In actual practice, defendants in Section 10b and Rule 10b-5 cases have tended to fall into four general categories: (1) insiders, (2) broker-dealers, (3) corporations whose stock is purchased or sold by plaintiffs, and (4) those who "aid and abet" or conspire with a party who falls into one of the first three categories. Accountants usually fall into the fourth category. Silence may constitute aiding and abetting. While there is no general duty on the part of all persons with knowledge of improper activities to report them, a duty to disclose may arise from the fact of a special relationship or set of circumstances, such as an accountant certifying financial statements.

The application of Section 10b and Rule 10b-5 is not limited to securities subject to the act. It applies to all sales of any security if the requisite fraud exists and the interstate aspect is established. The rule requires that those standing in a fiduciary relationship disclose all material facts before entering into transactions. This means that an officer, a director, or a controlling shareholder has a duty to disclose all material facts. Failure to do so is a violation, and lack of privity of contract is no defense.

Liability under Rule 10b-5 may be imposed even though the accountant performs only an unaudited write-up. An accountant is liable for errors in financial statements contained in a prospectus or other filed report even though unaudited if there are errors that he or she knew or should have known. Even when performing an unaudited write-up, an accountant is obligated to undertake at least a minimal investigation into the figures supplied to him or her and is not free to disregard suspicious circumstances.

Section 10b and Rule 10b-5 are usually referred to as the antifraud provisions of the act. A plaintiff seeking damages under the provisions must establish (1) the existence of a material misrepresentation or omission made in connection with the purchase or sale of a security, (2) the culpable state of mind of the defendant, (3) his or her reliance and due diligence, and (4) damage as a result of the reliance.

In determining whether the financial reports and statements are materially misleading, courts do not consider whether they comply with accounting norms, but whether the reports and statements fairly present the true financial position of the issuer to the untutored eye of an ordinary investor. Conformity with generally accepted accounting principles is not determinative of liability under the antifraud provisions of the Securities Exchange Act of 1934.

The concept of fraud encompasses not only untrue statements of material facts but the omission of material facts necessary to prevent the statements actually made from being misleading. In other words, a half-truth that misleads is fraudulent. Finally, a failure to correct a misleading impression left by statements already made or silence where there is a duty to speak gives rise to a violation of Rule 10b-5. As a result, an accountant has a duty to disclose subsequently acquired information if prior reports prepared for reliance by investors are false.

Suits by investors under the antifraud provisions require proof of intent to defraud or scienter. However, the cases take the modern view of scienter and hold that either actual knowledge or a reckless disregard for the truth equivalent to actual knowledge supply proof of this element. However, proof of negligence does not supply this element, as the following case illustrates.

CASE

Ernst & Ernst v. Hochfelder et al.
96 S.Ct. 1375 (1976)

POWELL, J.

The issue in this case is whether an action for civil damages may lie under § 10(b) of the Securities Exchange Act of 1934 (1934 Act) and Securities and Exchange Commission Rule 10b-5 in the absence of an allegation of intent to deceive, manipulate, or defraud on the part of the defendant. Petitioner, Ernst & Ernst, is an accounting firm. From 1946 through 1967 it was retained by First Securities Company of Chicago (First Securities), a small brokerage firm and member of the Midwest Stock Exchange and of the National Association of Securities Dealers, to perform periodic audits of the firm's books and records. In connection with these audits Ernst & Ernst prepared for filing with the Securities and Exchange Commission (the Commission) the annual reports required of First Securities under § 17(a) of the 1934 Act. It

also prepared for First Securities responses to the financial questionnaires of the Midwest Stock Exchange (the Exchange).

Respondents were customers of First Securities who invested in a fraudulent securities scheme perpetrated by Lestor B. Nay, president of the firm and owner of 92% of its stock. Nay induced the respondents to invest funds in "escrow" accounts that he represented would yield a high rate of return. Respondents did so from 1942 through 1966, with the majority of the transactions occurring in the 1950's. In fact, there were no escrow accounts as Nay converted respondent's funds to his own use immediately upon receipt. These transactions were not in the customary form of dealings between First Securities and its customers. The respondents drew their personal checks payable to Nay or a designated bank for his account. No such escrow accounts were reflected on the books and records of First Securities, and none was shown on its periodic accounting to respondents in connection with their other investments. Nor were they included in First Securities' filings with the Commission or the Exchange.

This fraud came to light in 1968 when Nay committed suicide, leaving a note that described First Securities as bankrupt and the escrow accounts as "spurious." Respondents subsequently filed this action for damages against Ernst & Ernst . . . under § 10(b) of the 1934 Act. The complaint charged that Nay's escrow scheme violated § 10(b) and Commission Rule 10b-5, and that Ernst & Ernst had "aided and abetted" Nay's violations by its "failure" to conduct proper audits of First Securities. As revealed through discovery, respondents' cause of action rested on a theory of negligent nonfeasance. The premise was that Ernst & Ernst had failed to utilize "appropriate auditing procedures" in its audits of First Securities, thereby failing to discover internal practices of the firm said to prevent an effective audit. The practice principally relied on was Nay's rule that only he could open mail addressed to him at First Securities or addressed to First Securities to his attention, even if it arrived in his absence. Respondents contended that if Ernst & Ernest had conducted a proper audit, it would have discovered this "mail rule." The existence of the rule then would have been disclosed in reports to the Exchange and to the Commission by Ernst & Ernst as an irregular procedure that prevented an effective audit. This would have led to an investigation of Nay that would have revealed the fraudulent scheme. Respondents specifically disclaimed the existence of fraud or intentional misconduct on the part of Ernst & Ernst.

After extensive discovery the District Court granted Ernst & Ernst's motion for summary judgment and dismissed the action. . . .

The Court of Appeals of the Seventh Circuit reversed and remanded, holding that one who breaches a duty of inquiry and disclosure owed another is liable in damages for aiding and abetting a third party's violation of Rule 10b-5 if the fraud would have been discovered or prevented but for the breach. . . .

We granted certiorari to resolve the question whether a private cause of action for damages will lie under § 10(b) and Rule 10b-5 in the absence of any allegation of "scienter"—intent to deceive, manipulate, or defraud. . . .

Federal regulation of transactions in securities emerged as part of the aftermath of the market crash in 1929. The Securities Act of 1933 (1933 Act) was designed to provide investors with full disclosure of material information concerning public offerings of securities in commerce, to protect investors against fraud and, through the imposition of specified civil liabilities, to promote ethical standards of honesty and fair dealing. The 1934 Act was intended principally to protect investors against manipulation of stock prices through regulation of transactions upon securities exchanges and in over-the-counter markets, and to impose regular reporting requirements on companies whose stock is listed on national securities exchanges. Although the Acts contain numerous carefully drawn express civil remedies and criminal penalties, Congress recognized that efficient regulation of securities trading could not be accomplished under a rigid statutory program. As part of the 1934 Act Congress created the Commission, which is provided with an arsenal of flexible enforcement powers.

Section 10 of the 1934 Act makes it "unlawful for any person . . . (b) [t]o use or employ, in connection with the purchase or sale of any security . . . any manipulative or deceptive device or contrivance in contravention of such rules and regulations as the Commission may perceive as necessary or appropriate in the public interest or for the protection of investors." In 1942, acting pursuant to the power conferred by § 10(b), the Commission promulgated Rule 10b-5, which now provides:

> Employment of manipulative and deceptive devices.
>
> It shall be unlawful for any person, directly or indirectly, by the use of any means or instrumentality of interstate commerce, or of the mails, or of any facility of any national securities exchange.
>
> 1. To employ any device, scheme, or artifice to defraud,
> 2. To make any untrue statement of a material fact or to omit to state a material fact necessary in order to make the statements made, in the light of the circumstances under which they were made, not misleading, or
> 3. To engage in any act, practice, or course of business which operates or would operate as a fraud or deceit upon any person, in connection with the purchase or sale of any security.

Although § 10(b) does not by its terms create an express civil remedy for its violation . . . the existence of a private cause of action for violations of the statute and the rule is now well established. During the 30-year period since a private cause of action was first implied under § 10(b) and Rule 10b-5, a substantial body of case law and commentary has developed as to its elements. Courts and commentators long have differed with regard to whether scienter is a necessary element of such a cause of action, or whether negligent conduct alone is sufficient. In addressing this question, we turn first to the language of § 10(b), for "[t]he starting point in every case involving construction of a statute is the language itself."

Section 10(b) makes unlawful the use of employment of "any manipulative or deceptive device or contrivance" in contravention of Commission rules. The words "manipulative or deceptive" used in conjunction with "device or contrivance" strongly suggest that § 10(b) was intended to proscribe knowing or intentional misconduct.

In its *amicus curiae* brief, however, the Commission contends that nothing in the language "manipulative or deceptive device or contrivance" limits its operation to knowing or intentional practices. In support of its view, the Commission cites the overall congressional purpose in the 1933 and 1934 Act to protect investors against false and deceptive practices that might injure them.

The Commission then reasons that since the "effect" upon investors of given conduct is the same regardless of whether the conduct is negligent or intentional, Congress must have intended to bar all such practices and not just those done knowingly or intentionally. . . . The argument simply ignores the use of the words "manipulative," "device," and "contrivance," terms that make unmistakable a congressional intent to proscribe a type of conduct quite different from negligence. Use of the word "manipulative" is especially significant. It is and was virtually a term of art when used in connection with securities markets. It connotes intentional or willful conduct designed to deceive or defraud investors by controlling or artificially affecting the price of securities. . . .

. . . When a statute speaks so specifically in terms of manipulation and deception, and of implementing devices and contrivances—the commonly understood terminology of intentional wrongdoing—and when its history reflects no more expansive intent, we are quite unwilling to extend the scope of the statute to negligent conduct.

■ *Reversed.*

CASE CONCEPTS REVIEW

1. What is the issue presented to the Supreme Court by this case?
2. The plaintiff-respondent makes what argument as to why the accounting firm "aided and abetted" the fraudulent activities of Nay?
3. What specific language of the 1934 Act does the court rely on to justify its conclusions that scienter (or intent) is a required element of proof to hold an accountant under §10(b) and Rule 10b-5?

12. Criminal Liability: Securities Laws

In recent years some accountants have been indicted for crimes allegedly committed in the practice of their profession. Section 24 of the 1933 Act declares that willful violations of its provisions constitute a crime. It in effect declares that fraud in the sale of a security is a crime punishable by a fine of $10,000 and five years in prison. The 1934 Act also provides for criminal sanctions for false and misleading statements. The law requires that such false statements be willfully and knowingly made. The fine for a violation is $100,000, and the maximum prison sentence is five years. Compliance with GAAP is not an absolute defense in a criminal case.

In addition to these criminal sanctions, Congress recently reiterated its concern with the vigorous enforcement of the securities law. In the Securities Enforcement Remedies and Penny Stock Reform Act of 1990, the SEC is authorized to seek civil (not criminal) fines against violators of the 1933 and 1934 Acts of up to $500,000 for an organization and $100,000 for an individual. The SEC also can seek a court order banning an individual found to have violated the 1934 Act from service as director or officer of an organization.

The usual defense asserted by accountants in criminal cases is lack of criminal intent. Mere mistakes or negligence is not usually considered to be criminal conduct.

In the leading case of *United States v. Natelli*, 527 F.2d 311 (1975), the United States Court of Appeals for the Second Circuit had occasion to discuss the element of criminal intent and the role of the jury in deciding if it exists. It noted that the failure to follow sound accounting practice is evidence that may prove criminal intent. It said in part,

It is hard to probe the intent of a defendant. Circumstantial evidence, particularly with proof of motive, where available, is often sufficient to convince a reasonable man of criminal intent beyond a reasonable doubt. When we deal with a defendant who is a professional accountant, it is even harder, at times, to distinguish between simple errors of judgment and errors made with sufficient criminal intent to support a conviction, especially when there is no financial gain to the accountant other than his legitimate fee. . . .

The arguments Natelli makes in this court as evidence of his innocent intent were made to the jury and presented fairly. There is no contention that Judge Tyler improperly excluded any factual evidence offered. While there is substance to some of Natelli's factual contentions for jury consideration, we cannot find, on the totality of the evidence, that he was improperly convicted.

The original action of Natelli in permitting the booking of unbilled sales after the close of the fiscal period in an amount sufficient to convert a loss into a profit was contrary to sound accounting practice, particularly when the cost of sales based on time spent by account executives in the fiscal period was a mere guess. When the uncollectibility, and indeed, the nonexistence of these large receivables was established in 1969, the revelation stood to cause Natelli severe criticism and possible liability. He had a motive, therefore, intentionally to conceal the write-offs that had to be made. . . .

Whether or not the deferred tax item was properly converted to a tax credit, the jury had a right to infer that "netting" the extraordinary item against ordinary earnings on the books in a special journal entry was, in the circumstances, motivated by a desire to conceal. . . .

We reject the argument of insufficient evidence as to Natelli, our function being limited to determining whether the evidence was sufficient for submission to the jury. We hold that it was.

13. Criminal Liability: Tax Preparation

Criminal sanctions are also applicable to accountants for their participation in falsifying tax returns. Tax crimes for which accountants may be held liable are contained in both the Internal Revenue Code (IRC) and the United States Criminal Code (Title 18). An accountant risks criminal prosecution if he or she willfully assists in the preparation of a false return.

It should always be kept in mind that whether or not the falsity or fraud is committed with the knowledge or consent of the client involved is irrelevant. Additionally, tax return preparers may be found guilty of assisting in the preparation of a false return when they utilize information furnished by the taxpayer that they know is false.

Certain conduct by accountants and others in the preparation of tax returns is frequently alleged to be a criminal conspiracy. Title 18 of the U.S. Code authorizes criminal penalties for anyone who conspires either to commit an offense against the United States or to defraud the United States, or any agency thereof. The penalty for a violation of this section includes a maximum fine of $10,000 and/or a maximum term of five years of imprisonment.

The United States Code also proscribes falsely swearing to the truth of any testimony or document for which a law of the United States authorizes an oath to be administered. The penalty for a violation of this section is a fine of not more than $2,000 or five years' imprisonment or both. This code is supplemented by a penalty for falsely verifying any statement that is within the purview of the tax law, IRC §7206(1). Thus, in effect, an accountant who commits perjury in the preparation of a tax return is subject to the sanctions of both of the foregoing provisions.

In summary, it should be recognized by all who participate in the preparation of tax returns and any related documents that criminal liability may be imposed for conduct that violates either the Internal Revenue Code or the United States Criminal Code. Accountants are prohibited from willfully assisting anyone in falsifying tax returns or claims. Furthermore, it is illegal for accountants to participate in conspiracies for the purpose of tax evasion. Additionally, false information given under oath may subject accountants to punishment on the grounds of perjury.

THE VIEW OF THE PROFESSION

The recent proliferation of lawsuits against accountants and the tremendous increase in the cost of malpractice insurance have caused many in the profession to examine the problem of accountants' liability in detail. Numerous articles have been written and many solutions suggested. The following discussion surveys the problem and offers some solutions. It was written by a recognized legal authority who is a major adviser to one of the world's leading accounting firms.

SPECIAL REPORT: ACCOUNTANTS' LIABILITY

Newton N. Minow

Chairman of the Arthur Andersen & Co. Public Review Board

. . . The immense number of plaintiffs in search of compensation for losses, allegedly at the hands of persons they sue, has put enormous pressure on elastic legal doctrines such as negligence and fault, which in earlier times limited recoveries to cases in which defendants' conduct was truly culpable. As applied by sympathetic judges and more so by juries, these doctrines of personal responsibility and fault have fallen to the notion that the highest good of a legal system is its capacity to shift losses to those with deep pockets or insurance, for which it is often assumed no one pays.

The movement away from rigorous conceptions of fault and toward a notion of "strict liability" affects many areas of the law. This movement began in the field of products liability. In that context, "strict liability means that whenever a particular product emerges from an assembly line in a defective condition, the manufacturer will be liable for any injury that the defect causes," regardless of whether there is a showing of specific fault in the manufacturing of the defective product. The intellectual underpinnings of this theory are that risks should be borne by society, rather than the individual, and that large, prosperous economic actors are effective risk bearers because they can plan and insure against the claimed damages.

The theory of strict product liability has been transferred by some courts to the area of professional liability as well. Lawsuits against professionals of all types are proceeding at an unprecedented pace and on legal theories that would have been unthinkable only a decade or two ago. Architects, doctors, lawyers, accountants—all face a steady stream of lawsuits. The suits seem premised on a view that the professionals' responsibilities extend to every possible occurrence.

continued

They appear to reflect a rejection of the notion that a professional may be living up to his or her own best professional ability and yet still be unable to prevent risk or misfortunes of patients or clients. . . .

It is in this context of unprecedented litigation and liability that sweeping new assertions of accountants' liability have occurred. The new theory seems to be that the accountant should be held responsible for a business that does not function properly.

Until the last decade, accountants were largely unaffected by these systematic changes, but the proliferation of lawsuits against them since the 1970s has drawn accountants into the midst of the legal thicket. Indeed, the accountants' relatively recent exposure to widening assertions of liability appears symptomatic of the system's larger predicament. The number of lawsuits against accountants has soared, the damages awarded have skyrocketed, and novel theories of liability are imposed by courts. Many more lawsuits have been filed against accountants in the last decade and a half than in the entire previous history of the profession. . . .

Recent decisions have imposed vast new liability on accountants. The concept of accountants' liability that has emerged in these cases is broad and expansive, almost limitless, as is the number and class of people to whom the accountant is held responsible. Some investors and creditors automatically sue accountants and their firms when businesses fail without regard to what caused the failure and whether the accountants were negligent in the performance of their audit responsibilities. There is an obvious lure in suing the accounting firms, for they are frequently the only solvent party left standing in the wake of corporate bankruptcy. Not coincidentally, the two great surges in litigation against accountants have occurred during times of enormous business failures—the recessions of the early 70s and 80s.

The great expansion of accountants' liability has proceeded through an erosion of rules of fault and causation now typical of many areas of the law. First there has been a broad expansion of the class of people to whom accountants are liable. The classic case on the subject had long been Judge Cardozo's opinion in *Ultramares*. Judge Cardozo held that accountants could not be held liable to third parties for negligence because it might "expose accountants to a liability in an indeterminate amount for an indeterminate time to an indeterminate class. The hazards of business conducted on these terms are so extreme as to enkindle doubt whether a flaw may not exist in the implication of a duty that exposes to these consequences."

In recent decisions, however, courts have held that accountants' liability extends to any investor or creditor who convinces a court or jury that the accountant, in hindsight, could have done something more than he did that would have revealed a business failure or corporate insider's fraud. The effect of these holdings is precisely to expose the accountants to the indeterminate liability feared by Judge Cardozo. Most importantly, the accountants can be held liable for the entire amount of the claimed loss even if their alleged negligence contributed to only a small portion of the total losses; the accountants, meanwhile, are given nothing more than a hollow right to try to recover some of the losses from the usually bankrupt corporation.

Second, in cases alleging fraud under the federal securities laws, courts have relaxed the requirement that plaintiffs actually have relied upon alleged misrepresentations by defendants, including accountants' reports on financial statements. Adopting the so-called "fraud-on-the-market" theory, a number of courts have ruled that investors could recover from defendants for alleged misrepresentations of which the investors were completely unaware, so long as reli-

continued

ance on the statements by other investors affected the price at which the plaintiff bought or sold the security.

In imposing this expansion of liability, courts have transferred the reasoning and analytical framework developed for products liability to accountants' liability. For instance, in rejecting the *Ultramares* concerns, the New Hampshire Supreme Court compared accountants and manufacturers to justify the broad, new liability:

> [A]n accountant, like the manufacturer under products liability law, is in the best position to regulate the effects of his conduct by controlling the degree of care exercised during the performance of his professional duty. The accountant, through the fee structure, can pass along to his clients the cost of insuring against financial loss sustained by them through reliance upon his negligent misstatement of fact.

Another state supreme court—New Jersey—recently came to a similar conclusion and applied similar reasoning:

> If recovery for defective products may include economic loss, why should such loss not be compensable if caused by negligent misrepresentation? The maker of the product and the person making the written representation with intent that it be relied upon are, respectively, impliedly holding out that the product is reasonably fit, suitable, and safe, and that the representation is reasonably sufficient, suitable, and accurate.

The New Jersey court further emphasized its view that accountants are effective and appropriate risk-bearers because they are able to plan and to insure:

> Independent auditors have apparently been able to obtain liability insurance covering these risks or otherwise to satisfy their financial obligation. We have no reason to believe they may not purchase malpractice insurance policies that cover their negligent acts leading to misstatements relied upon by persons who received the audit from the company pursuant to a proper business purpose. . . . Much of the additional costs incurred either because of more thorough auditing review or increased insurance premiums would be borne by the business entity and its stockholders or its customers.

The principles and conclusions derived from products liability are thus playing a major role in inspiring the current expansion of accountants' liability.

A third factor in the expansion of accountants' liability is the extreme broadening of the concept of accountants' negligence itself—a widening of the practices found negligent and legally actionable. Much of this expansion is rooted in a misperception of the accounting profession and its work product. Victor Earle, general counsel of Peat, Marwick, Mitchell & Co., precisely described this misperception with prescience 11 years ago:

> The misconceptions in the public mind are at least fivefold: first, as to *scope*—that auditors make a 100% examination of the company's records, which can be depended upon to uncover all errors or misconduct; second, as to *evaluation*—that auditors pass on the wisdom and legality of a company's multitudinous business decisions; third, as to *precision*—that the numbers set forth in a company's audited financial statements are immutable absolutes; fourth, as to *reducibility*—that the audited results of a company's operations for a year can be synthesized into a single number; and fifth, as to *approval*—that by expressing an opinion on a company's

continued

financial statement, the auditors "certify" its health and attractiveness for investment purposes.

In practical terms, the effect of these misconceptions is the failure of courts and juries to distinguish between an *audit failure* and a *business failure*. As a comprehensive treatise on the law governing accountants recently put it, "From [the public misperception of the auditor's duties] flows an erroneous legal supposition that [the auditor's] responsibility should be coextensive with that of the client." . . .

Taken together, these developments have the potential to create a crushing burden of limitless liability in which accountants become the insurers for all business failures—sometimes at treble damages. There is simply no justification to shift the normal risks of investment from the investor to accountants or, through accountants' liability insurance, to all investors or the public generally. The function of accounting is to provide information to those in the market who place capital at risk—not to guarantee all such risks. Business risks are properly borne by those who make the business and investment decisions, for they are the ones who reap the rewards of business successes and who can respond most efficiently to profit and loss and other market information. A "no-fault" or riskless capital market would deaden economic incentives and sap entrepreneurialism, because in a market or world with no losers there can be no winners.

Even assuming that some kind of investor insurance arrangement were desirable, it would be irrational to provide it through the cumbersome, costly, and time-consuming process of the courts. A straightforward scheme of investor insurance would have at least the advantages of candor and lower cost of administration. It should be obvious, moreover, that any such insurance or strict liability scheme would do little or nothing to deter those whose conduct caused the business failure, since they would have escaped liability, as they often do now.

Even if the expansion of accountants' liability stops short of insurance for all business risk, however, accountants are left in the dark about the nature and extent of their liability. They are left to the vagaries of each litigational outcome, to a situation of litigational roulette, and always subject to the proclivity of triers of fact to give plaintiffs relief at the expense of defendants' "deep pockets." There are many social costs to this situation, costs rarely considered in the decisions expanding accountants' liability. The general confusion about the extent of accountants' liability encourages frivolous litigation and clouds meritorious claims. Amorphous, expansive liability could also discourage the accounting profession from serving riskier enterprises—in other words, the kinds of new, daring entrepreneurial ventures that our economy so desperately needs, including experimental, high-technology companies. If accountants are asked to be the ultimate insurers for businesses, their natural response will be deep caution and reluctance about businesses whose prospects are less than certain.

Accountants might also undertake wasteful and redundant procedures as a defense against being second-guessed by judges and juries, much as physicians are encouraged to practice defense medicine by the threat of unexpected malpractice liability. Finally, accountants would be discouraged from innovations within their own practice, such as review of earnings forecasts, which, though potentially highly useful to the investing public, are necessarily speculative and pose obvious litigation risks to accountants in the present climate.

For all these reasons, the problem of accountants' liability should be carefully and deliberately reconsidered. . . . Perhaps the principal assumption which needs to be reanalyzed is the appropriateness of the products liability analogy in

continued

the context of accountants' liability. The accountant differs from the auto manufacturer in many important respects. An auditor does not have absolute knowledge of and control over a company's finances and records in the same way that an auto manufacturer has knowledge of and control over its production process. The auditor does have control over his or her examination of a client's financial statement, but the relationship between the statement and a claimed loss is far more indirect than the relationship between a defective product and a claimed harm. . . .

The equities are also very different in the products liability and accountants' liability contexts. Products liability litigation pits a consumer, expecting an adequate product, against a company with a stake in each product sold. Accountants' liability litigation, in contrast, pits sophisticated investors and creditors, risktakers who hope to reap financial profit from their investments but who are aware of the ever-present possibility of loss as well, against accountants—professionals who perform an attest service for a fee. Imposing broad liability on accountants reaps windfalls for investors and creditors: they alone obtain the fruits of successful investments and at the same time become insured against losses from those that fail if they can pin liability on accountants.

A most difficult challenge facing society and the professions is how to restore some reason to the way the legal system responds to the risks of everyday life, including the vagaries of investment. The first step must surely be to abandon the tendency, spawned in the products liability area, to translate every risk into a legal liability. That instinct has proven to be decidedly unsound in defining accountants' responsibility. Second, we must repair the legal doctrines governing liability that have become distorted by the quest for compensation for every loss. Liability doctrines affecting accountants must clearly distinguish business failures from audit failures, leaving the former to be borne by the investors who assumed such normal risks, or perhaps under appropriate circumstances to be recovered from the directors or managers of the failed enterprise who in some cases can be fairly held to account. Accountants' liability should be preserved where an actual audit failure has in fact caused injury.

One change in legal doctrine that might better maintain the distinction between compensable losses caused by audit failures and other business losses would be the adoption in accountants' liability cases of the doctrine of comparative negligence with limited, proportionate liability. Under comparative negligence, the extent to which a party is at fault is determined on a percentage basis by the judge or jury; under limited, proportionate liability, moreover, the amount that the party must pay cannot exceed the percentage of the damage reflecting that party's share of the fault. The principle guiding these concepts is that each should pay according to his fault, and no further. . . .

Perhaps a more basic problem, but one not readily cured, is the confusion regarding the standard of negligence itself—the wide gap between the expectations revealed by judges and juries and the reality of what accountants do. . . .

There are no easy answers to the problems of this "expectation gap." At a minimum, if there are areas of legitimate professional disagreement or latitude concerning either accounting principles or the standards for the performance of audits, the parameters of that latitude should be clarified and detailed. In addition, the American Institute of Certified Public Accountants should also undertake a broad project of public education about the profession, its work and its standards. . . .

Other reforms could also assist in restoring rational limits on accountants' liability litigation. Consideration might be given to creating "safe harbors"

continued

from liability for activities which, though beneficial to the public, are known to be accompanied by high risk, such as reports on earnings forecasts and financial statements of highly speculative enterprises. . . . More generally, our legal procedures governing class actions and pre-trial discovery of evidence should be reexamined with an eye to changes that would discourage frivolous or harassing suits without foreclosing legitimate claims. . . .

In a broader context, the problem of accountants' liability cannot be separated from the societal revolution of which it is a part. The nation is beginning a very fruitful debate on the direction and character of our legal system. . . .

There can be no progress, however, unless and until the legislatures, the courts, lawyers, and the public recognize that the legal system is not a means of spreading and compensating for every risk which comes with living in a complicated world. There is no way to have a "riskless" society and even the pursuit of such a society is extraordinarily costly. Not only are costs shifted to persons without fault, but enormous resources are consumed by the process itself, leaving delayed and unfulfilled the one purpose such a system seeks to serve.

Society properly should hold persons, including those in the professions, accountable for losses caused by their misconduct. Indeed, that concept of compensable wrongs is at the heart of our legal system. But the delusion current in the law that all risks must be recompensed by somebody else is eclipsing the principles of individual freedom and responsibility—which are the fundamental values our legal system is intended to preserve.

CHAPTER SUMMARY

Malpractice Theories

1. Accountants may be liable for breach of contract, the same as any other party, if they fail to perform as agreed.
2. The tort theories of fraud and negligence are often used in malpractice cases against accountants.
3. Negligent performance of a contract is a mixed tort and contract theory used to sue accountants.
4. Many malpractice cases are based on violations of federal and state statutes relating to the sale of securities.

Expert Testimony

1. Compliance with GAAP and GAAS does not necessarily eliminate liability.
2. GAAP and GAAS are evidence that the accountant was not negligent, but they are not conclusive.
3. The basic issue is whether or not the financial reports fairly present the facts.

NEGLIGENCE ACTIONS

Introduction

1. Professional persons must exercise that degree of care and caution that their professional calling requires. Failure to do so is negligence.
2. Negligence may consist of an act or an omission.

Liability to Clients

1. While an auditor has no duty to discover fraud or embezzlement, an auditor may be negligent in failing to discover them if following correct procedures would have disclosed fraud or embezzlement.
2. Failure to qualify financial statements may be negligence.

3. Contributory negligence and comparative negligence are usually not defenses for accountants sued by their clients.

Liability to Third Parties: The *Ultramares* Doctrine

1. Accountants are not liable to third parties for negligence in the absence of privity of contract or close relationship sufficiently equivalent to privity.

2. Liability to third parties would expose accountants to a liability in an indeterminate amount for an indeterminate time to an indeterminate class.

3. An accountant may be liable to a third party actually intended by the accountant to rely on the financial reports.

Modification of the *Ultramares* Doctrine

1. Section 552 of the *Restatement of Torts* extends liability in favor of third parties to whom the accountant intends to supply the information or knows the recipient intends to supply it.

2. Some courts have expanded the liability to actually foreseen third parties.

3. Others have gone further and expanded liability in favor of anyone that is reasonably foreseeable.

Exculpatory Clauses

1. An exculpatory clause seeks to avoid liability by contract even if a party is negligent.

2. Such clauses are often found to be against public policy, especially if there is unequal bargaining power.

3. Large accounting firms should not expect such clauses to be upheld by courts.

4. Exculpatory clauses are not binding on third parties.

STATUTORY LIABILITY

The 1933 Securities Act

1. Accountants are liable if there are material errors or omissions in registration statements and prospectuses.

2. The liability extends to third-party investors, and neither fraud nor negligence must be proved.

3. Due diligence is a defense, but the burden of proof is on the accountant.

4. Lack of materiality and the statute of limitations are other common defenses.

5. Actual reliance by a purchaser of a security need not be proved.

The 1934 Securities Exchange Act

1. Section 18 incorporates common-law fraud as a basis of liability, and gross negligence will supply scienter.

2. Most lawsuits are brought under §10b and Rule 10b-5 of the SEC, covering manipulative and deceptive devices and contrivances.

3. Accountants are usually accused of aiding and abetting insiders, brokers, or sellers of stock in 10b-5 cases.

4. Section 10b and Rule 10b-5 cover all securities, not just those subject to the act.

5. Accountants may be liable under 10b for errors in unaudited write-ups.

6. There is no liability for simple negligence. Scienter as an element of fraud must be proved.

Criminal Liability

1. Both the 1933 and 1934 Acts have provisions imposing criminal sanctions for willful violations of their provisions.

2. Fraud in the sale of a security is a crime.

3. Compliance with GAAP is not an absolute defense to a criminal charge.

4. The Internal Revenue Service Code and the United States Criminal Code contain provisions making it a crime to willfully assist in the preparation of a false tax return.

5. It is also a crime to defraud the United States government or to conspire with someone else to do so.

REVIEW QUESTIONS AND PROBLEMS

1. Albert charged $5,000 to audit the books of Bonnie's Dress Shop. Later it was discovered that Albert had failed to verify the accounts receivable. Is Bonnie entitled to recover the audit fee? Why or why not?

2. Harvey, a certified public accountant, is sued for malpractice by a client. Elrod, another CPA, testifies that in his opinion Harvey had followed generally accepted accounting principles in the performance of his duties. Does this evidence entitle Harvey to a directed verdict in his favor? Why or why not?

3. Don, a certified public accountant, conducted an audit for ABC Company. Due to a time limitation, Don did not verify the accuracy of the closing inventory but rather accepted the president of ABC's statement that the inventory was correct. Unknown to both Don and the president, the inventory was overstated by 33⅓ percent due to theft by employees. A bank that had loaned money to ABC on the strength of the financial statements sued Don on a theory of fraud. He defended, denying any intention to mislead. Is Don liable? Explain.

4. Amy, a certified public accountant, is sued by Jimmy, a client who alleges a violation of the Securities Act of 1933. Amy contends that she has exercised "due diligence" in the performance of her professional duties, while Jimmy contends that she failed to do so. Is "due diligence" a defense that will allow Amy to avoid liability? Who has the burden of proof on the issue? Explain.

5. Ollie, an accountant charged with a criminal violation of the securities laws, is found to be "not guilty" by a jury. Later Sam, the investor on whose testimony the criminal case was brought, filed a civil action against Ollie seeking dollar damages. Ollie sought to have the case dismissed because of the acquittal in the criminal case. Will the court do so? Why or why not?

6. Assume that a defendant accountant had deliberately closed his eyes to material facts that affected the financial statements of a company being audited. Will this evidence supply the criminal intent required to convict under the securities laws? Explain.

7. A lending company brought a negligence suit against a borrower's accountants after the borrower defaulted on its loans and went bankrupt. In order to obtain the loans, the borrower had given the lender financial statements prepared by the accountants that misrepresented the borrower's financial health. Should the plaintiff-creditor collect? Why or why not?

8. Action was brought against accountants who had audited the financial statements of a certain company. The plaintiffs, allegedly relying on the correctness of the audit, acquired common stock in the company in conjunction with the sale of their business to the company. That stock subsequently proved to be worthless after the financial statements were found to be fraudulent. Are the accountants liable? Why or why not?

9. A bank loaned money to a corporation on the strength of financial statements prepared by a certified public accountant. The statements overstated the corporation's net worth by $400,000. When the corporation went into receivership, the bank sued the accountant to recover the amount of the loan. Under what circumstances should the accountant be liable? Explain.

10. Plaintiff owned stock warrants in a corporation. On the financial statements prepared by the defendant CPA as part of an audit, loans were reported as income. Are the auditors guilty of fraud? Why or why not?

11. A promoter of a limited partnership venture in oil and gas used a tax opinion letter issued by the accounting firm as part of his sales pitch. The letter stated that a limited partner who contributed $65,000 in cash could deduct approximately $128,000 on his tax return. The tax opinion letter was in material error. Is the accounting firm liable for violating §10b of the 1934 Act? Why or why not?

CHAPTER

33

INTRODUCTION TO COMMERCIAL PAPER

CHAPTER PREVIEW

This chapter covers the law as it relates to contract obligations that are in the form of *commercial paper*. These principles are primarily found in Articles 3 and 4 of the Uniform Commercial Code. Such contracts are often referred to as *negotiable instruments*. These instruments are created to move freely in financial transactions as a substitute for money or to represent a credit transaction. For example, checks are negotiable instruments used instead of cash to pay for goods and services. When a person borrows money or purchases goods on credit, the usual practice is for that person to sign a promissory note payable to the lender or seller.

Chapters 34 through 36 cover the law as it relates to negotiable instruments and the rights and liabilities of the various parties to a commercial paper transaction. This chapter serves as an introduction to the relevant terminology and to the role of banks in these transactions involving commercial paper.

As treasurer of a large company, you are charged with overseeing all your company's relationships with financial institutions.

What procedures should you adopt with respect to the company checking account and bank statements?

CONCEPT OF NEGOTIABILITY

Negotiable instruments
Paper that serves as a substitute for money or as a credit transaction.

Negotiable instruments developed because of the commercial need for something that would be readily acceptable in lieu of money and would accordingly be readily transferable in trade or commerce. Substantial protection and assurance of payment must be given to any person to whom the paper might be transferred. To accomplish this protection, it is necessary to insulate the transferee from most of the defenses that a primary party, such as the maker of a note, might have against the payee. The purpose of the negotiability trait is to prevent the parties to an underlying contract from asserting defenses against the person to whom the paper is transferred.

To accomplish the foregoing, Article 3 of the Code provides that a person to whom negotiable paper is negotiated takes it free of personal defenses arising out of the agreement from which the negotiable paper was created.

This basic theory of negotiability can be further explained by noting the difference between the *assignment* of a contract and the *negotiation* of a negotiable instrument. Assume that a dealer owes a manufacturer $1,000 but has a counterclaim because the product was defective. If a third party such as a bank purchased the manufacturer's contract right to collect the $1,000 from the dealer, it would be subject to the dealer's defense of failure of consideration. The bank, as assignee, would secure no better right against the dealer than the original right held by the manufacturer, the assignor. The bank therefore could not collect the full $1,000 from the dealer.

In this example, if the evidence of the debt is not a simple contract for money but a negotiable promissory note given by the dealer to the manufacturer, and if it is properly negotiated, the bank is in a position superior to that which it occupied when it was an assignee. Assuming that it is a "holder in due course," the bank has a better title because it is free of the personal defenses that are available against the manufacturer, the original party to the paper. The dealer, therefore, cannot use the defense of failure of consideration, and the bank can collect the $1,000.

Transfer of the instrument free of personal defenses is the very essence of negotiability. Three requirements must be met before a transferee is free from personal defenses. First, the instrument must be negotiable; that is, it must comply with the statutory formalities and language requirements. An instrument that does not qualify is nonnegotiable, and any transfer is an assignment subject to all defenses. Second, the instrument must be properly *negotiated* to the transferee. If the instrument is not properly negotiated, the transfer is an assignment subject to all defenses. Third, the party to whom negotiable commercial paper is negotiated must be a *holder in due course* or have the rights of a holder in due course. Each of these concepts is discussed in detail in the following chapters.

The defenses that cannot be asserted against a holder in due course are called *personal defenses. Real defenses*, on the other hand, may be asserted against anyone, including a holder in due course. Real defenses are matters that go to the very existence of the instruments. Personal defenses such as failure of consideration involve less serious matters and usually relate to the transaction out of which the negotiable instrument arose, or events such as payment of the note. The following case illustrates the importance of obtaining the return of a negotiable instrument when payment is made.

CASE

Bank of Miami v. Florida City Express, Inc.
367 So.2d 683 (Fla. App. 1979)

SCHWARTZ, J.

. . . Florida City Express, Inc., the maker of negotiable promissory notes, must pay twice because the Bank of Miami, a holder in due course, was not paid once. That is the impact of the law of negotiable instruments, as now embodied in the Uniform Commercial Code, upon the undisputed facts of this case.

On November 1, 1974, Florida City Express, Inc., in return for merchandise, executed an ordinary "short form" promissory note for $3,292.12 payable to Latin American Tire Co.; the maturity date was February 3, 1975. On January 17, 1975, it gave Latin American a similar note for $3,500.00 due on March 3, 1975. On November 18, 1974 and January 30, 1975, respectively, Latin American indorsed and discounted the notes with the Bank of Miami. The bank took the notes before maturity for value, and without notice of the existence of any defenses to them; hence, it was indisputably a holder in due course of both instruments. At each maturity date, the bank, after making unsuccessful demands on Latin American, called upon Florida City Express, as the maker of the notes, to pay them. Therein lies the unhappy tale told by this case.

For Florida City had already paid all the amounts due to Latin American by virtue of payments made by several checks given both before and after the negotiation of the notes by Latin American to the bank. However, the maker had not required, as to the payments made before the transfer, that any notation of those payments be made on the notes themselves. Furthermore, it had not demanded that they be displayed or surrendered by Latin American when payments were made after the payee *had* negotiated them and when they were therefore no longer in Latin American's possession. When, however, the bank sued Florida City on the notes in this action, it raised the defense of payment. After a non-jury trial, the court below upheld that defense and entered judgment for the defendant. We disagree and reverse.

Our holding is based on the long familiar, universal rule, . . . that a holder in due course takes and holds a negotiable instrument free of all defenses of which he is not on notice. And it is very clear that this rule includes the defense of discharge or payment. . . .

When an instrument is paid in whole or in part before maturity, it is the duty of the party making payment to have the payment indorsed or to require surrender of the instrument, and if he omits these precautions and the instrument is transferred before maturity to a holder in due course without notice of the payments, he may not avail himself of the defense of prior payment against such a holder. Since the maker neither required an indorsement of its payments on the notes, nor demanded their surrender, it must therefore take the unpleasant consequences of that failure by making a second payment to the present holder.

Florida City argues that the bank should have given it notice of its acquisition of the notes. No authority is cited, because none exists, to support this proposition. The maker's claim that a double payment of over $6,000.00 could have been avoided had the bank used a 15-cent stamp has some obvious surface attraction. But we agree with the appellant that the imposition of a notice requirement would be contrary not only to every decided case on the subject but also to the important policy that negotiable instruments must flow freely and without such impediments in the stream of commerce.

■ *Reversed and remanded.*

1. What party signed the promissory notes as evidence of its promise to pay for the merchandise purchased?
2. What party received these notes as evidence of the money it was owed? What did this party do with the notes?
3. Why did Florida City Express refuse to pay Bank of Miami when the Bank sought collection of the amount stated in the notes?
4. Why does the court conclude that Florida City Express must pay the Bank of Miami?
5. What is the lesson to be learned from this case?

KINDS OF COMMERCIAL PAPER

1. Terminology

Article 3 of the Code, Commercial Paper, is restricted in its coverage to the negotiable note, certificate of deposit, draft, and check. A note is two-party paper, as is a certificate of deposit. The parties to a note are the *maker,* who promises to pay, and the *payee,* to whom the promise is made. The draft and the check are three-party instruments. A draft presupposes a debtor-creditor relationship between the *drawer* and the *drawee* or some other obligation on the part of the drawee in favor of the drawer. The drawee is the debtor; the drawer is the creditor. The drawer-creditor orders the drawee-debtor to pay money to a third party, who is the *payee*. The mere execution of the draft does not obligate the drawee on the paper. The drawee's liability on the paper arises when it formally *accepts* the obligation to pay in writing on the draft itself. By accepting, the drawee becomes primarily liable on the paper]3-410(1)[. Thereafter, the drawee is called an *acceptor,* and its liability is similar to the liability of the maker of a promissory note.

2. Notes

Bearer The person in possession of an instrument.

A *note* initially is a two-party instrument in which the issuer (the *maker*) promises to pay to the order of a *payee* or to **bearer.** A note is used to evidence an obligation to pay in the future and is typically employed in loan and secured sales transactions. Figure 33–1 is a sample of a simple note payable to the order of a specific payee.

FIGURE 33–1 ■ A Simple Note Payable to a Specific Payee

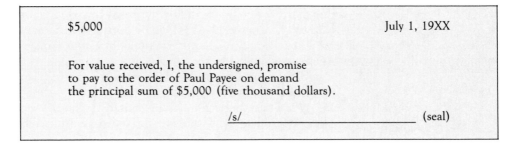

$5,000   July 1, 19XX

For value received, I, the undersigned, promise
to pay to the order of Paul Payee on demand
the principal sum of $5,000 (five thousand dollars).

/s/ _____ (seal)

3. Certificates of Deposit

A *certificate of deposit* (commonly called a CD) is a two-party, usually short-term, instrument in which a bank is the maker [3-104(2)(c)]. A CD is a bank's written acknowledgment of money on deposit that the bank promises to pay to the depositor or to his or her order or to some third person. The promise to repay distinguishes the CD from a deposit slip. A CD basically is a promissory note issued by a bank as a means of investment. People buy CDs to earn the interest they bear. The bank may pay higher rates of interest than on a savings account, since a CD may not be redeemed until the date specified without significant penalties. Figure 33–2 is an example of a negotiable CD.

FIGURE 33–2 ■ A Negotiable CD

CERTIFICATE OF DEPOSIT
First Athens Bank
Athens, GA

Has received on deposit and on <u>May 1, 1996</u> will pay to the order of <u>Darlene Depositor</u> <u>$20,000.00</u> (twenty thousand dollars) with interest at a rate of <u>ten</u> percent (<u>10%</u>) payable upon return of this certificate properly indorsed. No payment before maturity. No interest after maturity.

First Athens Bank

<u>May 1, 1993</u>
(date of issue)

/s/ _____
(authorized signature)

4. Drafts

A *draft* (sometimes called a bill of exchange) is a simple order to pay money [3-104(2)(a)]. It is addressed by one person (the *drawer*) to another person (the *payor* or *drawee*), requiring that person to pay on demand or at a fixed future time a definite amount to the order of a named person (the *payee* or *holder*) or to the bearer. A seller of goods or services may draw a draft on the buyer for purchase price of the goods, making the instrument payable to himself or herself. In this case, the seller is both the drawer and the payee, while the buyer is the drawee of the draft. In drawing this draft, the seller implicitly promises to pay its amount to any holder if it is not paid by the drawee [3-413(2)]. By putting the demand for payment in the stylized form of a draft, the seller thereby facilitates the transfer of his or her right to receive payment from the buyer.

Drafts may be payable on demand or at a fixed or determinable time. Usually demand drafts are presented to the drawee for payment and are said to be payable *on sight*. Time drafts may be presented to the drawee for payment or *acceptance*. They are said to be payable at a fixed time after sight.

5. Checks

A *check* is a demand draft drawn on a bank. A check drawn by a bank on itself is a *cashier's check.* *Travelers' checks* are like cashier's checks in that the financial institution issuing them is both the drawer and the drawee. Travelers' checks are negotiable when they have been completed by the identifying signature. A *bank draft* is a banker's check; that is, it is a check drawn by one bank on another bank, payable on demand.

A *certified check* is one that has been accepted by the drawee bank. Either the drawer or the holder of a check may present it to the drawee bank for certification. The bank will stamp "certified" on the check, and an official of the bank will sign it and date it. By certifying, the bank assumes responsibility for payment and sets aside funds from its customer's account to cover the check.

Certification may or may not change the legal liability of the parties on the instrument. When the *drawer* has a check certified, such a certification merely acts as additional security and does not relieve the drawer of any liability. On the other hand, when the *holder* of a check secures certification by the drawee bank, the holder thereby accepts the bank as the only party liable thereon. Such an act discharges the drawer and all prior indorsers from any liability]3-411(1)[. The effect of such certification is similar to a payment by the bank and redeposit by the holder.

The refusal of a bank to certify a check at the request of a holder is not a dishonor of the instrument. The bank owes the depositor a duty to pay but not necessarily the duty to certify checks that are drawn on it, unless there is a previous agreement to certify]3-411(2)[. A drawer cannot stop payment on a check after the bank has certified it.

BANK DEPOSITS AND COLLECTIONS

6. Terminology

Article 4 of the Code, Bank Deposits and Collections, provides uniform rules to govern the collection of checks and other instruments for the payment of money. These rules govern the relationship of banks with one another and with depositors in the collection and payment of items.

The following terminology of Section 4-105 of the Code is significant with regard to the designation of the various banks in the collection process for checks:

1. *Depositary bank* means the first bank to which an item is transferred for collection even though it is also the payor bank.
2. *Payor bank* means a bank by which an item is payable as drawn or accepted.
3. *Intermediary bank* means any bank to which an item is transferred in course of collection except the depositary or payor bank.
4. *Collecting bank* means any bank handling the item for collection except the payor bank.
5. *Presenting bank* means any bank presenting an item to a payor bank.
6. *Remitting bank* means any payor or intermediary bank remitting for an item.

A bank may occupy more than one status in the collection process. For example, a bank that receives a customer's deposit drawn on another bank is both a depositary and a collecting bank. A bank accepting a deposit of a check drawn by another customer is both a depositary and a payor bank.

Timing is important in the check collection process. Many of the technical rules of law refer to a *banking day,* which is defined as "that part of any day on which a bank is open to the public for carrying on substantially all of its banking functions" [4-104(1)(c)]. A bank is permitted to establish a cutoff hour of 2 P.M. or later, so the bank may have an opportunity to process items, prove balances, and make the necessary entries to determine its position for the day. If an item is received after the cutoff hour or after the close of the banking day, it may be treated as having been received at the opening of the next banking day [4-107]. The term *midnight deadline* with respect to a bank means midnight on its banking day following the banking day on which it receives a check or a notice regarding the check [4-104(1)(h)].

7. The Bank Collection Process

If a check is deposited in a bank other than the bank on which it is drawn, it must be sent to the payor bank for payment. This collection process may involve routing the item through a number of banks that typically credit or debit accounts they maintain with one another. In particular, the regional Federal Reserve Banks, with which most banks have accounts, play a major role in this process. An example may help you understand the collection process.

Suppose that Carson in Athens, Georgia, mails his check drawn on the First Athens Bank to Exxon in Houston, Texas, in payment of an obligation. Exxon deposits the check in the First National Bank of Houston, which forwards it to the Federal Reserve Bank of Houston, which sends it to the Federal Reserve Bank of Atlanta, which presents it to the First Athens Bank for payment. The relationship of these parties is depicted in Figure 33–3.

As Figure 33–3 indicates, the collection process begins when the customer (Exxon) deposits a check to its account. The account is provisionally credited by the bank. The check then passes through the collecting banks, each of which provisionally credits the account of the prior bank. When the check finally reaches the payor-drawee bank (First Athens Bank), that bank debits the drawer's (Carson's) account.

Clearinghouse An association of banks or other payors regularly clearing items.

Honor To pay or to accept the instrument.

Dishonor Acceptance or payment is refused or cannot be obtained.

Customer A person having an account with a bank or for whom a bank has agreed to collect items.

The payor bank then credits the account of the presenting bank, remits to it, or, if both belong to the same **clearinghouse,** includes the check in its balance there. If the payor bank **honors** the check, the settlement is final. Transactions prior to this final settlement by the payor bank are called "provisional settlements," because it is not known until final settlement whether the check is "good." If the payor bank **dishonors** the check, as in the case of an "N.S.F." (not sufficient funds) check, the presenting bank will revoke its provisional settlement and charge the item back to the account of the prior collecting bank. Likewise, other banks in the chain of collection will charge back. The final step is a chargeback to the **customer's** account by the depositary bank and the return of the check to the customer. Each of the collecting banks must return the item or send notification of the facts by its midnight deadline. The right to charge back by the depositary bank is not affected by the fact that the depositor may have drawn against the provisional credit.

FIGURE 33–3 ■ Process of Collecting Transit Item

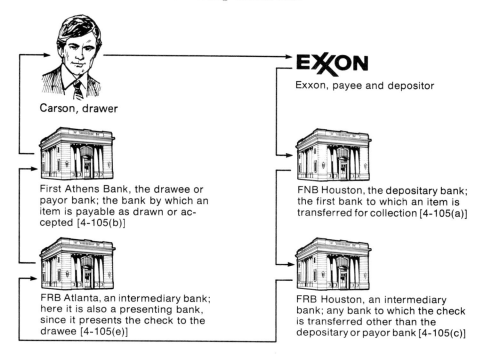

Carson, drawer

EXXON
Exxon, payee and depositor

First Athens Bank, the drawee or payor bank; the bank by which an item is payable as drawn or accepted [4-105(b)]

FNB Houston, the depositary bank; the first bank to which an item is transferred for collection [4-105(a)]

FRB Atlanta, an intermediary bank; here it is also a presenting bank, since it presents the check to the drawee [4-105(e)]

FRB Houston, an intermediary bank; any bank to which the check is transferred other than the depositary or payor bank [4-105(c)]

A depositor does not have the right to draw against uncollected funds. Accordingly, a depositor is not entitled to draw against an item payable by another bank until the provisional settlement his or her depositary bank has received becomes final [4-213(4)(a)].

AVAILABILITY OF FUNDS.   Because of complaints by customers that the check collection process allowed financial institutions to "hold" the availability of funds for excessive periods, Congress passed and President Ronald Reagan signed the Expedited Funds Availability Act. The regulations issued by the Federal Reserve Board have established when funds from deposited checks must be available to customers.

Funds from cashier's checks, certified checks, government checks, and electronic deposits must be available to the customer on the next business day after deposit. Funds from local checks (those written on financial institutions within the same Federal Reserve check-processing region as the depositary bank) must be made available within two business days after deposit. Finally, funds represented by out-of-town checks must be made available within five business days after deposit.

These time periods on making funds available do not apply to new accounts (those less than thirty days old) or to checks written for more than $5,000. Customers under these circumstances must inquire of their banks how long the check collection process will likely take. Of course, banks may allow their customers to draw against uncollected funds during a time period shorter than that just discussed.

Notwithstanding the foregoing general rules, the first $100 of any deposit must be available to the customer on the next day after the deposit is made. This $100-tomorrow exception is designed to ensure that a customer has some source of readily available funds.

Indorsement Writing one's name on paper for the purpose of transferring the title. When a payee of a negotiable instrument writes his or her name on the back of the instrument, the writing is an indorsement.

INDORSEMENTS. A customer who deposits an item for collection should indorse it, but quite frequently a customer forgets that signature. The depositary bank may supply the missing **indorsement.** If the bank states on the item that it was deposited by a customer or credited to his or her account, such a statement is as effective as the customer's indorsement. This is a practical rule intended to speed up the collection process by making it unnecessary to return to the depositor any items he or she may have failed to indorse [4-205]. The term *customer* is broadly construed and may include parties other than depositors.

8. Collecting Banks

Presentment A demand for acceptance or payment made on the maker, acceptor, drawee, or other payor by, or on behalf of, the holder.

Settle To pay in cash, by clearinghouse settlement, or by remittance or otherwise as instructed. A settlement may be either provisional or final.

When a bank has received a check for collection, it has the duty to use ordinary care in performing its collection operations. These operations include presenting the check to the drawee or forwarding it for **presentment,** sending notice of nonpayment if it occurs and returning the check after learning that it has not been paid, and **settling** for the check when it receives final payment. Failure of the collecting bank to use ordinary care in handling a check subjects the bank to liability to the depositor for any loss or damage sustained.

To act seasonably, a bank is generally required to take proper action before the midnight deadline following the receipt of a check, a notice, or a payment. Thus, if a collecting bank receives a check on Monday and presents it or forwards it to the next collecting bank anytime prior to midnight Tuesday, it has acted seasonably. If it fails to do so, it has liability unless it is excused by matters beyond its control.

The following case summarizes the duties of the collecting bank in the collection process.

CASE

Golden Gulf, Inc. v. AmSouth Bank, N.A.
565 So.2d 114 (Ala. 1990)

ALMON, J.

This is an appeal from a summary judgment entered in favor of AmSouth Bank, N.A. ("AmSouth"), and against Golden Gulf, Inc., and Starich, Inc. ("appellants")....

Richard White, Robert Underwood, and Terry Patrick were officers of an Alabama corporation, Golden Gulf. In January 1988, they opened a demand checking account at AmSouth on behalf of Golden Gulf. Shortly before this account was opened, a Utah corporation, Starich, had acquired substantially all of Golden Gulf's assets and had assumed substantially all of its liabilities. Thereafter, on April 21, 1988, Golden Gulf was dissolved and White, Underwood, and Patrick became employees of Starich. However, the Golden Gulf checking account at AmSouth was not closed and remained in use under that corporation's name.

On August 27, 1988, the appellants entered into a subscription agreement wherein Albert M. Rossini agreed

to pay Starich $250,000 for 250,000 shares of Starich common stock. Rossini tendered a check, drawn on the Mark Twain Bank in Kansas City, Missouri, to the appellants for that amount, made payable to "Golden Gulf/Starich, Inc." That check was deposited in the Golden Gulf checking account at AmSouth on August 30, 1988. On September 1, 1988, the appellants contacted AmSouth to ask if the $250,000 had been "collected." AmSouth answered that the funds had not been collected. On September 2, 1988, the appellants again contacted AmSouth and asked if the funds were "available." AmSouth told the appellants that the funds were available for use. The appellants then requested AmSouth to wire those funds to a bank in New York, for use by Starich in that State. AmSouth complied with that request.

On September 7, 1988, AmSouth received notice from the Mark Twain Bank that Rossini's check would not be paid, due to nonsufficient funds. On September 8, 1988, AmSouth notified the appellants that the check had been dishonored.... AmSouth thereafter revoked the credit it had given the Golden Gulf account, asserting that the credit had been only provisional. AmSouth then charged back to that account the amount of the provisional credit, resulting in an overdraft of $248,965.69.

On October 13, 1988, AmSouth filed a complaint against the appellants, alleging that they were liable for the amount of the overdraft. . . . The Circuit Court . . . entered a summary judgment for AmSouth, awarding it $257,641.97. . . . The appellants contend that . . . a final settlement had been made. AmSouth contends that only a provisional settlement had been made. . . .

The . . . issue is whether AmSouth's responses to the appellants' inquiries gave rise to a fact question as to the "provisional" or "final" nature of the settlement extended to the appellants' account. . . . There is a presumption . . . that the initial settlements extended by banks are provisional. If no evidence to rebut that presumption was before the trial court, AmSouth's right to charge back the amount credited to the appellants' account would be unaffected, and the summary judgment in favor of AmSouth would be proper. In order to resolve this issue, it is necessary to discuss the distinction between "provisional" and "final" settlements.

Upon receipt of a check, a depositary bank often extends a "provisional" credit to its customer's account, while reserving the right to charge back that amount if the check is dishonored. This credit allows the customer to make use of the funds represented by the deposited check. . . .

The settlement or credit extended will ordinarily remain provisional until the depositary bank receives payment from the payor bank. . . . It is undisputed that the payor bank, in this case the Mark Twain Bank, refused to pay the check. . . .

The appellants point to their evidence that AmSouth told them on September 2, 1988, that the funds were available for their use and argue that AmSouth thereby represented that the check had been paid. They argue further that that representation was equivalent to saying that a final settlement had been made. However, this argument is a misapprehension of the function and nature of provisional settlements. The mere availability of the funds represented by the check does not, by itself, confirm that the check had been finally paid. Instead, the bank allows its customer to make use of the funds while it awaits subsequent determination of whether the item will be finally paid. That is the very essence of provisional settlements. . . .

Section 7-4-212 gives collecting banks the right to charge back amounts credited to their customers' accounts if the deposit that is the basis of a provisional settlement is subsequently dishonored or suspended. . . .

Because the settlement involved in this case was provisional, AmSouth was entitled to charge back the amount of the dishonored check to the appellants' account. . . .

Therefore, the judgment is

■ *Affirmed.*

CASE CONCEPTS REVIEW

1. How would you describe AmSouth Bank in terms of the type of bank it is in this case?
2. Why did AmSouth sue to collect approximately $250,000?
3. Why does the court presume that the settlement given by AmSouth was provisional instead of final?
4. What impact did AmSouth's decision to make the funds available to its customers have on the nature of the provisional settlement?

9. Payor Banks

An item is finally paid by a payor bank when the bank (1) pays the item in cash, (2) settles for the item without reserving the right to revoke the settlement, (3) completes the process of posting the item, or (4) makes a provisional settlement and fails to revoke it within the time prescribed [4-213(1)]. Upon final payment, the payor bank is accountable for the item, and it has substituted its own obligation for that of the drawer. Final payment usually occurs whenever the payor bank makes a provisional settlement for the item (a credit) and then fails to revoke its credit within its midnight deadline after receipt of the item.

A payor bank that is not also the depositary bank must make a provisional settlement for an item on the banking day it is received. However, that bank has until final payment of the check—but not later than its midnight deadline—to decide whether or not the item is good [4-302(a)]. Within this time, the bank may revoke the settlement and return the item or, if this is not possible, send written notice of nonpayment. This enables the bank to defer posting until the next day.

When a check drawn by one customer of a bank is deposited by another customer of the same bank for credit on its books, the bank may return the item and revoke any credit given at any time prior to its midnight deadline [4-302(b)]. The deposit of an item on which the depositary bank is itself the payor bank becomes available for withdrawal on the opening of the second banking day following receipt of the item [4-213(4)(b)].

Failure of the payor-drawee bank to take action within the prescribed time limits may make it accountable to the person who deposited the check if the check is not paid. This liability is imposed if the bank (1) retains a check presented to it by another bank without settling for it by midnight of the banking day of receipt or (2) does not pay or return the check or send notice of dishonor within the period of its midnight deadline [4-302(a)].

Another problem relates to the *order of payment of checks*. There is no priority among checks drawn on a particular account and presented to a bank on any particular day. The checks and other items may be accepted, paid, certified, or charged to the indicated account of its customer in any order convenient to the bank [4-303(2)].

An item does not always proceed through the clearinghouse. It may be presented directly to the payor bank by a customer of that bank for payment over the counter. If the payor bank pays the item in cash, it may not later collect back the payments if its customer had insufficient funds on deposit [4-213(1)(a)].

BANKS AND THEIR CUSTOMERS

10. The Debtor-Creditor Relationship

Setoff The right of a creditor, such as a bank, to seize money from the account of a customer who is the debtor.

The legal relationship between a bank and its depositors is that of debtor and creditor. If the depositor is a borrower of the bank, the reverse relationship (creditor-debtor) also exists between the bank and its customers. The dual relationship provides the bank with a prompt and easy method of protecting itself in the event of a depositor's default or pending insolvency. A bank can "seize" bank deposits under its right of **setoff** if such action becomes necessary to protect its account receivable. The following case illustrates the right of setoff generally held by a bank.

CASE

Miracle Hills Centre Limited Partnership v. Nebraska National Bank of Omaha
434 N.W.2d 304 (Neb. 1989)

QUIST, J.

Plaintiff-appellee, Miracle Hills Centre Limited Partnership (Miracle Hills), sought an accounting from defendant-appellant, Nebraska National Bank of Omaha (bank), claiming the bank wrongfully converted funds deposited to an account that Financial Structures, Inc. (FSI), maintained with the bank. . . .

FSI maintained two checking accounts at the bank, a regular account and a payroll account. Deposits were made to the regular account, and checks were drawn on this account for payment of subcontractors on various projects, as well as for general overhead expenses. . . .

At the time of the transaction that is the subject of this dispute, FSI was indebted to the bank on a promissory note in the amount of $84,867.37, plus interest. The note was past due and in default.

One of the FSI projects was the Miracle Hills Shopping Center. Miracle Hills was the developer, with construction financing provided by Westmark Financial Corporation. On September 10, 1985, the bank received for deposit by FSI Westmark's check payable to FSI in the amount of $129,208. No special instructions or limitations accompanied the check. At that time FSI's regular account had a balance of $51.87, and checks in excess of that amount had been presented for payment.

Westmark's check was drawn on the Douglas County Bank in Omaha. On learning that there was an insufficient balance in Westmark's account to cover the check to FSI, checks presented for payment were returned. On September 11, Westmark wire-transferred $129,208 to the Financial Structures account, No. 4003276, at the bank. The bank then honored checks presented for payment on that account, and also set off against the account in the amount of $86,625.69 to pay the principal and interest on FSI's past-due note. Some 6 weeks later, Miracle Hills made demand for the amount set off. The bank refused, and Miracle Hills commenced this action. . . .

It is undisputed that FSI's indebtedness to the bank was past due at the time of the setoff. This court dealt with that issue in *First Nat. Bank v. Benedict Consol, Indus.*, 402 N.W.2d 259, 263 (1987), when we stated:

> We have long held that a bank may set off the funds of a depositor to pay a debt due the bank from the depositor, and, absent an agreement to the contrary or specific instructions from the debtor, a creditor may apply the proceeds to such debts and in such order as the creditor determines.

A party claiming that a deposit made in the ordinary course of business was a special deposit bears the burden of proving the special nature of the deposit by clear and satisfactory evidence. Until such a showing has been made, deposits made in the ordinary course of business are general deposits. Miracle Hills has failed to provide clear and satisfactory evidence that the deposit in question was not a general deposit.

Miracle Hills argues that under the circumstances a duty was imposed upon the bank to see to it that the proceeds of the Westmark deposit were applied only for the payment of subcontractors on the Miracle Hills Shopping Center project. Miracle Hills contends that the bank had actual knowledge of the ownership of the funds and, at a bare minimum, sufficient knowledge to put the bank on inquiry as to the ownership of the funds. . . .

However, a careful review of the evidence in this case established neither actual knowledge nor notice of facts sufficient to put the bank on inquiry as to any special ownership of the funds.

Westmark's wire transfer states, "Please forward [$129,208] and notify Nebr Natl Bank Omaha for Financial Structures #4003276." Clearly, the wire transfer calls for an unconditional payment to FSI's general checking account. Westmark placed no limitation on the deposit and gave no indication to the bank that the deposit was to be used solely for payments on the Miracle Hills project. Therefore, there was no express trust imposed on the deposit.

The bank was subject to the duties and liabilities of a payor bank under the Uniform Commercial Code. The record indicates the bank had no independent knowledge of which project any given check was connected with. If a trust were implied from these facts, the lack of such information would make it virtually impossible for the bank to meet its duties under the U.C.C. without subjecting itself to significant liability. Therefore, we find no implied trust existed.

Miracle Hills further argues that even if the bank did not have actual knowledge or inquiry notice, equitable principles would hold that the bank cannot set off the deposit when it has not changed its position and has no superior equities. In applying general equitable principles, it must be kept in mind that Miracle Hills is largely responsible for its own predicament. It failed to take steps which could have been taken to assure desired distribution of the funds. The simple expedient of issuing joint checks payable to FSI and the subcontractors or providing limitations or conditions on the deposit or account could have avoided the situation in which Miracle Hills now finds itself. . . .

■ *Reversed and remanded.*

CASE CONCEPTS REVIEW

1. What is the relationship between FSI and the bank?
2. What is the relationship among FSI, Miracle Hills, and Westmark?
3. What is the justification of the bank taking $86,625.69 from FSI's account?
4. Why does the court reject Miracle Hills' argument that the funds transferred to the bank by Westmark should be held for the benefit of Miracle Hills?

A bank is under a duty to honor properly payable checks drawn by its customer when there are sufficient funds in his or her account to cover the checks. A check is not properly payable if it has been altered or if it contains a forgery. If a bank pays a check that is not properly payable, the customer may insist on the account being recredited.

If there are insufficient funds, the bank may honor the properly payable checks, even though this action creates an overdraft. The customer is indebted to the bank for the overdraft and implicitly promises to reimburse the bank [4-401(1)]. While most overdrafts are dishonored, they are sometimes paid and the customer owes the bank for the check.

If a bank in good faith pays an altered check, it can charge the account of its customer only according to the original tenor of the check. Thus, if a check is raised, the bank can charge its customer's account only with the original amount of the check [4-401(2)(a)]. If a person signs his or her name to an incomplete check and it is thereafter completed and presented to the drawee bank that pays it, the bank can charge the customer's account for the full amount if it pays in good faith and does not know that the completion was improper [4-401(2)(b)]. The improperly completed check is not an altered check.

11. Wrongful Dishonor

If a bank wrongfully dishonors a check, it is liable to its customer for damages proximately caused by the wrongful dishonor. When the dishonor occurs by mistake, as distinguished from a malicious or willful dishonor, liability is limited to the *actual damages proved* [4-402]. These damages may include *consequential damages* proximately caused by the wrongful dishonor, damages such as for arrest or prosecution of the customer. If the wrongful dishonor is willful, punitive damages in addition to actual damages may be awarded. The Code rejects early common-law decisions holding that, if the dishonored item were drawn by a merchant, he or she was defamed in business because of the reflection on the merchant's credit. Consequently, a merchant cannot recover damages on the basis of defamation because of wrongful dishonor of a check.

Some cases have allowed customers to collect for mental suffering as a part of consequential damages. The following case is an example of this trend. Notice that the bank's customer also collected punitive damages.

CASE

Twin City Bank v. Isaacs
672 S.W.2d 651 (Ark. 1984)

HAYS, J.

Twin City Bank has appealed from a judgment entered on a jury verdict against it in favor of Kenneth and Vicki Isaacs for damages sustained from the bank's wrongful dishonor of the Isaacs' checks resulting in a hold order against their account for a period of approximately four years.

On Sunday, May 13, 1979, the Isaacs discovered that their checkbook was missing. They reported the loss to Twin City promptly on Monday, May 14, and later learned that two forged checks totalling $2,050 had been written on their account and honored by the bank on May 11 and 12. The sequence of events that followed is dis-

puted, but the end result was a decision by the bank to freeze the Isaacs' checking account which had contained approximately $2,500 before the forgeries occurred. A few checks cleared Monday morning before a hold order was issued leaving the balance at approximately $2,000. Mr. Isaacs had been convicted of burglary and the initial hold on the account was attributable to the bank's concern that the Isaacs were somehow involved with the two forged checks. The individual responsible for the forgeries was charged and convicted soon after the forgeries occurred and on May 30, 1979 the police told the bank there was nothing to connect the Isaacs with the person arrested. Two weeks later the police notified the bank a second time they could not connect the Isaacs to the forgeries. The bank maintains it continued to keep the account frozen on the advice of its attorneys. However that may be, the Isaacs were denied their funds for some four years. The

---

Isaacs filed suit in mid-June of 1979 for wrongful dishonor of their checks and wrongful withholding of their funds.

The jury awarded the Isaacs $18,500 in compensatory damages and $45,000 in punitive damages. . . .

On the issue of damages, the bank maintains there was insufficient evidence to support the $18,500 award for mental anguish, for loss of credit and loss of the bargain on a house, that the award of punitive damages should not have been given at all as there was not only insufficient proof of actual damages but insufficient evidence of malice or intent to oppress on the part of the bank. The bank does not challenge the sufficiency of the evidence of its wrongful dishonor, but contends only that there was no evidence to support an award of damages. These arguments cannot be sustained.

The statute upon which this suit was based is Ark. Stat. Ann. § 85-4-402.

> Bank's liability to customer for wrongful dishonor—A payor bank is liable to its customer for damages proximately caused by the wrongful dishonor of an item. When the dishonor occurs through mistake liability is limited to actual damages proved. If so proximately caused and proved damages may include damages for an arrest or prosecution of the customer or other consequential damages. Whether any consequential damages are proximately caused by the wrongful dishonor is a question of fact to be determined in each case.

The jury was instructed that if they found the bank liable they were to fix the amount of money which would compensate the Isaacs "for any of the following elements of damage sustained which were proximately caused by the conduct of Twin City Bank: 1) Any amounts of money wrongfully held by the defendant and remaining unpaid 2) any mental anguish and embarrassment suffered by the plaintiffs 3) any financial losses sustained by the [Isaacs]."

Initially, there can be no serious question as to certain losses: the $2,000 wrongfully withheld by the bank for four years, and the value of two vehicles repossessed because the Isaacs did not have access to their funds, resulting in a loss of approximately $2,200. . . . The bank does not refute these damages but argues there is no showing of any financial deprivation from loss of credit or loss of the bargain on a house the Isaacs wanted to buy, and insufficient proof of mental anguish. We find, however, that in addition to the losses previously mentioned, there was sufficient evidence to sustain damages for mental suffering, loss of credit, and sufficient demonstration of some loss attributable to the inability to pursue the purchase of a home.

Mental suffering under § 4-402 of the Uniform Commercial Code is relatively new and has not been frequently addressed by other courts, but of those a majority has allowed recovery. In general, the type of mental anguish suffered under § 4-402 does not need to rise to the higher standard of injury for intentional infliction of emotional distress. Wrongful dishonors tend to produce intangible injuries similar to those involved in defamation actions. . . .

In this case, prior to the forgery incident the Isaacs' credit reputation with Twin City Bank was described by the bank as "impeccable" and the freezing of their funds had a traumatic effect on their lives. They obviously lost their credit standing with Twin City, and were unable to secure credit commercially at other institutions because of their status at Twin City. The Isaacs had to borrow from friends and family, and were left in a precarious position financially. They did not have use of their $2,000 for four years. The allegation relative to the loss of a house resulted from the dishonor of an earnest money check for a home they were planning to buy, ending prospects for the purchase at that time. Though there may have been insufficient proof of loss of the bargain on the house, as the bank argues, nevertheless this evidence was admissible as an element of mental suffering. The denial of credit contributed to some monetary loss . . . in addition to its being a reasonable element of mental suffering. . . . There was also testimony that the financial strain contributed to marital difficulties leading at one point to the filing of a divorce suit. The suit was dropped but there was testimony that the difficulties caused by the bank's action caused substantial problems in the marriage. Finally, the Isaacs lost equities in two vehicles repossessed as a result of the withholding of their funds. One of these, a new van, was repossessed by Twin City in June, 1979, before a five day grace period for a current installment had expired.

We believe there was substantial evidence to support the verdict. . . .

The bank's objection to the award of punitive damages is . . . [that] the verdict of $45,000 was excessive. . . .

In *Holmes v. Hollingsworth*, 352 S.W.2d 96 (1961), we noted the elements that may be considered in assessing the amount of punitive damages, recognizing that the deterrent effect has some correlation to the financial condition of the party against whom punitive damages are allowed. In view of the circumstances in their entirety presented by this case, we cannot say the amount awarded was grossly excessive or prompted by passion or prejudice.

■ *Affirmed.*

CASE CONCEPTS REVIEW

1. Why did the Twin City Bank freeze the Isaacs' checking account?
2. How much money was there in the frozen account?

What was the amount of the jury's verdict in favor of the Isaacs?

3. What are five items of damages that the court uses to explain the jury's verdict?

4. Do you agree that bank customers might suffer mental anguish in similar factual situations?

5. How does the court justify the award of punitive damages?

12. Stop Payment Orders

A customer has the right to stop payment on checks drawn on his or her account. Only the drawer has this right; it does not extend to holders—payees or indorsers. To be effective, a stop payment order must be received at a time and in a manner that will afford the bank a reasonable opportunity to stop payment before it has taken other action on the item [4-403]. For example, if a check has been certified, the depositor cannot stop payment, whether the depositor or the payee procured the certification.

A bank must act reasonably in complying with a valid stop payment order. It cannot avoid liability by asserting immaterial differences between the check and the stop payment order. An oral stop order is binding on the bank for only fourteen days unless confirmed in writing within that period. Unless renewed in writing, a written stop order is effective for only six months [4-404].

A bank that honors a check on which payment has been stopped is liable to the drawer of the check for any loss the drawer suffers because of the bank's failure to obey the stop order. The burden is on the customer to establish the amount of the loss. Thus, if the drawer did not have a valid reason to stop payment, he or she cannot collect from a bank that fails to obey the stop payment order [4-403(3)]. Because of the concept of negotiability previously noted, a stop order on a check gives the drawer only limited protection. If the check is negotiated by the payee to a holder in due course, that holder can require payment of the amount by the drawer of the check, notwithstanding the stop order.

The bank cannot by agreement disclaim its responsibility for its failure to obey stop payment orders [4-303(1)]. Thus a form signed by a customer agreeing not to hold the bank responsible for failure to stop payment could not be enforced.

13. Banks' Rights and Duties

A bank is entitled, but not *obligated,* to pay a check that is over six months old, and it may charge the check to the customer's account [4-404]. Certified checks do not fall within the six-month rule; they are the primary obligation of the certifying bank, and the obligation runs directly to the holder of the check.

In paying *stale checks,* the bank must act in good faith and exercise ordinary care. It must ask questions, and if a reasonable person would be put on notice that something is wrong, it should contact the drawer for authority to pay the stale item.

As a general proposition, the death or incompetence of a person terminates the authority of others to act on that person's behalf. If this principle were applied to banks, a tremendous burden would be imposed on them to verify the continued life and competence of drawers. A bank's authority to pay checks therefore continues until it knows that a customer has died or has been judged incompetent and the bank has had a reasonable opportunity to act [4-405].

14. Depositors' Rights and Duties

Banks make available to their customers a statement of account and canceled checks. Within a reasonable time after they are received, the customer must examine them for forgeries and for alterations. The bank does not have the right to charge an account with forged or altered checks, but the customer's failure to examine the statement and to notify the bank will prevent the customer from asserting the forgery (or alteration) against the bank if the bank can establish that it suffered a loss because of this failure. The bank may be able to prove that prompt notification would have enabled it to recover from the forger [4-406(2)].

The Code does not specify the period of time within which the customer must report forgeries or alterations. It does specify that if the same wrongdoer commits successive forgeries or alterations, the customer must examine and notify the bank within fourteen days after the first item and statement were available to him or her. Otherwise, the customer cannot assert the same person's forgeries or alterations paid in good faith by the bank [4-406(2)(b)]. This rule is intended to prevent the wrongdoer from having the opportunity to repeat these misdeeds.

If the customer can establish that the bank itself was negligent in paying a forged or altered item, the bank cannot avail itself of a defense based on the customer's tardiness in examining and reporting [4-406(3)]. However, after a stated period elapses from the time the customer receives the statement containing the first evidence of what becomes a pattern of wrongdoing, the bank is relieved of liability even if it was negligent in paying the checks. These time periods stated in the UCC are one year after the statement is received by the customer if the forgery or alteration appears on the face of the instruments [4-406(4)]. The period of three years applies to forged indorsements found on the back of the instruments [4-406(4)]. Thus, an unreasonably long delay in the customer's examination of the statements sent results in the customer being liable regardless of the actions taken by the bank. If a payor bank, as a matter of policy or public relations, waives its defense of tardy notification by its customer, it cannot thereafter hold the collecting bank or any prior party liable for the forgery [4-406(5)]. The following case illustrates the application of these principles.

CASE

K & K Mfg. Inc. v. Union Bank
628 P.2d 44 (Ariz. 1981)

HATHAWAY, J.

. . . In this case we must apply articles three and four of the Uniform Commercial Code to determine who should bear the risk of loss when a dishonest employee forges her employer's name as drawer on a number of checks on his business and personal checking accounts, then appropriates the proceeds for her personal use.

Appellant Bill J. Knight is the president and majority stockholder of K & K Manufacturing, Inc. K & K Manufacturing employed only two persons when the events which form the basis of this action occurred. These two employees were Knight and a bookkeeper, Eleanor Garza. The bookkeeper's duties at K & K Manufacturing were very broad, including picking up the company mail and Knight's personal mail from a common post office box, preparing checks for Knight's signature to pay both company and personal bills, and making entries in a cash disbursement journal reflecting the expenses for which the checks were written. Most importantly, it was her responsibility to reconcile the monthly statements prepared and sent by appellee Union Bank, where Knight kept both his business and personal checking and savings accounts.

Between March 1977 and January 1978, Miss Garza forged Knight's signature on some 66 separate checks drawn on his personal or business accounts at Union Bank. The majority of these checks were made payable to her. The total amount of the forgeries on the K & K Manufacturing account was $49,859.31. The total on Knight's personal account was $11,350. The bank paid each such check and Miss Garza received or was credited with the proceeds.

Appellant brought this action against appellee for breach of contract, seeking repayment of the funds the bank paid out on checks with unauthorized signatures. After a court trial, judgment was entered in favor of appellant Knight for $5,500, representing the amount paid out of his personal account on forged checks from March 28 to May 20, 1977. This figure included eight forged checks paid by the bank prior to the mailing of its monthly statement containing a record of the payments and the checks themselves to Knight on May 6, plus a 14-day period. Since no forged checks on the K & K Manufacturing account were paid prior to May 20, judgment was entered for appellee against it. Both Knight and K & K Manufacturing have appealed.

We turn to the question of whether appellants met their burden of proof of demonstrating appellee did not exercise ordinary care in paying the bad checks. The issue is whether its method of ascertaining unauthorized signatures on its depositor's checks met the standard of care under the circumstances.

Implied in the debtor/creditor relationship between a bank and its checking account depositor is the contractual undertaking on the part of the bank that it will only discharge its obligations to the depositor upon his authorized signature. The mere fact that the bank has paid a forged check does not mean the bank has breached its duty of ordinary care, however.

At trial, an operations officer for appellee testified as to the methods employed during the period the forgeries occurred to discover unauthorized signatures on depositors' checks. She testified that checks were organized so that a bundle from the same account could be compared with the authorized signature on the bank's signature card. A staff of five filing clerks handled an average of approximately 1,000 checks each per hour in this manner. She testified it was common for a file clerk to become familiar with the drawer's signature in large accounts such as appellants'. An official of a large Arizona bank testified that tellers and file clerks are not trained to be handwriting experts. He testified that in his opinion, because most large banks have completely abandoned physical comparison of checks with the signature card, the system employed by appellee was better than the norm of the banking community in Southern Arizona.

In view of this and other evidence, we conclude that there was sufficient evidence to support . . . the judgment entered below. Similar methods of comparing drawer's signatures have been upheld as constituting ordinary care and being within reasonable commercial standards across the country. Appellant Knight and his controller admitted the forgeries were quite good. Appellants also argue that because the bank tellers recognized Miss Garza was cashing large checks made to herself and her boyfriend and that she was driving an expensive sports car, they had a further duty to check the validity of the drawer's signature. This evidence was balanced by testimony that Miss Garza thoroughly explained the reasons for the large checks as increased salary, bonuses, and payment of Knight's expenses while he was out of town. Knight and Miss Garza were in the bank together on a regular basis and the tellers knew Miss Garza was authorized to handle large amounts of Knight's money.

Finally, there was evidence that some K & K Manufacturing checks were forged with a rubber stamp facsimile of Knight's signature, which was only authorized for use with the Knight Foundry account. Appellants argue appellee fell below the standard of ordinary care in honoring these checks. The trial court personally examined appellee's expert witness on this subject. There was testimony that if facsimile signatures appear "all of a sudden" on the checks, the depositor may be contacted, but there was sufficient evidence that the piecemeal use of the stamp here, which was at times authorized by appellants, was not such that appellee should be held to bring it to their attention. The finding of fact that appellee's acts, including those regarding the facsimile signature, did not fall below ordinary care or reasonable commercial standards was not clearly erroneous.

■ *Affirmed.*

CASE CONCEPTS REVIEW

1. What is the relationship among Eleanor Garza, Bill Knight, and K & K Manufacturing, Inc.?
2. How was Miss Garza able to forge so many checks over a number of months without being detected?
3. What is the basis of Knight arguing that the bank was liable for these improperly payable checks?
4. Why does the court reject Knight's argument and conclude that he has the liability for Miss Garza's wrongdoing?

15. Funds Transfers

The occurrence of paperless transactions between banks and their customers has increased greatly during the past decade. Congress has passed the Electronic Fund Transfer Act to regulate the use of wire transfers in point-of-sale transactions and other consumer payments, such as automatic deposits and withdrawals from accounts. In 1989, the Commissioners on Uniform State Laws offered Article 4A of the UCC to the states for adoption. As of 1991, only Virginia had passed legislation to make this new Article a part of its laws.

You may want to study this new part of the UCC if it has become a part of your state's laws. The appendix includes the actual language of Article 4A as well as an explanation of why the Commissioners felt this addition to the UCC is necessary.

REVISED ARTICLES 3 AND 4

In 1990, the Commissioners on Uniform State Laws proposed new revisions of Articles 3 and 4 to the various states for adoption. In an attempt to balance between the lack of adoptions to date and the anticipation of widespread acceptance of these revisions, we highlight some of the changes proposed at the end of chapters 33 through 36. All references in these parts are to the revised articles.

The first question you might ask is, Why revise Articles 3 and 4? The answer lies in the significant changes that have occurred in how business is transacted and how banks process funds since the original Articles 3 and 4 were presented to the states for adoption beginning in 1952. For example, in the early 1950s, approximately 7 billion checks were processed by banks annually. The Federal Reserve Board estimated that 48 billion checks were written in 1988. Furthermore, the increased reliance on paperless wire transfers makes the paper-based assumptions of the original Articles 3 and 4 outdated.

Among the changes that are worthy of noting here is the renaming of Article 3. Instead of "Commercial Paper," revised Article 3 is entitled "Negotiable Instruments."

Whereas this chapter discusses four types of commercial paper, the revision recognizes two basic forms of negotiable instruments. An instrument is a *note* if it contains a promise; it is a *draft* if it contains an order [3-104(e)]. Checks in their various forms continue to be drafts drawn on banks [3-104(f)–(i)]. A certificate of deposit is a type of note with a bank as the maker [3-104(j)].

The meaning of the word *bank* is expanded to reflect the various types of financial institutions that offer banking services today. A bank means a person engaged in the business of banking, including a savings bank, savings and loan association, credit union, or trust company [4-105(1)].

With respect to when final payment is made by a payor bank, revised Article 4 deletes the reference to completing the process of posting. The payment in cash, the failure to reserve the right to revoke a provisional settlement, or the failure to revoke the provisional settlement in a timely fashion continues to represent final payment by a payor bank [4-215(a)].

Revised section 4-205 makes a depositary bank a holder of an instrument even if the necessary indorsement is missing. This bank does not have to provide the missing indorsement as it does under the original version.

The payor bank's liability for wrongfully dishonoring the customer's checks is clarified in revised section 4-402. There is no distinction between a mistaken and willful dishonor. The bank is liable for the customer's actual damages, and these may include damages for arrest or prosecution and other consequential damages [4-402(b)]. Whether punitive damages might be recovered against the bank is to be determined by state law other than the UCC. Therefore, the willfulness of the bank's dishonor may still become important if intent is determined to be important to the award of punitive damages.

Finally, the time period for the customer's examination of a checking statement is expanded from fourteen to thirty days [4-406(d)(2)]. Also, in the revised section 4-406 there is no reference to the customer's duty to search for and discover unauthorized indorsements. However, under revised section 4-111, the UCC still provides a three-year statute of limitations for a customer to seek a credit of an item bearing an unauthorized indorsement.

CHAPTER SUMMARY

CONCEPT OF NEGOTIABILITY

1. An assignee of a contract takes it subject to any defense the obligor may have against the assignor.
2. The goal of negotiability is to insulate a transferee from personal defenses that a primary party, such as a maker of a note, might have against the transferor.
3. For a holder to take an instrument free of personal defenses, the instrument must be negotiable, must be properly negotiated, and the holder must be a holder in due course.

KINDS OF COMMERCIAL PAPER

Notes
1. A promissory note is a two-party instrument in which the maker promises to pay a stated amount to the payee.

Certificates of Deposit
1. A certificate of deposit is a two-party instrument in which a financial institution such as a bank promises to repay a stated sum with interest on a certain date.

Drafts
1. A draft is a bill of exchange in which a drawer orders a drawee to pay a stated amount to a payee.

Checks
1. A check is a demand draft drawn on a bank.
2. A check drawn by a bank on itself is a cashier's check. Travelers' checks are cashier's checks in which the financial institution is both the drawer and the drawee.
3. A certified check is one that has been accepted by the drawee bank, and by the acceptance it assumes the obligation of the drawer. Certification at the request of a holder releases the drawer from any further liability. A bank has no duty to certify a check.

Terminology	1. Depositary bank—the first bank to which an item is transferred for collection.

Terminology

1. Depositary bank—the first bank to which an item is transferred for collection.
2. Payor bank—the bank by which an item is payable as drawn or accepted.
3. Intermediary bank—any bank to which an item is transferred in the course of collection, except the depositary or payor bank.
4. Collecting bank—any bank handling the item for collection, except the payor bank.
5. Presenting bank—any bank presenting an item to a payor bank.
6. Remitting bank—any payor or intermediary bank remitting an item.
7. A banking day is that part of the day in which a bank is open, and which usually ends at 2:00 P.M. so the bank may process items before it closes. Items received after 2:00 P.M. are generally posted the following day.
8. A midnight deadline is midnight on the banking day following the banking day the item or notice is received by the bank.

The Bank Collection Process

1. A check deposited in the account is a provisional settlement until the check is honored by the payor bank.
2. If the payor bank dishonors a check, provisional settlements are revoked. This must occur for each bank by its midnight deadline.
3. Depositors do not have the right to draw against provisional settlements, although many banks allow them to do so.
4. Items deposited for collection without indorsement may be indorsed by the depositary bank on behalf of its customer. The indorsement indicates that it was deposited to the account of the customer.
5. Depositary banks may not supply indorsements of persons who are not customers.

Collecting Banks

1. Banks have a duty to use ordinary care in the collection process. Failure to do so creates liability for losses sustained.
2. Banks must take action before the midnight deadline on checks, notices from other banks, and making payments.

Payor Banks

1. An item is paid by a payor bank when it actually pays the item, settles for it without reserving the right to revoke the settlement, completes the posting of the item, or makes a provisional settlement and does not revoke it within the time allowed.
2. A provisional settlement may be revoked until the midnight deadline.
3. If a check is drawn on the payor bank by a customer of the same bank, the bank may revoke the credit any time until the close of business the next day.
4. There is no priority in the order of paying checks presented on the same day.

BANKS AND THEIR CUSTOMERS

The Debtor-Creditor Relationship

1. The relationship between a bank and its depositors is that of debtor and creditor. If the depositor borrows money from the bank, the opposite relationship also exists.
2. A bank can seize deposits and set them off against debts to the bank.
3. A bank has a duty to honor checks when there are sufficient funds on deposit. It may also pay other checks and collect the amounts from its depositors.
4. A bank can charge a customer's account for an altered check only to the extent of the original amount of the check.
5. If an incomplete check is signed by a depositor and it is completed improperly, a bank can, in good faith, charge the account with the completed amount.

Wrongful Dishonor	1. A bank is liable for all damages caused by wrongful dishonor.
	2. If the dishonor is willfully wrong, punitive damages may be collected.
	3. Wrongful dishonor is not defamation of a merchant.
Stop Payment Orders	1. A customer has the right to stop payment on checks drawn on his or her account.
	2. The stop order must be received in a time and manner that will allow the bank a reasonable opportunity to stop payment.
	3. Oral stop orders expire in fourteen days unless confirmed in writing.
	4. Written stop orders are effective for only six months but may be renewed in writing.
	5. A bank that fails to stop payment upon proper notice is liable to the drawer of the check for any proven losses.
	6. A bank may not contractually disclaim liability for failure to obey a stop order.
Banks' Rights and Duties	1. A bank may pay a check more than six months old but need not do so.
	2. The death or incompetence of a customer terminates the bank's authority to honor checks written on the customer's account.
	3. Notice of these events must be given to the bank.
Depositors' Rights and Duties	1. Upon receipt of the statement of account and canceled checks, the depositor has a duty to examine them within a reasonable time for forged, unauthorized, or altered checks.
	2. Although the bank does not initially have the right to charge the customer's account for forged, unauthorized, or altered checks, the customer's failure to examine and notify may prevent him or her from asserting the improper charge to his or her account.
	3. If both the customer and the bank are at fault in allowing the forged, altered, or unauthorized check to be paid, the bank is liable.
	4. The customer cannot assert a forged, altered, or unauthorized check after one year from the time the canceled check or the statement of account was available for examination.
	5. Forged indorsements must be reported within three years.

REVIEW QUESTIONS AND PROBLEMS

1. Match each term in column A with the appropriate statement in Column B.

A	B
(1) Depositary bank	(a) Period after which a forged indorsement may no longer be asserted
(2) Personal defense	(b) Period after which written stop payment order expires
(3) Midnight deadline	(c) Period after which a forged check may no longer be asserted by depositor
(4) Six months	(d) The first bank to which an item is transferred for collection
(5) Fourteen days	(e) Part of next banking day
(6) Certification	(f) Period after which an oral stop payment order expires
(7) Real defense	(g) Precludes a bank from honoring a stop order
(8) One year	(h) May not be asserted against a holder in due course
(9) Three years	(i) May be asserted against a holder in due course
(10) Presenting bank	(j) Any bank presenting an item except a payor bank

2. Give the *name* of each of the following three *forms* and parties to the form.

```
┌─────────────────────────────────────────────────────────────┐
│ John E. Murray, Jr.                              NO. 157      │
│ School of Law                                                 │
│ Pittsburgh, PA                              8-26              │
│                          January 4, 19 XX   ────             │
│                                              430             │
│ PAY TO THE                                                    │
│ ORDER OF   George Harlis               $ 70.00               │
│  Seventy and  no/100  ──────────────────── DOLLARS           │
│ Pleasant Hills Office                                         │
│ MELLON BANK            John E. Murray Jr.                     │
│ :0430--0026:  243--7716:  0157  :00000000 7000:             │
└─────────────────────────────────────────────────────────────┘
```
(a)

```
┌─────────────────────────────────────────────────────────────┐
│            FIRST CITY BANK OF NEW YORK                        │
│   No. 4762      New York, New York      May 1, 19XX          │
│   THIS CERTIFIES THAT THERE HAS BEEN DEPOSITED with          │
│   the undersigned the sum of  $400,000.00                     │
│   four hundred thousand ───────────── DOLLARS                │
│   Payable to the order of Dina Oil Company on July 27,       │
│   1993           with interest only to maturity at the rate of│
│   TWELVE per cent (12%) per annum upon surrender of this     │
│   certificate properly indorsed.                             │
│                  FIRST CITY BANK OF NEW YORK BY:             │
│                  M. Hopkins, Vice President                  │
│                                      Authorized Signature    │
└─────────────────────────────────────────────────────────────┘
```
(b)

```
┌─────────────────────────────────────────────────────────────┐
│                        Moscow, Idaho  June 7, 19XX           │
│                                                               │
│   One year from date pay to the order of  Betty Stein        │
│    Four thousand ──────────────────────── Dollars            │
│                                                               │
│                         Andre Pelleer                        │
│                                                               │
│   To:  Robert Shaw                                            │
│        47 Peachtree Street                                    │
│        Atlanta, Georgia 30303                                 │
└─────────────────────────────────────────────────────────────┘
```
(c)

3. A check was issued payable jointly to Sam and Chuck. Sam indorsed the check and deposited it in his account with National Bank. Chuck did not indorse the check, nor has Chuck ever been a customer of National Bank. National Bank supplied Chuck's missing indorsement and forwarded the check to the drawee bank. Chuck sued National Bank for cashing the check without his indorsement. May the bank supply the missing indorsement of a joint payee who is not a customer-depositor with the bank? Explain.

4. Pearl is the holder of a check drawn by Sharpe on Washington State Bank. Pearl also maintains an account at Washington State Bank. The check is deposited at the bank on Monday. On that same day, Sharpe's account is overdrawn, but she promises to make a substantial deposit, so the bank holds the check until Thursday. Sharpe does not make the deposit, and the bank, on Friday, returns the check to Pearl marked "Insufficient Funds." Can Pearl require the bank to make good on the check? Why or why not?

5. Equipment Company bought equipment from Wells and paid him with a check drawn on Citizens Bank. When the equipment was not delivered the next day, Equipment Company stopped payment on the check. Wells cashed the check at his own bank, Fargo Bank. When the check was presented to Citizens Bank, it refused to honor the check because of the stop order. Can Fargo Bank successfully collect from Wells? Why or why not?

6. Fitting issued a check for $800. After writing the check, she had second thoughts and contacted the bank about the possibility of stopping payment. A bank employee advised Fitting to deliberately create an overdraft situation by withdrawing enough money so there would remain insufficient funds to cover the check in question. The bank employee indicated that in those circumstances the bank would not pay the check. Fitting proceeded to withdraw money from the account, leaving enough money to cover other checks she had written. The bank nevertheless paid the $800 check in question. Is Fitting liable for the overdraft? Why or why not?

7. On January 29, Edwards, a wholesale grocer, made a large deposit in cash to his account at Cattlemen's Bank. In error, Edwards's deposit was posted to the account of Edmunds, another depositor. On the following day, Nevins, a local producer jobber, deposited a check to his account at Watermill bank drawn on Cattlemen's Bank to Nevins's order by Edwards. When the check was presented for payment, Cattlemen's Bank refused to honor it and stamped it "Insufficient Funds." The check was promptly returned to Nevins by Watermill Bank. If Edwards's deposit on January 29 had been properly posted, his bank account balance would have been substantially greater than the amount of his check to Nevins. Edwards sues the Cattlemen's Bank for damages. What should this recovery be? Why? Should Edwards recover?

8. The facts are as in problem 7. Assume that Edwards's check had been given to Nevins in payment for a carload of produce that Edwards had arranged to resell at a large profit, that the bank was aware of this, that on dishonor of the check Nevins stopped the goods in transit, and that Edwards as a result lost his profit on the resale of the goods. May Edwards recover such lost profits from the bank? Explain.

9. Franklin, a depositor of the Milltown Bank, orally ordered the cashier of the bank to stop payment on a check he had issued. The check was issued in payment for goods that were not received. Franklin learned that the seller was a notorious confidence man. The cashier in turn notified the tellers that an oral stop order had been given. Ten days later one of the tellers, who was not paying much attention to his business, paid the seller's wife, who had been sent to the bank to cash the check for the seller. Franklin, while examining his canceled checks at the end of the month, discovered the error and promptly demanded that his account be credited for the amount of the check. Is he entitled to the credit? Why?

10. Men's Wear drew a check payable to Zino & Co. When Zino did not receive it in the mail, Men's Wear placed a stop payment order in writing with the Drawee Bank. Approximately one year later, Drawee Bank paid on the check to a collecting bank and charged Men's Wear's account. Men's Wear had not renewed its stop payment order. Is Drawee Bank liable to Men's Wear for failing to honor the stop payment order? Why or why not?

11. On June 30, 1990, Charles issued check number 2668 drawn on Community State Bank in the amount of $5,000 to Southern Masonry. Subsequently, Charles was advised by the payee that the check had been lost, and a replacement check was issued and cashed. In January, 1993, check number 2668 was deposited by the payee in its account at Community State Bank. Is the bank entitled to charge Charles's account? Why or why not?

12. Newton, a holder in due course, presented a check to the Marshall Bank, the drawee bank named on the face of the instrument. The bank examined the signature of the

drawer very carefully, but the signature was such an exact forgery of the drawer's signature that only a handwriting expert could have detected a difference. The bank therefore paid the check. Assume that the check was promptly returned to the drawer-depositor but that he did not discover the forgery until thirteen months after the check was returned to him. Can he compel the bank to credit his account for the loss? Why?

CHAPTER

34 NEGOTIABLE INSTRUMENTS AND NEGOTIATION

CHAPTER OUTLINE

GENERAL REQUIREMENTS
1. Writing Signed by a Maker or Drawer
2. Necessity of a Promise or Order
3. Unconditional Promise or Order
4. The Particular Fund Concept
5. Sum Certain in Money
6. Certain Time of Payment
7. Acceleration and Extension Clauses

THE MAGIC WORDS OF NEGOTIABILITY
8. Introduction
9. Order Paper
10. Bearer Paper

OTHER FACTORS AFFECTING NEGOTIABILITY
11. Terms and Omissions Not Affecting Negotiability
12. Incomplete Instruments
13. Ambiguous Terms and Rules of Construction

TRANSFER OF COMMERCIAL PAPER
14. Introduction
15. Transfer by Negotiation
16. Types of Indorsements
17. Blank Indorsements
18. Special Indorsements
19. Restrictive Indorsements

REVISED ARTICLE 3

CHAPTER PREVIEW

The preceding chapter introduced the four requirements that must be satisfied if a third party is to take commercial paper free of the defenses that arise from underlying contractual transactions. These four requirements may be stated so an affirmative response to each of the following questions must be given:

1. Does the paper meet the prerequisites of a negotiable instrument?
2. Has the negotiable instrument been properly negotiated?
3. Is the holder of the instrument in due course?
4. Are the defenses personal as opposed to real?

This chapter analyzes the first two of these four questions: The requirements of a negotiable instrument and its proper negotiation.

One of your responsibilities as an officer of a financial institution is to decide whether or not to purchase (at a discount) the promissory notes that are payable to your customers.

What criteria should you use in making your decision to purchase these notes?

GENERAL REQUIREMENTS

The negotiability of an instrument is determined by the terms written on the face of the instrument. To be negotiable, an instrument must satisfy four basic requirements: It must (1) be signed by the maker or drawer, (2) contain an unconditional promise or order to pay a sum certain in money, (3) be payable on demand or at a definite time, and (4) be payable to order or to bearer [3-104(1)].

1. Writing Signed by a Maker or Drawer

The first requirement is simply that there be a writing signed by the maker or drawer [3-104(1)(a)]. It is not required that any particular type or kind of writing be used, nor is it necessary that the signature be at any particular place on the instrument. The instrument may be in any form that includes "printing, typewriting, or any other intentional reduction to tangible form" [1-201(46)]. A symbol is a sufficient signature if "executed or adopted by a party with present intention to authenticate a writing" [1-201(39)]. The use of the word *authenticate* in the definition of *signed* makes it clear that a complete signature is not required. The authentication may be printed or written and may be placed on the instrument by stamp.

For purposes of internal control, many businesses and other organizations require that instruments be signed by at least two persons or that they be countersigned. When the agreement requires two signatures, the drawee may not pay on only one signature, even if the one signing is authorized. The authority is limited or divided; both must sign.

2. Necessity of a Promise or Order

A negotiable note must contain a *promise* to pay. Although the word *promise* is used in almost all notes, a word or words expressing an undertaking to pay may be substituted. The promise must be derived from the language of the instrument, not from the fact that a debt exists. A mere acknowledgment of a debt in writing (an IOU) does not contain a promise. Even though an IOU is a valid enforceable instrument on which recovery may be had, it is not negotiable.

Order A direction to pay that must be more than an authorization or request. It must, with reasonable certainty, identify the person to pay.

A draft must contain an **order** to pay. The purpose of the instrument is to order the drawee to pay money to the payee or his or her order. The drawer must use plain language to show an intention to make an order and to signify more than an authorization or request. It must be a direction to pay. Thus an instrument in the following form would not be negotiable: "To John Doe. I wish you would pay $1,000 to the order of Richard Roe. [Signed] Robert Lee." This would nevertheless be a valid authorization for John Doe to make payment to Richard Roe. The correct method to create an order to pay would be, "To John Doe. Pay $1,000 to the order of Richard Roe. [Signed] Robert Lee."

3. Unconditional Promise or Order

Negotiable instruments serve as a substitute for money and as a basis for short-term credit. If these purposes are to be served, it is essential that the instruments be readily received in lieu of money and freely transferable. Conditional promises or orders would defeat these purposes, for it would be necessary that every person determine whether or not the condition had been performed prior to taking the instrument. The instruments would not freely circulate. In recognition of these facts, the law requires that the promise or order be *unconditional*.

The question of whether or not the promise or order is conditional arises when the instrument contains language in addition to the promise or order to pay money. The promise or order is conditional if the language of the instrument provides that payment is controlled by, or is subject to, the terms of some other agreement [3-105(2)(a)]. Clearly, a promise or order is conditional if reference to some other agreement is *required* and if payment is *subject* to the terms of another contract. Such a reference imposes the terms of the other writing.

However, a mere reference to some other contract or document does not condition the promise or order and does not impair negotiability. Such reference simply gives information about the transaction that gave rise to the instrument. Thus the words *subject to contract* condition the promise or order, but the words *as per contract* do not render the promise or order conditional. The latter is informative rather than restrictive.

Statements of the consideration for which the instrument was given and statements of the transaction out of which the instrument arose are simply informative [3-105(1)(b)]. A draft may have been drawn under a letter of credit, and a reference to this fact does not impose a condition [3-105(1)(d)]. Notes frequently contain a statement that some sort of security has been given, such as a mortgage on property, or that title to goods has been retained as security for the payment of the note. In either case, the purpose is to make clear to the holder that the promise to pay is secured by something in addition to the general credit of the maker; and as a consequence, a mere reference to the security does not destroy negotiability [3-105(1)(e)].

Normally implied or constructive conditions in an agreement that underlies the instrument do not make the instrument conditional. For example, a promise that payment will be made when the contract is performed does not make the promise to pay conditional [3-105(1)(a)]. However, express conditions stated in the instrument itself can make the promise to pay conditional. The following case illustrates this rule and discusses the close relationship between an unconditional promise and the requirement that the time of payment be fixed.

CASE

Calfo v. D. C. Stewart Co.

717 P.2d 697 (Utah 1986)

ZIMMERMAN, J.

This case involves a suit by plaintiff Angelo Calfo upon a promissory note issued by defendant D. C. Stewart Co. ("Stewart"). The note was payable to the order of C. J. Realty and was sold to Calfo by an agent of C. J. Realty. The trial court granted Calfo a summary judgment enforcing the note. Stewart appealed. We hold that the note was not a negotiable instrument and reverse the trial court on that ground.

Stewart owned the Astro Motel in Cedar City, Utah. Defendant Roland Vance, a real estate agent for defendant C. J. Realty, approached Stewart about listing the motel for sale with C. J. Realty. The listing agreement was entered into, and Vance subsequently obtained a potential buyer for the motel.

On September 24, 1979, Stewart and the potential buyer entered into a lease agreement and option to purchase. The agreement provided that the lessees could exercise an option to purchase the motel on or before May 1, 1980. Also on September 24, 1979, Stewart executed a promissory note for $15,900 payable to C. J. Realty to secure the real estate commission to which C. J. Realty would be entitled if the lessees exercised their option to purchase. The promissory note provided that it would be payable as follows:

> Total due in full upon final closing between D. C. Stewart Co., Seller, and Wendell James Downward and Connie Downward, husband and wife, Buyers, which shall be on or before May 1, 1980, when Buyers exercise their option to purchase the Astro Motel in Cedar City, Utah.

On September 27, 1979, the promissory note was sold by Vance, acting on behalf of C. J. Realty, to the plaintiff Calfo for $12,720.

The lessees never exercised their option to purchase the Astro Motel. However, after May 1, 1980, Calfo made demand upon all of the defendants for payment of the note. When payment was not forthcoming, suit was brought on the note against Stewart, and against Vance as guarantor of the note. . . .

Stewart argues that trial court erred in finding the promissory note to be a negotiable instrument. To be negotiable under section 3-104(1) of the Uniform Commercial Code, an instrument must meet four criteria. Specifically, it must (i) evidence a signature by the maker or drawer, (ii) contain an unconditional promise or order to pay a sum certain in money, (iii) be payable on demand or at a definite time, and (iv) be payable to order or to bearer. Stewart and Calfo agree that the promissory note in question satisfies the first and fourth of these requirements. They disagree as to whether second and third are met.

Although the second and third requirements of negotiability are separately stated, in fact they are closely related. Both focus on whether the instrument is a clear and unconditional promise to pay. These concerns are central to the whole concept of negotiable instruments and that should be kept in mind in determining whether a document is entitled to be treated as a negotiable instrument under the Uniform Commercial Code. Two important functions of negotiable instruments are "to supplement the supply of currency" and to provide a present representation of "future payment of money."

> These currency and credit functions would be defeated by conditional promises, because the costly and time consuming investigations that would be required by such promises would impede circulation. Conditional paper would increase the risks of the holder, and discount rates would be increased commensurately. Substitutes for money must be capable of rapid circulation at minimum risks, and credit documents are feasible only when low discounting prevails. Obviously, then, negotiable instruments must be unconditional to serve the purposes for which they are created.

Because a negotiable instrument is a substitute for money or currency, both the promise to pay and the certainty of payment must be unequivocal.

For similar reasons, an instrument's negotiability must be determinable from what appears on its face and without reference to extrinsic facts. This requirement protects transferees from latent defenses to payment, *i.e.*, those defenses which are not readily apparent from the document. On the other hand, if the document evinces terms which should alert the transferee of possible defenses, then the transferee is not entitled to insulation from those apparent defenses.

> The whole purpose of the concept of a negotiable instrument under Article 3 is to declare that transferees in the ordinary course of business are only to be held liable for information appearing in the instrument itself and will not be expected to know of any limitations on negotiability, or changes of terms, etc., contained in any separate documents. The whole idea of the facilitation of easy transfer of notes and instruments requires that a transferee be able to trust what the instrument says, and be able to determine the validity of the note and its negotiability from the language in the note itself.

The present case involves a promissory note which is "due in full upon final closing between . . . seller and . . . buyers, which shall be on or before May 1, 1980, when buyers exercise their option to purchase the Astro Motel. . . ." In determining whether this promise to pay is conditional or indefinite, we are not aided by the trial court's summary finding that this is a "good note." The document specifically states that it is due only upon final closing "when buyers exercise their option to purchase." This language clearly places the holder on notice that the note will become due only upon a contingency which the holder cannot control, *i.e.*, the exercise by buyers of their option to purchase. As for definiteness, the date set forth, May 1, 1980, merely defines when the option to purchase expires and does not establish a time as to when the note will certainly become due. On these facts, we find the note to be both conditional and indefinite on its face. . . .

For the reasons stated, we hold that the promissory note sued upon is not a negotiable instrument and that judgment was improperly entered against Stewart. There appears to be no dispute in the record that the sale of the Astro Motel did not occur. Stewart's defenses of lack of consideration, non-maturity of the note, and failure of condition precedent seem to be absolute.

■ *Reversed and remanded.*

CASE CONCEPTS REVIEW

1. Who were the parties to the promissory note, and why was it created?
2. How did Calfo become the owner of this note?
3. Why did Stewart refuse to pay Calfo? What defense did Stewart assert?
4. In response to Calfo's claim to be a holder in due course of a negotiable instrument, Stewart argues the note is not a negotiable instrument. What is the basis of Stewart's argument?
5. Why does this court conclude that this note was nonnegotiable?

4. The Particular Fund Concept

A maker or drawer must engage or pledge his or her general credit, or the promise or order is conditional. A statement that an instrument is to be paid only out of a particular fund imposes a condition [3-105(2)(b)]. Such an instrument does not carry the general personal credit of the maker or drawer. It is contingent on the sufficiency of the fund on which it is drawn. For example, if a note states, "I promise to pay to the order of John only out of my corn profits," the note is conditioned on having corn profits. The promise is conditional, and the instrument is nonnegotiable. This result is due to the *particular fund concept*.

There are three exceptions to this concept. First, an instrument is not considered conditional merely because it makes reference to a particular source or fund from which payment is expected but not required. For example, although a check indicates it will be paid out of a particular account, it still may be negotiable. This conclusion with respect to checks is based on the fact that if the payor bank does not honor the check, the drawer remains personally liable for its payment. Thus, the reference to the checking account as the source of payment does not limit the payment to the resources of that particular fund or account.

The second exception involves an instrument that is issued by a government or governmental unit and is limited to payment out of a particular fund [3-105(1)(g)]. The third exception is when an unincorporated association, such as a partnership, trust, or an estate, limits its obligation to pay the instrument only from the assets of the organization and eliminates liability of the individual members, such as partners. The instrument may still be negotiable. For purposes of negotiability, the Code recognizes partnerships and other unincorporated associations as "commercial entities" that may execute negotiable instruments as an entity [3-105(1)(h)].

5. Sum Certain in Money

To be negotiable, an instrument must be payable in money. Instruments payable in chattels such as wheat or platinum are not payable in money. *Money* means a medium of exchange that is authorized or adopted by a domestic or foreign government as a part of its currency [1-201(24)]. The amount payable may be stated in foreign as well as domestic money [3-107(2)]. If the sum payable is stated in foreign currency, payment may be made in the dollar equivalent unless it is specified in the instrument that the foreign currency is the only medium of payment.

The language used in creating commercial paper must be certain with respect to the amount of money promised or ordered to be paid. Otherwise, its value at any period could not be definitely determined. If the principal sum to be paid is definite, negotiability is not affected by the fact that it is to be paid with interest, in installments, with exchange at a fixed or current rate, or with cost of collection and attorney's fees in case payment is not made at maturity [3-106].

If at any time during the term of the paper its full value can be ascertained, the requirement that the sum must be certain is satisfied. The obligation to pay costs and attorney's fees is part of the security contract, separate and distinct from the primary promise to pay money; therefore, it does not affect the required sum certain. The certainty of amount is not affected if the instrument specifies different rates of interest before and after default; nor is the certainty affected by a provision for a stated discount for early payment or an additional charge if payment is made after the date fixed [3-106(1)(c)]. The principal amount to be paid, however, must be certain for the note to be negotiable.

6. Certain Time of Payment

As a substitute for money, negotiable instruments would be of little value if the holder were unable to determine when he or she could demand payment. A negotiable instrument, therefore, must be payable on demand or at a definite time [3-104(1)(c)].

An instrument is payable on *demand* when it so states, when payable at sight or on presentation, or when no time of payment is stated [3-108]. In general, the words *payable on demand* are used in notes, and the words *at sight* in drafts. If nothing is said about the due date, the instrument is demand paper. A check is a good illustration of such an instrument. The characteristic of demand paper is that its holder can require payment at any time by making a demand on the person who is obligated on the paper.

Not every instrument that indicates no time of payment is a demand instrument. If the instrument provides for periodic payment of interest or contains an acceleration clause without specifying the actual due date, such instruments are nonnegotiable. The interest clauses and acceleration clauses clearly indicate an intent that it not be payable on demand. As the following case illustrates, such clauses must be carefully worded if negotiability is to be retained.

CASE

P. P., Inc. v. McGuire
509 F. Supp. 1079 (D. N.J. 1981)

McGuire bought Tursi's clothes boutique, paying $10,000 in cash and executing a promissory note for $65,000. The note had an acceleration clause and stated that "interest payments of $541.66 shall be due and payable at a rate of 10 percent per annum on the fifth day of October, November, and December, 1979." Tursi refused to close the sale to McGuire and sold the note to Parker in another deal. When Parker sued McGuire on the $65,000 note, McGuire defended on the basis of failure of consideration, since Tursi refused to close the sale of his boutique. Parker contended that failure of consideration on a negotiable instrument is not a defense against a holder in due course. McGuire responded that the note was not negotiable because the note was not payable on demand or at a definite time.

DEBEVOISE, J.

... It is not necessary to decide whether plaintiff meets the requisites of a holder in due course because the note on which he sues is clearly not a negotiable instrument. For an instrument to be negotiable, it must satisfy each of the requirements outlined in U.C.C. §3-104(1). It must:

(a) be signed by the maker or drawer; and
(b) contain an unconditional promise or order to pay a sum certain in money and no other promise, order, obligation or power given by the maker or drawer except as authorized by this Article; and
(c) be payable on demand or at a definite time; and
(d) be payable to order or bearer.

If any one of elements (a) through (d) is lacking, the instrument is not negotiable and Article 3 of the Uniform Commercial Code does not apply.

The McGuires' note upon which plaintiff seeks to recover fails of negotiability because it is not, on its face, payable either on demand or at a definite time. The note calls for three installments of interest to be paid on "the 5th day of October, November, and December, 1979." It also contains an acceleration clause given the holder the option of declaring the entire balance of principal, with interest, due and payable prior to maturity upon the makers' default on any installment of "principal or interest." Nowhere on the instrument's face, however, has a time for repayment of principal been specified.

Under U.C.C. §3-109:

An instrument is payable at a definite time if by its terms it is payable

(a) on or before a stated date or at a fixed period after a stated date; or
(b) at a fixed period after sight; or
(c) at a definite time subject to any acceleration; or
(d) at a definite time subject to extension at the option of the holder, or to extension to a further definite time at the option of the maker or acceptor or automatically upon or after a specified act or event.

This promissory note clearly contains none of the provisions necessary to make it payable at a definite time.

An instrument may also be negotiable if it is payable on demand. "Instruments payable on demand include those payable at sight or on presentation and those in which no time for payment is stated." If the note had merely stated that the McGuires promised to pay the Tursis $65,000 at a given rate of interest, there can be no question that the note would have been payable on demand. Here, however, it is apparent from the face of the instrument that the parties did not intend for this note to be payable on demand, nor would any reasonable person so interpret it. Were the note payable on demand, for example, there would be no need for an acceleration clause. Moreover, no note payable on demand would specify a fixed amount of interest payable for the following three months and make no provision for interest thereafter. One can speculate that the parties intended the note to mature at a definite time approximately three months after the date it was signed. Exactly what time was intended, however, is impossible to ascertain from the face of the note. When a note is payable only at an indefinite time in the future, and parol evidence is required to supplement its terms, the note is not a negotiable instrument within the meaning of Article 3 of the Uniform Commercial Code....

■ *Summary judgment denied.*

CASE CONCEPTS REVIEW

1. Who is the maker and who is the original payee in the promissory note?
2. Why does Tursi sell the note to Parker?
3. What defense does McGuire assert when Parker seeks to collect payment of the note?
4. On what basis does Parker, on behalf of P. P., Inc., argue that McGuire's defense is ineffective against its claim for payment?
5. Why does the court conclude in favor of allowing McGuire's defense?

The requirement of a definite time is in keeping with the necessity for certainty in instruments. It is important that the value of an instrument can always be determined. This value will be dependent on the ultimate maturity date of the instrument. If an instrument is payable only upon an act or event, the time of its occurrence being uncertain, the instrument is not payable at a definite time even though the act or event has occurred [3-109(2)]. Thus, an instrument payable "thirty days after my father's death" would not be negotiable.

The requirement of certainty as to the time of payment is satisfied if it is payable on or before a specified date [3-109(1)(a)]. Thus an instrument payable "on or before" June 1, 1993 is negotiable. The obligor on the instrument has the privilege of making payment prior to June 1, 1993 but is not required to pay until the specified date. An instrument payable at a fixed period after a stated date, or at a fixed period after sight, is payable at a definite time [3-109(1)(b)]. The expressions "one year after date" or "sixty days after sight" are definite as to time.

7. Acceleration and Extension Clauses

Two types of provisions appearing on the face of instruments may affect the definite time requirement. One, an *acceleration clause*, hastens or accelerates the maturity date of an instrument. Accelerating provisions may be of many different kinds. A typical one provides that in case of default in payment, the entire note shall become due and payable. Another kind gives the holder an option to declare the instrument due and payable when he or she feels insecure about ultimate payment. An instrument payable at a definite time subject to any acceleration is negotiable [3-109(1)(c)]. If, however, the acceleration provision permits the holder to declare the instrument due when he or she feels insecure, the holder must act in good faith in the honest belief that the likelihood of payment is impaired. The presumption is that the holder has acted in good faith, placing the burden on the obligor-payor to show that such act was not in good faith [1-208].

The second type of provision affecting time is an *extension clause*, the converse of the acceleration provision. It lengthens the time for payment beyond that specified in the instrument. A note payable in two years might provide that the maker has the right to extend the time of payment six months. An instrument is payable "at a definite time subject to extension at the option of the holder, or to extension to a further definite time at the option of the maker or acceptor" [3-109(1)(d)]. If an extension is at the option of the holder, no time limit is required. The holder always has a right to refrain from undertaking collection. An extension at the option of the maker or acceptor, however, must specify a definite time for ultimate payment or negotiability is destroyed.

THE MAGIC WORDS OF NEGOTIABILITY

8. Introduction

The *words of negotiability* express the intention to create negotiable paper. The usual words of negotiability are *order* and *bearer* [3-110, 3-111]. When these words are used, the maker or drawer has in effect stated that the instrument may be negotiated to another party. When the word *bearer* is used, it means that payment will be made to anyone who *bears* or possesses it. When the word *order* is used, it means that it will be paid to the designated payee or anyone to whom the payee orders it to be paid.

Other words of equivalent meaning may be used, but to ensure negotiability it is preferable to use the conventional words. If the instrument is not payable to order or to bearer, it is not negotiable, and all defenses are available in suits on the instrument. The following case illustrates how easy it is to overlook the magic words.

CASE

First Inv. Co. v. Andersen
621 P.2d 683 (Utah 1980)

Andersen gave promissory notes to Great Lakes in return for Great Lakes' promise to deliver 65,000 trees for Andersen's nursery business. The notes recited,

> For value received, Robert Andersen of Nephi, Utah, promises to pay to Great Lakes Nursery Corp. at Waukesha, Wisconsin, six thousand four hundred twelve dollars payable as follows: $100 per month beginning Oct. 1, 1965 for 24 months and then $111.30 per month for 36 months including interest computed at 7% per annum added to the principal amount of $4,750.00.

In return for a loan, Great Lakes transferred the notes to First Investment. When Great Lakes failed to deliver the trees, Andersen refused to pay First Investment. First Investment sued Andersen claiming that it was not subject to Andersen's defense of failure of consideration because the notes were negotiable. The trial court found for the defendant.

MAUGHAN, J.

... Defendants prevailed before the trial court on the ground the notes were not negotiable, and failure of consideration was a defense against any person not a holder in due course.

The primary issue is whether the two promissory notes were negotiable. A negotiable promissory note ... is an unconditional promise in writing made by one person to another, signed by the maker, engaging to pay on demand, or at a fixed or determinable future time, a sum certain in money, *to order or to bearer.*

An instrument to be negotiable ... must be payable to order or to bearer. An instrument is payable to order where it is drawn payable to the order of a specified person, or to him or his order.

Under ... the U.C.C. 70A-3-104(1)(d), one of the requirements to qualify a writing as a negotiable instrument is that it contain the time-honored "words of negotiability," such as "pay to the order" or "pay to the bearer." The mere promise to pay, absent the magic words "payable to order or to bearer" renders the note nonnegotiable, and the liability is determined as a matter of simple contract law.

In the instant case, the notes were payable simply to the payee, and were not payable to the order of the payee or to the payee or its order and were thus not negotiable instruments. Since the notes were not negotiable, the transfer by the Nursery to plaintiff must be deemed an assignment, and the assignee (plaintiff) stood in the shoes of the assignor and took subject to existing equities and defenses. . . .

■ *Affirmed.*

CASE CONCEPTS REVIEW

1. What was the reason Andersen signed promissory notes in favor of Great Lakes Nursery?
2. What did Great Lakes do with these notes?
3. Why does the court allow Andersen to assert the defense of Great Lakes' nonperformance when First Investment sued to collect the note?
4. What words are missing from these notes that would have changed the result of this case?

9. Order Paper

If the terms of an instrument provide that it is payable to the order or assigns of a person who is specified with reasonable certainty, the instrument is payable to order [3-110(1)]. The expressions "Pay to the order of John Doe" or "Pay to John Doe or order" or "Pay to John Doe or assigns" create order paper (see Figure 34-1).

FIGURE 34–1 ■ Order Paper Payable to the Order of John Doe [3-110(1)]. (It requires John Doe's indorsement if it is to be negotiated.)

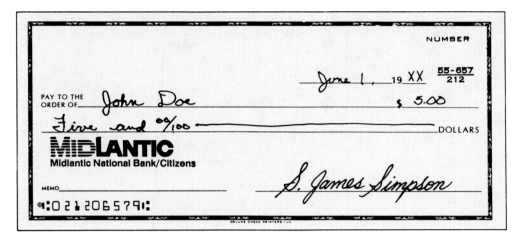

An instrument may be payable to the order of two or more payees together, such as A and B, or in the alternative, A or B. An instrument payable to the order of A and B must be indorsed by both. One payable to the order of A or B may be indorsed and negotiated by either [3-116].

An instrument may be payable to the order of an estate, a trust, or a fund. Such instruments are payable to the order of the representative of the estate, trust, or fund [3-110(1)(e)]. An instrument payable to the order of a partnership or an unincorporated association such as a labor union is payable to such partnership or association. It may be indorsed by any person authorized by the partnership or association [3-110(1)(g)].

10. Bearer Paper

The basic characteristic of bearer paper (see Figure 34–2) as distinguished from order paper is that it is payable to bearer when created if it is payable (1) to bearer, (2) to the order of bearer (as distinguished from the order of a specified person or bearer), (3) to a specified person or bearer (notice that it is not to *the order of* a specified person or bearer), or (4) to "cash" or "the order of cash," or any other indication that does not purport to designate any specific payee [3-111]. An instrument will be considered bearer paper only after it is determined that it cannot be order paper.

OTHER FACTORS AFFECTING NEGOTIABILITY

11. Terms and Omissions Not Affecting Negotiability

Some additional terms, usually for the benefit of the payee or other holder, may be included in commercial paper without impairing negotiability. Many instruments contain statements indicating that collateral has been given. These statements, in-

FIGURE 34–2 ■ Bearer Paper. (Its negotiation is effective without an indorsement [3-111].)

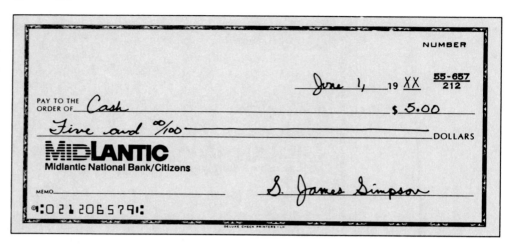

cluding provisions relating to the rights of the payee or holder in the collateral, do not affect negotiability [3-112(1)(b)(c)].

The drawer of a check or draft may include a provision that the payee, by indorsing or cashing it, acknowledges full satisfaction of an obligation of the drawer. The provision will not affect negotiability [3-112(1)(f)]. Checks or drafts drawn by insurance companies in settlement of claims usually contain such a provision.

Often, the consideration for which an instrument was given is set forth in the instrument, and it is common to include words such as "for value received" or "in payment for services rendered." The omission of words stating the consideration for which an instrument was given will not affect its negotiability. Nor is the negotiable character of an instrument otherwise negotiable impaired by omission of a statement of the place where the instrument is drawn or payable [3-112(1)(a)].

Whether there is no date, a wrong date, an antedate, or a postdate is not important from the standpoint of negotiability [3-114(1)]. Any date that does appear on the instrument is presumed correct until evidence is introduced to establish a contrary date [3-114(3)]. Any fraud or illegality connected with the date of the instrument does not affect its negotiability but merely gives a defense.

12. Incomplete Instruments

A person may sign an instrument that is incomplete in that it lacks one or more of the necessary elements of a complete instrument. Thus a paper signed by the maker or drawer, in which the payee's name or the amount is omitted, is incomplete.

An incomplete instrument cannot be enforced until it is completed [3-115(1)]. If the blanks are subsequently filled in by any person in accordance with the authority or instructions given by the party who signed the incomplete instrument, it is then effective as completed. A person might leave blank, signed checks with an employee who must pay for goods to be delivered. When the employee fills in the amounts and names of the payees, the checks are perfectly valid.

A date is not required for an instrument to be negotiable; however, if a date is necessary to ascertain maturity ("payable sixty days from date"), an undated instrument is an incomplete instrument. The date may be inserted by the holder. If an instrument is payable on demand or at a fixed period after date, the date that is put on the instrument controls, even though it is antedated or postdated {3-114(2)}.

13. Ambiguous Terms and Rules of Construction

In view of the millions of negotiable instruments that are made and drawn daily, it is to be expected that a certain number of them will be ambiguously worded. Accordingly, the code provides a number of rules to be applied in interpreting negotiable instruments.

Some instruments are drawn in such a manner that it is doubtful whether the instrument is a draft or a note. It may be directed to a third person but contain a promise to pay, rather than an order to pay. The holder may treat it as either a draft or a note and present it for payment to either the person who signed it or the apparent drawee. Where a draft is drawn on the drawer, it is treated as a note {3-118(a)}.

An instrument may contain handwritten terms, typewritten terms, or printed terms. Where there are discrepancies in the instrument, handwritten terms control typewritten and printed terms, and typewritten terms control printed terms {3-118(b)}. Thus a printed note form may state that it is payable on demand, but there may be typed or written on the note "payable thirty days from date." Such an instrument would be payable in thirty days.

There may also be a conflict between the words and the figures on an instrument. Thus a check may have the words "fifty dollars" and the figures "$5000." The words control, and the check would be for $50. If the words are ambiguous, the figures will control {3-118(c)}. In a check with the words "Five seventy-five dollars" and figures $5.75," the figures will control. In some cases, the ambiguity may arise from the context of the words.

If an instrument provides for the payment of interest but does not state the rate, the rate will be at the judgment rate at the place of payment. An unsatisfied money judgment bears interest at a rate specified by statute, and whatever this judgment rate is in a particular state will thus be applicable in this situation. Interest will run from the date of the instrument or, if it is undated, from the date of issue {3-118(d)}.

If two or more persons sign an instrument as maker, acceptor, drawer, or indorser as part of the same transaction, they are jointly and severally liable unless the instrument specifies otherwise. This means that the full amount of the obligation could be collected from any one of them or that all of them might be joined in a single action. Joint and several liability is imposed even though the instrument contains such words as "I promise to pay" {3-118(e)}.

14. Introduction

The general rule governing the transfer of almost all types of property is that a person can transfer no greater interest than he or she owns. *Assignments* follow that general rule. The general law of assignments is discussed in chapter 17. When one attempts to transfer rights by assignment, it is generally stated that the assignee steps into the shoes of the assignor. Thus, the transfer of an instrument by assignment vests in the assignee only those rights the assignor had.

By contrast, the key feature of negotiability is that a *negotiation* might confer on a transferee greater rights than were held by the transferor. If the transfer is by negotiation, the transferee becomes a *holder* [3-202(1)]. A holder has, for example, the legal power to transfer the instrument by assignment or negotiation; the holder can usually enforce it in his or her own name [3-301]; he or she can discharge the liability of any party in several ways (as we shall later explain); and he or she enjoys several procedural advantages. Moreover, the holder has the opportunity to become a *holder in due course* with rights not granted by the instrument.

Thus, in an *assignment*, only the rights of the transferor are passed to the transferee, but in a *negotiation*, there is the possibility of granting greater rights. Any contract can be assigned; only a negotiable instrument can be negotiated.

15. Transfer by Negotiation

Two methods of negotiating an instrument make the transferee a holder. If the instrument is payable to bearer, it may be negotiated by delivery alone; if it is order paper, indorsement and delivery are required [3-202(1)]. Although bearer paper can be negotiated without indorsement, the person to whom it is transferred will often require an indorsement. The reason for this is that an indorser has a greater liability than one who negotiates without indorsement. Also, if the instrument is dishonored, identification of the person who negotiated the paper becomes easier with an indorsement.

The indorsement must be placed on the instrument itself or on a paper so firmly affixed to it that it becomes a part thereof. The indorsement paper that is annexed is called an *allonge*. The indorsement must be made by the holder or by someone who has the authority to do so on behalf of the holder [3-202(2)]. If the payee is a corporation, an officer will indorse on its behalf. The indorsement should include the corporate name, but this is not actually required.

The indorsement, to be effective as a negotiation, must convey the entire instrument or any unpaid balance due on the instrument. If it purports to indorse less than the entire instrument, it will be effective only as a partial assignment [3-202(3)]. An indorsement reading "Pay to A one-half of this instrument" would not be a negotiation, and A's position would be that of an assignee.

The indorser may add to the indorsement words of assignment, condition, waiver, guarantee, or limitation or disclaimer of liability, and the like. The indorsement is nevertheless effective to negotiate the instrument [3-202(4)]. Thus if A, the payee of a negotiable instrument, signs his name on the reverse side with the words "I hereby assign this instrument to B," he has effectively indorsed the instrument, and upon delivery to B, B is a holder.

If the name of the payee is misspelled, the payee may negotiate by indorsing either the name appearing on the instrument or in his or her true name, or both. A person who pays the instrument or gives value for it may require that both names be indorsed [3-203]. The desirable practice is to indorse in both names when the name of the payee is misspelled.

Instruments payable to multiple parties must be indorsed by all parties to negotiate the instrument. If authorized, one party may sign for the other. A bank may supply missing indorsements for its depositors. If there is a joint account, it may add the indorsement of either party or both in the event an item is payable to both. Note the significance of this right for banks in the following case.

CASE

Beyer v. First Nat. Bank of Dillon
612 P.2d 1285 (Mont. 1980)

Fred Beyer and his wife Peggy Beyer opened a joint account at the defendant bank. Both deposited checks to the account and wrote checks on it. As a part of a settlement with an insurance company, they received a check payable to "Fred Beyer and Peggy Beyer." It was deposited to the joint account without indorsement. The bank negotiated the check after a bank employee stamped the check with the following indorsement:

Deposited to the account of the within named payee in accordance with payee's instruction. Absence of the indorsement guaranteed by the First National Bank of Dillon, Montana.

The Beyers had marital difficulties, and Peggy took all of the money out of the account. Fred sued the bank for the funds, alleging that it was liable to him for the check because he had not indorsed it.

The trial court held for the bank.

DALY, J.

. . . This check is governed by section 30-3-116, MCA which provides:

Instruments payable to two or more persons: An instrument payable to the order of two or more persons:
(a) *if in the alternative is payable to any one of them and may be negotiated, discharged or enforced by any of them who has possession of it;*
(b) *if not in the alternative is payable to all of them and may be negotiated, discharged, or enforced only by all of them.*

Since the check is payable only to "Fred Beyer and Peggy Beyer" together, subsection (b) applies and "both must endorse in order to negotiate the instrument, although one, of course, may be authorized to sign for the other." The mere fact that the copayees are husband and wife does not authorize one to sign for the other.:

Normally, when a check is made payable to husband and wife, it is considered to be payable to them jointly and the check must be endorsed by both of them. . . .

It is undisputed that neither Peggy Beyer nor Fred Beyer endorsed the $5,899 check and that it was deposited to Account No. 2-227-7 by Peggy Beyer and stamped with the Bank's guaranteed endorsement. As a general proposition, Courts in a number of cases have held or recognized that a cashing or collecting bank which pays a check drawn to joint payees, other than partners, without obtaining the authentic endorsement of all such payees, is liable to a nonsigning payee for the value of his interest in the check, unless the nonsigning payee has authorized or ratified such payment. . . .

Section 30-3-419(3), MCA, however, gives the depository or collecting bank a defense to a suit for conversion and limits the bank's liability where the bank acts in good faith and in accordance with reasonable commercial standards:

. . . a representative, including a depositary or collecting bank, who has in good faith and in accordance with the reasonable commercial standards applicable to the business of such representative dealt with an instrument or its proceeds on behalf of one who was not the true owner is not liable in conversion or otherwise to the true owner beyond the amount of any proceeds remaining in his hands.

Therefore, if the defendant-respondent, First National Bank of Dillon, acted in good faith and in accordance with reasonable commercial standards when it permitted Peggy Beyer to deposit the $5,899 check payable to "Fred Beyer and Peggy Beyer" in Checking Account No. 2-227-7 without the endorsement of either payee, the Bank would not be liable to Fred Beyer beyond the amount of any proceeds remaining in the Bank. Since the record indicates that neither the instrument itself nor any proceeds of it remained in the Bank at the time of suit, the Bank would not be liable at all if it acted in good faith and in accordance with reasonable commercial standards.

The Bank's good faith has not been challenged, and since the account to which the check was deposited was in fact the joint account of Fred and Peggy Beyer, as the trial court found, the Bank has complied with reasonable commercial standards.

■ *Affirmed.*

CASE CONCEPTS REVIEW

1. Why does Fred Beyer assert that the bank is liable to him for the amount of the insurance check?
2. To whom was this check made payable?
3. Who indorsed this check upon its deposit with the bank?
4. What standard of care is applicable to the bank's actions in this case? How was this standard established?

16. Types of Indorsements

The ordinary indorsements used in negotiating paper are either special or blank. If added terms condition the indorsement, it is also a restrictive indorsement, which limits the indorsee's use of the paper. Also, the indorser may *limit* or *qualify* his or her liability as an indorser by adding words such as "without recourse." This qualified indorsement has the effect of relieving the indorser of contractual liability as an indorser—that he or she will pay if the primary obligor refuses to do so. A qualified indorsement will also be a blank or a special indorsement. These indorsements are discussed in the following sections.

17. Blank Indorsements

A blank indorsement consists of the indorser's name written on the instrument. If an instrument drawn payable to order is indorsed in blank (see Figure 34–3), it becomes payable to bearer [3-204(2)]. After the blank indorsement, if it is indorsed

FIGURE 34–3 ■ Order Paper, Payable to the Order of Henry Smith. (With his blank indorsement, shown at right, the order paper becomes bearer paper, negotiable by mere delivery.)

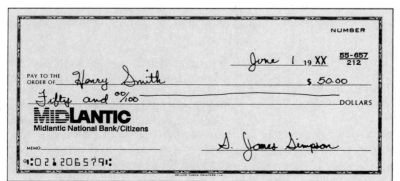
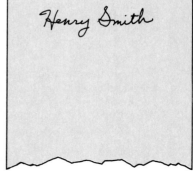

specially, it reverts to its status as order paper, and an indorsement is required for further negotiation [3-204(1)]. If a check, on its face payable to the order of Henry Smith, is indorsed "Henry Smith," it becomes bearer payable and can be negotiated by mere delivery. A thief or finder could pass title to the instrument.

18. Special Indorsements

A special indorsement specifies the person to whom or to whose order it makes the instrument payable (see Figure 34–4). When an instrument is specially indorsed, it becomes payable to the *order of* the special indorsee and requires his or her indorsement for further negotiation. Thus an indorsement "Pay to John Jones" or "Pay to the order of John Jones" is a special indorsement and requires the further indorsement by John Jones for negotiation. If a bearer instrument is indorsed specially, it requires further indorsement by the indorsee. This is true if the instrument was originally bearer paper or if it became bearer paper as the result of a blank indorsement. In other words, the last indorsement determines whether the instrument is order paper or bearer paper [3-204].

The holder of an instrument may convert a blank indorsement into a special indorsement by writing above the blank indorser's signature any contract consistent with the character of the indorsement [3-204(3)]. Thus Richard Roe, to whom an instrument has been indorsed in blank by John Doe, could write above Doe's signature, "Pay to Richard Roe." The paper would require Roe's indorsement for further negotiation.

FIGURE 34–4 ■ A Special Indorsement by Henry Smith. (For negotiation, it requires further indorsement by John Jones.)

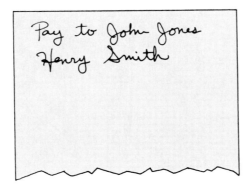

19. Restrictive Indorsements

A person who indorses an instrument may impose certain restrictions on the indorsement; that is, the indorser may protect or preserve certain rights in the paper and limit the rights of the indorsee. Of the four types of restrictive indorsement, one is conditional (for example, "Pay John Doe if Generator XK-711 arrives by June

1, 1993"). Or the indorsement may purport to prohibit further transfer of the instrument, such as "Pay to John Doe only" [3-205(a)(b)]. When a check is deposited in a bank and will be processed through bank collection, the indorsements "For collection," "For deposit only," and "Pay any bank" are restrictive [3-205(c)]. In the fourth type, the indorser stipulates that it is for the benefit or use of the indorser or some other person, such as "Pay John Doe in trust for Richard Roe" [3-205(d)].

A restrictive indorsement does not prevent further transfer or negotiation of the instrument [3-206(1)]. Thus, an instrument indorsed "Pay to John Doe only" could be negotiated by John Doe in the same manner as if it had been indorsed "Pay to John Doe."

The most common restrictive indorsement is "For deposit only" (see Figure 34–5). It is a common practice for payees of checks to use such an indorsement to safeguard checks. Once a check is stamped "For deposit only," a thief or finder of the check cannot cash it. The only action the bank can take is to deposit it into the indorser's account. If it fails to do so, it has liability to the indorser.

The effect of restrictive indorsements is substantially limited when applied to banks. An intermediary bank or a payor bank that is not a depositary bank can disregard any restrictive indorsement except that of the bank's immediate transferor. This limitation does not affect whatever rights the restrictive indorser may have against the bank of deposit or his or her right against parties outside the bank's collection process [3-206(2)]. Under a conditional indorsement or an indorsement for collection or deposit, a transferee (other than an intermediary bank) becomes a holder for value if it pays consistent with the indorsement [3-206(3)].

When the indorsement is for the benefit of the indorser or another person, such as "Pay to John Doe in trust for Richard Roe," only the first taker is required to act consistently with the restrictive indorsement [3-206(4)]. John Doe has the obligation to use the instrument or the proceeds from it for the benefit of Richard Roe. John Doe could negotiate the instrument to John Smith, who could qualify as a holder and ignore the restriction.

FIGURE 34–5 ■ A Restrictive Indorsement by Henry Smith. (Subsequent holders should be only the banks in the collection process.)

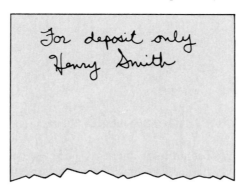

The fundamental aspects of what makes a negotiable instrument and how it is negotiated are not changed by the 1990 revision of Article 3. However, there are some important elements of the revision that are summarized here. The citations are to the Revised Article 3.

First, a note or draft containing a reference to payment being made from a particular fund or source does not destroy the unconditional nature of the promise or order [3-106(b)(ii)]. The drafters explain this change with the following comment:

> This reverses the result of former Section 3-105(2)(b). There is no cogent reason why the general credit of a legal entity must be pledged to have a negotiable instrument. Market forces determine the marketability of instruments of this kind. If potential buyers don't want promises or orders that are payable only from a particular source or fund, they won't take them, but Article 3 should apply.

Second, the phrase *sum certain* is replaced with the words *fixed amount* [3-104(a)]. Additionally, the Revised Article 3 clarifies that variable interest rates do not destroy the existence of a fixed amount [3-112(b)]. Thus, a note may still be negotiable if it contains the maker's promise to repay a fixed amount of money even though the interest to be paid is calculated based on a formula that may vary over the term of the payment.

Third, negotiability is not destroyed if the printed form of checks omits the word *order* [3-104(c)]. A check that reads "pay to Jane Doe" is negotiable and considered to be order paper. A similar exception to the requirement that the word *order* be present is not made for notes or drafts other than checks.

Fourth, a negotiable instrument may be made payable in such a way that creates confusion whether it is order or bearer paper. The original version of Article 3 presumed that order paper was preferable. The Revised Article 3 creates an opposite presumption. If the instrument says "Pay to the order of Jane Doe or bearer," it is bearer paper [3-109(a)(1) and (b)] and can be negotiated by delivery alone.

Fifth, banks are allowed to pay postdated checks even before the date written on the check [3-113(a) and 4-401(c)]. This rule is a part of the Revised Article 3 because of the reliance banks place on the mechanical processing of checks. A drawer is permitted to notify the payor bank that specific checks are postdated and require that the bank defer payment until the stated date. The effective time periods for this type of notice are the same as those periods applicable to stop payment orders (fourteen days for oral notice; six months for written notice).

Sixth, Revised Article 3 provides a definition for the term *indorsement*. The original article did not. An indorsement is defined from the perspective of its purpose in the negotiation process. An indorsement is a signature, other than that of the maker, drawer, or acceptor, that is made to (1) negotiate the instrument, (2) restrict payment of the instrument, or (3) incur the indorser's liability on the instrument [3-204(a)].

Chapter Summary

Signed Writing
1. The negotiable instrument must be signed by the maker or drawer.
2. The signature can be anything intended to authenticate the instrument, and it can be applied by mechanical means.

Promise or Order
1. A note must contain a promise, and a draft must contain an order.

Unconditional Promise or Order
1. The promise or order must be unconditional. A promise is conditional if reference to some other document is required or the instrument is subject to the terms of another document.
2. A recital of consideration does not destroy negotiability.

Particular Fund Concept
1. A promise that is limited to a particular fund is conditional, and the instrument is not negotiable.
2. Exceptions to the particular fund concept involve instruments specifying an account to be debited and instruments issued by governmental units, partnerships, or unincorporated associations.

Sum Certain in Money
1. The unconditional promise or order must involve a sum certain in money.
2. Money is any currency adopted by a government.
3. A sum certain is present if the amount of money involved can be calculated from the information contained on the face of the instrument.

Certain Time of Payment
1. An instrument to be negotiable must be payable on demand or at a definite time.
2. An instrument is payable on demand when no time of payment is stated.

Acceleration and Extension Clauses
1. An acceleration clause that changes the maturity date does not destroy negotiability.
2. An extension clause that extends the time of payment at the option of the maker or acceptor without specifying the time of ultimate payment destroys negotiability.
3. An extension clause exercised by the holder does not destroy negotiability.

Order Paper
1. To be negotiable, a note must be payable to the order of some person or to bearer. A note or check that is simply payable to a specified person is nonnegotiable.
2. An instrument payable to the order of two people must be indorsed by both.
3. An instrument payable to an estate, trust, or fund may be indorsed by the appropriate representative.

Bearer Paper
1. Bearer paper may be negotiated without indorsement by delivery.
2. An instrument is bearer paper if it specifies that it is payable to bearer or to cash.
3. Bearer paper may be negotiated by a finder or thief, and anyone in possession of it is entitled to collect.

Terms and Omissions Not Affecting Negotiability
1. Many terms do not affect negotiation. For example, a statement acknowledging satisfaction of an obligation on a check does not destroy negotiability.
2. An undated instrument is nevertheless negotiable as is a postdated instrument.

Incomplete Instruments
1. An incomplete instrument cannot be enforced until it is completed.
2. Instruments may be completed as authorized or unauthorized. Unauthorized completion is a personal defense that cannot be asserted against a holder in due course.

Ambiguous Terms and Rules of Construction

1. Handwritten terms prevail over typewritten terms or printed terms, and typewritten terms control printed terms.
2. If there is a conflict between words and figures, the words control.
3. If an instrument provides for interest without stating the rate, the rate on judgments will be followed.

TRANSFER OF COMMERCIAL PAPER

Negotiation

1. The term *negotiation* is used to describe the method of transferring a negotiable instrument in a manner that makes the transferee a holder.
2. A transfer that is not a proper negotiation is an assignment, and the assignee has the same rights as the assignor.
3. For proper negotiation, the whole instrument must be negotiated.
4. Bearer paper is negotiated by delivery. Order paper requires indorsement and delivery.

Blank Indorsements

1. A blank indorsement consists of the indorser's name, usually written on the back of the instrument.
2. A blank indorsement converts order paper to bearer paper.

Special Indorsements

1. Special indorsements indicate the person to whom the instrument is payable. Special indorsements require the indorsement of such person for further negotiation.

Restrictive Indorsements

1. Restrictive indorsements allow the indorser to preserve rights and limit the options of the indorsee.
2. The most common restrictive indorsement is "for deposit only." This means that the bank may not cash the check but must deposit the proceeds into the account of the indorser.
3. A restrictive indorsement when applied to banks does not prevent further negotiation and is applicable only to the immediate indorsee.

REVIEW QUESTIONS AND PROBLEMS

1. Match each term in column A with the appropriate statement in column B.

A	B
(1) IOU	(a) Varying exchange rates have no impact
(2) Particular fund concept	(b) A statement of the transaction out of which the instrument arose
(3) Sum certain in money	(c) Requires good faith in its execution
(4) Restrictive indorsement	(d) Without recourse
(5) Negotiability unaffected	(e) Not a promise
(6) Acceleration clause	(f) Does not destroy negotiability if a governmental unit is the maker or drawer
(7) Extension clause	(g) May or may not destroy negotiability
(8) Blank indorsement	(h) For deposit only
(9) Qualified indorsement	(i) Pay to John Jones./s/Paul Pringle
(10) Special indorsement	(j) A signature

2. Comment briefly on the provisions described in these instruments as to their bearing on negotiability. In each instance, the other portions of the instrument are in proper form.

   a. A bill of exchange drawn by Y on Z directs Z to pay $1,000 to the order of A and charge this amount to Y's "Book Fund."

b. The XYZ Company (a partnership) signed a note promising to pay $1,000 and bearing the notation "limited to payment out of the entire assets of the maker."

c. X signed a note promising to pay $5,000 or deliver 100 barrels of oil at the option of the holder.

d. One of the notes is payable "five days after the death of the maker."

e. A note containing the following notation: "with interest at bank rates."

3. Mary executed a note and a purchase money mortgage to Al. Al negotiated the note to Tiger Bank. The note contained the following stipulation: "This note with interest is secured by a mortgage on real estate, of even date herewith, made by the maker hereof in favor of the said payee. The terms of said mortgage are by this reference made a part hereof." Is the note negotiable? Explain.

4. Skyblast Freight executed a note that contained the following provisions: "This note is payable only from the proceeds of the sale of the Skyblast Freight Building." Is the note negotiable? Why or why not?

5. To finance construction of a public golf course, Sarpy County sold short-term, interest-bearing notes. The notes stated that they were "to be paid from funds gathered by property tax collections." When the company hired to build the golf course went out of business, the golf course project was abandoned. Holders of the notes sued the county. The county defended, claiming that the notes were nonnegotiable because they were payable out of a particular fund. The county further contended that since the notes were nonnegotiable, the holders took the notes subject to the defense of failure of consideration, since the golf course was not completed. Plaintiffs contend that the notes were negotiable and that they took the notes free of the defense of failure of consideration. Are notes issued by a governmental unit payable only out of a particular fund negotiable? Explain.

6. Employer gave Pension Fund and Company a note stating that Employer promises to pay Pension Fund Company "all current contributions as they become due under the collective bargaining agreement in addition to the sum of $15,606.44 with interest." Is this note negotiable? Why or why not?

7. Horace Brace has in his possession the following instrument:

November 1, 1992

I, Walter Forgel, hereby promise to pay Charles Smidlap ONE THOUSAND DOLLARS ($1,000.00) one year after date. This instrument was given for the purchase of FIVE HUNDRED (500) shares of Beefstake Mining Corporation. Interest at 10 percent.

Walter Forgel (Signature)

Horace Brace purchased the instrument from Charles Smidlap at a substantial discount. Smidlap specializes in the sale of counterfeit mining stock. Walter Forgel is one of his innocent victims. What are the rights of Brace against Forgel on the instrument? Explain.

8. Roberts was a holder in due course of a properly drawn check payable to "Bearer." He indorsed the check as follows:

Pay to the order of Wilson Hall without recourse.
/s/Peter Roberts

What type of indorsement did Roberts make? If Hall wishes to negotiate the instrument, what is required? Explain.

9. Casey held a negotiable instrument payable to his order. He transferred the instrument to Dale for value. At the time of transfer, Casey failed to indorse his name on the back of the instrument, and Dale accepted the instrument as given to him. What rights does Dale have on the instrument? Explain.

10. A caterer, holder of a check, wishes to protect herself against its loss or theft. It has been indorsed to her in blank. Describe two methods by which she may gain this protection. Explain.

11. Quincy signed a promissory note payable to the order of Unger, who indorsed the note in blank over to Pritchard. Pritchard then transferred the note to Truax by delivery. Is Truax a holder of the instrument? Why or why not?

12. Bob issued a check payable to the order of Gary, who lost it without indorsing it. Can a finder of the check negotiate it? Why or why not?

35 HOLDERS IN DUE COURSE AND DEFENSES

CHAPTER PREVIEW

*T*he questions introduced in chapter 34, which summarize the requirements to create commercial paper free of the defenses that arise from an underlying contract, are worthy of being repeated:

1. Does the paper meet the prerequisites of a negotiable instrument?
2. Has the negotiable instrument been properly negotiated?
3. Is the holder of the instrument in due course?
4. Are the defenses personal as opposed to real?

In the preceding chapter, the first two questions were examined and answered. This chapter considers questions 3 and 4 on holders in due course and on the types of defense.

You are the senior loan officer of your bank. Among your many customers is a mobile home dealer, whose inventory your bank finances. This dealer typically takes promissory notes from its customers. The dealer then indorses these notes to your bank as partial payment for its debt. A dissatisfied customer of the dealer refuses to pay your bank until the defects with the mobile home are corrected.

Can you successfully sue this dissatisfied customer of the mobile home dealer to collect on the note? What should you do?

STATUS OF THIRD PARTIES

The original party to whom an instrument is issued or drawn has the right to transfer the instrument to someone else. The party to whom it is transferred may be an *assignee*, a *holder*, or a *holder in due course*.

Assignee A third party who receives the right to have a contract performed. This party is viewed as "standing in the shoes" of the assignor. The assignee is not free from the defenses that could be asserted against the assignor's claim of performance. (See chapter 17 for a review of assignments.)

ASSIGNEE. A third party becomes an **assignee** of an instrument in one of two situations. First, if the instrument being transferred does not satisfy the elements of being negotiable, the third party receiving the instrument is an assignee. Second, if the instrument being transferred is negotiable but is not properly negotiated, the third party receiving the instrument is once again an assignee. As an assignee, the third party is subject to all the defenses that could have been asserted against the assignor had that party sought collection of the instrument.

HOLDER. If a negotiable instrument is properly negotiated, the party receiving it is a **holder.** If certain requirements are met, the holder may qualify as a **holder in due course** and have a special status [3-302]. If a holder does not qualify as a holder in due course, his or her position is equivalent to that of an assignee, and any defense available to the original parties may be asserted against the holder.

Holder The party to whom a negotiable instrument is issued or properly negotiated. The status as a holder is technically satisfied irrespective of the holder's actions or knowledge.

Either the original payee or a third party may qualify as a holder of an instrument and may transfer or negotiate it. A holder may legally discharge the instrument or enforce payment in his or her own name [3-301]. A thief or finder may qualify as a holder of a bearer instrument. As we will see later, a thief or finder cannot qualify as a holder in due course because he or she gave no value for the instrument.

The following case provides a further explanation of this status as a holder. Note in this case that the payees of a note are considered as the holders of the note, the parties who can discharge the makers' liability.

CASE

Edwards v. Mesch
763 P.2d 1169 (N.M. 1988)

SCARBOROUGH, C. J.

Defendants-appellants, Robert J. and Florence M. Mesch (Meshes), executed a promissory note in favor of plaintiffs-appellees, John E. and Jean M. Edwards (Edwards), as payees on March 14, 1986. The promissory note for the amount of $6,000.00 with interest at the rate of 10% per annum on the balance was for money the Edwards had loaned to the Meshes. The Meshes subsequently defaulted on the note after making a single payment, and the Edwards brought suit to collect all unpaid principal and accrued interest. After a trial on the merits on November 11, 1987, the district court entered judgment for the Edwards in the sum of $6,751.10, with interest on the principal balance accruing at the rate of 10% per annum, and awarded attorney's fees and costs to the Edwards. . . .

On appeal the Meshes argue that the Edwards have no enforceable rights in the note and were not the real party in interest at the time of the trial. During the trial the Edwards did not deny assigning their interests in the note to the Tres Santos Corp., a closely held corporation, 100% of whose shares are owned by plaintiff-appellee, John E. Edwards. The Meshes argued at trial, and again on appeal, that since the Edwards assigned their interests in the note to the Tres Santos Corp., it became the real party in interest, and thus an indispensable party to the lawsuit. This argument finds no support in legal authority.

The promissory note which the Meshes executed to the Edwards is a negotiable instrument, and as such is governed by the Uniform Commercial Code (UCC). According to the UCC, a "holder" of a negotiable instrument is "a person who is in possession of *** an instrument *** drawn, issued or indorsed to him or to his order or to bearer or in blank." NMSA 1978, § 55-1-201(20). Before a person can become a "holder", two conditions must be satisfied—(1) the obligation evidenced by the instrument must run to him and (2) he must have possession of the instrument. A negotiable instrument payee (the Edwards) is always a holder if the payee has the instrument in his possession because the payee is the person to whom the instrument was issued. "It is inherent in the character of negotiable paper that any person in possession of an instrument which by its terms runs to him is a holder, and that anyone may deal with him as a holder." NMSA 1978, § 55-3-207 Official Comment 2. . . .

The Edwards were payees and holders of the note and could enforce payment of the note after they had assigned it to the Tres Santos Corp. "The holder of an instrument *whether or not he is the owner* may *** enforce payment in his own name." NMSA 1978, § 55-3-301 (emphasis added). The Meshes' argument on appeal that the district court ruling exposes them to double liability is without merit. "The liability of any party is discharged to the extent of his payment or satisfaction to the holder even though it is made with knowledge of a claim of another person to the instrument ***." NMSA 1978, § 55-3-603(1). . . .

Rule 1-017 of Civil Procedure for the District Courts requires that "[e]very action shall be prosecuted in the name of the real party in interest ***. The capacity of an individual *** to sue or be sued shall be determined by the law of this state." This court has held that the test for determining who is the real party in interest is whether one is the owner of the right being enforced and is in a position to discharge the defendant from the liability being asserted in the suit. The Edwards in the instant case were the holders and payees on the promissory note and properly asserted their rights as plaintiffs at trial. . . . Furthermore, the Edwards were in a position at trial to discharge the Meshes from all liabilities to any third party from the promissory note. Therefore, the arguments that the Tres Santos Corp. was the real party in interest and an indispensable party at trial are without merit.

A review of the record below reveals the district judge expended commendable effort to explain the governing principles of law and his rulings in the instant case to the Meshes. We uphold the decision of the district court, and further hold that since the promissory note provides for costs and attorney's fees to payees for collection and enforcement of the note, the Edwards are entitled to recover reasonable attorney's fees on appeal. . . .

■ *Affirmed.*

CASE CONCEPTS REVIEW

1. Who are the makers of the promissory note? Who are the payees?
2. What procedural defense did the Meshes assert when the Edwards sued to collect payment?
3. How does the court describe the transfer of the note by Edwards to Tres Santos Corp.?
4. Should this case have been decided differently if the Edwards had negotiated the note to Tres Santos Corp. rather than merely having assigned their interest in the note?

Holder in due course
A party who is a holder of a negotiable instrument and who takes it for value, in good faith, and without notice of defenses. This party is free from the personal defenses on the contract that give rise to the commercial paper.

HOLDER IN DUE COURSE.   If there is no claim or defense to the instrument, it is immaterial whether the party seeking to enforce it is a holder or a holder in due course. The Code makes all holders the functional equivalent of holders in due course until a defense is claimed. The burden of proving a defense is on the party asserting it. When the defense is proved, the holder has the burden of proving that he or she is a holder in due course [3-307(3)]. If the holder can prove that, he or she can enforce payment, notwithstanding the presence of a personal defense to the instrument. (Later in this chapter we discuss both types of defenses: personal and real.) A holder in due course will not be able to enforce the instrument in the event that a real defense is proven. The preferred status of a holder in due course exists only where the defense to the instrument is a personal defense.

Issues as to whether or not a party is a holder in due course usually arise when the party seeks to collect on the instrument. But occasionally a party is sued on a negligence theory for losses incurred in transactions involving an instrument. To avoid liability, the defendant must establish that he or she is or was a holder in due course. Thus a holder in due course is free of claims and is not subject to personal defenses.

CONTRACT PROVISIONS.   Contract provisions frequently attempt to give a status equivalent to a holder in due course to an assignee of contract. These provisions purport to waive defenses if the contract is assigned. Some states have declared such provisions to be illegal as against public policy if the drawer or maker is a consumer. Other states have enforced waiver of defense clauses provided the assignee meets the requirements to qualify as a holder in due course and the defense waived is a personal defense. Thus the material in this chapter is significant for many non-negotiable contracts as well as negotiable instruments.

HOLDER IN DUE COURSE

1. Requirements

To qualify as a holder in due course, a holder must meet three basic requirements. He or she must take the instrument (1) for value, (2) in good faith, and (3) without notice that it is overdue, that it has been dishonored, or that any other person has a claim to it or defense against it [3-302(1)].

A payee may be a holder in due course if all the requirements are met. Most payees deal with the maker or drawer. However, a payee may be a holder in due course when the instrument is not delivered to the payee by the maker but is delivered by an intermediary or agent of the maker. A payee that participates in the transaction out of which the instrument arises cannot be a holder in due course.

When an instrument is acquired in a manner other than through the usual channels of negotiation or transfer, the holder will not be a holder in due course. Thus, if an instrument is obtained by an executor in taking over an estate, is purchased at a judicial sale, is obtained through legal process by an attaching creditor, or is acquired as a transaction not in the regular course of business, the party acquiring it is not a holder in due course [3-302(3)].

2. Value

A holder must have given *value* for an instrument to qualify as a holder in due course. A person to whom an instrument was transferred as a gift would not qualify as a holder in due course. *Value* does not have the same meaning as *consideration* in the law of contracts. A mere promise is consideration, but it is not value. As long as a promise is executory, the value requirement to be a holder in due course has not been met [3-303].

While a mere promise is not value, if the promise to pay is negotiable in form, it does constitute value [3-303(c)]. A drawer who issues a check in payment for a negotiable note that he or she is purchasing from the holder becomes a holder for value even before the check is cashed. A bank that cashes a check has given value, as the following case provides.

CASE

Trail Leasing, Inc. v. Drovers First American Bank
447 N.W.2d 190 (Minn. 1989)

SIMONETT, J.

... Plaintiff-respondent Trail Leasing, Inc., sues defendant-appellant Drovers First American Bank. Trail Leasing alleges Drovers negligently cashed certain checks drawn on plaintiff's checking account at Drovers. The facts are stipulated.

Over a period of about 2 1/2 years, Pamela Haas, employed as an assistant bookkeeper by Trail Leasing, embezzled funds from her employer. Haas had access to the check blanks for Trail Leasing's commercial account at Drovers. On April 11, 1983, she wrote out a check for $328.20 payable to Drovers First American State Bank. She then had two of Trail Leasing's authorized officers sign the check. (Three of Trail Leasing's officers were authorized by resolution to sign checks and this authorization was on file with the bank. Haas was not one of the three.) Haas went to Drovers and asked for cash for the check. She filled out and gave to the bank a "change order form," a form used by a bank's customers specifying the coins and bill denominations in which they wish to take cash for business operations. Haas did not endorse the check. Drovers paid the cash to Haas, who pocketed the money.

From April 11, 1983, to October 1985, every few weeks, Haas would repeat this transaction, the amounts of the checks varying from $67.97 to as much as $1,156.43, always, it seems, in some odd amount and always payable to the Drovers bank. By the time her scheme was discovered (through a discrepancy in one of the change orders), Haas had negotiated 55 checks for a total of $39,952.17. The stipulation of facts does not disclose how Haas was able to get the authorized officers of her company to sign the checks, nor how her scheme was able to evade whatever internal controls her employer might have had. The checks contained no notations as to their purpose....

Drovers did not participate in or know of the embezzlement scheme, and the parties stipulated that Drovers did not have notice of facts from which it could be inferred that Haas was acting contrary to her employer's interests. Drovers never contacted Trail Leasing to determine if Haas had authority to receive cash for these checks she brought to the bank. As already mentioned, Haas was not authorized by her employer to sign checks....

The trial court granted Drovers summary judgment, ruling that the bank was a holder in due course as a matter of law and, therefore, took the Haas checks free from all claims.

The court of appeals ... reversed ..., ruling that Drovers was not a holder in due course because "Drovers did not take the instrument for value." Rather, "Haas was simply withdrawing money from Trail Leasing's commercial account." ... We granted Drovers' petition for further review.... The dispositive issue before us ... is whether Drovers is a holder in due course.

The issue may be further narrowed. Under Minn. Stat. § 336.3-302 (1988), a holder in due course is anyone who takes the instrument "(a) for value; and (b) in good faith; and (c) without notice that it is overdue or has been dishonored or of any defense against or claim to it on the part of any person." Here it has been stipulated that Drovers took the Haas checks in good faith and without notice of any claims. The issue then becomes, as it did for the appeals panel, whether Drovers meets the third requirement of taking the checks "for value." This, too, is the issue raised in the petition for further review by Drovers.

We conclude that Drovers took the Haas checks "for value" and, therefore, was a holder in due course.

"A holder takes the instrument for value," says Minn. Stat. § 336.3-303(a), "to the extent that the agreed consideration has been performed or that he acquires a security interest in or lien on the instrument otherwise than by legal process." This provision eliminated a conflict in prior law by making clear that merely a promise to the transferor is not value until the promise has been performed. Here Drovers performed; it paid cash for the checks. Trail Leasing argues that at best Drovers gave only "conditional value" because it retained and exercised the right to debit Trail Leasing's commercial account. But even so, the bank first had to pay out its money before debiting Trail Leasing's account. As the comment to § 336.3-303 says, "Where an agreed sum of money is actually paid for an instrument *** the instrument is clearly taken 'for value' ***."

. . . The trial court's summary judgment in favor of the bank is reinstated.

■ *Reversed.*

CASE CONCEPTS REVIEW

1. How did Haas embezzle approximately $40,000 from Trail Leasing?
2. To whom were the checks that Haas used in her scheme made payable?
3. After Drovers Bank cashed checks and debited Trail Leasing's account, what was the basis of Trail Leasing's argument that the account should be recredited?
4. Drovers Bank claims to be a holder in due course free from Trail Leasing's argument or defense that it should have these checks paid from its account. How does Trail Leasing attempt to defeat the bank's holder-in-due-course status?
5. Why does the court find that the bank has given value?

A holder who takes an instrument in payment of an existing debt is a holder for value [3-303(b)]. Thus, if Ada owed Brenda $500 on a past-due account and transferred a negotiable instrument to Brenda in payment of such account, Brenda would qualify as a holder for value. The same holds true if the instrument is received as collateral for an existing debt, whether the debt is due or not.

A purchaser of a limited interest in paper can be a holder in due course only to the extent of the interest purchased [3-302(4)]. If a negotiable instrument is transferred as collateral for a loan, the transferee may be a holder in due course, but only to the extent of the debt that is secured by the pledge of the instrument. For example, George loans Gerry $2,500. To secure the loan, Gerry negotiates Ron's note in the amount of $4,000 to George. George is a holder in due course only to the extent of $2,500.

A person who purchases an instrument for less than its *face value* can be a holder in due course to the full amount of the instrument. Cora is the payee of a note for $1,000. She may discount the note and indorse it to Wick for $800. Wick has nevertheless paid value and is entitled to collect the full $1,000.

3. Good Faith

A holder must take the instrument in good faith to qualify as a holder in due course [3-302(1)]. *Good faith* is defined as "honesty in fact in the conduct or transaction concerned" [1-201(19)]. If a person takes an instrument under circumstances that clearly establish that there is a defense to the instrument, this person does not take it in good faith. Failure to follow accepted business practices or to act reasonably by commercial standards, however, does not establish lack of good faith. Good faith is a subjective rather than an objective determination. Honesty rather than diligence or negligence is the issue.

Taking a note on large discount does not in and of itself establish lack of good faith. A large discount may result from factors other than the existence of a defense to the instrument. The burden is on the party seeking to deny the holder-in-due-course status to prove lack of good faith. Good faith is presumed in the absence of facts to show bad faith.

4. Without Notice

Notice A person has "notice" of a fact when he or she (a) has actual knowledge of it; or (b) has received a notice or notification of it; or (c) has reason to know that it exists based on all the facts and circumstances known at the time in question.

Closely related to good faith is the requirement that the transferee must not have **notice** of any claim or defense to the instrument, that it is overdue, or that it has been dishonored [3-304]. A person has notice of a fact if he or she has actual knowledge of it, has received notification of it, or (from the facts and circumstances known to him or her) has "reason to know" that it exists [1-201(25)]. The law generally provides that a person has reason to know a fact if his or her information would indicate its existence to a person of ordinary intelligence (or of the intelligence of the person involved, if that is above the ordinary). A person also has reason to know the facts if they are so highly probable that a person exercising reasonable care will assume their existence. The following case illustrates these basic elements of the no-notice requirement for a holder to be in due course.

CASE

First National Bank in Lenox v. Creston Livestock Auction, Inc.
447 N.W.2d 132 (Ia. 1989)

HARRIS, J.

The controlling question is whether a bank's endorsement on a check affected the bank's status as a holder in due course. We agree with the trial court's determination that it did not.

Jerry Parker, a Union County farmer, had dealings with two banks. He first obtained a loan from the First National Bank in Lenox, Iowa (Lenox Bank). Lenox Bank took a security interest in all of Parker's livestock and livestock proceeds. Parker later obtained another loan from the First National Bank in Creston (Creston Bank) and that bank also took a security interest in Parker's livestock and livestock proceeds.

Sometime later Parker sold steers to Creston Livestock Auction, Inc. (Creston Livestock). There is no dispute that Lenox Bank held a perfected security interest in the steers at the time and had mailed notice of this fact to Creston Livestock.

Creston Livestock nevertheless paid for the steers by delivering to Parker a check made payable to Parker and Creston Bank. The back of the check contained the following language:

> . . . By endorsing this check the payee represents and warrants to the purchasers of said property that he is the sole owner thereof, and that said property is free and clear of all liens whatsoever. . . .

Parker endorsed the check and turned it over to Creston Bank in satisfaction of his indebtedness to it. Creston Bank endorsed the check, unaware of Lenox Bank's prior perfected security interest.

Lenox Bank brought a conversion action against Creston Livestock, claiming it was entitled to the funds received by Creston Livestock. Creston Livestock paid the amount of the check to Lenox Bank in settlement, then brought this cross-petition against Creston Bank for contribution.

The trial court determined that Creston Bank was a holder in due course. . . .

This determination is controlling of the question in the case because, if Creston Bank was the holder in due course, it held the check free and clear of the claims of Lenox Bank. If Creston Bank was not a holder in due course it held the check subject to all claims and defenses.

The Iowa Code defines a "holder in due course" as follows:

1. A holder in due course is a holder who takes the instrument
   (a) for value; and
   (b) in good faith; and
   (c) without notice that it is overdue or had been dishonored or of any defense against or claim to it on the part of any person.

Creston Livestock does not dispute Creston Bank's claim that it received the check for value, leaving only the questions of good faith and notice.

Notice and good faith, which are often interrelated, have been called "first cousins." There is a certain confusion concerning whether the tests of notice and of good faith are to be objective or subjective. We think the test for good faith is subjective. The test for notice is essentially objective. It is somewhat rare but entirely possible for a payee to be a holder in due course. It is somewhat unusual because a payee ordinarily has been involved in the transaction which gave rise to the check and hence will most often have actual knowledge of claims or defects in it. But it is participation in the transaction out of which the instrument arose, rather than the taking of the instrument, which precludes holder-in-due-course status. Creston Bank did not participate in the sale of the steers at the livestock auction. Its status as copayee does not prevent it from being a holder in due course.

In challenging the trial court findings, Creston Livestock points to the quoted language of the back of the check. It contends Creston Bank cannot be a holder in due course after endorsing the check as copayee, in view of the warranty that the livestock was "free and clear of all liens." The argument is that this endorsement is an acknowledgement of notice of Lenox Bank's claims. . . . It is agreed that Creston Bank had no actual knowledge of any claims against the check, and there is no assertion it received any notification of it. . . .

Under the Uniform Commercial Code "notice" has a specific statutory meaning:

> A person has "*notice*" of a fact when
> **a.** the person has actual knowledge of it; or
> **b.** the person has received a notice or notification of it; or
> **c.** from all the facts and circumstances known to the person at the time in question the person has reason to know that it exists. A person "knows" or has "knowledge" of the fact when that person has actual knowledge of it. "Discover" or "learn" or a word or phrase of similar import refers to knowledge rather than to reason to know. . . .

Creston Bank argues that it cannot be associated with the words on the back of the check, that the words themselves show they were intended for indorsement only by Parker, the farmer who sold the steers. . . .

Notwithstanding the livestock company's contention to the contrary, notice does not appear by way of a concession made by the bank in the indorsement on the back of the check. As the trial court pointed out, the language relied on expressly contradicts, rather than acknowledges, knowledge of any claim against or defect in the check. Even if the quoted language on the check can be ascribed to the bank, there is nothing in it which hints that Creston Bank had reason to know of Lenox Bank's claim.

We also agree with the trial court's findings that Creston Bank took the check in good faith. Good faith is "honesty in fact in the conduct or transaction concerned." The parties stipulated that when Creston Bank took the check it had "no actual knowledge of the Lenox Bank's security interest in Parker's livestock or the proceeds thereof." The record is devoid of any hint that Creston Bank considered the transaction as anything other than the routine collection of any honest debt.

We conclude that Creston Bank was a holder in due course. This being true, its rights do not yield to those of Lenox Bank's earlier perfected security interest. Creston Bank took the check free of the claims of Lenox Bank.

■ *Affirmed.*

CASE CONCEPTS REVIEW

1. What financial transaction did Jerry Parker conduct with the Lenox Bank?
2. Why is Creston Livestock writing a check payable to Parker and the Creston Bank?
3. Why did the Lenox Bank sue Creston Livestock? Why did Creston Livestock settle Lenox Bank's claim? Why did Creston Livestock then sue the Creston Bank?
4. Creston Bank asserts that it is a holder in due course of the check payable to it. What is the argument offered by Creston Livestock to defeat the holder-in-due-course status of Creston Bank?
5. What does the court conclude with respect to the application of the holder-in-due-course status? Why does the court reach this conclusion?

If there is visible evidence of forgery or alteration, a purchaser is put on notice of a claim or defense [3-304(1)(a)]. Certain irregularities on the face of an instrument also put a purchaser on notice that there may be a claim or defense to the instrument. Many are obvious, such as a signature that is obviously affixed by someone else.

If an instrument is incomplete in some important respect at the time it is purchased, notice is imparted [3-304(1)(a)]. Blanks in an instrument that do not relate to material terms do not give notice of a claim or defense; but if the purchaser has notice that the completion was improper, he or she is not a holder in due course [3-304(4)(d)].

Knowledge that a defense exists or that the instrument has been dishonored prohibits the status of a holder in due course. In some situations, knowledge of certain facts does *not*, of itself, give the purchaser notice of a defense or claim. Awareness that an instrument is antedated or postdated does not prevent a holder from taking in due course [3-304(4)(a)]. Knowledge of a separate contract is not notice. Although a defense will arise if the contract is not performed, such knowledge does not prevent one from becoming a holder in due course. Of course, if the purchaser is aware that the contract has been breached or repudiated, he or she will not qualify as a holder in due course.

Actual notice to prevent a party from being holder in due course must be received at a time and in a way that will give a reasonable opportunity to act on it [3-304(6)]. A notice received by the president of a bank one minute before the bank's teller cashes a check is not effective in preventing the bank from becoming a holder in due course.

5. Before Overdue

To be a holder in due course, a purchaser of an instrument must take it without notice that it is overdue [3-304(1)(c)]. A purchaser of overdue paper is charged with knowledge that some defense may exist. A purchaser has notice that an instrument is overdue if he or she has reason to know that any part of the principal amount is overdue [3-304(3)(a)]. Past-due interest does not impart notice to the holder [3-304(4)(f)]. The instrument itself will usually indicate if it is past due, as in the following case.

CASE

Richardson v. Girner
668 S.W.2d 523 (Ark. 1984)

Girner executed a $5,000 promissory note to First Realty Corporation on September 25, 1980. Monthly payments on the note were to commence on January 15, 1981. A schedule was printed on the back of the note. The note was assigned by First Realty to Imran Bohra in exchange for property. On July 27, 1981, Bohra transferred the note to his attorney, F. Eugene Richardson, in payment for legal services rendered by Richardson. At that time, there was no entry of any payment on the back of the note. Girner had claims against Bohra far in excess of the amount of the note. The trial court found for the defendant, and plaintiff appeals.

PURTLE, J.

... The trial court held that the appellant was not a holder in due course and took the note by assignment subject to the defense of set-off by the makers against an intervening assignee. . . .

The primary issue before us is whether appellant took the note without notice that it was overdue or was otherwise subject to defense on the part of any holder prior to appellant. Arkansas Stat. Ann. §85-3-302 defines a holder in due course to be one who in good faith takes an instrument for value and without notice that it is overdue or has been dishonored or is subject to any defense against or claim to it on the part of any person. The facts in this case clearly reveal that at the time appellant acquired the note no payments had been entered in the schedule on the back of the note. Six payments should have been made at the time of the transfer to appellant. Appellant found out during the meeting with Bohra, at the time of the assignment, that the note was past due. Appellant argues that the note was not declared to be in default until after he contacted the maker. It is not necessary to have the holder of the note declare that it is in default when this fact is obvious in other ways. Unless a person is a holder in due course the note is subject to all valid claims to it on the part of any person, and all defenses, counterclaims and set-offs.

According to Ark. Stat. Ann. §85-3-201(1) (Add. 1961), transfer of an instrument vests in the transferee such rights as a transferor possesses. In the present case Bohra knew that the Girners had claims against him far in excess of the amount of the note here in question. From the record there is an indication that Bohra had been told by the Girners, prior to assignment of the note to Richardson, that he should consider the note paid. He was given credit in the amount of the note by the Girners on their claim against him.

In view of the fact that appellant had notice that payments on the note were overdue at the time he took the note, he was not a holder in due course. Therefore, the note was subject to the defense by the Girners against Bohra. . . . It was proper for the court to . . . dismiss appellant's claim.

■ *Affirmed.*

CASE CONCEPTS REVIEW

1. Who is the maker of this promissory note? Who is the payee?

2. Which additional parties have been holders of this note?

3. What defense does Girner assert when Richardson seeks to collect payment?

4. Why does the court find that Richardson is not a holder in due course?

5. Although Richardson cannot recover from Girner, does Richardson have any claim against his transferor, Imran Bohra?

With respect to the holder having notice that the instrument is overdue, demand paper poses a special problem. This type of instrument does not have a fixed date of maturity. Purchasers of demand paper cannot be holders in due course if they have reason to know that they are taking it after a demand has been made, or if they take it more than a reasonable length of time after its issue [3-304(3)(c)]. What is a reasonable or an unreasonable time is determined on the basis of a number of factors—the kind of instrument, the customs and usages of the trade or business, and the particular facts and circumstances involved. In the case of a check, a reasonable time is presumed to be thirty days [3-304(3)(c)]. The thirty-day period is a presumption rather than an absolute rule.

6. Holder from a Holder in Due Course

A transferee may have the rights of a holder in due course, even though he or she personally does not meet all the requirements. Because a transferee obtains all the rights that the transferor had, a person who derives title through a holder in due course also has those rights. Code Section 3-201(1) states this principle, the *shelter provision,* which advances the marketability of commercial paper.

The main significance of the shelter provision is that it permits one who is not a holder in due course to share the shelter from claims and defenses enjoyed by the holder in due course from whom he or she got the instrument.

EXAMPLE Paul fraudulently induces Mary to execute and deliver a note to him. Paul then negotiates the note to Tom, who qualifies as a holder in due course. Tom makes a gift of the note to Al, who sells it to Bob, a friend of Paul's, who knew of Paul's fraud. Bob sells it to Carl after maturity. Is Carl a holder in due course? No. Were Bob and Al holders in due course when they owned the instrument? No. Is Carl subject to Mary's defense? No. While Al, Bob, and Carl are not and were not holders in due course, they have the rights of a holder in due course. They have Tom's rights and are free of the personal defense. Mary's defense was cut off by Tom's status as a holder in due course. (See Figure 35–1.)

FIGURE 35-1 ■ Example for Shelter Provision

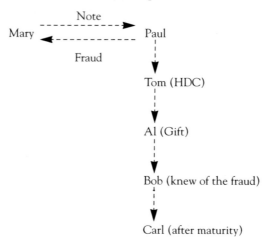

The shelter provision is subject to a limitation. A person who formerly held the paper cannot improve his or her position by later reacquiring it from a holder in due course. If a former holder was a party to any fraud or illegality affecting the instrument, or had notice of a defense or claim against it as a prior holder, he or she cannot claim the rights of a holder in due course by taking from a later holder in due course.

DEFENSES

7. Classifications

A holder in due course takes commercial paper free from the *personal defenses* of the parties to the paper [3-305]. One who is not a holder in due course or who does not have the rights of one under the shelter provision is subject to such defenses. All transferees, including holders in due course, are subject to what are referred to as *real defenses*.

In general, real defenses relate to the existence of any obligation on the part of the person who asserts them. The most obvious real defense is forgery of the signature of the maker of a note or the drawer of a check. The person whose signature was forged has not entered into any contract, and he or she has an absolute defense even against a holder in due course.

The Code generally specifies which defenses are real and which are personal. A few defenses—infancy being one—are real in some states and personal in others. Table 35-1 groups defenses according to their usual status. The basic aspects of most personal defenses are discussed in the materials on contracts in chapters 9 through 17.

TABLE 35-1 ■ Commercial Paper: Typical Defenses

PERSONAL DEFENSES	REAL DEFENSES
Lack or failure of consideration	Unauthorized signature
Nonperformance of a condition precedent	Material alteration
Nondelivery, conditional delivery, or delivery for a special purpose	Infancy, if it is a defense to a simple contract
Payment	Lack of capacity
	Illegality
Slight duress	Extreme duress
Fraud in the inducement	Fraud in the execution
Theft by the holder or one through whom the holder has taken	
Violation of a restrictive indorsement	Discharge in bankruptcy
Unauthorized completion	Discharge of which the holder has notice
Other defenses to a simple contract	
Any real defense where the party was negligent	

8. Personal Defenses

A distinction exists between *fraud in the inducement* and *fraud in the execution*. Inducement pertains to the consideration for which an instrument is given. The primary party intended to create an instrument but was fraudulently induced to do so. Such a defense is personal and is not available against a holder in due course. Fraud in the execution exists where a negotiable instrument is procured from a party when circumstances are such that the party does not know that he or she is giving a negotiable instrument. Fraud in the execution is a real defense [3-305(2)(c)]. The theory is that since the party primarily to be bound has no intention of creating an instrument, none is created. Such fraud is rare because persons are usually charged with knowledge of what they sign.

Another personal defense, acquisition of title by or through a thief, is easily preventable. Conversion of bearer paper to order paper precludes its negotiation by a thief or finder.

A holder in due course is not subject to the defense of unauthorized completion of an instrument [3-407(3)]. The defense is personal. The person who left the blank space must bear the risk of wrongful completion.

Negligence of a party, frequently present in situations of fraud and material alteration, will reduce a real defense to a personal defense [3-406]. A check written with a wide, blank space preceding the amount offers a wrongdoer an easy place to raise that amount. The negligent check writer reduces the defense of material alteration to a personal one. This negligence by the drawer typically means that the payor bank (drawee) does not have to recredit the drawer's account for the amount of the alteration. This bank, as a holder in due course, is free from the personal defense that resulted from the drawer's negligence.

9. Real Defenses

The real defense of unauthorized signature includes signatures by agents without authority and forgeries [3-404(1)]. It applies to indorsements as well as to the signature creating the instrument.

The most common example of a material alteration is the "raising" of a check [3-407]. A check drawn in the amount of $50 might be raised by alteration to $500. This creates a real defense to the extent of the alteration. A subsequent holder in due course could enforce the check only in the amount of its original $50.

The defense of lack of capacity is a real defense if the state law so provides. If it is a defense to a simple contract, it is a real defense [3-305(2)(a)]. The same is true for all forms of illegality. If a contract is merely voidable, the defense is personal; if the contract is void or unenforceable, the defense is a real one. If state law provides that usurious contracts are null and void, usury is a real defense.

EXCEPTIONS TO HOLDER-IN-DUE-COURSE STATUS

10. Introduction

The holder in due course concept was predicated on the need for commercial paper to move quickly, freely, and as "a courier without luggage" in the financial community. Negotiable instruments were intended to be the equivalent of money. Use of commercial paper was encouraged by freeing it of personal defenses if its holder is a holder in due course. Today, consumer advocates argue that protection of the consumer in credit transactions is more important than the reasons for the holder-in-due-course concept, and that all defenses should always be available to the consumer-debtor. They feel that the best protection for a consumer is the right to withhold payment if goods are defective or not delivered. The logic of this argument also has been extended to commercial credit transactions when there is a close business relationship between an original contracting party and the transferee that receives the negotiable instrument.

A number of states have enacted statutes prohibiting the use or enforcement of clauses that cut off defenses in contracts such as leases. Courts in many states have held that a holder was not a holder in due course when the finance company was closely connected with the seller. Courts have also strictly construed the application of the holder-in-due-course rule. Doubts about the negotiability of instruments have been resolved against negotiability. Several states have achieved this result by the enactment of the Uniform Consumer Credit Code, whose provisions are applicable to instruments other than checks. This code offers two alternative approaches to the problem. A state legislature can select the one it considers best suited to the needs of the state.

One alternative simply gives maximum protection to the consumer by allowing him or her to assert all claims and defenses against the assignee of any paper that he or she signed. The other alternative provides that the assignee can give written notice of the assignment to the debtor. The consumer is then given the right to assert defenses for three months. After the three-month period, the assignee is free of any defense, and the debtor's only remedy is against the seller.

11. FTC Rule

Since these state efforts were not universal, in 1976 the Federal Trade Commission (FTC), acting under its authority to prohibit unfair or deceptive methods of competition, adopted a rule that prohibits the use of the holder-in-due-course concept against consumers in credit transactions. It also provides that a clause purporting to cut off defenses is an unfair method of competition and illegal.

The FTC rule is designed to eliminate substantial abuses often inflicted on the purchaser of consumer goods. For example, assume that Carter purchases stereo equipment on credit from The Stereo Company. Carter intends to use this equipment in a personal, noncommercial manner. Carter signs a negotiable promissory note promising to pay the purchase price over a thirty-six-month period. The Stereo Company then sells this note to the First National Bank. The note is properly negotiated to the Bank. Now, what would happen if the equipment did not perform as Carter expected and The Stereo Company refuses or is unable to fix the equipment? Carter likely would refuse to make further payments on the note. The First National Bank might assert its right to payment against Carter. When Carter explains that the equipment is defective, the Bank argues that it is free from this personal defense since it is holder in due course. The impact of the Bank's status is that Carter would be liable to pay for merchandise that is defective. Carter's only recourse is against The Stereo Company, which already has indicated its willingness to correct the defective equipment. Carter, the consumer debtor, is caught between the uncooperative seller and the protected holder in due course.

The FTC rule is applicable to any sale or lease of goods or services to consumers in commerce. In such a transaction, it is an unfair or deceptive act or practice for a seller to receive a credit contract that does not contain the following provision in at least 10-point bold type:

NOTICE

**ANY HOLDER OF THIS CONSUMER CREDIT CONTRACT
IS SUBJECT TO ALL CLAIMS AND DEFENSES
WHICH THE DEBTOR COULD ASSERT AGAINST THE SELLER
OF GOODS OR SERVICES OBTAINED PURSUANT HERETO
OR WITH THE PROCEEDS HEREOF.**

Thus the holder could not be a holder in due course, because the holder agrees to be subject to all defenses.

To prevent sellers from sending buyers directly to the lender and thus circumventing the law, the rule has a special provision relating to lending institutions. It declares that it is an unfair or deceptive practice for a seller to accept in payment the proceeds of a purchase-money loan unless a similar notice is included in the loan agreement in 10-point bold type.

For the purpose of the foregoing rule, a purchase-money loan exists if the seller refers the consumer to the creditor or is affiliated with the creditor by common control, contract, or business arrangement. This means that if the lending institution regularly does business with the seller or has an understanding that its customers may obtain financing, the provision must be included in the loan contract. Again, it provides that all defenses are available to the consumer.

As a result of the FTC rule, if a consumer-purchaser has any defense against the seller, it may assert that defense against the bank or other financial institution that seeks to collect the debt. Thus, banks and other financial institutions must make sure that the seller stands behind the products sold. In addition, they must deal only with responsible parties on a recourse basis if losses are to be avoided.

12. Close Connectedness Doctrine

While the FTC rule applies only to consumer credit transactions, many arguments have been made that a similar result should occur in some commercial credit transactions. Continuing the preceding example, suppose that Carter purchased the stereo equipment for use in the reception area of a business. Are there situations when Carter, as a commercial debtor, should be free from the claims of the bank as a holder in due course?

Under a doctrine known as *close connectedness,* a transferee does not take an instrument in good faith when the transferee is so closely connected with the transferor that the transferee may be charged with knowledge of an infirmity in the underlying transaction. The rationale for the close connectedness doctrine is the basic philosophy of the holder-in-due-course concept: to encourage free negotiability of commercial paper by removing certain anxieties from one who takes the paper as an innocent purchaser, knowing no reason why the paper is not sound as its face would indicate. Therefore, the more the holder knows about the underlying transaction, and particularly the more he or she controls or participates or becomes involved in it, the less he or she fits the role of a good-faith purchaser for value. The closer the holder's relationship to the underlying agreement that is the source of the note, the less need there is for giving him or her the tension-free rights.

Among the factors that tend to establish the close connection are (1) drafting by the transferee of forms for the transferor; (2) approval of the transferor's procedures by the transferee (e.g., setting the interest rate); (3) an independent check by the transferee on the credit of the debtor; (4) heavy reliance by the transferor on the transferee (e.g., transfer by the transferor of all or substantial part of his or her paper to the transferee); and (5) common or connected ownership or management of the transferor and transferee.

Close connectedness exists also (1) when the transferee or assignee has substantial voice in, or control of, a vested interest in the underlying transaction, or (2) if the transferee has knowledge of the particular transaction or of the way the seller does business, so he or she knows of claims the buyer has against the seller. The basic question is whether the holder of the instrument is actually a party to the transaction.

As a result of the close connectedness doctrine, many courts have held that a transferee of a negotiable note does not take in "good faith" and is not a holder in due course of a note given in the sale of goods where the transferee is a finance company involved with the seller of the goods and has a pervasive knowledge of factors relating to the terms of the sale. As the following case illustrates, the issue of whether businesses are closely connected is one of fact for the jury to decide.

CASE

St. James v. Diversified Commercial Finance

714 P.2d 179 (Nev. 1986)

YOUNG, J.

On February 22, 1982, Denise E. B. St. James and Timothy T. B. St. James, dba Las Vegas Chiropractic Center (appellants), purchased a debt collection service from National Revenue Corporation (NRC). John Walker, an NRC employee, sold the service to appellants and had them sign two promissory notes payable to respondent Diversified Commercial Finance Corporation (Diversified) to finance the purchase.

Diversified acknowledges that it provides financing for NRC and facilitates that financing by supplying NRC with preprinted promissory notes for NRC's customers to sign. The promissory notes contained the following preprinted provision:

> Borrower recognizes and acknowledges that all funds borrowed on this Promissory Note will be paid to National Revenue Corporation (NRC). Borrower authorizes NRC to pay to Lender [Diversified] any credits or refunds that may become due Borrower to the extent of any outstanding principal amount and interest due under this Promissory Note, with any remaining balance from said credit or refund going to Borrower.

Appellants stopped making payments on the notes after several months because NRC allegedly was not providing the services promised. Diversified filed a complaint seeking the balance due on the notes ($3,940.00) plus interest, costs and attorney's fees. Appellants answered, setting forth as an affirmative defense failure of consideration, i.e., NRC's failure to provide the services promised in the service agreement. The district court granted Diversified's motion for summary judgment on February 1, 1985. The court concluded that Diversified was a holder in due course of the notes and therefore immune from the defenses available against the seller, NRC.

A holder in due course of an instrument is one who takes the instrument (1) for value, (2) in good faith and (3) without notice that it is overdue or has been dishonored or of any defenses or claims to it. Payees may be holders in due course. Holder in due course status operates to insulate the holder from certain defenses to the instrument of any party with whom the holder has not dealt.

However, § 3-305 makes the holder subject to all defenses of a party with whom the holder has dealt.

Appellants contend that they may assert the defense of failure of consideration against Diversified because they are a party with whom the holder—Diversified—has dealt. Under traditional analysis, however, appellants' argument fails because Diversified did fulfill its obligation on the contract: It paid NRC for the services NRC was to provide to appellants. There was no failure of consideration with respect to the transaction because Diversified was not obligated to perform the collection service but only to pay NRC. The failure of consideration allegedly arose in the transaction between appellants and NRC.

Many jurisdictions have broken with this traditional analysis of the holder in due course rule and have limited its application either by statutory enactment or judicial adoption of the close connection doctrine. . . .

The close connection doctrine holds lenders subject to the defenses that a buyer has against his seller where the lender and seller are closely connected. The Uniform Consumer Credit Code (U3C) and Federal Trade Commission (FTC) rules both contain provisions which make not only assignees of consumer credit paper but also direct lenders in consumer transactions subject to the consumer's claims and defenses against the seller.

The FTC rule would have easily disposed of the case at bar had it involved a consumer transaction. One commentator has noted that the omission of nonconsumer transactions from the rule is unfortunate since the reasons for the rule appear equally applicable in both kinds of transactions. We can discern no reason to limit the doctrine to consumer transactions; we therefore adopt the close connection doctrine with respect to all transactions where the buyer can demonstrate a close connection between the seller and lender.

Whether a lender and seller are closely connected will necessarily depend upon the facts of each case. We adopt the test articulated by the New Jersey Supreme Court in *Unico v. Owen*, 50 N.J. 101, 232 A.2d 405 (1967) for determining whether such a connection exists:

> [W]hen it appears from the totality of the arrangements between [seller] and financer that the financer has had a substantial voice in setting standards for the underlying transaction, or has approved the standards established by the [seller], and has agreed to take all or a predetermined or substantial quantity of the negotiable paper which is backed by such standards, the financer should be considered a participant in the original transaction and therefore not entitled to holder in due course status.

We conclude that the district court erred in granting summary judgment to Diversified. . . . The record in this case shows that a genuine issue of material fact, whether Diversified and NRC are closely connected, remains to be tried. The promissory notes themselves, as exhibits to the pleadings, indicate that Diversified may have been in reality a party to the service agreement. The notes were supplied to NRC by Diversified and provided in preprinted type that the money loaned by Diversified to appellants would be paid directly to NRC. In addition, the notes were prepared around the same time as the NRC service agreement by an NRC employee, John Walker. Walker's name appears in the upper right-hand corner of the notes as well as on the service agreement. Finally, in preprinted type the notes designate that a yellow copy should be kept by NRC. We conclude that the promissory notes on their face were sufficient to demonstrate that a material fact remained to be tried. Diversified was not, therefore, entitled to judgment as a matter of law. . . .

■ *Reversed and remanded.*

CASE CONCEPTS REVIEW

1. What is the relationship among the St. Jameses, the National Revenue Corporation, and the Diversified Commercial Finance Corporation?

2. Why did the St. Jameses stop making payments on the promissory notes they had signed?

3. Why does the FTC rule not resolve this case in favor of the St. Jameses?

4. What does the court mean by the close connectedness doctrine?

5. Does the court conclude that this doctrine definitely prevents Diversified from collecting payment from the St. Jameses? Explain.

REVISED ARTICLE 3

As with the material in the preceding chapter, the 1990 Revised Article 3 does not make drastic changes with respect to holders in due course and the personal or real nature of defenses. The following changes should be considered more of an effort to fine-tune the law and its application rather than a major overhaul. All references to UCC sections are to the Revised Article 3, unless stated otherwise.

The first change that bears on the material discussed in this chapter relates to the meaning of the phrase *holder in due course*. In addition to retaining the requirements that a holder gives value, is in good faith, and be without notice of defenses, Revised Article 3 contains a requirement with respect to the instrument. For a holder to be in due course, the instrument must not contain apparent evidence of a forgery or alteration or otherwise appear so irregular or incomplete as to call into question its authenticity [3-302(a)(1)]. This element of authenticity of the instrument is new as a requirement for holder-in-due-course status. A similar requirement may be found by the court interpreting the original Article 3, but such a finding would relate to a holder in due course being subject to the real defenses of forgery or alteration.

A second change clarifies the requirement that a holder in due course take the instrument "without notice." In original § 3-302(1)(c), the holder has to take without notice that the instrument is (1) overdue, (2) dishonored, or (3) subject to any defense. Revised Article 3 provides the following list of specific items of which that holder must not have notice: (1) Instrument is overdue, (2) instrument has been dishonored, (3) instrument is part of a series and there is an uncured defect with respect to payment of another instrument, (4) instrument contains an unauthorized signature, (5) instrument has been altered, (6) instrument is subject to defenses, (7) instrument is subject to any claim to the instrument, and (8) instrument is subject to any claim in recoupment [3-302(a)(2)].

A third change relates to the last two items just mentioned. Revised Article 3 expands defenses referred to in the original Article to include claims to an instrument [3-306] and claims in recoupment [3-305]. A *claim to the instrument* exists whenever a party has a claim of ownership, a lien, or other possessory interest in the instrument. This claim might include the right to rescind a negotiation and thereby reclaim the instrument.

A *claim in recoupment* arises when a maker of note or drawer of a draft receives merchandise from the payee and later discovers that the merchandise is defective. Rather than undoing the transaction and claiming the instrument, the maker or drawer expends money to correct the defect. When the payment for the merchandise is sought by the payee or a subsequent holder of the instrument, the maker or drawer claims a recoupment in an amount equal to the additional expenditures. A holder in due course takes free from the claims to the instrument [3-306] and the claims in recoupment [3-305(b)].

A fourth change in the Revised Article 3 with respect to this chapter's coverage relates to when a holder might have notice of the instrument being overdue. Whereas the original Article 3 creates a presumption that checks were overdue thirty days after the date of issue, Revised Article 3 substitutes a ninety-day presumption [3-304(a)(2)].

The Original Article 3 states that demand paper, other than checks, is overdue when taken more than a reasonable time after issuance. The Revised Article 3 requires a bit more of a holder taking demand paper. This holder must judge whether such instruments are overdue based on the circumstances of the particular case in light of the nature of the instrument and the usage of trade [3-304(a)(3)]. The determination of when the holder of demand paper, other than checks, has taken with notice that such instruments are overdue will be an issue for determination by a fact finder, like a jury.

Finally, the Revised Article 3 changes the meaning of *value* as it relates to the nonexistence of consideration. Whereas the original Article 3 states that an executory promise is not generally viewed as value, Revised Article 3 permits the holder to enjoy a freedom from defenses to the extent of the value of the performance that is rendered [3-303(b)]. For example, assume Debra issues a check for $250 to Pauline in return for Pauline having typed four term papers of equal length. Pauline negotiates this check to Terry in payment for Terry's promise to fix Pauline's printer next week. If Debra discovers that Pauline's typing is unacceptable (perhaps due to a printing problem), Debra has a defense that can be asserted against Terry since Terry did not give value for the check. Now suppose Terry performed $150 worth of labor on Pauline's printer before Debra discovers the defense of Pauline's defective performance. Terry can recover up to $150 against Debra, but Debra can assert the defense to defeat Terry's claim for the additional $100.

CHAPTER SUMMARY

Status Possibilities
1. A transferee of commercial paper may be an assignee, a holder, or a holder in due course.
2. An assignee is a transferee of a simple contract, or one to whom a negotiable instrument has not been properly negotiated.
3. A holder has a negotiable instrument that has been properly negotiated.
4. A holder that meets certain requirements is a holder in due course and takes instruments free of personal defenses.

Contract Provisions
1. Contracts often contain clauses that waive defenses in the event the contract is assigned.
2. Such clauses are illegal in some states and legal in others.
3. If legal, most states require that the assignee meet the same requirements as a holder in due course, and these states waive only personal defenses.

HOLDER IN DUE COURSE

Value
1. A holder in due course must take the instrument for value and not as a gift. A mere promise is not value, but a preexisting debt is value.

Good Faith
1. A holder in due course must take in good faith. Good faith is honesty in fact. If the holder knows that there is a defense, he or she is not a good-faith taker.

Without Notice
1. A holder in due course must take without notice that it is overdue, has been dishonored, or that there is a claim or defense to the instrument. A person has notice if he or she has actual knowledge or reason to know the fact.

Before Overdue
1. An instrument is overdue if it is demand paper and more than a reasonable length of time has passed. In the case of a check, this time period is thirty days.

Holder from a Holder in Due Course
1. A transferee from a holder in due course has the rights of a holder in due course and thus is free of personal defenses. A person may take by gift, with knowledge of a defense, or after maturity and still be able to collect on an instrument if it has passed through the hands of a holder in due course.
2. The shelter provision is not applicable to a reacquirer.

DEFENSES

Personal Defenses
1. A personal defense is one that arises out of the transaction that created the instrument. It is generally based on the law of contracts.
2. Payment is a very important personal defense.
3. Negligence reduces a real defense to a personal defense.

Real Defenses
1. A real defense may be asserted against any party, including a holder in due course.
2. Real defenses go to the essence of the instrument. The most important real defense is forgery.

EXCEPTIONS TO HOLDER-IN-DUE-COURSE STATUS

FTC Rule
1. The FTC rule prevents the use of the holder-in-due-course concept in a consumer credit transaction.
2. In such transactions involving consumers, the contract must contain a notice in 10-point bold type informing all holders that any defense available against the seller of goods can be asserted against the holder.
3. The same notice must be contained in purchase-money loan documents.

Close Connectedness Doctrine

1. To provide nonconsumer debtors similar protection to that given to consumers under the FTC rule, some courts conclude that a transferee lacks good faith if it is closely connected to the transferor.
2. Lacking good faith, this transferee cannot qualify as a holder in due course and thus is subject to the defenses the debtor has against the original seller-transferor.

REVIEW QUESTIONS AND PROBLEMS

1. Match each term in column A with the appropriate statement in column B.

A	B
(1) Shelter provision	(a) May be a real defense or a personal one depending on state law
(2) Value	(b) Prohibits consumers from holder-in-due-course status
(3) Good faith	(c) Always a real defense
(4) Holder	(d) Eliminates real defenses
(5) FTC rule	(e) Allows a transferee to have the rights of a holder in due course
(6) Fraud in the execution	(f) A mere promise does not qualify as this
(7) Infancy	(g) Has possession of a negotiable instrument that has been properly negotiated
(8) Negligence	(h) Honesty in fact

2. Siegman, a diamond merchant, issued a note for diamonds purchased. The seller indorsed the note to a bank "as collateral for his preexisting obligations to the banks and as collateral for the diamonds shipped to defendants." Did the bank give value so as to qualify as a holder in due course? Explain.

3. A bank received a check to deposit in Seve's account. Seve subsequently wrote checks withdrawing most of the proceeds of the deposited check. The bank paid these checks before receiving notice that the deposited check was dishonored. Does the bank qualify as a holder in due course? Explain.

4. Andrews owed Martin, his accountant, a fee for services rendered. Andrews drew a check on his bank payable to "Cash" and signed it. He left the amount blank because he was not sure of the exact amount owed. On his way to Martin's office, Andrews lost the check. Oliver found the check, filled it in for $500, and handed it to Ernest to satisfy a $500 debt that Oliver owed to Ernest. Ernest accepted the check in good faith as payment for the debt and immediately presented it to the drawee bank. The drawee bank refused to cash it because of a stop payment order. Is Andrews liable to Ernest for the $500? Why?

5. C&S Bank sued Johnson to collect a $50,000 note. Johnson had signed the note payable to Peek. Peek had transferred the note to the bank as security for a $20,000 loan. Johnson seeks to assert a defense of fraud and lack of consideration. Is the bank a holder in due course? Why or why not?

6. Ken Hessler was in the business of raising hogs for J and J Farms, Inc. JJ Farms would deliver the hogs to Hessler and require him to sign a promissory note payable to JJ Farms to cover the cost of the hogs and feed. After the hogs were raised, JJ Farms would take them to be sold at auction. The proceeds were applied to satisfy Hessler's notes and his fees for raising the hogs. Business went well until January 4, when JJ Farms' representative asked Hessler to sign his wife's name to the promissory note for the hogs delivered that week. Hessler signed his wife's name, and then placed his initials "K.H." after the signature. JJ Farms then immediately sold the note to Arcanum National

Bank. Unfortunately for Hessler, the hogs delivered to him on January 4 had previously been sold by JJ Farms to another buyer, who repossessed the hogs from Hessler. The note became due, and Arcanum demanded payment from Hessler. Arcanum claimed to be a holder in due course. Hessler contended that Arcanum was subject to the defense of lack of consideration since the note on its face gave notice of a defense. Does a promissory note in which the wife's name is signed by the husband followed by his initials constitute "notice" so as to preclude a buyer of the note from being a holder in due course? Explain.

7. Charles was appointed guardian for his seven-year-old son, Chad, who was the beneficiary of his grandfather's life insurance policy. The insurance company issued a check for $30,588.39 made payable to "Charles, Guardian of the Estate of Chad a Minor." Charles opened a personal account with the check and absconded with the proceeds. When the bank was sued by Chad, it claimed to be a holder in due course. Was it? Explain.

8. Nevers executed a note payable to the order of Young due on January 1, 1993. On March 1, 1993, Young negotiated the note to Glassen. Will Glassen be subject to the personal defenses of Nevers? Why?

9. Wells issued a check on its account at First National Bank payable to the order of Tayman in the amount of $4,200. Wells stopped payment on the check early the next banking day. Later that day, Tayman attempted to cash the check at First National, and when payment was refused, he took the check to his own bank, Second National, which cashed it. Is Second National a holder in due course? Why or why not?

10. Arthur purchased securities from William, giving William his check payable to William's order and drawn on Produce Bank in payment. William immediately indorsed the check to the order of Robert, and it was accepted by Robert in payment of a debt owed him by William. Robert indorsed the check in blank and delivered it to his son, Charles, as a birthday gift. Arthur has discovered that the securities sold him by William are worthless and has directed Produce Bank to stop payment. When Produce Bank refuses to pay Charles on the check and Charles sues Arthur, may Arthur assert the defense of failure of consideration against Charles? Explain.

11. Hilda executed a note payable to Home Improvements, Inc., for various improvements to her house. The company negotiated the note to a bank, which sued Hilda. If the bank is a holder in due course, can Hilda raise the defense that Home Improvements made several material misrepresentations in inducing her to sign the note? Explain.

12. Smith delivered to Janett his check drawn on National Bank payable to Janett. Janett had the check certified and delivered it to Cook as payment on account. The certification was stamped on the face of the check. It said "Certified payable as originally drawn." The original check was for $1,000. Janett had raised the amount to $4,000 prior to the certification. No one but an expert would have realized that the check had been raised. How much can Cook collect on the check? How much can the bank charge to Smith's account? Explain.

13. W. G. and Betty Ellis executed a promissory note for $25,000 in favor of Standard Finance Company for the purpose of getting a loan. Mr. Ellis took the money and left the vicinity. When the note was due, Mrs. Ellis refused payment. She contended that Mr. Ellis had tricked her into signing the note. She claimed that Mr. Ellis assured her that her signature was a mere "formality," that he alone was liable, and that the debt would be repaid without any participation by her. Standard Finance contended that Mrs. Ellis's defense was fraud in the inducement, a personal defense, which is ineffective to defeat the rights of a holder in due course. Is the fraud in this case a real or a personal defense? Explain.

14. Pam bought equipment from a dealer who was to supply additional equipment weekly. These additional items would permit Pam to make tapes that the dealer was to pur-

chase. Pam gave the dealer a note for the equipment; but the additional equipment was never delivered and the dealer went out of business. Before closing, the dealer discounted the note at a bank that had purchased other notes from the dealer. The bank had a very close relationship with the dealer and apparently knew of the dealer's shady business practices. The bank now sues Pam to collect the proceeds of the note. Is it a holder in due course? Why?

36 LIABILITY OF PARTIES TO COMMERCIAL PAPER

CHAPTER PREVIEW

The discussion in the previous two chapters is premised on the notion that one party has a valid defense to excuse nonperformance of the contract that gives rise to the commercial paper transaction. In this chapter, we examine the parties' liability for payment of the commercial paper itself. We assume there is no defense with respect to the underlying contract.

In this chapter, you will learn that a person must sign the commercial paper to be held liable for its payment. You will study the various types of liability the law imposes based on how a party signs the paper. Aspects of conditional liability and unconditional liability are discussed. One way to help simplify what may seem like complex material is to ask a series of questions: What party is expected to pay on the instrument? If that party does not pay, who else can you expect to pay? If the expected party does pay but later discovers it paid by mistake, can this party recover from any other party?

These questions are answered through the presentation of material in this chapter.

■ BUSINESS MANAGEMENT DECISION

You are the president of a closely held corporation that runs a retail clothing store. Your business has grown to the point where your store needs expanding and remodeling. This will cost $150,000, an amount you wish to borrow on behalf of the corporation.

How should you sign a promissory note on behalf of the corporation to avoid becoming personally liable?

LIABILITY BASED ON SIGNATURES

1. In General

A person's liability on commercial paper results from his or her signature on the instrument. The signature may be affixed as a maker, drawer, or acceptor on the face of the instrument, or it may be an indorsement on the back. Liability varies, based on the capacity of the signer. However, the signature generally must be genuine or signed by an authorized agent to impose liability on the signer. As with almost every general rule, this one is subject to exceptions, which are discussed in section 4.

2. Capacity of the Signature

The liability of makers of notes is different from the liability of drawers of drafts and checks, which is different from that of indorsers of commercial paper. The liability of these parties varies because of the different capacities in which they sign commercial paper. A person signing commercial paper may do so to assist or accommodate someone else. This signer may enjoy a special status insofar as liability is concerned. These various liabilities are described throughout this chapter.

The capacity in which a person signs is usually obvious because of the location of the signature. Makers and drawers usually sign in the lower right-hand corner of an instrument, and indorsers sign on the back of an instrument. A drawee normally places his or her signature of acceptance on the face of the instrument, but signing the back would clearly indicate that the drawee was signing as an acceptor unless he or she could establish otherwise. When the signature does not reveal the obligation of the party who signs, the signature is an indorsement [3-402].

3. Agency Principles

The general principles of the law of agency are applicable to commercial paper. A principal is bound when a duly authorized agent signs the principal's name on commercial paper. If the agent is not authorized to sign, the principal is not bound unless the principal (1) ratifies the signature or (2) is estopped from asserting lack of authority. An agent who fails to bind his or her principal because of lack of authority will usually be personally liable to third parties.

An agent is also personally liable if he or she fails to show representative capacity [3-403(2)(a)]. This may occur when the principal is not named on the instrument. Even if the principal's name appears on the instrument, the agent may fail to indicate that he or she is signing in a representative capacity. In such cases, the agent is also personally liable [3-403(2)(a)].

An agent can relieve himself or herself of liability to the person to whom the paper was issued by proving that such party knew the agent was acting only as an agent for his or her principal [3-403(2)(b)]. Between the parties, parol evidence is admissible to show the intent of the parties where the principal's name appears on the instrument and the status of the agent's signature is ambiguous. In the case of checks, the imprinting of the corporate name constitutes substantial evidence that the drawer signed in a representative capacity on behalf of the corporation. The payee of a corporate check expects less from the drawer than does the payee of a corporate note. It is common for creditors to demand the individual promise of corporate officers on notes, especially in the case of small corporations.

To avoid personal liability, the signer has the burden of establishing representative capacity. The proof may be an agreement, understanding, or course of dealing that shows an intent between the parties for the signer to act in a representative capacity. Failure to meet the burden of proof results in personal liability, as the following case demonstrates.

CASE

Thomas v. McNeill
448 N.W.2d 231 (S.D. 1989)

Daniel McNeill, James Thomas, and another individual formed a business known as F & M Enterprises (F & M). The initial capital contributions by these three owners totaled $100,000. Thomas paid one-third of this total for his ownership share in F & M. The original purpose for which F & M was formed did not materialize. However, the three owners decided to use the contributed capital for another purpose.

MILLER, J.
... In May of 1979 these funds were used to purchase a mobile home business which was named Nu-

Trend Homes, and which was to be a business owned by F & M.

Nu-Trend Homes lost money and McNeill and Thomas had some personal differences. These factors led to a discussion about terminating the business relationship. McNeill offered to buy out Thomas' interest in F & M and Thomas agreed if he could receive $5,000.00 cash immediately and a note for the balance of $28,300.00. McNeill accomplished the buy-out on September 15, 1980, by borrowing $5,000.00 under the corporate name issuing a Nu-Trend check on the Nu-Trend account to Thomas in the amount of $5,000.00, and executing a promissory note to Thomas for $28,300.00 with interest at twelve percent per annum. McNeill signed this September 15, 1980, promissory note (September Note). It neither named F & M, nor showed that McNeill signed in any type of representative capacity for F & M. Other than

McNeill's signature, the blanks provided on the note as to who promises to pay, where, and when, were left blank.

For a number of months after September 15, 1980, Thomas received interest payments on the September Note through Nu-Trend Home's business checks. There were no payments of principal on this note. After March of 1983, Thomas no longer received interest checks. In February, 1984, F & M stopped selling mobile homes and began to liquidate assets.

Thomas was scheduled to have surgery in the fall of 1984 and wanted his business affairs to be current before this time. He asked McNeill to execute a new promissory note reflecting the current debt with accrued interest, since only a portion of the interest payments and none of the principal payments had been made on the September Note. On October 5, 1984, McNeill executed a new promissory note to Thomas in the amount of $33,677.00, with interest at twelve percent per annum. Like the September Note, the October 5, 1984, note (October Note) was signed by McNeill without indication of any representative capacity, and the blanks provided on the note as to who promises to pay, where, and when, were left blank. There were no payments of interest or principal on the October Note.

In February 1987, Thomas brought suit against McNeill seeking payment on the October Note. McNeill answered by affirmatively denying personal liability on the note, alleging that the note was an obligation of F & M. . . . The trial court found as a matter of law that the October Note was a personal obligation on the part of McNeill. . . .

McNeill contends . . . that the trial court should have allowed him to adduce parol evidence to show the intention of the parties. Thomas claims that the intention of the parties is clear by looking at the October Note itself. . . .

The issue presented falls within the purview of the Uniform Commercial Code, and in particular within SDCL 57A-3-403(2)(a), which provides in pertinent part:

(2) An authorized representative who signs his own name to an instrument
   (a) Is personally obligated if the instrument neither names the person represented nor shows that the representative signed in a representative capacity;

McNeill, however, contends that SDCL 57A-3-403(2)(b) controls in this controversy. That section provides that an authorized representative who signs his own name to an instrument:

   (b) Except as otherwise established between the immediate parties, is personally obligated if the instrument names the person represented but does not show that the representative signed in a repre-

sentative capacity, or if the instrument does not name the person represented but does show that the representative signed in a representative capacity.

The deposition testimony of McNeill revealed that he signed the October Note and that the October Note neither named any person whom McNeill allegedly was representing nor showed that McNeill signed in any type of representative capacity. An examination of the note itself clearly reveals these undisputed facts. . . .

Courts all across the country have granted summary judgment to a plaintiff such as Thomas when presented with a similar factual scenario. . . .

Official Comment 3 to U.C.C. § 3-403 makes clear the drafter's intention that parol evidence be inadmissible to disestablish obligations such as the October Note. Official Comment 3 of U.C.C. § 3-403 indicates the results various signatures have upon the individual liability of an agent. We will paraphrase this example to show the same in this case.

Assuming that F & M is a principal and McNeill is its agent, a note might, for example, bear the following signatures affixed by the agent:

(a) "F & M," or
(b) "McNeill," or
(c) "F & M by McNeill, Agent,"
(d) "McNeill, Agent,"
(e) "F & M McNeill."

A signature in form (a) does not bind McNeill if authorized. A signature in (b) personally obligates McNeill, and parol evidence is inadmissible under SDCL 57A-3-403(2)(a) to disestablish his obligation. The unambiguous way to make clear that McNeill is signing in his representative capacity without personal liability is to sign as in (c). Any other definite indication is sufficient, as where the instrument reads "F & M promises to pay" and it is signed "McNeill, Agent." McNeill is not bound if he is authorized.

U.C.C. § 3-403(2)(b) adopts the New York's minority rule in cases such as (d); and adopts the majority rule in cases such as (e). "In both cases the section admits parol evidence in litigation between the immediate parties to prove signature by the agent in his representative capacity." U.C.C. § 3-403, Official Comment 3. . . .

The October Note, like example (b) above, neither names the person allegedly represented by McNeill nor shows that he signed in any type of representative capacity. In such a case there is no ambiguity created by the signature and the trial court can only look within the four corners of the promissory note to determine the intent of the parties.

Taking the undisputed facts of this case, the trial court had a definite basis upon which to grant Thomas' motion for summary judgment on his complaint and correctly found that there existed no genuine issue of material fact regarding McNeill's liability on the October Note.

■ *We affirm. . . .*

CASE CONCEPTS REVIEW

1. Daniel McNeill claims to be an agent in this case. Which party is McNeill's principal?

2. How did McNeill sign the October note payable to Thomas?

3. Why does the court conclude that McNeill was personally liable to Thomas?

4. Why does the court not accept McNeill's attempt to testify orally about his agency status?

5. Would this court have reached a different conclusion if the note in question had been the one signed in September?

4. Exceptions: Impostors and Fictitious Payees

An exception to the requirement that signatures be genuine arises when an instrument is made payable to an imposter or to a fictitious person. The drawer's signature is genuine, but the instrument is indorsed in the name of the person who is being impersonated or in the fictitious name.

In the imposter situation, one person poses as someone else and induces the drawer to issue a check payable to the order of the person being impersonated. In the fictitious payee case, the person who induces the issuance of the instrument simply provides the name of the payee while never intending for this payee to have any interest in the instrument. In both cases the instrument is then indorsed in the name of the person being impersonated or the name of the fictitious payee. The indorsement in the name of the payee is effective because it was made by the person that the drawer intended to indorse, and the named payee was not intended to have an interest in the check. The loss falls on the drawer rather than on the person who took the check or the bank that honored it [3-405(1)(a)].

If the check is intended for the party named but is diverted and forged by an employee, the indorsement is not effective because the instrument is not indorsed by the party intended by the drawer. This covers two factual situations. First, the imposter rule placing liability on the drawer does not apply if the imposter acts as an agent and has the check made payable to the principal. Second, the fictitious payee rule does not apply if the drawer's employee steals the check after it has been intended for the payee's benefit. In both of these situations, the liability would initially be on the drawee who accepted the forged indorsement.

A typical fictitious payee case involves a dishonest employee authorized to sign his employer's name to checks, or one who draws checks that he presents to his employer for the latter's signature. Thus, the employee may draw payroll checks or checks payable to persons with whom the employer would be expected to do business. He either signs the checks or obtains his employer's signature and then cashes the checks, indorsing the name of the payee. If he is in charge of the company's books, he is able to manipulate the books when the canceled checks are returned and may thus avoid detection. The Code imposes this loss on the employer; the dishonest employee can effectively indorse in the payee's name [3-405(1)(c)]. The following case is typical of those illustrating this very important principle. This case discusses that the bank's protection under § 3-405(1)(c) can be lost if the bank is shown to engage in the fraudulent scheme or otherwise acts in bad faith.

CASE

Prudential-Bache Securities, Inc. v. Citibank, N.A.

536 N.E.2d 1118 (N.Y. 1989)

KAYE, J.

For more than two years, a massive fraud went undetected within Prudential-Bache, involving the issuance of firm checks that were regular on their face but improperly made payable to fictitious customers actually under the control of a Prudential-Bache employee. This case is an attempt by Prudential-Bache to recoup a portion of its losses from defendant, Citibank, one of the banks through which the employee laundered the proceeds of those checks. . . .

Beginning about the summer of 1981, John Efler, former section manager of Prudential-Bache's Dividend Department . . . caused the issuance of Prudential-Bache checks drawn on its account at Banker's Trust Company, and made payable to companies that were not actual Prudential-Bache customers but had names like them. Efler apparently accomplished this by creating false records, misinforming coemployees that proper claims had been presented, himself both requisitioning and approving the checks, and violating other Prudential-Bache procedures. . . . Efler succeeded in embezzling approximately $18.9 million before the scheme was uncovered in October 1983. In two separate actions, Prudential-Bache has sought to recover its losses from the banks. At issue in this case is the approximately $3.7 million channeled through Citibank.

Between May and September 1983—the final months of the fraud—Efler induced Prudential-Bache to issue checks to M.N. Corporation and Harvard Corporation. M.N. and Harvard were not actual Prudential-Bache customers entitled to the dividends requisitioned for them by Efler, but shell corporations set up and controlled by Efler and his coconspirator, Lawrence Artese. Artese, not a Prudential-Bache employee, opened and maintained the accounts in the names of M.N. and Harvard at Citibank's Hudson Street branch for the purpose of depositing the checks and laundering the proceeds through them. To effect the scheme, the conspirators bribed two Citibank employees, Robert Hutchinson, an assistant manager, and Juanita Reyes, a customer service representative. . . .

Once the accounts were activated at Citibank's Hudson Street branch, Artese began a pattern of laundering funds there. Within the span of a few months at the branch, he personally moved more than $3.7 million in Prudential-Bache checks into the accounts and removed the funds in cash. . . . Prudential-Bache asserts that . . . Citibank employees, including managers, were aware of

these activities, through conversations with Artese on his near-daily visits to the branch and through cash distributions at teller windows. . . .

Prudential-Bache . . . commenced the present action against Citibank. . . .

Supreme Court concluded that Prudential-Bache's complaint should be dismissed because the claims were barred by UCC 3-405(1)(c). . . .

The Uniform Commercial Code, in its rules governing check fraud, assigns losses by the relative responsibility of the parties for the loss. Losses arising out of forged indorsements are allocated to the party best able to take precautions to prevent them.

Ordinarily, an unauthorized indorsement—that is, either a forged indorsement or one made by an agent exceeding authority (UCC 1-201 [43])—is ineffective to pass title or authorize the drawee bank to pay. The check is not properly payable because an unauthorized signature is inoperative as that of the person whose name is signed. Consequently, the drawee bank generally may not debit the drawer's account when it pays such a check. . . .

UCC 3-405(1)(c) creates an exception to the general principle that a drawer is not liable on an unauthorized indorsement. Known as the "fictitious payee" or "padded payroll" rule, UCC 3-405(1)(c) provides that an "indorsement by any person in the name of a named payee is effective if *** an agent or employee of the maker or drawer has supplied him with the name of the payee intending the latter to have no such interest." Thus, in the very particular factual circumstances described by UCC 3-405(1)(c), the indorsement is treated as effective even though it is technically unauthorized, and the loss is allocated to the drawer-employer.

UCC 3-405(1)(c) expresses a fundamental public policy determination. As explicated in the Comment, the principle embodied by UCC 3-405(1)(c) is that losses arising in the specific manner described by the statute are more business risks than banking risks. The employer is normally in a better position to prevent such forgeries by reasonable care in the selection or supervision of his employees, or, if he is not, is at least in a better position to cover the loss by fidelity insurance; and that the cost of such insurance is properly an expense of his business rather than of the business of the holder or drawee.

These assumptions evidence the degree to which the section was calculated by the Legislature to shift the balance in favor of the bank in situations in which the drawer's own employee has perpetrated the fraud or committed the crime giving rise to the loss. As has been widely acknowledged, UCC 3-405 is a banker's provision intended to narrow the liability of banks and broaden the responsibility of their customers.

The facts of this case fit comfortably within UCC 3-405(1)(c). It is undisputed that an "employee" (Efler) supplied the "maker or drawer" (Prudential-Bache) with the name of a "payee" (M.N. and Harvard). The payees, who were fictitious customers not entitled to the dividend payments, were intended "to have no such interest" in the instruments issued (UCC 3-405[1][c]). Contrary to plaintiff's assertion, the subsection is not limited to forged indorsements; it plainly covers situations, as here, where an employee starts the wheels of normal business procedure in motion to produce a check for a non-authorized transaction. Moreover, the practical, policy considerations that motivated UCC 3-405(1)(c) are evident in the facts of this case. There was no indebtedness from Prudential-Bache to M.N. or Harvard when the firm issues checks naming those entities as payees. As is plain simply from the chronology of undisputed facts, Prudential-Bache was in a position to prevent the massive losses in issue here, by supervising its employees, enforcing its rules and examining records relating to a fraud that had been in progress for nearly two years. Under UCC 3-405(1)(c), the loss occasioned by Efler's wrongdoing should thus fall to plaintiff, not Citibank. . . .

■ *Affirmed.*

CASE CONCEPTS REVIEW

1. How was an employee of Prudential-Bache able to embezzle in excess of $18 million?
2. What arrangements did Efler and Artese make with Citibank employees as a means of facilitating the embezzlement scheme?
3. Why does the court conclude that Citibank has no liability to Prudential-Bache under § 3-405(1)(c) of the UCC?

5. Classification of Parties

Primary party The one all other parties expect to pay. The maker of a note and the acceptor of a draft are the primary party to those instruments.

Secondary party A person who expects the primary party to pay but who becomes liable if the primary party does not pay and certain conditions are met. Drawers of drafts and indorsers are typically secondary parties.

For the purposes of liability, the Code divides the parties to commercial paper into two groups—primary parties and secondary parties. The classification of the parties is based on how they signed the paper. The capacity in which the party signed determines how that party is classified. The **primary parties** are the makers of notes and acceptors of drafts. These parties have incurred a definite obligation to pay and are the parties who, in the normal course of events, will *actually* pay the instrument. The acceptor of a draft normally is the drawee. Thus, the payor banks of checks are primary parties.

The **secondary parties** are drawers of drafts, drawers of checks, and indorsers of any instrument. These parties do not expect to pay the instrument but assume, rather, that the primary parties will fulfill their obligations. The drawer and indorsers expect that the acceptor will pay the draft. The indorsers of a note expect that the maker will pay when the note matures. Drawers and indorsers have a responsibility to pay if the primary parties do not, *provided* that certain conditions precedent are satisfied. The drawer and the indorser are, in effect, saying that they will pay if the primary party (acceptor or maker) does not, but only if the party entitled to payment has made proper demand on the primary party and due notice of the primary party's dishonor of the instrument has then been given to the secondary parties [3-413(2), 3-414(1)]. These conditions are described in detail in sections 7 through 12. A more thorough discussion of the liability of secondary parties is presented in sections 15 through 20.

6. Liability of Primary Parties

A primary party engages that he or she will pay the instrument according to its terms. The maker thus assumes an obligation to pay the note as it was worded at the time he or she executed it. The acceptor assumes responsibility for the draft as it was worded when he or she gave acceptance [3-413(1)].

If a maker signs an incomplete note, when the note is completed—even though the completion is unauthorized—it can be enforced against the maker by a holder in due course. On the other hand, if an instrument is materially altered after it is made, the maker has a real defense in the absence of negligence. The maker confirms to all subsequent parties the existence of the payee and the payee's capacity to indorse [3-413(3)].

Acceptance The written commitment that an instrument will be paid upon the holder's request for payment.

The drawee of a check or draft is not liable on the instrument until **acceptance.** Upon acceptance, the acceptor is primarily liable. An acceptance must be in writing on the draft and signed by the drawee-acceptor [3-410(1)]. Acceptance is usually made by the drawee's writing or stamping the word *accepted,* with the name and the date, across the face of the instrument. The usual means for accepting a check is to have it certified.

A party presenting a draft for acceptance is entitled to an unqualified acceptance by the drawee. Thus, when the drawee offers an acceptance that in any manner varies or changes the direct order to pay or accept, the holder may refuse the acceptance [3-412(1)]. The paper is dishonored; and upon notice of dishonor or protest, the holder may hold responsible all prior parties on the paper—back to, and including, the drawer.

You should understand that most checks are paid directly rather than accepted first. Typically, the collection process results in the payor bank making final payment. Sometimes the payee or other holder of a check might not want payment but does want an assurance that payment will be made later. Sellers in transactions involving large dollar amounts may request acceptance, rather than payments, before completing a delivery to the buyers.

CONDITIONAL LIABILITY

7. Introduction

The term *conditional liability* is used to describe the secondary liability that results from the status of parties as drawers or indorsers. The adjective *conditional* refers to the fact that certain conditions precedent must be fulfilled to establish liability [3-501]. The conditions precedent are *presentment, dishonor, notice of dishonor,* and in some instances *protest.* The importance of exact compliance with the conditions precedent cannot be overemphasized. Failure to comply may result in the discharge of the secondary parties.

8. Presentment: In General

Presentment The demand for payment or acceptance made on the primary party by a holder of an instrument.

Presentment is a demand made on a maker or drawee [3-504(1)]. In relation to a note, it is a demand for payment made by the holder on the maker. In the case of a draft, it may be either a demand for acceptance or a demand for payment.

The drawee of a draft is not bound on the instrument as a primary party until acceptance. The holder will usually wait until maturity and present the draft to the drawee for payment, but the holder may present it to the drawee for acceptance before maturity to give credit to the instrument during the period of its term. The drawee is under no legal duty to the holder to accept. If the acceptance is refused, the draft must be presented for payment. If dishonor occurs, liability may be passed to the indorsers and the drawer upon proper notice of dishonor.

In most instances, it is not necessary to present an instrument for acceptance. Presentment for payment alone is usually sufficient, but presentment for acceptance must be made to charge the drawer and indorsers of some drafts. For example, if the date of payment depends on presentment, as in the case of a draft payable after sight, presentment for acceptance is required to fix the maturity date of the instrument [3-501(1)(a)].

9. Presentment: How and Where

Presentment may be made by personally contacting the primary party and making a demand for acceptance or payment. Presentment may be made by mail or through a clearinghouse [3-504(2)(a)(b)]. Presentment by mail is effective when received. If the instrument specifies the place of acceptance or payment, presentment is made there. If no place is specified, presentment may be made at the place of business of the party to accept or to pay. Presentment is excused if neither the party to accept or pay nor anyone authorized to act for him or her is present or accessible at such place [3-504(2)(c)]. A draft accepted or a note made payable at a bank in the United States must be presented at that bank [3-504(4)]. Presentment of a check to the data processing center of the payor bank is effective if the records are maintained at the center. This is important when a bank has several branches, as occurred in the following case.

CASE

Chrysler Credit Corp. v. First Nat. Bank & Trust

582 F. Supp. 1436 (1984)

Plaintiff, Chrysler Credit Corporation, sues to recover the sum of $53,337.75 from First National Bank and Trust of Washington County, Pennsylvania (First National). Plaintiff and Al Barry, Inc. (dealer) executed financing agreements whereby plaintiff agreed to finance the purchase of new and used vehicles for sale by the dealer. Al Barry drew ten checks on January 18 and 19, 1979, payable to Chrysler Credit Corporation in the total sum of $53,337.75. The checks were drawn on the Barry account at the Charleroi branch office of First National. Chrysler deposited the checks in its account at the Monroeville branch of Mellon Bank on January 19, 1979. The checks were routed through the Federal Reserve and received at the main branch and data processing center of First National at Washington, Pennsylvania, on January 22, 1979.

The checks were processed by employees at the processing center, placed in a reader-sorter memory machine, and posted in a reject journal because they were drawn on uncollected funds. The checks were then withdrawn or pulled by employees of central operations.

On January 23, 1979, at approximately 10:30 A.M., the Charleroi branch received a copy of the posting reject journal by courier from the main branch. The branch manager made a decision to pay the checks the same day. However, on January 24, the branch manager reversed the decision, dishonored the checks, and notified the processing center. The central operations department returned the checks to plaintiff.

Chrysler Credit contends that the checks were "presented on and received by" the Charleroi branch within the meaning of the Uniform Commercial Code on January 22, 1979. Thus the bank is liable for the amount of each check because it failed to dishonor within twenty-four hours of presentment.

ZIEGLER, J.

. . . This case presents the question whether presentment of a check at the data processing center of a payor bank requires the bank to give notice of dishonor or return the check prior to midnight of the next banking day. . . . We conclude that when a check is received at the data processing center of the payor bank, where the bookkeeping services for the branch offices are conducted, the bank's failure to send notice of dishonor or return the check before midnight of the next business day renders the bank liable for the amount of a worthless check pursuant to 13 Pa.C.S.A. §4302....

The Uniform Commercial Code provides that a payor bank must pay, return or dishonor a check within the midnight deadline following presentment to or receipt by the bank.... These limitations require that payor banks make decisions on demand items to insure prompt payment to a chain of individuals and institutions in a fluid commercial transaction. Otherwise, a situation is created where a series of banks are extending credit to each other....

The foregoing policy determinations make clear that First National was required to pay, return or dishonor the 10 checks before midnight on the day following presentment. Failure to act renders the bank accountable. First National contends that the checks were "presented on and received by" the payor bank when the Charleroi branch received the posting reject journal on the morning of January 23, because the branch is treated as a separate bank for the purpose of computing the time within which action must be taken under the Commercial Code. Thus, according to defendant, the bank had until midnight on January 24 to meet its deadline. We disagree.... Presentment at a processing center operated by a bank, rather than the banking office where the check is drawn, is effective to trigger the time limits of the midnight deadline.

... This court must ... determine the definition of a "branch bank."... A branch (must) be judged by the functions it performs, without regard to where those functions are physically performed.... Because we interpret the intent of §4302 to favor the expeditious processing of commercial paper and because we find that the banking industry as a whole will benefit if all banks are held to a standard of prompt processing of checks, we hold that the midnight deadline of §4302 is to be measured from the time checks are presented to a payor bank's computer processing center, where the center is a designated place of presentment and where the center performs an integral and necessary check processing function.... We find that First National is accountable for the face value of the 10 checks in question, plus 6 percent interest calculated from January 23, 1979, when the bank failed to meet its statutory midnight deadline.

■ *So ordered.*

CASE CONCEPTS REVIEW

1. Which party is the drawer of the checks in this case?
2. What did Crysler Credit, as payee, do with the checks?
3. When and where were these checks received by the payor bank?
4. When did the manager of the Charleroi branch of First National finally decide not to pay these checks?
5. Why did the court determine that First National was liable on the checks?

To balance the liberal attitude regarding what will suffice as a presentment, Section 3-505(1) empowers the party on whom presentment is made to require

1. Exhibition of the instrument
2. Reasonable identification of the person making presentment
3. Evidence of authority if presentment is made for another
4. Production of the instrument at a place specified in it or (if none is specified) at any reasonable place
5. A signed receipt on the instrument for any partial or full payment and its surrender upon full payment

If the primary party does not avail himself or herself of these rights, the presentment is perfectly valid, no matter how or where the presentment is made. If the primary party does require proper presentment, a failure to comply invalidates the presentment, but the instrument is not dishonored. The requirement of identification of the presenting party applies to bearer paper as well as order paper [3-505].

10. Presentment: When

In general, an instrument must be presented for payment on the day of maturity. The presentment must be made at a reasonable hour and, if at a bank, during banking hours.

When an instrument is payable on demand, it must be presented or negotiated within a reasonable time after such secondary party became liable; for example, after his or her indorsement [3-503(1)(e)]. Thus, in the case of a demand note, an indorser would be discharged if presentment were not made within a reasonable time after he or she indorsed the note. A reasonable time for presentment is determined by the nature of the instrument, any usage of banking or trade, and the facts of the particular case [3-503(2)].

The drawer of a check is liable for it for a reasonable time, presumed to be thirty days after date or issue, whichever is later. In that time, a check should be presented for payment or the collection process should be initiated [3-504(2)(a)]. The presumed reasonable time for presentment to hold the indorser liable is seven days after the indorsement [3-503(2)(b)].

11. Dishonor

Dishonor The primary party's refusal to make payment or grant acceptance within the allocated time after presentment is properly made by a holder.

The party who presents an instrument is entitled to have the instrument paid or accepted. If the party to whom the instrument is presented refuses to pay or accept, the instrument is **dishonored** [3-507(1)]. The timing of the primary party's response to a presentment becomes crucial in determining whether dishonor occurs.

When a draft is presented to the drawee for *acceptance,* the drawee may wish to ascertain some facts from the drawer before assuming the obligation of an acceptor. As a result, the law allows the drawee to defer acceptance until the close of the next business day following presentment [3-506(1)]. If the drawee needs more time within which to obtain information, the holder can give the drawee one additional business day within which to accept. The secondary parties are not discharged by the one-day postponement. The holder who presents the draft for *acceptance* is seeking the drawee's obligation on the paper and will not receive payment until a later date. For this reason, the Code permits a longer period of time within which to accept a draft than is allowed when the draft is presented for payment.

When an instrument is presented for *payment,* the party to whom presentment is made is allowed a reasonable time to examine the instrument, to determine whether the instrument is properly payable, but payment must be made in any event on the same day that it is presented and before the close of business on that day [3-506(2)]. With respect to checks, to make this section of the UCC consistent with others, the use of the word *payment* on the day of the presentment must include a provisional payment or settlement that can be revoked within the payor bank's midnight deadline [4-302(a)]. If this provisional payment is not made by the payor bank on the day of presentment or if the bank revokes such a payment within its midnight deadline, a dishonor of the check occurs.

12. Notice of Dishonor

Notice of dishonor Notification that the primary party has dishonored the instrument by refusing payment or acceptance, whichever one was requested upon presentment.

When an instrument has been dishonored on proper presentment, the holder must give prompt **notice of the dishonor** to have a right of recourse against secondary parties [3-508(1)].

The timing for the delivery of an effective notice of dishonor is of the utmost importance. Except for banks, notice must be given before midnight of the third business day after dishonor [3-508(2)]. A person who has received notice of dishonor and wishes to notify other parties must do so before midnight of the third business day after receipt of the notice.

Banks must give any necessary notice before the bank's "midnight deadline"—before midnight of the next banking day following the day on which a bank receives the notice of dishonor [3-508(2)].

Notice may be given in any reasonable manner, including oral notice, notice by telephone, and notice by mail. The notice must identify the dishonored instrument and state that it has been dishonored. Written notice is effective when sent, even though it is not received, if it bears proper address and postage [3-508(4)].

13. Protest

Protest is a certificate stating the following: An instrument was presented for payment or acceptance, it was dishonored, and the reasons, if any, given for refusal to accept or pay [3-509]. It is a formal method for satisfying the conditions precedent and is required only for drafts that are drawn or payable outside the United States. The protest requirement is in conformity with foreign law in this respect. In other cases, protest is optional with the holder. Protest serves as evidence that presentment was made, dishonor occurred, and notice of dishonor was given. It creates a presumption that the conditions precedent were satisfied.

LIABILITY OF SECONDARY PARTIES

14. Introduction

So far in this chapter, we have studied which parties are classified as having secondary liability, and we have examined the conditions that generally must be satisfied to hold these secondary parties liable. In the following six sections, we will refine our understanding of the liability of the parties on commercial paper. After reading these sections, you should feel comfortable determining which parties are liable if the primary party does not pay the instrument and which parties are liable if the primary party pays by mistake.

15. Accommodation Parties

One who signs an instrument for the purpose of lending his or her name and credit to another party to an instrument is an *accommodation party* [3-415(1)]. He or she may sign as an indorser, maker, or acceptor or as a co-maker or co-acceptor. The accommodation party is liable in the capacity in which he or she signed [3-415(2)]. As an indorser, the accommodation party does not indorse for the purpose of transferring the paper, but rather to lend security to it.

Since any party, including a co-maker, may be an accommodation party, and accommodation parties are treated somewhat differently from other parties, issues as to the status of a party frequently arise. The intention of parties is the significant element in determining whether one who signs a note is an accommodation party or a principal maker. The primary factors to be considered in determining the intent of the parties are (1) whether or not the proceeds of the instrument are received by the party, and (2) whether the signature was required as a condition of the loan. If the party did not receive the proceeds but the creditor demanded the signature as a condition for the loan, the party signing is an accommodation party.

Suretyship The legal relationship whereby one person becomes a surety for the benefit of the creditor and debtor.

Surety A person who agrees to become liable to the creditor for the debtor's obligation in the event the debtor fails to perform as promised.

Whether the signature is as a co-maker or indorser, it should be recognized that the liability of an accommodation party is supported by the consideration that flows from the creditor to the principal debtor, and the fact that no consideration flowed directly to the accommodation party is no defense. Lack of benefit to a party does tend to show the status of the party, however.

The significance of being an accommodation party is found in the law of **suretyship.** An accommodation party is a **surety.** In some situations a surety is entitled to a discharge from liability where other parties are not. The right to discharge may be asserted against one who is not a holder in due course [3-415(3)]. Sureties have a right of contribution from co-sureties. Sureties are not liable to the party accommodated. If a surety is required to pay, he or she can obtain reimbursement from the accommodated party [3-415(5)]. The following case demonstrates the benefits of being an accommodation party.

CASE

Mobley v. Harmon
803 S.W.2d 900 (Ark. 1991)

BROWN, J.

The sole issue in this appeal is whether an accommodation maker who has paid off a promissory note owed a bank and been formally assigned that note can recover the amount paid against the co-maker of the note. . . .

Appellant Jeff Mobley and appellee John Harmon had been friends for a long time, and in 1981 Harmon asked Mobley to cosign a promissory note and assist him in getting a $10,000 loan from First National Bank of Russellville. The bank loan officer preferred to lend the money to Mobley, whom he knew, and have Harmon cosign the note. On October 20, 1981, both parties signed a note as makers in the amount of $10,000. The proceeds of the loan, in the form of a cashier's check, went solely to Harmon as payee. The note was due and payable in full on April 20, 1982. . . .

Harmon made payments on the loan and then defaulted, and Mobley subsequently assumed responsibility for the payments. These payments by both makers reduced the note principal to $6,776.77. The note was extended several times by the bank. The first four extension agreements were signed by both Harmon and Mobley. . . .

In January, 1984, Harmon moved to Texas. Also in 1984 Mobley had open heart surgery. After Harmon's move, four additional extension agreements were signed by Mobley and the bank without Harmon's consent. . . . In the case of each of those extensions, Mobley testified that he did not get Harmon's signature because "I either couldn't find him or he refused to come back [from

Texas], one or the other." Harmon testified that he refused to sign one of the extensions and "then he [Mobley] quit communicating with me.". . . Harmon returned to Arkansas in 1986.

The last extension agreement was signed by Mobley on January 7, 1986, and it extended the due date on the note to July 8, 1986. However, Mobley decided to pay off the note two days after signing the last extension and did so on January 9, 1986. On that same date the bank formally assigned its interest in the note to Mobley.

Mobley filed suit against Harmon on March 28, 1989, to recoup the amount paid to the Russellville bank. After a trial before the court, the judge held in favor of Harmon and dismissed Mobley's lawsuit on the basis that Harmon's liability was discharged under the Uniform Commercial Code. . . . [Mobley appealed.]

We begin by noting that Harmon and Mobley claim the same status as accommodation maker, and each party fervently asserts that the other was primary maker. It is true that the bank clearly wanted Mobley as the primary maker because it had had no dealings with Harmon. But Harmon received the full benefit of the loan, which was undoubtedly orchestrated for his benefit.

We have said in recent cases that the intention of the parties is the most significant element in determining accommodation status, and where a person receives no direct benefit from an executed note, it is likely that he will be regarded as the accommodation party. We therefore agree that the total circumstances support the trial court's determination that Mobley was the accommodation maker.

This case is then governed by the Uniform Commercial Code, and conflicting sections are involved. The Code first discusses liability between the accommodator and the person accommodated:

(5) An accommodation party is not liable to the party accommodated, and if he pays the instrument has a right of recourse on the instrument against such party.

Ark. Code Ann. § 4-3-415(5) (1987). This section would appear to give Mobley clear recourse against Harmon.

Yet in a subsequent section the Code impairs that right of recourse and discharges certain parties to the note, including note holders, under facts which exist in this case. The particular defense that inures to Harmon's benefit is discharged under the impairment-of-recourse section:

(1) The holder discharges any party to the instrument to the extent that without such party's consent the holder:

(a) Without express reservation of rights releases or agrees not to sue any person against whom the party has to the knowledge of the holder a right of recourse or agrees to suspend the right to enforce against such person the instrument or collateral or otherwise discharges such person. . . .

Ark. Code Ann. § 4-3-606(1)(a) (1987).

That is precisely what occurred in this case. The bank agreed to suspend the right to enforce its note against Harmon, when it looked only to Mobley to sign the last four extension agreements. . . . The Commercial Code is clear that the last extension agreed to by Harmon "authorized a single extension for not longer than the original period" unless otherwise specified. That would authorize an extension for six months, or until April 30, 1984. Beyond that date Harmon and Mobley were in default, and when the bank chose to extend the obligation four more times with only Mobley's agreement, it effectively released Harmon. This discharge defense was available to Harmon had the bank sought collection on the note. . . .

However, . . . the Russellville bank assigned the note to the accommodator, Mobley, who became holder of the note. Ordinarily a holder takes a note assignment subject to all defenses which the maker had against the bank. But the Code specifically gives an accommodation maker an independent cause of action against the party accommodated, as already shown in this opinion. Mobley therefore is not suing Harmon merely in his status as note holder, but is suing him under the authority of a separate Code provision which empowers him to do so. Because of this independent status under section 4-3-415(5), Mobley's right of recourse is unencumbered by any defenses Harmon held against the bank.

The policy behind this result is certainly sound and is best illustrated in the following commentary:

It also follows from the nature of the surety's undertaking that he is entitled to recover from the debtor any payment he is called on to make to the creditor. If a friend agrees to sign another's note and is ultimately made to pay that note to the creditor, curbstone equity tells us that he should have a cause of action against the person who actually benefited from the creditor's loan.

In light of this reasoning we cannot agree with the trial court that Harmon's liability was automatically discharged *against all parties* when the note was extended without his consent. As already noted the discharge was a defense available to Harmon against the bank. . . . But it was not a defense available against an accommodation party who is suing the party accommodated. . . .

■ *Reversed and remanded.*

CASE CONCEPTS REVIEW

1. How was the note, which was payable to the Russellville Bank, signed by Mobley and Harmon?
2. On what basis does the court determine that Mobley is an accommodation party?
3. Why does the court conclude that the Bank had no claim of payment against Harmon?
4. Why is Mobley allowed to recover against Harmon?

16. Guarantors

The liability of an accommodation party arises without express words. A guarantor's liability is based on words of guaranty. If the words *payment guaranteed* or their equivalent are added to a signature, the signer engages that if the instrument is not paid when due, he or she will pay it without previous resort by the holder to other parties on the paper [3-416(1)]. If the words *collection guaranteed* are added to a signature, the signer becomes liable only after the holder has reduced a claim against the maker or acceptor to judgment, and execution has been returned unsatisfied, or after the maker or acceptor has become insolvent or it is otherwise apparent that it is useless to proceed against him or her [3-416(2)].

A guarantor differs from other types of secondary parties in that the guarantor's liability is based on the primary party's failure to pay alone. The conditions precedent of presentment and notice of dishonor being given within reasonable times do not have to be satisfied to hold the guarantor liable on the guaranty [3-416(5)].

17. Drawers

Drawer's contract The implicit promise made when the drawer signs a negotiable draft. This promise states that the drawer generally will pay the amount of the instrument if the drawee dishonors it.

While drawers are secondary parties in the sense that they expect their drawees to pay, it is accurate to state that generally a drawer is going to be liable to pay if the drawee refuses to pay a properly drawn draft. There are two reasons that support this conclusion. First, most drawers are parties to the underlying contract that gives rise to the commercial paper. For example, if a buyer writes a check in payment for the goods or services received and the check is dishonored, that buyer remains liable to pay since such payment is the performance due under the sales or service contract.

A second reason that drawers generally are liable when their drafts are dishonored concerns the application of the UCC provisions. Under Article 3, anytime a person signs a negotiable draft (such as a check) as a drawer, that party implicitly makes a promise. This promise is known as the **drawer's contract.** By his or her signature, the drawer has committed to pay the draft if presentment is properly made, dishonor occurs, and notice of dishonor is timely given [3-413(2)]. A certificate of protest can substitute for proof that these conditions have occurred.

For the purposes of this drawer's contract, presentment must be made within thirty days of the draft's issuance [3-503(2)(a)]. The notice of dishonor is timely if it is delivered by a bank within its midnight deadline or by any other party before midnight of the third business day after dishonor occurred or that party received the notice of dishonor [3-508(2)]. These timely requirements make it appear that the drawer is discharged of liability under the drawer's contract if either presentment or notice of dishonor is delayed beyond these reasonable periods. However, this discharge occurs only if the delay in presentment or in delivery of notice of dishonor causes the drawer to lose money due to the drawee's insolvency [3-502(1)(b)]. Since payor banks seldom become insolvent and federal insurance protects the bank's customers in the event of such insolvency, a drawer of a check is likely to remain liable on the check even if there is an unreasonable delay in presentment or notice of dishonor being given. Therefore, while the UCC classifies the drawer as a secondary party, in reality the drawer's liability for checks is very similar to that of a primary party.

18. Indorsers

Indorser's contract The implicit promise that an indorser makes to pay the instrument if certain conditions are satisfied.

CONDITIONAL LIABILITY.   An indorser of a note, certificate of deposit, draft, or check implicitly creates a contract of liability by the indorsement. Like that of the drawer, this **indorser's contract** is based on the conditional liability of the indorser as a secondary party. In essence, by indorsing a negotiable instrument, the indorser is saying, "I will pay if this instrument is properly presented, dishonored, and notice of dishonor is timely given" [3-414(1)].

The relevant time period for presentment (or furtherance of the collection process) is within seven days after the indorsement [3-503(2)(b)]. The time period allowed for a proper delivery of notice of dishonor is the same as provided in the drawer's contract (midnight deadline for banks; third business day for other parties) [3-508(2)]. In contrast with the drawer, if either the presentment or notice of dishonor is unreasonably delayed, the indorser is relieved of all liability on the instrument [3-502(1)(1)].

EXAMPLE   David signs a $50 check payable to Paula. This check is in payment for Paula letting David use her car during the past weekend. Paula indorses the check to Terry in payment for Terry giving Paula a ride to an out-of-town concert. Terry keeps the check for two months before depositing it. When this check is presented, through the collection process, to David's bank, it is dishonored because David's account has insufficient funds. If notice of dishonor is appropriately given to all the banks in the collection process and if Terry's depositary bank gives Terry timely notice of dishonor, can Terry collect from Paula on her indorser's contract? The answer is no. Terry's unreasonable delay in making presentment or in initiating the collection process by depositing the check discharges Paula, as an indorser, from further liability on the check. *Note:* Terry can collect from David because the delay in presentment (and possible delay in delivering notice of dishonor) does not relieve David of liability. The payor bank was not insolvent in this example; hence, David has not lost any money due to Terry's delays.

Suppose that, in this preceding example, there had been a number of indorsers. In essence, because the collection process may involve several banks, there probably are numerous indorsers. Indorsers are liable in the order of their indorsements. An indorser who is required to pay the instrument will seek recovery from the preceding indorser. One indorser in the chain of negotiation may fail to deliver notice of dishonor to the preceding indorser within a reasonable time period. This indorser may still recover if he can show that notice of dishonor was received by the preceding indorser from another source. Proper notice operates for the benefit of all parties who have rights on the instrument against the party notified [3-508(8)]. Thus, it is necessary to notify a party only once for his or her liability to be fixed. Assume that A, B, C, and D are indorsers in that order.

- Holder gives notice to A and C only.
- C will not be required to give additional notice to A.
- If C is compelled to pay, C would have recourse against A.
- B and D are discharged if they are not notified by the holder or one of the indorsers.

WITHOUT RECOURSE.   The conditional liability of indorsers can be disclaimed if they indorse the negotiable instrument with the words *without recourse* [3-414(1)]. These words are interpreted to mean that even if the instrument is dishonored upon proper presentment and timely notice of dishonor is delivered, the indorser cannot be held liable to pay the instrument. The holder of the unpaid instrument then can attempt to hold another secondary party liable. Such a party might be an indorser who did not sign *without recourse* or the drawer.

Perhaps you are asking yourself, As a potential holder of the instrument, what good is it to have an indorsement which is qualified by the phrase *without recourse*? The answer is presented in the next subsection.

UNCONDITIONAL LIABILITY.   In addition to having conditional liability, all indorsers become unconditionally liable to pay the indorsed instrument under certain circumstances. This unconditional nature of the indorser's liability is designed to assist in allocating losses when a primary party pays an instrument by mistake. The following situations are covered by the indorser's unconditional liability:

1. A primary party pays an instrument that contains a forged indorsement.
2. A primary party pays an instrument that contains a forged maker's or drawer's signature.
3. A primary party pays an instrument that has been materially altered.

By indorsing the instrument, the indorser makes certain warranties. The existence of specific warranties depends on whether the party receiving the instrument is the primary party or simply another holder who is assisting in the collection process. An indorser who makes presentment to the primary party automatically warrants that the indorser has good title to the instrument, that the indorser has no knowledge of the drawer's or maker's signature being forged, and that the instrument has not been materially altered [3-417(1)]. An indorser who negotiates the instrument to a holder who is not the primary party warrants that the indorser has good title, that all signatures are genuine, that the instrument has not been materially altered, that there are no defenses good against the indorser, and that the indorser has no knowledge of any insolvency proceedings involving the maker, acceptor, or drawer [3-417(2)].

The reason for distinguishing between these two sets of warranties, depending on the status of the recipient, can best be explained by examining which parties to the commercial paper should be liable if the instrument contains a forgery. A discussion of situations 1 and 2 in the preceding list is presented in detail in sections 20 and 21. Prior to turning to that material, some additional points about these warranties need to be addressed.

Which party should be liable if an instrument that passes through numerous holders contains an alteration? The unconditional liability of the indorser's warranties would make the party that dealt with the alterer ultimately liable [3-417(1)(c) and (2)(c)]. In an example involving an altered check, the drawer would be able to have the payor bank recredit the account in the amount of the alteration since this check was not properly payable [4-401]. The payor bank can collect from the presenting bank, and it can collect from its predecessor and so on back up the chain of negotiation to the party that first took the altered check. Each party could correctly claim that the preceding party breached the warranty that the instrument was not materially altered.

The drafters of Article 4 included the same two sets of warranties in § 4-207 to make it very clear that customers of banks are treated the same way as indorsers who transfer the instrument outside the collection process.

What impact does a qualified indorsement (without recourse) have on the warranties? Remember, the phrase *without recourse* negated or disclaimed the indorser's conditional liability. A similar result does not occur with respect to the indorser's unconditional liability. An indorser who signs without recourse may still become liable for a breach of warranty. The only impact a qualified indorsement has on the warranties is to change this indorser's warranty about no defenses being good against him or her to a warranty that the indorser has *no knowledge* of any such defenses [3-417(3)].

19. Transferors without Indorsement

In the preceding subsection, our discussion was limited to warranties made by indorsers. In fact, these warranties arise whenever there is a transfer of an instrument. Even when bearer paper is negotiated by delivery alone, warranties are given by the transferor to the transferee. They are the same warranties an unqualified indorser makes, except that the warranties run only to the immediate transferee, whereas the indorser's warranties extend to all subsequent holders [3-417(2)].

20. Forgeries

Now we return to two situations in which the primary party has paid an instrument by mistake. When the mistake is based on the unauthorized signature of the drawer or of an indorser, the primary party once again looks to the warranties discussed in the preceding two sections.

Forgery False writing or alteration of an instrument with the fraudulent intent of deceiving and injuring another. Writing another's name on a check without consent.

Banks have a special problem in connection with **forgeries.** Checks presented to payor banks for payment may bear forged signatures of drawers or forged indorsements. If the drawer's signature is forged, the bank that honors the check has not followed the order of the drawer and cannot charge the account [4-401]. If charged, it must be recredited. Likewise, the bank will have to make restitution to the party whose name was forged on the check as an indorsement [3-419(1)(c)]. In either case, the loss initially is that of the bank that pays the instrument bearing the forgery.

In the case of a forged drawer's signature, the payor bank as a general rule cannot collect payment from the party who received the payment. This party simply warranted that he or she had no knowledge of the drawer's signature being forged. Assuming this party had no actual knowledge of the forgery, there is no breach of the warranty [3-417(1)(b) and 4-207(1)(b)]. The bank has the signature of the drawer on file and is charged with knowledge of the forgers. This general rule is subject to the exception that if the party receiving payment is the forger or dealt with the forger and was negligent in doing so, the payor may recover the payment. Thus, if a collecting bank was negligent, the payor bank that paid on a forged drawer's signature could recover from the collecting bank.

A payor bank who pays on a forged indorsement has greater rights in seeking to recover the payment than does the payor who pays on a forged drawer's signature. In the case of a forged indorsement, the payor has no way of knowing about the forgery, and thus it can collect from the person to whom payment was made, who in turn can collect from all prior parties back to the forger. The following case illustrates how banks utilize the warranties made within the collection process in the event that the instrument contains a forgery.

CASE

E.S.P., Inc. v. Midway National Bank
447 N.W.2d 882 (Minn. 1989)

KELLEY, J.

. . . Barr and Nelson, Inc. maintained a checking account with Midway. On February 3, 1981, Barr and Nelson, Inc.

issued a check for $30,000 payable to Mechanical Constructors and E.S.P. Heating as joint payees. That same day Mechanical Constructors deposited the check into its First Bank account. At the time of deposit, E.S.P., Inc.'s endorsement had apparently been forged on the back of the check. E.S.P., Inc.'s share of the $30,000 check was $17,600. On February 6, 1981, First Bank received payment of the $30,000 from Midway. E.S.P., Inc. claims it never received its portion of the proceeds.

More than four years later, on February 25, 1985, E.S.P., Inc. sent to Midway an affidavit of forgery. Upon receipt, Midway notified First Bank of the forgers claim and requested that First Bank remit to Midway the $17,600 claimed by E.S.P., Inc. First Bank disclaimed responsibility and failed to remit.

Nearly six years after Midway paid the check, on January 30, 1987, E.S.P., Inc. commenced this action against Midway. Its claim is based upon conversion under Minn. Stat. § 336.3-419(1)(c) (1988). Under Minnesota law, E.S.P., Inc. is prevented from suing First Bank directly even though First Bank was that bank which collected the check without verifying the endorsements. Minn. Stat. § 336.3-419(3) (1988) provides a depository or collecting bank with defenses in a direct suit by a payee; it does, however, permit a payee, such as E.S.P., Inc., to sue the payor bank for conversion because it converted the check when it paid on a forged endorsement. . . .

Although Midway, as payor bank, may be liable for conversion, it, in turn, may look to First Bank, the collecting and depositary bank, for restitution. The warranty of good title automatically arises as part of the interbank collection process. All banks in the collection chain are liable if that warranty is breached, but only the initial collecting or depositary bank has a duty to check endorsements. The purpose underlying the rule is to place the loss upon the party who last dealt with the wrongdoer. This party is best able to prevent the conversion by carefully checking endorsements. Therefore, First Bank, as the result of the warranty of title arising under Minn. Stat. § 336.4-207(1)(a), ultimately would be liable to Midway, the payor bank.

Because the Uniform Commercial Code places that ultimate responsibility for E.S.P., Inc.'s loss on First Bank, . . . Midway served upon First Bank this third-party action. In reply, First Bank argues that . . . Midway's action is barred by the statute of limitations because it was commenced more than six years after the statutory warranty was breached.

The question in this case is . . . when the six-year limitation period commences to run. First Bank argues that Midway's claim is for a breach of warranty and, therefore, the statute commenced to run at the time of the breach (February 6, 1981). In contrast, Midway argues that its action is for indemnity for the loss it may sustain as the result of First Bank's breach of statutory warranty of title. Because limitation statutes generally commence to run on indemnity claims at the time the indemnitee sustained a loss, and since Midway sustains no loss until it is compelled to pay E.S.P., Inc., the statute has not yet commenced to run. Accordingly, Midway asserts, its third party action is timely.

Both the trial court, when it granted First Bank summary judgment, and the court of appeals, when it af-

firmed that judgment, rejected Midway's argument. Both courts concluded that Midway's third-party action was premised on the breach of warranty, which, if it occurred at all, took place six years and six days before institution of this third-party action against First Bank. . . .

The court of appeals . . . opined that Midway received from E.S.P., Inc. in 1985 an affidavit of forgery and was put on notice of the potential claim, after which it could have commenced a declaratory judgment action against First Bank. Because it did not do so, the majority implied . . . that Midway cannot now complain if the six-year statute is now applied to bar its claim. . . . To require a payor bank, such as Midway, to commence suit before it has suffered a loss each time it receives an affidavit of forgery, although suit ultimately may never be brought against the bank for conversion, would create an intolerable burden on banks. Not only would such a requirement be burdensome on payor banks, but other banks as well in the collection chain who have not at the time of receiving the notice sustained a loss, or who may never sustain one as a result of the forged endorsement. It is likewise burdensome on the judicial system itself by imposing on it the processing of "litigation" which may never ripen into a case or controversy capable of judicial resolution. To employ a colloquialism, a rule requiring banks in the collection chain to take such precipitate action would be somewhat akin to "putting the cart before the horse." This we decline to do. . . .

We hold that the payor bank who seeks indemnity from the collecting and depositary bank . . . is not barred by the statute of limitations because the statute on that claim does not commence running until the payor bank has sustained loss.

In doing so, however, we emphasize the narrow application of today's holding. It is limited to actions by payor banks, or other banks in the collection chain, for indemnity arising from the breach of the warranty of title under the Uniform Commercial Code, and is specifically designed to further a major purpose of that code—the development of consistent and commercially reasonable rules of law to govern commercial transactions. . . .

■ *Reversed and remanded.*

CASE CONCEPTS REVIEW

1. Which party was the customer-depositor of Midway National Bank?
2. To whom did Barr and Nelson, Inc. write a $30,000 check?
3. Who's indorsement on this check is allegedly forged?
4. What bank is the depositary bank that assisted in the collection of this check with the forged indorsement?

5. Why does E.S.P., Inc. sue the Midway Bank, as the payor bank, instead of the depository bank?

6. What is the basis of Midway Bank asserting its claim against the depository bank?

21. Double Forgeries

Assume that a drawer's signature is forged and that there is no indorsement by the payee or that the payee's indorsement is also forged. Which party bears the loss if the check is paid by the drawee bank? If the rule applicable to forged drawer's signature is followed, the drawee bears the loss because of the prescription that it is familiar with the drawer's signature. If the loss allocation scheme for a check with a forged indorsement is followed, the loss would be on the party who dealt with the forger because that party was in the best position to notice the flaw in the indorsement and to verify the identity of the person forging the indorsement.

The courts that have faced this conflict have resolved it in favor of placing the loss on the drawee bank. A check bearing a double forgery is treated like a check bearing only a forged drawer's signature. This rationale is that in a double forgery situation, no true payee can make a legitimate claim to the check, so any loss suffered by the drawer is attributable to the forged drawer's signature rather than the forged indorsement. The fictitious payee rule is not applicable to cases of double forgeries because the forged indorsement does not cause the drawer's loss. The drawer did not intend payment to any payee, so no payee can appear and demand payment. It is irrelevant whether the payee is real or fictitious and whether the indorsement is forged, missing, or otherwise defective.

ADDITIONAL ASPECTS OF LIABILITY

22. Excuses for Failure to Perform Conditions Precedent

An unexcused delay in making any *necessary* presentment or in giving notice of dishonor discharges parties who are entitled to performance of the conditions precedent. Indorsers are completely discharged by such delay; and drawers, makers of notes payable at a bank, and acceptors of drafts payable at a bank are discharged to the extent of any loss caused by the delay [3-502]. Delay in making presentment, in giving notice of dishonor, or in making protest is excused when the holder has acted with reasonable diligence and the delay is not due to any fault of the holder. The holder must, however, comply with these conditions or attempt to do so as soon as the cause of the delay ceases to exist [3-511(1)].

The performance of the conditions precedent is entirely excused if the party to be charged has *waived* the condition. When such waiver is stated on the face of the instrument, it is binding on all parties; when it is written above the signature of the indorser, it binds only the indorser [3-511(6)]. Most promissory notes contain such a waiver.

The performance of the conditions precedent is also excused if the party to be charged has dishonored the instrument or has countermanded payment or otherwise has no reason to expect or right to require that the instrument be accepted or paid [3-511(2)(b)]. If a drawer of a check has stopped payment on the check, the drawer is not in a position to complain about slow presentment or any lack of notice of dishonor.

23. Discharge of Liability

The liability of various parties may be discharged in a variety of ways, many of them previously noted [3-601]. Certification of a check at the request of a holder discharges all prior parties [3-411]. Any ground for discharging a simple contract also discharges commercial paper [3-601(2)].

Payment usually discharges a party's liability. This is true even if the payor has knowledge of the claim of another person. Payment does not operate to discharge liability if the payor acts in bad faith and pays one who acquired the instrument by theft. Payment is also no defense if paid in violation of a restrictive indorsement [3-603].

A holder may discharge any party by intentionally canceling the instrument or by striking out or otherwise eliminating a party's signature. The surrender of the instrument to a party will also discharge that party [3-605].

If a holder agrees not to sue one party or agrees to release *collateral,* then all parties with rights against such party or against the collateral are discharged from liability. This assumes that there is no express reservation of rights by the holder and that the party claiming discharge did not consent to the holder's actions [3-606].

When an instrument is reacquired by a prior party, this party may cancel all intervening indorsements. In this event, all indorsements are canceled and the indorsers are discharged [3-208].

Fraudulent and material alteration of an instrument discharges any party whose liability is affected by the alteration. Of course, this is not true if the alteration is agreed to or if the party seeking to impose liability is a holder in due course [3-407]. In fact, no discharge is effective against a holder in due course unless he or she has notice of the discharge when taking the instrument [3-602].

REVISED ARTICLE 3

As in the conclusions to the preceding three chapters, we highlight here the more significant changes made in the 1990 Revised Article 3. The following discussion is presented in the order that the material appears in this chapter. As in the preceding three chapters, references to Code sections are to the Revised Article 3 unless stated otherwise.

With respect to agency principles, Revised Article 3 makes it easier for agents, regardless of how they sign an instrument, to establish that their principal should be the liable party. For example, principals that are undisclosed to the payee and subsequent holders are liable for their instruments once their existence and identity are disclosed. This liability continues regardless of how the agent signed the instrument [3-402(a)]. In another situation designed to protect the agent, Revised Article 3 allows a person who signs in an ambiguous manner to prove, with oral testimony or other evidence, that the original party to the instrument did not intend to hold this agent liable [3-402(b)(ii)]. This opportunity for the agent to prove the lack of personal responsibility does not apply when a holder in due course takes the instrument. Finally, an agent may sign a check written on the principal's account without indicating a representative capacity. If this check contains the principal's name, the agent is not liable [3-402(c)]. This rule seems logical since the preprinted form of the check gives the payee and holders notice that an agency relationship must exist.

Revised Article 3 broadens the imposter rule and holds the drawer, rather than the drawee, liable even when the check is written to a purported principal of the imposter. Thus, the imposter who is posing as an agent may provide an effective indorsement even though it is unauthorized [3-404(a)].

Under the revised fictitious payee rule, the indorsement needs to be substantially similar to the name of the payee on the instrument [3-405(c)]. The original Article 3 requires an indorsement that exactly matches the payee's name. A second change with the fictitious payee rule concerns an expansion of the rule to cover a broader range of activities by a fraudulent employee. For example, an employee of the drawer who steals a check that the drawer actually intended for the named payee can provide an indorsement, effectively shifting the loss to the employer/drawer and away from the drawee [3-405(a) and (b)].

Recognizing the utilization of modern means of communication, Revised Article 3 permits presentment [3-501(b)(1)] and notice of dishonor [3-503(b)] to be made by electronic means. Other methods of communication contained in the original Article 3 are still permissible.

Revised Article 3 continues the basic elements of conditional liability of secondary parties. However, the timing aspects of satisfying these conditions are relaxed. There is no explicit provision requiring presentment to be made within a stated time period. In essence, original § 3-503 is omitted. However, with respect to discharging the indorser's contract, a reference to presentment within thirty days is discussed later in this section. The timing for a bank to give an effective notice of dishonor continues to be within the applicable midnight deadline [3-503(c)(i)]. However, nonbanking entities have thirty days to give notice of dishonor rather than the original three business days [3-503(c)(ii)].

There has been some confusion about the legal distinction between an accommodation party and a guarantor under the original Article 3. The revision attempts to clarify this confusion by indicating that guarantors in essence are accommodating another party who may become liable for the instrument [3-419(c) and (d)].

One of the most significant changes in the Revised Article 3 concerns the drawer's contract. While presentment must be made and dishonor must occur before a drawer can be held liable for the draft, delivery of a notice of dishonor no longer needs to be made to the drawer [3-414(b)]. In this way, the drawer is viewed much more like a primarily liable party. This change seems sensible in light of the discussion in section 17 of how the drawer generally remains liable for payment of the drafts issued.

Revised Article 3 continues to permit discharge of an indorser's liability if notice of dishonor is not properly given [3-415(c)] or if presentment is not made in a timely manner [3-415(e)]. Changes are made with respect to the time periods allowed for the satisfaction of both these conditions. As stated earlier, persons other than banks have thirty days to deliver notice of dishonor [3-503(c)(ii)]. Whereas original § 3-503(2)(b) requires presentment to be made or collection furthered within seven days of the indorsement, the new time period is thirty days [3-415(e)].

Finally, Revised Article 3 attempts to simplify the language concerning the warranties made by any party transferring an instrument. This simplification and clarification is accomplished by creating two Code sections to replace original

§ 3-417. First, the same five warranties made to a transferee who is not the payor are called "Transfer Warranties" [3-416]. The three warranties made to obtain presentment of the instrument for payment are known as "Presentment Warranties" [3-417]. Similar sets of warranties are a part of Revised Article 4 [4-207 and 4-208].

In addition to separating the warranties based on to whom they are made, Revised Article 3 also provides three changes with respect to these warranties. First, the three presentment warranties (rights to enforce the instrument, no alteration, and no knowledge of the drawer's signature being forged) are made only to the drawee of an unaccepted draft. If a holder is seeking payment from (1) an indorser or the drawer of a dishonored draft or (2) a maker of a note, that holder warrants only that he or she has the right to enforce the instrument [3-417(d)]. The warranties of no alteration and no knowledge of the drawer's or maker's signature being forged are viewed as unnecessary to protect these paying parties. They should have as much, if not more, knowledge and ability to detect alterations and forged signatures as the holder seeking payment.

Second, any party (whether a transferee or a payor) asserting a claim for breach of warranty must have provided notice of such a claim within thirty days of learning of the breach [3-416(c) and 3-417(e)].

Third, the qualified indorsement made with the phrase *without recourse* has no impact whatsoever on the warranties made by the indorser of a check [3-416(c) and 3-417(e)]. The removal of this type of indorsement having any impact on the warranties allows banks in the collection process to rely on these warranties in passing liability to the wrongdoer or at least to the party who dealt with the wrongdoer.

CHAPTER SUMMARY

LIABILITY BASED ON SIGNATURES

In General	1. Signatures of makers, drawers, and acceptors are affixed to the front of an instrument. Indorsements generally are on the back of the paper.
	2. All signatures generally must be genuine to hold the signer liable.
Capacity of the Signature	1. Liability of the signer varies, depending on whether the signature is that of a maker, acceptor, drawer, or indorser.
	2. The signature also may indicate the accommodation nature of the signer.
	3. The capacity of the signature usually is reflected by its location.
	4. When the signature is not clear as to the capacity, the signature is an indorsement.
Agency Principles	1. No person is liable on an instrument unless his or her signature is on the instrument, but it may be affixed by an agent.
	2. A principal is bound by acts of his or her agent. If the agent is not authorized to sign, the principal is not bound unless he or she ratifies it or is estopped from asserting lack of authority.
	3. An agent is personally liable if he or she fails to show representative capacity or fails to bind the principal.
Exceptions: Impostors and Fictitious Payees	1. If a check is payable to an imposter or fictitious payee and indorsed by the impostor or by the person supplying the name of the fictitious person, the indorsement is effective as a negotiation. In such a case, the loss falls on the drawer and not the bank.
	2. These situations usually are a part of an embezzlement scheme, and the loss is placed on the employer who was in a position to prevent it from occurring.

Classification of Parties	1. Parties to commercial paper are either primarily or secondarily liable.
	2. Primary parties include makers of notes, drawees of drafts, and acceptors.
	3. Secondary parties include accommodation parties, guarantors, drawers of drafts, and indorsers.
Liability of Primary Parties	1. These parties agree to pay the instruments in accordance with their terms.
	2. The secondary parties and holders expect the primary party to make payment or grant acceptance, whichever is requested.

CONDITIONAL LIABILITY

Presentment	1. Presentment is a demand on a maker or drawee for payment or acceptance. Failure to make a proper presentment results in complete discharge of indorsers.
	2. Presentment by mail or through a clearinghouse is effective. It may also be made at the place of business of the party to accept or pay. The party on whom presentment is made has the power to require exhibition of the instrument.
	3. Presentment must be made on the day of maturity, or if payable on demand, it must be presented or negotiated within a reasonable time after such secondary party became liable.
	4. Drawer of a check is liable for thirty days after date or issue, whichever is later. An indorser is liable for seven days after indorsement. Presentment beyond these time periods releases indorsers, but the drawer may remain liable.
Dishonor	1. If an instrument is presented and not paid or accepted, it is dishonored.
	2. If presentment is for acceptance, the drawee has one additional day to act.
	3. If presentment is for payment, the drawee must act on the presentment that day.
Notice of Dishonor	1. When an instrument is dishonored, the presenting party has recourse against indorsers or other secondary parties, provided that he or she gives notice of dishonor.
	2. Notice of dishonor requires the holder to be prompt in order to have a right of recourse against unqualified indorsers. Except for a bank, the notice must be given before midnight of the third business day.
	3. Banks must give notice of dishonor before the bank's midnight deadline.
	4. Notice may be by any reasonable manner. It may be written, oral, or by phone.
Protest	1. Protest is a certificate stating the instrument was presented for payment, it was dishonored, and the reasons for refusal to accept or pay. It is used primarily in foreign transactions.

LIABILITY OF SECONDARY PARTIES

Accommodation Parties	1. An accommodation party is a surety. Such a party may sign as a maker, acceptor, or indorser.
	2. The nature of this party's signature determines whether the classification of primary or secondary party is more appropriate.
	3. As an indorser, this party does not indorse to negotiate but to lend credit to the instrument.
	4. An accommodation party may collect from co-makers and is not liable to the party accommodated.
Guarantors	1. These parties are identified by the nature of the language accompanying their signatures.
	2. These parties are classified as either payment guarantors or collection guarantors.
Drawers	1. Through the drawer's contract, these secondarily liable parties promise to pay the instrument if presentment is made, dishonor occurs, and notice of dishonor is given.
	2. Even when there is an unreasonable delay in satisfying these conditions, drawers generally remain liable to pay the instrument.

	3. In addition to their liability as parties on the commercial paper, drawers usually are liable as parties to the underlying contract.
Indorsers	**1.** Through the indorser's contract, these secondarily liable parties promise to pay the instrument if presentment is made, dishonor occurs, and notice of dishonor is given.
	2. If there is an unreasonable delay in presentment being made or in notice of dishonor being delivered, the indorsers are discharged from liability.
	3. Indorsers may disclaim the conditional nature of their liability by indorsing "without recourse."
	4. By their indorsements, these parties promise to the primary party that the indorsers have good title to the instrument and no knowledge of the maker's or drawer's signature being forged, and that the instrument is not materially altered.
	5. Indorsers warrant to holders other than the primary party that the indorsers have good title to the instrument, all signatures are genuine, the instrument is not materially altered, there are no good defenses, and there is no knowledge of insolvency proceedings involving the primary parties.
Transferors without Indorsement	**1.** Transferors who do not indorse, but who simply deliver the bearer paper, still make the unconditional warranties.
	2. These warranties bind the transferor only to the immediate transferee and not to subsequent holders.
Forgeries	**1.** A bank that pays on a forged signature of the drawer cannot charge the drawer's account.
	2. A bank paying on the forged signature of an indorser must return the instrument to the party whose name was forged.
	3. In the event of the forged signature of a drawer, the bank cannot collect from the party receiving payment unless that party is the forger or the party dealt with the forger negligently.
	4. A payor bank that pays on a forged indorsement can collect from the person to whom payment was made.
Double Forgeries	**1.** If both the drawer's signature and an indorsement are forged, the loss falls on the drawee.
	2. If the drawer's signature is forged, it is irrelevant whether the payee is real or fictitious and whether the indorsement is forged, missing, or otherwise defective.

ADDITIONAL ASPECTS OF LIABILITY

Excuses for Failure to Perform Conditions Precedent	**1.** Conditions precedent of notice of dishonor, presentment, or protest may be waived by the party to be charged. Such waivers are contained in most notes.
Discharge of Liability	**1.** Discharge of a party's liability may be accomplished by payment, cancellation of the instrument, surrender of the instrument, or fraudulent and material alteration of an instrument.

REVIEW QUESTIONS AND PROBLEMS

1. Match each term in column A with the appropriate statement in column B.

A	B
(1) Presentment	(a) One who signs an instrument for the purpose of lending his or her name and credit to another party
(2) Dishonor	(b) The secondary liability that results from the status of parties as drawers or unqualified indorsers

(3) Notice of dishonor

(4) Accommodation party

(5) Protest

(6) Primary party

(7) Acceptor

(8) Unconditional liability

(9) Conditional liability

(c) A person who agrees to pay an instrument according to its terms

(d) A person who is primarily liable on a draft

(e) The liability of one who negotiates by use of a qualified indorsement

(f) A refusal to pay or to accept

(g) A requirement for conditional liability

(h) A formal method of satisfying conditions precedent

(i) A demand made on a maker or drawee

2. Security Bank sued a corporate borrower, Fastwich, Inc., and certain guarantors of the note. The note was signed as follows:

[typed] FASTWICH, INC.
[/s/] John J. Smith II [/s/] Carolyn Smith
[/s/] Gary D. Smith [/s/] Cheryl J. Smith

Is the corporation bound on the note? Why or why not?

3. Lee executed and delivered a promissory note due November 1, 1993, to the plaintiff bank. The note was a consolidation of previous loans made to Village Homes, Inc., which were in default. The note was signed by Lee personally. "Village Homes, Inc." does not appear anywhere on the note. Is Lee personally liable on the note? Why or why not?

4. John Madera signed a promissory note payable to A. Duda & Sons, Inc., in the amount of $47,872. The note began "for value received, we promise to pay A. Duda & Sons, Inc. . . . ." Madera signed the note beneath the name and address of Tomatoes, Inc., as follows:

TOMATOES, INC.
3118 Produce Row
Houston, Texas 77023

/s/ John Madera

When the note was not paid, Duda & Sons filed suit against Tomatoes and against Madera individually, alleging that the two defendants were jointly and severally liable for the balance due on the note. Is Madera liable on the note in an individual capacity? Explain.

5. Alex was employed by a brokerage company. He devised a scheme to defraud his employer by issuing fraudulent orders to sell customers' securities. When the brokerage firm issued a check to the customer whose stock had been sold, Alex would obtain the check, forge the customer's indorsement, and pocket the money. When the fraud was discovered, the brokerage company sought to recover its losses from the bank on whom the checks were drawn. Is the bank liable for honoring the checks on a forged indorsement? Explain.

6. Anne loaned Donna's son David money to start a business, which later failed. David offered to sign a promissory note for the debt to prevent Anne from instituting legal proceedings against the remaining assets of the failed business. Anne agreed, but would only accept a note cosigned or indorsed by Donna. Donna signed the back of her son's note. Anne sued Donna to collect the note when David could not be located. Is Donna liable? Why?

7. A check in settlement of a lawsuit was made payable jointly to the client and to the attorney. The attorney indorsed it in blank and delivered it to the client. When the check was dishonored, the client sued the attorney to collect the face of the check. Is the attorney liable as an indorser? Why or why not?

8. The defendant received a check drawn on plaintiff's bank. The defendant indorsed the check and received payment from his bank. That bank sent the check for collection to the plaintiff bank, and the check was honored. Several days later, the bank discovered that the drawer of the check did not have an account and that it had mistakenly charged the check to another of its customers. Plaintiff then sought to recover from defendant as an indorser. He contended that the check had not been dishonored within the time allowed by law. Is he liable as an indorser? Why or why not?

9. Mark delivers a negotiable promissory note to Peter. Peter specially indorses it and delivers it to Art. Art adds his signature and delivers it to Bill. Bill, without signing it, delivers it to Carl. Carl indorses without recourse and delivers it to Dick. Dick presents the instrument to Mark, who replies, "I'm sorry, but I have no money." From whom can Dick collect the note? What must he do to collect? Explain.

10. The facts are as in problem 9, except Mark informs Dick that the signature on the note is a forgery. From whom can Dick collect the note? Explain.

11. Plaintiff forwarded two checks to defendant bank for collection. The checks were not honored because of insufficient funds. The drawee bank failed to give notice of dishonor by its midnight deadline. It claims to be excused because of a computer breakdown. The Code excuses delays by banks if caused by "emergency conditions or other circumstances beyond the control of the bank provided it exercises such diligence as the circumstances require." Is the payor bank excused from giving proper notice of dishonor? Explain.

12. On Thursday, May 15, Fox, the payee on a check drawn by Owens of Riverside Bank, indorsed the check to the order of Granger, who, on the same date, indorsed the check to the order of Hines, a mutual friend of Granger and Owens. On Friday, May 16, Hines presented the check for payment at the bank and payment was refused because of insufficient funds in Owens's account. Not wishing to embarrass Owens, Hines telephoned and advised Owens of the bank's refusal to pay and the reason therefor. Owens promised to make a deposit to his bank account on the following Monday and told Hines to again present the check at the bank on that day and it would be paid. Hines agreed but unexpectedly had to go out of town on business and could not again present the check for payment until the following Thursday, May 22. When Hines again presented the check at the bank, payment was again refused for the same reason. Hines thereupon promptly and properly notified Granger, Fox, and Owens of the dishonor of the check. It was later determined that Owens was insolvent. Does Hines have a cause of action against Granger and Fox? Explain. Assuming that Hines may recover from Granger and Fox and recovers from Fox only, may Fox recover from Granger? Explain.

13. Drawer issues a check "to the order of Payee" for $5,000. Forger steals the check from payee, forges payee's name on the check and sells the check to Jane, who deposits it in her account with Depositary Bank. The check proceeds through the bank collection process, where it is ultimately paid by drawee. Because the check was stolen, payee was not paid.
    a. May payee require drawer to issue another check? Why?
    b. Can drawer now require drawee to recredit his account for the first check that was stolen and forged? Why?
    c. Assume that payee seeks recovery from drawee, rather than requiring drawer to issue a new check. Will payee win? Why?
    d. If drawee has either recredited drawer's account or paid payee for conversion of the check, may drawee now recover from Depositary Bank? Why?
    e. Will Depositary Bank now be able to recover from Jane? Why?
    f. Can Jane now recover from forger? Why?

14. Winston Corporation purchased five $1,000 thirty-day notes of the Fubor Corporation. The notes were clever forgeries. The forger, William Claude, drew the notes to his own order and signed the name of Oscar Fubor to the notes as the maker. He then in-

dorsed them to Bernard Oldfield, signing his own name in blank. Oldfield negotiated them to Winston Corporation using a "without recourse" indorsement. What are the rights, if any, of Winston against Fubor, Claude, and Oldfield? Explain.

15. Sue indorsed a note. Above all indorsements was printed, "Notice of protest waived." The note was not paid when it became due. The holder sent notice to Sue's former address, and she did not receive it. Was she properly notified? Why or why not?

CHAPTER

37

INTRODUCTION TO ARTICLE 9: SECURED TRANSACTIONS

CHAPTER PREVIEW

With this chapter, we begin an in-depth examination of the *creditor-debtor* relationship. The creation of this relationship is one of the most common examples of contracts in our society today. The extension of credit occurs at every level of business as well as in our personal lives. For example, manufacturers finance raw materials and equipment; wholesalers and retailers finance inventory; and consumers finance their purchases. The common denominator in all these financial transactions is that the creditor wants to be paid.

Creditors often might feel uncomfortable relying only on the debtor's promise to repay a debt. Particularly when the dollar amount involved is large, creditors often insist on a second source of repayment in addition to the debtor's personal promise to repay. The second source may take several forms. Very often, if the debtor owns any real estate, it is mortgaged to secure a debt. The use of real estate as security is discussed in chapter 39. Another source of repayment is a second person's commitment to pay the debt. This source creates a *suretyship*, which is discussed in chapter 40. A third source is the use of the debtor's personal property as collateral. It is this use of personal property that is the subject matter of this chapter and the next one.

Article 9 of the Uniform Commercial Code provides for a *secured transaction*. This transaction involves a *security interest* in personal property or fixtures granted by a debtor to a creditor, which the creditor can use to obtain satisfaction of the debt in the event of nonpayment [9-102(1)(a)]. A *fixture* is an item of personal property that has become attached to real estate. Items of personal property and fixtures used as security are called *collateral* [9-105(1)(c)]. A creditor who is protected by a valid Article 9 security interest is known as a *secured creditor*. A creditor obtains a security interest by entering into a *security agreement* with the debtor. To be secured as to third parties, the creditor must *perfect* the security interest [9-301].

This chapter discusses the scope of Article 9, the creation of a security interest, and the perfection of such an interest.

■ BUSINESS MANAGEMENT DECISION

As president of a large bank, you are contacted by the president of your community's largest department store. This store seeks an open line of credit of $10 million to finance its inventory worth an estimated $15 million.

If you grant the line of credit, what should you require of the store?

1. Unsecured Creditors

Most debtors voluntarily repay their obligations, and most creditors depend only on the debtor's personal promise to pay. Such creditors are said to be *unsecured*. An unsecured creditor does not have any source other than the debtor from which to collect the debt. A credit sales transaction wherein the seller is unsecured is often called a sale on *open account* or *open credit*.

The danger facing unsecured creditors is illustrated by the steps an unsecured creditor must take if the debtor fails to repay voluntarily. The unsecured creditor must first sue the debtor and obtain a judgment. Then, as a *judgment creditor*, it may pursue the enforcement procedures available to a judgment creditor. These post-judgment procedures include obtaining a writ of execution—having a law enforcement official levy on the debtor's property and having the property sold at a public auction. The process of litigation and enforcement of the judgment are costly in terms of both time and money. More importantly, the debtor may not have any property that can be sold to pay the judgment, in which case the creditor will be unable to collect the debt. Many unsecured debts become simply uncollectible.

2. Secured Creditors

As stated in the introductory paragraphs to this chapter, an Article 9 secured creditor has an interest in one or more items of the debtor's personal property. When these secured creditors perfect their security interests, they are in a much more favorable position than unsecured creditors. For example, the secured creditor, upon the debtor's default, can seize the collateral and have the collateral applied to the payment of the debt. These rights of a secured creditor upon the debtor's default are explained further in chapter 38.

Secured creditors enjoy an advantage when a debtor becomes insolvent or files for bankruptcy. The secured creditor has personal property from which repayment may be obtained. By having a security interest in the debtor's personal property, a secured creditor, in effect, is given priority over unsecured creditors.

However, a perfected secured party is not assured that the debt will be repaid. As discussed in chapter 38, secured creditors may lose their claim to the property under a number of circumstances. Furthermore, the value of the debtor's personal property may be insufficient to satisfy the entire debt. It is the secured creditor's responsibility always to keep informed of the debtor's business practices and personal obligations.

SCOPE OF ARTICLE 9

3. In General

To gain an appreciation for how an Article 9 secured transaction protects creditors, our study is divided into five parts:

1. The scope of Article 9
2. The creation of a security interest
3. The perfection of a security interest
4. The priorities to the collateral
5. The creditor's rights and duties when a debtor defaults

The first three objectives are discussed in this chapter. Priority issues and the creditor's rights and duties on the debtor's default are discussed in chapter 38.

Although Article 9 deals primarily with secured transactions, it also covers outright sales of certain types of property, such as accounts receivable [9-102(1) (b)]. Thus, a sale of the accounts receivable of a business must comply with the Code requirements as if the accounts were security for a loan.

Except for sales such as those of accounts receivable, the main test to be applied in determining whether a given transaction falls within the purview of Article 9 is whether it was intended to have effect as security. Every transaction with such intent is covered [9-102(1)(a)]. A lease with option to buy may be considered a security transaction rather than a lease if the necessary intent is present.

Certain credit transactions are expressly excluded from Article 9 coverage [9-104]. In general, these exclusions involve transactions that are not of a commercial nature. Examples of common exclusions include a landlord's lien, an assignment of wages, and a transfer of an insurance policy. Another important exclusion is the lien created by state law in favor of those who service or repair personal property, such as automobiles. This lien, known as an *artisan's lien,* is discussed in more detail in chapter 40.

4. Classifications of Collateral

The broad application of Article 9 can best be seen by examining the various types of **collateral** covered by it. There is not an item of personal property that cannot be used as collateral in a secured transaction. The only limitation to what is acceptable as collateral is the creditor's willingness to accept an interest in a particular item of personal property.

Collateral may be classified according to its physical makeup into (1) tangible, physical property or goods; (2) documentary property that has physical existence, such as a negotiable instrument, but is simply representative of a contractual obligation; and (3) purely intangible property, such as an account receivable. Each type of collateral presents its own peculiar problems, and the framework of Article 9 is structured on the peculiarities of each type. Table 37–1 summarizes the various classifications of personal property that may be the collateral that is the subject of a security interest. The following three sections also discuss each of these three classifications.

5. Tangible Goods

In secured transactions under Article 9, four categories of *tangible* goods are established. These categories include the following:

1. Consumer goods
2. Equipment
3. Farm products
4. Inventory

TABLE 37–1 ■ Collateral Subject to a Security Interest

TANGIBLE PROPERTY (GOODS)	DOCUMENTARY COLLATERAL	INTANGIBLE PROPERTY
Any personal property that is movable at the time the security interest attaches or that is a fixture [9-105(1)(h)]. A fixture is a special type of article 9 collateral [9-313]. Goods are classified as one of the following: • Consumer goods [9-109(1)] • Equipment [9-109(2)] • Farm products [9-109(3)] • Inventory [9-109(4)]	Involves some indispensable piece of paper and has both tangible and intangible aspects. Documentary collateral is classified into one of the following: • Chattel paper [9-105(1)(b)] • Documents [9-105(1)(f)] • Instruments [9-105(1)(i)]	Not evidenced by an indispensable writing, which distinguishes it from documentary collateral. Intangible property consists of one of the following: • Account [9-106] • General intangibles [9-106]

In determining the classification of any particular item of goods, it is necessary to take into account not only the physical attributes of the collateral but also the status of the debtor who is buying the property or using it as security for a loan and the use the debtor will make of the goods. Keep in mind that the classification will determine the place of filing to perfect the security interest against third parties. It may also affect the rights of the debtor on default.

Consumer goods Goods that are used or bought for use primarily for personal, family, or household purposes.

CONSUMER GOODS. Goods fall into the **consumer goods** classification if they are used or bought primarily for personal, family, or household purposes [9-109(1)].

Equipment Goods that are used or bought for use primarily in business or by a debtor that is a nonprofit organization or a governmental subdivision or agency.

EQUIPMENT. Goods that are used or bought for use primarily in a business, in farming, in a profession, or by a nonprofit organization or governmental agency fall within the **equipment** category [9-109(2)]. The category is something of a catch-all, embracing goods that otherwise defy classification. Since equipment often is attached to realty and becomes a fixture, the discussion of fixtures later is especially significant for the equipment classification.

Farm products Crops or livestock used or produced in farming operations.

FARM PRODUCTS. The **farm products** category includes crops and livestock, supplies used or produced in farming operations, and the products of crops or livestock in their unmanufactured state (ginned cotton, wool, milk, and eggs), provided that the items are in the possession of a debtor who is engaged in farming operations [9-109(3)]. Farm products are *not* equipment or inventory. Note that goods cease to be farm products and must therefore be reclassified when (1) they are no longer in the farmer's possession or (2) they have been subjected to a manufacturing process. Thus, when the farmer delivers his or her farm products to a marketing agency for sale or to a frozen-food processor as raw materials, the products in the hands of the other party are inventory. Likewise, if the farmer maintained a canning operation, the canned product would be inventory, even though it remained in the farmer's possession.

Inventory Goods that a person holds for sale or lease or goods that are raw materials, work in process, or materials used or consumed in a business.

INVENTORY. **Inventory** consists of goods that are held by a person for sale or lease or are to be furnished under a contract of service. They may be raw materials, work in process, completed goods, or material used or consumed in a business [9-109(4)]. The basic test to be applied in determining whether goods are inventory is whether they are held for immediate or ultimate sale or lease. The reason for the inclusion of materials used or consumed in a business (e.g., supplies of fuel, boxes, and other containers for packaging the goods) is that they will soon be used in making an end product for sale.

The proper classification of goods is determined on the basis of their nature and intended use by the debtor. For example, a television set in a dealer's warehouse is inventory to the dealer. When the set is sold and delivered to a consumer customer, it becomes a consumer good. If an identical set were sold on the same terms to the owner of a tavern, to be used for entertaining customers, the set would be equipment in the hands of the tavern owner. The secured party generally cannot rely on the classification furnished by the debtor. The secured party must analyze all facts to ensure proper classification of the collateral and proper perfection of the security interest. The following case illustrates that collateral may fall into a different classification than might be apparent at first glance.

First State Bank v. Producers Livestock Marketing Association Non-Stock Cooperative

261 N.W.2d 854 (Neb. 1978)

BOSLAUGH, J.

This case involves a controversy concerning a security interest in cattle owned by James W. Faden. Faden, who died on January 12, 1971, was a farmer and rancher who lived in southern Banner County, Nebraska. On November 8, 1965, he executed and delivered a financing statement and security agreement to the plaintiff, First State Bank at Kimball, Nebraska. On that date he borrowed $12,200 from the bank. His total indebtedness to the bank was then $38,360. The financing statement and security agreement was filed in Banner County on November 9, 1965, and a continuation agreement was filed on August 14, 1970. At the time of his death Faden owed the bank nearly $150,000.

The security agreement secured future advances and granted a security interest in "livestock" including any "increase, additions, accessions and substitutions thereto.". . .

The defendant, Producers Livestock Marketing Association Non-Stock Cooperative, hereinafter referred to as Producers, operates a livestock auction business in Gering, Nebraska. In a series of six transactions between February 1, 1969, and March 28, 1970, Faden sold 112 head of cattle at the auction in Gering and deposited the proceeds in the Scottsbluff National Bank at Scottsbluff, Nebraska. The plaintiff claims these cattle were covered by the security agreement and that Producers is liable to the plaintiff for the proceeds from the sale of the cattle. . . .

The trial court found generally for the plaintiff on its petition. . . . The trial court found specifically that the plaintiff had a security interest in all the livestock owned by Faden and involved in this action. The defendant has appealed.

The first transaction which is in dispute took place on February 1, 1969. On that date Faden sold 2 head of cattle at Gering, through Producers for net proceeds of $719.35.

On May 17, 1969, Faden sold 5 head of cattle at Gering, through Producers for net proceeds of $1,199.55. The evidence does not show where the cattle sold on these two dates originated.

On December 19, 1969, Faden purchased 47 head of cattle at the Torrington Livestock Commission Com-

pany at Torrington, Wyoming, for $9,464.19 and paid for them with a check on the plaintiff bank. The cattle were shipped to Gering, Nebraska, and sold through Producers on December 20, 1969, for net proceeds of $8,326.88. Two days later Faden borrowed $9,500 from the plaintiff to cover his December 19, 1969, check.

On January 16, 1970, Faden purchased 37 head of cattle at Torrington for $8,079.77. The cattle were shipped to Gering and sold through Producers on the following day, January 17, 1970, for net proceeds of $7,496.72. Three days later, Faden borrowed $8,000 from the plaintiff bank to cover his check of January 16, 1970.

On February 20, 1970, Faden purchased 9 head of cattle at Torrington for $2,054. The cattle were shipped to Gering and sold the following day, February 21, 1970, through Producers for net proceeds of $1,883.48. On February 26, 1970, Faden borrowed $2,100 from the plaintiff bank to cover his check of February 20, 1970.

On March 26, 1970, Faden purchased 21 head of cattle at Torrington for $5,697. Twelve of these cattle were shipped to Gering and sold through Producers on March 28, 1970, for net proceeds of $2,850.65. On March 31, 1970, Faden borrowed $5,700 from the plaintiff bank to cover his check of March 26, 1970.

The defendant contends that the security agreement did not cover the cattle sold through Producers in the transactions described above because they were not "farm products." The defendant claims that Faden was actually engaged in two occupations and that in addition to being a farmer and rancher he was a cattle trader or speculator.

Under the Uniform Commercial Code, goods are classified as consumer goods, equipment, farm products, or inventory. Livestock used or produced in farming operations and in the possession of a debtor engaged in raising, fattening, grazing, or other farming operations are farm products. If goods are farm products they are neither equipment nor inventory.

Goods which are held for sale or lease are classified as inventory. The Comment to Section 9-109, U.C.C., states that the classifications are mutually exclusive and that the principal test to determine whether goods are inventory is whether they are held for immediate or ultimate sale. In borderline cases the principal use to which the property is put should be considered determinative.

As to the cattle which were sold on February 1, 1969, and May 17, 1969, there is no evidence as to their origin. In the absence of any evidence to show affirmatively that these cattle were not a part of the farming and ranching operation of Faden the trial court could have concluded that they were farm products.

As to the cattle which were sold on December 20, 1969, January 17, 1970, February 21, 1970, and March 28, 1970, the evidence shows affirmatively and without dispute that they were purchased in Torrington, Wyoming, 1 or 2 days before they were shipped to Gering, Nebraska, for sale. These cattle were goods held for immediate sale and there is nothing to indicate they had any connection whatsoever with Faden's farming and ranching operation in Banner County. Under the facts in this case these cattle were inventory as a matter of law.

It is clear from the terms of the security agreement that the plaintiff and Faden intended to create a security interest in livestock used or bought primarily for farming operations and not business operations. The bank may not have been aware of Faden's activities as a cattle trader but the record establishes that the transactions involved in this case were not isolated instances. . . .

The evidence in this case does not support the finding of the trial court that the plaintiff had a security interest in all the livestock owned by Faden and involved in this action. The judgment must, therefore, be

■ *Reversed and remanded.*

CASE CONCEPTS REVIEW

1. What type of collateral was described in the security agreement signed by Faden in favor of the First State Bank?

2. What is the basis for the bank's claim against Producers Livestock?

3. What classification did Producers Livestock contend was applicable to the cattle it sold for Faden?

4. How does the court classify the cattle that Faden sold through Producers Livestock?

6. Documentary Collateral

Chattel paper A writing that evidences both a monetary obligation and a security interest in, or a lease of, specific goods.

Account debtor The person who is obligated on an account, chattel paper, contract right, or general intangible.

Document of title Includes bill of lading, dock warrant, dock receipt, warehouse receipt, or order for the delivery of goods.

Bill of lading A document evidencing the receipt of goods for shipment, issued by a person engaged in the business of transporting or forwarding goods.

Warehouse receipt Issued by a person engaged in the business of storing goods for hire.

In secured transactions, three types of paper are considered to represent such valuable property interests that they are included as potential collateral. These items of paper property include chattel paper, documents of title, and instruments. These items comprise various categories of paper frequently used in commerce. These papers may be negotiable or nonnegotiable. Each of these items of potential collateral is evidenced by a writing, and each represents rights and duties of the parties who signed the writing.

CHATTEL PAPER. **Chattel paper** refers to a writing or writings that evidence both (1) an obligation to pay money and (2) a security interest in, or a lease of, specific goods [9-105(1)(b)]. The chattel paper is *itself* a security agreement. A security agreement in the form of a conditional sales contract, for example, is often executed in connection with a negotiable note or a series of notes. The group of writings (the contract plus the note) taken together as a composite constitutes *chattel paper*.

A typical situation involving chattel paper as collateral is one in which a secured party who has obtained it in a transaction with a customer may wish to borrow against it in his or her own financing. For example, a dealer sells an electric generator to a customer in a conditional sales contract, and the customer signs a negotiable installment note. At this point, the contract is the security agreement; the dealer is the secured party; the customer is the debtor; and the generator is the collateral (equipment). The dealer, needing funds for working capital, transfers the contract and the note to a financing agency as security for a loan. In the transaction between dealer and finance company, the contract and note are the collateral (chattel paper), the finance company is the secured party, the dealer is the debtor, and the customer is now designated as the **account debtor.**

DOCUMENTS OF TITLE. Included under the heading of **documents of title** are **bills of lading, warehouse receipts,** and any other document that in the regular course of business or financing is treated as sufficient evidence that the person in possession of it is entitled to receive, hold, and dispose of the document and the goods it covers [1-201(15)].

Instrument A writing that evidences an obligation to pay money, a negotiable instrument, or an investment security.

INSTRUMENTS.   As distinguished from chattel paper, an **instrument** means (1) negotiable instrument, (2) an investment security such as stocks and bonds, or (3) any other writing that evidences a right to the payment of money and is not itself a security agreement or lease [9-105(1)(i)]. To qualify as an instrument, the other writing must also be one that is in the ordinary course of business transferred by indorsement or assignment. Thus the classification includes, in addition to negotiable instruments, those that are recognized as having some negotiable attributes. Instruments are frequently used as collateral, and they present certain problems in this connection because of their negotiable character. These problems are discussed further in the part of this chapter concerning perfection. Due to the readily transferable nature of negotiable instruments, priority issues also are complicated when this type of collateral is used in a secured transaction. These complications are explained in the next chapter.

7. Intangible Collateral

In the law of secured transactions, there is a third basic classification of collateral called *intangibles*. This classification includes the following categories: (1) accounts and (2) general intangibles. These categories are distinguished from documentary collateral by virtue of the fact that they are not represented by a writing. In other words, these categories of potential collateral are truly lacking any physical characteristics.

Account A right to payment that is not evidenced by a writing.

ACCOUNTS.   An **account** is any right to payment arising out of a contract for the sale of goods or services if that right is not evidenced by a writing [9-106]. An account receivable, which arose from a sale on open credit, is a typical example of an account. These rights of payments may be a valuable business asset that a creditor is willing to take a security interest in as collateral for the business' debt.

General intangibles Any personal property (including things in action) other than goods, chattel paper, documents, instruments, and accounts.

GENERAL INTANGIBLES.   The **general intangibles** category is a catchall that includes miscellaneous intangible personal property that may be used as commercial security but does not fall within any of the preceding classifications of collateral. Examples of general intangibles include goodwill, literary rights, patents, and copyrights [9-106].

CREATION OF A SECURITY INTEREST

8. Introduction

Attachment A four-step process of creating an enforceable security interest.

The ultimate goal of the secured party is to have an enforceable, attached, and perfected security interest. The remainder of this chapter is devoted to these three concepts: *enforceability, attachment,* and *perfection.* Completing the steps as outlined in Section 9-203 causes a security interest to spring into existence. This moment of creation is called **attachment.** At the time of attachment, the security interest is also enforceable against the debtor and third parties [9-203(1), 9-201]. However, third parties may defeat the security interest if it is not perfected. Perfection is discussed later in this chapter.

The following steps are required of creditors to create a security interest:

1. Make a security agreement with the debtor.
2. Make sure the debtor has "rights in the collateral."
3. Give value.
4. Make the security interest enforceable either by putting the security agreement in writing, which the debtor signs, or by taking possession of the collateral pursuant to the agreement.

The four steps can occur in any order. A security agreement may be executed and the secured party may give value (such as a loan) before the debtor acquires rights in the collateral. Assume that Sewall, a small manufacturing company, is seeking a loan of $5,000 from a bank. Sewall intends to buy a Model 711 Reaper sewing machine, which will be the collateral. Assume that the following progressive steps occur:

1. *A security agreement is signed by Sewall, but not by the bank. Sewall has yet to deal with Reaper.* Only the debtor is required to sign this document.
2. *Now Sewall contracts with Reaper to buy the Model 711 machine.* According to Article 2, a buyer does not have any rights in the goods until the goods are identified to the contract [2-501(1)(b)].
3. *Reaper removes a Model 711 machine from its inventory and marks it for delivery to Sewall.* Now the goods are identified to the contract. Therefore the debtor, Sewall, has rights in the collateral [2-501].
4. *The bank, for the first time, makes a binding commitment to lend Sewall the $5,000.* The requirement that the secured party give value is met. Agreeing to lend money, as well as actually making a loan, is the giving of value [1-201(44)].

Not until step 4 is completed does an Article 9 security interest exist. Only after these four steps are completed has a security interest attached to the collateral (sewing machine). After step 4, we find a written security agreement signed by the debtor; the debtor has rights in the collateral; and the secured party has given value. Thus an attached and enforceable security interest comes into existence. The following three sections describe a few more rules about the elements of creating a valid security interest.

9. The Security Agreement

The basic instrument in a secured transaction is the *security agreement* [9-105(1)(l)]. It must be in writing unless the security arrangement is a possessory one and the secured party is in possession of the collateral [9-203(1)]. Allowing the creditor to possess the collateral is not always feasible. Indeed, most circumstances require that the debtor have possession of the collateral. In these situations, the security agreement must be in writing, and it must be signed by the debtor. Regardless of whether the security agreement is in oral or written form, this agreement must describe the collateral in a manner sufficient so it can be reasonably identified [9-110].

The following case provides one example of the acceptability of a general description of the collateral in the security agreement.

United Bank of Bismarck v. Selland

425 N.W.2d 921 (N.D. 1988)

VANDEWALLE, J.

... In March 1984 the Sellands received a $16,100 farm-operating loan from the Bank. The promissory note executed by the Sellands was due and payable December 15, 1984, and stated that the loan was secured by a security agreement covering "All Equipment, Machinery and Farm Products." The Sellands defaulted, and in September 1985 the Bank brought an action to recover the unpaid balance due on the note plus accrued interest. . . . The county court on November 19, 1986, entered judgment against the Sellands in the amount of $5,450.84 plus interest, and further granted the Bank "possession of the farm equipment and machinery pledged as security for the indebtedness owed to the plaintiff to the extent necessary to satisfy this judgment." The county court denied Larry Selland's motion to amend the judgment to delete the part granting possession of the farm machinery to the Bank. . . .

We believe the major issue implicitly raised by Selland in this appeal . . . (is) whether the security agreement contained an adequate description of the collateral. . . .

Selland asserts that the security agreement is defective because it does not list specific items of property, but merely gives the Bank a security interest in "all" farm machinery, equipment and farm products. We disagree. . . .

The purpose of a description of collateral in a security agreement is only to evidence the agreement of the parties and therefore it need only make possible the identification of the thing described. The Official Comment to U.C.C. § 9-110 explains that "⌊u⌋nder this rule courts should refuse to follow the holdings, often found in the older chattel mortgage cases, that descriptions are insufficient unless they are of the most exact and detailed nature. . ." Applying this reasoning, the vast majority of courts have held that descriptions of collateral virtually identical to that found in the security agreement in this case were sufficient. We believe the description in this case adequately fulfills the purpose ascribed to it under the Uniform Commercial Code and is not unacceptably vague in its designation of the property involved. . . .

The order of the county court is

■ *Affirmed.*

CASE CONCEPTS REVIEW

1. What collateral was identified by the language of the security agreement?
2. What is the debtor's (Selland's) argument about the description of the collateral?
3. What are the Code's requirements under §9-110 for describing the collateral in a security agreement?

When it is a written form, the security agreement usually will contain many other provisions in addition to the names of the parties, a grant of a security interest, and an identification of the collateral. The forms in general use include a statement of the amount of the obligation and the terms of repayment; the debtor's duties in respect to the collateral, such as insuring it; and the rights of the secured party on default. In general, the parties can include such terms and provisions as they may deem appropriate to their particular transactions.

10. Debtor's Rights in Collateral

Another requirement for attachment (or creation of a valid security interest) is that the debtor must have rights in the collateral. It is clear that the debtor-buyer gets rights in the collateral against the seller upon delivery of the goods. A number of recent cases have held that the buyer can acquire rights prior to shipment, the earliest time being when the seller identifies the goods to the contract. The rights acquired by the buyer are subject to the seller's right of reclamation if the buyer fails to pay or if the buyer's check bounces. If a security interest created by the buyer attaches to the goods prior to the seller exercising a right to reclaim, the secured party generally prevails over the unpaid seller holding the bounced check.

There are many situations in which a debtor grants a creditor an interest in collateral that the debtor is not acquiring under a contract. Typically, in these situations a debtor has rights in the collateral if the debtor has possession of the property. However, when does a commercial fisher have rights in the fish as inventory? When does a farmer have rights in the crops to be grown or in the unborn offspring of livestock? The best answers to these questions seem to be that the fisher has rights in the fish when they are caught and the farmer has rights in the crops when they are planted and in the offspring of livestock when they are conceived.

While the debtor's possession of the collateral is an important factor in considering the debtor's rights in the collateral, such possession cannot be viewed as conclusive. As the following case illustrates, a debtor's possession of personal property must be combined with the legal rights of ownership for a security interest to attach to the property.

CASE

Pleasant View Farms, Inc. v. Ness
455 N.W.2d 602 (S.D. 1990)

SABERS, J.

Pleasant View Farms (Pleasant View) claims the trial court erred when it concluded that Leroy Ness had sufficient rights in twenty-five calves to allow the security interest of Farmers Home Administration (FmHA) to attach thereto.

In the fall of 1985, Darold Tomsheck, an officer of Pleasant Valley, reached an agreement with Ness whereby Ness would provide the care and feeding of certain livestock belonging to Pleasant View in exchange for the entire 1986 calf crop. Although no written contract was ever executed by the parties, the trial court found that the oral agreement provided:

> Ness was to be liable for all death loss, from any cause whatsoever, exceeding two percent of the number delivered by Tomsheck. Ness was to compensate Pleasant View . . . for any and all death loss exceeding said two percent by replacing said death losses with heifer calves of Tomsheck's choosing from the 1986 calf crop.

During April 1986, a severe blizzard killed fifty-one of the heifer cows. The surviving herd produced twenty-five calves.

Prior to the agreement with Pleasant View, Ness granted FmHA a security interest in his presently owned and after-acquired livestock. FmHA perfected its security interest in Ness' livestock by filing financing statements.

The trial court concluded that Pleasant View was entitled to all twenty-five calves pursuant to the death loss provision of the agreement. However, the court concluded that Ness' rights in the twenty-five calves were sufficient

to enable the security interest of FmHA to attach to the calves. Consequently, FmHA's perfected security interest in the calves took priority over the interest of Pleasant View. Pleasant View appeals the decision giving FmHA priority over the calves. . . .

Before a security interest may attach to collateral, the debtor must have rights in the collateral. Full ownership by the debtor is not necessary, but the security interest will attach to the collateral only to the extent of the debtor's rights in the collateral. In that regard, mere possession of the collateral by the debtor is insufficient to enable a security interest to attach to the collateral. . . .

FmHA's security interest will attach to the calves only to the extent of Ness' interest therein. Pleasant View claims that Ness held the calves pursuant to a bailment, resulting in insufficient rights for a security interest to attach. However, the oral agreement between Pleasant View and Ness, as found by the trial court, provides otherwise.

Under the agreement, Ness was "to keep the entire 1986 calf crop," but he was required to *"compensate"* Pleasant View out of the calf crop for any death loss to the original herd. This arrangement indicates that the calf crop belongs to Ness because Pleasant View could not be "compensated" with something it presently owned. In other words, a calf belonged to Ness from conception until it was selected as a death loss replacement. Therefore, Ness' ownership of the calf crop provided sufficient rights in the collateral to enable FmHA's security interest to attach.

■ *Affirmed.*

CASE CONCEPTS REVIEW

1. Name the debtor and the secured creditor in this case. What is the position of Pleasant View Farms?

2. On what basis do FmHA and Pleasant View Farm each claim a superior interest in the calves in Ness's possession?

3. In this court's viewpoint, what rights does Ness have in these calves? How does this answer determine the legal positions of FmHA and Pleasant View Farms?

11. Creditor's Value

For purposes of attachment, *value* means that a secured party has furnished to the debtor any consideration sufficient to support a simple contract [1-201(44)]. When a creditor loans money, value is clearly given. Even when the creditor agrees to loan money in the future, perhaps by establishing a line of credit for the debtor, value is given. The executory nature of the creditor's promise to loan money in the future does not destroy the existence of value being given. Furthermore, value also is present when a creditor takes a security interest to secure a preexisting claim against the debtor.

PERFECTION OF A SECURITY INTEREST

12. Introduction

Perfection This process is essential to inform the public that a creditor has an interest in the debtor's personal property. Perfection may occur by filing a financing statement, by possession, by attachment, or by noting the security interest on a certificate of title.

Between the debtor and secured party, the security agreement protects the secured party's security interest. But the secured party also wants protection against third parties, who may later make claims against the secured collateral. **Perfection** of the security interest will give this desired protection to the secured party. Perfection is designed to give notice to third parties that financing is occurring on the basis of collateral described. In general, an unperfected secured party's claim is subordinate to the claims of others who acquire an interest in the collateral without knowledge of the unperfected security interest.

Article 9 provides numerous ways in which a security interest can be perfected. The methods of perfection include (1) filing a financing statement, (2) taking possession of the collateral, or (3) simply creating a security interest (automatic perfection). Several factors must be taken into account in determining which of the three methods is appropriate in any given transaction: (1) the kind of collateral in which security interest was created, (2) the use the debtor intends to make of the collateral, and (3) the status of the debtor in relation to the secured party.

13. Perfection by Filing

Financing statement The legal documentation that must be properly filed by the creditor to be perfected by filing. This statement includes the names and addresses of the parties, an identification of the collateral, and the debtor's signature.

The most common method of perfecting a security interest that arises out of a business-related loan transaction occurs when the creditor files in the appropriate public office. Several issues arise related to this type of filing. Among these issues are (1) what must be filed?; (2) where is the appropriate public office for the filing?; and (3) when should the filing occur?

WHAT MUST BE FILED?   The document that creditors file to perfect a security interest is known as a **financing statement.** This document includes the names and addresses of the creditor and debtor. It also contains a statement that identifies the collateral. If the collateral includes crops, timber, minerals, or fixtures, the financing statement needs to include a description of the real estate involved [9-402(1) and (5)]. This financing statement must indicate that the debtor and creditor have entered into a security agreement. Finally, the financing statement must be signed by the debtor. Simple forms, often referred to as a UCC-1 form, are available for use as a financing statement. These forms have spaces for additional provisions as agreed on by the parties. However, the basic information, as stated in this paragraph, is all that is necessary to have a valid financing statement.

The purpose of filing a financing statement is to give notice that the secured party has a security interest in the described collateral. Potential creditors are charged with the task of going to a public office to see if the proposed collateral is already encumbered. A person searching the records finds only minimal information and may seek more from the parties listed in the financing statement. The addresses of the creditor and debtor are available so interested third parties know the sources of the additional information.

The following case discusses this important purpose of filing. This case principally involves an airplane as collateral, which required the secured party to file with the Federal Aviation Administration (FAA). Keeping in mind that the special nature of this FAA filing does not change the purpose of the UCC financing statement, this case is a valuable illustration.

CASE

First National Bank v. First Interstate Bank
774 P.2d 645 (Wyo. 1990)

THOMAS, J.

... On August 7, 1981, Richard and Verlene Walker (Walkers) borrowed about $93,000 from the Riverton Bank. They gave the Riverton Bank a promissory note on that occasion which was secured by property identified as "Rigs." That note was renewed on July 27, 1982, at which time the Walkers owed the Riverton Bank about $77,000, and was secured by "2 Drilling Rigs." The next transaction is the critical one. On April 6, 1984, the Walkers asked to borrow an additional sum which was loaned by the bank upon a security agreement which encumbered the Walkers' 1979 Cessna airplane. The security agreement showed the principal amount as $7,328.35, but it also included the following statement:

> ... In addition to the Note, this security agreement secures all amounts I owe to the Bank, whether now or later. This means that every loan I have now or get later is secured by this security agreement, as well as any other amount I may owe to the Bank (such as an overdraft on my checking account).

... At that time, the Walkers owed the Riverton Bank $77,605.63, which was the balance due on the previous promissory note.

The Riverton Bank filed its security agreement with the County Clerk and Ex-Officio Register of Deeds in and for Fremont County, Wyoming on April 12, 1984. On May 9, 1984, the security agreement was also filed with the Federal Aviation Administration (FAA).

On August 7, 1984, Richard Walker, d/b/a R & R Drilling, obtained a loan from the Cortez Bank. That loan, in the amount of $58,836.73, was secured by the same Cessna airplane. ... The title examination also reflected the fact that the Cortez Bank recorded its security agreement with the FAA on September 14, 1984.

Subsequently, having obtained peaceful possession, the Riverton Bank sold the Cessna airplane. The sale was made in bulk with other collateral in the possession of the Riverton Bank for $70,000. The Riverton Bank retained the entire proceeds of the sale.

This action was instituted by the Cortez Bank seeking a declaratory judgment that it was entitled to the proceeds from the sale of the aircraft in excess of the sum of $7,328.35 specified in the security agreement recorded with the FAA on May 9, 1984 by the Riverton Bank. The district court ruled ... against the Cortez Bank, and this appeal was taken from that judgment.

The essence of the dispute ... is found in the claim of the Cortez Bank that it was misled by the amount recited in the security agreement and that, consequently, the security agreement is not effective with respect to any indebtedness other than that amount. The Riverton Bank argues ... that it gave value for the security interest it acquired in the Cessna airplane; that it properly perfected its security interest; and that it was properly entitled to priority with respect to its security interest.

If collateral is not in the possession of the secured party, it is necessary that the debtor sign a written security agreement containing a description of the collateral and manifesting the intention of the parties to create a security interest in that collateral. If value has been given, and the debtor has rights in the collateral, the security interest attaches and becomes enforceable against the debtor with respect to the collateral as soon as all of the minimal requirements have been met. Value includes total or partial satisfaction of a pre-existing claim. . . .

The security agreement specifically provided, as between the Walkers and the Riverton Bank, that all amounts owed to the bank, whether then existing or later advanced, were covered by the security agreement. The Cessna aircraft was described specifically as the collateral. . . . At the time the security agreement was made, the Walkers owed the Riverton Bank money on a previous promissory note made August 7, 1981. The agreement clearly manifests the intention of the parties that the aircraft served as collateral to secure the pre-existing debt. The Walkers had the rights of ownership in the Cessna airplane, and the security interest of the Riverton Bank attached when the security agreement was signed on April 6, 1984.

The security interest was perfected, according to law, on April 23, 1984 when the Riverton Bank filed the security agreement with the FAA. . . .

While, in this instance, the Riverton Bank recorded the security agreement, it was filed as a financing statement. . . . A financing statement is filed to give constructive notice of a security interest in property. . . . The formal requisites for financing statements are articulated in § 34-21-951. . . .

> The purpose of the filed statement or agreement is to give the minimum information necessary to put a searcher on inquiry. The section contemplates that the complete state of affairs will be learned only after such inquiry.

There is no question that the filed document in this section satisfied the requirements of § 34-21-951. . . .

Section 34-21-951, setting forth the requisites of a financing statement, does not require any statement of the amount secured. The same thing is true with respect to a security agreement. The law does not require that a security agreement recite the amount of the debt secured. These statutes contain minimal requirements with respect to the enforceability of and the attachment of the security interest and, if those requirements are met, nothing more need be done.

We find, in this instance, no question that the Walkers and the Riverton Bank intended that the Cessna aircraft serve as security for previously existing indebtedness. . . .

Under these circumstances, the Riverton Bank did everything that the law requires to perfect its security interest in the aircraft. The Cortez Bank had constructive, and perhaps actual, knowledge of the existence of a security interest in that aircraft. The theory of the Uniform Commercial Code is that, given that information, further inquiry is required in order to disclose the other facts that may be material to a subsequent purchaser or lender. Proper analysis and application of the Uniform Commercial Code leads to a conclusion that the judgment of the district court in this declaratory judgment suit be affirmed. . . .

■ *Affirmed.*

CASE CONCEPTS REVIEW

1. In the security agreement signed by the Walkers and granted to the Riverton Bank, what dollar amount of debt was specified?
2. How much indebtedness owed to Riverton was covered by the security agreement?
3. Why does the Cortez Bank claim it has an interest in the proceeds from the sale of the plane?
4. What notice did the Cortez Bank receive from the proper filing of the Riverton Bank?
5. What is the process that the Cortez Bank should have followed after receiving the notice of the Riverton Bank's filing?

At times, the issue of whether a financing statement can substitute for a security agreement, or vice versa, arises. Generally, a financing statement is not a substitute for a security agreement. A security agreement may be filed as a financing statement if it contains the required information and is signed by the debtor. However, a financing statement usually will not qualify as a security agreement. Most businesspeople use a separate financing statement, because filing a security agreement would make public some information the parties might prefer to keep confidential.

WHERE SHOULD IT BE FILED?   The Code allows the states to require that the financing statement be filed in a central filing system, a local filing system, or a combination [9-401]. A central filing system means that all filing is in the state capital except for fixtures, which are filed locally. Local filing means that filing is at the county level. Most states have enacted dual filing systems. The usual system requires local filing for fixtures, local filing for farm-related collateral and consumer goods, and central filing for other business-related collateral, such as inventory and equipment. If the appropriate office for filing is unclear, the secured party should file the financing statement in every office that might be considered proper.

The three proposed alternatives for a filing system create problems when the secured transaction involves parties and collateral in several states. Because the states' filing systems are not uniform, where a creditor should file becomes an important question. Suppose that the Nationwide Construction Company is headquartered in Chicago, Illinois and that it has a major construction project underway in Atlanta, Georgia. If Nationwide borrows money from Bank of America in San Francisco and grants this creditor a security interest in the equipment located on the Atlanta construction site, where would Bank of America file its financing statement? The proper location for filing is determined by the debtor's residence or principal place of business [9-103(3)(e)]. Therefore, Bank of America would look to the filing system established by the state of Illinois. Any other party with a potential interest in the construction equipment located in Atlanta would also look to the filing system in the state of Illinois to learn whether conflicting interests exist.

WHEN SHOULD IT BE FILED?   A secured party can file a financing statement before the security interest attaches to the collateral. In fact, since the filing serves as notice to third parties, it is wise for the secured party to file at the earliest possible moment. Nevertheless, the filing of a financing statement does not perfect a security interest until such interest is in existence by attachment [9-303(1)].

The financing statement may provide a maturity or expiration date, but more often it is silent on this point. In the absence of such data, the filing is effective for a period of five years, subject to being renewed by the filing of a continuation statement signed by the secured party [9-403(2)]. To be effective, a continuation statement must be filed within six months of the financing statement's termination. If it is properly renewed, the original financing statement continues to be valid for another five years [9-403(3)].

The presence in the records of a financing statement constitutes a burden on the debtor, since it reveals to all persons with whom the debtor may be dealing that his or her property is or may be subject to the claims of others. The Code therefore provides for the filing of a *termination statement* to clear the record when the secured party is no longer entitled to a security interest. Failure of the secured party to send a termination statement within ten days after written demand by the debtor subjects the secured party to a $100 penalty and makes him or her liable for any loss suffered by the debtor [9-404(1)].

CERTIFICATES OF TITLE.   Under certain circumstances, the filing of a financing statement does not perfect the creditor's security interest. The Code makes special provisions for goods such as motor vehicles that have a certificate of title. The filing requirements of the Code do not apply, and the usual method of indicating a security interest is to have it noted on the certificate of title [9-302(3)]. If the security interest is properly perfected on the certificate of title, the security interest is valid even though a substitute certificate of title fails to disclose the interest of the secured party. In most states, taking title in the name of the secured party is not a valid means of perfection. The following case explains the reason behind this rule of law.

CASE

Noble v. Bonnett
577 P.2d 248 (Ariz. 1978)

GORDON, J.

Contemporaneously with a loan of money and credit by Lila Bonnett, to her son, Louis, Louis transferred the title to his 1971 Dodge to Lila, the appellee herein. It was understood between the parties that Louis was to remain the owner of the car and that Lila was to hold the title in her name solely as a security device until Louis satisfied his obligations under the loans. Soon thereafter William and Virginia Noble, judgment creditors of Louis and appellants herein, levied upon the Dodge which Louis had retained in his possession. . . .

After the trial of appellee's claim, the trial judge determined that, although Louis was the owner of the Dodge, and hence had a property interest theoretically subject to execution by his judgment creditors, appellee had a security interest in the vehicle in an amount equal to its value that was superior to the claim of appellants. The Court of Appeals agreed that Louis had interests in the Dodge that were subject to execution. However, in a memorandum decision, it reversed holding that appellee did not have a valid security interest as a matter of law because she failed to properly perfect her interest. . . . We accepted review to resolve questions as to the proper method of perfecting a security interest in an automobile.

As a preliminary matter, it should be noted that the Uniform Commercial Code on Secured Transactions defers to any state statute that requires indication of a security interest on a certificate of title as the exclusive source of law under which a security interest can be perfected in property subject to that statute. For automobiles the special statute in Arizona states:

> No conditional sale contract, conditional lease, chattel mortgage or other lien or encumbrance, title retention instrument or other instrument affecting or evidencing title to, ownership of, or reservation of title to any registered vehicle, other than a lien dependent upon possession, is valid as against the creditors of an owner acquiring a lien by levy or attachment, or subsequent purchasers or encumbrancers without notice, until the requirements of this section have been complied with.

. . . [Other sections of the Arizona law] proceed to dictate a detailed process by which a security interest in an automobile is perfected. First, the secured party must deposit a copy of the instrument creating the security interest with the motor vehicle division along with the certificate of title last issued for the vehicle. If the vehicle has not yet been registered, the copy of the instrument creating the lien must be accompanied by the owner's application for an original registration and certificate of title.

When satisfied as to the genuineness of the application, the motor vehicle division issues a new certificate of title, listing the name of the owner and a statement of all encumbrances that have been certified to the division as existing against the vehicle. The issuance of a new certificate of title constitutes constructive notice to creditors or subsequent purchasers of all liens against the vehicle except those authorized by law that are dependent upon possession. . . .

It is clear that the appellee's unorthodox method of taking a security interest did not meet the requirements of . . . [the Arizona law]. Hence, the issue on appeal is reduced to whether her failure to do so automatically rendered her security interest invalid vis-à-vis the appellants.

It is appellee's contention . . . that the sole problem envisaged by the Legislature when drafting this provision was the situation where title to the vehicle is in the name of the owner and a secured creditor of the owner who has not recorded his interest in any manner attempts to assert that interest against a bona fide purchaser or subsequent creditor of the owner. By contrast, appellee contends that where the secured party takes title in her own name, there is no hidden interest and, hence, no potential for fraud because subsequent creditors are on notice of the interest of the secured party. . . .

Regardless of whether the Legislature considered the specific problem presented in this case, it is our view that the goal of preventing fraud in automobile transactions will be well served by our refusal to sanction the taking of title in the name of the secured party as a valid security device. If we were to approve of this method, there would always be the danger that the secured party, having the indicia of ownership, would defraud the true owner of the vehicle by transferring it to a bona fide purchaser. . . .

This case is remanded for proceedings not inconsistent with this opinion.

■ *So ordered.*

1. What interest did Lila have in Louis's car? What interest did the Nobles have in this same vehicle?

14. Perfection by Possession

Pledge Personal property, as security for a debt or other obligation, deposited or placed with a person called a pledgee.

The simplest way to give notice of a security interest is for the secured party to take possession of the collateral [9-305]. This transfer of the collateral's possession from the debtor to the secured party is called a **pledge.** Since a secured party's possession of the collateral gives notice of his or her security interest, no public filing is required. As noted previously, the possessory security interest is very easy to accomplish because a written security agreement is not required. However, the use of possession as perfection is quite limited because most debtors either need or want possession of the collateral.

Possession is the required method of perfection of a security interest in instruments. Filing a financing statement is deemed inappropriate, since instruments are created to be freely transferable in commercial transactions. Because a third party accepting an instrument as security or as payment would not think to check for the existence of a financing statement, the Code limits the method of perfection in instruments to possession.

Possession is an optional method of perfection if the collateral consists of goods, negotiable documents of title, and chattel paper [9-305]. Since intangible collateral lacks a physical existence, it cannot be possessed. Therefore, the filing of a financing statement is essential for perfection if the collateral is an account or a general intangible.

Although it usually is considered an alternative to filing, possession of the collateral is the only method whereby complete protection in documents and chattel paper can be obtained. The reason possession of documents is necessary for absolute perfection is that the rights of good-faith holders to whom a document has been negotiated by the debtor will prevail over the secured party, even though there has been a filing. Possession of chattel paper is necessary to prevent buyers who purchase chattel paper in the ordinary course of their business from obtaining a superior claim in the paper [9-308]. These situations involving issues of priority to the collateral are discussed in more detail in the next chapter.

15. Perfection by Attachment

Another method of perfection simply involves the attachment of the security interest to the collateral. In other words, in some situations, the creation of the security interest, which is attachment, is also perfection. In these situations, the secured party is automatically perfected by attachment. Two examples of when and why the Code permits perfection by attachment are discussed next. A third situation involving this type of perfection is presented in section 19.

PMSI IN CONSUMER GOODS.   Probably the most common example of perfection by attachment occurs when a creditor receives a purchase-money security interest in consumer goods as collateral. To understand why perfection by attachment is necessary in these situations, you must first appreciate what a purchase-money security interest is.

Purchase-money security interest A security interest that is taken or retained by the seller of the collateral to secure all or part of its price; or taken by a person who, by making a loan, gives value to enable the debtor to acquire rights in, or the use of, collateral.

There are two types of **purchase-money security interests** (often referred to as PMSI). The first one is called the seller's PMSI. This occurs when a seller of goods finances the purchase price and retains a security interest in the goods sold as collateral [9-107(1)(a)]. The second example of a PMSI involves the lender's PMSI. This situation arises when a lender advances money to enable a debtor to acquire the collateral, and the money is, in fact, used to buy the collateral [9-107(1)(b)].

Perfection by attachment is possible when a PMSI is created in any item of consumer goods [9-302]. Creditors are allowed to be automatically perfected when they have taken a PMSI in consumer goods because it would be very burdensome to have to file a financing statement after every consumer credit sales transaction. Furthermore, this perfection by attachment prevents the official record keepers from being overworked with a multitude of filings.

TEMPORARY PERFECTION BY ATTACHMENT.   For a variety of commercial reasons, it may be necessary or desirable that the secured party with a security interest perfected by possession not have this possession for a short period of time. For example, a debtor granting a new security interest in instruments or negotiable documents may not have these papers to hand to the creditor at the time the loan-related papers, such as the note and security agreement, are signed. The Code provides the secured party twenty-one days at the outset of this transaction to get possession of the instruments or negotiable documents used as collateral. During this initial twenty-one days, the secured party is automatically perfected by attachment [9-304(4)]. If the secured party fails to obtain possession of this collateral within this twenty-one days, that creditor is no longer perfected.

Even after obtaining possession of the collateral, a second party may find it necessary to release possession of the collateral to the debtor. Since the release is of short duration, it would be cumbersome to require a filing. The Code therefore provides that a security interest *remains perfected* for a period of twenty-one days without filing when a secured party having a perfected security interest releases the collateral to the debtor [9-304(5)]. This grace period applies only to (1) instruments, (2) negotiable documents, and (3) goods in the hands of a bailee not covered by a negotiable document of title.

If an *instrument* is temporarily released to the debtor, the purpose must be to enable the debtor to make a presentation of it, collect it, renew it, obtain registration of a transfer, or make an ultimate sale or exchange. The risks associated with such a release involve the debtor's improper or unauthorized negotiation of the instrument, or the debtor's sale of the instrument to a bona fide purchaser. If the debtor has possession of the instruments, these risks always are present.

The purposes for which *goods* or *documents* may be released to the debtor are limited. The release to the debtor of these items of collateral must be for the purpose of (1) ultimate sale or exchange or (2) loading, unloading, storing, shipping, transshipping, manufacturing, processing, or otherwise dealing with them in a manner preliminary to their sale or exchange [9-304(5)].

16. In General

Often a creditor may create a security interest in collateral that is likely to be sold by the debtor. This event is very common when the collateral is inventory. To remain secured, the creditor will want to create a *floating lien*. A floating lien is created when the security agreement describes the collateral as including property acquired in the future by the debtor [9-204(1)]. The security agreement may also provide that future advances made to the debtor will be covered [9-204(3)]. The secured party can also have a security interest in the proceeds of the sale of collateral in the debtor's ordinary course of business.

The secured party's floating lien is protected against the claims of third parties by virtue of the public notice that such a financing arrangement has been made. The amount of the debt and the actual collateral can be constantly changing if the security agreement is worded to include after-acquired property, future advances of money, and the proceeds of any sale. This sort of arrangement allows the secured party to tie up most of the assets of a debtor, a possibility considered acceptable in business financing but restricted toward consumers, as the next section indicates.

17. After-Acquired Property

The security agreement may provide that property acquired by the debtor at any later time shall also secure some or all of the debtor's obligation under the security agreement. Many security agreements contain an *after-acquired property clause* such as the following:

> The security interest of the secured party under this security agreement extends to all collateral of the type that is the subject of this agreement and is acquired by the debtor at any time during the continuation of this agreement.

Under this clause, as soon as the debtor acquires rights in new property, a security interest in the new property vests in favor of the secured party [9-204(1)].

This clause obviously binds a debtor severely. The Code limits the effect of after-acquired property clauses in relation to consumer goods, since the clauses seem best suited to commercial transactions and might work undue hardship on a consumer. Unless a consumer obtains goods within ten days after the secured party gives value, a security interest usually cannot attach under an after-acquired property clause in consumer goods contracts [9-204(2)].

The following case demonstrates that while courts are willing to enforce clearly worded after-acquired property clauses, uncertain or imprecise language will not necessarily protect the secured party.

CASE

Graphics Resources, Inc. v. Thiebauth
447 N.W.2d 28 (Neb. 1989)

GRANT, J.

. . . This case began as an action . . . brought by Graphic against Bruce E. Thiebauth to recover video equipment in Thiebauth's possession valued at $48,416. Kekeisen filed a petition to intervene, claiming a security interest in the equipment. On January 8, 1988, the court sustained Graphic's motion for summary judgment against the intervenor, Kekeisen, and dismissed the petition to intervene in the case. Kekeisen's motion for a new trial was denied, and he timely appealed, assigning seven errors, which may be summarized in Kekeisen's allegation that the trial court erred in finding that the word "additions" in Kekeisen's security agreement did not include after-acquired equipment as a matter of law. . . .

The record shows that on July 20, 1984, Kekeisen loaned $30,000 to Aircraft Video Marketing, Inc., and entered into a security agreement with Aircraft Video to cover items of equipment owned by Aircraft Video as of that date. Kekeisen later filed a financing statement perfecting his interest in the video equipment. The collateral was listed in the security agreement as follows: "All of Debtor's equipment, including replacement parts, additions, repairs, and accessories incorporated therein or affixed thereto. Without limitation the term 'equipment' includes all items used in recording, processing, playing back, or broadcasting moving or still pictures, by whatever process."

Additional video equipment was apparently purchased by Aircraft Video after the execution of the security agreement with Kekeisen. Kekeisen sums up the facts as follows: "In early 1985, Aircraft Video Marketing purchased the additional video equipment which is the subject of dispute in the instant action, for use with the existing video equipment in the business." Graphic's petition . . . listed specific equipment, and there is no argument but that the property listed in the petition was purchased by Aircraft Video after the execution of Kekeisen's security agreement.

On May 17, 1985, Graphic entered into a purchase agreement with Aircraft Video to purchase all of the assets of Aircraft Video with funds procured through a loan from First National Bank of Omaha. As security for the loan, First National took a security interest in all of Aircraft Video's assets, including all property "now owned or hereafter acquired" by Aircraft Video.

Use of after-acquired property clauses in security agreements are expressly allowed by Neb.U.C.C. § 9-204.

The only limitation on their use with which we are presently concerned relates to the sufficiency of the description of collateral. Neb. U.C.C. § 9-110 provides, "For the purposes of this article any description of personal property or real estate is sufficient whether or not it is specific if it reasonably identifies what is described."

The term "additions," as it is used in the security agreement, does not sufficiently describe in legal or lay terms the equipment acquired by Aircraft Video after the execution of the security agreement. "Addition" is defined in Black's Law Dictionary 35 (5th ed. 1979) as an "[e]xtension; increase, augmentation." This definition in no way contemplates that "additions" is sufficient to reasonably identify the after-acquired collateral.

Furthermore, considering the context in which "additions" is used in Kekeisen's security agreement, no reasonable interpretation could lead us to conclude that after-acquired property was intended as its meaning. The words used in the contract must be given their plain and ordinary meaning, as ordinary, average, or reasonable persons would understand them. "Additions" is not set out distinctly, but is listed among the words "replacement parts . . . repairs, and accessories," and, in its ordinary sense, clearly and unambiguously refers to items like replacement parts, repairs, and accessories, which can be incorporated in or affixed to the existing equipment. A written contract is not subject to interpretation or construction if it is expressed in clear and unambiguous language.

Had the parties chosen to do so, they could have easily included language clearly stating that after-acquired equipment would be included in the security agreement. While a description need not refer to the items of collateral with specificity, the description must, at a minimum, reasonably identify the after-acquired collateral. § 9-110. The security agreement presently before us contains no such language. . . .

Kekeisen's assignment of error is without merit because there was no genuine issue as to any material fact, and Graphic was entitled to judgment as a matter of law. The decision of the trial court is

■ *Affirmed.*

CASE CONCEPTS REVIEW

1. What is the relationship between Thiebauth, Aircraft Video, Kekeisen, Graphic Resources, and First National Bank?

2. What language did Kekeisen, as the secured party, use in the security agreement in an attempt to create an after-acquired property clause?

3. What is the basis for Graphic Resources to claim an interest in the video equipment held by Aircraft Video?

4. Relatively speaking, when did Kekeisen become a secured party and when did Graphic Resources purchase the assets of Aircraft Video?

5. Why does the court rule in favor of Graphic Resources and against Kekeisen?

18. Future Advances

A creditor may include in a security agreement that the collateral protects him or her with respect to future advances in addition to the original loan. Such a provision is usually referred to as a *dragnet clause*. Dragnet clauses are also used to pick up existing debts. A *future advance* occurs when the secured party makes another loan to the debtor. This additional loan is a future advance covered by a properly worded security agreement even if the secured party was not obligated to make the second loan. A problem that arises with future advances occurs in this context: SP-1 lends money, files a financing statement, and has perfected his security interest. SP-2 later lends money, files, and perfects his interest in the same collateral. SP-1 generally would have priority, since he was the first to file. But what happens when SP-1 lends additional money after SP-2 has filed and perfected? SP-1 still has priority.

If the future advance is made while a security interest is perfected, the secured party with priority to the original collateral has the same priority with respect to the future advance. Likewise, if a perfected secured party makes a commitment to lend money later, that party has the same priority regarding the future advance as he or she has with respect to the original collateral. These rules are justified by the necessity of protecting the filing system. In other words, a secured party that is perfected by filing remains perfected when future advances are made without having to check for filings made later than his or her financing statement.

19. Proceeds

Proceeds Whatever is received when collateral is sold, exchanged, collected, or otherwise disposed of.

The passing of the security interest from goods to the **proceeds** of the sale is an important part of the floating lien concept. A debtor may sell or otherwise dispose of the collateral, but the secured party may have an interest in the identifiable proceeds. These proceeds may take the form of cash or noncash proceeds. Examples of noncash proceeds include accounts receivable, instruments, chattel paper, documents of title, or any form of goods [9-306(1)]. Insurance payments also clearly are proceeds.

Two different factual situations concerning proceeds may arise. A debtor may have the authority to dispose of the collateral, as in a sale of inventory. Or the debtor may dispose of the collateral without authority to do so. In either situation, the secured party has an interest in the proceeds. In the former, the debtor loses security interest in the collateral that is sold in the ordinary course of business but retains an interest in the proceeds. If the debtor sells the collateral without authority, the secured party retains a security interest in the original collateral, and the secured party gains an interest in the proceeds [9-306(2)].

An interest in the proceeds from the sale of collateral may remain perfected even if the original financing statement does not specifically mention proceeds. This continuous perfection occurs if the original financing statement's description of collateral includes the type of collateral that covers the proceeds. For example, suppose that the original financing statement describes the collateral as inventory and accounts. If an item of inventory is sold on account, the proceed is an account receivable. The secured party is perfected with respect to this account by the original financing statement. However, suppose that the item of inventory is sold and the buyer signs a promissory note. This note, as an instrument, is not covered by the original financing statement. Indeed, to be perfected the secured party must take possession of this note. In this situation, the Code provides that the secured party is automatically perfected for ten days with regard to the proceeds not covered by the original financing statement. To remain perfected, the secured party must perfect the interest in these proceeds by some acceptable method during this ten-day period [9-306(3)].

Special provisions relate to the secured party's interest in proceeds if the debtor becomes involved in bankruptcy or other insolvency proceedings [9-306(4)]. In general, the secured party is entitled to reclaim from the trustee in bankruptcy proceeds that can be identified as relating to the original collateral. If the proceeds are no longer identifiable because they have been commingled or deposited in an account, the secured party nonetheless has a perfected security interest in an amount up to the proceeds received by the debtor within ten days prior to the commencement of the bankruptcy proceedings. Other priority issues are discussed in the next chapter.

CHAPTER SUMMARY

INTRODUCTION

Unsecured Creditors

1. An unsecured creditor has only the debtor to look to for payment of a debt or performance of a contractual promise.
2. If the debtor fails to perform, the unsecured creditor must file suit and try to collect.
3. An unsecured creditor who has obtained a judgment is a judgment creditor. This creditor must obtain a writ of execution, have the writ levied on the debtor's property, and have the property, if any, sold at public auction.

Secured Creditors

1. To avoid the time and expenses of seeking a judgment and having the debtor's property sold, creditors often seek an interest in collateral.
2. Collateral may take many forms. However, Article 9 is limited to the debtor's personal property and fixtures.
3. Secured creditors have many advantages in collecting unpaid debts over unsecured creditors.

SCOPE OF ARTICLE 9

In General

1. Article 9 includes any commercial transaction wherein the purpose is to use the debtor's personal property or fixtures as collateral.
2. Article 9 also covers transactions involving the outright sale of accounts receivable.
3. Article 9 does not govern transactions involving security interests that are not commercial in nature.
4. Such excluded transactions are the creation of a landlord's lien, an assignment of wages, and a transfer of an insurance policy.

Classifications of Collateral

1. Collateral is classified on the basis of its physical characteristics and on the basis of the debtor's use of the collateral.
2. Article 9 collateral can be classified as tangible goods, documentary collateral, or intangible collateral.
3. Tangible goods can be categorized as consumer goods, equipment, farm products, and inventory.
4. Documentary collateral can be subdivided into documents of title, chattel paper, and instruments.

5. Intangible collateral consists of accounts and general intangibles.

CREATION OF A SECURITY INTEREST

Introduction	**1.** To create a valid Article 9 security interest, the interest must attach to the collateral and become enforceable.
	2. This process is achieved by (a) the existence of a security agreement, (b) the debtor having rights in the collateral, (c) the creditor granting value, and (d) the debtor signing the agreement or the creditor taking possession of the collateral.
	3. These steps of attachment may occur in any order as long as all have occurred.
The Security Agreement	**1.** The agreement is the grant of a security interest by the debtor to the creditor.
	2. The agreement must name the parties and describe the collateral involved.
	3. The agreement may be oral if the creditor takes possession of the collateral. If possession remains with the debtor, this agreement must be in writing and signed by the debtor.
Debtor's Rights in Collateral	**1.** In general, a debtor has rights in the collateral when it is identified to a sales contract.
	2. Normally, the debtor has rights in the collateral when the debtor has possession. However, a debtor-lessee may not have sufficient rights in items possessed to create a security interest in these items.
Creditor's Value	**1.** Value is defined as consideration sufficient to support a contract.
	2. A creditor's executory promise to lend money is value.

PERFECTION OF A SECURITY INTEREST

Introduction	**1.** Perfection is the step that notifies the public that a creditor has an interest in the described collateral.
	2. Perfection generally gives a secured creditor priority to collateral over the claims of third parties.
Perfection by Filing	**1.** The most common method of perfection is filing a financing statement.
	2. The financing statement is a separate document from a security agreement. The debtor must sign a written financing statement.
	3. A financing statement is effective for five years unless a shorter time period is clearly stated or unless a continuation statement is filed to extend the statement's duration.
	4. To be valid, a financing statement must be filed in the appropriate office, as required by state law.
Perfection by Possession	**1.** Notice of the creditor's interest in collateral clearly is given if the creditor has possession of the collateral.
	2. Possession is an optional method of perfection if the collateral is tangible goods, negotiable documents, or chattel paper.
	3. Possession is mandatory if the collateral is instruments.
	4. An interest in intangible collateral cannot be perfected by possession. A financing statement must be filed when the collateral is intangible in form.
Perfection by Attachment	**1.** In some situations, the creation (or attachment) of a security interest automatically perfects the secured creditor.
	2. The most common example of perfection by attachment involves the secured party's PMSI in consumer goods.
	3. The twenty-one-day exceptions to the creditor's having possession of instruments, negotiable documents, or goods held by a bailee that are not under a negotiable document are other examples of perfection by attachment.

FLOATING LIENS

In General	**1.** A floating lien is created when a creditor's security interest covers after-acquired collateral, future advances, and proceeds.

2. This concept avoids the necessity of the secured party having to create a new security interest and file a new financing statement every time the debtor acquires additional property or borrows additional money.

After-Acquired Property

1. A clause granting the creditor an interest in new property acquired by the debtor may be included in the security agreement.

2. This clause's application is limited to a ten-day period if the property is consumer goods.

Future Advances

1. A security agreement may state that the security interest covers future loans made by the creditor.

2. In general, priority with respect to future advances made is determined by the date of original perfection.

Proceeds

1. A secured party's floating lien also gives that party's interest in the proceeds of a sale of collateral.

2. These proceeds may be in the form of cash or noncash collateral.

3. An interest in proceeds continues as perfected if the original financing statement included a description of the type of collateral that covers the proceeds. Otherwise, the secured party is perfected by attachment for a ten-day period.

REVIEW QUESTIONS AND PROBLEMS

1. Match each term in column A with the appropriate statement in column B.

A	B
(1) Unsecured creditor	(a) The essential element in the creation and enforceability of a security agreement
(2) Tangible goods	(b) Exists when either a seller or lender, as a secured party, lends the money that enables the debtor to buy the collateral
(3) Inventory	(c) A general classification of collateral that has a physical nature
(4) Chattel paper	(d) The document that must be filed to perfect a security interest
(5) General intangible	(e) A category of collateral held by a business debtor for resale
(6) Attachment	(f) A party whose only collateral is the debtor's promise to repay
(7) Security agreement	(g) A catchall category for collateral
(8) Financing statement	(h) Another name for perfection by attachment
(9) Automatic perfection	(i) A writing that evidences both an obligation to pay money and a security interest or lease
(10) Purchase-money security interest	(j) An essential document that must be signed by the debtor if he or she retains possession of the collateral if a security interest is to be created
(11) Floating lien	(k) Arises from the sale of collateral
(12) Proceeds	(l) Created when a creditor's security interest covers after-acquired collateral or future advances or both

2. Clark rented a TV from Rental Service. The rental agreement provided that Clark would lease the set for at least one week. Title would remain with Rental Service unless Clark rented the TV set for seventy-eight consecutive weeks and fulfilled all the terms of the agreement. After a few months, Rental Service repossessed the TV set. Clark contended the agreement was really an installment sales agreement disguised as a lease. Is this transaction a secured sale or a lease? Explain.

3. Classification of collateral is not always easy. Classify the following collateral:
   a. Burns Rentals leases and sells TV sets and cars. Burns obtains financing from City Bank, enabling him to buy twenty-five cars and 100 new TV sets.
   b. Burns has fifty cars on his lot for lease.
   c. Burns sells a truck to Boyce and retains a security interest in the truck. Boyce uses the truck exclusively for weekend camping and fishing trips.
   d. Burns assigns Boyce's promissory note and security agreement to City Bank as collateral for a loan.
   e. Burns Rentals buys 300 new Philco TV sets for his annual summer sale. Classify the TV sets in the hands of Philco; in Burns's possession. Virgil, owner of Virgil's Truck City and Bar, buys a TV set during the sale. The set is delivered to Virgil in its original carton and put in the back of his sixteen-wheeler. What type of goods did Virgil buy?
   f. When Philco sells TV sets to Burns, it packages them in special shipping cartons, using packaging materials such as Styrofoam and excelsior. Philco maintains a large supply of these materials.
   g. Burns has a large supply of diesel fuel and oil for his fleet of trucks.

4. Jim Gibbs purchased a used truck and delivered it to Vernie King for needed repairs. After one month, Gibbs was notified that the truck was repaired. The total cost of the repairs was more than Gibbs could afford. King agreed to lend Gibbs $1,250 as a partial payment for the repairs. Gibbs orally agreed to give King a security interest in the truck in return for the loan. However, no written security agreement was prepared or signed. Gibbs took possession of the truck and later defaulted on his repayment of the $1,250. King sought to repossess the truck as a secured creditor. Gibbs argued that King did not have a security interest in this truck. Can a creditor be secured on the basis of an oral security agreement if the debtor has possession of the collateral? Explain.

5. A bank entered into a security agreement with a farmer. It covered "all crops in bin or stored in commercial elevator" and "all crops growing or to be grown." The agreement did not include any description of the land concerned. The farmer harvested the grain and took it immediately to the grain company for sale, without prior storage. Is the grain subject to the bank's security interest? Why or why not?

6. Gil sold office furniture to Fireside Realty Company. To secure the sale, the parties executed a security agreement that described the collateral as "furniture as per the attached listing." No listing was attached, nor was any listing included in the financing statement. Does Gill have a security interest in the furniture? Explain.

7. Chapman entered into a franchise agreement with Senter, which provided for an initial inventory and assistance in opening an auto parts store. When Senter's check in payment of the inventory was dishonored, Chapman notified Senter that the franchise agreement was revoked and that Chapman was repossessing the inventory. Chapman had the locks changed on the store to effect its repossession. Senter then borrowed $4,500 from a bank using the inventory of the store as collateral. Chapman claims that this security interest never was perfected because it had never "attached" to the collateral. Is he correct? Why or why not?

8. Walker purchased Terminal Moving & Storage Company by making a small down payment and signing a promissory note for the remainder of the purchase price. On the same day, Walker, as sole owner, executed a security interest in all of the corporation's assets in favor of the seller. The seller later assigned the security interest and the note to a third party, who assigned them to Putnam. When the corporation filed for bankruptcy a few years later, the bankruptcy trustee contended that Putnam did not have a valid security interest. The trustee argued that the security interest was given without any consideration being given to the corporation itself. Therefore the security interest did not attach because no value had been given. Did Putnam have a valid security interest? Explain.

9. A financing statement listed the debtor as "Elite Boats, Division of Glasco, Inc." rather than as "Glasco, Inc.," the correct name of the company. Is the financing statement adequate to perfect a security interest? Why or why not?

10. Francis executed a security agreement and a financing statement securing a debt with his growing crops. Both documents described the farmland as "the southeast one-quarter of section 24, township 71 north, range 32 in Grant Township, Adams County, Iowa." That description was in error; the secured party had intended to refer not to section 24 but to section 25 (where Francis lived on a farm his father owned). Is the security interest in the crops perfected? Why or why not?

11. Paula, an accountant, lent money to a company that was already indebted to her for services rendered. As security for the loan and to secure payment for the services, the company assigned to Paula a portion of its expected recovery of a pending lawsuit. Paula did not file a financing statement with regard to the assignment. Subsequently, Debra was awarded a judgment against the company in another lawsuit. Debra, without knowledge of the assignment to Paula, had the sheriff levy against the company's property. At the sheriff's execution sale, all of the company's rights in the pending lawsuit were sold to Debra. When the lawsuit was settled, Paula claimed rights to the proceeds. Is Paula entitled to the proceeds of the lawsuit pursuant to her security interest? Explain.

12. Tom and Marie Shafer purchased a household washing machine and dishwasher on credit from the Georgia Power Company (GPC). GPC took purchase money security interests in each of these appliances that were perfected by attachment. Later, the Shafers granted security interests in these same appliances to Personal Thrift as collateral for a loan. Personal Thrift perfected its interests by filing a proper financing statement. The Shafers defaulted on all these loans, and Personal Thrift took possession of the appliances. GPC sued Personal Thrift, seeking to recover the two appliances. Personal Thrift argued that GPC's automatic perfection was unconstitutional as a violation of equal protection and due process. Is perfection by attachment constitutional? Explain.

13. Nelson, a farmer, signed a security agreement to Farmer's Bank covering his crops. The agreement contained a dragnet clause. Nelson had debts from a former crop year and later borrowed to plant his current crops. When he sold the crops to a grain elevator, the elevator used the proceeds to satisfy debts due it rather than pay the proceeds to Farmer's Bank as it had demanded. Farmer's Bank sues the elevator for the value of the crops. Is Farmer's Bank entitled to recover? Why?

14. Cable Services of Florida, Inc., purchased a backhoe and financed the purchase with ITT Industrial Credit Company. ITT prepared a security agreement that required Cable to insure the backhoe. Cable did acquire insurance through the Insurance Management Corporation (IMC), which agreed to lend Cable the money for the insurance premium. This insurance actually was issued by U.S.F.&G. Company. The backhoe was stolen, and the parties claimed the benefits under this insurance policy. IMC received a check from U.S.F.&G. as payment under the policy. ITT, as a secured party, claimed this insurance money as a proceed from the backhoe. IMC claimed a portion of these insurance benefits as payment of its loan to Cable for the insurance premiums. Is money paid under an insurance policy a proceed to which the secured party is entitled? Why or why not?

15. By answering the following, check your knowledge of the business decisions involved in secured transactions:
    a. Assume that you are a retailer with a large amount of outstanding accounts receivable and you are in need of cash to pay expenses. How might you raise the necessary cash? Explain.
    b. Assume that you are considering lending to Fred Tauber of Tauber & Sons and taking a security interest in certain property of Tauber & Sons. What should you do prior to lending the money? Explain.
    c. Assume that you are arranging to finance another's business. It will be a secured financing plan that works on a continuing basis. What provisions should you require for inclusion in the security agreement and in the financing statement? Explain.
    d. Assume that you are a secured party and are in doubt about whether you have to file and, if so, where to file. What do you do? Explain.

ISSUES IN ARTICLE 9 TRANSACTIONS

CHAPTER PREVIEW

The preceding chapter describes how an Article 9 security interest is created and perfected. In this chapter, we assume that these essential steps have been accomplished. Based on this assumption, two additional issues involving Article 9 transactions are examined. First, does a perfected secured creditor have priority over other parties claiming an interest in the personal property that is the collateral? By the word *priority*, we mean the party that is first in line to have its claim paid from the proceeds made from the sale of the collateral. The second issue presented in this chapter concerns the rights and duties of the secured creditor and the debtor when the debtor defaults.

■ BUSINESS MANAGEMENT DECISION

A customer of your bank operates an appliance store. This customer wants to borrow $500,000 to finance a new line of VCRs. As the chief commercial loan officer, you have the Article 9 records examined, and you learn that this customer has granted a security interest in the store's inventory to a competing financial institution. You believe that the new line of VCRs will be profitable to your customer.

    If you decide to approve the loan, what can you do to obtain a priority claim to the VCRs over that of the competing financial institution?

PRIORITY ISSUES IN GENERAL

Collateral is frequently the subject of conflicting claims. Two or more persons may claim a security interest in the same collateral, or a person may claim that he or she has a better right to the collateral than does the secured party. Interests that may compete with the secured party's claim of priority fall into the following two basic categories: (1) those who purchase the collateral from the debtor and (2) those who are creditors of the debtor. These creditors may be further subdivided into those who have a conflicting security interest in the same collateral and those who have some other lien on the collateral. Among the many ways in which conflicting claims to collateral may arise, the following are some of the more important situations:

1. A debtor sells the collateral to a good-faith purchaser who may or may not know of the security interest.
2. A debtor gives more than one security interest in the same collateral.
3. Collateral becomes attached to real property, so it is a fixture.
4. Collateral becomes attached to personal property that belongs to another or in which another has security interest.
5. Collateral has been processed (such as raw material, in which there is a security interest, being converted into a finished product).
6. The government or some other creditor claims a lien on the property.
7. Collateral has been repaired or improved by the services or materials of another.
8. A trustee in bankruptcy claims the collateral in connection with a bankruptcy case involving the debtor.

In all these situations, as well as in many others, it is necessary to sort out the conflicting interests and determine the priority among them. Keep in mind that the priority of a secured party's claim often is determined by whether or not the secured party has perfected his or her security interest. If it is not properly perfected, there is no priority. The general rule of Article 9 of the Uniform Commercial Code regarding priority is that after proper perfection, the secured party has priority over (1) those who purchase the collateral from the debtor, (2) those who are also creditors of the debtor, and (3) those who represent creditors in insolvency proceedings instituted by, or against, the debtor.

The bulk of the following material involves exceptions to this general rule. In addition to these exceptions, a secured party that has priority to collateral may agree, explicitly or implicitly, to subordinate its claim in preference to the rights of a third party. We assume in these discussions that this has not occurred.

SECURED PARTY VERSUS BUYERS OF COLLATERAL

1. General Rule

We now turn our attention to the secured party's priority when the collateral is sold or transferred to a third party. In general, the secured party's security interest continues in any collateral sold or transferred unless the security agreement authorizes such a sale or transfer free of the security interest. This general rule makes sense, since the secured party and the debtor are free to make any legal agreement they wish and a secured party may voluntarily give up the security interest. A more likely issue arises when the debtor sells the collateral without the secured party's approval. Under Section 9-306(2), if the debtor makes an unauthorized sale or transfer, the security interest usually continues in the collateral in the hands of the buyer, as was held in the following case.

CASE

Matteson v. Harper
682 P.2d 766 (Ore. 1984)

JONES, J.

Plaintiff sued defendant for a conversion of collateral in which plaintiff had a perfected security interest. The trial court granted summary judgment for plaintiff in the amount of $17,000, representing the fair market value of the equipment on the date of the conversion. The Court of Appeals reversed. . . .

Matteson, plaintiff, owned a bulldozer, which he purchased as an investment. He sold the bulldozer to the Thorson group and retained and perfected a security interest by filing a financing statement on October 6, 1980. The security agreement prohibited sale of the bulldozer without Matteson's written consent.

The Thorson group defaulted on payments and delivered, for sale, the bulldozer to Walker, an auctioneer who dealt in earth-moving equipment. In March, 1981, upon discovering that the Thorson group had made the delivery, Matteson wrote Walker:

> . . . Mr. Bob Thorson . . . has indicated that the John Deer [*sic*] 4500 he is purchasing from me is to be at an auction in Seattle on March 26, 1981.
>
> A minimum sales price must be $22,400.00, plus auctioneer's fee, any transportation costs, storage and handling fees, etc., or I cannot consent to the sale. . . .

Walker did not respond to the letter.

On April 18, 1981, defendant, Harper, purchased the bulldozer from Walker in Tigard, Oregon, for $20,500. Walker kept the proceeds of the sale and thereafter went bankrupt. Matteson demanded that Harper return the bulldozer to him. Harper refused and Matteson brought this action for conversion of property. . . .

Harper contends that Matteson's letter to Walker "authorized" the sale of the bulldozer . . . and, therefore, Matteson's security interest did not continue. . . .

Here, Matteson expressly conditioned the sale of the bulldozer requiring a sales price of at least $22,400 plus fees and costs. The sale of the bulldozer to Harper for $20,500 violated the condition imposed by Matteson and does not constitute an authorized sale. . . .

Defendant, Harper, contends that as a policy matter the secured party is in a better position to protect his interest in the collateral than is the buyer. Defendant suggests Matteson could have affixed a notice on the bulldozer at the place of sale, informing would-be buyers of Matteson's security interest. The purpose behind filing a financing statement to perfect a security interest is to inform potential buyers of the existing interest. . . .

Requiring the secured party to follow the collateral to every sale and post a notice to unwary buyers would undermine the simplicity, uniformity and reliability of the filing system.

The purpose of the Uniform Commercial Code generally and the secured transaction provisions specifically is. . .

to provide a simple and unified structure within which the immense variety of present-day secured financing transactions can go forward with less cost and with greater certainty.

This purpose is best served by providing a comprehensive system by which parties may perfect a security interest and on which they may rely.

The Court of Appeals is reversed and the trial court · is affirmed.

■ *So ordered.*

CASE CONCEPTS REVIEW

1. Who is the secured party? The debtor? What relationship does Walker have to these parties? What relationship does Harper have?

2. What is the basis for Matteson to claim that Harper had converted Matteson's interest in Bulldozer?

3. What does Harper argue that Matteson should have done to better protect his security interest?

4. Why does this court reject Harper's argument?

There are three situations in which the buyers take priority over the secured party, even though the sale was unauthorized. These situations are considered in the next three sections.

2. Buyers in the Ordinary Course of Business

Buyer in ordinary course of business A person who, in good faith and without knowledge that the sale is in violation of the ownership rights or security interest of a third party in the goods, buys in ordinary course from a person in the business of selling goods of that kind.

A **buyer in the ordinary course of business** takes free of a security interest created by his seller even though the security interest is perfected and even though the buyer knows of its existence [9-307(1)]. A buyer in the ordinary course of business is a buyer who buys goods from a seller who is in the business of selling goods of that kind [1-201(9)]. When you buy goods at the grocery store, department store, and gas station, you are a buyer in the ordinary course of business. In general, a transaction in the ordinary course of business involves the sale of a seller's inventory.

The reason for giving priority to a buyer in the ordinary course of business is obvious. When you buy goods from a professional seller, you expect to get clear title to the goods and would never think that they might be subject to a security interest. This rule, then, simply codifies the customary expectations of buyers in our society. It has been applied to buyers of new cars from a dealership and to a dealer buyer who buys from another dealer. Generally, this rule would not apply if you bought a used car from a car repair garage, since the garage is not in the business of selling cars on a daily basis. In other words, the garage does not sell cars in the ordinary course of its business. In the following case, the court makes it clear that the buyer who claims to be in the ordinary course of business has the burden to prove that the seller-debtor is also in the ordinary course of business with respect to the sale of the collateral. This issue usually is a factual one best left for the jury's decision.

CASE

Northern Commercial Company v. Cobb

778 P.2d 205 (Alas. 1989)

MATTHEWS, C. J.

Appellant Northern Commercial Company d/b/a N.C. Machinery Company ("NC") seeks possession of an item of collateral which its debtor sold to appellee Mallard Leasing Company ("Mallard"). The trial court granted summary judgment to Mallard . . . [NC appealed.] On appeal, Mallard asserts that it is . . . protected as a buyer in due course. . . .

    In September of 1983, NC sold to Les Cobb d/b/a Cobb Enterprises ("Cobb") a used Caterpillar D8K Tractor. NC loaned a portion of the purchase price to Cobb, and took a security interest in the tractor and in a Caterpillar 966C Wheel Loader, which NC had previously sold to Cobb. NC duly perfected its interest in these items by filing a financing statement in the public records.

    Cobb apparently sold the loader to Mallard in early 1986. Cobb thereafter defaulted on the terms of the security agreement by failing to make installment payments due for July, August, and September, 1986. NC then sought to accelerate the note and demanded possession of the loader. NC then filed suit and a motion for prejudgment attachment. All parties agreed to treat the motion as one for summary judgment. . . .

    Alaska Statute 45.09.307(a) provides that a buyer in the ordinary course of business takes his or her purchase free of a security interest created by the seller:

> A buyer in ordinary course of business . . . takes free of a security interest created by the seller even though the security interest is perfected and even though the buyer knows of its existence.

A "buyer in the ordinary course of business" is defined by AS 45.01.201(9) as:

> A person who, in good faith and without knowledge that the sale to that person is in violation of the ownership rights or security interest of a third party in the goods, buys in ordinary course from a person in the business of selling goods of that kind.

Mallard contends that it is a buyer in the ordinary course, and that AS 45.09.307(a) protects it from NC's security interest. In order to establish that this section applies, Mallard, as the buyer claiming to be protected, bears the burden of proving the necessary elements of that section of the statute. It must prove essentially two elements. First, that Cobb was in the business of selling goods of that kind. Second, that it acted in good faith, with no knowledge that the sale violated the security agreement.

    In order to claim the protection of AS 45.09.307(a) Mallard must show that Cobb was a dealer in heavy equipment. Mallard introduced as evidence an affidavit signed by Les Cobb. In the affidavit, Cobb stated that he had been a dealer in vehicles and equipment since approximately May, 1985. He further stated that during that time he had continuously displayed a large sign which reads "Cobb Truck and Equipment Sales-Rental-Lease" in a prominent location on his display lot; that he had periodically advertised in the classified advertisements section of the Fairbanks Daily News-Miner; and that he had obtained an Alaska Motor Vehicle Dealer Registration Certificate. Finally, he stated that he had sold fifteen to twenty other items before he sold the loader to Mallard, and continued to sell vehicles and equipment after the sale.

    Mallard also submitted the affidavit of William J. Beaman, president of Mallard Leasing Company. Beaman stated that before he purchased the loader he personally visited Cobb's business to ascertain whether Cobb was a dealer. Beaman stated that he relied on the aforementioned large sign, and the fact that Cobb had many pieces of equipment in inventory. In fact, Beaman stated that "[t]he inventory was larger than that of some other dealers with whom I have done business over the years."

    These affidavits do not resolve the issue of whether Cobb was a dealer in heavy equipment. The fact that Cobb was licensed as a motor vehicle dealer is not conclusive as to his dealership status. This is particularly so where the question is not whether Cobb was a dealer of motor vehicles, but whether he was a dealer in heavy equipment. The affidavits contain no specific facts which would prove or disprove that Cobb was a dealer. The statement that Cobb had sold fifteen to twenty "other items" does not necessarily lead to the conclusion that these items were similar to the loader, or that Cobb was a dealer in heavy equipment. Further, Beaman's affidavit is undermined by his own admissions in other contexts. In a deposition he admitted that he had conducted business in Fairbanks since 1973, but had never heard of Cobb's company. He also admitted to Tom Kleinschmidt that he had originally been leery about Cobb's status but that Cobb had produced a "piece of paper" as proof that he was a dealer.

    For these reasons, we find that a material question of fact exists as to whether Cobb was in fact a dealer in heavy equipment. Summary judgment therefore would be inappropriate on this issue. . . .

    As to Mallard's contention that it is protected as a buyer in due course, summary judgment is inappropriate. A material question of fact exists as to whether Cobb was a dealer in heavy equipment. . . .

■ *Reversed and remanded.*

2. What two elements must Mallard prove to establish he was a buyer in the ordinary course of business?

3. Why does the court conclude that a jury should decide the factual issue of whether Cobb was a dealer of heavy equipment?

1. What is the relationship between NC, Cobb, and Mallard?

The buyer-in-ordinary-course-of-business rule does not apply to a person buying farm products from a person engaged in farming operations [9-307(1)]. Typically, farmers or ranchers get loans and grant security interest in their crops or cattle. This rule allows the secured party to follow its security interest into the hands of a cattle buyer or a grain elevator or food processor. To understand the reason for this exception, you should recognize that most farmers borrow money to plant and raise their crops. These loans are repaid when the crops are sold. If the law did not grant priority to creditors of farmers, these farmers would not be able to function. Creditors of farmers and those who do business with farmers must keep this exception to the buyer-in-ordinary-course-of-business rule clearly in mind.

3. Buyers of Consumer Goods

The rule of continuing priority for the secured party does not apply when a consumer-buyer purchases consumer goods from a consumer-debtor. The consumer-debtor, by definition, cannot sell his or her property in the ordinary course of business. This is because, as a consumer, the seller is not engaged in a business activity. In chapter 37, we discuss that a secured party with a purchase-money security interest (PMSI) in consumer goods is automatically perfected when the security interest is created. In other words, a PMSI in consumer goods is perfected by attachment. Nevertheless, a secured party who relies on this automatic perfection may lose priority. As the next paragraph explains, a secured party with a PMSI in consumer goods has to file a financing statement to be assured of priority over a consumer-buyer of the collateral.

Section 9-307(2) allows a consumer-buyer of consumer goods from a consumer-debtor to take free of the PMSI unless prior to the purchase the secured party has filed a financing statement covering such goods. Suppose that Smith buys a sofa from Furniture Company and gives it a PMSI in the sofa for the unpaid purchase price. Furniture Company does not file a financing statement. A few months later, Smith sells the sofa to her next-door neighbor, Jones, who uses the sofa in his home. Although Furniture Company has an automatically perfected security interest in the sofa, the sale is free of that PMSI if Jones paid value, did not know of the PMSI, and uses the sofa for consumer purposes [9-307(2)]. If Furniture Company had filed a financing statement, Jones's purchase would be subject to the PMSI. In the alternative, if Jones had purchased this sofa from Smith for a resale in his used-furniture store, Jones's purchase would be subject to the Furniture Company's security interest even if the Furniture Company had not filed a financing statement. This result is because Jones would not be a consumer-buyer in this latter example.

4. Buyers of Chattel Paper and Instruments

In the preceding chapter, we note that perfection by attachment is possible with respect to an interest in instruments for twenty-one days and with respect to proceeds for ten days. Since security interests in chattel paper or instruments perfected by attachment may be in conflict with security interests in those items perfected by filing, Article 9 has priority rules to cover such conflicts. Perfection by attachment when the collateral is chattel paper or instruments is used in three situations:

1. The chattel paper or instruments or both are *proceeds* from the sale of *inventory* collateral.
2. The chattel paper or instruments or both are *proceeds* from the sale of *noninventory* collateral.
3. The instruments are the original collateral. (If chattel paper is the original collateral, the secured party must file a financing statement or take possession to perfect the interest in chattel paper. Perfection by attachment is not possible if the original collateral is chattel paper.)

PROCEEDS FROM SALE OF INVENTORY COLLATERAL.   To illustrate the first situation, assume that a retail merchant has financed its inventory with the First State Bank. This bank has a security interest in the merchant's inventory, and it has perfected this interest by filing a financing statement describing the inventory. As a part of its daily business, the merchant sells some of its inventory to a buyer who signs an installment sales contract, which grants the merchant a security interest in the items sold. This installment sales contract, as a proceed from the sale of inventory, is chattel paper. Further assume that another buyer simply signs a promissory note when buying some of the merchant's inventory. This transaction creates an instrument as a proceed. To replenish the inventory, the merchant sells within five days the chattel paper and instrument proceeds to the Second State Bank. Which bank has priority proceeds?

The First State Bank would claim to have priority with respect to these proceeds as a secured party perfected under the ten-day rule of automatic perfection. The Second State Bank would claim priority as a buyer who has possession of and who has paid value for these proceeds. *Answer:* A purchaser of chattel paper or an instrument who pays value and who takes possession of it in the ordinary course of business takes priority over a security interest in the chattel paper or instrument that is claimed merely as proceeds from the sale of inventory [9-308(b)]. This rule applies even if the purchaser had knowledge of the secured party's security interest in these proceeds. Thus, the Second State Bank has priority.

PROCEEDS FROM SALE OF NONINVENTORY COLLATERAL OR AS ORIGINAL COLLATERAL.   The rule that governs the other two situations is a little different. If the chattel paper or instruments were proceeds from the sale of noninventory collateral or if the instruments were the original collateral, a buyer of these items in the ordinary course of business has priority only if he or she does not have any knowledge of the secured party's security interest in the chattel paper or instruments [9-308(a)]. For example, suppose that the merchant granted to the First State Bank a security interest in equipment as well as inventory. Assume that this bank files a financing statement describing the collateral as inventory, equipment, and chattel paper. Now suppose that the merchant sells a piece of equipment in return for chattel paper and then sells the chattel paper to the Second State Bank. That bank is subject to the First State Bank's interest in the chattel paper, since Second State Bank had constructive knowledge of First State Bank's interest in chattel paper via the financing statement's being properly filed.

Of course, a financing statement describing the collateral as instruments does not protect a secured party. Remember, perfection in instruments can be achieved only through possession. Indeed, the real lesson of Section 9-308 and of this discussion is that a secured party has not *absolutely* perfected its interest in chattel paper as proceeds or in instruments as proceeds or original collateral until it has taken possession of these items of collateral.

SECURED PARTY VERSUS SECURED PARTY

5. General Rule

Two or more creditors may obtain security interests covering the same collateral. If the value of the collateral is less than the total of the claims it secures, upon the debtor's default it will be necessary to determine the priority of competing security interests.

Section 9-312 governs most secured party versus secured party priority contests. It contains special rules to be applied when the conflicting security interests are regular or when at least one of the interests is a purchase-money security interest. The general rule governing priority between regular perfected security interests in the same collateral is found in Section 9-312(5)(a) of the Code.

This section basically provides a *first-in-time rule.* In other words, the first creditor to file or to perfect, if filing is not required, will have priority. This rule emphasizes the special status of filing a financing statement. Remember, filing can occur at any time, even prior to attachment. The Code adopts a pure "race type" statute: The first to file or perfect wins. Knowledge is unimportant. The benefit of a race statute is that it provides for certainty and predictability. Whichever party wins the race has priority.

This first-in-time rule also makes it advantageous to be perfected by attachment. Suppose a retail merchant sold a refrigerator to Smith to be used in Smith's home. Assume the merchant sold this refrigerator to Smith on credit, and the merchant had Smith sign a security agreement. This merchant is automatically perfected by attachment, since he has a PMSI in consumer goods. If Smith then granted a security interest in this refrigerator to a bank in return for a loan, the bank must file a financing statement to be perfected. If Smith defaults on his payments to both the merchant and the bank, which party has priority to the refrigerator? The merchant has priority, since he was perfected before the bank filed. Section 9-312(5)(a) states that the creditor who files *or* perfects first has priority.

There are a number of exceptions to this general rule, and each is designed to meet the needs of a specific commercial situation. The next five sections examine some of these exceptions. For example, a secured party with a PMSI enjoys a preferred status in some situations.

6. PMSI in Inventory Collateral

To be really protected, a secured party with a security interest in inventory usually will insist on having the security agreement contain an after-acquired inventory clause. If that security interest is perfected by filing, the general rule is that this secured party will have priority over a later secured party, since he or she was first in time. However, what happens if the debtor wants to finance a new line of inventory? This general rule effectively stops the debtor unless the secured party is willing to make a future advance. For the purpose of allowing the debtor more control over his or her inventory, Section 9-312(3) creates an exception to this general rule.

For example, a bank lends a store money secured by all the store's inventory now owned or hereafter acquired. The bank properly files a financing statement. A year later, a loan company advances money to allow the store to acquire a new line of appliances. Before the new appliances arrive, the loan company properly files a financing statement covering the appliances. The loan company then notifies the bank that the loan company intends to finance the new appliances for the store on a PMSI. The loan company now has priority over the bank, but only in relation to the new appliances.

The requirements of Section 9-312(3) are rather simple. First, the PMSI secured party must perfect its PMSI and give the other secured party *written* notice that it has (or expects to have) a PMSI in certain described inventory. Perfection and notice must occur prior to the debtor's receiving the inventory. The purpose of the notice is to protect the first secured party so he or she will not make new loans based on the after-acquired inventory or otherwise rely on the new inventory as collateral.

It is not important whether the perfection of the PMSI or the notification to the preexisting secured party occurs first. What is important is that these steps must occur before the debtor takes possession of the new inventory. Proof of the time that each of the steps was accomplished is essential if the PMSI creditor is to have priority. In the following case, the matter was returned for a trial on the time issues. A paper trail showing compliance is essential for a lender financing inventory.

CASE

King's Appliance v. Citizens & Southern Bank

278 S.E.2d 733 (Ga. 1981)

CARLEY, J.

The instant appeal involves priority between conflicting security interests in the same collateral and interpretation of Code Ann. §109A-9-312. The relevant facts are as follows: On August 3, 1978, The Citizens and Southern Bank (C&S) filed a financing statement listing itself as the secured party and Randall B. Helton, d/b/a United TV (Helton) as the debtor. The financing statement covered the following types of property:

All equipment of the Debtor of every description used or useful in the conduct of the Debtor's business, now or hereafter existing or acquired, and all accessories, parts and equipment now or hereafter affixed thereto or used in connection therewith. All inventory, accounts receivable and contract rights of borrower whether now or hereafter existing or acquired; all chattel paper and instruments, whether now or hereafter existing or acquired, evidencing any obligation to borrow for payment of goods sold or leased or services rendered; and all products and proceeds of any of the foregoing.

On November 27, 1978, Helton entered into an "Inventory Financing Agreement" with Appliance Buyers Credit Corporation (ABCC) "to finance the acquisition by [Helton] of certain merchandise of inventory from time to time from" King's Appliance & Electronics, Inc. (King's Appliance). On November 29, 1978, ABCC filed a financing statement listing itself as the secured party and Helton as the debtor. The financing statement covered the following property:

Television sets, phonographs, stereos, radios and combinations, tape recorders, organs, pianos and other musical instruments, refrigerators, freezers, ice makers, dish and clothes washers and dryers, ranges, food waste disposers, trash compactors, dehumidifiers, humidifiers, room air conditioners, heating and air conditioning equipment, vacuum cleaners, and other types of mechanical or electrical, commercial, household or industrial equipment and accessories or replacement parts for any of such merchandise.

On December 1, 1978, pursuant to Code Ann. §109A-9-312(3)(d), ABCC sent notification to C&S

that it "has or expects to acquire a purchase money security interest in the inventory of [Helton]" and described the inventory by item or type.

Thereafter, King's Appliance apparently began to ship to Helton merchandise which had been financed by ABCC as well as certain merchandise on consignment. The security interest held by ABCC in that part of Helton's inventory financed under the agreement with ABCC was eventually assigned to King's Appliance. When Helton subsequently defaulted on his obligations to both C&S and King's Appliance, C&S took possession of all of Helton's inventory and gave notice of its intent to sell the inventory and apply the amount realized to Helton's indebtedness to it. King's Appliance, contending that as ABCC's assignee it held a perfected security interest in part of the inventory under Code Ann. §109A-9-302(2), filed a complaint seeking, in effect, a determination that its security interest in the inventory had priority over that of C&S under Code Ann. §109A-9-312(3). The trial court entered its order granting summary judgment to C&S and denying summary judgment to King's Appliance. The order was based upon the trial court's following interpretation of Code Ann. §109A-9-312:

> Subpart (3)(b)(i) absolutely requires the purchase money secured party to give notification in writing to the holder of the conflicting security interest *before* the date of the filing [of the financing statement] by the purchase money secured party.... The notice given C&S [dated December 1, 1978] was *after* the filing of the security interest of [ABCC on November 29, 1978].... Failure to give a timely notice prevents priority from being accorded the purchase money security interest....

King's Appliance appeals, urging that the trial court misconstrued Code Ann. §109A-9-312(3)(b) and that summary judgment was erroneously granted to C&S and denied to it....

Code Ann. §109A-9-312(3) provides that a perfected purchase money security interest in inventory has priority over a conflicting prior security interest in the same property if:

(a) The purchase money security is perfected at the time the debtor receives possession of the inventory; and

(b) The purchase money secured party gives written notice to those holders of conflicting prior security interests who have perfected their interest in the same types of inventory before the purchase money secured party perfects his; and

(c) The holder of the previously perfected security interest receives the notification no more than five years before the date the debtor receives possession of the inventory secured by the purchase money interest; and

(d) The notification states that a purchase money security interest in the debtor's inventory, described by item or type, has been or is expected to be acquired.

Insofar as the trial court in the instant case misconstrued Code Ann. §109A-9-312(3) and granted summary judgement to C&S on the basis of this misconstruction, the judgment must be reversed.

We conclude, however, that summary judgment for King's Appliance was not authorized under the evidence. Under the proper construction of Code Ann. §109A-9-312(3), even if C&S has been given proper notification in compliance with subsections (b) and (d), the record before us shows neither the date upon which Helton, the debtor, received possession of the inventory in which King's Appliance holds the assigned purchse money security interest nor the date that C&S received notification of that security interest. Under subsections (a) and (c) of the current Code Ann. §109A-9-312(3) the security interest of King's Appliance is entitled to priority only to that part of the inventory received by and in the possession of Helton (1) after the purchase money security interest therein was first perfected *and* (2) after C&S received notification. If Helton received possession of any items of inventory before a purchase money security interest therein was perfected *or* before C&S received notification of the conflicting purchase money security interest in Helton's inventory the purchase money security interest of King's Appliance in those items is not entitled to priority over the prior security interest of C&S in Helton's inventory. We conclude, therefore, that there remains genuine issues of material fact for jury resolution and it was not error to deny the motion of King's Appliances for summary judgment.

■ *Reversed.*

CASE CONCEPTS REVIEW

1. Which party was the first one to create and perfect a security interest in Helton's inventory?

2. What type of security interest did ABCC attempt to create?

3. How does King's Appliance become the secured creditor asserting a priority claim in Helton's inventory?

4. What steps must be accomplished by King's Appliance to defeat C&S's preexisting security interest in Helton's inventory?

7. PMSI in Noninventory Collateral

For collateral other than inventory, a purchase-money security interest is superior to conflicting security interests in the same collateral, provided the purchase-money security interest is perfected at the time the debtor receives the collateral or within ten days thereafter [9-312(4)]. Thus, prior notice to other secured parties is not required in cases of equipment if the security interest is perfected within ten days after the debtor receives the equipment. The prior notice requirement is limited to a PMSI in new inventory under Section 9-312(3).

Why is prior notice required for inventory but not other classifications of collateral? The answer is that secured parties are likely to rely on the debtor's inventory more than on other types of collateral as a primary source of repayment. In other words, the sale of inventory is much more likely to produce regular income from which debts can be paid. Therefore, the secured parties need to be informed more readily about the fact that they cannot rely on new inventory. The lack of prior notice about new equipment being purchased on credit, for example, does not create a problem for the preexisting secured parties, since their reliance on that equipment should be minimal.

A secured party with a purchase-money security interest in noninventory collateral is given a special status for ten days after the debtor receives the property. The protection during this period is limited. It gives priority over the rights of only (1) transferees in bulk (buyers of all or a substantial portion of a business) from the debtor and (2) lien creditors to the extent that such rights arise between the time the purchase-money security interest attaches and the time of filing [9-301(2)]. The purchase-money secured party is not protected against (1) a sale by the debtor to another party or (2) a secured transaction in which the collateral is given as security for a loan during the period prior to filing. Of course, to remain continuously perfected, the secured party must file a financing statement or otherwise perfect during this ten-day period.

8. Fixtures

Fixture An item of personal property that becomes so attached or incorporated into real estate that it is treated as an item of real property rather than as personal property.

Personal property that is collateral for a secured party may be annexed to real estate. This annexation transforms the personal property into a **fixture**. Examples of fixtures would include an installed heating/air-conditioning unit, a built-in kitchen appliance, and lighting and plumbing fixtures. The use of fixtures or potential fixtures as collateral raises a question of priority between the Article 9 secured party and one who has an interest in the real estate. These third parties with possible conflicting interests could include the owner of the real estate or a party who has a security interest in that real estate. (Chapter 39 discusses in detail the use of real property as security.)

The party that has priority is entitled, upon default, to remove the fixtures. This party is required to reimburse an encumbrancer or owner other than the debtor for the cost of repair of any physical damages caused by the removal [9-313(5)].

Building materials are clearly not classified as fixtures [9-313(2)]. The revised Code recognizes three categories of goods: (1) those that retain their chattel character and are not part of the real estate, (2) building materials that lose their chattel character entirely and are a part of the real estate, and (3) an intermediate class that becomes a part of the real estate for some purposes but may be a part of a secured transaction. The third category is *fixtures.*

The term **fixture filing** is used to require filing where a mortgage on real estate would be filed. The financing statement for fixture filing must (1) show that it covers fixtures, (2) recite that it is to be filed in the real estate records, (3) describe the real estate, and (4) show the name of the record owner if the debtor does not own the real estate. A creditor's failure to meet these requirements of a fixture filing destroys that creditor's claim of priority.

Fixture filing A creation of Article 9 that is required to be filed in lieu of a financing statement to perfect an interest in personal property that might become a fixture.

A mortgage may describe fixtures and thus be used as a financing statement. In such cases, the mortgage is exempt from the five-year limitation on financing statements.

Two basic priority rules are based on fixture filing. First, there is the general rule that governs the potential conflict between a nonpurchase-money security interest in fixtures and a real estate interest. This rule is another one based on the first-in-time principle. For example, if the Article 9 security interest is fixture-filed before a mortgage is recorded, the fixture filer has priority. Of course, if the mortgage is recorded first, it has priority [9-313(4)(b)]. The second rule concerns purchase-money security interest in fixtures. If the fixture filing for a PMSI occurs before the goods become fixtures or within ten days thereafter, the security interest is superior to any *earlier* realty interest, such as a prior recorded mortgage [9-313(4)(a)]. This rule giving the holder of a PMSI in fixtures ten days to get perfected is consistent with the rule discussed in section 7.

A special filing rule applies to *soft fixtures* (readily removable factory or office machines or readily removable replacements of domestic appliances). These fixtures can be perfected by any method allowed under Article 9, such as filing, taking possession, fixture filing, or automatic perfection. If you replace a stove (a fixture) in your house and give a PMSI to the seller, the PMSI in consumer goods (stove) would thus automatically be perfected. This perfected secured creditor (seller) of the soft fixture would have priority to that item of property over the preexisting holders of an interest in the real estate [9-313(4)(c)]. The logic of giving this "second-in-time" party priority is based on the fact that the "first-in-time" party (such as a mortgagee) would not be harmed substantially if the new machine or appliance were removed. The real estate without the new machine or appliance is no less valuable than it would have been with the old item, which likely was in poor repair.

A special priority provision for a construction loan gives it total priority [9-313(6)]. Thus, a security interest in fixtures added as part of new construction is always subordinate to the construction mortgage on file or to a mortgage given to refinance a construction mortgage.

9. Accessions

Accessions Items of personal property that become incorporated into other items of personal property.

In addition to being affixed to real estate, goods may be installed in or affixed to other goods. In general, this occurs when parts are added to personal property to repair that object. These parts are called **accessions.** When accessions are present, there is a possibility for conflict between a party with an interest in the repaired object and a party with an interest in the accessions. The confusing thing in determining which of these parties has priority is that the attachment (creation) of a security interest is as important as the perfection of that interest.

Two basic rules govern priority to accessions. First, a security interest that attaches to goods *before* they become accessions generally has priority over all persons' claims to the whole object. This rule applies regardless of whether the claims to the whole object arose before or after the accessions were installed [9-314(1)]. The second rule is applied when a security interest in goods attaches *after* they become accessions. In general, this security interest is superior to all subsequent claims to the whole object. However, preexisting claims to the whole object have priority over the security interest in the accessions [9-314(2)].

To help in your understanding of Section 9-314, consider the following:

EXAMPLE The Houston Oil Company owns a large air compressor that it uses in its oil and gas drilling operations. This compressor is part of the equipment in which the Bank of the Southwest has perfected a security interest. The basis of the bank's perfection is a financing statement. Last month, the oil company had the compressor repaired by the Hughes Tool Company. These repairs cost $30,000, and the oil company signed a security agreement granting to Hughes an interest in the parts installed in the compressor. If the oil company defaults on its payments to both the bank and Hughes, the aforementioned rules determine which party has priority to the accessions. If the Hughes Tool Company created its security interest before the repairs were made, it has priority. If the repairs were made and then the security interest was created (attached), the bank has priority. Upon the debtor's default, the secured party with priority can remove its collateral from the whole. However, this party must make payment for the cost of repair of any physical damage caused by removal [9-314(4)].

These general rules on priority to accessions are subject to two exceptions. First, any party with an interest in the whole object who has priority can consent to subordinate that interest in favor of the party with an interest in the accessions. To be binding, this consent must be in writing. The second exception is a bit more confusing, since it reintroduces the concept of perfection as the basis for priority. Notice that in the preceding example we never mentioned that Hughes had to perfect its interest in the parts to have priority over the bank. If Hughes does not perfect its interest by filing a financing statement, it can lose whatever priority it has to (1) a subsequent purchaser of the whole object, (2) a subsequent judgment creditor who levies on the whole object, and (3) a creditor with a prior perfected security interest to the extent that this creditor makes subsequent advances [9-314(3)]. Therefore, to be assured of priority to the parts installed, the repairer who extends credit must create and perfect its security interest in the parts (accessions) prior to installing them.

10. Commingled and Processed Goods

In a manufacturing process, several items—including raw materials and components, each of which may be subject to different security interests—may combine to make a finished product. The collateral to which the financing party is entitled will ultimately be the product that results from the combination of the materials in which that party has a security interest. If a security interest in the raw materials was perfected, the security interest continues in the product if the identity of the goods is lost *or* the original financing statement provided for a security interest that covered the "product" [9-315(1)]. In a situation in which component parts are assembled into a machine, the secured party would generally have a choice of claiming either (1) a security interest in the machine or (2) an interest in a component part as provided for security interests in accessions [9-314(1)]. If the secured party stipulates "product," he or she cannot claim an accession. When more than one security interest exists in the product, the secured parties share in the product in proportion to the costs of their materials used [9-315(2)].

SECURED PARTY VERSUS LIEN CREDITORS

11. General Rule

In addition to other secured parties and buyers of the collateral, a secured party's security interest can conflict with parties holding *liens* arising from operation of law. Four types of liens created by law may come into conflict with an Article 9 security interest: (1) federal tax lien; (2) laborer's, artisan's, or materialperson's lien; (3) judgment creditor's lien; and (4) the bankruptcy trustee's lien. In general, the rule determining priority between a secured party and a lienholder is the first-in-time rule. In other words, the party that is first to indicate its interest on the public record has priority.

For example, failure to pay federal taxes allows the Internal Revenue Service to file a notice of a tax lien on any property of the delinquent taxpayer. The property described in a federal tax lien may also be subject to an Article 9 security interest. The secured party has a priority claim to this property if the notice of the tax lien is filed *after* the security interest is perfected. If the notice of the tax lien is filed *before* the security interest is perfected, the Internal Revenue Service has priority.

Although the federal tax lien follows the first-in-time rule, other liens do create some exceptions to this general rule, as discussed in the following sections.

12. Laborer's, Artisan's, and Materialperson's Liens

Laborer's, artisan's, and *materialperson's liens* are discussed in detail in chapter 40. For now, it is sufficient to know that these liens may be created under common law or by statute. The *common-law lien* on goods—allowed for repair, improvement, storage, or transportation—is superior to a perfected security interest as long as the lien claimant retains possession of the property. *Statutory liens* also may have such priority. Even though a lien is second in point of time, it will be granted priority over a perfected security interest in the goods unless the statute creating the lien provides that it is subordinate [9-310]. The reason for giving superiority to a second-in-time lien is the presumption that the service rendered by the lienholder has added to or protected the value of the collateral.

13. Judgment Creditor's Lien

Lien creditor A creditor who has acquired a lien on property involved by attachment, levy, or the like.

Article 9 defines a **lien creditor** as a creditor who acquired a lien on the debtor's property by a sheriff's levy based on the creditor's judgment, or a trustee in bankruptcy [9-301(3)]. The lien creditor is more generally called a judgment creditor, as discussed in the introduction to chapter 37. This creditor, having obtained a judgment in a lawsuit, seeks to collect that judgment by levy, attachment, execution, or the like on the debtor's property. The Code provides a first-in-time rule. A secured party who perfects before the judicial lien creditor levies will prevail. Assume that a levy is made on October 3. If the secured party has perfected at any time prior to October 3, the secured party's security interest has priority over the judicial lien creditor. Priority goes to the lien creditor if the security interest is perfected after October 3.

There is one important exception to this general first-in-time rule. Under Section 9-301(2), the Code provides a ten-day grace period for filing a PMSI, regardless of the type of collateral. Assume that a secured party makes a PMSI loan to a debtor on May 1 and that the secured party files to perfect on May 8. Since filing was within the ten-day period, the security interest relates back to May 1 under Section 9-301(2). Therefore, if a lien is levied on May 3, the security interest is perfected and is superior to a lien creditor under Section 9-301(a)(b).

14. Bankruptcy Trustee's Lien

The subject of bankruptcy is covered in chapter 42. Bankruptcy is a remedy for financial difficulties granted by the federal Bankruptcy Reform Act of 1978. When a debtor (voluntarily or involuntarily) is put into bankruptcy, his or her nonexempt assets are required to be turned over to a trustee to be sold to satisfy the claims of unsecured creditors. If a secured party has a security interest in some of those assets, then the security interest is threatened. The bankruptcy trustee is another third party who may attempt to defeat certain Article 9 secured parties. It is the trustee's job to gather and liquidate the debtor's estate, reduce it to cash, and make a pro rata payment to the bankrupt-debtor's *unsecured* creditors.

The trustee will attempt to show that the Article 9 security interest is ineffective. If the attempt is successful, it will increase the available assets and, in turn, increase the pro rata distribution to the unsecured creditors. The acid test for an Article 9 security interest is said to be its ability to survive the trustee's attack. Several sections of the 1978 Bankruptcy Act give the trustee powers to avoid an Article 9 security interest; many of them—such as the power to avoid the security interest as a *preference* under Section 547—are considered in chapter 42. For now, we analyze one important right of the bankruptcy trustee in his or her quest to set aside a security interest.

The most frequent clash between the secured party and the trustee occurs when the security interest is not perfected. The trustee will prevail over an unperfected security interest by using the bankruptcy law and the Code. The trustee generally has the rights of a hypothetical lien creditor. This allows the trustee to pretend to be a lien creditor on the date the bankruptcy petition is filed. In essence, on this date, the trustee can assert the same rights that a lien creditor would have on that same date under Article 9. (See the preceding section for the rights of a lien creditor.) The following example illustrates that this rule is easy to apply.

Assume that the bankruptcy petition was filed on October 10, and the secured party filed a financing statement on October 11. As we already know, the lien creditor's levy has priority over an unperfected security interest but is inferior to a previously perfected security interest. Now apply that reasoning to the time the bankruptcy petition is filed. If before that date (October 10 in our example) the security interest is perfected, the trustee loses. But in our example, perfection occurred on October 11. Since the security interest was unperfected on October 10, the trustee will have priority.

15. Introduction

A debtor's default is the event that illustrates the real benefits of being an Article 9 secured party. Article 9 defines the rights and duties of both secured parties and debtors in default situations. The provisions of Part 5 of Article 9 permit the secured party to take possession of the collateral and dispose of it to satisfy the claim. This secured party may obtain the collateral by self-help (if this procedure does not breach the peace) or by court action [9-503]. Once the collateral is in hand, the secured party has two alternatives. The first one is to conduct a *foreclosure sale* with the proceeds to be applied to the unpaid debt. The second option is *strict foreclosure,* which occurs when the secured creditor retains the collateral in satisfaction of the debt. At any time before either alternative regarding disposition of the collateral becomes final, the debtor has the right to *redeem* his or her interest in the collateral by paying off the debt.

The first event that a secured party must establish is a *default* by the debtor. The security agreement will set forth the debtor's obligations, which, if breached, will constitute a default. A default may occur even though payments on the debt are current. For example, a note may require that the debtor insure the collateral. Failure to maintain proper insurance coverage may justify the creditor's repossessing the collateral and selling it according to the procedures described in the sections that follow. The next case illustrates this expansive view of what creates a default by the debtor.

CASE

Ash v. Peoples Bank of Greensboro
500 So.2d 5 (Ala. 1986)

ALMON, J.

David Ash appeals from summary judgments for the defendants in Ash's action arising from an allegedly wrongful repossession of his 1976 Ford van. Defendants are Peoples Bank of Greensboro, which financed Ash's purchase of the van; Roberts Union 76, which sold him the van and later towed it when it was repossessed; and Jessie Bell, who signed as guarantor on Ash's note to Peoples Bank. Peoples Bank repossessed the van because Ash failed to maintain insurance coverage. Ash claims damages for breach of contract and conversion.

Ash purchased the van from Roberts Union 76 on March 20, 1983. To pay for the van, Ash borrowed money from Peoples Bank, executing to the bank a promissory note and security agreement. The amount of the note was $3374.94, payable in 30 monthly installments. Peoples Bank required a co-signer before lending Ash the money. Jessie Bell co-signed.

Peoples Bank, following its practice in lending money secured by personal property, required Ash to insure the van. He applied for insurance and a policy insuring the van was issued by Dairyland Insurance Company.

Although Ash made all the monthly payments on the note, he defaulted on his insurance premiums on two occasions. His coverage thereby lapsed. On the first occasion coverage was reinstated. On the second occasion Dairyland notified Peoples Bank that its coverage had expired and that the van would not be insured after February 7, 1984. On February 14, the bank notified Ash of the lapse, but he did not respond. The bank attempted to communicate with Ash by telephone but was unable to reach him. On March 2, Jessie Bell went to Ash's residence, at the bank's request, and told him he would have to reinstate the insurance.

Ash claims that he paid the premiums due on February 27, but the bank telephoned his insurance agency on the afternoon of March 2 and on the morning of March 3 and was told on both occasions that Ash's coverage had not been reinstated.

On March 3, 1984, Peoples Bank sent Richard Roberts to Ash's residence to repossess the van. Although

Ash was in his house at the time, he did not answer Roberts's knock on his door. Receiving no answer from Ash, Roberts proceeded to take possession of the van, which was located on a public street. He transported it to Peoples Bank by wrecker.

After the repossession, Ash's mother and a friend of his went to the insurance agent and paid the premium for reinstatement. They took the receipt to Peoples Bank, whereupon the bank called Bell for instructions as to whether the van should be delivered to Ash. Bell told the bank to call the loan and refuse delivery of the van to Ash. Peoples Bank refused to deliver the van to Ash. It took the position that not only must the insurance be reinstated but also the entire balance must be paid before Ash could get the van. Ash was unable to pay the balance at that time, but he continued to make the monthly payments.

On May 7, 1984, Ash filed suit against Peoples Bank of Greensboro, Roberts Union 76, and Jessie Bell. The trial court entered judgments for the defendants.

The principle issue is whether Peoples Bank wrongfully repossessed the van and thereby became guilty of conversion.

Unless the parties have agreed otherwise, a secured party has the right to take possession of the collateral upon a default. The secured party can use self-help to repossess as long as he does not commit a breach of the peace.

It is without dispute that no breach of peace was committed. The question is, was there a default that warranted repossession? The failure of Ash to keep the van insured was the sole reason given by Peoples Bank for repossession. A representative of the bank testified on deposition:

Q. Did you repossess the van for failure to pay the monthly payments?

A. We repossessed the van because he failed to have insurance coverage.

The insurance clause in the security agreement required Ash to keep the van insured against loss by fire, theft, and collision. The default provisions gave Peoples Bank the right to require payment of the entire balance due on the loan if Ash breached any of the promises in the agreement.

Ash argues first that Peoples Bank is estopped from considering the lapse of insurance coverage as a default because the bank had previously failed to declare a default after such a lapse. The contract provides that the fact that the bank waives its rights in one instance does not mean it will waive them in other instances. Furthermore, Ash reinstated coverage in the first instance, but on the second occasion the bank determined from the insurance agency that he had not reinstated it as late as the morning of the repossession, which was nearly a month after the lapse and more than two weeks after the bank had sent Ash notice that he was required to reinstate coverage. Thus, the bank did not establish a pattern of allowing lapse of insurance coverage from which Ash could have been led to expect that such a lapse would not result in repossession. Ash's estoppel argument does not present reversible error. . . .

Because none of the arguments advanced by Ash presents any reversible error, the judgments of the trial court are due to be affirmed.

■ *Affirmed.*

CASE CONCEPTS REVIEW

1. What is the basis of the secured party (Peoples Bank) claiming that the debtor (Ash) had defaulted on his loan owed to Peoples Bank?
2. What is Ash's argument why the Bank should not be allowed to assert that Ash's failure to maintain insurance is a default?
3. Why does the court reject Ash's argument?

The following sections discuss the parties' rights and duties on the debtor's default from a chronological perspective. First, the secured party must take possession of the collateral. This act often is called *repossession,* since the secured party may have sold the collateral to the debtor. Next, the secured party must decide whether to sell the collateral or to keep it. Finally, the secured party must give the debtor the opportunity to exercise his or her rights to redeem.

Prior to discussing the secured party's ability to repossess the collateral, a special rule concerning some types of collateral should be noted. If the collateral is accounts, chattel paper, instruments, or general intangibles, repossession is not necessary because the secured party is already in possession of the collateral. The secured party can simply proceed to collect whatever may become due on the collateral. He or she may give reasonable notice to the person who owes the account receivable or instrument to make payment directly to the secured party [9-502(1)]. A failure to give reasonable notice prevents the secured party from collecting these debts from any party other than the original debtor.

16. Repossession of Collateral

Self-help A creditor's attempt to take possession of collateral without the court's assistance.

SELF-HELP.   Generally, a secured party will attempt "peaceable," **self-help** repossession, since it is swift and inexpensive. The main drawback is that self-help techniques must not result in a breach of the peace. Countless judicial options have considered whether self-help repossession is peaceable or not under particular situations.

The following three sets of circumstances usually are deemed peaceable in connection with a repossession. First, the secured party removes the collateral (a car) from the street or parking lot without the knowledge or objection of the debtor. More than likely, starting the car without the use of the ignition key will be considered peaceful. If the removal is from the debtor's open premises, such as a driveway, it is not objectionable. Second, removal without the debtor's consent (or even if debtor knows but does not make an express objection) is not a breach of the peace. Finally, removal of the collateral from the premises of a third party (such as a garage, parking lot, neighbor's yard) is lawful as long as neither the debtor nor third person expressly objects.

Breach of the peace This occurrence invalidates the creditor's legal right to take possession of the collateral without the assistance of a court. This event occurs whenever the possession by the creditor is accompanied by violence, deception, or an objection by the debtor.

In four situations, repossession will usually involve a **breach of the peace.** First, it is a breach to threaten or to appear to threaten violence to the debtor or other person who is present, whether or not any violence occurs. Second, removal of the collateral over the express objection of the debtor (even if there is no violence) is a breach of the peace. Most courts also find a breach of the peace when the removal is over the express objection of a third party in possession of the collateral. Third, the use of trickery is a breach of the peace. For example, posing as a police officer would be considered an illegal repossession. Fourth, unauthorized entry into the debtor's home, garage, or other building for the purpose of repossession is unlawful. The following case demonstrates the wide latitude generally given secured creditors in exercising their rights of repossession through the self-help method without committing a breach of the peace.

CASE

Collins v. Gulf Furniture Stores, Inc.
549 So.2d 6 (Ala. 1989)

ADAMS, J.

Carolyn Jeanette Collins appeals from the trial court's summary judgment for Gulf Furniture Stores, Inc., on her claims that Gulf Furniture trespassed and breached the peace while repossessing a gas range and vacuum cleaner that she had purchased on an installment payment plan. Collins does not dispute that she had defaulted on the payments.

Although Collins was not at home at the time of repossession, employees of Gulf Furniture entered her rented home with permission from her minor son and took possession of the range and vacuum cleaner from a storage closet in Collins's bedroom. Collins's son signed

his mother's name to a "voluntary release" form, and the employees left the premises; there is no evidence in the record of violence or intimidation during the repossession. Collins subsequently sued Gulf Furniture, alleging that she had not authorized the entering of her home to repossess the range and vacuum cleaner and that Gulf Furniture had breached the peace in its repossession, in violation of Ala. Code 1975, § 78-9-503 ("Secured party's right to take possession after default").

The trial court entered summary judgment for Gulf Furniture. . . . The issue for our review is whether the trial court erred in entering summary judgment against Collins's claims based on breach of the peace and trespass. In reviewing the disposition of a motion for summary judgment, we use the same standard as that of the trial court in determining whether the evidence made out a genuine issue of material fact. In other words, we test the sufficiency of the evidence to determine if any real {factual} issue exists.

Section 7-9-503 allows a secured party, after default, to take possession of collateral without judicial process, if it can do so peacefully, i.e., without risk of injury to the secured party, the debtor, or innocent bystanders. The secured party may repossess collateral at the secured party's own convenience, and neither a demand for possession nor the debtor's consent is required before the secured party is entitled to take possession.

Notwithstanding the evidence regarding her son's allowing Gulf Furniture employees to enter her home, Collins presented no evidence to prove that Gulf Furniture trespassed or breached the peace in repossessing the range and the vacuum cleaner. In light of evidence that no actual or constructive force was used in the repossession, the trial court properly entered summary judgment for Gulf Furniture.

■ *Affirmed.*

CASE CONCEPTS REVIEW

1. How did Gulf Furniture obtain entrance into Collins's house?
2. Why does the court conclude that this entry was not a breach of the peace?

JUDICIAL ACTION.   If a secured party cannot obtain possession of the collateral by the peaceful self-help method, a judicial action becomes necessary. Repossession by judicial action may be accomplished by several means. The secured party may bring a *replevin* action, which is a judicial action for the actual recovery of the possession of an item of personal property. Or the action may be for a personal judgment against the debtor, with that judgment being levied on the collateral. In some states, the judicial action may be brought to obtain a foreclosure sale of specific personal property.

Obviously, repossession by judicial action is more expensive than self-help; however, the Code does make the debtor liable for most court costs, including attorney's fees. The secured party is well advised to use the courts when the debtor will not part with the goods without a fight. Under the typical judicial action, the plaintiff files a complaint, makes an affidavit, and posts a required bond. Then the sheriff seizes the property. Unless the debtor objects within a specified time, the property is delivered to the secured party.

ALTERNATIVES TO REPOSSESSION.   By including specific provisions in the security agreement, secured parties can tailor their rights on the debtor's default to suit their particular needs. In other words, secured parties may provide for alternative remedies to the self-help repossession or the judicial action allowed by Article 9. The security agreement can, for instance, put the debtor to work. It can provide that the debtor assemble the collateral and make it available to the secured party at a place reasonably convenient to both parties [9-503]. If the debtor refuses, the secured party may use judicial help in requiring a debtor in possession of collateral that is spread out over a number of places to gather the collateral at one place.

In the case of collateral such as heavy equipment, the physical removal from the debtor's plant and storage elsewhere pending resale may be excessively expensive and, in some cases, impractical. Thus the Code allows the secured party, without removal, to render equipment unusable and to dispose of the collateral on the debtor's premises [9-503]. Any such action must, of course, be "commercially reasonable."

17. Rights and Duties of Secured Party in Possession

The secured party has certain rights against the debtor who has defaulted. First, any reasonable expenses incurred in connection with the collateral are chargeable to the debtor and are secured by the collateral [9-207(2)(a)]. Second, the risk of accidental loss or damage to the collateral is on the debtor to the extent that the loss is not covered by insurance [9-207(2)(b)]. Finally, the secured party is entitled to hold as additional security any increase in or profits received from the collateral, unless the increase or profit is money [9-207(2)(c)].

Once the secured party has obtained possession of the collateral, that party must decide what to do with the collateral. The secured party may sell the collateral and apply the sale proceeds to satisfy the debt. Or the secured party may decide to keep the collateral in satisfaction of the debt. Because of the potential harshness of strict foreclosure, there are situations when a debtor or other interested party can force the secured party to sell the collateral.

The Code imposes certain duties on a secured party in possession of the collateral [9-207]. The most important is to exercise reasonable care in the custody and preservation of the collateral. If the collateral is chattel paper or instruments, reasonable care includes taking steps to preserve rights against prior parties unless otherwise agreed.

EXAMPLE Debtor pledged its stock in ABC Corporation to creditor to secure a loan. While creditor was in possession, ABC issued rights to current stockholders to buy additional shares, which rights would expire if not exercised by a stated date. Knowing of this right, creditor failed to notify debtor about it before the expiration date. Creditor thus failed to exercise due care and would be liable to debtor for any loss caused by the failure to notify.

18. Foreclosure Sale

Foreclosure The forced sale of a defaulting debtor's property at the insistence of the creditor.

After default, a secured party may sell, lease, or otherwise dispose of the collateral [9-504]. The usual disposition is by public or private **foreclosure** sale. The primary goal is to get the best possible price on the resale, since that benefits both the debtor and the secured party. For example, the higher the foreclosure sale price, the greater the likelihood of a surplus for the debtor. Also, the likelihood of a deficiency is diminished.

The foreclosure sale can be public or private, and it can be by one or more contracts [9-504(3)]. A *public sale* is a sale by auction open to the general public. A public sale often occurs on the courthouse steps. A *private sale* is a sale through commercial channels to a buyer arranged by the secured party. Such a buyer could be a dealer who regularly buys and sells goods like the collateral.

Although the Code provides flexible rules for the foreclosure sale, it does not leave the debtor unprotected and at the secured party's mercy. Indeed, the Code imposes definite restrictions on the secured party, who must adhere to these restrictions or risk losing the remedies provided by the Code. Of these restrictions, three are the most important: (1) *reasonable notification* of the foreclosure sale given to the debtor by the secured party, (2) *reasonable timing* of the foreclosure sale, and (3) *commercial reasonableness* of every aspect of the foreclosure sale.

NOTICE REQUIRED. A secured party is not free to assume that repossession of the collateral serves as *notice* of a possible public or private foreclosure sale. The Code requires the secured party to give reasonable notice of either the time and place of any public sale or of the time after which a private sale may occur [9-504(3)]. This notice gives debtors a deadline within which to protect themselves in whatever manner they see fit.

When notification is required by the Code, it must be reasonable in all situations. Upon the failure to give reasonable notice of a foreclosure sale, the secured party usually is denied the right to sue the debtor for a deficiency judgment, although the other aforementioned approaches may be followed. It should be emphasized that this notice must be given, not necessarily received.

The notice must be sent to the debtor and (to be reasonable) must be sent in time for the debtor to take appropriate steps to protect his or her interests, if desired. The notice of resale need not be given if the debtor has signed *after default* a statement renouncing or modifying his or her right to notification of sale.

In the case of when the collateral is consumer goods, notice must be given only to the debtor. When the collateral is anything other than consumer goods, the Code requires that notice be sent to any other secured party from whom the secured party has received written notice of an interest.

Notification of an impending disposition is not required if the collateral is (1) perishable or (2) threatens to decline speedily in value or (3) is of a type customarily sold on a recognized market [9-504(3)]. Examples of goods sold on a recognized market include commodities or corporate stock sold on a public exchange. Used cars and similar items are not considered customarily sold in a recognized market, since there is no established price for these items.

TIME OF SALE.   In general, the Code does not establish any stated *time* limitation within which the foreclosure sale or disposition of collateral must occur. This absence of a stated time period for resale conforms to the Code philosophy of encouraging disposition by private sale through regular commercial channels. For example, it may not be wise to dispose of goods if the market collapses. Likewise, the sale of large amounts of inventory in parcels over time may be more reasonable than a forced sale of the entire amount in bulk. The foreclosure sale must be commercially reasonable. The secured party is not allowed to delay when no reason exists for not making a prompt sale.

An exception to this general rule of no time restriction does apply if the collateral is consumer goods and if the debtor has paid over 60 percent of the purchase price or loan amount. Under these circumstances, the consumer goods must be sold within ninety days after the secured party has taken possession of the collateral. This exception is necessary to protect the debtor, since, in most cases, a sale of the consumer goods will produce proceeds in excess of the debt.

COMMERCIAL REASONABLENESS.   Every aspect of the resale, including the *method, manner, time, place,* and *terms* must be commercially reasonable. The term *commercially reasonable* is not defined in the Code, but case law has developed some rules to assist in making the determination in future cases. First, the fact that a better price could have been obtained at another time or by another method is not of itself sufficient to establish that the resale was unreasonable. However, recent case law indicates that a resale at a price substantially under what might well have been received is not commercially reasonable. In particular, if the sale is followed by a second sale at a substantially greater price, it is not reasonable. If the secured party has not exerted much effort (as in failing to contact a number of prospective buyers), the sale may be held not commercially reasonable.

The Code allows the secured party to buy the collateral at any public sale, but the right to buy at a private sale is restricted. Only if the collateral is of a type normally sold in a recognized market or is subject to universal price quotations can the secured party buy at a private sale [9-504(3)]. This prohibition against the creditor's buying at a private sale acknowledges that creditors can overreach the debtor's

Sham sale A sales transaction arranged by the seller to benefit a buyer who pays an unreasonably low price for the item sold.

rights by conducting a sham sale. A **sham sale** occurs if the collateral is purchased by the creditor at an unreasonably low price that allows the creditor to make the debtor liable for a substantial deficiency. Obviously, this type of resale is commercially unreasonable.

A resale is recognized as commercially reasonable if the secured party either (1) sells the collateral in the customary manner in a recognized market or (2) sells at a price current in such market at the time of resale or (3) sells in conformity with reasonable commercial practices among dealers in the type of property sold.

CONSEQUENCES FOR NONCOMPLIANCE.   Nowhere does the Code specify the consequences of a creditor's failure to meet the requirements of proper notice and commercially reasonable disposition. Courts have reached varying results in cases where a creditor has failed to comply with the Code's provisions governing disposition of the collateral.

One line of authority holds that the creditor's failure to comply with the requirements governing disposition of repossessed collateral serves as an absolute bar to the creditor's right to a *deficiency judgment*. These courts view the Code's requirements as conditions precedent to the creditor's right to recover a deficiency judgment.

A second line of authority, adopted by only a few courts, permits the secured party to recover a deficiency judgment despite his or her noncompliance with the requirements subject to the debtor's rights to recover from the secured party any loss occasioned by the creditor's failure to comply with the Code. Under this approach, the debtor's claim for damages is generally asserted as a counterclaim in the creditor's action for a deficiency judgment.

The third approach on failure to follow the statute is that the failure is not an absolute bar to the recovery of a deficiency, but there is a presumption that the fair market value of collateral at the time of repossession was equal to the amount of the total debt that it secured. The presumption arises when it has been determined that the secured party has disposed of the collateral in a commercially unreasonable manner. The burden to prove that the fair market value of the collateral was less than the debt at that time is then on the secured party.

19. Rights of Parties after Foreclosure

The buyer of the collateral at a foreclosure sale receives it free of the security interest under which the sale was held. This buyer also is free of any inferior security interest [9-504(4)]. Thus the good-faith purchaser at a disposition sale receives substantial assurance that he or she will be protected in purchase.

After the sale has been made, the proceeds of the sale will be distributed and applied as follows. First, the expenses the secured party incurred in taking repossession and conducting the foreclosure sale will be paid. After these expenses are paid, the sale's proceeds are used to satisfy the debt owed to the secured party. Third, any indebtedness owed to persons who have inferior security interest in the collateral will be paid. Fourth and finally, any surplus remaining after all these debts are satisfied will be returned to the debtor [9-504(1)]. If the foreclosure sale is commercially reasonable in all respects but does not produce enough to satisfy all these charges, the debtor is liable for any deficiency [9-504(2)].

20. Strict Foreclosure

NOTICE REQUIRED.   The secured party who intends to keep the collateral in satisfaction of the debt rather than conduct a foreclosure sale must send written notice to the debtor indicating this intent [9-505(2)]. Like with the notice of resale, this notice is not required if the debtor has signed, after default, a statement modifying or renouncing the right to this notice. If the collateral is consumer goods, only the debtor needs to be given notice of the proposed **strict foreclosure.** Notice to other interested parties is not necessary when consumer goods are involved, since most of the secured parties claiming a conflicting interest will have PMSI and will be relying on perfection by attachment. Thus, the secured party proposing a strict foreclosure will not even know of conflicting interests.

Strict foreclosure The agreement by the creditor and debtor to allow the creditor to retain possession of the debtor's property in satisfaction of the creditor's claim.

When collateral other than consumer goods is involved, written notice proposing strict foreclosure must be sent to all persons who have filed a financing statement covering the collateral or who are known to have a security interest in it. Within the time period (discussed in the next subsection), the debtor or any interested party may object in writing to the proposed strict foreclosure. If no objections are received, the secured party can retain the collateral in satisfaction of the debt [9-505(2)].

PREVENTION OF STRICT FORECLOSURE.   Strict foreclosure is disallowed in two situations. First, special provisions relate to consumer transactions. Disposition of consumer goods may be *compulsory*, and, if so, a sale must be made within ninety days after possession is taken by the secured party. This resale of the collateral is mandatory when there exists either (1) a purchase-money security interest in consumer goods and 60 percent of the purchase price has been paid or (2) an interest in consumer goods to secure a nonpurchase-money loan and 60 percent of the loan has been repaid [9-505(1)]. As stated previously, these rules exist because there is a presumption that the resale will result in surplus proceeds. The resale within ninety days ensures that the consumer debtor will not be deprived of this surplus. Of course, it is possible that even though a large percentage of the purchase price or loan amount has been paid, the resale of the collateral clearly will not produce a surplus. Thus the consumer debtor is allowed to waive the right of mandatory resale. This waiver must be in writing and must be signed by the debtor after default [9-505(1)].

The second situation when strict foreclosure may be prevented involves an objection to the secured party keeping the collateral. As noted in the preceding subsection, the debtor and all other interested parties must be sent written notice that a strict foreclosure is proposed. Any of these parties may object to this proposal. This objection must be made in writing, and it must be received by the secured party's proposing the strict foreclosure within twenty-one days of the original notice's being sent. If these requirements for objecting to a strict foreclosure are met, the collateral must be sold [9-505(2)].

21. Debtor's General Remedies

Except for the ninety-day period for consumer goods, the secured party is not required to make disposition of the repossessed goods within any time limit. The debtor has the right to *redeem* or reinstate his or her interest in the collateral until (1) that property has been sold or contracted to be sold, or (2) the obligation has

Redemption To buy back. A debtor buys back or redeems his or her mortgaged property when paying the debt.

been satisfied by the retention of the property. The debtor must, as a condition of **redemption,** tender the full amount of the obligation secured by the collateral plus expenses incurred by the secured party in connection with the collateral and (if so provided in the security agreement) attorneys' fees and legal expenses [9-506].

If the secured party fails to comply with the provisions of the Code relating to default, a court may order disposition or restrain disposition, as the situation requires. If the sale has already taken place, the secured party is liable for any loss resulting from noncompliance and may lose the right to recover any deficiency. If the collateral is consumer goods, the consumer debtor is entitled to recover from the secured party (1) the credit service charge plus 10 percent of the principal amount of the debt or (2) the time-price differential plus 10 percent of the cash price, whichever is greater [9-507(1)]. The secured party who forecloses a security interest in consumer goods must be very careful to comply with the law as it relates to their sale.

Note that if the creditor fails to follow the compulsory sale of consumer goods under the 60 percent–ninety-day rule of Section 9-505(1), the debtor may recover in conversion or under the liability provisions of Section 9-507(1). Under the latter provision, the debtor may recover any loss caused by the secured party's failure to comply with Code provisions. In addition to recovering damages caused by the secured party, if consumer goods are involved, the debtor also can recover the Code penalty discussed in the preceding paragraph.

CHAPTER SUMMARY

SECURED PARTY VERSUS BUYERS OF COLLATERAL

General Rule

1. Secured parties who are perfected generally have priority over buyers of collateral. However, there are at least three exceptions.

Buyers in the Ordinary Course of Business

1. Such a buyer takes free from a perfected secured party's interest.
2. A buyer in the ordinary course of business is a buyer who buys goods from a seller who is in the business of selling goods of that kind from inventory.
3. This rule of priority does not apply when the collateral is farm products.

Buyers of Consumer Goods

1. A buyer of consumer goods from a consumer cannot make this purchase in the ordinary course of business, since the consumer is not in business.
2. A buyer of consumer goods from a consumer has priority over a secured party who has relied on perfection by attachment of a purchase-money security interest if the buyer has no knowledge of the security interest and if the buyer uses the goods as consumer goods.
3. A secured party can be assured of priority with respect to consumer goods if a financing statement is properly filed.

Buyers of Chattel Paper and Instruments

1. A buyer of chattel paper or instruments that are proceeds from the sale of inventory collateral has priority over a secured party even if that buyer has knowledge of the security interest. This buyer must make the purchase in the ordinary course of business for value and must take possession of the chattel paper or instruments.
2. A buyer of chattel paper or instruments that are proceeds from the sale of noninventory collateral takes priority over a secured party only if that secured party relies on the ten-day automatic perfection rule and if the buyer lacks knowledge of the security interest.
3. A buyer of instruments that were original collateral takes priority over a secured party only if that secured party relies on the twenty-one-day automatic perfection rules and if the buyer lacks knowledge of the security interest.

General Rule	1. The secured party who is first to file or perfect has priority to the described collateral. When PMSIs are involved, exceptions do exist.
PMSI in Inventory Collateral	1. A second-in-time secured party who has a PMSI in inventory may have priority over a preexisting secured party. 2. This purchase-money secured party must notify the preexisting secured party in writing and must file a financing statement before the debtor gets possession of the collateral.
PMSI in Noninventory Collateral	1. A second-in-time secured party who has a PMSI in noninventory collateral may have priority over a preexisting secured party. 2. This purchase-money secured party does not have to give notice of its PMSI. However, this party must file a financing statement before or within ten days after the debtor takes possession of the collateral.
Fixtures	1. The financing of fixtures or potential fixtures creates the possible conflict between an Article 9 secured party and a party with an interest in the real estate. 2. The Code requires a fixture filing. It specifically provides rules concerning priority in certain situations when a fixture-secured party and a real estate secured party have conflicting interests. 3. These situations include the financing of building materials, the financing of soft fixtures, the creation of PMSI and non-PMSI in fixtures, and the rights of construction mortgages.
Accessions	1. An *accession* is a good or part that is added to or installed in a larger good. Accessions typically arise in repairs of personal property. 2. A secured party who creates a security interest in accessions before they are affixed to the whole object has priority to the accessions. 3. If the security interest in accessions is created after the parts are added to the whole object, the party secured by the accessions has priority over anyone who subsequently takes an interest in the whole. However, this secured party's interest is inferior to parties who have a preexisting interest in the whole object. 4. To be assured of priority, the party who is secured by accessions should perfect as well as create the security interest *prior* to the parts being added to the whole object.
Commingled and Processed Goods	1. A creditor with a perfected security interest in raw materials or component parts generally has a security interest in the finished product as well. 2. Secured parties with conflicting interests in the finished products must share in proportion to the costs of the materials used in manufacturing the finished products.

SECURED PARTY VERSUS LIEN CREDITORS

General Rule	1. Whichever party, the secured party or the lien creditor, who is on record first in time has priority. 2. Federal tax liens follow this general rule. A tax lien is considered to be on record when the notice of the lien is filed.
Laborer's, Artisan's, and Materialperson's Liens	1. These liens may be of common-law or statutory origin. 2. Article 9 provides an exception to the general priority rule because it is presumed that the repairs increase the value of the collateral.
Judgment Creditor's Lien	1. These lienholders usually are subject to the aforementioned general rule. A judicial lien is on record when it is levied on the debtor's property. 2. A PMSI-secured party may defeat a preexisting judgment creditor's lien if the secured party perfects within ten days after debtor receives possession of collateral and if the judicial lien is levied between the time the security interest attaches and the time it is perfected.

Bankruptcy Trustee's Lien	1. The bankruptcy trustee is considered a hypothetical lien creditor. Therefore, the trustee is in the same priority position as the judgment creditor.
	2. The bankruptcy trustee's lien arises on the date the bankruptcy petition is filed.

RIGHTS AND DUTIES ON DEBTOR'S DEFAULT

Repossession of Collateral	1. The secured party's basic right on the debtor's default is to obtain possession of the collateral.
	2. The collateral may be possessed through peaceful self-help or through judicial action.
	3. This judicial action may take the form of a replevin action, a suit for judgment and levy, or a suit for an order of foreclosure.
	4. The secured party can include any legal provision in the security agreement providing an alternative remedy to repossession.
	5. These provisions can require the debtor to assemble all collateral in one location, or the secured party may be allowed to make heavy equipment unusable and sell it from the debtor's place of business.
Rights and Duties of Secured Party in Possession	1. The secured party can recover the cost of repossession from the debtor.
	2. Any increase in the collateral is additional security protecting the secured party.
	3. Once the secured party has possession of the collateral, that party must decide to conduct a foreclosure sale or to keep the collateral in satisfaction of the debt, which is called strict foreclosure.
	4. In general, the secured party must handle the collateral with reasonable care.
Foreclosure Sale	1. A foreclosure sale may be public or private. A public sale is open to the general public and usually is an auction.
	2. A private sale is arranged by the secured party who locates one or more buyers of the collateral.
	3. The secured party always must give the debtor notice of the foreclosure sale. This notice must include the time and place of a public sale. The notice need only inform the debtor of the time after which a private sale may occur.
	4. If the collateral is consumer goods, notice of resale needs to be given only to the debtor. If other types of collateral are involved, notice also must be given to the other secured parties who have notified the secured party arranging the sale of their interest.
	5. This type of notice is not required if the collateral is perishable, threatens to decline in value rapidly, or is sold on a recognized market.
	6. In general, there is no time limit within which a foreclosure sale must occur.
	7. The applicable standard is that the sale must occur within a reasonable time.
	8. All aspects of a foreclosure sale must be handled in a commercially reasonable manner.
	9. This standard has been and continues to be developed by case law, since the Code does not provide a definition of commercial reasonableness.
Rights of Parties after Foreclosure	1. A buyer at a commercially reasonable foreclosure sale takes the property free from the security interest of the seller and all inferior security interests.
	2. The proceeds of a resale of collateral will be distributed to the secured party to pay for the expenses of repossession and resale and for the debt. Any remaining proceeds will be paid to other parties secured by the same collateral. Any surplus is paid to the debtor. Any deficiency is owed by the debtor.
Strict Foreclosure	1. A secured party who proposes to keep the collateral in satisfaction of the debt must send the debtor written notice of this proposal unless the debtor has waived after default the right to such notice.
	2. If the collateral is not consumer goods, written notice of strict foreclosure also must be sent to all other known interested parties.

3. If the collateral is consumer goods and 60 percent of the purchase price or loan amount has been paid, the consumer goods must be sold within ninety days of the secured party's possession of them.

4. Any debtor or interested party may object to the strict foreclosure and force a foreclosure sale. This objection must be given in writing within twenty-one days of the secured party's notice of strict foreclosure being sent.

Debtor's General Remedies

1. The debtor has a right to redeem his or her interest in the collateral anytime prior to final action being taken by the secured party.

2. To redeem interests in default, the debtor must pay all amounts owed to the secured party.

3. If the secured party fails to comply with any Code provision, the debtor can sue for actual damages plus any applicable Code remedy.

REVIEW QUESTIONS AND PROBLEMS

1. Match each term in column A with the appropriate statement in column B.

A	B
(1) Buyer in the ordinary course of business	(a) May be of common-law or statutory origin
(2) Accession	(b) A judicial action seeking possession of personal property
(3) Laborer's lien	(c) The reinstatement of a defaulting debtor's interest in collateral
(4) Judicial lien	(d) A foreclosure sale involving an unreasonably low price
(5) Self-help	(e) A party who purchases an item from a seller in the business of selling such items
(6) Replevin	(f) A foreclosure when anyone may be the buyer
(7) Public sale	(g) The rights of a judgment creditor who levies on the debtor's property
(8) Sham sale	(h) A secured party's retention of collateral in satisfaction of the debt
(9) Strict foreclosure	(i) Personal property affixed to personal property
(10) Redemption	(j) A method of repossession that is available as long as it is peaceful

2. Assume that the following events occur. Answer each part based on these and any additional facts given.

The First National Bank agrees to lend $500,000 to Custom Sound Stereo and Television Company. To secure its position, the bank takes a security interest in Custom Sound's inventory, equipment, accounts, and chattel paper and in its after-acquired inventory, equipment, accounts, and chattel paper. A security agreement and financing statement is filed in the proper location to give the bank a perfected security interest.

a. Corliss purchases a TV set for her personal use. If Custom Sound defaults on its loan payments, who has priority between the bank and Corliss? Explain.

b. Deborah, a doctor, purchases a stereo for her office waiting room. If Custom Sound defaults on its loan payments, who has priority to the stereo between the bank and Deborah? Explain.

c. Suppose Deborah purchased her stereo on credit. She signed a promissory note, but not a security agreement. Does the bank have any interest in this note? If so, how is this interest perfected? Explain.

d. If Custom Sound sells Deborah's note to the Second Financial Institution three days after she signed it, who has priority to the note between the bank and the Institution? Explain.

e. Suppose Corliss purchased her TV set on credit. She signed a promissory note and a security agreement. What are all the ways that Custom Sound can perfect its interest in Corliss's TV set?

f. Assume Corliss, while still owing Custom Sound, sells the TV set to Freddie, a neighbor. Who has priority to the TV set between Custom Sound and Freddie if Corliss defaults on her payments to Custom Sound?

g. Suppose Custom Sound is in need of new computerized stereo testing equipment. It agrees to buy on credit new equipment worth $50,000 from Hi-Fi Diagnostic Corporation. This corporation wants to keep a security interest in the equipment sold to Custom Sound. What must Hi-Fi Diagnostic Corporation do to be sure of having priority to the equipment in case Custom Sound defaults?

3. Farmers' Bank had a perfected security interest in 1,280 pigs owned by Pigs Unlimited. Pigs Unlimited's basic business was that of buying and selling feeder pigs. The feeder pig enterprise consisted of purchasing newly weaned pigs and selling them to buyers in the pig-fattening business. Farmers in the pig-fattening business would bring the pigs up to a weight of 200 to 250 pounds and then sell them to a packing house. Often feeder pigs remained in the pens at Pigs Unlimited only a few days before a buyer picked them up. Sometimes, however, because of market conditions, a feeder pig would remain unsold and grow to the fattened stage before being sold. Pigs Unlimited sold the 1,280 pigs in question to Webel Feed Mill, a pig fattener. Pigs Unlimited then defaulted on its loan to Farmers' Bank. Farmers' Bank, relying on its security interest, sued Webel Feed Mill, claiming priorities to the pigs. Webel Feed Mill argued that because it was a buyer in the ordinary course of business, it took free of any security interest. Farmers' Bank argued that its security interest is intact because the pigs are farm products. Was Webel Feed Mill a buyer in the ordinary course of business of inventory or farm products? Why?

4. A dispute arose between two banks as to which one had the better rights to grain bins located on the debtor's real estate. The Bank of Rector had financed the debtor's purchase of the real estate involved and had recorded its mortgage. The Corning Bank had previously financed the grain bins and had filed a financing statement. This financing statement did not describe the real estate where the bins were located, nor was it referenced into the real estate records. When the debtor became insolvent, these banks sought a judicial determination establishing which one had priority to the grain bins. Does the filing of a financing statement prior to the records of a mortgage give the Corning Bank priority to the grain bins? Why?

5. Krueger left his car with Gomer for extensive repairs. State Bank has a perfected security interest in the car. Gomer's bill is $1,152, which Krueger cannot pay. Can Gomer sell the car to get his bill paid? Why or why not?

6. SP-1 takes a security interest in Don's inventory on February 1. Don files a bankruptcy petition on February 5. SP-1 files a financing statement on February 9 to perfect its security interest in Don's inventory. May the trustee prevail over SP-1's security interest? Would your answer change if SP-1's security interest were a PMSI? Explain.

7. Vernon J. Rumbaugh and his wife, Gladys, borrowed $30,000 from the Southwest Bank of Omaha. A security agreement and financing statement were prepared by the bank. The collateral described in these documents was inventory, fixtures, and accounts receivable in Rumbaugh's hardware business. The financing statement was not signed by Vernon J. Rumbaugh, who was the sole owner of the business. However, in the place for the debtor's signature appeared "By Gladys H. Rumbaugh." This financing statement was filed in the appropriate office. Later, Rumbaugh's hardware store voluntarily filed a petition in bankruptcy. The trustee in bankruptcy objected to the bank's claim of priority to Rumbaugh's inventory and fixtures. Does the bank have priority to the collateral when compared to the bankruptcy trustee? Explain.

8. To answer parts a through g of this problem, rely on the following situation: A debtor was in arrears in his auto payments. When he failed to respond to requests for payment from the secured party, the secured party sent an agent to repossess the car. Is the agent's repossession of the car peaceful in the following instances?
    a. When the agent repossesses, the car is parked in front of the debtor's house.
    b. The agent at 11:00 P.M. tows away the car from the parking lot at the apartment house complex where the debtor had an assigned space.
    c. The car is parked in the debtor's unlocked garage.
    d. The car is parked in the debtor's locked garage. The agent unlocks the garage door, removes the car, and locks the garage.
    e. The car is parked at a service station after a tuneup. The station owner permits the agent to remove the car.
    f. The car is parked on the road in front of the debtor's house. As the agent starts to enter the car, the debtor bursts from the door of his house, shouting epithets and demanding that his car not be moved. But the agent is able to start the car and drive away before the debtor can get to the car.
    g. The agent comes to the debtor's house and states that he is from the city water department and needs to check the debtor's pipe system. The agent then sneaks into the garage and drives the car away.

9. The Barnette Bank had a perfected security interest in the assets of Quest and Sea-Sky Travel Agency. Due to the debtor's delinquency in repaying a loan, the bank decided to take possession of the agency's assets. A bank official called the owner, Quest, who was at home sick. Nevertheless, this official asked Quest to come to her place of business so the bank could close it down. Quest asked for some time to retrieve some valuable papers in her office. The bank official agreed to her request. Despite this agreement, when Quest arrived at her office, bank employees already had removed most of the contents of her office. Indeed, Quest's records were scattered on the floor. Quest brought an action contending that the bank's self-help measures were a breach of the peace. Is the bank liable to Quest for its actions in taking possession of her travel agency's assets? Why?

10. Clark Equipment lent Armstrong Equipment Company $1,800,000. This loan was secured by heavy road-building equipment used by Armstrong in a five-state area. The security agreement signed by Armstrong contained a clause that allowed Clark to "require borrower to assemble the collateral and make it available at a place to be designated which is reasonably convenient to all parties." When Armstrong defaulted, Clark asked Armstrong to assemble the equipment. This request was ignored, and Armstrong continued to conduct work through all five states. Clark sued to enjoin Armstrong's operation and to force the assembling of the collateral. Armstrong argued that the injunction remedy is not provided for by the Code. Is Clark entitled to an injunction compelling Armstrong to assemble all the collateral in one location? Explain.

11. Scott Trucking purchased several trucks and financed the transaction through Mack Financial Corporation. Scott became delinquent and returned the trucks to Mack in February 1990. These trucks remained in Mack's possession until they were sold at a public auction on January 25, 1993. In February 1990, Scott owed Mack $127,600. In January 1993, the trucks were sold for $44,700. Is Scott Trucking liable for the deficiency? Why or why not?

12. Carol granted a security interest in her mobile home to the bank. When Carol defaulted on her payments, the bank sent a certified letter to her at her last known address. This letter contained notice of the time when and the place where the bank would be selling Carol's mobile home. Since Carol had moved, the letter was forwarded to her new address. Twice the post office attempted to deliver this certified letter, but no one would come to the door. Notices that a certified letter was at the post office were left in Carol's mailbox. Ultimately, the letter was returned to the bank. The mobile home was sold, and a deficiency balance remains. Is the bank entitled to collect it from Carol? Why or why not?

13. A furniture manufacturer, secured by a security agreement, sold furniture to Daniel on credit. When Daniel did not pay as agreed, the creditor repossessed the furniture. This creditor approached one possible buyer for the items but failed to sell them. The creditor then bought the collateral at a private sale and sued Daniel for a deficiency of $7,000. Daniel contends that he is entitled to credit for the full value of the repossessed goods because the private sale was improper. Is Daniel correct? Why or why not?

14. McIlroy Bank lent money to Seven Day Builders (SDB) to enable SDB to lease some equipment. This equipment was used as collateral to secure the bank that repayment would be made. When SDB defaulted, the bank took possession of the equipment. Although it never notified SDB of its intentions, the bank planned to retain possession of this equipment in satisfaction of the debt. SDB argued that the bank could not keep the collateral and that the bank was liable for damages caused to SDB. Did the bank fail to follow proper procedures such that it is liable to the debtor? Explain.

15. The secured party repossessed Crosby's personal pickup truck after Crosby had paid over 60 percent of the cash price. The secured party failed to sell the truck within the ninety days required by the Code. Crosby sued for the statutory penalty under Section 9-507(1). Is Crosby entitled to collect this penalty? How is this penalty calculated?

REAL PROPERTY AS SECURITY

CHAPTER PREVIEW

*T*he most valuable asset many individuals ever own is a piece of land, whether or not that land has an improvement (such as a house) on it. When a person has a legal interest in a piece of real estate, that person is said to have a real property interest. Creditors feel much more comfortable or secure that they will be able to collect the money owed them if they have an interest in their debtors' real property.

The preceding two chapters discuss how creditors are benefited by having security interests in items of personal property. This chapter concentrates on the use of real property as a means of providing security for creditors. In particular, the laws relating to real estate mortgages and to mechanic's liens are discussed.

> You operate a building supply business, and you have supplied on credit lumber and other materials for the construction of a large apartment complex. The general contractor of this project has been one of your best customers. However, sixty days have passed since you have received a payment, and the project is nearing completion.
>
> What should you do to protect your chances of being paid?

MORTGAGE TRANSACTIONS

1. Terminology

Mortgage A conveyance of an interest in real property for the purpose of creating a security for a debt.

A real estate **mortgage** is an interest in real property, an interest created for the purpose of securing the performance of an obligation, usually the payment of a debt. A mortgage is not a debt—only security for a debt. The owner of the land that is being used as security for the debt is called the *mortgagor,* since that owner is granting a mortgage interest to the creditor. This party to whom the interest in the real estate is conveyed is called the *mortgagee.*

2. Theories of Mortgages

TITLE THEORY.   Three distinct legal theories relate to mortgages. The first of these, the *title theory,* was developed under common law. Originally, a mortgage on land was an absolute conveyance of the title to the land by the owner to the mortgagee. However, title reverted to the mortgagor when the obligation was performed or the money was repaid. If the mortgagor failed to repay the debt, the property remained the property of the mortgagee. Under the title theory, the mortgagee could not be forced to sell the land to satisfy the debt. The process of not having a forced sale is known as *strict foreclosure.* Furthermore, any time after default, the mortgagor lost all rights to redeem the interest in the real property. Due to the harshness of its application, the title theory has very little support today.

LIEN (OR EQUITABLE) THEORY.   The second theory of mortgages is usually known as the *lien theory,* although it is sometimes called the *equitable theory.* Under this theory, a mortgage is not a conveyance of title, but only a method of creating a *lien* on the real estate. The lien or equitable theory avoids the harshness that results under the title theory. Under the lien theory, a mortgagee does not have title when the mortgagor defaults; the mortgagee simply has a lien that can be foreclosed. Upon foreclosure of the lien, any proceeds of the sale are used to pay the debt and the costs of the sale. Any excess from the proceeds remains the property of the mortgagor. In addition, the lien theory grants to the mortgagor a right to redeem his or her property after the default and foreclosure. These rights to redeem are discussed in section 12.

INTERMEDIATE THEORY.   Many states do not follow the title or the lien theory; they have reached a compromise between the two, an *intermediate theory*. Under it, a mortgage is a conveyance of title, but the equitable theories are applied to it. Mortgages must be foreclosed; and the mortgagor has the right to redeem the interest prior to the foreclosed sale. This right of redemption exists even though the mortgagee has "title."

3. Documents Involved

Remember that a mortgage is evidence of the interest a lender is receiving; it is not evidence of the loan being made. Therefore, typically there are two documents involved in the mortgage financing transaction.

The *promissory note* is the piece of paper that evidences the borrower's agreement to repay the amount of the loan. This note should include the principal borrowed, the interest rate charged, the term or the life of the loan, and the amount of the periodic payments.

In addition to the note, the *mortgage document* must be prepared. Since a mortgage is a contract, it must meet all the requirements of an enforceable agreement. A mortgage must be in writing and contain (1) the names of the mortgagor and mortgagee, (2) an accurate description of the mortgaged property, (3) the terms of the debt (incorporated from the note), and (4) the mortgagor's signature. This document must be executed with all the formalities of a deed.

So that the mortgagee may give notice to third parties that he or she has an interest in the real estate, it is necessary that the mortgage be recorded in the recording office of the county where the real estate is situated. Recording serves to notify subsequent parties of the lien or encumbrance of the mortgage.

4. Mortgage Clauses

In addition to the essential requirements just mentioned, mortgage documents are often several pages long because they contain many optional clauses. Some of the more typical mortgage provisions include an acceleration clause, a prepayment penalty clause, and a dragnet clause. These clauses are discussed next. A mortgage also usually contains provisions on the rights and duties of the mortgagor and mortgagee. These rights and duties are discussed in section 5.

ACCELERATION CLAUSES.   An acceleration clause enables the mortgagee to declare the entire outstanding balance of the loan immediately due and payable if stated conditions occur. For example, a *due-on-default clause* allows the mortgagee at his or her option to demand full payment if the mortgagor has failed to make a payment or a series of payments within a stated time period. A default may also occur whenever the mortgagor fails to comply with any other provision of the mortgage.

A *due-on-encumbrance clause* allows the mortgagee to accelerate the debt owed any time the mortgagor encumbers the real property without the mortgagee's consent. Examples of encumbering the property might include creating an easement in favor of a third party, agreeing to the application of restrictive covenants on the use of the land, failing to pay for work done to improve the property, or failing to pay taxes as they become due. The occurrence of any of these events entitles the mortgagee to demand full payment to protect the security interest the mortgagee already has.

The most controversial acceleration clause has been the *due-on-sale clause.* This type of clause permits the mortgagee to call the loan due whenever the mortgagor sells the collateral. The purpose of this clause originally was to protect the mortgage from purchasers with a questionable ability to repay the loan. In other words, with the due-on-sale acceleration clause, the mortgagee could prevent the assumption of the mortgage-secured loan by a buyer who was not creditworthy. Many states required proof of **impairment of the security** as a condition to enforcement of the clause.

During periods of rapidly increasing interest rates, the due-on-sale clause has been utilized by mortgagees to adjust their below-market interest rates to a higher level without proof of impairment of the security. This clause has been used to prevent assumptions without an upward adjustment of the interest rate being charged.

Regardless of the type of acceleration clause used by a creditor to call a loan due, courts have insisted on the mortgagee acting in an equitable manner. For example, the right of acceleration may be waived if it is not exercised within a reasonable time. In the following case, the court considers whether an acceleration of the amount due is equitable in light of the insignificance of the debtor's default.

Impairment of security
A decrease in the value of the collateral from which the debt may be collected or a decline in the likelihood that the debtor will repay the creditor.

CASE

Vonk v. Dunn
775 P.2d 1088 (Ariz. 1989)

FELDMAN, VICE C. J.

The Vonks brought this action to foreclose a mortgage that the Dunns had given to secure the purchase of land. . . .

The Dunns bought 160 acres in Cochise County from the Vonks in 1982 for $28,000. The Dunns paid $4,000 down and signed a promissory note for the $24,000 balance, securing the note with a mortgage on the property. The note ran at eight percent per annum and was payable in regular monthly installments on the first of each month. The note contained a ten-day grace period, which ran without notice from the first day of the month. The mortgage also required the Dunns to pay property taxes. The sanction for delinquent mortgage or property tax payments was acceleration and foreclosure at the Vonks' election. Finally, the mortgage required payment of the mortgagee's attorney's fees and costs in any collection proceeding.

For about three years, the Dunns made timely mortgage payments. For the first six months of 1986, however, the Dunns were late. The Vonks wrote the Dunns, putting them on notice that they must make their payments on time. The notice also called on the Dunns to pay delinquent property taxes. The Dunns acknowledged the reinstatement notice, paid the property taxes, and made timely payments for the rest of 1986.

However, the Dunns' bank mistakenly returned the February 1987 payment check marked "Insufficient Funds." The Vonks notified their attorney, who prepared to foreclose. The attorney learned that the Dunns had not paid their November 1986 property taxes. Without contacting the Dunns, the Vonks began foreclosure on February 27, 1987. The complaint alleged default for failure to make the February mortgage payment and the delinquent property taxes. At this point, the Dunns had paid nearly thirty-five percent of the purchase price.

After the Vonks filed their complaint on February 27, 1987, the Dunns obtained and sent to the Vonks a letter from their bank stating that it had mistakenly dishonored their check. Subsequently, the Vonks offered to dismiss the action if the Dunns brought the payments current *and* paid attorney's fees and costs incurred to that time: $932.65.

The Dunns rejected this offer, arguing that the Vonks could have avoided the entire matter by contacting the Dunns during the note's ten-day grace period. The Dunns, however, paid the delinquent taxes in March 1987. In addition, during the intervening months the

Dunns continued to make regular installment payments on the note, totalling $2,338, which the Vonks accepted. . . . Two months later, the trial court granted summary judgment to the Vonks. At the sheriff's sale, the Vonks purchased the property for the amount of their judgment.

On appeal, the Dunns argued the foreclosure was oppressive and unconscionable. The court of appeals . . . affirmed, reasoning that the Dunns' default in payment of the taxes justified acceleration of the note and foreclosure of the mortgage. The Dunns petitioned this court for review. . . .

The note and mortgage allowed the Vonks to accelerate and foreclose for tax delinquency. However, a mortgage foreclosure is an equitable proceeding. . . .

Because foreclosure is an equitable proceeding, the plaintiff must do more than merely establish that the defendant has violated the strict terms of the mortgage or note. The plaintiff must additionally show that some purpose of the [acceleration] clause is being circumvented or that the mortgagee's security is jeopardized. . . .

The Dunns owed no more than $66 in property taxes and the arrearage was not of long duration. . . . The property was not in danger of being lost for tax delinquency. We believe that with equitable considerations in mind, a factfinder could find that the Vonks' invocation of the acceleration clause was unnecessary to protect their security.

Further, the factfinder could have considered whether the breach of the tax obligation was trivial. Considering that the Dunns had already made forty-nine of the sixty note payments, paying nearly thirty-five percent of the purchase price, the $66 tax delinquency appears insignificant. The factfinder could conclude that given the Dunns' investment, including the $4,000 down payment and their improvements on the property, it was oppressive and unconscionable to accelerate and foreclose for a $66 tax arrearage without giving notice and an opportunity to cure. . . .

Finally, the factfinder could certainly infer that the delinquent tax payment was only a secondary issue to the Vonks. They decided to foreclose when the bank dishonored the Dunns' February check. After it became clear that the bank had wrongfully dishonored the Dunns' check, the Vonks' original reason for foreclosing dissipated, yet they maintained the action solely because of nonpayment of the $66 in taxes. . . .

We believe a reasonable factfinder could conclude that acceleration and foreclosure for the $66 tax delinquency was both oppressive and unconscionable. Because there was an issue of fact, the court of appeals improperly affirmed the grant of summary judgment. . . .

■ *Reversed and remanded.*

CASE CONCEPTS REVIEW

1. What party is the mortgagor, and which is the mortgagee?
2. What is the factual basis for the Vonks to accelerate the amount due from the Dunns?
3. What was the amount of overdue taxes?
4. Why does the court conclude that the granting of a summary judgment in the mortgagee's favor was erroneous?

PREPAYMENT PENALTY CLAUSE.   A mortgagor has the right without penalty to pay the loan off earlier than the agreed time unless the mortgage or note includes a prepayment penalty clause. This clause is used to protect the mortgagee when interest rates are falling. The prepayment penalty clause usually is limited to the situation where the mortgagor borrows funds at a lower rate to pay off the original loan. This clause is not applicable when the mortgagor prepays the loan due to the sale of the mortgaged property. This use would likely be prohibited as a restraint on the transferability of property.

If a mortgage contains both a due-on-sale and a prepayment penalty clause, the mortgagee probably is taking unfair advantage of the mortgagor—especially if the mortgagor is a consumer borrower. Most courts probably would refuse to allow the combined effect of these clauses. These clauses could be declared unenforceable as being unconscionable or contrary to public policy.

DRAGNET CLAUSE.   A mortgage may be created prior to the time when money is advanced to the mortgagor. Such a mortgage is called a *mortgage to secure future advances*. The clause in a mortgage that makes the security interest cover future advances is referred to as a *dragnet clause*. This clause gives the mortgagee a valid interest in the real property described in the mortgage as of the date the mortgage is recorded to the extent of the amount stated in the mortgage.

For example, assume Rick E. Olsen, an owner of real estate, signs a mortgage containing a dragnet clause naming First Federal Savings and Loan as the mortgagee. This mortgage secures a loan First Federal makes to Rick in the amount of $150,000 and is recorded on September 2, 1991. Suppose Second National Bank then lends Rick $50,000 and receives a mortgage describing the same land as that described in the mortgage protecting First Federal. Second National's mortgage is recorded on April 10, 1992. Further assume that as of today's date, Rick has paid off 20 percent of the loan he owes First Federal ($30,000 of the $150,000), and it lends him another $20,000 without taking any new security. If Rick defaults the next day and if his land is sold for $145,000, who gets what of the proceeds? *Answer:* First Federal would get the full $140,000 Rick owes it, and Second National would get the remaining $5,000 of the proceeds. Second National would then be unsecured with respect to the remainder of what Rick owed it. The lesson of this example is to beware of dragnet clauses unless they are protecting you.

The following case provides further illustration of the impact of a dragnet clause and additional advances by the mortgagee.

CASE

National Bank of Waterloo v. Moeller
434 N.W.2d 887 (Ia. 1989)

NEUMAN, J.

This litigation began as an action in equity to foreclose deeds of trust on two parcels of farm real estate. . . .

The Moellers owned a 328-acre farm known as "Davis Corners." Across the road was the Pierce farm. In January 1983, John Moeller was approached by Pierce's agent, Luke Kollasch, about buying the Pierce farm. Moeller was interested but at the time he was "asset rich and cash poor."

Pierce's financial position at the time was nothing less than precarious. He was buying his farm on contract, and he faced a balloon payment in excess of $500,000 due March 1, 1983. The National Bank of Waterloo held an assignment of Pierce's interest in the real estate contract as security for $70,000 in outstanding loans. Thus the bank was as eager as Pierce to unload the property before Pierce's interest in it was forfeited.

The bank agreed to lend Moeller the full purchase price of the Pierce farm (approximately $565,000) on the representation by sales agent Kollasch that Moeller's regular financier, the PCA, would subordinate its four mortgages on Moeller's Davis Corners property so that it could be given as additional collateral. The bank neither discussed this proposed subordination with Moeller nor made it part of the loan commitment. Nevertheless, Moeller became aware of the proposal through Kollasch, and discussed the idea with PCA.

PCA was amenable to the subordination as long as Moeller could furnish substitute collateral. That did not appear to be a problem in view of Moeller's extensive land holdings. A nearby Minnesota farm seemed a likely substitute.

In early March 1983, bank officer Willis Crees and PCA branch manager James Morrow discussed the proposed subordination by telephone. Confirming that conversation, Morrow wrote a letter to Crees on March 21 which stated, in pertinent part:

PCA is agreeable to the substitution and we are currently in the process of accomplishing this. As discussed, about 30 days will be required due to Minnesota procedural problems and the nature of the collateral being secured. Provided no unexpected problems arise, PCA will subordinate our position to the bank's mortgage sometime before the end of April.

No further communication between the bank and PCA occurred. The bank closed the Pierce/Moeller deal on March 30. Funds were disbursed to pay off the Pierce contract and Moeller executed deeds of trust in favor of the bank on both the Pierce and David Corners properties. Contrary to its usual policy, however, the bank made no postclosing title search to assure itself of the priority of its liens.

Eighteen months later, when Moeller had difficulty servicing this new debt, the bank learned that the proposed subordination had never materialized. . . . In the interim, PCA had lent Moeller an additional $275,000 in operating loans pursuant to future advances clauses in PCA's prior mortgages on the Davis Corners property. Thus when the bank foreclosed its deeds of trust on both the Pierce farm and Davis Corners in April 1985, a controversy arose over who was entitled to priority on Davis Corners, the bank or PCA. From a judgment entered in favor of the bank, PCA now appeals. . . .

It is undisputed that when Moeller gave the bank a deed of trust on his Davis Corners property, the PCA held four prior mortgages on the same ground securing an outstanding indebtedness of approximately $275,000. . . .

It is also undisputed that although the bank and PCA had no further communication relative to Moeller after the March 21 letter, by late Spring 1983 PCA learned of the bank's lien on the Davis Corners property through conversations with Moeller. Nevertheless, PCA continued to lend Moeller substantial sums for his farm operations pursuant to future advances clauses contained in its mortgages. The record reveals that the principal obligation on Moeller's operating loan was paid down to five dollars by December 1983, exclusive of accrued interest, while the balance on the term notes stood at $70,000. Further advances by PCA, however, thereafter increased Moeller's indebtedness to over $300,000 by the time the bank's foreclosure proceedings were initiated in April 1985.

Given this factual record, the district court sustained the bank's claim of priority by applying the following legal conclusion:

> Advances to a borrower by a lender holding a senior mortgage after that lender has actual knowledge of the existence of a junior mortgage, are junior to the intervening rights of the junior mortgagee unless the senior mortgagee's mortgage makes such advances obligatory.

. . . In *Freese Leasing,* our attention was focused on a priority question that turned on whether a lender and borrower intended the "dragnet clause" of two real estate mortgages to cover subsequent loans for the borrower's used car business. *Freese Leasing,* 253 N.W.2d at 925. We mentioned in passing the "prevailing rule" that as between competing lienholders, "[m]ere constructive notice" of a later encumbrance would not defeat the priority of future advances made by a first mortgagee, even after recording of the subsequent mortgage, inasmuch as the prior mortgage is "affected only by actual notice.". . .

We think that PCA had the right to rely on the priority of its mortgages, not only with respect to the original obligations secured thereby, but for future extensions of credit authorized by the language of the recorded instruments. Those advances may not have been obligatory, but they clearly related to the original transactions and were thus valid and enforceable under the standard adopted in *Freese Leasing.* Moreover, the mortgage documents gave PCA the absolute right to advance sums for the payment of delinquent taxes and insurance in order to protect the encumbered property. These contract terms, designed to benefit both the lender and the borrower, would be effectively defeated by the adoption of the "common-law" rule proposed by the bank. We find no merit, legal or equitable, in allowing such a result.

Accordingly, we reverse the judgment of the district court and remand the case for entry of judgment establishing the priority of PCA's liens on the Davis Corners property.

■ *Reversed and remanded.*

CASE CONCEPTS REVIEW

1. What is the nature of the dispute between the bank and PCA?
2. This dispute concerns the proceeds from the sale of Davis Corners. Why are these parties not arguing over the proceeds from the sale of the Pierce Farm?
3. Although PCA loaned $275,000 to Moeller after the bank had recorded its deed of trust, PCA argues it has priority to the foreclosure proceeds. What is the logic of PCA's argument?
4. Why was the telephone call and letter exchanged between officials of PCA and the bank not sufficient to give the bank a priority claim?

5. Rights and Duties of the Parties

Cloud on the title A defect, encumbrance, or other interest that exists in the record title to land.

Payment of the mortgage debt terminates the mortgage. Upon payment, the mortgagor is entitled to a release or satisfaction of the mortgage. This release should be recorded to clear the title to the land; otherwise, the unreleased mortgage will remain a **cloud on the title.** If the mortgagee refuses to give a release, he or she can be compelled to do so in a court of equity.

The mortgagor is entitled to retain possession of the real estate during the period of the mortgage unless a different arrangement is provided for in the mortgage. The mortgagor may not use the property in a manner that will materially reduce its value. Mining ore, pumping oil, or cutting timber are operations that cannot be conducted by the mortgagor during the period of the mortgage unless the right to do so is reserved in the mortgage agreement. The rights will be implied when they are being conducted at the time the mortgage is created.

Any parcel of real estate may be subject to more than one mortgage. In addition, mortgaged land may be subject to a lien for property taxes. A mortgagee has a right to pay off any superior mortgage to protect his or her security and can charge the amount so paid to the mortgagor. Likewise, the mortgagee may pay taxes or special assessments that are a lien on the land and recover the sum expended. The mortgagor is under a duty to protect the security; but should he or she fail to do so, the mortgagee has the right to make any reasonable expenditures necessary to protect the security for a debt.

The rights and duties of the parties may change when the mortgaged property is transferred. This situation, involving the transfer of the mortgage itself, is discussed in the next section.

6. Transfer of Mortgaged Property

The mortgagor may sell, will, or give away the mortgaged property, subject, however, to the rights of the mortgagee. A transferee from a mortgagor has no greater rights or duties than the mortgagor. For example, a grantee of the mortgagor's interest may redeem the land by paying off the debt. A grantee of mortgaged property is not personally liable for the mortgage debt unless he or she impliedly or expressly assumes and agrees to pay the mortgage. An assumption of a debt secured by a mortgage must be established by clear and convincing evidence. A purchase "subject to" a mortgage is usually considered not to be a legally enforceable assumption. If the grantee assumes the mortgage, the grantee becomes personally liable for the debt, even when the land is worth less than the mortgage.

To illustrate, assume that Berg purchases real estate worth $88,000, which is subject to a mortgage of $60,000. Berg pays the former owner $28,000 cash. If she assumes and agrees to pay the mortgage, Berg becomes personally liable for the $60,000 debt. If the property is sold at a foreclosure sale, Berg is liable for any deficiency. However, if she merely purchased the property "subject to" the mortgage when she paid the $28,000, Berg would have no liability for any deficiency on foreclosure.

If the grantee of the mortgaged property assumes and agrees to pay the indebtedness, he or she thereby becomes the person primarily liable for the debt. Between the grantee and the mortgagor, by virtue of the grantee's promise to the mortgagor to pay the debt, the grantee is the principal debtor, and the mortgagor is a surety. This assumption by the grantee does not relieve the mortgagor of the obligation to the mortgagee, and the mortgagor continues to be liable unless released from indebtedness by the mortgagee. Such a release must comply with all the requirements for a novation.

7. Alternatives to the Mortgage

Now that some of the basic principles of a mortgage have been discussed, at least three alternatives to the mortgage should be considered.

Deed of trust An instrument by which title to real property is conveyed to a trustee to hold as security for the holder of notes.

DEED OF TRUST.   A document known as a **deed of trust** or *trust deed* may be used as a substitute for a mortgage for the purpose of securing debts. Through this document, title to the real property is conveyed to a third party, who is the trustee, to be held for the benefit of the creditor. Whereas a mortgage involves two parties—the mortgagor (debtor) and the mortgagee (creditor)—the deed of trust involves three parties—the trustor (debtor), the trustee, and the beneficiary (creditor).

The trustee's title does not affect the debtor's use of the land as long as the loan is being repaid. If the debt is fully paid at the time required by the contract, the trustee reconveys the title to the debtor and releases the lien thereon. If there is a default, the trustee sells the property and applies the proceeds to the payment of the secured loan. Under this power of sale, the trustee transfers to the new purchaser all right, title, and interest that the debtor had at the time the deed trust was executed.

Deeds of trust are used instead of mortgages when the note is likely to be negotiated and when numerous notes are secured by the same property. The nature of the deed of trust is that the note secured by it can be freely transferred, separate and apart from the deed of trust. When the debtor pays the note, he or she surrenders it to the trustee under the trust deed, and the latter makes it a matter of record that the obligation has been satisfied.

DEED ABSOLUTE ON ITS FACE.   A second alternative concerns a deed absolute on its face (one that purports to be only a deed with no qualifications) that may be shown by parol evidence to be a mortgage. If such evidence indicates that the intention of the parties was to make the transfer as security for a loan, the deed will be construed as a mortgage. The grantor of the deed must prove by clear, precise, and positive evidence that it was the intention of the parties to use the deed for the purpose of securing a loan. The burden is often difficult to sustain.

8. A Third Alternative: Contract for a Deed

The third alternative to a mortgage occurs when the seller of real estate finances the transaction through a *contract for a deed* rather than with the use of a formal mortgage. It is actually a conditional sale of real estate in which the seller retains title to the land and the buyer makes payments for an extended period of time. In essence, the seller finances the sales transaction. A contract for a deed providing for payments over five, ten, or twenty years is not unusual. The buyer's right to a deed to the property is conditioned on all payments being made. The seller is protected against nonpayment, since he or she retains legal ownership of the property until all payments are made.

Sometimes this type of sales agreement is known as an *installment land contract*. Regardless of its name, this contract contains many of the usual provisions found in the traditional sales contract. In addition, the purchaser has the risk of loss if improvements are destroyed during the period of the contract, unless there is an agreement or state statute to the contrary.

Three other clauses found in most installment land contracts are of particular importance. The *acceleration clause*, like those discussed in section 4, allows the seller to declare the full amount of the contract due and payable in the event the buyer fails to make any of the payments or fails to perform any other of the contract's provisions as agreed.

FORFEITURE CLAUSE.   The *default* or *forfeiture clause* allows the seller, when the buyer is in default, to terminate the contract and to get the deed back from the escrow agent. The net effect of this clause is to allow the seller to keep all payments and improvements made as liquidated damages for breach of contract and to regain possession of the premises even if leased to a third party.

After a buyer has made substantial payments or has a substantial equity in the land, forfeiture of a contract for a deed might be inequitable. The principles discussed in chapter 9 that apply to liquidated damages and forfeitures are also applicable to these contracts because courts of equity abhor forfeitures. When the buyer's equity is substantial and forfeiture would be inequitable, a court, upon proper application, may prohibit the forfeiture. The court orders the property to be sold and the proceeds distributed to the seller, to the extent necessary to pay off the contract. The balance is paid to the buyer. No general rule can be stated to describe cases in which a forfeiture will be allowed or not. As a part of its equitable jurisdiction, the court will examine all the facts. If the buyer has paid only a small amount, forfeiture usually will be permitted. If the buyer has made only a slight default with regard to the amount and time of payment, or the amount of the unpaid purchase price is much less than the value of the property involved, forfeiture will be denied. Forfeiture clauses are easily waived, but usually a buyer must be notified if the clause is to be reinstated after he or she has defaulted without having been required to forfeit.

ESCROW ARRANGEMENT.   One of the problems with a sales contract that might be performed over a significant time period concerns the seller's ability to transfer title at any specific time.

Escrow An agreement under which a seller places the deed with a third person called an escrow agent. The performance of a condition or the happening of an event stated in the agreement permits the escrow holder to make delivery to the buyer.

An **escrow** provision is desirable because it is always possible for the seller to die or otherwise become incapacitated between the time of executing the contract and the date of delivery of possession and final payment. Therefore the deed should be executed concurrently with the contract. The deed is then delivered to a third person, known as the *escrowee* or *escrow agent*, to be delivered to the buyer upon final payment. If the seller dies in the meantime, the transaction can be closed without delay.

The escrow arrangement also prevents a claim of a creditor or the rights of a new spouse from interfering with the rights of the buyers if the creditor's claim arose or the marriage occurred after a contract was signed but before the closing. The escrow in effect removes title from the seller. In essence, the law presumes at the actual closing that the transfer of title relates back to the time the escrow was established. Although an escrow arrangement may be created as a separate contract, it is often included as part of the sales contract, especially when the time period until closing is long.

MORTGAGE FORECLOSURE

9. Introduction

The issue of how the mortgage really protects the mortgagee is based on the assumption that the mortgagor has defaulted or will default prior to the loan being paid fully. If no default occurs, the mortgagee will recover that which it wants—repayment of the loan. However, upon a default, the real property described in the

Foreclosure The forced sale of property, which is used as security, to satisfy the obligation of a defaulting debtor.

mortgage can be used as leverage to encourage the mortgagor to pay what is owed. If payment still is not forthcoming, **foreclosure** becomes the valuable, albeit last, means of collection. In the following sections, you will read about the methods of foreclosure, the priority of claims to the proceeds, the mortgagor's rights to redeem his interest in the real property, and the mortgagee's rights to seek a deficiency.

10. Types of Foreclosures

The statutes of the various states specify the procedure by which mortgages are foreclosed. The common types of foreclosure proceedings are strict foreclosure, foreclosure by judicial action, and foreclosure by exercise of the power of sale.

STRICT FORECLOSURE.   Strict foreclosure gives the mortgagee clear title to the land. A decree of strict foreclosure provides that if the debt is not paid by a certain date, the mortgagor loses the described real estate and the mortgagee takes it free from the rights of junior mortgagees and lienholders. It is used only where it is clear that the mortgaged property is not worth the mortgage indebtedness, the mortgagor is insolvent, and the mortgagee accepts the property in full satisfaction of the indebtedness. The substitution of the property for the debt has a historical basis in the United States in those states that followed the absolute title theory. Since the title theory has very little impact today, strict foreclosure seldom arises by operation of law.

Today the mortgagor may agree to transfer title to the mortgagee in satisfaction of a debt by use of a *deed in lieu of foreclosure*. Obtaining title by this deed is not synonymous with the strict foreclosure process. Unlike foreclosure, a deed in lieu of foreclosure does not extinguish all the junior liens that may be on the property. Therefore, the mortgagee who accepts a deed in lieu of foreclosure may become involved in legal disputes with other creditors. These disputes usually involve the issue of whether the mortgagee took advantage of a defaulting mortgagor and thereby received property of more value than the debt satisfied.

FORECLOSURE BY JUDICIAL ACTION.   The usual method of foreclosing a mortgage is a proceeding in a court of equity. If the mortgagor is in default, the court will authorize the sale of all the land at public auction. Following the sale, the purchaser receives a deed to the land. The funds received from the sale are used to pay court costs, the mortgage indebtedness, and inferior liens in the order of their priority. If any surplus remains, it is paid to the former owner of the property.

Statutes in many states provide a period of time after the sale within which the mortgagor or other persons having an interest are entitled to redeem the property. Where such statutes are in force, the purchaser is not entitled to a deed until after the expiration of the period within which redemption may be made. If the mortgagor remains in possession of the property sold, the purchaser may request that the court appoint a receiver and order the mortgagor to pay rent during the redemption period. The purchaser is entitled to the net rent during this period.

FORECLOSURE BY POWER OF SALE.   Particularly in states following the intermediate theory of mortgages, the mortgage often provides that, upon default by the mortgagor, the mortgagee may sell the real property without resorting to judicial action. This method of foreclosure can be made only in strict conformity with the mortgage's provisions. Such provisions usually require the mortgagee to advertise several times in the local newspaper the time and location of the public auction.

This type of power of sale makes the mortgagee the agent of the mortgagor for the purpose of selling the property. The power of sale creates in the mortgagee's favor an agency coupled with an interest, which means that the mortgagee's appointment as the mortgagor's agent is irrevocable. Therefore the mortgagor's death, insanity, bankruptcy, or withdrawal of consent does not destroy the validity of the power of sale. This type of agency and its termination are discussed in more detail in chapter 25.

As the mortgagor's agent, the mortgagee cannot purchase the property at the sale unless there is an explicit grant of such authority. Whoever the purchaser is at a foreclosure pursuant to a power of sale receives only the title the mortgagor had when he or she made the mortgage. In some states, a power of sale is expressly forbidden from appearing in a mortgage. In these jurisdictions, foreclosures can occur only after a judicial hearing.

11. Priority to Proceeds

A mortgage that holds senior priority on a property and that will be paid first in the event of default and foreclosure is known as a *first mortgage*. The amount of money that can be raised through a first mortgage is often less than the borrower needs to complete a purchase. In such cases *junior mortgages*—that is, second, third, and fourth mortgages, which are subordinate to the first mortgage—are sometimes used. Such mortgages carry more risk than first mortgages and usually are issued for shorter periods of time and at higher interest rates.

The priority given to various mortgages on the same real estate normally is determined by which mortgagee is the first to record the mortgage document with the public records. However, order of recording does not always determine priority. One mortgagee whose mortgage is already on record may agree to subordinate its priority to another mortgagee. For example, a mortgagee that holds a security interest on a vacant land probably would agree to let a second mortgagee who has lent funds for a construction project have priority if the construction of an improvement will increase the land's value by more than the amount of the additional mortgage.

Junior mortgages also are commonly used to help in the financing of the sale of an existing home or income properties. For example, a homeowner may be able to get a higher price for his or her house if the purchaser can assume an existing mortgage at an interest rate lower than those currently charged by banks. The required down payment may be larger than the buyer can pay, however, and the seller may be willing to take a second mortgage for part of the purchase price. Furthermore, second mortgages commonly are used for home-improvement loans. A family that wants to add a room or make extensive repairs to its home can usually get the money to do so at a lower rate through a junior mortgage than by taking out a personal installment loan.

A mortgage that is recorded before other interests may not have priority if its recording is defective. The following case involves a first-in-time mortgage that loses its right to priority because of a defective legal description of the land involved.

CASE

Poncelet v. English
795 P.2d 436 (Mont. 1990)

SHEEHY, J.

Appellant Greg Poncelet appeals from the determination of the District Court . . . granting summary judgment to Colonial Savings and Loan Association as to lien priority. . . .

Appellant raises the following issues:

1. Whether Colonial Savings and Loan and Whitecap International had notice of the appellant's prior recorded mortgage despite the error in its legal description.
2. Whether the District Court erred in precluding priority designation to appellant's prior recorded mortgage.

Respondent English executed a promissory note to appellant Poncelet, secured by a mortgage on real property in Polson, Lake County. The note and mortgage were recorded on June 2, 1986. The mortgage was drafted by Poncelet without benefit of any title insurance commitment. The description read:

> Lot "A" of the Amended Plat of Lots 11 and 12 in Block 6, City of Polson, Lake County, Montana, according to the official plat thereof on file and of record in the office of the County Clerk and Recorder of Lake County, Montana.

This legal description was in error since the appropriate description was:

> Lot "A" of the Amended Plat of Lots 11 and 12 of Block 6 of *Riverside Addition* to the City of Polson, Lake County, Montana, according to the official plat thereof on file and of record in the office of the County Clerk and Recorder of Lake County, Montana. (Emphasis added.)

On November 28, 1986, English executed and delivered a trust indenture to First American Title and Escrow of Polson as the trustee, and Whitecap International, Inc. as the beneficiary, to secure the payment of a loan of $79,926. The trust indenture was recorded on December 4, 1986, and later assigned to Colonial Savings and Loan Association.

Whitecap required the English loan to be secured by a mortgage on English's real property in Polson. Whitecap had First American examine the title to the real property. The record discloses that First American was aware of an existing mortgage on property belonging to English. . . .

Poncelet initiated the foreclosure on the note and mortgage given by English. . . . In his complaint, Poncelet sought the $32,545.05 balance on the note plus interest, a reformation by the court of the legal description to include the omitted language "of Riverside Addition," and all proceeds from the sale of the property, plus any deficiency which might remain.

Colonial Savings and Loan, a named defendant . . . which had been assigned the Whitecap note and trust indenture, raised as a counterclaim the inferior interest of Poncelet's mortgage due to the error in legal description, and sought a judicial declaration that it be declared null and void. . . .

The court determined that both the English-Whitecap-Colonial trust indenture and the English-Poncelet mortgage were valid, but that the latter was invalid, null, and void in relation to the former. The court granted Colonial's motion for summary judgment and denied Poncelet's motion. From this judgment, Poncelet appeals.

Poncelet maintains that Colonial and Whitecap had notice of the Poncelet mortgage through First American Title and Escrow of Polson, arguing that due to First American's actual notice of the Poncelet mortgage, Whitecap and its successor Colonial are thereby charged with notice.

The record discloses no evidence of actual notice of the Poncelet mortgage on the parts of Whitecap or Colonial. Such notice is crucial. Montana case law is clear on this point. The form of recording of conveyance is paramount unless a party has *actual* notice of a prior claim. While this rule may have an undeniably harsh effect where Poncelet is concerned, we cannot minimize the import of full compliance with proper legal descriptions for the purpose of constructive notice from recorded instruments. It was incumbent upon Poncelet to make certain that the recorded mortgage contained an accurate legal description of the property.

. . . In order to give a mortgage priority as against a subsequent mortgagee, the mortgage must describe the land covered by it with sufficient accuracy to enable one examining the record to identify the land. In the present case, . . . the mortgage described land other than the land intended to be mortgaged. The subsequent mortgagee had no duty to inquire further when the mortgage appeared on its face to describe some property but not specific property. . . .

Clearly, neither the title company nor Whitecap or Colonial had a duty to inquire further when the Poncelet mortgage appeared to describe property outside the Riverside Addition. Rather, the risk is and should be upon the first mortgagee to use care in correctly and properly describing the property to protect against subsequent purchasers or mortgagees. The District Court correctly held the Poncelet mortgage to be inferior in priority to the Whitecap-Colonial trust indenture.

■ *Affirmed.*

CASE CONCEPTS REVIEW

1. In this case, English granted a mortgage interest in its property to Poncelet. English also executed a deed of trust in favor of Whitecap International, Inc. as a beneficiary. How does Colonial Savings and Loan become involved in this litigation?
2. What is Colonial's argument as to why Poncelet's preexisting mortgage is inferior to the foreclosure proceeds?
3. Why does the court agree with Colonial's position?

Foreclosure of an inferior mortgage is made subject to all superior liens. In other words, the foreclosure of a second mortgage does not affect a first mortgage. The buyer at the foreclosure sale takes title, and the first mortgage remains a lien on the property. A foreclosure does cut off the enforceability of all inferior liens. For instance, the foreclosure of a first mortgage eliminates the rights of the second and subsequent mortgages.

12. Mortgagor's Rights of Redemption

Equity of redemption
The right a mortgagor has before final foreclosure to redeem or get back his or her property after it has been forfeited for nonpayment of the debt it secured.

EQUITABLE.   A mortgagor who is in default on a note secured by a mortgage can terminate the foreclosure process prior to its completion by exercising a right called the **equity of redemption.** Upon the mortgagor's payment of an amount equal to the debt then owing plus interest and any expenses incurred by the mortgagee, the mortgagor's interest in the property is restored. In other words, the debt and the mortgage will be reinstated if the mortgagor redeems his or her interest by making payment prior to the foreclosure sale.

Any person who acquires the mortgagor's interest while a default situation exists also acquires the right to redeem the property interest equitably prior to foreclosure. Because the mortgagee may have the right to accelerate the amount owed upon default, the entire debt may have to be paid to redeem the interest. Normally the mere payment of the amount in the default is not sufficient if the debt has been accelerated properly.

Statutory right of redemption The right of a mortgagor to redeem his or her interest in the property that has been sold at a foreclosure sale. The time period during which this right can be exercised is determined by statute.

STATUTORY.   In many states (including Alabama, Arizona, California, Colorado, Connecticut, Hawaii, Idaho, Illinois, Indiana, Iowa, Kansas, Kentucky, Maine, Michigan, Minnesota, Missouri, Montana, Nevada, New Jersey, North Dakota, Oregon, South Dakota, Utah, and Washington), the mortgagor is allowed to redeem his or her property even after foreclosure. This right to redeem property after a foreclosure sale is called the **statutory right of redemption.** The statutory redemption period varies from state to state, being as short as six months and as long as two years. In some states, the period is shortened if the mortgagee waives any right to a deficiency. The most common statutory period is one year. In states that have this statutory right of redemption, the purchaser at a foreclosure sale does not obtain full and clear title until the statutory period of redemption has passed.

13. Mortgagee's Right to a Deficiency Judgment

Deficiency judgment
The creditor's right to obtain a court order that the debtor owes the difference between the amount of the debt and the amount that the property was sold for at the foreclosure sale.

A person who executes the note or bond secured by the mortgage is personally liable for the debt. If the property that is the security for the debt does not sell for a sum sufficient to pay the indebtedness, the mortgagor remains liable for the deficiency, and a **deficiency judgment** may be entered for this unpaid balance. This judgment may be collected from the mortgagor's other property or income. In other words, additional assets of the mortgagor may be seized and sold by an officer of the court to satisfy the mortgagee's claim of deficiency.

Property that is sold at a foreclosure sale seldom brings a price that reflects the market value of the property under normal circumstances. During the Great Depression of the 1930s, prices at foreclosure sales fell to extremely low levels, often leaving debtors with large deficiency judgments against them even after they had lost their mortgaged property. As might be expected, a great deal of antideficiency legislation was passed during that period. To recover the full amount of a deficiency, the mortgagee must be able to prove the foreclosure sale was conducted according to commercially reasonable standards. Indeed, the mortgagee should have the foreclosure price approved by the appropriate court prior to or concurrent with the filing of a motion for a deficiency judgment. In the alternative, the mortgagee may waive the right to collect the amount of a deficiency.

To prevent imposing too great a hardship on mortgagors, different schemes have been devised to limit the amount of these parties' liability for deficiencies. Some states, including Nebraska, New Jersey, and Oregon, have simply outlawed all deficiency judgments. Many other states have antideficiency statutes that are applicable only to purchase-money mortgages. When a mortgage is given to secure payment of the balance of the purchase price of real property, the mortgagee is not entitled to a deficiency judgment. In these states, if the mortgage proceeds are not used to finance the purchase of the real property, deficiency judgments are allowed. The elimination of liability for deficiencies rests on several theories: that the mortgagee lent his or her money on the security of the real estate and not the personal credit of the purchaser; that a mortgagee should share with the mortgagor the risk of declining real estate values; and that if the real estate is the limit of the security, sounder loans and fewer inflationary ones will be made.

MECHANIC'S LIENS

14. Introduction

Mechanic's lien A lien for the value of material and labor expended in the construction of buildings and other improvements.

Mechanic's lien laws provide for the filing of liens on real estate that has been improved. An improvement is any addition to the land. While the term *improvement* does not always mean that the land's value has been increased, most improvements usually do increase the real estate's value. The purpose of a mechanic's lien is to protect contractors, suppliers, and laborers in the event of nonpayment of their accounts. This purpose is accomplished by state laws that grant to the unpaid party a lien against real estate. The nature of and protection provided by mechanic's liens are described in the following case.

CASE

Niagara Venture v. Sicoli & Massaro, Inc.

566 N.E.2d 648 (N.Y. 1990)

KAYE, J.

Are private improvement (or mechanics') liens valid against a property owner's interest in the *undeveloped* portion of a tract when, at the time the liens are filed, the owner has conveyed the *developed* portion of the tract to a third party? . . .

This controversy centers on the construction of a water theme park—"The Niagara Splash"—in the City of Niagara Falls. The project was initiated by a series of agreements among Niagara Venture (petitioner), the City of Niagara Falls (the City) and the Niagara Falls Urban Renewal Agency, and was funded in part by public grants and loans from the City. Pursuant to an agreement dated October 15, 1986, the City and the Urban Renewal Agency conveyed a total of 20.6 acres to petitioner. As provided in the agreement, the northerly portion of the parcel was to be the site of the theme park structures, and the southerly portion fronting on Rainbow Boulevard in the City was to become part of a previously approved hotel complex. The agreement further contemplated a later sale-and-leaseback between petitioner and the City.

In March 1987, petitioner entered into agreements with various contractors and suppliers, including respondents, for labor and materials to construct the theme park. It is undisputed that at the time of these arrangements, petitioner owned the unified 20.6 acre tract upon which the improvements were made.

On September 3, 1987, . . . petitioner conveyed the developed 16.1-acre portion of the tract, containing the theme park structures, to the City for a nominal amount, and retained the undeveloped 4.5-acre portion of the tract. The City thus became record owner of the 16.1 acres and leased it back to petitioner. . . .

In November 1987 and May 1988, respondents filed . . . mechanics' liens against the entire 20.6 acres. Petitioner soon after instituted the present proceeding . . . to discharge all liens against the property, on the theory that it was no longer the owner of the improvements.

The trial court . . . discharged the mechanics' liens to the extent they encumbered property owned by the City, and upheld the mechanics' liens on the 4.5 acres. On appeal of so much of the order as upheld the mechanics' liens as against the 4.5 acres, a divided Appellate Division reversed and discharged those liens, reasoning that petitioner retained no improved property that could be the subject of private improvement liens. We now reverse, agreeing . . . that the mechanics' liens were valid as against

the 4.5-acre balance of the tract still owned by petitioner at the time the liens were filed.

A first principle . . . is that a lien filed against a unified parcel operates against the owner's interest in the entire parcel even if improvements are physically made on only a portion of the property. Thus, had the liens been filed before petitioner conveyed away any portion of the parcel, those liens would have encumbered its interest in the entire parcel, including the 4.5 undeveloped acres. . . .

Our analysis centers on the Lien Law. . . . Section 3 provides that: "[A] contractor [or] subcontractor *** who performs labor or furnishes materials for the improvement of real property with the consent or at the request of the owner thereof *** shall have a lien for the principal and interest, of the value, or the agreed price, of such labor *** or materials upon the real property improved or to be improved and upon such improvement, from the time of filing a notice of such lien as prescribed in this chapter."

Petitioner contends that the statutory words "upon the real property improved" limit the scope of a lien to the precise site of an improvement—a reading of the statute that would immediately put it at variance with the long-accepted principle that a lien filed against a unified parcel operates against the entire parcel. . . .

It is the function of section 3 to define both who qualifies as a "mechanic" and the type of lien such a person secures. Section 3 does not purport to fix the extent of the lien; indeed, read literally, section 3 provides for a mechanic's lien to apply to an entire improved parcel, with no protection for a subsequent good-faith purchaser. Lien Law § 4, explicitly captioned "Extent of lien," defines the scope of the lien.

Section 4 provides that a mechanic's lien "shall extend to the owner's right, title or interest in the real property and improvements, existing at the time of filing the notice of lien." Petitioner urges that the words "real property and improvements" must be read in the conjunctive, that a lien can attach only to real property *and* improvements coexisting in the possession of the owner at the moment of filing. Again, petitioner's hypertechnical reading of the statute must be rejected. Section 4 explicitly creates a lien on the owner's "right, title or interest" in the real property, not in any particular segment of it. Petitioner's interest in the improved parcel was subject to the liens prior to the conveyance, and its remaining interest is still subject to those liens. . . .

The result we reach is fully consistent with both the letter of the Lien Law and the policy underlying the statute. The Lien Law may be said to have a dual purpose: first, to provide security for laborers and materialmen and second, to provide notice and a degree of certainty to subsequent purchasers. . . . Reading the statute as petitioner urges would be contrary to the first goal of the Lien Law and would not advance the second. But both statutory purposes are served when the lien is recognized as valid against the interest in the improved parcel remaining in the hands of the owner, and invalid against the portion conveyed to good-faith purchasers before the time of filing.

Applying those principles to the facts before us . . . to say that petitioner, simply by conveying the developed portion of the parcel, can free itself of all encumbrances relating to the improvements is wholly at odds with the intent of the Lien Law. That result is especially appropriate in the present case, where petitioner continues to enjoy significant benefits of ownership of the entire parcel. . . .

Accordingly, the order of the Appellate Division should be . . .

■ *Reversed.*

CASE CONCEPTS REVIEW

1. It is clearly established that the respondent, Sicoli & Massaro, contributed to the construction of The Niagara Splash water park. Why does the petitioner, Niagara Venture, argue that the mechanic's lien should be disallowed?

2. Why does the court reject this argument?

3. What are the two purposes of the Lien Law as discussed by this court?

4. Would the outcome of this case have been different if Niagara Venture did not have the opportunity to repurchase the improved property?

To gain an understanding of how mechanic's liens generally are used to secure payment for one who contributed to an improvement, the following sections discuss potential lienholders, the perfection and enforcement of liens, priority issues, and protection against liens.

15. Potential Lienholders

The persons usually entitled to a lien include those who (1) deliver material, fixtures, apparatus, machinery, or forms to be used in repairing, altering, or constructing a building on the premises; (2) fill, sod, or do landscape work in connection with the premises; (3) act as architect, engineer, or superintendent during the construction of a building; or (4) furnish labor for repairing, altering, or constructing a building.

Persons who contract with the owner, whether they furnish labor or material or agree to construct the building, are known as *contractors.* Thus, virtually any contract between the owner and another that has for its purpose the improvement of real estate gives rise to a lien on the premises in favor of those responsible for the improvement.

In addition to contractors, anyone to whom a distinct part of the contract has been sublet has a right to a lien. These parties are customarily referred to as *subcontractors.* Their rights differ slightly from those of contractors, and some of these differences are considered in later sections.

Those parties who furnish materials to a contractor or subcontractor and those who do the physical work also may have the right to mechanic's liens. These parties are known as *suppliers* and *laborers,* respectively.

The following case demonstrates that the potential lienholder generally must provide some direct contribution to the improvement of real estate. A supplier's supplier usually cannot obtain the protection of a mechanic's lien.

CASE

Logan Equipment v. Profile Construction Co., Inc.

585 A.2d 73 (R.I. 1991)

MURRAY, J.

... From May 1989 to September 1989, Logan leased several pieces of excavation equipment to the Lawrence Group, a subcontractor of appellee Profile Construction Co. (Profile). The equipment was for use on a construction site in the town of Coventry. When the Lawrence Group failed to pay over $33,000 in rental charges, Logan filed a notice of intention to claim a lien in the Land Evidence Records office in Coventry. The filing of this notice caused work on the project to cease, and Profile was therefore unable to obtain financing.

On September 15, 1989, Profile filed a complaint against Logan in Kent County Superior Court, alleging that Logan's notice of intention to claim a lien was damaging Profile's business and slandering its title to the property. Profile sought damages and requested that Logan be directed to remove the notice and enjoined from maintaining it. Subsequently Logan filed . . . a petition to enforce its lien.

After hearing arguments by the parties, the trial justice declared . . . the notice of intention to claim a lien . . . to be null and without effect. Taking judicial notice of Logan's petition to enforce its lien, the trial justice dismissed the petition. . . . The matters have been consolidated on appeal.

The issue before us is whether a lessor of excavation equipment may claim a mechanic's lien under G.L.1956 chapter 28 of title 34. Section 34-28-1 states:

> Whenever any building *** shall be constructed *** such building *** is hereby made liable and shall stand subject to liens for all the work done by any person *** and for the materials used *** which have been furnished by any person.

Profile contends that Logan did not do work or furnish materials in accordance with § 34-28-1 but merely leased equipment to the Lawrence Group and therefore may not claim a mechanic's lien. The mechanics' lien law in Rhode Island is intended to afford a liberal remedy to all who have contributed labor or material towards adding to the value of the property to which the lien attaches. There is little doubt that Logan contributed to the value of the construction project by leasing equipment to the Lawrence Group. The contribution of value, however, is not what the statute requires. Rather the furnishing of labor or materials forms the basis for a mechanic's lien.

Logan argues that the Legislature intended § 34-28-1 to be broadly construed so as to bring bare rentals of equipment within its purview. Although we agree that a broad construction will serve to afford a liberal remedy, we shall not construe the statute so broadly as to extend a remedy to claimant who has not first brought itself clearly within the terms of the statute. Once the claimant has established its right to a lien, then we may proceed to a liberal construction. In order to find in Logan's favor, we must determine that Logan provided "work" or "materials" by leasing equipment.

It is generally held under applicable lien laws that machinery not (a) totally depreciated by use on the property or (b) incorporated into the improvement, or (c) in connection with which labor was also supplied could not be the basis of a valid lien. The excavation equipment in question was not totally depreciated by its use, nor was it incorporated into the improvement. Therefore, it does not satisfy the definition of materials. . . .

Logan's appeal now turns on a contention that he did work. It is well settled that the rental or the value of the use of machinery cannot be the basis for the claim of a mechanic's lien. . . . Some jurisdictions have amended their statutes to include expressly the rental of equipment as the basis for a lien. But when the statute speaks only in terms of work done or materials furnished, as does our own law, jurisdictions generally deny recovery. . . .

Furthermore, Logan supplied no labor with the equipment. Courts that have denied mechanics' liens on bare leases of equipment have stated that they would hold otherwise if the lessors had also supplied someone to operate the equipment.

We therefore hold that under our present statute a bare rental of equipment will not serve as the basis for a mechanic's lien. We accept the proposition that this result may seem inequitable. After all, Logan's contribution of excavation equipment undoubtedly added to the value of the construction. We are not in the habit, however, of supplying new statutory meaning where the Legislature has not clearly spoken. If the Legislature wishes to extend the protection of the mechanic's lien statute to lessors of equipment, then the Legislature may amend the statute as other jurisdictions have done. Until then, this court is constrained by the present incarnation of the mechanics' lien law.

For the foregoing reasons Logan's appeal is denied and dismissed, the order of the Superior Court is

■ *Affirmed.*

1. The relationship of the parties is crucial to the decision of this court. Who is the general contractor? Who is the supplier of excavation equipment to the general contractor? Who provided (by lease) the equipment to this supplier?

2. Why does the court reject the lessor's claim of a mechanic's lien?

16. Perfection and Enforcement

In some states, a contractor has a lien as soon as the contract to repair or to improve the real estate is entered into. In others, the lien attaches as soon as the work is commenced. A supplier of materials usually has a lien as soon as the materials are furnished. A laborer has a lien when the work is performed. The statutes relating to mechanic's liens provide for the method of perfecting these mechanic's liens and for the time period during which they may be perfected. The time period begins when the work is substantially completed.

The usual procedure is that the party seeking to perfect a mechanic's lien files or records a notice of lien in the office of the county in which deeds to real estate are recorded. Some statutes provide for filing in the county of residence of the owner. A copy of the notice is sent to the owner of record and to the party contracting for the repair or improvement. This notice must be filed within the prescribed statutory period. The law then requires a suit to foreclose the lien and specifies that it be commenced within an additionally prescribed period, such as one year. Anything less than strict observance of the filing requirements eliminates the mechanic's lien, but not the debt.

Most mechanic's lien laws provide a relatively long period, such as one year, during which a contractor may file a mechanic's lien and proceed to enforce it against the property interest of the party with whom he or she contracted. This time period is relatively long because the obligation is known to the owner, and he or she is in no way prejudiced if the lien is not promptly filed.

A much shorter time period is set for subcontractors, suppliers, and laborers to file a mechanic's lien. The owner of the premises may not know the source of materials and may not know the names of all persons performing services on the premises. To this extent, the liens of subcontractors, suppliers, and laborers may be secret, and the owner may pay the wrong person. Therefore, the time period in which the statutory procedures must be followed is relatively short, such as sixty to ninety days.

If the property is sold or mortgaged, the existence of any mechanic's lien often would be unknown to the purchaser or mortgagee. For this reason the statutes on mechanic's liens usually specify the same short period of time for the perfection of the mechanic's lien—whether by a contractor, subcontractor, supplier, or laborer—if it is to be effective against good-faith purchasers of the property or subsequent mortgagees. Under these statutory provisions, a mechanic's lien that could be enforced against the property interest of the original contracting owner cannot be enforced against the property interest of the new owner or mortgagee after the expiration of the prescribed statutory period. Thus, during the relatively short statutory period, a mechanic's lien is good against innocent third parties even though it has not been properly perfected. Consequently, a purchaser of real estate should always ascertain if any repairs or improvements have been made to the premises within the time period for filing mechanic's liens. If it is determined that repairs or improvements have been made, the procedures outlined in the next section should be followed.

If a contractor, subcontractor, supplier of material, or laborer fails to file notice of lien within the appropriate prescribed time period or fails to commence suit within the additional period, the lien is lost.

Since a person entitled to a mechanic's lien has a prescribed period within which to file the lien, the date on which this time period starts to run is frequently quite important. Most statutes provide that in the case of a supplier, the time period starts to run from the date the materials are delivered; and in the case of a contractor or subcontractor performing services, the time for filing starts to run from the completion of the work. This latter concept requires further clarification, however.

Should a contractor or subcontractor be able to postpone the time for filing by performing additional services at a later date? Assume that a contractor has allowed the time for filing his lien to elapse. Should the time period start all over if he makes a minor repair, such as adjusting a doorknob or touching up a paint job? Common sense would say no, and most statutes provide that a contractor or subcontractor cannot extend the statutory period of time by performing minor, trifling repairs after the work has been substantially completed. In other words, trivial work done or materials furnished after the contract has been substantially completed will not extend the time in which a lien claim can be filed.

17. Priorities

Two basic situations create issues of priorities concerning mechanic's liens. The first concerns priority among similar mechanic's liens. The second situation involves the priority of a mechanic's lienholder compared with the rights of a mortgagee to the proceeds from the forced sale of the real estate.

AMONG MECHANIC'S LIENHOLDERS.   If there are several mechanic's liens filed as the result of the same improvement project, the liens are entitled to priority on the basis of when the lienholder began work on the project. If several liens are considered equal in priority and there are insufficient funds to satisfy all these claims, the lienholders must share the proceeds on a pro rata basis. Each lienholder is entitled to that portion of the proceeds that his or her work represented of the entire improvement.

BETWEEN MECHANIC'S LIENHOLDER AND MORTGAGEE.   When determining the priority of a mechanic's lien and a mortgage on the same property, the date of attachment is crucial. Nearly all states provide that a mortgage attaches when it is properly recorded. If the state where the land is located is one of the few providing that a mechanic's lien attaches when a notice of lien is filed, then priority is given to the creditor who is first to file.

The majority of states' laws on mechanic's liens say that these liens attach when work first begins or when supplies are first delivered. In these states a mortgage may be filed before a notice of lien is filed, and yet the lien has priority. A mortgagee must therefore make sure there are no potential mechanic's liens or obtain an agreement from contractors, laborers, and suppliers that their liens are subordinated to the mortgage. Without these actions, a mortgagee may lose all or at least part of the foreclosure proceeds to a mechanic's lienholder.

Still other states give priority to mechanic's liens over a previously recorded mortgage because the lienholder has increased the value of the real property. This added value should be evident in the greater proceeds obtained at the foreclosure sale. After the lienholder is paid, the mortgagee still has the remaining proceeds, which should be the same as if no improvement had been made. This priority given to the mechanic's lien may not apply if the items added to the real estate become inseparable from the entire improvement.

Some states by statute give priority to a construction mortgage over mechanic's liens. This preference is given because all the parties intend that the contractors and suppliers will be paid out of the proceeds of the construction loan. This priority is usually limited to the amounts that the construction mortgagee is obligated to advance. If the funds do not have to be advanced by the mortgagee, an unpaid perfected mechanic's lien will have priority over the prior mortgage.

18. Protection against Liens

Mechanic's lien statutes usually provide that an owner is not liable for more than the contract price if he or she follows the procedures outlined in the law. These usually require that the owner, prior to payment, obtain from the contractor a sworn statement setting forth all the creditors and the amounts due, or to become due, to each of them. It is then the duty of the owner to retain sufficient funds at all times to pay the amounts indicated by the sworn statements. In addition, if any liens have been filed by the subcontractors, it is the owner's duty to retain sufficient money to pay them. The owner is at liberty to pay any balance to the contractor.

An owner has a right to rely on the truthfulness of the sworn statement of the contractor. If the contractor misstates the facts and obtains a sum greater than that to which he or she is entitled, the loss falls on the subcontractors who dealt with the contractor rather than on the owner. Under such circumstances, the subcontractors may look only to the contractor for payment. Payments made by the owner, without first obtaining a sworn statement, may not be used to defeat the claims of subcontractors, suppliers, and laborers. Before making any payment, the owner has the duty to require the sworn statement and to withhold the amount necessary to pay the claims indicated.

The owner may also protect himself or herself by obtaining waivers of the contractor's lien and of the liens of subcontractors, suppliers, and laborers. A *waiver* is the voluntary relinquishment of the right to a lien before a notice of lien is filed. In a few states, a waiver of the lien by the contractor is also a waiver of the lien of the subcontractors, as they derive their rights through those of the contractor. However, in most states, lien waivers are effective only against those who agree not to claim a mechanic's lien and who execute a waiver.

Even after a notice of lien is filed, lienholders may extinguish their right to enforce the lien. This postfiling process is known as a *release* of the lien. Very often, the concept of waivers and that of releases is confused. A waiver occurs before a notice of lien is filed, whereas a release is used after there is a public filing. A mechanic's lien commonly is released when the landowner pays the lienholder after a notice of lien has been filed.

Chapter Summary

Terminology	1. A *mortgage* is the document wherein a borrower grants to a lender a security interest in the borrower's real estate.
	2. A *mortgagor* is the borrower who grants the security interest in real estate to the lender.
	3. A *mortgagee* is the lender who receives a security interest in real estate.
Theories of Mortgages	1. Originally, a mortgage conveyed legal title or ownership to the mortgagee.
	2. Today, the law of a state usually views a mortgage as creating only a lien on the real estate or, in the alternative, a mortgagee has title that is created as a lien for security purposes.
	3. These modern theories are known as the lien (or equity) theory and the intermediate theory, respectively.
Documents Involved	1. The borrower in a mortgage transaction usually signs a promissory note, which is evidence of the borrower's personal obligation to repay.
	2. The borrower also signs a mortgage, which is the document that grants the lender a security interest in described real estate.
Mortgage Clauses	1. Mortgages often include acceleration clauses that allow the mortgagee to make the entire debt due and payable upon the occurrence of certain events. These clauses may be classified as due on default, due on encumbrance, and due on sale.
	2. A prepayment penalty clause is often included in a mortgage. It allows the mortgagee to collect a penalty if the debt is paid off early without permission.
	3. A dragnet clause allows one mortgage to serve as security for any future loan the mortgagee grants to the mortgagor.
Rights and Duties of the Parties	1. Payment of the mortgage debt terminates the mortgage.
	2. Upon its termination, the mortgage must be marked satisfied in the public records.
	3. Generally, the mortgagor retains possession of the real estate during the mortgage's term.
	4. However, the mortgagor cannot use the real estate in a way that devalues it.
	5. The mortgagee has the right to protect the value of the real estate by paying off other claimants and charging the amount paid to the mortgagor.
Transfer of Mortgaged Property	1. When real estate and the mortgage describing such real estate are transferred, the question arises about whether the original mortgagor or the transferee or both are liable.
	2. The transferee who takes the property "subject to" the mortgage does not become personally liable for any deficiency should there be a foreclosure sale.
	3. The transferee who takes the property and who "assumes" the mortgage does become personally liable for any deficiency.
	4. In either of the two aforementioned situations, the original mortgagor remains personally liable for the debt unless there has been a novation.
Alternatives to the Mortgage	1. In many states, a three-party document, known as a deed of trust, is often used instead of a mortgage.
	2. A deed, which is absolute on its face, may be treated as a mortgage if the parties' intent was for the deed to serve as security and not as an outright conveyance.
Contract for a Deed	1. This is a conditional sales contract of real estate.
	2. The seller finances the transaction and retains title as security.
	3. Payments are made over a substantial time period.
	4. An escrow arrangement is essential in such contracts.

Types of Foreclosures	1. Strict foreclosure occurs when a mortgagee simply keeps title to the real estate rather than conducting a foreclosure sale. This process was most closely associated with the title theory. Due to the rejection of the title theory, strict foreclosure seldom is allowed today.
	2. Foreclosure by judicial action requires court approval to conduct a sale of the mortgaged real estate. In states that follow a lien theory of mortgages, this type of foreclosure is most common.
	3. Foreclosure by the power of sale usually is allowed in states that have adopted an intermediate theory of mortgages if the mortgage contains a power-of-sale clause.
Priority to Proceeds	1. Mortgagees have priority to the proceeds of a sale in the same order in which their mortgages were recorded.
	2. An exception to this order occurs if a mortgagee with a superior priority subordinates its claim to an inferior mortgagee.
	3. Upon the foreclosure of a superior mortgage, all inferior mortgages are extinguished. However, the buyer at a foreclosure sale of an inferior mortgage takes subject to all superior mortgages.
Mortgagor's Rights of Redemption	1. A mortgagor in default has the right to redeem or reinstate his or her interest in the real estate by paying the debt plus necessary expenses.
	2. All mortgagors may exercise the equitable right of redemption prior to the foreclosure sale.
	3. Even after the foreclosure sale, some states allow the mortgagor to exercise a statutory right of redemption. This statutory right is more likely to exist in states recognizing the lien theory of mortgages.
Mortgagee's Right to a Deficiency Judgment	1. After a foreclosure sale that has not produced proceeds equal to the debt, the mortgagee may sue the mortgagor for the deficiency.
	2. To recover a deficiency judgment, the mortgagee must prove that the foreclosure sale was commercially reasonable.
	3. A few states have abolished this right to collect a deficiency judgment, particularly when a purchase-money mortgage is involved.

MECHANIC'S LIENS

Introduction	1. A mechanic's lien gives security to any party who has contributed to an improvement of real estate.
	2. An improvement does not necessarily increase the value of real estate.
Potential Lienholders	1. Those parties who contract directly or indirectly with an owner for an improvement are potential lienholders. Typically, these parties include general contractors and subcontractors.
	2. Suppliers of materials and laborers who provide work also are potential lienholders.
Perfection and Enforcement	1. Since mechanic's liens are created by state law, each state's requirements for a valid lien vary to some degree.
	2. In general, a lienholder must file a notice of a lien within a statutory time period after work is completed.
	3. In addition to the notice of lien, a lawsuit must be filed within the time provided.
	4. As a result of the lawsuit, a court may order that the improved real estate be sold to satisfy the lienholder's claim for payment.
Priorities	1. Among mechanic's lienholders, priority usually is determined by the beginning of that lienholder's work or delivery of materials.

2. If lienholders are equal in priority, they share the proceeds on a pro rata basis. Each should receive the same percentage of the proceeds that his or her work contributed to the whole improvement.

3. The priority between mechanic's liens and mortgages depends on the state's law and the time each claim attached to the real estate.

Protection against Liens

1. A real estate owner who is improving his or her land should obtain a sworn statement from the contractor prior to making any payment. This statement should explain who are potential lienholders. The owner can then take steps to satisfy these parties' claims.

2. An owner generally can prevent claims by making payment to the lienholders or by having these lienholders waive or release their rights to a mechanic's lien.

REVIEW QUESTIONS AND PROBLEMS

1. Match each term in column A with the appropriate statement in column B.

A	B
(1) Mortgagee	(a) A clause that allows one mortgage to secure future advances
(2) Mortgagor	(b) Allows the mortgagor to reinstate his or her interest after a foreclosure sale has occurred
(3) Lien theory	(c) A clause found in a mortgage that permits the mortgagee to conduct a foreclosure sale without court approval
(4) Due on default	(d) The party who lends money and is secured by an interest in real estate
(5) Dragnet	(e) The voluntary relinquishment of the right to a mechanic's lien prior to a notice of lien being filed
(6) Strict foreclosure	(f) A view of mortgages that does not involve the conveyance of title
(7) Power of sale	(g) A seldom-used process whereby the mortgagee gets to keep mortgaged property regardless of the property's value and the amount of the debt
(8) Equitable right of redemption	(h) The voluntary relinquishment of a mechanic's lien after the notice of lien has been filed
(9) Statutory right of redemption	(i) The filing of this is a required step in the perfection and enforcement of a mechanic's lien
(10) Notice of a lien	(j) A type of acceleration clause often included in a mortgage
(11) Waiver	(k) A borrower of money who grants the creditors a security interest in real estate
(12) Release	(l) Allows the mortgagor to reinstate his or her interest after default but before a foreclosure sale occurs

2. Mort owned real estate that he had mortgaged. Mort sold this property to Pat, who agreed to take it "subject to" the mortgage. Pat ascertained the balance of the debt Mort owed at the date of purchase of the land. When Pat failed to make payments, the mortgage was foreclosed. What does the term *taking subject to a mortgage* mean? Explain. Is Mort liable for the balance due? Why or why not?

3. Johnson was heavily in debt. He deeded his land to a state bank and leased it back for one year with an option to repurchase it. For the deed he received cash to apply to his debts in an amount equal to approximately one-half the value of the land. Johnson sued the state bank to have the deed declared to be a mortgage. Is he likely to succeed? Why or why not?

4. Richard Hammer borrowed $7,000 from the Danvers Savings Bank and executed a promissory note in favor of the bank. The note was secured by land in Boxford, Massachusetts. After the defendant defaulted, the bank foreclosed on his property. No potential buyers attended the foreclosure sale except bank representatives. They purchased the defendant's real estate for $100, and later resold it for $2,025. The bank sought a $10,040.02 deficiency judgment against Hammer, consisting of the sum of the $7,000 principal due under the note, $1,523.55 in accrued interest, $1,237.88 in taxes, $709.50 for legal notices of the foreclosure sale, $150 for an auctioneer, and $1,444.09 for legal fees and expenses, less a credit of $2,025, the resale price. Hammer argued that the price paid for his land was so inadequate that the sale should be invalidated. Is the bank entitled to this deficiency judgment? Why?

5. Garland paid $72,000 down and signed a purchase-money mortgage note for the $287,000 balance due on realty. When Garland defaulted, over $300,000 in principal and interest was still owing. At a public auction, Hill, the mortgagee, bid $25,000 for the property and agreed to forgive the balance of principal and interest due. Garland filed suit to enjoin the sale on the equitable ground that the price was "shockingly inadequate." May an inadequate purchase price be made adequate by the mortgagee's waiver of his right to claim a deficiency against the mortgagor? Explain.

6. Bay Side, Inc., borrowed money from the MFS Service Corporation and secured the loan by signing a mortgage that contained a due-on-default acceleration clause. When Bay Side failed to make a loan payment, MFS declared the entire amount due and payable. MFS also began foreclosure proceedings to sell the real estate described in the mortgage. Bay Side sought to terminate the foreclosure proceedings by paying MFS the amount of the original default plus expenses. When MFS refused to withdraw the foreclosure action, Bay Side appealed. After a mortgage-secured debt has been accelerated due to the debtor's default, can the equity of redemption be exercised by a partial payment? Why?

7. Johnson, a surveyor, was employed by Barnhill to survey, plat, and lay out 194 acres of land. A dispute arose as to payment, and Johnson filed a mechanic's lien and instituted this action to foreclose it. Barnhill moved to dismiss the action on the ground that the work done by Johnson did not entitle him to a mechanic's lien since the real estate had not been improved. Is the surveyor entitled to a mechanic's lien? Why or why not?

8. At the time Bill bought a new home, his attorney examined the recorded documents affecting interests in the property. No mechanic's liens were revealed. A short time after Bill had bought this home, Ralph, a roofer, demanded payment for a roof installed prior to Bill's purchase. Is it possible that Ralph has any rights against Bill's property? Why?

9. On November 10, 1992, an architect signed a certificate acknowledging the substantial completion of the construction of a building. Thereafter, the contractor continued to do finishing work until January 2, 1993. A mechanic's lien was filed March 11, 1993. The state law required that mechanic's liens be filed within ninety days after the completion of any building. Does the contractor have a valid lien? Why or why not?

10. The Graffs, plaintiffs, brought this action to invalidate a mechanic's lien claimed against their property by Boise Cascade on the grounds that the notice of lien was invalid because it did not set forth the name of the person who requested the materials and because it was not properly verified. The defendant, Boise Cascade Corporation, argued that the omissions were inconsequential and that the notice of the lien complied with the statutory requirements. Are the statutory requirements that the notice of lien contain the name of the person to whom the material was furnished and a proper verifi-

cation of the claim mandatory conditions precedent to the creation and existence of a lien? Explain.

11. William A. Mead was a trustee for a trust that owned adjacent parcels of real property in Maricopa County. Smith Pipe & Steel Company sold and furnished construction materials to Flood Plumbing Company, a licensed plumbing subcontractor, for use in the construction of structures and improvements on the *south* parcel of the adjacent lots. Flood completed the work but subsequently went bankrupt and failed to pay Smith for the materials. Smith then recorded a Notice and Claim of Lien. The Notice and Claim of Lien, however, gave the legal description of the *north* parcel instead of the south parcel on which the improvements were made. After Smith filed a complaint to foreclose the lien, Mead moved for summary judgment, arguing that the erroneous description rendered the lien invalid. May a lien claimant perfect its lien when the Notice and Claim of Lien contain erroneous legal descriptions of the land involved? Explain.

12. Carver Lumber filed a suit to foreclose a mechanic's lien. Commercial Bank, which held a purchase-money mortgage on the same property, claimed priority over Carver Lumber's lien. Commercial Bank's mortgage was recorded after Carver Lumber began work on the property. Is the bank correct? What assumptions have you made in reaching your answer? Explain.

13. Swann contracted with Diver Company for the construction of a house on his property. Upon completion, Swann made a substantial payment to Diver and instructed him to pay Materials, Inc., for building material supplied for the house. Diver delivered a $3,400 check and a $3,400 promissory note to Materials in exchange for its waiver of lien. But the check and the note proved to be worthless, and Materials informed Swann that the waiver was rescinded. Is Materials entitled to a mechanic's lien? Why or why not?

ADDITIONAL LAWS ASSISTING CREDITORS

CHAPTER PREVIEW

*T*he preceding chapter discusses how creditors can obtain an interest in a debtor's real property as a method of feeling secure that the amount owed can be collected. Chapters 37 and 38 discuss the taking of a security interest in personal property as another way a creditor can feel secure when extending credit.

This chapter examines two more legal transactions designed to assist creditors in their collection of debts: artisan's liens and suretyship. The first transaction covers one party performing work or adding value to another party's personal property. This lien against the personal property is analogous to mechanic's liens against real property.

The second area involves the use of a third party's commitment to a creditor that the debtor will perform as promised or the third party becomes liable. This chapter continues the discussion of how creditors can obtain security or a source, in addition to the debtor, from which the debt can be collected.

As a commercial loan officer for the First Bank, you are responsible for the bank's relationship with its business debtors. The Hi-Fashion Clothing Store, Inc. is one of your best customers, and it currently owes the bank $1.5 million. The repayment of this loan is guaranteed by Paul Dress, the founder and former chairman of Hi-Fashion. Mr. Dress is retired and is no longer actively involved in the day-to-day operations of Hi-Fashion.

The current chief financial officer of Hi-Fashion has asked you to arrange extending the term of this loan from five to eight years. This extension would allow Hi-Fashion to reduce its current monthly payment. The bank is inclined to approve this request, upon your recommendation.

What must you do to ensure that Mr. Dress continues to be liable?

ARTISAN'S LIENS

Artisan's lien The claim against an item of personal property that arises when one has expended labor on, or added to, the property. This person is entitled to possession of the property as security until paid for the value of labor or material.

An **artisan's lien** is a security interest in personal property in favor of one who has performed services on the personal property. Such services often take the form of a repair. From a very early date, the common law permitted one who expended labor or materials on the personal property of another to retain possession of the property as security for compensation. This right to possession creates a lien against the owner's personal property when the task is completed. By court decisions, such a lien typically has been interpreted to exist in favor of public warehousepeople and common carriers of goods entrusted to their care. Today, in almost every state, the artisan's lien has been extended by statute to cover all cases of storage or repair. However, the artisan's lien generally is considered to be personal to the party who performs the services. The lien is not assignable.

Because the artisan's lien is perfected by possession, voluntary surrender of the property generally terminates the lien. If the artisan parts with possession, reacquisition of the goods involved will not re-create the lien. As exceptions to the general rule that the lienholder must maintain possession to have perfection of the artisan's lien, two points are emphasized. First, a lienholder may temporarily surrender possession, with an agreement that the lien will continue. However, if rights of a third party arise while the lienholder is not in possession of the property, the lien is inferior to the third party's rights. Also, surrender of possession of part of the goods will not affect the lien on the remaining goods.

Second, the release of possession will not terminate the lien if a notice of lien is recorded in accordance with state lien and recording statutes prior to surrender of possession of the goods. Notice of an artisan's lien in the public records serves as an adequate substitute for possession. The concept of a filing in the public records has been adopted by some states as an essential step in perfecting an artisan's lien.

In the following case, this filing requirement narrows the protection available to the lienholder.

CASE

Cool v. Sahling Trucks, Inc.
466 N.W.2d 796 (Neb. 1991)

WHITE, J.

For the purposes of this opinion, the following facts are relevant: . . . Appellant Cool, on April 8, 1987, filed an artisan's lien . . . alleging that parts and labor to the value of $22,065.34 were furnished for the Kenworth tractor for the period beginning August 23, 1985, and ending when the last item was furnished, February 17, 1987, less than 60 days from the filing. . . .

The trial court found that the appellant was entitled to a lien for only the value of materials and parts furnished in the immediate past 60 days prior to the filing in the amount of $64.53, for which sum and costs appellant was awarded judgment.

It is obvious that the major repairs necessitated by an accident . . . had been completed a considerable time before the 60-day period prior to the filing of the lien. The truck was returned for service, and from time to time thereafter, materials and labor were furnished. We note, for example, the entry of November 1, 1986, "2 front tires 400.00"; the next entry, of January 13, 1987, "repaint hood 60.00"; and three entries of February 17, 1987, totaling the amount of the court's award. There was no evidence that the services were performed as part of one continuous contract, but, rather, they appear to have been a periodic as-needed series of repair orders, unconnected one to the other.

Section 52-202 provides:

Any person who makes, alters, repairs or in any way enhances the value of any vehicle, automobile, machinery, farm implement or tool, or shoes a horse or horses, or mule or mules at the request of or with the consent of the owner or owners thereof shall have a lien upon such vehicle, automobile, machinery, farm implement or tool, horse or horses, mule or mules, in cases where he has parted with the possession thereof, for his reasonable or agreed charges, for work done or material furnished; *Provided*, the person making such repairs or furnishing such material or performing such work shall file in the office of the clerk of the county in which such work was done, or material furnished, or in which such property is kept, within sixty days after performing such work or furnishing such material, a verified statement. . . .

We affirm, though we reject the trial court's narrow construction of § 52-202. It seems to us that . . . the artisan's lien attaches if the necessary documents are filed within 60 days of the furnishing of an item of labor or material which is part of a single contract or undertaking. This is the construction our court has uniformly placed on materialmen's and laborers' contracts pursuant to §§ 52-101 et seq. In this case it is clear that the labor and/or materials furnished by Cool were not part of a single contract, but were furnished separately as the vehicle needed servicing.

The judgment is

■ *Affirmed.*

CASE CONCEPTS REVIEW

1. During what time period did Cool perform work on the Kenworth tractor?
2. Cool was required to file a statement of his lien within sixty days of furnishing material or performing service. Did Cool do so?
3. How many contracts for repairs were made by Cool and Sahling?

Under common law, the lienholder had to retain the property until a judgment was obtained; then he or she levied execution on the property. Modern statutes permit the lienholder to have the property sold to satisfy the claim. These statutes usually require notice to the owner prior to the sale. With respect to the proceeds of a forced sale, the artisan generally has a superior claim when compared with a preexisting Article 9 secured party. The lienholder has priority because the law presumes that the work of improvement done on the personal property has increased that property's value at least in an amount equal to the lienholder's claim. Therefore, the secured creditor has not been damaged by having inferior status. Any surplus proceeds left after all claims against the property are satisfied are paid to the owner of the property.

1. Introduction

Suretyship The relationship created between the debtor, creditor, and third party when that third party promises the creditor that the debtor will perform the promises made or, in the alternative, the third party will perform.

Suretyship provides security for a creditor without involving an interest in property. In suretyship, the security for the creditor is provided by a third person's promise to be responsible for the debtor's obligation.

Suretyship may have commenced with the beginning of civilization. Although there is evidence of surety contracts as far back as 2750 B.C., and in the Code of Hammurabi, about 2250 B.C., the earliest written contract of suretyship that has been found dates to 670 B.C. By A.D. 150, the Romans had developed a highly technical law of suretyship. The concept of a corporate surety did not evolve until the Industrial Revolution. Today, suretyship plays a major role in many business transactions, especially construction contracts. Suretyship also is involved in a substantial percentage of loan transactions.

2. Terminology

A *principal,* or *principal debtor,* or *obligor* is the party who borrows money or assumes direct responsibility to perform a contractual obligation. The party entitled to receive payment or performance is called the *creditor* or *obligee.* Any party who promises the creditor to be liable for a principal's payment of performance is either a *surety* or *guarantor.* The word *party* includes individuals as well as all types of business organizations.

What is the difference between a surety and a guarantor? Historically, the distinction has involved the difference between a third party being primarily and secondarily liable. Also involved is the distinction between assuring a creditor that the principal will perform a noncredit contractual promise and that the principal will repay money borrowed.

SURETY.   A surety's promise to be liable for a principal's obligation is created as a part of and dependent on the principal's agreement to perform. In a narrow sense, a surety is considered primarily liable for the principal's performance. In other words, a creditor could demand performance from the surety rather than the principal. From this concept came the general rule that no notice of the principal's default had to be given for the creditor to hold the surety liable. This notice requirement and its ramifications are discussed in section 7.

Since a surety's promise is part of the creditor-debtor relationship, a creditor may sue the surety simultaneously when action is taken against the principal. Finally, a surety's obligation can be summarized as being a promise to do what the principal agreed to do.

GUARANTOR.   On the other hand, a guarantor's promise to be liable for a principal's obligation is created separate from and independent of the principal's agreement to perform. In other words, a guarantor's promise is only related to, but not an essential part of, the principal's obligation. A guarantor will become liable to the creditor only when the principal has defaulted. Therefore, the principal is primarily liable and the guarantor is secondarily liable. Historically, this concept has required the creditor to give the guarantor notice of the debtor's default before action could be commenced against the guarantor. Furthermore, a creditor, if necessary, must bring two legal actions—first against the principal and, second and separately, against the guarantor. To summarize—a guarantor promises that the principal will do what the principal promised to do.

GUARANTY AGREEMENTS.   There are two types of guaranty agreements: general and special. A *general guarantor* is a party whose promise is not limited to a single transaction or to a single creditor. For example, a principal may have an open line of credit and may borrow from the creditor many times within the overall credit limitation. A guarantor who promises to be liable upon the principal's default regardless of the number of transactions within the credit line is called a general guarantor. The general guarantor has significant potential liability.

A *special guarantor* is a party who limits the promise made to a single transaction or to a single creditor or both. A special guarantor's obligation would not protect a creditor to the full extent of an open line of credit if the initial loan transaction was for a lesser amount. In addition, a creditor cannot assign the special guarantor's promise to a new creditor, as the following case discusses. This case also provides an example of the language of a guaranty agreement.

CASE

Flying J, Inc. v. Booth
773 P.2d 144 (Wyo. 1989)

Elvin and Jacqueline Booth owned one-half of the shares of Booth Livestock, Inc. (BL). The other half of BL's stock was owned by Paul and Joan Gillett. BL ran a truck stop under the name Husky Super Stop. Husky Oil Company (Husky) sold diesel fuel and other products necessary for the operation of the truck stop. BL sought to purchase these products from Husky on credit. Before beginning to extend credit to BL in 1974, Husky required the Booths to sign a guaranty, which stated in part:

> THE UNDERSIGNED, jointly and severally (herein called Guarantor . . .), do hereby guarantee and agree to pay any and all indebtedness of any nature whatsoever incurred by BOOTH LIVE-STOCK, INC. (herein called Debtor) a corporation . . . unto HUSKY OIL COMPANY OF DELA-WARE (herein called Husky).

> The guaranty herein is given in consideration of future extension of credit to Debtor by Husky. This guaranty covers any indebtedness incurred by Debtor prior to or subsequent to the date hereof. Guarantor covenants and agrees that this guaranty is absolute, unconditional, and unlimited as to such indebtedness and any charges or interest thereon, and any costs of collection, including attorneys' fees and court costs. . . .

For nearly ten years, Husky supplied merchandise to BL. In 1983, the Booths sold their interest in BL to the Gilletts. Husky continued to sell items to BL on credit. In 1984, Husky sold its business to a subsidiary of Flying J, Inc., which continued to do business with BL. Thereafter, BL defaulted on its obligation. Flying J, Inc. sued the Booths to recover under the guaranty agreement signed in 1974. The Gilletts were not sued because Paul had died and Joan had filed bankruptcy.

The Booths, appellees, moved for a summary judgment on the grounds that they had signed a special guaranty that could not be assigned by Husky to Flying J, Inc. The trial court granted this motion, and Flying J, Inc. appealed.

URBIGKIT, J.

. . . Appellant launches a two-pronged attack with initial contention that summary judgment was improperly granted against it because the district court erred in holding this instrument to be an unassignable special guaranty. Alternatively, appellant then argues that even if we agree that this is a special guaranty, we should follow the states that allow a modification of the common law to permit assignment and enforcement of any special guaranty where there has been no material change in the obligation to the guarantor. We disagree with appellant on both bases.

A general guaranty is drawn to address all potential creditors in general such as "to whom it may concern," and effectively promises all those creditors that the principal's obligations will be performed. By limitation, a special guaranty is drawn with reference to only one creditor such as a particular person, firm, or corporation. The appellees' guaranty in the instant case specifically refers to only one creditor, Husky. Therefore, the district court did not err in finding a special guaranty intent by the parties.

Our second inquiry is assignability. At common law, a general guaranty is assignable or transferable, but a special guaranty is not. . . . The rationale supporting the common law rule is that when a written instrument names only a specific creditor, there is no demonstration of an intent to make the instrument enforceable by someone not named within it. . . .

Essentially, appellant argues that appellees' guaranty is ambiguous with respect to assignability because the instrument purports to be "absolute, unconditional, and unlimited," and contains no provision which expressly forbids assignments. . . .

There is nothing ambiguous about the guaranty executed by appellees. The guaranty was drafted and given "in consideration of future extension of credit to Debtor by Husky," the sole and specific obligee. That language expressly and clearly indicates that the relationship and intent of these parties was rooted in appellees' reliance on Husky's ability and willingness to perform its contract with BL. A guaranty expressly given in consideration of the extension of future credit by a specific individual is generally held to be nontransferable. This is expressly the situation here where future sales were anticipated. Even where obligee sells his business and his successors continue to extend credit, the guarantor is liable only for debts resulting which accrued prior to the transfer of the original obligee's assets but not after. Unquestionably, in the instant case, all the disputed debts occurred after appellees transferred BL wholly to the Gilletts and discontinued their participation. . . .

Appellant asks us to join those courts which permit the assignment of special guaranties in the absence of actual prejudice to the guarantor. While some courts may have modified the common law approach, we decline to follow them. . . . Appellant provides no compelling reason for us to abandon a position that has existed unchanged in nearly eighty-seven years in Wyoming jurisprudence. Consequently, we determine that lacking any genuine issue of material fact or error of law, the district court did not err in granting summary judgment.

■ *Affirmed.*

CASE CONCEPTS REVIEW

1. Which party is the original debtor? Which is the original creditor? Who are the original guarantors?
2. How does the Flying J, Inc. become involved in this litigation?
3. What are the two arguments made by Flying J, Inc., as to why it should be allowed to enforce the guaranty agreement?
4. Why does the court reject both these arguments?

Guaranty agreements also are classified as absolute or conditional. Under an *absolute guaranty,* a creditor can go directly to the guarantor to collect. In a *conditional guaranty,* the creditor must have made reasonable but unsuccessful attempts to collect from the principal before the guarantor can be held liable.

LEGAL SIGNIFICANCE BETWEEN SURETY AND GUARANTOR. Fortunately, today the distinction between a surety and a guaranty has very little significance. This result is due in large part to the *Restatement of Security,* a legal treatise on the subject of suretyship. Although the *Restatement* is not the law, its influence on the law is quite substantial. Those scholars who prepared the *Restatement of Security* considered *surety* to be interchangeable with *guarantor.* Therefore, unless stated otherwise, the general principles presented next are applicable to sureties as well as guarantors. Keep in mind that the statute of frauds applies only to guaranty contracts involving secondary promises and not to contracts involving a primary promise.

3. Suretyship versus Indemnity

A contract of suretyship should be distinguished from a contract of *indemnity.* Both contracts ultimately provide protection that what has been promised will be performed. However, the approach to accomplishing this purpose is vitally different. A surety makes a promise to a person (creditor) who is *to receive* the performance of an act or payment of a debt by another (principal). In a contract of indemnity, the assurance of performance is made to the party (principal) who is promising *to do* an act or *to pay* a debt. Whereas suretyship provides security to creditors, indemnity provides security to principal debtors. In other words, indemnity is a promise to the debtor, or obligor, to hold that debtor harmless from any loss incurred as a result of nonpayment of a debt or nonperformance of a promise. Most insurance contracts are examples of indemnification agreements between the insurer and the insured.

The following case provides a discussion of the surety-indemnity distinction while also illustrating the similarities.

CASE

United States Fidelity and Guaranty Company v. Hathaway
394 S.E.2d 764 (W. Va. 1990)

MILLER, J.

United States Fidelity and Guaranty Company (USF & G) appeals from an order ... which granted Vivian M. Hathaway's motion to dismiss. ...

Orion M. Hathaway and Vivian M. Hathaway are husband and wife. Mr. Hathaway was the sole proprietor of a construction business called Hathaway Construction Company (the Company). As is common in the construction business, the Company had to acquire performance bonds (bonds) which guaranteed completion of each new job. USF & G agreed to issue bonds on behalf of the Company, thus acting as the Company's surety, if both Mr. and Mrs. Hathaway agreed to indemnify USF & G. On March 23, 1976, both Mr. and Mrs. Hathaway signed what was termed a master surety agreement (the agreement) in which they both agreed to indemnify USF & G if the company defaulted on one of its construction jobs, and USF & G had to pay the Company's creditors pursuant to the terms of the bond.

During 1976 through 1979, USF & G apparently provided several bonds on behalf of the Company, a sole proprietorship. In 1979, the Company incorporated under the same name (the Corporation). The agreement was not amended to reflect the change in legal status.

On December 1, 1983, USF & G issued a bond to insure completion of the Courtland Acres housing project for the elderly in Thomas, West Virginia. On July 9, 1985, the Corporation defaulted on the Courtland Acres project, and pursuant to the terms of the bond, USF & G paid the Corporation's creditors a total of $264,106.06.

Subsequently, USF & G sought indemnification from Mr. and Mrs. Hathaway. When the Hathaways refused to compensate USF & G, it commenced a civil action on December 6, 1985, against them. In addition to

their answer to the complaint, the Hathaways filed a motion to dismiss Mrs. Hathaway as a party defendant on the ground that she did not have an interest in the Corporation. The motion to dismiss further alleged that dismissal was appropriate because the bond guaranteeing performance on the Courtland Acres project was executed on behalf of the business after it had incorporated, and the agreement only required Mrs. Hathaway to indemnify losses for bonds issued on behalf of the sole proprietorship. The trial court granted Mrs. Hathaway's motion to dismiss by an order dated September 29, 1986.

USF & G argues that it was error for the trial court to grant Mrs. Hathaway's motion to dismiss for failure to state a claim upon which relief could be granted. ...

When we consider dismissal under summary judgment, the inquiry is whether there were any genuine issues of material fact. ...

Mrs. Hathaway maintains that she was a gratuitous surety because she received no consideration for signing the agreement. ... A gratuitous surety is favored by the law, and, if there is any material modification in the suretyship contract without the surety's consent, the gratuitous surety is relieved of liability. Mrs. Hathaway argues that there was a material modification in the agreement when USF & G acted as surety on the Corporation's construction contracts because she had only agreed to indemnify USF & G on bonds issued on behalf of the sole proprietorship.

From a purely technical standpoint, Mrs. Hathaway was not a surety. Courts have held that contracts similar to that executed by Mr. and Mrs. Hathaway are indemnity agreements. ... We explained the distinction between suretyship and indemnity in *State ex rel. Copley v. Carey*, 91 S.E.2d 461, 467 (1956):

There is a vital distinction between a contract of suretyship and a contract of indemnity. In a contract of suretyship the obligation of the principal and his surety is original, primary and direct and the surety is liable for the debt, default or miscarriage of his principal. A contract of indemnity is likewise an original undertaking and creates a primary obligation, but the promise of the indemnitor, in a contract of indemnity against loss sustained by the person indemnified, is not to answer for the debt, default or miscarriage of another person but is to make good the loss which results to the person indemnified from such debt, default, or miscarriage.

Even though Mrs. Hathaway is an indemnitor, she has much the same defense as if she were a surety: If there is a material change by the indemnitee in the undertaking indemnified without the consent of the indemnitor that increases the risk to or prejudices the indemnitor, then the indemnitor may be discharged from liability.

In the present case, there was a genuine issue of material fact as to whether USF & G's issuance of surety bonds to the Corporation substantially prejudiced Mrs. Hathaway who only agreed to act as an indemnitor for the Company when it was a sole proprietorship. . . .

The chief inquiry that must be made on remand is whether Mrs. Hathaway, as an indemnitor, was subject to an increased risk of harm or prejudice as a result of USF & G's continuing to write performance bonds for the business after its incorporation.

Accordingly, we reverse the trial court's decision granting Mrs. Hathaway's motion to dismiss and remand the case for further proceedings consistent with this opinion.

■ *Reversed and remanded.*

CASE CONCEPTS REVIEW

1. What are the original relationships between the sole proprietorship, USF & G, and Mr. and Mrs. Hathaway?
2. What event occurred in 1979 that, at least arguably, changed these original relationships?
3. Technically speaking, what is the distinction between a surety and an indemnitor?
4. As a practical matter, does this distinction make a difference in the outcome of this appeal?

4. Creation of Suretyship Contracts

Two basic situations exist when a surety's promise would benefit the creditor: (1) when the creditor is concerned about the principal's ability to repay a loan and (2) when the creditor is concerned about the principal's completion of a contractual promise other than repayment.

Typically, a surety's promise to the creditor to pay the principal's loan is made gratuitously. The consideration (or money) given to the principal is sufficient consideration to make the surety's promise enforceable. Such sureties are generally known as *uncompensated sureties,* and their liabilities may be limited by law.

Performance bonds and fidelity bonds are also examples of suretyship. A *performance bond* provides protection against losses that may result from the failure of a contracting party to perform the contract as agreed. The surety (bonding company) promises the party entitled to performance to pay losses caused by nonperformance by the principal in an amount not to exceed the face of the bond. *Fidelity bonds* give protection against the dishonest acts of a person. In other words, such a bonding company promises to repay the employer any loss, not to exceed a stated amount, caused by the covered employees' embezzlement. Bonding companies are sureties in the sense that the term *surety* includes security either for the payment of money or for the faithful performance of some other duty. Bonding companies usually are *compensated sureties.*

Whereas uncompensated sureties are given special protection as favorites of the law, compensated sureties are perceived as being able to take care of themselves. This difference is illustrated in the interpretation of the contract. Ambiguous provisions of surety agreements are construed in favor of the unpaid surety and against the creditor. Ambiguous provisions of surety agreements involving compensated sureties are resolved against the surety. This distinction results from the fact that ambiguous language is generally construed against the party writing it. In the case of unpaid sureties, the language is usually framed by the creditor and signed by the surety. In the case of compensated sureties, the contract is usually prepared by the surety.

Suretyship agreements are usually express written contracts, whereby the surety assumes responsibility for the principal's performance for the creditor. The surety agrees to pay or to perform in case the principal defaults.

Contracts of suretyship also may result by operation of law. Assume that Jones sells his retail lumber business to Smith, who assumes and agrees to pay, as part of the purchase price, all of Jones's outstanding liabilities. Between Smith and Jones, Smith has now become the primary debtor. Jones is a surety and secondarily liable. As soon as the creditors are notified of the sale, they are obligated to respect the new relationship by attempting to recover from Smith before looking to Jones for payment.

5. Liability of the Parties in General

The surety's liability is dependent on the many factors that exist in a three-party relationship. Therefore the following discussion is divided into three parts, each based on the following relationships:

1. Creditor-surety (sections 6 through 8)
2. Creditor-principal (sections 9 through 13)
3. Principal-surety (sections 14 through 16)

CREDITOR-SURETY RELATIONSHIP

6. Fiduciary Aspects

The suretyship relationship has some fiduciary aspects. It requires good faith and fair dealing. For this reason, a creditor possessing information affecting the risk must communicate such information to the surety before the contract is made. This duty applies only to information that is *significant* to the risk. It does not cover *all* matters that might affect the risk. If some facts make the risk a materially greater one than the surety intends to assume, and if the creditor knows this, the creditor has a duty to disclose those facts to the surety. The duty to disclose exists only if the creditor has reason to believe that the surety does not know the facts and the creditor has a reasonable opportunity to communicate them to the surety. The following case held that a failure to communicate facts to the surety creates a defense for the surety.

CASE

Camp v. First Financial Federal S. & L.
772 S.W.2d 602 (Ark. 1989)

DUDLEY, J.

Appellant, Worth Camp, Jr., co-signed a $25,000 promissory note payable to appellee, First Financial Federal Sav-
ings and Loan Association. The purpose of the transaction was to establish a line of credit for an inventory of used cars to be resold by Rusty Jones, a used car dealer who was the other co-signor. The note was renewed three (3) times and, during that time, the amount of the note was increased to $50,000. Jones defaulted, suit was filed, and judgment was entered against Jones and appel-

lant. . . . [Camp appeals, but] Jones is not involved in this appeal. . . .

Ark. Code Ann. § 4-3-415(1) . . . defines an accommodation party as "one who signs the instrument in any capacity for the purpose of lending his name to another party to it." The comment to this section provides in part that the "essential characteristic is that the accommodation party is a surety. . . ." Thus, an accommodation party may appear on the instrument as a co-maker. Under the facts of this case, appellant is an accommodation party and a surety.

Sureties may have simple contract defenses. One of the defenses involves the creditor's failure to disclose facts which materially increase a surety's risk. A number of courts have adopted Section 124(1) of the Restatement of Security (1940), to define the creditor's duty to disclose. We also adopt the section which provides:

§ 124. Non-Disclosure by Creditor.

(1) Where before the surety has undertaken his obligation the creditor knows facts unknown to the surety that materially increase the risk beyond that which the creditor has reason to believe the surety intends to assume, and the creditor also has reason to believe that these facts are unknown to the surety and has a reasonable opportunity to communicate them to the surety, failure of the creditor to notify the surety of such facts is a defense to the surety.

. . . In this case, the original note was executed on August 2, 1984, and the renewals were executed on January 25, 1985, September 11, 1985, and March 15, 1986. The appellant testified that on August 15, 1985, just before the September 1985 renewal, the loan officer of appellee "advised me the note was coming up for renewal and he advised me that the interest had been paid.". . . In truth, interest payments were four (4) months delinquent. Appellant testified that he would not have executed the September 11, 1985, renewal if he had known that interest was not current. . . .

Appellee's conduct toward appellant was even more egregious in a different regard. All of the witnesses agreed that appellee would not make the loan to Jones alone.

Appellee's president testified that "the loan would not have been made without Mr. Camp as the co-borrower." However, once appellant signed as a co-maker, and the loan limits were practically reached, the appellee began making side loans, or personal loans, to Jones. For example, when $24,861 of the guaranteed $25,000 line of credit had been reached, appellee made a side loan to Jones of $3,250. When $48,019 of the $50,000 guaranteed line of credit had been reached the appellee made side loans to Jones of almost $10,000. These side loans to Jones amounted to $25,038, and were repaid from cars which were mortgaged to appellee. Yet, all parties understood that the loans which appellant co-signed were to be repaid by the sale of the car inventory. Appellant knew nothing of the side loans and naturally thought that Jones' used car business was making payments only on the loans which he co-signed. . . .

Both of these actions, the failure to disclose and the secret side loans, materially increased the surety's contemplated risk, and the creditor was aware of the surety's ignorance of the facts. Yet, the creditor, appellee, chose to misrepresent the truth about the currency of the interest payments and to secret the side loans.

As a result of the actions, the surety assumed a risk well beyond that which he intended. The appellee was aware of the facts, and although given the opportunity, failed to communicate them to the surety. Such actions by a creditor discharge a surety. Accordingly, the judgment is reversed and the complaint is dismissed.

■ *Reversed and dismissed.*

CASE CONCEPTS REVIEW

1. Which parties were the principal debtor, the creditor, and the surety?
2. Camp was not a guarantor of this loan transaction. How did he become a surety?
3. What factual happenings between the debtor and creditor was Camp unaware of?
4. What impact did the lack of disclosure have on the liability of Camp as a surety?

When we concentrate on a typical loan transaction, the surety generally will have as much, if not more, knowledge about the principal than will the creditor. Therefore, the fiduciary duty of disclosure will seldom arise if the surety is a relative of or otherwise related in a business sense to the principal. However, in keeping with conservative lending practices—when in doubt about its appropriateness—the creditor should disclose what it knows about the principal when the surety inquires.

Since the contract is between the surety and the creditor, any misconduct of the principal that induces a party to become a surety does not allow that surety to avoid the contract. At the time of the contract, however, a creditor who is aware of the principal's misrepresentation is obligated to inform the surety of the misrepresentation. This duty to inform probably occurs most frequently when a creditor learns that a principal has misrepresented its financial condition to a prospective surety. Particularly when the surety does not have access to the principal's records and books, the creditor is obligated to warn the surety of the increased risk. In this situation, a creditor's failure to warn the surety will release that surety from liability.

Perhaps the most common application of these fiduciary duties occurs when a financial institution is bonding its employees. An employer who knows of an employee's past financial transgressions (such as embezzlement) must inform the bonding company of this fact at the time a bond is sought. Furthermore, an employer who discovers that a bonded employee has been guilty of misappropriation of funds should immediately discharge the employee unless the surety assents to his or her continued employment. To allow the employee to continue subjects the surety to a risk not contemplated. Rehabilitation of the employee by giving him or her a second chance can be undertaken only with the consent of the surety. If the surety does not consent, and if the employee is guilty of misappropriation a second time, the surety is not liable on the surety bond.

7. Principal's Default: Notice

By the nature of the agreement, a surety has no obligation to the creditor unless the principal fails to perform. Although no performance is owed prior to that time, a surety is liable to the creditor *as soon as* the principal defaults. This simple-sounding rule means that the creditor usually does not have to exhaust his or her remedies against the principal before seeking to recover from the surety. Additionally, a creditor may take action against the surety without having to give notice to the surety that the principal has defaulted. The action will provide the notice. The rule that notice need not be given the surety is subject to the following three exceptions:

1. The contract may require notice to the surety.
2. A surety who is a drawer or indorser of commercial paper is entitled to notice unless waived in the paper.
3. A surety who only guarantees collection is entitled to notice.

SURETY-CREDITOR AGREEMENT.   A surety may insist on including a clause in the contract with the creditor requiring the notice of the principal's default be given within a specified time. Whenever such a clause is included, courts will enforce it. If such a clause is binding on the parties, the creditor's failure to notify the surety of the principal's default discharges the surety from liability. However, the notice requirement must be reasonably, and not strictly, interpreted, as occurred in the following case.

CASE

Local No. 1179 v. Merchants Mutual Bonding Co.
613 P.2d 944 (Kan. 1980)

The Floor Covering Association agreed with Local Union No. 1179 to fund certain health, welfare, pension, and other fringe benefits payments. As a part of their collective bargaining agreement, the Association was required to furnish a surety bond covering the agreed-on payments. Merchants Mutual Bonding Company signed a bond covering up to $10,000 of the Association's fringe benefits payment. This bond contained a requirement that Merchants Mutual be notified within thirty days of the Association's failure to perform. In March 1975, Driscoll, a member of the Association, defaulted on making its fringe benefits payments. In March or April, an agent of the union orally told Merchants Mutual that there may be a claim filed on the bond. Formal written notice of a claim was not sent until September 1975. The union, as a creditor, filed suit against Merchants Mutual. This defendant argued it was not liable since the bond's notice requirement had not been satisfied. Furthermore, there had been no action taken against the defaulting Association.

HERD, J.

. . . The Association was formed, according to its articles of incorporation, for the primary purpose of negotiating, entering into, and administering collective bargaining agreements with the employees of the member firms. This is borne out by the testimony of the officers of the Association. The Association itself had no employees; it simply presented a united front, a single entity for the purpose of negotiating and entering into a collective bargaining agreement with the Union. The Union represented its members, the employees; the Association represented management, its member floor covering contractors.

The Association itself paid no wages and no fringe benefits. Each member firm paid to its workmen the union scale provided by the April 1, 1973, collective bargaining agreement or the later amendments thereto, and each remitted monthly to the Union and the trustees the amounts required for vacation pay, health and welfare, pension, and other fringe benefits. The Association had no financial dealings with plaintiffs; it was a nonprofit corporation, was not authorized to issue capital stock, and there is no evidence that it had any assets. The Association was acting as an agent for its member contractors when it negotiated and signed the collective bargaining agreement and when it applied for and secured the surety bond required by that agreement. The bond makes reference to and incorporates the terms of the collective bargaining agreement insofar as it requires payment of dues, vacation and holiday pay, health, welfare, and pension contributions and other fringe benefits.

The union proceeded against Driscoll, the actual employer who was obligated to make the fringe benefit payments, and it secured a judgment against him. Looking through form to substance, as we are required to do, it is obvious that the bond was intended to protect the plaintiffs from default by Driscoll or the other member contractors in the payment of fringe benefits. A surety bond is to be construed in the light of the circumstances in which it is given, so as to effectuate its purpose. . . . The bond provides that in the event of default, the obligees (plaintiffs) shall notify the surety within 30 days after the obligees shall have had knowledge of such default. No penalty is provided in the bond for failure to give prompt notice.

The evidence, outlined above, is that Driscoll was obligated to pay fringe benefits for his employees by early March, 1975, and that he did not do so. The plaintiffs then knew that Driscoll was in default. In either March or April, the Union notified the resident agent of the surety by telephone, of the default and the possibility that a claim would be made on the bond. A formal written claim was made in September. There was no evidence that the surety was disadvantaged or that its position was adversely affected because of delay in the giving of notice. We agree with the trial court that "there was substantial compliance with the notice requirement. . . ."

In *School District v. McCurley*, 142 P. 1077 (1914) we held that bonding companies engaged in the business of insuring the performance of contracts of others for pay are not "favorites of the law" in the sense the term is applied to accommodation sureties; that such companies are in fact insurers; and that the failure of the obligee to give notice of the principal's default in strict compliance with the terms of the bond does not relieve the surety of liability when the failure to notify resulted in no actual loss or prejudice to the surety. We said:

> The breach of a condition precedent in a bond given by an insurer for pay will not relieve the insurer from liability for any loss for which he would otherwise be liable unless such breach contributed to the loss.

We conclude that under no construction of the evidence is the surety entitled to discharge in this case. . . .

■ *Affirmed.*

CASE CONCEPTS REVIEW

1. When did the Union, as creditor, learn of the principal's (Driscoll's) default?
2. When was the Bonding Company, as surety, notified of this default?
3. What did the bonding contract call for with respect to notice of the principal's default?
4. Why did the court conclude that this notice requirement had been satisfied so the surety was not discharged?

SURETY AS DRAWER OR INDORSER OF COMMERCIAL PAPER. Any drawer of a draft (check) and any indorser of a note, draft, or certificate of deposit becomes liable on the instrument signed if (1) presentment for payment or acceptance was made within a reasonable time, (2) dishonor occurred, and (3) notice of dishonor was given within the time allowed. Since this notice of dishonor must be given, parties who become a surety through their status as an accommodating drawer or indorser or both are entitled to be notified of the principal's (primary party's) default (dishonor). Chapter 36, on the liability of parties to commercial paper, gives further details of the notice requirement in this exception.

SURETY AS COLLECTION GUARANTOR.   Chapter 36 also explains that a collection guarantor under the terms of the Uniform Commercial Code assures the creditor that collection can be obtained from the guarantor if all efforts to collect from the principal prove unsuccessful. Due to the nature of this assurance, equity requires that the guarantor's potential liability not be unresolved indefinitely while the creditor pursues its claim against the principal.

To the extent that a collection guarantor suffers from a lack of notice, that guarantor is discharged. For example, assume that a creditor attempts to collect a debt owed by the principal for two years without notifying that collection guarantor of any such actions. Then the creditor seeks to collect from the guarantor. Also assume that the guarantor can prove that two years before, the guarantor could have recovered 75 percent of the obligation owed from the principal, but now the guarantor can recover nothing. The creditor's lack of notice relieves the guarantor of 75 percent of the original obligation.

The collection guarantor is not damaged by a lack of notice if that guarantor is aware of what actions the creditor is taking to collect from the principal. In the preceding example, if the guarantor knew of the creditor's efforts despite no notice being received, that guarantor has not been prejudiced in any way. In other words, the guarantor could have satisfied its potential obligation at any time and pursued its rights against the principal. Therefore, in this situation, the collection guarantor remains liable for 100 percent of the obligation.

8. Surety's Performance and Subrogation Rights

In general, when a principal defaults, the surety immediately becomes liable to the creditor. The surety can satisfy its obligation to the creditor by performing as promised or by showing that it has a valid excuse for not performing. The following sections present several situations in which the surety is relieved of liability. However, for the time being, assume that upon the principal's default, the surety does perform as promised. When performance has been completed, the surety's most important right involves the concept of **subrogation.**

Subrogation The substitution of one person in another's place, whether as a creditor or as the possessor of any lawful right, so the substituted person may succeed to the rights, remedies, or proceeds of the claim.

The term *subrogation* literally means the substitution of one person in the place of another. The surety who fully performs the obligation of the principal is subrogated to the creditor's rights against the principal. The surety who pays the principal's debt becomes entitled to any security interest the principal has granted to the creditor regarding the debt paid. Furthermore, whenever the creditor obtains a judgment against the principal, the surety receives the benefit of this judgment when the surety satisfies the principal's debts.

Because of the right of subrogation, a creditor in possession of collateral given to him or her by the principal is not at liberty to return it without the consent of the surety. Any surrender of security releases the surety to the extent of its value, with the loss of subrogation damaging the surety to that extent. Failure of the creditor to make use of the security, however, does not release the surety, since the latter is free to pay the indebtedness and to obtain the security for his or her own protection. If the creditor loses the benefit of collateral by inactivity—failure to record a mortgage or notify an indorser—the surety is released to the extent that he or she is injured. In general, if the person who is entitled to protection under the contract of suretyship does anything that will materially prejudice the rights of the surety, the surety will, to that extent at least, be discharged.

The right of subrogation protects the creditor as well as the surety. In other words, a creditor has the right to step into the shoes of the surety and to enforce the surety's rights against the principal. Assume that the principal delivered corporate stock to the surety to protect the surety in the event of the principal's default. The creditor, to the extent of the claim, may substitute his or her position for that of the surety with reference to the stock. In the event of the return of the stock by the surety to the principal, the creditor is entitled to follow the stock into the hands of the debtor and subject it to a lien. The creditor may also secure an injunction against return of the stock to the principal, thus having it impounded by the court until the principal debt falls due, at which time the stock may be sold for the benefit of the creditor.

CREDITOR-PRINCIPAL RELATIONSHIP

9. Introduction

As has been stated previously, a surety generally becomes liable only when the principal defaults. Therefore, if the principal does not default, the surety never becomes liable to the creditor; no default occurs if the principal performs as promised. However, there may be other situations in which the principal has not defaulted because he or she has a valid excuse for nonperformance. These situations may involve a defense the principal can assert against the creditor, a release of the principal by the creditor, or a modification of the creditor-principal relationship. Any of these possible situations may have an impact on the surety's liability.

10. Principal's Defenses

In general, any defense the principal can use to reduce liability to the creditor may also be used by a surety to reduce liability. This idea of making the principal's defenses available to the surety is not conditioned on the principal's utilizing the defense first. The surety is protected by the defense regardless of whether or not the principal is relieved of liability.

One important defense is that of lack of a primary obligation. In other words, the surety is not bound if the principal is not bound. This may occur when the principal fails to sign a contract, although expected to do so. Other common examples of defenses that may be available to the principal and surety include mutual mistake, fraud, duress, undue influence, illegality, impossibility, and lack or failure of consideration.

Setoffs and counterclaims of both the principal and the surety may be used as a defense by the surety under certain circumstances. The surety can set off any claim it has against the creditor and use the setoff to reduce or eliminate the liability. If the principal is insolvent, if the principal and surety are sued jointly, or if the surety has taken an assignment of the claim of the principal, the surety is entitled to use as a defense any setoff that could be used by the principal debtor in a suit by the creditor.

There are three important exceptions to the general rule that defenses available to the principal may be used by the surety to avoid liability to the surety; (1) the principal's lack of capacity, (2) the principal's discharge in bankruptcy, and (3) the principal's performance excused due to the statute of limitations having run.

LACK OF CAPACITY AND DISCHARGE IN BANKRUPTCY. Lack of capacity and discharge in bankruptcy are not available to the surety as defenses because the surety promised in the first instance to protect the creditor against the principal's inability to perform. Most creditors, particularly those in loan transactions, anticipate the principal's lack of capacity or discharge in bankruptcy. A creditor is likely to protect against the consequences of these possible events by insisting that a surety becomes involved.

When a principal who lacks capacity avoids a contract and fails to return the consideration that was received from the creditor, the surety is required to make up any deficiency between the value of whatever the principal has performed and the complete performance. If, on the other hand, the principal returns all or some of the consideration received from the creditor, the surety's liability is reduced by the value of the consideration returned.

STATUTE OF LIMITATIONS. The principal's defense that the statute of limitations prevents collection by the creditor may not be used by the surety. The principal and the surety have separate time periods for which they remain liable to the creditor, and that period may be longer for the surety. For example, the principal may be liable only on the basis of an oral promise (two-year statute of limitations, for instance). The surety's obligation may be based on a written agreement subject to a six-year statute of limitations. Obviously, the creditor who waits for three years after the principal's default cannot recover from the principal. Nevertheless, in this situation, the surety remains liable.

11. Releases

In general, a creditor who voluntarily releases the principal from liability also releases the surety. The logic of this general rule is based on the fact that the surety becomes liable only upon the principal's default. If the principal never defaults since the creditor relinquishes its claim against the principal, the surety never becomes liable either. Any conclusion to the contrary would mean the creditor could indirectly require the principal's performance even after a release. If a creditor could hold the surety liable, the surety could seek reimbursement from the principal. Therefore, the creditor would indirectly be requiring the principal's performance.

As always, we must consider some exceptions to this general rule. The following three are discussed here: (1) A surety that consents to a principal's release is not released; (2) a creditor that reserves rights against a surety does not release that surety; and (3) a release obtained by that principal's fraud does not release the surety if the creditor rescinds the release prior to the surety's reliance on the release.

THE SURETY'S CONSENT. It is hard to imagine why any commercial surety would voluntarily consent to remain liable when a principal is released from liability. Indeed, most situations involving a surety's consent to remain personally liable probably will involve a friendship or kinship between the surety and the principal. For example, a surety may wish to help a friend or relative by improving that principal's financial record. To achieve this result, the surety may actually seek the principal's release by consenting to remain liable.

Furthermore, a surety may be secured by the principal in return for acting as a surety. We could assume that a business, as principal, granted its president, as surety, a security interest in all its accounts and general intangibles. A creditor may be willing to take the surety's security interest in full satisfaction of the performance owed. The creditor might agree to release the principal from further personal liability if the surety consents to the creditor's having the right to pursue its claim against the accounts and general intangibles. The basis for this conclusion is the creditor's right of subrogation, discussed in section 8.

RESERVATION OF RIGHTS.   Even a nonconsenting surety is not released when a principal is released if the creditor reserves rights against the surety. In essence, the creditor's reservation of rights is interpreted to be a promise by the creditor that the principal will not be sued. The creditor can still hold the surety liable, and the surety can seek reimbursement from the principal upon the surety's performance. Therefore, in essence, the principal ultimately remains liable despite the prior release. The creditor really has promised only that the creditor will not sue the principal. To protect the surety's potential claim against the principal, the surety may perform for the creditor any time after that creditor has released the principal and has reserved rights against the surety. Due to its vital importance and its impact on the surety's liability, notice of the reservation of rights against a surety should be given in writing to both the surety and the principal.

PRINCIPAL'S FRAUD.   With the use of false financial statements, the principal may induce a creditor to accept less than full performance from the principal or no performance at all in return for the creditor's release. Once that creditor learns of this fraudulent scheme by the principal, the creditor may rescind its release agreement. What impact these events have on a surety's liability depends on the factual situation. Normally a surety (that has not consented and has not had rights reserved against it) is released when the principal is released. However, if the release is obtained by fraud by the principal, the creditor would be greatly disadvantaged if the surety is released altogether. Therefore, if the surety had no knowledge of the fraud, that surety is released only to the extent it has relied on the release and the changed legal position as a result of the release. If the surety had knowledge of the principal's wrongful acts, the surety is not justified in relying on the release. In this latter situation, the creditor still may hold the surety liable for the principal's uncompleted performance.

12. Extensions of Time for Payment

Before discussing the rules regarding the surety's liability, we need to have a clear understanding of what is meant by an extension of time for performance. To affect the surety's liability, the extension agreement must be a binding, enforceable contract. As such, it must be for a definite time and supported by consideration. In other words, the principal must induce the creditor to extend the time originally involved by promising something in addition to what the principal is already obligated to do. A principal's consideration for an extension may take the form of a refinancing agreement or an advance payment of interest. Merely promising to pay the original debt at a future date will not supply the consideration, because performance of a preexisting obligation is not consideration.

The creditor's gratuitous indulgence or passive permission to the principal to take more time than the contract provides has no impact on the surety's liability. Such conduct by the creditor does not injure the surety in any way. Upon the principal's default, the surety is free to perform at any time and pursue all available remedies.

If there is a formalized agreement between creditor and principal whereby the time for performance is extended to a definite time, a nonconsenting, uncompensated surety is discharged from liability. This rule is necessary, since the extension of time delays any potential default by the principal. Such a delay could adversely affect the surety's ability to recover from the principal if the surety has to perform. During the extension, the principal's financial condition could worsen, which could increase the surety's ultimate risk of loss.

The following case discusses these legal principles related to whether a surety is discharged upon an extension of time for payment versus a period of leniency on the creditor's collection.

CASE

Bier Pension Plan Trust v. Estate of Schneierson
545 N.E.2d 1212 (N.Y. 1989)

SIMONS, J.

Plaintiff brought this action against defendant, the estate of the surety of one Lieberman, to recover on a guarantee of Lieberman's debt. The estate's answer raised several defenses but on this appeal we are concerned only with the contention that it has been released from its undertaking because plaintiff altered the original contract with Lieberman.

Plaintiff alleges in its complaint that on November 1, 1983 it loaned Marvin Lieberman $280,000 for three months at 12% interest and that Joel Schneierson, defendant's testator, guaranteed payment. Lieberman failed to pay the debt at maturity despite repeated requests that he do so. On May 28, 1985 he confessed judgment and, on July 11, 1986, plaintiff entered judgment on the confession for $344,500. Plaintiff then demanded defendant satisfy the judgment and commenced this action when it failed to do so. Plaintiff acknowledges that it did not proceed against Lieberman immediately and that Lieberman paid interest after maturity. However, it asserts in its motion papers that: "Plaintiff's accommodation to the principal obligor to permit him additional time to make the payment did not prejudice or effect [*sic*] the defendant or its guarantee in any manner."

Defendant contends that the "accommodation" was a new agreement between plaintiff and Lieberman, extending the loan and that plaintiff received payments of interest at 12% after the original debt had matured. It asserts that this extension . . . changed the original three-month contract to one continuing the loan for a reasonable time and discharged it from its undertaking on the original note. Based on these facts, the parties made cross motions for summary judgment. Special Term denied both motions. Only defendant appealed to the Appellate Division, which reversed the order insofar as appealed from, and granted summary judgment to defendant. We granted leave to appeal. . . .

Under general contract rules, an obligation may not be altered without the consent of the party who assumed the obligation. Suretyship is a contractual relation and thus the rule is stated that the creditor and the principal debtor may not alter the surety's undertaking to cover a different obligation without the surety's consent. If they do so the surety is discharged because the parties have substituted a new contract, to which it never agreed, for the original. If the surety is to remain liable on its undertaking, its right to make payment of the debt upon maturity of the indebtedness and, by subrogation to the creditor's rights, to proceed against the principal debtor to obtain repayment may not be affected without its consent.

An obligation is altered when the debtor is discharged from the original contract and a new contract is substituted in its place. The test is whether there is a new contract which will be enforced by the courts. Obviously, if the debtor can assert a new contract in defense to an action on the original contract the surety may do so also and, since it did not guarantee performance of the new agreement, it cannot be held answerable for the principal debtor's default. Conversely, if the principal debtor is bound by the original contract (because the new agreement is unenforceable for lack of consideration or fraudulently induced, for example) the original debt remains undischarged, the surety is answerable for the principal debtor's default and the surety's right of subrogation against the debtor in accordance with the terms of the original contract is preserved.

If the creditor and principal debtor agree to extend maturity, then under the general rule the surety is discharged even if the term is extended only a few days. Indulgence or leniency in enforcing a debt when due is not an alteration of the contract, however. An unenforceable agreement to give time is merely revocable permission to defer performance. If the creditor retains the right to demand payment of the debt according to its original terms the surety is not discharged.

Applying these rules to the present case, we conclude there are questions of fact whether plaintiff and Lieberman made an enforceable agreement to extend the terms of the debt. . . .

Assuming interest at 12% was in fact paid, we believe that . . . the acceptance of contract interest, even if it is higher than the prevailing legal rate of interest, should not bind the parties to extend the loan for a reasonable additional time. . . . [This] rule has been the law of this State for over 100 years and has the force of precedent and long acceptance by the business community. It is also supported by sound policy considerations, for any other rule would require a creditor to declare default and institute legal proceedings to collect the debt when the loan matures if payment is not made immediately. Even a delay of a day or two could risk loss of the surety's undertaking. A lenient creditor's only safe alternative would be to forego postmaturity interest, a result which penalizes forbearance and is contrary to the law's preference for voluntary resolution of disputes. Conversely, the surety is not without remedies. It may protect itself against forbearance by reserving in the original contract the right to demand immediate default or, if it feels prejudiced by delay in enforcing the debt, it may pay the debt upon default and proceed by way of subrogation against the principal debtor to enforce repayment.

Accordingly, the order of the Appellate Division should be reversed, with costs, and defendant's motion for summary judgment denied.

■ *Order reversed.*

CASE CONCEPTS REVIEW

1. When Lieberman failed to repay the loan owed to the Pension Plan, what action was taken to collect this debt?
2. With respect to the surety's continuing liability, what is the distinction between the creditor extending the debtor's time for payment and the creditor simply being lenient in enforcing the obligation?
3. Why does the court hold that after default the creditor accepting a rate of interest higher than the legal rate of interest does not necessarily result in an extension of time for payment?
4. How can the surety protect itself from the creditor's leniency after the principal has defaulted?

As with releases, this general rule of releasing the surety upon the creditor granting a formal extension of time does not apply if the surety consents to the extension. Furthermore, a surety is not discharged by a formal extension of time if the creditor expressly reserves rights against the surety. This reservation of rights must be a part of the extension agreement. The creditor's stipulation that rights are reserved against the surety does not bind the surety to the extension agreement. Thus, the surety may proceed to satisfy the creditor's claim and sue the principal for reimbursement at any time. The principal, therefore, is not really protected by an extension agreement that includes the creditor's reservation of rights against the surety. This type of extension agreement simply is a limited promise by the creditor not to sue the principal during the extension period.

Finally, a formalized extension of the time for performance discharges a compensated surety only to the extent that surety is injured by the extension. Of course, this rule assumes that the surety does not consent to the extension agreement. A compensated surety is perceived as being capable of protecting itself by anticipating possible extension agreements and charging a premium in accordance with expectations.

13. Other Modifications

In addition to an extension of the time for payment, any other modification of the creditor-principal agreement generally discharges the surety. The logic behind this general rule is that a surety should not be liable for the performance of some agreement made after the surety's commitment to the creditor. A modification agreed to by creditor and principal is a novation that relieves the surety from its obligation. In general, evidence of a renewed obligation is not considered to be a modification that relieves the surety of liability. However, if the renewal note increases the principal's obligation, the surety is relieved of further liability unless the surety consents to the renewal agreement.

An examination of the exceptions or qualifications to this general rule may make the philosophy behind it clearer. These exceptions include the following: (1) A surety that consents to the modification is not discharged; (2) an uncompensated but nonconsenting surety is not discharged to the extent that the modification benefits the surety; and (3) a compensated surety is not discharged if the modification does not materially increase the surety's risk.

SURETY'S CONSENT. As in other areas of suretyship, the parties can override the application of the general rule on modification by this agreement. A surety who consents to remain liable is not discharged by a modification to the creditor-principal agreement. This exception is applicable regardless of when the surety consents. Whether consent to modifications occurs before, at the time of, or after the modification, the consenting surety remains liable to the creditor.

If the surety's consent is not a part of the original agreement signed by the surety, the creditor has the responsibility to notify the surety of the modification and to obtain the surety's consent. Failure to obtain this consent upon full notice of the modification automatically discharges the surety.

UNCOMPENSATED SURETIES. The surety who is not paid is a favorite of the law. In fact, the uncompensated surety is so protected in some states that any modification to the principal's obligation results in an absolute discharge of this surety, assuming no consent.

Courts in some states have disliked the harshness of the rule that discharges an uncompensated surety whenever any modification is made without that surety's consent. Therefore, there are decisions that hold that an uncompensated (and nonconsenting) surety should not be discharged if the creditor-principal modification benefits the surety. This benefit must be so obvious that there is no way to doubt its beneficial nature. Typically, such a modification occurs only when the creditor agrees to reduce the amount due or the rate of interest. In some states, a change in interest rates (up or down) does not discharge a continuing surety. Since interest rates are expected to change in today's economy, that change should not discharge the continuing surety.

COMPENSATED SURETIES. Sureties that receive consideration (separate from that received by the principal) in return for their promises are *not* protected by the law to the same extent as uncompensated sureties. Thus, with respect to the impact of creditor-principal modifications, a compensated surety is discharged altogether only if that surety's risk has materially increased. If the increased risk to the surety cannot be readily determined, it is immaterial. To the extent that a compensated surety's risk is increased only slightly by the modification, that surety is discharged only to the extent of the increased risk. And if the compensated surety's risk is not affected by the modification, the surety remains liable as promised.

Why is an extension of time for payment treated differently from other modifications? This distinction in treatment basically is due to the creditor's ability to reserve rights against the surety upon an extension of the time of performance. In this discussion of modification, there has been no mention of reservation of rights. A creditor cannot reserve rights against a surety when a general modification of the principal's agreement is made.

PRINCIPAL-SURETY RELATIONSHIP

14. Surety's Duty to Account

Not only does the principal owe a duty to perform to the creditor, but the principal also owes that same duty to the surety. This duty arises by express agreement or by implication. Whenever a surety is present, the principal owes the duty to protect that surety from liability regardless of whether the surety has a contract with that principal or with the creditor. The only exception to this general rule is when the principal is relieved of liability due to a defense assertable against the creditor's claim. It is this general duty the principal owes the surety that justifies the surety's right to be reimbursed by the principal after the surety has satisfied the creditor's claim.

The surety owes a duty to account to the principal for any profits obtained after the surety performs. For example, suppose a principal gave a creditor a security interest in some equipment. And assume that a surety personally paid $100,000 to satisfy the principal's delinquent obligation. As noted previously, the surety has the right to the security interest via subrogation. If the surety sold the equipment for $175,000, that surety would have to return $75,000 to the principal. This surety's duty to account emphasizes that the surety is liable for the principal's performance of an obligation. In essence, the surety should be liable for no more than, and should not benefit from, the commitment made.

15. Surety's Right to Reimbursement

Generally, after the surety has performed, the surety is entitled to be reimbursed by the principal. As you have come to expect, this general rule on the surety's right to be reimbursed is subject to at least two exceptions. First, a principal may inform a surety of a valid defense that a principal can assert to deny the creditor's claim. If the surety fails to use this defense as a means of reducing liability, the surety is not entitled to be reimbursed by the principal. Basically, the law requires the principal to bear the burden of informing the surety of available defenses. However, this requirement to inform does not apply when the principal's defense cannot be asserted by the surety. For example, the principal's defenses of (1) lack of capacity, (2) discharge in bankruptcy, and (3) expiration of the statute of limitations cannot be asserted by the surety. Regardless of whether a surety knows of these defenses, that surety cannot force the principal to reimburse expenses after the surety has satisfied the creditor's claim. In other words, these defenses extinguish the principal's liability altogether.

A second exception to the principal's duty to reimburse occurs when a surety has performed for a creditor after a principal has been released. A surety that performs is not entitled to be reimbursed by the principal if the principal has been released by the creditor's agreement. This rule makes logical sense, since it would be fraudulent for a creditor of a discharged or released principal to seek performance from a surety. If a surety does perform under the circumstances, the surety has a right to have the value of performance returned from the creditor.

This rule relieving the principal of the duty to reimburse the surety is not applicable when the creditor releasing the principal reserves rights against the surety. As discussed in sections 11 and 12, a surety remains liable to perform the principal's obligations if the creditor reserves rights against the surety. If the surety must perform for the creditor, it is only fair that the surety be reimbursed by the principal. The use of the concept of reservation of rights is allowed when a principal is released by a creditor or when time for payment is extended formally. In both cases, the principal debtor remains liable to the surety.

16. Liability of Co-Sureties

Throughout this chapter, there has been an implicit assumption that only one surety was involved in protecting the creditor. This assumption is too simplistic to reflect the actual situation in the marketplace. In any contract, a creditor may insist on or otherwise be benefited by the existence of two or more sureties. Generally, these sureties may exist as co-sureties or as subsureties. *Co-sureties* are jointly and severally liable to the creditor. The term *joint and several* means the creditor may sue the co-sureties jointly for the performance promised or may sue each surety separately for the entire performance due. A *subsurety* promises to be liable only in the event that the surety refuses to perform and thereby defaults. A subsurety is a surety's surety. Unless the sureties involved in a transaction agree otherwise, they are considered co-sureties. A subsuretyship normally must be created by the agreement of the parties, whereas a co-suretyship may be created by implication.

Numerous legal principles govern the rights of all the parties involved in a transaction with two or more sureties. In general, all the basic rules and exceptions discussed in this chapter remain applicable. For example, a release of the principal is a release of the surety if the surety does not consent to the release and if the creditor does not reserve rights against the surety. When a creditor releases one surety but not the other sureties, the general rule is that the remaining sureties are released to the extent that they cannot seek contribution against the released surety. Once again, this rule is not applicable if the remaining sureties consent or if the creditor reserves rights against the remaining sureties.

In addition to the applicability of the aforementioned legal principles, there are rules that govern the liability of co-sureties one to another. Similar to the surety's right to be reimbursed by the principal, the fundamental rule among co-sureties is their right of contribution. This right is how co-sureties work out among themselves their fair share of the performance completed for the creditor. Whereas a creditor can hold one surety liable for all of the principal's obligation, that surety is liable for only a pro rata share (among the co-sureties) of the performance rendered. The right of contribution works to allocate the liability 50–50 among two co-sureties, 33⅓–33⅓–33⅓ among three co-sureties, and so forth. Before one co-surety can collect from another, proof of payment of the obligation is required. In general, any recovery does not include attorneys' fees, although interest calculated at the statutory rate may be recovered.

CHAPTER SUMMARY

1. Artisan's liens are the right to possess, for leverage in the collection process, personal property that one has serviced or repaired.
2. The "improved" personal property must be possessed at all times.
3. If possession is surrendered voluntarily, the lien is lost unless a claim of lien is filed in the public records.
4. Artisan's liens are personal and cannot generally be assigned.
5. The property is sold and the proceeds are used to satisfy the lienholder's claim.
6. In general, artisan's lienholders have priority to the sale proceeds.

SURETYSHIP IN GENERAL

Terminology
1. A principal is a debtor or one who is obligated to perform a contractual promise.
2. A creditor is the party to whom money is owed or who is entitled to some other contractual performance.
3. A surety is a party who assures the creditor that the principal will perform as promised.
4. The term *surety* should be compared and contrasted with *guarantor* and *indemnitor*.

Creation of Suretyship Contracts
1. These contracts usually arise in relationship to the principal's obligation to repay a debt or to complete some other promised performance.
2. These contracts may be created as expressed written agreements or by operation of law.

CREDITOR-SURETY RELATIONSHIP

Fiduciary Aspects
1. A suretyship is based on trust and confidence.
2. Both creditor and surety must share any information that may adversely affect that party's potential liability.

Principal's Default: Notice
1. A surety becomes liable to the creditor when the principal defaults.
2. In general, the creditor does not have to give notice of default to hold the surety liable.
3. However, notice of default is required if the creditor-surety agreement requires it, if the surety is a drawer or indorser of commercial paper, of if the surety is a collection guarantor.

Surety's Performance and Subrogation Rights
1. A surety satisfies its obligation upon performance.
2. Having performed, the surety is entitled to any rights of the creditor.
3. Likewise, the creditor is entitled to be protected by any rights held by the surety.

CREDITOR-PRINCIPAL RELATIONSHIP

Principal's Defenses
1. Sureties generally can utilize any defense a principal has against the creditor to reduce liability.
2. The principal's defenses of lack of capacity, discharge in bankruptcy, and expiration of the statute of limitations cannot be asserted by the surety.

Releases
1. In general, a creditor who releases a principal from liability also releases any surety.
2. The principal's release does not relieve the surety of liability if the surety consents to the release, if the creditor reserves rights against the surety, or if the release is obtained by the principal's fraud.

Extensions of Time for Payment
1. An extension must be a valid agreement supported by consideration if it is to have an impact on the surety's liability.
2. A formal extension does discharge the surety's liability unless the surety consents, unless the creditor reserves rights against the surety, or unless the surety is compensated and not injured by the extension.

| Other Modifications | 1. In general, any modification of the creditor-principal relationship discharges the surety. |
| | 2. Exceptions to this general rule include the surety's consent to the modification, the uncompensated surety to the extent of any benefit, and the compensated surety as long as the modification does not materially increase that surety's risk. |

PRINCIPAL-SURETY RELATIONSHIP

Surety's Duty to Account	1. The surety must account to the principal for any benefits the surety receives from performance.
Surety's Right to Reimbursement	1. In general, after performance a surety is entitled to be reimbursed by the principal. This right of the surety is based on the principal's obligation not to default.
	2. The surety's right to reimbursement does not apply if the principal has informed the surety of a valid defense that would defeat the creditor's claim of performance.
	3. The right to reimbursement is also lacking if the surety performs after the principal has been discharged or released by the creditor, unless the creditor reserves rights against the surety.
Liability of Co-Sureties	1. In general, the liability of co-sureties is based on the same principles as the liability of one surety.
	2. Co-sureties are jointly and severally liable. Generally, the right of contribution assures that co-sureties share liability on a pro rata basis.

REVIEW QUESTIONS AND PROBLEMS

1. Match each term in column A with the appropriate statement in column B.

A	B
(1) Artisan's lien	(a) Literally means "to stand in the place of another"
(2) Surety	(b) A method by which a creditor can continue to hold a surety liable
(3) Indemnity	(c) A surety's right against a principal
(4) Subrogation	(d) Not created when a repairperson agrees to do work on credit
(5) Uncompensated surety	(e) The right that exists between co-sureties
(6) Reservation of rights	(f) In modern law, another term for a guarantor
(7) Reimbursement	(g) A promise to hold someone harmless
(8) Contribution	(h) Viewed as a favorite of law

2. Mary took her car to the local Chevrolet dealer for service and necessary repairs. After the dealer performed the desired work, Mary paid the bill in full. However, the dealer refused to relinquish possession of her car, since Mary had not paid for repairs previously made on the same car. Does the dealer have a lien on her car so Mary cannot regain possession of it? Why or why not?

3. Plaintiff, known as 660 Syndicate, owned an airplane that had been leased to Wyoming Airlines. The Wyoming Airlines had Rocky Mountain Turbines (R.M.T.) service and repair the airplane. Although it had not been paid, R.M.T. returned the airplane to Wyoming Airlines. After it could not collect the money it was owed, R.M.T. reacquired possession of the repaired airplane. R.M.T. planned to enforce its lien by selling the airplane. Plaintiff filed suit claiming that it was entitled to possession of the airplane. Plaintiff argued that R.M.T.'s lien was unenforceable. Was R.M.T.'s lien on the plane made valid by the subsequent acquisition of the plane? Explain.

4. Sam wrote a letter of guaranty to Carl on behalf of Rex, a retailer. The letter stated that Sam "does guarantee payment of any credit granted by you not to exceed ten thousand dollars ($10,000)." Rex was involved in a series of individual transactions with Carl, of

which none exceeded $10,000. Rex failed to pay, but Sam contends that his total liability is limited to one transaction. Is Sam correct? Why or why not?

5. The Damsel Corporation sought financing from Chemical Bank. To receive the financing, the officers of the corporation were required to execute personal guaranty contracts with the bank. The identical instruments provided that they were continuing guaranties and that they were to remain in effect irrespective of any interruptions in the business relations of Damsel with the bank. The officers had the right to terminate the guaranties by giving written notice at any time.

   Damsel had paid off its debt to Chemical Bank. However, the bank continued to factor accounts receivable for several of Damsel's suppliers. As a result of this arrangement, Damsel wrote hundreds of checks to the bank. Some of the checks were dishonored. Damsel filed for bankruptcy protection under a Chapter 11 reorganization proceeding. In an attempt to collect the dishonored checks, the bank sued the Damsel officers on their personal guaranties. These officers argued that Damsel's repayment of the original debt had terminated their guaranty agreements. Did the personal guaranties of the Damsel officers survive the corporation's payment of the original debt? Explain.

6. Lee signed as guarantor of a promissory note signed by Akins and payable to Vaughn. Lee expressly inserted a provision into the note that if the principal debtor defaulted, Lee must be notified promptly if he was to be liable. After the maker defaulted, no notice was given of that fact by Vaughn to Lee. When Vaughn sued Lee for payment, Lee contended that the lack of notice discharged this liability. When a surety contract expressly requires notice of the default, is the surety liable on the note if the payee does not promptly notify the surety? Why or why not?

7. Owens hired Terry, a general contractor, to build a house. Terry, in turn, hired Paint-It-All, a subcontractor, to paint the house. Being concerned about Paint-It-All's reputation, Terry required that a performance bond be obtained. Paint-It-All paid the Aetna Insurance Company to assure its performance. Paint-It-All failed to do the job, and Terry brought an action against Aetna alone. May he do so? Explain.

8. Donald Dunwoody borrowed money from the First National Bank and in return granted a security interest in his office equipment. In addition to this security, the bank required that Donald's sister, Sarah, sign as surety of her brother's performance. Donald did default on his payment. Sarah paid the loan in full and now claims to have rights in her brother's office equipment. Is she correct? Explain.

9. Lamar and Carolyn Upshaw guaranteed payment up to $4,000 on a loan from First State Bank to James Chaney. The Upshaws gave the bank a mortgage to a parcel of property they owned as security for payment. Subsequently, Chaney signed a new note with the bank renewing his obligations and canceling all prior notes. Chaney defaulted, and the bank seeks to foreclose on the Upshaw realty. Could the bank foreclose on the Upshaw property based on their surety agreement in the original note? Explain.

10. A newspaper entered into a contract with Alan by the terms of which Alan was to purchase newspapers at wholesale and deliver them to residential buyers. Alan's father agreed to serve as accommodation surety. Although the contract called for weekly payments by Alan, the newspaper allowed him to pay monthly. Did this allowance relieve Alan's father from any liability as surety? Why or why not?

11. Panworld purchased bicycles on credit from Heide. AMR corporation guaranteed Panworld's debt as a compensated surety. Later Panworld and Heide modified the original contract without the consent of the surety. No injury to AMR resulted from the modifications. Is AMR still liable? Explain.

CHAPTER

41 LAWS ASSISTING DEBTORS AND CONSUMERS

CHAPTER PREVIEW

The four preceding chapters discuss laws designed to assist creditors in the collection of debts. Numerous laws also attempt to protect consumers from financial and physical harm. These laws seek to protect consumers in their contracts, especially those that involve credit, and from injury caused by products.

Debtor and consumer protection involves all branches of government. There are protection statutes enacted by federal and state governments. Courts have also extended protection to consumers. The demise of privity of contract in breach-of-warranty cases is an example of judicial consumer protection. Finally, administrative agencies such as the Federal Trade Commission and Federal Reserve Board have responsibilities to assist in the protection of consumer-debtors.

The law aids debtors and consumers for several reasons. Debtors and consumers frequently have less bargaining power than creditors and sellers. Many are financially unsophisticated, easily deceived, and lack information needed to make intelligent decisions. Therefore, much of the consumer movement has been directed at providing all the relevant information so borrowers and purchasers will be able to make reasonably intelligent decisions in the marketplace. Other laws are aimed at equalizing the bargaining power between buyer and seller. This equalization is often accomplished by declaring contract provisions illegal if they would not be agreed to by a party with equal bargaining power.

This chapter covers the laws regulating both debtor and consumer protection. The concerns for debtors and consumers are so interrelated that many laws were enacted specifically to protect consumer-debtors. Sections 1 through 14 concentrate on the laws that assist such debtors. The last portion of this chapter deals with laws that protect consumers who are not necessarily debtors.

■ BUSINESS MANAGEMENT DECISION

As the general manager of a collection agency, you are told by one of your collectors that a debtor does not want to be contacted again. This debtor informed your collector that the debtor has retained a lawyer.

What guidance should you give your collector?

DEBTOR PROTECTION IN GENERAL

Since this chapter examines laws and regulations related to consumer credit transactions, it is appropriate to begin with a clarification of terminology. First, the word *consumer* applies to those individuals involved in transactions concerning personal, family, or household needs as opposed to commercial or business purposes. The term *credit* describes any situation in which money is lent with repayment to be made in the future.

In this chapter, unless stated otherwise, the legal principles discussed are applicable to all consumer credit transactions regardless of whether the lender is a secured or unsecured creditor. If the creditor is secured, the form of security (by personal property, real property, or a surety's promise) generally does not change the force of the laws and regulations discussed.

The following sections (1 through 14) are arranged in the chronology that they become applicable in the creditor-debtor relationship. For example, the steps and legal requirements of the credit application are discussed first. Then the actual credit transaction is presented, and finally the creditor's options in collecting the debt are reviewed.

1. Equal Credit Opportunity Act

The Equal Credit Opportunity Act (ECOA) originally prohibited discrimination in credit transactions on the basis of sex or marital status. The ECOA was enacted in response to findings of studies that indicated that women had a much more difficult time borrowing money than did their male counterparts. Later the ECOA was amended to add age, race, color, religion, national origin, receipt of public assistance benefits, and the good-faith exercise of any right under the Consumer Credit Protection Act as categories of prohibited discrimination in credit transactions.

A *creditor* subject to the ECOA is an individual or a business organization, in the ordinary course of business, participating in a decision whether or not to extend credit. Creditors include financial institutions, retail stores, and credit card issuers. *Discrimination* occurs when an applicant is treated less favorably than other applicants. An *applicant* is any individual or business organization requesting or receiving an extension of credit from a creditor. An *application* is defined as an oral or written request for an extension of credit made in accordance with procedures established by a creditor for the type of credit requested. The terms and the provisions of the ECOA are applicable to lease transactions as well as sales transactions if credit decisions are involved, as was held in the following case.

CASE

Brothers v. First Leasing
724 F.2d 789 (9th Cir. 1984)

REINHARDT, J.

The district court dismissed plaintiff's claim that her application for an automobile lease had been denied on the basis of sex or marital status in violation of the Equal Credit Opportunity Act (ECOA). The sole issue on appeal is whether the ECOA applies to consumer leases. We hold that it does.

In January 1982, plaintiff-appellant, Patricia Ann Brothers, attempted to lease an automobile for her personal use from defendant-appellant, First Leasing. First Leasing required Brothers to submit a completed "Application for Lease Credit," which was to provide First Leasing with information with which to evaluate her financial condition.

Brothers informed First Leasing that she intended to lease the automobile in her own name rather than jointly with her husband, Jamesd A. Garske. Nonetheless, First Leasing insisted that Brothers include on the "Application for Lease Credit" information concerning Mr. Garske's financial history. In addition, First Leasing required Mr. Garske, as well as Brothers, to sign the application. Brothers submitted the application, signed by her husband, with the requested information about his finances. First Leasing then obtained TRW Credit Reports on Brothers and her husband. Mr. Garske's credit report indicated that he previously had filed for bankruptcy.

In a form entitled "Statement of Credit Denial, Termination, or Change," which complies with the requirements of the ECOA, and is almost identical to the form suggested in the ECOA regulations, First Leasing rejected Brothers' application. The "principal reason" given for the denial of Brothers' lease credit application was her husband's previous bankruptcy. The form used by First Leasing also contained a statement that the ECOA bars "creditors from discriminating against credit applicants on the basis of sex [or] marital status."

Brothers filed a claim against First Leasing that alleged that (1) the requirement that Mr. Garske sign her lease credit application, and (2) the denial of *her* application because of *his* credit record, constituted unlawful discrimination on the basis of sex or marital status under the ECOA. Contending that the ECOA does not apply to leases, First Leasing moved to dismiss the action for failure to state a claim upon which relief can be granted. The district court held that the lease was not covered by the ECOA and granted the motion. . . .

The use of the broad term "credit transactions" in the ECOA does not, by itself, answer the question whether consumer leases are covered by the Act, although a literal reading of the language supports the view that they are. On the one hand, the lease obligation that Brothers would have incurred under the automobile lease falls within the ECOA's definition of "credit." So would the obligations incurred under most consumer leases. Moreover, the credit investigation engaged in by First Leasing is specifically included within the Federal Reserve Board's definition of "credit transaction."

Although "credit transactions" might in some contexts lend itself to a narrow interpretation, we cannot give it such a construction in the ECOA in view of the overriding national policy against discrimination that underlies the Act and in view of the current structure of the Consumer Credit Protection Act, the umbrella statute. We must construe the literal language of the ECOA in light of the clear, strong purpose evidenced by the Act and adopt an interpretation that will serve to effectuate that purpose....

The purpose of the ECOA is to eradicate credit discrimination waged against women, especially married women whom creditors traditionally refused to consider for individual credit. Congress reaffirmed the goal of antidiscrimination in credit in the 1976 amendments to the ECOA by adding race, color, religion, national origin, and age to sex and marital status as characteristics that may not be considered in deciding whether to extend credit.

In enacting and amending the ECOA, Congress recognized that a prohibition against discrimination in credit provides a much-needed addition to the previously existing strict prohibitions against discrimination in employment, housing, voting, education, and numerous other areas. The ECOA is simply one more tool to be used in our vigorous national effort to eradicate invidious discrimination "root and branch" from our society.

In view of the strong national commitment to the eradication of discrimination in our society, we see no reason why Congress would have wanted to subject the leasing of durable consumer goods to regulation under the disclosure provisions of the Consumer Credit Protection Act, but to exclude those transactions from the scope of the antidiscrimination provisions of that Act. Certainly, abolishing discrimination in the affording of credit is at least as important as compelling the disclosure of information regarding finance charges. To conclude that discrimination in consumer leasing transactions is exempt from the ECOA simply because Congress did not add express language covering consumer leases when it amended the ECOA for entirely unrelated reasons would be inconsistent with the broad purpose of the statute and the liberal construction we must give it. It is far more reasonable to conclude that Congress thought that an express amendment was unnecessary because the ECOA on its face applies to all credit transactions and, therefore, the language already in the Act was broad enough to cover consumer leases.

In enacting the Consumer Leasing Act, Congress explicitly recognized the "recent trend toward leasing automobiles and other durable goods for consumer use as an alternative to installment credit sales." Prospective lessors run extensive credit checks on consumer lease applicants just as they do in the case of credit sales applicants.... Therefore, interpreting "credit transactions" so that the ECOA applies to lease transactions, as well as to credit sales and loans, is essential to the accomplishment of the Act's antidiscriminatory goal....

Finally, to interpret the term "credit transactions" narrowly, so as to exclude consumer leases, would nullify Congress' use of flexible language necessary "to insure the effective application of legislative policy to changing circumstances."

Because the language of the ECOA is broad and its antidiscriminatory purpose is overriding, ... we conclude that the ECOA applies to consumer leases.

The district court's order dismissing appellant's claim is reversed and the case is remanded.

■ *So ordered.*

CASE CONCEPTS REVIEW

1. What did First Leasing require of Ms. Brothers upon her application for credit?
2. Why did Ms. Brothers not want to use her husband as a co-borrower?
3. What is the basis of Ms. Brothers's complaint? What is the basis of First Leasing's defense?
4. Why did the court reject this defense and find that Ms. Brothers was entitled to have her complaint tried?

The ECOA allows suits for dollar damages by victims of credit discrimination. Individual victims are entitled to recover actual damages, which can include a recovery for embarrassment and mental distress. In addition to actual damages, victims can sue for attorney's fees, other legal costs, and punitive damages up to $10,000. Punitive damages may be awarded even in the absence of actual damages being proved. In addition to these private remedies, governmental entities may bring suit to enjoin violations of the ECOA and to assess civil penalties. Punitive damages may not be recovered by the government.

Generally any action to enforce the ECOA must be begun within two years from the date the violation occurred. An exception to this statute of limitations arises if an administrative agency or the attorney general begins enforcement action within two years of the violation's occurrence. Any applicant who has been a victim of wrongful discrimination then has one year after the governmental enforcement action is commenced to bring a civil action to enforce the ECOA.

2. Discrimination Prohibited

A creditor must not advertise the availability of credit in any way that implicitly discriminates. For example, a picture of potential applicants must not include only males or females, whites or blacks, young or old, and so on. Such a picture must be representative of all potential applicants. Furthermore, an ad campaign must not be directed to a target audience that could result in possible discrimination due to the makeup of the target audience. Advertising must be directed to the entire community in a nondiscriminatory manner. A creditor found guilty of discriminatory advertising may be ordered to conduct an affirmative advertising campaign specifically aimed at the group suffering from past discrimination.

In addition to concerns about advertising, creditors must be aware of what information can be properly requested on an application. Recall that the purpose of the ECOA is to prohibit discrimination when extending credit on the basis of the applicant's race, color, religion, national origin, sex, marital status, age, receipt of income from a public assistance program, or exercise of a right under the law. The best way to avoid discrimination is not to request any information on which a discrimination charge can be based. With respect to the application form, the following are six general rules regarding information that should *not* be requested from the applicant:

1. A creditor should not inquire about an applicant's spouse or former spouse.
2. A creditor should not inquire about the applicant's marital status when the applicant will be individually liable.
3. A creditor should not inquire whether an applicant's income is derived from alimony, child support, or separate maintenance payments.
4. A creditor should not inquire about the sex of an applicant.
5. A creditor should not inquire about the applicant's birth control practices, capacity to bear children, or intention to have children.
6. A creditor should not inquire about an applicant's race, color, religion, or national origin.

3. Fair Credit Reporting Act

Shortly after an applicant has applied for a loan, the creditor normally will check on the applicant's credit history. This check may be conducted simply by examining the applicant's past record with this creditor. Or the creditor may contact a third party for a credit report. When this latter step occurs, the First Credit Reporting Act (FCRA) must be followed. The basic reason for the FCRA's enactment was to prevent abuses in credit-reporting systems. Furthermore, with this law, Congress provided a means to protect all individuals' privacy and to ensure accuracy with respect to the information in the reports covered.

The FCRA covers the compilation, distribution, and utilization of credit reports on consumers. Reports on businesses are not within the scope of this law. The FCRA governs the activities of both the consumer reporting agencies and the users of information provided by such agencies. The term **consumer reporting agency** includes any person who or entity that regularly collects information on consumers and furnishes it to third parties. In essence, these agencies are in the business of selling consumer reports for a fee. A **consumer report** is a written or oral communication relating to a consumer's creditworthiness, credit standing, credit capacity, character, general reputation, personal characteristics, or mode of living.

From these definitions, it is clear that a report containing information solely about transactions or experiences between the consumer and the party making the report is not covered by the FCRA. For example, a financial institution may be asked about its credit experience with one of its customers. If that institution reports only its experience with the customer, a consumer report, as defined in the FCRA, is not involved. The FCRA covers only consumer reporting agencies.

Consumer Reporting Agency The person or organization covered by the requirements of the Federal Credit Reporting Act because information on consumers is collected and sold.

Consumer report Any document that is sold by a consumer reporting agency.

4. Consumer Reporting Agencies

To be covered, a consumer report must be for use in connection with at least one of the following:

1. Extending credit
2. Hiring, transferring, promoting, or firing an employee
3. Selling insurance
4. Issuing a license, particularly one of a professional nature
5. Determining eligibility for governmental financial assistance

A reporting agency must take steps not to include obsolete information. In general, adverse information over seven years old is obsolete and should not be included in a consumer report. Information on bankruptcy cases over ten years old also is considered obsolete. Furthermore, all consumer reporting agencies must establish procedures that, when implemented, will prevent improper or inaccurate information from being included in a consumer report.

5. Users of Information

Those parties that decide whether a consumer will be extended credit, sold insurance, employed, or licensed may use information from two sources other than themselves. These two outside sources of information are consumer reporting agencies or someone else. Users of this information have an obligation to disclose the source of such information to the consumer. However, the duty to disclose and the extent of such disclosure depend on the source of information.

First, assume that adverse action was taken regarding a consumer's credit, insurance, or employment application because of some information contained in a consumer report. When the user of this information notifies the consumer of the adverse action, the user automatically must disclose the name and address of the consumer reporting agency that furnished the report. Without this requirement, the consumer would find it difficult to determine whether the information in the report was accurate.

Second, again assume that adverse action was because of some information furnished to the user by a party other than a consumer reporting agency. Before the FCRA requires the user to disclose the information relied on, that user and the consumer must follow several steps: (1) At the time notice of adverse action is given, the user also must notify the consumer that he or she has the right to request in writing the reasons for the adverse action being taken; (2) within sixty days after receiving the user's notice, the consumer must make a written request for an explanation of why this adverse action was taken; (3) after receiving the consumer's request for an explanation, the user must disclose the information on which the adverse decision was based.

These preceding paragraphs help clarify that the FCRA regulates users of consumer reports as well as the consumer reporting agency that compiles the report. In the following case, the issue of the user's liability focuses on what is a consumer report. The court had to resolve whether the FCRA became applicable when the information in the report was sought for a proper purpose or only when the report was used for a specific statutory purpose.

CASE

St. Paul Guardian Insurance Company v. Johnson
884 F.2d 881 (5th Cir. 1989)

JOHNSON, J.

In 1986, the appellant, Charles Johnson, (hereinafter Johnson) filed a claim with St. Paul Guardian Insurance Company (hereinafter St. Paul) for losses incurred as a result of an alleged theft at Johnson's rural home near Hardin, Texas. During the course of St. Paul's investigation of the claim, St. Paul investigators visited Johnson's home and became suspicious of Johnson's claim. The investigators noted in particular that the large number of items reported as stolen by Johnson could not have been easily contained in Johnson's small house. Additionally, the investigators got the impression that Johnson did not live in the house. Acting on their suspicions, the investigators undertook a more comprehensive investigation to determine whether the house was indeed Johnson's residence, as required by St. Paul's policy, and whether Johnson owned the items that he had reported as stolen.

During the course of the ensuing investigation, St. Paul investigators sought and obtained a copy of Johnson's credit report for investigative purposes. Ostensibly, the credit report had been secured in order to determine whether the house was Johnson's primary residence, and whether Johnson owned the items reportedly stolen. Ultimately, after the St. Paul investigators completed their investigation, the company denied Johnson's claim.

St. Paul then filed an action . . . seeking a declaratory judgment that St. Paul was not liable under the policy for Johnson's claim. Johnson counterclaimed alleging that St. Paul, during its investigation and denial of Johnson's claim, had violated provisions of the Fair Credit Reporting Act (FCRA). . . . The district court granted St. Paul's motion for a directed verdict against Johnson on the FCRA . . . claim. The jury returned a verdict in favor of St. Paul on Johnson's claim under the policy, finding that no theft had occurred. Thereafter, Johnson appealed the district court's directed verdict on Johnson's FCRA claim only. . . .

The FCRA was the product of Congressional concern over abuses in the credit reporting industry. The legislative history of the FCRA reveals that it was crafted to "protect an individual from inaccurate or arbitrary information . . . in a consumer report . . . ," and "to establish credit reporting practices that utilize accurate, relevant, and current information in a confidential and responsible manner." The FCRA defines a consumer report as

> . . . any written, oral, or other communication of any information by a consumer reporting agency bearing on a consumer's credit worthiness, credit standing, credit capacity, character, general reputation, personal characteristics, or mode of living which is used or expected to be used or collected in whole or in part for the purpose of serving as a factor in establishing the consumer's eligibility for (1) credit or insurance to be used primarily for personal, family, or household purposes, or (2) employment

purposes, or (3) other purposes authorized under section 1681b of this title.

In the instant case, St. Paul contends that because it did not "use" the information contained in Johnson's credit report for any of the enumerated purposes, . . . the credit report was not a consumer report within the meaning of the FCRA. Thus, St. Paul contends that its conduct with regard to its use of Johnson's credit report during the course of the investigation of Johnson's claim was not governed by the strictures of the FCRA. Johnson, on the other hand, argues that it is the "purpose" for which the information contained in the credit report was collected rather than its ultimate "use" which should control whether it should be deemed a consumer report under the FCRA or not. Our resolution of these two divergent positions will necessarily decide whether, in the instant case, the credit report obtained by St. Paul was a "consumer report" under the FCRA, and if so, whether St. Paul was obligated to comply with the provisions of the FCRA. . . .

The information contained in Johnson's credit report was not collected "solely for use" in evaluating Johnson's claim against St. Paul. Rather, the record indicates that St. Paul merely obtained a copy of a pre-existing credit report on Johnson containing information which had already been collected for purposes other than St. Paul's investigation of Johnson's claim. Although St. Paul did not ultimately use Johnson's credit report for one of the FCRA's enumerated purposes, the information in the report nevertheless was "collected in whole or in part" by a credit reporting agency for FCRA enumerated purposes. Thus, under a plain reading of § 1681a(d), the report obtained by St. Paul is a "consumer report" to which the provisions of the FCRA apply.

St. Paul's reading of the FCRA also creates irreconcilable conflicts between its statutory provisions. One of the central purposes of the FCRA was to restrict the purposes for which consumer reports may be used, for the simple reason that such reports may contain sensitive information about consumers that can easily be misused. To illustrate the untenable nature of St. Paul's construction of the FCRA in this context, suppose X secured Y's credit report for the sole purpose of disclosing it to embarrass Y. Under St. Paul's reasoning, focusing solely on X's "use" of the report, the report would not be a credit report under the FCRA and thus Y would not be afforded FCRA protections. Not only would this result run contrary to congressional intent, it would render meaningless FCRA section 1681b which allows for the release of credit reports only for certain purposes.

Under St. Paul's reasoning, credit reports would be releasable under all circumstances. If used for non-FCRA purposes, a credit report would be releasable because it did not fall with the FCRA definition of a consumer report. If used for FCRA purposes, a credit report would likewise be releasable because it would meet the definition of a consumer report. We simply cannot conclude that Congress intended such an illogical result. Accordingly, we reject St. Paul's argument that the definition of a "consumer report" under the FCRA depends on the use to which the information contained therein is put and conclude that the purpose for which the information was collected governs whether that report is a "consumer report" under the FCRA. We therefore hold that St. Paul was bound to comply with FCRA provisions in the handling of Johnson's credit report. . . .

We conclude that Johnson has standing to pursue his FCRA claim against St. Paul. . . .

■ *Reversed and remanded.*

CASE CONCEPTS REVIEW

1. Why did St. Paul obtain a consumer report on Johnson?
2. What is the argument asserted by St. Paul as to why it is not subject to the FCRA?
3. What is the argument asserted by Johnson as to why this case is within the scope of the FCRA?
4. Do you agree with the court's conclusion? Why?

6. Rights of Consumers

Any consumer has the right to and the consumer reporting agency has the duty to disclose the following items contained in that consumer's file:

1. The nature and substance of all information except medical records
2. The sources of that information
3. The parties receiving a consumer report for employment purposes within the prior two years and the parties receiving a consumer report for any other purposes within the prior six months

Before disclosing the information contained in the consumer's file, the consumer reporting agency must ask the consumer to provide proper identification.

When information from the consumer's file is made available to the consumer, he or she has the right to have the information explained by a competently trained employee of the consumer reporting agency.

The consumer has a right to the information in his or her file without any charge if the request is made within thirty days after the consumer receives either (1) notice of adverse action on an application for credit, insurance, or employment or (2) notice from a debt collection agency that his or her credit rating may be adversely affected. In other situations, consumers may be charged a reasonable fee when examining the contents of their files. This fee is collected by the consumer reporting agency.

Another important protection of consumers is their right to challenge the accuracy of information contained in the file. For instance, suppose that a consumer examines his or her file and has a justifiable reason to dispute the correctness or relevance of some information. The consumer must communicate this dispute's existence to the consumer reporting agency. Upon receiving this notice of dispute, the agency must reinvestigate the appropriateness of this information being in the consumer's file. As a result of such a reinvestigation, one of two steps must be followed.

First, if the consumer reporting agency determines that the information is inaccurate or cannot be verified, such information must be deleted from the file. Second, the reinvestigation may result in a finding that the disputed information is accurate and relevant. This second finding by the consumer reporting agency means that the dispute is not resolved. In this event, the consumer must be allowed to write a brief statement describing his or her position, to be included in that consumer's file. This statement may be limited to 100 words if the consumer reporting agency provides assistance to the consumer regarding the writing of the statement.

The consumer has the right to insist that this or some similar statement be included in any future consumer report furnished by the agency. Furthermore, upon the consumer's request, the agency must give notice that information has been deleted or give notice of a statement of the consumer's position to any user of a consumer report if that user received (1) a report related to an employment purpose within a two-year period or (2) a report related to any other purpose within a six-month period prior to the consumer's request.

To encourage enforcement of its provisions, the FCRA provides for both civil and criminal sanctions. Regarding civil liability, any consumer reporting agency or user of credit reports that *negligently* fails to comply with FCRA is liable to the consumer for that person's actual damages plus costs of the action and reasonable attorney's fees. Additionally, if the consumer reporting agency or user is shown to have *willfully* violated the FCRA's provisions, that party is liable for any punitive damages the court might award. Civil actions must be filed within two years of the date the violation occurred. If the violation involves misrepresentation of information, the statute of limitations begins running when the misrepresentation is discovered.

In the cases in which someone obtains information about a consumer from a consumer reporting agency under false pretenses, criminal sanctions may be imposed. When false pretenses are knowingly and willfully utilized, the perpetrator may be fined up to $5,000 or confined for up to one year or both.

The decision to extend the applicant credit also creates a number of legal requirements that must be satisfied. These requirements are found in the federal Truth-in-Lending Act and in the Uniform Consumer Credit Code if your state has adopted this code.

7. Truth-in-Lending Act: General Approach

The Truth-in-Lending Act (TILA) and Regulation Z issued by the Federal Reserve Board to implement the statute apply to any individual or business organization offering or extending credit. They apply whenever the following four conditions are met:

1. The applicant for credit is an individual consumer as contrasted with a corporation or other business organization.
2. Credit is offered or extended on a regular basis, which means the creditor extended consumer credit more than twenty-five times during the previous calendar year. If the creditor extended consumer credit secured by a dwelling at least five times, the regularity requirement is met.
3. The repayment of the credit extended is subject to a finance charge or is evidenced by a written agreement that allows for more than four installments.
4. Finally, the credit is for family, household, or personal uses. This fourth element of TILA's coverage once again emphasizes the consumer versus business nature of the loan covered by the act.

Consumer credit transactions are exempt from the act if the amount of credit extended exceeds $25,000. The reason for this exemption seems to be that consumer debtors who borrow over $25,000 have the sophistication to protect themselves. However, even untrained and inexperienced consumers borrow substantially more than $25,000 when they purchase a personal residence and use that residence as security. Therefore, mortgage transactions involving personal residences are not exempted from the Act's requirements regardless of the dollar amount involved.

8. Disclosures Required

The basic purpose of TILA has been, and continues to be, to encourage potential consumer debtors to shop for credit. To facilitate this comparison shopping, the Act requires the creditor to disclose certain items of information. Although there are numerous and technical disclosure requirements, the most important items to be revealed include the following:

1. The identity of the creditor
2. The amount financed
3. An itemization of the amount financed
4. The finance charge
5. The annual percentage rate
6. The payment schedule
7. The total amount of all payments

Of these, items 2, 4, 5, and 7 frequently are the most important.

AMOUNT FINANCED.   The amount financed by the creditor is calculated by taking the amount of the loan's principal, adding other amounts financed by the creditor that are not a part of the finance charge, and then subtracting the amount of any prepaid finance charge. This amount must be stated as a dollar figure and must be clearly marked as the "Amount Financed."

FINANCE CHARGE.   This item is considered one of the most important, and it is one of the most complex to calculate. Once again, this disclosure is in the form of a dollar figure. This finance charge figure quickly shows the consumer applicant what this credit transaction is costing over its term. In essence, this figure includes all charges paid by the consumer applicant when securing the extension of credit. This dollar figure is more than the total amount of all interest payments. The finance charge also includes all fees charged by the creditor as a cost of extending credit. Especially in long-term, mortgage-secured loans, it is not unusual for the finance charge to be greater than the amount financed.

ANNUAL PERCENTAGE RATE.   Along with the finance charge, the annual percentage rate (APR) is the second part of the all-important disclosure requirement of TILA. The APR can be used by consumer applicants to compare the cost of obtaining credit. This cost is expressed in terms of a percentage rate rather than in dollars, as with the finance charge. The APR is the cost of the credit expressed as a yearly rate. This rate is a measure that relates the amount and timing of the credit received by the consumer applicant to the amount and timing of the payments to be made by the applicant. The complex method of calculating the APR is beyond our purpose in this chapter. However, since the finance charge includes items in addition to interest payments, the APR is almost always higher than the quoted interest rate.

TOTAL AMOUNT OF ALL PAYMENTS.   Under the heading "Total Amount of All Payments," the creditor must disclose in a dollar figure the total amount the consumer debtor will have paid after all the payments have been made. A simple way to check the accuracy of this figure is to add the amount financed and the finance charge. This addition should equal the total amount of all payments. If the consumer applicant desires to do so, this figure can be a helpful source in comparing credit opportunities.

TILA also protects borrowers by prohibiting misleading advertising, such as representing lower down payments and lower installment payments than are actually available. If an advertisement contains any details of a credit plan, it must also include as disclosures substantial information on finance charges, rates, cash price, down payment, and other information included in the specific regulations used to enforce the law.

9. Sanctions for Truth-in-Lending Violations

TILA provides for both civil and criminal sanctions against creditors that fail to comply with the applicable provisions. For example, in a civil suit based on the creditor's failure to make all necessary disclosures, an individual plaintiff may recover two times the finance charge subject to a minimum of $100 and a maximum of $1,000. In a class action for improper disclosures, there is no limit on an individual's claim, but the class can recover only the lesser of $500,000 or 1 percent of the creditor's net worth.

Not all improper disclosures result in civil liability. Creditors that make bona fide errors in their disclosures are not necessarily liable. A bona fide error may include an inaccurate disclosure due to clerical, printing, or computer malfunctions.

Technical but immaterial violations do not create a ground to hold creditors liable for dollar damages.

Although it is rare, the Justice Department can bring criminal charges against a creditor for violating TILA. To be a crime, failure to make adequate and accurate disclosures must be done knowingly and willfully. The criminal violation is punishable by up to a $5,000 fine or up to one year in confinement or some combination of the two.

The TILA allows consumer-debtors to rescind the credit transaction if they have granted to the creditor a mortgage-type interest in their personal residence. This right of rescission is a part of the law as a method of protecting the debtor's interest in the residence. The creditor must give the debtor notice of this right of rescission, and this notice must state the duration of the rescission period.

Typically, if all TILA disclosures are made properly, the period of rescission expires at midnight of the third business day after the credit transaction is completed. If disclosures, including notice of the right of rescission, are not made or are defective, the period of rescission extends for three years after the transaction is completed. The following case illustrates the potential impact of the debtor's right to rescind the credit transaction.

CASE

Jackson v. Grant
890 F.2d 118 (9th Cir. 1989)

CANBY, J.

Edna Jackson appeals the district court's judgment denying her rescission under the Federal Truth in Lending Act, ("TILA"). Jackson seeks to rescind a loan transaction entered into with Union Home Loans ("Union"), a real estate loan broker. She contends that notice of her right to cancel the loan was not properly given. . . .

On February 18, 1983, Jackson received, read and executed the following documents:

(1) TILA Disclosure Statement;

(2) Mortgage Loan Disclosure Statement;

(3) Summary and Acknowledgement of the Terms of the Loan Transaction (hereinafter "Summary of Loan Terms");

(4) Deed of Trust;

(5) Promissory Note;

(6) Notice of Right to Cancel.

The TILA Disclosure Statement listed the annual percentage rate, the finance charge, the amount financed, the total payments, and the payment schedule for the loan. The Mortgage Loan Disclosure Statement and the Statement of Loan Terms informed Jackson that Union will not be the lender, that the lender is presently not known and that Jackson was not guaranteed a loan. The name of the lender was left blank on the Promissory Note and Deed of Trust. The Notice of Right to Cancel specified March 1, 1983 as the last date for cancellation.

Unable to find another lender, on April 28, 1983, Union sent a letter to Jackson advising her that the "loan will be made with funds owned or controlled by Union Home Loans." The terms of the loan were set out in the note and deed of trust executed, and the Disclosure Statement presented, on February 18, 1983, except that Jackson was required to pay an additional $700.00 and to delete credit life insurance from the loan. Jackson agreed to these changes and the loan closed on April 29, 1983.

On February 7, 1986, Jackson notified Sid and Belle G. Grant, assignees of the loan made by Union, of her election to cancel the loan transaction pursuant to the TILA. She filed a complaint seeking rescission on February 10, 1986. . . . Jackson argued that the loan transaction was not "consummated" until April of 1983 and that she therefore did not receive proper notice of her right to cancel the transaction within three business days following consummation. . . .

The TILA was enacted by Congress to "avoid the uninformed use of credit." In order to effectuate this purpose, the TILA has been liberally construed in this circuit. Even technical or minor violations of the TILA impose liability on the creditor.

Section 125(a) of the TILA provides that in credit transactions in which a security interest in a consumer's residence is retained:

the [consumer] shall have the right to rescind the transaction until midnight of the third business day following the consummation of the transaction or the delivery of the information and rescission forms required under this section together with a statement containing the material disclosures required under this subchapter, whichever is later.

This right of rescission is further explained in Regulation Z of the Federal Reserve Board:

The consumer may exercise the right to rescind until midnight of the third business day following consummation, delivery of the notice [of the right to rescind], or delivery of all material disclosures, whichever occurs last. If the required notice or material disclosures are not delivered, the right to rescind shall expire 3 years after consummation.

Notice of the right to rescind must specify the date the rescission period expires. Jackson argues that because the loan transaction was not consummated until late April, the rescission period expired three business days after that date. Accordingly, the Notice of the Right to Cancel delivered to Jackson in February listed an incorrect expiration date of March 1, prior to the actual consummation of her loan. Therefore, the "required notice" was never delivered and the right to rescind the transaction extended until three years after the April consummation date.

Jackson's argument has merit. Under Regulation Z, consummation "means the time that a consumer becomes contractually obligated on a credit transaction.". . . If an essential element of the contract is reserved for the future agreement of both parties, there is generally no legal obligation created until such an agreement is entered into. It is essential not only that the parties to the contract exist, but that it is possible to identify them.

In the present case, on February 18, 1983, Jackson executed a series of documents which designated herself as the borrower and Union as the "broker" or "arranger of credit." Several documents . . . explicitly state that Union

is not the lender and that Jackson was not guaranteed a loan by signing the loan documents. . . . While it is not necessary to decide what, if any, binding agreement was created by and between Jackson and Union on February 18, one conclusion is inescapable. No one, including Union, had agreed to extend credit to Jackson as of that date and no loan transaction was "consummated." The lender is unidentifiable and therefore no valid loan contract existed.

At most, the February 18 documents constituted an offer by Jackson to accept a loan under the terms specified. That offer was not "accepted" until Union agreed to fund Jackson's loan itself. Because no contract existed, Jackson was not "contractually obligated.". . .

Because the loan transaction was not consummated until late April and Jackson received no notice of her TILA cancellation right and the expiration date at that time, Jackson's right to rescind extended three years and her request for rescission several months before her balloon payment was due was timely. We reach this conclusion without great enthusiasm, for Jackson received many of the benefits of the agreement she is now rescinding. Nevertheless, Congress did not intend for TILA to apply only to sympathetic consumers; Congress designed the law to apply to all consumers, who are inherently at a disadvantage in loan and credit transactions.

■ *Reversed and remanded.*

CASE CONCEPTS REVIEW

1. When did Jackson receive notice that she could rescind the credit transaction? What date was given as the duration of this right of rescission?
2. When did Jackson and Union complete their credit transaction?
3. When did Jackson give notice that she was rescinding this transaction?
4. Why does this court conclude that Jackson's rescission was made on a timely basis?

10. Uniform Consumer Credit Code

All the federal laws discussed in this chapter do not preempt state consumer credit protection laws as long as these state laws do not narrow the protection provided by Congress. Because of the diversity among the states concerning protection of consumers in credit transactions, the Commissioners on Uniform State Laws have prepared a proposed uniform law similar to many of the federal laws. The Uniform Consumer Credit Code (UCCC) attempts to protect consumers by utilizing the technique of full disclosure of all pertinent facts about the credit transaction to buyers. The UCCC is applicable to virtually every transaction involving credit: retail installment sales, consumer credit, small loans, and usury.

The UCCC does not fix rates of interest but rather sets maximums that may be charged. When the amount financed is $300 or less, the maximum is 36 percent per year; and when the amount is more than $300 but less than $1,000, it is 21 percent per year. The credit code has detailed provisions covering matters such as delinquency charges, deferral charges, service charges on refinancing or loan consolidation, and revolving charge accounts. It also prohibits most deficiency judgments when goods sold as a part of a consumer credit sale are repossessed.

The UCCC requires a written disclosure that *conspicuously* sets forth the required facts prior to a sale or loan. Just as in the Truth-in-Lending Act, the annual percentage rate is the key fact that must be disclosed. The difference between the cash price and the credit price is also essential as a part of the disclosure. The provisions on advertising generally require that the ad include the rate of the credit service charge as well as the amount of the charge.

In addition to regulating the cost of credit, the UCCC prohibits certain types of agreements. It prohibits the use of the holder-in-due course concept and outlaws agreements cutting off defenses. It prohibits the use of multiple agreements to obtain higher interest. It also prohibits *balloon payments.* If any scheduled payment is more than twice as large as the average payment, the buyer has the right to refinance the balloon payment, without penalty, on terms no less favorable than the original terms. The balloon-payment provision is not applicable to a sale for agricultural purposes or one pursuant to a revolving charge account.

The UCCC prohibits debtors from assigning their earnings as part of a credit sale. In addition, lenders are not allowed to take an assignment of earnings for payment of a debt arising out of a consumer loan. The UCCC also prohibits referral sales schemes in which the buyer is given credit on a purchase for furnishing the names of other possible purchasers.

Violations of the UCCC may be punished criminally. In addition, debtors are relieved of their obligation to pay the finance charge, and they are entitled to recover, from creditors who violate the law, up to three times the finance charge actually paid. Of course, debtors are not obligated to pay charges in excess of those allowable by the act. If a debtor entitled to a refund is refused a refund, the debtor is entitled to recover the total amount of the credit service charge or ten times the excess charge, whichever is greater. If the excess charge was in deliberate violation of the act, the penalty may be recovered even if the excess has been repaid.

This UCCC proposal has received modest approval, being adopted by only nine states: Colorado, Idaho, Indiana, Iowa, Kansas, Maine, Oklahoma, Utah, and Wyoming. South Carolina and Wisconsin have legislation substantially similar to the UCCC.

DEBT COLLECTION

11. Fair Credit Billing Act

From the creditor's perspective, after credit has been extended the next stage of the transaction is collection from the debtor. Prior to being able to collect an amount owed, the creditor must inform the consumer-debtor what is owed. This information is conveyed through a *billing.* Due to the problem a mistake in a billing could cause, the Fair Credit Billing Act (FCBA) was enacted. The FCBA is applicable only to open-ended consumer credit transactions. A billing error associated with any business loan or with a consumer closed-end transaction is *not* covered by the FCBA.

DEFINITIONS.   The term *billing error*, as used in the FCBA, can consist of a periodic statement containing any of the following: (1) a reflection of credit not actually extended, (2) a reflection of credit extended of which the debtor seeks clarification, (3) a reflection of the cost of goods and services not received by the debtor or by an authorized agent, (4) a reflection of a computational error made by the creditor, (5) a failure to reflect a payment made by the debtor, and (6) a failure to reflect the type of transaction involved. A billing error also occurs when the creditor fails to send the periodic statement to the borrower's last known address if that address has been given to the creditor at least twenty days before the end of a billing cycle.

A *billing error notice* is a written notice received by a creditor from a consumer-debtor. This notice must contain the consumer-debtor's statement that a billing error exists, and there must be a statement as to why the consumer believes such error exists. Furthermore, this notice must enable the creditor to identify the following items: (1) the consumer-debtor's name, (2) the account number, and (3) the type, date, and amount of the billing error. Finally, this notice must be received by the creditor within sixty days after the first periodic statement containing the error was sent by the creditor for the provisions of the act to apply.

CREDITOR'S GENERAL DUTIES.   If a creditor receives a billing error notice, that creditor must, first of all, acknowledge in writing to the consumer-debtor the receipt of the notice within thirty days of its actual receipt. Second, the creditor, within two billing cycles but not more than ninety days after the notice is received, must either (1) correct the error, credit the account for the correct amount, and send a notice of the correction made; or (2) send a written statement of clarification to the consumer-debtor as to why the creditor believes no error has been made.

Until a billing error has been corrected or until an explanation of the billing's accuracy has been sent and received, the creditor cannot (1) restrict the credit available to the consumer-debtor, (2) close that account, and (3) report or even threaten to report the consumer-debtor's nonpayment to a credit rating organization. A report to a credit-reporting agency may be made after the creditor has sent an explanation of why there is no billing error and after the time for payment has passed if the consumer-debtor has not reasserted the billing error's existence. If a dispute continues to exist, the creditor may make a credit report if the following steps are satisfied: (1) The report must indicate that the amount or account is in dispute, (2) the creditor must mail or otherwise deliver to the consumer-debtor a written notice of the name and address of all persons receiving the credit report, and (3) the creditor promptly must make a report of any subsequent resolution of the dispute to all those who received the original report.

The FCBA also regulates some of the accounting practices of creditors. For example, prompt posting of all payments is required to prevent additional finance charges being billed to the consumer-debtor's account. Furthermore, creditors of revolving charge accounts cannot impose finance charges on a new purchase made by the consumer-debtor unless a statement including the amount on which the finance charge for that period is based is mailed at least fourteen days before the date the finance charge will be imposed if full payment is not made.

12. Credit Card Protection

Lost or stolen credit cards are often used for unauthorized purchases, resulting in a loss to (1) the business that dealt with the wrong person, (2) the credit card company, which may be the same as (1), as in the case of an oil company's gasoline credit card, or (3) the actual cardholder. TILA seeks to limit the cardholder's loss and to impose most of the losses on the issuer of the card. For example, the law prohibits the issuance of credit cards except upon application or upon the renewal of an existing card. Thus, the person to whom a card is issued has no liability for unauthorized purchases if that card was issued without being requested.

TILA further provides that a cardholder is liable only up to the lesser of the amount charged or $50 for the unauthorized use of a credit card, and then only if all the following conditions are met:

1. The credit card is an accepted card, one that the cardholder had requested.
2. The charge is made prior to the cardholder's giving notice to the issuer that the card was lost or stolen.
3. Within two years before the unauthorized use, the issuer warned the cardholder of his or her potential liability for unauthorized use.
4. The issuer had provided the cardholder with a preaddressed notice form that may be mailed to the issuer in the event the card is lost or stolen.

The warning to the cardholder mentioned in condition 3 may be given by printing it on the card. This notice must state that the liability in the case of loss or theft shall not exceed $50. The cardholder also must be informed in a clear manner that the notice of loss or theft may be given orally as well as in writing.

Finally, no cardholder is liable unless the issuer has provided a method whereby the user of the card can be identified as the person authorized to use it. This identification traditionally has been by the cardholder's signature, photograph, or fingerprint on the card. To reduce the problem of counterfeiting credit cards, the means of identifying the cardholder has shifted to mechanical and electronic devices.

13. Fair Debt Collection Practices Act

The Fair Debt Collection Practices Act (FDCPA) was adopted to prevent the use of abusive, deceptive, and unfair debt collection practices by debt collectors. This law is also intended to ensure the competitiveness of those debt collectors that are not utilizing abusive tactics.

The FDCPA is directed toward those that are in the business of collecting debts owed to someone else. For example, creditors are not subject to the FDCPA's provisions unless they attempt to collect a debt by using a name that does not reveal that creditor's identity. Creditors are exempt from this law because it is believed that creditors will not engage in unfair debt collection practices with their customers. This belief is based on the fact that creditors will not jeopardize their goodwill with their debtors by using questionable practices.

The FDCPA is applicable only to the collection of consumers' debts. The law presumes that business debtors are able to protect themselves from unfair debt collection practices.

The law permits a bill collector to communicate with third parties, such as neighbors or employers of the debtor, but it limits the contact. Third parties may not be informed that the consumer owes a debt. When an attorney represents the debtor and the bill collector knows it, the collector may not get in touch with anyone else except the attorney, unless the attorney fails to respond to the collector's communication.

The Act also restricts the methods that may be used in the collection process. The collector may not (1) physically threaten the debtor, (2) use obscene language, (3) pretend to be an attorney, (4) threaten the debtor with arrest or garnishment unless the collector or creditor is legally entitled to such action and intends to take it, or (5) telephone the debtor repeatedly with intent to annoy. In telephoning the debtor, the collector must make a meaningful disclosure of his or her identity and may not telephone collect or call before 8:00 A.M. or after 9:00 P.M. In addition to these specific prohibitions, the Act forbids the collector from using any "unfair or unconscionable" means to collect the debt.

If a debtor desires to stop repeated contacts, he or she need only notify the collector in writing of this wish. Any further contact by the collector following such notification violates the Act. The collector's sole remedy in such cases is to sue the debtor. Violations of the law entitle the debtor to sue the collector for actual damages, including damages for invasion of privacy and infliction of mental distress, court costs, and attorney's fees. In the absence of actual damages, the court may still order the collector to pay the debtor up to $1,000 for violations.

The FDCPA requires that the collector give notice to the debtor that this collector will be attempting to collect the debt instead of the creditor. This notice must let the debtor know that any information obtained will be used for the purposes of collection. The notice also must inform the debtor of the statutory rights to have the debt verified. Upon the debtor's written request for verification of the debt, collection practices must stop until the verification is forthcoming. The following case illustrates the court's concern about the format of this notice.

CASE

Miller v. Payco-General American Credits, Inc.
943 F.2d 482 (4th Cir. 1991)

WILKINSON, J.

This case examines whether a form letter used by a debt collection agency observed the rights of consumers under the Fair Debt Collection Practices Act....

Lenvil Miller owed $2,501.61 to the Star Bank of Cincinnati. Star Bank referred collection of Miller's account to Payco-General American Credits, Inc. ("Payco"), a debt collection agency. Payco then sent to Miller the collection form which is the source of the controversy.

Across the top of the one page form is the title, "DEMAND FOR PAYMENT," in large, red, boldface type. After the title follows information as to the creditor, the amount owed, and Payco's address. In the middle of the page, again in large, red, boldface type, is the statement, "THIS IS A DEMAND FOR IMMEDIATE FULL PAYMENT OF YOUR DEBT." That statement is followed by these sentences in black boldface type: YOUR SERIOUSLY PAST DUE ACCOUNT HAS BEEN GIVEN TO US FOR IMMEDIATE ACTION. YOU HAVE HAD AMPLE TIME TO PAY YOUR DEBT, BUT YOU HAVE NOT. IF THERE IS A VALID REASON, PHONE US AT [telephone number] TODAY. IF NOT, PAY US—NOW. The bottom third of the document is almost completely filled by the single word, "NOW," in white letters nearly two inches tall against a red background.

At the very bottom of the page, in the smallest type to appear on the form (letters one-eighth of an inch high), is the statement, "NOTICE: SEE REVERSE SIDE FOR IMPORTANT INFORMATION." The notice is printed in white against a red background. On the reverse of the document are four paragraphs printed in gray ink. The last three paragraphs contain the validation notice—that is, statements required by the Fair Debt Collection Practices Act (FDCPA) that inform the consumer how to obtain verification of the debt.

Miller brought suit against Payco . . . on the ground that the validation notice did not comply with the FDCPA. Miller did not dispute that Payco included all the debt validation information required by the FDCPA. Rather, Miller charged that the validation notice was contradicted by other parts of the collection letter, that it was overshadowed by the demands for immediate payment, and that it was not effectively conveyed to the consumer. The district court granted summary judgment for Payco, concluding that the company had complied with the FDCPA by printing the validation notice on the back of the document and referring to it on the front.

Miller now appeals.

Section 1692g requires collector to send a consumer, either in its initial communication or within five days of its initial communication, a written notice containing: 1) the debt amount; 2) the name of the current creditor; 3) a statement that if the consumer disputes the debt in writing within thirty days, the collector will send verification of the debt to the consumer; 4) a statement that if the consumer does not dispute the debt within thirty days, the collector will assume the debt to be valid; 5) a statement that the collector will send the name of the original creditor, upon written request within thirty days. If the consumer, in writing, disputes the debt or requests the name of the original creditor, then the collector must halt all collection efforts until it mails verification of the debt or the creditor's name to the consumer.

In interpreting the demands of the FDCPA, we bear in mind that the statute was enacted "to eliminate abusive debt collection practices" which "contribute to the number of personal bankruptcies, to marital instability, to the loss of jobs, and to invasions of individual privacy." Congress included the debt validation provisions in order to guarantee that consumers would receive adequate notice of their legal rights. Thus, a debt collector does not comply with § 1692g merely by inclusion of the required debt validation notice; the notice Congress required must be conveyed effectively to the debtor. For example, a validation notice printed on the back of a form letter where the front of the letter contains no reference at all to the notice does not comply with § 1692g. Furthermore, in order to be effective, the notice must not be overshadowed or contra-

dicted by other messages or notices appearing in the initial communication from the collection agency.

We agree with Miller that the form he received from Payco both contradicted and overshadowed the required validation notice, preventing the notice's effective communication. The front of the Payco form demands "IMMEDIATE FULL PAYMENT" and commands the consumer to "PHONE US TODAY," emphasized by the word "NOW" emblazoned in white letters nearly two inches tall against a red background. The message conveyed by those statements on the face of the form flatly contradicts the information contained on the back.

A consumer who wished to obtain validation of his debt could lose his rights under the statute if he followed the commands to telephone. Section 1692g guarantees that validation will be sent and collection activities will cease only when the consumer disputes the debt in writing. If a consumer attempted to exercise his statutory rights by making the requested telephone call, Payco would be under no obligation to comply with section 1692g's directives to verify the debt and to cease collection efforts. The language on the front of the form emphatically instructs consumers to dispute their debt by telephone, in opposition to the statutory requirements.

The emphasis on immediate action also stands in contradiction to the FDCPA, which provides consumers a thirty day period to decide to request validation. A consumer who received Payco's form could easily be confused between the commands to respond "immediately," "now," and "today," and the thirty day response time contemplated by the statute. . . .

The manner of Payco's presentation plainly undercuts and overshadows the message of the validation notice. Screaming headlines, bright colors and huge lettering all point to a deliberate policy on the part of the collector to evade the spirit of the notice statute, and mislead the debtor into disregarding the notice. We do not believe on these facts that Payco effectively conveyed the validation notice to Miller. . . .

■ *Reversed and remanded.*

CASE CONCEPTS REVIEW

1. Upon reading the front side of the letter Payco sent Miller, what impression would the reader likely form?

2. Did this form letter contain an accurate description of Miller's rights under the law?

3. Why does the court conclude that the FDCPA has been violated in this factual situation?

14. Limitations on Garnishment

A logical source from which a debt can be collected from a consumer-debtor is that person's earnings. Legal action may be taken to use the debtor's earnings to pay a debt. This legal process is known as *garnishment*. Because garnishment may adversely affect the consumer's employment and his or her family's welfare, Congress has statutorily limited the amount of earnings that can be subject to garnishment.

Disposable earnings are that part of a consumer's earnings left after all withholdings required by law are deducted from the earnings. In general, the federal maximum amount of the total disposable earnings subject to garnishment in any week may not exceed the *lesser* of the following: (1) 25 percent of the disposable earnings for the week or (2) the amount by which the disposable earnings for that week exceed thirty times the federal minimum hourly wage prescribed by the Fair Labor Standards Act. For example, suppose that a consumer-debtor has disposable earnings of $500 per week and these earnings are subject to garnishment. What is the federal limit on the amount garnished? The answer is $125. The calculation of 25 percent of disposable earnings is $125, whereas this amount of disposable earnings exceeding thirty times the minimum wage ($4.25 per hour) is $127.50. Since $125 is the lesser of the amounts calculated, it is the garnishment limit.

In the past some employers have discharged employees when their earnings were garnished. The federal law now prohibits this discharge on the basis that the employee's earnings have been subject to garnishment for only one indebtedness. (By implication, the law seems to permit the dismissal of an employee from employment if there are garnishments involving two or more indebtednesses owed by that employee.) If an employer violates this provision limiting the discharge of employees, the employer may be fined up to $1,000 or imprisoned up to one year, or any combination of these two sentences.

The federal law does not preempt the field of garnishment or affect any state law. Many state laws exempt larger amounts than does the federal law, and the net effect of the federal law is to exempt the larger amount that either provides. Both the state and the federal laws illustrate a public policy against using a wage earner's income to pay judgment debts. In some states, the amount exempt is left to the courts, to avoid undue hardship on the debtor.

OTHER CONSUMER PROTECTION LAWS

15. Magnuson-Moss Warranty Act

In the past, warranties have been written in language so technical and misleading that many so-called warranties on products were actually disclaimers of warranties. Prior to the adoption of the federal law on warranties and the Federal Trade Commission (FTC) rules designed to accomplish its goals, a wide gap separated what the consumer was led to believe and what the manufacturer and seller would do under a warranty. To alleviate this problem, to provide consumers with adequate information about express warranties, and to prevent deceptive warranties, Congress enacted the Magnuson-Moss Warranty Act. This law and the FTC rules adopted under it are applicable to the sale of all consumer products costing over $5. The law is not applicable to service contracts or to leases.

This law does not require that a warranty be given. However, if a warranty is made by the seller, that warranty must satisfy the requirements stated in the following paragraphs. Specifically, the Magnuson-Moss Act provides guidance concerning express warranties, implied warranties, and mechanisms for resolving disputes.

EXPRESS WARRANTIES.   The first requirement of the law is that a warrantor of a consumer product must, by means of a written warranty, fully and conspicuously disclose in simple and readily understood language the terms and conditions of the warranty. The law and the rules then specify what must be included in the written warranty. Such a warranty must include, among other things, a statement of what the warrantor will do in the event of a defect or breach of warranty, at whose expense, and for what period of time. Furthermore, the warranty must set forth the step-by-step procedure the consumer is to follow to obtain performance of the warranty.

Any exceptions or limitations of the warranty must be indicated. A warrantor may not exclude or limit consequential damages for breach of any warranty unless the exclusion or limitation appears conspicuously on the face of the warranty.

The law also requires that each warranty be labeled "full" or "limited" if the product sells for over $15. A *full warranty* must indicate its duration. Products covered by a full warranty must be repaired or replaced by the seller without charge and within a reasonable time in the event there is a defect, malfunction, or failure to conform to the written warranty. A purchaser of a *limited warranty* is put on notice to find out its limits.

To assist the consumer in making an intelligent purchase decision, sellers are required to make available all information about the warranties. Prior to the sale, this information must be clearly and conspicuously displayed in close connection with the warranted product. If the contract involves a used car, the FTC has issued specific rules that must be complied with to provide consumers with accurate warranty information.

IMPLIED WARRANTIES.   Under the federal law, a warrantor may not impose any limitation on the duration of any implied warranty. No supplier may disclaim or modify any implied warranty if there is a written warranty or if, at the time of sale or within ninety days, the supplier enters into a service contract with the buyer. The latter restriction does not prevent a seller from limiting the time period of a written warranty. The time period of the warranty must also be set forth in clear and unmistakable language on the face of the warranty.

MECHANISMS TO RESOLVE DISPUTES.   A significant aspect of the federal law deals with informal mechanisms for the resolution of consumer disputes. The law does not require such mechanisms, but it strongly encourages sellers to use them. If a seller establishes a procedure for an independent or government entity to resolve disputes with its buyers, the consumer must resort to the procedure before filing suit against the seller. Consumers are given access to these informal dispute procedures free of charge.

Violations of the warranty law subject the business to a suit for damages. This cause of action is in addition to a suit under the Uniform Commercial Code. The law also authorizes class action suits for damages for breach of warranty if at least

100 persons are affected. The law also allows consumers to collect attorney's fees if legal counsel is required to enforce a warranty. This makes litigation a reasonable alternative even though the cost of the product is not substantial. Without the provision authorizing attorney's fees, consumer suits in breach of warranty cases would rarely be the subject of litigation.

16. Housing Warranties

Due to the nature of the transaction, the buyer of real estate normally will have had very little opportunity to inspect the real estate and its improvements prior to the signing of a contract. Therefore, during the time prior to the closing, the buyer should make an effort to inspect the property thoroughly. A smart buyer would seek the assistance of experts to inspect, when applicable, the roof, the air-conditioning and heating unit, the plumbing, the electrical wiring, and other major appliances and utilities. Even after such inspections, the buyer may not discover some substantial defect that adversely affects the property's value.

Buyers have been allowed to rescind purchases on the ground of fraud or misrepresentation, but historically warranties were found to exist only when specifically included in the contract. In other words, the seller of housing was not held responsible for the habitability of the structure or the quality of workmanship and materials. In recent years, most states have changed the law as it relates to the sale of housing but have retained the doctrine of *caveat emptor* for vacant real estate. The courts in these states have imposed liability on sellers and builders of housing by use of a variety of theories. Some courts have held that there is an implied warranty against structural defects, similar to the implied warranty of fitness in the sale of personal property, and that there is no rational basis for differentiating between the sale of a newly constructed house by the builder-vendor and the sale of any other manufactured product. These courts usually have not extended the warranty against structural defects to the individual who builds a house and later decides to sell it. Casual sales and resales are not included because the warranty arises when the seller is in the business of selling housing. Furthermore, warranties of habitability usually are not implied in the sale of vacant land.

Other courts have created an implied warranty that a home is built and constructed in a reasonably workmanlike manner and that it is fit for its intended purpose—habitation. In one case, there was no water supply, and the subdivider-seller was held liable for breach of this warranty. In another case, the air-conditioning system did not work properly, and the seller was held to have breached an implied warranty. In some cases, the buyer is entitled to damages. If the breach is so great that the home is unfit for habitation, rescission is an available remedy. However, the theory of implied warranty does not impose on the builder an obligation to build a perfect house.

The issue of whether the builder's liability is limited to the first purchaser or extends to subsequent purchasers has caused courts a great deal of difficulty. Some courts have held that subsequent purchasers are protected by the builder's implied warranty. Other courts have ruled that the subsequent purchaser can recover when it is proved the builder was negligent. The distinctions between implied warranty and negligence theories are subtle and at times confusing, as is illustrated in the following case.

CASE

Cosmopolitan Homes, Inc. v. Weller
663 P.2d 1041 (Colo. 1983)

DUBOFSKY, J.

We granted certiorari to review the Court of Appeals' holding in *Weller v. Cosmopolitan Homes, Inc.*, which allowed subsequent purchasers of a home to assert a claim for property damage to the structure allegedly caused by the negligence of the homebuilder. We affirm the judgment of the Court of Appeals but limit the negligence claim to latent defects which the purchaser was unable to discover prior to purchase.

The plaintiffs, Shirley Mae Weller and William S. Weller, are the fourth owners of a house designed, built and sold in 1973 by the defendants Cosmopolitan Homes, Inc., Hutchinson Construction Company, and Builders' Research Engineering Company (the builders). Although the Wellers seek to recover for deficiencies in workmanship, design and materials in the house attributable to negligent design and construction by the defendants, the facts alleged in the complaint relate to cracking in the foundation from movement or settling of the house which had not occurred at the time the Wellers made their purchase on January 4, 1977.

The district court dismissed the Wellers' complaint on the ground that there was no privity of contract between the defendants and the Wellers because the Wellers were not the first purchasers or users of the house, and therefore the defendants did not owe the Wellers a duty of reasonable care. The Court of Appeals reversed the district court ruling, holding that regardless of lack of privity of contract, the purchaser of a used home may recover for property damage caused by the negligence of the builder.

On certiorari review, the defendants argue that a claim for negligence against a builder is indistinguishable as a matter of proof from a claim of breach of implied warranty of habitability. The defendants therefore assert that the builder should not be held liable in a negligence action brought by a subsequent purchaser because case law in Colorado has limited an implied warranty's protection to first purchasers. We disagree with the defendants' assertion. An obligation to act without negligence in the construction of a home is independent of contractual obligations such as an implied warranty of habitability. . . .

The policy supporting the extension of the negligence remedy to a subsequent purchaser is based on many of the reasons for implying a warranty of habitability to the first purchaser. . . .

[G]iven the mobility of most potential home owners, it is foreseeable that a house will be sold to subsequent purchasers, and any structural defects are as certain to harm the subsequent purchaser as the first. We see no reason for disallowing a subsequent purchaser to state a claim in negligence.

Although some states have allowed both a claim for negligence against a builder and a claim for implied warranty to be brought by subsequent purchasers, and despite the claim of the builder here that the two claims are indistinguishable as a matter of proof, we conclude that there are a number of differences between the two claims and therefore they should be treated differently. Some overlap in elements of proof of such actions may occur, but the scope of duty differs and the basis for liability is distinguishable. The implied warranty of habitability and fitness arises from the contractual relation between the builder and the purchaser. Proof of a defect due to improper construction, design, or preparation is sufficient to establish liability in the builder-vendor. Negligence, however, requires that a builder or contractor be held to a standard of reasonable care in the conduct of its duties to the foreseeable users of the property. Negligence in tort must establish defects in workmanship, supervision, or design as a responsibility of the individual defendant. Proof of defect alone is not enough to establish the claim. Foreseeability limits the scope of the duty, and the passage of time following construction makes causation difficult to prove. Moreover, in the context of the purchase of a used home, the owner must demonstrate that the defect is latent or hidden, and must show that the defect was caused by the builder.

The reason for allowing recovery only for latent or hidden defects, which have been defined as "those manifesting themselves after purchase and which are not discoverable through reasonable inspection," is to prevent an action where mere deterioration or loss of a bargain is claimed. Often a buyer is willing to accept certain deficiencies in a house in exchange for a lower purchase price. However, a buyer cannot be expected to discover structural defects which remain latent at the time of purchase.

■ *Affirmed.*

CASE CONCEPTS REVIEW

1. What is the basis of the Wellers' complaint against the builders of their home?
2. Why did the trial court dismiss this complaint? What was the ruling of the court of appeals?
3. What distinctions does this court make between a negligence claim and breach of warranty claim?
4. Why does this court limit the Wellers' claim to that for those defects that were latent or hidden when the Wellers purchased this house?

This issue of how to protect subsequent purchasers may be of less importance today because of the variety of builder-supported programs that give the buyers of new homes an express warranty for a stated period. These warranties require the builder or an insurance company to repair major defects discovered within the period of coverage. Actually these warranties can be positive selling points for the property, since they can be transferred during the time provided. Express warranty programs as well as court-adopted remedies involving implied warranties and negligence make it clear that consumer protection has been extended to housing.

17. Consumer Product Safety Act

The Consumer Product Safety Act created the Consumer Product Safety Commission and a Product Safety Advisory Council. This law imposes safety standards on manufacturing and commercial operations relating to consumer products and, with a few exceptions, identifies and regulates almost all aspects of safety in products sold to the public. Since there is no requirement that the goods be sold, the law covers free samples and products sold to others but used by consumers. The breadth of the law is apparent from its definition of *consumer product*. The term includes any article produced or distributed for sale to, or use by, a consumer in or around a permanent or temporary household or residence, a school, in recreation, or otherwise.

Manufacturers of consumer products are required to furnish information about their products to the commission. This information may include technical data; it must include all information on new products. The law also requires manufacturers to notify the commission whenever they learn that a product is defective or fails to meet applicable standards. Notice also must be given to the general public and to known purchasers whenever it is found that a product is defective or in violation of a safety rule.

Once a product safety rule has been adopted, a variety of private and public enforcement procedures are available. Courts are authorized to issue injunctions, which may result in the removal of a product from the market. The law provides a penalty of $2,000 for each violation, up to a maximum of $500,000 for each product involved in a violation. A consumer is authorized to sue in federal courts for injuries caused by a product if the manufacturer is knowingly in violation of a product safety rule, provided the claim meets the jurisdictional amount ($50,000) of the federal courts.

18. Unfair Business Practices

By federal statute, the Federal Trade Commission is responsible for preventing unfair or deceptive acts or practices in commerce. As a result of this law, the FTC has a Bureau of Consumer Protection actively engaged in regulating advertising and the sale of goods. Advertising is unfair or deceptive if it has a tendency or capacity to mislead consumers.

The FTC has found numerous unfair and deceptive promotional devices and advertisements. One ad violated the law by comparing the seller's price with a higher "regular" price or a manufacturer's list price. It is deceptive to refer to a "regular price" unless the seller usually and recently sold the items at that price in the regular course of business. Also, it has been held deceptive to refer to the "manufacturer's list price" when that list price is not the ordinary and customary retail sales price of the item in the locality. Bait and switch promotions are another violation of the FTC Act. In a *bait and switch* sales technique, a product is advertised at a low price that will bring in customers whom the advertiser then tries to switch to other products.

Ads that are false or misleading about the quality of a product or its source are also unfair and deceptive. Disparaging the product of a competitor may be stopped by the FTC on the ground that such ads are unfair. Words that are technically not false may be held to be deceptive if they give the wrong impression to consumers. The words *guaranteed for life* were held to be deceptive when the seller intended the life to be the life of the product, and consumers thought that the guarantee was for the life of the purchaser of the product.

Many states have laws designed to aid and protect consumers in a multitude of transactions. These laws, which are enacted pursuant to the police power, are usually enforced by the state attorney general, but they may be enforced by consumers and class-action suits.

19. Home Solicitation

Under its authority to prevent unfair deceptive business practices, the Federal Trade Commission has regulated door-to-door selling. The FTC rule covers any sale, lease, or rental of consumer goods with a purchase price of $25 or more at places of business other than the normal place of business of the seller. It does not cover mail-order or telephone sales or sales in which the buyer has requested the seller to visit his home.

The law requires the seller to furnish the buyer with a copy of the contract in the same language—for example, Spanish—used in the oral presentation. The contract must, in 10-point type, notify the buyer that the transaction may be canceled at any time prior to midnight of the third business day after the date of the transaction. The seller is required to furnish the buyer with a form to be used to cancel, so all the buyer is required to do is to sign the form and send it to the seller. The seller also must orally inform the buyer of the right to cancel.

The law requires the seller to honor the notice of cancellation within ten days, refund all payments made and all property traded in, and return any instruments assigned by the buyer. If the purchase is canceled, all security arrangements are null and void. If the goods have been delivered to the buyer prior to cancellation, the seller must, within ten days, notify the buyer whether the seller intends to repossess or to abandon the goods.

20. Real Estate Settlement Procedures Act

Since the purchase of a home is the most significant transaction ever entered into by most people, the law contains provisions aimed at assisting buyers with this transaction. At one time, the amount of settlement costs or closing costs in real estate transactions often came as a surprise, if not a shock, to many purchasers. To aid home buyers and borrowers, Congress, in 1974, enacted a law requiring the disclosure of all costs to buyers and borrowers prior to the consummation of a real estate transaction. The law assumes that the disclosure of the total cost will allow buyers and borrowers to shop for credit and thus reduce the settlement costs in many cases. The disclosure statement also gives advance notice of the cash required at settlement.

The law requires the use of a standard form for advance disclosure of closing costs and for recording the actual charges incurred at settlement in all covered transactions. Some settlement costs are typically paid by sellers; others are the obligation of buyers. The form covers both categories of expenses. Among the common items disclosed are loan origination fees, loan discount points, appraisal fees, attorney's fees, inspection fees, title charges, and the cost of surveys.

The law also outlaws certain practices that are contrary to the interest of the home-buying public. Among these are giving kickbacks for referring a borrower to a lender, charging or accepting a fee for something other than services actually performed, and requiring that a home seller purchase title insurance from any particular title company. For the title insurance violation, there is a liability equal to three times the cost of the title insurance.

In addition to the foregoing, this law prevents a lender from requiring that an unreasonable amount be paid in advance for the purposes of paying real property taxes and insurance when they are due. These payments generally are known as *escrow* payments. A lender can require the borrower to pay at closing, as escrow, the amount equal to the number of months between the closing date and the last time the bill was paid. In addition, the lender can collect at closing a cushion of two months of the total estimated bill for taxes and insurance.

Chapter Summary

DEBTOR PROTECTION IN GENERAL

1. The federal government has enacted into law numerous statutes designed to protect the consumer-debtor in credit transactions.
2. A consumer-debtor is an individual involved in a credit transaction for the purpose of satisfying personal, family, or household needs.
3. Credit is applicable to any transaction in which money is lent with repayment to be made in the future.

CREDIT APPLICATIONS

Equal Credit Opportunity Act
1. This law prevents discrimination in granting credit on the basis of sex, race, color, age, religion, national origin, the receipt of welfare, or the exercise of any right under the law.
2. Victims of illegal discrimination may collect actual damages, attorney's fees, other legal expenses, and punitive damages.
3. The ECOA prohibits discriminatory advertising concerning the availability of credit.
4. The creditor must take care not to request on a credit application any information that may lead to discrimination in the extension of credit.

Fair Credit Reporting Act
1. This law was designed to prevent abuses in the credit reporting industry and to ensure a person's right to privacy.

	2. The FCRA's protection is limited to reports on consumers. Businesses are presumed to be able to protect themselves.
	3. The FCRA regulates those who distribute reports on consumers and the users of such reports.
Consumer Reporting Agencies	1. Such an agency exists when it regularly collects information on consumers and furnishes it to third parties.
	2. These agencies must make certain that consumer reports are used for a justifiable purpose.
	3. These agencies also must take precautions to ensure the accuracy of the information distributed. Such information must not be obsolete.
Users of Information	1. Whenever a user of a consumer report takes adverse action on a consumer's credit, insurance, employment, or license application, that user must disclose from which reporting agency the information was obtained.
Rights of Consumers	1. A consumer has the right to inspect the report an agency has compiled on that consumer.
	2. This consumer may challenge the accuracy of any information.
	3. If the information is retained by the consumer reporting agency, the consumer may prepare and require the agency to include in any report a written statement about the dispute.

CREDIT TRANSACTIONS

Truth-in-Lending Act	1. TILA is applicable only if the credit transaction involves a consumer-debtor who will repay a debt that is payable in more than four installments or is subject to a finance charge.
	2. TILA attempts to encourage consumer-debtors to shop for the best credit opportunities. This purpose is accomplished through disclosure requirements that provide the information to make comparison possible.
Disclosures Required	1. TILA's most important required disclosures are the amount financed, the finance charge, the annual percentage rate, and the total amount of all payments.
Sanctions for Violations	1. Failure to make these disclosures accurately exposes the creditor to liability for twice the finance charge within the range of $100 to $1,000.
Uniform Consumer Credit Code	1. This law has been adopted by a few states.
	2. It does not fix interest rates but does set maximum rates of interest.
	3. This law prohibits certain types of transactions such as those requiring balloon payments after the end of a relatively short period of time.
	4. The law prohibits a seller from taking a wage assignment from a consumer.

DEBT COLLECTION

Fair Credit Billing Act	1. This law specifies the rights of consumer-debtors and the duties of creditors if there is a billing error in an open-ended credit transaction.
	2. After a consumer-debtor has submitted a billing error notice, the creditor must respond by correcting the error or explaining why the bill is accurate.
	3. The FCBA establishes criteria for how the creditor is to treat the consumer-debtor during the resolution of a dispute.
	4. This law also provides creditors with accounting principles that must be followed when a payment is credited to the consumer-debtor's bill.
Credit Card Protection	1. A cardholder is liable only up to $50 for the unauthorized use of a credit card.

	2. There is no liability for unauthorized purchases by credit card that were not requested by the cardholder.
	3. There is no liability unless the card has a method for identification of the user.
Fair Debt Collection Practices Act	**1.** The FDCPA was passed to prevent the abuses that may occur in the debt collection process.
	2. This law regulates only third parties who act as debt collectors. Creditors who collect from their own debtors are exempt.
	3. The FDCPA covers only the collection of consumer debts. Again, businesses are presumed to be able to protect themselves.
	4. A number of collection practices are allowed and a number are considered illegal under the FDCPA.
	5. Any person abused during a third party's efforts to collect a consumer debt may recover actual damages, attorney's fees, and other legal expenses.
Limitations on Garnishment	**1.** Both federal and state governments limit the amount of wages that can be used to pay debts.
	2. The federal law limits garnishment to 25 percent of take-home pay or the amount that disposable earnings exceed thirty times the federal minimum wage, whichever is less.
	3. Employers may not discharge an employee because one garnishment proceeding has been instituted against that employee.

OTHER CONSUMER PROTECTION LAWS

Magnuson-Moss Warranty Act	**1.** Warranties of consumer products must be in writing and must fully and conspicuously disclose in simple, readily understood language the terms of the warranty.
	2. The warranty must include a statement of what the warrantor will do in the event of a breach of warranty, at whose expense, and for what time period.
	3. The warranty must inform the consumer of the steps to be followed to obtain performance.
	4. Warranties must be labeled full or limited, and information about warranties must be readily available.
	5. A warrantor may exclude or limit consequential damages only in conspicuous writing on the face of the warranty.
	6. Informal procedures established by the warrantor to resolve disputes concerning warranties must be followed by the customers.
Housing Warranties	**1.** Prior to closing, the buyer should inspect the real property thoroughly for possible problems.
	2. To protect buyers from the hard-to-discover defects, courts have held that builders implicitly warrant that a residence is habitable.
	3. Many builders have begun to give express warranties that houses are free from structural defects.
Consumer Product Safety Act	**1.** The Consumer Product Safety Commission imposes safety standards on manufacturers of consumer products. Manufacturers are required to furnish information to the commission.
	2. There are sanctions in addition to common-law liability, and the statute allows suits in the federal courts in the event that product safety rules are violated.
Unfair Business Practices	**1.** The Federal Trade Commission may prohibit deceptive business practices by issuing cease and desist orders.
	2. State statutes also attempt to prohibit deception of consumers. They generally create liability not only to consumers but also to competitors for false and deceptive advertising.

Home Solicitation

1. The Federal Trade Commission has rules regulating door-to-door selling. These cover goods costing $25 or more.
2. The rules require written contracts in at least 10-point type, and the contract must allow cancellation anytime prior to midnight of the third business day after the transaction.
3. The buyer must be orally informed of the right to cancel and obtain a refund.

Real Estate Settlement Procedures Act

1. This law applies to the purchase of homes. It requires the disclosure of all costs to buyers and borrowers in advance of the closing of the transaction.
2. The buyer is furnished a completed standard form informing him or her as to the amount of such costs and which party is expected to pay them.

REVIEW QUESTIONS AND PROBLEMS

1. Match each term in column A with the appropriate statement in column B.

A	B
(1) Consumer-debtor	(a) A third party who collects information on consumers and furnishes it to creditors, insurers, employers, and similar parties
(2) Equal Credit Opportunity Act	(b) Designed to inform buyers of closing costs
(3) Fair Credit Reporting Act	(c) Enacted to encourage consumer applicants to shop for the best credit opportunity
(4) Consumer reporting agency	(d) Exists to ensure that buyers of housing are protected against defects
(5) Truth-in-Lending Act	(e) An individual involved in a credit transaction for the purposes of satisfying personal, family, or household needs
(6) Billing error	(f) Passed to prevent abuses that may occur in the debt collection process
(7) Fair Debt Collection Practices Act	(g) Law that regulates those parties that either distribute or use information on consumers
(8) Housing warranties	(h) Regulated by the Federal Trade Commission and state laws
(9) Magnuson-Moss Warranty Act	(i) Law enacted to prevent discrimination based on several factors in the granting of credit
(10) Consumer Product Safety Act	(j) The federal law that establishes requirements concerning manufacturers' warranties
(11) Unfair business practices	(k) A mistake in an open-ended credit statement.
(12) Real Estate Settlement Procedures Act	(l) Enacted to impose safety standards on manufacturers of consumer products

2. The Equal Credit Opportunity Act was passed to prevent discrimination in the credit extension transaction. What are the criteria on which the credit decision cannot be legally based?

3. An application for a federally insured home loan was initially denied on the basis of the mortgage reports supplied by a credit-reporting agency to the mortgage company. Although the reporting agency accurately reported the information supplied to it by the applicant's creditors, certain information supplied by the creditors was inaccurate. The applicant sued the reporting agency for negligence. Are credit-reporting agencies that

accurately report inaccurate information furnished by creditors liable for damages under the Fair Credit Reporting Act? Why?

4. Lamb's automobile insurance policy was canceled due to information in a report furnished by Equifax Services, Inc. (Equifax), to the insurance company. Lamb contacted Equifax to discover the contents of the report. He was verbally told the contents but was not given a copy. Lamb disputed the following two items contained in the report: (1) the reason for his first divorce and (2) information concerning an arrest. Because of the dispute, Equifax reinvestigated Lamb's background and issued a new report. It deleted the first disputed item but retained the second based on a verification by police records. Lamb was given a copy of this second report, and he took no exception to it. The second report was furnished to another source, but Lamb was not told this fact. When he learned that Equifax had reported the information about his arrest, Lamb instituted this suit alleging defamation and violation of the FCRA. Did Equifax violate the disclosure requirements of the FCRA? Explain.

5. Friendly Finance held a mortgage on Dandy's six-unit apartment building. Dandy fell behind on his payments and, to avoid foreclosure, agreed to execute a mortgage on his home in favor of Friendly. This second mortgage secured a note for the amount that Dandy was in arrears on his payments. When the second mortgage was entered, Friendly did not comply with the Truth-in-Lending law. Dandy now sues Friendly for his actual damages plus twice the amount of the finance charge. Should Dandy succeed? Why?

6. Marjorie Dehning purchased consumer goods from Wise Furniture on four separate occasions. Each sales contract refinanced the previous contract and retained a security interest in all the goods purchased. Dehning defaulted on the last contract with an outstanding balance of $811.23 due. Dehning had made payments of $947.55 prior to default. Dehning then brought this action alleging that Wise had violated the Truth-in-Lending Act and Regulation Z by failing to disclose adequately its finance charge and retained security interests. Did Wise's failure to disclose its finance charge and failure to unequivocally describe its retained security interests violate the Truth-in-Lending Act? Explain.

7. A salesman for Plumbing Company sold a water-softening unit to Baker. The sales agreement included a "referral sale" credit. For every sale to a buyer Baker had referred to Plumbing, Baker would get a $40 credit toward payment for Baker's unit. Is this a valid sales agreement? Explain.

8. Plaintiff, a former credit card holder, alleged a violation of the Fair Credit Billing Act. The credit card was issued to a corporation for a company account with the plaintiff, as president, authorized to use it, and he agreed to be jointly liable. Later a dispute arose over the account and the card was canceled. Is this dispute subject to the Fair Credit Billing Act? Why or why not?

9. The Charge-It Company issued a credit card to Albert at his request. Albert's card was stolen, and he immediately notified Charge-It. The thief used Albert's card for motel and gasoline purchases. Who bears the loss in this situation? Why?

10. Mr. Boudreaux owed the Allstate Company $985, payable in twenty-four monthly installments. When Boudreaux became unemployed, he fell behind in his payments. Allstate hired the Debtor's Collection Agency to collect the amount owed by Boudreaux. This agency began calling his neighbors repeatedly, since the Boudreaux phone was disconnected. It used insulting language in speaking to these neighbors about Boudreaux. Mrs. Boudreaux also was insulted when an agent attempted to collect the amount owed. Does Boudreaux have any recourse against the agency for these debt collection actions? Explain.

11. Harry, a wage earner, earns $700 per week. His employer witholds 20 percent for income and FICA taxes. A garnishment proceeding is commenced against Harry and his

employer to collect a judgment owed by Harry. Under the applicable federal law, how much of Harry's wages may be garnished each week? Explain your calculations.

12. Tom purchased a BMW that was warranted for 36,000 miles or three years. Within the warranty period, the engine failed. The seller contended that the failure was caused by buyer abuse. Tom sued under the Magnuson-Moss Warranty Act and the Uniform Commercial Code. Are both remedies available? Explain. Why would a plaintiff want to use both?

42

BANKRUPTCY

CHAPTER PREVIEW

The law of bankruptcy provides possible solutions to problems that arise when a person, partnership, corporation, farmer, or municipality is unable, or finds it difficult to satisfy obligations to creditors. Bankruptcy has its roots in the law of the Roman Empire and has been a part of English jurisprudence since 1542. The bankruptcy laws in the United States have been amended periodically. The last major revision is known as the Bankruptcy Reform Act of 1978. This law became effective on October 1, 1979. Additional amendments to it occurred in 1984, 1986, 1988, and 1990. From these dates, you can begin to understand that a highly technical area of law, like bankruptcy, is developed over a period of time.

The basic concept underlying bankruptcy is to allow a debtor who is in a difficult financial situation a fresh financial start. In other words, the bankruptcy laws permit a deserving debtor the opportunity to come out from under overwhelming financial burdens and to begin life anew. However, this "fresh start" is not granted without the debtor's paying something for the opportunity. In essence, the bankruptcy laws have always attempted to balance the rights of the debtor with the rights of the creditors. To protect the creditors, the debtor must turn over his or her assets to court supervision. Loss of every asset would deprive the debtor of the opportunity for a fresh financial start. Therefore, the debtor may exempt certain items from the bankruptcy estate and retain them as the basis for a new beginning.

As you study this chapter, keep in mind that the bankruptcy laws provide an acceptable alternative for debtors in financial difficulty. Filing for bankruptcy is no longer socially unacceptable or an admission of failure. More than ever before, bankruptcy has become an acceptable solution to the financial distress individuals or businesses could not otherwise overcome.

This chapter discusses the types of bankruptcy proceedings, some procedural aspects of a bankruptcy case, and rights and duties of the parties involved in a bankruptcy case.

■ BUSINESS MANAGEMENT DECISION

Your company, which is self-insured, faces thousands of products liability suits. The potential liability could reach hundreds of millions of dollars. Other than these suits, your company is financially sound and profitable.

Should your company consider filing for bankruptcy protection?

TERMINOLOGY

Debtor The party who files a bankruptcy petition or against whom such a petition is filed.

Claim A creditor's right to payment in a bankruptcy case.

At the outset of your study of this chapter, you should be familiar with some of the more common terms used in bankruptcy proceedings. A **debtor** is the individual, business organization, municipality, or farmer that a bankruptcy proceeding involves. A **claim** is a right to payment from the debtor. Claims are held and asserted by creditors. An **order of relief** is entered by the bankruptcy judge when he or she finds that the debtor is entitled to the protection of the bankruptcy law. A **discharge** is an order by the bankruptcy judge that a debtor is relieved of paying specific debts. Finally, the **trustee** is the person responsible for managing the debtor's assets and for satisfying the creditor's claim to the extent possible.

1. In General

Order of relief The ruling by a bankruptcy judge that a particular case is properly before the bankruptcy court.

Discharge An order by a bankruptcy court that a debt is no longer valid; in essence, the debtor's obligation is forgiven.

Trustee The person named to handle the assets and obligations of the debtor during the bankruptcy proceeding.

The federal bankruptcy laws have two distinct approaches to the problems of debtors. One approach is to liquidate debts. The liquidation approach recognizes that misfortune and poor judgment often create a situation in which debtors will never be able to pay their debts by their own efforts, or at least it will be very difficult to do so.

The second approach is to postpone the time of payment of debts or to reduce some of them to levels that make repayment possible. This approach is found in the reorganization sections for businesses and in the adjustment of debts provisions for municipalities, farmers, and individuals with regular incomes. The reorganization and adjustment provisions are aimed at rehabilitation of debtors. These procedures, if utilized, prevent harassment of debtors and spare them undue hardship while enabling most creditors eventually to obtain some repayment.

There are five types of bankruptcy proceedings, each identified by a chapter of the statute: Chapter 7, Liquidation; Chapter 9, Adjustment of Debts of a Municipality; Chapter 11, Reorganization; Chapter 12, Adjustment of Debts of a Family Farmer; Chapter 13, Adjustment of Debts of an Individual with Regular Income. Chapter 9 adjustment proceedings recognize the financial plight of many governmental units such as New York City and Cleveland, Ohio. A municipal governmental entity may be a debtor under Chapter 9 if state law or a public official authorized by state law permits it. The municipality must be unable to meet its debts as they mature, and it must desire to effect a plan to adjust its debts. Because of the special and limited use of this proceeding, it will not be discussed further in this text.

2. Liquidation Proceedings

Liquidation The process of winding up the affairs of a corporation or firm for the purpose of paying its debts and disposing of its assets.

Liquidation proceedings are used to eliminate most of the debts of a debtor. In exchange for having the debts declared uncollectible, the debtor must allow many, if not most, of his or her assets to be used to satisfy creditors' claims. Cases under Chapter 7 of the statute may involve individuals, partnerships, or corporations, but only individuals may receive a discharge from the court. A discharge voids any judgment against the debtor to the extent that it creates a personal liability. A discharge covers all scheduled debts that arose before the date of the order for relief. It is irrelevant whether or not a claim was filed or allowed. A discharge also operates as an injunction against all attempts to collect the debt—by judicial proceedings, telephone calls, letters, personal contacts, or other efforts. Under all types of proceedings, once they are commenced, creditors are prohibited from attempting to collect their debts.

The debts of partnerships and corporations that go through liquidation proceedings are not discharged. These businesses are still technically liable for their debts; however, the lack of discharge is immaterial unless the partnership or corporation acquires assets later. This lack of discharge stops people from using "shell" businesses after bankruptcy for other purposes.

Certain businesses are denied the right to liquidation proceedings. Railroads, insurance companies, banks, savings and loan associations, homestead associations, and credit unions may not be debtors under Chapter 7 of the Bankruptcy

Act. These organizations are subject to the jurisdiction of administrative agencies that handle all aspects of such organizations, including problems related to insolvency. Under this arrangement, there are alternative legal provisions for their liquidation.

Chapter 7 has special provisions relating to liquidation proceedings involving stockbrokers and commodity brokers. These special provisions are necessary to protect their customers, because bankruptcies of this kind usually involve large indebtedness and substantial assets. Stockbrokers and commodity brokers are subject only to Chapter 7. Chapter 11 and Chapter 13 proceedings are not available to them.

3. Reorganization Proceedings

Reorganization proceedings are utilized when debtors wish to restructure their finances and attempt to pay creditors over an extended period, as required by a court-approved plan. Such cases almost always involve a business as the debtor. Chapter 11 of the 1978 Bankruptcy Act contains detailed provisions on all aspects of the plan of reorganization and its execution.

As soon as practicable after the order for relief, a committee of creditors holding unsecured claims is formed. The committee ordinarily consists of persons with the seven largest claims, and it may employ attorneys, accountants, or other agents to assist it. Working with the trustee and the debtor concerning the administration of the case, it represents the interests of the creditors. It may investigate the financial condition of the debtor and will assist in the formulation of the reorganization plan.

The court in reorganization cases will usually appoint a trustee before approval of the plan of reorganization. If the court does not appoint a trustee, it will appoint an examiner who conducts an investigation into the affairs of the debtor, including any mismanagement or irregularities.

After the trustee or the examiner conducts the investigation of the acts, conduct, assets, liabilities, financial conditions, and other relevant aspects of the debtor, a written report of this investigation is filed with the court. The trustee may file a plan of reorganization if the debtor does not, or it may recommend conversion of the case to liquidation proceedings. The trustee will also file tax returns for the debtor, file reports with the court, and may even operate the debtor's business unless the court orders otherwise. The debtor may file a plan of reorganization with the voluntary petition or later, in an attempt to extricate the business from its financial difficulties and help it to survive. The plan will classify claims, and all claims within a class will be treated the same. All unsecured claims for less than a specified amount may be classified together. The plan will designate those classes of claims that are unimpaired under the plan and will specify the treatment to be given claims that are impaired.

The plan must provide a means for its execution. It may provide that the debtor will retain all or part of the property of the estate. It may also propose that property be sold or transferred to creditors or other entities. Mergers and consolidations may be proposed. In short, the plan will deal with all aspects of the organization of the debtor, its property, and its debts. Some debts will be paid in full, some will be partially paid over an extended period of time, and others may not be paid at all. The only limitation is that all claimants must receive as much as they would receive in liquidation proceedings.

Holders of claims or interests in the debtor's property are allowed to vote and to accept or reject the proposed plan of reorganization. A class of claims has accepted a plan if at least two-thirds in amount and more than half in number of claims vote yes. Acceptance by a class of interests such as equity holders requires a two-thirds yes vote.

A hearing is held on the confirmation of a plan, to determine if it is fair and equitable. The statute specifies several conditions, such as good faith, which must be met before the plan is approved. Also before approval, it must be established that each holder of a claim or interest has either accepted the plan or will receive as much under the reorganization plan as would be received in liquidation proceedings. For secured creditors, this means that they will receive the value of their security either by payment or by delivery of the property. Confirmation of the plan makes it binding on the debtor, equity security holders, and creditors. Confirmation vests the property of the estate in the debtor and releases the debtor from any payment not specified in the reorganization plan.

As a general rule, any debtor subject to liquidation under the statute (Chapter 7) is also subject to reorganization (Chapter 11). An exception exists for railroads. The public interest in railroads prevents their liquidation, but the law recognizes that financial reorganization of railroads is not only possible but often desirable.

4. Adjustment of Individuals' Debts

Chapter 13 proceedings are used to adjust the debts of individuals with regular income whose debts are small enough and whose income is significant enough that substantial repayment is feasible. Such persons often seek to avoid the stigma of bankruptcy. Unsecured debts of individuals utilizing Chapter 13 proceedings cannot exceed $100,000, and the secured debts cannot exceed $350,000. Persons utilizing Chapter 13 are usually employees earning a salary, but persons engaged in business also qualify. Self-employed persons who incur trade debts are considered to be engaged in business.

The debtor files a plan that provides for the use of all or a portion of future earnings or income for the payment of debts. The income is under the supervision and control of the trustee. Except as provided in the plan, the debtor keeps possession of his or her property. If the debtor is engaged in business, the debtor continues to operate the business. The plan must provide for the full payment of all claims entitled to priority unless the creditors with priority agree to a different treatment. If a plan divides unsecured claims into classes, all claims within a class must be given the same treatment.

Unsecured claims not entitled to priority may be repaid in full or reduced to a level not lower than the amount that would be paid upon liquidation. Since this amount is usually zero, any payment to unsecured creditors will satisfy the law. The secured creditors may be protected by allowing them to retain their lien, by payment of the secured claim in full, or by the surrender of the property to the secured claimant. The usual plan will provide for payments over three years, but the court may extend the payment period up to a total of five years. A typical plan allocates one-fourth of a person's take-home pay to repay debts.

The plan may modify the rights of holders of secured and unsecured claims, except that the rights of holders or real estate mortgages may not be modified.

Claims arising after the filing of the petition may be included in the plan. This is a realistic approach, because all the debts of the debtor must be taken into account if the plan is to accomplish its objectives.

When the court conducts a hearing on the confirmation of the plan, if it is satisfied that the debtor will be able to make all payments to comply with it, the plan will be approved. Of course, the plan must be proposed in good faith, be in compliance with the law, and be in the best interest of the creditors.

As soon as the debtor completes all payments under the plan, the court grants the debtor a discharge of all debts, unless the debtor waives the discharge or the debts are not legally dischargeable (see sections 8 and 9).

Courts, after a hearing, may also grant a discharge, even though all payments have not been made, if the debtor's failure to complete the payments is due to circumstances for which the debtor should not justly be held accountable. In such cases, the payments under the plan must be not less than those that would have been paid on liquidation, and modification must not be practicable.

5. Adjustment of Family Farmers' Debts

In 1986, the dire economic plight of the nation's farmers prompted Congress to enact Chapter 12 of the bankruptcy law. Chapter 12 is a reorganization and adjustment law designed to help family farmers stay in business. Without it Congress feared that tens of thousands of farmers would be forced off their farms notwithstanding the fact that farmers may not be put into Chapter 7 involuntarily. This exemption from involuntary bankruptcy is discussed further in section 12 of this chapter.

Chapter 12 of the bankruptcy law is directed at both the short-term and long-term debt of farmers. Under Chapter 12, farmers with as much as $1.5 million in debt are allowed to write down the debt to the current value of their collateral—forcing lenders to write off the difference between a loan's face value and the depressed value of most farm assets. This became necessary because land values had declined sharply, and thus the value of collateral was often less than the debt. If a farmer obtained a discharge in bankruptcy, the creditor would only receive the value of the collateral anyway, so Congress decided to keep the farmers on the farm and to limit the secured creditors to what they would receive in liquidation proceedings.

Under the provisions of Chapter 12, a farmer must file a reorganization plan within ninety days after filing a bankruptcy petition. The plan includes a statement of the farmer's opinion of the current market value of his or her land and other collateral. Secured creditors have an opportunity to challenge the farmer's estimate of collateral value. Once the plan is approved by the court, creditors cannot veto it.

The farmer must use all of his or her income that is not needed to support the farm family and current operating expenses for the next three to five years to pay off unsecured creditors, such as feed and fuel dealers. If these debts are not paid after five years, they are forgiven. The farmer must pay secured creditors the current market value of the collateral in installments. This will usually be over the life of the original loan.

The net effect of the law is to reduce the amount of the yearly payments from that originally agreed on to whatever it takes to amortize the new value of the collateral. In a sense, the farmer is repurchasing the farm at its new and lower value.

Chapter 12 may make it more difficult for farmers to get new loans or to renew them. It may make cash flow more important than collateral in many loan decisions. It may also give a farmer seeking to renew a loan a negotiating tool. If the loan is not renewed, the farmer threatens to file under Chapter 12, and this would force some write-off of the loan.

GENERAL PRINCIPLES

6. Property of the Estate

The *bankruptcy estate* consists of all legal or equitable interests of the debtor in property, wherever located. The property may be tangible or intangible and includes causes of action. All property is included in the estate to begin with, but the debtor may exempt portions entitled to exemption, as discussed in the next section.

The estate includes property that the trustee recovers by using his or her power to avoid prior transactions. It also includes property inherited by the debtor or received as a beneficiary of life insurance within 180 days of the petition. Proceeds, products, offspring, rents, and profits generated by or coming from property in the estate are also part of the estate.

In general, property acquired by the debtor after commencement of the case—including earnings from employment—belongs to the debtors. Property held in trust for the benefit of the debtor under a *spendthrift trust* does not become a part of the estate. In essence, the trustee in bankruptcy acquires the same interest with the same restrictions as the debtor had at the time the bankruptcy petition was filed. However, the trustee can require creditors to turn over possession of assets that were held by the creditors at the time the petition was filed. In return, the trustee must provide adequate protection for these creditors' claims. These concepts apply to the IRS and other government agencies, as the following case illustrates.

CASE

United States v. Whiting Pools, Inc.
103 S.Ct. 2309 (1983)

Whiting Pools, Inc., sold, installed, and serviced swimming pools. When the corporation became obligated for $92,000 in FICA taxes, the IRS seized all of the corporation's tangible personal property. The estimated liquidation value of the property seized was $35,000 at most, but its estimated going concern value in Whiting's hands was $162,876. One day after the seizure, Whiting filed a Chapter 11 bankruptcy petition. The Bankruptcy Court ruled that the seized assets were property of the debtor's estate. It ordered the IRS to turn the property over to the bankruptcy trustee on the condition that the trustee provide the IRS with protection for its interests. The Supreme Court granted certiorari to decide what property becomes part of the debtor's estate.

BLACKMUN, J.

. . . By virtue of its tax lien, the Service holds a secured interest in Whiting's property. We first examine whether §542(a) of the Bankruptcy Code generally authorizes the turnover of a debtor's property seized by a secured creditor prior to the commencement of reorganization proceedings. Section 542(a) requires an entity in possession of "property that the trustee may use, sell, or lease . . ." to deliver that property to the trustee. . . .

In proceedings under the reorganization provisions of the Bankruptcy Code, a troubled enterprise may be restructured to enable it to operate successfully in the future. Until the business can be reorganized pursuant to a plan, . . . the trustee or debtor-in-possession is authorized to manage the property of the estate and to continue the operation of the business. By permitting reorganization, Congress anticipated that the business would continue to provide jobs, to satisfy creditors' claims, and to produce a return for its owners. Congress presumed that the assets of the debtor would be more valuable if used in a rehabilitated business than if "sold for scrap." The reorganization effort would have small chance of success, however, if property essential to running the business were excluded from the estate. Thus, to facilitate the rehabilitation of the debtor's business, all the debtor's property must be included in the reorganization estate.

This authorization extends even to property of the estate in which a creditor has a secured interest. Although Congress might have safeguarded the interests of secured creditors outright by excluding from the estate any property subject to a secured interest, it chose instead to include such property in the estate and to provide secured creditors with "adequate protection" for their interests. At the secured creditor's insistence, the bankruptcy court must place such limits or conditions on the trustee's power to sell, use, or lease property as are necessary to protect the creditor. The creditor with a secured interest in property included in the estate must look to this provision for protection, rather than to the nonbankruptcy remedy of possession.

Both the congressional goal of encouraging reorganizations and Congress' choice of methods to protect secured creditors suggest that Congress intended a broad range of property to be included in the estate.

The statutory language reflects this view of the scope of the estate.... [Section] 541 (a) provides that the "estate is comprised of all the following property, wherever located: . . . all legal or equitable interests of the debtor in property as of the commencement of the case.".... Most important, in the context of this case, §541(a)(1) is intended to include in the estate any property made available to the estate by other provisions of the Bankruptcy Code. Several of these provisions bring into the estate property in which the debtor did not have a possessory interest at the time the bankruptcy proceedings commenced.

Section 542(a) is such a provision. It requires an entity (other than a custodian) holding any property of the debtor that the trustee can use to turn that property over to the trustee. Given the broad scope of the reorganization estate, property of the debtor repossessed by a secured

creditor falls within this rule, and therefore may be drawn into the estate. . . .

As does all bankruptcy law, §542(a) modifies the procedural rights available to creditors to protect and satisfy their liens. In effect, §542(a) grants to the estate a possessory interest in certain property of the debtor that was not held by the debtor at the commencement of reorganization proceedings. The Bankruptcy Code provides secured creditors various rights, including the right to adequate protection, and these rights replace the protection afforded by possession. . . .

We conclude that the reorganization estate includes property of the debtor that has been seized by a creditor prior to the filing of a petition for reorganization.

We see no reason why a different result should obtain when the IRS is the creditor. The Service is bound by §542(a) to the same extent as any other secured creditor. The Bankruptcy Code expressly states that the term "entity," used in §542(a), includes a governmental unit. Moreover, Congress carefully considered the effect of the new Bankruptcy Code on tax collection and decided to provide protection to tax collectors, such as the IRS, through grants of enhanced priorities for unsecured tax claims and by the nondischarge of tax liabilities. . . . Nothing in the Bankruptcy Code or its legislative history indicates that Congress intended a special exception for the tax collector in the form of an exclusion from the estate of property seized to satisfy a tax lien.

The judgment of the Court of Appeals is affirmed.

■ *So ordered.*

CASE CONCEPTS REVIEW

1. Which type of bankruptcy proceeding is involved in this case?
2. What is the difference between the liquidation value and the going concern value of the property seized by the IRS?
3. What does §542(a) require the secured party to do with the debtor's assets held by the secured party?
4. What is required of the trustee to protect a secured party's right to payment when that secured party turns the debtor's assets over to the trustee?

7. Exemptions

Technically, all property of the debtor becomes property of the bankruptcy estate, but an individual debtor is then permitted to claim some of it as exempt from the proceedings. That property is then returned to the debtor. Exemptions are granted by federal, state, and local laws. The 1978 Bankruptcy Act, as it has been amended, allows the following exemptions in the debtor's property:

1. Real property used as a residence, up to $7,500
2. The debtor's interest, not to exceed $1,200, in one motor vehicle
3. The debtor's interest, not to exceed $200 in any particular item or $4,000 in aggregate value, in household furnishings, wearing apparel, appliances, books, animals, crops, or musical instruments that are held primarily for the personal family or household use of the debtor and his dependents
4. The debtor's interest in jewelry, not to exceed $500
5. The debtor's interest in other property, not to exceed $400, plus up to $3,750 of any unused real property exemption
6. The debtor's interest, not to exceed $750, in any implements, professional books, or tools of the trade of the debtor, or the trade of his or her dependents
7. Unmatured life insurance contracts
8. The cash value of life insurance, not to exceed $4,000
9. Professionally prescribed health aids
10. The debtor's right to receive benefits such as social security, unemployment compensation, public assistance, disability benefits, alimony, child support and separate maintenance reasonably necessary, and current payments of pension, profit sharing, annuity, or similar plans
11. The debtor's right to receive payment traceable to the wrongful death of an individual on whom the debtor was dependent or to life insurance on the life of such a person or to payments for personal injury, not to exceed $7,500

The 1984 amendments placed a cap of $4,000 on the total amount of household items that can be exempt. These amendments also restrict tenants to an additional amount of $3,750 when exempting personal property under exemption 5. Prior to this change, debtors who did not own a residence could use the entire real estate exemption of $7,500 (see exemption 1) to exempt additional personal property not exempted by another provision of the federal exemptions. Creditors have praised these amendments as a more equitable balance of debtors' and creditors' rights.

Every state has enacted statutes granting exemptions to debtors domiciled there, but these exemptions vary greatly from state to state. For example, some state exemptions exceed those provided by the federal bankruptcy laws. Other state exemptions are too small to give a debtor a real chance at a fresh financial start. Debtors may claim the larger exemptions offered by their state if it is to their advantage to do so. To encourage some states to raise their exemptions, the 1978 Act provides that the federal exemptions will be available to debtors unless the state specifically passes a law denying its residents the federal exemptions. Over half the states have adopted laws denying debtors the use of the federal exemptions; however, these states have substantially increased their own exemptions. The following case demonstrates the broad protection that is given by some state exemption statutes.

CASE

In Re Siegmann
757 P.2d 820 (Okl. 1988)

LAVENDER, J.

The United States Bankruptcy Court for the Western District of Oklahoma has certified the following question to this Court pursuant to the Oklahoma Uniform Certification of Questions of Law Act:

> Does the term "tools, apparatus . . . used in any trade . . ." include all types of equipment, regardless of size, source of power, mobility, value or mode of operation, needed by a person in pursuit of a trade?

Accompanying the question the bankruptcy court has certified the following findings of fact:

The debtor owns a 1979 Ford tractor, a front end loader, a box blade, and a 6 × 14 flat bed trailer. This property is subject to a properly perfected nonpurchase money security interest in favor of a creditor, Northwest Bank of Enid. The debtor has claimed this as exempt property. . . .

The debtor is a contractor and must use the tractor and related equipment to perform various tasks which are part of his duties. Thus, the tractor and related equipment are necessary to enable the debtor to pursue his trade. . . .

The question as posed by the bankruptcy court calls for the interpretation of 31 O.S. Supp.1987 § 1(A) (6) which provides:

The following property shall be reserved to every person residing in the state, exempt from attachment or execution and every other species of forced sale for the payment of debts, except as herein provided:

. . . Tools, apparatus and books used in any trade or profession of such person or a dependent of such person; . . .

The intent and purpose of the statute in question is apparent on its face. The statute reflects an intent to insure that the items necessary to allow a person to continue to work to support himself are secured to that person exempt from seizure and sale. The statute reflects no limitation in terms of type of equipment, size, source of power, mobility or mode of operation in regard to the tools or apparatus which would come within the coverage of this limitation. . . .

In its brief . . . the creditor, Northwest Bank of Enid, has argued that the proper construction of the tools of the trade exemption should be narrow and, as the language of the exemption has not been materially changed in regard to the coverage since the beginning of the present century, should not be read to include property beyond the contemplation of those who first drafted the language. In regard to this latter argument we find the Supreme Court of Montana to have given an excellent response in the course of receding from a prior pronouncement which limited that State's tools of the trade exemption to tools and implements capable of being used by hand:

. . . Today a tool is still a powered or unpowered item designed to be used by mechanics or artisans to perform a task and is manageable in size and weight so that in its normal operation it can be maneuvered or used by the operator's physical strength alone without the aid of independent motive powers and it is liable to be more expensive and require more skill. The definition includes common hand tools and common powered hand tools such as drills, wrenches, saws, but also includes larger industrial items that may be mounted on a dolly or are pushed around on wheels or are stationary in normal operations such as table saws, lathes, and welders.

Implements include tools but also more. An implement is a powered or unpowered item designed to be used by a mechanic or artisan to perform a task. It may include an item that cannot be in its normal operation maneuvered by the operator's physical strength but must be used with the aid of independent motor powers.

The Montana Supreme Court went on to find that a backhoe and trailer came within the coverage of the tools of the trade exemption. . . .

We now hold that the tools of the trade exemption under 31 O.Supp.1987 § 1(A) (6) applies to any property which comes within the scope of the terms tools, apparatus or books, is used in the trade or profession of the debtor or a dependent of the debtor, and is reasonably necessary, convenient or suitable for production of work in that trade or profession regardless of size, source of power, mobility or mode of operation. . . .

■ *So ordered.*

CASE CONCEPTS REVIEW

1. What law governs which assets of the debtor are exempt from the creditor's claim in bankruptcy?
2. What kinds of assets are the subject of this exempt property issue?
3. What conclusion does the court reach with respect to whether or not these assets are exempt?

As a general rule, exempt property is not subject to any debts that arise before the commencement of the case. Exceptions to the general rule apply to tax claims, alimony, child support, and separate maintenance. Exempt property can be used to collect such debts after the proceeding. The discharge in bankruptcy does not prevent enforcement of valid liens against exempt property; however, judicial liens and nonpossessory, nonpurchase-money security interests in household goods, wearing apparel, professional books, tools, and professionally prescribed health aids may be avoided. A debtor may redeem such tangible personal property from a lien securing a dischargeable consumer debt by paying the lienholder the amount of the secured claim. Exempt property is free of such liens after the proceedings. Waivers of exemptions are unenforceable, to prevent creditors from attempting to deny debtors the necessary property to gain a fresh start.

8. Debts That Are Not Discharged

A debt is a liability on a claim. A claim may be based on the right to payment that could be enforced in a proceeding at law, or it may be based on the right to an equitable remedy for breach of performance if the breach gives a right to payment. Claims based on equitable remedies may be dischargeable the same as those based on legal remedies, as the following case indicates. Note what the court did not hold as well as what it held.

CASE

Ohio v. Kovacs

105 S.Ct. 705 (1985)

Kovacs operated a hazardous waste disposal business in Ohio. The state filed suit against Kovacs for polluting public waters in violation of environmental laws. Kovacs settled the suit by agreeing to stop the pollution, clean up the waste site, and pay the state $75,000. The agreement was made part of an injunction.

When Kovacs did not clean up the waste site or pay the $75,000, the state had a receiver appointed who took possession of the property. Kovacs then filed a petition in bankruptcy. The state contended that the cost of the cleanup was not dischargeable in bankruptcy. The lower courts held that the obligation was dischargeable.

WHITE, J.

. . . The question before us is whether, in the circumstances present here, Kovacs' obligation under the injunction is a "debt" or "liability on a claim" subject to discharge under the Bankruptcy Code.

Except for the nine kinds of debts saved from discharge by 11 U.S.C. § 523(a), a discharge in bankruptcy discharges the debtor from all debts that rose before bankruptcy. It is not claimed here that Kovacs' obligation under the injunction fell within any of the categories of debts excepted from discharge by § 523. Rather, the State submits that the obligation to clean up the Chem-Dyne site is not a debt at all within the meaning of the bankruptcy law.

For bankruptcy purposes, a debt is a liability on a claim. § 101(11). A claim is defined by § 101(4) as follows:

(4) "claim" means—
(A) right to payment, whether or not such right is reduced to judgment, liquidated, unliquidated, fixed, contingent, matured, unmatured, disputed, undisputed, legal, equitable, secured, or unsecured; or
(B) right to an equitable remedy for breach of performance if such breach gives rise to a right to payment, whether or not such right to an equitable remedy is reduced to judgment, fixed, contingent, matured, unmatured, disputed, undisputed, secured, or unsecured.

The provision at issue here is § 101(4)(B). For the purposes of that section, there is little doubt that the State had the right to an equitable remedy under state law and that the right has been reduced to judgment in the form of an injunction ordering the cleanup. The State argues, however, that the injunction it has secured is not a claim against Kovacs for bankruptcy purposes because (1) Kovacs' default was a breach of the statute, not a breach of an ordinary commercial contract which concededly would give rise to a claim; and (2) Kovacs' breach of his obligation under the injunction did not give rise to a right to payment within the meaning of § 101(4)(B). We are not persuaded by either submission.

There is no indication in the language of the statute that the right to performance cannot be a claim unless it arises from a contractual arrangement. The State resorted to the courts to enforce its environmental laws against Kovacs and secured a negative order to cease polluting, an affirmative order to clean up the site, and an order to pay a sum of money to recompense the State for damage done to the fish population. Each order was one to remedy an alleged breach of Ohio law; and if Kovacs' obligation to pay $75,000 to the State is a debt dischargeable in bankruptcy, which the State freely concedes, it makes little sense to assert that because the cleanup order was entered to remedy a statutory violation, it cannot likewise constitute a claim for bankruptcy purposes. Furthermore, it is apparent that Congress desired a broad definition of a "claim" and knew how to limit the application of a provision to contracts when it desired to do so. . . .

The injunction surely obliged Kovacs to clean up the site. But when he failed to do so, rather than prosecute Kovacs under the environmental laws or bring civil or criminal contempt proceedings, the State secured the appointment of a receiver, who was ordered to take possession of all of Kovacs' nonexempt assets . . . and to comply with the injunction entered against Kovacs. As wise as this course may ahve been, it dispossessed Kovacs, removed his authority over the site, and divested him of assets that might have been used by him to clean up the property. . . . Although Kovacs had been ordered to "cooperate" with the receiver, he was disabled by the receivership from personally taking charge of and carrying out the removal of wastes from the property. What the receiver wanted from Kovacs after bankruptcy was the money to defray cleanup costs. At oral argument in this Court, the State's counsel conceded that after the receiver was appointed, the only performance sought from Kovacs was the payment of money. Had Kovacs furnished the necessary funds, either before or after bankruptcy, there seems little doubt that the receiver and the State would have been satisfied. On the facts before it, and with the receiver in control of the site, we cannot fault the Court of Appeals for concluding that the cleanup order had been converted into an obligation to pay money, an obligation that was dischargeable in bankruptcy.

It is well to emphasize what we have not decided. First, we do not suggest that Kovacs' discharge will shield him from prosecution for having violated the environmental laws of Ohio or for criminal contempt for not performing his obligations under the injunction prior to bankruptcy. Second, had a fine or monetary penalty for violation of state law been imposed on Kovacs prior to bankruptcy, § 523(a)(7) forecloses any suggestion that his obligation to pay the fine or penalty would be discharged in bankruptcy. Third, we do not address what the legal consequences would have been had Kovacs taken bankruptcy before a receiver had been appointed and a trustee had been designated with the usual duties of a bankruptcy trustee. Fourth, we do not hold that the injunction against bringing further toxic wastes on the premises or against any conduct that will contribute to the pollution of the site or the State's waters is dischargeable in bankruptcy; we here address, as did the Court of Appeals, only the affirmative duty to clean up the site and the duty to pay money to that end. Finally, we do not question that anyone in possession of the site—whether it is Kovacs or another in the event the receivership is liquidated and the trustee abandons the property, or a vendee from the receiver or the bankruptcy trustee—must comply with the environmental laws of the State of Ohio. Plainly, that person or firm may not maintain a nuisance, pollute the waters of the State, or refuse to remove the source of such conditions. As the case comes to us, however, Kovacs has been dispossessed and the State seeks to enforce his cleanup obligation by a money judgment.

■ *Affirmed.*

CASE CONCEPTS REVIEW

1. On what debt is the court deciding the issue of dischargeability?
2. What factual situation and court order gave rise to this debt?
3. Why does the court decide that this debt is dischargeable?

As the court noted in the preceding case, not all debts are discharged in Chapter 7 cases. A discharge in bankruptcy does not discharge an individual debtor from the following debts:

1. Certain taxes and customs duties
2. Debts for obtaining money, property, services, or credit by false pretenses, false representations, or actual fraud
3. Consumer debts over $500 for luxury goods and services incurred within forty days of the order of relief
4. Cash advances over $1,000 that are extensions of consumer credit under an open-end credit plan within twenty days of the order of relief
5. Unscheduled debts
6. Debts for fraud or defalcation while acting in a fiduciary capacity and debts created by embezzlement or larceny

7. Alimony, child support, and separate maintenance
8. Liability for willful and malicious torts
9. Tax penalties if the tax is not dischargeable
10. Student loans less than five years old
11. Debts incurred as a result of an accident caused by driving while intoxicated
12. Debts owed before a previous bankruptcy to which discharge was denied for grounds other than the six-year rule
13. Fines and penalties payable to and for the benefit of governmental units that are not compensation for actual pecuniary losses

The taxes that are not discharged are the same ones that receive priority under the second, third, and seventh categories discussed in section 23 of this chapter. If debtors fail to file a return, file it beyond its last due date, or file a fraudulent return, those taxes are not discharged. One of the most common tax liabilities that is not discharged in bankruptcy is the one for unpaid withholding and social security taxes.

Items 3 and 4, which were added by the 1984 amendments, now prevent the debtor from going on a spending spree or "loading up" at creditors' expense just before filing a bankruptcy petition. The phrase "luxury goods and services" is defined as not including goods or services acquired for the support or maintenance of the debtor or his or her dependents.

The denial of a discharge of debts that are not properly scheduled on the bankruptcy petition means that the claim of any creditor who is not listed or who does not learn of the proceedings in time to file a claim continues to be valid. The debtor, under such circumstances, remains liable to pay the creditor unless the debtor can prove that the creditor did have knowledge of the proceeding in time to file a claim. Proof of actual knowledge is required, and although such knowledge often exists, care should be taken to list all creditors so all claims are subject to being discharged.

Typically, for a debt to be denied discharge because of fraud, the creditor must have placed reasonable reliance on a false written statement. One issue involving the use of fraud to deny a discharge of the underlying debt has concerned the creditor's burden of proof in establishing that the fraud exists. In the following case, the Supreme Court resolves this issue.

CASE

Grogan v. Garner
111 S.Ct. 654 (1991)

STEVENS, J.

Section 523(a) of the Bankruptcy Code provides that a discharge in bankruptcy shall not discharge an individual debtor from certain kinds of obligations, including those for money obtained by "actual fraud." The question in this case is whether the statute requires a defrauded creditor to prove his claim by clear and convincing evidence in order to preserve it from discharge.

Petitioners brought an action against respondent alleging that he had defrauded them in connection with the sale of certain corporate securities. Following the trial court's instructions that authorized a recovery based on the preponderance of the evidence, a jury returned a verdict in favor of petitioners and awarded them actual and punitive damages. Respondent appealed from the judgment on the verdict, and, while his appeal was pending, he filed a petition for relief under Chapter 11 of the Bankruptcy Code, listing the fraud judgment as a dischargeable debt.

The Court of Appeals . . . affirmed the fraud judgment. . . . Petitioners then filed a complaint in the bankruptcy proceeding requesting a determination that their claim based on the fraud judgment should be exempted from discharge pursuant to § 523.... The Bankruptcy Court found that all of the elements required to establish actual fraud under § 523 had been proved and that ... the debt was therefore not dischargeable.

Respondent ... has consistently argued that ... the jury instructions in the first trial merely required that fraud be proved by a preponderance of the evidence, whereas § 523 requires proof by clear and convincing evidence. Both the Bankruptcy Court and the District Court rejected this argument.

The Court of Appeals, however, reversed. It recognized that the "Bankruptcy Code is silent as to the burden of proof necessary to establish an exception to discharge under section 523(a), including the exception for fraud," but concluded that two factors supported the imposition of a "clear and convincing" standard, at least in fraud cases. First, the court stated that the higher standard had generally been applied in both common-law fraud litigation and in resolving dischargeability issues before § 523(a) was enacted, and reasoned that it was unlikely that Congress had intended silently to change settled law. Second, the court opined that the general "fresh start" policy that undergirds the Bankruptcy Code militated in favor of a broad construction favorable to the debtor.

The Eighth Circuit holding is consistent with rulings in most other Circuits, but conflicts with recent decisions by the Third and Fourth Circuits. The conflict, together with the importance of the issue, prompted us to grant certiorari....

We have previously held that a debtor has no constitutional or "fundamental" right to a discharge in bankruptcy. We also do not believe that, in the context of provisions designed to exempt certain claims from discharge, a debtor has an interest in discharge sufficient to require a heightened standard of proof.

We are unpersuaded by the argument that the clear-and-convincing standard is required to effectuate the "fresh start" policy of the Bankruptcy Code. This Court has certainly acknowledged that a central purpose of the Code is to provide a procedure by which certain insolvent debtors can reorder their affairs, make peace with their creditors, and enjoy a new opportunity in life with a clear field for future effort, unhampered by the pressure and discouragement of preexisting debt. But in the same breath that we have invoked this "fresh start" policy, we have been careful to explain that the Act limits the opportunity for a completely unencumbered new beginning to the honest but unfortunate debtor.

The statutory provisions governing nondischargeability reflect a congressional decision to exclude from the general policy of discharge certain categories of debts—such as child support, alimony, and certain unpaid educational loans and taxes, as well as liabilities for fraud. Congress evidently concluded that the creditors' interest in recovering full payment of debts in these categories outweighed the debtors' interest in a complete fresh start. We think it unlikely that Congress, in fashioning the standard of proof that governs the applicability of these provisions, would have favored the interest in giving perpetrators of fraud a fresh start over the interest in protecting victims of fraud. Requiring the creditor to establish by a preponderance of the evidence that his claim is not dischargeable reflects a fair balance between these conflicting interests.

Our conviction that Congress intended the preponderance standard to apply to the discharge exceptions is reinforced by the structure of § 523(a).... Because it seems clear that a preponderance of the evidence is sufficient to establish the nondischargeability of some of the types of claims covered by § 523(a), it is fair to infer that Congress intended the ordinary preponderance standard to govern the applicability of all the discharge exceptions....

A final consideration supporting our conclusion that the preponderance standard is the proper one is that ... application of that standard will permit exception from discharge of all fraud claims creditors have successfully reduced to judgment. This result accords with the historical development of the discharge exceptions.... The 1898 Bankruptcy Act provided that "judgments" sounding in fraud were exempt from discharge. In the 1903 revisions, Congress substituted the term "liabilities" for "judgments." This alteration was intended to broaden the coverage of the fraud exceptions. Absent a clear indication from Congress of a change in policy, it would be inconsistent with this earlier expression of congressional intent to construe the exceptions to allow some debtors facing fraud judgments to have those judgments discharged.

For these reasons, we hold that the standard of proof for the dischargeability exceptions in 11 U.S.C. § 523(a) is the ordinary preponderance-of-the-evidence standard.

The judgment of the Court of Appeals is

■ *Reversed.*

CASE CONCEPTS REVIEW

1. Petitioner (Grogan) established that the respondent (Garner) engaged in fraud in a securities transaction. What burden of proof did the petitioner satisfy at the trial level?

2. Why does respondent argue that this debt based on the proven fraud is still allowed to be discharged?

3. What are at least two reasons why the court concludes that the fraud-induced debt is exempt from being discharged if proven by a preponderance of the evidence?

Tort liability claims based on negligence are discharged. Tort liability claims arising from willful and malicious acts are not discharged. A judgment arising out of an assault and battery is not discharged. Item 11 was added by the 1984 amendments. The logic behind making this tort liability nondischargeable indicates support in the battle to discourage drunk driving. A 1990 amendment made it clear that this policy of nondischargeability extends to injuries arising out of the operation of a motor vehicle under the influence of alcohol, drugs, or other substances.

The provision generally denying discharge to student loans was added in the 1978 revision. It seeks to give creditors and the government five years to collect student loans. There is an exception if the debtor is able to convince the court that undue hardship will result on him or her and dependents if the student loan debt is not discharged. If the debtor fails to prove the undue hardship caused by the student loan, a general discharge will not relieve the debtor of the obligation to pay that student loan. Student loans are not discharged automatically. A person seeking a discharge of them must prove undue hardship in the bankruptcy court.

As a result of item 13, criminals will not be able to use the bankruptcy laws to avoid fines that have been levied. The Supreme Court has extended this nondischargeable debt to include restitution obligations imposed on debtors in state criminal proceedings. Great deference is given to state criminal proceedings, and amounts owed to accomplish the penal goals of a state such as the deterrence of crime are not dischargeable.

9. Grounds for Denying Discharge

A discharge in bankruptcy is a privilege, not a right. Therefore, in addition to providing that certain debts are not discharged, the 1978 Bankruptcy Act specifies the following grounds for denying an individual debtor a discharge:

1. Fraudulent transfers
2. Inadequate records
3. Commission of a bankruptcy crime
4. Failure to explain a loss of assets or deficiency of assets
5. Refusing to testify in the proceedings or to obey a court order
6. Any of the above within one year in connection with another bankruptcy case of an insider
7. Another discharge within six years
8. Approval by the court of a waiver of discharge

The first three grounds for denying discharge are predicated on wrongful conduct by the debtor in connection with the case. Fraudulent transfers involve such acts as removing, destroying, or concealing property with the intent to hinder, delay, or defraud creditors or the trustee. The conduct must occur within one year preceding the case, or it may occur after the case is commenced.

A debtor is also denied a discharge if he or she has concealed, destroyed, mutilated, falsified, or failed to keep or preserve any books and records relating to his or her financial condition. A debtor is required to keep records from which his or her financial condition may be ascertained, unless the failure is justified.

Bankruptcy crimes are generally related to the proceedings. They include a false oath, the use or presentation of a false claim, or bribery in connection with the proceedings and with the withholding of records.

The six-year rule, which allows a discharge only if another discharge has not been ordered within six years, extends to Chapter 11 and Chapter 13 proceedings, as well as to those under Chapter 7. Confirmation of a plan under Chapter 11 or 13 does not have the effect of denying a discharge within six years if all the unsecured claims were paid in full, or if 70 percent of them were paid and the debtor has used his or her best efforts to pay the debts.

Either a creditor or the trustee may object to the discharge. The court may order the trustee to examine the facts to see if grounds for the denial of the discharge exist. Courts are also granted the authority to revoke a discharge within one year if it was obtained by fraud on the court.

PROCEDURAL STEPS

10. Introduction

Chapter 3 of the 1978 Bankruptcy Reform Act is concerned with procedural aspects and administration of all types of bankruptcy cases, regardless of the chapter under which the case is filed. The provisions of Chapter 3 give guidance in how to and who can file a case, in how the automatic stay prohibits any action against the debtor, and in how creditors are informed of the debtor's status. These provisions are discussed in the next five sections. The most technical portion of Chapter 3 is entitled "administrative powers." These provisions grant the bankruptcy court and the trustee a wide range of powers to accomplish the purposes of the bankruptcy law. Sections 16 through 20 present a more detailed examination of these powers and duties.

11. Voluntary Commencement

A debtor may voluntarily instigate a bankruptcy case under any appropriate chapter by filing a petition with the bankruptcy court. In recognition of the fact that husbands and wives often owe the same debts, a joint case may be filed. A *joint case* is a voluntary one concerning a husband and wife, and it requires only one petition. The petition must be signed by both spouses, since one spouse cannot take the other into bankruptcy without the other's consent. Insolvency is not a condition precedent to any form of voluntary bankruptcy action.

All petitioners must pay a filing fee of $60, in installments if they prefer. Only one filing fee is required in a joint case. A petition filed by a partnership as a firm is not a petition on behalf of the partners as individuals. If they intend to obtain individual discharges, separate petitions are required.

The petition contains lists of secured and unsecured creditors, all property owned by the debtor, property claimed by the debtor to be exempt, and a statement of affairs of the debtor. This statement includes current income and expenses, so the judge can dismiss a case if he or she believes that a substantial abuse of the bankruptcy code has occurred. This is an important consideration when a debtor's liabilities do not exceed assets and the filing is based on some fact other than that the debtor cannot pay debts as they come due. The statement of affairs of a debtor engaged in business is much more detailed than the one filed by a debtor not in business.

In general, the filing of a voluntary petition constitutes an order of relief indicating that the debtor is entitled to the bankruptcy court's protection. This concept of an automatic order of relief upon the debtor's filing caused creditors to argue that some debtors were filing voluntary petitions when the debtor did not need the court's protection. In 1984, Congress amended Chapter 7 to allow the bankruptcy judge, on his or her own initiative, to dismiss a case filed voluntarily if the debtor's obligations are primarily consumer debts and if the order of relief would be an abuse of the bankruptcy law. However, there is a presumption in favor of granting the relief requested by the debtor.

12. Involuntary Commencement

Involuntary cases are commenced by one or more creditors filing a petition. If there are twelve or more creditors, the petition must be signed by at least three creditors whose unsecured claims are not contingent and aggregate at least $5,000. If there are fewer than twelve creditors, only one need sign the petition, but the $5,000 amount must still be met. Employees, insiders, and transferees of voidable transfers are not counted in determining the number of creditors. "Insiders" are persons such as relatives, partners of the debtor, and directors and officers of the corporation involved. The subject of voidable transfers is discussed later in this chapter.

Creditors may commence involuntary proceedings to harass the debtor. To protect the debtor, the court may require the petitioning creditors to file a bond to indemnify the debtor. This bond will cover the amounts for which the petitioning creditors may have liability to the debtor. The liability may include court costs, attorney's fees, and damages caused by taking the debtor's property.

Until the court enters an order for relief in an involuntary case, the debtor may continue to operate his or her business and to use, acquire, and dispose of property. However, the court may order an interim trustee appointed to take possession of the property and to operate the business. If the case is a liquidation proceeding, the appointment of the interim trustee is mandatory unless the debtor posts a bond guaranteeing the value of the property in his or her estate.

Since some debtors against whom involuntary proceedings are commenced are, in fact, not bankrupt, the debtor has a right to file an answer to the petition of the creditors and to deny the allegations of the petition. If the debtor does not file an answer, the court orders relief against the debtor. If an answer is filed, the court conducts a trial on the issues raised by the petition and the answer. A court will order relief in an involuntary proceeding against the debtor only if it finds that the debtor is generally not paying debts as they become due. Insolvency in the balance sheet sense (liabilities exceeding assets) is not required. Relief may also be ordered if, within 120 days before the filing of the petition, a custodian, receiver, or agent has taken possession of property of the debtor for the purpose of enforcing a lien against the debtor.

The statute specifies which debtors under each chapter are subject to involuntary proceedings. Farmers and not-for-profit corporations are not subject to involuntary proceedings, under either Chapter 7 or Chapter 11. A *farmer* is defined as a person who receives more than 80 percent of gross income for the taxable year preceding the bankruptcy case from a farming operation he or she owns and operates. The term *farming operation* includes tillage of the soil; dairy farming; ranching; production or raising of crops, poultry, or livestock; and production of poultry or livestock products in an unmanufactured state.

Creditors also are prohibited from forcing any debtor into a Chapter 13 proceeding. The reason for this rule is that a Chapter 13 debtor is required to pay off his or her debts pursuant to an approved plan. To force an individual debtor to work to pay debts is equivalent to involuntary servitude, which violates the Thirteenth Amendment of the Constitution.

13. Conversion of Cases

Because a case may be filed voluntarily or involuntarily under the various chapters, the issue arises as to whether the debtor or the creditors can convert a filing to another type of proceeding. If the original filing is under Chapter 7, the debtor can request a conversion to a Chapter 11 or 13 proceeding. Creditors can have a Chapter 7 case converted to Chapter 11, but not to Chapter 13. If the case was filed voluntarily as a Chapter 11 reorganization proceeding, the debtor may request that the case be converted to a Chapter 7 or 13 proceeding. However, if the Chapter 11 proceeding was begun involuntarily, the creditors must consent to a conversion to Chapter 7. Creditors may seek to convert a Chapter 11 proceeding to Chapter 7 as long as the debtor is neither a farmer nor a nonprofit corporation. Creditors cannot convert a case from Chapter 11 to Chapter 13 without the debtor's consent.

In general, a debtor may convert a Chapter 13 proceeding to Chapter 7 or 11, whichever is more appropriate. Creditors also may ask the court to convert a case filed under Chapter 13 to Chapter 7 or 11 unless the debtor is a farmer. If the debtor is a farmer, any conversion must be agreed to by that farmer before that conversion will occur.

The following case discusses a variety of issues concerning the conversion of cases. Principally involved is the question of whether an individual debtor may proceed with a Chapter 11 case.

CASE

Toibb v. Radloff
111 S.Ct. 2197 (1991)

BLACKMUN, J.

In this case we must decide whether an individual debtor not engaged in business is eligible to reorganize under Chapter 11 of the Bankruptcy Code.

From March 1983 until April 1985, petitioner Sheldon Baruch Toibb, a former staff attorney with the Federal Energy Regulatory Commission, was employed as a consultant by Independence Electric Corporation (IEC), a company he and two others organized to produce and market electric power. Petitioner owns 24 percent of the company's shares. After IEC terminated his employment, petitioner was unable to find work as a consultant

in the energy field; he has been largely supported by his family and friends since that time.

On November 18, 1986, petitioner filed in the United States Bankruptcy Court . . . a voluntary petition for relief under Chapter 7 of the Code. The Schedule of Assets and Liabilities accompanying petitioner's filing disclosed . . . unsecured debts of $170,605. Petitioner listed as nonexempt assets his IEC shares and a possible claim against his former business associates. He stated that the market value of each of these assets was unknown.

On August 6, 1987, the Chapter 7 Trustee . . . notified the creditors that the Board of Directors of IEC had offered to purchase petitioner's IEC shares for $25,000. When petitioner became aware that this stock had such value, he decided to avoid its liquidation by moving to convert his Chapter 7 case to one under the reorganization provisions of Chapter 11.

The Bankruptcy Court granted petitioner's conversion motion, and on February 1, 1988, petitioner filed a plan of reorganization. Under the plan, petitioner proposed to pay his unsecured creditors $25,000 less administrative expenses and priority tax claims, a proposal that would result in a payment of approximately 11 cents on the dollar. He further proposed to pay the unsecured creditors, for a period of six years, 50 percent of any dividends from IEC or of any proceeds from the sale of the IEC stock, up to full payment of the debts.

On March 8, 1988, the Bankruptcy Court on its own motion ordered petitioner to show cause why his petition should not be dismissed because petitioner was not engaged in business and, therefore, did not qualify as a Chapter 11 debtor. . . . Petitioner . . . argued that Chapter 11 should be available to an individual debtor not engaged in an ongoing business. On August 1, the Bankruptcy Court ruled that . . . petitioner failed to qualify for relief under Chapter 11.

The . . . District Court . . . upheld the Bankruptcy Court's dismissal of petitioner's Chapter 11 case. The . . . Court of Appeals . . . affirmed. . . . We granted certiorari. . . .

In our view, the plain language of the Bankruptcy Code disposes of the question before us. Section 109 defines who may be a debtor under the various chapters of the Code. Section 109(d) provides: "Only a person that may be a debtor under chapter 7 of this title, except a stockbroker or a commodity broker, and a railroad may be a debtor under chapter 11 of this title. . . ." The Code defines "person" as used in Title 11 to "include [an] individual." Under the express terms of the Code, therefore, petitioner is "a person who may be a debtor under chapter 7" and satisfies the statutory requirements for a Chapter 11 debtor.

The Code contains no ongoing business requirement for reorganization under Chapter 11, and we are loath to infer the exclusion of certain classes of debtors from the protections of Chapter 11, because Congress took care in § 109 to specify who qualifies—and who does not qualify—as a debtor under the various chapters of the Code. . . . Congress knew how to restrict recourse to the avenues of bankruptcy relief; it did not place Chapter 11 reorganization beyond the reach of a nonbusiness individual debtor. . . .

We are not persuaded by the contention that Chapter 11 is unavailable to a debtor without an ongoing business because many of the Chapter's provisions do not apply to a nonbusiness debtor. There is no doubt that Congress intended that a business debtor be among those who might use Chapter 11. Code provisions . . . certainly are designed to aid in the rehabilitation of a business. It does not follow, however, that a debtor whose affairs do not warrant recourse to these provisions is ineligible for Chapter 11 relief. Instead, these provisions . . . reflect an understandable expectation that Chapter 11 would be used primarily by debtors with ongoing businesses; they do not constitute an additional prerequisite for Chapter 11 eligibility beyond those established in § 109(d).

Although the foregoing analysis is dispositive of the question presented, we deal briefly with . . . policy considerations . . . inferring a congressional intent to preclude a nonbusiness debtor from reorganizing under Chapter 11. . . . Petitioner suggests, . . . and we agree, that Chapter 11 . . . embodies the general Code policy of maximizing the value of the bankruptcy estate. Under certain circumstances a consumer debtor's estate will be worth more if reorganized under Chapter 11 than if liquidated under Chapter 7. Allowing such a debtor to proceed under Chapter 11 serves the congressional purpose of deriving as much value as possible from the debtor's estate. . . .

Section 1129(a)(7) provides that a reorganization plan may not be confirmed unless all the debtor's creditors accept the plan or will receive not less than they would receive under a Chapter 7 liquidation. Because creditors cannot be expected to approve a plan in which they would receive less than they would from an immediate liquidation of the debtor's assets, it follows that a Chapter 11 reorganization plan usually will be confirmed only when creditors will receive at least as much as if the debtor were to file under Chapter 7. Absent some showing of harm to the creditors of a nonbusiness debtor allowed to reorganize under Chapter 11, we see nothing in the allocation of "burdens" and "benefits" of Chapter 11 that warrants an inference that Congress intended to exclude a consumer debtor from its coverage. . . .

The plain language of the Bankruptcy Code permits individual debtors not engaged in business to file for relief under Chapter 11. Although the structure and legislative history of Chapter 11 indicate that this Chapter was intended primarily for the use of business debtors, the Code contains no "ongoing business" requirement for Chapter 11 reorganization, and we find no basis for imposing one. Accordingly, the judgment of the Court of Appeals is

■ *Reversed.*

CASE CONCEPTS REVIEW

1. What type of bankruptcy proceeding was utilized initially by the debtor?
2. What motivated the debtor to convert the initial case to a Chapter 11 proceeding?
3. The lower courts all agreed on the proper outcome of this case. What was that judgment?
4. Why does the Supreme Court reverse these judgments? Discuss at least three reasons for this conclusion.

14. Automatic Stay

Bankruptcy cases operate to **stay** other judicial or administrative proceedings against the debtor. These stays of proceedings may operate to the detriment of a creditor or third party. For example, a stay would prevent a utility company from shutting off service. Despite this potential harm to creditors, the stay automatically becomes applicable immediately upon the bankruptcy petition being filed.

The stay provision often works to the disadvantage of secured creditors; especially in reorganization cases under Chapter 11. If the value of the property securing the debt does not cover the full debt, the creditor will lose because he or she cannot sell the property during the period of the stay. Creditors whose collateral is worth less than the loan amount are not entitled to compensation for the period of the stay in the bankruptcy court.

When the trustee continues to operate the debtor's business, it is frequently necessary to use, sell, or lease property of the debtor. To prevent irreparable harm to creditors and other third parties as a result of stays, a trustee may be required to provide "adequate protection" to third parties. In some cases, adequate protection requires that the trustee make periodic cash payments to creditors. In others, the trustee may be required to provide a lien to the creditor. When the sale, lease, or rental of the debtor's property may decrease the value of an entity's interest in property held by the trustee, a creditor may be entitled to a lien on the proceeds of any sale, lease, or rental. The court is empowered to determine if the trustee has furnished adequate protection; and when the issue is raised, the burden of proof is on the trustee.

The automatic stay is designed to protect both debtor and creditor. The stay provides the debtor time and freedom from financial pressures to attempt repayment or to develop a plan of reorganization. Creditors are protected by the stay, since it forces them to comply with the orderly administration of the debtor's estate. In other words, the stay prevents some creditors from grabbing all the debtor's assets while other creditors receive nothing. It also allows for orderly trials of claims such as those for personal injury or wrongful death. Such claims are tried in the federal district courts and not in the bankruptcy courts.

Despite these advantages of staying all proceedings against the debtor who files a bankruptcy petition, there are exceptions to the application of the automatic stay. These exceptions apply to proceedings that are not directly related to the debtor's financial situation. Proceedings that are not automatically stayed when a bankruptcy petition is filed include (1) criminal actions against the debtor; (2) the collection of alimony, maintenance, or support from property that is not part of the estate; and (3) the commencement or continuation of an action by a governmental unit to enforce that governmental unit's police power. Although these actions are not stayed automatically by the filing of a bankruptcy petition, the trustee may seek to enjoin these actions if they harm the debtor's estate.

15. Meeting of Creditors

In a voluntary case, the debtor has filed the required schedules with the petition. In an involuntary case, if the court orders relief, the debtor will be required to complete the same schedules as the debtor in a voluntary proceeding. From this point, the proceedings are identical. All parties are given notice of the order for relief. If the debtor owns real property, notice is usually filed in the public records of the county where the land is situated. The notice to creditors will include the date by which all claims are to be filed and the date of a meeting of the creditors with the debtor. This meeting of creditors must be within a reasonable time after the order for relief. The debtor appears at the meeting with the creditors, and the creditors are allowed to question the debtor under oath. The court may also order a meeting of any equity security holders of the debtor.

At the meeting of creditors, the debtor may be examined by the creditors to ascertain if property has been omitted from the list of assets, if property has been conveyed in defraud of creditors, and other matters that may affect the right of the debtor to have his or her obligations discharged.

In liquidation cases, the first meeting of creditors includes the important step of electing a *permanent trustee*. This trustee will replace the interim trustee appointed by the court at the time the order for relief was entered. The unsecured creditors who are not insiders elect this permanent trustee. To have a valid election, creditors representing at least 20 percent of the amount of unsecured claims held against the debtor must vote. The election is then determined by a majority of the unsecured creditors voting.

TRUSTEE AND CASE ADMINISTRATION

16. Trustee and the Estate

The trustee may be an individual or a corporation that has the capacity to perform the duties of a trustee. In a case under Chapter 7 or 13 of the Act, an individual trustee must reside or have an office and the corporate trustee must have an office in the judicial district in which the case is pending or in an adjacent district. Prior to becoming a trustee in a particular case, the trustee must file with the court a bond in favor of the United States. This bond may be used as a source of collection if the trustee should fail to faithfully perform his or her duties.

The trustee is the representative of the estate and has the capacity to sue and to be sued. Trustees are authorized to employ professional persons such as attorneys, accountants, appraisers, and auctioneers and to deposit or invest the money of the estate during the proceedings. In making deposits or investments, the trustee must seek the maximum reasonable net return, taking into account the safety of the deposit or investment.

The statute has detailed provisions on the responsibilities of the trustee under the tax laws. As a general rule, the trustee has responsibility for filing tax returns for the estate. After the order for relief, income received by the estate is taxable to it and not to an individual debtor. The estate of a partnership or a corporation debtor is not a separate entity for tax purposes. While the technical requirements of the tax laws are beyond the scope of this text, it should be remembered that the bankruptcy laws contain detailed rules complementary to the Internal Revenue Code in bankruptcy cases, and both must be followed by the trustee.

17. General Duties and Powers

The statutory duties of the trustees in liquidation proceedings are to (1) collect and reduce to money the property of the estate; (2) account for all property received; (3) investigate the financial affairs of the debtor, (4) examine proofs of claims and object to the allowance of any claim that is improper; (5) oppose the discharge of the debtor if advisable; (6) furnish information required by a party in interest; (7) file appropriate reports with the court and the taxing authorities, if a business is operated; and (8) make a final report and account and file it with the court.

A trustee that is authorized to operate the business of the debtor is authorized to obtain unsecured credit and to incur debts in the ordinary course of business. These debts are paid as administrative expenses.

A trustee in bankruptcy has several rights and powers with respect to the property of the debtor. First, the trustee has a judicial lien on the property, just as if the trustee were a creditor. Second, the trustee has the rights and powers of a judgment creditor who obtained a judgment against the debtor on the date of the adjudication of bankruptcy and who had an execution issued that was returned unsatisfied.

Third, the trustee has the rights of a bona fide purchaser of the real property of the debtor as of the date of the petition. Finally, the trustee has the rights of an actual unsecured creditor to avoid any transfer of the debtor's property and to avoid any obligation incurred by the debtor that is voidable under any federal or state law. As a result of these rights, the trustee is able to set aside transfers of property and to eliminate the interests of other parties where creditors or the debtor could do so.

The trustee also has the power to avoid certain liens of others on the property of the debtor. Liens that first become effective on the bankruptcy or insolvency of the debtor are voidable. As a general rule, liens that are not perfected or enforceable against a bona fide purchaser of the property are also voidable. Assume that a seller or creditor has an unperfected lien on goods in the hands of the debtor on the date the petition is filed. The lien is perfected later. That lien is voidable if it could not be asserted against a good-faith purchaser of the goods. Liens for rent and for distress for rent are also voidable.

The law imposes certain limitations on all these rights and powers of the trustee. A purchase-money security interest under Article 9 of the Code may be perfected after the petition is filed if it is perfected within ten days of delivery of the property. Such a security interest cannot be avoided by the trustee if properly perfected.

The rights and powers of the trustee are subject to those of a seller of goods in the ordinary course of business who has the right to reclaim goods if the debtor was insolvent when the debtor received them. The seller must demand the goods back within ten days, and the right to reclaim is subject to any superior rights of secured creditors. Courts may deny reclamation and protect the seller by giving his or her claim priority as an administrative expense.

18. Executory Contracts and Unexpired Leases

Debtors are frequently parties to contracts that have not been performed. Also, there are often lessees of real property, and the leases usually cover long periods of time. As a general rule, the trustee is authorized, subject to court approval, to assume or to reject an executory contract or unexpired lease. If the contract or lease is rejected, the other party has a claim subject to some statutory limitations. A rejection by the trustee creates a prepetition claim for the rejected contract or lease debt subject to these limitations.

If the contract or lease is assumed, the trustee will perform the contract or assign it to someone else, and the estate will presumably receive the benefits. If the trustee assumes a contract or lease, he or she must cure any default by the debtor and provide adequate assurance of future performance. In shopping-center leases, adequate assurance includes protection against declines in percentage rents and preservation of the tenant mix, among other things.

A trustee may not assume an executory contract that requires the other party to make a loan, deliver equipment, or issue a security to the debtor. A party to a contract based on the financial strength of the debtor is not required to extend new credit to a debtor in bankruptcy.

Contracts and leases often have clauses prohibiting assignment. The law also prohibits the assignment of certain contract rights, such as those that are personal in nature. The trustee in bankruptcy is allowed to assume contracts, notwithstanding a clause prohibiting the assumption or assignment of the contract or lease. The trustee is not allowed to assume a contract if applicable nonbankruptcy law excuses the other party from performance to someone other than the debtor, unless the other party consents to the assumption.

The statute invalidates contract clauses that automatically terminate contracts or leases upon filing of a petition in bankruptcy or upon the assignment of the lease or contract. The law also invalidates contract clauses that give a party other than the debtor the right to terminate the contract upon assumption by the trustee or assignment by the debtor. Such clauses hamper rehabilitation efforts and are against public policy. They are not needed, because the court can require the trustee to provide adequate protection and can ensure that the other party receives the benefit of its bargain.

Debtors are sometimes lessors instead of lessees. If the trustee rejects an unexpired lease of a debtor lessor, the tenant may treat the lease as terminated or may remain in possession for the balance of the lease. There is a similar provision for contract purchasers of real estate. They may treat the rejection as a termination, or they may remain in possession and make the payments due under the contract. A purchaser that treats a contract as terminated has a lien on the property to the extent of the purchase price paid.

If the trustee assigns a contract to a third party and the third party later breaches the contract, the trustee has no liability. This is a change of the common law in which an assignor is not relieved of liability by an assignment. An assignment by a trustee in bankruptcy is, in effect, a novation if the assignment is valid.

In 1984, the United States Supreme Court held that the trustee's power gave the trustee the right to terminate employees who were working under a collective bargaining contract. Unions were so upset by this ruling that they convinced Congress that the court's decision had to be changed by legislation. Indeed, the union's efforts were a major reason that the 1984 amendments were passed by Congress and signed by President Ronald Reagan. When an employer files a petition under Chapter 11, the amended law requires the trustee to apply to the court to reject the collective bargaining contract. After the application is filed, the trustee and the employees' representative must negotiate about how the collective bargaining contract can be changed to allow the debtor-employer to reorganize successfully. If these negotiations are unsuccessful in reaching a mutual agreement, the trustee may seek the bankruptcy court's approval to reject the collective bargaining contract. The court must conduct a hearing within fourteen days after the trustee filed an application to reject the contract. The court's ruling on this application must be announced within thirty days of the hearing.

In 1988, Congress provided a mechanism allowing a debtor in a Chapter 11 proceeding, through its trustee, to modify the payments of insurance benefits to retired employees. Retiree benefits are those "payments to any entity or person for the purpose of providing or reimbursing payments for retired employees and their spouses and dependents, for medical, surgical, or hospital care benefits, or benefits in the event of sickness, accident, disability, or death under any plan, fund, or program maintained or established in whole or in part by the debtor prior to filing a petition commencing under this title."

A proposed modification is to be made to the authorized representative of the retirees. If this modification is rejected, an application for modification of retiree benefits can be filed with the bankruptcy court. A hearing within fourteen days of the application being filed allows all interested parties to express their views. The bankruptcy court is supposed to rule on the requested modification within ninety days of the hearing's commencement.

19. Voidable Preferences

Preference If an insolvent debtor pays some creditors a greater percentage of the debts than other creditors in the same class, and if the payments are made within ninety days prior to filing a bankruptcy petition, those payments constitute illegal and voidable preference. An intention to prefer such creditors must be shown.

One of the goals of bankruptcy proceedings is to provide an equitable distribution of a debtor's property among creditors. To achieve this goal, the trustee in bankruptcy is allowed to recover transfers that constitute a **preference** of one creditor over another. As one judge said, "A creditor who dips his hand in a pot which he knows will not go round must return what he receives, so that all may share." To constitute a recoverable preference, the transfer must (1) have been made by an insolvent debtor; (2) have been made to a creditor for, or on account of, an antecedent debt owed by the debtor before the transfer; (3) have been made within ninety days of the filing of the bankruptcy petition; and (4) enable the creditor to receive a greater percentage of the claim than he or she would receive under a distribution from the bankruptcy estate in a liquidation proceeding.

Insofar as the time period is concerned, there is an exception when the transfer is to an insider. In this case, the trustee may avoid the transfer if it occurred within one year of the date of filing the petition, provided the insider had reasonable cause to believe the debtor was insolvent at the time of the transfer.

A debtor is presumed to be insolvent during the ninety-day period prior to the filing of the petition. Any person contending that the debtor was solvent has the burden of coming forward with evidence to prove solvency. Once credible evidence is introduced, the party with the benefit of the presumption of insolvency has the burden of persuasion on the issue.

Recoverable preferences include not only payments of money but also the transfer of property as payment of, or as security for, a prior indebtedness. Since the law is limited to debts, payments by the debtor of tax liabilities are exempt from the preference provision and are not recoverable. A mortgage or pledge may be set aside as readily as direct payments. A pledge or mortgage can be avoided if received within the immediate ninety-day period prior to the filing of the petition in bankruptcy, provided it was obtained as security for a previous debt. The effective date of a transfer or a mortgage of real property may be questioned if the date the legal documents are signed is different from the date these documents are recorded. A logical solution to this potential problem seems to be to rely on the date the document is recorded in the public records.

Payment of a fully secured claim does not constitute a preference and therefore may not be recovered. Transfers of property for a contemporaneous consideration may not be set aside, because there is a corresponding asset for the new liability. A mortgage given to secure a contemporaneous loan is valid even when the mortgagee took the security with knowledge of the debtor's insolvency. An insolvent debtor has a right to attempt to extricate himself or herself, as far as possible, from financial difficulty. If the new security is personal property, it must be perfected within ten days after the security interest attaches. The trustee's power to avoid a preference does not apply in a case filed by an individual debtor whose debts are primarily consumer debts if the aggregate value of the property subject to the preferential transfer is less than $600.

The law also creates an exception for transfers in the ordinary course of business or in the ordinary financial affairs of persons not in business. The payment of such debts is not recoverable by the trustee. This exception covers ordinary debt payments such as utility bills. The law on preferences is directed at unusual transfers and payments, not those occurring promptly in the ordinary course of the debtor's affairs. The following case discusses the issue of whether payments on long-term debt can be made in the ordinary course of business or whether this exception to the trustee's power to avoid preferential payment is limited to short-term debt.

CASE

Union Bank v. Wolas
112 S.Ct. 527 (1991)

STEVENS, J.

Section 547(b) of the Bankruptcy Code authorizes a trustee to avoid certain property transfers made by a debtor within 90 days before bankruptcy. The Code makes an exception, however, for transfers made in the ordinary course of business, § 547(c)(2). The question presented is whether payments on long-term debt may qualify for that exception.

On December 17, 1986, ZZZZ Best Co., Inc. (Debtor) borrowed seven million dollars from petitioner, Union Bank (Bank). On July 8, 1987, the Debtor filed a voluntary petition under Chapter 7 of the Bankruptcy Code. During the preceding 90-day period, the Debtor had made two interest payments totalling approximately $100,000 and had paid a loan commitment fee of about $2,500 to the Bank. After his appointment as trustee of the Debtor's estate, respondent filed a complaint against the Bank to recover payments pursuant to § 547(b).

The Bankruptcy Court found that the loans had been made "in the ordinary course of business or financial affairs" of both the Debtor and the Bank, and that both interest payments as well as the payment of the loan commitment fee had been made according to ordinary business terms and in the ordinary course of business. . . . The Bankruptcy Court concluded that the payments . . . were not avoidable by the trustee. The District Court affirmed. . . .

The Court of Appeals held that the ordinary course of business exception to avoidance of preferential transfers was not available to long-term creditors. . . . [Thus, the District Court's decision was reversed.] The importance of the question of law . . . persuaded us to grant the Bank's petition for certiorari.

. . . In subsection 547(b), Congress broadly authorized bankruptcy trustees to "avoid any transfer of an interest of the debtor in property" if five conditions are satisfied and unless one of seven exceptions defined in subsection (c) is applicable. In brief, the five characteristics of a voidable preference are that it (1) benefit a creditor; (2) be on account of antecedent debt; (3) be made while the debtor was insolvent; (4) be within 90 days before bankruptcy; and (5) enable the creditor to receive a larger share of the estate than if the transfer had not been made. Section 547 also provides that the debtor is presumed to have been insolvent during the 90-day period preceding bankruptcy. In this case, it is undisputed that all five of the foregoing conditions were satisfied and that the interest and loan commitment fee payments were voidable preferences unless excepted by subsection (c)(2).

The most significant feature of subsection (c)(2) that is relevant to this case is the absence of any language distinguishing between long-term debt and short-term debt. That subsection provides:

> The trustee may not avoid under this section a transfer—
>
> ... (2) to the extent that such transfer was—
>
> (A) in payment of a debt incurred by the debtor in the ordinary course of business or financial affairs of the debtor and the transferee;
>
> (B) made in the ordinary course of business or financial affairs of the debtor and the transferee; and
>
> (C) made according to ordinary business terms.

Instead of focusing on the term of the debt for which the transfer was made, subsection (c)(2) focuses on whether the debt was incurred, and payment made, in the "ordinary course of business or financial affairs" of the debtor and transferee. Thus, the text provides no support for respondent's contention that § 547(c)(2)'s coverage is limited to short-term debt, such as commercial paper or trade debt. . . .

The Bank and the trustee agrees that § 547 is intended to serve two basic policies that are fairly described in the House Committee Report. The Committee explained:

> A preference is a transfer that enables a creditor to receive payment of a greater percentage of his claim against the debtor than he would have received if the transfer had not been made and he had participated in the distribution of the assets of the bankrupt estate. The purpose of the preference section is two-fold. First, by permitting the trustee to avoid prebankruptcy transfers that occur within a short period before bankruptcy, creditors are discouraged from racing to the courthouse to dismember the debtor during his slide into bankruptcy. The protection thus afforded the debtor often enables him to work his way out of a difficult financial situation through cooperation with all of his creditors. Second, and more important, the preference provisions facilitate the prime bankruptcy policy of equality of distribution among creditors of the debtor. Any creditor that received a greater payment than others of his class is required to disgorge so that all may share equally. The operation of the preference section to deter 'the face of diligence' of creditors to dismember the debtor before bankruptcy furthers

the second goal of the preference section—that of equality of distribution.

As this comment demonstrates, the two policies are not entirely independent. On the one hand, any exception for a payment on account of an antecedent debt tends to favor the payee over other creditors and therefore may conflict with the policy of equal treatment. On the other hand, the ordinary course of business exception may benefit all creditors by deterring the "race to the courthouse" and enabling the struggling debtor to continue operating its business.

Respondent places primary emphasis, as did the Court of Appeals, on the interest in equal distribution. When a debtor is insolvent, a transfer to one creditor necessarily impairs the claims of the debtor's other unsecured and undersecured creditors. By authorizing the avoidance of such preferential transfers, § 547(b) empowers the trustee to restore equal status to all creditors. Respondent thus contends that the ordinary course of business exception should be limited to short-term debt so the trustee may order that preferential long-term debt payments be returned to the estate to be distributed among all of the creditors.

But the statutory text—which makes no distinction between short-term debt and long-term debt—precludes an analysis that divorces the policy of favoring equal distribution from the policy of discouraging creditors from racing to the courthouse to dismember the debtor. Long-term creditors, as well as trade creditors, may seek a head start in that race. Thus, even if we accept the Court of Appeals' conclusion that the availability of the ordinary business exception to long-term creditors does not directly further the policy of equal treatment, we must recognize that it does further the policy of deterring the race to the courthouse and, as the House Report recognized, may indirectly further the goal of equal distribution as well. Whether Congress has wisely balanced the sometime conflicting policies underlying § 547 is not a question that we are authorized to decide.

In sum, we hold that payments on long-term debt, as well as payments on short-term debt, may qualify for the ordinary course of business exception to the trustee's power to avoid preferential transfers. . . .

■ *Reversed and remanded.*

CASE CONCEPTS REVIEW

1. What payments by the debtor (ZZZZ Best Co.) are challenged by the trustee (Wolas) as being preferential and thus voidable?
2. What five elements must the trustee prove to justify the finding that a payment is a preference?
3. Petitioner (Union Bank) argues that the payments

made by the debtor fall within the scope of what exception to the voidable preferences?

4. How does the respondent (Wolas, as trustee) respond to the application of this exception?

5. What does this court conclude about the application of the ordinary course of business exception to voidable preferences?

20. Fraudulent Transfers

A transfer of property by a debtor may be fraudulent under federal or state law. The trustee may proceed under either to set aside a fraudulent conveyance. Under federal law, a *fraudulent conveyance* is a transfer within one year of the filing of the petition, with the intent to hinder, delay, or defraud creditors. Under state law, the period may be longer and is usually within the range of two to five years.

Fraudulent intent may be inferred from the fact that the consideration is unfair, inadequate, or nonexistent. Solvency or insolvency at the time of the transfer is significant, but it is not controlling. Fraudulent intent exists when the transfer makes it impossible for the creditors to be paid in full or for the creditors to use legal remedies that would otherwise be available.

The intent to hinder, delay, or defraud creditors may also be implied. Such is the case when the debtor is insolvent and makes a transfer for less than a full and adequate value. Fraudulent intent is present if the debtor was insolvent on the date of the transfer or if the debtor becomes insolvent as a result of the transfer.

If the debtor is engaged in business or is about to become so, the fraudulent intent will be implied when the transfer leaves the businessperson with an unreasonably small amount of capital. The businessperson may be solvent; nevertheless, he or she has made a fraudulent transfer if the net result of the transfer leaves him or her with an unreasonably small amount of capital, provided the transfer was without fair consideration. Whether or not the remaining capital is unreasonably small is a question of fact.

The trustee may also avoid a transfer made in contemplation of incurring obligations beyond the debtor's ability to repay as they mature. Assume that a woman is about to enter business and that she plans to incur debts in the business. Because of her concern that she may be unable to meet these potential obligations, she transfers all her property to her husband, without consideration. Such a transfer may be set aside as fraudulent. The requisite intent is supplied by the factual situation at the time of the transfer and the state of mind of the transferor. The actual financial condition of the debtor in such a case is not controlling but does shed some light on the intent factor and state of mind of the debtor.

The trustee of a partnership debtor may avoid transfers of partnership property to partners if the debtor was or thereby became insolvent. This rule was made to prevent a partnership's preferring partners who are also creditors over other partners. Such transfers may be avoided if they occurred within one year of the date of filing the petition.

If a transferee is liable to the trustee only because the transfer was to defraud creditors, the law limits the transferee's liability. To the extent that the transferee does give value in good faith, the transferee has a lien on the property. For the purpose of defining value in the fraudulent transfer situation, the term includes property or the satisfaction or securing of a present or existing debt. It does not include an unperformed promise to support the debtor or a relative of a debtor.

21. Creditors and Claims

Creditors are required to file proof of their claims if they are to share in the debtor's estate. Filed claims are allowed unless a party in interest objects. If an objection is filed, the court conducts a hearing to determine the validity of the claim. A claim may be disallowed if it is (1) unenforceable because of usury, unconscionability, or failure of consideration, (2) for unmatured interest, (3) an insider's or attorney's claim and exceeds the reasonable value of the services rendered, (4) for unmatured alimony or child support, (5) for rent, and (6) for breach of an employment contract. These latter two claims may be disallowed to the extent that they exceed the statutory limitations for such claims.

Illegality can be raised, because any defense available to the debtor is available to the trustee. Postpetition interest is not collectible, because interest stops accruing at the date of filing the petition. Bankruptcy operates as an acceleration of the principal due. From the date of filing, the amount of the claim is the total principal plus interest to that date.

Unreasonable attorney's fees and claims of insiders are disallowed because they encourage concealing assets or returning them to the debtor. Since alimony claims are not dischargeable in bankruptcy, there is no reason to allow a claim for postpetition alimony and child support.

The amount of rent that may be included in a claim is limited. The law is designed to compensate the landlord for his or her loss, but not to allow the claim to be so large that other creditors will not share in the estate. A landlord's damages are limited to the rent for the greater of one year or 15 percent of the remaining lease term, not to exceed three years. In liquidation cases, the time is measured from the earlier of the date of filing the petition and the date of surrender of possession. In cases filed under Chapters 9, 11, and 13 of the Act, the claim is limited to three years' rent. Of course, these limitations are not applicable to rent owed by the trustee, an administrative expense for which the estate is liable.

Landlords often have a security deposit for rent. To the extent that the security deposit exceeds the rent allowed as a claim, it must be paid over to the trustee to be a part of the bankruptcy estate. If the security deposit is less than the claim, the landlord keeps the security deposit, and it will be applied in satisfaction of the claim. The limitations on claims for rent are applicable to bona fide leases, not to leases of real property that are financing or security leases.

The limitation for damages resulting from termination of employment contracts is similar to the one for rent. Damages are limited to compensation for the year following the earlier of the date of the petition and that of the termination of employment.

Claims are sometimes contingent or otherwise unliquidated and uncertain. Personal injury and wrongful death claims against a debtor that cannot be settled are tried in federal district courts and not in bankruptcy courts. The law authorizes the bankruptcy court to estimate and to fix the amount of such claims, if necessary, to avoid undue delay in closing the estate or approving of a plan of reorganization. The same is true of equitable remedies such as specific performance. Courts will convert such remedies to dollar amounts and proceed to close the estate or approve the plan.

If a secured claim is undersecured—that is, if the debt exceeds the value of the collateral—the claim is divided into two parts. The claim is secured to the extent of the value of the collateral. It is an unsecured claim for the balance.

22. Right of Setoff

Any creditor who also owes the debtor money may have a right of *setoff*. In essence, this creditor is allowed to cancel out these obligations. For example, suppose that a bank lends a debtor $2,000 and that this debtor has $1,500 on deposit at the bank. If the debtor fails to make payment on the $2,000 loan, the bank can use the deposit to reduce the amount of the debtor's loan.

If a debtor files a bankruptcy petition and the creditor exercises the right of setoff, the issue of a preference arises. In our example, the bank becomes a preferred creditor to the extent of the $1,500 setoff, but the bank generally is legally entitled to this preference if the amount of the deposit has not increased during the ninety days preceding the filing of the petition in bankruptcy. However, this preference would be nullified if the deposit was made or increased just before the bankruptcy petition was filed for the purpose of preferring the bank over other creditors. In that case, the deposit becomes a part of the debtor's estate, and the setoff is disallowed.

Since the filing of the petition in bankruptcy operates as a stay of all proceedings, the right of setoff operates at the time of final distribution of the estate. Since the law allows the trustee to use the funds of the debtor with court approval, parties who wish to exercise the right of setoff should seek "adequate protection."

The right to setoff will usually be exercised by a creditor against a deposit that has been made within ninety days of the filing of a petition in bankruptcy. Quite frequently, there are several such deposits, and there may also have been several payments on the debt during the ninety-day period. As a result of these variables, the application of setoff principles is sometimes difficult.

The law seeks to prohibit a creditor from improving his or her position during the ninety-day period. It does so by allowing the trustee to recover that portion of the setoff that would be considered a preference. This amount recoverable by the trustee is the insufficiency between the amount owed and the amount on deposit on the first day of the ninety-day period preceding the filing of a bankruptcy petition that a deficiency occurred to the extent that this insufficiency is greater than the insufficiency existing on the day the petition is filed. If the deposit on the first day of the preceding ninety-day period exceeds the creditor's claim, look for the first insufficiency during the ninety-day period and calculate the setoff based on the first insufficiency.

Assume that a bankruptcy petition was filed on September 2. Throughout the ninety days prior to this filing, the debtor owes $2,000 to the creditor. On June 4, the debtor has on deposit with the creditor $1,500. On July 15, the amount on deposit is reduced to $700. On September 1, the debtor's balance is increased to $1,800. At the time of the filing, the creditor seeks to use the entire $1,800 on deposit to set off its claim against the debtor. The trustee would be able to recover $300 of this attempted setoff, since there was a greater insufficiency of that amount on the first day of the ninety-day period prior to the petition's being filed. In other words, the creditor's setoff would be limited to $1,500.

23. Priorities

The bankruptcy law establishes certain priorities in the payment of claims. After secured creditors have had the opportunity to benefit from a security interest in collateral, the general order of priority is as follows:

1. Administrative expenses
2. Involuntary GAP creditors
3. Wages, salaries, and commissions
4. Contributions to employee benefit plans
5. Suppliers of grain to a grain storage facility or of fish to a fish produce storage or processing facility
6. Consumer deposits
7. Governmental units for certain taxes

Administrative expenses include all costs of administering the debtor's estate, including taxes incurred by the estate. Typical costs include attorney's fees, appraiser's fees, and wages paid to persons employed to help preserve the estate.

The term *involuntary GAP creditor* describes a person who extends credit to the estate after the filing of an involuntary petition under Chapter 11 and before a trustee is appointed or before the order for relief is entered. Such claims include taxes incurred as the result of the conduct of business in this period.

The third class of priority is limited to amounts earned by an individual within ninety days of the filing of the petition or the cessation of the debtor's business, whichever occurred first. The priority is limited to $2,000 for each individual, but it includes vacation, severance, and sick leave pay as well as regular earnings. The employee's share of employment taxes is included in the third priority category, provided the wages and the employee's share of taxes have been paid in full. The category does not include fees paid to independent contractors.

The fourth priority recognizes that fringe benefits are an important part of many labor-management contracts. The priority is limited to claims for contributions to employee benefit plans, arising from services rendered within 120 days before commencement of the case or cessation of the debtor's business, whichever occurs first. The priority is limited to $2,000 multiplied by the number of employees less the amount paid under priority 3. The net effect is to limit the total priority for wages and employee benefits to $2,000 per employee.

The fifth priority was included in the 1984 amendments. It is designed to protect the farmer who raises grain and the fisherman if their grain or fish are held by the owner of a production or storage facility. If the farmers or fishermen have not been paid for the grain or fish transferred, they have a priority claim to the extent of $2,000 per creditor.

The sixth priority was added in 1978 as an additional method of consumer protection. It protects consumers who have deposited money in connection with the purchase, lease, or rental of property or the purchase of services for personal, family, or household use that were not delivered or provided. The priority is limited to $900 per consumer.

The seventh priority is for certain taxes. Priority is given to income taxes for a taxable year that ended on or before the date of filing the petition. The last due date of the return must have occurred not more than three years before the filing. Employment taxes and transfer taxes such as gift, estate, sale, and excise taxes are also given sixth-class priority. Again the transaction or event that gave rise to the tax must precede the petition date, and the return must have been due within three years. The bankruptcy laws have several very technical aspects relating to taxation, and they must be reviewed carefully for tax returns filed by the trustee and claims for taxes.

In liquidation cases, the property available is first distributed among the priority claimants in the order just discussed. Then the property is distributed to general unsecured creditors who file their claims on time. Next, payment is made to unsecured creditors who tardily file their claims. Thereafter distribution is made to holders of penalty, forfeiture, or punitive damage claims. Punitive penalties, including tax penalties, are subordinated to the first three classes of claims, as a matter of policy. Regular creditors should be paid before windfalls to persons and entities collecting penalties. Finally, postpetition interest on prepetition claims is paid if any property is available to do so. After the interest is paid, any surplus goes to the debtor. Claims within a particular class are paid pro rata if the trustee is unable to pay them in full.

CHAPTER SUMMARY

1. Of major importance today is the Bankruptcy Reform Act of 1978 as it has been amended in 1984, 1986, 1988, and 1990.
2. The basic purpose of the bankruptcy law is to give a debtor in financial difficulty an opportunity to overcome this problem.
3. Terms to remember include *debtor, claim, order of relief, discharge,* and *trustee*.

TYPES OF PROCEEDINGS

In General

1. The bankruptcy law has two basic approaches to resolving a debtor's financial problems—one is liquidation and the other is reorganization.

Liquidation Proceedings

1. This proceeding is governed by Chapter 7 of the statute.
2. In general, a debtor surrenders all assets from which creditors are paid as much as possible.
3. Individual debtors generally have all unpaid debts discharged or forgiven. Technically, a business organization's debts are not discharged.

Reorganization Proceedings

1. This proceeding is governed by Chapter 11 of the statute.
2. In essence, the debtor attempts to restructure the financial situation so creditors can be substantially paid over time.
3. The key to a successful reorganization is the court's approval of a reasonable confirmation plan.

Adjustment of Individuals' Debts

1. This proceeding is governed by Chapter 13 of the statute.
2. The debtor must be an individual who has regular income and who has unsecured debts not exceeding $100,000 and secured debts not exceeding $350,000.
3. Again, a plan of repayment must be approved. The unsecured creditors must receive at least as much as they would under a Chapter 7 liquidation proceeding.

Adjustment of Family Farmers' Debts

1. This proceeding is governed by Chapter 12 of the statute.
2. A farmer may have debts reduced to the value of his or her collateral.

3. Farmers must use all income that is not required for support to pay off unsecured debts. Any debts not paid within five years are discharged.

4. Periodic payments are paid on secured debts to pay off the value of the collateral.

GENERAL PRINCIPLES

Property of the Estate

1. All the property interests of a debtor are used to create an estate.
2. The trustee, in essence, has whatever interests a debtor had at the time a bankruptcy petition was filed.

Exemptions

1. To enhance the debtor's fresh start, the debtor may exempt certain property from the estate.
2. These exemptions are governed by either federal or state law, whichever the state law provides.

Debts That Are Not Discharged

1. Certain debts are not discharged; therefore they survive the bankruptcy case and remain payable to the creditor.

Grounds for Denying Discharge

1. There also are grounds for denying a discharge.
2. Basically, in its balancing process, the drafters of the law decided that debts created in certain situations should not be forgiven.

PROCEDURAL STEPS

Voluntary Commencement

1. Any proceeding may be started by a debtor filing a petition in bankruptcy.
2. The voluntary filing acts as an order of relief unless the bankruptcy judge decides that a consumer debtor is not entitled to Chapter 7 protection.

Involuntary Commencement

1. In general, cases may also be started by creditors with at least $5,000 in claims filing a petition. This creditor-commenced action is known as an *involuntary case*.
2. In an involuntary case, the bankruptcy judge must decide whether an order of relief is appropriate.
3. An involuntary case cannot be filed under Chapter 13 of the statute regardless of who the debtor is. An involuntary case under Chapters 7 and 11 cannot be filed when the debtor is a farmer or a nonprofit corporation.

Automatic Stay

1. The filing of a bankruptcy petition protects the debtor against any action taken by creditors.
2. This stay is automatic even before the creditors learn of the petition's being filed.
3. The stay remains in effect until the bankruptcy judge permits actions by creditors.

Meeting of Creditors

1. After the order of relief is entered, a meeting of the creditors will be scheduled. At this meeting, creditors can question the debtor and examine documents.
2. Also at this meeting, unsecured creditors will elect a permanent trustee.

TRUSTEE AND CASE ADMINISTRATION

Trustee and the Estate

1. The trustee must satisfy statutory prerequisites before he, she, or it is qualified.
2. The trustee has the responsibility for preserving the estate for the benefit of all creditors.
3. The trustee must fulfill the administrative duties with regard to taxes and similar matters.
4. In general, the trustee is a fiduciary of the estate.

General Duties and Powers

1. The trustee may employ professionals in representing the estate. The trustee also may sue and be sued in a representative capacity.
2. The trustee has several statutory duties designed to ensure the proper workings of the bankruptcy law.

3. The trustee may operate the business of the debtor and may incur expenses associated with such an operation.

4. The trustee may assume the position of a lienholder or a good-faith purchaser if such positions enhance the estate.

5. The trustee also may avoid certain liens on the debtor's property.

Executory Contracts and Unexpired Leases

1. The trustee has the general power to perform or avoid executory contracts and unexpired leases, regardless of what the agreement may state about the debtor's right to assign.

2. The trustee's power to avoid or modify a collective bargaining contract has been limited, but not removed, by the 1984 amendments.

3. The 1988 amendment added a mechanism whereby the obligation to pay insurance benefits to retired employees might be modified.

Voidable Preferences

1. To keep all creditors on an equal basis, the trustee can avoid any transfer or payment to a creditor if such was made within ninety days of the petition being filed, if such was made to satisfy all or part of antecedent debts, if such was made while the debtor was insolvent, and if such was indeed a preference.

2. The debtor is presumed to be insolvent during the ninety days prior to the petition's being filed.

3. If the preferred creditor is an insider, the time period of concern is one year, not ninety days, before the petition was filed.

Fraudulent Transfers

1. A transfer of property may be fraudulent under either federal or state law.

2. In general, any transfer within a statutory time period prior to the filing of a bankruptcy petition is fraudulent if the debtor intended to hinder, delay, or defraud creditors.

3. The trustee has the power to declare these transfers invalid to protect the estate for the creditors' benefit.

CREDITORS

Creditors and Claims

1. Creditors must be able to prove their claims to be paid from the debtor's estate.

2. There are numerous reasons why a claim may be disallowed altogether or otherwise limited.

Right of Setoff

1. Because the debtor may have a claim against the creditor, that creditor can set off the amount owed to the debtor against the claims the creditor makes on the debtor's estate.

2. This setoff must not give an unreasonable preference to the creditor. The trustee will examine all events during the ninety days prior to the filing of the bankruptcy to determine the proper amount of the setoff.

Priorities

1. The creditors' claims are subject to payment according to the priority established by the bankruptcy law.

2. Seven categories of priority claims must be paid before the first general unsecured creditor's claim is paid.

REVIEW QUESTIONS AND PROBLEMS

1. Match each term in column A with the appropriate statement in column B.

A	B
(1) Liquidation	(a) A creditor's right to payment

(2)	Reorganization	(b)	Entered by bankruptcy judge whenever debtor is entitled to the court's protection
(3)	Claim	(c)	The creditor's right to reduce the amount of its claim by the amount it owes the debtor
(4)	Discharge	(d)	The type of proceeding pursued under Chapter 7
(5)	Order of relief	(e)	A transfer that gives a creditor an unfair advantage over other creditors
(6)	Meeting of creditors	(f)	The legal forgiveness of a debt
(7)	Voidable preference	(g)	The type of proceeding pursued under Chapter 11
(8)	Right of setoff	(h)	The event when, among other things, a permanent trustee is elected

2. The bankruptcy court approved a repayment plan proposed by debtors, Eddie and Angela Freeman, pursuant to Chapter 13. Under the plan, the Freemans agreed to pay their secured creditors in full, but their unsecured creditors were to receive nothing. Public Finance is an unsecured creditor and appeals the affirmation of the plan, arguing that a plan that proposes no payment to unsecured creditors fails to meet the good-faith requirement of the bankruptcy law. Does "good faith" exist only when the debtor proposes payment to unsecured creditors? Explain.

3. Pauline lives in a state that exempts $800 for an automobile owned by a debtor in a bankruptcy proceeding. Pauline's car was worth more than $800, so she sought to recover $800 of the sales price when the court sold the car to satisfy her debts. Her creditors contend that she is not entitled to any exemption for a car worth more than $800. Who is correct? Explain.

4. Clark, a 43-year-old licensed family therapist, filed a Chapter 7 petition in bankruptcy and claimed an exemption for his Keogh retirement plan. Contributions to such a plan are tax deductible, and income tax on the fund and its earnings is deferred until withdrawn. Funds may be withdrawn when a participant becomes 59½, dies, or is disabled. If funds are withdrawn before these events, the participant must pay a penalty tax of 10 percent in addition to regular income taxes and is barred from making contributions to the plan for five years. Is the Keogh plan asset exempt? Explain.

5. A state court awarded a wife $100,000 in alimony. The husband did not pay it and later filed a petition under Chapter 7 of the bankruptcy law. He proved that his ex-wife did not need the money, as she was now gainfully employed and was in fact quite wealthy. Is this debt dischargeable? Explain.

6. Taylor borrowed money pursuant to the Guaranteed Student Loan Program. Three years later he filed a petition in voluntary bankruptcy and included his student loans on his list of debts. Taylor was given a general discharge in bankruptcy. Is he still liable for his student loans? Why or why not?

7. Robinson pleaded guilty to larceny in the second degree. The charge was based on her wrongful receipt of $9,932.95 in welfare benefits from the state of Connecticut. As a part of her sentence, Robinson was required to make restitution at the rate of $100 per month during her probationary period. Robinson filed a Chapter 7 bankruptcy petition. She sought to have her obligation to make restitution discharged. Although they received notice of the Chapter 7 petition, the staff members of the Connecticut Department of Income Maintenance and of the Probation Office did not respond. Robinson's obligation to make restitution was discharged. Later the Probation Office objected when the restitution payments ceased. Robinson filed this action to have the discharge affirmed. Were the restitution payments, as required as a condition of Robinson's probation, dischargeable in a Chapter 7 bankruptcy proceeding? Why?

8. Fred Murray owns 350 acres of farmland on which he raises cattle, pigs, and other livestock. He also grows hay and has a large garden. In addition to these responsibilities related to his farming operations, Fred works for the state labor department. In fact, 50 percent of his income comes from his salary paid by the state. Through mismanagement, Fred became involved in financial difficulties and was not paying his debts as they became due. His creditors commenced an involuntary bankruptcy proceeding against him. Is the creditors' action proper? Explain.

9. On September 8, 1992, William and Katherine Arens filed a voluntary petition in bankruptcy. The notice of bankruptcy was not issued until September 10, 1992. On September 9, United Northwest Federal Credit Union sued the Arenses to recover money and foreclose its security interest on their mobile home. The Arenses were notified of this suit when they received a summons from the sheriff on September 16. No further action was taken on the credit union's lawsuit in state court until after the bankruptcy court dismissed the debtors' petition on May 4, 1993, for their failure to appear in court. On May 11, the state trial court entered a default judgment against the couple in the credit union's lawsuit. Mr. and Mrs. Arens now challenge the entry of a default judgment against them as contrary to the bankruptcy law's automatic stay provision. May a creditor begin a lawsuit against a debtor when a bankruptcy petition has been filed? Explain.

10. The Chocolate Cookie Company entered into a twenty-year lease at an annual rental of $4,000 a year. This lease contained a clause that the lease was not assignable without the lessor's consent. Eighteen months after the lease was signed, the Chocolate Cookie Company commenced voluntary liquidation proceedings. The trustee sought to enforce the lease, despite the nonassignability clause. May the trustee enforce the lease as written? Why?

11. With the facts as in problem 10, how much could the lessor claim in the bankruptcy proceeding if the trustee terminated the lease six months after the petition was filed (after two years of the lease term had passed)? Explain.

12. Despite financial difficulties, Barney bought two suits for $500. When he received a bill for the suits, two weeks later, he was insolvent, but he fully paid this bill in cash. One month later he filed a petition in bankruptcy. The appointed trustee sued to recover the $500 paid, contending that the payment was a preferential transfer. Was the trustee correct? Why?

13. Tracy filed a bankruptcy petition on November 2. The State Bank seeks to establish its right to setoff, based on the following facts. For the six months prior to the petition's being filed, Tracy owed the bank $2,000 at all times. Tracy had a savings account that had the following balances:

July 1–August 30	$3,000.00
August 31–September 15	1,000.00
September 16–October 2	500.00
October 3–November 2	2,000.00

What is the maximum amount of setoff to which the bank is entitled? Why? Would your answer change if the balance on November 2 were only $500.00? Explain.

14. The trustee in bankruptcy seeks to avoid a transfer of real property by the debtor to the Jerrolds on the basis that the transfer was a preference. A warranty deed was signed by the debtor and delivered to the Jerrolds on May 25. For some unexplained reason, the deed was not recorded until August 17. A Chapter 7 voluntary petition was filed on September 10. Therefore, the deed involved in the disputed transfer was delivered more than ninety days before the date of the filing of the debtor's petition in bankruptcy. However, the deed was filed for registration within the ninety-day period. For the purposes of determining whether a transfer of real property is voidable as preferential, is a deed effective on the date of delivery or on the date of recording? Why?

15. After filing for Chapter 11 reorganization, an employer continued to pay wages to its employees and to withhold the required amounts of FICA and income taxes from their paychecks. However, it did not pay the withheld amount to the IRS. Subsequently, the bankruptcy court appointed a trustee to supervise the liquidation of the estate. The government filed a claim for the taxes due from the reorganization period. Which priority claim does the government have? Explain.

CHAPTER

43

INTRODUCTION TO THE LAW OF PROPERTY

CHAPTER PREVIEW

While most people tend to think of property as a thing owned or possessed by someone, this is not the way the law thinks of and analyzes property. In the law, property is thought of as "a bundle of rights" that one or more persons may have with respect to a thing. These rights may include the right to physically control the thing (possession); the right to transfer the thing to another by sale, gift, or will; or even the right to destroy it. The *bundle of rights* concept means that property is a series of legal relationships in which some people have rights and all others have duties that are negative in character. For example, each of us has a duty not to interfere with another's use and enjoyment of his or her property. As you study chapters 43 through 45, keep in mind the bundle of rights concept.

The concept of property as a bundle of rights is meaningless unless it is associated with people or with legal entities that qualify as persons. Some of the terms frequently used in expressing this association are *ownership, title,* and *possession.* The word *owner* usually describes someone who possesses all the rights or interest associated with the thing involved. The word *title* often is thought to be synonymous with *ownership. Title* is also used to signify the method by which ownership is acquired, as by a transfer of title. It may also be used to indicate the evidence by which ownership is established—a written instrument called a title, as a car title. Thus the word *title* has a variety of meanings, depending on the context.

The word *possession* is equally difficult to define accurately. Its meaning is also dependent somewhat on the context in which it is used. Possession implies the concept of physical control by a person over property and the personal and mental relationship to it. While it is physically possible to possess a watch or a ring, it is obviously physically impossible to possess 1,000 acres of land in the same manner. Yet the word *possession* as a legal term is used in both instances. Possession describes not only physical control but the power to obtain physical control by legal sanctions, if necessary. In general, the concepts of possession and title should be kept separate and distinct. In other words, having possession of property does not mean the possessor also has title. The reverse is also true—a person who has title to property does not always have possession of that property. For example, a landlord of an apartment building owns (has title to) each unit; the tenants have physical control (possession) of the premises.

The next two chapters concentrate on various transactions involving property, but this chapter is concerned with some introductory principles of property. In particular, this chapter discusses the distinction among categories of property, the property status of personal property added to land (called *fixtures*), the variety of ownership interests that may be held in land, and legal restrictions to these interests.

■ BUSINESS MANAGEMENT DECISION

You are a commercial loan officer at a local financial institution. You commit to loan $1,000,000 to an investor who plans to buy an apartment complex. In addition to having an interest in the land and the buildings, you want the heating and air-conditioning units, the carpeting, and the appliances to be part of your security.

What should you do to make certain you have the interests as security you desire?

1. Real versus Personal Property

Real property The legal interests in land and things attached to or growing on land.

Personal property The rights, powers, and privileges a person has in things that are not real property.

From the standpoint of its physical characteristics, property is classified as either **real property** or **personal property.** When describing property, the adjective *real* refers to land and things attached to the land. Therefore, land as part of the earth's surface, buildings, fences, and trees are examples of things classified as *real property. Personal property* consists of all other things that are not real property. By definition, all items of property are classified as either real or personal property, although lawyers sometimes refer to *mixed property* to describe such things as real estate leases.

2. Real Property

The legal terms *real property* and *real estate* are very similar and frequently confused. In fact, these terms are often used interchangeably. However, there is a technical distinction between real property and real estate. The term *real estate* refers to the physical aspects of land and its attachments. For example, the dirt on the land is real estate, as are any actual improvements, such as buildings, roads, fences, and landscaping. Also included in the definition of real estate are the spaces above and below the land's surface. Included in these spaces are mineral, water, and air rights. Historically, real estate included unlimited subsurface (mineral rights) and air rights. Today, these rights are limited to a reasonable distance. Despite this limitation, these rights still have great value to the landowner. Indeed, interference with mineral and air rights is treated similarly to trespass on the land's surface.

The term *real property* is used to describe the legal rights that a person can have in real estate. For instance, the ownership interest a person may have in land and its improvements is classified as a real property interest. Because the distinction between real property and real estate is a subtle one, the text and cases included in this book use the terms as synonyms.

The three most important areas of the law of real property concern (1) ownership interests, (2) methods of acquiring title, and (3) transactions. The various ownership interests that can be created in land are discussed in this chapter. The next chapter discusses the methods used to acquire real property. Transactions involving leases are reviewed in chapter 45.

3. Personal Property

Tangible Describes property that is physical in character and capable of being moved.

Intangible Something that represents value but has no physical nature.

Personal property may be classified as **tangible** or **intangible.** The term *tangible personal property* includes objects such as goods. The term *intangible personal property* refers to things such as accounts receivable, goodwill, patents, and trademarks. Intangible personal property has value, as tangible property has, and each can be transferred.

The term *chattel* is used to describe personal property generally, but chattels may also be classified as chattels real and chattels personal. *Chattels real* describes an interest in land, such as a leasehold; *chattels personal* is applied to movable personal property. When the term *chattel* is used in connection with intangible personal property, the property is referred to as chattels personal in action. A *chattel personal in action*—or *chose in action,* as it is frequently called—is something to which one has a right to possession, but concerning which one may be required to bring some legal action ultimately to enjoy possession. A contract right may be said to be a chose in action because a lawsuit may be necessary to obtain the rights under the contract. A negotiable instrument such as a note or check is a common form of chose in action. Although the instrument itself may be said to be property, in reality it is simply evidence of a right to money, and it may be necessary to maintain an action to reduce the money to possession.

In this text, three aspects of personal property are considered most important. First, what happens if an item of personal property becomes permanently attached to real estate? This question is answered in sections 6 through 10 of this chapter, dealing with fixtures. Second, how does a person acquire or transfer ownership of personal property? This issue is discussed in chapter 44. Third, what transactions involving personal property are most important? Chapter 45 concentrates on personal property transactions, especially the legal aspects of bailments.

4. Reasons for Distinguishing between Real and Personal Property

The distinction between real and personal property appears to be obvious. However, this distinction may become difficult to make in a number of factual settings. Reasons why the law distinguishes between these broad categories of property are discussed in this section. Examples of how this distinction becomes confused are presented in sections 6 through 10.

CONFLICT OF LAWS PRINCIPLES.   When property becomes involved in a multiple-state transaction, the law that governs the property rights may depend on whether that property is real or personal. Sorting out which state's laws are applicable may be determined by the conflict of laws principle. Chapter 1 may be reviewed for an overview of conflicts of laws problems.

Situs "Place, situation." The place where a thing is located. The situs of land is the state or county where it is located.

As a general rule, conflict of laws principles provide that the law of the **situs**—the law of the state where real property is located—determines all legal questions concerning real property. Legal issues concerning conflict of laws relating to personal property are not so easily resolved. Conflict of laws rules may refer to the law of the owner's domicile to resolve some questions and to the law of the state with the most significant contacts with the property to resolve others. The law of the situs of the property is also used to resolve some legal issues. Therefore, the description of property as real or personal has a significant impact on the determination of the body of substantive law used to decide legal issues concerning the property.

TRANSFER OF PROPERTY.   During the lifetime of the owner, the distinction between real and personal property is significant, since the methods of transferring them are substantially different. Formal instruments such as deeds are required to transfer an interest in land, whereas few formalities are required in the case of personal property. A bill of sale may be used in selling personal property; but it is not generally required, and it does not, in any event, involve the technicalities of a deed. The transfer of personal property is, as a rule, quite simply accomplished (a motor vehicle transfer may require the delivery of a certificate of title), whereas formality is required to transfer real property.

When the owner of property dies, how the transfer of title is accomplished may depend on whether the owner had a will. If no will is found, ownership of real property typically passes to a court-appointed administrator who determines who is entitled to the real property under the terms of the state law. Title to personal property generally passes directly to the heirs of the deceased owner. A valid will can simplify this need to distinguish between real and personal property.

TAXES.   Systems for taxing real estate are different from those for taxing personal property in many states. Property taxes on real estate are significant in every state, while personal property taxes often are less significant. Typical of the issues that may arise are those relating to mobile homes. Is a mobile home that is placed on a foundation real estate and thus subject to real estate taxation, or is it personal property? Similar questions make it apparent that parties to various transactions and courts are frequently called on to label property as real or personal. If the issue is likely to arise, it should always be covered in agreements.

5. The Doctrine of Equitable Conversion

In contracts for the sale of real estate, there is frequently a substantial time lag between the execution of the contract and its performance. During this period, one or more of the parties may die, the property may be destroyed, or the original parties may enter into other transactions, such as an assignment of the contract. The legal effect of these events and transactions is not determined by legal title to the property involved. Rather, the interest is determined by equitable principles and a doctrine known as the doctrine of **equitable conversion.** The doctrine of equitable conversion operates on the execution of a contract involving real estate and converts the interest of the seller who has legal title to real property to an interest in personal property, and it converts the interest of the buyer who owes money to an interest in real estate. In other words, after the execution of a contract, the law considers that the seller's interest in the transaction is personal property and that the buyer's interest is real property. This result comes from the concept that equity regards the transaction as being completed.

To illustrate the foregoing, assume that your Aunt Agatha, in her will, leaves all her real estate to you and all her personal property to me. Aunt Agatha then enters into a contract to sell her house for $50,000 but dies before receiving the money. Although Aunt Agatha has legal title to the real estate at the time of her death, the doctrine of equitable conversion converts that to personal property, and the $50,000 would be paid to me, not you, under Agatha's will.

Equitable conversion
An equitable principle that, for certain purposes, permits real property to be converted into personal property and vice versa.

FIXTURES

6. What Is a Fixture?

The classification of property as real or personal may be very difficult at times, and it may change from time to time. For example, when a dishwasher is purchased at an appliance store, it is clearly personal property. However, what is its status if it is

Fixture An item of personal property that has become attached or annexed to real estate. Fixtures generally are treated as part of the real estate.

built into your kitchen cabinets? Does this dishwasher remain an item of personal property, or has it become a part of the real estate? The answers to these questions are determined by the *law of fixtures*. A **fixture** is personal property that has become a part of real estate.

To understand better what a fixture is, it is helpful to review the reasons for distinguishing between personal and real property. Also important is being able to know when personal property is likely to have become a fixture. There are three tests, discussed in sections 8 through 10, that courts have used to determine fixture status. These are often called the annexation, adaptation, and intention tests. As you read the following sections, keep in mind that once personal property becomes a fixture, it is treated as a part of the real estate. The tests are not cumulative, and their use depends on the factual situation.

7. Reasons for Determining Fixture Status

The question of whether or not an item is a fixture and thus part of the real estate arises in determining (1) the value of real estate for tax purposes; (2) whether or not a sale of the real estate includes the item of property in question; (3) whether or not the item of property is a part of the security given by a mortgagor of the real estate to a mortgagee; and (4) whether the item belongs to the owner of the building or to the tenant on termination of a lease.

If property is a fixture, (1) it is included in the value of real estate for tax purposes; (2) it is sold, and title passes with the real estate; (3) it is a part of the security covered by a mortgage; and (4) it belongs to the landlord owner, not to the tenant on termination of a lease.

Fixture issues also arise under Article 9 of the Uniform Commercial Code in disputes between secured creditors and persons with an interest in the land. The UCC provides that no security interest exists in goods incorporated into a structure in the manner of lumber, bricks, tile, cement, glass, metal work and the like. A party with a security interest in such goods loses it when the goods are incorporated into the real estate.

8. Annexation Test

The degree of attachment of personal property to the real estate is the essence of the annexation test. Furthermore, whether the article can be removed without material injury to the article, building, and land are important considerations in determining whether the article is a fixture.

The common law required the chattel to be "let into" or "united" to the land. The test of annexation alone is inadequate, for many things attached to the soil or buildings are not fixtures, and many things not physically attached to the soil or buildings are considered fixtures. Articles of furniture substantially fastened but easily removed are not necessarily fixtures. Physical annexation may be only for the purpose of more convenient use. On the other hand, machinery that has been annexed but detached for repairs or other temporary reasons may still be considered a fixture, although severed.

Doors, windows, screens, and storm windows, although readily detachable, are generally considered fixtures because they are an integral part of the building and pertain to its function. Electric ranges connected to a building by a plug or vent pipe generally are not fixtures. The removal of wainscoting, wood siding, fireplace mantels, and water systems would cause a material injury to the building and land; therefore, these items usually are fixtures.

9. Adaptation Test

Because the annexation test alone is inadequate to determine what is a fixture, the adaptation test has been developed. Adaptation means that the article is used in promoting the purpose for which the land is used. Thus, if an article is placed on, or annexed to, land to improve it, make it more valuable, and extend its use, it is a fixture. Pipes, pumps, and electric motors for an irrigation system are chattels that may be adapted to become fixtures. This test alone is not adequate, because rarely is an article attached or placed on land except to advance the purpose for which the land is to be used.

10. Intention Test

Because of the inherent weaknesses with the annexation and adaptation tests, it is always best for parties to specify their intentions concerning the issue of fixtures. However, when the parties' intent is not clear, in addition to annexation and adaptation, the following situations and circumstances may be useful in determining the parties' intent: (1) the kind and character of the article affixed; (2) the purpose and use for which the annexation has been made; and (3) the relation and situation of the parties making the annexation. The relation of landlord and tenant suggests that items such as showcases, acquired and used by the tenant, are not intended to become permanently part of the real property. Such property, called **trade fixtures,** is an exception to the general rule of fixtures because they are generally intended to be removed by the tenant at the end of the lease. Trade fixtures continue to be classified as personal property.

Trade fixtures Personal property placed on or annexed to real estate leased by a tenant for the purpose of carrying on a trade or business. The tenant generally is allowed to remove this property at the end of the lease.

The most important factor to consider in determining whether personal property has become a fixture is the intent of the parties. In other words, as between a buyer and seller of real estate, those parties may clearly state in their contract that an attached ceiling fan will be removed by the seller. Likewise, mortgage documents, security agreements, and leases should all be written in a way to indicate whether the parties intend the property to be treated as personal property or as a fixture. If the parties neglect to state their intentions, courts have turned to the annexation and adaptation tests as a way to predict what the parties' intent really was. However, when the parties' intent is clear, courts have used this factor as the controlling one in determining fixture status.

In the following case, notice the evidence the court used to determine that there existed a factual issue as to whether the personal property had become a fixture.

CASE

Marsh v. Binstock
462 N.W.2d 172 (N.D. 1990)

LEVINE, J.

Martin Decker, Jr., appeals from a summary judgment awarding damages for conversion to Steven and Bertha Marsh [hereinafter collectively "Marsh"] against Decker and Myron Binstock. . . .

Marsh sold Binstock certain farm real estate on a contract for deed which was properly recorded. The sale included a dairy barn which housed milking equipment, composed of a six-hundred gallon tank, a washer, and an air compressor. The equipment was affixed to the barn by screws, electrical wiring, water pipes, and freon pipes.

Binstock defaulted on the contract for deed and eventually deeded the property back to Marsh. Before doing so, however, Binstock sold the milking equipment to Decker for $1,900. The equipment was removed from the barn by Binstock and Decker, and Decker has since disposed of some of the equipment.

Marsh commenced this action against Binstock and Decker for conversion of the equipment, asserting that the various items were fixtures and that Marsh retained an interest in fixtures under the contract for deed. Binstock and Decker denied that the items were fixtures, arguing that the milking equipment was personal property, or, in the alternative, that Marsh had granted Binstock authority to sell the milking equipment. On Marsh's motion for summary judgment, the county court held that there were no remaining issues of material fact and that the items of milking equipment were fixtures as a matter of law. Because Decker had disposed of some of the equipment, making its return impossible, the court awarded Marsh damages of $1,900 plus interest. . . . Decker has appealed. . . .

The dispositive issue on appeal is whether the county court erred in determining that there was no issue of material fact on the status of the milking equipment as fixtures. The parties agree that if the milking equipment was personal property, rather than fixtures, Decker did not commit conversion when he purchased the equipment from Binstock. . . .

In the motion for summary judgment, Marsh asserted that the equipment constituted fixtures as a matter of law, relying upon the manner of its annexation to the realty and upon the documentation evidencing the sale between Marsh and Binstock.

"Fixture" is defined in Section 47-01-05, N.D.C.C.:

A thing is deemed to be affixed to land when it is attached to it by roots, as in the case of trees, vines, or shrubs, or imbedded in it, as in the case of walls, or permanently resting upon it, as in the case of buildings, or permanently attached to what is thus permanent, as by means of cement, plaster, nails, bolts, or screws.

We have stated that, in determining whether an item is a fixture under the statute, relevant considerations include the intent of the person making the annexation to the realty, the manner in which it is annexed, and its adaptation to the use of the realty.

Taking these factors into consideration, it is clear that the items of milking equipment were, at least at one time, fixtures. They were permanently attached to the barn by screws, electrical wiring, and separate piping for water and freon. They had been installed by Marsh in 1978, and remained permanently in place until removed by Decker and Binstock in 1989. They clearly were specifically adapted to the use of the realty, i.e., a barn used in a milking operation. Finally, all outward manifestations suggest that it was Marsh's intent, as the person annexing these items to the realty, that they would be fixtures.

Our inquiry, however, does not end there. Notwithstanding the physical characteristics of a fixture, parties may agree to give it the legal character of personality. Such an agreement follows the well-established principle that when an owner of realty and fixtures sells the fixtures separate from the real estate, a constructive severance occurs and the fixtures become personal property. The determination whether there has been an agreement to treat fixtures as personalty is a question of fact.

The documents evidencing the sale to Binstock arguably create an inference that the parties intended to treat the milking equipment as personal property. The contract for deed allocated the $136,000 purchase price as follows: single family home—$54,000; milking equipment—$8,000; and land and other improvements—$74,000. The statement of full consideration filed with the State Board of Equalization stated that personal property valued at $8,000 was included in the sale. Marsh testified at his deposition that no other personal property was included in the sale which might account for the $8,000 claim on the tax statement. In addition, the contract for deed describes the property to be sold as the described land "TOGETHER WITH MILKING EQUIPMENT ATTACHED TO OR A PART OF BUILDINGS ON SAID PREMISES AS WELL AS ALL FIXTURES." Although this language may be subject to differing interpretations, it can be read as indicating that the items of milking equipment were not fixtures. This would lend further support to the assertion that the parties intended to give the milking equipment the legal characteristics of personal property.

The foregoing evidence, viewed in a light most favorable to Decker, raises an issue of material fact on the existence of an agreement between Marsh and Binstock to treat the milking equipment as personalty. Marsh, as the moving party, has failed to establish that there is no dispute of material fact, making summary judgment inappropriate. . . .

■ *Reversed and remanded.*

CASE CONCEPTS REVIEW

1. Which parties were the original seller and buyer of the farm involved in this case?
2. How did Decker become involved in this litigation?
3. What occurred so the original seller had legal title to the farm and its improvements?
4. What ruling of the trial court forms the basis of this appeal?
5. Why does the court conclude that the trial court's ruling was erroneous?

REAL PROPERTY OWNERSHIP INTERESTS

11. Bundle of Rights

We have emphasized that property interests are best defined as the bundle of rights a person has in a thing. Property is an object or a thing over which someone exercises legal rights.

Defining property interests as a bundle of rights enables courts and the law to develop a variety of such interests in property. A person may possess all of the bundle of rights in relation to a thing, in which case he or she is the only owner. On the other hand, the bundle of rights may be divided among several people, in which case there is multiple ownership of the rights. For example, the owner of a tract of land may authorize the local public utility companies to install power and telephone lines through the land. The utility companies are granted what is called an *easement,* which is a property right. As a result, the owner has less than the full bundle of rights, and the rights of others result in what is known as an **encumbrance.**

Encumbrance A burden on the title to land. A mortgage or other lien is an encumbrance on the title.

Furthermore, this bundle-of-rights concept allows owners of real property to create a variety of ownership interests. In essence, the type of real property ownership interest is determined by the rights of an owner to possess, use, and transfer the land. To understand the possible variations of ownership interests, keep in mind that the complete bundle of rights must be accounted for at all times.

12. Fee Simple Estates

Fee simple absolute The most complete interest a person may have in land. Such an estate is not qualified by any other interest, and it passes upon the death of the owners to the heirs, free from any conditions. It includes the entire bundle of rights.

When used in connection with land, the legal term *estate* is synonymous with ownership interests. *Fee simple estates* are those interests classified as either absolute or qualified present interests. *Present interests* are those that allow the owner to possess the land now. In the alternative, the owner of a present interest may transfer the right of possession to another party. A **fee simple absolute** is the most complete ownership interest possible. It contains the largest bundle of rights of any estate in land. The fee simple absolute is the interest usually received by the grantee in a real estate sales transaction. The language used to create this unlimited interest does not contain words of limitation. A fee simple interest that may be defeated in the future by the occurrence or nonoccurrence of a stated event or condition is called a *qualified* or *conditional fee simple.*

The possible variations of these fee simple estates are complex and beyond the scope of this text. It is sufficient for you to keep two points in mind about qualified fee simple estates. First, these interests do not contain the complete bundle of rights that exists with every piece of land. Therefore, there is a future ownership interest that may become possessory, causing the holder of this future interest to gain superior title relative to the owner of the qualified fee simple interest. Second, these qualified interests usually are less valuable when compared with a fee simple absolute interest. Thus, you should always be aware of the ownership interest involved in a real estate transaction. Generally, you would not be willing to pay as much for a qualified fee simple as you would for a fee simple absolute interest. A gift of land "to my grandson as long as he remains married" is an example of a qualified or conditional fee simple interest.

13. Life Estates

Life estate An interest in real property that lasts only as long as a designated person lives.

One of the most widely used ownership interests in estate planning is the **life estate.** When properly used, the life estate enables landowners to provide for those they desire while reducing both income and estate taxes. The life estate interest may be created either by will or by deed. A life estate may be for the life of the grantee, or it may be created for the duration of the life of some other designated person. It may be conditional upon the happening of an event, such as the marriage of the life tenant. A husband may convey property to his wife for life or until she remarries. Unless the instrument that creates the life estate places limitations on it, the interest can be sold or mortgaged like any other interest in real estate. The buyer or mortgagee must, of course, take into consideration the fact that the life estate may be terminated at any time by the death of the person for whose life it was created.

Waste Damage to the real property, so its value is impaired.

Trust A legal device whereby property is transferred from one person to another for the benefit of a third person.

The life tenant is obligated to use reasonable care to maintain the property in the condition in which it was received, ordinary wear and tear excepted. There is a duty to repair, to pay taxes, and, out of the income received, to pay interest on any mortgage that may have been outstanding at the time the life estate was created. The life tenant has no right to **waste** the property or to do anything that tends to deplete the value of the property. A life tenant would have no right to drill for oil, mine coal, or cut timber from the land, unless those operations were being conducted at the time the life estate was created. If the extraction of minerals is begun by a life tenant, the proceeds are put into a **trust**. The income of the trust is paid to the life tenant, and upon the death of the life tenant, the principal of the trust estate is paid to the person who has the future interest that follows the life estate. Likewise, a life tenant has no duty to make lasting improvements to the property. If such improvements are made, the holder of the future interest cannot be required to contribute to their cost.

14. Remainders and Reversions

Because a life estate represents less than the complete bundle of rights, there must be a future interest accompanying every life estate. After the termination of a life estate, the remaining estate may be transferred to someone else or it may go back to the original owner or to his or her heirs. If the estate is to be given to someone else upon the termination of a life estate, it is called an *estate in remainder.* If it is to go back to the original owner, it is called a *reversion.* When a reversion exists and the original owner of that interest is dead, the property reverts to the heirs of that original owner. Regardless of whether a remainder or a reversion follows a life estate, these future interests may be sold, mortgaged, or otherwise transferred as if they were any other real property interest. This right to transfer these interests exists even before the life estate ends and the remainder or reversion becomes present possessory interests. Upon the death of the life tenant, the remainder or reversion generally converts into a fee simple absolute interest once again.

Since the owners of remainders and reversions have a valuable real property interest, they have the right to enforce the life tenant's duty not to waste the land's value. The timing for filing a suit to recover damages for or to enjoin waste depends on the type of waste occurring. For example, the holder of a life estate may actively destroy an improvement on the real estate or it may only be passive—the neglect of an improvement, allowing it to deteriorate. In general, the statute of limitations for filing an action against waste begins to run when active waste occurs and when the life tenant dies if the passive type of waste has occurred.

15. Easements and Licenses

Easement An easement is an interest in land—a right that one person has to some profit, benefit, or use in or over the land of another. Such right is created by a deed, or it may be acquired by prescription (the continued use of another's land for a statutory period) or by implication.

License (privilege) A mere personal privilege given by the owner to another to do designated acts on the land of the owner.

An **easement** is a right granted for the use of real property. The grantor may convey to the grantee a right of way over his or her land, the right to erect a building that may shut off light or air, the right to lay drain tile under the land, or the right to extend utilities over the land. If these rights of easement are reserved in the deed conveying the property or granted by a separate deed, they pass along with the property to the next grantee and are burdens on the land. An easement made by special contract is binding only on the immediate parties to the agreement. If a right to use another's land is given orally, it is not an easement but a **license.** The owner of the land may revoke a license at any time unless it has become irrevocable by conduct constituting estoppel. An easement given by grant cannot be revoked except by deed, since such a right of way is considered a right in real property; nor can it be modified without the consent of the owner of the easement.

An owner of land may create an easement for the benefit of another by deed. Usually, a party desiring an easement purchases it from the owner of the *servient land* (the land on which the easement exists). Or a seller of real estate may reserve an easement in his or her favor when deeding the property to someone else. This situation will occur when a party sells only part of his or her land and the portion retained requires the easement. Assume that Farmer Brown sells half of his farm to a neighbor. Since the half sold borders on the only road touching the farm, Farmer Brown will need to reserve an easement for the entering and exiting of the land retained. This land retained is often called the *dominant land,* and the land transferred subject to an easement is called the *servient estate.*

Easements may be obtained through adverse use. Such easements are known as *easements by prescription.* These concepts of adverse use or possession are developed more fully in the next chapter. For now, suffice it to say that if a party uses an easement for a long period of time, the owner of the land may not deny the existence of the easement.

Easements may also be obtained through judicial proceedings in certain cases. Since the law takes the position that an owner of land should be entitled to access to that land, owners of land that would otherwise be landlocked may be entitled to an *easement by necessity*. Such an easement is, in effect, granted by the owner of the servient land to the owner of the other land by implication. The following discusses three essential requirements that must be found before a court agrees to establish an easement by implication.

CASE

Russakoff v. Scruggs
400 S.E.2d 529 (Va. 1991)

LACY, J.

The issue we must decide on this appeal is whether lot owners established an easement for access to and use of a lake.

In the 1960s, Richmond Real Estate Developers, Inc. . . . began constructing Canterbury East subdivision. . . . The subdivision included a man-made lake with a waterline at the contour line of about the 136' elevation. . . . Richard L. and Diane Y. Russakoff, Edward E. Haddock, and Edwin M. Lohmann (collectively Russakoff), each own a lot in Canterbury East subdivision. Their rear lot lines abut the 140' contour, thus leaving a strip of land approximately 20 feet wide, between the lots and the lake. This strip was reserved for flood plains, sewer lines, and water lines.

Richmond Real Estate Developers ceased paying taxes on the lake property. . . . A tax sale was held on September 16, 1983, where Kerry I. and Doris J. Scruggs (collectively Scruggs) were the highest bidders. On May 25, 1984 the Commonwealth conveyed the lake property to Scruggs pursuant to the tax sale. Scruggs then posted "no trespassing" signs, erected a fence around the lake, and sent all homeowners surrounding the lake a letter offering them use of the lake by renting or purchasing shares. . . .

By bill of complaint . . . Russakoff alleged a right to use the lake by virtue of . . . [an] easement by implication. . . . The trial court ruled that Russakoff was not entitled to any easement or other rights to use Canterbury Lake. The court dismissed the action, and Russakoff appeals. . . .

Easements are not ownership interests in the servient tract but the privilege to use the land of another in a particular manner for a particular purpose. Easements are appurtenant to, and run with, the dominant tract if they benefit the owner in his use and enjoyment of that tract.

There are a number of ways an easement can be created. Easements may be created by express grant or reser-

vation, by implication, by estoppel or by prescription. In the case of easements over streets and roads, we have recognized the creation of an easement by reference in the deed to a plat showing the road. . . . Within the category of easements created by implication, we have recognized easements created by necessity, and by pre-existing use (also referred to as quasi-easements).

Russakoff claims . . . an easement arising by implication. Such an easement is based on the legal principle that when one conveys land, he is presumed to transfer all that is necessary to the use and enjoyment of the land conveyed. While one cannot have an easement on land he owns, if, before severance, one part of the land was used for the benefit of another part, a "quasi-easement" exists over the "quasi-servient" portion of the land. That easement is conveyed by implication when the dominant tract is severed; the grantee of the dominant tract obtains an easement over the servient tract, based on the previous use.

While the extent of the easement right is determined by the circumstances surrounding the conveyance which divides the single ownership, the existence of the easement is established on a showing that (1) the dominant and servient tracts originated from a common grantor, (2) the use was in existence at the time of the severance, and that (3) the use is apparent, continuous, and reasonably necessary for the enjoyment of the dominant tract.

It is clear from the record before us that Russakoff's lots (dominant tracts), and the lake property (servient tract), were originally part of a single tract, thereby satisfying the first prong of the test. Next, the record is equally clear that, at the time Russakoff's predecessors in title took possession of the dominant tracts, the servient tract was a lake. . . .

Turning to the question of apparent and continuous use, the trial court identified Russakoff's use of a pump for lawn watering as the only use of the lake. This use, the trial court held, was not sufficient to establish an easement. Russakoff asserts that this holding is erroneous and that the record supports a finding that the use of the lake and strip of land to gain access to the lake was sufficient to establish an easement. We agree.

The record reflects that Russakoff and previous owners of the lots used the lake openly and continuously, through the construction of docks, piers, and sprinkler systems, and by using the lake for boating and ice skating. . . .

Our review of this record shows that the trial judge's finding that the only use of the lake was Russakoff's lawn sprinkler system, which he found to be insufficient to support an easement, is clearly erroneous. Rather, the record supports a contrary conclusion that use of the lake was continuous and apparent.

The third prong of the test also requires that the easement be reasonably necessary to the use and enjoyment of the dominant tract. . . .

Here, we hold that a purchaser of a lot would have a legitimate expectation of the right to access and use the lake where a visual inspection and reference to the plat incorporated in the deed of conveyance showed the existence of a lake within 20 feet of one's lot line, and where investigation would disclose that the 20-foot strip between the lake and the lot line was retained solely for certain utility and flood plain uses. The Canterbury East developers contemplated enjoyment of the lake, as a lake, by purchasers of the lots surrounding the lake. Under these circumstances, the easement at issue was reasonably necessary to the use and enjoyment of the lakeside lots.

. . . The evidence in this case supports a finding of a use which was apparent, continuous, and reasonably necessary to the enjoyment of the dominant tract. The record also clearly shows Scruggs' knowledge of the use. . . . Scruggs testified that shortly after purchasing the lake, he traversed the lake in a canoe and disconnected at least two of the existing sprinkler systems which used the lake water for lawn watering purposes, and Scruggs' actions show that the use of the lake by surrounding property owners was apparent, and that he was aware of the use.

At the time Scruggs purchased the lake, its use was apparent, continuous, and reasonably necessary to the enjoyment of property surrounding the lake. Therefore, we conclude that an easement by implication was established in favor of Russakoff for access to and use of Canterbury Lake. . . .

■ *Reversed.*

CASE CONCEPTS REVIEW

1. How did the Scruggs acquire title to the lake and the 20-foot strip of land bordering the lake?
2. What is the legal basis for the plaintiffs/appellants to claim a right to use the lake?
3. What three elements of easement by implication must be established for such an easement to exist?
4. How did the plaintiffs/appellants satisfy each of these elements?

OWNERSHIP AMONG MULTIPLE PARTIES

16. Introduction

In the preceding four sections, there has been an assumption that each real property ownership interest is owned by only one person. In reality, these interests can be, and often are, owned by two or more parties. There are three distinct methods by which two or more people may own property at the same time: tenancy in common, joint tenancy, and tenancy by the entirety. The first two types of co-ownership are applicable to every kind of property, real or personal. However, *tenancy by the entirety* is a type of joint tenancy held by spouses in real estate only. Several states have modified the common-law characteristics of these forms of ownership, so it is essential that each state's law be consulted for the technicalities of these tenancies.

The next three sections discuss these three common forms of multiple ownership. Section 20 then discusses two types of joint ownership often used in multiple-family housing complexes or in office buildings.

17. Tenancy in Common

Tenancy in common
The most usual method of two or more persons owning property at the same time. None of the formalities or unities required for other specialized forms of co-ownership are essential for this method.

Most states presume that the ownership interest in property held by two or more people is a **tenancy in common.** These co-owners, known as tenants in common, may acquire their interests at different times. Their percentage of ownership interests does not have to be equal. They may transfer their interests during their lifetime or upon their death to whomever they desire.

Tenants in common do have the right to possess the entire item of property subject to the co-owners' rights. However, the degree of control each owner has over the property and over who might become a future co-owner is limited when compared to that possessed by co-owners under the forms of multiple ownership.

Joint tenancy Two or more persons that own property in such manner that they have "one and the same interest, accruing by one and the same conveyance, commencing at one and the same time, and held by one and the same undivided possession." Upon the death of one joint tenant, his or her property passes to the survivor or survivors.

18. Joint Tenancy

The basic distinction between a tenancy in common and a **joint tenancy** is that the latter involves the right of survivorship. In the event of the death of a tenant in common, his or her share in the property passes to the executor named in the will or to the administrator of the deceased's estate. If property is held in joint tenancy, the interest of a deceased owner automatically passes to the surviving joint owner. Such property is not subject to probate or to the debts of the deceased joint tenant. Thus, joint tenancy with the right of survivorship passes the title of the deceased by operation of law to the survivor or survivors, free of the claims of anyone else except for taxes that may be due. The case following demonstrates the impact of the death of a joint tenant on the beneficiaries named in that joint tenant's will.

CASE

Gladson v. Gladson
800 S.W.2d 709 (Ark. 1990)

GLAZE, J.

Ilene Gladson, now deceased, had two accounts with Dean Witter Reynolds that she held as joint tenant with right of survivorship with her husband and daughter, Vickie. Sometime after the accounts were opened, Mrs. Gladson's husband died, but the accounts otherwise remained unchanged. However, Mrs. Gladson did subsequently execute a will nominating Vickie as executrix of her estate and bequeathing, among other things, $5,000 from each of the two accounts to her son, John Gladson, Jr.

After Mrs. Gladson died, Vickie petitioned to admit her mother's will to probate. Because she claimed ownership to the two Dean Witter accounts as the surviving joint tenant, Vickie did not list those accounts in the inventory of Mrs. Gladson's estate. John disagreed with his sister's claim and requested that Vickie account for the funds in the accounts that their mother bequeathed him.

The two parties submitted their dispute to the probate judge on stipulations and briefs, and the judge responded, holding in Vickie's favor. We affirm the trial judge's decision.

In his argument, John . . . argues his mother's mere opening of the Dean Witter accounts was not conclusive of her intent to establish them as joint tenancies with right of survivorship. Instead, he contends the trial court should have considered Mrs. Gladson's will as controlling of her intent which reflected that the accounts should be included in her estate so her bequests to John could be fulfilled.

John's argument ignores the manner in which the parties submitted this case to the court below. Both parties stipulated that the two Dean Witter accounts created joint tenancies with right of survivorship in Mrs. Gladson, her husband and Vickie. In other words, they agreed Mrs. Gladson had opened the accounts with the intent to create joint accounts with the right of survivorship. The only issue submitted to the trial court was whether Mrs. Gladson's will and bequest to her son can be said to have terminated the previously established accounts to which

Vickie lays claim as the surviving tenant. The trial judge said no, and that being the only issue properly presented in this appeal, we agree.

Our court apparently has not addressed this issue. However, we considered with approval the Arizona Supreme Court's discussion of the history of joint tenancy and that part of the discussion relevant here reads as follows:

> Another characteristic of joint tenancy is that it is not testamentary but "is a present estate in which both joint tenants are seized in the case of real estate, and possession in case of personal property, per my et per tout," that is, such joint tenant is seized by the half as well as by the whole. The right of survivorship in a joint tenancy therefore does not pass anything from the deceased to the surviving joint tenant. Inasmuch as both cotenants in a joint tenancy are possessors and owners per tout, *i.e.*, of the whole, the title of the first joint tenant who dies merely terminated and the survivor continues to possess and own the whole of the estate as before.

Consistent with the foregoing, the rule appears well settled that a devise by a joint tenant, who is survived by other joint tenants, is not effective to pass any title to the real estate in joint tenancy for the reason that the title passes by operation of law to the survivor or survivors. Such a rule applies in full measure to personal property. In sum, title to property held in joint tenancy takes precedence over the claim of a devisee, legatee or heir, as the case may be.

As previously noted, Vickie was the sole surviving tenant of the survivorship accounts she held with her mother and father. As a consequence, Vickie acquired ownership to those funds by operation of law upon her mother's death. That ownership could not be terminated by Mrs. Gladson's will and bequests of funds contained in those accounts to John. Therefore, we affirm the trial court's holding that Vickie owns both accounts free and clear of any claim John has asserted by virtue of their mother's will and specific bequests.

■ *Affirmed.*

CASE CONCEPTS REVIEW

1. On what basis does Vickie Gladson claim to have the ownership interest in the Dean Witter Reynolds accounts?
2. On what basis does John Gladson claim an interest in these same accounts?
3. What is the basis for the court's determination of rights between Vickie and John?

To establish a valid joint tenancy, certain requirements must be satisfied. These requirements are known as the four unities of time, title, interest, and possession. The *unity of time* requires that the joint tenants' ownership be created in the same conveyance. To have the *unity of title*, each owner must have the same estate, such as a fee simple absolute, a remainder, or any other estate, which is created by the same conveyance. The *unity of interest* exists when each owner has the same percentage interest subject to the other owners' interest. For example, two joint tenants must each own 50 percent of the undivided property, three own 33 percent each, four own 25 percent each, and so forth. Finally, the *unity of possession* is present when each joint tenant has the right to possess all the property subject to the other owners' rights of possession.

When there is a question about which form of ownership exists in any specific case, the law usually favors tenancy in common and property passing by will or intestacy, rather than its passing by right of survivorship. Courts do not find that property is held in joint tenancy with the right of survivorship unless there is a contract between the two co-owners clearly stating that such is the case and that the right of survivorship is to apply. Bank signature cards' and stock certificates that use the term *joint tenancy* or "with the right of survivorship" create such a contract, as does the language "as joint tenants and not as tenants in common." In most states, the contract must be signed by both parties to be effective. Failure to use the proper language or have a properly executed contract results in a tenancy in common.

Several additional aspects of holding property in joint tenancy frequently result in litigation. First, joint tenancy is often used as a substitute for a will. A party wishing to leave property to another on death sometimes puts the property in joint tenancy. Is a present gift intended? Does the new joint tenant have the right to share in the income of the property prior to the death of the original owner? Such issues are frequently litigated, and the answers depend on the intent of the parties.

A similar issue arises when one person in ill health or incapacitated adds another person's name to a savings or a checking account to allow the latter to pay bills and handle the former's business transactions. The signature card often provides for a joint tenancy. Was a joint tenancy or mere agency intended? Joint tenancy arrangements are frequently challenged successfully on the ground that the right of survivorship was not intended.

Another difficulty involves describing the property held in joint tenancy. Frequently, a contract covering a safe deposit box will provide that it be held in joint tenancy. Does such a contract cover the contents of the box as well? The following case is typical of those involving this issue.

CASE

Newton County v. Davison
790 S.W.2d 810 (Ark. 1986)

HOLT, J.

. . . The decedent, Mrs. Morak, died on July 8, 1984, intestate and with no known heirs. On January 4, 1985, Dwight and Kathleen Davison, appellees, filed a petition alleging they were joint tenants with a right of survivorship in the contents of a safe deposit box which Mrs. Morak had rented on June 11, 1981. The lock box contained U.S. savings bonds worth $324,987.35 and $4,020 in currency. The bonds show Mrs. Morak and various members of her family, all of whom are apparently deceased, as the owners. The administrator of the estate filed an answer alleging that the agreement of joint tenancy with right of survivorship between the appellees and the decedent was merely for the use of the box and not for the disposition of the contents.

The chancellor found that the appellees and Mrs. Morak were good friends and neighbors and that the Davisons took care of Mrs. Morak and her family for several years prior to her death. The court further found that about three years prior to Mrs. Morak's death, she and the Davisons agreed to lease a safe deposit box as joint tenants with right of survivorship so that each would be a joint owner of all of the contents of the box and the survivors would be the complete owners of those contents.

Although we do not set aside such findings of fact by a chancellor unless they are clearly erroneous, we find that the agreement between the parties was only for the rental of the safe deposit box and not for the disposition of its contents.

The only evidence offered indicating that the Davisons had a right to the contents of the lock box was provided by the Davisons. Mr. Davison testified that Mrs. Morak told him he and his wife were to become joint owners of what was in the box. He also stated, however, that he did not know what the box contained, that he never entered the box during Mrs. Morak's lifetime, he and his wife were not to receive any benefits from the contents of the box until after Mrs. Morak's death, and Mrs. Morak was to receive all benefits from the bonds during her life. Mr. Davison admitted there was no agreement as to the use of the bonds themselves. There was further evidence that Mrs. Morak stated her intention to make a will but she died before she was able to do so.

Based on the foregoing evidence we are unable to say that Mrs. Morak clearly intended to make a gift to the Davisons of the contents of the safe deposit box. In *Black v. Black*, 199 Ark. 609, 135 S.W.2d 837 (1940), we noted that there is a presumption of ownership in favor of the surviving lessee of a safe deposit box which can be rebutted by testimony to the contrary. In that case, however, the lease agreement signed by the parties renting the box specifically stated that the property placed in the box is joint property and upon the death of either joint tenant the property passes to the survivor. Such an agreement as to the contents is missing here. . . .

Other courts have held that the deposit of articles in a jointly leased safe deposit box of itself works no change in title, absent an express agreement that the contents of the box shall be joint property. This is so even if the language in the lease describes a joint tenancy with the right of survivorship, unless it specifically refers to the contents. Similarly, it is generally held that a joint lease of a safe deposit box in and of itself is insufficient to support the contention that a gift has been made of the contents.

In finding the language of the lease and Mr. Davison's testimony insufficient to establish ownership of the contents of the lock box, we announce our intention to require an affirmative showing that the owner of a lock box intended to give the contents of the lock box to another. Such an intention cannot be demonstrated without a specific written reference to the disposition of the contents of a lock box and is not indicated by an agreement only to rent the box in two or more names with a right of survivorship. . . .

■ *Reversed.*

CASE CONCEPTS REVIEW

1. How were Mrs. Morak and the Davisons listed on the rental card describing the safety deposit box?
2. What is the position of the administrator of Mrs. Morak's estate with respect to how the signature card is to be interpreted?
3. The trial court ruled in favor of the Davisons. What is the rationale for this court reversing this ruling?

What is the effect of a mortgage by one joint tenant that purports to cover all the property held in joint tenancy? In some states, the mortgage operates to sever the joint tenancy, and the mortgage is valid against the undivided interest of the mortgagor. This result is not reached in states that treat a mortgage as merely a lien. In these states, there is no severance, and upon the death of the mortgagor, the property is free of the mortgage. In almost every state, the courts have held that one joint tenant cannot encumber the interest of the other co-tenant without consent. A grantor can only give what he or she owns, and a grantee can only receive what the grantor is entitled to convey. A mortgagee's claim is thus limited to the interest of the mortgagor.

Another disadvantage of the joint tenancy arrangement is the ease with which it may be severed or terminated. Each joint tenant has the power to terminate the right of survivorship by a simple transfer or conveyance of interest to a third party. The severance of the unities of time, title, interest, or possession converts the joint tenancy to a tenancy in common. This severance may occur either by one of the co-owner's actions or by order of a court in a suit for partition of the owners' interests.

19. Tenancy by the Entirety

If the owners are related by marriage and the state law so provides, a conveyance to a husband and wife creates a specialized joint tenancy, which is called *tenancy by the entireties*. A tenancy by the entirety in states that authorize such common ownership of real estate can exist only between husband and wife. A conveyance of real estate to a husband and wife in these states is automatically a tenancy by the entirety if all four of the aforementioned unities are present. Neither tenant can unilaterally sever or end the tenancy. It may be terminated only by divorce, a joint transfer to a third party, or a conveyance by one spouse to the other. The inability of either spouse to terminate the tenancy unilaterally is the primary difference between a joint tenancy and a tenancy by the entireties, as the basic characteristic of each is the right of survivorship.

In most states that authorize tenancy by the entireties, not only is there a prohibition on one tenant making a voluntary transfer of his or her share, but there are also severe restrictions on the rights of creditors to collect an individual debt from one tenant of the property. Suppose a husband and wife own their home as tenants by the entireties. A creditor has a judgment for $10,000 against the husband alone. In most states, the creditor could not cause a sale of the house to collect the debt. Of course, if the creditor had a judgment against both husband and wife, the creditor could collect from a judicial sale of the property.

20. Condominiums and Cooperatives

A *condominium* is an individually owned apartment, town house, or office in a multiunit structure such as an apartment building or in a complex. As a method of owning and transferring property, it possesses some of the characteristics of individual ownership and some of multiple ownership. In addition to the individual apartment, town house, or office, the owner has an undivided interest in the common areas of the building and land, such as hallways, entrances, yard, recreation, and other public areas. Thus, the deed to a condominium covers the housing unit involved and undivided fractional interest in the common areas. Taxes, expenses, and liabilities arising from these common areas usually are divided on a proportional basis, using each owner's fractional interests in the undivided common areas.

Condominiums are of growing importance in commercial offices as well as residential uses. Due to their structural nature, a determination of an owner's full rights and duties requires an understanding of not only the law of property but also the law of business organizations. In a condominium complex there is an organization created to operate the common areas, to make repairs, and to make improvements. This organization usually is a corporation. Each owner of a unit has one vote in an election of a board of directors or governors. This board of the owners' association operates the development subject to the owners' approval.

There is a distinction between a *condominium* and a *cooperative* insofar as the ownership of real estate is concerned. A *cooperative* venture may involve an activity such as a retail store, or it may involve the ownership and operation of a residential development. If a person buys an interest in a cooperative, he or she is purchasing a share of a not-for-profit corporation. Strictly speaking, the owner of an interest in a cooperative does not own real estate but personal property—his or her share of the cooperative. The cooperative would pay taxes and upkeep out of the assessments to its members. A condominium contains multiple units for taxing purposes; the cooperative is a single unit. The same may be said for financing. Each owner of a condominium may mortgage his or her own portion. In a cooperative, if there is financing, there will be only one mortgage. In both the condominium and the cooperative there is a special form of business organization to coordinate the operation of the property.

21. Introduction

There can be no property rights without a government and a legal system to create and enforce them. Private property rights cannot exist without some method of keeping the bundle of rights for the true owner and for restoring these rights if he or she is deprived of them. It should also be recognized that no one person has a totally unrestricted bundle of rights. To some extent, the law always limits private property rights and the use of private property to protect the public's interest.

There are two basic methods of restricting ownership interests in land. First, governing bodies at the federal, state, and local levels may require an owner to sell land so it may be utilized for a public purpose. These governing bodies may also regulate the use of land through statutes and ordinances. For example, there are many environmental protection laws designed to control the use of land. Furthermore, zoning regulations are typical of the ordinances intended as land-use controls. Collectively, governmental regulations of an ownership interest are called *public restrictions*.

The second method of restricting ownership interests is referred to as *private restrictions*. By *private*, we mean that nongovernmental parties limit an owner's use and enjoyment of the land. Examples of private restrictions, discussed in section 23, include easements, licenses, conditions, and covenants. Although these items may be considered to be interests in the hands of those that can enforce them, they are restrictions on the ownership interests on which they exist. They restrict the bundle of rights and create rights in others.

22. Public Restrictions: Eminent Domain

Eminent domain The right that resides in the United States, state, county, city, or other public body to take private property for public use upon payment of just compensation.

One of the inherent rights the founders of our nation recognized was the right of individuals to own property. Indeed, the United States Constitution, in the Fifth Amendment, states that property shall not be taken from any person for a public use without just compensation. This language has been interpreted to be applicable to all levels of government. In essence, the Constitution not only protects the property owner, it also gives the governing body the power to buy private property when two conditions are satisfied. First, the property being acquired must be needed for the public's use and benefit. Second, the property owner must be justly compensated. This constitutional power is known as the power of **eminent domain.** In other words, the government may terminate an owner's interest by acquiring it for a public purpose upon payment of the fair market value.

Without question, the public-use requirement is satisfied when land is needed for the construction of a public highway, park, hospital, school, or airport. Indeed, in similar cases, the issue of public use for the condemned land is seldom litigated. However, more recently there has been an expansion of the public-use doctrine. For example, the exercise of the eminent domain power has been justified even when the property taken was not actually to be used by the public, as occurred in the following case.

CASE

Poletown Neighborhood Council v. City of Detroit
304 N.W.2d 455 (Mich. 1981)

PER CURIAM

This case arises out of a plan by the Detroit Economic Development Corporation to acquire, by condemnation if necessary, a large tract of land to be conveyed to General Motors Corporation as a site for construction of an assembly plant. The plaintiffs, a neighborhood association and several individual residents of the affected area, brought suit . . . to challenge the project. . . .

Defendants' motions for summary judgment were denied pending trial on a single question of fact: whether the city abused its discretion in determining that condemnation of plaintiffs' property was necessary to complete the project.

The trial lasted 10 days and resulted in a judgment for defendants and an order on December 9, 1980, dismissing plaintiffs' complaint. The plaintiffs file a claim of appeal. . . .

This case raises a question of paramount importance to the future welfare of this state and its residents: Can a municipality use the power of eminent domain . . . to condemn property for transfer to a private corporation to build a plant to promote industry and commerce, thereby adding jobs and taxes to the economic base of the municipality and state? . . .

The term "public use" has not received a narrow or inelastic definition by this Court in prior cases. Indeed, this Court has stated that "'[a] public use changes with changing conditions of society'" and that "'[t]he right of the public to receive and enjoy the benefit of the use determines whether the use is public or private.'" . . .

[T]he legislature has authorized municipalities to acquire property by condemnation in order to provide industrial and commercial sites and the means of transfer from the municipality to private users.

Plaintiffs-appellants do not challenge the declaration of the legislature that programs to alleviate and prevent conditions of unemployment and to preserve and develop industry and commerce are essential public purposes. Nor do they challenge the proposition that legislation to accomplish this purpose falls within the Constitutional grant of general legislative power to the legislature. . . .

What plaintiffs-appellants do challenge is the constitutionality of using the power of eminent domain to condemn one person's property to convey it to another private person in order to bolster the economy. They argue that whatever incidental benefit may accrue to the public, assembling land to General Motors' specifications for conveyance to General Motors for its uncontrolled use in profit making is really a taking for private use and not a public use because General Motors is the primary beneficiary of the condemnation.

The defendants-appellees contend, on the other hand, that the controlling public purpose in taking this land is to create an industrial site which will be used to alleviate and prevent conditions of unemployment and fiscal distress. The fact that it will be conveyed to and ultimately used by a private manufacturer does not defeat this predominant public purpose.

There is no dispute about the law. All agree that condemnation for a public use or purpose is permitted. All agree that condemnation for a private use or purpose is forbidden. Similarly, condemnation for a private use cannot be authorized whatever its incidental public benefit and condemnation for a public purpose cannot be forbidden whatever the incidental private gain. The heart of this dispute is whether the proposed condemnation is for the primary benefit of the public or the private user. . . .

In the court below, the plaintiffs-appellants challenged the necessity for the taking of the land for the proposed project. In this regard the city presented substantial evidence of the severe economic conditions facing the residents of the city and state, the need for new industrial development to revitalize local industries, the economic boost the proposed project would provide, and the lack of other adequate available sites to implement the project.

When there is such public need, "[t]he abstract right [of an individual] to make use of his own property in his own way is compelled to yield to the general comfort and protection of community, and to a proper regard to relative rights in others." Eminent domain is an inherent power of the sovereign of the same nature as, albeit more severe than, the power to regulate the use of land through zoning or the prohibition of public nuisances.

In the instant case the benefit to be received by the municipality invoking the power of eminent domain is a clear and significant one and is sufficient to satisfy this Court that such a project was an intended and a legitimate object of the Legislature when it allowed municipalities to exercise condemnation powers even though a private party will also, ultimately, receive a benefit as an incident thereto.

The power of eminent domain is to be used in this instance primarily to accomplish the essential public purposes of alleviating unemployment and revitalizing the economic base of the community. The benefit to a private interest is merely incidental.

Our determination that this project falls within the public purpose, as stated by the Legislature, does not mean that every condemnation proposed by an economic development corporation will meet with similar acceptance simply because it may provide some jobs or add to the industrial or commercial base. If the public benefit was not so clear and significant, we would hesitate to sanction approval of such a project. The power of eminent domain is restricted to furthering public uses and purposes and is not to be exercised without substantial proof that the public is primarily to be benefited. Where, as here, the condemnation power is exercised in a way that benefits specific and identifiable private interests, a court inspects with heightened scrutiny the claim that the public interest is the predominant interest being advanced. Such public

benefit cannot be speculative or marginal but must be clear and significant if it is to be within the legitimate purpose as stated by the Legislature. We hold this project is warranted on the basis that its significance for the people of Detroit and the state has been demonstrated.

■ *Affirmed.*

CASE CONCEPTS REVIEW

1. Why is the City of Detroit, through its Economic Development Corporation, condemning the land involved in this case?
2. What question creates an expression of the legal issue presented to the court?
3. How does the court justify its conclusion that this land is being taken for a public use?

Today, the more difficult issue to resolve when property is being condemned is how much is just compensation. Indeed, the question of property's fair market value usually is the basic factual issue to be answered by the court in eminent domain cases. Expert appraisers are called to testify, and the final determination of what is just compensation frequently is left to a jury. With respect to the concept of just compensation, you should realize it is not equal to full compensation. Although some statutes have been adopted by legislatures defining the items a property owner must be paid for, the Constitution does not require that the owner be reimbursed for attorneys' fees, expert witnesses' fees, costs of relocating, or loss of business goodwill.

The Supreme Court has given new vigor to the Fifth Amendment rights of property owners. Previously, the Supreme Court had refused to decide whether a demand for just compensation could be a remedy sought by a landowner claiming to have had land taken by the application of an excessive land-use regulation. In a 1987 decision, the Supreme Court held that any temporary taking of property requires just compensation. If the state occupies your property for even a short period, it must pay rental. The case involved a church summer camp whose buildings were destroyed by a flood. The state restricted all use of the land because it was in a flood plain. A state court lifted the restriction but denied compensation to the owners for the loss of use prior to the decision. The Supreme Court said the state had to pay for the time the restriction was in effect. Any governmental action that even temporarily denies a landowner use of land is a taking requiring just compensation within the Fifth Amendment.

A second case involved a landowner seeking a building permit. The state conditioned granting the permit on the owner's creating an easement on his land for the public to pass across his property to reach the beach. This condition was held by the Supreme Court to be a taking and unconstitutional without just compensation. If state and local governments attach conditions to building permits that are unrelated to the purpose of the development, the result is a taking for which the government must compensate the landowners. The issuance of building permits cannot be used to achieve unrelated goals. The law recognizes that the government's power to forbid particular land uses under the police power includes the power to condition such uses on some concession by the owner as long as the concession furthers the same governmental purpose advanced to justify prohibiting the use.

23. Public Restrictions: Zoning Regulations

The primary method local governments use to restrict a landowner's interest is the adoption of a *zoning ordinance*. These ordinances typically divide a community into zones and regulate the use of land within each zone. The type and intensity of the land's use in these zones can be classified as open space, residential, commercial, or industrial. Within each classification there can be several categories that further regulate the owner's use of the land. For example, property zoned R-1 might be reserved for single-family residences with lot sizes of not under one-half acre. R-5 could represent that zone wherein multiple-family residences (apartments or condominiums) are permitted.

A community's comprehensive zoning plan also restricts the use of land regarding the density of development allowed. Restrictions on buildings' height and bulk are not uncommon. Height limitations usually restrict the maximum height of buildings in feet or stories. Bulk regulations control the percentage of the lot the building may occupy. Setback and lot size requirements are examples of typical bulk restrictions.

The overall purpose of zoning ordinances is to provide a more aesthetically pleasing environment for all citizens of the community. Few people want their residence located in or near the site of a major industrial facility. Although it is a restriction on ownership interests, properly designed and implemented zoning regulations can enhance property values. Despite these benefits, you should know that there are methods for changing zoning classifications when they become unreasonable. In other words, in most communities the local zoning ordinances are subject to a continuous review process.

24. Private Restrictions: Conditions and Covenants

An ownership interest in land may be restricted by *conditions* or *covenants*. In section 12, qualified fee simple estates are discussed. In essence, these interests are conditioned on the occurrence of a stated event. For example, land may be conveyed by a grantee, Albert, on the condition that he marry before his twenty-fifth birthday. If Albert does not satisfy the condition of marriage, he loses all ownership interest in the property conveyed. In other words, a breach of a stated condition may result in termination of all interests previously held.

Quite often a grantor of land may wish to restrict the use of the land conveyed, but not wish to use the harshness of stated conditions. Restrictive covenants give such a grantor an alternative. These restrictions may be contained in the deed, or they may be made applicable to several tracts of land by attaching them to a plat of a subdivision. A *plat* is a diagram of the lot lines contained in a subdivision. This plat often is recorded in the public records so reference can be made to it. Where such restrictions are contained in a plat, they are binding on all subsequent purchasers, and they supplement the applicable zoning laws.

The typical restrictions contained in a plat or a deed may provide that the land shall be used exclusively for residential purposes, that the style and cost of the residence must meet certain specifications, and that certain restrictions inserted in the deed are covenants or promises on the part of the grantee to observe them and are said to run with the land. Even though the grantee fails to include them in a subsequent deed made by him or her, any new owner is nevertheless subject to them. They remain indefinitely as restrictions against the use of the land, although they may not be enforced if conditions change substantially after the inception of the covenants.

Most of these covenants are inserted for the benefit of surrounding property. They may be enforced by surrounding owners, particularly when the owner of a sub-division inserts similar restrictions in each deed or in the plat. The owner of any lot subject to the restrictions is permitted to enforce the restrictions against other lot owners in the same subdivision.

Restrictions in a deed, however, are strictly construed against the party seeking to enforce them. Doubts about restrictions are resolved in favor of freedom of the land from servitude, as a matter of public policy.

Occasionally, a covenant is inserted for the personal benefit of the grantor and will not run with the land. If a grantee, as part of the consideration, covenants to repair a dam on land owned by the grantor, the covenant will not run with the land and will not place a duty on a subsequent grantee. The promise neither touches nor concerns the land; it is only a personal covenant for the benefit of the grantor.

It should be emphasized that covenants and conditions that discriminate on the grounds of race, creed, color, or national origin are unconstitutional as a denial of equal protection of the laws. Such covenants were common at one time, and many are still incorporated in restrictions that accompany plats. When challenged, they have been held to be unconstitutional. They should be considered void.

CHAPTER SUMMARY

INTRODUCTION

1. *Ownership* is synonymous with *title*.
2. *Title* means the right or legal interest an owner has in a property item.
3. *Possession* represents the physical control a person may exert over property.

CLASSIFICATIONS OF PROPERTY

Real Property

1. The legal interests a person may have in land and things attached to or growing on the land are real property interests.
2. These interests may include the right to the use and benefit of the land's surface, air space, subsurface area, or any combination of these.

Personal Property

1. This is the legal interest in all property other than real property.
2. Personal property may be tangible, such as a car or book.
3. Personal property also includes intangible items, such as accounts receivables, goodwill, and rights to enforce contracts.
4. A name for personal property in general is *chattel*.

Reasons for Distinguishing between Real and Personal Property	1. Conflict-of-laws principles apply differently, depending on the type of property. 2. Real and personal property may be treated differently when the owner dies. 3. Transactions involving real property generally are more formal than personal property transactions. 4. These types of property are treated differently from the standpoint of taxation.
The Doctrine of Equitable Conversion	1. Courts of equity often treat an interest in real estate as personal property, and vice versa. 2. This doctrine is important when there is a lag between making a contract and performing it.

FIXTURES

What Is a Fixture?	1. A fixture is an item of personal property that has become part of the land.
Reasons for Determining Fixture Status	1. Fixtures increase the value of real estate. 2. Fixtures generally are included in the sale of real property—personal property can be retained by the seller. 3. Fixtures generally are part of the security given to the creditor taking real property as security. Personal property items are excluded from this security. 4. Fixtures usually remain as the landlord's property at the end of a lease, whereas personal property can often be taken by the tenant.
Tests	1. The annexation test states that the more firmly personal property is attached to real estate, the more likely it is to be a fixture. 2. The adaptation test states that the more the personal property item is used to promote the use and enjoyment of the land, the more likely it is to be a fixture. 3. The intention test, which is the most important, relies on the parties involved to agree whether an item is a fixture or whether it remains as personal property.

REAL PROPERTY OWNERSHIP INTERESTS

Bundle of Rights	1. The rights described by the bundle of rights theory may be held by one person, or they may be divided among two or more people. 2. How these rights are divided determines the ownership interests that may be created. Regardless of how many interests are created, the entire bundle of rights must be accountable with respect to each piece of land.
Fee Simple Estates	1. The basic types of interests presently held by the owner. 2. A fee simple absolute represents the most complete bundle of rights possible. 3. Qualified or conditional fee simple ownership interests may be defeated by the future occurrence of a stated event.
Life Estates	1. The life estate is an important tool in estate planning. 2. This type of ownership interest will terminate upon the death of a designated person. 3. The life tenant has a duty to preserve the value of the real property and not to waste the land's resources or improvements. 4. A life estate must be followed by a future interest known as a *remainder* or *reversion*.
Remainders and Reversions	1. A remainder is held by a third party, and a reversion is held by the grantor of the life estate.
Easements and Licenses	1. An easement is the right of one person to use the land owned by another person. Usually an easement is thought of as a permanent restriction that passes from one owner to the next. 2. A license is a less permanent grant of use of land as compared with an easement.

Introduction	1. Property may be owned by two or more persons as tenants in common, as joint tenants, or as tenants by the entireties.
Tenancy in Common	1. This is the most common form of multiple ownership. It is presumed by the courts unless the co-owners clearly state otherwise.
	2. These co-owners may acquire their interests at any time. They do not have to have equal ownership percentages. They may transfer their interests during their lives or upon their death to whomever they desire.
Joint Tenancy	1. This form of multiple ownership is characterized by the right of survivorship.
	2. The unities of time, title, interest, and possession must exist to create a joint tenancy.
	3. The right of survivorship may be severed by one of the co-owners, while alive, transferring his or her interest to a new party.
Tenancy by the Entirety	1. This is a specialized form of joint tenancy that must satisfy the four unities.
	2. This form of multiple ownership is limited to real property interests jointly held by a husband and wife.
	3. Generally, the right of survivorship cannot be severed without the consent of both spouses.
Condominiums and Cooperatives	1. A condominium is an individually owned apartment or town house in a multiunit complex.
	2. In addition to the individual unit, a condominium owner has an undivided interest in the common areas.
	3. A person with an interest in a cooperative owns at least one share in a corporation that owns the real property. This personal property interest allows the owner to lease a portion of the real estate.

RESTRICTIONS ON OWNERSHIP INTERESTS

Public Restrictions	1. The power of eminent domain allows a government body to take private property for the public use upon the payment of just compensation.
	2. Through its zoning regulations, a local community can restrict the use of land. Typically the zones include open space, residential, commercial, and industrial uses.
Private Restrictions	1. Restrictive covenants are commonly seen in subdivisions. Their purpose is to enhance the value of neighboring property by having all owners agree not to use their land in destructive or unpleasing ways.
	2. These covenants must be distinguished from conditions. A breach of a covenant may make the owner liable for damages. However, a breach of a condition usually causes the loss of the ownership interest.

REVIEW QUESTIONS AND PROBLEMS

1. Match each term in column A with the appropriate statement in column B.

A	B
(1) Title	(a) The legal interests a person may have in land and things attached to or growing on the land
(2) Possession	(b) This power allows the government to take private property for public use upon the payment of just compensation

(3) Real property	(c) An item of personal property that has become attached to land and is treated as real property
(4) Chattel	(d) The legal interest in property; synonymous with ownership
(5) Fixture	(e) The most important method for determining fixture status
(6) Intention test	(f) Another name for personal property
(7) Fee simple absolute	(g) The most complete ownership interest in real property
(8) Remainder	(h) A permanent right of one person to use the land of another person
(9) Easement	(i) The right to physical control of the use and enjoyment of property
(10) Joint tenancy	(j) The future interest that follows a life estate and is held by a third party
(11) Tenancy by the entirety	(k) A special method of ownership whereby spouses can own real property with a right of survivorship
(12) Eminent domain	(l) A method of ownership of personal or real property that is accompanied by the right of survivorship

2. The state of New Jersey sought to tax as real property cranes used in the loading and unloading of ships designed to carry freight in containers. These large cranes were mounted and movable on tracks at the pier. Each crane weighed 1,000,000 pounds and required special concrete piles for the base of the piers. Each crane was 50 feet wide and stood 170 feet above the rail. The boom could be raised to 245 feet. Complex electrical systems were required for operation of the cranes. The cranes were movable by barge. Were the cranes fixtures and thus taxable as part of the real estate? Explain.

3. Turner owned and operated a comprehensive cable TV system that contained about 630 miles of feeder cable. The cable was annexed to telephone poles owned by the telephone company, under a lease that required removal if the telephone company should need the space for its own service needs. The county assessed the TV cable system as real property, contending that the cable is a fixture under common law principles. Should the TV cable be classified as as fixture? Why or why not?

4. Following an oral agreement with Marley, the owner and operator of Marley's Store, The Oil Company installed gasoline pumps and storage tanks. The agreement included a clause that the equipment would remain on the property as long as Marley purchased gasoline solely from The Oil Company. Marley sold the property to Clarence, who decided to purchase gasoline from another source. The Oil Company offered to sell the equipment to Clarence or remove it. Clarence claimed that the equipment was firmly annexed to the property and was a part of the real estate he purchased. Was Clarence correct? Explain.

5. Mr. and Mrs. Causby owned land near a military airport. On this land, Causby had a home and several chicken houses. Because the Causby land was near the end of a runway, military airplanes passed directly over it. The planes' glide path caused them to fly at an altitude of only 83 feet over Causby's land. This resulted in the planes being 67 feet above Causby's house, 63 feet above the barn, and 18 feet above the tallest tree. Due to the loud noise of these planes, Causby lost many chickens when they flew into the walls. Ultimately, Causby had to quit raising chickens. Mr. and Mrs. Causby lost sleep, became nervous, and suffered from fright that a plane would crash. Are Mr. and Mrs. Causby entitled to be compensated for the damages caused by these airplanes passing through their air space? Why?

6. A husband willed certain land to his wife for life, with the remainder to their children. After the husband's death, his wife leased the property to a coal company, which strip-mined the land. Is it legal for a holder of a life estate to transfer her interest? Do the children have a good cause of action against the coal company? Why or why not?

7. At her husband's death, Ada was given a life estate in some farmland that contained a house. The remainder interests were left to Dorothy and Kent, children of Ada. Ada lived in or rented the farmhouse for three years. From then until her death ten years later, the house was unoccupied, and as a result, it slowly deteriorated. Due to poor family relationships, the remaindermen were estranged from Ada. Although they checked on the house from time to time, the remaindermen took no official action to stop the ongoing waste. However, Dorothy did mention to her mother many times the need to fix up the farmhouse. At Ada's death, Dorothy and Kent filed a claim against Ada's estate for $16,159, the amount of damage done to the house during the life estate. The representative of Ada's estate did not deny that waste had occurred. Instead, she asserted the defense that the remaindermen were barred from filing a claim since they unreasonably delayed taking action to prevent Ada's waste. Under these circumstances, was the remaindermen's suit for damages timely filed? Explain.

8. Harris, by will, devised land to his wife for the duration of her life with the remainder to pass to the Audubon Society to be used as a "wildlife refuge" on her death. On the property there is a commercially operated kennel for cats and dogs that is leased to a third party. This lease produces about $3,600 a year in rental income for the life tenant. The Department of Health inspected the kennel and ordered improvements to the kennel facility as a condition of license renewal. The cost of these improvements is estimated at $28,570. Is the remainder interest responsible for paying any of the cost of the improvements? Why or why not?

9. Marguerite sold land to Joe reserving her right of free egress and ingress over the private road. Joe sold the land to Kim, but the deed did not mention that Kim was taking the land subject to the easement contained in the conveyance by Marguerite to Joe. Is the easement effective against Kim? Why or why not?

10. James and Bessie Egan had a life estate in a tract of land, and Melford Egan owned the remainder. An agreement between these parties provided for a fifty-fifty division of the proceeds of any sale of the property. Under a threat of condemnation, these parties signed a contract and a deed to the state of Missouri. On October 5, this contract and deed were placed in escrow to be held until a check for the purchase price was received. On October 25, James and Bessie were killed in an accident. On November 9, the state delivered its check to the escrow agent. A dispute arose concerning who was entitled to the sales proceeds. Was the delivery of the signed deed to an escrow agent on October 5 effective to pass title to the state, so that James and Bessie were entitled to half the proceeds? Why?

11. A school district condemned a parcel of land. On the land there was a propane storage tank that was cradled on concrete piers. The piers were four feet high and were buried approximately six feet beneath the surface of the ground. They were constructed of steel and concrete. Related equipment consisting of an electric motor, pump, and various valves to load and unload propane was welded in place and attached to a concrete foundation and to an electric conduit on the site. The tank and related equipment weigh approximately twelve to fourteen tons. Must the school district pay for the propane tank and its related equipment and foundation? Why or why not?

12. Alan owned land in a subdivision and planned to construct two apartment buildings on the land. Some residents of the subdivision brought suit for an injunction, contending that the construction would violate the covenants contained in the subdivision plat, which restrict buildings to single-family residences. Alan claimed that the covenant was no longer effective because the land had been rezoned for multifamily buildings. Should the restrictive covenant remain enforceable? Why or why not?

13. Terry planned to construct an apartment building on land he owned in a subdivision. The plat of the subdivision contained a restrictive covenant prohibiting use of its land for business purposes. Some residents of the subdivision contended this covenant prohibited Terry's plans. Terry sought a court decision determining the impact of the covenant on his proposal. Should the covenant be interpreted to prevent the construction of an apartment building? Explain.

14. Hanna owned four lots in the Browncroft Extension residential neighborhood. He planned to construct duplexes on these lots. Malley, the owner of one lot in this neighborhood, filed suit to enjoin Hanna's construction plans. Malley argued that Hanna's plans, if allowed, would violate a restrictive covenant found in both Hanna's and Malley's chain of title. This restrictive covenant, originally placed in the deeds from the developer to the parties' predecessors in title, stated the following:

> Each lot in the Browncroft tract shall be used for residence purposes only and no double house, Boston flat, or apartment house, shall ever be built upon any lot in said tract.

Hanna asserted that Malley lacked the right to enforce the restrictive covenant. Should Malley be allowed to enforce the restrictive covenant? Why?

ACQUIRING TITLE TO PROPERTY

CHAPTER PREVIEW

In addition to the general legal principles of property discussed in chapter 43, it is important to understand how title to both personal and real property is acquired. This understanding of acquiring title to property will allow you to study more thoroughly transactions involving property.

The legal requirements for obtaining an ownership interest differ greatly, depending on whether the property involved is personal or real. Therefore, this chapter examines the methods of acquiring title to personal property. It then concentrates on both voluntary and involuntary transfers of real property. Also, issues related to transferring title to personal and real property at the owner's death are discussed. Finally, the chapter concludes with an examination of how a party proves the existence of title to land.

■ BUSINESS MANAGEMENT DECISION

As the property manager employed by a large wood products company, you learn that a business located adjacent to a piece of your company's timberland is using a portion of your company's land to park vehicles.

Should you be concerned? If so, why? What should you do?

ACQUIRING TITLE TO PERSONAL PROPERTY

1. Methods: Original Possession

Title to personal property may be acquired through any of the following methods: *original possession, transfer, accession,* or *confusion.* Original possession is a method of extremely limited applicability. It may be used to obtain title over wild animals and fish or things that are available for appropriation by individuals. Property that is in its native state and over which no one as yet has taken full and complete control belongs to the first person who reduces such property to his or her exclusive possession. Property once reduced to ownership, but later abandoned, belongs to the first party next taking possession.

In addition, it might be said that property created through mental or physical labor belongs to the creator unless he or she has agreed to create it for someone else for compensation. Books, inventions, and trademarks would be included under this heading. This kind of property is usually protected by the government through means of copyrights, patents, and trademarks.

2. Title by Transfer: In General

As a general rule, a transferee receives the rights of the transferor, and a transferee takes no better title than the transferor had. If the transferor of the personal property did not have title to the property, the transferee would not have title either, even though the transferee believes that the transferor had a good title. Suppose

Pastor Jones purchases a new stereo set for a church from parishioner Tithe. Unknown to Pastor Jones, Tithe had stolen the stereo from the Bulldog Music Store. The stereo set still belongs to Bulldog Music, and the church has no title to it. An innocent purchaser from a thief obtains no title to the property purchased, and no subsequent purchaser stands in any better position. Because the thief had no title or ownership, persons who acquired the property from or through the thief have no title or ownership.

In chapter 18, section 12, we discuss the concept of a good-faith purchaser of personal property. We emphasize that if the transferor of the property has a voidable title, and sells property to an innocent purchaser, the transferee may obtain good title to the property. Assume that through fraudulent representations, Fred acquires title to Sam's property. Sam could avoid the transaction with Fred and obtain a return of his property. If Fred sells the property to Ann, and she does not know about his fraudulent representations, Sam cannot disaffirm against Ann. Ann has good title to the property, since she is a good-faith purchaser for value.

Title to personal property may be transferred by sale, will, gift, or operation of law. Since it is probably most relevant in business transactions, the law relating to transfer by sale is discussed in chapters 18 and 19 on Article 2 of the Uniform Commercial Code. Transfer of title by gift is discussed in the next section of this chapter. Finally, transfer of title to personal property may occur by the operation of law. Sections 4 through 6 discuss some examples of how the law affects the transfer of title to personal property. Title to personal property also may be transferred at the owner's death through the provisions of a will or by intestate succession. Legal issues related to wills and descent are described in sections 19 through 24.

3. Transfer by *Inter Vivos* Gift

The phrase *inter vivos* refers to gifts made voluntarily during the life of the party transferring title. A testamentary gift is one that is effective only at the owner's death.

REQUIREMENTS.   Generally, there are just two people required to accomplish an *inter vivos* gift. The *donor* is the party making the gift. The *donee* is the one receiving or acquiring title to the property. The law requires that three elements be satisfied to have a valid *inter vivos* gift. These elements are (1) the donor's intent to make a gift, (2) delivery of possession by the donor, and (3) acceptance of the gift by the donee. From a legal standpoint, the element of *delivery* usually is most important. Unless a contrary intent is clear and obvious, the physical change of possession of personal property creates a presumption that both the donor and donee consent to a gift. However, in the event there is a dispute over the true ownership of personal property, all three elements must be established to have a valid gift.

The delivery can be actual or constructive or symbolic, if the situation demands. Thus, if the property is in storage, the donor could make a delivery by giving the donee the warehouse receipt. A donor may also accomplish delivery by giving the donee something that is a token representing the donee's dominion and control. A delivery of the keys to an automobile may be a valid symbolic delivery, although a symbolic or constructive delivery will not suffice if actual delivery is reasonably possible.

The following case discusses the essential elements of an *inter vivos* gift and finds them to be lacking.

CASE

Young v. Young

393 S.E.2d 398 (Va. 1990)

RUSSELL, J.

This dispute concerns the ownership of stock in a closely held corporation. It turns on the law of *inter vivos* gifts.

In the 1930's, Lehman H. Young, Sr. (Young, Sr.), established a printing business. . . . He was sole owner of the business and operated it as a sole proprietorship for about 33 years. In 1970, Young, Sr. formed a corporation . . . to which he contributed all the assets of the printing business in exchange for all the shares of . . . stock. Later, Young, Sr., transferred most of his shares to his sister . . . to hold in trust for himself. . . . He retained only a few shares in his own name.

In 1980, and in each succeeding year through 1984, Young, Sr., directed his sister to transfer some of the shares she held in trust for him to his two daughters, Deborah Young Harris and Pamela Young Walker, and to his son, Lehman H. Young, Jr. (Young, Jr.). Each such transfer was represented by a new certificate issued in the donee child's name. The corporation issued new certificates for 29 shares given to each child in the years 1980, 1981, and 1982; for 27 shares given to each child in 1983 and 1984; and for an additional 100 shares given to each daughter in 1984. . . .

The new certificates were registered in the corporate stock transfer ledger, but Young, Sr., retained possession of all the certificates, except those which represented the initial gifts in 1980. On each occasion of a purported gift to a daughter, Young, Sr., acknowledged receipt of the certificate's delivery by signing the daughter's name in the receipt space of the stock transfer ledger and by making the notation, "L H Young Sr. Atty." It is undisputed that neither daughter ever appointed Young, Sr., her attorney in fact, that neither daughter ever received delivery of a stock certificate after 1980, and that, except for the 1980 gifts, neither daughter knew of the purported annual gifts when Young, Sr., attempted to make them.

In 1987, a dispute arose between father and son concerning the business. . . . In October 1987, Young, Sr., caused 254 shares of stock to be transferred on the stock transfer ledger from his daughters' names to his own. . . . This . . . gave him voting control. . . .

In June 1988, Young, Jr., filed this proceeding. . . . He asked for . . . [a] judicial determination of the proper shareholders and their respective interests. . . . The court concluded that the attempt of Young, Sr., to recapture the daughters' shares was void and ineffectual. The court established a revised list of shareholders, showing Young, Jr., in voting control. . . .

We granted Young, Sr., an appeal. . . .

The ownership of stock as reflected in the corporate records is *prima facie* correct. . . . It is undisputed that the 254 shares in question were initially the subject of a valid original issue to Young, Sr., who paid value for them in order to capitalize the corporation. The dispositive question is whether they were ever validly transferred from him to his daughters. Because the daughters paid no consideration for them, principles governing gifts *inter vivos* apply.

In order to establish a gift *inter vivos*, the following elements must be shown:

(1) The gift must be of personal property;

(2) possession of the property must be delivered at the time of the gift to the donee, or some other for him and the gift must be accepted by the donee; and

(3) the title of the property must vest in the donee at the time of the gift.

Further, the gift is effective only if the donor has donative intent at the time of the gift and if there is such actual or constructive delivery as divests the donor of all dominion and control over the property and invests it in the donee.

At common law, the securities could be the subject of a valid *inter vivos* gift to the daughters only if delivered either to them, or to someone designated by them, in such manner as to "divest the donor of all dominion and control" over the securities. Further, the daughters must "accept" them. Under the UCC, the daughters must "acquire possession" of the certificates, or such possession must be acquired by a "person designated by" the daughters. The prerequisite elements of delivery to, and acceptance by, the daughters, are entirely lacking on the present facts. Because the disputed securities were never delivered to the daughters nor to anyone designated by the daughters to receive them, no *inter vivos* gift was ever made. These undisputed facts were more than sufficient to overcome the *prima facie* showing of ownership made by the corporate records. . . .

Young, Jr., argues on appeal that Young, Sr., having caused the corporate records to reflect annual gifts of stock to the daughters, should now be estopped to deny the validity of such gifts. We reject that argument for two reasons. First, the daughters, having no knowledge of the purported gifts, made no change of position in reliance on them and suffered no disadvantage because of them. Therefore, an essential element of estoppel is lacking. Second, the daughters are not contesting Young, Sr.'s apparent change of mind; the contest is made only by Young, Jr. As a stranger to the purported gifts, he had no standing to enforce them. . . .

■ *Reversed.*

1. This case involves a number of purported gifts of corporate stock. Who is the donor? Who are the donees?

2. Which purported gifts are the subject matter of this litigation?

3. Why does the donor revoke these "gifts" and reclaim ownership of the corporate stock?

4. What essential element of an *inter vivos* gift is found to be lacking in this case?

5. What is the immediate impact of the court's ruling that an *inter vivos* gift has not been made?

GENERAL RULES AND EXCEPTION.   There are two general rules that you should keep in your mind concerning *inter vivos* gifts. First, an executory promise to make a gift is not enforceable, since the donee typically has not given consideration to support the donor's promise. Second, an executed or completed gift cannot be rescinded by the donor. This latter general rule is subject to one important exception.

Gift *causa mortis*   A gift made in anticipation of death. If the donor survives, the gift is revocable.

Gifts *causa mortis* constitute this exception to the general rule on the finality of completed gifts. A gift *causa mortis* is made in contemplation of death. This gift arises out of the situation in which a person is, or believes he or she is, facing death and makes a gift on the assumption that death is imminent. A person about to embark on a perilous trip or to undergo a serious operation or one who has an apparently incurable and fatal illness might make a gift and deliver the item to the donee on the assumption that he or she may soon die. If this donor returns safely or does not die, he or she is allowed to revoke the gift and recover the property from the donee.

4. Title by Accession

Accession literally means "adding to." In the law of personal property, accession has two basic meanings. First, it refers to an owner's right to all that his or her property produces. The owner of a cow is also the owner of each calf born, and the owner of lumber is the owner of a table made from the lumber by another. *Accession* is also the legal term used to signify the acquisition of title to personal property when it is incorporated into other property or joined with other property.

When accession occurs, who has title is frequently in issue. The general rule is that when the goods of two different owners are united without the willful misconduct of either party, the title to the resulting product goes to the owner of the major portion of the goods. This rule is based on the principle that personal property permanently added to other property and forming a minor portion of the finished product becomes part of the larger unit. Since title can be in only one party, it is in the owner of the major portion. The owner of the minor portion might recover damages if his or her portion were wrongfully taken. The law of accession simply prevents the owner of the minor portion from recovering the property itself.

The law of accession distinguishes between the rights of innocent and willful trespassers, although both are wrongful. An *innocent* trespasser to personal property is one who acts through mistake or conduct that is not intentionally wrongful. A *willful* trespasser cannot obtain title against the original owner under any circumstances because of the wrongful intent.

Suppose that Garrod owns some raw materials, and that Durham inadvertently uses these materials to manufacture a product. The product belongs to Garrod. If Durham also adds some raw materials of his own, the manufactured product belongs to the party who contributed the major portion of the materials. If

FIGURE 44-1 ■ An Illustration of the Law of Accession

	NO ADDITION	MINOR ADDITION	MAJOR ADDITION
INNOCENT WRONGDOER	Garrod	Garrod	Durham
INTENTIONAL WRONGDOER	Garrod	Garrod	Garrod

Durham becomes the owner, Garrod is entitled to recover her damages. If Garrod is the owner, Durham is not entitled to anything, since he used Garrod's materials without authority to do so. If Durham had knowingly used Garrod's raw materials, Durham could not recover the completed product under any circumstances due to his willful misconduct.

To make this example an even clearer illustration of the law of accession, suppose that each of the labels on the chart in Figure 44-1 describes actions by Durham. The owner of the finished product is indicated in each box. As you can see, the real distinction occurs when Durham makes a major addition to Garrod's raw materials. It is under these circumstances that the innocent or intentional nature of Durham's trespass becomes most important.

Similar issues arise when unauthorized repairs are made to an owner's personal property and when property subject to an accession is sold. In general, the owner is entitled to goods as repaired, irrespective of the repair's value, unless the parts added during the repair can be severed without damaging the original goods. If the property that is the subject of accession is sold to a good-faith purchaser, the rights and liabilities of this third party are the same as those of the seller. If the seller is a willful trespasser, he or she has no title and can convey none. The true owner can recover the property without any liability to the third party. If the innocent third party made improvements or repairs, he or she has the right to remove the additions if they can be removed without damaging the original goods.

5. Title by Confusion

Property of such a character that one unit may not be distinguished from another unit and that is usually sold by weight or measure is known as *fungible property.* Grain, hay, logs, wine, oil, and similar property are of this nature. When personal property belongs to various parties, it may be mixed by intention, accident, mistake, or wrongful misconduct of an owner of some of the goods. Confusion of fungible property belonging to various owners, assuming that no misconduct (confusion by consent, accident, or mistake) is involved, results in an undivided ownership of the total mass. For example, grain is stored in a public warehouse by many parties. Each owner holds an undivided interest in the total mass, his or her particular interest being dependent on the amount stored. Should there be a partial destruction of the total mass, the loss would be divided proportionately.

Confusion of goods that results from the wrongful conduct of one of the parties causes the title to the total mass to pass to the innocent party. If the mixture is divisible, an exception exists. The wrongdoer, if able to show that the resultant mass is equal in value per unit to that of the innocent party, is able to recover his or her share. If the new mixture is worth no less per unit than that formerly belonging to the innocent party, the wrongdoer may claim his or her portion of the new mass by presenting convincing evidence of the amount added. If two masses are added together and the wrongdoer can only establish his or her proportion of one mass, that party is only entitled to that proportion of the combined mass.

For example, Farmers Smith and Jones grow corn on adjoining property. Farmer Smith agrees to store Jones's corn in return for 25 percent of the corn stored. Without measuring the amount of corn stored for Jones, Smith adds this corn to a silo containing corn grown by Smith. Since there is no certainty as to how much corn belongs to Jones, a court would probably award him 75 percent of all the corn stored. Smith is limited to a one-fourth interest of even his corn, since he wrongfully commingled a fungible product. This result is necessary to ensure that Jones recovers at least his share of the corn.

6. Abandoned, Lost, and Mislaid Property

Property is said to be *abandoned* whenever it is discarded by the true owner who, at that time, has no intention of reclaiming it. The property belongs to the first individual again reducing it to possession.

Property is *lost* whenever, as a result of negligence, accident, or some other cause, it is found at some place other than that chosen by the owner. Title to lost property continues to rest with the true owner. However, until this owner has been ascertained, the finder may keep the property found. The finder's title is good against everyone except the true owner. The rights of the finder are superior to those of the person in charge of the property on which the lost article is found unless the finder is a trespasser. Occasionally, state statutes provide for newspaper publicity concerning articles that have been found. If the owner cannot be located, the found property or a portion of it reverts to the state or county if the property's value exceeds an established minimum. Otherwise, it goes to the finder.

Property is *mislaid* or *misplaced* if its owner has intentionally placed it at a certain spot but the manner of placement indicates that he or she has forgotten to pick it up. The presumption is that the owner will eventually remember where he or she left it and return for it. The finder must turn it over to the owner of the premises, who may hold it until the owner is located. The distinctions between abandoned, lost, and mislaid property are subtle and frequently litigated. As the following case illustrates, the factual situations in such cases are amazing and seem more fictional than real.

CASE

Ritz v. Selma United Methodist Church
467 N.W.2d 266 (Ia. 1991)

CARTER, J.

Ruth E. Ritz and several other named plaintiffs appeal from an adverse determination by the court in a declaratory judgment action seeking to adjudicate adverse claims to buried money. Plaintiffs are the beneficiaries and heirs of Charles and Rosa Nelson, husband and wife, and Opal Nelson, the only daughter of Charles and Rosa. Charles and Rosa, and later Opal, owned a dwelling house and lot in Selma, Iowa. The Nelson family's ownership of this property spanned a period extending from 1922 until Opal's death in 1981.

The property was abandoned by Opal's personal representative at the time of the final settlement of her estate because of substantial unpaid real estate taxes and other clouds on the title. Van Buren County ultimately gained title to the property at a tax sale. The defendant, Selma United Methodist Church (the Church), purchased the property from Van Buren County in 1987.

When the Church razed the house and garage on the property, a substantial sum of paper money and coins was found buried in the ground in tin cans and glass jars. Several silver half-dollars included in this cash hoard antedated 1900. Also included among the money discovered were several twenty-dollar and ten-dollar gold certificates circa 1928. The face amount of the coins and currency totaled $24,547.74. . . .

The district court found that Charles Nelson was the true owner of the money and had buried it at the location where it was found by the agents of the Church. The court . . . concluded, however, that any claims of the plaintiffs to this cash hoard had to be brought within five years of the order of final settlement in Opal Nelson's estate. Because more than five years had transpired between the time of that settlement order and the finding of the money, the court found plaintiffs were barred from asserting ownership. From this premise, the court determined that title to the money vested in the Church, as finder. . . .

Plaintiffs have appealed. They contend that, as heirs or beneficiaries of the true owner of the money, they have a superior claim against the present owners of the real property where it was found. They further urge that Opal Nelson's estate can be reopened more than five years after final settlement in order to administer this newly discovered property. . . .

The rights of finders of property vary according to the characterization of the property found. . . . The general rule is that the finder of lost property becomes the owner thereof against the whole world other than the true owner. Property is lost when the owner unintentionally and involuntarily parts with its possession and does not know where it is.

Mislaid property is that which the owner has voluntarily placed somewhere and then forgets that it is there. The right of possession of mislaid property is in the owner of the premises upon which it is found, as against all persons other than the true owner. . . .

Abandoned property is that to which the owner has voluntarily relinquished all right, title, and interest with the intention of terminating his ownership. The finder who reduces abandoned property to possession acquires absolute title as against the former owner.

Although the real estate was abandoned by Opal's estate, we believe that it would be a completely unwarranted inference to conclude that the money found by the Church had been abandoned by its owner. The fact that it was buried in jars and tin cans indicates that the owner was attempting to preserve it. . . . It is fairly to be classified as the type of property to which the true owner retains ownership as against the finder or the owner of the property where it is found.

In applying the rules of ownership relating to lost or mislaid property, courts are in general agreement that if the original owner is deceased that person's heirs or legatees are entitled to lay claim to the property. . . .

Although the district court found that Charles Nelson had been the owner of the found money and that his interest therein had passed to Opal, it concluded that plaintiffs were barred from claiming by, through, or under Opal. It based this conclusion on the five-year limitation which section 633.488 places on reopening a final settlement in an estate. . . .

Section 633.488 contemplates a reopening of matters which have been previously considered in the final accounting, distribution, and settlement order. Section 633.489, on the other hand, is aimed at reopening a closed estate for the purpose of administering property omitted from the inventory or performing other necessary acts which were not performed during the original administration. Section 633.489 does not place any time limitation on reopening for such purposes.

Based on the district court's findings as to Charles Nelson's ownership and Opal's succession thereto, the bills and coins were property of Opal which were not administered in her estate. This is a circumstance which allows reopening of that estate for purposes of administering these assets and making distribution to her legatees in their proportionate share. These legatees are the rightful owners of the money rather than the finder. This is true even though Opal was not aware of the buried money at the time of her death. The district court erred in concluding otherwise. . . .

■ *Reversed and remanded.*

CASE CONCEPTS REVIEW

1. What property is discovered on the land formerly owned by the Nelsons?
2. What is the basis for the Church's claim to the money? What is the basis for the claim of the Nelsons' heirs?
3. Why does the court conclude that this property is either lost or mislaid as opposed to abandoned?
4. Which party has a superior claim to lost or mislaid property?
5. Why does the court conclude that Opal's beneficiaries and heirs can reopen her estate despite the passage of a significant amount of time?

7. Introduction

Title to real property may be acquired (1) by original entry, called title by occupancy; (2) by a deed from the owner; (3) by judicial sale; (4) by benefit of the period of the statue of limitations, called *adverse possession*; (5) by accretion, which may happen when a river, lake, or other body of water creates new land by depositing soil; and (6) by will or descent under intestacy statues. The first five methods listed are discussed throughout the next 11 sections of this chapter. Sections 19 through 24 discuss issues with respect to transfer by will or descent.

8. Original Entry

Original entry refers to a title obtained from the sovereign. Except in those portions of the United States where the original title to the land was derived from grants that were issued by the king of England and other sovereigns who took possession of the land by conquest, title to all the land in the United States was derived from the United States government. Private individuals who occupied land for the period of time prescribed by federal statue and met other conditions established by law acquired title by patent from the federal government.

Delivery of a valid deed is the most common method of voluntarily transferring real property ownership interests. Sections 9 through 15 examine the essential requirements and types of deeds frequently used. Thereafter, this chapter discusses some of the ways in which title to land may be lost by the owner involuntarily. These topics include transfers by judicial sale, adverse possession, and accretion.

9. Transfer by Deed: Legal Descriptions

Deed A written instrument in a special form, signed, sealed, delivered, and used to pass the legal title of real property from one person to another.

A **deed** is the legal document that is issued to transfer the ownership interest in or title to land. Although there are other essential elements of deeds, one of the most important parts of any deed is the legal description of the land involved. By reference to the deed, people must be able to get the information that allows them to determine the exact location of the land described. This description is based on one of the following acceptable systems: (1) the metes and bounds system, (2) the rectangular survey system, or (3) the plat system.

METES AND BOUNDS.   The *metes and bounds* system establishes boundary lines by reference to natural or artificial monuments, that is, to fixed points, such as roads, streams, fences, trees. A metes and bounds description starts with a monument, determines the angle of the line and the distance to the next monument, and so forth, until the tract is fully enclosed and described. Because surveyors may not always agree, the law of metes and bounds creates an order of precedence. Reference to monuments controls over courses (angles), and courses control over distances. In general, the least important factor to consider is the amount of acres or area contained in a description.

RECTANGULAR SURVEY.   The term *rectangular survey* refers to a system of describing land by using a known baseline and principal meridians. The baseline runs from

FIGURE 44-2 ■ Division of a Section in the Rectangular Survey

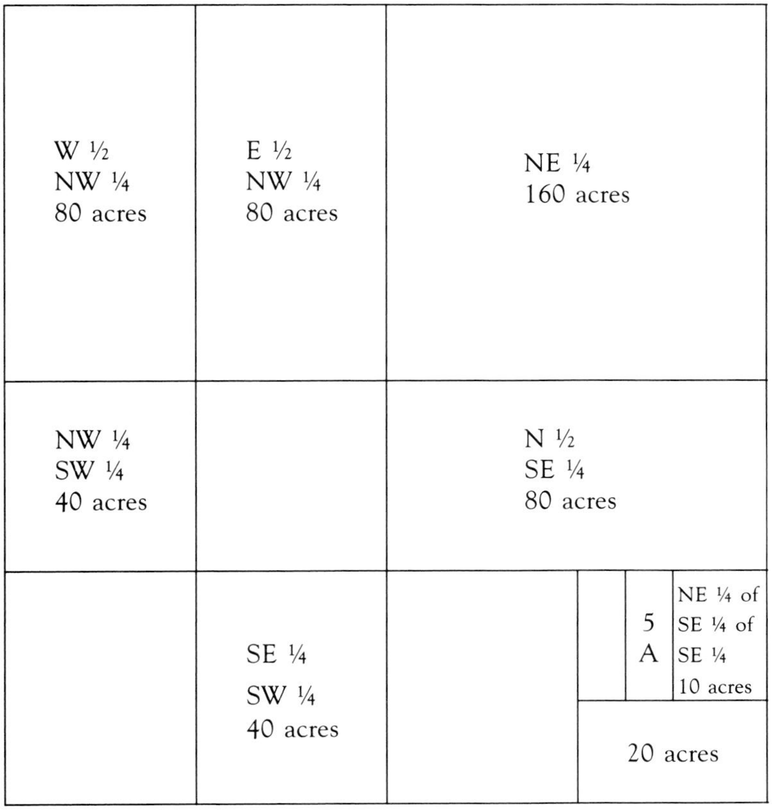

W ½ NW ¼ 80 acres	E ½ NW ¼ 80 acres	NE ¼ 160 acres		
NW ¼ SW ¼ 40 acres		N ½ SE ¼ 80 acres		
	SE ¼ SW ¼ 40 acres		5 A	NE ¼ of SE ¼ of SE ¼ 10 acres
			20 acres	

east to west, and principal meridians run from north to south. Townships are thus located in relation to these lines. For example, a township may be described as 7 North, Range 3 East of the third Principal Meridian. This township is seven townships north of the baseline and three east of the third principal meridian. The townships, then, would be divided into thirty-six sections, each section being one square mile, which consists of 640 acres. Parts of the section are described by their locations within it, as Figure 44–2 illustrates.

PLAT.   A *plat* is a recorded document dividing a tract described by metes and bounds or rectangular survey into streets, blocks, and lots. The land may thereafter be described in relation to the recorded plat simply by giving the lot number, block, and subdivision name. Lot 8 in Block 7 of Ben Johnson's Subdivision in the City of Emporia, Kansas, might describe real property located in that municipality.

10. Other Essential Requirements of All Deeds

The statutes of the various states provide the necessary form, language, and execution requirements of deeds. For example, these statutes usually require that the parties involved be identified at the beginning of the deed. Often these parties are

Grantor A person who executes the deed, thereby transferring title.

Grantee A person to whom a grant is made; one named in a deed to receive title.

Notary public A public officer authorized to administer oaths.

Escrow agent A third party other than the grantor and grantee who holds the signed deed until the buyer has paid the full purchase price. For a review of escrow arrangements, see chapter 39, section 8.

referred to as the **grantor** and **grantee.** All deeds must contain language that indicates the type of ownership interest being conveyed. Also, the deed must state clearly that this interest is being transferred to the grantee. A properly drafted deed needs to be signed by the grantor and, in some states, sealed, witnessed, or acknowledged in the presence of a **notary public.** Finally, the deed must be delivered.

A deed is not effective until it is delivered—that is, placed entirely out of the control of the grantor. This delivery usually occurs by the handing of the instrument to the grantee or to some third party known as an **escrow agent.** The delivery by the grantor must occur during the lifetime of the grantor. It cannot be delivered by someone else after the grantor's death, even if the grantor has ordered the delivery.

So the owner of real estate may notify all persons of the change in title to the property, the statutes of the various states provide that deeds shall be recorded in the recording office of the county in which the land is located. Failure to record a deed by a new owner makes it possible for the former owner to convey and pass good title to the property to an innocent third party, although the former owner has no right to do so and would be liable to the first grantee in such a case.

Although the recording of a deed is necessary to give public notice of a change of ownership, the recording is not necessary to pass title as between the grantor and grantee.

However, when a deed is recorded there exists a very strong presumption that the deed was delivered by the grantor. The court's discussion in the following case illustrates the weight given to the recording of a deed.

CASE

Gross v. Gross
781 P.2d 284 (Mont. 1989)

Richard Gross is the son of Peter Gross. Peter's wife (Richard's mother) died in 1980. Peter was 80 years old at the time. Sometime after his wife's death, Peter suffered a stroke which prompted a discussion between father and son concerning the father putting his affairs in order. Shortly after this discussion, the father executed and recorded three warranty deeds that transferred property from the father to the father and son as joint tenants. The father retained the deeds in his possession, continued to occupy and maintain the property and pay all expenses associated with the property.

After the father executed and recorded the deeds, he told his son that he had put the property into a joint tenancy with the son. It is undisputed that the father executed these deeds to avoid probate. Subsequently the father remarried and asked the son to reconvey the property. The son refused. The father sued to have the deeds declared null and void. The trial court entered summary judgment in favor of the father. It held that the father presented sufficient evidence to overcome the presumption of delivery raised by the recording of the deeds. The son appealed.

HARRISON, J.

. . . When a deed is executed a presumption arises that delivery occurred and that recording the deed strengthens that presumption. We conclude that this presumption can only be overcome by clear and convincing evidence.

In assessing whether the grantor has presented clear and convincing evidence, the general rule is that the grantor's self-serving statements are not enough to overcome the presumption of delivery. Also the fact that the grantor has retained possession of the deeds and continued to occupy and control the land will not rebut the presumption when a close relationship exists between the grantor and grantee.

The father testified that he did not intend to create a present interest and argued in essence that his actions subsequent to recording the deeds were inconsistent with the intention to create a present interest. The District Court held that the father had presented sufficient evidence to overcome the presumption of delivery. In reaching its conclusion, the District Court relied on the father's dominion and control of the property along with his paying all of the expenses such as taxes and insurance.

We do not agree that the father presented the kind of clear and convincing evidence required to rebut the presumption of delivery. . . . The evidence relied on by the District Court to determine that the father did not intend to create a present interest in the son cannot be used to rebut the presumption of delivery given the close relationship between father and son. . . .

A grantor's self-serving statement will not overcome the presumption of delivery raised by recording. No independent third party testimony exists to corroborate the father's testimony regarding his intent.

The undisputed evidence in the record establishes that the father intended to avoid probate. As to his property, he chose to accomplish that purpose by executing and recording deeds that granted his son a joint tenancy in the property. This intentional act constituted unrebutted evidence of his intention to create a present interest in the son which upon the death of the father would automatically pass full title to the son. The father testified that he did not intend to pass a present interest to the son and that he retained deeds and controlled the property. But . . . the father's self-serving statements and those particular subsequent acts, by law, cannot rebut the presumption.

The father must present clear and convincing evidence other than his own statements and other than those particular subsequent acts. He has not presented any other clear evidence. . . .

■ *Reversed.*

CASE CONCEPTS REVIEW

1. What is the relationship between the parties in this litigation?
2. Who is the grantor? Who are the grantees?
3. Who had possession of the deeds that created a joint tenancy between the father and son after these deeds had been recorded?
4. What evidence does the father offer to rebut the presumption that the deeds were not delivered to the son?
5. Why does the court refuse to give substantial weight to this evidence?

11. Optional Elements of Deeds

In addition to the essential requirements of all deeds, a deed may contain all, some, or none of the optional elements referred to as *covenants* or *warranties*. These covenants or warranties are promises or guarantees made by the grantor pertaining to the land and the grantor's bundle of rights with respect to it. These covenants may include a promise that (1) at the time of making the deed, the grantor has fee simple title and the right and power to convey it (*covenant of seizin*); (2) the property is free from all encumbrances except those noted in the deed (*covenant against encumbrances*); (3) the grantee and his successors will have the quiet and peaceful enjoyment of the property (*covenant of quiet enjoyment*); and (4) the grantor will defend the title of the grantee if anyone else should claim the property (*covenant of further assurances*).

Many different kinds of deeds are used throughout the United States, the statutes of each state providing for the various types. The common types are the *warranty deed*, the *grant deed*, the *bargain and sale deed*, and the *quitclaim deed*. There are also special types of deeds used when the grantor holds a special legal position at the time of conveyance. Special deeds are used by the executors and administrators of estates, by guardians, and by sheriffs or other court officials executing deeds in their official capacity. The major distinction among types of deeds relates to the covenants or warranties the grantor of the deed makes to the grantee. A deed may contain several warranties or none at all, depending on the type of deed and the language used.

12. Warranty Deed

From the grantee's perspective, the *warranty deed* provides the broadest protection that the grantor is conveying clear title to the land described in the deed. This protection is provided because the warranty deed contains all four of the aforementioned covenants. Therefore, the warranty deed is the type of deed grantees usually insist on in traditional real estate sales transactions.

The covenant of seizin is breached when the grantor's title is inferior to another person's ownership interest. The warranty against encumbrances is the one that is most likely to be breached. All real estate is encumbered at least to the extent of taxes that are a lien. Moreover, unsatisfied judgments against the owners constitute an encumbrance in most states, as do both visible and recorded easements. In fact, there is a breach of warranty even if the grantee has knowledge of the encumbrance and it is not an exception in the deed. Therefore, the deed must be carefully prepared and must except all encumbrances or there will be liability for breach of warranty.

Whether public restrictions on ownership interests, such as zoning ordinances, constitute an encumbrance has created some controversy. In general, the mere existence of a public restriction on the use of real estate does not constitute an encumbrance. However, an existing violation of a public restriction is an encumbrance within the meaning of the covenant against encumbrances.

The lawyer drafting a deed must ascertain which encumbrances actually exist and except them in the deed. A typical deed might provide that the conveyance is "subject to accrued general taxes, visible easements, and easements and restrictions of record." If there is an outstanding mortgage, it would also be included as an exception to the warranty against encumbrances. The warranty of quiet enjoyment and the covenant of further assurances are promises by the grantor to defend the title in legal proceedings if someone else claims it. Such defense includes paying court costs and attorneys' fees.

13. Grant Deed

In some states (California being one), a deed known as a grant deed is in more common use than is the warranty deed. In a *grant deed,* the grantor covenants that no interest in the property has been conveyed to another party, that the property has not been encumbered except as noted, and that any title to the property the grantor might receive in the future will be transferred to the grantee. A grantor under a grant deed has liability only as a result of encumbrances or claims that arose while the property was owned by the grantor. A grant deed does not protect the grantee against encumbrances that existed prior to the grantor taking title. As a result, the grant deed is much narrower than the warranty deed in the promises made to the grantee.

14. Bargain and Sale Deed

A *bargain and sale deed* warrants that the grantor has title to the property and the right to convey, but it does not contain any express covenants as to the title's validity. This deed also is sometimes called a *warranty deed without covenants.* The bargain and sale deed simply states that the grantor "does hereby grant, bargain, sell, and convey" his or her interest in the real property to the grantee. In states that authorize a bargain and sale deed, a grantee who desires the covenants and warranties of a warranty deed must require that the sales contract state that a warranty deed will be delivered by the grantor. If the sales contract is silent about the type of deed, the grantor is obligated only to sign and deliver a bargain and sale deed.

15. Quitclaim Deed

A grantor who does not wish to make warranties with respect to the title may execute a *quitclaim deed*, merely transferring all the "right, title, and interest" of the grantor to the grantee. Whatever title the grantor has, the grantee receives, but the grantor makes no warranties. A quitclaim deed is used when the interest of the grantor is not clear; for example, where a deed will clear a defective title. It is also used to eliminate possible conflicting interests or when, in fact, there may be no interest in the grantor.

The grantee who takes property under a quitclaim deed must understand that he or she may be receiving nothing at all. A person could give a quitclaim deed to the Brooklyn Bridge to anyone willing to pay for it. The grantee obviously is not given anything at all by such a deed. The grantor simply conveyed all of his or her interest in the bridge, without assurances that any rights of ownership did, in fact, exist. To transfer all of a person's rights in someone else's property is to transfer nothing at all.

The amount of protection each deed gives to the grantee is the most important distinction to remember. The order in which these types of deeds are discussed is also the order of the amount of protection provided. The warranty deed contains the greatest protection for the grantee. The grant deed protects the grantee from encumbrances placed on the land's title by the grantor but not by others. The bargain and sale deed simply states that the grantor has the right to convey the title involved, but all other covenants and warranties are missing. Finally, the grantor who gives a quitclaim deed does not even promise that he or she has any rights in the land at all.

ACQUIRING TITLE TO REAL PROPERTY: INVOLUNTARY TRANSFERS

16. Transfer by Judicial Sale

Judicial sale A sale authorized by a court that has jurisdiction to grant such authority. Such sales are conducted by an officer of the court.

Title to land may be acquired by a purchaser at a sale conducted by a sheriff or other proper official and made under the jurisdiction or a court having competent authority to order the sale. To raise money to pay a judgment obtained against an owner, a **judicial sale** of that owner's property may be necessary. To collect unpaid taxes, land owned by a delinquent taxpayer is sold at a public *tax sale*. The purchaser at a tax sale acquires a tax title. A mortgage foreclosure sale is a proceeding in equity by which a mortgagee obtains, by judicial sale, money to pay the obligation secured by the mortgage. The word *foreclosure* is also applied to the proceedings for enforcing other types of liens, such as mechanic's liens, assessments against realty to pay public improvements, and other statutory liens. The character of title acquired by a purchaser at a judicial sale is determined by state statute.

17. Title by Adverse Possession

Adverse possession Acquisition of legal title to another's land by being in continuous possession during a period prescribed in the statute.

Although the concepts of title and possession usually are treated as separate and distinct, physical control of land may result in the possessor's acquiring title under the principle known as **adverse possession.** A person who enters into actual possession of land and remains thereon openly and notoriously for the period of time prescribed in the statute of limitations, claiming title in denial of, and adversely to, the superior title of another, will at the end of the statutory period acquire legal title.

The owner's knowledge that his or her land is occupied adversely is not essential to the claim, but possession must be of a nature that would charge a reasonably diligent legal owner with knowledge of the adverse claim. In other words, the possessor must not try to hide his or her present use of the land. Indeed, any time the legal owner or anyone else asserts rights to the land, the possessor must deny that claim and be steadfast in his or her right to the property's use.

CLAIM OF RIGHT.   The possessor's claim to be the owner of land must be based on some legal right. Obviously, some mistake leads to the application of the principles of adverse possession. The possessor must be more than a squatter. The possessor must believe that he or she has a *claim of right* as the true owner of the property. *Color of title* is an expression that refers to a title that has a defect but is otherwise good. A mistake in a deed does not convey clear title but does convey color of title. In many states adverse possession by one with color of title who pays real estate taxes will ripen into title in a much shorter period than is required for adverse possession without color of title. For example, a state with a twenty-year requirement may require only ten years if there is color of title and payment of the taxes. This use of adverse possession is very important in clearing defective titles. Errors can be ignored after the statutory period if there is adverse possession.

Adverse possession may still be one method by which a landowner of a large tract involuntarily "transfers" an ownership interest in that tract. However, today the bulk of reported adverse possession cases deal with boundary disputes involving strips of land just a few feet wide. This factual situation frequently arises when neighbors discover that a fence or hedge has been located on their common boundary for a number of years. As the following case illustrates, the location of a fence that is not on the actual boundary may result in title being obtained by adverse possession.

CASE

Sashinger v. Wynn
571 So.2d 1065 (Ala. 1990)

ADAMS, J.

Mrs. Arthurine Sashinger appeals from a judgment holding that an existing fence between her property and the property of Lonnie B. Wynn is the true dividing line between their two parcels of land. . . .

The record reveals the following relevant facts: Arthurine Sashinger . . . has actually resided on the Holcombe tract for the past 15 years. Portions of this large tract were periodically sold so that the tract is now owned by several landowners. Lonnie B. Wynn purchased his portion of the Holcombe tract in 1963 from John E. Henson, Jr. At that time, a fence surrounded the property that was not described in the deed to Wynn. However, Wynn believed that the fence was the true dividing line and that he

owned the land inside its border. Virtually all of the surrounding landowners also considered the fence to be the true dividing line and that the land inside the fence belonged to Wynn. . . . From the time he purchased the land in 1963, Wynn has maintained the fence and has cultivated the land inside its borders. Until 1986, no one had ever disputed Wynn's possession of the land inside the fence or asserted a claim against the property.

In 1986, the remainder of the Holcombe tract was divided among several persons by a final judgment in the case of *J.C. Skinner v. Elzadie Holcombe, et al.* Sashinger was awarded two parcels in that judgment. Pursuant to that judgment, a survey of the land was conducted. The survey revealed that the fence line separating Sashinger's property and Wynn's property was not the dividing line described in Wynn's deed. Apparently, the fence bore no relationship to the property line described in Wynn's deed. Until this point, no one in the community, including Sashinger, had ever questioned that the fence was the true property line or that the land inside the fence belonged to Wynn. However, once the surveyor's marks were placed, Sashinger noticed that the fence encroached onto one of her newly acquired parcels.

On October 9, 1987, Sashinger filed an action to resolve the boundary dispute. She asked the trial court to judicially establish the boundary between her property and Wynn's property. Wynn, in his answer and counterclaim, asserted that he held title to the land inside of and up to the fence by adverse possession. He maintained that he and his predecessors had been in adverse possession for more than 20 years and that the land inside the fence had been enclosed by the fence for more than 20 years.

The case was heard without a jury. After hearing the evidence, the trial judge ruled that the fence line represented the true dividing line between the parcel owned by Wynn and the parcel owned by Sashinger. The judge held that Wynn had acquired title to the land up to the fence by adverse possession. Sashinger now asks this Court to reverse the findings of the trial court. . . .

Wynn's claim of adverse possession is supported under either of two methods of adverse possession recognized by this Court. First, because Wynn had possessed the land for 23 years with the belief that he owned it, he clearly met the traditional 20-year possession. Moreover, the community, including Sashinger, regarded the land as his. Second, this Court has consistently held that where a case involves a boundary dispute between coterminous landowners, title may be acquired by an adverse possession period of only 10 years. One claiming by adverse possession must show, in addition to the fact that he has held the land for 10 years, all of the traditional adverse possession elements to open, hostile, notorious, continuous, and exclusive possession. Wynn has clearly satisfied the requirement of a 10-year holding period, as well as the traditional elements of adverse possession. Wynn's possession of the land inside the fence has continued for 23 years. Moreover, the use and maintenance of the fence and the land inside the fence had been so open and notorious that the surrounding landowners unequivocally rec-

ognized that the land belonged to Wynn. Thus, under either the traditional 20-year holding period or the hybrid "coterminous boundary" 10-year holding period, Wynn has acquired title to the land up to the fence line.

Sashinger argues that the title acquired through adverse possession may be lost just as title to any other property may be lost. Specifically, she argues that the final judgment in *J.C. Skinner v. Elzadie Holcombe* divested Wynn of his title in the land inside of and up to the fence. While Mrs. Sashinger is correct that a final judgment may divest title, the final judgment in the *Skinner* case did not have that effect.

Under either theory of adverse possession applicable to this case, the traditional prescriptive theory or the "coterminous boundary" theory, Holcombe lost title to the land in question to Wynn by adverse possession before the court in *Skinner* purported to give it to Mrs. Sashinger. Applying the traditional prescriptive 20-year holding period, Wynn acquired title in 1983, and, applying the "coterminous boundary" 10-year holding period, Wynn acquired title in 1973. Therefore, as the land did not belong to Holcombe at the time of the final judgment in *Skinner* and was no longer part of the Holcombe tract, the circuit court's final judgment had no effect on Wynn's title.

For the reasons set out in this opinion, the judgment of the circuit court is

■ *Affirmed.*

CASE CONCEPTS REVIEW

1. When did Lonnie Wynn begin to possess the property in dispute?
2. When did the dispute over this property arise?
3. What two types of adverse possession does the court discuss?
4. Why does it not make any difference which of these two theories of adverse possession applies in this case?

TACKING.   In our mobile society, it is a fact that residential property typically is transferred every few years. Therefore, the issue of how the statutory period of adverse possession is satisfied often arises. The answer to this issue is found in the principle of *tacking*. Tacking allows successive owners to add their time periods of ownership together to satisfy the long statutory period required for adverse possession. For tacking to occur, successive owners must claim under the same chain of title. In other words, a buyer may be able to tack to the seller's period of ownership. Likewise, an heir may tack to his or her ancestor's ownership period.

Although adverse possession does occur among private owners of land, it has been held that a municipal corporation or other governmental body cannot lose its interests in land to one claiming to be the owner, regardless of how long that person has possessed the land. In other words, governmental land cannot be adversely possessed.

18. Title by Accretion

Accretion Gradual, imperceptible accumulation of land by natural causes, usually next to a stream or river.

Soil added to land by action of water is an **accretion.** If a shore or bank is extended by gradual addition of sand or mud deposited by water, the extension also is called an *alluvion.* If water recedes and exposes more land, the increase in the shore or bank is a *reliction.*

A sudden deposit of land such as that caused by a flood does not make a change in ownership or boundary lines; but if the change is slow and gradual by alluvion or reliction, the newly formed land belongs to the owner of the bed of the stream in which the new land was formed. If opposite banks of a private stream belong to different persons, it is a general rule that each owns the bed to the middle of the stream; however, title to lands created by accretion may be acquired by adverse possession. In public waters, such as navigable streams, lakes, and the sea, the title of the bed of water, in the absence of special circumstances, is in the United States. Accretion to the land belongs to the **riparian** owner; islands created belong to the government.

Riparian A person is a riparian owner if his or her land is situated beside a stream or other body of water, either flowing over or along the border of the land.

ACQUIRING TITLE TO PERSONAL AND REAL PROPERTY: WILLS AND INTESTATE SUCCESSION

19. Terminology

Will The formal instrument by which a person makes disposition of his or her property, to take effect on his or her death.

Guardian A person appointed by the court to look after the property rights and person of a minor.

Testator A person who has died leaving a will.

Executor (of an estate) The person whom the testator names or appoints to administer his or her estate on his or her death and to dispose of according to the testator's intention.

A **will** is a document that expresses a person's intention as to the disposition of his or her property on death. It also serves several additional functions. It designates the personal representative who is to be responsible for settling the affairs of the deceased. A will may make provision for the appointment of **guardians** of the person and the estate of a minor child. Indeed, for young parents who have not yet amassed much financial wealth, the appointment of a guardian for their minor children usually is the most important reason to have a will. Many wills also provide for payment of taxes that may be due on the death of the deceased and for matters such as whether or not the personal representative should be required to have sureties on the official bond.

A person who dies leaving a valid will is said to die *testate.* This person, upon signing a will, generally is referred to as the **testator.** The personal representative of a testator is an **executor.** A person who dies without leaving a valid will dies *intestate.* The personal representative of a person who dies intestate is called an **administrator.** This personal representative (whether an executor or an administrator) is in charge of gathering the deceased's assets, paying the lawful debts, and distributing the assets to the appropriate persons. A *guardian* is the personal representative in charge of the well-being of a minor's person or property or both. A *conservator* may be appointed when the care of a mentally incompetent adult is involved. Some states use the term *guardian* as well.

A gift by will of real estate usually is called a *devise;* a gift of personal property other than money is called a *bequest;* and a gift of money is referred to as a *legacy.*

Administrator A person to whom letters of administration have been issued by a probate court, giving such person authority to administer, manage, and close the estate of a person who died intestate.

Devises, bequests, and legacies are further classified as specific, general, or residuary. A *specific gift* (devise, bequest, or legacy) is a gift of particular property described to identify and distinguish it from all other parts of the deceased's property. If property described in a specific gift is not owned by the testator at death, the gift fails or is said to be *adeemed*. A *general gift* is one that does not describe any particular property, and it may be satisfied by delivery of any property of the general kind described. A gift of a specified sum of money is a general legacy. A *residuary gift* is one that includes all the property not included in the specific or general devises, bequests, or legacies. All of these terms are important in the payment and distribution of the shares of an estate and in determining which party actually receives a specific item of property.

20. Testamentary Capacity

Testamentary capacity Persons are said to have testamentary capacity when they understand the nature of their business and the value of their property, know those persons who are natural objects of their bounty, and comprehend the manner in which they have provided for the distribution of their property.

Testamentary capacity does not require a perfect mind or average intelligence. Testamentary capacity does require a minimum age, such as eighteen years. Persons executing a will must have sufficient mental capacity to comprehend and remember who are the natural objects of their affection, to comprehend the kind and character of their property, and to understand that they are engaged in making a will. Less mental capacity is required to execute a will than is required to execute ordinary business transactions and contracts. Since many people at the time of making a will are in poor health, the law recognizes that many testators will not be of perfect mind, and all that is required is a minimum capacity to understand the nature and extent of one's property and to formulate the plan involved in making the will.

21. Formalities of Execution

In general, the testator must sign the will. In the alternative, since many people who are physically incapacitated may not be able to sign the will, it may be signed by someone else in the presence and at the direction of the testator. It will not be set aside simply by proving that the signature on it is not that of the deceased.

In most states, the testator need not sign in the presence of witnesses if acknowledging to them that the instrument is his or her own and that it bears his or her signature. The witnesses need not be informed that the document is a will, but only that it is the testator's instrument. The signature aspect of attestation is that the testator must watch the witnesses sign, and in most states it is essential that the witnesses testify that the testator watched them sign as attesting witnesses.

Credible witnesses are those who are competent to testify in support of the will. If the witnesses are interested parties because they take something under the will, such witnesses generally will not be allowed to receive any more property as a result of the will than they would have received had there been no will. In other words, witnesses to the will cannot profit or gain any property as a result of the will. They will be required to testify and will lose whatever the will gives them in excess of their intestate share of the deceased's estate.

The most important thing to remember about executing a will is that the number of credible witnesses and the formalities required vary from state to state. Consultation with a lawyer licensed in the state involved is always recommended.

22. Grounds for Challenging a Will's Validity

Very often a disinherited or disappointed party will challenge the validity of a will by proving that a testator lacked the mental capacity to make that will. Another challenge might be that the formal requirements of signing and witnessing the will were not met. In addition, the validity of a testator's will may be challenged on the grounds that the testator was unduly influenced to make a will that provides for a distribution scheme contrary to that testator's expected wishes and desires. This ground for challenging a will is defined as influence that overpowers the mind of the testator and deprives him or her of free agency in the execution of the will. It is the equivalent of saying, "This is not my wish, but I must do it." It is more than mere persuasion, for here there is an exercise of independent judgment and deliberation. A presumption of undue influence is often found to exist where there is a fiduciary relationship between a testator and a beneficiary who takes substantial benefits from the will. This is especially true if the beneficiary is a nonrelated dominant party and the testator a dependent party and the will is written, or its preparation procured, by the beneficiary.

23. Revocation, Republication, Revival, and Renunciation

A will is said to be *ambulatory*, or not effective, until the death of the testator. It may be revoked at any time. Among the common methods of revoking a will are physical destruction, making a will declaring the revocation, a later will that is inconsistent with the prior will, marriage, and divorce. In many states, divorce revokes the will only to the extent of bequests or devises to the former spouse. Marriage revokes a will because it is presumed that the testator would want a different plan of distribution as the result of the marriage. It is therefore important that whenever there is a marriage or a divorce, the law of the state of the domicile be consulted to determine its effect on a prior will.

State laws usually prohibit partial revocation of a will except by a duly signed and attested instrument. Additions, alterations, substitutions, interlineations, and deletions on the face of a will are therefore ineffective, and the will stands as originally executed. The law prohibits partial revocation because of the ease with which such minor changes could be made by third parties even after the death of the person whose will is involved.

Unless a provision is made for a child born after the execution of the will, or unless the will by clear and convincing language indicates that after-born children are to be disinherited, in most states the after-born child takes from the estate whatever he or she would have received had there been no will. A legal adoption has the same effect. This stipulation is based on the assumption that the testator at the time of the execution of the original will would not have considered the after-born child and that a provision would have been included had the child been considered.

In most states, a will that is in any manner totally revoked can be revived only by the republication or reexecution of the will or by a written instrument which declares the revival and is executed in the same manner as a new will. For example, suppose that a person during his or her lifetime has executed four wills, each specifically revoking the former. None of these wills has been destroyed until the testator, shortly before death, physically destroyed Will Number 4. Is Number 3 then valid?

In most states, the answer is no. Wills are not stacked one on the other so that the revocation of the latest will revives the earlier will. In the situation described, the person would die without a will.

Some states have recognized an exception to the general rule that a revoked will is ineffective unless the testator's intent indicates otherwise. This exception is known as the *doctrine of dependent relative revocation*. In essence, this doctrine applies when the testator intends to revoke one will and substitute a new will in its place. If the new will is not made or is not valid for some reason, this doctrine allows the previously revoked will to remain valid. In order for the doctrine to apply, it must be proved that the testator intended the revocation of an old will to be conditioned on the validity of a new will. Usually the nature of a deceased person's intent is very difficult to prove. Therefore, the doctrine of dependent relative revocation will be applied to a very narrow factual situation. As a practical matter, an old will should not be destroyed prior to the execution of a new one.

Codicil An addition to, or a change in, an executed last will and testament. It is a part of the original will and must be executed with the same formality as the original will.

A similar issue as to a will's validity arises when a person executes a **codicil** or a minor change to a will. When a codicil is executed and it specifically refers to a former will, it has the effect of bringing the former will down to the date of the codicil, and the will is then construed as of the date of the codicil. A codicil can validate a previously invalid will. It can also validate a will that has been revoked by marriage or divorce.

The law in most states gives a spouse certain rights that cannot be denied by will. These rights include support during the period of administration, with a statutory minimum usually provided. The court will determine the exact amount, based on the size of the estate and the standard of living of the surviving spouse. A spouse may also *renounce* a will and take a statutory share in lieu of provisions made by the will. In other words, one spouse cannot completely prevent his or her property from passing to a surviving spouse by making different provisions in the will. In many states, a spouse receives one-half the estate upon renunciation, irrespective of the provisions of the will. It should be recognized that the right to renounce usually exits for spouses only—children can be completely disinherited.

24. Intestate Succession

Intestate Succession The transfer by operation of law of all rights and obligations of a deceased person to those who are entitled to them.

As stated previously, a person who dies without leaving a valid will is said to die *intestate*. When a person dies intestate, the state law provides how the deceased's property will be distributed. In this sense, a state's **intestate succession** law acts as an alternative to a will. Although all of the states attempt to provide a scheme of distribution that a reasonable person likely would have intended, the statutes of intestacy do vary from state to state. To complicate matters, the intestate laws of two or more states may have to be used in settling the estate of a person who dies without a will. For example, when real estate is a part of the deceased's estate, the appropriate intestate statute is that of the state in which the land is located. When personal property is to be distributed, the law of the deceased's domicile generally controls.

The typical intestate succession statute provides that the deceased's assets are to be inherited by the deceased's closest living relatives. However, the intestate succession statute in one state may provide that a spouse of the deceased receives the entire estate if there are no surviving children. In another state, under similar circumstances the intestate statute may require that the property be divided between the deceased's spouse and parents. If a person is survived by a spouse and children, most states provide that the estate is divided among the spouse and children. Often this is an undesirable result, because of the unmarketability of property owned by minors. This problem arises due to the fact that minors generally can void contractual transactions prior to reaching the age of majority.

Everyone over the legal age of testamentary capacity should be aware of his or her state's scheme of intestate succession. If that scheme contradicts a person's desires for distributing assets, that person should have a valid will prepared and executed. Indeed, as an alternative to a valid will that can be personalized to the testator's specific needs, the intestate succession scheme is considered inferior as an estate planning tool.

EVIDENCE OF TITLE

25. Abstract of Title

Ownership of real estate is a matter of public record. Every deed, mortgage, judgment, lien, or other transaction that affects the title to real estate must be made a matter of public record in the county in which the real estate is located. Deeds and other documents are usually recorded in the county recorder's office. The records of the probate court furnish the public documents necessary to prove title by will or descent. Divorce proceedings and other judicial proceedings that affect the title to real estate are also part of the public record.

To establish title to real estate, it is necessary to examine all the public records that may affect the title. In a few states, lawyers actually examine all the public records to establish the title to real estate. Because it is extremely difficult for an individual or his or her attorney to examine all the records, in most states businesses have been formed for the express purpose of furnishing the appropriate records for any given parcel of real estate. These *abstract companies* are usually well-established firms that have maintained tract indexes for many years and keep them current on a daily basis. Upon request, an abstract company prepares an abstract of the records that sets forth the history of the parcel in question and all matters that may affect the title. The abstract of title is examined by an attorney, who writes an opinion concerning the title, setting forth any defects in the title as well as encumbrances against it. The abstract of title must be brought up to date each time the property is transferred or proof of title is required, so the chain of title will be complete. The opinion on title will be useless unless all court proceedings, such as foreclosures, partitions, transfers by deed, and probate proceedings, are shown. It should be noted that an attorney's opinion on title is just that—an opinion. If the attorney makes a mistake—his or her opinion states that a client has title to Blackacre when in fact the client does not have title to Blackacre—the client does not have title. The client's recourse would be a malpractice suit against the attorney.

26. Title Insurance

Because of limited resources, many lawyers are unable to respond in damages to pay losses caused by their mistakes. Therefore, the abstract of title and attorney's opinion as a means of protecting owners are often not satisfactory. There may be title defects that do not appear in the record and that the attorney does not cover in the title opinion. An illegitimate child may be an unknown heir with an interest in property, as may a spouse in a secret marriage. To protect owners against such hidden claims and to offset the limited resources of most lawyers, *title insurance* has developed.

Title insurance is, in effect, an opinion of the title company instead of the lawyer. The opinion of the title company is backed up to the extent of the face value of the title insurance policy. If the purported owner loses property, he or she collects the insurance just as if it were life insurance and the insured had died. Title insurance can cover matters beyond those in a title opinion. It has the financial backing of the issuing company, which is financially more secure than any law firm. Modern real estate practice uses title policies rather than abstracts and title opinions. Title insurance companies usually maintain their own tract records, thus eliminating the cost of bringing the abstract up to date. Generally, title insurance companies issue a *title commitment letter* at the seller's request. This commitment becomes the basis of the title insurance policy issued to protect the buyer. Title insurance companies that are negligent in searching a title become liable for the damages caused. The following case involves the issue of whether the title insurance's liability is based on a breach of contract or a breach of a duty owed in tort law.

CASE

Erskine Florida Properties, Inc. v. First American Title Insurance Co.

557 So.2d 859 (Fla. 1989)

SHAW, J.

This case presents the following issue: When a party conducts a title search of a piece of property and searches only the direct and indirect alphabetical indexes, can it be held liable for failing to discover an improperly indexed claim? We conclude that under the facts here it can.

First American Title Insurance Company contracted with Erskine to provide a title search on property that Erskine was interested in purchasing. In conducting the search, First American searched only the names provided by Erskine in the direct and indirect alphabetical indexes maintained in the county clerk's office. Because of a clerical error by the clerk's office, the limited search did not reveal a superior claim of interest in the property. Relying on the search, Erskine purchased and resold the property and was successfully sued by the true owner. Erskine sued First American in a third-party action for conducting an improper title search, and the trial court held First American liable. It concluded that First American was wrong to rely solely on the alphabetical indexes for the following reasons. First, it should have used all available public facilities, including a parcel identification index. According to the court, this index was used by other abstracters in the community as a backup in their

searches, and First American knew of its existence. And second, First American should have searched the title according to the property's legal description. The district court reversed, relying on a negligence standard of care . . . grounded in tort. The court ruled that Erskine had failed to introduce expert testimony concerning an abstracter's standard of care in the county.

We conclude that sufficient evidence exists to support the trial court's finding of liability. The liability of a title abstracter lies in contract, not tort:

> An abstracter is liable in damages for injuries resulting from wrongful or negligent errors, defects or omissions in an abstract prepared and furnished by him. It was settled in an early case, which has been followed in nearly all the decisions on this question, that his liability is not in tort, but is contractual, and must be based upon a breach of his express or implied contract with his customer or client to furnish him with a true and correct abstract. It is therefore measured by the nature, extent and terms of his undertaking or employment.

. . . The general nature of the contractual duty involved: "[T]he abstracter's contractual duty [is] to perform the service skillfully and diligently."

The parcel identification index was available to the public, and First American's title searcher testified that she was aware of it. The county clerk testified that although her office cautions abstracters not to rely solely on the index because the identification numbers are assigned by the tax assessor's office, abstracters do rely on the index "as a security check." If the proper identification numbers are assigned and entered into the computer, she testified, the resulting search is reliable. "If they [First American] had been running the parcel ID number for this piece of property they would have picked it [the superior interest] up."

We agree with the court's statement in *Williams v. Polgar*, 215 N.W.2d 149, 157 (1974):

> Because an abstracter is hired to determine what is in the public record, misstatements of, or failure to include, relevant items contained in that record are obviously examples of acts constituting failure to perform abstracting services in a diligent and reasonably skillful workmanlike manner.

The evidence supports the trial court's finding that First American failed to conduct an adequate search. No expert testimony on Erskine's behalf was necessary. We note, however, that First American was free to introduce its own experts to show that it conducted a skillful and diligent search. We quash the decision of the district court below and remand for reinstatement of the trial court's judgment.

■ *It is so ordered.*

CASE CONCEPTS REVIEW

1. What is the issue presented to the court in this litigation?
2. The trial court found First American liable. The district court, upon review, concluded the opposite. What legal basis did the district court utilize to reach its conclusion?
3. What did Erskine fail to prove to satisfy its burden of proof according to the district court?
4. Why does this court quash the district court's decision and reinstate the trial court's judgment?

27. Torrens System

Another method used to prove ownership in some localities is known as the *Torrens System*, based on a registered title that can be transferred only on the official registration records. The original registration of any title usually requires a judicial determination as to the current owner, and then all subsequent transfers merely involve the surrender of the registered title, in much the same way that an automobile title is transferred. The Torrens system is a much simpler system to use after a title has once been registered, but the high cost of obtaining the original registration has prevented it from replacing abstracts and title policies as proof of title in most areas.

CHAPTER SUMMARY

ACQUIRING TITLE TO PERSONAL PROPERTY

Methods: Original Possession	1. Original possession is a method of acquiring title that has limited application.
	2. It is utilized to determine ownership of property in its native state, such as wild animals or fish.
Title by Transfer: In General	1. The most common way title to personal property is transferred is by an Article 2 sales transaction (see chapters 18 and 19).
	2. Title to personal property also may be transferred by will at the owner's death.
	3. Title to personal property also can be transferred as a gift or by operation of law.
Transfer by *Inter Vivos* Gift	1. An *inter vivos* gift is one made voluntarily during the life of the giver.
	2. The person making a gift is called a *donor*. The *donee* is the person receiving the gift.
	3. To have a valid *inter vivos* gift, there must be donative intent, delivery, and acceptance.
	4. In general, a promise to make a gift is not enforceable. However, once the gift is made, it generally cannot be revoked. A gift *causa mortis* is an exception to the irrevocability of completed gifts.

Title by Accession	1. This literally means "adding to."
	2. This concept governs the acquisition of title to personal property when it is incorporated into or joined with other property.
	3. The principles of accession depend on whether the wrongdoer was an innocent or willful trespasser.
Title by Confusion	1. *Fungible property* usually is sold by weight or measure. One unit of this type of property cannot be distinguished from another unit.
	2. Confusion or commingling of fungible property may cause title to all or some portion of the property to pass from a wrongdoer to an innocent party.
Abandoned, Lost, and Mislaid Property	1. Abandoned property is discarded by the true owner who has no intent to reclaim it. The first person to take possession of abandoned property is considered the new owner.
	2. Lost property is that found in some place other than that chosen by the owner. The person who finds lost property has superior rights to everyone except for the true owner.
	3. Mislaid property are those items that the owner has forgotten to pick up. The owner of the real estate on which the mislaid property is discovered holds the property subject to the claims of the true owner.

ACQUIRING TITLE TO REAL PROPERTY: VOLUNTARY TRANSFERS

Original Entry	1. Title is obtained from the government by a patent. It seldom occurs today.
Transfer by Deed	1. A deed is the legal document that represents title to land.
	2. A valid deed must contain an accurate legal description based on the metes and bounds, the rectangular survey, or the reference to the plats system of describing land's boundaries.
Other Essential Requirements of All Deeds	1. A valid deed must also identify the parties involved, contain language transferring an ownership interest, be signed by the grantor, and be delivered to the grantee in the grantor's lifetime.
Optional Elements of Deeds	1. By including or deleting optional covenants or warranties, various types of deeds can be created.
	2. Deeds vary in the amount of protection they give to the grantee. From the most to least protection provided, these deeds include the warranty deed, the grant deed, the bargain and sale deed, and the quitclaim deed.

ACQUIRING TITLE TO REAL PROPERTY: INVOLUNTARY TRANSFERS

Transfer by Judicial Sale	1. A court with proper jurisdiction may order that real property be sold to satisfy the owner's creditors.
	2. Examples of judicial sales include tax sales and foreclosures of mortgages, mechanic's liens, assessment for public improvements, and other statutory liens.
Title by Adverse Possession	1. Adverse possession is an example of when possession may result in legal title.
	2. The essential elements of adverse possession are satisfied if a person possesses land openly, notoriously, hostilely, and continuously for the statutory period under a claim of right.
	3. In essence, the record owner is prevented from claiming title if possession has adversely continued for the statutory time period.
Title by Accretion	1. Soil added to land by the action of a body of water.
	2. The gradual extension of a shoreline by matter being deposited by water is called *alluvion*.
	3. If more land is exposed by the water receding, *reliction* occurs.
	4. The gradual increase in land belongs to the owner of the streambed in which the new land was formed.

ACQUIRING TITLE TO PERSONAL AND REAL PROPERTY: WILLS AND INTESTATE SUCCESSION

Terminology

1. A person who leaves a valid will dies *testate*. This person is known as a *testator*.

2. An *executor* settles the estate of a person dying testate. An *administrator* is appointed by a court to settle the estate of a person dying intestate. A *guardian* is the personal representative of the person of a minor and his estate. A *conservator* is the personal representative of a person who is not competent to handle his or her own affairs.

3. A gift of real property as a term of the will is a *devise*. A *bequest* is a gift of personal property in general under a will. A *legacy* is a gift of a specific amount of money.

Testamentary Capacity

1. A testator must be the minimum statutory age, such as 18.

2. A testator must have the capacity to know the kind and character of his or her property, to know and remember the natural objects of his or her affection, and to make a scheme of distribution.

Formalities of Execution

1. A will must be signed by the testator or by someone else in the presence and at the direction of the testator.

2. A will must be attested in the presence of the testator by two or three (depending on the state) disinterested and competent witnesses.

Grounds for Challenging a Will's Validity

1. The lack of the testator's capacity to make a will and the lack of proper execution are two grounds for having a will declared void.

2. Proof that the testator was unduly influenced, which means his or her true desires were not followed, is another important method for challenging a will.

Revocation, Republication, Revival, and Renunciation

1. A will is ambulatory and can be changed at any time during the testator's life.

2. A will may be revoked by destruction, a later will, marriage, or divorce.

3. Once a will is revoked, it cannot be revived automatically. To be valid, a revoked will must be republished.

4. A spouse may renounce a will and claim a statutory interest against the estate.

Intestate Succession

1. A person who dies without leaving a valid will is said to die *intestate*.

2. In such a case, the deceased person's property is distributed according to the scheme of distribution provided by state statute.

EVIDENCE OF TITLE

1. The seller typically is required to transfer marketable title.

2. To establish the marketability of the seller's title, a lawyer's title opinion letter or a title insurance policy should be obtained.

3. A few states allow a title registration, known as the Torrens system, as an alternative method of showing marketable title.

REVIEW QUESTIONS AND PROBLEMS

1. Match each term in column A with the appropriate statement in Column B.

A	B
(1) *Inter vivos* gift	(a) Discarded by the owner with no intent to reclaim it
(2) Accession	(b) An example of when possession of real property may result in legal title
(3) Fungible property	(c) Legal documents that represent title to real property
(4) Abandoned property	(d) Usually sold by weight or measure; subject to confusion

(5) Mislaid property

(6) Deeds

(7) Rectangular survey system

(8) Warranty deed

(9) Adverse possession

(10) Reliction

(e) The deed that assures the grantee of the most protection possible

(f) This concept governs the acquisition of title to personal property when it is incorporated into or joined with other property

(g) Made voluntarily during the life of the donor

(h) Occurs when land is exposed by water receding

(i) A method used to describe accurately the boundaries of real estate

(j) Held by the owner of the real estate on which it is found, subject to the true owner's claims

2. Aunt Bee bought ten lottery tickets, each representing a chance to win an automobile. She wrote her minor niece's name on the back of one of these tickets and mailed it to her niece's mother. The niece was never informed that this ticket was received. At the drawing for the car, the niece's ticket was selected. Aunt Bee claimed the car belonged to her since the niece had not accepted the gift. Is Aunt Bee correct? Explain.

3. Vivian lived with and cared for her uncle, Mr. Evans, throughout the last years of his life. One month before he died, Mr. Evans went to his bank and examined the contents of his safe deposit box. He asked for both keys to this box. Upon arriving home, he gave Vivian one of these keys and told her that the contents belonged to her when he died. The safe deposit box contained stocks, bonds, and other items worth approximately $800,000. Although Vivian had a key, she could not have obtained access to its contents, since the box remained registered in Mr. Evans's name alone. When Mr. Evans died, his heirs claimed the contents of his deposit box. Vivian argued that she was the donee of an *inter vivos* gift of the box's contents. Which element of an *inter vivos* gift is an issue? Make the arguments for each side and indicate the likely outcome of the case.

4. An automobile owned by Perkins was stolen. The thief installed a new engine and sold the car to a used-car dealer. The dealer, in turn, sold the car to Moseley, who added a sun visor, seat covers, and a gasoline tank. May Perkins reclaim the automobile and keep the items added? Explain.

5. Troop, who is in the oil business, is the sole owner of a well named Gusher. Troop also is in partnership with Wright, and together they have equal interests in Spindletop. These parties have agreed that Troop will store the oil produced by Spindletop and will make monthly reports to Wright. After several months passed without a report, Wright discovered that Troop was storing oil produced from Gusher and Spindletop in the same holding tank. If Troop has not kept accurate records of both wells' production, how much of the stored oil is Wright entitled to, if any? Explain.

6. Bernice rented a safe deposit box from the Old Orchard Bank. In May, while examining the contents of her own box, Bernice discovered $6,325 in cash on a chair that was pushed under an examination table. Bernice turned this money over to the bank, which sent a notice to its safe deposit box customers that property had been discovered in the safety vault. No one responded to this ad, and on July 1, Bernice claimed that she was entitled to this lost money. The bank refused to give her the money since it argued that the money had been mislaid. Bernice filed a suit to recover the cash. Who is entitled to the $6,325? Explain.

7. Zibton purchased numerous file cabinets from First National Bank of Chicago. Some of the cabinets were locked and some had miscellaneous papers in them. Zibton sold four cabinets to Strayve, who gave one to Michael. Six weeks later, while Michael was moving the cabinet, it fell over, and several of the locked drawers opened, revealing stacks of certificates of deposit, seven of which were unpaid and valid and totaled over $6 million. Six of the CDs were payable to bearer. Michael called the FBI, which took possession of the CDs. Michael sued for a declaratory judgment to determine owner-

ship of the CDs. Michael argued that First National Bank had abandoned any ownership interest in these CDs. Were the CDs abandoned by the bank? Why?

8. Campbell entered into a sales contract to buy real estate from Storer. To complete this transaction, a warranty deed was delivered to Campbell in 1990. Although he received it, Campbell failed to record this deed. In 1993, Storer conveyed by deed the same land to a third person. When he discovered he no longer was the record owner, Campbell sued Storer for damages. Storer defended his second conveyance on the grounds that Campbell's failure to record his deed prevented him from acquiring legal title to the real estate. Did Campbell acquire legal title in 1990? Why or why not?

9. Bryan and Linda contracted to have Pioneer Homes build a house. In return for $52,000, Pioneer Homes deeded a house and lot to them. The deed delivered specifically stated the title conveyed was good, marketable, and free of all encumbrances. Later, Bryan and Linda decided to sell this house and lot. It was then that they discovered their house was only 3.5 feet from the side boundary. This location of the house violated the local minimum side-lot requirement of 15 feet. To resolve this violation, Bryan and Linda purchased a strip of land for $1,500. They then sued Pioneer Homes for breach of the covenant against encumbrances. Did Pioneer Homes breach this covenant? Why or why not?

10. Lockhart agreed to purchase a parcel of real property located in Phenix City from Phenix City Investment Company. A warranty deed conveying title to the property was executed by Phenix City Investment Company to Lockhart. This deed contained the following covenants of warranty:

   And, we do for ourselves and for our heirs, executors, administrators and assigns, covenant with the said Grantee, his heirs and assigns, that we are lawfully seized in fee simple of said premises; that they are free from all encumbrances, unless otherwise noted above; that we have a good right to sell and convey the same as aforesaid; that we will and our heirs, executors, administrators, and assigns, shall warrant and defend the same to the said Grantee, his heirs and assigns, forever, against the lawful claims of all persons.

   At the same time, Lockhart signed a note payable to Phenix City Investment Company in the principal amount of $18,000, payable in monthly installments. As security for this note, he executed a purchase money mortgage on the real property. This statement appeared on the mortgage: "This is a second mortgage subject to the first mortgage executed to the American Federal Savings and Loan Association of Columbus, Georgia."

   Later, Lockhart learned that he would have to pay $16,000 to satisfy the first mortgage held by American Federal Savings and Loan. Lockhart sued Phenix City Investment Company for breach of its covenant against encumbrances. Phenix City argued that since Lockhart had knowledge of the first mortgage, no express exception of this encumbrance had to be noted in the warranty deed. Does a covenant against encumbrance protect the grantee against an encumbrance the grantee knew or should have known about? Why?

11. In 1977, J. G. Head's Farms, Inc., conveyed Lot 12, Block 8 of Unit A to Lottie Morrison. Lottie failed to record and then lost her deed. In 1990, J. G. Head's Farms, Inc., signed and delivered a quitclaim deed covering all the land it owned in Unit A to the Miami Holding Corporation. In 1993, J. G. Head's Farms, Inc., conveyed Lot 12 of Block 8 to Lottie Morrison by quitclaim deed. This deed, which replaced the 1977 warranty deed that had been lost, was recorded on March 4, 1993. Lottie Morrison then conveyed Lot 12 to Matthews. Thereafter, a dispute arose between Matthews and the Miami Holding Corporation as to who had superior title to Lot 12. Who does have superior title to Lot 12? Explain.

12. Dick and Dan owned adjoining property. By an honest mistake, Dick built a fence that was 5 feet onto Dan's property. Both owners recognized the fence as the boundary. Twenty-five years after the fence was built, Dan had his property surveyed. The survey

revealed the fence's improper location. Dan sought to have the fence removed, but Dick sued, claiming that he now owned the disputed 5-foot strip through adverse possession. Should Dick be declared to own this land? Why? (Assume a twenty-year statutory period.)

13. Paul Malinak owned 640 acres of land in Montana. During his ownership, St. Regis Paper Company acquired rights to timber on this land. Malinak mistakenly believed these rights expired in 1990. During early 1992, Malinak agreed to sell his land, and he requested a title insurance commitment from Safeco Title Insurance Company. This commitment deleted any mention of possible rights of St. Regis. Although that sale of the land fell through, Malinak sold his land to Lowell Novy in late 1992. Relying on the title commitment previously received, Malinak warranted the title to Novy without timber reservations. Safeco issued a title insurance policy to Novy that also made no mention of St. Regis's timber rights. Shortly after the sales transaction was closed, St. Regis notified Novy of its plans to cut timber. Novy sued Safeco under the title policy. Safeco notified Malinak that it would seek to recover from him if the company was liable to Novy. Malinak argued that Safeco was liable to him for his expenses in defending the title transferred to Novy. Malinak asserted that his warranty of clear title was based on Safeco's title commitment. Is the seller (Malinak) protected by a title insurance company's (Safeco's) commitment? Explain.

CHAPTER

45

LEASES
AND BAILMENTS

CHAPTER PREVIEW

There are many ways to classify transactions involving property interests. One way is to look at real property versus personal property transactions. Another way is to examine the interest transferred. We have chosen to use the latter method in this chapter. In chapters 18 and 19, we focus on Article 2's coverage of the *sale* of movable personal property. In the preceding chapter, our concentration is on how title to property is transferred. In sales transactions, the seller transfers both ownership and possession of the property to the buyer.

In this chapter, we cover those transactions involving real and personal property in which possession but not ownership is transferred. In particular, leases of real estate and bailments of personal property are examined.

You are president of a company that owns several apartment complexes. Your company rents mainly to college students. Due to a number of news reports, you become concerned about your company's liability for excessive drinking and drug use by your tenants. You desire to have the opportunity to inspect the apartments from time to time.

What should you do to accomplish this goal?

LEASES OF REAL PROPERTY

1. In General

Lease A contract by which one person divests himself or herself of possession of land and grants such possession to another for a period of time.

A **lease** is a transfer of possession of real estate from a landlord (lessor) to a tenant (lessee) for a consideration called rent. A lease may be oral or written, expressed, or simply implied from the facts and circumstances. A lease differs from a mere *license*, which is a privilege granted by one person to another to use land for some particular purpose. A license is not an interest in the land. A license to the licensee is personal and not assignable.

2. Classification of Leases

A lease may be a tenancy for a stated period, from period to period, at will, or at sufferance.

STATED PERIOD. As its name implies, a *tenancy for a stated period* lasts for the specific time stated in the lease. The statute of frauds requires a written lease if the period exceeds one year. The lease for a stated period terminates without notice at the end of the period. It is not affected by the death of either party during the period. A lease of land for a stated period is not terminated by destruction of the improvements during the period unless the lease so provides. If a lease covers *only* the improvements on land, destruction of them creates impossibility of performance.

PERIOD TO PERIOD. A *tenancy from period to period* may be created by the terms of the lease. A lease may run from January 1, 1993 to December 31, 1993, and from year to year thereafter unless terminated by the parties. Many leases from period to period arise when the tenant, with the consent of the landlord, holds over after the end of a lease for a stated period. When a *holdover* occurs, the landlord may object and evict the former tenant as a trespasser. Or the landlord may continue to treat the tenant as a tenant; in which case the lease continues from period to period, with the period being identical to that of the original lease, not to exceed one year.

The one-year limitation results from the language of the statute of frauds. The amount of rent is identical to that of the original lease.

Leases from year to year or from month to month can be terminated only upon giving proper notice. The length of the notice is usually prescribed by state statute—usually thirty days for a month-to-month lease and sixty to ninety days for one that is year to year. Statutes usually provide the time of the notice, such as on the day the rent is due. Farm leases usually have a special notice period so the tenant will have notice before planting the next year's crops.

AT WILL.   A *tenancy at will*, by definition, has no fixed period and can be terminated by either party at any time upon giving the prescribed statutory notice. A few states do not require notice, but if legal action is necessary to obtain possession for the lessor, a time lag will be automatically imposed.

AT SUFFERANCE.   A *tenancy at sufferance* occurs when a tenant holds over without the consent of the landlord. Until the landlord decides to evict the tenant or to allow him or her to stay, he or she is a tenant at sufferance.

3. Tenants: Rights and Duties

The rights and duties of the parties to the lease are determined by the lease itself and by the statutes of the state in which the real property is located. Several rights of tenants are frequently misunderstood. For example, the tenant is entitled to exclusive possession and control of the premises unless the lease provides to the contrary. The landlord has no right to go on the premises except to collect rent. This means that the owner of an apartment building cannot go into the leased apartments and inspect them unless the lease specifically reserves the right to do so. At the end of the lease, the landlord may retake possession of the premises and inspect for damage. A landlord may also retake possession for purposes of protecting the property if the tenant abandons the premises.

Unless the lease so provides, a tenant has no duty to make improvements or substantial repairs. A tenant is not obligated to replace a worn-out heating or air-conditioning system, but it is his or her duty to make minor repairs such as replacing a broken window. Because of the difficulty in classifying repairs, the lease should spell out the exact obligations of both parties. If the lease obligates the tenant to make repairs, the obligation includes significant items such as replacing a rotten floor or a defective furnace. The duty to repair usually does not extend to replacing the whole structure if it is destroyed.

An important right in many leases of commercial property is the tenant's right to remove *trade fixtures* that he or she has installed during the lease period. Remember the distinction between fixtures and trade fixtures. The former become a part of the real estate and belong to the owner of the land. The latter remain personalty and belong to the tenant. The right of removal terminates with the lease, and unremoved trade fixtures become the property of the landlord.

Another important right of the tenant relates to his or her corresponding duty to pay rent. The duty to pay rent is subject to setoffs for violations of the provisions of the lease by the landlord. The duty to pay rent is released in the event of an **eviction,** actual or constructive. *Constructive eviction* occurs when the premises become untenantable, not because of any fault of the tenant, or when some act of the landlord deprives the tenant of quiet enjoyment of the premises. (One example of

Eviction An action by a landlord to expel a tenant.

such an act involves the landlord's breach of an implied warranty of habitability, which is discussed in section 5.) Assume that Joe College rents a basement apartment on campus. A spring rain floods the apartment and makes it uninhabitable. Joe has been constructively evicted. He may move out, and his duty to pay rent is released. Failure to vacate the premises is a waiver of constructive eviction grounds, however. A tenant who continues in possession despite grounds for constructive eviction must continue to pay rent unless this duty is relieved by statute.

Some states and cities in recent years have enacted laws in an attempt to force landlords to maintain their property in a tenantable condition. These laws allow tenants to withhold rent where the premises are in such disrepair that the health and safety of the tenant is jeopardized. Such laws protect low-income tenants from slum landlords.

Unless prohibited by the lease, a tenant may assign the lease or sublet the premises without the consent of the landlord. In an *assignment,* the assignee becomes liable to the landlord for the rent (of course, the assignor remains liable also). In a *sublease,* the sublessee is liable to the tenant, and the tenant is liable to the landlord. An assignment transfers the original leasehold to the assignee. A sublease creates a new leasehold estate. Ordinarily, an assignment is for the balance of the original lease, whereas a sublease is only for part of the term.

If a lease prohibits assignment, it does not necessarily prevent a sublease; if a lease prohibits subleasing, it does not necessarily prevent assignment; if both are to be prohibited, the lease should so provide. Most leases provide that any assignment or sublease must have the approval of the landlord. Whether the landlord can withhold consent arbitrarily is an issue that has frequently arisen. Historically, the landlord's consent to a proposed assignment or sublease could be withheld without any reason. However, the trend now is to require that the landlord's lack of consent be reasonable under the factual circumstances. This is based on the requirement of good faith and commercial reasonableness.

4. Landlords: Rights and Duties

Lien The right of one person, usually a creditor, to keep possession, or control, of the property of another for the purpose of satisfying a debt.

Distress for rent The taking of personal property of a tenant in payment of rent.

The landlord's foremost right is to collect payment for rent. In many states and by the express terms of many leases, the landlord has a **lien** for unpaid rent on the personal property of the tenant physically located on the premises. This lien right is exercised in a statutory proceeding known as **distress for rent.** By following the prescribed procedures, the landlord is able to physically hold personalty on the premises until the rent is paid. If not paid, the tenant's personal property may be sold pursuant to court order. The proceeds of the sale, after deducting court costs, are applied to the rent.

A second basic right belonging to the landlord is to have the tenant vacate the premises upon termination of the tenancy. If the tenancy is terminated lawfully, the landlord's right to possession is absolute. The tenant may not deny the landlord's title. Furthermore, tenants have a duty to redeliver physical control of the premises in the same condition as received, ordinary wear and tear excepted. The motive of the landlord in terminating the lease usually is immaterial. However, because of federal statutes, a landlord may not discriminate in leasing or terminating a lease on the basis of race, color, religion, sex, or national origin.

The landlord's right to regain possession from the tenant is subject to the equitable positions of these parties. As the following case illustrates, a landlord cannot terminate a lease if the tenant's breach is relatively insignificant.

CASE

Fellows v. Martin
584 A.2d 458 (Conn. 1991)

SHEA, J.

The defendant tenant appeals from a judgment for the plaintiff landlord in a summary process action seeking possession of the leased premises for nonpayment of rent. The dispositive issue on appeal is whether the trial court erred in refusing to prevent the forfeiture of the lease on equitable grounds when the lessor's loss was small, the default slight, and the hardship to the tenant great. . . .

The trial court found the following facts. On March 4, 1983, the landlord leased a duplex apartment in East Hartford to the tenant for a term of ninety-nine years. The terms of the lease required the tenant to make a down payment in cash ($9900 paid at the execution of the lease), monthly payments for forty years on a promissory note ($419.57 per month), and monthly payments for the property tax ($54.48 per month) and insurance ($25.96 per month). The lease also required the tenant to pay the landlord's actual costs of exterior maintenance. The trial court found that the total amount of "rent" due was $500.01. The tenant withheld $25 from her rent check in April, 1988, because of a dispute over her parking accommodations. The landlord served the tenant with a notice to quit and commenced a summary process action to evict her from the premises.

The trial court rejected the tenant's special defenses of estoppel, based on the landlord's prior acceptance of amounts less than the full amount of rent, and satisfaction, based on the prior payment of $9900. In addition to her special defenses, the tenant also raised two counterclaims, seeking, . . . denial of the summary process action on equitable grounds. Counsel agreed at oral argument, and the transcript and trial briefs clearly show, that the trial court heard and considered the tenant's arguments in equity. . . .

"'Equity abhors . . . a forfeiture.'" It is well settled that equity will relieve against the forfeiture of a lease for nonpayment of rent. . . .

Connecticut Appellate and Superior Courts have applied the ancient equitable doctrine against forfeitures to summary process actions for nonpayment of rent and have occasionally, on the particular facts of each case, granted relief to the tenant. . . .

The factors considered by these courts in deciding whether to grant equitable relief in nonpayment cases are those suggested by Justice Story in his learned treatise, namely, (1) whether, in the absence of equitable relief, one party will suffer a loss "*wholly disproportionate to the in-*jury to the other party*" (emphasis added) and (2) whether the injury to the other party is reparable. . . .

A court of equity will apply the doctrine of clean hands to a tenant seeking such equitable relief; thus, a tenant whose breach was "willful" or "grossly negligent" will not be entitled to relief.

Applying these considerations to the undisputed facts of this case, we conclude that eviction of the tenant would work a forfeiture "wholly disproportionate to the injury suffered." In essence, the trial court ruled that for want of a $25.01 payment, withheld because of a dispute over a parking space, the tenant must forfeit a ninety-nine year lease and an advance rental payment of $9900. Although we ordinarily are reluctant to interfere with a trial court's equitable discretion, we will reverse where we find that a trial court acting as a court of equity could not reasonably have concluded as it did. This case presents just such a situation. Applying the maxim "de minimis non curat lex," we find that under the circumstances presented, the underpayment of $25.01 is insufficient, as a matter of law, to justify such a forfeiture.

We need not decide whether a tenant who deliberately refuses to pay rent may yet claim relief under the equitable doctrine against forfeitures where the forfeiture is as grossly disproportionate as it is in this case. Here, the trial court found that the tenant withheld the rent in a dispute over her parking accommodations. She apparently believed that she had the right to withhold rent if her landlord breached the lease. While her belief was erroneous, her misconception amounts to a mistake of law, rather than the type of "wilfulness" disapproved by . . . other authorities. Indeed, we have specifically held that a court of equity may grant relief from a forfeiture when the defendant's omission was caused by an error of law. The doctrine against forfeitures applies to a failure to pay rent in full when that failure is accompanied by a good faith intent to comply with the lease or a good faith dispute over the meaning of a lease.

Although the trial court's judgment must be set aside, we are mindful that the equitable doctrine against forfeitures presupposes that the landlord's injury is repairable—that is, the landlord's injury can be remedied by money instead of forfeiture of the tenancy.

Here, the tenant admits that her payment was $25.01 short of the amount the trial court found to be the rent due, $500.01. The record suggests that after service of the notice to quit, she resumed monthly payments of a sum in excess of that amount, that is, $525.01, the sum the landlord initially claimed. On remand, the trial court should hear evidence concerning this issue. . . .

■ *Reversed and remanded.*

1. What was the stated duration of the lease between the landlord and tenant?

2. How much did the tenant pay at the commencement of the lease? What was the monthly rent?

3. What was the dispute between the landlord and tenant about? How much did the tenant withhold from the rent?

4. Why does the court determine that the landlord is not entitled to recover possession of the leased premises?

A landlord also is entitled to recover from either the tenant or third parties for injuries to or waste of property. Tenants may not make any material changes or improvements without the landlord's permission. They may not move walls, install new ones, or do anything else that would constitute a material change in the premises without permission.

Tenants sometimes vacate the premises and refuse to pay any further rent prior to the expiration of the lease's full term. This is especially true in long-term commercial leases. What are the rights and duties of the parties when the tenant breaches the lease contract by abandoning the premises? Does the landlord have a duty to seek a new tenant? The answer to these questions depends on state law. In some states a landlord need not seek a new tenant, and the full obligation of the tenant remains. In these states, the tenant can look for someone to take over the lease, but the lessor need not. The modern view is that the landlord has a duty to mitigate the tenant's damages. If the landlord fails to attempt to mitigate the damages, the tenant's liability is eliminated. What types of damages might the landlord recover from the tenant who is breaching the lease? The following case discusses this issue and concludes that in addition to lost rent, consequential damages may be recovered if they are foreseeable.

CASE

Hornwood v. Smith's Food King No. 1
772 P.2d 1284 (Nev. 1989)

PER CURIAM

On June 2, 1975, Smith's Food King No. 1 (Smith's) entered into a thirty year lease of shopping center property owned by Sanford and Rita Hornwoods' (Hornwoods) predecessor in interest. Smith's leased approximately 28,000 square feet of space at 27 cents per square foot. The lease called for approximately $92,398 minimum annual rent and approximately 2.7 million dollars in total rent over the thirty year span of the lease. In addition, the agreement required Smith's to pay "percentage rent" calculated at 1.5 percent of sales generated by Smith's during the previous calendar year, less the aggregate amount of minimum rent paid during that calendar year. Smith's paid percentage rent for 1979 and 1980, but has not paid percentage rent since 1980 due to insufficient sales volume.

On November 1, 1986, Smith's closed its business at the leased premises and ceased its retail grocery operations. The closure occurred without any prior notice to the Hornwoods. The Hornwoods allege that Smith's closed its store at the leased premises because a new Smith's, built a short distance away, directly competed with the store Smith's operated at the leased premises. However, Smith's alleges that it closed its store as a result of various market studies, lost profits, and increased competition. Smith's further claims that it failed to give notice of the closure to the Hornwoods due to company policy. The policy is allegedly a result of previous experience with diminished employee morale, pilfering, and other attendant problems when notice of closure is given.

Smith's retained possession of the demised premises and continued to pay minimum rent after closing the store. The Hornwoods took no action to evict Smith's, instead choosing to allow Smith's to retain the premises and locate suitable subtenants. In May 1987, Smith's subleased 18,128 square feet to HUB Distributing, Inc., d/b/a Millers Outpost. Smith's subleased the remaining 10,000 square feet to Video Tyme in early 1988.

On December 4, 1986, the Hornwoods filed a complaint against Smith's charging that Smith's breached its lease by ceasing operations and vacating the demised premises prior to the expiration of the lease. After trial, the district court held that Smith's breached an implied covenant of continuous operation by ceasing operations with approximately twenty years remaining on the thirty year lease. However, the district court held that, because Smith's has continued to pay minimum rent, the Hornwoods were not entitled to an award of compensatory damages for breach of lease.

Additionally, the district court refused to award damages to the Hornwoods on any of their consequential damages theories. The Hornwoods sought consequential damages based on the diminution in value of the shopping center, lost future percentage rents from Smith's and the other tenants of the shopping center, and lost rent and other expenses associated with the other tenants. The court ruled that all of the alleged consequential damages were unforeseeable as a matter of law.

Furthermore, the Hornwoods claimed tort damages, alleging that Smith's acted in bad faith by closing its store, thereby breaching the implied covenant of good faith and fair dealing. The district court refused to impose tort liability upon Smith's ruling that Smith's did not breach its duty of good faith and fair dealing. . . .

The district court found that the lease contained an implied covenant to continuously operate as a grocery store. . . . Furthermore, the district court found that Smith's breached the implied covenant of continuous operation by ceasing to operate its grocery store located at the demised premises. However, the district court did not award the Hornwoods compensatory or consequential damages resulting from this breach. The Hornwoods do not contest the district court's ruling on compensatory damages. However, the Hornwoods argue that the diminution in value of the shopping center occurring when Smith's breached the lease is a recoverable consequential damage. We agree.

Damages from a breach of contract should be such as may fairly and reasonably be considered as arising naturally, or were reasonably contemplated by both parties at the time they made the contract. The Hornwoods argue that the diminution in value of the shopping center both arose naturally and foreseeably as a result of the termination of operations by Smith's.

The Hornwoods presented substantial evidence to support their argument. Mr. Maury Abrams, developer of the center, testified that anchor tenants, (i.e., Smith's) draw the largest amount of customers, attract other "satel-lite" tenants, and are necessary for long-term financing. Mr. Joe Abdenour, the leasing agent for the shopping center, testified that when an anchor tenant leaves, the rental value of the shopping center immediately decreases, thereby decreasing the overall value of the shopping center. Further, the Hornwoods presented evidence that Smith's attracted approximately 40,000 customers a month into the shopping center. On the other hand, the Hornwoods showed that Millers Outpost, a subtenant of Smith's, generated only 4,500 customers per month. Additionally, Mr. K. Donald Dunn, a certified real estate appraiser, stated that the value of the center decreased by $1,425,000 during the year following the departure of Smith's.

The district court found that the shopping center decreased in value in excess of one million dollars after Smith's ceased operations. However, the court concluded that the diminution of property value to the shopping center as a result of the departure of Smith's was unforeseeable and not compensable as a matter of law. We disagree.

Smith's is a sophisticated business entity. Smith's knew that its presence as the anchor tenant had a critical impact on the shopping center's success. Without an anchor tenant, obtaining long-term financing and attracting satellite tenants is nearly impossible for a shopping center. Perhaps most importantly, the anchor tenant insures the financial viability of the center by providing the necessary volume of customer traffic to the shopping center. Therefore, we find that the district court clearly erred in concluding, as a matter of law, that the diminution in value of the Hornwoods' shopping center was unforeseeable. Accordingly, we reverse that portion of the district court's ruling and remand to the district court for an assessment of the Hornwoods' damages as a consequence of the loss of their anchor tenant. . . .

■ *Reversed and remanded.*

CASE CONCEPTS REVIEW

1. For how long did Smith's Food King agree to rent the anchor space in the shopping center now owned by the Hornwoods?

2. At what point in this term did Smith's Food King cease to operate as a grocery store?

3. Why were the Hornwoods not entitled to compensatory damages?

4. Why does the court conclude that Smith's is liable to the Hornwoods for consequential damages?

It is common practice for a landlord to require that the tenant deposit a stated sum of money, such as one month's rent, as security for the lease. This security deposit covers nonpayment of rent and possible damage to the premises. Many landlords have been reluctant to return these security deposits, contending in most cases that damages were present, requiring repairs. As a result, many tenants have refused to pay the last month's rent, demanding that the security deposit be applied. Such practices by landlords and tenants have created a great deal of animosity and litigation. To alleviate this problem, the legislatures of many states have passed laws governing lease security deposits. Such laws usually require that the landlord pay interest on the deposits and itemize the cost of any repairs that were made from the deposit. They further require the landlord to return the deposit promptly and prohibit the landlord from using it to repair conditions caused by normal wear and tear. In the event a tenant is required to sue the landlord to recover the deposit, the tenant is entitled to collect attorney's fees. Finally, under these statutes, the tenant usually is not allowed to set off the deposit against the last month's rent.

Tort liability is sometimes imposed on landlords for injuries to their tenants. Such liability only exists where there is a duty owed by the landlord to the tenant and the duty is breached. For example, the modern view is that the owner of a residential dwelling unit, who leases it to a tenant for residential purposes, has a duty to reasonably inspect the premises before allowing the tenant to take possession, and to make the repairs necessary to transfer a reasonably safe dwelling unit to the tenant unless defects are waived by the tenant. This duty may be modified by agreement of the parties.

After the tenant takes possession, the landlord has a continuing duty to exercise reasonable care to repair dangerous defective conditions upon notice of their existence by the tenant, unless waived by the tenant. In most states, a landlord has no duty to maintain in a safe condition any part of the premises under the tenant's exclusive control. The landlord does, however, have a duty to use ordinary care to maintain in a reasonably safe condition any part of the leased premises that was reserved for the common use of all tenants. Further, if the landlord, after delivering possession of the premises to a tenant, enters to make repairs or improvements, the landlord must use reasonable care in making them.

5. Warranty of Habitability

In recent years, courts have been called on to decide if there is an implied *warranty of habitability* in a lease of residential property. (This is similar to the issue of warranties on the sale of new housing and is part of the broadened protection given the consuming public, which is discussed more fully in chapter 41.) Some courts have held in all housing leases that there is an implied warranty of habitability. One court held that the fact that a tenant knew of a substantial number of defects when he rented the premises and that rent was accordingly reduced did not remove the tenant from protection of the warranty. The court reasoned that permitting that type of bargaining would be contrary to public policy and the purpose of the doctrine of implied warranty of habitability. In determining the kinds of defects that will be deemed to constitute a breach of warranty of habitability, several factors are considered. Among the common factors are (1) the violation of any applicable housing code or building or sanitary regulations; (2) whether the nature of the deficiency affects a vital facility; (3) the potential or actual effect on safety and sanitation; and (4) whether the tenant was in any way responsible for the defect. A breach of this warranty may allow a tenant to terminate the lease. It may serve as a defense to a suit for rent and as a means to obtain a rent reduction.

Defects in vital portions of the premises that may affect health are more important than defects in extras such as swimming pools or recreational facilities, which are not likely to render the premises uninhabitable. It should be kept in mind that not all states recognize an implied warranty of habitability in residential leases. Also, most states have not extended implied warranties to commercial leases. In general, implied warranties of habitability are created either by courts on a case-by-case basis or by statutory enactment.

6. Liability to Third Parties

Difficult legal questions arise in cases involving the landlord's and tenant's liability for injuries to persons on the premises. As a general rule, a landlord makes no warranty that the premises are safe or suitable for the intended use by the tenant, and third persons are on the premises at their own peril. A landlord owes no greater duty to a tenant's guests than is owed to the tenant. A landlord does have a duty to give notice of latent defects of which he or she has knowledge, and some states add unknown defects of which the landlord should have knowledge in the exercise of ordinary care. In recent years, the liability of landlords under this view has expanded, but there still must be a duty that is breached before there is liability.

Knowing that business invitees of the tenant will be constantly entering the premises to transact business, the owner of business property has an increased responsibility known as the *public-use* exception to the general rule. The basis of the exception is that the landlord leases premises on which he or she knows or should know that there are conditions likely to cause injury to persons, that the purpose for which the premises are leased involve the fact that people will be invited on the premises as patrons of the tenant, and that the landlord knows or should know that the tenant cannot reasonably be expected to remedy or guard against injury from the defect. Thus, a landlord of a business owes a higher duty than does the landlord of essentially private premises. Moreover, landlords of business premises often undertake to care for the common areas. In such cases, they have a duty to inspect, repair, and maintain common areas in a reasonably safe condition.

Many suits against lessors by third persons result from falls on the premises, often associated with ice, snow, or waxed floors. Historically, a landlord had no duty to remove ice and snow. In recent years, many courts have changed this rule as it is applied to multiple-family dwellings and businesses. Many tenants are simply unequipped to perform the task of snow and ice removal. They sometimes lack the physical wherewithal, capability, or the equipment (and storage space) necessary to the task. Even in those states that do not require removal of ice and snow, if the landlord does undertake to remove snow and ice, he or she must do so with ordinary care, taking into account dangerous conditions caused by subsequent thawing and freezing of snow placed near the walkway.

7. Uniform Residential Landlord and Tenant Act

The National Conference of Commissioners on Uniform State Laws has proposed that state legislatures adopt the Uniform Residential Landlord and Tenant Act (URLTA). To date, at least nineteen states have followed this recommendation.

The URLTA or a substantially similar version has been adopted and is law in Alaska, Arizona, Connecticut, Florida, Hawaii, Iowa, Kansas, Kentucky, Michigan, Montana, Nebraska, New Mexico, Oklahoma, Oregon, Rhode Island, South Carolina, Tennessee, Virginia, and Washington.

In addition to making the laws governing residential lease transactions simpler, clearer, and more uniform, URLTA attempts to assure equal bargaining power between landlord and tenant. Many of the rights and duties already discussed are part of URLTA. For example, the landlord cannot collect a security deposit that exceeds one month's rent. Failure to return this deposit without justification makes the landlord liable for twice the amount of this deposit, plus the tenant's attorney's fees. The landlord must deliver possession of the premises at the beginning of the lease term, and the landlord must maintain the premises in a habitable condition.

A tenant's basic responsibilities are to pay rent, to keep the dwelling safe and clean, and to allow the landlord to enter the premises under reasonable circumstances. Examples of when the landlord must be allowed to enter would include the making of periodic inspections, repairs, or improvements. The tenant also must cooperate in showing the premises to potential buyers or tenants. URLTA provides the landlord with the right to enter in all emergency situations.

URLTA also contains an article on the remedies available to either tenant or landlord when the other party breaches the lease agreement. For the most part, URLTA adopts the common-law remedies and defenses, such as constructive and retaliatory eviction, previously discussed. Furthermore, provisions allow the tenant to make minor repairs and deduct the cost from the rent if the landlord fails to make the repair after being notified of the defect. A minor repair is defined as one costing less than $100 or one-half the periodic rent, whichever amount is greater. The common-law remedy available to the landlord known as distress for rent (see section 4 on page 991) is abolished. However, if the tenant holds over in bad faith after the lease expires, the landlord can sue for possession and three times the actual damages suffered or three months' rent, whichever is greater.

BAILMENTS OF PERSONAL PROPERTY

8. Required Elements

Bailment Delivery of personal property to another for a special purpose. Delivery is made under a contract, either expressed or implied, that upon the completion of the special purpose, the property shall be redelivered to the bailor or placed at his or her disposal.

Possession of personal property is often temporarily surrendered by the owner to another person. The person to whom the goods are delivered may perform some service pertaining to the goods, such as a repair, after which the goods are returned to the owner. Or someone may borrow or lease an article from its owner. Another temporary transfer of possession occurs when the owner causes the goods to be stored in a warehouse. In general, the provisions of the Uniform Commercial Code are applicable to these transactions involving the temporary transfer of possession of personal property.

An agreement whereby possession of personal property is surrendered by the owner with provision for its return at a later time is known as a **bailment.** The owner of the goods is called the *bailor.* The one receiving possession is called the *bailee.* There are three distinct requirements for a bailment: retention of title by the bailor, possession and temporary control of the property by the bailee, and ultimate possession to revert to the bailor or to someone designated by the bailor.

9. Types of Bailments

Bailments can be categorized naturally into three classes: bailments for the benefit of the bailor, bailments for the benefit of the bailee, and bailments for the mutual benefit of bailor and bailee. Typical of the first group are those cases in which the bailor leaves goods in the safekeeping of the bailee without any provision for paying the bailee for caring for the article. Because the bailee is not to use the goods or to be paid in any manner, the bailment is for the exclusive benefit of the bailor.

A bailment for the benefit of the bailee is best illustrated by a loan of some article by the bailor to the bailee without any compensation to the bailor. Assume a student borrows a professor's automobile for a weekend date. The bailment is one for the sole benefit of the student, the bailee.

The most common type of bailment is the one in which both parties are to benefit. Contracts for repair, carriage, storage, or pledge of property fall within this class. The bailor receives the benefit of some service; the bailee benefits by the receipt of certain agreed compensation. Thus both parties benefit as a result of the bailment.

To constitute a bailment for mutual benefit, it is not essential that the bailee actually receive compensation in money or tangible property. If the bailment is an incident of the business in which the bailee makes a profit, or it was accepted because of benefits expected to accrue, it is a mutual benefit bailment.

10. Degree of Care Owed by Bailor

Property leased by a bailor to a bailee (a mutual benefit bailment) must be reasonably fit for the intended purpose. For this reason, it is the duty of the bailor to notify the bailee of all defects in the property leased of which the bailor might reasonably have been aware. The bailor is responsible for any damage suffered by the bailee as the result of such defects, unless the notice is given. This rule holds even though the bailor is not aware of the defect if, by the exercise of reasonable diligence, the defect could have been discovered.

If, on the other hand, an article is merely loaned to a bailee—a bailment for the benefit of the bailee—the bailor's duty is to notify the bailee only of known defects. A bailor who fails to give the required notice of a known defect is liable to any person who might be expected to use the defective article as a result of the bailment. Employees of the bailee and members of the bailee's family may recover from the bailor for injuries received as a consequence of known defects.

BAILEES: RIGHTS AND DUTIES

11. Degree of Care Owed by Bailees

Provided that proper care has been exercised by the bailee, any loss or damage to the property bailed falls on the bailor. Each type of bailment requires a different degree of care by the bailee. In a bailment for the benefit of the bailor, the bailee is required to exercise only slight care. In a bailment for the benefit of the bailee, extraordinary care is required. A bailment for the mutual benefit of the parties demands ordinary care on the part of the bailee. *Ordinary care* is defined as care that the average individual usually exercises over his or her own property. The following case is typical of those distinguishing among the three types of bailments and the duties owed by the bailee to the bailor.

CASE

Morris v. Hamilton
302 S.E.2d 51 (Va. 1983)

STEPHENSON, J.

In this appeal involving a bailment, we must decide what standard of care is imposed upon the bailee by the relationship.

... Marsha Hamilton and Andrea Morris were guests at a dinner party attended by approximately 25 people. The party began about 7:00 P.M. and ended approximately 1:00 A.M. the following morning. Alcoholic beverages were served throughout the evening.

Approximately 11:30, while working in the kitchen, Hamilton removed her wristwatch and placed it on a counter. About midnight, the water in the house "went off," and Hamilton left the kitchen. Since she intended to resume her work when the water came on again, she left her watch on the counter. Hamilton went outside, where she had an after-dinner drink with several other guests. After 10 to 15 minutes, she became ill and fled to a bathroom.

Shortly after Hamilton left the kitchen, Morris saw the watch on the counter. Fearing for its safety, she picked it up and carried it in her hand as she looked for Hamilton. Morris was unable to find Hamilton and cannot recall what she did with the watch. She thought she either gave it to Hamilton's fiance or put it somewhere in the house for safekeeping....

The following day, Hamilton discovered she did not have her watch and returned to the house to retrieve it. A maid who was in the kitchen when Hamilton arrived told her she had not seen the watch. Although the house was searched thoroughly, the watch was never recovered.

Hamilton sued Morris alleging Morris was the bailee of the watch and that she negligently lost it while it was in her possession. Morris concedes she was a bailee. She contends, however, she acted gratuitously and therefore owed Hamilton a duty of only slight care. The trial court, sitting without a jury rejected the bailment theory, instead finding for Hamilton on a pure negligence theory. The court ruled Morris had violated her duty to exercise ordinary or reasonable care of the watch, and that her negligence was the proximate cause of its loss.

Acting upon Morris' concession that she was a bailee, we decide the case with reference to bailment principles. Ordinarily, in order to establish a bailment, there must be a delivery by the bailor and an acceptance by the bailee. However, no formal contract or actual meeting of the minds is necessary. Indeed, "it is the element of lawful possession, however created, and duty to account for the thing as the property of another that creates the bailment, regardless of whether or not such possession is based on contract in the ordinary sense." For an alleged bailee to have possession, he must have both physical control over the property and an intent to exercise that control.

When, as here, one comes into possession of a chattel and exercises physical control over it, a bailment is created by operation of law. It is known as a constructive or quasi-bailment.

The evidence shows that Morris acted solely for the benefit of Hamilton. She therefore was a gratuitous bailee....

A bailee who acts gratuitously is not held to the same standard of care as one who enters upon the same undertaking for pay. The latter owes a duty of reasonable or ordinary care, while a gratuitous bailee owes only a duty of slight care. Thus, in order for a bailor to recover from a gratuitous bailee, he must prove the bailee was guilty of gross negligence.

We hold, therefore, the trial court erred in ruling no bailment existed and in holding Morris to a standard of ordinary or reasonable care. Morris is liable for the loss of the watch only if she was guilty of gross negligence.

"[G]ross negligence is that degree of negligence which shows indifference to others as constitutes an utter disregard of prudence.... It must be such a degree of negligence as would shock fair minded persons...." Ordinarily, gross negligence is an issue for decision by the factfinder. It becomes a question of law only when reasonable minds cannot differ about the conclusion to be reached from the evidence.

Viewing the evidence and all reasonable inferences in the light most favorable to Hamilton, we hold as a matter of law that Morris' conduct was not sufficient to constitute gross negligence. Therefore, we will reverse the judgment of the trial court and enter final judgment for the appellant.

■ *Reversed.*

1. What article of property is the subject matter of this litigation?
2. Who owned this article? Who found it?
3. What happened to the article after it was found?
4. What type of bailment does the court decide existed?
5. What degree of care does this bailee owe to this bailor?

The amount of care demanded of a bailee varies with the nature and value of the article bailed. The care found to be sufficient in the case of a carpenter's tool chest would probably not be ample for a diamond ring worth $10,000. A higher standard of protection is required for valuable articles. Moreover, when damages are assessed against a bailee, they are based on retail replacement value, not the wholesale cost to a bailee. Figure 45-1 depicts the degrees of care owed by the bailor and bailee depending on the type of bailment.

In addition to the duty to exercise due care, the bailee promises to return the property to the bailor undamaged upon termination of the bailment. This promise can be used to create a prima facie case of negligence. A bailor who proves that property delivered in good condition was returned from the bailee in bad condition establishes a presumption of negligence, and that bailor is entitled to recover from the bailee unless the presumption is rebutted. If there is no other evidence, the bailor will win the suit. The bailee may rebut this prima facie case by introducing evidence to establish that there was no negligence on its part, but the bailee has the burden of proving that it has used reasonable care and caution after the prima facie case has been established. This prima facie case of negligence exists only if all elements of a bailment are present. If there is no bailment, there is no prima facie case upon nondelivery or damage to the goods. The following case demonstrates the application of this prima facie case concept.

FIGURE 45-1 ■ Degrees of Care and Duties in Bailments

TYPE OF BAILMENT	BAILOR'S CARE	BAILEE'S CARE	BAILEE'S NEGLIGENCE THAT BREACHES DUTY OF CARE
Sole benefit of bailor	Warn of known defects and those that should be known	Slight care	Extraordinary negligence
Mutual benefit	Warn of known defects and those that should be known	Ordinary care	Ordinary negligence
Sole benefit of bailee	Warn of known defects	Extraordinary care	Slight negligence

Volvo White Truck Corp. v. Vineyard

387 S.E.2d 763 (Va. 1990)

STEPHENSON, J.

In this appeal, a case involving a bailment for the mutual benefit of a bailor and a bailee, we determine when, and under what circumstances, the bailee (1) has the burden of persuasion on the issue of his negligence, and (2) has the burden of going forward with the evidence on the negligence issue.

Lowell Phillip Vineyard, the plaintiff/bailor, sued Volvo White Truck Corporation (Volvo), the defendant/bailee. Vineyard claimed that he delivered his tractor to Volvo for routine maintenance and that Volvo returned the tractor in a damaged condition. Vineyard's motion for judgment contained two counts. In the first, a tort count, he alleged that the damage to the tractor was caused by Volvo's negligence. In the second, a contract count, Vineyard alleged that Volvo breached the bailment contract. . . .

The jury returned a verdict in Vineyard's favor in the amount of $15,261.00. The trial court ruled that the verdict was excessive and ordered a remittitur to reduce the amount of the judgment to $9,107.80.

Vineyard owned a 1978 Kenworth, cab-over-engine style, tractor. With this style tractor, the entire cab pivots up and forward on hinges located on the front of the chassis. Access to the engine is gained by pivoting the cab.

A large fiberglass engine cover is located across the floor of the cab and is hidden from view by vinyl upholstery. This engine cover is called a "doghouse."

Under normal operating conditions, the rear of the cab rests upon a U-shaped collar bolted to the chassis. A hydraulically-operated hood on the back of the cab latches to the collar and fastens the rear of the cab to the chassis. If an attempt is made to raise the cab when the hook is latched, the doghouse can be damaged.

On July 23, 1985, Vineyard took the tractor to Volvo . . . for routine maintenance in preparation for hauling a trailer of goods to the West Coast. Volvo agreed to perform the service and to return the tractor the following day.

The next day, when Vineyard returned to Volvo to pick up the tractor, he observed that the cab was in the raised position. The U-shaped collar was not bolted to the chassis in its normal position but was held aloft by the cab's rear hood.

Upon starting the tractor's engine, Vineyard noticed that it sounded unusually loud. He also noticed that the upholstery covering the doghouse was stretched. When Vineyard pulled the upholstery back, he saw a large crack in the doghouse that, according to Vineyard, had not been present when the tractor was delivered to Volvo. This is the damage that prompted this litigation.

Vineyard immediately called the damage to the attention of Volvo's personnel, but they denied that they had caused the damage. . . .

Over Volvo's objection, the trial court granted jury instructions 4 and 5 which placed upon Volvo the burden of proving, by the greater weight of the evidence, that the tractor's damage was not caused by Volvo's failure to exercise reasonable care. Volvo contends on appeal that, in granting these instructions, the trial court committed reversible error. . . .

When a bailment is for the mutual benefit of the bailor and bailee, the bailee must use ordinary care for the protection, preservation, and return of the bailed property. If the bailee fails to use ordinary care, he is liable to the bailor for any loss or damage to the property resulting from the bailee's failure.

When the plaintiff/bailor's cause of action is based upon the alleged negligence of the defendant/bailee, the burden is on the plaintiff throughout the case to prove the defendant's negligence. This burden is called the burden of persuasion, and it always remains with the plaintiff in a negligence case.

However, when the bailor proves that the property was delivered to the bailee in good condition and was returned damaged in such a way as does not usually occur by the exercise of proper care, there arises a presumption that the bailee was negligent. This presumption operates to shift to the bailee the burden of going forward with evidence tending to rebut the presumption. The presumption, however, does not operate to shift to the bailee the burden of persuasion, *i.e.*, the burden of proving by a preponderance of the evidence that he was not negligent.

A different set of principles pertains, however, when the plaintiff/bailor brings a contract action based upon the bailee's alleged breach of a bailment contract. In such an action, we have adopted the so-called "modern rule." . . .

In a contract action, . . . the burden of persuasion also rests with the plaintiff throughout the trial. This burden, however, is merely the burden of showing the bailment contract and the bailee's failure to perform the contract by failing to return the property in an undamaged condition. When, however, the bailee seeks to defend the contract action by asserting the affirmative defense that the property was damaged without negligence on his part, the bailee has the burden of proving his own freedom from negligence, or, as otherwise stated, that he exercised due care to prevent the damage. Thus, with respect to the affirmative defense, the bailee has the burden of persuasion.

In the present case . . . a tort action and a contract

action were tried to the jury. The evidence pertaining to each action conflicted such that reasonable minds could differ about the conclusions to be reached. In both actions, therefore, jury issues were presented.

Accordingly, it was incumbent upon the trial court to instruct the jury fully and clearly on the principles of law governing both actions. Instructions 4 and 5 fail in that regard. . . . The jury instructions must differentiate between the two actions and the parties' burdens of proof in each action. . . .

■ *Reversed and remanded.*

CASE CONCEPTS REVIEW

1. Who is the bailor? Who is the bailee? What type of bailment is involved in this case?
2. What is the defect or the damage to the Kenworth tractor?
3. What is the plaintiff's burden if the bailee is sued for negligence?
4. How does this burden change if the suit is based on the bailee's breach of the bailment contract?
5. Why is the trial court's judgment reversed?

12. Disclaimers of Liability by Bailees

Bailees frequently attempt to disclaim liability for damage to property while it is in their possession. Such a clause in a contract is known as an *exculpatory clause.* Dry cleaners' tickets often bear statements disclaiming liability for damage to property delivered to them for cleaning. An exculpatory clause disclaiming liability for negligence is illegal if the bailee is a quasi-public institution, because such contracts are against public policy. This improper use of exculpatory clauses is discussed in chapter 13.

More and more bailees are being classified as quasi-public businesses because of the inequality of bargaining power between many bailors and their bailees. Not all exculpatory clauses seek to eliminate liability completely; some seek to limit the amount of damages. Contracts limiting the amount of damages are looked on more favorably than absolute disclaimers because it is fair for both parties to know the value of the property and the risk present. In accordance with this theory, the Uniform Commercial Code provides that the **warehouse receipt** or storage agreement may limit the amount of liability in case of loss or damage to the covered property, but the agreement cannot disclaim the obligation of reasonable care.

Carriers also attempt to limit their liability. A carrier may not contract away its liability for goods damaged in shipment, but it may limit the liability to a stated amount. A carrier may also, where lower rates are granted, relieve itself from the consequences of causes or conduct over which it has no control.

Because a carrier may limit liability to an agreed valuation, the shipper is limited in recovery to the value asserted in the bill of lading. The rate charged for transportation will vary with the value of the property shipped. For this reason, the agreed valuation is binding.

Warehouse receipt An instrument showing that the signer has in his or her possession certain described goods for storage. It obligates the signer, the warehouseperson, to deliver the goods to a specified person or to that person's order or bearer upon the return of the instrument.

Carrier A natural person or a corporation who receives goods under a contract to transport for a consideration from one place to another.

13. Other Rights and Duties of Bailees

The bailment agreement governs the rights and duties of the bailee. If the bailee treats the property in a different manner or uses it for some purpose other than that contemplated by the bailment contract, the bailee becomes liable for any loss or damage to the property, even though the damage can in no sense be attributed to the conduct of the bailee. Let us assume that Murray stores a car for the winter in Plante's public garage. Because of a crowded condition, Plante has the car temporarily moved to another garage without Murray's consent. As a result of a tornado, the car is destroyed while at the second location. The loss falls on Plante, who breached the terms of the bailment contract. In a restricted sense, the bailee is guilty of conversion of the bailor's property during the period in which the contract terms are being violated.

The bailee has no right to deny the title of the bailor unless the bailee has yielded possession to one having a better title than the bailor. The bailee has no right to retain possession of the property merely because he or she is able to prove that the bailor does not have legal title to the goods. To defeat the bailor's right to possession, the bailee must show that the property has been turned over to someone having better title or that the bailee is holding the property under an agreement with the true owner.

14. Common Carriers as Bailees

Common carrier One who is engaged in the business of transporting personal property from one place to another for compensation. Such person is bound to carry for all who tender their goods and the price for transportation. A common carrier operates as a public utility and is subject to state and federal regulations.

The contract for carriage of goods constitutes a mutual benefit bailment, but the care required of the carrier greatly exceeds that of the ordinary bailee. A **common carrier** is an absolute insurer of the safe delivery of the goods to their destination. Proof of delivery to a carrier of a shipment in good condition and its arrival at the destination in a damaged condition creates a prima facie case against the carrier.

This absolute liability of a common carrier is subject to only five exceptions. Any loss or damage must fall on the shipper if it results from (1) an act of God, (2) action of an alien enemy, (3) order of public authority, (4) inherent nature of the goods, or (5) misconduct of the shipper. Thus, any loss that results from an accident or the willful misconduct of some third party must be borne by the carrier. A person who wanted to injure a certain railway company set fire to several boxcars loaded with freight. Losses due to damage to the goods fell on the carrier. On the other hand, if lightning, an act of God, had set fire to the cars, the loss would have fallen on the shipper. However, the defense of an act of God is narrowly construed to include only events that were not foreseeable.

The shipper must suffer any damage to goods in shipment if damage results from the very nature of the goods, improper crating, or failure to protect the property. Thus, if a dog dies because its crate was poorly ventilated, the shipper is unable to recover from the carrier. Remember, though, that the carrier has the burden of proving that it was free from negligence and that the damage falls within one of the exceptions to the rule establishing the carrier's liability as an insurer of the shipment.

The burden is on the shipper to prove that the goods were in good condition at the time and place of shipment. Although proof that the goods were in good condition when delivered to the carrier and that they were damaged when delivered by the carrier creates a prima facie case of liability, there is no presumption that the goods were in good condition when delivered to the carrier. Actual proof is required.

Consignee A person to whom a shipper usually directs a carrier to deliver goods.

Warehouseperson A person engaged in the business of storing goods for hire.

The liability of the carrier attaches as soon as the goods are delivered. The extreme degree of care required of the carrier may be terminated before the goods are actually delivered to the **consignee.** Three views in the United States determine when the relationship of the carrier ceases. Some states hold that the duties of the carrier end, and those of a **warehouseperson** begin, as soon as the local shipment is unloaded from the car into the freight house. Others hold the carrier to strict liability until the consignee has had a reasonable time in which to inspect and remove the shipment. Still other states hold that the consignee is entitled to notice—and that he or she has reasonable time after notice— which to remove the goods before the liability of the carrier as a carrier is terminated. For example, assume that the goods arrive at their destination and are unloaded and placed in the freight house. Before the consignee has had time to take them away, the goods are destroyed by fire, although the carrier has exercised ordinary care. Under the first of these views, the loss would fall on the shipper because at the time of the fire, the railway was no longer a carrier but a warehouseperson. Under the other two views, the loss would fall on the carrier, whose liability as a carrier had not yet terminated because no time had been given for delivery.

The following case illustrates this relationship between a common carrier and a warehouseperson. In this case, the carrier's delivery of the shipper's merchandise was refused by the consignee. While the carrier has the goods and is awaiting further instructions from the shipper, does it owe the higher standard of care of a common carrier or the ordinary care of a warehouseperson?

CASE

Fisher Corporation v. Consolidated Freightways, Inc.
434 N.W.2d 17 (Neb. 1989)

CAPORALE, J.

Plaintiff-appellant, Fisher Corporation, a manufacturer of electronic equipment, seeks to recover the value of certain video cassette recorders stolen while in the possession of defendant-appellee, Consolidated Freightways, Inc., a transporter of goods. The district court, in accordance with verdicts, dismissed Fisher's action. Fisher appeals asserting . . . that the district court erred in ruling the evidence sufficient to support the verdicts. . . .

In its original petition, Fisher pled that it was entitled to recover on the theory that at the time of the theft, Consolidated was serving as a warehouser, or alternatively, on the theory that at the relevant time, Consolidated was serving as a common carrier. A warehouser, that is, one engaged in the business of storing goods for hire, is, in the absence of a contrary agreement, liable for goods lost while in its possession only if . . . the loss occurred through its negligence. A common carrier, on the other hand, is an insurer against loss from whatever cause, except an act of nature, of the public enemy, or of the owner of the goods. . . .

The record reveals that in June of 1984, Fisher, under a "standard bill of lading," delivered to Consolidated, at Fisher's warehouse in California, 132 recorders for shipment to World Radio, Inc., an electronics retailer, at Council Bluffs, Iowa. Consolidated divided the shipment into two parts, tendering delivery to World Radio of 60 recorders on June 29 and 72 recorders on July 6. World Radio rejected each tender as duplicative of earlier shipments.

. . . Once a common carrier tenders delivery of the consigned goods to a consignee which refuses delivery, the carrier loses its status as a common carrier and becomes a warehouser. Where a common carrier turned warehouser, acting as a bailee, accepts instructions from the bailor to ship goods to a specified location, its status as a warehouser again changes to that of common carrier.

. . . The record discloses that after each rejected tender, Consolidated returned the recorders to its terminal at Sarpy County, Nebraska, for storage, pending receipt of Fisher's further instructions. On the day after the second rejection, Consolidated loaded all 132 recorders onto a trailer, sealed but did not padlock the trailer doors, and placed the trailer at the south end of its terminal yard. Padlocks were not used on any trailer doors so as not to call attention to a trailer containing expensive cargo; rather, all trailers were sealed. The doors of the trailer faced away from the terminal, toward the south end of a Cyclone fence which encircled the yard.

In accordance with its usual practice, Consolidated sent Fisher a form letter notifying it of World Radio's rejection of the shipments and indicating that after 3 days, Fisher would be charged for storage unless Consolidated received disposition instructions.

At 7 a.m. on July 17, a Tuesday, Consolidated's employees discovered that 54 of the recorders were missing from the trailers. They also discovered that a large, 3-foot by 5-foot hole had been cut in the chain-link fence at the terminal's south end, and a smaller hole had been cut in the east fence. The recorders were never recovered. The exact time the theft occurred is unknown. . . .

At some point, Fisher notified Consolidated to return the rejected recorders to Fisher in California, but the record is not clear as to when that occurred. . . .

All that was clear at the close of all the evidence was that at some point 54 of the recorders in Consolidated's possession were stolen and that at some point Fisher telephoned Consolidated with authorization to return all 132 recorders. However, the evidence is such that reasonable minds could reach different conclusions as to when the theft occurred and as to when Consolidated received Fisher's return instruction. . . .

Consequently, the evidence is sufficient to sustain the jury's special finding that Consolidated did not receive Fisher's return authorization until after the theft had taken place, thereby making Consolidated a warehouser at the time of the loss rather than a common carrier. Moreover, the evidence concerning the manner in which Consolidated stored the recorders does not compel but does support the finding implicit in the general verdict that Consolidated had not been negligent. . . .

The judgment of the district court is

■ *Affirmed.*

CASE CONCEPTS REVIEW

1. Which party is the shipper of goods in this case? Which party is the common carrier?
2. What is the basis for this common carrier's argument that it is not an insurer of the safety of the stolen goods?
3. In light of the fact that the evidence as to when the goods were stolen and as to when the order of reshipment was delivered is not clear, why does the court affirm the district court's judgment?
4. Who ultimately bears the loss of the goods?

A common carrier, while not an insurer of its passengers' safety, owes the highest degree of care to them. In other words, a common carrier will be liable to passengers for injuries caused by even the slightest negligence. To persons who are on the premises, but not actually on board the carrier, the carrier owes only ordinary care. Passengers who are in the process of boarding or exiting are considered to be on board and are protected by the carrier's duty to exercise extraordinary care.

15. Innkeepers as Bailees

Issues similar to those involved with common carriers frequently arise in suits against hotel and motel operators. Under common law, an innkeeper was an insurer of the safety of the goods of its guests. The law imposed liability as a matter of public policy because the innkeeper and his or her employees had easy access to the guests' rooms. Exceptions to this general rule relieved the innkeeper from liability for loss caused by an act of God, a public enemy, an act of public authority, the inherent nature of the property, or the fault of the guest.

Most states have enacted statutes pertaining to hotel or motel operators' liability. These statutes usually provide that if the operator appropriately notifies guests that a safe or lockbox is maintained for their use, there is no liability if guests' property is stolen from their rooms. Such laws usually cover property of "small compass," which includes money, negotiable instruments, jewelry, and precious stones. The requirement that notice of the availability of the safe be given with notice of the liability limitation is usually strictly enforced.

Some states also have laws that limit the maximum liability of hotel and motel operators to a stated amount, such as $500. Others have changed the liability from that of an insurer to that of a bailee of a mutual benefit bailment (ordinary care as the duty). In all states, the liability of the innkeeper is limited to the value of the property. There is no liability for consequential damages that may flow from the loss of the property. The following case illustrates the typical factual situation and legal analysis involving an innkeeper's liability for personal property.

CASE

Grimes v. M.H.M., Inc.
776 S.W.2d 336 (Ark. 1989)

NEWBERN, J.

The appellant, H.D. Grimes, is the owner of a coin and pawnshop in Conway, Arkansas. He checked in as a guest at the Camelot Hotel in Little Rock where a coin show was to be held and he was to display merchandise. He took his luggage, which consisted of some nine items loaded on a dolly he had brought with him, to his sleeping room. His luggage included a briefcase and a larger briefcase, like a salesman's sample case, which, together, contained coins and jewelry he had brought for sale. The items in those two briefcases were, according to Mr. Grimes's deposition testimony, worth approximately $110,000. He left his luggage in his room unattended for a few minutes while he returned to the lobby to learn when the display area for the show would be ready. When he returned to his room the briefcases containing the coins and jewelry were missing. He brought this action against appellees, M.H.M., Inc. and Kinark Corporation, which were doing business as the Camelot Hotel. The appellees will be referred to here as "the Camelot." Grimes's complaint alleged the Camelot was liable as an insurer of his loss and, alternatively, for negligence resulting in the loss.

A summary judgment, resulting from a motion made by the Camelot, was rendered in favor of Grimes for $300. . . .

The $300 judgment was based on the limitation of an innkeeper's liability as provided in Ark. Code Ann. § 20-26-302. We must reverse because there is an issue of fact remaining as to whether the statute applies.

. . . At common law an innkeeper was an "insurer" of the safety of baggage or other things brought into the inn by a guest except in cases of acts of God or "the public enemy." . . .

Subsections (a), (b), and (c) of § 20-26-302, which have undergone only minor changes since their original enactment as parts of Act 217, provide in relevant part:

> (a) No hotel proprietor shall be liable for the loss of or injury to baggage or other articles of property of his guest, unless the baggage or other articles of property shall have been actually delivered by the guest to the hotel proprietor or to his servants for safekeeping, or unless the loss or injury occurred through the negligence of the hotel proprietor, or by his servants or employees in the hotel.

> (b) No . . . hotelkeeper, . . . who constantly has in his . . . hotel a metal safe or suitable vault in good order and fit for the custody of money, . . . jewelry, articles of gold and silver, precious stones, personal ornaments, . . . and who keeps on the doors of the sleeping rooms used by the guests suitable locks or bolts, and on the transoms and windows of the rooms suitable fastenings, and who keeps a copy of this section printed in distinct type constantly and conspicuously posted in not less than ten (10) conspicuous places in the hotel . . . , shall be liable for the loss . . . suffered by any guest unless the guest has offered to deliver the baggage or other articles or property to the . . . hotelkeeper for custody in the metal safe or vault, and the . . . hotelkeeper has omitted or refused to take it and deposit it in the safe or vault for custody, and to give the guest a receipt therefor.

> (c) The keeper of any . . . hotel shall not be obliged to receive from any one (1) guest for deposit in a safe or vault any property hereinbefore described exceeding a total value of three hundred dollars ($300) and shall not be liable for any excess of the property, whether received or not.

All the merchandise inside the stolen briefcases fell within one of the categories enumerated in § 20-26-302(b). It is undisputed that Grimes made no effort to check the cases and that there were lock box facilities available to him. His argument, however, is that the Camelot is not entitled to this limitation on liability because its security vaults or lock boxes were unsuitable for deposit of his goods, that the locks on the doors to the Camelot rooms were unsuitable because there were numerous keys which were unaccounted for which would open the rooms, and that the Camelot had not posted the required copies of the statutory section in "ten conspicuous places in the hotel."

With respect to at least one of the conditions set out in subsection (b) of § 20-26-302 a question of fact remains. The Camelot presented no evidence showing it had posted the required copies of the statutory section in ten conspicuous places. The Camelot argues that Grimes had presented no evidence to show that the requirement was not met. Summary judgment may not be rendered, however, unless the pleadings, depositions, answers to interrogatories and admissions on file, together with the affidavits, if any, show that there is no genuine issue as to any material fact and that the moving party is entitled to a judgment as a matter of law. The only item before the trial court on the point was Grimes's deposition in which he testified he had hired a private detective who photographed the notices on the facts of the sleeping room doors in the Camelot, which were not copies of the statute, and who reported that there were no postings elsewhere in the Camelot of the required notice.

The burden of showing there is no remaining genuine issue of fact is on the party moving for summary judgment, and we view all the proof submitted in a light most favorable to the party resisting the motion. The Camelot has made no showing whatever that it complied with at least one of the prerequisites stated for limiting its liability, and thus the burden it assumed in making its summary judgment motion has not been met.

The Camelot argues, however, that subsection (c) of the statute would limit its liability regardless of the conditions stated in (b) because it provides that the innkeeper is not obliged to receive more than $300 in value of the property "hereinbefore described" and is not liable for any "excess of the property, whether received or not." That argument separates subsections (b) and (c) for consideration despite the fact that the only property "hereinbefore described" is that described in subsection (b). The two subsections must be interpreted together. It is apparent that the $300 limitation which appears in subsection (c) applies only where the innkeeper has complied with subsection (b)....

■ *Reversed and remanded.*

CASE CONCEPTS REVIEW

1. What items were stolen from Mr. Grimes?
2. Under what factual circumstances were these items stolen? (Who do you think is the thief?)
3. What limitation does the Arkansas law place on the innkeeper's liability?
4. Why is the trial court award only $300 in damages reversed? What legal ruling of the trial court is under review?

DOCUMENTS OF TITLE

16. General Concepts and Definitions

A *document of title* is broadly defined as any "document which in the regular course of business or financing is treated as adequately evidencing that the person in possession of it is entitled to receive, hold and dispose of the document *and the goods it covers*" [1-201(15)]. Such a document must indicate that it was issued by a bailee or directed to a bailee and that it covers goods in the bailee's possession.

Documents of title are covered by Article 7 of the Uniform Commercial Code. Numerous other statutes, both state and federal, also regulate the business of carriers and warehousers. The federal Bills of Lading Act, for example, controls bills of lading covering foreign exports and interstate shipments of goods. The Code does not displace such statutes. Article 7 deals only with rights related to documents of title, not to the regulation of the services rendered by carriers or warehousers.

Documents of title can serve a dual function. They may serve as receipts for goods stored or shipped, and they may be representative of the goods. In the representative capacity, they are most useful in financing commercial transactions.

Some other common terms may be defined as follows:

- *Warehouse receipt:* An acknowledgement issued by a person engaged in the business of storing goods for hire [1-201(45)]
- *Bill of lading:* A document evidencing receipt of goods for shipment
- *Issuer:* A bailee who prepares the document of title.
- *Consignor:* The person named in a bill of lading as the person from whom the goods have been received for shipment.
- *Consignee:* The person named in a bill of lading as the one to whom delivery is to be made.

Documents of title may be negotiable or nonnegotiable. The concept of negotiability for a document of title is similar to that of negotiability discussed in connection with commercial paper. The holder of a negotiable document is in a much more favorable position than he or she would be with a nonnegotiable document. The holder of a negotiable document obtains the direct obligation of the issuer to hold or deliver the goods free from most defenses and claims. In essence, the holder is so well protected that he or she can almost regard the document as the equivalent of the goods it represents.

17. Negotiation and Transfer

A warehouse receipt, bill of lading, or other document is negotiable if, by its terms, the goods are to be delivered to the bearer or to the "order of" a named person. A document not containing these "words of negotiability" is not negotiable. Thus, a bill of lading that states that goods are consigned to John Doe would not be negotiable.

Both negotiable and nonnegotiable documents can be transferred, but the method of transfer is different. A nonnegotiable document can be *assigned;* then the assignee acquires only the rights of the assignor and is subject to all defenses that are available against the assignor. The assignee is burdened with all defects in the assignor's title. *Negotiation* of a negotiable document places the transferee in a much more favorable position. If there is "due negotiation," the transferee is free from the defects of the transferor's title and the claims of third persons.

The method of negotiating a document of title depends on whether it is an order document or a bearer document. The *order* document is negotiated by indorsement and delivery; the *bearer* document, by delivery alone. The effects of blank and special indorsements are the same as those for commercial paper, and the last indorsement controls. See chapter 34 for a further discussion of indorsements.

For the holder of a negotiable document of title to have the preferred status, there must have been a due negotiation. This means not only any necessary indorsement and delivery but also that the holder must satisfy certain requirements similar to those of a holder in due course of commercial paper. The holder must have purchased the document in good faith, without notice of a defense against it or claim to it on the part of any person. He or she must have paid value for it, and the negotiation must have been in the regular course of business or financing. One to whom a document is negotiated in satisfaction or payment of a prior debt has not paid value.

If there has been due negotiation, the holder acquires title to the document, title to the goods, and the direct obligation of the issuer to hold or deliver the goods according to the terms of the document. The holder's rights cannot be defeated by any stoppage of the goods or surrender of them by the bailee. His or her rights are not impaired even if the negotiation or any prior negotiation constituted a breach of duty; even if any person has been deprived of possession of the document by misrepresentation, fraud, accident, mistake, duress, loss, theft, or conversion; and even if a previous sale or other transfer of the goods or document has been made to a third person [7-502(2)].

18. Liability of Indorsers and Transferors

The *indorser* or *transferor* of a document of title makes three warranties to the immediate purchaser. He or she warrants that

1. The document is genuine. One who purchases a forged document of title may, upon discovery of the forgery, recover from the person who sold it.
2. The indorser or transferor has no knowledge of any facts that would impair the document's validity or worth.
3. The sale of the document is rightful and fully effective with respect to the title to the document and the goods it represents. However, unless the indorser has also sold the goods, he or she does not make any additional warranties concerning the goods. If the indorser is also the seller of the goods, he or she makes the usual seller's warranties. The indorser of a document of title does not warrant performance by the bailee.

The warranties are satisfied when the purchaser obtains a good right against the warehouseperson or carrier. If the bailee has misappropriated the goods or refuses to surrender them, the holder of the document's only recourse is an action against the bailee who issued the document.

If a bank or other person has been authorized to deliver a document of title, acting as an agent for this purpose, the delivery of the document creates no warranty by the agent as to the document itself. Thus, no liability would be assumed by any such agent if the document were not genuine.

19. Obligations of Bailees under Documents of Title

A public warehouse that issues a negotiable receipt is not at liberty to surrender the goods to the original bailor unless he or she surrenders the receipt for cancellation. The receipt represents the goods and must be surrendered before the goods may be obtained. A warehouse that surrenders goods without the return of the receipt may be called on for the goods by someone who has purchased the document. The goods should be delivered only to the person who possesses the receipt, and then only if the receipt has been properly indorsed when such indorsement is required.

A bailee can refuse to deliver the goods called for by the document until payment of just charges has been made. Applicable law may actually prohibit delivery without payment.

If a receipt was complete when issued but was later altered without authority, the warehouse's liability is determined by the original terms of the document. If a receipt was issued with blanks, a good-faith purchaser of the completed receipt may recover from the warehouse that issued the incomplete receipt.

A warehouse receipt, even though it has been properly negotiated, will in one situation be inferior to the rights of a buyer of the goods represented by the receipt. When a buyer in the ordinary course of business buys fungible goods from a warehouseperson who is also engaged in the business of buying and selling such fungible goods, he or she takes the goods free of any claim under the receipt. A typical case might involve the purchase of grain from an elevator. The holder of a receipt for grain stored would have no claim to grain purchased by a person from the owner of the elevator if the owner became insolvent and unable to deliver to the receipt holder.

LEASES OF PERSONAL PROPERTY

Sections 1 through 7 of this chapter dealt with lease transactions involving real property interests. Sections 8 through 15 examined the bailment of personal property. Historically, the lease of personal property has been a transaction that courts have analyzed as being similar to leases of real property, bailments of personal property, or even sales of goods (as discussed in chapters 18 and 19). While these analogies are imperfect, the lack of volume of personal property leases kept the law from developing with such leases specifically in mind.

In recent years, the substitution of lease transactions for sales transactions has increased dramatically. Perhaps this change in how business is conducted is best illustrated by the way people interact with automobile dealers today. To make increasingly expensive cars affordable, more and more lease opportunities are offered to the public. Because of this development in the number of lease transactions, the members of the National Conference of Commissioners on Uniform State Laws drafted a new part to the Uniform Commercial Code. This draft has become Article 2A.

A detailed discussion of Article 2A is beyond the scope of this book. Nevertheless, a brief explanation of why Article 2A is likely to be adopted widely is in order. The actual language of this article is part of the UCC in the Appendix. As of 1991, seven states already have adopted Article 2A—California, Minnesota, Nevada, Oklahoma, Oregon, South Dakota, and Utah. It is anticipated that Article 2A will become a part of every state's law—like the UCC in general.

Article 2A applies to all leases regardless of the form used [2A-102]. A *lease* is a transfer of the right of possession and use of goods for a term in return for consideration [2A-103(1)(j)]. Several observations about this definition can be made. First, a gratuitous bailment is not covered by Article 2A. Second, the word *goods* here basically has the same meaning as in Article 2: items of movable personal property and fixtures. Third, sales on approval and sales or return transactions are not covered; they remain subject to sections 2-326 and 2-327. Finally, the creation of a security interest in personal property is governed by Article 9 and is not to be confused with the Article 2A provisions on leases.

While the definition of a lease is broad enough to cover all types of personal property lease transactions, some of the Article 2A sections deal with two types of specific leases. A *consumer lease* occurs anytime the lessee is an individual who enters into the lease primarily for a personal, family, or household purpose [2A-103(1)(e)]. A *finance lease,* like those used in most automobile transactions, involves a lessor that does not select, manufacture, or supply the goods [2A-103(1)(g)].

In general, Article 2A provides aspects of the law that previously had to be borrowed from other areas. Specifically, the provisions in Part 2 of Article 2A include how the personal property is formed and how it should be interpreted. The effect of a lease of goods on the lessor, lessee, sublessee, lienholders, and creditors is discussed in Part 3. Issues related to performance of the lease agreement (Part 4) and questions that might arise upon the lessor's or lessee's default (Part 5) are also resolved.

It is anticipated that Article 2A's influence will increase as both consumer and commercial transactions continue to rely more heavily on the transfer of possession of property (leases) without a transfer of title (sales).

CHAPTER SUMMARY

Classification of Leases
1. A tenancy for a stated period lasts for the time specified in the lease.
2. A tenancy from period to period may run from month to month or year to year. Such a lease often is created when a tenant holds over, with the landlord's consent, after a lease for a stated period.
3. A tenancy at will has no definite duration and can be terminated by either the landlord or tenant after proper notice is given.
4. A tenancy at sufferance occurs when a tenant holds over without the landlord's consent.

Tenants: Rights and Duties
1. In general, the tenant has the right to exclusive possession free from interference.
2. Tenant has the right to have the premises suitable for the intended use.
3. Unless the lease provides otherwise, the tenant is free to assign or sublease his or her interest to a third party. (Note that leases frequently require the landlord's approval prior to such transfer.)
4. The tenant's basic duty is to pay the rent and to return possession at the end of the lease term.

Landlords: Rights and Duties
1. The landlord has the right to expect the tenants to pay rent.
2. The landlord has legal remedies, such as distress for rent and eviction powers, to encourage the tenant's performance.
3. The landlord generally has the duty to maintain the premises. Although tenants may be liable for damages caused, the landlord cannot unreasonably retain a security deposit.

Warranty of Habitability
1. Many courts have held that landlords implicitly warrant that residential property is habitable.
2. A breach of this warranty allows the tenant to reduce rental payments or to terminate the lease without further liability.

Liability to Third Parties
1. In general, a landlord has no greater duty to protect third parties from injuries than is owed to the tenants.
2. The public-use exception means that a landlord of a business owes a higher duty to third parties than does a landlord of private premises.

Uniform Residential Landlord and Tenant Act
1. This act is an attempt to make all state laws uniform in the area of residential leases.
2. At least nineteen states have adopted substantial portions of this Act.

Required Elements
1. A bailment involves the temporary transfer of possession of personal property with the understanding that possession must be returned. There is no transfer of ownership interests.
2. A *bailor* is the owner who transfers physical possession to another person. A *bailee* is the person receiving possession who understands that the possession will be returned to the bailor or a designated party.

Types of Bailments
1. A bailment for the sole benefit of the bailor usually occurs when a bailee is not compensated.
2. A bailment for the sole benefit of the bailee is illustrated by a bailee borrowing some item of personal property.
3. A bailment for the mutual benefit of the parties is the most common in commercial transactions. Rental agreements, warehouse arrangements, and shipping contracts are examples of this third type of bailment.

Degree of Care Owed by Bailor	1. This duty of care depends on the type of bailment.
	2. In bailments for the sole benefit of the bailee, bailor must give notice of any defects of which he or she is aware.
	3. In other types of bailment, the bailor must inspect the personal property and give notice of those defects known or those that should have been discovered.

BAILEES: RIGHTS AND DUTIES

Degree of Care Owed by Bailees	1. This degree of care depends on the type of bailment.
	2. In bailments for the sole benefit of the bailor, bailees owe only slight care.
	3. In bailments for the sole benefit of the bailee, bailees owe extraordinary care.
	4. In bailments for the mutual benefit of the parties, bailees owe ordinary reasonable care.
	5. Regardless of type of bailment, the bailee must return possession to the bailor or there is a presumption of negligence.
Disclaimers of Liability by Bailees	1. Courts tend to declare disclaimers of liability, known as exculpatory clauses, invalid as against public policy.
	2. Clauses limiting a bailee's liability are viewed more favorably and are often enforced.
Other Rights and Duties of Bailees	1. A bailee is liable if the bailed property is treated in a manner contrary to the bailment agreement.
	2. A bailee may deny the bailor the property only if the bailee can prove someone else has better title to the property.
Common Carriers as Bailees	1. As a bailee, a common carrier owes a duty of absolute assurance of the property's safe delivery.
	2. A common carrier's liability is limited by five exceptions. These are damage to the property being caused by (a) an act of God, (b) an action of an alien enemy, (c) an order of public authority, (d) the inherent nature of the property, and (e) the misconduct of the shipper.
Innkeepers as Bailees	1. Originally, innkeepers were considered absolute insurers of the safety of guests and the guests' belongings.
	2. Today, most states have statutes that limit the innkeeper's liability with respect to guests' personal property.

DOCUMENTS OF TITLE

Concepts and Definitions	1. A document of title evidences the right to possess the personal property described in the document.
	2. Typical examples are bills of lading and warehouse receipts.
	3. These documents facilitate the sale and financing of personal property.
	4. Documents may be negotiable or nonnegotiable in form, with negotiable documents generally being preferable.
Negotiation and Transfer	1. A negotiable document of title may be an order document or a bearer document.
	2. Order documents are negotiated by proper indorsement and delivery.
	3. Bearer documents are negotiated by delivery alone.
Liability of Indorsers and Transferors	1. An indorser or transferor of a document of title makes three warranties.
	2. If the purchaser of the document fails to obtain the goods described in the document from the bailee, that purchaser has a cause of action against the indorser or transferor for breach of the warranties made.
	3. An agent of the bailee, indorser, or transferor makes no warranties under which the holder of the document could make the agent personally liable.

Obligations of Bailees

1. A bailee that issued a negotiable document of title can properly deliver the goods only to the person who holds a properly negotiated document.
2. A bailee may require full payment of charges prior to honoring the document of title.

LEASES OF PERSONAL PROPERTY

1. The increase in the number of lease transactions in personal property has caused Article 2A to be added to the UCC.
2. While only a few states have adopted this new article, its widespread acceptance is anticipated.
3. A lease is any transfer of possession and use of goods for a period of time in which some consideration is paid.
4. Specifically, although not limited to these types of transactions, Article 2A recognizes the increased importance of consumer leases and finance leases.

REVIEW QUESTIONS AND PROBLEMS

1. Match each term in column A with the appropriate statement in column B.

A	B
(1) Tenancy for a stated period	(a) Occurs when a tenant holds over without the landlord's consent
(2) Tenancy at will	(b) The transfer of possession but not ownership of personal property
(3) Tenancy at sufferance	(c) An absolute insurer of safe delivery of goods being transported
(4) Distress for rent	(d) A lease for a specific period of time
(5) Bailment	(e) One of the landlord's legal remedies when a tenant refuses to pay rent
(6) Bailor	(f) The owner of personal property who transfers possession to a bailee
(7) Ordinary care	(g) A lease with no stated duration that can be terminated by either the landlord or the tenant after proper notice is given
(8) Exculpatory clause	(h) A disclaimer of liability
(9) Common carrier	(i) The degree of care owed by the bailee in a bailment for the mutual benefit of the parties
(10) Document of title	(j) Properly negotiated by indorsement and delivery
(11) Order document	(k) Evidences the right to possess the described personal property

2. Lambert owned an apartment building and leased an apartment to Tammy. While Tammy was out of town, Lambert entered the apartment and found some illegal drugs. When Tammy returned, Lambert asked her to move out or face criminal prosecution. Tammy sued, claiming that Lambert had trespassed. Was Lambert guilty of trespass? Why?

3. Pearl leased a farm for cash rent to Melvin for ten years. The lease provided that "the Lessee shall have the right and privilege of subleasing or assigning this instrument provided that the consent of the Lessor is first obtained." Later when the lessee attempted to sublease the land, the lessor responded that she could "not allow a sublease of any type" and declared that she did "not intend to allow a sublease of this property." The lessee subleased anyway, and the lessor sought to terminate the lease. Is she entitled to do so? Why or why not?

4. The Kroger Company opened a supermarket as one of the original tenants of a shopping center owned by Developer's Unlimited. Kroger signed a ten-year lease. However, due to declining sales, Kroger subleased the store space to Thomas, who operated a discount department store. Thomas agreed to assume all of Kroger's obligations under the original lease. Developer's claims that Kroger's sublease to Thomas is inconsistent with the terms of the original lease. Assuming there is no clause in the lease concerning Kroger's right to assign or sublease, does Developer's have any basis for denying Thomas the right to use the store space? Explain.

5. Grocers, Inc., as a tenant, entered into a five-year lease with Properties, Unltd., as a landlord. The leased property was to be used as a grocery store. Grocers, Inc., had financial difficulties and vacated the premises when it closed the store. The landlord listed the premises with a broker, but it asked for an annual rent of $33,600, which was $12,600 greater than the rent provided in the original lease with Grocers, Inc. When the premises were not relet at the higher rent, Properties, Unltd., sued Grocers, Inc., for accrued rent. Is this landlord entitled to accrued rent? Explain.

6. Jeff and four friends leased a house owned by Amanda Hogg. At the commencement of the lease, each tenant gave Ms. Hogg $100 as a security deposit. When the lease term legally expired, these tenants asked that their deposits be returned to Jeff. Ms. Hogg was given Jeff's forwarding address. Ms. Hogg failed to send a list of damages with itemized repair costs within thirty days after the premises were vacated. Ms. Hogg also refused to refund any of the tenants' security deposits. Are these tenants entitled to receive their deposits plus damages? Why or why not?

7. Stewart, while walking on the sidewalk, tripped and fell. The sidewalk was dilapidated and in a bad state of repair. An antiques store abutted the sidewalk. Stewart sued the owner of the store for his injuries. Should Stewart recover from this store owner? Explain.

8. Miller's car was parked in a large self-service parking garage owned by the Central Parking System. The parking garage is the type where a machine automatically gives a ticket to a driver before he or she enters the garage. The driver then parks in a place of his or her choice, leaves the car, and takes the keys. The only employee on duty is the attendant who collects the money from the driver upon exiting. Miller parked his car in the garage following this procedure. The wheels were stolen from his car. Is the garage company liable for the stolen wheels without a showing of negligence? Why?

9. Noble ordered a CD player, which was delivered by United Parcel Service to his apartment building. Paulette, the receptionist/switchboard operator, signed the appropriate receipt for and received the player, and she placed it on a shelf in a small room next to her desk where packages for tenants were kept. Later the player was stolen. Noble sued the landlord for the value of his property. Has he made a prima facie case? Explain.

10. Patrick left some of his clothes at Douglas Dry Cleaners, Inc. Through no negligence of Douglas, an arsonist started a fire that destroyed the company's building and its contents. Patrick is suing to recover the value of his clothes. Should he recover? Why?

11. Lloyd Groat was licensed as a common carrier. Arnold Albrecht, a logger, hired Groat to transport a 45-ton crawler log loader from one job site to another. Some of Albrecht's employees accompanied Groat during this transfer. While the equipment was being moved, the truck carrying the loader bogged down on a steep, freshly graveled logging road. Groat and Albrecht's employees used a Caterpillar bulldozer to extract the truck from the mire. While the truck was being pulled free, the log loader came loose from the trailer. The loader cascaded down an embankment, where it came to rest in a damaged condition. Albrecht filed suit, claiming Groat was strictly liable for the damage to the log loader, since he was a common carrier. Groat contended he should be able to reduce his liability due to the negligence of Albrecht's employees, which contributed to the damaging of the loader. Is strict liability the proper standard of liability of a common carrier? Explain.

12. Core Company shipped by railroad four carloads of apples from Seattle, Washington, to Washington, D.C. The apples arrived spoiled, and Core brought suit, alleging that the negligence of the railroad caused the apples to arrive in improper condition. An employee of Core, who was not present when the apples were inspected or shipped, testified that the apples were in good condition when delivered to the carrier. His testimony was based on inspection reports of the Department of Agriculture, which were prepared six weeks prior to shipment. Should the railroad be held liable? Explain.

13. Carey was a passenger on a bus owned and operated by Jack Rabbit Lines, Inc. She was seventy-nine years old at the time she was a passenger. Upon arrival, the bus was parked twelve to eighteen inches from a curb. The area where the passengers were to unload was dimly lit. As Carey stepped off the bus, she stepped into a gutter instead of on the sidewalk, resulting in a fall. She suffered injuries to her shoulder and wrist, resulting in some permanent physical impairment. The bus driver parked twelve to eighteen inches from the curb for convenience in unloading baggage. He did not warn passengers of the danger in disembarking from the bus. Did the bus driver provide a reasonably safe place for disembarking passengers? Why?

14. Bob Baylor stored ten valuable Oriental rugs with the Bailey Warehouse Corporation. Bob received a negotiable warehouse receipt at the time the rugs were stored. Bob then transferred this receipt to Nancy by properly indorsing it. To whom is Bailey now obligated to return the rugs? Why?

THE UNIFORM COMMERCIAL CODE

ARTICLE 1 / General Provisions

Part 1   Short Title, Construction, Application and Subject Matter of the Act

§ 1-101.   Short Title. This Act shall be known and may be cited as Uniform Commercial Code.

§ 1-102.   Purposes; Rules of Construction; Variation by Agreement.

(1) This Act shall be liberally construed and applied to promote its underlying purposes and policies.

(2) Underlying purposes and policies of this Act are

   (a) to simplify, clarify and modernize the law governing commercial transactions;

   (b) to permit the continued expansion of commercial practices through custom, usage and agreement of the parties;

   (c) to make uniform the law among the various jurisdictions.

(3) The effect of provisions of this Act may be varied by agreement, except as otherwise provided in this Act and except that the obligations of good faith, diligence, reasonableness and care prescribed by this Act may not be disclaimed by agreement but the parties may by agreement determine the standards by which the performance of such obligations is to be measured if such standards are not manifestly unreasonable.

(4) The presence in certain provisions of this Act of the words "unless otherwise agreed" or words of similar import does not imply that the effect of other provisions may not be varied by agreement under subsection (3).

(5) In this Act unless the context otherwise requires

   (a) words in the singular number include the plural, and in the plural include the singular;

   (b) words of the masculine gender include the feminine and the neuter, and when the sense so indicates words of the neuter gender may refer to any gender.

§ 1-103.   Supplementary General Principles of Law Applicable. Unless displaced by the particular provisions of this Act, the principles of law and equity, including the law merchant and the law relative to capacity to contract, principal and agent, estoppel, fraud, misrepresentation, duress, coercion, mistake, bankruptcy, or other validating or invalidating cause shall supplement its provisions.

§ 1-104.   Construction Against Implicit Repeal. This Act being a general act intended as a unified coverage of its subject matter, no part of it shall be deemed to be impliedly repealed by subsequent legislation if such construction can reasonably be avoided.

§ 1-105.   Territorial Application of the Act; Parties' Power to Choose Applicable Law.

(1) Except as provided hereafter in this section, when a transaction bears a reasonable relation to this state and also to another state or nation the parties may agree that the law either of this state or of such other state or nation shall govern their rights and duties. Failing such agreement this Act applies to transactions bearing an appropriate relation to this state.

(2) Where one of the following provisions of this Act specifies the applicable law, that provision governs and a contrary agreement is effective only to the extent permitted by the law (including the conflict of laws rules) so specified:

   Rights of creditors against sold goods.   Section 2-402.

   Applicability of the Article on Leases.   Sections 2A-105 and 2A-106.

   Applicability of the Article on Bank Deposits and Collections.   Section 4-102.

   Governing law in the Article on Funds Transfers.   Section 4A-507.

   Bulk sales subject to the Article on Bulk Sales.   Section 6-103.

   Applicability of the Article on Investment Securities. Section 8-106.

Perfection provisions of the Article on Secured
Transactions.   Section 9-103.

As amended in 1972, 1987, 1988 and 1989.

§ 1-106.   Remedies to Be Liberally Administered.

(1) The remedies provided by this Act shall be liberally administered to the end that the aggrieved party may be put in
as good a position as if the other party had fully performed
but neither consequential or special nor penal damages may
be had except as specifically provided in this Act or by other
rule of law.

(2) Any right or obligation declared by this Act is enforceable by action unless the provision declaring it specifies a different and limited effect.

§ 1-107.   Waiver or Renunciation of Claim or Right
After Breach. Any claim or right arising out of an alleged
breach can be discharged in whole or in part without consideration by a written waiver or renunciation signed and delivered by the aggrieved party.

§ 1-108.   Severability. If any provision or clause of this Act
or application thereof to any person or circumstances is held
invalid, such invalidity shall not affect other provisions or applications of the Act which can be given effect without the invalid provision or application, and to this end the provisions
of this Act are declared to be severable.

§ 1-109.   Section Captions. Section captions are parts of
this Act.

Part 2   General Definitions and Principles of Inter-
pretation

§ 1-201.   General Definitions. Subject to additional defi-
nitions contained in the subsequent Articles of this Act
which are applicable to specific Articles or Parts thereof, and
unless the context otherwise requires, in this Act:

(1) "Action" in the sense of a judicial proceeding includes
recoupment, counterclaim, set-off, suit in equity and any
other proceedings in which rights are determined.

(2) "Aggrieved party" means a party entitled to resort to a
remedy.

(3) "Agreement" means the bargain of the parties in fact as
found in their language or by implication from other circumstances including course of dealing or usage of trade or course
of performance as provided in this Act (Sections 1-205 and
2-208). Whether an agreement has legal consequences is determined by the provisions of this Act, if applicable; otherwise by the law of contracts (Section 1-103). (Compare
"Contract".)

(4) "Bank" means any person engaged in the business of
banking.

(5) "Bearer" means the person in possession of an instrument, document of title, or certificated security payable to
bearer or indorsed in blank.

(6) "Bill of lading" means a document evidencing the receipt
of goods for shipment issued by a person engaged in the business of transporting or forwarding goods, and includes an
airbill. "Airbill" means a document serving for air transporta-

tion as a bill of lading does for marine or rail transportation,
and includes an air consignment note or air waybill.

(7) "Branch" includes a separately incorporated foreign
branch of a bank.

(8) "Burden of establishing" a fact means the burden of per-
suading the triers of fact that the existence of the fact is more
probable than its non-existence.

(9) "Buyer in ordinary course of business" means a person
who in good faith and without knowledge that the sale to him
is in violation of the ownership rights or security interest of a
third party in the goods buys in ordinary course from a person
in the business of selling goods of that kind but does not include a pawnbroker. All persons who sell minerals or the like
(including oil and gas) at wellhead or minehead shall be
deemed to be persons in the business of selling goods of that
kind. "Buying" may be for cash or by exchange of other property or on secured or unsecured credit and includes receiving
goods or documents of title under a pre-existing contract for
sale but does not include a transfer in bulk or as security for
or in total or partial satisfaction of a money debt.

(10) "Conspicuous": A term of clause is conspicuous when
it is so written that a reasonable person against whom it is to
operate ought to have noticed it. A printed heading in capitals (as: NON-NEGOTIABLE BILL OF LADING) is conspicuous. Language in the body of a form is "conspicuous" if
it is in larger or other contrasting type or color. But in a telegram any stated term is "conspicuous". Whether a term or
clause is "conspicuous" or not is for decision by the court.

(11) "Contract" means the total legal obligation which results from the parties' agreement as affected by this Act and
any other applicable rules of law. (Compare "Agreement".)

(12) "Creditor" includes a general creditor, a secured creditor, a lien creditor and any representative of creditors, including an assignee for the benefit of creditors, a trustee in
bankruptcy, a receiver in equity and an executor or administrator of an insolvent debtor's or assignor's estate.

(13) "Defendant" includes a person in the position of defendant in a cross-action or counterclaim.

(14) "Delivery" with respect to instruments, documents of
title, chattel paper, or certificated securities means voluntary
transfer of possession.

(15) "Document of title" includes bill of lading, dock warrant, dock receipt, warehouse receipt or order for the delivery
of goods, and also any other document which in the regular
course of business or financing is treated as adequately evidencing that the person in possession of it is entitled to receive, hold and dispose of the document and the goods it
covers. To be a document of title a document must purport to
be issued by or addressed to a bailee and purport to cover
goods in the bailee's possession which are either identified or
are fungible portions of an identified mass.

(16) "Fault" means wrongful act, omission or breach.

(17) "Fungible" with respect to goods or securities means
goods or securities of which any unit is, by nature or usage of
trade, the equivalent of any other like unit. Goods which are
not fungible shall be deemed fungible for the purposes of this
Act to the extent that under a particular agreement or document unlike units are treated as equivalents.

(18) "Genuine" means free of forgery or counterfeiting.

(19) "Good faith" means honesty in fact in the conduct or transaction concerned.

(20) "Holder," with respect to a negotiable instrument, means the person in possession if the instrument is payable to bearer or, in the case of an instrument payable to an identified person, if the identified person is in possession. "Holder" with respect to a document of title means the person in possession if the goods are deliverable to bearer or to the order of the person in possession.

(21) To "honor" is to pay or to accept and pay, or where a credit so engages to purchase or discount a draft complying with the terms of the credit.

(22) "Insolvency proceedings" includes any assignment for the benefit of creditors or other proceedings intended to liquidate or rehabilitate the estate of the person involved.

(23) A person is "insolvent" who either has ceased to pay his debts in the ordinary course of business or cannot pay his debts as they become due or is insolvent within the meaning of the federal bankruptcy law.

(24) "Money" means a medium of exchange authorized or adopted by a domestic or foreign government and includes a monetary unit of account established by an intergovernmental organization or by agreement between two or more nations.

(25) A person has "notice" of a fact when

(a) he has actual knowledge of it; or

(b) he has received a notice or notification of it; or

(c) from all the facts and circumstances known to him at the time in question he has reason to know that it exists.

A person "knows" or has "knowledge" of a fact when he has actual knowledge of it. "Discover" or "learn" or a word or phrase of similar import refers to knowledge rather than to reason to know. The time and circumstances under which a notice or notification may cease to be effective are not determined by this Act.

(26) A person "notifies" or "gives" a notice or notification to another by taking such steps as may be reasonably required to inform the other in ordinary course whether or not such other actually comes to know of it. A person "receives" a notice or notification when

(a) it comes to his attention; or

(b) it is duly delivered at the place of business through which the contract was made or at any other place held out by him as the place for receipt of such communications.

(27) Notice, knowledge or a notice or notification received by an organization is effective for a particular transaction from the time when it is brought to the attention of the individual conducting that transaction, and in any event from the time when it would have been brought to his attention if the organization had exercised due diligence. An organization exercises due diligence if it maintains reasonable routines for communicating significant information to the person conducting the transaction and there is reasonable compliance with the routines. Due diligence does not require an individual acting for the organization to communicate information unless such communication is part of his regular duties or unless he has reason to know of the transaction and that the transaction would be materially affected by the information.

(28) "Organization" includes a corporation, government or governmental subdivision or agency, business trust, estate, trust, partnership or association, two or more persons having a joint or common interest, or any other legal or commercial entity.

(29) "Party", as distinct from "third party", means a person who has engaged in a transaction or made an agreement within this Act.

(30) "Person" includes an individual or an organization (See Section 1-102).

(31) "Presumption" or "presumed" means that the trier of fact must find the existence of the fact presumed unless and until evidence is introduced which would support a finding of its nonexistence.

(32) "Purchase" includes taking by sale, discount, negotiation, mortgage, pledge, lien, issue or re-issue, gift or any other voluntary transaction creating an interest in property.

(33) "Purchaser" means a person who takes by purchase.

(34) "Remedy" means any remedial right to which an aggrieved party is entitled with or without resort to a tribunal.

(35) "Representative" includes an agent, an officer of a corporation or association, and a trustee, executor or administrator of an estate, or any other person empowered to act for another.

(36) "Rights" includes remedies.

(37) "Security interest" means an interest in personal property or fixtures which secures payment or performance of an obligation. The retention or reservation of title by a seller of goods notwithstanding shipment or delivery to the buyer (Section 2-401) is limited in effect to a reservation of a "security interest". The term also includes any interest of a buyer of accounts or chattel paper which is subject to Article 9. The special property interest of a buyer of goods on identification of those goods to a contract for sale under Section 2-401 is not a "security interest", but a buyer may also acquire a "security interest" by complying with Article 9. Unless a consignment is intended as security, reservation of title thereunder is not a "security interest", but a consignment in any event is subject to the provisions on consignment sales (Section 2-326).

Whether a transaction creates a lease or security interest is determined by the facts of each case; however, a transaction creates a security interest if the consideration the lessee is to pay the lessor for the right to possession and use of the goods is an obligation for the term of the lease not subject to termination by the lessee, and

(a) the original term of the lease is equal to or greater than the remaining economic life of the goods,

(b) the lessee is bound to renew the lease for the remaining economic life of the goods or is bound to become the owner of the goods,

(c) the lessee has an option to renew the lease for the remaining economic life of the goods for no additional consideration or nominal additional consideration upon compliance with the lease agreement, or

(d) the lessee has an option to become the owner of the goods for no additional consideration or nominal additional consideration upon compliance with the lease agreement.

A transaction does not create a security interest merely because it provides that

(a) the present value of the consideration the lessee is obligated to pay the lessor for the right to possession and use of the goods is substantially equal to or is greater than the fair market value of the goods at the time the lease is entered into,

(b) the lessee assumes risk of loss of the goods, or agrees to pay taxes, insurance, filing, recording, or registration fees, or service or maintenance costs with respect to the goods,

(c) the lessee has an option to renew the lease or to become the owner of the goods,

(d) the lessee has an option to renew the lease for a fixed rent that is equal to or greater than the reasonably predictable fair market rent for the use of the goods for the term of the renewal at the time the option is to be performed, or

(e) the lessee has an option to become the owner of the goods for a fixed price that is equal to or greater than the reasonably predictable fair market value of the goods at the time the option is to be performed.

For purposes of this subsection (37):

(x) Additional consideration is not nominal if (i) when the option to renew the lease is granted to the lessee the rent is stated to be the fair market rent for the use of the goods for the term of the renewal determined at the time the option is to be performed, or (ii) when the option to become the owner of the goods is granted to the lessee the price is stated to be the fair market value of the goods determined at the time the option is to be performed. Additional consideration is nominal if it is less than the lessee's reasonably predictable cost of performing under the lease agreement if the option is not exercised;

(y) "Reasonably predictable" and "remaining economic life of the goods" are to be determined with reference to the facts and circumstances at the time the transaction is entered into; and

(z) "Present value" means the amount as of a date certain of one or more sums payable in the future, discounted to the date certain. The discount is determined by the interest rate specified by the parties if the rate is not manifestly unreasonable at the time the transaction is entered into; otherwise, the discount is determined by a commercially reasonable rate that takes into account the facts and circumstances of each case at the time the transaction was entered into.

(38) "Send" in connection with any writing or notice means to deposit in the mail or deliver for transmission by any other usual means of communication with postage or cost of transmission provided for and properly addressed and in the case of an instrument to an address specified thereon or otherwise agreed, or if there be none to any address reasonable under the circumstances. The receipt of any writing or notice within the time at which it would have arrived if properly sent has the effect of a proper sending.

(39) "Signed" includes any symbol executed or adopted by a party with present intention to authenticate a writing.

(40) "Surety" includes guarantor.

(41) "Telegram" includes a message transmitted by radio, teletype, cable, any mechanical method of transmission, or the like.

(42) "Term" means that portion of an agreement which relates to a particular matter.

(43) "Unauthorized" signature means one made without actual, implied, or apparent authority and includes a forgery.

(44) "Value". Except as otherwise provided with respect to negotiable instruments and bank collections (Sections 3-303, 4-208 and 4-209) a person gives "value" for rights if he acquires them

(a) in return for a binding commitment to extend credit or for the extension of immediately available credit whether or not drawn upon and whether or not a charge-back is provided for in the event of difficulties in collection; or

(b) as security for or in total or partial satisfaction of a pre-existing claim; or

(c) by accepting delivery pursuant to a pre-existing contract for purchase; or

(d) generally, in return for any consideration sufficient to support a simple contract.

(45) "Warehouse receipt" means a receipt issued by a person engaged in the business of storing goods for hire.

(46) "Written" or "writing" includes printing, typewriting or any other intentional reduction to tangible form.

As amended in 1962, 1972, 1977, 1987 and 1990.

§ 1-202. **Prima Facie Evidence by Third Party Documents.** A document in due form purporting to be a bill of lading, policy or certificate of insurance, official weigher's or inspector's certificate, consular invoice, or any other document authorized or required by the contract to be issued by a third party shall be prima facie evidence of its own authenticity and genuineness and of the facts stated in the document by the third party.

§ 1-203. **Obligation of Good Faith.** Every contract or duty within this Act imposes an obligation of good faith in its performance or enforcement.

§ 1-204. **Time; Reasonable Time; "Seasonably".**

(1) Whenever this Act requires any action to be taken within a reasonable time, any time which is not manifestly unreasonable may be fixed by agreement.

(2) What is a reasonable time for taking any action depends on the nature, purpose and circumstances of such action.

(3) An action is taken "seasonably" when it is taken at or within the time agreed or if no time is agreed at or within a reasonable time.

§ 1-205. **Course of Dealing and Usage of Trade.**

(1) A course of dealing is a sequence of previous conduct between the parties to a particular transaction which is fairly to be regarded as establishing a common basis of understanding for interpreting their expressions and other conduct.

(2) A usage of trade is any practice or method of dealing hav-

ing such regularity of observance in a place, vocation or trade as to justify an expectation that it will be observed with respect to the transaction in question. The existence and scope of such a usage are to be proved as facts. If it is established that such a usage is embodied in a written trade code or similar writing the interpretation of the writing is for the court.

(3) A course of dealing between parties and any usage of trade in the vocation or trade in the vocation or trade in which they are engaged or of which they are or should be aware give particular meaning to and supplement or qualify terms of an agreement.

(4) The express terms of an agreement and an applicable course of dealing or usage of trade shall be construed wherever reasonable as consistent with each other; but when such construction is unreasonable express terms control both course of dealing and usage of trade and course of dealing controls usage of trade.

(5) An applicable usage of trade in the place where any part of performance is to occur shall be used in interpreting the agreement as to that part of the performance.

(6) Evidence of a relevant usage of trade offered by one party is not admissible unless and until he has given the other party such notice as the court finds sufficient to prevent unfair surprise to the latter.

§ 1-206. Statute of Frauds for Kinds of Personal Property Not Otherwise Covered.

(1) Except in the cases described in subsection (2) of this section a contract for the sale of personal property is not enforceable by way of action or defense beyond five thousand dollars in amount or value of remedy unless there is some writing which indicates that a contract for sale has been made between the parties at a defined or stated price, reasonably identifies the subject matter, and is signed by the party against whom enforcement is sought or by his authorized agent.

(2) Subsection (1) of this section does not apply to contracts for the sale of goods (Section 2-201) nor of securities (Section 8-319) nor to security agreements (Section 9-203).

§ 1-207. Performance or Acceptance Under Reservation of Rights.

(1) A party who, with explicit reservation of rights performs or promises performance or assents to performance in a manner demanded or offered by the other party does not thereby prejudice the rights reserved. Such words as "without prejudice", "under protest" or the like are sufficient.

(2) Subsection (1) does not apply to an accord and satisfaction.

As amended in 1990.

§ 1-208. Option to Accelerate at Will. A term providing that one party or his successor in interest may accelerate payment or performance or require collateral or additional collateral "at will" or "when he deems himself insecure" or in words of similar import shall be construed to mean that he shall have power to do so only if he in good faith believes that the prospect of payment or performance is impaired. The burden of establishing lack of good faith is on the party against whom the power has been exercised.

§ 1-209. Subordinated Obligations. An obligation may be issued as subordinated to payment of another obligation of the person obligated, or a creditor may subordinate his right to payment of an obligation by agreement with either the person obligated or another creditor of the person obligated. Such a subordination does not create a security interest as against either the common debtor or a subordinated creditor. This section shall be construed as declaring the law as it existed prior to the enactment of this section and not as modifying it. Added 1966.

Note: *This new section is proposed as an optional provision to make it clear that a subordination agreement does not create a security interest unless so intended.*

ARTICLE 2 / Sales

Part 1   Short Title, General Construction and Subject Matter

§ 2-101. Short Title. This Article shall be known and may be cited as Uniform Commercial Code—Sales.

§ 2-102. Scope; Certain Security and Other Transactions Excluded From This Article. Unless the context otherwise requires, this Article applies to transactions in goods; it does not apply to any transaction which although in the form of an unconditional contract to sell or present sale is intended to operate only as a security transaction nor does this Article impair or repeal any statute regulating sales to consumers, farmers or other specified classes of buyers.

§ 2-103. Definitions and Index of Definitions.

(1) In this Article unless the context otherwise requires

(a) "Buyer" means a person who buys or contracts to buy goods.
(b) "Good faith" in the case of a merchant means honesty in fact and the observance of reasonable commercial standards of fair dealing in the trade.
(c) "Receipt" of goods means taking physical possession of them.
(d) "Seller" means a person who sells or contracts to sell goods.

(2) Other definitions applying to this Article or to specified Parts thereof, and the sections in which they appear are:

"Acceptance".   Section 2-606.
"Banker's credit".   Section 2-325.
"Between merchants".   Section 2-104.
"Cancellation".   Section 2-106(4).
"Commercial unit".   Section 2-105.
"Confirmed credit".   Section 2-325.
"Conforming to contract".   Section 2-106.
"Contract for sale".   Section 2-106.
"Cover".   Section 2-712.
"Entrusting".   Section 2-403.
"Financing agency".   Section 2-104.
"Future goods".   Section 2-105.
"Goods".   Section 2-105.
"Identification".   Section 2-501.
"Installment contract".   Section 2-612.
"Letter of Credit".   Section 2-325.

"Lot".   Section 2-105.
"Merchant".   Section 2-104.
"Overseas".   Section 2-323.
"Person in position of seller".   Section 2-707.
"Present sale".   Section 2-106.
"Sale".   Section 2-106.
"Sale on approval".   Section 2-326.
"Sale or return".   Section 2-326.
"Termination".   Section 2-106.

(3) The following definitions in other Articles apply to this Article:

"Check".   Section 3-104.
"Consignee".   Section 7-102.
"Consignor".   Section 7-102.
"Consumer goods".   Section 9-109.
"Dishonor".   Section 3-507.
"Draft".   Section 3-104.

(4) In addition Article 1 contains general definitions and principles of construction and interpretation applicable throughout this Article.

§ 2-104. Definitions: "Merchant"; "Between Merchants"; "Financing Agency".

(1) "Merchant" means a person who deals in goods of the kind or otherwise by his occupation holds himself out as having knowledge or skill peculiar to the practices or goods involved in the transaction or to whom such knowledge or skill may be attributed by his employment of an agent or broker or other intermediary who by his occupation holds himself out as having such knowledge or skill.

(2) "Financing agency" means a bank, finance company or other person who in the ordinary course of business makes advances against goods or documents of title or who by arrangement with either the seller or the buyer intervenes in ordinary course to make or collect payment due or claimed under the contract for sale, as by purchasing or paying the seller's draft or making advances against it or by merely taking it for collection whether or not documents of title accompany the draft. "Financing agency" includes also a bank or other person who similarly intervenes between persons who are in the position of seller and buyer in respect to the goods (Section 2-707).

(3) "Between merchants" means in any transaction with respect to which both parties are chargeable with the knowledge or skill of merchants.

§ 2-105. Definitions: Transferability; "Goods"; "Future" Goods; "Lot"; "Commercial Unit".

(1) "Goods" means all things (including specially manufactured goods) which are movable at the time of identification to the contract for sale other than the money in which the price is to be paid, investment securities (Article 8) and things in action. "Goods" also includes the unborn young of animals and growing crops and other identified things attached to realty as described in the section on goods to be severed from realty (Section 2-107).

(2) Goods must be both existing and identified before any interest in them can pass. Goods which are not both existing and identified are "future" goods. A purported present sale of future goods or of any interest therein operates as a contract to sell.

(3) There may be a sale of a part interest in existing identified goods.

(4) An undivided share in an identified bulk of fungible goods is sufficiently identified to be sold although the quantity of the bulk is not determined. Any agreed proportion of such a bulk or any quantity thereof agreed upon by number, weight or other measure may to the extent of the seller's interest in the bulk be sold to the buyer who then becomes an owner in common.

(5) "Lot" means a parcel or a single article which is the subject matter of a separate sale or delivery, whether or not it is sufficient to perform the contract.

(6) "Commercial unit" means such a unit of goods as by commercial usage is a single whole for purposes of sale and division of which materially impairs its character or value on the market or in use. A commercial unit may be a single article (as a machine) or a set of articles (as a suite of furniture or an assortment of sizes) or a quantity (as a bale, gross, or carload) or any other unit treated in use or in the relevant market as a single whole.

§ 2-106. Definitions: "Contract"; "Agreement"; "Contract for Sale"; "Sale"; "Present Sale"; "Conforming" to Contract; "Termination"; "Cancellation".

(1) In this Article unless the context otherwise requires "contract" and "agreement" are limited to those relating to the present or future sale of goods. "Contract for sale" includes both a present sale of goods and a contract to sell goods at a future time. A "sale" consists in the passing of title from the seller to the buyer for a price (Section 2-401). A "present sale" means a sale which is accomplished by the making of the contract.

(2) Goods or conduct including any part of a performance are "conforming" or conform to the contract when they are in accordance with the obligations under the contract.

(3) "Termination" occurs when either party pursuant to a power created by agreement or law puts an end to the contract otherwise than for its breach. On "termination" all obligations which are still executory on both sides are discharged but any right based on prior breach or performance survives.

(4) "Cancellation" occurs when either party puts an end to the contract for breach by the other and its effect is the same as that of "termination" except that the cancelling party also retains any remedy for breach of the whole contract or any unperformed balance.

§ 2-107. Goods to Be Severed From Realty: Recording.

(1) A contract for the sale of minerals or the like (including oil and gas) or a structure or its materials to be removed from realty is a contract for the sale of goods within this Article if they are to be severed by the seller but until severance a purported present sale thereof which is not effective as a transfer of an interest in land is effective only as a contract to sell.

(2) A contract for the sale apart from the land of growing crops or other things attached to realty and capable of severance without material harm thereto but not described in subsection (1) or of timber to be cut is a contract for the sale of goods within this Article whether the subject matter is to be

severed by the buyer or by the seller even though it forms part of the realty at the time of contracting, and the parties can by identification effect a present sale before severance.

(3) The provisions of this section are subject to any third party rights provided by the law relating to realty records, and the contract for sale may be executed and recorded as a document transferring an interest in land and shall then constitute notice to third parties of the buyer's rights under the contract for sale.

As amended in 1972.

Part 2 Form, Formation and Readjustment of Contract

§ 2-201. Formal Requirements; Statute of Frauds.
(1) Except as otherwise provided in this section a contract for the sale of goods for the price of $500 or more is not enforceable by way of action or defense unless there is some writing sufficient to indicate that a contract for sale has been made between the parties and signed by the party against whom enforcement is sought or by his authorized agent or broker. A writing is not insufficient because it omits or incorrectly states a term agreed upon but the contract is not enforceable under this paragraph beyond the quantity of goods shown in such writing.

(2) Between merchants if within a reasonable time a writing in confirmation of the contract and sufficient against the sender is received and the party receiving it has reason to know its contents, it satisfies the requirements of subsection (1) against such party unless written notice of objection to its contents is given within 10 days after it is received.

(3) A contract which does not satisfy the requirements of subsection (1) but which is valid in other respects is enforceable

   (a) if the goods are to be specially manufactured for the buyer and are not suitable for sale to others in the ordinary course of the seller's business and the seller, before notice of repudiation is received and under circumstances which reasonably indicate that the goods are for the buyer, has made either a substantial beginning of their manufacture or commitments for their procurement; or

   (b) if the party against whom enforcement is sought admits in his pleading, testimony or otherwise in court that a contract for sale was made, but the contract is not enforceable under this provision beyond the quantity of goods admitted; or

   (c) with respect to goods for which payment has been made and accepted or which have been received and accepted (Sec. 2-606).

§ 2-202. Final Written Expression: Parol or Extrinsic Evidence.
Terms with respect to which the confirmatory memoranda of the parties agree or which are otherwise set forth in a writing intended by the parties as a final expression of their agreement with respect to such terms as are included therein may not be contradicted by evidence of any prior agreement or of a contemporaneous oral agreement but may be explained or supplemented

(a) by course of dealing or usage of trade (Section 1-205) or by course of performance (Section 2-208); and

(b) by evidence of consistent additional terms unless the court finds the writing to have been intended also as a complete and exclusive statement of the terms of the agreement.

§ 2-203. Seals Inoperative.
The affixing of a seal to a writing evidencing a contract for sale or an offer to buy or sell goods does not constitute the writing a sealed instrument and the law with respect to sealed instruments does not apply to such a contract or offer.

§ 2-204. Formation in General.
(1) A contract for sale of goods may be made in any manner sufficient to show agreement, including conduct by both parties which recognizes the existence of such a contract.

(2) An agreement sufficient to constitute a contract for sale may be found even though the moment of its making is undetermined.

(3) Even though one or more terms are left open a contract for sale does not fail for indefiniteness if the parties have intended to make a contract and there is a reasonably certain basis for giving an appropriate remedy.

§ 2-205. Firm Offers.
An offer by a merchant to buy or sell goods in a signed writing which by its terms gives assurance that it will be held open is not revocable, for lack of consideration, during the time stated or if no time is stated for a reasonable time, but in no event may such period of irrevocability exceed three months; but any such term of assurance on a form supplied by the offeree must be separately signed by the offeror.

§ 2-206. Offer and Acceptance in Formation of Contract.
(1) Unless otherwise unambiguously indicated by the language or circumstances

   (a) an offer to make a contract shall be construed as inviting acceptance in any manner and by any medium reasonable in the circumstances;

   (b) an order or other offer to buy goods for prompt or current shipment shall be construed as inviting acceptance either by a prompt promise to ship or by the prompt or current shipment of conforming or non-conforming goods, but such a shipment of non-conforming goods does not constitute an acceptance if the seller seasonably notifies the buyer that the shipment is offered only as an accommodation to the buyer.

(2) Where the beginning of a requested performance is a reasonable mode of acceptance an offeror who is not notified of acceptance within a reasonable time may treat the offer as having lapsed before acceptance.

§ 2-207. Additional Terms in Acceptance or Confirmation.
(1) A definite and seasonable expression of acceptance or a written confirmation which is sent within a reasonable time operates as an acceptance even though it states terms additional to or different from those offered or agreed upon, unless acceptance is expressly made conditional on assent to the additional or different terms.

(2) The additional terms are to be construed as proposals for addition to the contract. Between merchants such terms become part of the contract unless:

(a) the offer expressly limits acceptance to the terms of the offer;

(b) they materially alter it; or

(c) notification of objection to them has already been given or is given within a reasonable time after notice of them is received.

(3) Conduct by both parties which recognizes the existence of a contract is sufficient to establish a contract for sale although the writings of the parties do not otherwise establish a contract. In such case the terms of the particular contract consist of those terms on which the writings of the parties agree, together with any supplementary terms incorporated under any other provisions of this Act.

§ 2-208. Course of Performance or Practical Construction.

(1) Where the contract for sale involves repeated occasions for performance by either party with knowledge of the nature of the performance and opportunity for objection to it by the other, any course of performance accepted or acquiesced in without objection shall be relevant to determine the meaning of the agreement.

(2) The express terms of the agreement and any such course of performance, as well as any course of dealing and usage of trade, shall be construed whenever reasonable as consistent with each other; but when such construction is unreasonable, express terms shall control course of performance and course of performance shall control both course of dealing and usage of trade (Section 1-205).

(3) Subject to the provisions of the next section on modification and waiver, such course of performance shall be relevant to show a waiver or modification of any term inconsistent with such course of performance.

§ 2-209. Modification, Rescission and Waiver.

(1) An agreement modifying a contract within this Article needs no consideration to be binding.

(2) A signed agreement which excludes modification or rescission except by a signed writing cannot be otherwise modified or rescinded, but except as between merchants such a requirement on a form supplied by the merchant must be separately signed by the other party.

(3) The requirements of the statute of frauds section of this Article (Section 2-201) must be satisfied if the contract as modified is within its provisions.

(4) Although an attempt at modification or rescission does not satisfy the requirements of subsection (2) or (3) it can operate as a waiver.

(5) A party who has made a waiver affecting an executory portion of the contract may retract the waiver by reasonable notification received by the other party that strict performance will be required of any term waived, unless the retraction would be unjust in view of a material change of position in reliance on the waiver.

§ 2-210. Delegation of Performance; Assignment of Rights.

(1) A party may perform his duty through a delegate unless otherwise agreed or unless the other party has a substantial interest in having his original promisor perform or control the acts required by the contract. No delegation of performance relieves the party delegating of any duty to perform or any liability for breach.

(2) Unless otherwise agreed all rights of either seller or buyer can be assigned except where the assignment would materially change the duty of the other party, or increase materially the burden or risk imposed on him by his contract, or impair materially his chance of obtaining return performance. A right to damages for breach of the whole contract or a right arising out of the assignor's due performance of his entire obligation can be assigned despite agreement otherwise.

(3) Unless the circumstances indicate the contrary a prohibition of assignment of "the contract" is to be construed as barring only the delegation to the assignee of the assignor's performance.

(4) An assignment of "the contract" or of "all my rights under the contract" or an assignment in similar general terms is an assignment of rights and unless the language or the circumstances (as in an assignment for security) indicate the contrary, it is a delegation of performance of the duties of the assignor and its acceptance by the assignee constitutes a promise by him to perform those duties. This promise is enforceable by either the assignor or the other party to the original contract.

(5) The other party may treat any assignment which delegates performance as creating reasonable grounds for insecurity and may without prejudice to his rights against the assignor demand assurances from the assignee (Section 2-609).

Part 3 General Obligation and Construction of Contract

§ 2-301. General Obligations of Parties. The obligation of the seller is to transfer and deliver and that of the buyer is to accept and pay in accordance with the contract.

§ 2-302. Unconscionable Contract or Clause.

(1) If the court as a matter of law finds the contract or any clause of the contract to have been unconscionable at the time it was made the court may refuse to enforce the contract, or it may enforce the remainder of the contract without the unconscionable clause, or it may so limit the application of any unconscionable clause as to avoid any unconscionable result.

(2) When it is claimed or appears to the court that the contract or any clause thereof may be unconscionable the parties shall be afforded a reasonable opportunity to present evidence as to its commercial setting, purpose and effect to aid the court in making the determination.

§ 2-303. Allocation or Division of Risks. Where this Article allocates a risk or a burden as between the parties "unless otherwise agreed", the agreement may not only shift the allocation but may also divide the risk or burden.

§ 2-304. Price Payable in Money, Goods, Realty, or Otherwise.

(1) The price can be made payable in money or otherwise. If it is payable in whole or in part in goods each party is a seller of the goods which he is to transfer.

(2) Even though all or part of the price is payable in an inter-

est in realty the transfer of the goods and the seller's obligations with reference to them are subject to this Article, but not the transfer of the interest in realty or the transferor's obligations in connection therewith.

§ 2-305. Open Price Term.

(1) The parties if they so intend can conclude a contract for sale even though the price is not settled. In such a case the price is a reasonable price at the time for delivery if

(a) nothing is said as to price; or

(b) the price is left to be agreed by the parties and they fail to agree; or

(c) the price is to be fixed in terms of some agreed market or other standard as set or recorded by a third person or agency and it is not so set or recorded.

(2) A price to be fixed by the seller or by the buyer means a price for him to fix in good faith.

(3) When a price left to be fixed otherwise than by agreement of the parties fails to be fixed through fault of one party the other may at his option treat the contract as cancelled or himself fix a reasonable price.

(4) Where, however, the parties intend not to be bound unless the price be fixed or agreed and it is not fixed or agreed there is no contract. In such a case the buyer must return any goods already received or if unable so to do must pay their reasonable value at the time of delivery and the seller must return any portion of the price paid on account.

§ 2-306. Output, Requirements and Exclusive Dealings.

(1) A term which measures the quantity by the output of the seller or the requirements of the buyer means such actual output or requirements as may occur in good faith, except that no quantity unreasonably disproportionate to any stated estimate or in the absence of a stated estimate to any normal or otherwise comparable prior output or requirements may be tendered or demanded.

(2) A lawful agreement by either the seller or the buyer for exclusive dealing in the kind of goods concerned imposes unless otherwise agreed an obligation by the seller to use best efforts to supply the goods and by the buyer to use best efforts to promote their sale.

§ 2-307. Delivery in Single Lot or Several Lots. Unless otherwise agreed all goods called for by a contract for sale must be tendered in a single delivery and payment is due only on such tender but where the circumstances give either party the right to make or demand delivery in lots the price if it can be apportioned may be demanded for each lot.

§ 2-308. Absence of Specified Place for Delivery. Unless otherwise agreed

(a) the place for delivery of goods is the seller's place of business or if he has none his residence; but

(b) in a contract for sale of identified goods which to the knowledge of the parties at the time of contracting are in some other place, that place is the place for their delivery; and

(c) documents of title may be delivered through customary banking channels.

§ 2-309. Absence of Specific Time Provisions; Notice of Termination.

(1) The time for shipment or delivery or any other action under a contract if not provided in this Article or agreed upon shall be a reasonable time.

(2) Where the contract provides for successive performances but is indefinite in duration it is valid for a reasonable time but unless otherwise agreed may be terminated at any time by either party.

(3) Termination of a contract by one party except on the happening of an agreed event requires that reasonable notification be received by the other party and an agreement dispensing with notification is invalid if its operation would be unconscionable.

§ 2-310. Open Time for Payment or Running of Credit; Authority to Ship Under Reservation. Unless otherwise agreed

(a) payment is due at the time and place at which the buyer is to receive the goods even though the place of shipment is the place of delivery; and

(b) if the seller is authorized to send the goods he may ship them under reservation, and may tender the documents of title, but the buyer may inspect the goods after their arrival before payment is due unless such inspection is inconsistent with the terms of the contract (Section 2-513); and

(c) if delivery is authorized and made by way of documents of title otherwise than by subsection (b) then payment is due at the time and place at which the buyer is to receive the documents regardless of where the goods are to be received; and

(d) where the seller is required or authorized to ship the goods on credit the credit period runs from the time of shipment but post-dating the invoice or delaying its dispatch will correspondingly delay the starting of the credit period.

§ 2-311. Options and Cooperation Respecting Performance.

(1) An agreement for sale which is otherwise sufficiently definite (subsection (3) of Section 2-204) to be a contract is not made invalid by the fact that it leaves particulars of performance to be specified by one of the parties. Any such specification must be made in good faith and within limits set by commercial reasonableness.

(2) Unless otherwise agreed specifications relating to assortment of the goods are at the buyer's option and except as otherwise provided in subsections (1)(c) and (3) of Section 2-319 specifications or arrangements relating to shipment are at the seller's option.

(3) Where such specification would materially affect the other party's performance but is not seasonably made or where one party's cooperation is necessary to the agreed performance of the other but is not seasonably forthcoming, the other party in addition to all other remedies

(a) is excused for any resulting delay in his own performance; and

(b) may also either proceed to perform in any reasonable manner or after the time for a material part of his own performance treat the failure to specify or to cooperate as a breach by failure to deliver or accept the goods.

§ 2-312. Warranty of Title and Against Infringement; Buyer's Obligation Against Infringement.

(1) Subject to subsection (2) there is in a contract for sale a warranty by the seller that

(a) the title conveyed shall be good, and its transfer rightful; and

(b) the goods shall be delivered free from any security interest or other lien or encumbrance of which the buyer at the time of contracting has no knowledge.

(2) A warranty under subsection (1) will be excluded or modified only by specific language or by circumstances which give the buyer reason to know that the person selling does not claim title in himself or that he is purporting to sell only such right or title as he or a third person may have.

(3) Unless otherwise agreed a seller who is a merchant regularly dealing in goods of the kind warrants that the goods shall be delivered free of the rightful claim of any third person by way of infringement or the like but a buyer who furnishes specifications to the seller must hold the seller harmless against any such claim which arises out of compliance with the specifications.

§ 2-313. Express Warranties by Affirmation, Promise, Description, Sample.

(1) Express warranties by the seller are created as follows:

(a) Any affirmation of fact or promise made by the seller to the buyer which relates to the goods and becomes part of the basis of the bargain creates an express warranty that the goods shall conform to the affirmation or promise.

(b) Any description of the goods which is made part of the basis of the bargain creates an express warranty that the goods shall conform to the description.

(c) Any sample or model which is made part of the basis of the bargain creates an express warranty that the whole of the goods shall conform to the sample or model.

(2) It is not necessary to the creation of an express warranty that the seller use formal words such as "warrant" or "guarantee" or that he have a specific intention to make a warranty, but an affirmation merely of the value of the goods or a statement purporting to be merely the seller's opinion or commendation of the goods does not create a warranty.

§ 2-314. Implied Warranty: Merchantability; Usage of Trade.

(1) Unless excluded or modified (Section 2-316), a warranty that the goods shall be merchantable is implied in a contract for their sale if the seller is a merchant with respect to goods of that kind. Under this section the serving for value of food or drink to be consumed either on the premises or elsewhere is a sale.

(2) Goods to be merchantable must be at least such as

(a) pass without objection in the trade under the contract description; and

(b) in the case of fungible goods, are of fair average quality within the description; and

(c) are fit for the ordinary purposes for which such goods are used; and

(d) run, within the variations permitted by the agreement, of even kind, quality and quantity within each unit and among all units involved; and

(e) are adequately contained, packaged, and labeled as the agreement may require; and

(f) conform to the promise or affirmations of fact made on the container or label if any.

(3) Unless excluded or modified (Section 2-316) other implied warranties may arise from course of dealing or usage of trade.

§ 2-315. Implied Warranty: Fitness for Particular Purpose.

Where the seller at the time of contracting has reason to know any particular purpose for which the goods are required and that the buyer is relying on the seller's skill or judgment to select or furnish suitable goods, there is unless excluded or modified under the next section an implied warranty that the goods shall be fit for such purpose.

§ 2-316. Exclusion or Modification of Warranties.

(1) Words or conduct relevant to the creation of an express warranty and words or conduct tending to negate or limit warranty shall be construed wherever reasonable as consistent with each other; but subject to the provisions of this Article on parol or extrinsic evidence (Section 2-202) negation or limitation is inoperative to the extent that such construction is unreasonable.

(2) Subject to subsection (3), to exclude or modify the implied warranty of merchantability or any part of it the language must mention merchantability and in case of a writing must be conspicuous, and to exclude or modify any implied warranty of fitness the exclusion must be by a writing and conspicuous. Language to exclude all implied warranties of fitness is sufficient if it states, for example, that "There are no warranties which extend beyond the description on the face hereof."

(3) Notwithstanding subsection (2)

(a) unless the circumstances indicate otherwise, all implied warranties are excluded by expressions like "as is", "with all faults" or other language which in common understanding calls the buyer's attention to the exclusion of warranties and makes plain that there is no implied warranty; and

(b) when the buyer before entering into the contract has examined the goods or the sample or model as fully as he desired or has refused to examine the goods there is no implied warranty with regard to defects which an examination ought in the circumstances to have revealed to him; and

(c) an implied warranty can also be excluded or modified by course of dealing or course of performance or usage of trade.

(4) Remedies for breach of warranty can be limited in accordance with the provisions of this Article on liquidation or limitation of damages and on contractual modification of remedy (Sections 2-718 and 2-719).

§ 2-317. Cumulation and Conflict of Warranties Express or Implied.

Warranties whether express or implied shall be construed as consistent with each other and as cumulative, but if such construction is unreasonable the intention of the parties shall determine which warranty is dominant. In ascertaining that intention the following rules apply:

(a) Exact or technical specifications displace an inconsistent sample or model or general language of description.

(b) A sample from an existing bulk displaces inconsistent general language of description.

(c) Express warranties displace inconsistent implied warranties other than an implied warranty of fitness for a particular purpose.

§ 2-318. Third Party Beneficiaries of Warranties Express or Implied.

Note: *If this Act is introduced in the Congress of the United States this section should be omitted. (States to select one alternative.)*

Alternative A

A seller's warranty whether express or implied extends to any natural person who is in the family or household of his buyer or who is a guest in his home if it is reasonable to expect that such person may use, consume or be affected by the goods and who is injured in person by breach of the warranty. A seller may not exclude or limit the operation of this section.

Alternative B

A seller's warranty whether express or implied extends to any natural person who may reasonably be expected to use, consume or be affected by the goods and who is injured in person by breach of the warranty. A seller may not exclude or limit the operation of this section.

Alternative C

A seller's warranty whether express or implied extends to any person who may reasonably be expected to use, consume or be affected by the goods and who is injured by breach of the warranty. A seller may not exclude or limit the operation of this section with respect to injury to the person of an individual to whom the warranty extends.

As amended in 1966.

§ 2-319. F.O.B. and F.A.S. Terms.

(1) Unless otherwise agreed the term F.O.B. (which means "free on board") at a named place, even though used only in connection with the stated price, is a delivery term under which

(a) when the term is F.O.B. the place of shipment, the seller must at that place ship the goods in the manner provided in this Article (Section 2-504) and bear the expense and risk of putting them into the possession of the carrier; or

(b) when the term is F.O.B. the place of destination, the seller must at his own expense and risk transport the goods to that place and there tender delivery of them in the manner provided in this Article (Section 2-503);

(c) when under either (a) or (b) the term is also F.O.B. vessel, car or other vehicle, the seller must in addition at his own expense and risk load the goods on board. If the term is F.O.B. vessel the buyer must name the vessel and in an appropriate case the seller must comply with the provisions of this Article on the form of bill of lading (Section 2-323).

(2) Unless otherwise agreed the term F.A.S. vessel (which means "free alongside") at a named port, even though used only in connection with the stated price, is a delivery term under which the seller must

(a) at his own expense and risk deliver the goods alongside the vessel in the manner usual in that port or on a dock designated and provided by the buyer; and

(b) obtain and tender a receipt for the goods in exchange for which the carrier is under a duty to issue a bill of lading.

(3) Unless otherwise agreed in any case falling within subsection (1)(a) or (c) or subsection (2) the buyer must seasonably give any needed instructions for making delivery, including when the term is F.A.S. or F.O.B. the loading berth of the vessel and in an appropriate case its name and sailing date. The seller may treat the failure of needed instructions as a failure of cooperation under this Article (Section 2-311). He may also at his option move the goods in any reasonable manner preparatory to delivery or shipment.

(4) Under the term F.O.B. vessel or F.A.S. unless otherwise agreed the buyer must make payment against tender of the required documents and the seller may not tender nor the buyer demand delivery of the goods in substitution for the documents.

§ 2-320. C.I.F. and C. & F. Terms.

(1) The term C.I.F. means that the price includes in a lump sum the cost of the goods and the insurance and freight to the named destination. The term C. & F. or C.F. means that the price so includes cost and freight to the named destination.

(2) Unless otherwise agreed and even though used only in connection with the stated price and destination, the term C.I.F. destination or its equivalent requires the seller at his own expense and risk to

(a) put the goods into the possession of a carrier at the port for shipment and obtain a negotiable bill or bills of lading covering the entire transportation to the named destination; and

(b) load the goods and obtain a receipt from the carrier (which may be contained in the bill of lading) showing that the freight has been paid or provided for; and

(c) obtain a policy or certificate of insurance, including any war risk insurance, of a kind and on terms then current at the port of shipment in the usual amount, in the currency of the contract, shown to cover the same goods covered by the bill of lading and providing for payment of loss to the order of the buyer or for the account of whom it may concern; but the seller may add to the price the amount of the premium for any such war risk insurance; and

(d) prepare an invoice of the goods and procure any other documents required to effect shipment or to comply with the contract; and

(e) forward and tender with commercial promptness all

the documents in due form and with any indorsement necessary to perfect the buyer's rights.

(3) Unless otherwise agreed the term C. & F. or its equivalent has the same effect and imposes upon the seller the same obligations and risks as a C.I.F. term except the obligation as to insurance.

(4) Under the term C.I.F. or C. & F. unless otherwise agreed the buyer must make payment against tender of the required documents and the seller may not tender nor the buyer demand delivery of the goods in substitution for the documents.

§ 2-321. C.I.F. or C. & F.: "Net Landed Weights"; "Payment on Arrival"; Warranty of Condition on Arrival. Under a contract containing a term C.I.F. or C. & F.

(1) Where the price is based on or is to be adjusted according to "net landed weights", "delivered weights", "out turn" quantity or quality or the like, unless otherwise agreed the seller must reasonably estimate the price. The payment due on tender of the documents called for by the contract is the amount so estimated, but after final adjustment of the price a settlement must be made with commercial promptness.

(2) An agreement described in subsection (1) or any warranty of quality or condition of the goods on arrival places upon the seller the risk of ordinary deterioration, shrinkage and the like in transportation but has no effect on the place or time of identification to the contract for sale or delivery or on the passing of the risk of loss.

(3) Unless otherwise agreed where the contract provides for payment on or after arrival of the goods the seller must before payment allow such preliminary inspection as is feasible; but if the goods are lost delivery of the documents and payment are due when the goods should have arrived.

§ 2-322. Delivery "Ex-Ship".

(1) Unless otherwise agreed a term for delivery of goods "ex-ship" (which means from the carrying vessel) or in equivalent language is not restricted to a particular ship and requires delivery from a ship which has reached a place at the named port of destination where goods of the kind are usually discharged.

(2) Under such a term unless otherwise agreed

(a) the seller must discharge all liens arising out of the carriage and furnish the buyer with a direction which puts the carrier under a duty to deliver the goods; and

(b) the risk of loss does not pass to the buyer until the goods leave the ship's tackle or are otherwise properly unloaded.

§ 2-323. Form of Bill of Lading Required in Overseas Shipment; "Overseas".

(1) Where the contract contemplates overseas shipment and contains a term C.I.F. or C. & F. or F.O.B. vessel, the seller unless otherwise agreed must obtain a negotiable bill of lading stating that the goods have been loaded in board or, in the case of a term C.I.F. or C. & F., received for shipment.

(2) Where in a case within subsection (1) a bill of lading has been issued in a set of parts, unless otherwise agreed if the documents are not to be sent from abroad the buyer may demand tender of the full set; otherwise only one part of the bill

of lading need be tendered. Even if the agreement expressly requires a full set

(a) due tender of a single part is acceptable within the provisions of this Article on cure of improper delivery (subsection (1) of Section 2-508); and

(b) even though the full set is demanded, if the documents are sent from abroad the person tendering an incomplete set may nevertheless require payment upon furnishing an indemnity which the buyer in good faith deems adequate.

(3) A shipment by water or by air or a contract contemplating such shipment is "overseas" insofar as by usage of trade or agreement it is subject to the commercial, financing or shipping practices characteristic of international deep water commerce.

§ 2-324. "No Arrival, No Sale" Term. Under a term "no arrival, no sale" or terms of like meaning, unless otherwise agreed,

(a) The seller must properly ship conforming goods and if they arrive by any means he must tender them on arrival but he assumes no obligation that the goods will arrive unless he has caused the non-arrival; and

(b) where without fault of the seller the goods are in part lost or have so deteriorated as no longer to conform to the contract or arrive after the contract time, the buyer may proceed as if there had been casualty to identified goods (Section 2-613).

§ 2-325. "Letter of Credit" Term; "Confirmed Credit".

(1) Failure of the buyer seasonably to furnish an agreed letter of credit is a breach of the contract for sale.

(2) The delivery to seller of a proper letter of credit suspends the buyer's obligation to pay. If the letter of credit is dishonored, the seller may on seasonable notification to the buyer require payment directly from him.

(3) Unless otherwise agreed the term "letter of credit" or "banker's credit" in a contract for sale means an irrevocable credit issued by a financing agency of good repute and, where the shipment is overseas, of good international repute. The term "confirmed credit" means that the credit must also carry the direct obligation of such an agency which does business in the seller's financial market.

§ 2-326. Sale on Approval and Sale or Return; Consignment Sales and Rights of Creditors.

(1) Unless otherwise agreed, if delivered goods may be returned by the buyer even though they conform to the contract, the transaction is

(a) a "sale on approval" if the goods are delivered primarily for use, and

(b) a "sale or return" if the goods are delivered primarily for resale.

(2) Except as provided in subsection (3), goods held on approval are not subject to the claims of the buyer's creditors until acceptance; goods held on sale or return are subject to such claims while in the buyer's possession.

(3) Where goods are delivered to a person for sale and such person maintains a place of business at which he deals in goods of the kind involved, under a name other than the

name of the person making delivery, then with respect to claims of creditors of the person conducting the business the goods are deemed to be on sale or return. The provisions of this subsection are applicable even though an agreement purports to reserve title to the person making delivery until payment or resale or uses such words as "on consignment" or "on memorandum". However, this subsection is not applicable if the person making delivery

(a) complies with an applicable law providing for a consignor's interest or the like to be evidenced by a sign, or

(b) establishes that the person conducting the business is generally known by his creditors to be substantially engaged in selling the goods of others, or

(c) complies with the filing provisions of the Article on Secured Transactions (Article 9).

(4) Any "or return" term of a contract for sale is to be treated as a separate contract for sale within the statute of frauds section of this Article (Section 2-201) and as contradicting the sale aspect of the contract within the provisions of this Article on parol or extrinsic evidence (Section 2-202).

§ 2-327. Special Incidents of Sale on Approval and Sale or Return.

(1) Under a sale on approval unless otherwise agreed

(a) although the goods are identified to the contract the risk of loss and the title do not pass to the buyer until acceptance; and

(b) use of the goods consistent with the purpose of trial is not acceptance but failure seasonably to notify the seller of election to return the goods is acceptance, and if the goods conform to the contract acceptance of any part is acceptance of the whole; and

(c) after due notification of election to return, the return is at the seller's risk and expense but a merchant buyer must follow any reasonable instructions.

(2) Under a sale or return unless otherwise agreed

(a) the option to return extends to the whole or any commercial unit of the goods while in substantially their original condition, but must be exercised seasonably; and

(b) the return is at the buyer's risk and expense.

§ 2-328. Sale by Auction.

(1) In a sale by auction if goods are put up in lots each lot is the subject of a separate sale.

(2) A sale by auction is complete when the auctioneer so announces by the fall of the hammer or in other customary manner. Where a bid is made while the hammer is falling in acceptance of a prior bid the auctioneer may in his discretion reopen the bidding or declare the goods sold under the bid on which the hammer was falling.

(3) Such a sale is with reserve unless the goods are in explicit terms put up without reserve. In an auction with reserve the auctioneer may withdraw the goods at any time until he announces completion of the sale. In an auction without reserve, after the auctioneer calls for bids on an article or lot, that article or lot cannot be withdrawn unless no bid is made within a reasonable time. In either case a bidder may retract his bid until the auctioneer's announcement of completion of the sale, but a bidder's retraction does not revive any previous bid.

(4) If the auctioneer knowingly receives a bid on the seller's behalf or the seller makes or procures such a bid, and notice has not been given that liberty for such bidding is reserved, the buyer may at his option avoid the sale or take the goods at the price of the last good faith bid prior to the completion of the sale. This subsection shall not apply to any bid at a forced sale.

Part 4 Title, Creditors and Good Faith Purchasers

§ 2-401. Passing of Title; Reservation for Security; Limited Application of This Section.
Each provision of this Article with regard to the rights, obligations and remedies of the seller, the buyer, purchasers or other third parties applies irrespective of title to the goods except where the provisions refers to such title. Insofar as situations are not covered by the other provisions of this Article and matters concerning title become material the following rules apply:

(1) Title to goods cannot pass under a contract for sale prior to their identification to the contract (Section 2-501), and unless otherwise explicitly agreed the buyer acquires by their identification a special property as limited by this Act. Any retention or reservation by the seller of the title (property) in goods shipped or delivered to the buyer is limited in effect to a reservation of a security interest. Subject to these provisions and to the provisions of the Article on Secured Transactions (Article 9), title to goods passes from the seller to the buyer in any manner and on any conditions explicitly agreed on by the parties.

(2) Unless otherwise explicitly agreed title passes to the buyer at the time and place at which the seller completes his performance with reference to the physical delivery of the goods, despite any reservation of a security interest and even though a document of title is to be delivered at a different time or place; and in particular and despite any reservation of a security interest by the bill of lading

(a) if the contract requires or authorizes the seller to send the goods to the buyer but does not require him to deliver them at destination, title passes to the buyer at the time and place of shipment; but

(b) if the contract requires delivery at destination, title passes on tender there.

(3) Unless otherwise explicitly agreed where delivery is to be made without moving the goods,

(a) if the seller is to deliver a document of title, title passes at the time when and the place where he delivers such documents; or

(b) if the goods are at the time of contracting already identified and no documents are to be delivered, title passes at the time and place of contracting.

(4) A rejection or other refusal by the buyer to receive or retain the goods, whether or not justified, or a justified revocation of acceptance revests title to the goods in the seller. Such revesting occurs by operation of law and is not a "sale".

§ 2-402. Rights of Seller's Creditors Against Sold Goods.

(1) Except as provided in subsections (2) and (3), rights of unsecured creditors of the seller with respect to goods which have been identified to a contract for sale are subject to the

buyer's rights to recover the goods under this Article (Sections 2-502 and 2-716).

(2) A creditor of the seller may treat a sale or an identification of goods to a contract for sale as void if as against him a retention of possession by the seller is fraudulent under any rule of law of the state where the goods are situated, except that retention of possession in good faith and current course of trade by a merchant-seller for a commercially reasonable time after a sale or identification is not fraudulent.

(3) Nothing in this Article shall be deemed to impair the rights of creditors of the seller

(a) under the provisions of the Article on Secured Transactions (Article 9); or

(b) Where identification to the contract or delivery is made not in current course of trade but in satisfaction of or as security for a pre-existing claim for money, security or the like and is made under circumstances which under any rule of law of the state where the goods are situated would apart from this Article constitute the transaction a fraudulent transfer or voidable preference.

§ 2-403. Power to Transfer; Good Faith Purchase of Goods; "Entrusting".

(1) A purchaser of goods acquires all title which his transferor had or had power to transfer except that a purchaser of a limited interest acquires rights only to the extent of the interest purchased. A person with voidable title has power to transfer a good title to a good faith purchaser for value. When goods have been delivered under a transaction of purchase the purchaser has such power even though

(a) the transferor was deceived as to the identity of the purchaser, or

(b) the delivery was in exchange for a check which is later dishonored, or

(c) it was agreed that the transaction was to be a "cash sale", or

(d) the delivery was procured through fraud punishable as larcenous under the criminal law.

(2) Any entrusting of possession of goods to a merchant who deals in goods of that kind gives him power to transfer all rights of the entruster to a buyer in ordinary course of business.

(3) "Entrusting" includes any delivery and any acquiescence in retention of possession regardless of any condition expressed between the parties to the delivery or acquiescence and regardless of whether the procurement of the entrusting or the possessor's disposition of the goods have been such as to be larcenous under the criminal law.

Note: *If a state adopts the repealer of Article 6—Bulk Transfers (Alternative A), subsection (4) should read as follows:*

(4) The rights of other purchasers of goods and of lien creditors are governed by the Articles on Secured Transactions (Article 9) and Documents of Title (Article 7).

Note: *If a state adopts Revised Article 6—Bulk Sales (Alternative B), subsection (4) should read as follows:*

(4) The rights of other purchasers of goods and of lien creditors are governed by the Articles on Secured Transactions (Article 9), Bulk Sales (Article 6) and Documents of Title (Article 7).

As amended in 1988.

Part 5 Performance

§ 2-501. Insurable Interest in Goods; Manner of Identification of Goods.

(1) The buyer obtains a special property and an insurable interest in goods by identification of existing goods as goods to which the contract refers even though the goods so identified are non-conforming and he has an option to return or reject them. Such identification can be made at any time and in any manner explicitly agreed to by the parties. In the absence of explicit agreement identification occurs

(a) when the contract is made if it is for the sale of goods already existing and identified;

(b) if the contract is for the sale of future goods other than those described in paragraph (c), when goods are shipped, marked or otherwise designated by the seller as goods to which the contract refers;

(c) when the crops are planted or otherwise become growing crops or the young are conceived if the contract is for the sale of unborn young to be born within twelve months after contracting or for the sale of crops to be harvested within twelve months or the next normal harvest season after contracting whichever is longer.

(2) The seller retains an insurable interest in goods so long as title to or any security interest in the goods remains in him and where the identification is by the seller alone he may until default or insolvency or notification to the buyer that the identification is final substitute other goods for those identified.

(3) Nothing in this section impairs any insurable interest recognized under any other statute or rule of law.

§ 2-502. Buyer's Right to Goods on Seller's Insolvency.

(1) Subject to subsection (2) and even though the goods have not been shipped a buyer who has paid a part or all of the price of goods in which he has a special property under the provisions of the immediately preceding section may on making and keeping good a tender of any unpaid portion of their price recover them from the seller if the seller becomes insolvent within ten days after receipt of the first installment on their price.

(2) If the identification creating his special property has been made by the buyer he acquires the right to recover the goods only if they conform to the contract for sale.

§ 2-503. Manner of Seller's Tender of Delivery.

(1) Tender of delivery requires that the seller put and hold conforming goods at the buyer's disposition and give the buyer any notification reasonably necessary to enable him to take delivery. The manner, time and place for tender are determined by the agreement and this Article, and in particular

(a) tender must be at a reasonable hour, and if it is of goods they must be kept available for the period reasonably necessary to enable the buyer to take possession; but

(b) unless otherwise agreed the buyer must furnish facilities reasonably suited to the receipt of the goods.

(2) Where the case is within the next section respecting shipment tender requires that the seller comply with its provisions.

(3) Where the seller is required to deliver at a particular destination tender requires that he comply with subsection (1)

and also in any appropriate case tender documents as described in subsections (4) and (5) of this section.

(4) Where goods are in the possession of a bailee and are to be delivered without being moved

(a) tender requires that the seller either tender a negotiable document of title covering such goods or procure acknowledgement by the bailee of the buyer's right to possession of the goods; but

(b) tender to the buyer of a non-negotiable document of title or of a written direction to the bailee to deliver is sufficient tender unless the buyer seasonably objects, and receipt by the bailee of notification of the buyer's rights fixes those rights as against the bailee and all third persons; but risk of loss of the goods and of any failure by the bailee to honor the non-negotiable document of title or to obey the direction remains on the seller until the buyer has had a reasonable time to present the document or direction, and a refusal by the bailee to honor the document or to obey the direction defeats the tender.

(5) Where the contract requires the seller to deliver documents

(a) he must tender all such documents in correct form, except as provided in this Article with respect to bills of lading in a set (subsection (2) of Section 2-323); and

(b) tender through customary banking channels is sufficient and dishonor of a draft accompanying the documents constitutes non-acceptance or rejection.

§ 2-504. Shipment by Seller.
Where the seller is required or authorized to send the goods to the buyer and the contract does not require him to deliver them at a particular destination, then unless otherwise agreed he must

(a) put the goods in the possession of such a carrier and make such a contract for their transportation as may be reasonable having regard to the nature of the goods and other circumstances of the case; and

(b) obtain and promptly deliver or tender in due form any document necessary to enable the buyer to obtain possession of the goods or otherwise required by the agreement or by usage of trade; and

(c) promptly notify the buyer of the shipment.

Failure to notify the buyer under paragraph (c) or to make a proper contract under paragraph (a) is a ground for rejection only if material delay or loss ensues.

§ 2-505. Seller's Shipment Under Reservation.
(1) Where the seller has identified goods to the contract by or before shipment:

(a) his procurement of a negotiable bill of lading to his own order or otherwise reserves in him a security interest in the goods. His procurement of the bill to the order of a financing agency or of the buyer indicates in addition only the seller's expectation of transferring that interest to the person named.

(b) a non-negotiable bill of lading to himself or his nominee reserves possession of the goods as security but except in a case of conditional delivery (subsection (2) of Section 2-507) a non-negotiable bill of lading naming the buyer as consignee reserves no security interest even though the seller retains possession of the bill of lading.

(2) When shipment by the seller with reservation of a security interest is in violation of the contract for sale it constitutes an improper contract for transportation within the preceding section but impairs neither the rights given to the buyer by shipment and identification of the goods to the contract nor the seller's powers as a holder of a negotiable document.

§ 2-506. Rights of Financing Agency.
(1) A financing agency by paying or purchasing for value a draft which relates to a shipment of goods acquires to the extent of the payment or purchase and in addition to its own rights under the draft and any document of title securing it any rights of the shipper in the goods including the right to stop delivery and the shipper's right to have the draft honored by the buyer.

(2) The right to reimbursement of a financing agency which has in good faith honored or purchased the draft under commitment to or authority from the buyer is not impaired by subsequent discovery of defects with reference to any relevant document which was apparently regular on its face.

§ 2-507. Effect of Seller's Tender; Delivery on Condition.
(1) Tender of delivery is a condition to the buyer's duty to accept the goods and, unless otherwise agreed, to his duty to pay for them. Tender entitles the seller to acceptance of the goods and to payment according to the contract.

(2) Where payment is due and demanded on the delivery to the buyer of goods or documents of title, his right as against the seller to retain or dispose of them is conditional upon his making the payment due.

§ 2-508. Cure by Seller of Improper Tender or Delivery; Replacement.
(1) Where any tender or delivery by the seller is rejected because non-conforming and the time for performance has not yet expired, the seller may seasonably notify the buyer of his intention to cure and may then within the contract time make a conforming delivery.

(2) Where the buyer rejects a non-conforming tender which the seller had reasonable grounds to believe would be acceptable with or without money allowance the seller may if he seasonably notifies the buyer have a further reasonable time to substitute a conforming tender.

§ 2-509. Risk of Loss in the Absence of Breach.
(1) Where the contract requires or authorizes the seller to ship the goods by carrier

(a) if it does not require him to deliver them at a particular destination, the risk of loss passes to the buyer when the goods are duly delivered to the carrier even though the shipment is under reservation (Section 2-505); but

(b) if it does require him to deliver them at a particular destination and the goods are there duly tendered while in the possession of the carrier, the risk of loss passes to the buyer when the goods are there duly so tendered as to enable the buyer to take delivery.

(2) Where the goods are held by a bailee to be delivered without being moved, the risk of loss passes to the buyer

(a) on his receipt of a negotiable document of title covering the goods; or

(b) on acknowledgment by the bailee of the buyer's right to possession of the goods; or

(c) after his receipt of a non-negotiable document of title or other written direction to deliver, as provided in subsection (4)(b) of Section 2-503.

(3) In any case not within subsection (1) or (2), the risk of loss passes to the buyer on his receipt of the goods if the seller is a merchant; otherwise the risk passes to the buyer on tender of delivery.

(4) The provisions of this section are subject to contrary agreement of the parties and to the provisions of this Article on sale on approval (Section 2-327) and on effect of breach on risk of loss (Section 2-510).

§ 2-510. Effect of Breach on Risk of Loss.

(1) Where a tender or delivery of goods so fails to conform to the contract as to give a right of rejection the risk of their loss remains on the seller until cure or acceptance.

(2) Where the buyer rightfully revokes acceptance he may to the extent of any deficiency in his effective insurance coverage treat the risk of loss as having rested on the seller from the beginning.

(3) Where the buyer as to conforming goods already identified to the contract for sale repudiates or is otherwise in breach before risk of their loss has passed to him, the seller may to the extent of any deficiency in his effective insurance coverage treat the risk of loss as resting on the buyer for a commercially reasonable time.

§ 2-511. Tender of Payment by Buyer; Payment by Check.

(1) Unless otherwise agreed tender of payment is a condition to the seller's duty to tender and complete any delivery.

(2) Tender of payment is sufficient when made by any means or in any manner current in the ordinary course of business unless the seller demands payment in legal tender and gives any extension of time reasonably necessary to procure it.

(3) Subject to the provisions of this Act on the effect of an instrument on an obligation (Section 3-310), payment by check is conditional and is defeated as between the parties by dishonor of the check on due presentment.

§ 2-512. Payment by Buyer Before Inspection.

(1) Where the contract requires payment before inspection nonconformity of the goods does not excuse the buyer from so making payment unless

(a) the non-conformity appears without inspection; or

(b) despite tender of the required documents the circumstances would justify injunction against honor under the provisions of this Act (Section 5-114).

(2) Payment pursuant to subsection (1) does not constitute an acceptance of goods or impair the buyer's right to inspect or any of his remedies.

§ 2-513. Buyer's Right to Inspection of Goods.

(1) Unless otherwise agreed and subject to subsection (3), where goods are tendered or delivered or identified to the contract for sale, the buyer has a right before payment or acceptance to inspect them at any reasonable place and time and in any reasonable manner. When the seller is required or authorized to send the goods to the buyer, the inspection may be after their arrival.

(2) Expenses of inspection must be borne by the buyer but may be recovered from the seller if the goods do not conform and are rejected.

(3) Unless otherwise agreed and subject to the provisions of this Article on C.I.F. contracts (subsection (3) of Section 2-321), the buyer is not entitled to inspect the goods before payment of the price when the contract provides

(a) for delivery "C.O.D." or on other like terms; or

(b) for payment against documents of title, except where such payment is due only after the goods are to become available for inspection.

(4) A place or method of inspection fixed by the parties is presumed to be exclusive but unless otherwise expressly agreed it does not postpone identification or shift the place for delivery or for passing the risk of loss. If compliance becomes impossible, inspection shall be as provided in this section unless the place or method fixed was clearly intended as an indispensable condition failure of which avoids the contract.

§ 2-514. When Documents Deliverable on Acceptance; When on Payment.
Unless otherwise agreed documents against which a draft is drawn are to be delivered to the drawee on acceptance of the draft if it is payable more than three days after presentment; otherwise, only on payment.

§ 2-515. Preserving Evidence of Goods in Dispute.
In furtherance of the adjustment of any claim or dispute

(a) either party on reasonable notification to the other and for the purpose of ascertaining the facts and preserving evidence has the right to inspect, test and sample the goods including such of them as may be in the possession or control of the other; and

(b) the parties may agree to a third party inspection or survey to determine the conformity or condition of the goods and may agree that the findings shall be binding upon them in any subsequent litigation or adjustment.

Part 6 Breach, Repudiation and Excuse

§ 2-601. Buyer's Rights on Improper Delivery.
Subject to the provisions of this Article on breach in installment contracts (Section 2-612) and unless otherwise agreed under the sections on contractual limitations of remedy (Sections 2-718 and 2-719), if the goods or the tender of delivery fail in any respect to conform to the contract, the buyer may

(a) reject the whole; or

(b) accept the whole; or

(c) accept any commercial unit or units and reject the rest.

§ 2-602. Manner and Effect of Rightful Rejection.

(1) Rejection of goods must be within a reasonable time after their delivery or tender. It is ineffective unless the buyer seasonably notifies the seller.

(2) Subject to the provisions of the two following sections on rejected goods (Sections 2-603 and 2-604),

(a) after rejection any exercise of ownership by the buyer with respect to any commercial unit is wrongful as against the seller; and

(b) if the buyer has before rejection taken physical possession of goods in which he does not have a security interest under the provisions of this Article (subsection (3) of Section 2-711), he is under a duty after rejection to hold them with reasonable care at the seller's disposition for a time sufficient to permit the seller to remove them; but

(c) the buyer has no further obligations with regard to goods rightfully rejected.

(3) The seller's rights with respect to goods wrongfully rejected are governed by the provisions of this Article on Seller's remedies in general (Section 2-703).

§ 2-603. Merchant Buyer's Duties as to Rightfully Rejected Goods.

(1) Subject to any security interest in the buyer (subsection (3) of Section 2-711), when the seller has no agent or place of business at the market of rejection a merchant buyer is under a duty after rejection of goods in his possession or control to follow any reasonable instructions received from the seller with respect to the goods and in the absence of such instructions to make reasonable efforts to sell them for the seller's account if they are perishable or threaten to decline in value speedily. Instructions are not reasonable if on demand indemnity for expenses is not forthcoming.

(2) When the buyer sells goods under subsection (1), he is entitled to reimbursement from the seller or out of the proceeds for reasonable expenses of caring for and selling them, and if the expenses include no selling commission then to such commission as is usual in the trade or if there is none to a reasonable sum not exceeding ten per cent on the gross proceeds.

(3) In complying with this section the buyer is held only to good faith and good faith conduct hereunder is neither acceptance nor conversion nor the basis of an action for damages.

§ 2-604. Buyer's Options as to Salvage of Rightfully Rejected Goods.
Subject to the provisions of the immediately preceding section on perishables if the seller gives no instructions within a reasonable time after notification of rejection the buyer may store the rejected goods for the seller's account or reship them to him or resell them for the seller's account with reimbursement as provided in the preceding section. Such action is not acceptance or conversion.

§ 2-605. Waiver of Buyer's Objections by Failure to Particularize.

(1) The buyer's failure to state in connection with rejection a particular defect which is ascertainable by reasonable inspection precludes him from relying on the unstated defect to justify rejection or to establish breach

(a) where the seller could have cured it if stated seasonably; or

(b) between merchants when the seller has after rejection made a request in writing for a full and final written statement of all defects on which the buyer proposes to rely.

(2) Payment against documents made without reservation of rights precludes recovery of the payment for defects apparent on the face of the documents.

§ 2-606. What Constitutes Acceptance of Goods.

(1) Acceptance of goods occurs when the buyer

(a) after a reasonable opportunity to inspect the goods signifies to the seller that the goods are conforming or that he will take or retain them in spite of their nonconformity; or

(b) fails to make an effective rejection (subsection (1) of Section 2-602), but such acceptance does not occur until the buyer has had a reasonable opportunity to inspect them; or

(c) does any act inconsistent with the seller's ownership; but if such act is wrongful as against the seller it is an acceptance only if ratified by him.

(2) Acceptance of a part of any commercial unit is acceptance of that entire unit.

§ 2-607. Effect of Acceptance; Notice of Breach; Burden of Establishing Breach After Acceptance; Notice of Claim or Litigation to Person Answerable Over.

(1) The buyer must pay at the contract rate for any goods accepted.

(2) Acceptance of goods by the buyer precludes rejection of the goods accepted and if made with knowledge of a nonconformity cannot be revoked because of it unless the acceptance was on the reasonable assumption that the nonconformity would be seasonably cured but acceptance does not of itself impair any other remedy provided by this Article for non-conformity.

(3) Where a tender has been accepted

(a) the buyer must within a reasonable time after he discovers or should have discovered any breach notify the seller of breach or be barred from any remedy; and

(b) if the claim is one for infringement or the like (subsection (3) of Section 2-312) and the buyer is sued as a result of such a breach he must so notify the seller within a reasonable time after he receives notice of the litigation or be barred from any remedy over for liability established by the litigation.

(4) The burden is on the buyer to establish any breach with respect to the goods accepted.

(5) Where the buyer is sued for breach of a warranty or other obligation for which his seller is answerable over

(a) he may give his seller written notice of the litigation. If the notice states that the seller may come in and defend and that if the seller does not do so he will be bound in any action against him by his buyer by any determination of fact common to the two litigations, then unless the seller after seasonable receipt of the notice does come in and defend he is so bound.

(b) if the claim is one for infringement or the like (subsection (3) of Section 2-312) the original seller may demand in writing that his buyer turn over to him control of the litigation including settlement or else be barred from any remedy over and if he also agrees to bear all expense and to satisfy any adverse judgment, then unless the buyer after seasonable receipt of the demand does turn over control the buyer is so barred.

(6) The provisions of subsections (3), (4) and (5) apply to any obligation of a buyer to hold the seller harmless against infringement or the like (subsection (3) of Section 2-312).

§ 2-608. Revocation of Acceptance in Whole or in Part.

(1) The buyer may revoke his acceptance of a lot or commercial unit whose non-conformity substantially impairs its value to him if he has accepted it

(a) on the reasonable assumption that its non-conformity would be cured and it has not been seasonably cured; or

(b) without discovery of such non-conformity if his acceptance was reasonably induced either by the difficulty of discovery before acceptance or by the seller's assurances.

(2) Revocation of acceptance must occur within a reasonable time after the buyer discovers or should have discovered the ground for it and before any substantial change in condition of the goods which is not caused by their own defects. It is not effective until the buyer notifies the seller of it.

(3) A buyer who so revokes has the same rights and duties with regard to the goods involved as if he had rejected them.

§ 2-609. Right to Adequate Assurance of Performance.

(1) A contract for sale imposes an obligation on each party that the other's expectation of receiving due performance will not be impaired. When reasonable grounds for insecurity arise with respect to the performance of either party the other may in writing demand adequate assurance of due performance and until he receives such assurance may if commercially reasonable suspend any performance for which he has not already received the agreed return.

(2) Between merchants the reasonableness of grounds for insecurity and the adequacy of any assurance offered shall be determined according to commercial standards.

(3) Acceptance of any improper delivery or payment does not prejudice the aggrieved party's right to demand adequate assurance of future performance.

(4) After receipt of a justified demand failure to provide within a reasonable time not exceeding thirty days such assurance of due performance as is adequate under the circumstances of the particular case is a repudiation of the contract.

§ 2-610. Anticipatory Repudiation.

When either party repudiates the contract with respect to a performance not yet due the loss of which will substantially impair the value of the contract to the other, the aggrieved party may

(a) for a commercially reasonable time await performance by the repudiating party; or

(b) resort to any remedy for breach (Section 2-703 or Section 2-711), even though he has notified the repudiating party that he would await the latter's performance and has urged retraction; and

(c) in either case suspend his own performance or proceed in accordance with the provisions of this Article on the seller's right to identify goods to the contract notwithstanding breach or to salvage unfinished goods (Section 2-704).

§ 2-611. Retraction of Anticipatory Repudiation.

(1) Until the repudiating party's next performance is due he can retract his repudiation unless the aggrieved party has since the repudiation cancelled or materially changed his position or otherwise indicated that he considers the repudiation final.

(2) Retraction may be by any method which clearly indicates to the aggrieved party that the repudiating party intends to perform, but must include any assurance justifiably demanded under the provisions of this Article (Section 2-609).

(3) Retraction reinstates the repudiating party's rights under the contract with due excuse and allowance to the aggrieved party for any delay occasioned by the repudiation.

§ 2-612. "Installment Contract"; Breach.

(1) An "installment contract" is one which requires or authorizes the delivery of goods in separate lots to be separately accepted, even though the contract contains a clause "each delivery is a separate contract" or its equivalent.

(2) The buyer may reject any installment which is non-conforming if the non-conformity substantially impairs the value of that installment and cannot be cured or if the non-conformity is a defect in the required documents; but if the non-conformity does not fall within subsection (3) and the seller gives adequate assurance of its cure the buyer must accept that installment.

(3) Whenever non-conformity or default with respect to one or more installments substantially impairs the value of the whole contract there is a breach of the whole. But the aggrieved party reinstates the contract if he accepts a non-conforming installment without seasonably notifying of cancellation or if he brings an action with respect only to past installments or demands performance as to future installments.

§ 2-613. Casualty to Identified Goods.

Where the contract requires for its performance goods identified when the contract is made, and the goods suffer casualty without fault of either party before the risk of loss passes to the buyer, or in a proper case under a "no arrival, no sale" term (Section 2-324) then

(a) if the loss is total the contract is avoided; and

(b) if the loss is partial or the goods have so deteriorated as no longer to conform to the contract the buyer may nevertheless demand inspection and at his option either treat the contract as avoided or accept the goods with due allowance from the contract price for the deterioration or the deficiency in quantity but without further right against the seller.

§ 2-614. Substituted Performance.

(1) Where without fault of either party the agreed berthing, loading, or unloading facilities fail or an agreed type of carrier becomes unavailable or the agreed manner of delivery otherwise becomes commercially impracticable but a commercially reasonable substitute is available, such substitute performance must be tendered and accepted.

(2) If the agreed means or manner of payment fails because of domestic or foreign governmental regulation, the seller may withhold or stop delivery unless the buyer provides a means or manner of payment which is commercially a sub-

stantial equivalent. If delivery has already been taken, payment by the means or in the manner provided by the regulation discharges the buyer's obligation unless the regulation is discriminatory, oppressive or predatory.

§ 2-615. Excuse by Failure of Presupposed Conditions.
Except so far as a seller may have assumed a greater obligation and subject to the preceding section on substituted performance:

(a) Delay in delivery or non-delivery in whole or in part by a seller who complies with paragraphs (b) and (c) is not a breach of his duty under a contract for sale if performance as agreed has been made impracticable by the occurrence of a contingency the non-occurrence of which was a basic assumption on which the contract was made or by compliance in good faith with any applicable foreign or domestic governmental regulation or order whether or not it later proves to be invalid.

(b) Where the causes mentioned in paragraph (a) affect only a part of the seller's capacity to perform, he must allocate production and deliveries among his customers but may at his option include regular customers not then under contract as well as his own requirements for further manufacture. He may so allocate in any manner which is fair and reasonable.

(c) The seller must notify the buyer seasonably that there will be delay or non-delivery and, when allocation is required under paragraph (b), of the estimated quota thus made available for the buyer.

§ 2-616. Procedure on Notice Claiming Excuse.

(1) Where the buyer receives notification of a material or indefinite delay or an allocation justified under the preceding section he may by written notification to the seller as to any delivery concerned, and where the prospective deficiency substantially impairs the value of the whole contract under the provisions of this Article relating to breach of installment contracts (Section 2-612), then also as to the whole,

  (a) terminate and thereby discharge any unexecuted portion of the contract; or

  (b) modify the contract by agreeing to take his available quota in substitution.

(2) If after receipt of such notification from the seller the buyer fails so to modify the contract within a reasonable time not exceeding thirty days the contract lapses with respect to any deliveries affected.

(3) The provisions of this section may not be negated by agreement except in so far as the seller has assumed a greater obligation under the preceding section.

Part 7   Remedies

§ 2-701. Remedies for Breach of Collateral Contracts Not Impaired.
Remedies for breach of any obligation or promise collateral or ancillary to a contract for sale are not impaired by the provisions of this Article.

§ 2-702. Seller's Remedies on Discovery of Buyer's Insolvency.

(1) Where the seller discovers the buyer to be insolvent he may refuse delivery except for cash including payment for all goods theretofore delivered under the contract, and stop delivery under this Article (Section 2-705).

(2) Where the seller discovers that the buyer has received goods on credit while insolvent he may reclaim the goods upon demand made within ten days after the receipt, but if misrepresentation of solvency has been made to the particular seller in writing within three months before delivery the ten day limitation does not apply. Except as provided in this subsection the seller may not base a right to reclaim goods on the buyer's fraudulent or innocent misrepresentation of solvency or of intent to pay.

(3) The seller's right to reclaim under subsection (2) is subject to the rights of a buyer in ordinary course or other good faith purchaser under this Article (Section 2-403). Successful reclamation of goods excludes all other remedies with respect to them.

As amended in 1966.

§ 2-703. Seller's Remedies in General.
Where the buyer wrongfully rejects or revokes acceptance of goods or fails to make a payment due on or before delivery or repudiates with respect to a part or the whole, then with respect to any goods directly affected and, if the breach is of the whole contract (Section 2-612), then also with respect to the whole undelivered balance, the aggrieved seller may

(a) withhold delivery of such goods;

(b) stop delivery by any bailee as hereafter provided (Section 2-705);

(c) proceed under the next section respecting goods still unidentified to the contract;

(d) resell and recover damages as hereafter provided (Section 2-706);

(e) recover damages for non-acceptance (Section 2-708) or in a proper case the price (Section 2-709);

(f) cancel.

§ 2-704. Seller's Right to Identify Goods to the Contract Notwithstanding Breach or to Salvage Unfinished Goods.

(1) An aggrieved seller under the preceding section may

  (a) identify to the contract conforming goods not already identified if at the time he learned of the breach they are in his possession or control;

  (b) treat as the subject of resale goods which have demonstrably been intended for the particular contract even though those goods are unfinished.

(2) Where the goods are unfinished an aggrieved seller may in the exercise of reasonable commercial judgment for the purposes of avoiding loss and of effective realization either complete the manufacture and wholly identify the goods to the contract or cease manufacture and resell for scrap or salvage value or proceed in any other reasonable manner.

§ 2-705. Seller's Stoppage of Delivery in Transit or Otherwise.

(1) The seller may stop delivery of goods in the possession of a carrier or other bailee when he discovers the buyer to be insolvent (Section 2-702) and may stop delivery of carload, truckload, planeload or larger shipments of express or freight when the buyer repudiates or fails to make a payment due before delivery or if for any other reason the seller has a right to withhold or reclaim the goods.

(2) As against such buyer the seller may stop delivery until

    (a) receipt of the goods by the buyer; or

    (b) acknowledgment to the buyer by any bailee of the goods except a carrier that the bailee holds the goods for the buyer; or

    (c) such acknowledgment to the buyer by a carrier by reshipment or as warehouseman; or

    (d) negotiation to the buyer of any negotiable document of title covering the goods.

(3)(a) To stop delivery the seller must so notify as to enable the bailee by reasonable diligence to prevent delivery of the goods.

    (b) After such notification the bailee must hold and deliver the goods according to the directions of the seller but the seller is liable to the bailee for any ensuing charges or damages.

    (c) If a negotiable document of title has been issued for goods the bailee is not obliged to obey a notification to stop until surrender of the document.

    (d) A carrier who has issued a non-negotiable bill of lading is not obliged to obey a notification to stop received from a person other than the consignor.

§ 2-706. Seller's Resale Including Contract for Resale.

(1) Under the conditions stated in Section 2-703 on seller's remedies, the seller may resell the goods concerned or the undelivered balance thereof. Where the resale is made in good faith and in a commercially reasonable manner the seller may recover the difference between the resale price and the contract price together with any incidental damages allowed under the provisions of this Article (Section 2-710), but less expenses saved in consequence of the buyer's breach.

(2) Except as otherwise provided in subsection (3) or unless otherwise agreed resale may be at public or private sale including sale by way of one or more contracts to sell or of identification to an existing contract of the seller. Sale may be as a unit or in parcels and at any time and place and on any terms but every aspect of the sale including the method, manner, time, place and terms must be commercially reasonable. The resale must be reasonably identified as referring to the broken contract, but it is not necessary that the goods be in existence or that any or all of them have been identified to the contract before the breach.

(3) Where the resale is at private sale the seller must give the buyer reasonable notification of his intention to resell.

(4) Where the resale is at public sale

    (a) only identified goods can be sold except where there is a recognized market for a public sale of futures in goods of the kind; and

    (b) it must be made at a usual place or market for public sale if one is reasonably available and except in the case of goods which are perishable or threaten to decline in value speedily the seller must give the buyer reasonable notice of the time and place of the resale; and

    (c) if the goods are not to be within the view of those attending the sale the notification of sale must state the place where the goods are located and provide for their reasonable inspection by prospective bidders; and

    (d) the seller may buy.

(5) A purchaser who buys in good faith at a resale takes the goods free of any rights of the original buyer even though the seller fails to comply with one or more of the requirements of this section.

(6) The seller is not accountable to the buyer for any profit made on any resale. A person in the position of a seller (Section 2-707) or a buyer who has rightfully rejected or justifiably revoked acceptance must account for any excess over the amount of his security interest, as hereinafter defined (subsection (3) of Section 2-711).

§ 2-707. "Person in the Position of a Seller".

(1) A "person in the position of a seller" includes as against a principal an agent who has paid or become responsible for the price of goods of his principal or anyone who otherwise holds a security interest or other right in goods similar to that of a seller.

(2) A person in the position of a seller may as provided in this Article withhold or stop delivery (Section 2-705) and resell (Section 2-706) and recover incidental damages (Section 2-710).

§ 2-708. Seller's Damages for Non-acceptance or Repudiation.

(1) Subject to subsection (2) and to the provisions of this Article with respect to proof of market price (Section 2-723), the measure of damages for non-acceptance or repudiation by the buyer is the difference between the market price at the time and place for tender and the unpaid contract price together with any incidental damages provided in this Article (Section 2-710), but less expenses saved in consequence of the buyer's breach.

(2) If the measure of damages provided in subsection (1) is inadequate to put the seller in as good a position as performance would have done then the measure of damages is the profit (including reasonable overhead) which the seller would have made from full performance by the buyer, together with any incidental damages provided in this Article (Section 2-710), due allowance for costs reasonably incurred and due credit for payments or proceeds of resale.

§ 2-709. Action for the Price.

(1) When the buyer fails to pay the price as it becomes due the seller may recover, together with any incidental damages under the next section, the price

    (a) of goods accepted or of conforming goods lost or damaged within a commercially reasonable time after risk of their loss has passed to the buyer; and

    (b) of goods identified to the contract if the seller is unable after reasonable effort to resell them at a reasonable price or the circumstances reasonably indicate that such effort will be unavailing.

(2) Where the seller sues for the price he must hold for the buyer any goods which have been identified to the contract and are still in his control except that if resale becomes possible he may resell them at any time prior to the collection of the judgment. The net proceeds of any such resale must be credited to the buyer and payment of the judgment entitles him to any goods not resold.

(3) After the buyer has wrongfully rejected or revoked acceptance of the goods or has failed to make a payment due or has repudiated (Section 2-610), a seller who is held not entitled to the price under this section shall nevertheless be awarded damages for non-acceptance under the preceding section.

§ 2-710. Seller's Incidental Damages. Incidental damages to an aggrieved seller include any commercially reasonable charges, expenses or commissions incurred in stopping delivery, in the transportation, care and custody of goods after the buyer's breach, in connection with return or resale of the goods or otherwise resulting from the breach.

§ 2-711. Buyer's Remedies in General; Buyer's Security Interest in Rejected Goods.

(1) Where the seller fails to make delivery or repudiates or the buyer rightfully rejects or justifiably revokes acceptance then with respect to any goods involved, and with respect to the whole if the breach goes to the whole contract (Section 2-612), the buyer may cancel and whether or not he has done so may in addition to recovering so much of the price as has been paid

(a) "cover" and have damages under the next section as to all the goods affected whether or not they have been identified to the contract; or

(b) recover damages for non-delivery as provided in this Article (Section 2-713).

(2) Where the seller fails to deliver or repudiates the buyer may also

(a) if the goods have been identified recover them as provided in this Article (Section 2-502); or

(b) in a proper case obtain specific performance or replevy the goods as provided in this Article (Section 2-716).

(3) On rightful rejection or justifiable revocation of acceptance a buyer has a security interest in goods in his possession or control for any payments made on their price and any expenses reasonably incurred in their inspection, receipt, transportation, care and custody and may hold such goods and resell them in like manner as an aggrieved seller (Section 2-706).

§ 2-712. "Cover"; Buyer's Procurement of Substitute Goods.

(1) After a breach within the preceding section the buyer may "cover" by making in good faith and without unreasonable delay any reasonable purchase of or contract to purchase goods in substitution for those due from the seller.

(2) The buyer may recover from the seller as damages the difference between the cost of cover and the contract price together with any incidental or consequential damages as hereinafter defined (Section 2-715), but less expenses saved in consequence of the seller's breach.

(3) Failure of the buyer to effect cover within this section does not bar him from any other remedy.

§ 2-713. Buyer's Damages for Non-delivery or Repudiation.

(1) Subject to the provisions of this Article with respect to proof of market price (Section 2-723), the measure of damages for non-delivery or repudiation by the seller is the difference between the market price at the time when the buyer learned of the breach and the contract price together with any incidental and consequential damages provided in this Article (Section 2-715), but less expenses saved in consequence of the seller's breach.

(2) Market price is to be determined as of the place for tender or, in cases of rejection after arrival or revocation of acceptance, as of the place of arrival.

§ 2-714. Buyer's Damages for Breach in Regard to Accepted Goods.

(1) Where the buyer has accepted goods and given notification (subsection (3) of Section 2-607) he may recover as damages for any non-conformity of tender the loss resulting in the ordinary course of events from the seller's breach as determined in any manner which is reasonable.

(2) The measure of damages for breach of warranty is the difference at the time and place of acceptance between the value of the goods accepted and the value they would have had if they had been as warranted, unless special circumstances show proximate damages of a different amount.

(3) In a proper case any incidental and consequential damages under the next section may also be recovered.

§ 2-715. Buyer's Incidental and Consequential Damages.

(1) Incidental damages resulting from the seller's breach include expenses reasonably incurred in inspection, receipt, transportation and care and custody of goods rightfully rejected, any commercially reasonable charges, expenses or commissions in connection with effecting cover and any other reasonable expense incident to the delay or other breach.

(2) Consequential damages resulting from the seller's breach include

(a) any loss resulting from general or particular requirements and needs of which the seller at the time of contracting had reason to know and which could not reasonably be prevented by cover or otherwise; and

(b) injury to person or property proximately resulting from any breach of warranty.

§ 2-716. Buyer's Right to Specific Performance or Replevin.

(1) Specific performance may be decreed where the goods are unique or in other proper circumstances.

(2) The decree for specific performance may include such terms and conditions as to payment of the price, damages, or other relief as the court may deem just.

(3) The buyer has a right of replevin for goods identified to the contract if after reasonable effort he is unable to effect cover for such goods or the circumstances reasonably indicate that such effort will be unavailing or if the goods have been shipped under reservation and satisfaction of the security interest in them has been made or tendered.

§ 2-717. Deduction of Damages From the Price. The buyer on notifying the seller of his intention to do so may deduct all or any part of the damages resulting from any breach of the contract from any part of the price still due under the same contract.

§ 2-718. Liquidation or Limitation of Damages; Deposits.

(1) Damages for breach by either party may be liquidated in the agreement but only at an amount which is reasonable in the light of the anticipated or actual harm caused by the breach, the difficulties of proof of loss, and the inconvenience or nonfeasibility of otherwise obtaining an adequate remedy. A term fixing unreasonably large liquidated damages is void as a penalty.

(2) Where the seller justifiably withholds delivery of goods because of the buyer's breach, the buyer is entitled to restitution of any amount by which the sum of his payments exceeds

    (a) the amount to which the seller is entitled by virtue of terms liquidating the seller's damages in accordance with subsection (1), or

    (b) in the absence of such terms, twenty per cent of the value of the total performance for which the buyer is obligated under the contract or $500, whichever is smaller.

(3) The buyer's right to restitution under subsection (2) is subject to offset to the extent that the seller establishes

    (a) a right to recover damages under the provisions of this Article other than subsection (1), and

    (b) the amount or value of any benefits received by the buyer directly or indirectly by reason of the contract.

(4) Where a seller has received payment in goods their reasonable value or the proceeds of their resale shall be treated as payments for the purposes of subsection (2); but if the seller has notice of the buyer's breach before reselling goods received in part performance, his resale is subject to the conditions laid down in this Article on resale by an aggrieved seller (Section 2-706).

§ 2-719. Contractual Modification or Limitation of Remedy.

(1) Subject to the provisions of subsections (2) and (3) of this section and of the preceding section on liquidation and limitation of damages,

    (a) the agreement may provide for remedies in addition to or in substitution for those provided in this Article and may limit or alter the measure of damages recoverable under this Article, as by limiting the buyer's remedies to return of the goods and repayment of the price or to repair and replacement of nonconforming goods or parts; and

    (b) resort to a remedy as provided is optional unless the remedy is expressly agreed to be exclusive, in which case it is the sole remedy.

(2) Where circumstances cause an exclusive or limited remedy to fail of its essential purpose, remedy may be had as provided in this Act.

(3) Consequential damages may be limited or excluded unless the limitation or exclusion is unconscionable. Limitation of consequential damages for injury to the person in the case of consumer goods is prima facie unconscionable but limitation of damages where the loss is commercial is not.

§ 2-720. Effect of "Cancellation" or "Rescission" on Claims for Antecedent Breach.

Unless the contrary intention clearly appears, expressions of "cancellation" or "rescission" of the contract or the like shall not be construed as a renunciation or discharge of any claim in damages for an antecedent breach.

§ 2-721. Remedies for Fraud.

Remedies for material misrepresentation or fraud include all remedies available under this Article for non-fraudulent breach. Neither rescission or a claim for rescission of the contract for sale nor rejection or return of the goods shall bar or be deemed inconsistent with a claim for damages or other remedy.

§ 2-722. Who Can Sue Third Parties for Injury to Goods.

Where a third party so deals with goods which have been identified to a contract for sale as to cause actionable injury to a party to that contract

    (a) a right of action against the third party is in either party to the contract for sale who has title to or a security interest or a special property or an insurable interest in the goods; and if the goods have been destroyed or converted a right of action is also in the party who either bore the risk of loss under the contract for sale or has since the injury assumed that risk as against the other;

    (b) if at the time of the injury the party plaintiff did not bear the risk of loss as against the other party to the contract for sale and there is no arrangement between them for disposition of the recovery, his suit or settlement is, subject to his own interest, as a fiduciary for the other party to the contract;

    (c) either party may with the consent of the other sue for the benefit of whom it may concern.

§ 2-723. Proof of Market Price: Time and Place.

(1) If an action based on anticipatory repudiation comes to trial before the time for performance with respect to some or all of the goods, any damages based on market price (Section 2-708 or Section 2-713) shall be determined according to the price of such goods prevailing at the time when the aggrieved party learned of the repudiation.

(2) If evidence of a price prevailing at the times or places described in this Article is not readily available the price prevailing within any reasonable time before or after the time described or at any other place which in commercial judgment or under usage of trade would serve as a reasonable substitute for the one described may be used, making any proper allowance for the cost of transporting the goods to or from such other place.

(3) Evidence of a relevant price prevailing at a time or place other than the one described in this Article offered by one party is not admissible unless and until he has given the other party such notice as the court finds sufficient to prevent unfair surprise.

§ 2-724. Admissibility of Market Quotations.

Whenever the prevailing price or value of any goods regularly bought and sold in any established commodity market is in issue, reports in official publications or trade journals or in newspapers or periodicals of general circulation published as the reports of such market shall be admissible in evidence. The circumstances of the preparation of such a report may be shown to affect its weight but not its admissibility.

§ 2-725. Statute of Limitations in Contracts for Sale.

(1) An action for breach of any contract for sale must be commenced within four years after the cause of action has accrued. By the original agreement the parties may reduce the

period of limitation to not less than one year but may not extend it.

(2) A cause of action accrues when the breach occurs, regardless of the aggrieved party's lack of knowledge of the breach. A breach of warranty occurs when tender of delivery is made, except that where a warranty explicitly extends to future performance of the goods and discovery of the breach must await the time of such performance the cause of action accrues when the breach is or should have been discovered.

(3) Where an action commenced within the time limited by subsection (1) is so terminated as to leave available a remedy by another action for the same breach such other action may be commenced after the expiration of the time limited and within six months after the termination of the first action unless the termination resulted from voluntary discontinuance or from dismissal for failure or neglect to prosecute.

(4) This section does not alter the law on tolling of the statute of limitations nor does it apply to causes of action which have accrued before this Act becomes effective.

ARTICLE 3 / Commercial Paper

Part 1 Short Title, Form and Interpretation

§ 3-101. Short Title. This article shall be known and may be cited as Uniform Commercial Code—Commercial Paper.

§ 3-102. Definitions and Index of Definitions.

(1) In this Article unless the context otherwise requires

(a) "Issue" means the first delivery of an instrument to a holder or a remitter.

(b) An "order" is a direction to pay and must be more than an authorization or request. It must identify the person to pay with reasonable certainty. It may be addressed to one or more such persons jointly or in the alternative but not in succession.

(c) A "promise" is an undertaking to pay and must be more than an acknowledgment of an obligation.

(d) "Secondary party" means a drawer or endorser.

(e) "Instrument" means a negotiable instrument.

(2) Other definitions applying to this Article and the sections in which they appear are:

"Acceptance."   Section 3-410.
"Accommodation party."   Section 3-415.
"Alteration."   Section 3-407.
"Certificate of deposit."   Section 3-104.
"Certification."   Section 3-411.
"Check."   Section 3-104.
"Definite time."   Section 3-109.
"Dishonor."   Section 3-507.
"Draft."   Section 3-104.
"Holder in due course."   Section 3-302.
"Negotiation."   Section 3-202.
"Note."   Section 3-104.
"Notice of dishonor."   Section 3-508.
"On demand."   Section 3-108.
"Presentment."   Section 3-504.
"Protest."   Section 3-509.
"Restrictive Indorsement."   Section 3-205.
"Signature."   Section 3-401.

(3) The following definitions in other Articles apply to this Article:

"Account."   Section 4-104.
"Banking Day."   Section 4-104.
"Clearing house."   Section 4-104.
"Collecting bank."   Section 4-105.
"Customer."   Section 4-104.
"Depositary Bank."   Section 4-105.
"Documentary Draft."   Section 4-104.
"Intermediary Bank."   Section 4-105.
"Item."   Section 4-104.
"Midnight deadline."   Section 4-104.
"Payor bank."   Section 4-105.

(4) In addition Article 1 contains general definitions and principles of construction and interpretation applicable throughout this Article.

§ 3-103. Limitations on Scope of Article.

(1) This Article does not apply to money, documents of title or investment securities.

(2) The provisions of this Article are subject to the provisions of the Article on Bank Deposits and Collections (Article 4) and Secured Transactions (Article 9).

§ 3-104. Form of Negotiable Instruments: "Draft"; "Check"; "Certificate of Deposit"; "Note."

(1) Any writing to be a negotiable instrument within this Article must

(a) be signed by the maker or drawer; and

(b) contain an unconditional promise or order to pay a sum certain in money and no other promise, order, obligation or power given by the maker or drawer except as authorized by this Article; and

(c) be payable on demand or at a definite time; and

(d) be payable to order or to bearer.

(2) A writing which complies with the requirements of this section is

(a) a "draft" ("bill of exchange") if it is an order;

(b) a "check" if it is a draft drawn on a bank and payable on demand;

(c) a "certificate of deposit" if it is an acknowledgment by a bank of receipt of money with an engagement to repay it;

(d) a "note" if it is a promise other than a certificate of deposit.

(3) As used in other Articles of this Act, and as the context may require, the terms "draft," "check," "certificate of deposit" and "note" may refer to instruments which are not negotiable within this Article as well as to instruments which are so negotiable.

§ 3-105. When Promise or Order Unconditional.

(1) A promise or order otherwise unconditional is not made conditional by the fact that the instrument

(a) is subject to implied or constructive conditions; or

(b) states its consideration, whether performed or promised, or the transaction which gave rise to the instrument, or that the promise or order is made or the instrument matures in accordance with or "as per" such transaction; or

(c) refers to or states that it arises out of a separate agreement or refers to a separate agreement for rights as to pre-payment or acceleration; or

(d) states that it is drawn under a letter of credit; or

(e) states that it is secured, whether by mortgage, reservation of title or otherwise; or

(f) indicates a particular account to be debited or any other fund or source from which reimbursement is expected; or

(g) is limited to payment out of a particular fund or the proceeds of a particular source, if the instrument is issued by a government or governmental agency or unit; or

(h) is limited to payment out of the entire assets of a partnership, unincorporated association, trust or estate by or on behalf of which the instrument is issued.

(2) A promise or order is not unconditional if the instrument

(a) states that it is subject to or governed by any other agreement; or

(b) states that it is to be paid only out of a particular fund or source except as provided in this section.

§ 3-106. Sum Certain.

(1) The sum payable is a sum certain even though it is to be paid

(a) with stated interest or by stated installments; or

(b) with stated different rates of interest before and after default or a specified date; or

(c) with a stated discount or addition if paid before or after the date fixed for payment; or

(d) with exchange or less exchange, whether at a fixed rate or at the current rate; or

(e) with costs of collection or an attorney's fee or both upon default.

(2) Nothing in this section shall validate any term which is otherwise illegal.

§ 3-107. Money.

(1) An instrument is payable in money if the medium of exchange in which it is payable is money at the time the instrument is made. An instrument payable in "currency" or "current funds" is payable in money.

(2) A promise or order to pay a sum stated in a foreign currency is for a sum certain in money and, unless a different medium of payment is specified in the instrument, may be satisfied by payment of that number of dollars which the stated foreign currency will purchase at the buying sight rate for that currency on the day on which the instrument is payable or, if payable on demand, on the day of demand. If such an instrument specifies a foreign currency as the medium of payment the instrument is payable in that currency.

§ 3-108. Payable on Demand.

Instruments payable on demand include those payable at sight or on presentation and those in which no time for payment is stated.

§ 3-109. Definite Time.

(1) An instrument is payable at a definite time if by its terms it is payable

(a) on or before a stated date or at a fixed period after a stated date; or

(b) at a fixed period after sight; or

(c) at a definite time subject to any acceleration; or

(d) at a definite time subject to extension at the option of the holder, or to extension to a further definite time at the option of the maker or acceptor or automatically upon or after a specified act or event.

(2) An instrument which by its terms is otherwise payable only upon an act or event uncertain as to time of occurrence is not payable at a definite time even though the act or event has occurred.

§ 3-110. Payable to Order.

(1) An instrument is payable to order when by its terms it is payable to the order or assigns of any person therein specified with reasonable certainty, or to him or his order, or when it is conspicuously designated on its face as "exchange" or the like and names a payee. It may be payable to the order of

(a) the maker or drawer; or

(b) the drawee; or

(c) a payee who is not maker, drawer or drawee; or

(d) two or more payees together or in the alternative; or

(e) an estate, trust or fund, in which case it is payable to the order of the representative of each estate, trust or fund or his successors; or

(f) an office, or an officer by his title as such in which case it is payable to the principal but the incumbent of the office or his successors may act as if he or they were the holder; or

(g) a partnership or unincorporated association, in which case it is payable to the partnership or association and may be indorsed or transferred by any person thereto authorized.

(2) An instrument not payable to order is not made so payable by such words as "payable upon return of this instrument properly indorsed."

(3) an instrument made payable both to order and to bearer is payable to order unless the bearer words are handwritten or typewritten.

§ 3-111. Payable to Bearer. An instrument is payable to bearer when by its terms it is payable to

(a) bearer or the order of bearer; or

(b) a specified person or bearer; or

(c) "cash" or the order of "cash," or any other indication which does not purport to designate a specific payee.

§ 3-112. Terms and Omissions Not Affecting Negotiability.

(1) The negotiability of an instrument is not affected by

(a) the omission of a statement of any consideration or of the place where the instrument is drawn or payable; or

(b) a statement that collateral has been given to secure obligations either on the instrument or otherwise of an obligor on the instrument or that in case of default on those obligations the holder may realize on or dispose of the collateral; or

(c) a promise or power to maintain or protect collateral or to give additional collateral; or

(d) a term authorizing a confession of judgment on the instrument if it is not paid when due; or

(e) a term purporting to waive the benefit of any law intended for the advantage or protection of any obligor; or

(f) a term in a draft providing that the payee by indorsing or cashing it acknowledges full satisfaction of an obligation of the drawer; or

(g) a statement in a draft drawn in a set of parts (Section 3-801) to the effect that the order is effective only if no other part has been honored.

(2) Nothing in this section shall validate any term which is otherwise illegal.

§ 3-113. Seal.
An instrument otherwise negotiable is within this Article even though it is under a seal.

§ 3-114. Date, Antedating, Postdating.

(1) The negotiability of an instrument is not affected by the fact that it is undated, antedated or postdated.

(2) Where an instrument is antedated or postdated the time when it is payable is determined by the stated date if the instrument is payable on demand or at a fixed period after date.

(3) Where the instrument or any signature thereon is dated, the date is presumed to be correct.

§ 3-115. Incomplete Instruments.

(1) When a paper whose contents at the time of signing show that it is intended to become an instrument is signed while still incomplete in any necessary respect it cannot be enforced until completed.

(2) If the completion is unauthorized the rules as to material alteration apply (Section 3-407), even though the paper was not delivered by the maker or drawer; but the burden of establishing that any completion is unauthorized is on the party so asserting.

§ 3-116. Instruments Payable to Two or More Persons.
An instrument payable to the order of two or more persons

(a) if in the alternative is payable to any one of them and may be negotiated, discharged or enforced by any of them who has possession of it;

(b) if not in the alternative is payable to all of them and may be negotiated, discharged or enforced only by all of them.

§ 3-117. Instruments Payable with Words of Description.
An instrument made payable to a named person with the addition of words describing him

(a) as agent or officer of a specified person is payable to his principal but the agent or officer may act as if he were the holder;

(b) as any other fiduciary for a specified person or purpose is payable to the payee and may be negotiated, discharged or enforced by him;

(c) in any other manner is payable to the payee unconditionally and the additional words are without effect on subsequent parties.

§ 3-118. Ambiguous Terms and Rules of Construction.
The following rules apply to every instrument:

(a) Where there is doubt whether the instrument is a draft or a note the holder may treat it as either. A draft drawn on the drawer is effective as a note.

(b) Handwritten terms control typewritten and printed terms, and typewritten control printed.

(c) Words control figures except that if the words are ambiguous figures control.

(d) Unless otherwise specified a provision for interest means interest at the judgment rate at the place of payment from the date of the instrument, or if it is undated from the date of issue.

(e) Unless the instrument otherwise specifies two or more persons who sign as maker, acceptor or drawer or indorser and as a part of the same transaction are jointly and severally liable even though the instrument contains such words as "I promise to pay."

(f) Unless otherwise specified consent to extension authorizes a single extension for not longer than the original period. A consent to extension, expressed in the instrument, is binding on secondary parties and accommodation makers. A holder may not exercise his option to extend an instrument over the objection of a maker or acceptor or other party who in accordance with Section 3-604 tenders full payment when the instrument is due.

§ 3-119. Other Writings Affecting Instrument.

(1) As between the obligor and his immediate obligee or any transferee the terms of an instrument may be modified or affected by any other written agreement executed as a part of the same transaction, except that a holder in due course is not affected by any limitation of his rights arising out of the separate written agreement if he had no notice of the limitation when he took the instrument.

(2) A separate agreement does not affect the negotiability of an instrument.

§ 3-120. Instruments "Payable Through" Bank.
An instrument which states that it is "payable through" a bank or the like designates that bank as a collecting bank to make presentment but does not of itself authorize the bank to pay the instrument.

§ 3-121. Instruments Payable at Bank.

Note: *If this Act is introduced in the Congress of the United States this section should be omitted.*
(States to select either alternative)

Alternative A

A note or acceptance which states that it is payable at a bank is the equivalent of a draft drawn on the bank payable when it falls due out of any funds of the maker or acceptor in current account or otherwise available for such payment.

Alternative B

A note or acceptance which states that it is payable at a bank is not of itself an order or authorization to the bank to pay it.

§ 3-122. Accrual of Cause of Action.

(1) A cause of action against a maker or an acceptor accrues

(a) in the case of a time instrument on the day after maturity;

(b) in the case of a demand instrument upon its date or, if no date is stated, on the date of issue.

(2) A cause of action against the obligor of a demand or time certificate of deposit accrues upon demand, but demand on a

time certificate may not be made until on or after the date of maturity.

(3) A cause of action against a drawer of a draft or an indorser of any instrument accrues upon demand following dishonor of the instrument. Notice of dishonor is a demand.

(4) Unless an instrument provides otherwise, interest runs at the rate provided by law for a judgment

    (a) in the case of a maker, acceptor or other primary obligor of a demand instrument, from the date of demand;

    (b) in all other cases from the date of accrual of the cause of action.

Part 2   Transfer and Negotiation

§ 3-201.   Transfer: Right to Indorsement.

(1) Transfer of an instrument vests in the transferee such rights as the transferor has therein, except that a transferee who has himself been a party to any fraud or illegality affecting the instrument or who as a prior holder had notice of a defense or claim against it cannot improve his position by taking from a later holder in due course.

(2) A transfer of a security interest in an instrument vests the foregoing rights in the transferee to the extent of the interest transferred.

(3) Unless otherwise agreed any transfer for value of an instrument not then payable to bearer gives the transferee the specifically enforceable right to have the unqualified indorsement of the transferor. Negotiation takes effect only when the indorsement is made and until that time there is no presumption that the transferee is the owner.

§ 3-202.   Negotiation.

(1) Negotiation is the transfer of an instrument in such form that the transferee becomes a holder. If the instrument is payable to order it is negotiated by delivery with any necessary indorsement; if payable to bearer it is negotiated by delivery.

(2) An indorsement must be writted by or on behalf of the holder and on the instrument or on a paper so firmly affixed thereto as to become a part thereof.

(3) An indorsement is effective for negotiation only when it conveys the entire instrument or any unpaid residue. If it purports to be of less it operates only as a partial assignment.

(4) Words of assignment, condition, waiver, guaranty, limitation or disclaimer of liability and the like accompanying an indorsement do not affect its character as an indorsement.

§ 3-203.   Wrong or Misspelled Name.

Where an instrument is made payable to a person under a misspelled name or one other than his own he may indorse in that name or his own or both; but signature in both names may be required by a person paying or giving value for the instrument.

§ 3-204.   Special Indorsement; Blank Indorsement.

(1) A special indorsement specifies the person to whom or to whose order it makes the instrument payable. Any instrument specially indorsed becomes payable to the order of the special indorsee and may be further negotiated only by his indorsement.

(2) An indorsement in blank specifies no particular indorsee and may consist of a mere signature. An instrument payable to order and indorsed in blank becomes payable to bearer and may be negotiated by delivery alone until specially indorsed.

(3) The holder may convert a blank indorsement into a special indorsement by writing over the signature of the indorser in blank any contract consistent with the character of the indorsement.

§ 3-205.   Restrictive Indorsements.

An indorsement is restrictive which either

    (a) is conditional; or

    (b) purports to prohibit further transfer of the instrument; or

    (c) includes the words "for collection," "for deposit," "pay any bank" or like terms signifying a purpose of deposit or collection; or

    (d) otherwise states that it is for the benefit or use of the indorser or of another person.

§ 3-206.   Effect of Restrictive Indorsement.

(1) No restrictive indorsement prevents further transfer or negotiation of the instrument.

(2) An intermediary bank, or a payor bank which is not the depositary bank, is neither given notice nor otherwise affected by a restrictive indorsement of any person except the bank's immediate transferor or the person presenting for payment.

(3) Except for an intermediary bank, any transferee under an indorsement which is conditional or includes the words "for collection," "for deposit," "pay any bank," or like terms (subparagraphs (a) and (c) of Section 3-205) must pay or apply any value given by him for or on the security of the instrument consistently with the indorsement and to the extent that he does so he becomes a holder for value. In addition such transferee is a holder in due course if he otherwise complies with the requirements of Section 3-302 on what constitutes a holder in due course.

(4) The first taker under an indorsement for the benefit of the indorser of another person (subparagraph (d) of Section 3-205) must pay or apply any value given by him for or on the security of the instrument consistently with the indorsement and to the extent that he does so he becomes a holder for value. In addition such taker is a holder in due course if he otherwise complies with the requirements of Section 3-302 on what constitutes a holder in due course. A later holder for value is neither given notice nor otherwise affected by such restrictive indorsement unless he has knowledge that a fiduciary or other person has negotiated the instrument in any transaction for his own benefit or otherwise in breach of duty (subsection (2) of Section 3-304).

§ 3-207.   Negotiation Effective Although It May Be Rescinded.

(1) Negotiation is effective to transfer the instrument although the negotiation is

    (a) made by an infant, a corporation exceeding its power, or any other person without capacity; or

    (b) obtained by fraud, duress or mistake of any kind; or

    (c) part of an illegal transaction; or

    (d) made in breach of duty.

(2) Except as against a subsequent holder in due course such negotiation is in an appropriate case subject to rescission, the

declaration of a constructive trust or any other remedy permitted by law.

§ 3-208.   Reacquisition. Where an instrument is returned to or reacquired by a prior party he may cancel any indorsement which is not necessary to his title and reissue or further negotiate the instrument, but any intervening party is discharged as against the reacquiring party and subsequent holders not in due course and if his indorsement has been cancelled is discharged as against subsequent holders in due course as well.

Part 3   Rights of a Holder

§ 3-301.   Rights of a Holder.

The holder of an instrument whether or not he is the owner may transfer or negotiate it and, except as otherwise provided in Section 3-603 on payment or satisfaction, discharge it or enforce payment in his own name.

§ 3-302.   Holder in Due Course.

(1) A holder in due course is a holder who takes the instrument

(a) for value; and

(b) in good faith; and

(c) without notice that it is overdue or has been dishonored or of any defense against or claim to it on the part of any person.

(2) A payee may be a holder in due course.

(3) A holder does not become a holder in due course of an instrument:

(a) by purchase of it at judicial sale or by taking it under legal process; or

(b) by acquiring it in taking over an estate; or

(c) by purchasing it as part of a bulk transaction not in regular course of business of the transferor.

(4) A purchaser of a limited interest can be a holder in due course only to the extent of the interest purchased.

§ 3-303.   Taking for Value. A holder takes the instrument for value

(a) to the extent that the agreed consideration has been performed or that he acquires a security interest in or a lien on the instrument otherwise than by legal process; or

(b) when he takes the instrument in payment of or as security for an antecedent claim against any person whether or not the claim is due; or

(c) when he gives a negotiable instrument for it or makes an irrevocable commitment to a third person.

§ 3-304.   Notice to Purchaser.

(1) The purchaser has notice of a claim or defense if

(a) the instrument is so incomplete, bears such visible evidence of forgery or alteration, or is otherwise so irregular as to call into question its validity, terms or ownership or to create an ambiguity as the party to pay; or

(b) the purchaser has notice that the obligation of any party is voidable in whole or in part, or that all parties have been discharged.

(2) The purchaser has notice of a claim against the instrument when he has knowledge that a fiduciary has negotiated the instrument in payment of or as security for his own debt or in any transaction for his own benefit or otherwise in breach of duty.

(3) The purchaser has notice that an instrument is overdue if he has reason to know

(a) that any part of the principal amount is overdue or that there is an uncured default in payment of another instrument of the same series; or

(b) that acceleration of the instrument has been made; or

(c) that he is taking a demand instrument after demand has been made or more than a reasonable length of time after its issue. A reasonable time for a check drawn and payable within the states and territories of the United States and the District of Columbia is presumed to be thirty days.

(4) Knowledge of the following facts does not of itself give the purchaser notice of a defense of claim

(a) that the instrument is antedated or postdated;

(b) that it was issued or negotiated in return for an executory promise or accompanied by a separate agreement, unless the purchaser has notice that a defense or claim has arisen from the terms thereof;

(c) that any party has signed for accommodation;

(d) that an incomplete instrument has been completed, unless the purchaser has notice of any improper completion;

(e) that any person negotiating the instrument is or was a fiduciary;

(f) that there has been default in payment of interest on the instrument or in payment of any other instrument, except one of the same series.

(5) The filing or recording of a document does not of itself constitute notice within the provisions of this Article to a person who would otherwise be a holder in due course.

(6) To be effective notice must be received at such time and in such manner as to give a reasonable opportunity to act on it.

§ 3-305.   Rights of a Holder in Due Course. To the extent that a holder is a holder in due course he takes the instrument free from

(1) all claims to it on the part of any person; and

(2) all defenses of any party to the instrument with whom the holder has not dealt except

(a) infancy, to the extent that it is a defense to a simple contract; and

(b) such other incapacity, or duress, or illegality of the transaction, as renders the obligation of the party a nullity; and

(c) such misrepresentation as has induced the party to sign the instrument with neither knowledge nor reasonable opportunity to obtain knowledge of its character or its essential terms; and

(d) discharge in insolvency proceedings; and

(e) any other discharge of which the holder has notice when he takes the instrument.

§ 3-306. Rights of One Not Holder in Due Course. Unless he has the rights of a holder in due course any person takes the instrument subject to

(a) all valid claims to it on the part of any person; and
(b) all defenses of any party which would be available in an action on a simple contract; and
(c) the defenses of want or failure of consideration, nonperformance of any condition precedent, non-delivery, or delivery for a special purpose (Section 3-408); and
(d) the defense that he or a person through whom he holds the instrument acquired it by theft, or that payment or satisfaction to such holder would be inconsistent with the terms of a restrictive indorsement. The claim of any third person to the instrument is not otherwise available as a defense to any party liable thereon unless the third person himself defends the action for such party.

§ 3-307. Burden of Establishing Signatures, Defenses and Due Course.

(1) Unless specifically denied in the pleadings each signature on an instrument is admitted. When the effectiveness of a signature is put in issue

(a) the burden of establishing it is on the party claiming under the signature; but
(b) the signature is presumed to be genuine or authorized except where the action is to enforce the obligation of a purported signer who has died or become incompetent before proof is required.

(2) When signatures are admitted or established, production of the instrument entitles a holder to recover on it unless the defendant establishes a defense.
(3) After it is shown that a defense exists a person claiming the rights of a holder in due course has the burden of establishing that he or some person under whom he claims is in all respects a holder in due course.

Part 4   Liability of Parties

§ 3-401. Signature.

(1) No person is liable on an instrument unless his signature appears thereon.
(2) A signature is made by use of any name, including any trade or assumed name, upon an instrument, or by any word or mark used in lieu of a written signature.

§ 3-402. Signature in Ambiguous Capacity. Unless the instrument clearly indicates that a signature is made in some other capacity it is an indorsement.

§ 3-403. Signature of Authorized Representative.

(1) A signature may be made by an agent or other representative, and his authority to make it may be established as in other cases of representation. No particular form of appointment is necessary to establish such authority.
(2) An authorized representative who signs his own name to an instrument

(a) is personally obligated if the instrument neither names the person represented nor shows that the representative signed in a representative capacity;
(b) except as otherwise established between the immedi-

ate parties, is personally obligated if the instrument names the person represented but does not show that the representative signed in a representative capacity, or if the instrument does not name the person represented but does show that the representative signed in a representative capacity.

(3) Except as otherwise established the name of an organization preceded or followed by the name and office of an authorized individual is a signature made in a representative capacity.

§ 3-404. Unauthorized Signatures.

(1) Any unauthorized signature is wholly inoperative as that of the person whose name is signed unless he ratifies it or is precluded from denying it; but it operates as the signature of the unauthorized signer in favor of any person who in good faith pays the instrument or takes it for value.
(2) Any unauthorized signature may be ratified for all purposes of this Article. Such ratification does not of itself affect any rights of the person ratifying against the actual signer.

§ 3-405. Impostors; Signature in Name of Payee.

(1) An indorsement by any person in the name of a named payee is effective if

(a) an impostor by use of the mails or otherwise has induced the maker or drawer to issue the instrument to him or his confederate in the name of the payee; or
(b) a person signing as or on behalf of a maker or drawer intends the payee to have no interest in the instrument; or
(c) an agent or employee of the maker or drawer has supplied him with the name of the payee intending the latter to have no such interest.

(2) Nothing in this section shall affect the criminal or civil liability of the person so indorsing.

§ 3-406. Negligence Contributing to Alteration or Unauthorized Signature. Any person who by his negligence substantially contributes to a material alteration of the instrument or to the making of an unauthorized signature is precluded from asserting the alteration or lack of authority against a holder in due course or against a drawee or other payor who pays the instrument in good faith and in accordance with the reasonable commercial standards of the drawee's or payor's business.

§ 3-407. Alteration.

(1) Any alteration of an instrument is material which changes the contract of any party thereto in any respect, including any such change in

(a) the number or relations of the parties; or
(b) an incomplete instrument, by completing it otherwise than as authorized; or
(c) the writing as signed, by adding to it or by removing any part of it.

(2) As against any person other than a subsequent holder in due course

(a) alteration by the holder which is both fraudulent and material discharges any party whose contract is thereby changed unless that party assents or is precluded from asserting the defense;

(b) no other alteration discharges any party and the instrument may be enforced according to its original tenor, or as to incomplete instruments according to the authority given.

(3) A subsequent holder in due course may in all cases enforce the instrument according to its original tenor, and when an incomplete instrument has been completed, he may enforce it as completed.

§ 3-408. Consideration.
Want or failure of consideration is a defense as against any person not having the rights of a holder in due course (Section 3-305), except that no consideration is necessary for an instrument or obligation thereon given in payment of or as security for an antecedent obligation of any kind. Nothing in this section shall be taken to displace any statute outside this Act under which a promise is enforceable notwithstanding lack or failure of consideration. Partial failure of consideration is a defense pro tanto whether or not the failure is in an ascertained or liquidated amount.

§ 3-409. Draft Not an Assignment.

(1) A check or other draft does not of itself operate as an assignment of any funds in the hands of the drawee available for its payment, and the drawee is not liable on the instrument until he accepts it.

(2) Nothing in this section shall affect any liability in contract, tort or otherwise arising from any letter of credit or other obligation or representation which is not an acceptance.

§ 3-410. Definition and Operation of Acceptance.

(1) Acceptance is the drawee's signed engagement to honor the draft as presented. It must be written on the draft, and may consist of his signature alone. It becomes operative when completed by delivery or notification.

(2) A draft may be accepted although it has not been signed by the drawer or is otherwise incomplete or is overdue or has been dishonored.

(3) Where the draft is payable at a fixed period after sight and the acceptor fails to date his acceptance the holder may complete it by supplying a date in good faith.

§ 3-411. Certificate of a Check.

(1) Certification of a check is acceptance. Where a holder procures certification the drawer and all prior indorsers are discharged.

(2) Unless otherwise agreed a bank has no obligation to certify a check.

(3) A bank may certify a check before returning it for lack of proper indorsement. If it does so the drawer is discharged.

§ 3-412. Acceptance Varying Draft.

(1) Where the drawee's proffered acceptance in any manner varies the draft as presented the holder may refuse the acceptance and treat the draft as dishonored in which case the drawee is entitled to have his acceptance cancelled.

(2) The terms of the draft are not varied by an acceptance to pay at any particular bank or place in the United States, unless the acceptance states that the draft is to be paid only at such bank or place.

(3) Where the holder assents to an acceptance varying the terms of the draft each drawer and indorser who does not affirmatively assent is discharged.

§ 3-413. Contract of Maker, Drawer and Acceptor.

(1) The maker or acceptor engages that he will pay the instrument according to its tenor at the time of his engagement or as completed pursuant to Section 3-115 on incomplete instruments.

(2) The drawer engages that upon dishonor of the draft and any necessary notice of dishonor or protest he will pay the amount of the draft to the holder or to any indorser who takes it up. The drawer may disclaim this liability by drawing without recourse.

(3) By making, drawing or accepting the party admits as against all subsequent parties including the drawee the existence of the payee and his then capacity to indorse.

§ 3-414. Contract of Indorser; Order of Liability.

(1) Unless the indorsement otherwise specifies (as by such words as "without recourse") every indorser engages that upon dishonor and any necessary notice of dishonor and protest he will pay the instrument according to its tenor at the time of his indorsement to the holder or to any subsequent indorser who takes it up, even though the indorser who takes it up was not obligated to do so.

(2) Unless they otherwise agree indorsers are liable to one another in the order in which they indorse, which is presumed to be the order in which their signatures appear on the instrument.

§ 3-415. Contract of Accommodation Party.

(1) An accommodation party is one who signs the instrument in any capacity for the purpose of lending his name to another party to it.

(2) When the instrument has been taken for value before it is due the accommodation party is liable in the capacity in which he has signed even though the taker knows of the accommodation.

(3) As against a holder in due course and without notice of the accommodation oral proof of the accommodation is not admissible to give the accommodation party the benefit of discharges dependent on his character as such. In other cases the accommodation character may be shown by oral proof.

(4) An indorsement which shows that it is not in the chain of title is notice of its accommodation character.

(5) An accommodation party is not liable to the party accommodated, and if he pays the instrument has a right of recourse on the instrument against such party.

§ 3-416. Contract of Guarantor.

(1) "Payment guaranteed" or equivalent words added to a signature means that the signer engages that if the instrument is not paid when due he will pay it according to its tenor without resort by the holder to any other party.

(2) "Collection guaranteed" or equivalent words added to a signature mean that the signer engages that if the instrument is not paid when due he will pay it according to its tenor, but only after the holder has reduced his claim against the maker or acceptor to judgment and execution has been returned unsatisfied, or after the maker or acceptor has become insol-

vent or it is otherwise apparent that it is useless to proceed against him.

(3) Words of guaranty which do not otherwise specify guarantee payment.

(4) No words of guaranty added to the signature of a sole maker or acceptor affect his liability on the instrument. Such words added to the signature of one of two or more makers or acceptors create a presumption that the signature is for the accommodation of the others.

(5) When words of guaranty are used presentment, notice of dishonor and protest are not necessary to charge the user.

(6) Any guaranty written on the instrument is enforcible notwithstanding any statute of frauds.

§ 3-417. Warranties on Presentment and Transfer.

(1) Any person who obtains payment or acceptance and any prior transferor warrants to a person who in good faith pays or accepts that

(a) he has a good title to the instrument or is authorized to obtain payment or acceptance on behalf of one who has a good title; and

(b) he has no knowledge that the signature of the maker or drawer is unauthorized, except that this warranty is not given by a holder in due course acting in good faith

(i) to a maker with respect to the maker's own signature; or

(ii) to a drawer with respect to the drawer's own signature, whether or not the drawer is also the drawee; or

(iii) to an acceptor of a draft if the holder in due course took the draft after the acceptance or obtained the acceptance without knowledge that the drawer's signature was unauthorized; and

(c) the instrument has not been materially altered, except that this warranty is not given by a holder in due course acting in good faith

(i) to the maker of a note; or

(ii) to the drawer of a draft whether or not the drawer is also the drawee; or

(iii) to the acceptor of a draft with respect to alteration made prior to the acceptance, even though the acceptance provided "payable as originally drawn" or equivalent terms; or

(iv) to the acceptor of a draft with respect to an alteration made after the acceptance.

(2) Any person who transfers an instrument and receives consideration warrants to his transferee and if the transfer is by indorsement to any subsequent holder who takes the instrument in good faith that

(a) he has a good title to the instrument or is authorized to obtain payment or acceptance on behalf of one who has a good title and the transfer is otherwise rightful; and

(b) all signatures are genuine or authorized; and

(c) the instrument has not been materially altered; and

(d) no defense of any party is good against him; and

(e) he has no knowledge of any insolvency proceeding instituted with respect to the maker or acceptor or the drawer of an unaccepted instrument.

(3) By transferring "without recourse" the transferor limits the obligation stated in subsection (2) (d) to a warranty that he has no knowledge of such a defense.

(4) A selling agent or broker who does not disclose the fact that he is acting only as such gives the warranties provided in this section, but if he makes such disclosure warrants only his good faith and authority.

§ 3-418. Finality of Payment or Acceptance.
Except for recovery of bank payments as provided in the Article on Bank Deposits and Collections (Article 4) and except for liability for breach of warranty on presentment under the preceding section, payment or acceptance of any instrument is final in favor of a holder in due course, or a person who has in good faith changed his position in reliance on the payment.

§ 3-419. Conversion of Instrument; Innocent Representative.

(1) An instrument is converted when

(a) a drawee to whom it is delivered for acceptance refuses to return it on demand; or

(b) any person to whom it is delivered for payment refuses on demand either to pay or to return it; or

(c) it is paid on a forged indorsement.

(2) In an action against a drawee under subsection (1) the measure of the drawee's liability is the face amount of the instrument. In any other action under subsection (1) the measure of liability is presumed to be the face amount of the instrument.

(3) Subject to the provisions of this Act concerning restrictive indorsements a representative, including a depositary or collecting bank, who has in good faith and in accordance with the reasonable commercial standards applicable to the business of such representative dealt with an instrument or its proceeds on behalf of one who was not the true owner is not liable in conversion or otherwise to the true owner beyond the amount of any proceeds remaining in his hands.

(4) An intermediary bank or payor bank which is not a depositary bank is not liable in conversion solely by reason of the fact that proceeds of an item indorsed restrictively (Sections 3-205 and 3-206) are not paid or applied consistently with the restrictive indorsement of an indorser other than its immediate transferor.

Part 5 Presentment, Notice of Dishonor and Protest

§ 3-501. When Presentment, Notice of Dishonor, and Protest Necessary or Permissible

(1) Unless excused (Section 3-511) presentment is necessary to charge secondary parties as follows:

(a) presentment for acceptance is necessary to charge the drawer and indorsers of a draft where the draft so provides, or is payable elsewhere than at the residence or place of business of the drawee, or its date of payment depends upon such presentment. The holder may at his option present for acceptance any other draft payable at a stated date;

(b) presentment for payment is necessary to charge any indorser;

(c) in the case of any drawer, the acceptor of a draft payable at a bank or the maker of a note payable at a bank, presentment for payment is necessary, but failure to make presentment discharges such drawer, acceptor or maker only as stated in Section 3-502(1) (b).

(2) Unless excused (Section 3-511)

(a) notice of any dishonor is necessary to charge any indorser;

(b) in the case of any drawer, the acceptor of a draft payable at a bank or the maker of a note payable at a bank, notice of any dishonor is necessary, but failure to give such notice discharges such drawer, acceptor or maker only as stated in Section 3-502(1) (b).

(3) Unless excused (Section 3-511) protest of any dishonor is necessary to charge the drawer and indorsers of any draft which on its face appears to be drawn or payable outside of the states and territories of the United States and the District of Columbia. The holder may at his option make protest of any dishonor of any other instrument and in the case of a foreign draft may on insolvency of the acceptor before maturity make protest for a better security.

(4) Notwithstanding any provision of this section, neither presentment nor notice of dishonor nor protest is necessary to charge an indorser who has indorsed an instrument after maturity.

§ 3-502. Unexcused Delay; Discharge.

(1) Where without excuse any necessary presentment or notice of dishonor is delayed beyond the time when it is due

(a) any indorser is discharged; and

(b) any drawer or the acceptor of a draft payable at a bank or the maker of a note payable at a bank who because the drawee or payor bank becomes insolvent during the delay is deprived of funds maintained with the drawee or payor bank to cover the instrument may discharge his liability by written assignment to the holder of his rights against the drawee or payor bank in respect of such funds, but such drawer, acceptor or maker is not otherwise discharged.

(2) Where without excuse a necessary protest is delayed beyond the time when it is due any drawer or indorser is discharged.

§ 3-503. Time of Presentment.

(1) Unless a different time is expressed in the instrument the time for any presentment is determined as follows:

(a) where an instrument is payable at or a fixed period after a stated date any presentment for acceptance must be made on or before the date it is payable;

(b) where an instrument is payable after sight it must either be presented for acceptance or negotiated within a reasonable time after date or issue whichever is later;

(c) where an instrument shows the date on which it is payable presentment for payment is due on that date;

(d) where an instrument is accelerated presentment for payment is due within a reasonable time after the acceleration;

(e) with respect to the liability of any secondary party presentment for acceptance or payment of any other instrument is due within a reasonable time after such party becomes liable thereon.

(2) A reasonable time for presentment is determined by the nature of the instrument, any usage of banking or trade and the facts of the particular case. In the case of an uncertified check which is drawn and payable within the United States and which is not a draft drawn by a bank the following are presumed to be reasonable periods within which to present for payment or to initiate bank collection:

(a) with respect to the liability of the drawer, thirty days after date or issue whichever is later and

(b) with respect to the liability of an indorser, seven days after his indorsement.

(3) Where any presentment is due on a day which is not a full business day for either the person making presentment or the party to pay or accept, presentment is due on the next following day which is a full business day for both parties.

(4) Presentment to be sufficient must be made at a reasonable hour, and if at a bank during its banking day.

§ 3-504. How Presentment Made.

(1) Presentment is a demand for acceptance or payment made upon the maker, acceptor, drawee or other payor by or on behalf of the holder.

(2) Presentment may be made

(a) by mail, in which even the time of presentment is determined by the time or receipt of the mail; or

(b) through a clearing house; or

(c) at the place of acceptance or payment specified in the instrument or if there be none at the place of business or residence of the party to accept or pay. If neither the party to accept or pay nor anyone authorized to act for him is present or accessible at such place presentment is excused.

(3) It may be made

(a) to any one of two or more makers, acceptors, drawees or other payors; or

(b) to any person who has authority to make or refuse the acceptance or payment.

(4) A draft accepted or a note made payable at a bank in the United States must be presented at such bank.

(5) In the cases described in Section 4-210 presentment may be made in the manner and with the result stated in that section.

§ 3-505. Rights of Party to Whom Presentment Is Made.

(1) The party to whom presentment is made may without dishonor require

(a) exhibition of the instrument; and

(b) reasonable identification of the person making presentment and evidence of his authority to make it if made for another; and

(c) that the instrument be produced for acceptance or payment at a place specified in it, or if there be none at any place reasonable in the circumstances; and

(d) a signed receipt on the instrument for any partial or full payment and its surrender upon full payment.

(2) Failure to comply with any such requirement invalidates the presentment but the person presenting has a reasonable time in which to comply and the time for acceptance or payment runs from the time of compliance.

§ 3-506. Time Allowed for Acceptance or Payment.

(1) Acceptance may be deferred without dishonor until the close of the next business day following presentment. The holder may also in good faith effort to obtain acceptance and without either dishonor of the instrument or discharge of secondary parties allow postponement of acceptance for an additional business day.

(2) Except as a longer time is allowed in the case of documentary drafts drawn under a letter of credit, and unless an earlier time is agreed to by the party to pay, payment of an instrument may be deferred without dishonor pending reasonable examination to determine whether it is properly payable, but payment must be made in any event before the close of business on the day of presentment.

§ 3-507. Dishonor; Holder's Right of Recourse; Term Allowing Representment.

(1) An instrument is dishonored when

(a) a necessary or optional presentment is duly made and due acceptance or payment is refused or cannot be obtained within the prescribed time or in case of bank collections the instrument is seasonably returned by the midnight deadline (Section 4-301); or

(b) presentment is excused and the instrument is not duly accepted or paid.

(2) Subject to any necessary notice of dishonor and protest, the holder has upon dishonor an immediate right of recourse against the drawers and indorsers.

(3) Return of an instrument for lack of proper indorsement is not dishonor.

(4) A term in a draft or an indorsement thereof allowing a stated time for representment in the event of any dishonor of the draft by nonacceptance if a time draft or by nonpayment if a sight draft gives the holder as against any secondary party bound by the term an option to waive the dishonor without affecting the liability of the secondary party and he may present again up to the end of the stated time.

§ 3-508. Notice of Dishonor.

(1) Notice of dishonor may be given to any person who may be liable on the instrument by or on behalf of the holder or any party who has himself received notice, or any other party who can be compelled to pay the instrument. In addition an agent or bank in whose hands the instrument is dishonored may give notice to his principal or customer or to another agent or bank from which the instrument was received.

(2) Any necessary notice must be given by a bank before its midnight deadline and by any other person before midnight of the third business day after dishonor or receipt of notice of dishonor.

(3) Notice may be given in any reasonable manner. It may be oral or written and in any terms which identify the instrument and state that it has been dishonored. A misdescription which does not mislead the party notified does not vitiate the notice. Sending the instrument bearing a stamp, ticket or writing stating that acceptance or payment has been refused or sending a notice of debit with respect to the instrument is sufficient.

(4) Written notice is given when sent although it is not received.

(5) Notice to one partner is notice to each although the firm has been dissolved.

(6) When any party is in insolvency proceedings instituted after the issue of the instrument notice may be given either to the party or to the representative of his estate.

(7) When any party is dead or incompetent notice may be sent to his last known address or given to his personal representative.

(8) Notice operates for the benefit of all parties who have rights on the instrument against the party notified.

§ 3-509. Protest; Noting for Protest.

(1) A protest is a certificate of dishonor made under the hand and seal of a United States consul or vice consul or a notary public or other person authorized to certify dishonor by the law of the place where dishonor occurs. It may be made upon information satisfactory to such person.

(2) The protest must identify the instrument and certify either that due presentment has been made or the reason why it is excused and that the instrument has been dishonored by a nonacceptance or nonpayment.

(3) The protest may also certify that notice of dishonor has been given to all parties or to specified parties.

(4) Subject to subsection (5) any necessary protest is due by the time that notice of dishonor is due.

(5) If, before protest is due, an instrument has been noted for protest by the officer to make protest, the protest may be made at any time thereafter as of the date of the noting.

§ 3-510. Evidence of Dishonor and Notice of Dishonor.

The following are admissible as evidence and create a presumption of dishonor and of any notice or dishonor therein shown:

(a) a document regular in form as provided in the preceding section which purports to be a protest;

(b) the purported stamp or writing of the drawee, payor bank or presenting bank on the instrument or accompanying it stating that acceptance or payment has been refused for reasons consistent with dishonor;

(c) any book or record of the drawee, payor bank, or any collecting bank kept in the usual course of business which shows dishonor, even though there is no evidence of who made the entry.

§ 3-511. Waived or Excused Presentment, Protest or Notice of Dishonor or Delay Therein.

(1) Delay in presentment, protest or notice of dishonor is excused when the party is without notice that it is due or when the delay is caused by circumstances beyond his control and he exercises reasonable diligence after the cause of the delay ceases to operate.

(2) Presentment or notice or protest as the case may be is entirely excused when

(a) the party to be charged has waived it expressly or by implication either before or after it is due; or

(b) such party has himself dishonored the instrument or has countermanded payment or otherwise has no reason to expect or right to require that the instrument be accepted or paid; or

(c) by reasonable diligence the presentment or protest cannot be made or the notice given.

(3) Presentment is also entirely excused when

(a) the maker, acceptor or drawee of any instrument except a documentary draft is dead or in insolvency proceedings instituted after the issue of the instrument; or
(b) acceptance or payment is refused but not for want of proper presentment.

(4) Where a draft has been dishonored by nonacceptance a later presentment for payment and any notice of dishonor and protest for nonpayment are excused unless in the meantime the instrument has been accepted.

(5) A waiver of protest is also a waiver of presentment and of notice of dishonor even though protest is not required.

(6) Where a waiver of presentment or notice or protest is embodied in the instrument itself it is binding upon all parties; but where it is written above the signature of an indorser it binds him only.

Part 6 Discharge

§ 3-601. Discharge of Parties.

(1) The extent of the discharge of any party from liability on an instrument is governed by the section on

(a) payment or satisfaction (Section 3-603; or
(b) tender of payment (Section 3-604); or
(c) cancellation or renunciation (Section 3-605); or
(d) impairment of right of recourse or of collateral (Section 3-606); or
(e) reacquisition of the instrument by a prior party (Section 3-208); or
(f) fraudulent and material alteration (Section 3-407); or
(g) certification of a check (Section 3-411); or
(h) acceptance varying a draft (Section 3-412); or
(i) unexcused delay in presentment or notice of dishonor or protest (Section 3-502).

(2) Any party is also discharged from his liability on an instrument to another party by any other act or agreement with such party which would discharge his simple contract for the payment of money.

(3) The liability of all parties is discharged when any party who has himself no right of action or recourse on the instrument

(a) reacquires the instrument in his own right; or
(b) is discharged under any provision of this Article, except as otherwise provided with respect to discharge for impairment of recourse or of collateral (Section 3-606).

§ 3-602. Effect of Discharge Against Holder in Due Course.
No discharge of any party provided by this Article is effective against a subsequent holder in due course unless he has notice thereof when he takes the instrument.

§ 3-603. Payment or Satisfaction.

(1) The liability of any party is discharged to the extent of his payment or satisfaction to the holder even though it is made with knowledge of a claim of another person to the instrument unless prior to such payment or satisfaction the person making the claim either supplies indemnity deemed adequate by the party seeking the discharge or enjoins payment or satisfaction by order of a court of competent jurisdiction in an action in which the adverse claimant and the

holder are parties. This subsection does not, however, result in the discharge of the liability

(a) of a party who in bad faith pays or satisfies a holder who acquired the instrument, by theft or who (unless having the rights of a holder in due course) holds through one who so acquired it; or
(b) of a party (other than an intermediary bank or a payor bank which is not a depositary bank) who pays or satisfies the holder of an instrument which has been restrictively indorsed in a manner not consistent with the terms of such restrictive indorsement.

(2) Payment or satisfaction may be made with the consent of the holder by any person including a stranger to the instrument. Surrender of the instrument to such a person gives him the rights of a transferee (Section 3-201).

§ 3-604. Tender of Payment.

(1) Any party making tender of full payment to a holder when or after it is due is discharged to the extent of all subsequent liability for interest, costs and attorney's fees.

(2) The holder's refusal of such tender wholly discharges any party who has a right or recourse against the party making the tender.

(3) Where the maker or acceptor of an instrument payable otherwise than on demand is able and ready to pay at every place of payment specified in the instrument when it is due, it is equivalent to tender.

§ 3-605. Cancellation and Renunciation.

(1) The holder of an instrument may even without consideration discharge any party

(a) in any manner apparent on the face of the instrument or the indorsement, as by intentionally cancelling the instrument or the party's signature by destruction or mutilation, or by striking out the party's signature; or
(b) by renouncing his rights by a writing signed and delivered or by surrender of the instrument to the party to be discharged.

(2) Neither cancellation nor renunciation without surrender of the instrument affects the title thereto.

§ 3-606. Impairment of Recourse or of Collateral.

(1) The holder discharges any party to the instrument to the extent that without such party's consent the holder

(a) without express reservation of rights releases or agrees not to sue any person against whom the party has to the knowledge of the holder a right of recourse or agrees to suspend the right to enforce against such person the instrument or collateral or otherwise discharges such person, except that failure or delay in effecting any required presentment, protest or notice of dishonor with respect to any such person does not discharge any party as to whom presentment, protest or notice of dishonor is effective or unnecessary; or
(b) unjustifiably impairs any collateral for the instrument given by or on behalf of the party or any person against whom he has a right of recourse.

(2) By express reservation of rights against a party with a right of recourse the holder preserves

(a) all his rights against such party as of the time when the instrument was originally due; and

(b) the right of the party to pay the instrument as of that time; and

(c) all rights of such party to recourse against others.

Part 7   Advice of International Sight Draft

§ 3-701.   Letter of Advice of International Sight Draft.

(1) A "letter of advice" is a drawer's communication to the drawee that a described draft has been drawn.

(2) Unless otherwise agreed when a bank receives from another bank a letter of advice of an international sight draft the drawee bank may immediately debit the drawer's account and stop the running of interest pro tanto. Such a debit and any resulting credit to any account covering outstanding drafts leaves in the drawer full power to stop payment or otherwise dispose of the amount and creates no trust or interest in favor of the holder.

(3) Unless otherwise agreed and except where a draft is drawn under a credit issued by the drawee, the drawee of an international sight draft owes the drawer no duty to pay an unadvised draft but if it does so and the draft is genuine, may appropriately debit the drawer's account.

Part 8   Miscellaneous

§ 3-801.   Drafts in a Set.

(1) Where a draft is drawn in a set of parts, each of which is numbered and expressed to be an order only if no other part has been honored, the whole of the parts constitutes one draft but a taker of any part may become a holder in due course of the draft.

(2) Any person who negotiates, indorses or accepts a single part of a draft drawn in a set thereby becomes liable to any holder in due course of that part as if it were the whole set, but as between different holders in due course to whom different parts have been negotiated the holder whose title first accrues has all rights to the draft and its proceeds.

(3) As against the drawee the first presented part of a draft drawn in a set is the part entitled to payment, or if a time draft to acceptance and payment. Acceptance of any subsequently presented part renders the drawee liable thereon under subsection (2). With respect both to a holder and to the drawer payment of a subsequently presented part of a draft payable at sight has the same effect as payment of a check notwithstanding an effective stop order (Section 4-407).

(4) Except as otherwise provided in this section, where any part of a draft in a set is discharged by payment or otherwise the whole draft is discharged.

§ 3-802.   Effect of Instrument on Obligation for Which It Is Given.

(1) Unless otherwise agreed where an instrument is taken for an underlying obligation

(a) the obligation is pro tanto discharged if a bank is drawer, maker or acceptor of the instrument and there is no recourse on the instrument against the underlying obligor; and

(b) in any other case the obligation is suspended pro tanto until the instrument is due or if it is payable on demand until its presentment. If the instrument is dishonored action may be maintained on either the instrument or the obligation; discharge of the underlying obligor on the instrument also discharges him on the obligation.

(2) The taking in good faith of a check which is not postdated does not of itself so extend the time on the original obligation as to discharge a surety.

§ 3-803.   Notice to Third Party.

Where a defendant is sued for breach of an obligation for which a third person is answerable over under this Article he may give the third person written notice of the litigation, and the person notified may then give similar notice to any other person who is answerable over to him under this Article. If the notice states that the person notified may come in and defend and that if the person notified does not do so he will in any action against him by the person giving the notice be bound by any determination of fact common to the two litigations, then unless after seasonable receipt of the notice the person notified does come in and defend he is so bound.

§ 3-804.   Lost, Destroyed or Stolen Instruments. The owner of an instrument which is lost, whether by destruction, theft or otherwise, may maintain an action in his own name and recover from any party liable thereon upon due proof of his ownership, the facts which prevent his production of the instrument and its terms. The court may require security indemnifying the defendant against loss by reason of further claims on the instrument.

§ 3-805.   Instruments Not Payable to Order or to Bearer. This Article applies to any instrument whose terms do not preclude transfer and which is otherwise negotiable within this Article but which is not payable to order to bearer, except that there can be no holder in due course of such an instrument.

ARTICLE 4 / Bank Deposits and Collections

Part 1   General Provisions and Definitions

§ 4-101.   Short Title. This Article shall be known and may be cited as Uniform Commercial Code—Bank Deposits and Collections.

§ 4-102.   Applicability.

(1) To the extent that items within this Article are also within the scope of Articles 3 and 8, they are subject to the provisions of those Articles. In the event of conflict the provisions of this Article govern those of Article 3 but the provisions of Article 8 govern those of this Article.

(2) The liability of a bank for action or non-action with respect to any item handled by it for purposes of presentment, payment or collection is governed by the law of the place where the bank is located. In the case of action or non-action by or at a branch or separate office of a bank, its liability is governed by the law of the place where the branch or separate office is located.

§ 4-103. Variation by Agreement; Measure of Damages; Certain Action Constituting Ordinary Care.

(1) The effect of the provisions of this Article may be varied by agreement except that no agreement can disclaim a bank's responsibility for its own lack of good faith or failure to exercise ordinary care or can limit the measure of damages for such lack or failure; but the parties may by agreement determine the standards by which such responsibility is to be measured if such standards are not manifestly unreasonable.

(2) Federal Reserve regulations and operating letters, clearing house rules, and the like, have the effect of agreements under subsection (1), whether or not specifically assented to by all parties interested in items handled.

(3) Action or non-action approved by this Article or pursuant to Federal Reserve regulations or operating letters constitutes the exercise of ordinary care and, in the absence of special instructions, action or non-action consistent with clearing house rules and the like or with a general banking usage not disapproved by this Article, prima facie constitutes the exercise of ordinary care.

(4) The specification or approval of certain procedures by this Article does not constitute disapproval of other procedures which may be reasonable under the circumstances.

(5) The measure of damages for failure to exercise ordinary care in handling an item is the amount of the item reduced by an amount which could not have been realized by the use of ordinary care, and where there is bad faith it includes other damages, if any, suffered by the party as a proximate consequence.

§ 4-104. Definitions and Index of Definitions.

(1) In this Article unless the context otherwise requires

   (a) "Account" means any account with a bank and includes a checking, time, interest or savings account;

   (b) "Afternoon" means the period of a day between noon and midnight;

   (c) "Banking day" means that part of any day on which a bank is open to the public for carrying on substantially all of its banking functions;

   (d) "Clearing house" means any association of banks or other payors regularly clearing items;

   (e) "Customer" means any person having an account with a bank or for whom a bank has agreed to collect items and includes a bank carrying an account with another bank;

   (f) "Documentary draft" means any negotiable or non-negotiable draft with accompanying documents, securities or other papers to be delivered against honor of the draft;

   (g) "Item" means any instrument for the payment of money even though it is not negotiable but does not include money;

   (h) "Midnight deadline" with respect to a bank is midnight on its next banking day following the banking day on which it receives the relevant item or notice or from which the time for taking action commences to run, whichever is later;

   (i) "Properly payable" includes the availability of funds for payment at the time of decision to pay or dishonor;

   (j) "Settle" means to pay in cash, by clearing house settlement, in a charge or credit or by remittance, or otherwise as instructed. A settlement may be either provisional or final;

   (k) "Suspends payments" with respect to a bank means that it has been closed by order of the supervisory authorities, that a public officer has been appointed to take it over or that it ceases or refuses to make payments in the ordinary course of business.

(2) Other definitions applying to this Article and the sections in which they appear are:

   "Collecting bank."   Section 4-105.
   "Depositary bank."   Section 4-105.
   "Intermediary bank."   Section 4-105.
   "Payor bank."   Section 4-105.
   "Presenting bank."   Section 4-105.
   "Remitting bank."   Section 4-105.

(3) The following definitions in other Articles apply to this Article:

   "Acceptance."   Section 3-410.
   "Certificate of deposit."   Section 3-104.
   "Certification."   Section 3-411.
   "Check."   Section 3-104.
   "Draft."   Section 3-104.
   "Holder in due course."   Section 3-302.
   "Notice of dishonor."   Section 3-508.
   "Presentment."   Section 3-504.
   "Protest."   Section 3-509.
   "Secondary party."   Section 3-102.

(4) In addition Article 1 contains general definitions and principles of construction and interpretation applicable throughout this Article.

§ 4-105. "Depositary Bank"; "Intermediary Bank"; "Collecting Bank"; "Payor Bank"; "Presenting Bank"; "Remitting Bank."

In this Article unless the context otherwise requires

   (a) "Depositary bank" means the first bank to which an item is transferred for collection even though it is also the payor bank;

   (b) "Payor bank" means a bank by which an item is payable as drawn or accepted;

   (c) "Intermediary bank" means any bank to which an item is transferred in course of collection except the depositary or payor bank;

   (d) "Collecting bank" means any bank handling the item for collection except the payor bank;

   (e) "Presenting bank" means any bank presenting an item except a payor bank;

   (f) "Remitting bank" means any payor or intermediary bank remitting for an item.

§ 4-106. Separate Office of a Bank.
A branch or separate office of a bank [maintaining its own deposit ledgers] is a separate bank for the purpose of computing the time within which and determining the place at or to which action may be taken or notices or orders shall be given under this Article and under Article 3.

Note: *The words in Brackets are optional.*

§ 4-107. Time of Receipt of Items.

(1) For the purpose of allowing time to process items, prove balances and make the necessary entries on its books to determine its position for the day, a bank may fix an afternoon hour of two P.M. or later as a cut-off hour for the handling of money and items and the making of entries on its books.

(2) Any item or deposit of money received on any day after a cut-off hour so fixed or after the close of the banking day may be treated as being received at the opening of the next banking day.

§ 4-108. Delays.

(1) Unless otherwise instructed, a collecting bank in a good faith effort to secure payment may, in the case of specific items and with or without the approval of any person involved, waive, modify or extend time limits imposed or permitted by this Act for a period not in excess of an additional banking day without discharge of secondary parties and without liability to its transferor or any prior party.

(2) Delay by a collecting bank or payor bank beyond time limits prescribed or permitted by this Act or by instructions is excused if caused by interruption of communication facilities, suspension of payments by another bank, war, emergency conditions or other circumstances beyond the control of the bank provided it exercises such diligence as the circumstances require.

§ 4-109. Process of Posting.
The "process of posting" means the usual procedure followed by a payor bank in determining to pay an item and in recording the payment including one or more of the following or other steps as determined by the bank:

(a) verification of any signature;
(b) ascertaining that sufficient funds are available;
(c) affixing a "paid" or other stamp;
(d) entering a charge or entry to a customer's account;
(e) correcting or reversing an entry or erroneous action with respect to the item.

Part 2 Collection of Items: Depositary and Collecting Banks

§ 4-201. Presumption and Duration of Agency Status of Collecting Banks and Provisional Status of Credits; Applicability of Article; Item Indorsed "Pay any Bank."

(1) Unless a contrary intent clearly appears and prior to the time that a settlement given by a collecting bank for an item is or becomes final (subsection (3) of Section 4-211 and Sections 4-212 and 4-213) the bank is an agent or sub-agent of the owner of the item and any settlement given for the item is provisional. This provision applies regardless of the form of indorsement or lack of indorsement and even though credit given for the item is subject to immediate withdrawal as of right or is in fact withdrawn; but the continuance of ownership of an item by its owner and any rights of the owner to proceeds of the item are subject to rights of a collecting bank such as those resulting from outstanding advances on the item and valid rights of setoff. When an item is handled by banks for purposes of presentment, payment and collection, the relevant provisions of this Article apply even though action of parties clearly establishes that a particular bank has purchased the item and is the owner of it.

(2) After an item has been indorsed with the words "pay any bank" or the like, only a bank may acquire the rights of a holder

(a) until the item has been returned to the customer initiating collection; or
(b) until the item has been specially indorsed by a bank to a person who is not a bank.

§ 4-202. Responsibility for Collection; When Action Seasonable.

(1) A collecting bank must use ordinary care in

(a) presenting an item or sending it for presentment; and
(b) sending notice of dishonor or nonpayment or returning an item other than a documentary draft to the bank's transferor]or directly to the depositary bank under subsection (2) of Section 4-212] (*see note to Section 4-212*) after learning that the item has not been paid or accepted, as the case may be; and
(c) settling for an item when the bank receives final settlement; and
(d) making or providing for any necessary protest; and
(e) notifying its transferor of any loss or delay in transit within a reasonable time after discovery thereof.

(2) A collecting bank taking proper action before its midnight deadline following receipt of an item, notice or payment acts seasonably; taking proper action within a reasonably longer time may be seasonable but the bank has the burden of so establishing.

(3) Subject to subsection (1) (a), a bank is not liable for the insolvency, neglect, misconduct, mistake or default of another bank or person or for loss or destruction of an item in transit or in the possession of others.

§ 4-203. Effect of Instructions.
Subject to the provisions of Article 3 concerning conversion of instruments (Section 3-429) and the provisions of both Article 3 and this Article concerning restrictive indorsements only a collecting bank's transferor can give instructions which affect the bank or constitute notice to it and a collecting bank is not liable to prior parties for any action taken pursuant to such instructions or in accordance with any agreement with its transferor.

§ 4-204. Methods of Sending and Presenting; Sending Direct to Payor Bank.

(1) A collecting bank must send items by reasonably prompt method taking into consideration any relevant instructions, the nature of the item, the number of such items on hand, and the cost of collection involved and the method generally used by it or others to present such items.

(2) A collecting bank may send

(a) any item direct to the payor bank;
(b) any item to any non-bank payor if authorized by its transferor; and
(c) any item other than documentary drafts to any non-bank payor, if authorized by Federal Reserve regulation or operating letter, clearing house rule or the like.

(3) Presenting may be made by a presenting bank at a place where the payor bank has requested that presentment be made.

§ 4-205. Supplying Missing Indorsement; No Notice from Prior Indorsement.

(1) A depositary bank which has taken an item for collection may supply any indorsement of the customer which is necessary to title unless the item contains the words "payee's indorsement required" or the like. In the absence of such a requirement a statement placed on the item by the depositary bank to the effect that the item was deposited by a customer or credited to his account is effective as the customer's indorsement.

(2) An intermediary bank, or payor bank which is not a depositary bank, is neither given notice nor otherwise affected by a restrictive indorsement of any person except the bank's immediate transferor.

§ 4-206. Transfer Between Banks.
Any agreed method which identifies the transferor bank is sufficient for the item's further transfer to another bank.

§ 4-207. Warranties or Customer and Collecting Bank on Transfer or Presentment of Items; Time for Claims.

(1) Each customer or collecting bank who obtains payment or acceptance of an item and each prior customer and collecting bank warrants to the payor bank or other payor who in good faith pays or accepts the item that

    (a) he has a good title to the item or is authorized to obtain payment of acceptance on behalf of one who has a good title and the transfer is otherwise rightful; and

    (b) he has no knowledge that the signature of the maker or drawer is unauthorized, except that this warranty is not given by any customer or collecting bank that is a holder in due course and acts in good faith

        (i) to a maker with respect to the maker's own signature; or

        (ii) to a drawer with respect to the drawer's own signature, whether or not the drawer is also the drawee; or

        (iii) to an acceptor of an item if the holder in due course took the item after the acceptance or obtained the acceptance without knowledge that the drawer's signature was unauthorized; and

    (c) the time has not been materially altered, except that this warranty is not given by any customer or collecting bank that is a holder in due course and acts in good faith

        (i) to the maker of a note; or

        (ii) to the drawer of a draft whether or not the drawer is also the drawee; or

        (iii) to the acceptor of an item with respect to an alteration made prior to the acceptance if the holder in due course took the item after the acceptance provided "payable as originally drawn" or equivalent terms; or

        (iv) to the acceptor of an item with respect to an alteration made after the acceptance.

(2) Each customer and collecting bank who transfers an item and receives a settlement or other consideration for it warrants to his transferee and to any subsequent collecting bank who takes the item in good faith that

    (a) he has a good title to the item or is authorized to obtain payment or acceptance on behalf of one who has a good title and the transfer is otherwise rightful; and

    (b) all signatures are genuine or authorized; and

    (c) the item has not been materially altered; and

    (d) no defense of any party is good against him; and

    (e) he has no knowledge of any insolvency proceeding instituted with respect to the maker or acceptor or the drawer of an unaccepted item.

In addition each customer and collecting bank so transferring an item and receiving a settlement or other consideration engages that upon dishonor and any necessary notice of dishonor and protest he will take up the item.

(3) The warranties and the engagement to honor set forth in the two preceding subsections arise notwithstanding the absence of indorsement or words of guaranty or warranty in the transfer or presentment and a collecting bank remains liable for their breach despite remittance to its transferor. Damages for breach of such warranties or engagement to honor shall not exceed the consideration received by the customer or collecting bank responsible plus finance charges and expenses related to the item, if any.

(4) Unless a claim for breach of warranty under this section is made within a reasonable time after the person claiming learns of the breach, the person liable is discharged to the extent of any loss caused by the delay in making claim.

§ 4-208. Security Interest of Collecting Bank in Items, Accompanying Documents and Proceeds.

(1) A bank has a security interest in an item and any accompanying documents or the proceeds of either

    (a) in case of an item deposited in an account to the extent to which credit given for the item has been withdrawn or applied;

    (b) in case of an item for which it has given credit available for withdrawal as of right, to the extent of the credit given whether or not the credit is drawn upon and whether or not there is a right of charge-back; or

    (c) if it makes an advance on or against the item.

(2) When credit which has been given for several items received at one time or pursuant to a single agreement is withdrawn or applied in part the security interest remains upon all the items, any accompanying documents or the proceeds of either. For the purpose of this section, credits first given are first withdrawn.

(3) Receipt by a collecting bank of a final settlement for an item is a realization on its security interest in the item, accompanying documents and proceeds. To the extent and so long as the bank does not receive final settlement for the item or give up possession of the item or accompanying documents for purposes other than collection, the security interest continues and is subject to the provisions of Article 9 except that

    (a) no security agreement is necessary to make the security interest enforceable (subsection (1) (b) of Section 9-203); and

    (b) no filing is required to perfect the security interest; and

    (c) the security interest has priority over conflicting perfected security interests in the item, accompanying documents or proceeds.

§ 4-209. When Bank Gives Value for Purposes of Holder in Due Course.
For purposes of determining its status as a holder in due course, the bank has given value to the extent that it has a security interest in an item provided that the bank otherwise complies with the requirements of Section 3-302 on what constitutes a holder in due course.

§ 4-210. Presentment by Notice of Item Not Payable by, through or at a Bank; Liability of Secondary Parties.

(1) Unless otherwise instructed, a collecting bank may present an item not payable by, through or at a bank by sending to the party to accept or pay a written notice that the bank holds the item for acceptance or payment. The notice must be sent in time to be received on or before the day when presentment is due and the bank must meet any requirement of the party to accept or pay under Section 3-505 by the close of the bank's next banking day after it knows of the requirement.

(2) Where presentment is made by notice and neither honor nor request for compliance with a requirement under Section 3-505 is received by the close of business on the day after maturity or in the case of demand items by the close of business on the third banking day after notice was sent, the presenting bank may treat the item as dishonored and charge any secondary party by sending him notice of the facts.

§ 4-211. Media or Remittance; Provisional and Final Settlement in Remittance Cases.

(1) A collecting bank may take in settlement of an item

(a) a check of the remitting bank or of another bank on any bank except the remitting bank; or

(b) a cashier's check or similar primary obligation of a remitting bank which is a member of or clears through a member of the same clearing house or group as the collecting bank; or

(c) appropriate authority to charge an account of the remitting bank or of another bank with the collecting bank; or

(d) if the item is drawn upon or payable by a person other than a bank, a cashier's check, certified check or other bank check or obligation.

(2) If before its midnight deadline the collecting bank properly dishonors a remittance check or authorization to charge on itself or presents or forwards for collection a remittance instrument of or on another bank which is of a kind approved by subsection (1) or has not been authorized by it, the collecting bank is not liable to prior parties in the event of the dishonor of such check, instrument or authorization.

(3) A settlement for an item by means of a remittance instrument or authorization to charge is or becomes a final settlement as to both the person making and the person receiving the settlement

(a) if the remittance instrument or authorization to charge is of a kind approved by subsection (1) or has not been authorized by the person receiving the settlement and in either case the person receiving the settlement acts seasonably before its midnight deadline in presenting, forwarding for collection or paying the instrument or authorization is finally paid by the payor by which it is payable;

(b) if the person receiving the settlement has authorized remittance by a non-bank check or obligation or by a cashier's check or similar primary obligation of or a check

upon the payor or other remitting bank which is not of a kind approved by subsection (1) (b),—at the time of the receipt of such remittance check or obligation; or

(c) if in case not covered by sub-paragraphs (a) or (b) the person receiving the settlement fails to seasonably present, forward for collection, pay or return a remittance instrument of authorization to it to charge before its midnight deadline,—at such midnight deadline.

§ 4-212. Right of Charge-Back or Refund.

(1) If a collecting bank has made provisional settlement with its customer for an item and itself fails by reason of dishonor, suspension of payments by a bank or otherwise to receive a settlement for the item which is or becomes final, the bank may revoke the settlement given by it, charge back the amount of any credit given for the item to its customer whether or not it is able to return the items if by its midnight deadline or within a longer reasonable time after it learns the facts it returns the item or sends notification of the facts. These rights to revoke, charge-back and obtain refund terminate if and when a settlement for the item received by the bank is or becomes final (subsection (3) of Section 4-211 and subsections (2) and (3) of Section 4-213).

[(2) Within the time and manner prescribed by this section and Section 4-301, an intermediary or payor bank, as the case may be, may return an unpaid item directly to the depositary bank and may send for collection a draft on the depositary bank and obtain reimbursement. In such case, if the depositary bank has received provisional settlement for the item, it must reimburse the bank drawing the draft and any provisional credits for the item between banks shall become and remain final.]

Note: *Direct returns is recognized as an innovation that is not yet established bank practice, and therefore, Paragraph 2 has been bracketed. Some lawyers have doubted whether it should be included in legislation or left to development by agreement.*

(3) A depositary bank which is also the payor may charge-back the amount of an item to its customer's account or obtain refund in accordance with the section governing return of an item received by a payor bank for credit on its books (Section 4-301).

(4) The right to charge-back is not affected by

(a) prior use of the credit given for the item; or

(b) failure by any bank to exercise ordinary care with respect to the item but any bank so failing remains liable.

(5) A failure to charge-back or claim refund does not affect other rights of the bank against the customer or any other party.

(6) If credit is given in dollars as the equivalent of the value of an item payable in a foreign currency the dollar amount of any charge-back or refund shall be calculated on the basis of the buying site rate for the foreign currency prevailing on the day when the person entitled to the charge-back or refund learns that it will not receive payment in ordinary course.

§ 4-213. Final Payment of Item by Payor Bank; When Provisional Debits and Credits Become Final; When Certain Credits Become Available for Withdrawal.

(1) An item is finally paid by a payor bank when the bank has done any of the following whichever happens first:

(a) paid the item in cash; or

(b) settled for the item without reserving a right to revoke the settlement and without having such right under statute, clearing house rule or agreement; or

(c) completed the process of posting the item to the indicated account of the drawer, maker or other person to be charged therewith; or

(d) made a provisional settlement for the item and failed to revoke the settlement in the time and manner permitted by statute, clearing house rule or agreement.

Upon a final payment under subparagraphs (b), (c) or (d) the payor bank shall be accountable for the amount of the item.

(2) If provisional settlement for an item between the presenting and payor banks is made through a clearing house or by debits or credits in an account between them, then to the extent that provisional debits or credits for the item are entered in accounts between the presenting and payor banks or between the presenting and successive prior collecting banks seratim, they become final upon final payment of the item by the payor bank.

(3) If a collecting bank receives a settlement for an item which is or becomes final (subsection (3) of Section 4-211, subsection (2) of Section 4-213) the bank is accountable to its customer for the amount of the item and any provisional credit given for the item in an account with its customer becomes final.

(4) Subject to any right of the bank to apply the credit to an obligation of the customer, credit given by a bank for an item in an account with its customer becomes available for withdrawal as of right

(a) in any case where the bank has received a provisional settlement for the item,—when such settlement becomes final and the bank has had a reasonable time to learn that the settlement is final;

(b) in any case where the bank is both a depositary bank and a payor bank and the item is finally paid,—at the opening of the bank's second banking day following receipt of the item.

(5) A deposit of money in a bank is final when made but, subject to any right of the bank to apply the deposit to an obligation of the customer, the deposit becomes available for withdrawal as of right at the opening of the bank's next banking day following receipt of the deposit.

§ 4-214. Insolvency and Preference.

(1) Any item in or coming into the possession of a payor or collecting bank which suspends payment and which item is not finally paid shall be returned by the receiver, trustee or agent in charge of the closed bank to the presenting bank or the closed bank's customer.

(2) If a payor bank finally pays an item and suspends payments without making a settlement for the item with its customer or the presenting bank which settlement is or becomes final, the owner of the item has a preferred claim against the payor bank.

(3) If a payor bank gives or a collecting bank gives or receives a provisional settlement for an item and thereafter suspends payments, the suspension does not prevent or interfere with

the settlement becoming final if such finality occurs automatically upon the lapse of certain time or the happening of certain events (subsection (3) of Section 4-211, subsections (1)(d), (2) and (3) of Section 4-213).

(4) If a collecting bank receives from subsequent parties settlement for an item which settlement is or becomes final and suspends payments without making a settlement for the item with its customer which is or becomes final, the owner of the item has a preferred claim against such collecting bank.

Part 3 Collection of Items: Payor Banks

§ 4-301. Deferred Posting; Recovery of Payment by Return of Items; Time of Dishonor.

(1) Where an authorized settlement for a demand item (other than a documentary draft) received by a payor bank otherwise than for immediate payment over the counter has been made before midnight of the banking day of receipt the payor bank may revoke the settlement and recover any payment if before it has made final payment (subsection (1) of Section 4-213) and before its midnight deadline it

(a) returns the item; or

(b) sends written notice of dishonor or nonpayment if the item is held for protest or is otherwise unavailable for return.

(2) If a demand item is received by a payor bank for credit on its books it may return such item or send notice of dishonor and may revoke any credit given or recover the amount thereof withdrawn by its customer, if it acts within the time limit and in the manner specified in the preceding subsection.

(3) Unless previous notice of dishonor has been sent an item is dishonored at the time when for purposes of dishonor it is returned or notice sent in accordance with this section.

(4) An item is returned:

(a) as to an item received through a clearing house, when it is delivered to the presenting or last collecting bank or to the clearing house or is sent or delivered in accordance with its rules; or

(b) in all other cases, when it is sent or delivered to the bank's customer or transferor or pursuant to his instructions.

§ 4-302. Payor Bank's Responsibility for Late Return of Item. In the absence of a valid defense such as breach of a presentment warranty (subsection (1) of Section 4-207), settlement effected or the like, if an item is presented on and received by a payor bank the bank is accountable for the amount of

(a) a demand item other than a documentary draft whether properly payable or not if the bank, in any case where it is not also the depositary bank, retains the item beyond midnight of the banking day of receipt without settling for it or, regardless of whether it is also the depositary bank, does not pay or return the item or send notice of dishonor until after its midnight deadline; or

(b) any other properly payable item unless within the time allowed for acceptance or payment of that item the bank either accepts or pays the item or returns it and accompanying documents.

§ 4-303. When Items Subject to Notice, Stop-Order, Legal Process or Setoff; Order in which Items May Be Charged or Certified.

(1) Any knowledge, notice or stop-order received by, legal process served upon or setoff exercised by a payor bank, whether or not effective under other rules of law to terminate, suspend or modify the bank's right or duty to pay an item or to charge its customer's account for the item, comes too late to so terminate, suspend or modify such right or duty if the knowledge, notice, stop-order or legal process is received or served and a reasonable time for the bank to act thereon expires or the setoff is exercised after the bank has done any of the following:

(a) accepted or certified the item;
(b) paid the item in cash;
(c) settled for the item without reserving the right to revoke the settlement and without having such right under statute, clearing house rule or agreement;
(d) completed the process of posting the item to the indicated account of the drawer, maker or other person to be charged therewith or otherwise has evidenced by examination of such indicated account and by action its decision to pay the item; or
(e) become accountable for the amount of the item under subsection (1) (d) of Section 4-213 and Section 4-302 dealing with the payor bank's responsibility for late return of items.

(2) Subject to the provisions of subsection (1) items may be accepted, paid, certified or charged to the indicated account of its customer in any order convenient to the bank.

Part 4   Relationship Between Payor Bank and Its Customer

§ 4-401. When Bank May Charge Customer's Account.

(1) As against its customer, a bank may charge against his account any item which is otherwise properly payable from that account even though the charge creates an overdraft.
(2) A bank which in good faith makes payment to a holder may charge the indicated account of its customer according to

(a) the original tenor of his altered item; or
(b) the tenor of his completed item, even though the bank knows the item has been completed unless the bank has notice that the completion was improper.

§ 4-402. Bank's Liability to Customer for Wrongful Dishonor.
A payor bank is liable to its customer for damages proximately caused by the wrongful dishonor of an item. When the dishonor occurs through mistake liability is limited to actual damages proved. If so proximately caused and proved damages may include damages for an arrest or prosecution of the customer or other consequential damages. Whether any consequential damages are proximately caused by the wrongful dishonor is a question of fact to be determined in each case.

§ 4-403. Customer's Right to Stop Payment; Burden of Proof of Loss.

(1) A customer may by order to his bank stop payment of any item payable for his account but the order must be received at such time and in such manner as to afford the bank a reasonable opportunity to act on it prior to any action by the bank with respect to the item described in Section 4-303.
(2) An oral order is binding upon the bank only for fourteen calendar days unless confirmed in writing within that period. A written order is effective for only six months unless renewed in writing.
(3) The burden of establishing the fact and amount of loss resulting from the payment of an item contrary to a binding stop payment order is on the customer.

§ 4-404. Bank Not Obligated to Pay Check More Than Six Months Old.
A bank is under no obligation to a customer having a checking account to pay a check, other than a certified check, which is presented more than six months after its date, but it may charge its customer's account for a payment made thereafter in good faith.

§ 4-405. Death or Incompetence of Customer.

(1) A payor or collecting bank's authority to accept, pay or collect an item or to account for proceeds of its collection if otherwise effective is not rendered ineffective by incompetence of a customer of either bank existing at the time the item is issued or its collection is undertaken if the bank does not know of an adjudication of incompetence. Neither death nor incompetence of a customer revokes such authority to accept, pay, collect or account until the bank knows of the fact of death or of an adjudication of incompetence and has reasonable opportunity to act on it.
(2) Even with knowledge a bank may for ten days after the date of death pay or certify checks drawn on or prior to that date unless ordered to stop payment by a person claiming an interest in the account.

§ 4-406. Customer's Duty to Discover and Report Unauthorized Signature or Alteration.

(1) When a bank sends to its customer a statement of account accompanied by items paid in good faith in support of the debit entries or holds the statement and items pursuant to a request or instructions of its customer or otherwise in a reasonable manner makes the statement and items available to the customer, the customer must exercise reasonable care and promptness to examine the statement and items to discover his unauthorized signature or any alteration on an item and must notify the bank promptly after discovery thereof.
(2) If the bank establishes that the customer failed with respect to an item to comply with the duties imposed on the customer by subsection (1) the customer is precluded from asserting against the bank

(a) his unauthorized signature or any alteration on the item if the bank also establishes that it suffered a loss by reason of such failure; and
(b) an unauthorized signature or alteration by the same wrongdoer on any other item paid in good faith by the bank after the first item and statement was available to the customer for a reasonable period not exceeding fourteen

calendar days and before the bank receives notification from the customer of any such unauthorized signature or alteration.

(3) The preclusion under subsection (2) does not apply if the customer establishes lack of ordinary care on the part of the bank in paying the item(s).

(4) Without regard to care or lack of care of either the customer or the bank a customer who does not within one year from the time the statement and items are made available to the customer (subsection (1)) discover and report his unauthorized signature or any alteration on the face or back of the item or does not within three years from that time discover and report any unauthorized indorsement is precluded from asserting against the bank such unauthorized signature or indorsement or such alteration.

(5) If under this section a payor bank has a valid defense against a claim of a customer upon or resulting from payment of an item and waives or fails upon request to assert the defense the bank may not assert against any collecting bank or other prior party presenting or transferring the item a claim based upon the unauthorized signature or alteration giving rise to the customer's claim.

§ 4-407. Payor Bank's Right to Subrogation on Improper Payment.
If a payor bank has paid an item over the stop payment order of the drawer or maker, or otherwise under circumstances giving a basis for objection by the drawer or maker, to present unjust enrichment and only to the extent necessary to prevent loss to the bank by reason of its payment of the item, the payor bank shall be subrogated to the rights

(a) of any holder in due course on the item against the drawer or maker; and

(b) of the payee or any other holder of the item against the drawer or maker either on the item or under the transaction out of which the item arose; and

(c) of the drawer or maker against the payee or any other holder of the item with respect to the transaction out of which the item arose.

Part 5 Collection of Documentary Drafts

§ 4-501. Handling of Documentary Drafts; Duty to Send for Presentment and to Notify Customer of Dishonor.
A bank which takes a documentary draft for collection must present or send the draft and accompanying documents for presentment and upon learning that the draft has not been paid or accepted in due course must seasonably notify its customer of such fact even though it may have discounted or bought the draft or extended credit available for withdrawal as if right.

§ 4-502. Presentment of "On Arrival" Drafts.
When a draft or the relevant instructions require presentment "on arrival," "when goods arrive" or the like, the collecting bank need not present until in its judgment a reasonable time for arrival of the goods has expired. Refusal to pay or accept because the goods have not arrived is not dishonor; the bank must notify its transferor of such refusal but need not present the draft again until it is instructed to do so or learns of the arrival of the goods.

§ 4-503. Responsibility of Presenting Bank for Documents and Goods; Report or Reasons for Dishonor; Referee in Case of Need.
Unless otherwise instructed and except as provided in Article 5 a bank presenting a documentary draft

(a) must deliver the documents to the drawee on acceptance of the draft if it is payable more than three days after presentment; otherwise, only on payment; and

(b) upon dishonor, either in the case of presentment for acceptance or presentment for payment, may seek and follow instructions from any referee in case of need designated in the draft or if the presenting bank does not choose to utilize his services it must use diligence and good faith to ascertain the reason for dishonor, must notify its transferor of the dishonor and of the results of its effort to ascertain the reasons therefor and must request instructions.

But the presenting bank is under no obligation with respect to goods represented by the documents except to follow any reasonable instructions seasonably received; it has a right to reimbursement for any expense incurred in following instructions and to prepayment of or indemnity for such expenses.

§ 4-504. Privilege of Presenting Bank to Deal with Goods, Security Interest for Expenses.

(1) A presenting bank which, following the dishonor of a documentary draft, has seasonably requested instructions but does not receive them within a reasonable time may store, sell, or otherwise deal with the goods in any reasonable manner.

(2) For its reasonable expenses incurred by action under subsection (1) the presenting bank has a lien upon the goods or their proceeds, which may be foreclosed in the same manner as an unpaid seller's lien.

ARTICLE 5 / Letters of Credit

§ 5-101. Short Title.
This Article shall be known and may be cited as Uniform Commercial Code—Letters of Credit.

§ 5-102. Scope.

(1) This Article applies

(a) to a credit issued by a bank if the credit requires a documentary draft or a documentary demand for payment; and

(b) to a credit issued by a person other than a bank if the credit requires that the draft or demand for payment be accompanied by a document of title; and

(c) to a credit issued by a bank or other person if the credit is not within subparagraphs (a) or (b) but conspicuously states that it is a letter of credit or is conspicuously so entitled.

(2) Unless the engagement meets the requirements of subsection (1), this Article does not apply to engagements to make advances or to honor drafts or demands for payment, to authorities to pay or purchase, to guarantees or to general agreements.

(3) This Article deals with some but not all of the rules and concepts of letters of credit as such rules or concepts have de-

veloped prior to this act or may hereafter develop. The fact that this Article states a rule does not by itself require, imply or negate application of the same or a converse rule to a situation not provided for or to a person not specified by this Article.

§ 5-103. Definitions.

(1) In this Article unless the context otherwise requires

(a) "Credit" or "letter of credit" means an engagement by a bank or other person made at the request of a customer and of a kind within the scope of this Article (Section 5-102) that the issuer will honor drafts or other demands for payment upon compliance with the conditions specified in the credit. A credit may be either revocable or irrevocable. The engagement may be either an agreement to honor or a statement that the bank or other person is authorized to honor.

(b) A "documentary draft" or a "documentary demand for payment" is one honor of which is conditioned upon the presentation of a document or documents. "Document" means any paper including document of title, security, invoice, certificate, notice of default and the like.

(c) An "issuer" is a bank or other person issuing a credit.

(d) A "beneficiary" of a credit is a person who is entitled under its terms to draw or demand payment.

(e) An "advising bank" is a bank which gives notification of the issuance of a credit by another bank.

(f) A "confirming bank" is a bank which engages either that it will itself honor a credit already issued by another bank or that such a credit will be honored by the issuer or a third bank.

(g) A "customer" is a buyer or other person who causes an issuer to issue a credit. The term also includes a bank which procures issuance or confirmation on behalf of that bank's customer.

(2) Other definitions applying to this Article and the section sin which they appear are:

"Notation Credit". Section 5-108.
"Presenter". Section 5-112(3).

(3) Definitions in other Articles applying to this Article and the sections in which they appear are:

"Accept" or "Acceptance". Section 3-410.
"Contract for sale". Section 2-106.
"Draft". Section 30104.
"Holder in due course". Section 3-302.
"Midnight deadline". Section 4-104.
"Security". Section 8-102.

(4) In addition, Article 1 contains general definitions and principles of construction and interpretation applicable throughout this Article.

§ 5-104. Formal Requirements; Signing.

(1) Except as otherwise required in subsection (1)(c) of Section 5-102 on scope, no particular form of phrasing is required for a credit. A credit must be in writing and signed by the issuer and a confirmation must be in writing and signed by the confirming bank. A modification of the terms of a credit or confirmation must be signed by the issuer or confirming bank.

(2) A telegram may be a sufficient signed writing if it identifies its sender by an authorized authentication. The authentication may be in code and the authorized naming of the issuer in an advice of credit is a sufficient signing.

§ 5-105. Consideration. No consideration is necessary to establish a credit or to enlarge or otherwise modify its terms.

§ 5-106. Time and Effect of Establishment of Credit.

(1) Unless otherwise agreed a credit is established

(a) as regards the customer as soon as a letter of credit is sent to him or the letter of credit or an authorized written advice of its issuance is sent to the beneficiary; and

(b) as regards the beneficiary when the receives a letter of credit or an authorized written advice of its issuance.

(2) Unless otherwise agreed once an irrevocable credit is established as regards the customer it can be modified or revoked only with the consent of the customer and once it is established as regards the beneficiary it can be modified or revoked only with his consent.

(3) Unless otherwise agreed after a revocable credit is established it may be modified or revoked by the issuer without notice to or consent from the customer or beneficiary.

(4) Notwithstanding any modification or revocation of a revocable credit any person authorized to honor or negotiate under the terms of the original credit is entitled to reimbursement for or honor of any draft or demand for payment duly honored or negotiated before receipt of notice of the modification or revocation and the issuer in turn is entitled to reimbursement from its customer.

§ 5-107. Advice of Credit; Confirmation; Error in Statement of Terms.

(1) Unless otherwise specified an advising bank by advising a credit issued by another bank does not assume any obligation to honor drafts drawn or demands for payment made under the credit but it does assume obligation for the accuracy of its own statement. (2) A confirming bank by confirming a credit becomes direct obligated on the credit to the extent of its confirmation as thought it were its issuer and acquires the rights of an issuer.

(3) Even though an advising bank incorrectly advises the terms of a credit it has been authorized to advise the credit is established as against the issuer to the extent of its original terms.

(4) Unless otherwise specified the customer bears as against the issuer all risks of transmission and reasonable translation or interpretation of any message relating to a credit.

§ 5-108. "Notation Credit"; Exhaustion of Credit.

(1) A credit which specifies that any person purchasing or paying drafts drawn or demands for payment made under it must note the amount of the draft or demand on the letter or advice of credit is a "notation credit".

(2) Under a notation credit

(a) a person paying the beneficiary or purchasing a draft or demand for payment from his acquires a right to honor only if the appropriate notation is made and by transferring or forwarding for honor the documents under the credit such a person warrants to the issuer that the notation has been made, and

(b) unless the credit or a signed statement that an appropriate notation has been made accompanies the draft or demand for payment the issuer may delay honor until evidence of notation has been procured which is satisfactory to it but its obligation and that of its customer continue for a reasonable time not exceeding thirty days to obtain such evidence.

(3) If the credit is not a notation credit

(a) the issuer may honor complying drafts or demands for payment presented to it in the order in which they are presented and is discharged pro tanto by honor of any such draft or demand;

(b) as between competing good faith purchasers of complying drafts or demands the person first purchasing has priority over a subsequent purchaser even though the later purchased draft or demand has been first honored.

§ 5-109. Issuer's Obligation to Its Customer.

(1) An issuer's obligation to its customer includes good faith and observance of any general banking usage but unless otherwise agreed does not include liability or responsibility

(a) for performance of the underlying contract for sale or other transaction between the customer and the beneficiary; or

(b) for any act or omission of any person other than itself or its own branch or for loss of destruction of a draft, demand or document in transit or in the possession of others; or

(c) based on knowledge or lack of knowledge of any usage of any particular trade.

(2) An issuer must examine documents with care so as to ascertain that on their face they appear to comply with the terms of the credit but unless otherwise agreed assumes no liability or responsibility for the genuineness, falsification or effect of any document which appears on such examination to be regular on its face.

(3) A non-bank issuer is not bound by any banking usage of which it has no knowledge.

§ 5-110. Availability of Credit in Portions; Presenter's Reservation of Lien or Claim.

(1) Unless otherwise specified a credit may be used in portions in the discretion of the beneficiary.

(2) Unless otherwise specified a person by presenting a documentary draft or demand for payment under a credit relinquishes upon its honor all claims to the documents and a person by transferring such draft or demand or causing such presentment authorizes such relinquishment. An explicit reservation of claim makes the draft or demand non-complying.

§ 5-111. Warranties on Transfer and Presentment.

(1) Unless otherwise agreed the beneficiary by transferring or presenting a documentary draft or demand for payment warrants to all interested parties that the necessary conditions of the credit have been complied with. This is in addition to any warranties arising under Articles 3, 4, 7 and 8.

(2) Unless otherwise agreed a negotiating, advising, confirming, collecting or issuing bank presenting or transferring a draft or demand for payment under a credit warrants only the matters warranted by a collecting bank under Article 4

and any such bank transferring a document warrants only the matters warranted by an intermediary under Articles 7 and 8.

§ 5-112. Time Allowed for Honor or Rejection; Withholding Honor or Rejection by Consent; "Presenter".

(1) A bank to which a documentary draft or demand for payment is presented under a credit may without dishonor of the draft, demand or credit

(a) defer honor until the close of the third banking day following receipt of the documents; and

(b) further defer honor if the presenter has expressly or impliedly consented thereto.

Failure to honor within the time here specified constitutes dishonor of the draft or demand and of the credit [except as otherwise provided in subsection (4) of Section 5-114 on conditional payment].

Note: *The bracketed language in the last sentence of subsection (1) should be included only if the optional provisions of Section 5-114(4) and (5) are included.*

(2) Upon dishonor the bank may unless otherwise instructed fulfill its duty to return the draft or demand and the documents by holding them at the disposal of the presenter and sending him an advice to that effect.

(3) "Presenter" means any person presenting a draft or demand for payment for honor under a credit even though that person is a confirming bank or other correspondent which is acting under an issuer's authorization.

§ 5-113. Indemnities.

(1) A bank seeking to obtain (whether for itself or another) honor, negotiation or reimbursement under a credit may give an indemnity to induce such honor, negotiation or reimbursement.

(2) An indemnity agreement inducing honor, negotiation or reimbursement

(a) unless otherwise explicitly agreed applies to defects in the documents but not in the goods; and

(b) unless a longer time is explicitly agreed expires at the end of ten business days following receipt of the documents by the ultimate customer unless notice of objection is sent before such expiration date. The ultimate customer may send notice of objection to the person from whom he received the documents and any bank receiving such notice is under a duty to send notice to its transferor before its midnight deadline.

§ 5-114. Issuer's Duty and Privilege to Honor; Right to Reimbursement.

(1) An issuer must honor a draft or demand for payment which complies with the terms of the relevant credit regardless of whether the goods or documents conform to the underlying contract for sale or other contract between the customer and the beneficiary. The issuer is not excused from honor of such a draft or demand by reason of an additional general term that all documents must be satisfactory to the issuer, but an issuer may require that specified documents must be satisfactory to it.

(2) Unless otherwise agreed when documents appear on their fact to comply with the terms of a credit but a required document does not in fact conform to the warranties made

on negotiation or transfer of a document of title (Section 7-507) or of a certificated security (Section 8-306) or is forged or fraudulent or there is fraud in the transaction:

(a) the issuer must honor the draft or demand for payment if honor is demanded by a negotiating bank or other holder of the draft or demand which has taken the draft or demand under the credit and under circumstances which would make it a holder in due course (Section 3-302) and in an appropriate case would make it a person to whom a document of title has been duly negotiated (Section 7-502) or a bona fide purchaser of a certificated security (Section 8-302); and

(b) in all other cases as against its customer, an issuer acting in good faith may honor the draft or demand for payment despite notification from the customer of fraud, forgery or other defect not apparent on the face of the documents but a court of appropriate jurisdiction may enjoin such honor.

(3) Unless otherwise agreed an issuer which has duly honored a draft or demand for payment is entitled to immediate reimbursement of any payment made under the credit and to be put in effectively available funds not later than the day before maturity of any acceptance made under the credit.

[(4) When a credit provides for payment by the issuer on receipt of notice that the required documents are in the possession of a correspondent or other agent of the issuer

(a) any payment made on receipt of such notice is conditional; and

(b) the issuer may reject documents which do not comply with the credit if it does so within three banking days following its receipt of the documents; and

(c) in the event of such rejection, the issuer is entitled by charge back or otherwise to return of the payment made.]

[(5) In the case covered by subsection (4) failure to reject documents within the time specified in sub-paragraph (b) constitutes acceptance of the documents and makes the payment final in favor of the beneficiary.]

Note: *Subsections (4) and (5) are bracketed as optional. If they are included the bracketed language in the last sentence of Section 5-112(1) should also be included.*

As amended in 1977.

§ 5-115. Remedy for Improper Dishonor or Anticipatory Repudiation.

(1) When an issuer wrongfully dishonors a draft or demand for payment presented under a credit the person entitled to honor has with respect to any documents the rights of a person in the position of a seller (Section 2-707) and may recover from the issuer the face amount of the draft or demand together with incidental damages under Section 2-710 on seller's incidental damages and interest but less any amount realized by resale or other use or disposition of the subject matter of the transaction. In the event no resale or other utilization is made the documents, goods or other subject matter involved in the transaction must be turned over to the issuer on payment of judgment.

(2) When an issuer wrongfully cancels or otherwise repudiates a credit before presentment of a draft or demand for payment drawn under it the beneficiary has the rights of a seller

after anticipatory repudiation by the buyer under Section 2-610 if he learns of the repudiation in time reasonably to avoid procurement of the required documents. Otherwise the beneficiary has an immediate right of action for wrongful dishonor.

§ 5-116. Transfer and Assignment.

(1) The right to draw under a credit can be transferred or assigned only when the credit is expressly designated as transferable or assignable.

(2) Even though the credit specifically states that it is nontransferable or nonassignable the beneficiary may before performance of the conditions of the credit assign his right to proceeds. Such an assignment is an assignment of an account under Article 9 on Second Transactions and is governed by that Article except that

(a) the assignment is ineffective until the letter of credit or advice of credit is delivered to the assignee which delivery constitutes perfection of the security interest under Article 9; and

(b) the issuer may honor drafts or demands for payment drawn under the credit until it receives a notification of the assignment signed by the beneficiary which reasonably identifies the credit involved in the assignment and contains a request to pay the assignee; and

(c) after what reasonably appears to be such a notification has been received the issuer may without dishonor refuse to accept or pay even to a person otherwise entitled to honor until the letter of credit or advice of credit is exhibited to the issuer.

(3) Except where the beneficiary has effectively assigned his right to draw or his right to proceeds, nothing in this section limits his right to transfer or negotiate drafts or demands drawn under the credit.

As amended in 1972.

§ 5-117. Insolvency of Bank Holding Funds for Documentary Credit.

(1) Where an issuer or an advising or confirming bank or a bank which has for a customer procured issuance of a credit by another bank becomes insolvent before final payment under the credit and the credit is one to which this Article is made applicable by paragraphs (a) or (b) of Section 5-102(1) on scope, the receipt or allocation of funds or collateral to secure or meet obligations under the credit shall have the following results:

(a) to the extent of any funds or collateral turned over after or before the insolvency as indemnity against or specifically for the purpose of payment of drafts or demands for payment drawn under the designated credit, the drafts or demands are entitled to payment in preference over depositors or other general creditors of the issuer or bank; and

(b) on expiration of the credit or surrender of the beneficiary's rights under it unused any person who has given such funds or collateral is similarly entitled to return thereof; and

(c) a charge to a general or current account with a bank if specifically consented to for the purpose of indemnity against or payment of drafts or demands for payment drawn under the designated credit falls under the same rules as if the funds had been drawn out in cash and then turned over with specific instructions.

(2) After honor or reimbursement under this section the customer or other person for whose account the insolvent bank has acted is entitled to receive the documents involved.

REPEALER OF ARTICLE 6 / Bulk Transfers and Revised Article 6 Bulk Sales (States to Select One Alternative)

Alternative A

§ 1. **Repeal.** Article 6 and Section 9-111 of the Uniform Commercial Code are hereby repealed, effective _____ .

§ 2. **Amendment.** Section 1-105(2) of the Uniform Commercial Code is hereby amended to read as follows:
(2) Where one of the following provisions of this Act specifies the applicable law, that provision governs and a contrary agreement is effective only to the extent permitted by the law (including the conflict of laws rules) so specified:

Rights of creditors against sold goods.   Section 2-402.
Applicability of the Article on Leases.   Sections 2A-105 and 2A-106.
Applicability of the Article on Bank Deposits and Collections.   Section 4-102.
Applicability of the Article on Investment Securities.   Section 8-106.
Perfection provisions of the Article on Secured Transactions.   Section 9-103.

§ 3. **Amendment.** Section 2-403(4) of the Uniform Commercial Code is hereby amended to read as follows:
(4) The rights of other purchasers of goods and of lien creditors are governed by the Articles on Secured Transactions (Article 9), and Documents of Title (Article 7).

§ 4. **Savings Clause.** Rights and obligations that arose under Article 6 and Section 9-111 of the Uniform Commercial Code before their repeal remain valid and may be enforced as though those statutes had not been repealed.]
[End Of Alternative A]

Alternative B

§ 6-101. Short Title.
This Article shall be known and may be cited as Uniform Commercial Code—Bulk Sales.

§ 6-102. Definitions and Index of Definitions.
(1) In this Article, unless the context otherwise requires:
(a) "Assets" means the inventory that is the subject of a bulk sale and any tangible and intangible personal property used or held for use primarily in, or arising from, the seller's business and sold in connection with that inventory, but the term does not include:
(i) fixtures (Section 9-313(1)(a)) other than readily removable factory and office machines;
(ii) the lessee's interest in a lease of real property; or
(iii) property to the extent it is generally exempt from creditor process under nonbankruptcy law.

(b) "Auctioneer" means a person whom the seller engages to direct, conduct, control, or be responsible for a sale by auction.
(c) "Bulk sale" means:
(i) in the case of a sale by auction or a sale or series of sales conducted by a liquidator on the seller's behalf, a sale or series of sales not in the ordinary course of the seller's business of more than half of the seller's inventory, as measured by value on the date of the bulk-sale agreement, if on that date the auctioneer or liquidator has notice, or after reasonable inquiry would have had notice, that the seller will not continue to operate the same or a similar kind of business after the sale or series of sales; and
(ii) in all other cases, a sale not in the ordinary course of the seller's business of more than half the seller's inventory, as measured by value on the date of the bulk-sale agreement, if on that date the buyer has notice, or after reasonable inquiry would have had notice, that the seller will not continue to operate the same or a similar kind of business after the sale.

(d) "Claim" means a right to payment from the seller, whether or not the right is reduced to judgment, liquidated, fixed, matured, disputed, secured, legal, or equitable. The term includes costs of collection and attorney's fees only to the extent that the laws of this state permit the holder of the claim to recover them in an action against the obligor.
(e) "Claimant" means a person holding a claim incurred in the seller's business other than:
(i) an unsecured and unmatured claim for employment compensation and benefits, including commissions and vacation, severance, and sick-leave pay;
(ii) a claim for injury to an individual or to property, or for breach of warranty, unless:
(A) a right of action for the claim has accrued;
(B) the claim has been asserted against the seller; and
(C) the seller knows the identity of the person asserting the claim and the basis upon which the person has asserted it; and
(States to Select One Alternative)

Alternative A
[(iii) a claim for taxes owing to a governmental unit.]

Alternative B
[(iii) a claim for taxes owing to a governmental unit, if:
(A) a statute governing the enforcement of the claim permits or requires notice of the bulk sale to be given to the governmental unit in a manner other than by compliance with the requirements of this Article; and
(B) notice is given in accordance with the statute.]
(f) "Creditor" means a claimant or other person holding a claim.
(g) (i) "Date of the bulk sale" means:
(A) if the sale is by auction or is conducted by a liquidator on the seller's behalf, the date on which more than ten percent of the net proceeds is paid to or for the benefit of the seller; and

(B) in all other cases, the later of the date on which:
(I) more than ten percent of the net contract price is paid to or for the benefit of the seller; or
(II) more than ten percent of the assets, as measured by value, are transferred to the buyer.
(ii) For purposes of this subsection:
(A) Delivery of a negotiable instrument (Section 3-104(1)) to or for the benefit of the seller in exchange for assets constitutes payment of the contract price pro tanto;
(B) To the extent that the contract price is deposited in an escrow, the contract price is paid to or for the benefit of the seller when the seller acquires the unconditional right to receive the deposit or when the deposit is delivered to the seller or for the benefit of the seller, whichever is earlier; and
(C) An asset is transferred when a person holding an unsecured claim can no longer obtain through judicial proceedings rights to the asset that are superior to those of the buyer arising as a result of the bulk sale. A person holding an unsecured claim can obtain those superior rights to a tangible asset at least until the buyer has an unconditional right, under the bulk-sale agreement, to possess the asset, and a person holding an unsecured claim can obtain those superior rights to an intangible asset at least until the buyer has an unconditional right, under the bulk-sale agreement, to use the asset.

(h) "Date of the bulk-sale agreement" means:
(i) in the case of a sale by auction or conducted by a liquidator (subsection (c)(i)), the date on which the seller engages the auctioneer or liquidator; and
(ii) in all other cases, the date on which a bulk-sale agreement becomes enforceable between the buyer and the seller.
(i) "Debt" means liability on a claim.
(j) "Liquidator" means a person who is regularly engaged in the business of disposing of assets for businesses contemplating liquidation or dissolution.
(k) "Net contract price" means the new consideration the buyer is obligated to pay for the assets less:
(i) the amount of any proceeds of the sale of an asset, to the extent the proceeds are applied in partial or total satisfaction of a debt secured by the asset; and
(ii) the amount of any debt to the extent it is secured by a security interest or lien that is enforceable against the asset before and after it has been sold to a buyer. If a debt is secured by an asset and other property of the seller, the amount of the debt secured by a security interest or lien that is enforceable against the asset is determined by multiplying the debt by a fraction, the numerator of which is the value of the new consideration for the asset on the date of the bulk sale and the denominator of which is the value of all property securing the debt on the date of the bulk sale.
(l) "Net proceeds" means the new consideration received for assets sold at a sale by auction or a sale conducted by a liquidator on the seller's behalf less:
(i) commissions and reasonable expenses of the sale;
(ii) the amount of any proceeds of the sale of an asset,

to the extent the proceeds are applied in partial or total satisfaction of a debt secured by the asset; and
(iii) the amount of any debt to the extent it is secured by a security interest or lien that is enforceable against the asset before and after it has been sold to a buyer. If a debt is secured by an asset and other property of the seller, the amount of the debt secured by a security interest or lien that is enforceable against the asset is determined by multiplying the debt by a fraction, the numerator of which is the value of the new consideration for the asset on the date of the bulk sale and the denominator of which is the value of all property securing the debt on the date of the bulk sale.
(m) A sale is "in the ordinary course of the seller's business" if the sale comports with usual or customary practices in the kind of business in which the seller is engaged or with the seller's own usual or customary practices.
(n) "United States" includes its territories and possessions and the Commonwealth of Puerto Rico.
(o) "Value" means fair market value.
(p) "Verified" means signed and sworn to or affirmed.
(2) The following definitions in other Articles apply to this Article:
(a) "Buyer."   Section 2-103(1)(a).
(b) "Equipment."   Section 9-109(2).
(c) "Inventory."   Section 9-109(4).
(d) "Sale."   Section 2-106(1).
(e) "Seller."   Section 2-103(1)(d).

(3) In addition, Article 1 contains general definitions and principles of construction and interpretation applicable throughout this Article.

§ 6-103.   Applicability of Article

(1) Except as otherwise provided in subsection (3), this Article applies to a bulk sale if:
(a) the seller's principal business is the sale of inventory from stock; and
(b) on the date of the bulk-sale agreement the seller is located in this state or, if the seller is located in a jurisdiction that is not a part of the United States, the seller's major executive office in the United States is in this state.

(2) A seller is deemed to be located at his [or her] place of business. If a seller has more than one place of business, the seller is deemed located at his [or her] chief executive office.
(3) This Article does not apply to:

(a) a transfer made to secure payment or performance of an obligation;
(b) a transfer of collateral to a secured party pursuant to Section 9-503;
(c) a sale of collateral pursuant to Section 9-504;
(d) retention of collateral pursuant to Section 9-505;
(e) a sale of an asset encumbered by a security interest or lien if (i) all the proceeds of the sale are applied in partial or total satisfaction of the debt secured by the security interest or lien or (ii) the security interest or lien is enforceable against the asset after it has been sold to the buyer and the net contract price is zero;
(f) a general assignment for the benefit of creditors or to a subsequent transfer by the assignee;

(g) a sale by an executor, administrator, receiver, trustee in bankruptcy, or any public officer under judicial process;
(h) a sale made in the course of judicial or administrative proceedings for the dissolution or reorganization of an organization;
(i) a sale to a buyer whose principal place of business is in the United States and who:

  (i) not earlier than 21 days before the date of the bulk sale, (A) obtains from the seller a verified and dated list of claimants of whom the seller has notice three days before the seller sends or delivers the list to the buyer or (B) conducts a reasonable inquiry to discover the claimants;
  (ii) assumes in full the debts owed to claimants of whom the buyer has knowledge on the date the buyer receives the list of claimants from the seller or on the date the buyer completes the reasonable inquiry, as the case may be;
  (iii) is not insolvent after the assumption; and
  (iv) gives written notice of the assumption not later than 30 days after the date of the bulk sale by sending or delivering a notice to the claimants identified in subparagraph (ii) or by filing a notice in the office of the [Secretary of State];

(j) a sale to a buyer whose principal place of business is in the United States and who:

  (i) assumes in full the debts that were incurred in the seller's business before the date of the bulk sale;
  (ii) is not insolvent after the assumption; and
  (iii) gives written notice of the assumption not later than 30 days after the date of the bulk sale by sending or delivering a notice to each creditor whose debt is assumed or by filing a notice in the office of the [Secretary of State];

(k) a sale to a new organization that is organized to take over and continue the business of the seller and that has its principal place of business in the United States if:

  (i) the buyer assumes in full the debts that were incurred in the seller's business before the date of the bulk sale;
  (ii) the seller receives nothing from the sale except an interest in the new organization that is subordinate to the claims against the organization arising from the assumption; and
  (iii) the buyer gives written notice of the assumption not later than 30 days after the date of the bulk sale by sending or delivering a notice to each creditor whose debt is assumed or by filing a notice in the office of the [Secretary of State];

(1) a sale of assets having:

  (i) a value, net of liens and security interests, of less than $10,000. If a debt is secured by assets and other property of the seller, the net value of the assets is determined by subtracting from their value an amount equal to the product of the debt multiplied by a fraction, the numerator of which is the value of the assets on the date of the bulk sale and the denominator of which is the value of all property securing the debt on the date of the bulk sale; or

  (ii) a value of more than $25,000,000 on the date of the bulk-sale agreement; or

(m) a sale required by, and made pursuant to, statute.

(4) The notice under subsection (3)(i)(iv) must state: (i) that a sale that may constitute a bulk sale has been or will be made; (ii) the date or prospective date of the bulk sale; (iii) the individual, partnership, or corporate names and the addresses of the seller and buyer; (iv) the address to which inquiries about the sale may be made, if different from the seller's address; and (v) that the buyer has assumed or will assume in full the debts owed to claimants of whom the buyer has knowledge on the date the buyer receives the list of claimants from the seller or completes a reasonable inquiry to discover the claimants.

(5) The notice under subsections (3)(j)(iii) and (3)(k)(iii) must state: (i) that a sale that may constitute a bulk sale has been or will be made; (ii) the date or prospective date of the bulk sale; (iii) the individual, partnership, or corporate names and the addresses of the seller and buyer; (iv) the address to which inquiries about the sale may be made, if different from the seller's address; and (v) that the buyer has assumed or will assume the debts that were incurred in the seller's business before the date of the bulk sale.

(6) For purposes of subsection (3)(1), the value of assets is presumed to be equal to the price the buyer agrees to pay for the assets. However, in a sale by auction or a sale conducted by a liquidator on the seller's behalf, the value of assets is presumed to be the amount the auctioneer or liquidator reasonably estimates the assets will bring at auction or upon liquidation.

§ 6-104. Obligations of Buyer.

(1) In a bulk sale as defined in Section 6-102(1)(c)(ii) the buyer shall:

  (a) obtain from the seller a list of all business names and addresses used by the seller within three years before the date the list is sent or delivered to the buyer;
  (b) unless excused under subsection (2), obtain from the seller a verified and dated list of claimants of whom the seller has notice three days before the seller sends or delivers the list to the buyer and including, to the extent known by the seller, the address of and the amount claimed by each claimant;
  (c) obtain from the seller or prepare a schedule of distribution (Section 6-106(1));
  (d) give notice of the bulk sale in accordance with Section 6-105;
  (e) unless excused under Section 6-106(4), distribute the net contract price in accordance with the undertakings of the buyer in the schedule of distribution; and
  (f) unless excused under subsection (2), make available the list of claimants (subsection (1)(b)) by:

    (i) promptly sending or delivering a copy of the list without charge to any claimant whose written request is received by the buyer no later than six months after the date of the bulk sale;
    (ii) permitting any claimant to inspect and copy the list at any reasonable hour upon request received by the buyer no later than six months after the date of the bulk sale; or

(iii) filing a copy of the list in the office of the [Secretary of State] no later than the time for giving a notice of the bulk sale (Section 6-105(5)). A list filed in accordance with this subparagraph must state the individual, partnership, or corporate name and a mailing address of the seller.

(2) A buyer who gives notice in accordance with Section 6-105(2) is excused from complying with the requirements of subsections (1)(b) and (1)(f).

§ 6-105. Notice to Claimants.

(1) Except as otherwise provided in subsection (2), to comply with Section 6-104(1)(d), the buyer shall send or deliver a written notice of the bulk sale to each claimant on the list of claimants (Section 6-104(1)(b)) and to any other claimant of whom the buyer has knowledge at the time the notice of the bulk sale is sent or delivered.

(2) A buyer may comply with Section 6-104(1)(d) by filing a written notice of the bulk sale in the office of the [Secretary of State] if:

(a) on the date of the bulk-sale agreement the seller has 200 or more claimants, exclusive of claimants holding secured or matured claims for employment compensation and benefits, including commissions and vacation, severance, and sick-leave pay; or

(b) the buyer has received a verified statement from the seller stating that, as of the date of the bulk-sale agreement, the number of claimants, exclusive of claimants holding secured or matured claims for employment compensation and benefits, including commissions and vacation, severance, and sick-leave pay, is 200 or more.

(3) The written notice of the bulk sale must be accompanied by a copy of the schedule of distribution (Section 6-106(1)) and state at least:

(a) that the seller and buyer have entered into an agreement for a sale that may constitute a bulk sale under the laws of the State of _____ ;

(b) the date of the agreement;

(c) the date on or after which more than ten percent of the assets were or will be transferred;

(d) the date on or after which more than ten percent of the net contract price was or will be paid, if the date is not stated in the schedule of distribution;

(e) the name and a mailing address of the seller;

(f) any other business name and address listed by the seller pursuant to Section 6-104(1)(a);

(g) the name of the buyer and an address of the buyer from which information concerning the sale can be obtained;

(h) a statement indicating the type of assets or describing the assets item by item;

(i) the manner in which the buyer will make available the list of claimants (Section 6-104(1)(f)), if applicable; and

(j) if the sale is in total or partial satisfaction of an antecedent debt owed by the seller, the amount of the debt to be satisfied and the name of the person to whom it is owed.

(4) For purposes of subsections (3)(e) and (3)(g), the name of a person is the person's individual, partnership, or corporate name.

(5) The buyer shall give notice of the bulk sale not less than 45 days before the date of the bulk sale and, if the buyer gives notice in accordance with subsection (1), not more than 30 days after obtaining the list of claimants.

(6) A written notice substantially complying with the requirements of subsection (3) is effective even though it contains minor errors that are not seriously misleading.

(7) A form substantially as follows is sufficient to comply with subsection (3):

Notice of Sale

(1) _____ , whose address is _____ , is described in this notice as the "seller."

(2) _____ , whose address is _____ , is described in this notice as the "buyer."

(3) The seller has disclosed to the buyer that within the past three years the seller has used other business names, operated at other addresses, or both, as follows: _____ .

(4) The seller and the buyer have entered into an agreement dated _____ , for a sale that may constitute a bulk sale under the laws of the state of _____ .

(5) The date on or after which more than ten percent of the assets that are the subject of the sale were or will be transferred is _____ , and [if not stated in the schedule of distribution] the date on or after which more than ten percent of the net contract price was or will be paid is _____ .

(6) The following assets are the subject of the sale: _____ .

(7) [If applicable] The buyer will make available to claimants of the seller a list of the seller's claimants in the following manner: _____ .

(8) [If applicable] The sale is to satisfy $_____ of an antecedent debt owed by the seller to _____ .

(9) A copy of the schedule of distribution of the net contract price accompanies this notice.

[End of Notice]

§ 6-106. Schedule of Distribution.

(1) The seller and buyer shall agree on how the net contract price is to be distributed and set forth their agreement in a written schedule of distribution.

(2) The schedule of distribution may provide for distribution to any person at any time, including distribution of the entire net contract price to the seller.

(3) The buyer's undertakings in the schedule of distribution run only to the seller. However, a buyer who fails to distribute the net contract price in accordance with the buyer's undertakings in the schedule of distribution is liable to a creditor only as provided in Section 6-107(1).

(4) If the buyer undertakes in the schedule of distribution to distribute any part of the net contract price to a person other than the seller, and, after the buyer has given notice in accordance with Section 6-105, some or all of the anticipated net contract price is or becomes unavailable for distribution as a consequence of the buyer's or seller's having complied with an order of court, legal process, statute, or rule of law, the buyer is excused from any obligation arising under this Article or under any contract with the seller to distribute the

net contract price in accordance with the buyer's undertakings in the schedule if the buyer:

(a) distributes the net contract price remaining available in accordance with any priorities for payment stated in the schedule of distribution and, to the extent that the price is insufficient to pay all the debts having a given priority, distributes the price pro rata among those debts shown in the schedule as having the same priority;

(b) distributes the net contract price remaining available in accordance with an order of court;

(c) commences a proceeding for interpleader in a court of competent jurisdiction and is discharged from the proceeding; or

(d) reaches a new agreement with the seller for the distribution of the net contract price remaining available, sets forth the new agreement in an amended schedule of distribution, gives notice of the amended schedule, and distributes the net contract price remaining available in accordance with the buyer's undertakings in the amended schedule.

(5) The notice under subsection (4)(d) must identify the buyer and the seller, state the filing number, if any, of the original notice, set forth the amended schedule, and be given in accordance with subsection (1) or (2) of Section 6-105, whichever is applicable, at least 14 days before the buyer distributes any part of the net contract price remaining available.

(6) If the seller undertakes in the schedule of distribution to distribute any part of the net contract price, and, after the buyer has given notice in accordance with Section 6-105, some or all of the anticipated net contract price is or becomes unavailable for distribution as a consequence of the buyer's or seller's having complied with an order of court, legal process, statute, or rule of law, the seller and any person in control of the seller are excused from any obligation arising under this Article or under any agreement with the buyer to distribute the net contract price in accordance with the seller's undertakings in the schedule if the seller:

(a) distributes the net contract price remaining available in accordance with any priorities for payment stated in the schedule of distribution and, to the extent that the price is insufficient to pay all the debts having a given priority, distributes the price pro rata among those debts shown in the schedule as having the same priority;

(b) distributes the net contract price remaining available in accordance with an order of court;

(c) commences a proceeding for interpleader in a court of competent jurisdiction and is discharged from the proceeding; or

(d) prepares a written amended schedule of distribution of the net contract price remaining available for distribution, gives notice of the amended schedule, and distributes the net contract price remaining available in accordance with the amended schedule.

(7) The notice under subsection (6)(d) must identify the buyer and the seller, state the filing number, if any, of the original notice, set forth the amended schedule, and be given in accordance with subsection (1) or (2) of Section 6-105,

whichever is applicable, at least 14 days before the seller distributes any part of the net contract price remaining available.

§ 6-107. Liability for Noncompliance.

(1) Except as provided in subsection (3), and subject to the limitation in subsection (4):

(a) a buyer who fails to comply with the requirements of Section 6-104(1)(e) with respect to a creditor is liable to the creditor for damages in the amount of the claim, reduced by any amount that the creditor would not have realized if the buyer had complied; and

(b) a buyer who fails to comply with the requirements of any other subsection of Section 6-104 with respect to a claimant is liable to the claimant for damages in the amount of the claim, reduced by any amount that the claimant would not have realized if the buyer had complied.

(2) In an action under subsection (1), the creditor has the burden of establishing the validity and amount of the claim, and the buyer has the burden of establishing the amount that the creditor would not have realized if the buyer had complied.

(3) A buyer who:

(a) made a good faith and commercially reasonable effort to comply with the requirements of Section 6-104(1) or to exclude the sale from the application of this Article under Section 6-103(3); or

(b) on or after the date of the bulk-sale agreement, but before the date of the bulk sale, held a good faith and commercially reasonable belief that this Article does not apply to the particular sale is not liable to creditors for failure to comply with the requirements of Section 6-104. The buyer has the burden of establishing the good faith and commercial reasonableness of the effort or belief.

(4) In a single bulk sale the cumulative liability of the buyer for failure to comply with the requirements of Section 6-104(1) may not exceed an amount equal to:

(a) if the assets consist only of inventory and equipment, twice the net contract price, less the amount of any part of the net contract price paid to or applied for the benefit of the seller or a creditor; or

(b) if the assets include property other than inventory and equipment, twice the net value of the inventory and equipment less the amount of the portion of any part of the net contract price paid to or applied for the benefit of the seller or a creditor which is allocable to the inventory and equipment.

(5) For the purposes of subsection (4)(b), the "net value" of an asset is the value of the asset less (i) the amount of any proceeds of the sale of an asset, to the extent the proceeds are applied in partial or total satisfaction of a debt secured by the asset and (ii) the amount of any debt to the extent it is secured by a security interest or lien that is enforceable against the asset before and after it has been sold to a buyer. If a debt is secured by an asset and other property of the seller, the amount of the debt secured by a security interest or lien that

is enforceable against the asset is determined by multiplying the debt by a fraction, the numerator of which is the value of the asset on the date of the bulk sale and the denominator of which is the value of all property securing the debt on the date of the bulk sale. The portion of a part of the net contract price paid to or applied for the benefit of the seller or a creditor that is "allocable to the inventory and equipment" is the portion that bears the same ratio to that part of the net contract price as the net value of the inventory and equipment bears to the net value of all of the assets.

(6) A payment made by the buyer to a person to whom the buyer is, or believes he [or she] is, liable under subsection (1) reduces pro tanto the buyer's cumulative liability under subsection (4).

(7) No action may be brought under subsection (1)(b) by or on behalf of a claimant whose claim is unliquidated or contingent.

(8) A buyer's failure to comply with the requirements of Section 6-104(1) does not (i) impair the buyer's rights in or title to the assets, (ii) render the sale ineffective, void, or voidable, (iii) entitle a creditor to more than a single satisfaction of his [or her] claim, or (iv) create liability other than as provided in this Article.

(9) Payment of the buyer's liability under subsection (1) discharges pro tanto the seller's debt to the creditor.

(10) Unless otherwise agreed, a buyer has an immediate right of reimbursement from the seller for any amount paid to a creditor in partial or total satisfaction of the buyer's liability under subsection (1).

(11) If the seller is an organization, a person who is in direct or indirect control of the seller, and who knowingly, intentionally, and without legal justification fails, or causes the seller to fail, to distribute the net contract price in accordance with the schedule of distribution is liable to any creditor to whom the seller undertook to make payment under the schedule for damages caused by the failure.

§ 6-108. Bulk Sales by Auction; Bulk Sales Conducted by Liquidator.

(1) Sections 6-104, 6-105, 6-106, and 6-107 apply to a bulk sale by auction and a bulk sale conducted by a liquidator on the seller's behalf with the following modifications:

(a) "buyer" refers to auctioneer or liquidator, as the case may be;

(b) "net contract price" refers to net proceeds of the auction or net proceeds of the sale, as the case may be;

(c) the written notice required under Section 6-105(3) must be accompanied by a copy of the schedule of distribution (Section 6-106(1)) and state at least:

(i) that the seller and the auctioneer or liquidator have entered into an agreement for auction or liquidation services that may constitute an agreement to make a bulk sale under the laws of the State of _____ ;

(ii) the date of the agreement;

(iii) the date on or after which the auction began or will begin or the date on or after which the liquidator began or will begin to sell assets on the seller's behalf;

(iv) the date on or after which more than ten percent

of the net proceeds of the sale were or will be paid, if the date is not stated in the schedule of distribution;

(v) the name and a mailing address of the seller;

(vi) any other business name and address listed by the seller pursuant to Section 6-104(1)(a);

(vii) the name of the auctioneer or liquidator and an address of the auctioneer or liquidator from which information concerning the sale can be obtained;

(viii) a statement indicating the type of assets or describing the assets item by item;

(ix) the manner in which the auctioneer or liquidator will make available the list of claimants (Section 6-104(1)(f), if applicable; and

(x) if the sale is in total or partial satisfaction of an antecedent debt owed by the seller, the amount of the debt to be satisfied and the name of the person to whom it is owed; and

(d) in a single bulk sale the cumulative liability of the auctioneer or liquidator for failure to comply with the requirements of this section may not exceed the amount of the net proceeds of the sale allocable to inventory and equipment sold less the amount of the portion of any part of the net proceeds paid to or applied for the benefit of a creditor which is allocable to the inventory and equipment.

(2) A payment made by the auctioneer or liquidator to a person to whom the auctioneer or liquidator is, or believes he [or she] is, liable under this section reduces pro tanto the auctioneer's or liquidator's cumulative liability under subsection (1)(d).

(3) A form substantially as follows is sufficient to comply with subsection (1)(c):

Notice of Sale

(1) _____ , whose address is _____ , is described in this notice as the "seller."

(2) _____ , whose address is _____ , is described in this notice as the "auctioneer" or "liquidator."

(3) The seller has disclosed to the auctioneer or liquidator that within the past three years the seller has used other business names, operated at other addresses, or both, as follows: _____ .

(4) The seller and the auctioneer or liquidator have entered into an agreement dated _____ for auction or liquidation services that may constitute an agreement to make a bulk sale under the laws of the State of _____ .

(5) The date on or after which the auction began or will begin or the date on or after which the liquidator began or will begin to sell assets on the seller's behalf is _____ , and [if not stated in the schedule of distribution] the date on or after which more than ten percent of the net proceeds of the sale were or will be paid is _____ .

(6) The following assets are the subject of the sale: _____ .

(7) [If applicable] The auctioneer or liquidator will make available to claimants of the seller a list of the seller's claimants in the following manner: _____ .

(8) [If applicable] The sale is to satisfy $_____ of an antecedent debt owed by the seller to _____ .

(9) A copy of the schedule of distribution of the net proceeds accompanies this notice.
[End of Notice]

(4) A person who buys at a bulk sale by auction or conducted by a liquidator need not comply with the requirements of Section 6-104(1) and is not liable for the failure of an auctioneer or liquidator to comply with the requirements of this section.

§ 6-109. What Constitutes Filing; Duties of Filing Officer; Information From Filing Officer.

(1) Presentation of a notice or list of claimants for filing and tender of the filing fee or acceptance of the notice or list by the filing officer constitutes filing under this Article.

(2) The filing officer shall:

(a) mark each notice or list with a file number and with the date and hour of filing;

(b) hold the notice or list or a copy for public inspection;

(c) index the notice or list according to each name given for the seller and for the buyer; and

(d) note in the index the file number and the addresses of the seller and buyer given in the notice or list.

(3) If the person filing a notice or list furnishes the filing officer with a copy, the filing officer upon request shall note upon the copy the file number and date and hour of the filing of the original and send or deliver the copy to the person.

(4) The fee for filing and indexing and for stamping a copy furnished by the person filing to show the date and place of filing is $_____ for the first page and $_____ for each additional page. The fee for indexing each name more than two is $_____ .

(5) Upon request of any person, the filing officer shall issue a certificate showing whether any notice or list with respect to a particular seller or buyer is on file on the date and hour stated in the certificate. If a notice or list is on file, the certificate must give the date and hour of filing of each notice or list and the name and address of each seller, buyer, auctioneer, or liquidator. The fee for the certificate is $_____ if the request for the certificate is in the standard form prescribed by the [Secretary of State] and otherwise is $_____ . Upon request of any person, the filing officer shall furnish a copy of any filed notice or list for a fee of $_____ .

(6) The filing officer shall keep each notice or list for two years after it is filed.

§ 6-110. Limitation of Actions.

(1) Except as provided in subsection (2), an action under this Article against a buyer, auctioneer, or liquidator must be commenced within one year after the date of the bulk sale.

(2) If the buyer, auctioneer, or liquidator conceals the fact that the sale has occurred, the limitation is tolled and an action under this Article may be commenced within the earlier of (i) one year after the person bringing the action discovers that the sale has occurred or (ii) one year after the person bringing the action should have discovered that the sale has occurred, but no later than two years after the date of the bulk sale. Complete noncompliance with the requirements of this Article does not of itself constitute concealment.

(3) An action under Section 6-107(11) must be commenced within one year after the alleged violation occurs.]

ARTICLE 7 / Warehouse Receipts, Bills of Lading and Other Documents of Title

Part 1 General

§ 7-101. Short Title. This Article shall be known and may be cited as Uniform Commercial Code—Documents of Title.

§ 7-102. Definitions and Index of Definitions.

(1) In this Article, unless the context otherwise requires:

(a) "Bailee" means the person who by a warehouse receipt, bill of lading or other document of title acknowledges possession of goods and contracts to deliver them.

(b) "Consignee" means the person named in a bill to whom or to whose order the bill promises delivery.

(c) "Consignor" means the person named in a bill as the person from whom the goods have been received for shipment.

(d) "Delivery order" means a written order to deliver goods directed to a warehouseman, carrier or other person who in the ordinary course of business issues warehouse receipts or bills of lading.

(e) "Document" means document of title as defined in the general definitions in Article 1 (Section 1-201).

(f) "Goods" means all things which are treated as movable for the purposes of a contract of storage or transportation.

(g) "Issuer" means a bailee who issues a document except that in relation to an unaccepted delivery order it means the person who orders the possessor of goods to deliver. Issuer includes any person for whom an agent or employee purports to act in issuing a document if the agent or employee has real or apparent authority to issue documents, notwithstanding that the issuer received no goods or that the goods were misdescribed or that in any other respect the agent or employee violated his instructions.

(h) "Warehouseman" is a person engaged in the business of storing goods for hire.

(2) Other definitions applying to this Article or to specified Parts thereof, and the sections in which they appear are:

"Duly negotiate". Section 7-501.
"Person entitled under the document." Section 7-403(4).

(3) Definitions in other Articles applying to this Article and the sections in which they appear are:

"Contract for sale". Section 2-106.
"Overseas". Section 2-323.
"Receipt" of goods. Section 2-103.

(4) In addition Article 1 contains general definitions and principles of construction and interpretation applicable throughout this Article.

§ 7-103. Relation of Article to Treaty, Statute, Tariff, Classification or Regulation. To the extent that any treaty or statute of the United States, regulatory statute of this State or tariff, classification or regulation filed or issued pursuant thereto is applicable, the provisions of this Article are subject thereto.

§ 7-104. Negotiable and Non-negotiable Warehouse Receipt, Bill of Lading or Other Document of Title.

(1) A warehouse receipt, bill of lading or other document of title is negotiable

    (a) if by its terms the goods are to be delivered to bearer or to the order of a named person; or

    (b) where recognized in overseas trade, if it runs to a named person or assigns.

(2) Any other document is non-negotiable. A bill of lading in which it is stated that the goods are consigned to a named person is not made negotiable by a provision that the goods are to be delivered only against a written order signed by the same or another named person.

§ 7-105. Construction Against Negative Implication.
The omission from either Part 2 or Part 3 of this Article of a provision corresponding to a provision made in the other Part does not imply that a corresponding rule of law is not applicable.

Part 2 Warehouse Receipts: Special Provisions

§ 7-201. Who May Issue a Warehouse Receipt; Storage Under Government Bond.

(1) A warehouse receipt may be issued by any warehouseman.

(2) Where goods including distilled spirits and agricultural commodities are stored under a statute requiring a bond against withdrawal or a license for the issuance of receipts in the nature of warehouse receipts, a receipt issued for the goods has like effect as a warehouse receipt even though issued by a person who is the owner of the goods and is not a warehouseman.

§ 7-202. Form of Warehouse Receipt; Essential Terms; Optional Terms.

(1) A warehouse receipt need not be in any particular form.

(2) Unless a warehouse receipt embodies within its written or printed terms each of the following, the warehouseman is liable for damages caused by the omission to a person injured thereby:

    (a) the location of the warehouse where the goods are stored;

    (b) the date of issue of the receipt;

    (c) the consecutive number of the receipt;

    (d) a statement whether the goods received will be delivered to the bearer, to a specified person, or to a specified person or his order;

    (e) the rate of storage and handling charges, except that where goods are stored under a field warehousing arrangement a statement of that fact is sufficient on a non-negotiable receipt;

    (f) a description of the goods or of the packages containing them;

    (g) the signature of the warehouseman, which may be made by his authorized agent;

    (h) if the receipt is issued for goods of which the warehouseman is owner, either solely or jointly or in common with others, the fact of such ownership; and

    (i) a statement of the amount of advances made and of liabilities incurred for which the warehouseman claims a lien or security interest (Section 7-209). If the precise amount of such advances made or of such liabilities incurred is, at the time of the issue of the receipt, unknown to the warehouseman or to his agent who issues it, a statement of the fact that advances have been made or liabilities incurred and the purpose thereof is sufficient.

(3) A warehouseman may insert in his receipt any other terms which are not contrary to the provisions of this Act and do not impair his obligation of delivery (Section 7-403) or his duty of care (Section 7-204). Any contrary provisions shall be ineffective.

§ 7-203. Liability for Non-receipt or Misdescription. A
party to or purchaser for value in good faith of a document of title other than a bill of lading relying in either case upon the description therein of the goods may recover from the issuer damages caused by the non-receipt or misdescription of the goods, except to the extent that the document conspicuously indicates that the issuer does not know whether any part or all of the goods in fact were received or conform to the description, as where the description is in terms of marks or labels or kind, quantity or condition, or the receipt or description is qualified by "contents, condition and quality unknown", "said to contain" or the like, if such indication be true, or the party or purchaser otherwise has notice.

§ 7-204. Duty of Care; Contractual Limitation of Warehouseman's Liability.

(1) A warehouseman is liable for damages for loss of or injury to the goods caused by his failure to exercise such care in regard to them as a reasonably careful man would exercise under like circumstances but unless otherwise agreed he is not liable for damages which could not have been avoided by the exercise of such care.

(2) Damages may be limited by a term in the warehouse receipt or storage agreement limiting the amount of liability in case of loss or damage, and setting forth a specific liability per article or item, or value per unit of weight, beyond which the warehouseman shall not be liable; provided, however, that such liability may on written request of the bailor at the time of signing such storage agreement or within a reasonable time after receipt of the warehouse receipt be increased on part or all of the goods thereunder, in which event increased rates may be charged based on such increased valuation, but that no such increase shall be permitted contrary to a lawful limitation of liability contained in the warehouseman's tariff, if any. No such limitation is effective with respect to the warehouseman's liability for conversion to his own use.

(3) Reasonable provisions as to the time and manner of presenting claims and instituting actions based on the bailment may be included in the warehouse receipt or tariff.

(4) This section does not impair or repeal . . .

Note: *Insert in subsection (4) a reference to any statute which imposes a higher responsibility upon the warehouseman or invalidates contractual limitations which would be permissible under this Article.*

§ 7-205. Title Under Warehouse Receipt Defeated in Certain Cases. A buyer in the ordinary course of business of fungible goods sold and delivered by a warehouseman who is also in the business of buying and selling such goods takes free of any claim under a warehouse receipt even though it has been duly negotiated.

§ 7-206. Termination of Storage at Warehouseman's Option.

(1) A warehouseman may on notifying the person on whose account the goods are held and any other person known to claim an interest in the goods require payment of any charges and removal of the goods from the warehouse at the termination of the period of storage fixed by the document, or, if no period is fixed, within a stated period not less than thirty days after the notification. If the goods are not removed before the date specified in the notification, the warehouseman may sell them in accordance with the provisions of the section on enforcement of a warehouseman's lien (Section 7-210).

(2) If a warehouseman in good faith believes that the goods are about to deteriorate or decline in value to less than the amount of his lien within the time prescribed in subsection (1) for notification, advertisement and sale, the warehouseman may specify in the notification any reasonable shorter time for removal of the goods and in case the goods are not removed, may sell them at public sale held not less than one week after a single advertisement or posting.

(3) If as a result of a quality or condition of the goods of which the warehouseman had no notice at the time of deposit the goods are a hazard to other property or to the warehouse or to persons, the warehouseman may sell the goods at public or private sale without advertisement on reasonable notification to all persons known to claim an interest in the goods. If the warehouseman after a reasonable effort is unable to sell the goods he may dispose of them in any lawful manner and shall incur no liability by reason of such disposition.

(4) The warehouseman must deliver the goods to any person entitled to them under this Article upon due demand made at any time prior to sale or other disposition under this section.

(5) The warehouseman may satisfy his lien from the proceeds of any sale or disposition under this section but must hold the balance for delivery on the demand of any person to whom he would have been bound to deliver the goods.

§ 7-207. Goods Must Be Kept Separate; Fungible Goods.

(1) Unless the warehouse receipt otherwise provides, a warehouseman must keep separate the goods covered by each receipt so as to permit at all times identification and delivery of those goods except that different lots of fungible goods may be commingled.

(2) Fungible goods so commingled are owned in common by the persons entitled thereto and the warehouseman is severally liable to each owner for that owner's share. Where because of overissue a mass of fungible goods is insufficient to meet all the receipts which the warehouseman has issued against it, the persons entitled include all holders to whom overissued receipts have been duly negotiated.

§ 7-208. Altered Warehouse Receipts.
Where a blank in a negotiable warehouse receipt has been filled in without authority, a purchaser for value and without notice of the want of authority may treat the insertion as authorized. Any other unauthorized alteration leaves any receipt enforceable against the issuer according to its original tenor.

§ 7-209. Lien of Warehouseman.

(1) A warehouseman has a lien against the bailor on the goods covered by a warehouse receipt or on the proceeds thereof in his possession for charges for storage or transportation (including demurrage and terminal charges), insurance, labor, or charges present or future in relation to the goods, and for expenses necessary for preservation of the goods or reasonably incurred in their sale pursuant to law. If the person on whose account the goods are held is liable for like charges or expenses in relation to other goods whenever deposited and it is stated in the receipt that a lien is claimed for charges and expenses in relation to other goods, the warehouseman also has a lien against him for such charges and expenses whether or not the other goods have been delivered by the warehouseman. But against a person to whom a negotiable warehouse receipt is duly negotiated a warehouseman's lien is limited to charges in an amount or at a rate specified on the receipt or if no charges are so specified then to a reasonable charge for storage of the goods covered by the receipt subsequent to the date of the receipt.

(2) The warehouseman may also reserve a security interest against the bailor for a maximum amount specified on the receipt for charges other than those specified in subsection (1), such as for money advanced and interest. Such a security interest is governed by the Article on Secured Transactions (Article 9).

(3)

(a) A warehouseman's lien for charges and expenses under subsection (1) or a security interest under subsection (2) is also effective against any person who so entrusted the bailor with possession of the goods that a pledge of them by him to a good faith purchaser for value would have been valid but is not effective against a person as to whom the document confers no right in the goods covered by it under Section 7-503.

(b) A warehouseman's lien on household goods for charges and expenses in relation to the goods under subsection (1) is also effective against all persons if the depositor was the legal possessor of the goods at the time of deposit. "Household goods" means furniture, furnishings and personal effects used by the depositor in a dwelling.

(4) A warehouseman loses his lien on any goods which he voluntarily delivers or which he unjustifiably refuses to deliver.

As amended in 1966.

§ 7-210. Enforcement of Warehouseman's Lien.

(1) Except as provided in subsection (2), a warehouseman's lien may be enforced by public or private sale of the goods in block or in parcels, at any time or place and on any terms which are commercially reasonable, after notifying all persons known to claim an interest in the goods. Such notification must include a statement of the amount due, the nature of the proposed sale and the time and place of any public sale. The fact that a better price could have been obtained by a sale at a different time or in a different method from that selected by the warehouseman is not of itself sufficient to establish that the sale was not made in a commercially reasonable manner. If the warehouseman either sells the goods in the usual

manner in any recognized market therefor, or if he sells at the price current in such market at the time of his sale, or if he has otherwise sold in conformity with commercially reasonable practices among dealers in the type of goods sold, he has sold in a commercially reasonable manner. A sale of more goods than apparently necessary to be offered to insure satisfaction of the obligation is not commercially reasonable except in cases covered by the preceding sentence.

(2) A warehouseman's lien on goods other than goods stored by a merchant in the course of his business may be enforced only as follows:

(a) All persons known to claim an interest in the goods must be notified.

(b) The notification must be delivered in person or sent by registered or certified letter to the last known address of any person to be notified.

(c) The notification must include an itemized statement of the claim, a description of the goods subject to the lien, a demand for payment within a specified time not less than ten days after receipt of the notification, and a conspicuous statement that unless the claim is paid within that time the goods will be advertised for sale and sold by auction at a specified time and place.

(d) The sale must conform to the terms of the notification.

(e) The sale must be held at the nearest suitable place to that where the goods are held or stored.

(f) After the expiration of the time given in the notification, an advertisement of the sale must be published once a week for two weeks consecutively in a newspaper of general circulation where the sale is to be held. The advertisement must include a description of the goods, the name of the person on whose account they are being held, and the time and place of the sale. The sale must take place at least fifteen days after the first publication. If there is no newspaper of general circulation where the sale is to be held, the advertisement must be posted at least ten days before the sale in not less than six conspicuous places in the neighborhood of the proposed sale.

(3) Before any sale pursuant to this section any person claiming a right in the goods may pay the amount necessary to satisfy the lien and the reasonable expenses incurred under this section. In that event the goods must not be sold, but must be retained by the warehouseman subject to the terms of the receipt and this Article.

(4) The warehouseman may buy at any public sale pursuant to this section.

(5) A purchaser in good faith of goods sold to enforce a warehouseman's lien takes the goods free of any rights of persons against whom the lien was valid, despite noncompliance by the warehouseman with the requirements of this section.

(6) The warehouseman may satisfy his lien from the proceeds of any sale pursuant to this section but must hold the balance, if any, for delivery on demand to any person to whom he would have been bound to deliver the goods.

(7) The rights provided by this section shall be in addition to all other rights allowed by law to a creditor against his debtor.

(8) Where a lien is on goods stored by a merchant in the course of his business the lien may be enforced in accordance with either subsection (1) or (2).

(9) The warehouseman is liable for damages caused by failure to comply with the requirements for sale under this section and in case of willful violation is liable for conversion.

As amended in 1962.

Part 3 Bills of Lading: Special Provisions

§ 7-301. Liability for Non-receipt or Misdescription; "Said to Contain"; "Shipper's Load and Count"; Improper Handling.

(1) A consignee of a non-negotiable bill who has given value in good faith or a holder to whom a negotiable bill has been duly negotiated relying in either case upon the description therein of the goods, or upon the date therein shown, may recover from the issuer damages caused by the misdating of the bill or the non-receipt or misdescription of the goods, except to the extent that the document indicates that the issuer does not know whether any part or all of the goods in fact were received or conform to the description, as where the description is in terms of marks or labels or kind, quantity, or condition or the receipt or description is qualified by "contents or condition of contents of packages unknown", "said to contain", "shipper's weight, load and count" or the like, if such indication be true.

(2) When goods are loaded by an issuer who is a common carrier, the issuer must count the packages of goods if package freight and ascertain the kind and quantity if bulk freight. In such cases "shipper's weight, load and count" or other words indicating that the description was made by the shipper are ineffective except as to freight concealed by packages.

(3) When bulk freight is loaded by a shipper who makes available to the issuer adequate facilities for weighing such freight, an issuer who is a common carrier must ascertain the kind and quantity within a reasonable time after receiving the written request of the shipper to do so. In such cases "shipper's weight" or other words of like purport are ineffective.

(4) The issuer may be inserting in the bill the words "shipper's weight, load and count" or other words of like purport indicate that the goods were loaded by the shipper; and if such statement be true the issuer shall not be liable for damages caused by the improper loading. But their omission does not imply liability for such damages.

(5) The shipper shall be deemed to have guaranteed to the issuer the accuracy at the time of shipment of the description, marks, labels, number, kind, quantity, condition and weight, as furnished by him; and the shipper shall indemnify the issuer against damage caused by inaccuracies in such particulars. The right of the issuer to such indemnity shall in no way limit his responsibility and liability under the contract of carriage to any person other than the shipper.

§ 7-302. Through Bills of Lading and Similar Documents.

(1) The issuer of a through bill of lading or other document embodying an undertaking to be performed in part by persons acting as its agents or by connecting carriers is liable to anyone entitled to recover on the document for any breach by such other persons or by a connecting carrier of its obligation under the document but to the extent that the bill covers an

undertaking to be performed overseas or in territory not contiguous to the continental United States or an undertaking including matters other than transportation this liability may be varied by agreement of the parties.

(2) Where goods covered by a through bill of lading or other document embodying an undertaking to be performed in part by persons other than the issuer are received by any such person, he is subject with respect to his own performance while the goods are in his possession to the obligation of the issuer. His obligation is discharged by delivery of the goods to another such person pursuant to the document, and does not include liability for breach by any other such persons or by the issuer.

(3) The issuer of such through bill of lading or other document shall be entitled to recover from the connecting carrier or such other person in possession of the goods when the breach of the obligation under the document occurred, the amount it may be required to pay to anyone entitled to recover on the document therefor, as may be evidenced by any receipt, judgment, or transcript thereof, and the amount of any expense reasonably incurred by it in defending any action brought by anyone entitled to recover on the document therefor.

§ 7-303. Diversion; Reconsignment; Change of Instructions.

(1) Unless the bill of lading otherwise provides, the carrier may deliver the goods to a person or destination other than that stated in the bill or may otherwise dispose of the goods on instructions from

  (a) the holder of a negotiable bill; or
  (b) the consignor on a non-negotiable bill notwithstanding contrary instructions from the consignee; or
  (c) the consignee on a non-negotiable bill in the absence of contrary instructions from the consignor, if the goods have arrived at the billed destination or if the consignee is in possession of the bill; or
  (d) the consignee on a non-negotiable bill if he is entitled as against the consignor to dispose of them.

(2) Unless such instructions are noted on a negotiable bill of lading, a person to whom the bill is duly negotiated can hold the bailee according to the original terms.

§ 7-304. Bills of Lading in a Set.

(1) Except where customary in overseas transportation, a bill of lading must not be issued in a set of parts. The issuer is liable for damages caused by violation of this subsection.

(2) Where a bill of lading is lawfully drawn in a set of parts, each of which is numbered and expressed to be valid only if the goods have not been delivered against any other part, the whole of the parts constitute one bill.

(3) Where a bill of lading is lawfully issued in a set of parts and different parts are negotiated to different persons, the title of the holder to whom the first due negotiation is made prevails as to both the document and the goods even though any later holder may have received the goods from the carrier in good faith and discharged the carrier's obligation by surrender of his part.

(4) Any person who negotiates or transfers a single part of a bill of lading drawn in a set is liable to holders of that part as if it were the whole set.

(5) The bailee is obliged to deliver in accordance with Part 4 of this Article against the first presented part of a bill of lading lawfully drawn in a set. Such delivery discharges the bailee's obligation on the whole bill.

§ 7-305. Destination Bills.

(1) Instead of issuing a bill of lading to the consignor at the place of shipment a carrier may at the request of the consignor procure the bill to be issued at destination or at any other place designated in the request.

(2) Upon request of anyone entitled as against the carrier to control the goods while in transit and on surrender of any outstanding bill of lading or other receipt covering such goods, the issuer may procure a substitute bill to be issued at any place designated in the request.

§ 7-306. Altered Bills of Lading.
An unauthorized alteration or filling in of a blank in a bill of lading leaves the bill enforceable according to its original tenor.

§ 7-307. Lien of Carrier.

(1) A carrier has a lien on the goods covered by a bill of lading for charges subsequent to the date of its receipt of the goods for storage or transportation (including demurrage and terminal charges) and for expenses necessary for preservation of the goods incident to their transportation or reasonably incurred in their sale pursuant to law. But against a purchaser for value of a negotiable bill of lading a carrier's lien is limited to charges stated in the bill or the applicable tariffs, or if no charges are stated then to a reasonable charge.

(2) A lien for charges and expenses under subsection (1) on goods which the carrier was required by law to receive for transportation is effective against the consignor or any person entitled to the goods unless the carrier had notice that the consignor lacked authority to subject the goods to such charges and expenses. Any other lien under subsection (1) is effective against the consignor and in any person who permitted the bailor to have control or possession of the goods unless the carrier had notice that the bailor lacked such authority.

(3) A carrier loses his lien on any goods which he voluntarily delivers or which he unjustifiably refuses to deliver.

§ 7-308. Enforcement of Carrier's Lien.

(1) A carrier's lien may be enforced by public or private sale of the goods, in block or in parcels, at any time or place and on any terms which are commercially reasonable, after notifying all persons known to claim an interest in the goods. Such notification must include a statement of the amount due, the nature of the proposed sale and the time and place of any public sale. The fact that a better price could have been obtained by a sale at a different time or in a different method from that selected by the carrier is not of itself sufficient to establish that the sale was not made in a commercially reasonable manner. If the carrier either sells the goods in the usual manner in any recognized market therefor or if he sells at the price current in such market at the time of his sale or if he has otherwise sold in conformity with commercially rea-

sonable practices among dealers in the type of goods sold he has sold in a commercially reasonable manner. A sale of more goods than apparently necessary to be offered to ensure satisfaction of the obligation is not commercially reasonable except in cases covered by the preceding sentence.

(2) Before any sale pursuant to this section any person claiming a right in the goods may pay the amount necessary to satisfy the lien and the reasonable expenses incurred under this section. In that event the goods must not be sold, but must be retained by the carrier subject to the terms of the bill and this Article.

(3) The carrier may buy at any public sale pursuant to this section.

(4) A purchaser in good faith of goods sold to enforce a carrier's lien takes the goods free of any rights of persons against whom the lien was valid, despite noncompliance by the carrier with the requirements of this section.

(5) The carrier may satisfy his lien from the proceeds of any sale pursuant to this section but must hold the balance, if any, for delivery on demand to any person to whom he would have been bound to deliver the goods.

(6) The rights provided by this section shall be in addition to all other rights allowed by law to a creditor against his debtor.

(7) A carrier's lien may be enforced in accordance with either subsection (1) or the procedure set forth in subsection (2) of Section 7-210.

(8) The carrier is liable for damages caused by failure to comply with the requirements for sale under this section and in case of willful violation is liable for conversion.

§ 7-309. Duty of Care; Contractual Limitation of Carrier's Liability.

(1) A carrier who issues a bill of lading whether negotiable or non-negotiable must exercise the degree of care in relation to the goods which a reasonably careful man would exercise under like circumstances. This subsection does not repeal or change any law or rule of law which imposes liability upon a common carrier for damages not caused by its negligence.

(2) Damages may be limited by a provision that the carrier's liability shall not exceed a value stated in the document if the carrier's rates are dependent upon value and the consignor by the carrier's tariff is afforded an opportunity to declare a higher value or a value as lawfully provided in the tariff, or where no tariff is filed he is otherwise advised of such opportunity; but no such limitation is effective with respect to the carrier's liability for conversion to its own use.

(3) Reasonable provisions as to the time and manner of presenting claims and instituting actions based on the shipment may be included in a bill of lading or tariff.

Part 4   Warehouse Receipts and Bills of Lading: General Obligations

§ 7-401.   Irregularities in Issue of Receipt or Bill or Conduct of Issuer. The obligations imposed by this Article on an issuer apply to a document of title regardless of the fact that

(a) the document may not comply with the requirements of this Article or of any other law or regulation regarding its issue, form or content; or

(b) the issuer may have violated laws regulating the conduct of his business; or

(c) the goods covered by the document were owned by the bailee at the time the document was issued; or

(d) the person issuing the document does not come within the definition of warehouseman if it purports to be a warehouse receipt.

§ 7-402.   Duplicate Receipt or Bill; Overissue. Neither a duplicate nor any other document of the title purporting to cover goods already represented by an outstanding document of the same issuer confers any right in the goods, except as provided in the case of bills in a set, overissue of documents for fungible goods and substitutes for lost, stolen or destroyed documents. But the issuer is liable for damages caused by his overissue or failure to identify a duplicate document as such by conspicuous notation on its face.

§ 7-403.   Obligation of Warehouseman or Carrier to Deliver; Excuse.

(1) The bailee must deliver the goods to a person entitled under the document who complies with subsections (2) and (3), unless and to the extent that the bailee establishes any of the following:

(a) delivery of the goods to a person whose receipt was rightful as against the claimant;

(b) damage to or delay, loss or destruction of the goods for which the bailee is not liable], but the burden of establishing negligence in such cases is on the person entitled under the document];

Note: *The brackets in (1)(b) indicate that State enactments may differ on this point without serious damage to the principle of uniformity.*

(c) previous sale or other disposition of the goods in lawful enforcement of a lien or on warehouseman's lawful termination of storage;

(d) the exercise by a seller of his right to stop delivery pursuant to the provisions of the Article on Sales (Section 2-705);

(e) a diversion, reconsignment or other disposition pursuant to the provisions of this Article (Section 7-303) or tariff regulating such right;

(f) release, satisfaction or any other fact affording a personal defense against the claimant;

(g) any other lawful excuse.

(2) A person claiming goods covered by a document of title must satisfy the bailee's lien where the bailee so requests or where the bailee is prohibited by law from delivering the goods until the charges are paid.

(3) Unless the person claiming is one against whom the document confers no right under Sec. 7-503(1), he must surrender for cancellation or notation of partial deliveries any outstanding negotiable document covering the goods, and the bailee must cancel the document or conspicuously note the partial delivery thereon or be liable to any person to whom the document is duly negotiated.

(4) "Person entitled under the document" means holder in the case of a negotiable document, or the person to whom delivery is to be made by the terms of or pursuant to written instructions under a non-negotiable document.

§ **7-404.** **No Liability for Good Faith Delivery Pursuant to Receipt or Bill.** A bailee who in good faith including observance of reasonable commercial standards has received goods and delivered or otherwise disposed of them according to the terms of the document of title or pursuant to this Article is not liable therefor. This rule applies even though the person from whom he received the goods had no authority to procure the document or to dispose of the goods and even though the person to whom he delivered the goods had no authority to receive them.

Part 5 **Warehouse Receipts and Bills of Lading: Negotiation and Transfer**

§ **7-501.** **Form of Negotiation and Requirements of "Due Negotiation".**

(1) A negotiable document of title running to the order of a named person is negotiated by his indorsement and delivery. After his indorsement in blank or to bearer any person can negotiate it by delivery alone.

(2)

    (a) A negotiable document of title is also negotiated by delivery alone when by its original terms it runs to bearer.

    (b) When a document running to the order of a named person is delivered to him the effect is the same as if the document had been negotiated.

(3) Negotiation of a negotiable document of title after it has been indorsed to a specified person requires indorsement by the special indorsee as well as delivery.

(4) A negotiable document of title is "duly negotiated" when it is negotiated in the manner stated in this section to a holder who purchases it in good faith without notice of any defense against or claim to it on the part of any person and for value, unless it is established that the negotiation is not in the regular course of business or financing or involves receiving the document in settlement or payment of a money obligation.

(5) Indorsement of a non-negotiable document neither makes it negotiable nor adds to the transferee's rights.

(6) The naming in a negotiable bill of a person to be notified of the arrival of the goods does not limit the negotiability of the bill nor constitute notice to a purchaser thereof of any interest of such person in the goods.

§ **7-502.** **Rights Acquired by Due Negotiation.**

(1) Subject to the following section and to the provisions of Section 7-205 on fungible goods, a holder to whom a negotiable document of title has been duly negotiated acquires thereby:

    (a) title to the document;

    (b) title to the goods;

    (c) all rights accruing under the law of agency or estoppel, including rights to goods delivered to the bailee after the document was issued; and

    (d) the direct obligation of the issuer to hold or deliver the goods according to the terms of the document free of any defense or claim by him except those arising under the terms of the document or under this Article. In the case of a delivery order the bailee's obligation accrues only upon

acceptance and the obligation acquired by the holder is that the issuer and any indorser will procure the acceptance of the bailee.

(2) Subject to the following section, title and rights so acquired are not defeated by any stoppage of the goods represented by the document or by surrender of such goods by the bailee, and are not impaired even though the negotiation or any prior negotiation or any prior negotiation constituted a breach of duty or even though any person has been deprived of possession of the document by misrepresentation, fraud, accident, mistake, duress, loss, theft or conversion, or even though a previous sale or other transfer of the goods or document has been made to a third person.

§ **7-503.** **Document of Title to Goods Defeated in Certain Cases.**

(1) A document of title confers no right in goods against a person who before issuance of the document had a legal interest or a perfected security interest in them and who neither

    (a) delivered or entrusted them or any document of title covering them to the bailor or his nominee with actual or apparent authority to ship, store or sell or with power to obtain delivery under this Article (Section 7-403) or with power of disposition under this Act (Sections 2-403 and 9-307) or other statute or rule of law; nor

    (b) acquiesced in the procurement by the bailor or his nominee of any document of title.

(2) Title to goods based upon an unaccepted delivery order is subject to the rights of anyone to whom a negotiable warehouse receipt or bill of lading covering the goods has been duly negotiated. Such a title may be defeated under the next section to the same extent as the rights of the issuer or a transferee from the issuer.

(3) Title to goods based upon a bill of lading issued to a freight forwarder is subject to the rights of anyone to whom a bill issued by the freight forwarder is duly negotiated; but delivery by the carrier in accordance with Part 4 of this Article pursuant to its own bill of lading discharges the carrier's obligation to deliver.

§ **7-504.** **Rights Acquired in the Absence of Due Negotiation; Effect of Diversion; Seller's Stoppage of Delivery.**

(1) A transferee of a document, whether negotiable or non-negotiable, to whom the document has been delivered but not duly negotiated, acquires the title and rights which his transferor had or had actual authority to convey.

(2) In the case of a non-negotiable document, until but not after the bailee receives notification of the transfer, the rights of the transferee may be defeated

    (a) by those creditors of the transferor who could treat the sale as void under Section 2-402; or

    (b) by a buyer from the transferor in ordinary course of business if the bailee has delivered the goods to the buyer or received notification of his rights; or

    (c) as against the bailee by good faith dealings of the bailee with the transferor.

(3) A diversion or other change of shipping instructions by the consignor in a non-negotiable bill of lading which causes

the bailee not to deliver to the consignee defeats the consignee's title to the goods if they have been delivered to a buyer in ordinary course of business and in any event defeats the consignee's rights against the bailee.

(4) Delivery pursuant to a non-negotiable document may be stopped by a seller under Section 2-705, and subject to the requirement of due notification there provided. A bailee honoring the seller's instructions is entitled to be indemnified by the seller against any resulting loss or expense.

§ 7-505. Indorser Not a Guarantor for Other Parties.
The indorsement of a document of title issued by a bailee does not make the indorser liable for any default by the bailee or by previous indorsers.

§ 7-506. Delivery Without Indorsement: Right to Compel Indorsement.
The transferee of a negotiable document of title has a specifically enforceable right to have his transferor supply any necessary indorsement but the transfer becomes a negotiation only as of the time the indorsement is supplied.

§ 7-507. Warranties on Negotiation or Transfer of Receipt or Bill.
Where a person negotiates or transfers a document of title for value otherwise than as a mere intermediary under the next following section, then unless otherwise agreed he warrants to his immediate purchaser only in addition to any warranty made in selling the goods

(a) that the document is genuine; and
(b) that he has no knowledge of any fact which would impair its validity or worth; and
(c) that his negotiation or transfer is rightful and fully effective with respect to the title to the document and the goods it represents.

§ 7-508. Warranties of Collecting Bank as to Documents.
A collecting bank or other intermediary known to be entrusted with documents on behalf of another or with collection of a draft or other claim against delivery of documents warrants by such delivery of the documents only its own good faith and authority. This rule applies even though the intermediary has purchased or made advances against the claim or draft to be collected.

§ 7-509. Receipt or Bill: When Adequate Compliance With Commercial Contract.
The question whether a document is adequate to fulfill the obligations of a contract for sale or the conditions of a credit is governed by the Articles on Sales (Article 2) and on Letters of Credit (Article 5).

Part 6 Warehouse Receipts and Bills of Lading: Miscellaneous Provisions

§ 7-601. Lost and Missing Documents.
(1) If a document has been lost, stolen or destroyed, a court may order delivery of the goods or issuance of a substitute document and the bailee may without liability to any person comply with such order. If the document was negotiable the claimant must post security approved by the court to indemnify any person who may suffer loss as a result of non-surrender of the document. If the document was not

negotiable, such security may be required at the discretion of the court. The court may also in its discretion order payment of the bailee's reasonable costs and counsel fees.

(2) A bailee who without court order delivers goods to a person claiming under a missing negotiable document is liable to any person injured thereby, and if the delivery is not in good faith becomes liable for conversion. Delivery in good faith is not conversion if made in accordance with a filed classification or tariff or, where no classification or tariff is filed, if the claimant posts security with the bailee in an amount at least double the value of the goods at the time of posting to indemnify any person injured by the delivery who files a notice of claim within one year after the delivery.

§ 7-602. Attachment of Goods Covered by a Negotiable Document.
Except where the document was originally issued upon delivery of the goods by a person who had no power to dispose of them, no lien attaches by virtue of any judicial process to goods in the possession of a bailee for which a negotiable document of title is outstanding unless the document be first surrendered to the bailee or its negotiation enjoined, and the bailee shall not be compelled to deliver the goods pursuant to process until the document is surrendered to him or impounded by the court. One who purchases the document for value without notice of the process or injunction takes free of the lien imposed by judicial process.

§ 7-603. Conflicting Claims; Interpleader.
If more than one person claims title or possession of the goods, the bailee is excused from delivery until he has had a reasonable time to ascertain the validity of the adverse claims or to bring an action to compel all claimants to interplead and may compel such interpleader, either in defending an action for non-delivery of the goods, or by original action, whichever is appropriate.

ARTICLE 8 / Investment Securities

Part 1 Short Title and General Matters

§ 8-101. Short Title.
This Article shall be known and may be cited as Uniform Commercial Code—Investment Securities.

§ 8-102. Definitions and Index of Definitions.
(1) In this Article, unless the context otherwise requires:

(a) A "certificated security" is a share, participation, or other interest in property of or an enterprise of the issuer or an obligation of the issuer which is

(i) represented by an instrument issued in bearer or registered form;
(ii) of a type commonly dealt in on securities exchanges or markets or commonly recognized in any area in which it is issued or dealt in as a medium for investment; and
(iii) either one of a class or series or by its terms divisible into a class or series of shares, participations, interests, or obligations.

(b) An "uncertificated security" is a share, participation, or other interest in property or an enterprise of the issuer or an obligation of the issuer which is

    (i) not represented by an instrument and the transfer of which is registered upon books maintained for that purpose by or on behalf of the issuer;

    (ii) of a type commonly dealt in on securities exchanges or markets; and

    (iii) either one of a class or series or by its terms divisible into a class or series of shares, participations, interests, or obligations.

(c) A "security" is either a certificated or an uncertificated security. If a security is certificated, the terms "security" and "certificated security" may mean either the intangible interest, the instrument representing that interest, or both, as the context requires. A writing that is a certificated security is governed by this Article and not by Article 3, even though it also meets the requirements of that Article. This Article does not apply to money. If a certificated security has been retained by or surrendered to the issuer or its transfer agent for reasons other than registration of transfer, other temporary purpose, payment, exchange, or acquisition by the issuer, that security shall be treated as an uncertificated security for purposes of this Article.

(d) A certificated security is in "registered form" if

    (i) it specifies a person entitled to the security or the rights it represents; and

    (ii) its transfer may be registered upon books maintained for that purpose by or on behalf of the issuer, or the security so states.

(e) A certificated security is in "bearer form" if it runs to bearer according to its terms and not by reason of any indorsement.

(2) A "subsequent purchaser" is a person who takes other than by original issue.

(3) A "clearing corporation" is a corporation registered as a "clearing agency" under the federal securities laws or a corporation:

    (a) at least 90 percent of whose capital stock is held by or for one or more organizations, none of which, other than a national securities exchange or association, holds in excess of 20 percent of the capital stock of the corporation, and each of which is

        (i) subject to supervision or regulation pursuant to the provisions of federal or state banking laws or state insurance laws,

        (ii) a broker or dealer or investment company registered under the federal securities laws, or

        (iii) a national securities exchange or association registered under the federal securities laws; and

    (b) any remaining capital stock of which is held by individuals who have purchased it at or prior to the time of their taking office as directors of the corporation and who have purchased only so much of the capital stock as is necessary to permit them to qualify as directors.

(4) A "custodian bank" is a bank or trust company that is supervised and examined by state or federal authority having supervision over banks and is acting as custodian for a clearing corporation.

(5) Other definitions applying to this Article or to specified Parts thereof and the sections in which they appear are:

    "Adverse claim".   Section 8-302.
    "Bona fide purchaser".   Section 8-302.
    "Broker".   Section 8-303.
    "Debtor".   Section 9-105.
    "Financial intermediary".   Section 8-313.
    "Guarantee of the signature".   Section 8-402.
    "Initial transaction statement".   Section 8-408.
    "Instruction".   Section 8-308.
    "Intermediary bank".   Section 4-105.
    "Issuer".   Section 8-201.
    "Overissue".   Section 8-104.
    "Secured Party".   Section 9-105.
    "Security Agreement".   Section 9-105.

(6) In addition, Article 1 contains general definitions and principles of construction and interpretation applicable throughout this Article.

As amended in 1962, 1973 and 1977.

§ 8-103. Issuer's Lien.

A lien upon a security in favor of an issuer thereof is valid against a purchaser only if:

(a) the security is certificated and the right of the issuer to the lien is noted conspicuously thereon; or

(b) the security is uncertificated and a notation of the right of the issuer to the lien is contained in the initial transaction statement sent to the purchaser or, if his interest is transferred to him other than by registration of transfer, pledge, or release, the initial transaction statement sent to the registered owner or the registered pledgee.

As amended in 1977.

§ 8-104. Effect of Overissue; "Overissue".

(1) The provisions of this Article which validate a security or compel its issue or reissue do not apply to the extent that validation, issue, or reissue would result in overissue; but if:

    (a) an identical security which does not constitute an overissue is reasonably available for purchase, the person entitled to issue or validation may compel the issuer to purchase the security for him and either to deliver a certificated security or to register the transfer of an uncertificated security to him, against surrender of any certificated security he holds; or

    (b) a security is not so available for purchase, the person entitled to issue or validation may recover from the issuer the price he or the last purchaser for value paid for it with interest from the date of his demand.

(2) "Overissue" means the issue of securities in excess of the amount the issuer has corporate power to issue.

As amended in 1977.

§ 8-105. Certificated Securities Negotiable; Statements and Instructions Not Negotiable; Presumptions.

(1) Certificated securities governed by this Article are negotiable instruments.

(2) Statements (Section 8-408), notices, or the like, sent by the issuer of uncertificated securities and instructions (Sec-

tion 8-308) are neither negotiable instruments nor certificated securities.

(3) In any action on a security:

(a) unless specifically denied in the pleadings, each signature on a certificated security, in a necessary indorsement, on an initial transaction statement, or on an instruction, is admitted;

(b) if the effectiveness of a signature is put in issue, the burden of establishing it is on the party claiming under the signature, but the signature is presumed to be genuine or authorized;

(c) if signatures on a certificated security are admitted or established, production of the security entitles a holder to recover on it unless the defendant establishes a defense or a defect going to the validity of the security;

(d) if signatures on an initial transaction statement are admitted or established, the facts stated in the statement are presumed to be true as of the time of its issuance; and

(e) after it is shown that a defense or defect exists, the plaintiff has the burden of establishing that he or some person under whom he claims is a person against whom the defense or defect is ineffective (Section 8-202).

As amended in 1977.

§ 8-106. Applicability.
The law (including the conflict of laws rules) of the jurisdiction of organization of the issuer governs the validity of a security, the effectiveness of registration by the issuer, and the rights and duties of the issuer with respect to:

(a) registration of transfer of a certificated security;

(b) registration of transfer, pledge, or release of an uncertificated security; and

(c) sending of statements of uncertificated securities.

As amended in 1977.

§ 8-107. Securities Transferable; Action for Price.

(1) Unless otherwise agreed and subject to any applicable law or regulation respecting short sales, a person obligated to transfer securities may transfer any certificated security of the specified issue in bearer form or registered in the name of the transferee, or indorsed to him or in blank, or he may transfer an equivalent uncertificated security to the transferee or a person designated by the transferee.

(2) If the buyer fails to pay the price as it comes due under a contract of sale, the seller may recover the price of:

(a) certificated securities accepted by the buyer;

(b) uncertificated securities that have been transferred to the buyer or a person designated by the buyer; and

(c) other securities if efforts at their resale would be unduly burdensome or if there is no readily available market for their resale.

As amended in 1977.

§ 8-108. Registration of Pledge and Release of Uncertificated Securities.
A security interest in an uncertificated security may be evidenced by the registration of pledge to the secured party or a person designated by him. There can be no more than one registered pledge of an uncertificated security at any time. The registered owner of an uncertificated security is the person in whose name the security is registered, even if the security is subject to a registered pledge. The rights of a registered pledgee of an uncertificated security under this Article are terminated by the registration of release.

As added in 1977.

Part 2 Issue—Issuer

§ 8-201. "Issuer".

(1) With respect to obligations on or defenses to a security, "issuer" includes a person who:

(a) places or authorizes the placing of his name on a certificated security (otherwise than as authenticating trustee, registrar, transfer agent, or the like) to evidence that it represents a share, participation, or other interest in his property or in an enterprise, or to evidence his duty to perform an obligation represented by the certificated security;

(b) creates shares, participations, or other interests in his property or in an enterprise or undertakes obligations, which shares, participations, interests, or obligations are uncertificated securities;

(c) directly or indirectly creates fractional interests in his rights or property, which fractional interests are represented by certificated securities; or

(d) becomes responsible for or in place of any other person described as an issuer in this section.

(2) With respect to obligations on or defenses to a security, a guarantor is an issuer to the extent of his guaranty, whether or not his obligation is noted on a certificated security or on statements of uncertificated securities sent pursuant to Section 8-408.

(3) With respect to registration of transfer, pledge, or release (Part 4 of this Article), "issuer" means a person on whose behalf transfer books are maintained.

As amended in 1977.

§ 8-202. Issuer's Responsibility and Defenses; Notice of Defect or Defense.

(1) Even against a purchaser for value and without notice, the terms of a security include:

(a) if the security is certificated, those stated on the security;

(b) if the security is uncertificated, those contained in the initial transaction statement sent to such purchaser or, if his interest is transferred to him other than by registration of transfer, pledge, or release, the initial transaction statement sent to the registered owner or registered pledgee; and

(c) those made part of the security by reference, on the certificated security or in the initial transaction statement, to another instrument, indenture, or document or to a constitution, statute, ordinance, rule, regulation, order or the like, to the extent that the terms referred to do not conflict with the terms stated on the certificated security or contained in the statement. A reference under this paragraph does not of itself charge a purchaser for value with notice of a defect going to the validity of the security, even though the certificated security or statement expressly states that a person accepting it admits notice.

(2) A certificated security in the hands of a purchaser for value or an uncertificated security as to which an initial transaction statement has been sent to a purchaser for value, other than a security issued by a government or governmental agency or unit, even though issued with a defect going to its validity, is valid with respect to the purchaser if he is without notice of the particular defect unless the defect involves a violation of constitutional provisions, in which case the security is valid with respect to a subsequent purchaser for value and without notice of the defect. This subsection applies to an issuer that is a government or governmental agency or unit only if either there has been substantial compliance with the legal requirements governing the issue or the issuer has received a substantial consideration for the issue as a whole or for the particular security and a stated purpose of the issue is one for which the issuer has power to borrow money or issue the security.

(3) Except as provided in the case of certain unauthorized signatures (Section 8-205), lack of genuineness of a certificated security or an initial transaction statement is a complete defense, even against a purchaser for value and without notice.

(4) All other defenses of the issuer of a certificated or uncertificated security, including nondelivery and conditional delivery of a certificated security, are ineffective against a purchaser for value who has taken without notice of the particular defense.

(5) Nothing in this section shall be construed to affect the right of a party to a "when, as and if issued" or a "when distributed" contract to cancel the contract in the event of a material change in the character of the security that is the subject of the contract or in the plan or arrangement pursuant to which the security is to be issued or distributed.

As amended in 1977.

§ 8-203. Staleness as Notice of Defects or Defenses.

(1) After an act or event creating a right to immediate performance of the principal obligation represented by a certificated security or that sets a date on or after which the security is to be presented or surrendered for redemption or exchange, a purchaser is charged with notice of any defect in its issue or defense of the issuer if:

(a) the act or event is one requiring the payment of money, the delivery of certificated securities, the registration of transfer of uncertificated securities, or any of these on presentation or surrender of the certificated security, the funds or securities are available on the date set for payment or exchange, and he takes the security more than one year after that date; and

(b) the act or event is not covered by paragraph (a) and he takes the security more than 2 years after the date set for surrender or presentation or the date on which performance became due.

(2) A call that has been revoked is not within subsection (1).

As amended in 1977.

§ 8-204. Effect of Issuer's Restrictions on Transfer. A restriction on transfer of a security imposed by the issuer, even if otherwise lawful, is ineffective against any person without actual knowledge of it unless:

(a) the security is certificated and the restriction is noted conspicuously thereon; or

(b) the security is uncertificated and a notation of the restriction is contained in the initial transaction statement sent to the person or, if his interest is transferred to him other than by registration of transfer, pledge, or release, the initial transaction statement sent to the registered owner or the registered pledgee.

As amended in 1977.

§ 8-205. Effect of Unauthorized Signature on Certificated Security or Initial Transaction Statement. An unauthorized signature placed on a certificated security prior to or in the course of issue or placed on an initial transaction statement is ineffective, but the signature is effective in favor of a purchaser for value of the certificated security or a purchaser for value of an uncertificated security to whom the initial transaction statement has been sent, if the purchaser is without notice of the lack of authority and the signing has been done by:

(a) an authenticating trustee, registrar, transfer agent, or other person entrusted by the issuer with the signing of the security, of similar securities, or of initial transaction statements of the immediate preparation for signing of any of them; or

(b) an employee of the issuer, or of any of the foregoing, entrusted with responsible handling of the security or initial transaction statement.

As amended in 1977.

§ 8-206. Completion or Alteration of Certificated Security or Initial Transaction Statement.

(1) If a certificated security contains the signatures necessary to its issue or transfer but is incomplete in any other respect:

(a) any person may complete it by filling in the blanks as authorized; and

(b) even though the blanks are incorrectly filled in, the security as completed is enforceable by a purchaser who took it for value and without notice of the incorrectness.

(2) A complete certificated security that has been improperly altered, even though fraudulently, remains enforceable, but only according to its original terms.

(3) If an initial transaction statement contains the signatures necessary to its validity, but is incomplete in any other respect:

(a) any person may complete it by filling in the blanks as authorized; and

(b) even though the blanks are incorrectly filled in, the statement as completed is effective in favor of the person to whom it is sent if he purchased the security referred to therein for value and without notice of the incorrectness.

(4) A complete initial transaction statement that has been improperly altered, even though fraudulently, is effective in favor of a purchaser to whom it has been sent, but only according to its original terms.

As amended in 1977.

§ 8-207. Rights and Duties of Issuer With Respect to Registered Owners and Registered Pledgees.

(1) Prior to due presentment for registration of transfer of a certificated security in registered form, the issuer or indenture trustee may treat the registered owner as the person exclusively entitled to vote, to receive notifications, and otherwise to exercise all the rights and powers of an owner.

(2) Subject to the provisions of subsections (3), (4), and (6), the issuer or indenture trustee may treat the registered owner of an uncertificated security as the person exclusively entitled to vote, to receive notifications, and otherwise to exercise all the rights and powers of an owner.

(3) The registered owner of an uncertificated security that is subject to a registered pledge is not entitled to registration of transfer prior to the due presentment to the issuer of a release instruction. The exercise of conversion rights with respect to a convertible uncertificated security is a transfer within the meaning of this section.

(4) Upon due presentment of a transfer instruction from the registered pledgee of an uncertificated security, the issuer shall:

(a) register the transfer of the security to the new owner free of pledge, if the instruction specifies a new owner (who may be the registered pledgee) and does not specify a pledgee;

(b) register the transfer of the security to the new owner subject to the interest of the existing pledgee, if the instruction specifies a new owner and the existing pledgee; or

(c) register the release of the security from the existing pledge and register the pledge of the security to the other pledgee, if the instruction specifies the existing owner and another pledgee.

(5) Continuity of perfection of a security interest is not broken by registration of transfer under subsection (4)(b) or by registration of release and pledge under subsection (4)(c), if the security interest is assigned.

(6) If an uncertificated security is subject to a registered pledge:

(a) any uncertificated securities issued in exchange for or distributed with respect to the pledged security shall be registered subject to the pledge;

(b) any certificated securities issued in exchange for or distributed with respect to the pledged security shall be delivered to the registered pledgee; and

(c) any money paid in exchange for or in redemption of part or all of the security shall be paid to the registered pledgee.

(7) Nothing in this Article shall be construed to affect the liability of the registered owner of a security for calls, assessments, or the like.

As amended in 1977.

§ 8-208. Effect of Signature of Authenticating Trustee, Registrar, or Transfer Agent.

(1) A person placing his signature upon a certificated security or an initial transaction statement as authenticating trustee, registrar, transfer agent, or the like, warrants to a purchaser for value of the certificated security or a purchaser for value of an uncertificated security to whom the initial transaction statement has been sent, if the purchaser is without notice of the particular defect, that:

(a) the certificated security or initial transaction statement is genuine;

(b) his own participation in the issue or registration of the transfer, pledge, or release of the security is within his capacity and within the scope of the authority received by him from the issuer; and

(c) he has reasonable grounds to believe the security is in the form and within the amount the issuer is authorized to issue.

(2) Unless otherwise agreed, a person by so placing his signature does not assume responsibility for the validity of the security in other respects.

As amended in 1962 and 1977.

Part 3 Transfer

§ 8-301. Rights Acquired by Purchaser.

(1) Upon transfer of a security to a purchaser (Section 8-313), the purchaser acquires the rights in the security which his transferor had or had actual authority to convey unless the purchaser's rights are limited by Section 8-302(4).

(2) A transferee of a limited interest acquires rights only to the extent of the interest transferred. The creation or release of a security interest in a security is the transfer of a limited interest in that security.

As amended in 1977.

§ 8-302. "Bona Fide Purchaser"; "Adverse Claim"; Title Acquired by Bona Fide Purchaser.

(1) A "bona fide purchaser" is a purchaser for value in good faith and without notice of any adverse claim:

(a) who takes delivery of a certificated security in bearer form or in registered form, issued or indorsed to him or in blank;

(b) to whom the transfer, pledge, or release of an uncertificated security is registered on the books of the issuer; or

(c) to whom a security is transferred under the provisions of paragraph (c), (d)(i), or (g) of Section 8-313(1).

(2) "Adverse claim" includes a claim that a transfer was or would be wrongful or that a particular adverse person is the owner of or has an interest in the security.

(3) A bona fide purchaser in addition to acquiring the rights of a purchaser (Section 8-301) also acquires his interest in the security free of any adverse claim.

(4) Notwithstanding Section 8-301(1), the transferee of a particular certificated security who has been a party to any fraud or illegality affecting the security, or who as a prior holder of that certificated security had notice of an adverse claim, cannot improve his position by taking from a bona fide purchaser.

As amended in 1977.

§ 8-303. "Broker". "Broker" means a person engaged for all or part of his time in the business of buying and selling securities, who in the transaction concerned acts for, buys a security from, or sells a security to, a customer. Nothing in this

Article determines the capacity in which a person acts for purposes of any other statute or rule to which the person is subject.

§ 8-304. Notice to Purchaser of Adverse Claims.

(1) A purchaser (including a broker for the seller or buyer, but excluding an intermediary bank) of a certificated security is charged with notice of adverse claims if:

    (a) the security, whether in bearer or registered form, has been indorsed "for collection" or "for surrender" or for some other purpose not involving transfer; or

    (b) the security is in bearer form and has on it an unambiguous statement that it is the property of a person other than the transferor. The mere writing of a name on a security is not such a statement.

(2) A purchaser (including a broker for the seller or buyer, but excluding an intermediary bank) to whom the transfer, pledge, or release of an uncertificated security is registered is charged with notice of adverse claims as to which the issuer has a duty under Section 8-403(4) at the time of registration and which are noted in the initial transaction statement sent to the purchaser or, if his interest is transferred to him other than by registration of transfer, pledge, or release, the initial transaction statement sent to the registered owner or the registered pledgee.

(3) The fact that the purchaser (including a broker for the seller or buyer) of a certificated or uncertificated security has notice that the security is held for a third person or is registered in the name of or indorsed by a fiduciary does not create a duty of inquiry into the rightfulness of the transfer or constitute constructive notice of adverse claims. However, if the purchaser (excluding an intermediary bank) has knowledge that the proceeds are being used or that the transaction is for the individual benefit of the fiduciary or otherwise in breach of duty, the purchaser is charged with notice of adverse claims.

As amended in 1977.

§ 8-305. Staleness as Notice of Adverse Claims.
An act or event that creates a right to immediate performance of the principal obligation represented by a certificated security or sets a date on or after which a certificated security is to be presented or surrendered for redemption or exchange does not itself constitute any notice of adverse claims except in the case of a transfer:

(a) after one year from any date set for presentment or surrender for redemption or exchange; or

(b) after 6 months from any date set for payment of money against presentation or surrender of the security if funds are available for payment on that date.

As amended in 1977.

§ 8-306. Warranties on Presentment and Transfer of Certificated Securities; Warranties of Originators of Instructions.

(1) A person who presents a certificated security for registration of transfer or for payment or exchange warrants to the issuer that he is entitled to the registration, payment, or exchange. But, a purchaser for value and without notice of adverse claims who receives a new, reissued, or re-registered certificated security on registration of transfer or receives an initial transaction statement confirming the registration of transfer of an equivalent uncertificated security to him warrants only that he has no knowledge of any unauthorized signature (Section 8-311) in a necessary indorsement.

(2) A person by transferring a certificated security to a purchaser for value warrants only that:

    (a) his transfer is effective and rightful;

    (b) the security is genuine and has not been materially altered; and

    (c) he knows of no fact which might impair the validity of the security.

(3) If a certificated security is delivered by an intermediary known to be entrusted with delivery of the security on behalf of another or with collection of a draft or other claim against delivery, the intermediary by delivery warrants only his own good faith and authority, even though he has purchased or made advances against the claim to be collected against the delivery.

(4) A pledgee or other holder for security who redelivers a certificated security received, or after payment and on order of the debtor delivers that security to a third person, makes only the warranties of an intermediary under subsection (3).

(5) A person who originates an instruction warrants to the issuer that:

    (a) he is an appropriate person to originate the instruction; and

    (b) at the time the instruction is presented to the issuer he will be entitled to the registration of transfer, pledge, or release.

(6) A person who originates an instruction warrants to any person specially guaranteeing his signature (subsection 8-312(3)) that:

    (a) he is an appropriate person to originate the instruction; and

    (b) at the time the instruction is presented to the issuer

        (i) he will be entitled to the registration of transfer, pledge, or release; and

        (ii) the transfer, pledge, or release requested in the instruction will be registered by the issuer free from all liens, security interests, restrictions, and claims other than those specified in the instruction.

(7) A person who originates an instruction warrants to a purchaser for value and to any person guaranteeing the instruction (Section 8-312(6)) that:

    (a) he is an appropriate person to originate the instruction;

    (b) the uncertificated security referred to therein is valid; and

    (c) at the time the instruction is presented to the issuer

        (i) the transferor will be entitled to the registration of transfer, pledge, or release;

        (ii) the transfer, pledge, or release requested in the instruction will be registered by the issuer free from all liens, security interests, restrictions, and claims other than those specified in the instruction; and

        (iii) the requested transfer, pledge, or release will be rightful.

(8) If a secured party is the registered pledgee or the registered owner of an uncertificated security, a person who originates an instruction of release or transfer to the debtor or, after payment and on order of the debtor, a transfer instruction to a third person, warrants to the debtor or the third person only that he is an appropriate person to originate the instruction and, at the time the instruction is presented to the issuer, the transferor will be entitled to the registration of release or transfer. If a transfer instruction to a third person who is a purchaser for value is originated on order of the debtor, the debtor makes to the purchaser the warranties of paragraphs (b), (c)(ii) and (c)(iii) of subsection (7).

(9) A person who transfers an uncertificated security to a purchaser for value and does not originate an instruction in connection with the transfer warrants only that:

(a) his transfer is effective and rightful; and

(b) the uncertificated security is valid.

(10) A broker gives to his customer and to the issuer and a purchaser the applicable warranties provided in this section and has the rights and privileges of a purchaser under this section. The warranties of and in favor of the broker, acting as an agent are in addition to applicable warranties given by and in favor of his customer.

As amended in 1962 and 1977.

§ 8-307. Effect of Delivery Without Indorsement; Right to Compel Indorsement.

If a certificated security in registered form has been delivered to a purchaser without a necessary indorsement he may become a bona fide purchaser only as of the time the indorsement is supplied; but against the transferor, the transfer is complete upon delivery and the purchaser has a specifically enforceable right to have any necessary indorsement supplied.

As amended in 1977.

§ 8-308. Indorsements; Instructions.

(1) An indorsement of a certificated security in registered form is made when an appropriate person signs on it or on a separate document an assignment or transfer of the security or a power to assign or transfer it or his signature is written without more upon the back of the security.

(2) An indorsement may be in blank or special. An indorsement in blank includes an indorsement to bearer. A special indorsement specifies to whom the security is to be transferred, or who has power to transfer it. A holder may convert a blank indorsement into a special indorsement.

(3) An indorsement purporting to be only of part of a certificated security representing units intended by the issuer to be separately transferable is effective to the extent of the indorsement.

(4) An "instruction" is an order to the issuer of an uncertificated security requesting that the transfer, pledge, or release from pledge of the uncertificated security specified therein be registered.

(5) An instruction originated by an appropriate person is:

(a) a writing signed by an appropriate person; or

(b) a communication to the issuer in any form agreed upon in a writing signed by the issuer and an appropriate person.

If an instruction has been originated by an appropriate person but is incomplete in any other respect, any person may complete it as authorized and the issuer may rely on it as completed even though it has been completed incorrectly.

(6) "An appropriate person" in subsection (1) means the person specified by the certificated security or by special indorsement to be entitled to the security.

(7) "An appropriate person" in subsection (5) means:

(a) for an instruction to transfer or pledge an uncertificated security which is then not subject to a registered pledge, the registered owner; or

(b) for an instruction to transfer or release an uncertificated security which is then subject to a registered pledge, the registered pledgee.

(8) In addition to the persons designated in subsections (6) and (7), "an appropriate person" in subsections (1) and (5) includes:

(a) if the person designated is described as a fiduciary but is no longer serving in the described capacity, either that person or his successor;

(b) if the persons designated are described as more than one person as fiduciaries and one or more are no longer serving in the described capacity, the remaining fiduciary or fiduciaries, whether or not a successor has been appointed or qualified;

(c) if the person designated is an individual and is without capacity to act by virtue of death, incompetence, infancy, or otherwise, his executor, administrator, guardian, or like fiduciary;

(d) if the persons designated are described as more than one person as tenants by the entirety or with right of survivorship and by reason of death all cannot sign, the survivor or survivors;

(e) a person having power to sign under applicable law or controlling instrument; and

(f) to the extent that the person designated or any of the foregoing persons may act through an agent, his authorized agent.

(9) Unless otherwise agreed, the indorser of a certificated security by his indorsement or the originator of an instruction by his origination assumes no obligation that the security will be honored by the issuer but only the obligations provided in Section 8-306.

(10) Whether the person signing is appropriate is determined as of the date of signing and an indorsement made by or an instruction originated by him does not become unauthorized for the purposes of this Article by virtue of any subsequent change of circumstances.

(11) Failure of a fiduciary to comply with a controlling instrument or with the law of the state having jurisdiction of the fiduciary relationship, including any law requiring the fiduciary to obtain court approval of the transfer, pledge, or release, does not render his indorsement or an instruction originated by him unauthorized for the purposes of this Article.

As amended in 1962 and 1977.

§ 8-309. Effect of Indorsement Without Delivery.

An indorsement of a certificated security, whether special or in blank, does not constitute a transfer until delivery of the certificated security on which it appears or, if the indorsement is on a separate document, until delivery of both the document and the certificated security.

As amended in 1977.

§ **8-310. Indorsement of Certificated Security in Bearer Form.** An indorsement of a certificated security in bearer form may give notice of adverse claims (Section 8-304) but does not otherwise affect any right to registration the holder possesses.

As amended in 1977.

§ **8-311. Effect of Unauthorized Indorsement or Instruction.** Unless the owner or pledgee has ratified an unauthorized indorsement or instruction or is otherwise precluded from asserting its ineffectiveness:

(a) he may assert its ineffectiveness against the issuer or any purchaser, other than a purchaser for value and without notice of adverse claims, who has in good faith received a new, reissued, or re-registered certificated security on registration of transfer or received an initial transaction statement confirming the registration of transfer, pledge, or release of an equivalent uncertificated security to him; and

(b) an issuer who registers the transfer of a certificated security upon the unauthorized indorsement or who registers the transfer, pledge, or release of an uncertificated security upon the unauthorized instruction is subject to liability for improper registration (Section 8-404).

As amended in 1977.

§ **8-312. Effect of Guaranteeing Signature, Indorsement or Instruction.**

(1) Any person guaranteeing a signature of an indorser of a certificated security warrants that at the time of signing:

(a) the signature was genuine;

(b) the signer was an appropriate person to indorse (Section 8-308); and

(c) the signer had legal capacity to sign.

(2) Any person guaranteeing a signature of the originator of an instruction warrants that at the time of signing:

(a) the signature was genuine;

(b) the signer was an appropriate person to originate the instruction (Section 8-308) if the person specified in the instruction as the registered owner or registered pledgee of the uncertificated security was, in fact, the registered owner or registered pledgee of the security, as to which fact the signature guarantor makes no warranty;

(c) the signer had legal capacity to sign; and

(d) the taxpayer identification number, if any, appearing on the instruction as that of the registered owner or registered pledgee was the taxpayer identification number of the signer or of the owner or pledgee for whom the signer was acting.

(3) Any person specially guaranteeing the signature of the originator of an instruction makes not only the warranties of a signature guarantor (subsection (2)) but also warrants that at the time the instruction is presented to the issuer:

(a) the person specified in the instruction as the regis-

tered owner or registered pledgee of the uncertificated security will be the registered owner or registered pledgee; and

(b) the transfer, pledge, or release of the uncertificated security requested in the instruction will be registered by the issuer free from all liens, security interests, restrictions, and claims other than those specified in the instruction.

(4) The guarantor under subsections (1) and (2) or the special guarantor under subsection (3) does not otherwise warrant the rightfulness of the particular transfer, pledge, or release.

(5) Any person guaranteeing an indorsement of a certificated security makes not only the warranties of a signature guarantor under subsection (1) but also warrants the rightfulness of the particular transfer in all respects.

(6) Any person guaranteeing an instruction requesting the transfer, pledge, or release of an uncertificated security makes not only the warranties of a special signature guarantor under subsection (3) but also warrants the rightfulness of the particular transfer, pledge, or release in all respects.

(7) No issuer may require a special guarantee of signature (subsection (3)), a guarantee of indorsement (subsection (5)), or a guarantee of instruction (subsection (6)) as a condition to registration of transfer, pledge, or release.

(8) The foregoing warranties are made to any person taking or dealing with the security in reliance on the guarantee, and the guarantor is liable to the person for any loss resulting from breach of the warranties.

As amended in 1977.

§ **8-313. When Transfer to Purchaser Occurs; Financial Intermediary as Bona Fide Purchaser; "Financial Intermediary".**

(1) Transfer of a security or a limited interest (including a security interest) therein to a purchaser occurs only:

(a) at the time he or a person designated by him acquires possession of a certificated security;

(b) at the time the transfer, pledge, or release of an uncertificated security is registered to him or a person designated by him;

(c) at the time his financial intermediary acquires possession of a certificated security specially indorsed to or issued in the name of the purchaser;

(d) at the time a financial intermediary, not a clearing corporation, sends him confirmation of the purchase and also by book entry or otherwise identifies as belonging to the purchaser

(i) a specific certificated security in the financial intermediary's possession;

(ii) a quantity of securities that constitute or are part of a fungible bulk of certificated securities in the financial intermediary's possession or of uncertificated securities registered in the name of the financial intermediary; or

(iii) a quantity of securities that constitute or are part of a fungible bulk of securities shown on the account of the financial intermediary on the books of another financial intermediary;

(e) with respect to an identified certificated security to be delivered while still in the possession of a third person, not a financial intermediary, at the time that person acknowledges that he holds for the purchaser;

(f) with respect to a specific uncertificated security the pledge or transfer of which has been registered to a third person, not a financial intermediary, at the time that person acknowledges that he holds for the purchaser;

(g) at the time appropriate entries to the account of the purchaser or a person designated by him on the books of a clearing corporation are made under Section 8-320;

(h) with respect to the transfer of a security interest where the debtor has signed a security agreement containing a description of the security, at the time a written notification, which, in the case of the creation of the security interest, is signed by the debtor (which may be a copy of the security agreement) or which, in the case of the release or assignment of the security interest created pursuant to this paragraph, is signed by the secured party, is received by

  (i) a financial intermediary on whose books the interest of the transferor in the security appears;
  (ii) a third person, not a financial intermediary, in possession of the security, if it is certificated;
  (iii) a third person, not a financial intermediary, who is the registered owner of the security, if it is uncertificated and not subject to a registered pledge; or
  (iv) a third person, not a financial intermediary, who is the registered pledgee of the security, if it is uncertificated and subject to a registered pledge;

(i) with respect to the transfer of a security interest where the transferor has signed a security agreement containing a description of the security, at the time new value is given by the secured party; or

(j) with respect to the transfer of a security interest where the secured party is a financial intermediary and the security has already been transferred to the financial intermediary under paragraphs (a), (b), (c), (d), or (g), at the time the transferor has signed a security agreement containing a description of the security and value is given by the secured party.

(2) The purchaser is the owner of a security held for him by a financial intermediary, but cannot be a bona fide purchaser of a security so held except in the circumstances specified in paragraphs (c), (d)(i), and (g) of subsection (1). If a security so held is part of a fungible bulk, as in the circumstances specified in paragraphs (d)(ii) and (d)(iii) of subsection (1), the purchaser is the owner of a proportionate property interest in the fungible bulk.

(3) Notice of an adverse claim received by the financial intermediary or by the purchaser after the financial intermediary takes delivery of a certificated security as a holder for value or after the transfer, pledge, or release of an uncertificated security has been registered free of the claim to a financial intermediary who has given value is not effective either as to the financial intermediary or as to the purchaser. However, as between the financial intermediary and the purchaser the purchaser may demand transfer of an equivalent security as to which no notice of adverse claim has been received.

(4) A "financial intermediary" is a bank, broker, clearing corporation, or other person (or the nominee of any of them) which in the ordinary course of its business maintains security accounts for its customers and is acting in that capacity. A financial intermediary may have a security interest in securities held in account for its customer.

As amended in 1962 and 1977.

§ 8-314. Duty to Transfer, When Completed.

(1) Unless otherwise agreed, if a sale of a security is made on an exchange or otherwise through brokers:

  (a) the selling customer fulfills his duty to transfer at the time he:
    (i) places a certificated security in the possession of the selling broker or a person designated by the broker;
    (ii) causes an uncertificated security to be registered in the name of the selling broker or a person designated by the broker;
    (iii) if requested, causes an acknowledgement to be made to the selling broker that a certificated or uncertificated security is held for the broker; or
    (iv) places in the possession of the selling broker or of a person designated by the broker a transfer instruction for an uncertificated security, providing the issuer does not refuse to register the requested transfer if the instruction is presented to the issuer for registration within 30 days thereafter; and

  (b) the selling broker, including a correspondent broker acting for a selling customer, fulfills his duty to transfer at the time he:
    (i) places a certificated security in the possession of the buying broker or a person designated by the buying broker;
    (ii) causes an uncertificated security to be registered in the name of the buying broker or a person designated by the buying broker;
    (iii) places in the possession of the buying broker or of a person designated by the buying broker a transfer instruction for an uncertificated security, providing the issuer does not refuse to register the requested transfer if the instruction is presented to the issuer for registration within 30 days thereafter; or
    (iv) effects clearance of the sale in accordance with the rules of the exchange on which the transaction took place.

(2) Except as provided in this section or unless otherwise agreed, a transferor's duty to transfer a security under a contract of purchase is not fulfilled until he:

  (a) places a certificated security in form to be negotiated by the purchaser in the possession of the purchaser or of a person designated by the purchaser;
  (b) causes an uncertificated security to be registered in the name of the purchaser or a person designated by the purchaser; or
  (c) if the purchaser requests, causes an acknowledgment to be made to the purchaser that a certificated or uncertificated security is held for the purchaser.

(3) Unless made on an exchange, a sale to a broker pur-

chasing for his own account is within subsection (2) and not within subsection (1).

As amended in 1977.

§ 8-315. Action Against Transferee Based Upon Wrongful Transfer.

(1) Any person against whom the transfer of a security is wrongful for any reason, including his incapacity, as against anyone except a bona fide purchaser, may:

(a) reclaim possession of the certificated security wrongfully transferred;

(b) obtain possession of any new certificated security representing all or part of the same rights;

(c) compel the origination of an instruction to transfer to him or a person designated by him an uncertificated security constituting all or part of the same rights; or

(d) have damages.

(2) If the transfer is wrongful because of an unauthorized indorsement of a certificated security, the owner may also reclaim or obtain possession of the security or a new certificated security, even from a bona fide purchaser, if the ineffectiveness of the purported indorsement can be asserted against him under the provisions of this Article on unauthorized indorsements (Section 8-311).

(3) The right to obtain or reclaim possession of a certificated security or to compel the origination of a transfer instruction may be specifically enforced and the transfer of a certificated or uncertificated security enjoined and a certificated security impounded pending the litigation.

As amended in 1977.

§ 8-316. Purchaser's Right to Requisites for Registration of Transfer, Pledge, or Release on Books.
Unless otherwise agreed, the transferor of a certificated security or the transferor, pledgor, or pledgee of an uncertificated security on due demand must supply his purchaser with any proof of his authority to transfer, pledge, or release or with any other requisite necessary to obtain registration of the transfer, pledge, or release of the security; but if the transfer, pledge, or release is not for value, a transferor, pledgor, or pledgee need not do so unless the purchaser furnishes the necessary expenses. Failure within a reasonable time to comply with a demand made gives the purchaser the right to reject or rescind the transfer, pledge, or release.

As amended in 1977.

§ 8-317. Creditors' Rights.

(1) Subject to the exceptions in subsections (3) and (4), no attachment or levy upon a certificated security or any share or other interest represented thereby which is outstanding is valid until the security is actually seized by the officer making the attachment or levy, but a certificated security which has been surrendered to the issuer may be reached by a creditor by legal process at the issuer's chief executive office in the United States.

(2) An uncertificated security registered in the name of the debtor may not be reached by a creditor except by legal process at the issuer's chief executive office in the United States.

(3) The interest of a debtor in a certificated security that is in the possession of a secured party not a financial intermediary or in an uncertificated security registered in the name of a secured party not a financial intermediary (or in the name of a nominee of the secured party) may be reached by a creditor by legal process upon the secured party.

(4) The interest of a debtor in a certificated security that is in the possession of or registered in the name of a financial intermediary or in an uncertificated security registered in the name of a financial intermediary may be reached by a creditor by legal process upon the financial intermediary on whose books the interest of the debtor appears.

(5) Unless otherwise provided by law, a creditor's lien upon the interest of a debtor in a security obtained pursuant to subsection (3) or (4) is not a restraint on the transfer of the security, free of the lien, to a third party for new value; but in the event of a transfer, the lien applies to the proceeds of the transfer in the hands of the secured party or financial intermediary, subject to any claims having priority.

(6) A creditor whose debtor is the owner of a security is entitled to aid from courts of appropriate jurisdiction, by injunction or otherwise, in reaching the security or in satisfying the claim by means allowed at law or in equity in regard to property that cannot readily be reached by ordinary legal process.

As amended in 1977.

§ 8-318. No Conversion by Good Faith Conduct.
An agent or bailee who in good faith (including observance of reasonable commercial standards if he is in the business of buying, selling, or otherwise dealing with securities) has received certificated securities and sold, pledged, or delivered them or has sold or caused the transfer or pledge of uncertificated securities over which he had control according to the instructions of his principal, is not liable for conversion or for participation in breach of fiduciary duty although the principal had no right so to deal with the securities.

As amended in 1977.

§ 8-319. Statute of Frauds.
A contract for the sale of securities is not enforceable by way of action or defense unless:

(a) there is some writing signed by the party against whom enforcement is sought or by his authorized agent or broker, sufficient to indicate that a contract has been made for sale of a stated quantity of described securities at a defined or stated price;

(b) delivery of a certificated security or transfer instruction has been accepted, or transfer of an uncertificated security has been registered and the transferee has failed to send written objection to the issuer within 10 days after receipt of the initial transaction statement confirming the registration, or payment has been made, but the contract is enforceable under this provision only to the extent of the delivery, registration, or payment;

(c) within a reasonable time a writing in confirmation of the sale or purchase and sufficient against the sender under paragraph (a) has been received by the party against whom enforcement is sought and he has failed to send written objection to its contents within 10 days after its receipt; or

(d) the party against whom enforcement is sought admits in his pleading, testimony, or otherwise in court that a contract was made for the sale of a stated quantity of described securities at a defined or stated price.

As amended in 1977.

§ 8-320. Transfer or Pledge Within Central Depository System.

(1) In addition to other methods, a transfer, pledge, or release of a security or any interest therein may be effected by the making of appropriate entries on the books of a clearing corporation reducing the account of the transferor, pledgor, or pledgee and increasing the account of the transferee, pledgee, or pledgor by the amount of the obligation or the number of shares or rights transferred, pledged, or released, if the security is shown on the account of a transferor, pledgor, or pledgee on the books of the clearing corporation; is subject to the control of the clearing corporation; and

(a) if certificated,

(i) is in the custody of the clearing corporation, another clearing corporation, a custodian bank, or a nominee of any of them; and

(ii) is in bearer form or indorsed in blank by an appropriate person or registered in the name of the clearing corporation, a custodian bank, or a nominee of any of them; or

(b) if uncertificated, is registered in the name of the clearing corporation, another clearing corporation, a custodian bank, or a nominee of any of them.

(2) Under this section entries may be made with respect to like securities or interests therein as a part of a fungible bulk and may refer merely to a quantity of a particular security without reference to the name of the registered owner, certificate or bond number, or the like, and, in appropriate cases, may be on a net basis taking into account other transfers, pledges, or releases of the same security.

(3) A transfer under this section is effective (Section 8-313) and the purchaser acquires the rights of the transferor (Section 8-301). A pledge or release under this section is the transfer of a limited interest. If a pledge or the creation of a security interest is intended, the security interest is perfected at the time when both value is given by the pledgee and the appropriate entries are made (Section 8-321). A transferee or pledgee under this section may be a bona fide purchaser (Section 8-302).

(4) A transfer or pledge under this section is not a registration of transfer under Part 4.

(5) That entries made on the books of the clearing corporation as provided in subsection (1) are not appropriate does not affect the validity or effect of the entries or the liabilities or obligations of the clearing corporation to any person adversely affected thereby.

As added in 1962 and amended in 1977.

§ 8-321. Enforceability, Attachment, Perfection and Termination of Security Interests.

(1) A security interest in a security is enforceable and can attach only if it is transferred to the secured party or a person designated by him pursuant to a provision of Section 8-313(1).

(2) A security interest so transferred pursuant to agreement by a transferor who has rights in the security to a transferee who has given value is a perfected security interest, but a security interest that has been transferred solely under paragraph (i) of Section 8-313(1) becomes unperfected after 21 days unless, within that time, the requirements for transfer under any other provision of Section 8-313(1) are satisfied.

(3) A security interest in a security is subject to the provisions of Article 9, but:

(a) no filing is required to perfect the security interest; and

(b) no written security agreement signed by the debtor is necessary to make the security interest enforceable, except as provided in paragraph (h), (i), or (j) of Section 8-313(1). The secured party has the rights and duties provided under Section 9-207, to the extent they are applicable, whether or not the security is certificated, and, if certificated, whether or not it is in his possession.

(4) Unless otherwise agreed, a security interest in a security is terminated by transfer to the debtor or a person designated by him pursuant to a provision of Section 8-313(1). If a security is thus transferred, the security interest, if not terminated, becomes unperfected unless the security is certificated and is delivered to the debtor for the purpose of ultimate sale or exchange or presentation, collection, renewal, or registration of transfer. In that case, the security interest becomes unperfected after 21 days unless, within that time, the security (or securities for which it has been exchanged) is transferred to the secured party or a person designated by him pursuant to a provision of Section 8-313(1).

As added in 1977.

Part 4 Registration

§ 8-401. Duty of Issuer to Register Transfer, Pledge, or Release.

(1) If a certificated security in registered form is presented to the issuer with a request to register transfer or an instruction is presented to the issuer with a request to register transfer, pledge, or release, the issuer shall register the transfer, pledge, or release as requested if:

(a) the security is indorsed or the instruction was originated by the appropriate person or persons (Section 8-308);

(b) reasonable assurance is given that those indorsements or instructions are genuine and effective (Section 8-402);

(c) the issuer has no duty as to adverse claims or has discharged the duty (Section 8-403);

(d) any applicable law relating to the collection of taxes has been complied with; and

(e) the transfer, pledge, or release is in fact rightful or is to a bona fide purchaser.

(2) If an issuer is under a duty to register a transfer, pledge, or release of a security, the issuer is also liable to the person presenting a certificated security or an instruction for registration or his principal for loss resulting from any unreasonable delay in registration or from failure or refusal to register the transfer, pledge, or release.

As amended in 1977.

§ 8-402. Assurance That Indorsements and Instructions Are Effective.

(1) The issuer may require the following assurance that each necessary indorsement of a certificated security or each instruction (Section 8-308) is genuine and effective:

(a) in all cases, a guarantee of the signature (Section 8-312(1) or (2)) of the person indorsing a certificated security or originating an instruction including, in the case of an instruction, a warranty of the taxpayer identification number or, in the absence thereof, other reasonable assurance of identity;

(b) if the indorsement is made or the instruction is originated by an agent, appropriate assurance of authority to sign;

(c) if the indorsement is made or the instruction is originated by a fiduciary, appropriate evidence of appointment or incumbency;

(d) if there is more than one fiduciary, reasonable assurance that all who are required to sign have done so; and

(e) if the indorsement is made or the instruction is originated by a person not covered by any of the foregoing, assurance appropriate to the case corresponding as nearly as may be to the foregoing.

(2) A "guarantee of the signature" in subsection (1) means a guarantee signed by or on behalf of a person reasonably believed by the issuer to be responsible. The issuer may adopt standards with respect to responsibility if they are not manifestly unreasonable.

(3) "Appropriate evidence of appointment or incumbency" in subsection (1) means:

(a) in the case of a fiduciary appointed or qualified by a court, a certificate issued by or under the direction or supervision of that court or an officer thereof and dated within 60 days before the date of presentation for transfer, pledge, or release; or

(b) in any other case, a copy of a document showing the appointment or a certificate issued by or on behalf of a person reasonably believed by the issuer to be responsible or, in the absence of that document or certificate, other evidence reasonably deemed by the issuer to be appropriate. The issuer may adopt standards with respect to the evidence if they are not manifestly unreasonable. The issuer is not charged with notice of the contents of any document obtained pursuant to this paragraph (b) except to the extent that the contents relate directly to the appointment or incumbency.

(4) The issuer may elect to require reasonable assurance beyond that specified in this section, but if it does so and, for a purpose other than that specified in subsection (3)(b), both requires and obtains a copy of a will, trust, indenture, articles of co-partnership, by-laws, or other controlling instrument, it is charged with notice of all matters contained therein affecting the transfer, pledge, or release.

As amended in 1977.

§ 8-403. Issuer's Duty as to Adverse Claims.

(1) An issuer to whom a certificated security is presented for registration shall inquire into adverse claims if:

(a) a written notification of an adverse claim is received at a time and in a manner affording the issuer a reasonable opportunity to act on it prior to the issuance of a new, reissued, or reregistered certificated security, and the notification identifies the claimant, the registered owner, and the issue of which the security is a part, and provides an address for communications directed to the claimant; or

(b) the issuer is charged with notice of an adverse claim from a controlling instrument it has elected to require under Section 8-402(4).

(2) The issuer may discharge any duty of inquiry by any reasonable means, including notifying an adverse claimant by registered or certified mail at the address furnished by him or, if there be no such address, at his residence or regular place of business that the certificated security has been presented for registration of transfer by a named person, and that the transfer will be registered unless within 30 days from the date of mailing the notification, either:

(a) an appropriate restraining order, injunction, or other process issues from a court of competent jurisdiction; or

(b) there is filed with the issuer an indemnity bond, sufficient in the issuer's judgment to protect the issuer and any transfer agent, registrar, or other agent of the issuer involved from any loss it or they may suffer by complying with the adverse claim.

(3) Unless an issuer is charged with notice of an adverse claim from a controlling instrument which it has elected to require under Section 8-402(4) or receives notification of an adverse claim under subsection (1), if a certificated security presented for registration is indorsed by the appropriate person or persons the issuer is under no duty to inquire into adverse claims. In particular:

(a) an issuer registering a certificated security in the name of a person who is a fiduciary or who is described as a fiduciary is not bound to inquire into the existence, extent, or correct description of the fiduciary relationship; and thereafter the issuer may assume without inquiry that the newly registered owner continues to be the fiduciary until the issuer receives written notice that the fiduciary is no longer acting as such with respect to the particular security;

(b) an issuer registering transfer on an indorsement by a fiduciary is not bound to inquire whether the transfer is made in compliance with a controlling instrument or with the law of the state having jurisdiction of the fiduciary relationship, including any law requiring the fiduciary to obtain court approval of the transfer; and

(c) the issuer is not charged with notice of the contents of any court record or file or other recorded or unrecorded document even though the document is in its possession and even though the transfer is made on the indorsement of a fiduciary to the fiduciary himself or to his nominee.

(4) An issuer is under no duty as to adverse claims with respect to an uncertificated security except:

(a) claims embodied in a restraining order, injunction, or other legal process served upon the issuer if the process was served at a time and in a manner affording the issuer a reasonable opportunity to act on it in accordance with the requirements of subsection (5);

(b) claims of which the issuer has received a written notification from the registered owner or the registered pledgee if the notification was received at a time and in a manner affording the issuer a reasonable opportunity to act on it in accordance with the requirements of subsection (5);

(c) claims (including restrictions on transfer not imposed

by the issuer) to which the registration of transfer to the present registered owner was subject and were so noted in the initial transaction statement sent to him; and

(d) claims as to which an issuer is charged with notice from a controlling instrument it has elected to require under Section 8-402(4).

(5) If the issuer of an uncertificated security is under a duty as to an adverse claim, he discharges that duty by:

(a) including a notation of the claim in any statements sent with respect to the security under Sections 8-408(3), (6), and (7); and

(b) refusing to register the transfer or pledge of the security unless the nature of the claim does not preclude transfer or pledge subject thereto.

(6) If the transfer or pledge of the security is registered subject to an adverse claim, a notation of the claim must be included in the initial transaction statement and all subsequent statements sent to the transferee and pledgee under Section 8-408.

(7) Notwithstanding subsections (4) and (5), if an uncertificated security was subject to a registered pledge at the time the issuer first came under a duty as to a particular adverse claim, the issuer has no duty as to that claim if transfer of the security is requested by the registered pledgee or an appropriate person acting for the registered pledgee unless:

(a) the claim was embodied in legal process which expressly provides otherwise;

(b) the claim was asserted in a written notification from the registered pledgee;

(c) the claim was one as to which the issuer was charged with notice from a controlling instrument it required under Section 8-402(4) in connection with the pledgee's request for transfer; or

(d) the transfer requested is to the registered owner.

As amended in 1977.

§ 8-404. Liability and Non-liability for Registration.

(1) Except as provided in any law relating to the collection of taxes, the issuer is not liable to the owner, pledgee, or any other person suffering loss as a result of the registration of a transfer, pledge, or release of a security if:

(a) there were on or with a certificated security the necessary indorsements or the issuer had received an instruction originated by an appropriate person (Section 8-308); and

(b) the issuer had no duty as to adverse claims or has discharged the duty (Section 8-403).

(2) If an issuer has registered a transfer of a certificated security to a person not entitled to it, the issuer on demand shall deliver a like security to the true owner unless:

(a) the registration was pursuant to subsection (1);

(b) the owner is precluded from asserting any claim for registering the transfer under Section 8-405(1); or

(c) the delivery would result in overissue, in which case the issuer's liability is governed by Section 8-104.

(3) If an issuer has improperly registered a transfer, pledge, or release of an uncertificated security, the issuer on demand from the injured party shall restore the records as to the in-

jured party to the condition that would have obtained if the improper registration had not been made unless:

(a) the registration was pursuant to subsection (1); or

(b) the registration would result in overissue, in which case the issuer's liability is governed by Section 8-104.

As amended in 1977.

§ 8-405. Lost, Destroyed, and Stolen Certificated Securities.

(1) If a certificated security has been lost, apparently destroyed, or wrongfully taken, and the owner fails to notify the issuer of that fact within a reasonable time after he has notice of it and the issuer registers a transfer of the security before receiving notification, the owner is precluded from asserting against the issuer any claim for registering the transfer under Section 8-404 or any claim to a new security under this section.

(2) If the owner of a certificated security claims that the security has been lost, destroyed, or wrongfully taken, the issuer shall issue a new certificated security or, at the option of the issuer, an equivalent uncertificated security in place of the original security if the owner:

(a) so requests before the issuer has notice that the security has been acquired by a bona fide purchaser;

(b) files with the issuer a sufficient indemnity bond; and

(c) satisfies any other reasonable requirements imposed by the issuer.

(3) If, after the issue of a new certificated or uncertificated security, a bona fide purchaser of the original certificated security presents it for registration of transfer, the issuer shall register the transfer unless registration would result in overissue, in which event the issuer's liability is governed by Section 8-104. In addition to any rights on the indemnity bond, the issuer may recover the new certificated security from the person to whom it was issued or any person taking under him except a bona fide purchaser or may cancel the uncertificated security unless a bona fide purchaser or any person taking under a bona fide purchaser is then the registered owner or registered pledgee thereof.

As amended in 1977.

§ 8-406. Duty of Authenticating Trustee, Transfer AGent, or Registrar.

(1) If a person acts as authenticating trustee, transfer agent, registrar, or other agent for an issuer in the registration of transfers of its certificated securities or in the registration of transfers, pledges, and releases of its uncertificated securities, in the issue of new securities, or in the cancellation of surrendered securities:

(a) he is under a duty to the issuer to exercise good faith and due diligence in performing his functions; and

(b) with regard to the particular functions he performs, he has the same obligation to the holder or owner of a certificated security or to the owner or pledgee of an uncertificated security and has the same rights and privileges as the issuer has in regard to those functions.

(2) Notice to an authenticating trustee, transfer agent, registrar or other agent is notice to the issuer with respect to the functions performed by the agent.

As amended in 1977.

§ 8-407. Exchangeability of Securities.

(1) No issuer is subject to the requirements of this section unless it regularly maintains a system for issuing the class of securities involved under which both certificated and uncertificated securities are regularly issued to the category of owners, which includes the person in whose name the new security is to be registered.

(2) Upon surrender of a certificated security with all necessary indorsements and presentation of a written request by the person surrendering the security, the issuer, if he has no duty as to adverse claims or has discharged the duty (Section 8-403), shall issue to the person or a person designated by him an equivalent uncertificated security subject to all liens, restrictions, and claims that were noted on the certificated security.

(3) Upon receipt of a transfer instruction originated by an appropriate person who so requests, the issuer of an uncertificated security shall cancel the uncertificated security and issue an equivalent certificated security on which must be noted conspicuously any liens and restrictions of the issuer and any adverse claims (as to which the issuer has a duty under Section 8-403(4) to which the uncertificated security was subject. The certificated security shall be registered in the name of and delivered to:

(a) the registered owner, if the uncertificated security was not subject to a registered pledge; or

(b) the registered pledgee, if the uncertificated security was subject to a registered pledge.

As added in 1977.

§ 8-408. Statements of Uncertificated Securities.

(1) Within 2 business days after the transfer of an uncertificated security has been registered, the issuer shall send to the new registered owner and, if the security has been transferred subject to a registered pledge, to the registered pledgee a written statement containing:

(a) a description of the issue of which the uncertificated security is a part;

(b) the number of shares or units transferred;

(c) the name and address and any taxpayer identification number of the new registered owner and, if the security has been transferred subject to a registered pledge, the name and address and any taxpayer identification number of the registered pledgee;

(d) a notation of any liens and restrictions of the issuer and any adverse claims (as to which the issuer has a duty under Section 8-403(4)) to which the uncertificated security is or may be subject at the time of registration or a statement that there are none of those liens, restrictions, or adverse claims; and

(e) the date the transfer was registered.

(2) Within 2 business days after the pledge of an uncertificated security has been registered, the issuer shall send to the registered owner and the registered pledgee a written statement containing:

(a) a description of the issue of which the uncertificated security is a part;

(b) the number of shares or units pledged;

(c) the name and address and any taxpayer identification number of the registered owner and the registered pledgee;

(d) a notation of any liens and restrictions of the issuer and any adverse claims (as to which the issuer has a duty under Section 8-403(4)) to which the uncertificated security is or may be subject at the time of registration or a statement that there are none of those liens, restrictions, or adverse claims; and

(e) the date the pledge was registered.

(3) Within 2 business days after the release from pledge of an uncertificated security has been registered, the issuer shall send to the registered owner and the pledgee whose interest was released a written statement containing:

(a) a description of the issue of which the uncertificated security is a part;

(b) the number of shares or units released from pledge;

(c) the name and address and any taxpayer identification number of the registered owner and the pledgee whose interest was released;

(d) a notation of any liens and restrictions of the issuer and any adverse claims (as to which the issuer has a duty under Section 8-403(4)) to which the uncertificated security is or may be subject at the time of registration or a statement that there are none of those liens, restrictions, or adverse claims; and

(e) the date the pledge was registered.

(4) An "initial transaction statement" is the statement sent to:

(a) the new registered owner and, if applicable, to the registered pledgee pursuant to subsection (1);

(b) the registered pledgee pursuant to subsection (2); or

(c) the registered owner pursuant to subsection (3).

Each initial transaction statement shall be signed by or on behalf of the issuer and must be identified as "Initial Transaction Statement".

(5) Within 2 business days after the transfer of an uncertificated security has been registered, the issuer shall send to the former registered owner and the former registered pledgee, if any, a written statement containing:

(a) a description of the issue of which the uncertificated security is a part;

(b) the number of shares or units transferred;

(c) the name and address and any taxpayer identification number of the former registered owner and of any former registered pledgee; and

(d) the date the transfer was registered.

(6) At periodic intervals no less frequent than annually and at any time upon the reasonable written request of the registered owner, the issuer shall send to the registered owner of each uncertificated security a dated written statement containing:

(a) a description of the issue of which the uncertificated security is a part;

(b) the name and address and any taxpayer identification number of the registered owner;

(c) the number of shares or units of the uncertificated security registered in the name of the registered owner on the date of the statement;

(d) the name and address and any taxpayer identification number of any registered pledgee and the number of shares or units subject to the pledge; and

(e) a notation of any liens and restrictions of the issuer and any adverse claims (as to which the issuer has a duty under Section 8-403(4) to which the uncertificated security is or may be subject or a statement that there are none of those liens, restrictions, or adverse claims.

(7) At periodic intervals no less frequent than annually and at any time upon the reasonable written request of the registered pledgee, the issuer shall send to the registered pledgee of each uncertificated security a dated written statement containing:

(a) a description of the issue of which the uncertificated security is a part;

(b) the name and address and any taxpayer identification number of the registered owner;

(c) the name and address and any taxpayer identification number of the registered pledgee;

(d) the number of shares or units subject to the pledge; and

(e) a notation of any liens and restrictions of the issuer and any adverse claims (as to which the issuer has a duty under Section 8-403(4) to which the uncertificated security is or may be subject or a statement that there are none of those liens, restrictions, or adverse claims.

(8) If the issuer sends the statements described in subsections (6) and (7) at periodic intervals no less frequent than quarterly, the issuer is not obliged to send additional statements upon request unless the owner or pledgee requesting them pays to the issuer the reasonable cost of furnishing them.

(9) Each statement sent pursuant to this section must bear a conspicuous legend reading substantially as follows: "This statement is merely a record of the rights of the addressee as of the time of its issuance. Delivery of this statement, of itself, confers no rights on the recipient. This statement is neither a negotiable instrument nor a security."

As added in 1977.

ARTICLE 9 / Secured Transactions; Sales of Accounts and Chattel Paper

Part 1   Short Title, Applicability and Definitions

§ 9-101.   **Short Title.** This Article shall be known and may be cited as Uniform Commercial Code—Secured Transactions.

§ 9-102.   **Policy and Subject Matter of Article.**

(1) Except as otherwise provided in Section 9-104 on excluded transactions, this Article applies

(a) to any transaction (regardless of its form) which is intended to create a security interest in personal property or fixtures including goods, documents, instruments, general intangibles, chattel paper or accounts; and also

(b) to any sale of accounts or chattel paper.

(2) This Article applies to security interests created by contract including pledge, assignment, chattel mortgage, chattel trust, trust deed, factor's lien, equipment trust, conditional sale, trust receipt, other lien or title retention contract and lease or consignment intended as security. This Article does not apply to statutory liens except as provided in Section 9-310.

(3) The application of this Article to a security interest in a secured obligation is not affected by the fact that the obligation is itself secured by a transaction or interest to which this Article does not apply.

As amended in 1972.

§ 9-103.   **Perfection of Security Interest in Multiple State Transactions.**

(1) Documents, instruments and ordinary goods.

(a) This subsection applies to documents and instruments and to goods other than those covered by a certificate of title described in subsection (2), mobile goods described in subsection (3), and minerals described in subsection (5).

(b) Except as otherwise provided in this subsection, perfection and the effect of perfection or non-perfection of a security interest in collateral are governed by the law of the jurisdiction where the collateral is when the last event occurs on which is based the assertion that the security interest is perfected or unperfected.

(c) If the parties to a transaction creating a purchase money security interest in goods in one jurisdiction understand at the time that the security interest attaches that the goods will be kept in another jurisdiction, then the law of the other jurisdiction governs the perfection and the effect of perfection or nonperfection of the security interest from the time it attaches until thirty days after the debtor receives possession of the goods and thereafter if the goods are taken to the other jurisdiction before the end of the thirty-day period.

(d) When collateral is brought into and kept in this state while subject to a security interest perfected under the law of the jurisdiction from which the collateral was removed, the security interest remains perfected, but if action is required by Part 3 of this Article to perfect the security interest.

(i) if the action is not taken before the expiration of the period of perfection in the other jurisdiction or the end of four months after the collateral is brought into this state, whichever period first expires, the security interest becomes unperfected at the end of that period and is thereafter deemed to have been unperfected as against a person who became a purchaser after removal;

(ii) if the action is taken before the expiration of the period specified in subparagraph (i), the security interest continues perfected thereafter;

(iii) for the purpose of priority over a buyer of consumer goods (subsection (2) of Section 9-307), the period of the effectiveness of a filing in the jurisdiction from which the collateral is removed is governed by the rules with respect to perfection in subparagraphs (i) and (ii).

(2) Certificate of title.

(a) This subsection applies to goods covered by a certificate of title issued under a statute of this state or of another jurisdiction under the law of which indication of a security interest on the certificate is required as a condition of perfection.

(b) Except as otherwise provided in this subsection, perfection and the effect of perfection or non-perfection of the security interest are governed by the law (including the conflict of laws rules) of the jurisdiction issuing the certificate until four months after the goods are removed from that jurisdiction and thereafter until the goods are registered in another jurisdiction, but in any event not beyond surrender of the certificate. After the expiration of that period, the goods are not covered by the certificate of title within the meaning of this section.

(c) Except with respect to the rights of a buyer described in the next paragraph, a security interest, perfected in another jurisdiction otherwise than by notation on a certificate of title, in goods brought into this state and thereafter covered by a certificate of title issued by this state is subject to the rules stated in paragraph (d) of subsection (1).

(d) If goods are brought into this state while a security interest therein is perfected in any manner under the law of the jurisdiction from which the goods are removed and a certificate of title is issued by this state and the certificate does not show that the goods are subject to the security interest or that they may be subject to security interests not shown on the certificate, the security interest is subordinate to the rights of a buyer of the goods who is not in the business of selling goods of that kind to the extent that he gives value and receives delivery of the goods after issuance of the certificate and without knowledge of the security interest.

(3) Accounts, general intangibles and mobile goods.

(a) This subsection applies to accounts (other than an account described in subsection (5) on minerals) and general intangibles (other than uncertificated securities) and to goods which are mobile and which are of a type normally used in more than one jurisdiction, such as motor vehicles, trailers, rolling stock, airplanes, shipping containers, road building and construction machinery and commercial harvesting machinery and the like, if the goods are equipment or are inventory leased or held for lease by the debtor to others, and are not covered by a certificate of title described in subsection (2).

(b) The law (including the conflict of laws rules) of the jurisdiction in which the debtor is located governs the perfection and the effect of perfection or non-perfection of the security interest.

(c) If, however, the debtor is located in a jurisdiction which is not a part of the United States, and which does not provide for perfection of the security interest by filing or recording in that jurisdiction, the law of the jurisdiction in the United States in which the debtor has its major executive office in the United States governs the perfection and the effect of perfection or non-perfection of the security interest through filing. In the alternative, if the debtor is located in a jurisdiction which is not a part of the United States or Canada and the collateral is accounts or general intangibles for money due or to become due, the security interest may be perfected by notification to the account debtor. As used in this paragraph, "United States" includes its territories and possessions and the Commonwealth of Puerto Rico.

(d) A debtor shall be deemed located at his place of business if he has one, at his chief executive office if he has more than one place of business, otherwise at his residence. If, however, the debtor is a foreign air carrier under the Federal Aviation Act of 1958, as amended, it shall be deemed located at the designated office of the agent upon whom service of process may be made on behalf of the foreign air carrier.

(e) A security interest perfected under the law of the jurisdiction of the location of the debtor is perfected until the expiration of four months after a change of the debtor's location to another jurisdiction, or until perfection would have ceased by the law of the first jurisdiction, whichever period first expires. Unless perfected in the new jurisdiction before the end of that period, it becomes unperfected thereafter and is deemed to have been unperfected as against a person who became a purchaser after the change.

(4) Chattel paper.

The rules stated for goods in subsection (1) apply to a possessory security interest in chattel paper. The rules stated for accounts in subsection (3) apply to a non-possessory security interest in chattel paper, but the security interest may not be perfected by notification to the account debtor.

(5) Minerals.

Perfection and the effect of perfection or non-perfection of a security interest which is created by a debtor who has an interest in minerals or the like (including oil and gas) before extraction and which attaches thereto as extracted, or which attaches to an account resulting from the sale thereof at the wellhead or minehead are governed by the law (including the conflict of laws rules) of the jurisdiction wherein the wellhead or minehead is located.

(6) Uncertificated securities.

The law (including the conflict of laws rules) of the jurisdiction of organization of the issuer governs the perfection and the effect of perfection or non-perfection of a security interest in uncertificated securities.

As amended in 1972 and 1977.

§ 9-104. Transactions Excluded From Article. This Article does not apply

(a) to a security interest subject to any statute of the United States, to the extent that such statute governs the rights of parties to and third parties affected by transactions in particular types of property; or

(b) to a landlord's lien; or

(c) to a lien given by statute or other rule of law for services or materials except as provided in Section 9-310 on priority of such liens; or

(d) to a transfer of a claim for wages, salary or other compensation of an employee; or

(e) to a transfer by a government or governmental subdivision or agency; or

(f) to a sale of accounts or chattel paper as part of a sale of the business out of which they arose, or an assignment of accounts or chattel paper which is for the purpose of collection only, or a transfer of a right to payment under a contract to an assignee who is also to do the performance under the contract or a transfer of a single account to an assignee in whole or partial satisfaction of a preexisting indebtedness; or

(g) to a transfer of an interest in or claim in or under any policy of insurance, except as provided with respect to proceeds (Section 9-306) and priorities in proceeds (Section 9-312); or

(h) to a right represented by a judgment (other than a judgment taken on a right to payment which was collateral); or

(i) to any right of set-off; or

(j) except to the extent that provision is made for fixtures in Section 9-313, to the creation or transfer of an interest in or lien on real estate, including a lease or rents thereunder; or

(k) to a transfer in whole or in part of any claim arising out of tort; or

(l) to a transfer of an interest in any deposit account (subsection (1) of Section 9-105), except as provided with respect to proceeds (Section 9-306) and priorities in proceeds (Section 9-312).

As amended in 1972.

§ 9-105. Definitions and Index of Definitions.

(1) In this Article unless the context otherwise requires:

(a) "Account debtor" means the person who is obligated on an account, chattel paper or general intangible;

(b) "Chattel paper" means a writing or writings which evidence both a monetary obligation and a security interest in or a lease of specific goods, but a charter or other contract involving the use or hire of a vessel is not chattel paper. When a transaction is evidenced both by such a security agreement or a lease and by an instrument or a series of instruments, the group of writings taken together constitutes chattel paper;

(c) "Collateral" means the property subject to a security interest, and includes accounts and chattel paper which have been sold;

(d) "Debtor" means the person who owes payment or other performance of the obligation secured, whether or not he owns or has rights in the collateral, and includes the seller of accounts or chattel paper. Where the debtor and the owner of the collateral are not the same person, the term "debtor" means the owner of the collateral in any provision of the Article dealing with the collateral, the obligor in any provision dealing with the obligation, and may include both where the context so requires;

(e) "Deposit account" means a demand, time, savings, passbook or like account maintained with a bank, savings and loan association, credit union or like organization, other than an account evidenced by a certificate of deposit;

(f) "Document" means document of title as defined in the general definitions of Article 1 (Section 1-201), and a receipt of the kind described in subsection (2) of Section 7-201;

(g) "Encumbrance" includes real estate mortgages and other liens on real estate and all other rights in real estate that are not ownership interests;

(h) "Goods" includes all things which are movable at the time the security interest attaches or which are fixtures (Section 9-313), but does not include money, documents, instruments, accounts, chattel paper, general intangibles, or minerals or the like (including oil and gas) before extraction. "Goods" also includes standing timber which is to be cut and removed under a conveyance or contract for sale, the unborn young of animals, and growing crops;

(i) "Instrument" means a negotiable instrument (defined in Section 3-104), or a certificated security (defined in Section 8-102) or any other writing which evidences a right to the payment of money and is not itself a security agreement or lease and is of a type which is in ordinary course of business transferred by delivery with any necessary indorsement or assignment;

(j) "Mortgage" means a consensual interest created by a real estate mortgage, a trust deed on real estate, or the like;

(k) An advance is made "pursuant to commitment" if the secured party has bound himself to make it, whether or not a subsequent event of default or other event not within his control has relieved or may relieve him from his obligation;

(l) "Security agreement" means an agreement which creates or provides for a security interest;

(m) "Secured party" means a lender, seller or other person in whose favor there is a security interest, including a person to whom accounts or chattel paper have been sold. When the holders of obligations issued under an indenture of trust, equipment trust agreement or the like are represented by a trustee or other person, the representative is the secured party;

(n) "Transmitting utility" means any person primarily engaged in the railroad, street railway or trolley bus business, the electric or electronics communications transmission business, the transmission of goods by pipeline, or the transmission or the production and transmission of electricity, steam, gas or water, or the provision of sewer service.

(2) Other definitions applying to this Article and the sections in which they appear are:

"Account".   Section 9-106.
"Attach".   Section 9-203.
"Construction mortgage".   Section 9-313(1).
"Consumer goods".   Section 9-109(1).
"Equipment".   Section 9-109(2).
"Farm products".   Section 9-109(3).
"Fixture".   Section 9-313(1).
"Fixture filing".   Section 9-313(1).
"General intangibles".   Section 9-106.
"Inventory".   Section 9-109(4).
"Lien creditor".   Section 9-301(3).
"Proceeds".   Section 9-306(1).
"Purchase money security interest".   Section 9-107.
"United States".   Section 9-103.

(3) The following definitions in other Articles apply to this Article:

"Check".   Section 3-104.
"Contract for sale".   Section 2-106.
"Holder in due course".   Section 3-302.
"Note".   Section 3-104.
"Sale".   Section 2-106.

(4) In addition Article 1 contains general definitions and principles of construction and interpretation applicable throughout this Article.

As amended in 1966, 1972 and 1977.

§ 9-106.   Definitions: "Account"; "General Intangibles". "Account" means any right to payment for goods sold or leased or for services rendered which is not evidenced by an instrument or chattel paper, whether or not it has been earned by performance. "General intangibles" means any personal property (including things in action) other than goods, accounts, chattel paper, documents, instruments, and money. All rights to payment earned or unearned under a charter or other contract involving the use or hire of a vessel and all rights incident to the charter or contract are accounts.

As amended in 1966 and 1972.

§ 9-107.   Definitions: "Purchase Money Security Interest". A security interest is a "purchase money security interest" to the extent that it is

(a) taken or retained by the seller of the collateral to secure all or part of its price; or
(b) taken by a person who by making advances or incurring an obligation gives value to enable the debtor to acquire rights in or the use of collateral if such value is in fact so used.

§ 9-108.   When After-Acquired Collateral Not Security for Antecedent Debt. Where a secured party makes an advance, incurs an obligation, releases a perfected security interest, or otherwise gives new value which is to be secured in whole or in part by after-acquired property his security interest in the after-acquired collateral shall be deemed to be taken for new value and not as security for an antecedent debt if the debtor acquires his rights in such collateral either in the ordinary course of his business or under a contract of purchase made pursuant to the security agreement within a reasonable time after new value is given.

§ 9-109.   Classification of Goods: "Consumer Goods"; "Equipment"; "Farm Products"; "Inventory". Goods are
(1) "consumer goods" if they are used or bought for use primarily for personal, family or household purposes;
(2) "equipment" if they are used or bought for use primarily in business (including farming or a profession) or by a debtor who is a nonprofit organization or a governmental subdivision or agency or if the goods are not included in the definitions of inventory, farm products or consumer goods;
(3) "farm products" if they are crops or livestock or supplies used or produced in farming operations or if they are products of crops or livestock in their unmanufactured states (such as ginned cotton, woolclip, maple syrup, milk and eggs), and if they are in the possession of a debtor engaged in raising, fattening, grazing or other farming operations. If goods are farm products they are neither equipment nor inventory;
(4) "inventory" if they are held by a person who holds them for sale or lease or to be furnished under contracts of service

or if he has so furnished them, or if they are raw materials, work in process or materials used or consumed in a business. Inventory of a person is not to be classified as his equipment.

§ 9-110.   Sufficiency of Description. For the purposes of this Article any description of personal property or real estate is sufficient whether or not it is specific if it reasonably identifies what is described.

§ 9-111.   Applicability of Bulk Transfer Laws. The creation of a security interest is not a bulk transfer under Article 6 (see Section 6-103).

§ 9-112.   Where Collateral Is Not Owned by Debtor. Unless otherwise agreed, when a secured party knows that collateral is owned by a person who is not the debtor, the owner of the collateral is entitled to receive from the secured party any surplus under Section 9-502(2) or under Section 9-504(1), and is not liable for the debt or for any deficiency after resale, and he has the same right as the debtor

(a) to receive statements under Section 9-208;
(b) to receive notice of and to object to a secured party's proposal to retain the collateral in satisfaction of the indebtedness under Section 9-505;
(c) to redeem the collateral under Section 9-506;
(d) to obtain injunctive or other relief under Section 9-507(1); and
(e) to recover losses caused to him under Section 9-208(2).

§ 9-113.   Security Interests Arising Under Article on Sales or Under Article on Leases. A security interest arising solely under the Article on Sales (Article 2) or the Article on Leases (Article 2A) is subject to the provisions of this Article except that to the extent that and so long as the debtor does not have or does not lawfully obtain possession of the goods

(a) no security agreement is necessary to make the security interest enforceable; and
(b) no filing is required to perfect the security interest; and
(c) the rights of the secured party on default by the debtor are governed (i) by the Article on Sales (Article 2) in the case of a security interest arising solely under such Article or (ii) by the Article on Leases (Article 2A) in the case of a security interest arising solely under such Article.

As amended in 1987.

§ 9-114.   Consignment.

(1) A person who delivers goods under a consignment which is not a security interest and who would be required to file under this Article by paragraph (3)(c) of Section 2-326 has priority over a secured party who is or becomes a creditor of the consignee and who would have a perfected security interest in the goods if they were the property of the consignee, and also has priority with respect to identifiable cash proceeds received on or before delivery of the goods to a buyer, if

(a) the consignor complies with the filing provision of the Article on Sales with respect to consignments (paragraph (3)(c) of Section 2-326) before the consignee receives possession of the goods; and
(b) the consignor gives notification in writing to the holder of the security interest if the holder has filed a fi-

nancing statement covering the same types of goods before the date of the filing made by the consignor; and

(c) the holder of the security interest receives the notification within five years before the consignee receives possession of the goods; and

(d) the notification states that the consignor expects to deliver goods on consignment to the consignee, describing the goods by item or type.

(2) In the case of a consignment which is not a security interest and in which the requirements of the preceding subsection have not been met, a person who delivers goods to another is subordinate to a person who would have a perfected security interest in the goods if they were the property of the debtor.

As added in 1972.

Part 2   Validity of Security Agreement and Rights of Parties Thereto

§ 9-201.   General Validity of Security Agreement.
Except as otherwise provided by this Act a security agreement is effective according to its terms between the parties, against purchasers of the collateral and against creditors. Nothing in this Article validates any charge or practice illegal under any statute or regulation thereunder governing usury, small loans, retail installment sales, or the like, or extends the application of any such statute or regulation to any transaction not otherwise subject thereto.

§ 9-202.   Title to Collateral Immaterial.
Each provision of this Article with regard to rights, obligations and remedies applies whether title to collateral is in the secured party or in the debtor.

§ 9-203.   Attachment and Enforceability of Security Interest; Proceeds; Formal Requisites.
(1) Subject to the provisions of Section 4-208 on the security interest of a collecting bank, Section 8-321 on security interests in securities and Section 9-113 on a security interest arising under the Article on Sales, a security interest is not enforceable against the debtor or third parties with respect to the collateral and does not attach unless:

(a) the collateral is in the possession of the secured party pursuant to agreement, or the debtor has signed a security agreement which contains a description of the collateral and in addition, when the security interest covers crops growing or to be grown or timber to be cut, a description of the land concerned;

(b) value has been given; and

(c) the debtor has rights in the collateral.

(2) A security interest attaches when it becomes enforceable against the debtor with respect to the collateral. Attachment occurs as soon as all of the events specified in subsection (1) have taken place unless explicit agreement postpones the time of attaching.

(3) Unless otherwise agreed a security agreement gives the secured party the rights to proceeds provided by Section 9-306.

(4) A transaction, although subject to this Article, is also subject to _____ *, and in the case of conflict between the provisions of this Article and any such statute, the provisions of such statute control. Failure to comply with any applicable statute has only the effect which is specified therein.

Note: At* in subsection (4) insert reference to any local statute regulating small loans, retail installment sales and the like.

As amended in 1972 and 1977.

§ 9-204.   After-Acquired Property; Future Advances.
(1) Except as provided in subsection (2), a security agreement may provide that any or all obligations covered by the security agreement are to be secured by after-acquired collateral.

(2) No security interest attaches under an after-acquired property clause to consumer goods other than accessions (Section 9-314) when given as additional security unless the debtor acquires rights in them within ten days after the secured party gives value.

(3) Obligations covered by a security agreement may include future advances or other value whether or not the advances or value are given pursuant to commitment (subsection (1) of Section 9-105).

As amended in 1972.

§ 9-205.   Use or Disposition of Collateral Without Accounting Permissible.
A security interest is not invalid or fraudulent against creditors by reason of liberty in the debtor to use, commingle or dispose of all or part of the collateral (including returned or repossessed goods) or to collect or compromise accounts or chattel paper, or to accept the return of goods or make repossessions, or to use, commingle or dispose of proceeds, or by reason of the failure of the secured party to require the debtor to account for proceeds or replace collateral. This section does not relax the requirements of possession where perfection of a security interest depends upon possession of the collateral by the secured party or by a bailee.

As amended in 1972.

§ 9-206.   Agreement Not to Assert Defenses Against Assignee; Modification of Sales Warranties Where Security Agreement Exists.
(1) Subject to any statute or decision which establishes a different rule for buyers or lessees of consumer goods, an agreement by a buyer or lessee that he will not assert against an assignee any claim or defense which he may have against the seller or lessor is enforceable by an assignee who takes his assignment for value, in good faith and without notice of a claim or defense, except as to defenses of a type which may be asserted against a holder in due course of a negotiable instrument under the Article on Commercial Paper (Article 3). A buyer who as part of one transaction signs both a negotiable instrument and a security agreement makes such an agreement.

(2) When a seller retains a purchase money security interest in goods the Article on Sales (Article 2) governs the sale and any disclaimer, limitation or modification of the seller's warranties.

As amended in 1962.

§ 9-207. Rights and Duties When Collateral Is in Secured Party's Possession.

(1) A secured party must use reasonable care in the custody and preservation of collateral in his possession. In the case of an instrument or chattel paper reasonable care includes taking necessary steps to preserve rights against prior parties unless otherwise agreed.

(2) Unless otherwise agreed, when collateral is in the secured party's possession

(a) reasonable expenses (including the cost of any insurance and payment of taxes or other charges) incurred in the custody, preservation, use or operation of the collateral are chargeable to the debtor and are secured by the collateral;

(b) the risk of accidental loss or damage is on the debtor to the extent of any deficiency in any effective insurance coverage;

(c) the secured party may hold as additional security any increase or profits (except money) received from the collateral, but money so received, unless remitted to the debtor, shall be applied in reduction of the secured obligation;

(d) the secured party must keep the collateral identifiable but fungible collateral may be commingled;

(e) the secured party may repledge the collateral upon terms which do not impair the debtor's right to redeem it.

(3) A secured party is liable for any loss caused by his failure to meet any obligation imposed by the preceding subsections but does not lose his security interest.

(4) A secured party may use or operate the collateral for the purpose of preserving the collateral or its value or pursuant to the order of a court of appropriate jurisdiction or, except in the case of consumer goods, in the manner and to the extent provided in the security agreement.

§ 9-208. Request for Statement of Account or List of Collateral.

(1) A debtor may sign a statement indicating what he believes to be the aggregate amount of unpaid indebtedness as of a specified date and may send it to the secured party with a request that the statement be approved or corrected and returned to the debtor. When the security agreement or any other record kept by the secured party identifies the collateral a debtor may similarly request the secured party to approve or correct a list of the collateral.

(2) The secured party must comply with such a request within two weeks after receipt by sending a written correction or approval. If the secured party claims a security interest in all of a particular type of collateral owned by the debtor he may indicate that fact in his reply and need not approve or correct an itemized list of such collateral. If the secured party without reasonable excuse fails to comply he is liable for any loss caused to the debtor thereby; and if the debtor has properly included in his request a good faith statement of the obligation or a list of the collateral or both the secured party may claim a security interest only as shown in the statement against persons misled by his failure to comply. If he no longer has an interest in the obligation or collateral at the time the request is received he must disclose the name and address of any successor in interest known to him and he is li-

able for any loss caused to the debtor as a result of failure to disclose. A successor in interest is not subject to this section until a request is received by him.

(3) A debtor is entitled to such a statement once every six months without charge. The secured party may require payment of a charge not exceeding $10 for each additional statement furnished.

Part 3 Rights of Third Parties; Perfected and Unperfected Security Interests; Rules of Priority

§ 9-301. Persons Who Take Priority Over Unperfected Security Interests; Rights of "Lien Creditor".

(1) Except as otherwise provided in subsection (2), an unperfected security interest is subordinate to the rights of

(a) persons entitled to priority under Section 9-312;

(b) a person who becomes a lien creditor before the security interest is perfected;

(c) in the case of goods, instruments, documents, and chattel paper, a person who is not a secured party and who is a transferee in bulk or other buyer not in ordinary course of business or is a buyer of farm products in ordinary course of business, to the extent that he gives value and receives delivery of the collateral without knowledge of the security interest and before it is perfected;

(d) in the case of accounts and general intangibles, a person who is not a secured party and who is a transferee to the extent that he gives value without knowledge of the security interest and before it is perfected.

(2) If the secured party files with respect to a purchase money security interest before or within ten days after the debtor receives possession of the collateral, he takes priority over the rights of a transferee in bulk or of a lien creditor which arise between the time the security interest attaches and the time of filing.

(3) A "lien creditor" means a creditor who has acquired a lien on the property involved by attachment, levy or the like and includes an assignee for benefit of creditors from the time of assignment, and a trustee in bankruptcy from the date of the filing of the petition or a receiver in equity from the time of appointment.

(4) A person who becomes a lien creditor while a security interest is perfected takes subject to the security interest only to the extent that it secures advances made before he becomes a lien creditor or within 45 days thereafter or made without knowledge of the lien or pursuant to a commitment entered into without knowledge of the lien.

As amended in 1972.

§ 9-302. When Filing Is Required to Perfect Security Interest; Security Interests to Which Filing Provisions of This Article Do Not Apply.

(1) A financing statement must be filed to perfect all security interests except the following:

(a) a security interest in collateral in possession of the secured party under Section 9-305;

(b) a security interest temporarily perfected in instruments or documents without delivery under Section 9-304 or in proceeds for a 10 day period under Section 9-306;

(c) a security interest created by an assignment of a beneficial interest in a trust or a decedent's estate;

(d) a purchase money security interest in consumer goods; but filing is required for a motor vehicle required to be registered; and fixture filing is required for priority over conflicting interests in fixtures to the extent provided in Section 9-313;

(e) an assignment of accounts which does not alone or in conjunction with other assignments to the same assignee transfer a significant part of the outstanding accounts of the assignor;

(f) a security interest of a collecting bank (Section 4-208) or in securities (Section 8-321) or arising under the Article on Sales (see Section 9-113) or covered in subsection (3) of this section;

(g) an assignment for the benefit of all the creditors of the transferor, and subsequent transfers by the assignee thereunder.

(2) If a secured party assigns a perfected security interest, no filing under this Article is required in order to continue the perfected status of the security interest against creditors of and transferees from the original debtor.

(3) The filing of a financing statement otherwise required by this Article is not necessary or effective to perfect a security interest in property subject to

(a) a statute or treaty of the United States which provides for a national or international registration or a national or international certificate of title or which specifies a place of filing different from that specified in this Article for filing of the security interest; or

(b) the following statutes of this state; [list any certificate of title statute covering automobiles, trailers, mobile homes, boats, farm tractors, or the like, and any central filing statute.]; but during any period in which collateral is inventory held for sale by a person who is in the business of selling goods of that kind, the filing provisions of this Article (Part 4) apply to a security interest in that collateral created by him as debtor; or

(c) a certificate of title statute of another jurisdiction under the law of which indication of a security interest on the certificate is required as a condition of perfection (subsection (2) of Section 9-103).

(4) Compliance with a statute or treaty described in subsection (3) is equivalent to the filing of a financing statement under this Article, and a security interest in property subject to the statute or treaty can be perfected only by compliance therewith except as provided in Section 9-103 on multiple state transactions. Duration and renewal of perfection of a security interest perfected by compliance with the statute or treaty are governed by the provisions of the statute or treaty; in other respects the security interest is subject to this Article.

As amended in 1972 and 1977.

§ 9-303.   When Security Interest Is Perfected; Continuity of Perfection.

(1) A security interest is perfected when it has attached and when all of the applicable steps required for perfection have been taken. Such steps are specified in Sections 9-302, 9-304, 9-305 and 9-306. If such steps are taken before the security interest attaches, it is perfected at the time when it attaches.

(2) If a security interest is originally perfected in any way permitted under this Article and is subsequently perfected in some other way under this Article, without an intermediate period when it was unperfected, the security interest shall be deemed to be perfected continuously for the purposes of this Article.

§ 9-304.   Perfection of Security Interest in Instruments, Documents, and Goods Covered by Documents; Perfection by Permissive Filing; Temporary Perfection Without Filing or Transfer of Possession.

(1) A security interest in chattel paper or negotiable documents may be perfected by filing. A security interest in money or instruments (other than certificated securities or instruments which constitute part of chattel paper) can be perfected only by the secured party's taking possession, except as provided in subsections (4) and (5) of this section and subsections (2) and (3) of Section 9-306 on proceeds.

(2) During the period that goods are in the possession of the issuer of a negotiable document therefore, a security interest in the goods is perfected by perfecting a security interest in the document, and any security interest in the goods otherwise perfected during such period is subject thereto.

(3) A security interest in goods in the possession of a bailee other than one who has issued a negotiable document therefore is perfected by issuance of a document in the name of the secured party or by the bailee's receipt of notification of the secured party's interest or by filing as to the goods.

(4) A security interest in instruments (other than certificated securities) or negotiable documents is perfected without filing or the taking of possession for a period of 21 days from the time it attaches to the extent that it arises for new value given under a written security agreement.

(5) A security interest remains perfected for a period of 21 days without filing where a secured party having a perfected security interest in an instrument (other than a certificated security), a negotiable document or goods in possession of a bailee other than one who has issued a negotiable document therefor

(a) makes available to the debtor the goods or documents representing the goods for the purpose of ultimate sale or exchange or for the purpose of loading, unloading, storing, shipping, transshipping, manufacturing, processing or otherwise dealing with them in a manner preliminary to their sale or exchange, but priority between conflicting security interests in the goods is subject to subsection (3) of Section 9-312; or

(b) delivers the instrument to the debtor for the purpose of ultimate sale or exchange or of presentation, collection, renewal or registration of transfer.

(6) After the 21 day period in subsections (4) and (5) perfection depends upon compliance with applicable provisions of this Article.

As amended in 1972 and 1977.

§ 9-305.   When Possession by Secured Party Perfects Security Interest Without Filing. A security interest in letters of credit and advices of credit (subsection (2)(a) of Section 5-116), goods, instruments (other than certificated securities), money, negotiable documents, or chattel paper may be

perfected by the secured party's taking possession of the collateral. If such collateral other than goods covered by a negotiable document is held by a bailee, the secured party is deemed to have possession from the time the bailee receives notification of the secured party's interest. A security interest is perfected by possession from the time possession is taken without a relation back and continues only so long as possession is retained, unless otherwise specified in this Article. The security interest may be otherwise perfected as provided in this Article before or after the period of possession by the secured party.

As amended in 1972 and 1977.

§ 9-306. "Proceeds"; Secured Party's Rights on Disposition of Collateral.

(1) "Proceeds" includes whatever is received upon the sale, exchange, collection or other disposition of collateral or proceeds. Insurance payable by reason of loss or damage to the collateral is proceeds, except to the extent that it is payable to a person other than a party to the security agreement. Money, checks, deposit accounts, and the like are "cash proceeds". All other proceeds are "non-cash proceeds".

(2) Except where this Article otherwise provides, a security interest continues in collateral notwithstanding sale, exchange or other disposition thereof unless the disposition was authorized by the secured party in the security agreement or otherwise, and also continues in any identifiable proceeds including collections received by the debtor.

(3) The security interest in proceeds is a continuously perfected security interest if the interest in the original collateral was perfected but it ceases to be a perfected security interest and becomes unperfected ten days after receipt of the proceeds by the debtor unless

(a) a filed financing statement covers the original collateral and the proceeds are collateral in which a security interest may be perfected by filing in the office or offices where the financing statement has been filed and, if the proceeds are acquired with cash proceeds, the description of collateral in the financing statement indicates the types of property constituting the proceeds; or

(b) a filed financing statement covers the original collateral and the proceeds are identifiable cash proceeds; or

(c) the security interest in the proceeds is perfected before the expiration of the ten day period.

Except as provided in this section, a security interest in proceeds can be perfected only by the methods or under the circumstances permitted in this Article for original collateral of the same type.

(4) In the event of insolvency proceedings instituted by or against a debtor, a secured party with a perfected security interest in proceeds has a perfected security interest only in the following proceeds:

(a) in identifiable non-cash proceeds and in separate deposit accounts containing only proceeds;

(b) in identifiable cash proceeds in the form of money which is neither commingled with other money nor deposited in a deposit account prior to the insolvency proceedings;

(c) in identifiable cash proceeds in the form of checks

and the like which are not deposited in a deposit account prior to the insolvency proceedings; and

(d) in all cash and deposit accounts of the debtor in which proceeds have been commingled with other funds, but the perfected security interest under this paragraph (d) is

(i) subject to any right to set-off; and

(ii) limited to an amount not greater than the amount of any cash proceeds received by the debtor within ten days before the institution of the insolvency proceedings less the sum of (I) the payments to the secured party on account of cash proceeds received by the debtor during such period and (II) the cash proceeds received by the debtor during such period to which the secured party is entitled under paragraphs (a) through (c) of this subsection (4).

(5) If a sale of goods results in an account or chattel paper which is transferred by the seller to a secured party, and if the goods are returned to or are repossessed by the seller or the secured party, the following rules determine priorities:

(a) If the goods were collateral at the time of sale, for an indebtedness of the seller which is still unpaid, the original security interest attaches again to the goods and continues as a perfected security interest if it was perfected at the time when the goods were sold. If the security interest was originally perfected by a filing which is still effective, nothing further is required to continue the perfected status; in any other case, the secured party must take possession of the returned or repossessed goods or must file.

(b) An unpaid transferee of the chattel paper has a security interest in the goods against the transferor. Such security interest is prior to a security interest asserted under paragraph (a) to the extent that the transferee of the chattel paper was entitled to priority under Section 9-308.

(c) An unpaid transferee of the account has a security interest in the goods against the transferor. Such security interest is subordinate to a security interest asserted under paragraph (a).

(d) A security interest of an unpaid transferee asserted under paragraph (b) or (c) must be perfected for protection against creditors of the transferor and purchasers of the returned or repossessed goods.

As amended in 1972.

§ 9-307. Protection of Buyers of Goods.

(1) A buyer in ordinary course of business (subsection (9) of Section 1-201) other than a person buying farm products from a person engaged in farming operations takes free of a security interest created by his seller even though the security interest is perfected and even though the buyer knows of its existence.

(2) In the case of consumer goods, a buyer takes free of a security interest even though perfected if he buys without knowledge of the security interest, for value and for his own personal, family or household purposes unless prior to the purchase the secured party has filed a financing statement covering such goods.

(3) A buyer other than a buyer in ordinary course of business (subsection (1) of this section) takes free of a security interest to the extent that it secures future advances made after

the secured party acquires knowledge of the purchase, or more than 45 days after the purchase, whichever first occurs, unless made pursuant to a commitment entered into without knowledge of the purchase and before the expiration of the 45 day period.

As amended in 1972.

§ 9-308. Purchase of Chattel Paper and Instruments.
A purchaser of chattel paper or an instrument who gives new value and takes possession of it in the ordinary course of his business has priority over a security interest in the chattel paper or instrument

(a) which is perfected under Section 9-304 (permissive filing and temporary perfection) or under Section 9-306 (perfection as to proceeds) if he acts without knowledge that the specific paper or instrument is subject to a security interest; or

(b) which is claimed merely as proceeds of inventory subject to a security interest (Section 9-306) even though he knows that the specific paper or instrument is subject to the security interest.

As amended in 1972.

§ 9-309. Protection of Purchasers of Instruments, Documents, and Securities.
Nothing in this Article limits the rights of a holder in due course of a negotiable instrument (Section 3-302) or a holder to whom a negotiable document of title has been duly negotiated (Section 7-501) or a bona fide purchaser of a security (Section 8-302) and the holders or purchasers take priority over an earlier security interest even though perfected. Filing under this Article does not constitute notice of the security interest to such holders or purchasers.

As amended in 1977.

§ 9-310. Priority of Certain Liens Arising by Operation of Law.
When a person in the ordinary course of his business furnishes services or materials with respect to goods subject to a security interest, a lien upon goods in the possession of such person given by statute or rule of law for such materials or services takes priority over a perfected security interest unless the lien is statutory and the statute expressly provides otherwise.

§ 9-311. Alienability of Debtor's Rights: Judicial Process.
The debtor's rights in collateral may be voluntarily or involuntarily transferred (by way of sale, creation of a security interest, attachment, levy, garnishment or other judicial process) notwithstanding a provision in the security agreement prohibiting any transfer or making the transfer constitute a default.

§ 9-312. Priorities Among Conflicting Security Interests in the Same Collateral.

(1) The rules of priority stated in other sections of this Part and in the following sections shall govern when applicable: Section 4-208 with respect to the security interests of collecting banks in items being collected, accompanying documents and proceeds; Section 9-103 on security interests related to other jurisdictions; Section 9-114 on consignments.

(2) A perfected security interest in crops for new value given to enable the debtor to produce the crops during the production season and given not more than three months before the crops become growing crops by planting or otherwise takes priority over an earlier perfected security interest to the extent that such earlier interest secures obligations due more than six months before the crops become growing crops by planting or otherwise, even though the person giving new value had knowledge of the earlier security interest.

(3) A perfected purchase money security interest in inventory has priority over a conflicting security interest in the same inventory and also has priority in identifiable cash proceeds received on or before the delivery of the inventory to a buyer if

(a) the purchase money security interest is perfected at the time the debtor receives possession of the inventory; and

(b) the purchase money secured party gives notification in writing to the holder of the conflicting security interest if the holder had filed a financing statement covering the same types of inventory (i) before the date of the filing made by the purchase money secured party, or (ii) before the beginning of the 21 day period where the purchase money security interest is temporarily perfected without filing or possession (subsection (5) of Section 9-304); and

(c) the holder of the conflicting security interest receives the notification within five years before the debtor receives possession of the inventory; and

(d) the notification states that the person giving the notice has or expects to acquire a purchase money security interest in inventory of the debtor, describing such inventory by item or type.

(4) A purchase money security interest in collateral other than inventory has priority over a conflicting security interest in the same collateral or its proceeds if the purchase money security interest is perfected at the time the debtor receives possession of the collateral or within ten days thereafter.

(5) In all cases not governed by other rules stated in this section (including cases of purchase money security interests which do not qualify for the special priorities set forth in subsections (3) and (4) of this section), priority between conflicting security interests in the same collateral shall be determined according to the following rules:

(a) Conflicting security interests rank according to priority in time of filing or perfection. Priority dates from the time a filing is first made covering the collateral or the time the security interest is first perfected, whichever is earlier, provided that there is no period thereafter when there is neither filing nor perfection.

(b) So long as conflicting security interests are unperfected, the first to attach has priority.

(6) For the purposes of subsection (5) a date of filing or perfection as to collateral is also a date of filing or perfection as to proceeds.

(7) If future advances are made while a security interest is perfected by filing, the taking of possession, or under Section 8-321 on securities, the security interest has the same priority for the purposes of subsection (5) with respect to the future advances as it does with respect to the first advance. If a com-

mitment is made before or while the security interest is so perfected, the security interest has the same priority with respect to advances made pursuant thereto. In other cases a perfected security interest has priority from the date the advance is made.

As amended in 1972 and 1977.

§ 9-313. Priority of Security Interests in Fixtures.

(1) In this section and in the provisions of Part 4 of this Article referring to fixture filing, unless the context otherwise requires

(a) goods are "fixtures" when they become so related to particular real estate that an interest in them arises under real estate law

(b) a "fixture filing" is the filing in the office where a mortgage on the real estate would be filed or recorded of a financing statement covering goods which are or are to become fixtures and conforming to the requirements of subsection (5) of Section 9-402

(c) a mortgage is a "construction mortgage" to the extent that it secures an obligation incurred for the construction of an improvement on land including the acquisition cost of the land, if the recorded writing so indicates.

(2) A security interest under this Article may be created in goods which are fixtures or may continue in goods which become fixtures, but no security interest exists under this Article in ordinary building materials incorporated into an improvement on land.

(3) This Article does not prevent creation of an encumbrance upon fixtures pursuant to real estate law.

(4) A perfected security interest in fixtures has priority over the conflicting interest of an encumbrancer or owner of the real estate where

(a) the security interest is a purchase money security interest, the interest of the encumbrancer or owner arises before the goods become fixtures, the security interest is perfected by a fixture filing before the goods become fixtures or within ten days thereafter, and the debtor has an interest of record in the real estate or is in possession of the real estate; or

(b) the security interest is perfected by a fixture filing before the interest of the encumbrancer or owner is of record, the security interest has priority over any conflicting interest of a predecessor in title of the encumbrancer or owner, and the debtor has an interest of record in the real estate or is in possession of the real estate; or

(c) the fixtures are readily removable factory or office machines or readily removable replacements of domestic appliances which are consumer goods, and before the goods become fixtures the security interest is perfected by any method permitted by this Article; or

(d) the conflicting interest is a lien on the real estate obtained by legal or equitable proceedings after the security interest was perfected by any method permitted by this Article.

(5) A security interest in fixtures, whether or not perfected, has priority over the conflicting interest of an encumbrancer or owner of the real estate where

(a) the encumbrancer or owner has consented in writing

to the security interest or has disclaimed an interest in the goods as fixtures; or

(b) the debtor has a right to remove the goods as against the encumbrancer or owner. If the debtor's right terminates, the priority of the security interest continues for a reasonable time.

(6) Notwithstanding paragraph (a) of subsection (4) but otherwise subject to subsections (4) and (5), a security interest in fixtures is subordinate to a construction mortgage recorded before the goods become fixtures if the goods become fixtures before the completion of the construction. To the extent that it is given to refinance a construction mortgage, a mortgage has this priority to the same extent as the construction mortgage.

(7) In cases not within the preceding subsections, a security interest in fixtures is subordinate to the conflicting interest of an encumbrancer or owner of the related real estate who is not the debtor.

(8) When the secured party has priority over all owners and encumbrancers of the real estate, he may, on default, subject to the provisions of Part 5, remove his collateral from the real estate but he must reimburse any encumbrancer or owner of the real estate who is not the debtor and who has not otherwise agreed for the cost of repair of any physical injury, but not for any diminution in value of the real estate caused by the absence of the goods removed or by any necessity of replacing them. A person entitled to reimbursement may refuse permission to remove until the secured party gives adequate security for the performance of this obligation.

As amended in 1972.

§ 9-314. Accessions.

(1) A security interest in goods which attaches before they are installed in or affixed to other goods takes priority as to the goods installed or affixed (called in this section "accessions") over the claims of all persons to the whole except as stated in subsection (3) and subject to Section 9-315(1).

(2) A security interest which attaches to goods after they become part of a whole is valid against all persons subsequently acquiring interests in the whole except as stated in subsection (3) but is invalid against any person with an interest in the whole at the time the security interest attaches to the goods who has not in writing consented to the security interest or disclaimed an interest in the goods as part of the whole.

(3) The security interests described in subsections (1) and (2) do not take priority over

(a) a subsequent purchaser for value of any interest in the whole; or

(b) a creditor with a lien on the whole subsequently obtained by judicial proceedings; or

(c) a creditor with a prior perfected security interest in the whole to the extent that he makes subsequent advances

if the subsequent purchase is made, the lien by judicial proceedings obtained or the subsequent advance under the prior perfected security interest is made or contracted for without knowledge of the security interest and before it is perfected. A purchaser of the whole at a foreclosure sale other than the holder of a perfected security interest purchasing at his own foreclosure sale is a subsequent purchaser within this section.

(4) When under subsections (1) or (2) and (3) a secured party has an interest in accessions which has priority over the claims of all persons who have interests in the whole, he may on default subject to the provisions of Part 5 remove his collateral from the whole but he must reimburse any encumbrancer or owner of the whole who is not the debtor and who has not otherwise agreed for the cost of repair of any physical injury but not for any diminution in value of the whole caused by the absence of the goods removed or by any necessity for replacing them. A person entitled to reimbursement may refuse permission to remove until the secured party gives adequate security for the performance of this obligation.

§ 9-315. Priority When Goods Are Commingled or Processed.

(1) If a security interest in goods was perfected and subsequently the goods or a part thereof have become part of a product or mass, the security interest continues in the product or mass if

(a) the goods are so manufactured, processed, assembled or commingled that their identity is lost in the product or mass; or

(b) a financing statement covering the original goods also covers the product into which the goods have been manufactured, processed or assembled.

In a case to which paragraph (b) applies, no separate security interest in that part of the original goods which has been manufactured, processed or assembled into the product may be claimed under Section 9-314.

(2) When under subsection (1) more than one security interest attaches to the product or mass, they rank equally according to the ratio that the cost of the goods to which each interest originally attached bears to the cost of the total product or mass.

§ 9-316. Priority Subject to Subordination. Nothing in this Article prevents subordination by agreement by any person entitled to priority.

§ 9-317. Secured Party Not Obligated on Contract of Debtor. The mere existence of a security interest or authority given to the debtor to dispose of or use collateral does not impose contract or tort liability upon the secured party for the debtor's acts or omissions.

§ 9-318. Defenses Against Assignee; Modification of Contract After Notification of Assignment; Term Prohibiting Assignment Ineffective; Identification and Proof of Assignment.

(1) Unless an account debtor has made an enforceable agreement not to assert defenses or claims arising out of a sale as provided in Section 9-206 the rights of an assignee are subject to

(a) all the terms of the contract between the account debtor and assignor and any defense or claim arising therefrom; and

(b) any other defense or claim of the account debtor against the assignor which accrues before the account debtor receives notification of the assignment.

(2) So far as the right to payment or a part thereof under an assigned contract has not been fully earned by performance, and notwithstanding notification of the assignment, any modification of or substitution for the contract made in good faith and in accordance with reasonable commercial standards is effective against an assignee unless the account debtor has otherwise agreed but the assignee acquires corresponding rights under the modified or substituted contract. The assignment may provide that such modification or substitution is a breach by the assignor.

(3) The account debtor is authorized to pay the assignor until the account debtor receives notification that the amount due or to become due has been assigned and that payment is to be made to the assignee. A notification which does not reasonably identify the rights assigned is ineffective. If requested by the account debtor, the assignee must seasonably furnish reasonable proof that the assignment has been made and unless he does so the account debtor may pay the assignor.

(4) A term in any contract between an account debtor and an assignor is ineffective if it prohibits assignment of an account or prohibits creation of a security interest in a general intangible for money due or to become due or requires the account debtor's consent to such assignment or security interest.

As amended in 1972.

Part 4   Filing

§ 9-401. Place of Filing; Erroneous Filing; Removal of Collateral.

First Alternative Subsection (1)

(1) The proper place to file in order to perfect a security interest is as follows:

(a) when the collateral is timber to be cut or is minerals or the like (including oil and gas) or accounts subject to subsection (5) of Section 9-103, or when the financing statement is filed as a fixture filing (Section 9-313) and the collateral is goods which are or are to become fixtures, then in the office where a mortgage on the real estate would be filed or recorded;

(b) in all other cases, in the office of the [Secretary of State].

Second Alternative Subsection (1)

(1) The proper place to file in order to perfect a security interest is as follows:

(a) when the collateral is equipment used in farming operations, or farm products, or accounts or general intangibles arising from or relating to the sale of farm products by a farmer, or consumer goods, then in the office of the _____ in the county of the debtor's residence or if the debtor is not a resident of this state then in the office of the _____ in the county where the goods are kept, and in addition when the collateral is crops growing or to be grown in the office of the _____ in the county where the land is located;

(b) when the collateral is timber to be cut or is minerals or the like (including oil and gas) or accounts subject to subsection (5) of Section 9-103, or when the financing statement is filed as a fixture filing (Section 9-313) and the collateral is goods which are or are to become fixtures, then in the office where a mortgage on the real estate would be filed or recorded;

(c) in all other cases, in the office of the [Secretary of State].

Third Alternative Subsection (1)

(1) The proper place to file in order to perfect a security interest is as follows:

(a) when the collateral is equipment used in farming operations, or farm products, or accounts or general intangibles arising from or relating to the sale of farm products by a farmer, or consumer goods, then in the office of the _____ in the county of the debtor's residence or if the debtor is not a resident of this state then in the office of the _____ in the county where the goods are kept, and in addition when the collateral is crops growing or to be grown in the office of the _____ in the county where the land is located;

(b) when the collateral is timber to be cut or is minerals or the like (including oil and gas) or accounts subject to subsection (5) of Section 9-103, or when the financing statement is filed as a fixture filing (Section 9-313) and the collateral is goods which are or are to become fixtures, then in the office where a mortgage on the real estate would be filed or recorded;

(c) in all other cases, in the office of the [Secretary of State] and in addition, if the debtor has a place of business in only one county of this state, also in the office of _____ of such county, or, if the debtor has no place of business in this state, but resides in the state, also in the office of _____ of the county in which he resides.

Note: *One of the three alternatives should be selected as subsection (1).*

(2) A filing which is made in good faith in an improper place or not in all of the places required by this section is nevertheless effective with regard to any collateral as to which the filing complied with the requirements of this Article and is also effective with regard to collateral covered by the financing statement against any person who has knowledge of the contents of such financing statement.

(3) A filing which is made in the proper place in this state continues effective even though the debtor's residence or place of business or the location of the collateral or its use, whichever controlled the original filing, is thereafter changed.

Alternative Subsection (3)

[(3) A filing which is made in the proper county continues effective for four months after a change to another county of the debtor's residence or place of business or the location of the collateral, whichever controlled the original filing. It becomes ineffective thereafter unless a copy of the financing statement signed by the secured party is filed in the new county within said period. The security interest may also be perfected in the new county after the expiration of the four-month period; in such case perfection dates from the time of perfection in the new county. A change in the use of the collateral does not impair the effectiveness of the original filing.]

(4) The rules stated in Section 9-103 determine whether filing is necessary in this state.

(5) Notwithstanding the preceding subsections, and subject to subsection (3) of Section 9-302, the proper place to file in order to perfect a security interest in collateral, including fixtures, of a transmitting utility is the office of the [Secretary of State]. This filing constitutes a fixture filing (Section 9-313) as to the collateral described therein which is or is to become fixtures.

(6) For the purposes of this section, the residence of an organization is its place of business if it has one or its chief executive office if it has more than one place of business.

Note: *Subsection (6) should be used only if the state chooses the Second or Third Alternative Subsection (1).*

As amended in 1962 and 1972.

§ 9-402. Formal Requisites of Financing Statement; Amendments; Mortgage as Financing Statement.

(1) A financing statement is sufficient if it gives the names of the debtor and the secured party, is signed by the debtor, gives an address of the secured party from which information concerning the security interest may be obtained, gives a mailing address of the debtor and contains a statement indicating the types, or describing the items, of collateral. A financing statement may be filed before a security agreement is made or a security interest otherwise attaches. When the financing statement covers crops growing or to be grown, the statement must also contain a description of the real estate concerned. When the financing statement covers timber to be cut or covers minerals or the like (including oil and gas) or accounts subject to subsection (5) of Section 9-103, or when the financing statement is filed as a fixture filing (Section 9-313) and the collateral is goods which are or are to become fixtures, the statement must also comply with subsection (5). A copy of the security agreement is sufficient as a financing statement if it contains the above information and is signed by the debtor. A carbon, photographic or other reproduction of a security agreement or a financing statement is sufficient as a financing statement if the security agreement so provides or if the original has been filed in this state.

(2) A financing statement which otherwise complies with subsection (1) is sufficient when it is signed by the secured party instead of the debtor if it is filed to perfect a security interest in

(a) collateral already subject to a security interest in another jurisdiction when it is brought into this state, or when the debtor's location is changed to this state. Such a financing statement must state that the collateral was brought into this state or that the debtor's location was changed to this state under such circumstances; or

(b) proceeds under Section 9-306 if the security interest in the original collateral was perfected. Such a financing statement must describe the original collateral; or

(c) collateral as to which the filing has lapsed; or

(d) collateral acquired after a change of name, identity or corporate structure of the debtor (subsection (7)).

(3) A form substantially as follows is sufficient to comply with subsection (1):

Name of debtor (or assignor) _____

Address _____

Name of secured party (or assignee) _____
Address _____

1. This financing statement covers the following types (or items) of property:

   (Describe) _____

2. (If collateral is crops) The above described crops are growing or are to be grown on:

   (Describe Real Estate) _____

3. (If applicable) The above goods are to become fixtures on

   (Describe Real Estate) _____ and this financing statement is to be filed [for record] in the real estate records. (If the debtor does not have an interest of record) The name of a record owner is

   _____

4. (If products of collateral are claimed) Products of the collateral are also covered.

   (use   . . . .
   whichever   Signature of Debtor (or Assignor)
   is   . . . .
   applicable)   Signature of Secured Party (or Assignee)

(4) A financing statement may be amended by filing a writing signed by both the debtor and the secured party. An amendment does not extend the period of effectiveness of a financing statement. If any amendment adds collateral, it is effective as to the added collateral only from the filing date of the amendment. In this Article, unless the context otherwise requires, the term "financing statement" means the original financing statement and any amendments.

(5) A financing statement covering timber to be cut or covering minerals or the like (including oil and gas) or accounts subject to subsection (5) of Section 9-103, or a financing statement filed as a fixture filing (Section 9-313) where the debtor is not a transmitting utility, must show that it covers this type of collateral, must recite that it is to be filed [for record] in the real estate records, and the financing statement must contain a description of the real estate [sufficient if it were contained in a mortgage of the real estate to give constructive notice of the mortgage under the law of this state]. If the debtor does not have an interest of record in the real estate, the financing statement must show the name of a record owner.

(6) A mortgage is effective as a financing statement filed as a fixture filing from the date of its recording if

   (a) the goods are described in the mortgage by item or type; and
   (b) the goods are or are to become fixtures related to the real estate described in the mortgage; and
   (c) the mortgage complies with the requirements for a financing statement in this section other than a recital that it is to be filed in the real estate records; and
   (d) the mortgage is duly recorded.

No fee with reference to the financing statement is required other than the regular recording and satisfaction fees with respect to the mortgage.

(7) A financing statement sufficiently shows the name of the debtor if it gives the individual, partnership or corporate name of the debtor, whether or not it adds other trade names

or names of partners. Where the debtor so changes his name or in the case of an organization its name, identity or corporate structure that a filed financing statement becomes seriously misleading, the filing is not effective to perfect a security interest in collateral acquired by the debtor more than four months after the change, unless a new appropriate financing statement is filed before the expiration of that time. A filed financing statement remains effective with respect to collateral transferred by the debtor even though the secured party knows of or consents to the transfer.

(8) A financing statement substantially complying with the requirements of this section is effective even though it contains minor errors which are not seriously misleading.

Note: *Language in brackets is optional.*

Note: *Where the state has any special recording system for real estate other than the usual grantor-grantee index (as, for instance, a tract system or a title registration or Torrens system) local adaptations of subsection (5) and Section 9-403(7) may be necessary. See Mass.Gen.Laws Chapter 106, Section 9-409.*

As amended in 1972.

§ 9-403. What Constitutes Filing; Duration of Filing; Effect of Lapsed Filing; Duties of Filing Officer.

(1) Presentation for filing of a financing statement and tender of the filing fee or acceptance of the statement by the filing officer constitutes filing under this Article.

(2) Except as provided in subsection (6) a filed financing statement is effective for a period of five years from the date of filing. The effectiveness of a filed financing statement lapses on the expiration of the five year period unless a continuation statement is filed prior to the lapse. If a security interest perfected by filing exists at the time insolvency proceedings are commenced by or against the debtor, the security interest remains perfected until termination of the insolvency proceedings and thereafter for a period of sixty days or until expiration of the five year period, whichever occurs later. Upon lapse the security interest becomes unperfected, unless it is perfected without filing. If the security interest becomes unperfected upon lapse, it is deemed to have been unperfected as against a person who became a purchaser or lien creditor before lapse.

(3) A continuation statement may be filed by the secured party within six months prior to the expiration of the five year period specified in subsection (2). Any such continuation statement must be signed by the secured party, identify the original statement by file number and state that the original statement is still effective. A continuation statement signed by a person other than the secured party of record must be accompanied by a separate written statement of assignment signed by the secured party of record and complying with subsection (2) of Section 9-405, including payment of the required fee. Upon timely filing of the continuation statement, the effectiveness of the original statement is continued for five years after the last date to which the filing was effective whereupon it lapses in the same manner as provided in subsection (2) unless another continuation statement is filed prior to such lapse. Succeeding continuation statements may be filed in the same manner to continue the effectiveness of the original statement. Unless a statute on disposition of public records provides otherwise, the filing officer may re-

move a lapsed statement from the files and destroy it immediately if he has retained a microfilm or other photographic record, or in other cases after one year after the lapse. The filing officer shall so arrange matters by physical annexation of financing statements to continuation statements or other related filings, or by other means, that if he physically destroys the financing statements of a period more than five years past, those which have been continued by a continuation statement or which are still effective under subsection (6) shall be retained.

(4) Except as provided in subsection (7) a filing officer shall mark each statement with a file number and with the date and hour of filing and shall hold the statement or a microfilm or other photographic copy thereof for public inspection. In addition the filing officer shall index the statement according to the name of the debtor and shall note in the index the file number and the address of the debtor given in the statement.

(5) The uniform fee for filing and indexing and for stamping a copy furnished by the secured party to show the date and place of filing for an original financing statement or for a continuation statement shall be $_____ if the statement is in the standard form prescribed by the [Secretary of State] and otherwise shall be $_____ , plus in each case, if the financing statement is subject to subsection (5) of Section 9-402, $_____ . The uniform fee for each name more than one required to be indexed shall be $_____ . The secured party may at his option show a trade name for any person and an extra uniform indexing fee of $_____ shall be paid with respect thereto.

(6) If the debtor is a transmitting utility (subsection (5) of Section 9-401) and a filed financing statement so states, it is effective until a termination statement is filed. A real estate mortgage which is effective as a fixture filing under subsection (6) of Section 9-402 remains effective as a fixture filing until the mortgage is released or satisfied of record or its effectiveness otherwise terminates as to the real estate.

(7) When a financing statement covers timber to be cut or covers minerals or the like (including oil and gas) or accounts subject to subsection (5) of Section 9-103, or is filed as a fixture filing, [it shall be filed for record and] the filing officer shall index it under the names of the debtor and any owner of record shown on the financing statement in the same fashion as if they were the mortgagors in a mortgage of the real estate described, and, to the extent that the law of this state provides for indexing of mortgages under the name of the mortgagee, under the name of the secured party as if he were the mortgagee thereunder, or where indexing is by description in the same fashion as if the financing statement were a mortgage of the real estate described.

Note: *In states in which writings will not appear in the real estate records and indices unless actually recorded the bracketed language in subsection (7) should be used.*

As amended in 1972.

§ 9-404. Termination Statement.

(1) If a financing statement covering consumer goods is filed on or after _____ , then within one month or within ten days following written demand by the debtor after there is no outstanding secured obligation and no commitment to make advances, incur obligations or otherwise give value, the secured party must file with each filing officer with whom the financing statement was filed, a termination statement to the effect that he no longer claims a security interest under the financing statement, which shall be identified by file number. In other cases whenever there is no outstanding secured obligation and no commitment to make advances, incur obligations or otherwise give value, the secured party must on written demand by the debtor send the debtor, for each filing officer with whom the financing statement was filed, a termination statement to the effect that he no longer claims a security interest under the financing statement, which shall be identified by file number. A termination statement signed by a person other than the secured party of record must be accompanied by a separate written statement of assignment signed by the secured party of record complying with subsection (2) of Section 9-405, including payment of the required fee. If the affected secured party fails to file such a termination statement as required by this subsection, or to send such a termination statement within ten days after proper demand therefor, he shall be liable to the debtor for one hundred dollars, and in addition for any loss caused to the debtor by such failure.

(2) On presentation to the filing officer of such a termination statement he must note it in the index. If he has received the termination statement in duplicate, he shall return one copy of the termination statement to the secured party stamped to show the time of receipt thereof. If the filing officer has a microfilm or other photographic record of the financing statement, and of any related continuation statement, statement of assignment and statement of release, he may remove the originals from the files at any time after receipt of the termination statement, or if he has no such record, he may remove them from the files at any time after one year after receipt of the termination statement.

(3) If the termination statement is in the standard form prescribed by the [Secretary of State], the uniform fee for filing and indexing the termination statement shall be $_____ , and otherwise shall be $_____ , plus in each case an additional fee of $_____ for each name more than one against which the termination statement is required to be indexed.

Note: *The date to be inserted should be the effective date of the revised Article 9.*

As amended in 1972.

§ 9-405. Assignment of Security Interest; Duties of Filing Officer; Fees.

(1) A financing statement may disclose an assignment of a security interest in the collateral described in the financing statement by indication in the financing statement of the name and address of the assignee or by an assignment itself or a copy thereof on the face or back of the statement. On presentation to the filing officer of such a financing statement the filing officer shall mark the same as provided in Section 9-403(4). The uniform fee for filing, indexing and furnishing filing data for a financing statement so indicating an assignment shall be $_____ if the statement is in the standard form prescribed by the [Secretary of State] and otherwise shall be $_____ , plus in each case an additional fee of

$_____ for each name more than one against which the financing statement is required to be indexed.

(2) A secured party may assign of record all or part of his rights under a financing statement by the filing in the place where the original financing statement was filed of a separate written statement of assignment signed by the secured party of record and setting forth the name of the secured party of record and the debtor, the file number and the date of filing of the financing statement and the name and address of the assignee and containing a description of the collateral assigned. A copy of the assignment is sufficient as a separate statement if it complies with the preceding sentence. On presentation to the filing officer of such a separate statement, the filing officer shall mark such separate statement with the date and hour of the filing. He shall note the assignment on the index of the financing statement, or in the case of a fixture filing, or a filing covering timber to be cut, or covering minerals or the like (including oil and gas) or accounts subject to subsection (5) of Section 9-103, he shall index the assignment under the name of the assignor as grantor and, to the extent that the law of this state provides for indexing the assignment of a mortgage under the name of the assignee, he shall index the assignment of the financing statement under the name of the assignee. The uniform fee for filing, indexing and furnishing filing data about such a separate statement of assignment shall be $_____ if the statement is in the standard form prescribed by the [Secretary of State] and otherwise shall be $_____ , plus in each case an additional fee of $_____ for each name more than one against which the statement of assignment is required to be indexed. Notwithstanding the provisions of this subsection, an assignment of record of a security interest in a fixture contained in a mortgage effective as a fixture filing (subsection (6) of Section 9-402) may be made only by an assignment of the mortgage in the manner provided by the law of this state other than this Act.

(3) After the disclosure or filing of an assignment under this section, the assignee is the secured party of record.

As amended in 1972.

§ 9-406. Release of Collateral; Duties of Filing Officer; Fees.

A secured party of record may by his signed statement release all or a part of any collateral described in a filed financing statement. The statement of release is sufficient if it contains a description of the collateral being released, the name and address of the debtor, the name and address of the secured party, and the file number of the financing statement. A statement of release signed by a person other than the secured party of record must be accompanied by a separate written statement of assignment signed by the secured party of record and complying with subsection (2) of Section 9-405, including payment of the required fee. Upon presentation of such a statement of release to the filing officer he shall mark the statement with the hour and date of filing and shall note the same upon the margin of the index of the filing of the financing statement. The uniform fee for filing and noting such a statement of release shall be $_____ if the statement is in the standard form prescribed by the [Secre-

tary of State] and otherwise shall be $_____ , plus in each case an additional fee of $_____ for each name more than one against which the statement of release is required to be indexed.

As amended in 1972.

§ 9-407. Information From Filing Officer.

[(1) If the person filing any financing statement, termination statement, statement of assignment, or statement of release, furnishes the filing officer a copy thereof, the filing officer shall upon request note upon the copy the file number and date and hour of the filing of the original and deliver or send the copy to such person.]

[(2) Upon request of any person, the filing officer shall issue his certificate showing whether there is on file on the date and hour stated therein, any presently effective financing statement naming a particular debtor and any statement of assignment thereof and if there is, giving the date and hour of filing of each such statement and the names and addresses of each secured party therein. The uniform fee for such a certificate shall be $_____ if the request for the certificate is in the standard form prescribed by the [Secretary of State] and otherwise shall be $_____ . Upon request the filing officer shall furnish a copy of any filed financing statement or statement of assignment for a uniform fee of $_____ per page.]

Note: *This section is proposed as an optional provision to require filing officers to furnish certificates. Local law and practices should be consulted with regard to the advisability of adoption.*

As amended in 1972.

§ 9-408. Financing Statements Covering Consigned or Leased Goods.
A consignor or lessor of goods may file a financing statement using the terms "consignor," "consignee," "lessor," "lessee" or the like instead of the terms specified in Section 9-402. The provisions of this Part shall apply as appropriate to such a financing statement but its filing shall not of itself be a factor in determining whether or not the consignment or lease is intended as security (Section 1-201(37)). However, if it is determined for other reasons that the consignment or lease is so intended, a security interest of the consignor or lessor which attaches to the consigned or leased goods is perfected by such filing.

As added in 1972.

Part 5 Default

§ 9-501. Default; Procedure When Security Agreement Covers Both Real and Personal Property.

(1) When a debtor is in default under a security agreement, a secured party has the rights and remedies provided in this Part and except as limited by subsection (3) those provided in the security agreement. He may reduce his claim to judgment, foreclose or otherwise enforce the security interest by any available judicial procedure. If the collateral is documents the secured party may proceed either as to the documents or as to the goods covered thereby. A secured party in possession has the rights, remedies and duties provided in Section 9-207. The rights and remedies referred to in this subsection are cumulative.

(2) After default, the debtor has the rights and remedies provided in this Part, those provided in the security agreement and those provided in Section 9-207.

(3) To the extent that they give rights to the debtor and impose duties on the secured party, the rules stated in the subsections referred to below may not be waived or varied except as provided with respect to compulsory disposition of collateral (subsection (3) of Section 9-504 and Section 9-505) and with respect to redemption of collateral (Section 9-506) but the parties may by agreement determine the standards by which the fulfillment of these rights and duties is to be measured if such standards are not manifestly unreasonable:

    (a) subsection (2) of Section 9-502 and subsection (2) of Section 9-504 insofar as they require accounting for surplus proceeds of collateral;

    (b) subsection (3) of Section 9-504 and subsection (1) of Section 9-505 which deal with disposition of collateral;

    (c) subsection (2) of Section 9-505 which deals with acceptance of collateral as discharge of obligation;

    (d) Section 9-506 which deals with redemption of collateral; and

    (e) subsection (1) of Section 9-507 which deals with the secured party's liability for failure to comply with this Part.

(4) If the security agreement covers both real and personal property, the secured party may proceed under this Part as to the personal property or he may proceed as to both the real and the personal property in accordance with his rights and remedies in respect of the real property in which case the provisions of this Part do not apply.

(5) When a secured party has reduced his claim to judgment the lien of any levy which may be made upon his collateral by virtue of any execution based upon the judgment shall relate back to the date of the perfection of the security interest in such collateral. A judicial sale, pursuant to such execution, is a foreclosure of the security interest by judicial procedure within the meaning of this section, and the secured party may purchase at the sale and thereafter hold the collateral free of any other requirements of this Article.

As amended in 1972.

§ 9-502. Collection Rights of Secured Party.

(1) When so agreed and in any event on default the secured party is entitled to notify an account debtor or the obligor on an instrument to make payment to him whether or not the assignor was theretofore making collections on the collateral, and also to take control of any proceeds to which he is entitled under Section 9-306.

(2) A secured party who by agreement is entitled to charge back uncollected collateral or otherwise to full or limited recourse against the debtor and who undertakes to collect from the account debtors or obligors must proceed in a commercially reasonable manner and may deduct his reasonable expenses of realization from the collections. If the security agreement secures an indebtedness, the secured party must account to the debtor for any surplus, and unless otherwise agreed, the debtor is liable for any deficiency. But, if the underlying transaction was a sale of accounts or chattel paper, the debtor is entitled to any surplus or is liable for any deficiency only if the security agreement so provides.

As amended in 1972.

§ 9-503. Secured Party's Right to Take Possession After Default.
Unless otherwise agreed a secured party has on default the right to take possession of the collateral. In taking possession a secured party may proceed without judicial process if this can be done without breach of the peace or may proceed by action. If the security agreement so provides the secured party may require the debtor to assemble the collateral and make it available to the secured party at a place to be designated by the secured party which is reasonably convenient to both parties. Without removal a secured party may render equipment unusable, and may dispose of collateral on the debtor's premises under Section 9-504.

§ 9-504. Secured Party's Right to Dispose of Collateral After Default; Effect of Disposition.

(1) A secured party after default may sell, lease or otherwise dispose of any or all of the collateral in its then condition or following any commercially reasonable preparation or processing. Any sale of goods is subject to the Article on Sales (Article 2). The proceeds of disposition shall be applied in the order following to

    (a) the reasonable expenses of retaking, holding, preparing for sale or lease, selling, leasing and the like and, to the extent provided for in the agreement and not prohibited by law, the reasonable attorneys' fees and legal expenses incurred by the secured party;

    (b) the satisfaction of indebtedness secured by the security interest under which the disposition is made;

    (c) the satisfaction of indebtedness secured by any subordinate security interest in the collateral if written notification of demand therefor is received before distribution of the proceeds is completed. If requested by the secured party, the holder of a subordinate security interest must seasonably furnish reasonable proof of his interest, and unless he does so, the secured party need not comply with his demand.

(2) If the security interest secures an indebtedness, the secured party must account to the debtor for any surplus, and, unless otherwise agreed, the debtor is liable for any deficiency. But if the underlying transaction was a sale of accounts or chattel paper, the debtor is entitled to any surplus or is liable for any deficiency only if the security agreement so provides.

(3) Disposition of the collateral may be by public or private proceedings and may be made by way of one or more contracts. Sale or other disposition may be as a unit or in parcels and at any time and place and on any terms but every aspect of the disposition including the method, manner, time, place and terms must be commercially reasonable. Unless collateral is perishable or threatens to decline speedily in value or is of a type customarily sold on a recognized market, reasonable notification of the time and place of any public sale or reasonable notification of the time after which any private sale or other intended disposition is to be made shall be sent by the secured party to the debtor, if he has not signed after default a statement renouncing or modifying his right to notification of sale. In the case of consumer goods no other notification need be sent. In other cases notification shall be sent to any other secured party from whom the secured party has received (before sending his notification to the debtor or

before the debtor's renunciation of his rights) written notice of a claim of an interest in the collateral. The secured party may buy at any public sale and if the collateral is of a type customarily sold in a recognized market or is of a type which is the subject of widely distributed standard price quotations he may buy at private sale.

(4) When collateral is disposed of by a secured party after default, the disposition transfers to a purchaser for value all of the debtor's rights therein, discharges the security interest under which it is made and any security interest or lien subordinate thereto. The purchaser takes free of all such rights and interests even though the secured party fails to comply with the requirements of this Part or of any judicial proceedings

   (a) in the case of a public sale, if the purchaser has no knowledge of any defects in the sale and if he does not buy in collusion with the secured party, other bidders or the person conducting the sale; or
   (b) in any other case, if the purchaser acts in good faith.

(5) A person who is liable to a secured party under a guaranty, indorsement, repurchase agreement or the like and who receives a transfer of collateral from the secured party or is subrogated to his rights has thereafter the rights and duties of the secured party. Such a transfer of collateral is not a sale or disposition of the collateral under this Article.

As amended in 1972.

§ 9-505. Compulsory Disposition of Collateral; Acceptance of the Collateral as Discharge of Obligation.

(1) If the debtor has paid sixty per cent of the cash price in the case of a purchase money security interest in consumer goods or sixty per cent of the loan in the case of another security interest in consumer goods, and has not signed after default a statement renouncing or modifying his rights under this Part a secured party who has taken possession of collateral must dispose of it under Section 9-504 and if he fails to do so within ninety days after he takes possession the debtor at his option may recover in conversion or under Section 9-507(1) on secured party's liability.

(2) In any other case involving consumer goods or any other collateral a secured party in possession may, after default, propose to retain the collateral in satisfaction of the obligation. Written notice of such proposal shall be sent to the debtor if he has not signed after default a statement renouncing or modifying his rights under this subsection. In the case of consumer goods no other notice need be given. In other cases notice shall be sent to any other secured party from whom the secured party has received (before sending his notice to the debtor or before the debtor's renunciation of his rights) written notice of a claim of an interest in the collateral. If the secured party receives objection in writing from a person entitled to receive notification within twenty-one days after the notice was sent, the secured party must dispose of the collateral under Section 9-504. In the absence of such written objection the secured party may retain the collateral in satisfaction of the debtor's obligation.

As amended in 1972.

§ 9-506. Debtor's Right to Redeem Collateral. At any time before the secured party has disposed of collateral or entered into a contract for its disposition under Section 9-504 or before the obligation has been discharged under Section 9-505(2) the debtor or any other secured party may unless otherwise agreed in writing after default redeem the collateral by tendering fulfillment of all obligations secured by the collateral as well as the expenses reasonably incurred by the secured party in retaking, holding and preparing the collateral for disposition, in arranging for the sale, and to the extent provided in the agreement and not prohibited by law, his reasonable attorneys' fees and legal expenses.

§ 9-507. Secured Party's Liability for Failure to Comply With This Part.

(1) If it is established that the secured party is not proceeding in accordance with the provisions of this Part disposition may be ordered or restrained on appropriate terms and conditions. If the disposition has occurred the debtor or any person entitled to notification or whose security interest has been made known to the secured party prior to the disposition has a right to recover from the secured party any loss caused by a failure to comply with the provisions of this Part. If the collateral is consumer goods, the debtor has a right to recover in any event an amount not less than the credit service charge plus ten per cent of the principal amount of the debt or the time price differential plus 10 per cent of the cash price.

(2) The fact that a better price could have been obtained by a sale at a different time or in a different method from that selected by the secured party is not of itself sufficient to establish that the sale was not made in a commercially reasonable manner. If the secured party either sells the collateral in the usual manner in any recognized market therefor or if he sells at the price current in such market at the time of his sale or if he has otherwise sold in conformity with reasonable commercial practices among dealers in the type of property sold he has sold in a commercially reasonable manner. The principles stated in the two preceding sentences with respect to sales also apply as may be appropriate to other types of disposition. A disposition which has been approved in any judicial proceeding or by any bona fide creditors' committee or representative of creditors shall conclusively be deemed to be commercially reasonable, but this sentence does not indicate that any such approval must be obtained in any case nor does it indicate that any disposition not so approved is not commercially reasonable.

B ADDITIONS AND REVISIONS TO THE UNIFORM COMMERCIAL CODE

ARTICLE 2A / Leases

Part 1 General Provisions

§ 2A-101. Short Title.

This Article shall be known and may be cited as the Uniform Commercial Code—Leases.

§ 2A-102. Scope.

This Article applies to any transaction, regardless of form, that creates a lease.

§ 2A-103. Definitions and Index of Definitions.

(1) In this Article unless the context otherwise requires:

(a) "Buyer in ordinary course of business" means a person who in good faith and without knowledge that the sale to him [or her] is in violation of the ownership rights or security interest or leasehold interest of a third party in the goods buys in ordinary course from a person in the business of selling goods of that kind but does not include a pawnbroker. "Buying" may be for cash or by exchange of other property or on secured or unsecured credit and includes receiving goods or documents of title under a pre-existing contract for sale but does not include a transfer in bulk or as security for or in total or partial satisfaction of a money debt.

(b) "Cancellation" occurs when either party puts an end to the lease contract for default by the other party.

(c) "Commercial unit" means such a unit of goods as by commercial usage is a single whole for purposes of lease and division of which materially impairs its character or value on the market or in use. A commercial unit may be a single article, as a machine, or a set of articles, as a suite of furniture or a line of machinery, or a quantity, as a gross or carload, or any other unit treated in use or in the relevant market as a single whole.

(d) "Conforming" goods or performance under a lease contract means goods or performance that are in accordance with the obligations under the lease contract.

(e) "Consumer lease" means a lease that a lessor regularly engaged in the business of leasing or selling makes to a lessee who is an individual and who takes under the lease primarily for a personal, family, or household purpose [, if the total payments to be made under the lease contract, excluding payments for options to renew or buy, do not exceed $_____].

(f) "Fault" means wrongful act, omission, breach, or default.

(g) "Finance lease" means a lease with respect to which:

(i) the lessor does not select, manufacture, or supply the goods;

(ii) the lessor acquires the goods or the right to possession and use of the goods in connection with the lease; and

(iii) one of the following occurs:

(A) the lessee receives a copy of the contract by which the lessor acquired the goods or the right to possession and use of the goods before signing the lease contract;

(B) the lessee's approval of the contract by which the lessor acquired the goods or the right to possession and use of the goods is a condition to effectiveness of the lease contract;

(C) the lessee, before signing the lease contract, receives an accurate and complete statement designating the promises and warranties, and any disclaimers of warranties, limitations or modifications of remedies, or liquidated damages, including those of a third party, such as the manufacturer of the goods, provided to the lessor by the person supplying the goods in connection with or as part of the contract by which the lessor acquired the goods or the right to possession and use of the goods; or

(D) if the lease is not a consumer lease, the lessor, before the lessee signs the lease contract, informs the lessee in writing (a) of the identity of the person supplying the goods to the lessor, unless the lessee has selected that person and directed the lessor to acquire

1104

the goods or the right to possession and use of the goods from that person, (b) that the lessee is entitled under this Article to the promises and warranties, including those of any third party, provided to the lessor by the person supplying the goods in connection with or as part of the contract by which the lessor acquired the goods or the right to possession and use of the goods, and (c) that the lessee may communicate with the person supplying the goods to the lessor and receive an accurate and complete statement of those promises and warranties, including any disclaimers and limitations of them or of remedies.

(h) "Goods" means all things that are movable at the time of identification to the lease contract, or are fixtures (Section 2A-309), but the term does not include money, documents, instruments, accounts, chattel paper, general intangibles, or minerals or the like, including oil and gas, before extraction. The term also includes the unborn young of animals.

(i) "Installment lease contract" means a lease contract that authorizes or requires the delivery of goods in separate lots to be separately accepted, even though the lease contract contains a clause "each delivery is a separate lease" or its equivalent.

(j) "Lease" means a transfer of the right to possession and use of goods for a term in return for consideration, but a sale, including a sale on approval or a sale or return, or retention or creation of a security interest is not a lease. Unless the context clearly indicates otherwise, the term includes a sublease.

(k) "Lease agreement" means the bargain, with respect to the lease, of the lessor and the lessee in fact as found in their language or by implication from other circumstances including course of dealing or usage of trade or course of performance as provided in this Article. Unless the context clearly indicates otherwise, the term includes a sublease agreement.

(l) "Lease contract" means the total legal obligation that results from the lease agreement as affected by this Article and any other applicable rules of law. Unless the context clearly indicates otherwise, the term includes a sublease contract.

(m) "Leasehold interest" means the interest of the lessor or the lessee under a lease contract.

(n) "Lessee" means a person who acquires the right to possession and use of goods under a lease. Unless the context clearly indicates otherwise, the term includes a sublessee.

(o) "Lessee in ordinary course of business" means a person who in good faith and without knowledge that the lease to him [or her] is in violation of the ownership rights or security interest or leasehold interest of a third party in the goods, leases in ordinary course from a person in the business of selling or leasing goods of that kind but does not include a pawnbroker. "Leasing" may be for cash or by exchange of other property or on secured or unsecured credit and includes receiving goods or documents of title under a pre-existing lease contract but does not include a transfer in bulk or as security for or in total or partial satisfaction of a money debt.

(p) "Lessor" means a person who transfers the right to possession and use of goods under a lease. Unless the context clearly indicates otherwise, the term includes a sublessor.

(q) "Lessor's residual interest" means the lessor's interest in the goods after expiration, termination, or cancellation of the lease contract.

(r) "Lien" means a charge against or interest in goods to secure payment of a debt or performance of an obligation, but the term does not include a security interest.

(s) "Lot" means a parcel or a single article that is the subject matter of a separate lease or delivery, whether or not it is sufficient to perform the lease contract.

(t) "Merchant lessee" means a lessee that is a merchant with respect to goods of the kind subject to the lease.

(u) "Present value" means the amount as of a date certain of one or more sums payable in the future, discounted to the date certain. The discount is determined by the interest rate specified by the parties if the rate was not manifestly unreasonable at the time the transaction was entered into; otherwise, the discount is determined by a commercially reasonable rate that takes into account the facts and circumstances of each case at the time the transaction was entered into.

(v) "Purchase" includes taking by sale, lease, mortgage, security interest, pledge, gift, or any other voluntary transaction creating an interest in goods.

(w) "Sublease" means a lease of goods the right to possession and use of which was acquired by the lessor as a lessee under an existing lease.

(x) "Supplier" means a person from whom a lessor buys or leases goods to be leased under a finance lease.

(y) "Supply contract" means a contract under which a lessor buys or leases goods to be leased.

(z) "Termination" occurs when either party pursuant to a power created by agreement or law puts an end to the lease contract otherwise than for default.

(2) Other definitions applying to this Article and the sections in which they appear are:

"Accessions".   Section 2A-310(1).
"Construction mortgage".   Section 2A-309(1)(d).
"Encumbrance".   Section 2A-309(1)(e).
"Fixtures".   Section 2A-309(1)(a).
"Fixture filing".   Section 2A-309(1)(b).
"Purchase money lease".   Section 2A-309(1)(c).

(3) The following definitions in other Articles apply to this Article:

"Account".   Section 9-106.
"Between merchants".   Section 2-104(3).
"Buyer".   Section 2-103(1)(a).
"Chattel paper".   Section 9-105(1)(b).
"Consumer goods".   Section 9-109(1).
"Document".   Section 9-105(1)(f).
"Entrusting".   Section 2-403(3).
"General intangibles".   Section 9-106.
"Good faith".   Section 2-103(1)(b).
"Instrument".   Section 9-105(1)(i).
"Merchant".   Section 2-104(1).
"Mortgage".   Section 9-105(1)(j).

"Pursuant to commitment".   Section 9-105(1)(k).
"Receipt".   Section 2-103(1)(c).
"Sale".   Section 2-106(1).
"Sale on approval".   Section 2-326.
"Sale or return".   Section 2-326.
"Seller".   Section 2-103(1)(d).

(4) In addition Article 1 contains general definitions and principles of construction and interpretation applicable throughout this Article.

§ 2A-104.   Leases Subject to Other Law.

(1) A lease, although subject to this Article, is also subject to any applicable:

(a) certificate of title statute of this State: (list any certificate of title statutes covering automobiles, trailers, mobile homes, boats, farm tractors, and the like);

(b) certificate of title statute of another jurisdiction (Section 2A-105); or

(c) consumer protection statute of this State, or final consumer protection decision of a court of this State existing on the effective date of this Article.

(2) In case of conflict between this Article, other than Sections 2A-105, 2A-304(3), and 2A-305(3), and a statute or decision referred to in subsection (1), the statute or decision controls.

(3) Failure to comply with an applicable law has only the effect specified therein.

§ 2A-105.   Territorial Application of Article to Goods Covered by Certificate of Title.

Subject to the provisions of Sections 2A-304(3) and 2A-305(3), with respect to goods covered by a certificate of title issued under a statute of this State or of another jurisdiction, compliance and the effect of compliance or noncompliance with a certificate of title statute are governed by the law (including the conflict of laws rules) of the jurisdiction issuing the certificate until the earlier of (a) surrender of the certificate, or (b) four months after the goods are removed from that jurisdiction and thereafter until a new certificate of title is issued by another jurisdiction.

§ 2A-106.   Limitation on Power of Parties to Consumer Lease to Choose Applicable Law and Judicial Forum.

(1) If the law chosen by the parties to a consumer lease is that of a jurisdiction other than a jurisdiction in which the lessee resides at the time the lease agreement becomes enforceable or within 30 days thereafter or in which the goods are to be used, the choice is not enforceable.

(2) If the judicial forum chosen by the parties to a consumer lease is a forum that would not otherwise have jurisdiction over the lessee, the choice is not enforceable.

§ 2A-107.   Waiver or Renunciation of Claim or Right After Default.

Any claim or right arising out of an alleged default or breach of warranty may be discharged in whole or in part without consideration by a written waiver or renunciation signed and delivered by the aggrieved party.

§ 2A-108.   Unconscionability.

(1) If the court as a matter of law finds a lease contract or

any clause of a lease contract to have been unconscionable at the time it was made the court may refuse to enforce the lease contract, or it may enforce the remainder of the lease contract without the unconscionable clause, or it may so limit the application of any unconscionable clause as to avoid any unconscionable result.

(2) With respect to a consumer lease, if the court as a matter of law finds that a lease contract or any clause of a lease contract has been induced by unconscionable conduct or that unconscionable conduct has occurred in the collection of a claim arising from a lease contract, the court may grant appropriate relief.

(3) Before making a finding of unconscionability under subsection (1) or (2), the court, on its own motion or that of a party, shall afford the parties a reasonable opportunity to present evidence as to the setting, purpose, and effect of the lease contract or clause thereof, or of the conduct.

(4) In an action in which the lessee claims unconscionability with respect to a consumer lease:

(a) If the court finds unconscionability under subsection (1) or (2), the court shall award reasonable attorney's fees to the lessee.

(b) If the court does not find unconscionability and the lessee claiming unconscionability has brought or maintained an action he [or she] knew to be groundless, the court shall award reasonable attorney's fees to the party against whom the claim is made.

(c) In determining attorney's fees, the amount of the recovery on behalf of the claimant under subsections (1) and (2) is not controlling.

§ 2A-109.   Option to Accelerate at Will.

(1) A term providing that one party or his [or her] successor in interest may accelerate payment or performance or require collateral or additional collateral "at will" or "when he [or she] deems himself [or herself] insecure" or in words of similar import must be construed to mean that he [or she] has power to do so only if he [or she] in good faith believes that the prospect of payment or performance is impaired.

(2) With respect to a consumer lease, the burden of establishing good faith under subsection (1) is on the party who exercised the power; otherwise the burden of establishing lack of good faith is on the party against whom the power has been exercised.

Part 2   Formation and Construction of Lease Contract

§ 2A-201.   Statute of Frauds.

(1) A lease contract is not enforceable by way of action or defense unless:

(a) the total payments to be made under the lease contract, excluding payments for options to renew or buy, are less than $1,000; or

(b) there is a writing, signed by the party against whom enforcement is sought or by that party's authorized agent, sufficient to indicate that a lease contract has been made between the parties and to describe the goods leased and the lease term.

(2) Any description of leased goods or of the lease term is sufficient and satisfies subsection (1)(b), whether or not it is specific, if it reasonably identifies what is described.

(3) A writing is not insufficient because it omits or incorrectly states a term agreed upon, but the lease contract is not enforceable under subsection (1)(b) beyond the lease term and the quantity of goods shown in the writing.

(4) A lease contract that does not satisfy the requirements of subsection (1), but which is valid in other respects, is enforceable:

(a) if the goods are to be specially manufactured or obtained for the lessee and are not suitable for lease or sale to others in the ordinary course of the lessor's business, and the lessor, before notice of repudiation is received and under circumstances that reasonably indicate that the goods are for the lessee, has made either a substantial beginning of their manufacture or commitments for their procurement;

(b) if the party against whom enforcement is sought admits in that party's pleading, testimony or otherwise in court that a lease contract was made, but the lease contract is not enforceable under this provision beyond the quantity of goods admitted; or

(c) with respect to goods that have been received and accepted by the lessee.

(5) The lease term under a lease contract referred to in subsection (4) is:

(a) if there is a writing signed by the party against whom enforcement is sought or by that party's authorized agent specifying the lease term, the term so specified;

(b) if the party against whom enforcement is sought admits in that party's pleading, testimony, or otherwise in court a lease term, the term so admitted; or

(c) a reasonable lease term.

§ 2A-202. Final Written Expression: Parol or Extrinsic Evidence.

Terms with respect to which the confirmatory memoranda of the parties agree or which are otherwise set forth in a writing intended by the parties as a final expression of their agreement with respect to such terms as are included therein may not be contradicted by evidence of any prior agreement or of a contemporaneous oral agreement but may be explained or supplemented:

(a) by course of dealing or usage of trade or by course of performance; and

(b) by evidence of consistent additional terms unless the court finds the writing to have been intended also as a complete and exclusive statement of the terms of the agreement.

§ 2A-203. Seals Inoperative.

The affixing of a seal to a writing evidencing a lease contract or an offer to enter into a lease contract does not render the writing a sealed instrument and the law with respect to sealed instruments does not apply to the lease contract or offer.

§ 2A-204. Formation in General.

(1) A lease contract may be made in any manner sufficient to show agreement, including conduct by both parties which recognizes the existence of a lease contract.

(2) An agreement sufficient to constitute a lease contract may be found although the moment of its making is undetermined.

(3) Although one or more terms are left open, a lease contract does not fail for indefiniteness if the parties have intended to make a lease contract and there is a reasonably certain basis for giving an appropriate remedy.

§ 2A-205. Firm Offers.

An offer by a merchant to lease goods to or from another person in a signed writing that by its terms gives assurance it will be held open is not revocable, for lack of consideration, during the time stated or, if no time is stated, for a reasonable time, but in no event may the period of irrevocability exceed 3 months. Any such term of assurance on a form supplied by the offeree must be separately signed by the offeror.

§ 2A-206. Offer and Acceptance in Formation of Lease Contract.

(1) Unless otherwise unambiguously indicated by the language or circumstances, an offer to make a lease contract must be construed as inviting acceptance in any manner and by any medium reasonable in the circumstances.

(2) If the beginning of a requested performance is a reasonable mode of acceptance, an offeror who is not notified of acceptance within a reasonable time may treat the offer as having lapsed before acceptance.

§ 2A-207. Course of Performance or Practical Construction.

(1) If a lease contract involves repeated occasions for performance by either party with knowledge of the nature of the performance and opportunity for objection to it by the other, any course of performance accepted or acquiesced in without objection is relevant to determine the meaning of the lease agreement.

(2) The express terms of a lease agreement and any course of performance, as well as any course of dealing and usage of trade, must be construed whenever reasonable as consistent with each other; but if that construction is unreasonable, express terms control course of performance, course of performance controls both course of dealing and usage of trade, and course of dealing controls usage of trade.

(3) Subject to the provisions of Section 2A-208 on modification and waiver, course of performance is relevant to show a waiver or modification of any term inconsistent with the course of performance.

§ 2A-208. Modification, Rescission and Waiver.

(1) An agreement modifying a lease contract needs no consideration to be binding.

(2) A signed lease agreement that excludes modification or rescission except by a signed writing may not be otherwise modified or rescinded, but, except as between merchants, such a requirement on a form supplied by a merchant must be separately signed by the other party.

(3) Although an attempt at modification or rescission does not satisfy the requirements of subsection (2), it may operate as a waiver.

(4) A party who has made a waiver affecting an executory portion of a lease contract may retract the waiver by reasonable notification received by the other party that strict per-

formance will be required of any term waived, unless the retraction would be unjust in view of a material change of position in reliance on the waiver.

§ 2A-209. Lessee Under Finance Lease as Beneficiary of Supply Contract.

(1) The benefit of a supplier's promises to the lessor under the supply contract and of all warranties, whether express or implied, including those of any third party provided in connection with or as part of the supply contract, extends to the lessee to the extent of the lessee's leasehold interest under a finance lease related to the supply contract, but is subject to the terms of the warranty and of the supply contract and all defenses or claims arising therefrom.

(2) The extension of the benefit of a supplier's promises and of warranties to the lessee (Section 2A-209(1)) does not: (i) modify the rights and obligations of the parties to the supply contract, whether arising therefrom or otherwise, or (ii) impose any duty or liability under the supply contract on the lessee.

(3) Any modification or rescission of the supply contract by the supplier and the lessor is effective between the supplier and the lessee unless, before the modification or rescission, the supplier has received notice that the lessee has entered into a finance lease related to the supply contract. If the modification or rescission is effective between the supplier and the lessee, the lessor is deemed to have assumed, in addition to the obligations of the lessor to the lessee under the lease contract, promises of the supplier to the lessor and warranties that were so modified or rescinded as they existed and were available to the lessee before modification or rescission.

(4) In addition to the extension of the benefit of the supplier's promises and of warranties to the lessee under subsection (1), the lessee retains all rights that the lessee may have against the supplier which arise from an agreement between the lessee and the supplier or under other law.

§ 2A-210. Express Warranties.

(1) Express warranties by the lessor are created as follows:

(a) Any affirmation of fact or promise made by the lessor to the lessee which relates to the goods and becomes part of the basis of the bargain creates an express warranty that the goods will conform to the affirmation or promise.

(b) Any description of the goods which is made part of the basis of the bargain creates an express warranty that the goods will conform to the description.

(c) Any sample or model that is made part of the basis of the bargain creates an express warranty that the whole of the goods will conform to the sample or model.

(2) It is not necessary to the creation of an express warranty that the lessor use formal words, such as "warrant" or "guarantee," or that the lessor have a specific intention to make a warranty, but an affirmation merely of the value of the goods or a statement purporting to be merely the lessor's opinion or commendation of the goods does not create a warranty.

§ 2A-211. Warranties Against Interference and Against Infringement; Lessee's Obligation Against Infringement.

(1) There is in a lease contract a warranty that for the lease term no person holds a claim to or interest in the goods that arose from an act or omission of the lessor, other than a claim by way of infringement or the like, which will interfere with the lessee's enjoyment of its leasehold interest.

(2) Except in a finance lease there is in a lease contract by a lessor who is a merchant regularly dealing in goods of the kind a warranty that the goods are delivered free of the rightful claim of any person by way of infringement or the like.

(3) A lessee who furnishes specifications to a lessor or a supplier shall hold the lessor and the supplier harmless against any claim by way of infringement or the like that arises out of compliance with the specifications.

§ 2A-212. Implied Warranty of Merchantability.

(1) Except in a finance lease, a warranty that the goods will be merchantable is implied in a lease contract if the lessor is a merchant with respect to goods of that kind.

(2) Goods to be merchantable must be at least such as

(a) pass without objection in the trade under the description in the lease agreement;

(b) in the case of fungible goods, are of fair average quality within the description;

(c) are fit for the ordinary purposes for which goods of that type are used;

(d) run, within the variation permitted by the lease agreement, of even kind, quality, and quantity within each unit and among all units involved;

(e) are adequately contained, packaged, and labeled as the lease agreement may require; and

(f) conform to any promises or affirmations of fact made on the container or label.

(3) Other implied warranties may arise from course of dealing or usage of trade.

§ 2A-213. Implied Warranty of Fitness for Particular Purpose.

Except in a finance lease, if the lessor at the time the lease contract is made has reason to know of any particular purpose for which the goods are required and that the lessee is relying on the lessor's skill or judgment to select or furnish suitable goods, there is in the lease contract an implied warranty that the goods will be fit for that purpose.

§ 2A-214. Exclusion or Modification of Warranties.

(1) Words or conduct relevant to the creation of an express warranty and words or conduct tending to negate or limit a warranty must be construed wherever reasonable as consistent with each other; but, subject to the provisions of Section 2A-202 on parol or extrinsic evidence, negation or limitation is inoperative to the extent that the construction is unreasonable.

(2) Subject to subsection (3), to exclude or modify the implied warranty of merchantability or any part of it the language must mention "merchantability", be by a writing, and be conspicuous. Subject to subsection (3), to exclude or modify any implied warranty of fitness the exclusion must be by a writing and be conspicuous. Language to exclude all implied warranties of fitness is sufficient if it is in writing, is conspicuous and states, for example, "There is no warranty that the goods will be fit for a particular purpose".

(3) Notwithstanding subsection (2), but subject to subsection (4),

(a) unless the circumstances indicate otherwise, all implied warranties are excluded by expressions like "as is," or "with all faults," or by other language that in common understanding calls the lessee's attention to the exclusion of warranties and makes plain that there is no implied warranty, if in writing and conspicuous;

(b) if the lessee before entering into the lease contract has examined the goods or the sample or model as fully as desired or has refused to examine the goods, there is no implied warranty with regard to defects that an examination ought in the circumstances to have revealed; and

(c) an implied warranty may also be excluded or modified by course of dealing, course of performance, or usage of trade.

(4) To exclude or modify a warranty against interference or against infringement (Section 2A-211) or any part of it, the language must be specific, be by a writing, and be conspicuous, unless the circumstances, including course of performance, course of dealing, or usage of trade, give the lessee reason to know that the goods are being leased subject to a claim or interest of any person.

§ 2A-215. Cumulation and Conflict of Warranties Express or Implied.

Warranties, whether express or implied, must be construed as consistent with each other and as cumulative, but if that construction is unreasonable, the intention of the parties determines which warranty is dominant. In ascertaining that intention the following rules apply:

(a) Exact or technical specifications displace an inconsistent sample or model or general language of description.

(b) A sample from an existing bulk displaces inconsistent general language of description.

(c) Express warranties displace inconsistent implied warranties other than an implied warranty of fitness for a particular purpose.

§ 2A-216. Third-Party Beneficiaries of Express and Implied Warranties.

Alternative A

A warranty to or for the benefit of a lessee under this Article, whether express or implied, extends to any natural person who is in the family or household of the lessee or who is a guest in the lessee's home if it is reasonable to expect that such person may use, consume, or be affected by the goods and who is injured in person by breach of the warranty. This section does not displace principles of law and equity that extend a warranty to or for the benefit of a lessee to other persons. The operation of this section may not be excluded, modified, or limited, but an exclusion, modification, or limitation of the warranty, including any with respect to rights and remedies, effective against the lessee is also effective against any beneficiary designated under this section.

Alternative B

A warranty to or for the benefit of a lessee under this Article, whether express or implied, extends to any natural person who may reasonably be expected to use, consume, or be affected by the goods and who is injured in person by breach of the warranty. This section does not displace principles of law

and equity that extend a warranty to or for the benefit of a lessee to other persons. The operation of this section may not be excluded, modified, or limited, but an exclusion, modification, or limitation of the warranty, including any with respect to rights and remedies, effective against the lessee is also effective against the beneficiary designated under this section.

Alternative C

A warranty to or for the benefit of a lessee under this Article, whether express or implied, extends to any person who may reasonably be expected to use, consume, or be affected by the goods and who is injured by breach of the warranty. The operation of this section may not be excluded, modified, or limited with respect to injury to the person of an individual to whom the warranty extends, but an exclusion, modification, or limitation of the warranty, including any with respect to rights and remedies, effective against the lessee is also effective against the beneficiary designated under this section.

§ 2A-217. Identification.

Identification of goods as goods to which a lease contract refers may be made at any time and in any manner explicitly agreed to by the parties. In the absence of explicit agreement, identification occurs:

(a) when the lease contract is made if the lease contract is for a lease of goods that are existing and identified;

(b) when the goods are shipped, marked, or otherwise designated by the lessor as goods to which the lease contract refers, if the lease contract is for a lease of goods that are not existing and identified; or

(c) when the young are conceived, if the lease contract is for a lease of unborn young of animals.

§ 2A-218. Insurance and Proceeds.

(1) A lessee obtains an insurable interest when existing goods are identified to the lease contract even though the goods identified are nonconforming and the lessee has an option to reject them.

(2) If a lessee has an insurable interest only by reason of the lessor's identification of the goods, the lessor, until default or insolvency or notification to the lessee that identification is final, may substitute other goods for those identified.

(3) Notwithstanding a lessee's insurable interest under subsections (1) and (2), the lessor retains an insurable interest until an option to buy has been exercised by the lessee and risk of loss has passed to the lessee.

(4) Nothing in this section impairs any insurable interest recognized under any other statute or rule of law.

(5) The parties by agreement may determine that one or more parties have an obligation to obtain and pay for insurance covering the goods and by agreement may determine the beneficiary of the proceeds of the insurance.

§ 2A-219. Risk of Loss.

(1) Except in the case of a finance lease, risk of loss is retained by the lessor and does not pass to the lessee. In the case of a finance lease, risk of loss passes to the lessee.

(2) Subject to the provisions of this Article on the effect of default on risk of loss (Section 2A-220), if risk of loss is to pass to the lessee and the time of passage is not stated, the following rules apply:

(a) If the lease contract requires or authorizes the goods to be shipped by carrier

(i) and it does not require delivery at a particular destination, the risk of loss passes to the lessee when the goods are duly delivered to the carrier; but

(ii) if it does require delivery at a particular destination and the goods are there duly tendered while in the possession of the carrier, the risk of loss passes to the lessee when the goods are there duly so tendered as to enable the lessee to take delivery.

(b) If the goods are held by a bailee to be delivered without being moved, the risk of loss passes to the lessee on acknowledgment by the bailee of the lessee's right to possession of the goods.

(c) In any case not within subsection (a) or (b), the risk of loss passes to the lessee on the lessee's receipt of the goods if the lessor, or, in the case of a finance lease, the supplier, is a merchant; otherwise the risk passes to the lessee on tender of delivery.

§ 2A-220. Effect of Default on Risk of Loss.

(1) Where risk of loss is to pass to the lessee and the time of passage is not stated:

(a) If a tender or delivery of goods so fails to conform to the lease contract as to give a right of rejection, the risk of their loss remains with the lessor, or, in the case of a finance lease, the supplier, until cure or acceptance.

(b) If the lessee rightfully revokes acceptance, he [or she], to the extent of any deficiency in his [or her] effective insurance coverage, may treat the risk of loss as having remained with the lessor from the beginning.

(2) Whether or not risk of loss is to pass to the lessee, if the lessee as to conforming goods already identified to a lease contract repudiates or is otherwise in default under the lease contract, the lessor, or, in the case of a finance lease, the supplier, to the extent of any deficiency in his [or her] effective insurance coverage may treat the risk of loss as resting on the lessee for a commercially reasonable time.

§ 2A-221. Casualty to Identified Goods.

If a lease contract requires goods identified when the lease contract is made, and the goods suffer casualty without fault of the lessee, the lessor or the supplier before delivery, or the goods suffer casualty before risk of loss passes to the lessee pursuant to the lease agreement or Section 2A-219, then:

(a) if the loss is total, the lease contract is avoided; and

(b) if the loss is partial or the goods have so deteriorated as to no longer conform to the lease contract, the lessee may nevertheless demand inspection and at his [or her] option either treat the lease contract as avoided or, except in a finance lease that is not a consumer lease, accept the goods with due allowance from the rent payable for the balance of the lease term for the deterioration or the deficiency in quantity but without further right against the lessor.

Part 3 Effect of Lease Contract

§ 2A-301. Enforceability of Lease Contract.

Except as otherwise provided in this Article, a lease contract is effective and enforceable according to its terms between the parties, against purchasers of the goods and against creditors of the parties.

§ 2A-302. Title to and Possession of Goods.

Except as otherwise provided in this Article, each provision of this Article applies whether the lessor or a third party has title to the goods, and whether the lessor, the lessee, or a third party has possession of the goods, notwithstanding any statute or rule of law that possession or the absence of possession is fraudulent.

§ 2A-303. Alienability of Party's Interest Under Lease Contract or of Lessor's Residual Interest in Goods; Delegation of Performance; Transfer of Rights.

(1) As used in this section, "creation of a security interest" includes the sale of a lease contract that is subject to Article 9, Secured Transactions, by reason of Section 9-102(1)(b).

(2) Except as provided in subsections (3) and (4), a provision in a lease agreement which (i) prohibits the voluntary or involuntary transfer, including a transfer by sale, sublease, creation or enforcement of a security interest, or attachment, levy, or other judicial process, of an interest of a party under the lease contract or of the lessor's residual interest in the goods, or (ii) makes such a transfer an event of default, gives rise to the rights and remedies provided in subsection (5), but a transfer that is prohibited or is an event of default under the lease agreement is otherwise effective.

(3) A provision in a lease agreement which (i) prohibits the creation or enforcement of a security interest in an interest of a party under the lease contract or in the lessor's residual interest in the goods, or (ii) makes such a transfer an event of default, is not enforceable unless, and then only to the extent that, there is an actual transfer by the lessee of the lessee's right of possession or use of the goods in violation of the provision or an actual delegation of a material performance of either party to the lease contract in violation of the provision. Neither the granting nor the enforcement of a security interest in (i) the lessor's interest under the lease contract or (ii) the lessor's residual interest in the goods is a transfer that materially impairs the prospect of obtaining return performance by, materially changes the duty of, or materially increases the burden or risk imposed on, the lessee within the purview of subsection (5) unless, and then only to the extent that, there is an actual delegation of a material performance of the lessor.

(4) A provision in a lease agreement which (i) prohibits a transfer of a right to damages for default with respect to the whole lease contract or of a right to payment arising out of the transferor's due performance of the transferor's entire obligation, or (ii) makes such a transfer an event of default, is not enforceable, and such a transfer is not a transfer that materially impairs the prospect of obtaining return performance by, materially changes the duty of, or materially increases the burden or risk imposed on, the other party to the lease contract within the purview of subsection (5).

(5) Subject to subsections (3) and (4):

(a) if a transfer is made which is made an event of default under a lease agreement, the party to the lease contract not making the transfer, unless that party waives the default or otherwise agrees, has the rights and remedies described in Section 2A-501(2);

(b) if paragraph (a) is not applicable and if a transfer is made that (i) is prohibited under a lease agreement or (ii) materially impairs the prospect of obtaining return performance by, materially changes the duty of, or materially increases the burden or risk imposed on, the other party to the lease contract, unless the party not making the transfer agrees at any time to the transfer in the lease contract or otherwise, then, except as limited by contract, (i) the transferor is liable to the party not making the transfer for damages caused by the transfer to the extent that the damages could not reasonably be prevented by the party not making the transfer and (ii) a court having jurisdiction may grant other appropriate relief, including cancellation of the lease contract or an injunction against the transfer.

(6) A transfer of "the lease" or of "all my rights under the lease", or a transfer in similar general terms, is a transfer of rights and, unless the language or the circumstances, as in a transfer for security, indicate the contrary, the transfer is a delegation of duties by the transferor to the transferee. Acceptance by the transferee constitutes a promise by the transferee to perform those duties. The promise is enforceable by either the transferor or the other party to the lease contract.

(7) Unless otherwise agreed by the lessor and the lessee, a delegation of performance does not relieve the transferor as against the other party of any duty to perform or of any liability for default.

(8) In a consumer lease, to prohibit the transfer of an interest of a party under the lease contract or to make a transfer an event of default, the language must be specific, by a writing, and conspicuous.

§ 2A-304. Subsequent Lease of Goods by Lessor.

(1) Subject to Section 2A-303, a subsequent lessee from a lessor of goods under an existing lease contract obtains, to the extent of the leasehold interest transferred, the leasehold interest in the goods that the lessor had or had power to transfer, and except as provided in subsection (2) and Section 2A-527(4), takes subject to the existing lease contract. A lessor with voidable title has power to transfer a good leasehold interest to a good faith subsequent lessee for value, but only to the extent set forth in the preceding sentence. If goods have been delivered under a transaction of purchase, the lessor has that power even though:

(a) the lessor's transferor was deceived as to the identity of the lessor;
(b) the delivery was in exchange for a check which is later dishonored;
(c) it was agreed that the transaction was to be a "cash sale"; or
(d) the delivery was procured through fraud punishable as larcenous under the criminal law.

(2) A subsequent lessee in the ordinary course of business from a lessor who is a merchant dealing in goods of that kind to whom the goods were entrusted by the existing lessee of that lessor before the interest of the subsequent lessee became enforceable against that lessor obtains, to the extent of

the leasehold interest transferred, all of that lessor's and the existing lessee's rights to the goods, and takes free of the existing lease contract.

(3) A subsequent lessee from the lessor of goods that are subject to an existing lease contract and are covered by a certificate of title issued under a statute of this State or of another jurisdiction takes no greater rights than those provided both by this section and by the certificate of title statute.

§ 2A-305. Sale or Sublease of Goods by Lessee.

(1) Subject to the provisions of Section 2A-303, a buyer or sublessee from the lessee of goods under an existing lease contract obtains, to the extent of the interest transferred, the leasehold interest in the goods that the lessee had or had power to transfer, and except as provided in subsection (2) and Section 2A-511(4), takes subject to the existing lease contract. A lessee with a voidable leasehold interest has power to transfer a good leasehold interest to a good faith buyer for value or a good faith sublessee for value, but only to the extent set forth in the preceding sentence. When goods have been delivered under a transaction of lease the lessee has that power even though:

(a) the lessor was deceived as to the identity of the lessee;
(b) the delivery was in exchange for a check which is later dishonored; or
(c) the delivery was procured through fraud punishable as larcenous under the criminal law.

(2) A buyer in the ordinary course of business or a sublessee in the ordinary course of business from a lessee who is a merchant dealing in goods of that kind to whom the goods were entrusted by the lessor obtains, to the extent of the interest transferred, all of the lessor's and lessee's rights to the goods, and takes free of the existing lease contract.

(3) A buyer or sublessee from the lessee of goods that are subject to an existing lease contract and are covered by a certificate of title issued under a statute of this State or of another jurisdiction takes no greater rights than those provided both by this section and by the certificate of title statute.

§ 2A-306. Priority of Certain Liens Arising by Operation of Law.

If a person in the ordinary course of his [or her] business furnishes services or materials with respect to goods subject to a lease contract, a lien upon those goods in the possession of that person given by statute or rule of law for those materials or services takes priority over any interest of the lessor or lessee under the lease contract or this Article unless the lien is created by statute and the statute provides otherwise or unless the lien is created by rule of law and the rule of law provides otherwise.

§ 2A-307. Priority of Liens Arising by Attachment or Levy on, Security Interests in, and Other Claims to Goods.

(1) Except as otherwise provided in Section 2A-306, a creditor of a lessee takes subject to the lease contract.

(2) Except as otherwise provided in subsections (3) and (4) and in Sections 2A-306 and 2A-308, a creditor of a lessor takes subject to the lease contract unless:

(a) the creditor holds a lien that attached to the goods before the lease contract became enforceable,

(b) the creditor holds a security interest in the goods and the lessee did not give value and receive delivery of the goods without knowledge of the security interest; or

(c) the creditor holds a security interest in the goods which was perfected (Section 9-303) before the lease contract became enforceable.

(3) A lessee in the ordinary course of business takes the leasehold interest free of a security interest in the goods created by the lessor even though the security interest is perfected (Section 9-303) and the lessee knows of its existence.

(4) A lessee other than a lessee in the ordinary course of business takes the leasehold interest free of a security interest to the extent that it secures future advances made after the secured party acquires knowledge of the lease or more than 45 days after the lease contract becomes enforceable, whichever first occurs, unless the future advances are made pursuant to a commitment entered into without knowledge of the lease and before the expiration of the 45-day period.

§ 2A-308. Special Rights of Creditors.

(1) A creditor of a lessor in possession of goods subject to a lease contract may treat the lease contract as void if as against the creditor retention of possession by the lessor is fraudulent under any statute or rule of law, but retention of possession in good faith and current course of trade by the lessor for a commercially reasonable time after the lease contract becomes enforceable is not fraudulent.

(2) Nothing in this Article impairs the rights of creditors of a lessor if the lease contract (a) becomes enforceable, not in current course of trade but in satisfaction of or as security for a pre-existing claim for money, security, or the like, and (b) is made under circumstances which under any statute or rule of law apart from this Article would constitute the transaction a fraudulent transfer or voidable preference.

(3) A creditor of a seller may treat a sale or an identification of goods to a contract for sale as void if as against the creditor retention of possession by the seller is fraudulent under any statute or rule of law, but retention of possession of the goods pursuant to a lease contract entered into by the seller as lessee and the buyer as lessor in connection with the sale or identification of the goods is not fraudulent if the buyer bought for value and in good faith.

§ 2A-309. Lessor's and Lessee's Rights When Goods Become Fixtures.

(1) In this section:

(a) goods are "fixtures" when they become so related to particular real estate that an interest in them arises under real estate law;

(b) a "fixture filing" is the filing, in the office where a mortgage on the real estate would be filed or recorded, of a financing statement covering goods that are or are to become fixtures and conforming to the requirements of Section 9-402(5);

(c) a lease is a "purchase money lease" unless the lessee has possession or use of the goods or the right to possession or use of the goods before the lease agreement is enforceable;

(d) a mortgage is a "construction mortgage" to the extent it secures an obligation incurred for the construction of an improvement on land including the acquisition cost of the land, if the recorded writing so indicates; and

(e) "encumbrance" includes real estate mortgages and other liens on real estate and all other rights in real estate that are not ownership interests.

(2) Under this Article a lease may be of goods that are fixtures or may continue in goods that become fixtures, but no lease exists under this Article of ordinary building materials incorporated into an improvement on land.

(3) This Article does not prevent creation of a lease of fixtures pursuant to real estate law.

(4) The perfected interest of a lessor of fixtures has priority over a conflicting interest of an encumbrancer or owner of the real estate if:

(a) the lease is a purchase money lease, the conflicting interest of the encumbrancer or owner arises before the goods become fixtures, the interest of the lessor is perfected by a fixture filing before the goods become fixtures or within ten days thereafter, and the lessee has an interest of record in the real estate or is in possession of the real estate; or

(b) the interest of the lessor is perfected by a fixture filing before the interest of the encumbrancer or owner is of record, the lessor's interest has priority over any conflicting interest of a predecessor in title of the encumbrancer or owner, and the lessee has an interest of record in the real estate or is in possession of the real estate.

(5) The interest of a lessor of fixtures, whether or not perfected, has priority over the conflicting interest of an encumbrancer or owner of the real estate if:

(a) the fixtures are readily removable factory or office machines, readily removable equipment that is not primarily used or leased for use in the operation of the real estate, or readily removable replacements of domestic appliances that are goods subject to a consumer lease, and before the goods become fixtures the lease contract is enforceable; or

(b) the conflicting interest is a lien on the real estate obtained by legal or equitable proceedings after the lease contract is enforceable; or

(c) the encumbrancer or owner has consented in writing to the lease or has disclaimed an interest in the goods as fixtures; or

(d) the lessee has a right to remove the goods as against the encumbrancer or owner. If the lessee's right to remove terminates, the priority of the interest of the lessor continues for a reasonable time.

(6) Notwithstanding subsection (4)(a) but otherwise subject to subsections (4) and (5), the interest of a lessor of fixtures, including the lessor's residual interest, is subordinate to the conflicting interest of an encumbrancer of the real estate under a construction mortgage recorded before the goods become fixtures if the goods become fixtures before the completion of the construction. To the extent given to refinance a construction mortgage, the conflicting interest of an encumbrancer of the real estate under a mortgage has this priority to the same extent as the encumbrancer of the real estate under the construction mortgage.

(7) In cases not within the preceding subsections, priority between the interest of a lessor of fixtures, including the lessor's residual interest, and the conflicting interest of an encumbrancer or owner of the real estate who is not the lessee is determined by the priority rules governing conflicting interests in real estate.

(8) If the interest of a lessor of fixtures, including the lessor's residual interest, has priority over all conflicting interests of all owners and encumbrancers of the real estate, the lessor or the lessee may (i) on default, expiration, termination, or cancellation of the lease agreement but subject to the agreement and this Article, or (ii) if necessary to enforce other rights and remedies of the lessor or lessee under this Article, remove the goods from the real estate, free and clear of all conflicting interests of all owners and encumbrancers of the real estate, but the lessor or lessee must reimburse any encumbrancer or owner of the real estate who is not the lessee and who has not otherwise agreed for the cost of repair of any physical injury, but not for any diminution in value of the real estate caused by the absence of the goods removed or by any necessity of replacing them. A person entitled to reimbursement may refuse permission to remove until the party seeking removal gives adequate security for the performance of this obligation.

(9) Even though the lease agreement does not create a security interest, the interest of a lessor of fixtures, including the lessor's residual interest, is perfected by filing a financing statement as a fixture filing for leased goods that are or are to become fixtures in accordance with the relevant provisions of the Article on Secured Transactions (Article 9).

§ 2A-310. Lessor's and Lessee's Rights When Goods Become Accessions.

(1) Goods are "accessions" when they are installed in or affixed to other goods.

(2) The interest of a lessor or a lessee under a lease contract entered into before the goods became accessions is superior to all interests in the whole except as stated in subsection (4).

(3) The interest of a lessor or a lessee under a lease contract entered into at the time or after the goods became accessions is superior to all subsequently acquired interests in the whole except as stated in subsection (4) but is subordinate to interests in the whole existing at the time the lease contract was made unless the holders of such interests in the whole have in writing consented to the lease or disclaimed an interest in the goods as part of the whole.

(4) The interest of a lessor or a lessee under a lease contract described in subsection (2) or (3) is subordinate to the interest of

    (a) a buyer in the ordinary course of business or a lessee in the ordinary course of business of any interest in the whole acquired after the goods became accessions; or

    (b) a creditor with a security interest in the whole perfected before the lease contract was made to the extent that the creditor makes subsequent advances without knowledge of the lease contract.

(5) When under subsections (2) or (3) and (4) a lessor or a lessee of accessions holds an interest that is superior to all interests in the whole, the lessor or the lessee may (a) on default, expiration, termination, or cancellation of the lease contract by the other party but subject to the provisions of the lease contract and this Article, or (b) if necessary to en-

force his [or her] other rights and remedies under this Article, remove the goods from the whole, free and clear of all interests in the whole, but he [or she] must reimburse any holder of an interest in the whole who is not the lessee and who has not otherwise agreed for the cost of repair of any physical injury but not for any diminution in value of the whole caused by the absence of the goods removed or by any necessity for replacing them. A person entitled to reimbursement may refuse permission to remove until the party seeking removal gives adequate security for the performance of this obligation.

§ 2A-311. Priority Subject to Subordination.

Nothing in this Article prevents subordination by agreement by any person entitled to priority.

Part 4 Performance of Lease Contract: Repudiated, Substituted and Excused

§ 2A-401. Insecurity: Adequate Assurance of Performance.

(1) A lease contract imposes an obligation on each party that the other's expectation of receiving due performance will not be impaired.

(2) If reasonable grounds for insecurity arise with respect to the performance of either party, the insecure party may demand in writing adequate assurance of due performance. Until the insecure party receives that assurance, if commercially reasonable the insecure party may suspend any performance for which he [or she] has not already received the agreed return.

(3) A repudiation of the lease contract occurs if assurance of due performance adequate under the circumstances of the particular case is not provided to the insecure party within a reasonable time, not to exceed 30 days after receipt of a demand by the other party.

(4) Between merchants, the reasonableness of grounds for insecurity and the adequacy of any assurance offered must be determined according to commercial standards.

(5) Acceptance of any nonconforming delivery or payment does not prejudice the aggrieved party's right to demand adequate assurance of future performance.

§ 2A-402. Anticipatory Repudiation.

If either party repudiates a lease contract with respect to a performance not yet due under the lease contract, the loss of which performance will substantially impair the value of the lease contract to the other, the aggrieved party may:

    (a) for a commercially reasonable time, await retraction of repudiation and performance by the repudiating party;

    (b) make demand pursuant to Section 2A-401 and await assurance of future performance adequate under the circumstances of the particular case; or

    (c) resort to any right or remedy upon default under the lease contract or this Article, even though the aggrieved party has notified the repudiating party that the aggrieved party would await the repudiating party's performance and assurance and has urged retraction. In addition, whether or not the aggrieved party is pursuing one of the foregoing remedies, the aggrieved party may suspend performance or, if the aggrieved party is the lessor, proceed in accordance with the provisions of this Article on the lessor's right to identify goods to the lease contract notwithstanding default or to salvage unfinished goods (Section 2A-524).

§ 2A-403. Retraction of Anticipatory Repudiation.

(1) Until the repudiating party's next performance is due, the repudiating party can retract the repudiation unless, since the repudiation, the aggrieved party has cancelled the lease contract or materially changed the aggrieved party's position or otherwise indicated that the aggrieved party considers the repudiation final.

(2) Retraction may be by any method that clearly indicates to the aggrieved party that the repudiating party intends to perform under the lease contract and includes any assurance demanded under Section 2A-401.

(3) Retraction reinstates a repudiating party's rights under a lease contract with due excuse and allowance to the aggrieved party for any delay occasioned by the repudiation.

§ 2A-404. Substituted Performance.

(1) If without fault of the lessee, the lessor and the supplier, the agreed berthing, loading, or unloading facilities fail or the agreed type of carrier becomes unavailable or the agreed manner of delivery otherwise becomes commercially impracticable, but a commercially reasonable substitute is available, the substitute performance must be tendered and accepted.

(2) If the agreed means or manner of payment fails because of domestic or foreign governmental regulation:

(a) the lessor may withhold or stop delivery or cause the supplier to withhold or stop delivery unless the lessee provides a means or manner of payment that is commercially a substantial equivalent; and

(b) if delivery has already been taken, payment by the means or in the manner provided by the regulation discharges the lessee's obligation unless the regulation is discriminatory, oppressive, or predatory.

§ 2A-405. Excused Performance.

Subject to Section 2A-404 on substituted performance, the following rules apply:

(a) Delay in delivery or nondelivery in whole or in part by a lessor or a supplier who complies with paragraphs (b) and (c) is not a default under the lease contract if performance as agreed has been made impracticable by the occurrence of a contingency the nonoccurrence of which was a basic assumption on which the lease contract was made or by compliance in good faith with any applicable foreign or domestic governmental regulation or order, whether or not the regulation or order later proves to be invalid.

(b) If the causes mentioned in paragraph (a) affect only part of the lessor's or the supplier's capacity to perform, he [or she] shall allocate production and deliveries among his [or her] customers but at his [or her] option may include regular customers not then under contract for sale or lease as well as his [or her] own requirements for further manufacture. He [or she] may so allocate in any manner that is fair and reasonable.

(c) The lessor seasonably shall notify the lessee and in the case of a finance lease the supplier seasonably shall notify the lessor and the lessee, if known, that there will be delay or nondelivery and, if allocation is required under paragraph (b), of the estimated quota thus made available for the lessee.

§ 2A-406. Procedure on Excused Performance.

(1) If the lessee receives notification of a material or indefinite delay or an allocation justified under Section 2A-405, the lessee may by written notification to the lessor as to any goods involved, and with respect to all of the goods if under an installment lease contract the value of the whole lease contract is substantially impaired (Section 2A-510):

(a) terminate the lease contract (Section 2A-505(2)); or

(b) except in a finance lease that is not a consumer lease, modify the lease contract by accepting the available quota in substitution, with due allowance from the rent payable for the balance of the lease term for the deficiency but without further right against the lessor.

(2) If, after receipt of a notification from the lessor under Section 2A-405, the lessee fails so to modify the lease agreement within a reasonable time not exceeding 30 days, the lease contract lapses with respect to any deliveries affected.

§ 2A-407. Irrevocable Promises: Finance Leases.

(1) In the case of a finance lease that is not a consumer lease the lessee's promises under the lease contract become irrevocable and independent upon the lessee's acceptance of the goods.

(2) A promise that has become irrevocable and independent under subsection (1):

(a) is effective and enforceable between the parties, and by or against third parties including assignees of the parties; and

(b) is not subject to cancellation, termination, modification, repudiation, excuse, or substitution without the consent of the party to whom the promise runs.

(3) This section does not affect the validity under any other law of a covenant in any lease contract making the lessee's promises irrevocable and independent upon the lessee's acceptance of the goods.

Part 5 Default

A. In General

§ 2A-501. Default: Procedure.

(1) Whether the lessor or the lessee is in default under a lease contract is determined by the lease agreement and this Article.

(2) If the lessor or the lessee is in default under the lease contract, the party seeking enforcement has rights and remedies as provided in this Article and, except as limited by this Article, as provided in the lease agreement.

(3) If the lessor or the lessee is in default under the lease contract, the party seeking enforcement may reduce the party's claim to judgment, or otherwise enforce the lease contract by self-help or any available judicial procedure or nonjudicial procedure, including administrative proceeding, arbitration, or the like, in accordance with this Article.

(4) Except as otherwise provided in Section 1-106(1) or this Article or the lease agreement, the rights and remedies referred to in subsections (2) and (3) are cumulative.

(5) If the lease agreement covers both real property and goods, the party seeking enforcement may proceed under this Part as to the goods, or under other applicable law as to both the real property and the goods in accordance with that party's rights and remedies in respect of the real property, in which case this Part does not apply.

§ 2A-502. Notice After Default.

Except as otherwise provided in this Article or the lease agreement, the lessor or lessee in default under the lease contract is not entitled to notice of default or notice of enforcement from the other party to the lease agreement.

§ 2A-503. Modification or Impairment of Rights and Remedies.

(1) Except as otherwise provided in this Article, the lease agreement may include rights and remedies for default in addition to or in substitution for those provided in this Article and may limit or alter the measure of damages recoverable under this Article.

(2) Resort to a remedy provided under this Article or in the lease agreement is optional unless the remedy is expressly agreed to be exclusive. If circumstances cause an exclusive or limited remedy to fail of its essential purpose, or provision for an exclusive remedy is unconscionable, remedy may be had as provided in this Article.

(3) Consequential damages may be liquidated under Section 2A-504, or may otherwise be limited, altered, or excluded unless the limitation, alteration, or exclusion is unconscionable. Limitation, alteration, or exclusion of consequential damages for injury to the person in the case of consumer goods is prima facie unconscionable but limitation, alteration, or exclusion of damages where the loss is commercial is not prima facie unconscionable.

(4) Rights and remedies on default by the lessor or the lessee with respect to any obligation or promise collateral or ancillary to the lease contract are not impaired by this Article.

§ 2A-504. Liquidation of Damages.

(1) Damages payable by either party for default, or any other act or omission, including indemnity for loss or diminution of anticipated tax benefits or loss or damage to lessor's residual interest, may be liquidated in the lease agreement but only at an amount or by a formula that is reasonable in light of the then anticipated harm caused by the default or other act or omission.

(2) If the lease agreement provides for liquidation of damages, and such provision does not comply with subsection (1), or such provision is an exclusive or limited remedy that circumstances cause to fail of its essential purpose, remedy may be had as provided in this Article.

(3) If the lessor justifiably withholds or stops delivery of goods because of the lessee's default or insolvency (Section 2A-525 or 2A-526), the lessee is entitled to restitution of any amount by which the sum of his [or her] payments exceeds:

(a) the amount to which the lessor is entitled by virtue of terms liquidating the lessor's damages in accordance with subsection (1); or

(b) in the absence of those terms, 20 percent of the then present value of the total rent the lessee was obligated to pay for the balance of the lease term, or, in the case of a consumer lease, the lesser of such amount or $500.

(4) A lessee's right to restitution under subsection (3) is subject to offset to the extent the lessor establishes:

(a) a right to recover damages under the provisions of this Article other than subsection (1); and

(b) the amount or value of any benefits received by the lessee directly or indirectly by reason of the lease contract.

§ 2A-505. Cancellation and Termination and Effect of Cancellation, Termination, Rescission, or Fraud on Rights and Remedies.

(1) On cancellation of the lease contract, all obligations that are still executory on both sides are discharged, but any right based on prior default or performance survives, and the cancelling party also retains any remedy for default of the whole lease contract or any unperformed balance.

(2) On termination of the lease contract, all obligations that are still executory on both sides are discharged but any right based on prior default or performance survives.

(3) Unless the contrary intention clearly appears, expressions of "cancellation," "rescission," or the like of the lease contract may not be construed as a renunciation or discharge of any claim in damages for an antecedent default.

(4) Rights and remedies for material misrepresentation or fraud include all rights and remedies available under this Article for default.

(5) Neither rescission nor a claim for rescission of the lease contract nor rejection or return of the goods may bar or be deemed inconsistent with a claim for damages or other right or remedy.

§ 2A-506. Statute of Limitations.

(1) An action for default under a lease contract, including breach of warranty or indemnity, must be commenced within 4 years after the cause of action accrued. By the original lease contract the parties may reduce the period of limitation to not less than one year.

(2) A cause of action for default accrues when the act or omission on which the default or breach of warranty is based is or should have been discovered by the aggrieved party, or when the default occurs, whichever is later. A cause of action for indemnity accrues when the act or omission on which the claim for indemnity is based is or should have been discovered by the indemnified party, whichever is later.

(3) If an action commenced within the time limited by subsection (1) is so terminated as to leave available a remedy by another action for the same default or breach of warranty or indemnity, the other action may be commenced after the expiration of the time limited and within 6 months after the termination of the first action unless the termination resulted from voluntary discontinuance or from dismissal for failure or neglect to prosecute.

(4) This section does not alter the law on tolling of the statute of limitations nor does it apply to causes of action that have accrued before this Article becomes effective.

§ 2A-507. Proof of Market Rent: Time and Place.

(1) Damages based on market rent (Section 2A-519 or 2A-528) are determined according to the rent for the use of the goods concerned for a lease term identical to the remaining

lease term of the original lease agreement and prevailing at the times specified in Sections 2A-519 and 2A-528.

(2) If evidence of rent for the use of the goods concerned for a lease term identical to the remaining lease term of the original lease agreement and prevailing at the times or places described in this Article is not readily available, the rent prevailing within any reasonable time before or after the time described or at any other place or for a different lease term which in commercial judgment or under usage of trade would serve as a reasonable substitute for the one described may be used, making any proper allowance for the difference, including the cost of transporting the goods to or from the other place.

(3) Evidence of a relevant rent prevailing at a time or place or for a lease term other than the one described in this Article offered by one party is not admissible unless and until he [or she] has given the other party notice the court finds sufficient to prevent unfair surprise.

(4) If the prevailing rent or value of any goods regularly leased in any established market is in issue, reports in official publications or trade journals or in newspapers or periodicals of general circulation published as the reports of that market are admissible in evidence. The circumstances of the preparation of the report may be shown to affect its weight but not its admissibility.

B. Default by Lessor

§ 2A-508. Lessee's Remedies.

(1) If a lessor fails to deliver the goods in conformity to the lease contract (Section 2A-509) or repudiates the lease contract (Section 2A-402), or a lessee rightfully rejects the goods (Section 2A-509) or justifiably revokes acceptance of the goods (Section 2A-517), then with respect to any goods involved, and with respect to all of the goods if under an installment lease contract the value of the whole lease contract is substantially impaired (Section 2A-510), the lessor is in default under the lease contract and the lessee may:

(a) cancel the lease contract (Section 2A-505(1));

(b) recover so much of the rent and security as has been paid and is just under the circumstances;

(c) cover and recover damages as to all goods affected whether or not they have been identified to the lease contract (Sections 2A-518 and 2A-520), or recover damages for nondelivery (Sections 2A-519 and 2A-520);

(d) exercise any other rights or pursue any other remedies provided in the lease contract.

(2) If a lessor fails to deliver the goods in conformity to the lease contract or repudiates the lease contract, the lessee may also:

(a) if the goods have been identified, recover them (Section 2A-522); or

(b) in a proper case, obtain specific performance or replevy the goods (Section 2A-521).

(3) If a lessor is otherwise in default under a lease contract, the lessee may exercise the rights and pursue the remedies provided in the lease contract, which may include a right to cancel the lease, and in Section 2A-519(3).

(4) If a lessor has breached a warranty, whether express or implied, the lessee may recover damages (Section 2A-519(4)).

(5) On rightful rejection or justifiable revocation of acceptance, a lessee has a security interest in goods in the lessee's possession or control for any rent and security that has been paid and any expenses reasonably incurred in their inspection, receipt, transportation, and care and custody and may hold those goods and dispose of them in good faith and in a commercially reasonable manner, subject to Section 2A-527(5).

(6) Subject to the provisions of Section 2A-407, a lessee, on notifying the lessor of the lessee's intention to do so, may deduct all or any part of the damages resulting from any default under the lease contract from any part of the rent still due under the same lease contract.

§ 2A-509. Lessee's Rights on Improper Delivery; Rightful Rejection.

(1) Subject to the provisions of Section 2A-510 on default in installment lease contracts, if the goods or the tender or delivery fail in any respect to conform to the lease contract, the lessee may reject or accept the goods or accept any commercial unit or units and reject the rest of the goods.

(2) Rejection of goods is ineffective unless it is within a reasonable time after tender or delivery of the goods and the lessee seasonably notifies the lessor.

§ 2A-510. Installment Lease Contracts: Rejection and Default.

(1) Under an installment lease contract a lessee may reject any delivery that is nonconforming if the nonconformity substantially impairs the value of that delivery and cannot be cured or the nonconformity is a defect in the required documents; but if the nonconformity does not fall within subsection (2) and the lessor or the supplier gives adequate assurance of its cure, the lessee must accept that delivery.

(2) Whenever nonconformity or default with respect to one or more deliveries substantially impairs the value of the installment lease contract as a whole there is a default with respect to the whole. But, the aggrieved party reinstates the installment lease contract as a whole if the aggrieved party accepts a nonconforming delivery without seasonably notifying of cancellation or brings an action with respect only to past deliveries or demands performance as to future deliveries.

§ 2A-511. Merchant Lessee's Duties as to Rightfully Rejected Goods.

(1) Subject to any security interest of a lessee (Section 2A-508(5)), if a lessor or a supplier has no agent or place of business at the market of rejection, a merchant lessee, after rejection of goods in his [or her] possession or control, shall follow any reasonable instructions received from the lessor or the supplier with respect to the goods. In the absence of those instructions, a merchant lessee shall make reasonable efforts to sell, lease, or otherwise dispose of the goods for the lessor's account if they threaten to decline in value speedily. Instructions are not reasonable if on demand indemnity for expenses is not forthcoming.

(2) If a merchant lessee (subsection (1)) or any other lessee (Section 2A-512) disposes of goods, he [or she] is entitled to reimbursement either from the lessor or the supplier or out of the proceeds for reasonable expenses of caring for and disposing of the goods and, if the expenses include no disposition

commission, to such commission as is usual in the trade, or if there is none, to a reasonable sum not exceeding 10 percent of the gross proceeds.

(3) In complying with this section or Section 2A-512, the lessee is held only to good faith. Good faith conduct hereunder is neither acceptance or conversion nor the basis of an action for damages.

(4) A purchaser who purchases in good faith from a lessee pursuant to this section or Section 2A-512 takes the goods free of any rights of the lessor and the supplier even though the lessee fails to comply with one or more of the requirements of this Article.

§ 2A-512. Lessee's Duties as to Rightfully Rejected Goods.

(1) Except as otherwise provided with respect to goods that threaten to decline in value speedily (Section 2A-511) and subject to any security interest of a lessee (Section 2A-508(5)):

(a) the lessee, after rejection of goods in the lessee's possession, shall hold them with reasonable care at the lessor's or the supplier's disposition for a reasonable time after the lessee's seasonable notification of rejection;

(b) if the lessor or the supplier gives no instructions within a reasonable time after notification of rejection, the lessee may store the rejected goods for the lessor's or the supplier's account or ship them to the lessor or the supplier or dispose of them for the lessor's or the supplier's account with reimbursement in the manner provided in Section 2A-511; but

(c) the lessee has no further obligations with regard to goods rightfully rejected.

(2) Action by the lessee pursuant to subsection (1) is not acceptance or conversion.

§ 2A-513. Cure by Lessor of Improper Tender or Delivery; Replacement.

(1) If any tender or delivery by the lessor or the supplier is rejected because nonconforming and the time for performance has not yet expired, the lessor or the supplier may seasonably notify the lessee of the lessor's or the supplier's intention to cure and may then make a conforming delivery within the time provided in the lease contract.

(2) If the lessee rejects a nonconforming tender that the lessor or the supplier had reasonable grounds to believe would be acceptable with or without money allowance, the lessor or the supplier may have a further reasonable time to substitute a conforming tender if he [or she] seasonably notifies the lessee.

§ 2A-514. Waiver of Lessee's Objections.

(1) In rejecting goods, a lessee's failure to state a particular defect that is ascertainable by reasonable inspection precludes the lessee from relying on the defect to justify rejection or to establish default:

(a) if, stated seasonably, the lessor or the supplier could have cured it (Section 2A-513); or

(b) between merchants if the lessor or the supplier after rejection has made a request in writing for a full and final written statement of all defects on which the lessee proposes to rely.

(2) A lessee's failure to reserve rights when paying rent or other consideration against documents precludes recovery of the payment for defects apparent on the face of the documents.

§ 2A-515. Acceptance of Goods.

(1) Acceptance of goods occurs after the lessee has had a reasonable opportunity to inspect the goods and

(a) the lessee signifies or acts with respect to the goods in a manner that signifies to the lessor or the supplier that the goods are conforming or that the lessee will take or retain them in spite of their nonconformity; or

(b) the lessee fails to make an effective rejection of the goods (Section 2A-509(2)).

(2) Acceptance of a part of any commercial unit is acceptance of that entire unit.

§ 2A-516. Effect of Acceptance of Goods; Notice of Default; Burden of Establishing Default After Acceptance; Notice of Claim or Litigation to Person Answerable Over.

(1) A lessee must pay rent for any goods accepted in accordance with the lease contract, with due allowance for goods rightfully rejected or not delivered.

(2) A lessee's acceptance of goods precludes rejection of the goods accepted. In the case of a finance lease, if made with knowledge of a nonconformity, acceptance cannot be revoked because of it. In any other case, if made with knowledge of a nonconformity, acceptance cannot be revoked because of it unless the acceptance was on the reasonable assumption that the nonconformity would be seasonably cured. Acceptance does not of itself impair any other remedy provided by this Article or the lease agreement for nonconformity.

(3) If a tender has been accepted:

(a) within a reasonable time after the lessee discovers or should have discovered any default, the lessee shall notify the lessor and the supplier, if any, or be barred from any remedy against the party not notified;

(b) except in the case of a consumer lease, within a reasonable time after the lessee receives notice of litigation for infringement or the like (Section 2A-211) the lessee shall notify the lessor or be barred from any remedy over for liability established by the litigation; and

(c) the burden is on the lessee to establish any default.

(4) If a lessee is sued for breach of a warranty or other obligation for which a lessor or a supplier is answerable over the following apply:

(a) The lessee may give the lessor or the supplier, or both, written notice of the litigation. If the notice states that the person notified may come in and defend and that if the person notified does not do so that person will be bound in any action against that person by the lessee by any determination of fact common to the two litigations, then unless the person notified after seasonable receipt of the notice does come in and defend that person is so bound.

(b) The lessor or the supplier may demand in writing that the lessee turn over control of the litigation including settlement if the claim is one for infringement or the like (Section 2A-211) or else be barred from any remedy over.

If the demand states that the lessor or the supplier agrees to bear all expense and to satisfy any adverse judgment, then unless the lessee after seasonable receipt of the demand does turn over control the lessee is so barred.

(5) Subsections (3) and (4) apply to any obligation of a lessee to hold the lessor or the supplier harmless against infringement or the like (Section 2A-211).

§ 2A-517.   Revocation of Acceptance of Goods.

(1) A lessee may revoke acceptance of a lot or commercial unit whose nonconformity substantially impairs its value to the lessee if the lessee has accepted it:

(a) except in the case of a finance lease, on the reasonable assumption that its nonconformity would be cured and it has not been seasonably cured; or

(b) without discovery of the nonconformity if the lessee's acceptance was reasonably induced either by the lessor's assurances or, except in the case of a finance lease, by the difficulty of discovery before acceptance.

(2) Except in the case of a finance lease that is not a consumer lease, a lessee may revoke acceptance of a lot or commercial unit if the lessor defaults under the lease contract and the default substantially impairs the value of that lot or commercial unit to the lessee.

(3) If the lease agreement so provides, the lessee may revoke acceptance of a lot or commercial unit because of other defaults by the lessor.

(4) Revocation of acceptance must occur within a reasonable time after the lessee discovers or should have discovered the ground for it and before any substantial change in condition of the goods which is not caused by the nonconformity. Revocation is not effective until the lessee notifies the lessor.

(5) A lessee who so revokes has the same rights and duties with regard to the goods involved as if the lessee had rejected them.

§ 2A-518.   Cover; Substitute Goods.

(1) After a default by a lessor under the lease contract of the type described in Section 2A-508(1), or, if agreed, after other default by the lessor, the lessee may cover by making any purchase or lease of or contract to purchase or lease goods in substitution for those due from the lessor.

(2) Except as otherwise provided with respect to damages liquidated in the lease agreement (Section 2A-504) or otherwise determined pursuant to agreement of the parties (Sections 1-102(3) and 2A-503), if a lessee's cover is by a lease agreement substantially similar to the original lease agreement and the new lease agreement is made in good faith and in a commercially reasonable manner, the lessee may recover from the lessor as damages (i) the present value, as of the date of the commencement of the term of the new lease agreement, of the rent under the new lease agreement applicable to that period of the new lease term which is comparable to the then remaining term of the original lease agreement minus the present value as of the same date of the total rent for the then remaining lease term of the original lease agreement, and (ii) any incidental or consequential damages, less expenses saved in consequence of the lessor's default.

(3) If a lessee's cover is by lease agreement that for any rea-

son does not qualify for treatment under subsection (2), or is by purchase or otherwise, the lessee may recover from the lessor as if the lessee had elected not to cover and Section 2A-519 governs.

§ 2A-519.   Lessee's Damages for Non-delivery, Repudiation, Default, and Breach of Warranty in Regard to Accepted Goods.

(1) Except as otherwise provided with respect to damages liquidated in the lease agreement (Section 2A-504) or otherwise determined pursuant to agreement of the parties (Sections 1-102(3) and 2A-503), if a lessee elects not to cover or a lessee elects to cover and the cover is by lease agreement that for any reason does not qualify for treatment under Section 2A-518(2), or is by purchase or otherwise, the measure of damages for non-delivery or repudiation by the lessor or for rejection or revocation of acceptance by the lessee is the present value, as of the date of the default, of the then market rent minus the present value as of the same date of the original rent, computed for the remaining lease term of the original lease agreement, together with incidental and consequential damages, less expenses saved in consequence of the lessor's default.

(2) Market rent is to be determined as of the place for tender or, in cases of rejection after arrival or revocation of acceptance, as of the place of arrival.

(3) Except as otherwise agreed, if the lessee has accepted goods and given notification (Section 2A-516(3)), the measure of damages for nonconforming tender or delivery or other default by a lessor is the loss resulting in the ordinary course of events from the lessor's default as determined in any manner that is reasonable together with incidental and consequential damages, less expenses saved in consequence of the lessor's default.

(4) Except as otherwise agreed, the measure of damages for breach of warranty is the present value at the time and place of acceptance of the difference between the value of the use of the goods accepted and the value if they had been as warranted for the lease term, unless special circumstances show proximate damages of a different amount, together with incidental and consequential damages, less expenses saved in consequence of the lessor's default or breach of warranty.

§ 2A-520.   Lessee's Incidental and Consequential Damages.

(1) Incidental damages resulting from a lessor's default include expenses reasonably incurred in inspection, receipt, transportation, and care and custody of goods rightfully rejected or goods the acceptance of which is justifiably revoked, any commercially reasonable charges, expenses or commissions in connection with effecting cover, and any other reasonable expense incident to the default.

(2) Consequential damages resulting from a lessor's default include:

(a) any loss resulting from general or particular requirements and needs of which the lessor at the time of contracting had reason to know and which could not reasonably be prevented by cover or otherwise; and

(b) injury to person or property proximately resulting from any breach of warranty.

§ 2A-521. Lessee's Right to Specific Performance or Replevin.

(1) Specific performance may be decreed if the goods are unique or in other proper circumstances.

(2) A decree for specific performance may include any terms and conditions as to payment of the rent, damages, or other relief that the court deems just.

(3) A lessee has a right of replevin, detinue, sequestration, claim and delivery, or the like for goods identified to the lease contract if after reasonable effort the lessee is unable to effect cover for those goods or the circumstances reasonably indicate that the effort will be unavailing.

§ 2A-522. Lessee's Right to Goods on Lessor's Insolvency.

(1) Subject to subsection (2) and even though the goods have not been shipped, a lessee who has paid a part or all of the rent and security for goods identified to a lease contract (Section 2A-217) on making and keeping good a tender of any unpaid portion of the rent and security due under the lease contract may recover the goods identified from the lessor if the lessor becomes insolvent within 10 days after receipt of the first installment of rent and security.

(2) A lessee acquires the right to recover goods identified to a lease contract only if they conform to the lease contract.

C. Default by Lessee

§ 2A-523. Lessor's Remedies.

(1) If a lessee wrongfully rejects or revokes acceptance of goods or fails to make a payment when due or repudiates with respect to a part or the whole, then, with respect to any goods involved, and with respect to all of the goods if under an installment lease contract the value of the whole lease contract is substantially impaired (Section 2A-510), the lessee is in default under the lease contract and the lessor may:

(a) cancel the lease contract (Section 2A-505(1));

(b) proceed respecting goods not identified to the lease contract (Section 2A-524);

(c) withhold delivery of the goods and take possession of goods previously delivered (Section 2A-525);

(d) stop delivery of the goods by any bailee (Section 2A-526);

(e) dispose of the goods and recover damages (Section 2A-527), or retain the goods and recover damages (Section 2A-528), or in a proper case recover rent (Section 2A-529).

(f) exercise any other rights or pursue any other remedies provided in the lease contract.

(2) If a lessor does not fully exercise a right or obtain a remedy to which the lessor is entitled under subsection (1), the lessor may recover the loss resulting in the ordinary course of events from the lessee's default as determined in any reasonable manner, together with incidental damages, less expenses saved in consequence of the lessee's default.

(3) If a lessee is otherwise in default under a lease contract, the lessor may exercise the rights and pursue the remedies provided in the lease contract, which may include a right to cancel the lease. In addition, unless otherwise provided in the lease contract:

(a) if the default substantially impairs the value of the lease contract to the lessor, the lessor may exercise the rights and pursue the remedies provided in subsections (1) or (2); or

(b) if the default does not substantially impair the value of the lease contract to the lessor, the lessor may recover as provided in subsection (2).

§ 2A-524. Lessor's Right to Identify Goods to Lease Contract.

(1) After default by the lessee under the lease contract of the type described in Section 2A-523(1) or 2A-523(3)(a) or, if agreed, after other default by the lessee, the lessor may:

(a) identify to the lease contract conforming goods not already identified if at the time the lessor learned of the default they were in the lessor's or the supplier's possession or control; and

(b) dispose of goods (Section 2A-527(1)) that demonstrably have been intended for the particular lease contract even though those goods are unfinished.

(2) If the goods are unfinished, in the exercise of reasonable commercial judgment for the purposes of avoiding loss and of effective realization, an aggrieved lessor or the supplier may either complete manufacture and wholly identify the goods to the lease contract or cease manufacture and lease, sell, or otherwise dispose of the goods for scrap or salvage value or proceed in any other reasonable manner.

§ 2A-525. Lessor's Right to Possession of Goods.

(1) If a lessor discovers the lessee to be insolvent, the lessor may refuse to deliver the goods.

(2) After a default by the lessee under the lease contract of the type described in Section 2A-523(1) or 2A-523(3)(a) or, if agreed, after other default by the lessee, the lessor has the right to take possession of the goods. If the lease contract so provides, the lessor may require the lessee to assemble the goods and make them available to the lessor at a place to be designated by the lessor which is reasonably convenient to both parties. Without removal, the lessor may render unusable any goods employed in trade or business, and may dispose of goods on the lessee's premises (Section 2A-527).

(3) The lessor may proceed under subsection (2) without judicial process if it can be done without breach of the peace or the lessor may proceed by action.

§ 2A-526. Lessor's Stoppage of Delivery in Transit or Otherwise.

(1) A lessor may stop delivery of goods in the possession of a carrier or other bailee if the lessor discovers the lessee to be insolvent and may stop delivery of carload, truckload, planeload, or larger shipments of express or freight if the lessee repudiates or fails to make a payment due before delivery, whether for rent, security or otherwise under the lease contract, or for any other reason the lessor has a right to withhold or take possession of the goods.

(2) In pursuing its remedies under subsection (1), the lessor may stop delivery until

(a) receipt of the goods by the lessee;

(b) acknowledgment to the lessee by any bailee of the

goods, except a carrier, that the bailee holds the goods for the lessee; or

(c) such an acknowledgment to the lessee by a carrier via reshipment or as warehouseman.

(3)(a) To stop delivery, a lessor shall so notify as to enable the bailee by reasonable diligence to prevent delivery of the goods.

(b) After notification, the bailee shall hold and deliver the goods according to the directions of the lessor, but the lessor is liable to the bailee for any ensuing charges or damages.

(c) A carrier who has issued a nonnegotiable bill of lading is not obliged to obey a notification to stop received from a person other than the consignor.

§ 2A-527.   Lessor's Rights to Dispose of Goods.

(1) After a default by a lessee under the lease contract of the type described in Section 2A-523(1) or 2A-523(3)(a) or after the lessor refuses to deliver or takes possession of goods (Section 2A-525 or 2A-526), or, if agreed, after other default by a lessee, the lessor may dispose of the goods concerned or the undelivered balance thereof by lease, sale, or otherwise.

(2) Except as otherwise provided with respect to damages liquidated in the lease agreement (Section 2A-504) or otherwise determined pursuant to agreement of the parties (Sections 1-102(3) and 2A-503), if the disposition is by lease agreement substantially similar to the original lease agreement and the new lease agreement is made in good faith and in a commercially reasonable manner, the lessor may recover from the lessee as damages (i) accrued and unpaid rent as of the date of the commencement of the term of the new lease agreement, (ii) the present value, as of the same date, of the total rent for the then remaining lease term of the original lease agreement minus the present value, as of the same date, of the rent under the new lease agreement applicable to that period of the new lease term which is comparable to the then remaining term of the original lease agreement, and (iii) any incidental damages allowed under Section 2A-530, less expenses saved in consequence of the lessee's default.

(3) If the lessor's disposition is by lease agreement that for any reason does not qualify for treatment under subsection (2), or is by sale or otherwise, the lessor may recover from the lessee as if the lessor had elected not to dispose of the goods and Section 2A-528 governs.

(4) A subsequent buyer or lessee who buys or leases from the lessor in good faith for value as a result of a disposition under this section takes the goods free of the original lease contract and any rights of the original lessee even though the lessor fails to comply with one or more of the requirements of this Article.

(5) The lessor is not accountable to the lessee for any profit made on any disposition. A lessee who has rightfully rejected or justifiably revoked acceptance shall account to the lessor for any excess over the amount of the lessee's security interest (Section 2A-508(5)).

§ 2A-528.   Lessor's Damages for Non-acceptance, Failure to Pay, Repudiation, or Other Default.

(1) Except as otherwise provided with respect to damages liquidated in the lease agreement (Section 2A-504) or other-

wise determined pursuant to agreement of the parties (Sections 1-102(3) and 2A-503), if a lessor elects to retain the goods or a lessor elects to dispose of the goods and the disposition is by lease agreement that for any reason does not qualify for treatment under Section 2A-527(2), or is by sale or otherwise, the lessor may recover from the lessee as damages for a default of the type described in Section 2A-523(1) or 2A-523(3)(a), or, if agreed, for other default of the lessee, (i) accrued and unpaid rent as of the date of default if the lessee has never taken possession of the goods, or, if the lessee has taken possession of the goods, as of the date the lessor repossesses the goods or an earlier date on which the lessee makes a tender of the goods to the lessor, (ii) the present value as of the date determined under clause (i) of the total rent for the then remaining lease term of the original lease agreement minus the present value as of the same date of the market rent at the place where the goods are located computed for the same lease term, and (iii) any incidental damages allowed under Section 2A-530, less expenses saved in consequence of the lessee's default.

(2) If the measure of damages provided in subsection (1) is inadequate to put a lessor in as good a position as performance would have, the measure of damages is the present value of the profit, including reasonable overhead, the lessor would have made from full performance by the lessee, together with any incidental damages allowed under Section 2A-530, due allowance for costs reasonably incurred and due credit for payments or proceeds of disposition.

§ 2A-529.   Lessor's Action for the Rent.

(1) After default by the lessee under the lease contract of the type described in Section 2A-523(1) or 2A-523(3)(a) or, if agreed, after other default by the lessee, if the lessor complies with subsection (2), the lessor may recover from the lessee as damages:

(a) for goods accepted by the lessee and not repossessed by or tendered to the lessor, and for conforming goods lost or damaged within a commercially reasonable time after risk of loss passes to the lessee (Section 2A-219), (i) accrued and unpaid rent as of the date of entry of judgment in favor of the lessor, (ii) the present value as of the same date of the rent for the then remaining lease term of the lease agreement, and (iii) any incidental damages allowed under Section 2A-530, less expenses saved in consequence of the lessee's default; and

(b) for goods identified to the lease contract if the lessor is unable after reasonable effort to dispose of them at a reasonable price or the circumstances reasonably indicate that effort will be unavailing, (i) accrued and unpaid rent as of the date of entry of judgment in favor of the lessor, (ii) the present value as of the same date of the rent for the then remaining lease term of the lease agreement, and (iii) any incidental damages allowed under Section 2A-530, less expenses saved in consequence of the lessee's default.

(2) Except as provided in subsection (3), the lessor shall hold for the lessee for the remaining lease term of the lease agreement any goods that have been identified to the lease contract and are in the lessor's control.

(3) The lessor may dispose of the goods at any time before collection of the judgment for damages obtained pursuant to

subsection (1). If the disposition is before the end of the remaining lease term of the lease agreement, the lessor's recovery against the lessee for damages is governed by Section 2A-527 or Section 2A-528, and the lessor will cause an appropriate credit to be provided against a judgment for damages to the extent that the amount of the judgment exceeds the recovery available pursuant to Section 2A-527 or 2A-528.

(4) Payment of the judgment for damages obtained pursuant to subsection (1) entitles the lessee to the use and possession of the goods not then disposed of for the remaining lease term of and in accordance with the lease agreement.

(5) After default by the lessee under the lease contract of the type described in Section 2A-523(1) or Section 2A-523(3)(a) or, if agreed, after other default by the lessee, a lessor who is held not entitled to rent under this section must nevertheless be awarded damages for non-acceptance under Section 2A-527 or Section 2A-528.

§ 2A-530. Lessor's Incidental Damages.

Incidental damages to an aggrieved lessor include any commercially reasonable charges, expenses, or commissions incurred in stopping delivery, in the transportation, care and custody of goods after the lessee's default, in connection with return or disposition of the goods, or otherwise resulting from the default.

§ 2A-531. Standing to Sue Third Parties for Injury to Goods.

(1) If a third party so deals with goods that have been identified to a lease contract as to cause actionable injury to a party to the lease contract (a) the lessor has a right of action against the third party, and (b) the lessee also has a right of action against the third party if the lessee:

(i) has a security interest in the goods;

(ii) has an insurable interest in the goods; or

(iii) bears the risk of loss under the lease contract or has since the injury assumed that risk as against the lessor and the goods have been converted or destroyed.

(2) If at the time of the injury the party plaintiff did not bear the risk of loss as against the other party to the lease contract and there is no arrangement between them for disposition of the recovery, his [or her] suit or settlement, subject to his [or her] own interest, is as a fiduciary for the other party to the lease contract.

(3) Either party with the consent of the other may sue for the benefit of whom it may concern.

§ 2A-532. Lessor's Rights to Residual Interest

In addition to any other recovery permitted by this Article or other law, the lessor may recover from the lessee an amount that will fully compensate the lessor for any loss of or damage to the lessor's residual interest in the goods caused by the default of the lessee.

REVISED ARTICLE 3 / Negotiable Instruments

Part 1 General Provisions and Definitions

§ 3-101. Short Title.

This Article may be cited as Uniform Commercial Code—Negotiable Instruments.

§ 3-102. Subject Matter.

(a) This Article applies to negotiable instruments. It does not apply to money, to payment orders governed by Article 4A, or to securities governed by Article 8.

(b) If there is conflict between this Article and Article 4 or 9, Articles 4 and 9 govern.

(c) Regulations of the Board of Governors of the Federal Reserve System and operating circulars of the Federal Reserve Banks supersede any inconsistent provision of this Article to the extent of the inconsistency.

§ 3-103. Definitions.

(a) In this Article:

(1) "Acceptor" means a drawee who has accepted a draft.

(2) "Drawee" means a person ordered in a draft to make payment.

(3) "Drawer" means a person who signs or is identified in a draft as a person ordering payment.

(4) "Good faith" means honesty in fact and the observance of reasonable commercial standards of fair dealing.

(5) "Maker" means a person who signs or is identified in a note as a person undertaking to pay.

(6) "Order" means a written instruction to pay money signed by the person giving the instruction. The instruction may be addressed to any person, including the person giving the instruction, or to one or more persons jointly or in the alternative but not in succession. An authorization to pay is not an order unless the person authorized to pay is also instructed to pay.

(7) "Ordinary care" in the case of a person engaged in business means observance of reasonable commercial standards, prevailing in the area in which the person is located, with respect to the business in which the person is engaged. In the case of a bank that takes an instrument for processing for collection or payment by automated means, reasonable commercial standards do not require the bank to examine the instrument if the failure to examine does not violate the bank's prescribed procedures and the bank's procedures do not vary unreasonably from general banking usage not disapproved by this Article or Article 4.

(8) "Party" means a party to an instrument.

(9) "Promise" means a written undertaking to pay money signed by the person undertaking to pay. An acknowledgment of an obligation by the obligor is not a promise unless the obligor also undertakes to pay the obligation.

(10) "Prove" with respect to a fact means to meet the burden of establishing the fact (Section 1-201(8)).

(11) "Remitter" means a person who purchases an instrument from its issuer if the instrument is payable to an identified person other than the purchaser.

(b) Other definitions applying to this Article and the sections in which they appear are:

"Acceptance"   Section 3-409
"Accommodated party"   Section 3-419
"Accommodation party"   Section 3-419
"Alteration"   Section 3-407
"Anomalous indorsement"   Section 3-205
"Blank indorsement"   Section 3-205
"Cashier's check"   Section 3-104
"Certificate of deposit"   Section 3-104

"Certified check"   Section 3-409
"Check"   Section 3-104
"Consideration"   Section 3-303
"Draft"   Section 3-104
"Holder in due course"   Section 3-302
"Incomplete instrument"   Section 3-115
"Indorsement"   Section 3-204
"Indorser"   Section 3-204
"Instrument"   Section 3-104
"Issue"   Section 3-105
"Issuer"   Section 3-105
"Negotiable instrument"   Section 3-104
"Negotiation"   Section 3-201
"Note"   Section 3-104
"Payable at a definite time"   Section 3-108
"Payable on demand"   Section 3-108
"Payable to bearer"   Section 3-109
"Payable to order"   Section 3-109
"Payment"   Section 3-602
"Person entitled to enforce"   Section 3-301
"Presentment"   Section 3-501
"Reacquisition"   Section 3-207
"Special indorsement"   Section 3-205
"Teller's check"   Section 3-104
"Transfer of instrument"   Section 3-203
"Traveler's check"   Section 3-104
"Value"   Section 3-303

(c) The following definitions in other Articles apply to this Article:

"Bank"   Section 4-105
"Banking day"   Section 4-104
"Clearing house"   Section 4-104
"Collecting bank"   Section 4-105
"Depositary bank"   Section 4-105
"Documentary draft"   Section 4-104
"Intermediary bank"   Section 4-105
"Item"   Section 4-104
"Payor bank"   Section 4-105
"Suspends payments"   Section 4-104

(d) In addition, Article 1 contains general definitions and principles of construction and interpretation applicable throughout this Article.

§ 3-104. Negotiable Instrument.

(a) Except as provided in subsections (c) and (d), "negotiable instrument" means an unconditional promise or order to pay a fixed amount of money, with or without interest or other charges described in the promise or order, if it:

(1) is payable to bearer or to order at the time it is issued or first comes into possession of a holder;

(2) is payable on demand or at a definite time; and

(3) does not state any other undertaking or instruction by the person promising or ordering payment to do any act in addition to the payment of money, but the promise or order may contain (i) an undertaking or power to give, maintain, or protect collateral to secure payment, (ii) an authorization or power to the holder to confess judgment or realize on or dispose of collateral, or (iii) a waiver of the benefit of any law intended for the advantage or protection of an obligor.

(b) "Instrument" means a negotiable instrument.

(c) An order that meets all of the requirements of subsection (a), except paragraph (1), and otherwise falls within the definition of "check" in subsection (f) is a negotiable instrument and a check.

(d) A promise or order other than a check is not an instrument if, at the time it is issued or first comes into possession of a holder, it contains a conspicuous statement, however expressed, to the effect that the promise or order is not negotiable or is not an instrument governed by this Article.

(e) An instrument is a "note" if it is a promise and is a "draft" if it is an order. If an instrument falls within the definition of both "note" and "draft," a person entitled to enforce the instrument may treat it as either.

(f) "Check" means (i) a draft, other than a documentary draft, payable on demand and drawn on a bank or (ii) a cashier's check or teller's check. An instrument may be a check even though it is described on its face by another term, such as "money order."

(g) "Cashier's check" means a draft with respect to which the drawer and drawee are the same bank or branches of the same bank.

(h) "Teller's check" means a draft drawn by a bank (i) on another bank, or (ii) payable at or through a bank.

(i) "Traveler's check" means an instrument that (i) is payable on demand, (ii) is drawn on or payable at or through a bank, (iii) is designated by the term "traveler's check" or by a substantially similar term, and (iv) requires, as a condition to payment, a countersignature by a person whose specimen signature appears on the instrument.

(j) "Certificate of deposit" means an instrument containing an acknowledgment by a bank that a sum of money has been received by the bank and a promise by the bank to repay the sum of money. A certificate of deposit is a note of the bank.

§ 3-105.   Issue of Instrument.

(a) "Issue" means the first delivery of an instrument by the maker or drawer, whether to a holder or nonholder, for the purpose of giving rights on the instrument to any person.

(b) An unissued instrument, or an unissued incomplete instrument that is completed, is binding on the maker or drawer, but nonissuance is a defense. An instrument that is conditionally issued or is issued for a special purpose is binding on the maker or drawer, but failure of the condition or special purpose to be fulfilled is a defense.

(c) "Issuer" applies to issued and unissued instruments and means a maker or drawer of an instrument.

§ 3-106.   Unconditional Promise or Order.

(a) Except as provided in this section, for the purposes of Section 3-104(a), a promise or order is unconditional unless it states (i) an express condition to payment, (ii) that the promise or order is subject to or governed by another writing, or (iii) that rights or obligations with respect to the promise or order are stated in another writing. A reference to another writing does not of itself make the promise or order conditional.

(b) A promise or order is not made conditional (i) by a reference to another writing for a statement of rights with respect to collateral, prepayment, or acceleration, or (ii) because payment is limited to resort to a particular fund or source.

(c) If a promise or order requires, as a condition to payment, a countersignature by a person whose specimen signature appears on the promise or order, the condition does not make the promise or order conditional for the purposes of Section 3-104(a). If the person whose specimen signature appears on an instrument fails to countersign the instrument, the failure to countersign is a defense to the obligation of the issuer, but the failure does not prevent a transferee of the instrument from becoming a holder of the instrument.

(d) If a promise or order at the time it is issued or first comes into possession of a holder contains a statement, required by applicable statutory or administrative law, to the effect that the rights of a holder or transferee are subject to claims or defenses that the issuer could assert against the original payee, the promise or order is not thereby made conditional for the purposes of Section 3-104(a); but if the promise or order is an instrument, there cannot be a holder in due course of the instrument.

§ 3-107. Instrument Payable in Foreign Money.

Unless the instrument otherwise provides, an instrument that states the amount payable in foreign money may be paid in the foreign money or in an equivalent amount in dollars calculated by using the current bank-offered spot rate at the place of payment for the purchase of dollars on the day on which the instrument is paid.

§ 3-108. Payable on Demand or at Definite Time.

(a) A promise or order is "payable on demand" if it (i) states that it is payable on demand or at sight, or otherwise indicates that it is payable at the will of the holder, or (ii) does not state any time of payment.

(b) A promise or order is "payable at a definite time" if it is payable on elapse of a definite period of time after sight or acceptance or at a fixed date or dates or at a time or times readily ascertainable at the time the promise or order is issued, subject to rights of (i) prepayment, (ii) acceleration, (iii) extension at the option of the holder, or (iv) extension to a further definite time at the option of the maker or acceptor or automatically upon or after a specified act or event.

(c) If an instrument, payable at a fixed date, is also payable upon demand made before the fixed date, the instrument is payable on demand until the fixed date and, if demand for payment is not made before that date, becomes payable at a definite time on the fixed date.

§ 3-109. Payable to Bearer or to Order.

(a) A promise or order is payable to bearer if it:

    (1) states that it is payable to bearer or to the order of bearer or otherwise indicates that the person in possession of the promise or order is entitled to payment;

    (2) does not state a payee; or

    (3) states that it is payable to or to the order of cash or otherwise indicates that it is not payable to an identified person.

(b) A promise or order that is not payable to bearer is payable to order if it is payable (i) to the order of an identified person or (ii) to an identified person or order. A promise or order that is payable to order is payable to the identified person.

(c) An instrument payable to bearer may become payable to an identified person if it is specially indorsed pursuant to Section 3-205(a). An instrument payable to an identified person may become payable to bearer if it is indorsed in blank pursuant to Section 3-205(b).

§ 3-110. Identification of Person to Whom Instrument Is Payable.

(a) The person to whom an instrument is initially payable is determined by the intent of the person, whether or not authorized, signing as, or in the name or behalf of, the issuer of the instrument. The instrument is payable to the person intended by the signer even if that person is identified in the instrument by a name or other identification that is not that of the intended person. If more than one person signs in the name or behalf of the issuer of an instrument and all the signers do not intend the same person as payee, the instrument is payable to any person intended by one or more of the signers.

(b) If the signature of the issuer of an instrument is made by automated means, such as a check-writing machine, the payee of the instrument is determined by the intent of the person who supplied the name or identification of the payee, whether or not authorized to do so.

(c) A person to whom an instrument is payable may be identified in any way, including by name, identifying number, office, or account number. For the purpose of determining the holder of an instrument, the following rules apply:

    (1) If an instrument is payable to an account and the account is identified only by number, the instrument is payable to the person to whom the account is payable. If an instrument is payable to an account identified by number and by the name of a person, the instrument is payable to the named person, whether or not that person is the owner of the account identified by number.

    (2) If an instrument is payable to:

        (i) a trust, an estate, or a person described as trustee or representative of a trust or estate, the instrument is payable to the trustee, the representative, or a successor of either, whether or not the beneficiary or estate is also named;

        (ii) a person described as agent or similar representative of a named or identified person, the instrument is payable to the represented person, the representative, or a successor of the representative;

        (iii) a fund or organization that is not a legal entity, the instrument is payable to a representative of the members of the fund or organization; or

        (iv) an office or to a person described as holding an office, the instrument is payable to the named person, the incumbent of the office, or a successor to the incumbent.

(d) If an instrument is payable to two or more persons alternatively, it is payable to any of them and may be negotiated, discharged, or enforced by any or all of them in possession of the instrument. If an instrument is payable to two or more persons not alternatively, it is payable to all of them and may be negotiated, discharged, or enforced only by all of them. If an instrument payable to two or more persons is ambiguous as to whether it is payable to the persons alternatively, the instrument is payable to the persons alternatively.

§ 3-111. Place of Payment.

Except as otherwise provided for items in Article 4, an instrument is payable at the place of payment stated in the instrument. If no place of payment is stated, an instrument is payable at the address of the drawee or maker stated in the instrument. If no address is stated, the place of payment is the place of business of the drawee or maker. If a drawee or maker has more than one place of business, the place of payment is any place of business of the drawee or maker chosen by the person entitled to enforce the instrument. If the drawee or maker has no place of business, the place of payment is the residence of the drawee or maker.

§ 3-112. Interest.

(a) Unless otherwise provided in the instrument, (i) an instrument is not payable with interest, and (ii) interest on an interest-bearing instrument is payable from the date of the instrument.

(b) Interest may be stated in an instrument as a fixed or variable amount of money or it may be expressed as a fixed or variable rate or rates. The amount or rate of interest may be stated or described in the instrument in any manner and may require reference to information not contained in the instrument. If an instrument provides for interest, but the amount of interest payable cannot be ascertained from the description, interest is payable at the judgment rate in effect at the place of payment of the instrument and at the time interest first accrues.

§ 3-113. Date of Instrument.

(a) An instrument may be antedated or postdated. The date stated determines the time of payment if the instrument is payable at a fixed period after date. Except as provided in Section 4-401(c), an instrument payable on demand is not payable before the date of the instrument.

(b) If an instrument is undated, its date is the date of its issue or, in the case of an unissued instrument, the date it first comes into possession of a holder.

§ 3-114. Contradictory Terms of Instrument.

If an instrument contains contradictory terms, typewritten terms prevail over printed terms, handwritten terms prevail over both, and words prevail over numbers.

§ 3-115. Incomplete Instrument.

(a) "Incomplete instrument" means a signed writing, whether or not issued by the signer, the contents of which show at the time of signing that it is incomplete but that the signer intended it to be completed by the addition of words or numbers.

(b) Subject to subsection (c), if an incomplete instrument is an instrument under Section 3-104, it may be enforced according to its terms if it is not completed, or according to its terms as augmented by completion. If an incomplete instrument is not an instrument under Section 3-104, but, after completion, the requirements of Section 3-104 are met, the instrument may be enforced according to its terms as augmented by completion.

(c) If words or numbers are added to an incomplete instrument without authority of the signer, there is an alteration of the incomplete instrument under Section 3-407.

(d) The burden of establishing that words or numbers were added to an incomplete instrument without authority of the signer is on the person asserting the lack of authority.

§ 3-116. Joint and Several Liability; Contribution.

(a) Except as otherwise provided in the instrument, two or more persons who have the same liability on an instrument as makers, drawers, acceptors, indorsers who indorse as joint payees, or anomalous indorsers are jointly and severally liable in the capacity in which they sign.

(b) Except as provided in Section 3-419(e) or by agreement of the affected parties, a party having joint and several liability who pays the instrument is entitled to receive from any party having the same joint and several liability contribution in accordance with applicable law.

(c) Discharge of one party having joint and several liability by a person entitled to enforce the instrument does not affect the right under subsection (b) of a party having the same joint and several liability to receive contribution from the party discharged.

§ 3-117. Other Agreements Affecting Instrument.

Subject to applicable law regarding exclusion of proof of contemporaneous or previous agreements, the obligation of a party to an instrument to pay the instrument may be modified, supplemented, or nullified by a separate agreement of the obligor and a person entitled to enforce the instrument, if the instrument is issued or the obligation is incurred in reliance on the agreement or as part of the same transaction giving rise to the agreement. To the extent an obligation is modified, supplemented, or nullified by an agreement under this section, the agreement is a defense to the obligation.

§ 3-118. Statute of Limitations.

(a) Except as provided in subsection (e), an action to enforce the obligation of a party to pay a note payable at a definite time must be commenced within six years after the due date or dates stated in the note or, if a due date is accelerated, within six years after the accelerated due date.

(b) Except as provided in subsection (d) or (e), if demand for payment is made to the maker of a note payable on demand, an action to enforce the obligation of a party to pay the note must be commenced within six years after the demand. If no demand for payment is made to the maker, an action to enforce the note is barred if neither principal nor interest on the note has been paid for a continuous period of 10 years.

(c) Except as provided in subsection (d), an action to enforce the obligation of a party to an unaccepted draft to pay the draft must be commenced within three years after dishonor of the draft or 10 years after the date of the draft, whichever period expires first.

(d) An action to enforce the obligation of the acceptor of a certified check or the issuer of a teller's check, cashier's check, or traveler's check must be commenced within three years after demand for payment is made to the acceptor or issuer, as the case may be.

(e) An action to enforce the obligation of a party to a certificate of deposit to pay the instrument must be commenced within six years after demand for payment is made to the maker, but if the instrument states a due date and the maker is not required to pay before that date, the six-year period begins when a demand for payment is in effect and the due date has passed.

(f) An action to enforce the obligation of a party to pay an accepted draft, other than a certified check, must be commenced (i) within six years after the due date or dates stated in the draft or acceptance if the obligation of the acceptor is payable at a definite time, or (ii) within six years after the date of the acceptance if the obligation of the acceptor is payable on demand.

(g) Unless governed by other law regarding claims for indemnity or contribution, an action (i) for conversion of an instrument, for money had and received, or like action based on conversion, (ii) for breach of warranty, or (iii) to enforce an obligation, duty, or right arising under this Article and not governed by this section must be commenced within three years after the [cause of action] accrues.

§ 3-119. Notice of Right to Defend Action.

In an action for breach of an obligation for which a third person is answerable over pursuant to this Article or Article 4, the defendant may give the third person written notice of the litigation, and the person notified may then give similar notice to any other person who is answerable over. If the notice states (i) that the person notified may come in and defend and (ii) that failure to do so will bind the person notified in an action later brought by the person giving the notice as to any determination of fact common to the two litigations, the person notified is so bound unless after seasonable receipt of the notice the person notified does come in and defend.

Part 2 Negotiation, Transfer, and Indorsement

§ 3-201. Negotiation.

(a) "Negotiation" means a transfer of possession, whether voluntary or involuntary, of an instrument by a person other than the issuer to a person who thereby becomes its holder.

(b) Except for negotiation by a remitter, if an instrument is payable to an identified person, negotiation requires transfer of possession of the instrument and its indorsement by the holder. If an instrument is payable to bearer, it may be negotiated by transfer of possession alone.

§ 3-202. Negotiation Subject to Rescission.

(a) Negotiation is effective even if obtained (i) from an infant, a corporation exceeding its powers, or a person without capacity, (ii) by fraud, duress, or mistake, or (iii) in breach of duty or as part of an illegal transaction.

(b) To the extent permitted by other law, negotiation may be rescinded or may be subject to other remedies, but those remedies may not be asserted against a subsequent holder in due course or a person paying the instrument in good faith and without knowledge of facts that are a basis for rescission or other remedy.

§ 3-203. Transfer of Instrument; Rights Acquired by Transfer.

(a) An instrument is transferred when it is delivered by a person other than its issuer for the purpose of giving to the person receiving delivery the right to enforce the instrument.

(b) Transfer of an instrument, whether or not the transfer is a negotiation, vests in the transferee any right of the transferor to enforce the instrument, including any right as a holder in due course, but the transferee cannot acquire rights of a holder in due course by a transfer, directly or indirectly, from a holder in due course if the transferee engaged in fraud or illegality affecting the instrument.

(c) Unless otherwise agreed, if an instrument is transferred for value and the transferee does not become a holder because of lack of indorsement by the transferor, the transferee has a specifically enforceable right to the unqualified indorsement of the transferor, but negotiation of the instrument does not occur until the indorsement is made.

(d) If a transferor purports to transfer less than the entire instrument, negotiation of the instrument does not occur. The transferee obtains no rights under this Article and has only the rights of a partial assignee.

§ 3-204. Indorsement.

(a) "Indorsement" means a signature, other than that of a signer as maker, drawer, or acceptor, that alone or accompanied by other words is made on an instrument for the purpose of (i) negotiating the instrument, (ii) restricting payment of the instrument, or (iii) incurring indorser's liability on the instrument, but regardless of the intent of the signer, a signature and its accompanying words is an indorsement unless the accompanying words, terms of the instrument, place of the signature, or other circumstances unambiguously indicate that the signature was made for a purpose other than indorsement. For the purpose of determining whether a signature is made on an instrument, a paper affixed to the instrument is a part of the instrument.

(b) "Indorser" means a person who makes an indorsement.

(c) For the purpose of determining whether the transferee of an instrument is a holder, an indorsement that transfers a security interest in the instrument is effective as an unqualified indorsement of the instrument.

(d) If an instrument is payable to a holder under a name that is not the name of the holder, indorsement may be made by the holder in the name stated in the instrument or in the holder's name or both, but signature in both names may be required by a person paying or taking the instrument for value or collection.

§ 3-205. Special Indorsement; Blank Indorsement; Anomalous Indorsement.

(a) If an indorsement is made by the holder of an instrument, whether payable to an identified person or payable to bearer, and the indorsement identifies a person to whom it makes the instrument payable, it is a "special indorsement." When specially indorsed, an instrument becomes payable to the identified person and may be negotiated only by the indorsement of that person. The principles stated in Section 3-110 apply to special indorsements.

(b) If an indorsement is made by the holder of an instrument and it is not a special indorsement, it is a "blank indorsement." When indorsed in blank, an instrument becomes payable to bearer and may be negotiated by transfer of possession alone until specially indorsed.

(c) The holder may convert a blank indorsement that consists only of a signature into a special indorsement by writing, above the signature of the indorser, words identifying the person to whom the instrument is made payable.

(d) "Anomalous indorsement" means an indorsement made by a person who is not the holder of the instrument. An anomalous indorsement does not affect the manner in which the instrument may be negotiated.

§ 3-206. Restrictive Indorsement.

(a) An indorsement limiting payment to a particular person or otherwise prohibiting further transfer or negotiation of the instrument is not effective to prevent further transfer or negotiation of the instrument.

(b) An indorsement stating a condition to the right of the indorsee to receive payment does not affect the right of the indorsee to enforce the instrument. A person paying the instrument or taking it for value or collection may disregard the condition, and the rights and liabilities of that person are not affected by whether the condition has been fulfilled.

(c) If an instrument bears an indorsement (i) described in Section 4-201(b), or (ii) in blank or to a particular bank using the words "for deposit," "for collection," or other words indicating a purpose of having the instrument collected by a bank for the indorser or for a particular account, the following rules apply:

(1) A person, other than a bank, who purchases the instrument when so indorsed converts the instrument unless the amount paid for the instrument is received by the indorser or applied consistently with the indorsement.

(2) A depositary bank that purchases the instrument or takes it for collection when so indorsed converts the instrument unless the amount paid by the bank with respect to the instrument is received by the indorser or applied consistently with the indorsement.

(3) A payor bank that is also the depositary bank or that takes the instrument for immediate payment over the counter from a person other than a collecting bank converts the instrument unless the proceeds of the instrument are received by the indorser or applied consistently with the indorsement.

(4) Except as otherwise provided in paragraph (3), a payor bank or intermediary bank may disregard the indorsement and is not liable if the proceeds of the instrument are not received by the indorser or applied consistently with the indorsement.

(d) Except for an indorsement covered by subsection (c), if an instrument bears an indorsement using words to the effect that payment is to be made to the indorsee as agent, trustee, or other fiduciary for the benefit of the indorser or another person, the following rules apply:

(1) Unless there is notice of breach of fiduciary duty as provided in Section 3-307, a person who purchases the instrument from the indorsee or takes the instrument from the indorsee for collection or payment may pay the proceeds of payment or the value given for the instrument to the indorsee without regard to whether the indorsee violates a fiduciary duty to the indorser.

(2) A subsequent transferee of the instrument or person who pays the instrument is neither given notice nor otherwise affected by the restriction in the indorsement unless the transferee or payor knows that the fiduciary dealt with the instrument or its proceeds in breach of fiduciary duty.

(e) The presence on an instrument of an indorsement to which this section applies does not prevent a purchaser of the instrument from becoming a holder in due course of the instrument unless the purchaser is a converter under subsection (c) or has notice or knowledge of breach of fiduciary duty as stated in subsection (d).

(f) In an action to enforce the obligation of a party to pay the instrument, the obligor has a defense if payment would violate an indorsement to which this section applies and the payment is not permitted by this section.

§ 3-207. Reacquisition.

Reacquisition of an instrument occurs if it is transferred to a former holder, by negotiation or otherwise. A former holder who reacquires the instrument may cancel indorsements made after the reacquirer first became a holder of the instrument. If the cancellation causes the instrument to be payable to the reacquirer or to bearer, the reacquirer may negotiate the instrument. An indorser whose indorsement is canceled is discharged, and the discharge is effective against any subsequent holder.

Part 3   Enforcement of Instruments

§ 3-301.   Person Entitled to Enforce Instrument.

"Person entitled to enforce" an instrument means (i) the holder of the instrument, (ii) a nonholder in possession of the instrument who has the rights of a holder, or (iii) a person not in possession of the instrument who is entitled to enforce the instrument pursuant to Section 3-309 or 3-418(d). A person may be a person entitled to enforce the instrument even though the person is not the owner of the instrument or is in wrongful possession of the instrument.

§ 3-302.   Holder in Due Course.

(a) Subject to subsection (c) and Section 3-106(d), "holder in due course" means the holder of an instrument if:

(1) the instrument when issued or negotiated to the holder does not bear such apparent evidence of forgery or alteration or is not otherwise so irregular or incomplete as to call into question its authenticity; and

(2) the holder took the instrument (i) for value, (ii) in good faith, (iii) without notice that the instrument is overdue or has been dishonored or that there is an uncured default with respect to payment of another instrument issued as part of the same series, (iv) without notice that the instrument contains an unauthorized signature or has been altered, (v) without notice of any claim to the instrument described in Section 3-306, and (vi) without notice that any party has a defense or claim in recoupment described in Section 3-305(a).

(b) Notice of discharge of a party, other than discharge in an insolvency proceeding, is not notice of a defense under subsection (a), but discharge is effective against a person who became a holder in due course with notice of the discharge. Public filing or recording of a document does not of itself constitute notice of a defense, claim in recoupment, or claim to the instrument.

(c) Except to the extent a transferor or predecessor in interest has rights as a holder in due course, a person does not acquire rights of a holder in due course of an instrument taken (i) by legal process or by purchase in an execution, bankruptcy, or creditor's sale or similar proceeding, (ii) by purchase as part of a bulk transaction not in ordinary course of business of the transferor, or (iii) as the successor in interest to an estate or other organization.

(d) If, under Section 3-303(a)(1), the promise of performance that is the consideration for an instrument has been partially performed, the holder may assert rights as a holder in due course of the instrument only to the fraction of the amount payable under the instrument equal to the value of the partial performance divided by the value of the promised performance.

(e) If (i) the person entitled to enforce an instrument has only a security interest in the instrument and (ii) the person obliged to pay the instrument has a defense, claim in recoupment, or claim to the instrument that may be asserted against the person who granted the security interest, the person entitled to enforce the instrument may assert rights as a holder in due course only to an amount payable under the instrument which, at the time of enforcement of the instrument, does not exceed the amount of the unpaid obligation secured.

(f) To be effective, notice must be received at a time and in a manner that gives a reasonable opportunity to act on it.

(g) This section is subject to any law limiting status as a holder in due course in particular classes of transactions.

§ 3-303. Value and Consideration.

(a) An instrument is issued or transferred for value if:

(1) the instrument is issued or transferred for a promise of performance, to the extent the promise has been performed;

(2) the transferee acquires a security interest or other lien in the instrument other than a lien obtained by judicial proceeding;

(3) the instrument is issued or transferred as payment of, or as security for, an antecedent claim against any person, whether or not the claim is due;

(4) the instrument is issued or transferred in exchange for a negotiable instrument; or

(5) the instrument is issued or transferred in exchange for the incurring of an irrevocable obligation to a third party by the person taking the instrument.

(b) "Consideration" means any consideration sufficient to support a simple contract. The drawer or maker of an instrument has a defense if the instrument is issued without consideration. If an instrument is issued for a promise of performance, the issuer has a defense to the extent performance of the promise is due and the promise has not been performed. If an instrument is issued for value as stated in subsection (a), the instrument is also issued for consideration.

§ 3-304. Overdue Instrument.

(a) An instrument payable on demand becomes overdue at the earliest of the following times:

(1) on the day after the day demand for payment is duly made;

(2) if the instrument is a check, 90 days after its date; or

(3) if the instrument is not a check, when the instrument has been outstanding for a period of time after its date which is unreasonably long under the circumstances of the particular case in light of the nature of the instrument and usage of the trade.

(b) With respect to an instrument payable at a definite time the following rules apply:

(1) If the principal is payable in installments and a due date has not been accelerated, the instrument becomes overdue upon default under the instrument for nonpayment of an installment, and the instrument remains overdue until the default is cured.

(2) If the principal is not payable in installments and the due date has not been accelerated, the instrument becomes overdue on the day after the due date.

(3) If a due date with respect to principal has been accelerated, the instrument becomes overdue on the day after the accelerated due date.

(c) Unless the due date of principal has been accelerated, an instrument does not become overdue if there is default in payment of interest but no default in payment of principal.

§ 3-305. Defenses and Claims in Recoupment.

(a) Except as stated in subsection (b), the right to enforce the obligation of a party to pay an instrument is subject to the following:

(1) a defense of the obligor based on (i) infancy of the obligor to the extent it is a defense to a simple contract, (ii) duress, lack of legal capacity, or illegality of the transaction which, under other law, nullifies the obligation of the obligor, (iii) fraud that induced the obligor to sign the instrument with neither knowledge nor reasonable opportunity to learn of its character or its essential terms, or (iv) discharge of the obligor in insolvency proceedings;

(2) a defense of the obligor stated in another section of this Article or a defense of the obligor that would be available if the person entitled to enforce the instrument were enforcing a right to payment under a simple contract; and

(3) a claim in recoupment of the obligor against the original payee of the instrument if the claim arose from the transaction that gave rise to the instrument; but the claim of the obligor may be asserted against a transferee of the instrument only to reduce the amount owing on the instrument at the time the action is brought.

(b) The right of a holder in due course to enforce the obligation of a party to pay the instrument is subject to defenses of the obligor stated in subsection (a)(1), but is not subject to defenses of the obligor stated in subsection (a)(2) or claims in recoupment stated in subsection (a)(3) against a person other than the holder.

(c) Except as stated in subsection (d), in an action to enforce the obligation of a party to pay the instrument, the obligor may not assert against the person entitled to enforce the instrument a defense, claim in recoupment, or claim to the instrument (Section 3-306) of another person, but the other person's claim to the instrument may be asserted by the obligor if the other person is joined in the action and personally asserts the claim against the person entitled to enforce the instrument. An obligor is not obliged to pay the instrument if the person seeking enforcement of the instrument does not have rights of a holder in due course and the obligor proves that the instrument is a lost or stolen instrument.

(d) In an action to enforce the obligation of an accommodation party to pay an instrument, the accommodation party may assert against the person entitled to enforce the instrument any defense or claim in recoupment under subsection (a) that the accommodated party could assert against the person entitled to enforce the instrument, except the defenses of discharge in insolvency proceedings, infancy, and lack of legal capacity.

§ 3-306. Claims to an Instrument.

A person taking an instrument, other than a person having rights of a holder in due course, is subject to a claim of a property or possessory right in the instrument or its proceeds, including a claim to rescind a negotiation and to recover the instrument or its proceeds. A person having rights of a holder in due course takes free of the claim to the instrument.

§ 3-307. Notice of Breach of Fiduciary Duty.

(a) In this section:

(1) "Fiduciary" means an agent, trustee, partner, corporate officer or director, or other representative owing a fiduciary duty with respect to an instrument.

(2) "Represented person" means the principal, beneficiary, partnership, corporation, or other person to whom the duty stated in paragraph (1) is owed.

(b) If (i) an instrument is taken from a fiduciary for payment or collection or for value, (ii) the taker has knowledge of the fiduciary status of the fiduciary, and (iii) the represented person makes a claim to the instrument or its proceeds on the basis that the transaction of the fiduciary is a breach of fiduciary duty, the following rules apply:

(1) Notice of breach of fiduciary duty by the fiduciary is notice of the claim of the represented person.

(2) In the case of an instrument payable to the represented person or the fiduciary as such, the taker has notice of the breach of fiduciary duty if the instrument is (i) taken in payment of or as security for a debt known by the taker to be the personal debt of the fiduciary, (ii) taken in a transaction known by the taker to be for the personal benefit of the fiduciary, or (iii) deposited to an account other than an account of the fiduciary, as such, or an account of the represented person.

(3) If an instrument is issued by the represented person or the fiduciary as such, and made payable to the fiduciary personally, the taker does not have notice of the breach of fiduciary duty unless the taker knows of the breach of fiduciary duty.

(4) If an instrument is issued by the represented person or the fiduciary as such, to the taker as payee, the taker has notice of the breach of fiduciary duty if the instrument is (i) taken in payment of or as security for a debt known by the taker to be the personal debt of the fiduciary, (ii) taken in a transaction known by the taker to be for the personal benefit of the fiduciary, or (iii) deposited to an account other than an account of the fiduciary, as such, or an account of the represented person.

§ 3-308. Proof of Signatures and Status as Holder in Due Course.

(a) In an action with respect to an instrument, the authenticity of, and authority to make, each signature on the instrument is admitted unless specifically denied in the pleadings. If the validity of a signature is denied in the pleadings, the burden of establishing validity is on the person claiming validity, but the signature is presumed to be authentic and authorized unless the action is to enforce the liability of the purported signer and the signer is dead or incompetent at the time of trial of the issue of validity of the signature. If an action to enforce the instrument is brought against a person as the undisclosed principal of a person who signed the instrument as a party to the instrument, the plaintiff has the burden of establishing that the defendant is liable on the instrument as a represented person under Section 3-402(a).

(b) If the validity of signatures is admitted or proved and there is compliance with subsection (a), a plaintiff producing the instrument is entitled to payment if the plaintiff proves entitlement to enforce the instrument under Section 3-301, unless the defendant proves a defense or claim in recoupment. If a defense or claim in recoupment is proved, the right to payment of the plaintiff is subject to the defense or claim, except to the extent the plaintiff proves that the plaintiff has rights of a holder in due course which are not subject to the defense or claim.

§ 3-309. Enforcement of Lost, Destroyed, or Stolen Instrument.

(a) A person not in possession of an instrument is entitled to enforce the instrument if (i) the person was in possession of the instrument and entitled to enforce it when loss of possession occurred, (ii) the loss of possession was not the result of a transfer by the person or a lawful seizure, and (iii) the person cannot reasonably obtain possession of the instrument because the instrument was destroyed, its whereabouts cannot be determined, or it is in the wrongful possession of an unknown person or a person that cannot be found or is not amenable to service of process.

(b) A person seeking enforcement of an instrument under subsection (a) must prove the terms of the instrument and the person's right to enforce the instrument. If that proof is made, Section 3-308 applies to the case as if the person seeking enforcement had produced the instrument. The court may not enter judgment in favor of the person seeking enforcement unless it finds that the person required to pay the instrument is adequately protected against loss that might occur by reason of a claim by another person to enforce the instrument. Adequate protection may be provided by any reasonable means.

§ 3-310. Effect of Instrument on Obligation for Which Taken.

(a) Unless otherwise agreed, if a certified check, cashier's check, or teller's check is taken for an obligation, the obligation is discharged to the same extent discharge would result if an amount of money equal to the amount of the instrument were taken in payment of the obligation. Discharge of the obligation does not affect any liability that the obligor may have as an indorser of the instrument.

(b) Unless otherwise agreed and except as provided in subsection (a), if a note or an uncertified check is taken for an obligation, the obligation is suspended to the same extent the obligation would be discharged if an amount of money equal to the amount of the instrument were taken, and the following rules apply:

(1) In the case of an uncertified check, suspension of the obligation continues until dishonor of the check or until it is paid or certified. Payment or certification of the check results in discharge of the obligation to the extent of the amount of the check.

(2) In the case of a note, suspension of the obligation continues until dishonor of the note or until it is paid. Payment of the note results in discharge of the obligation to the extent of the payment.

(3) Except as provided in paragraph (4), if the check or note is dishonored and the obligee of the obligation for which the instrument was taken is the person entitled to enforce the instrument, the obligee may enforce either the instrument or the obligation. In the case of an instrument of a third person which is negotiated to the obligee by the obligor, discharge of the obligor on the instrument also discharges the obligation.

(4) If the person entitled to enforce the instrument taken for an obligation is a person other than the obligee, the obligee may not enforce the obligation to the extent the obligation is suspended. If the obligee is the person entitled to enforce the instrument but no longer has possession of it because it was lost, stolen, or destroyed, the obligation may not be enforced to the extent of the amount payable on the instrument, and to that extent the obligee's rights against the obligor are limited to enforcement of the instrument.

(c) If an instrument other than one described in subsection (a) or (b) is taken for an obligation, the effect is (i) that stated in subsection (a) if the instrument is one on which a bank is liable as maker or acceptor, or (ii) that stated in subsection (b) in any other case.

§ 3-311. Accord and Satisfaction by Use of Instrument.

(a) If a person against whom a claim is asserted proves that (i) that person in good faith tendered an instrument to the claimant as full satisfaction of the claim, (ii) the amount of the claim was unliquidated or subject to a bona fide dispute, and (iii) the claimant obtained payment of the instrument, the following subsections apply.

(b) Unless subsection (c) applies, the claim is discharged if the person against whom the claim is asserted proves that the instrument or an accompanying written communication contained a conspicuous statement to the effect that the instrument was tendered as full satisfaction of the claim.

(c) Subject to subsection (d), a claim is not discharged under subsection (b) if either of the following applies:

(1) The claimant, if an organization, proves that (i) within a reasonable time before the tender, the claimant sent a conspicuous statement to the person against whom

the claim is asserted that communications concerning disputed debts, including an instrument tendered as full satisfaction of a debt, are to be sent to a designated person, office, or place, and (ii) the instrument or accompanying communication was not received by that designated person, office, or place.

(2) The claimant, whether or not an organization, proves that within 90 days after payment of the instrument, the claimant tendered repayment of the amount of the instrument to the person against whom the claim is asserted. This paragraph does not apply if the claimant is an organization that sent a statement complying with paragraph (1)(i).

(d) A claim is discharged if the person against whom the claim is asserted proves that within a reasonable time before collection of the instrument was initiated, the claimant, or an agent of the claimant having direct responsibility with respect to the disputed obligation, knew that the instrument was tendered in full satisfaction of the claim.

§ 3-312. Lost, Destroyed, or Stolen Cashier's Check, Teller's Check, or Certified Check.

(a) In this section:

(1) "Check" means a cashier's check, teller's check, or certified check.

(2) "Claimant" means a person who claims the right to receive the amount of a cashier's check, teller's check, or certified check that was lost, destroyed, or stolen.

(3) "Declaration of loss" means a written statement, made under penalty of perjury, to the effect that (i) the declarer lost possession of a check, (ii) the declarer is the drawer or payee of the check, in the case of a certified check, or the remitter or payee of the check, in the case of a cashier's check or teller's check, (iii) the loss of possession was not the result of a transfer by the declarer or a lawful seizure, and (iv) the declarer cannot reasonably obtain possession of the check because the check was destroyed, its whereabouts cannot be determined, or it is in the wrongful possession of an unknown person or a person that cannot be found or is not amenable to service of process.

(4) "Obligated bank" means the issuer of a cashier's check or teller's check or the acceptor of a certified check.

(b) A claimant may assert a claim to the amount of a check by a communication to the obligated bank describing the check with reasonable certainty and requesting payment of the amount of the check, if (i) the claimant is the drawer or payee of a certified check or the remitter or payee of a cashier's check or teller's check, (ii) the communication contains or is accompanied by a declaration of loss of the claimant with respect to the check, (iii) the communication is received at a time and in a manner affording the bank a reasonable time to act on it before the check is paid, and (iv) the claimant provides reasonable identification if requested by the obligated bank. Delivery of a declaration of loss is a warranty of the truth of the statements made in the declaration. The warranty is made to the obligated bank and any person entitled to enforce the check. If a claim is asserted in compliance with this subsection, the following rules apply:

(1) The claim becomes enforceable at the later of (i) the time the claim is asserted, or (ii) the 90th day following the date of the check, in the case of a cashier's check or teller's check, or the 90th day following the date of the acceptance, in the case of a certified check.

(2) Until the claim becomes enforceable, it has no legal effect and the obligated bank may pay the check or, in the case of a teller's check, may permit the drawee to pay the check. Payment to a person entitled to enforce the check discharges all liability of the obligated bank with respect to the check.

(3) If the claim becomes enforceable before the check is presented for payment, the obligated bank is not obligated to pay the check.

(4) When the claim becomes enforceable, the obligated bank becomes obliged to pay the amount of the check to the claimant if payment of the check has not been made to a person entitled to enforce the check. Subject to Section 4-302(a)(1), payment to the claimant discharges all liability of the obligated bank with respect to the check.

(c) If the obligated bank pays the amount of a check to a claimant under subsection (b)(4) and, after the claim became enforceable, the check is presented for payment by a person having rights of a holder in due course, the claimant is obliged to (i) refund the payment to the obligated bank if the check is paid, or (ii) pay the amount of the check to the person having rights of a holder in due course if the check is dishonored.

(d) If a claimant has the right to assert a claim under subsection (b) and is also a person entitled to enforce a cashier's check, teller's check, or certified check which is lost, destroyed, or stolen, the claimant may assert rights with respect to the check either under this section or Section 3-309.

Part 4 Liability of Parties

§ 3-401. Signature.

(a) A person is not liable on an instrument unless (i) the person signed the instrument, or (ii) the person is represented by an agent or representative who signed the instrument and the signature is binding on the represented person under Section 3-402.

(b) A signature may be made (i) manually or by means of a device or machine, and (ii) by the use of any name, including a trade or assumed name, or by a word, mark, or symbol executed or adopted by a person with present intention to authenticate a writing.

§ 3-402. Signature by Representative.

(a) If a person acting, or purporting to act, as a representative signs an instrument by signing either the name of the represented person or the name of the signer, the represented person is bound by the signature to the same extent the represented person would be bound if the signature were on a simple contract. If the represented person is bound, the signature of the representative is the "authorized signature of the represented person" and the represented person is liable on the instrument, whether or not identified in the instrument.

(b) If a representative signs the name of the representative to an instrument and the signature is an authorized signature of the represented person, the following rules apply:

(1) If the form of the signature shows unambiguously that the signature is made on behalf of the represented person who is identified in the instrument, the representative is not liable on the instrument.

(2) Subject to subsection (c), if (i) the form of the signature does not show unambiguously that the signature is made in a representative capacity or (ii) the represented person is not identified in the instrument, the representative is liable on the instrument to a holder in due course that took the instrument without notice that the representative was not intended to be liable on the instrument. With respect to any other person, the representative is liable on the instrument unless the representative proves that the original parties did not intend the representative to be liable on the instrument.

(c) If a representative signs the name of the representative as drawer of a check without indication of the representative status and the check is payable from an account of the represented person who is identified on the check, the signer is not liable on the check if the signature is an authorized signature of the represented person.

§ 3-403. Unauthorized Signature.

(a) Unless otherwise provided in this Article or Article 4, an unauthorized signature is ineffective except as the signature of the unauthorized signer in favor of a person who in good faith pays the instrument or takes it for value. An unauthorized signature may be ratified for all purposes of this Article.

(b) If the signature of more than one person is required to constitute the authorized signature of an organization, the signature of the organization is unauthorized if one of the required signatures is lacking.

(c) The civil or criminal liability of a person who makes an unauthorized signature is not affected by any provision of this Article which makes the unauthorized signature effective for the purposes of this Article.

§ 3-404. Impostors; Fictitious Payees.

(a) If an impostor, by use of the mails or otherwise, induces the issuer of an instrument to issue the instrument to the impostor, or to a person acting in concert with the impostor, by impersonating the payee of the instrument or a person authorized to act for the payee, an indorsement of the instrument by any person in the name of the payee is effective as the indorsement of the payee in favor of a person who, in good faith, pays the instrument or takes it for value or for collection.

(b) If (i) a person whose intent determines to whom an instrument is payable (Section 3-110(a) or (b)) does not intend the person identified as payee to have any interest in the instrument, or (ii) the person identified as payee of an instrument is a fictitious person, the following rules apply until the instrument is negotiated by special indorsement:

(1) Any person in possession of the instrument is its holder.

(2) An indorsement by any person in the name of the payee stated in the instrument is effective as the indorsement of the payee in favor of a person who, in good faith, pays the instrument or takes it for value or for collection.

(c) Under subsection (a) or (b), an indorsement is made in the name of a payee if (i) it is made in a name substantially similar to that of the payee or (ii) the instrument, whether or not indorsed, is deposited in a depository bank to an account in a name substantially similar to that of the payee.

(d) With respect to an instrument to which subsection (a) or (b) applies, if a person paying the instrument or taking it for value or for collection fails to exercise ordinary care in paying or taking the instrument and that failure substantially contributes to loss resulting from payment of the instrument, the person bearing the loss may recover from the person failing to exercise ordinary care to the extent the failure to exercise ordinary care contributed to the loss.

§ 3-405. Employer's Responsibility for Fraudulent Indorsement by Employee.

(a) In this section:

(1) "Employee" includes an independent contractor and employee of an independent contractor retained by the employer.

(2) "Fraudulent indorsement" means (i) in the case of an instrument payable to the employer, a forged indorsement purporting to be that of the employer, or (ii) in the case of an instrument with respect to which the employer is the issuer, a forged indorsement purporting to be that of the person identified as payee.

(3) "Responsibility" with respect to instruments means authority (i) to sign or indorse instruments on behalf of the employer, (ii) to process instruments received by the employer for bookkeeping purposes, for deposit to an account, or for other disposition, (iii) to prepare or process instruments for issue in the name of the employer, (iv) to supply information determining the names or addresses of payees of instruments to be issued in the name of the employer, (v) to control the disposition of instruments to be issued in the name of the employer, or (vi) to act otherwise with respect to instruments in a responsible capacity. "Responsibility" does not include authority that merely allows an employee to have access to instruments or blank or incomplete instrument forms that are being stored or transported or are part of incoming or outgoing mail, or similar access.

(b) For the purpose of determining the rights and liabilities of a person who, in good faith, pays an instrument or takes it for value or for collection, if an employer entrusted an employee with responsibility with respect to the instrument and the employee or a person acting in concert with the employee makes a fraudulent indorsement of the instrument, the indorsement is effective as the indorsement of the person to whom the instrument is payable if it is made in the name of that person. If the person paying the instrument or taking it for value or for collection fails to exercise ordinary care in paying or taking the instrument and that failure substantially contributes to loss resulting from the fraud, the person bearing the loss may recover from the person failing to exercise ordinary care to the extent the failure to exercise ordinary care contributed to the loss.

(c) Under subsection (b), an indorsement is made in the name of the person to whom an instrument is payable if (i) it is made in a name substantially similar to the name of that person or (ii) the instrument, whether or not indorsed, is deposited in a depository bank to an account in a name substantially similar to the name of that person.

§ 3-406. Negligence Contributing to Forged Signature or Alteration of Instrument.

(a) A person whose failure to exercise ordinary care substantially contributes to an alteration of an instrument or to the making of a forged signature on an instrument is precluded from asserting the alteration or the forgery against a person who, in good faith, pays the instrument or takes it for value or for collection.

(b) Under subsection (a), if the person asserting the preclusion fails to exercise ordinary care in paying or taking the instrument and that failure substantially contributes to loss, the loss is allocated between the person precluded and the person asserting the preclusion according to the extent to which the failure of each to exercise ordinary care contributed to the loss.

(c) Under subsection (a), the burden of proving failure to exercise ordinary care is on the person asserting the preclusion. Under subsection (b), the burden of proving failure to exercise ordinary care is on the person precluded.

§ 3-407. Alteration.

(a) "Alteration" means (i) an unauthorized change in an instrument that purports to modify in any respect the obligation of a party, or (ii) an unauthorized addition of words or numbers or other change to an incomplete instrument relating to the obligation of a party.

(b) Except as provided in subsection (c), an alteration fraudulently made discharges a party whose obligation is affected by the alteration unless that party assents or is precluded from asserting the alteration. No other alteration discharges a party, and the instrument may be enforced according to its original terms.

(c) A payor bank or drawee paying a fraudulently altered instrument or a person taking it for value, in good faith and without notice of the alteration, may enforce rights with respect to the instrument (i) according to its original terms, or (ii) in the case of an incomplete instrument altered by unauthorized completion, according to its terms as completed.

§ 3-408. Drawee Not Liable on Unaccepted Draft.

A check or other draft does not of itself operate as an assignment of funds in the hands of the drawee available for its payment, and the drawee is not liable on the instrument until the drawee accepts it.

§ 3-409. Acceptance of Draft; Certified Check.

(a) "Acceptance" means the drawee's signed agreement to pay a draft as presented. It must be written on the draft and may consist of the drawee's signature alone. Acceptance may be made at any time and becomes effective when notification pursuant to instructions is given or the accepted draft is delivered for the purpose of giving rights on the acceptance to any person.

(b) A draft may be accepted although it has not been signed by the drawer, is otherwise incomplete, is overdue, or has been dishonored.

(c) If a draft is payable at a fixed period after sight and the acceptor fails to date the acceptance, the holder may complete the acceptance by supplying a date in good faith.

(d) "Certified check" means a check accepted by the bank on which it is drawn. Acceptance may be made as stated in subsection (a) or by a writing on the check which indicates that the check is certified. The drawee of a check has no obligation to certify the check, and refusal to certify is not dishonor of the check.

§ 3-410. Acceptance Varying Draft.

(a) If the terms of a drawee's acceptance vary from the terms of the draft as presented, the holder may refuse the acceptance and treat the draft as dishonored. In that case, the drawee may cancel the acceptance.

(b) The terms of a draft are not varied by an acceptance to pay at a particular bank or place in the United States, unless the acceptance states that the draft is to be paid only at that bank or place.

(c) If the holder assents to an acceptance varying the terms of a draft, the obligation of each drawer and indorser that does not expressly assent to the acceptance is discharged.

§ 3-411. Refusal to Pay Cashier's Checks, Teller's Checks, and Certified Checks.

(a) In this section, "obligated bank" means the acceptor of a certified check or the issuer of a cashier's check or teller's check bought from the issuer.

(b) If the obligated bank wrongfully (i) refuses to pay a cashier's check or certified check, (ii) stops payment of a teller's check, or (iii) refuses to pay a dishonored teller's check, the person asserting the right to enforce the check is entitled to compensation for expenses and loss of interest resulting from the nonpayment and may recover consequential damages if the obligated bank refuses to pay after receiving notice of particular circumstances giving rise to the damages.

(c) Expenses or consequential damages under subsection (b) are not recoverable if the refusal of the obligated bank to pay occurs because (i) the bank suspends payments, (ii) the obligated bank asserts a claim or defense of the bank that it has reasonable grounds to believe is available against the person entitled to enforce the instrument, (iii) the obligated bank has a reasonable doubt whether the person demanding payment is the person entitled to enforce the instrument, or (iv) payment is prohibited by law.

§ 3-412. Obligation of Issuer of Note or Cashier's Check.

The issuer of a note or cashier's check or other draft drawn on the drawer is obliged to pay the instrument (i) according to its terms at the time it was issued or, if not issued, at the time it first came into possession of a holder, or (ii) if the issuer signed an incomplete instrument, according to its terms when completed, to the extent stated in Sections 3-115 and 3-407. The obligation is owed to a person entitled to enforce the instrument or to an indorser who paid the instrument under Section 3-415.

§ 3-413. Obligation of Acceptor.

(a) The acceptor of a draft is obliged to pay the draft (i) according to its terms at the time it was accepted, even though the acceptance states that the draft is payable "as originally drawn" or equivalent terms, (ii) if the acceptance varies the terms of the draft, according to the terms of the draft as varied, or (iii) if the acceptance is of a draft that is an incomplete instrument, according to its terms when completed, to the extent stated in Sections 3-115 and 3-407. The obligation is owed to a person entitled to enforce the draft or to the drawer or an indorser who paid the draft under Section 3-414 or 3-415.

(b) If the certification of a check or other acceptance of a draft states the amount certified or accepted, the obligation of the acceptor is that amount. If (i) the certification or acceptance does not state an amount, (ii) the amount of the instrument is subsequently raised, and (iii) the instrument is then negotiated to a holder in due course, the obligation of the acceptor is the amount of the instrument at the time it was taken by the holder in due course.

§ 3-414. Obligation of Drawer.

(a) This section does not apply to cashier's checks or other drafts drawn on the drawer.

(b) If an unaccepted draft is dishonored, the drawer is obliged to pay the draft (i) according to its terms at the time it was issued or, if not issued, at the time it first came into possession of a holder, or (ii) if the drawer signed an incomplete instrument, according to its terms when completed, to the extent stated in Sections 3-115 and 3-407. The obligation is owed to a person entitled to enforce the draft or to an indorser who paid the draft under Section 3-415.

(c) If a draft is accepted by a bank, the drawer is discharged, regardless of when or by whom acceptance was obtained.

(d) If a draft is accepted and the acceptor is not a bank, the obligation of the drawer to pay the draft if the draft is dishonored by the acceptor is the same as the obligation of an indorser under Section 3-415(a) and (c).

(e) If a draft states that it is drawn "without recourse" or otherwise disclaims liability of the drawer to pay the draft, the drawer is not liable under subsection (b) to pay the draft if the draft is not a check. A disclaimer of the liability stated in subsection (b) is not effective if the draft is a check.

(f) If (i) a check is not presented for payment or given to a depositary bank for collection within 30 days after its date, (ii) the drawee suspends payments after expiration of the 30-day period without paying the check, and (iii) because of the suspension of payments, the drawer is deprived of funds maintained with the drawee to cover payment of the check, the drawer to the extent deprived of funds may discharge its obligation to pay the check by assigning to the person entitled to enforce the check the rights of the drawer against the drawee with respect to the funds.

§ 3-415. Obligation of Indorser.

(a) Subject to subsections (b), (c), and (d) and to Section 3-419(d), if an instrument is dishonored, an indorser is obliged to pay the amount due on the instrument (i) according to the terms of the instrument at the time it was indorsed, or (ii) if the indorser indorsed an incomplete instrument, according to its terms when completed, to the extent stated in Sections 3-115 and 3-407. The obligation of the indorser is owed to a person entitled to enforce the instrument or to a subsequent indorser who paid the instrument under this section.

(b) If an indorsement states that it is made "without recourse" or otherwise disclaims liability of the indorser, the indorser is not liable under subsection (a) to pay the instrument.

(c) If notice of dishonor of an instrument is required by Section 3-503 and notice of dishonor complying with that section is not given to an indorser, the liability of the indorser under subsection (a) is discharged.

(d) If a draft is accepted by a bank after an indorsement is made, the liability of the indorser under subsection (a) is discharged.

(e) If an indorser of a check is liable under subsection (a) and the check is not presented for payment, or given to a depositary bank for collection, within 30 days after the day the indorsement was made, the liability of the indorser under subsection (a) is discharged.

§ 3-416. Transfer Warranties.

(a) A person who transfers an instrument for consideration warrants to the transferee and, if the transfer is by indorsement, to any subsequent transferee that:

(1) the warrantor is a person entitled to enforce the instrument;

(2) all signatures on the instrument are authentic and authorized;

(3) the instrument has not been altered;

(4) the instrument is not subject to a defense or claim in recoupment of any party which can be asserted against the warrantor; and

(5) the warrantor has no knowledge of any insolvency proceeding commenced with respect to the maker or acceptor or, in the case of an unaccepted draft, the drawer.

(b) A person to whom the warranties under subsection (a) are made and who took the instrument in good faith may recover from the warrantor as damages for breach of warranty an amount equal to the loss suffered as a result of the breach, but not more than the amount of the instrument plus expenses and loss of interest incurred as a result of the breach.

(c) The warranties stated in subsection (a) cannot be disclaimed with respect to checks. Unless notice of a claim for breach of warranty is given to the warrantor within 30 days after the claimant has reason to know of the breach and the identity of the warrantor, the liability of the warrantor under subsection (b) is discharged to the extent of any loss caused by the delay in giving notice of the claim.

(d) A [cause of action] for breach of warranty under this section accrues when the claimant has reason to know of the breach.

§ 3-417. Presentment Warranties.

(a) If an unaccepted draft is presented to the drawee for payment or acceptance and the drawee pays or accepts the draft, (i) the person obtaining payment or acceptance, at the time of presentment, and (ii) a previous transferor of the draft, at the time of transfer, warrant to the drawee making payment or accepting the draft in good faith that:

(1) the warrantor is, or was, at the time the warrantor transferred the draft, a person entitled to enforce the draft or authorized to obtain payment or acceptance of the draft on behalf of a person entitled to enforce the draft;

(2) the draft has not been altered; and

(3) the warrantor has no knowledge that the signature of the drawer of the draft is unauthorized.

(b) A drawee making payment may recover from any warrantor damages for breach of warranty equal to the amount paid by the drawee less the amount the drawee received or is entitled to receive from the drawer because of the payment. In addition, the drawee is entitled to compensation for expenses and loss of interest resulting from the breach. The right of the drawee to recover damages under this subsection is not affected by any failure of the drawee to exercise ordinary care in making payment. If the drawee accepts the draft, breach of warranty is a defense to the obligation of the acceptor. If the acceptor makes payment with respect to the draft, the acceptor is entitled to recover from any warrantor for breach of warranty the amounts stated in this subsection.

(c) If a drawee asserts a claim for breach of warranty under subsection (a) based on an unauthorized indorsement of the draft or an alteration of the draft, the warrantor may defend by proving that the indorsement is effective under Section 3-404 or 3-405 or the drawer is precluded under Section 3-406 or 4-406 from asserting against the drawee the unauthorized indorsement or alteration.

(d) If (i) a dishonored draft is presented for payment to the drawer or an indorser or (ii) any other instrument is presented for payment to a party obliged to pay the instrument, and (iii) payment is received, the following rules apply:

(1) The person obtaining payment and a prior transferor of the instrument warrant to the person making payment in good faith that the warrantor is, or was, at the time the warrantor transferred the instrument, a person entitled to enforce the instrument or authorized to obtain payment on behalf of a person entitled to enforce the instrument.

(2) The person making payment may recover from any warrantor for breach of warranty an amount equal to the amount paid plus expenses and loss of interest resulting from the breach.

(e) The warranties stated in subsections (a) and (d) cannot be disclaimed with respect to checks. Unless notice of a claim for breach of warranty is given to the warrantor within 30 days after the claimant has reason to know of the breach and the identity of the warrantor, the liability of the warrantor under subsection (b) or (d) is discharged to the extent of any loss caused by the delay in giving notice of the claim.

(f) A [cause of action] for breach of warranty under this section accrues when the claimant has reason to know of the breach.

§ 3-418. Payment or Acceptance by Mistake.

(a) Except as provided in subsection (c), if the drawee of a draft pays or accepts the draft and the drawee acted on the mistaken belief that (i) payment of the draft had not been stopped pursuant to Section 4-403 or (ii) the signature of the drawer of the draft was authorized, the drawee may recover the amount of the draft from the person to whom or for whose benefit payment was made or, in the case of acceptance, may revoke the acceptance. Rights of the drawee under this subsection are not affected by failure of the drawee to exercise ordinary care in paying or accepting the draft.

(b) Except as provided in subsection (c), if an instrument has been paid or accepted by mistake and the case is not covered by subsection (a), the person paying or accepting may, to the extent permitted by the law governing mistake and restitution, (i) recover the payment from the person to whom or for whose benefit payment was made or (ii) in the case of acceptance, may revoke the acceptance.

(c) The remedies provided by subsection (a) or (b) may not be asserted against a person who took the instrument in good faith and for value or who in good faith changed position in reliance on the payment or acceptance. This subsection does not limit remedies provided by Section 3-417 or 4-407.

(d) Notwithstanding Section 4-215, if an instrument is paid or accepted by mistake and the payor or acceptor recovers payment or revokes acceptance under subsection (a) or (b), the instrument is deemed not to have been paid or accepted and is treated as dishonored, and the person from whom payment is recovered has rights as a person entitled to enforce the dishonored instrument.

§ 3-419. Instruments Signed for Accommodation.

(a) If an instrument is issued for value given for the benefit of a party to the instrument ("accommodated party") and another party to the instrument ("accommodation party") signs the instrument for the purpose of incurring liability on the instrument without being a direct beneficiary of the value given for the instrument, the instrument is signed by the accommodation party "for accommodation."

(b) An accommodation party may sign the instrument as maker, drawer, acceptor, or indorser and, subject to subsection (d), is obliged to pay the instrument in the capacity in which the accommodation party signs. The obligation of an accommodation party may be enforced notwithstanding any statute of frauds and whether or not the accommodation party receives consideration for the accommodation.

(c) A person signing an instrument is presumed to be an accommodation party and there is notice that the instrument is signed for accommodation if the signature is an anomalous indorsement or is accompanied by words indicating that the signer is acting as surety or guarantor with respect to the obligation of another party to the instrument. Except as provided in Section 3-605, the obligation of an accommodation party to pay the instrument is not affected by the fact that the person enforcing the obligation had notice when the instrument was taken by that person that the accommodation party signed the instrument for accommodation.

(d) If the signature of a party to an instrument is accompanied by words indicating unambiguously that the party is guaranteeing collection rather than payment of the obligation of another party to the instrument, the signer is obliged to pay the amount due on the instrument to a person entitled to enforce the instrument only if (i) execution of judgment against the other party has been returned unsatisfied, (ii) the other party is insolvent or in an insolvency proceeding, (iii) the other party cannot be served with process, or (iv) it is otherwise apparent that payment cannot be obtained from the other party.

(e) An accommodation party who pays the instrument is entitled to reimbursement from the accommodated party and is entitled to enforce the instrument against the accommodated party. An accommodated party who pays the instrument has no right of recourse against, and is not entitled to contribution from, an accommodation party.

§ 3-420. Conversion of Instrument.

(a) The law applicable to conversion of personal property applies to instruments. An instrument is also converted if it is taken by transfer, other than a negotiation, from a person not entitled to enforce the instrument or a bank makes or obtains payment with respect to the instrument for a person not entitled to enforce the instrument or receive payment. An action for conversion of an instrument may not be brought by (i) the issuer or acceptor of the instrument or (ii) a payee or indorsee who did not receive delivery of the instrument either directly or through delivery to an agent or a co-payee.

(b) In an action under subsection (a), the measure of liability is presumed to be the amount payable on the instrument, but recovery may not exceed the amount of the plaintiff's interest in the instrument.

(c) A representative, other than a depositary bank, who has in good faith dealt with an instrument or its proceeds on behalf of one who was not the person entitled to enforce the instrument is not liable in conversion to that person beyond the amount of any proceeds that it has not paid out.

Part 5 Dishonor

§ 3-501. Presentment.

(a) "Presentment" means a demand made by or on behalf of a person entitled to enforce an instrument (i) to pay the instrument made to the drawee or a party obliged to pay the instrument or, in the case of a note or accepted draft payable at a bank, to the bank, or (ii) to accept a draft made to the drawee.

(b) The following rules are subject to Article 4, agreement of the parties, and clearing-house rules and the like:

(1) Presentment may be made at the place of payment of the instrument and must be made at the place of payment if the instrument is payable at a bank in the United States; may be made by any commercially reasonable means, including an oral, written, or electronic communication; is effective when the demand for payment or acceptance is received by the person to whom presentment is made; and is effective if made to any one of two or more makers, acceptors, drawees, or other payors.

(2) Upon demand of the person to whom presentment is made, the person making presentment must (i) exhibit the instrument, (ii) give reasonable identification and, if presentment is made on behalf of another person, reasonable evidence of authority to do so, and (. . .) sign a receipt on the instrument for any payment made or surrender the instrument if full payment is made.

(3) Without dishonoring the instrument, the party to whom presentment is made may (i) return the instrument for lack of a necessary indorsement, or (ii) refuse payment or acceptance for failure of the presentment to comply with the terms of the instrument, an agreement of the parties, or other applicable law or rule.

(4) The party to whom presentment is made may treat

presentment as occurring on the next business day after the day of presentment if the party to whom presentment is made has established a cut-off hour not earlier than 2 p.m. for the receipt and processing of instruments presented for payment or acceptance and presentment is made after the cut-off hour.

§ 3-502. Dishonor.

(a) Dishonor of a note is governed by the following rules:

(1) If the note is payable on demand, the note is dishonored if presentment is duly made to the maker and the note is not paid on the day of presentment.

(2) If the note is not payable on demand and is payable at or through a bank or the terms of the note require presentment, the note is dishonored if presentment is duly made and the note is not paid on the day it becomes payable or the day of presentment, whichever is later.

(3) If the note is not payable on demand and paragraph (2) does not apply, the note is dishonored if it is not paid on the day it becomes payable.

(b) Dishonor of an unaccepted draft other than a documentary draft is governed by the following rules:

(1) If a check is duly presented for payment to the payor bank otherwise than for immediate payment over the counter, the check is dishonored if the payor bank makes timely return of the check or sends timely notice of dishonor or nonpayment under Section 4-301 or 4-302, or becomes accountable for the amount of the check under Section 4-302.

(2) If a draft is payable on demand and paragraph (1) does not apply, the draft is dishonored if presentment for payment is duly made to the drawee and the draft is not paid on the day of presentment.

(3) If a draft is payable on a date stated in the draft, the draft is dishonored if (i) presentment for payment is duly made to the drawee and payment is not made on the day the draft becomes payable or the day of presentment, whichever is later, or (ii) presentment for acceptance is duly made before the day the draft becomes payable and the draft is not accepted on the day of presentment.

(4) If a draft is payable on elapse of a period of time after sight or acceptance, the draft is dishonored if presentment for acceptance is duly made and the draft is not accepted on the day of presentment.

(c) Dishonor of an unaccepted documentary draft occurs according to the rules stated in subsection (b)(2), (3), and (4), except that payment or acceptance may be delayed without dishonor until no later than the close of the third business day of the drawee following the day on which payment or acceptance is required by those paragraphs.

(d) Dishonor of an accepted draft is governed by the following rules:

(1) If the draft is payable on demand, the draft is dishonored if presentment for payment is duly made to the acceptor and the draft is not paid on the day of presentment.

(2) If the draft is not payable on demand, the draft is dishonored if presentment for payment is duly made to the acceptor and payment is not made on the day it becomes payable or the day of presentment, whichever is later.

(e) In any case in which presentment is otherwise required for dishonor under this section and presentment is excused under Section 3-504, dishonor occurs without presentment if the instrument is not duly accepted or paid.

(f) If a draft is dishonored because timely acceptance of the draft was not made and the person entitled to demand acceptance consents to a late acceptance, from the time of acceptance the draft is treated as never having been dishonored.

§ 3-503. Notice of Dishonor.

(a) The obligation of an indorser stated in Section 3-415(a) and the obligation of a drawer stated in Section 3-414(d) may not be enforced unless (i) the indorser or drawer is given notice of dishonor of the instrument complying with this section or (ii) notice of dishonor is excused under Section 3-504(b).

(b) Notice of dishonor may be given by any person; may be given by any commercially reasonable means, including an oral, written, or electronic communication; and is sufficient if it reasonably identifies the instrument and indicates that the instrument has been dishonored or has not been paid or accepted. Return of an instrument given to a bank for collection is sufficient notice of dishonor.

(c) Subject to Section 3-504(c), with respect to an instrument taken for collection by a collecting bank, notice of dishonor must be given (i) by the bank before midnight of the next banking day following the banking day on which the bank receives notice of dishonor of the instrument, or (ii) by any other person within 30 days following the day on which the person receives notice of dishonor. With respect to any other instrument, notice of dishonor must be given within 30 days following the day on which dishonor occurs.

§ 3-504. Excused Presentment and Notice of Dishonor.

(a) Presentment for payment or acceptance of an instrument is excused if (i) the person entitled to present the instrument cannot with reasonable diligence make presentment, (ii) the maker or acceptor has repudiated an obligation to pay the instrument or is dead or in insolvency proceedings, (iii) by the terms of the instrument presentment is not necessary to enforce the obligation of indorsers or the drawer, (iv) the drawer or indorser whose obligation is being enforced has waived presentment or otherwise has no reason to expect or right to require that the instrument be paid or accepted, or (v) the drawer instructed the drawee not to pay or accept the draft or the drawee was not obligated to the drawer to pay the draft.

(b) Notice of dishonor is excused if (i) by the terms of the instrument notice of dishonor is not necessary to enforce the obligation of a party to pay the instrument, or (ii) the party whose obligation is being enforced waived notice of dishonor. A waiver of presentment is also a waiver of notice of dishonor.

(c) Delay in giving notice of dishonor is excused if the delay was caused by circumstances beyond the control of the person giving the notice and the person giving the notice exercised reasonable diligence after the cause of the delay ceased to operate.

§ 3-505. Evidence of Dishonor.

(a) The following are admissible as evidence and create a presumption of dishonor and of any notice of dishonor stated:

(1) a document regular in form as provided in subsection (b) which purports to be a protest;

(2) a purported stamp or writing of the drawee, payor bank, or presenting bank on or accompanying the instrument stating that acceptance or payment has been refused unless reasons for the refusal are stated and the reasons are not consistent with dishonor;

(3) a book or record of the drawee, payor bank, or collecting bank, kept in the usual course of business which shows dishonor, even if there is no evidence of who made the entry.

(b) A protest is a certificate of dishonor made by a United States consul or vice consul, or a notary public or other person authorized to administer oaths by the law of the place where dishonor occurs. It may be made upon information satisfactory to that person. The protest must identify the instrument and certify either that presentment has been made or, if not made, the reason why it was not made, and that the instrument has been dishonored by nonacceptance or nonpayment. The protest may also certify that notice of dishonor has been given to some or all parties.

Part 6 Discharge and Payment

§ 3-601. Discharge and Effect of Discharge.

(a) The obligation of a party to pay the instrument is discharged as stated in this Article or by an act or agreement with the party which would discharge an obligation to pay money under a simple contract.

(b) Discharge of the obligation of a party is not effective against a person acquiring rights of a holder in due course of the instrument without notice of the discharge.

§ 3-602. Payment.

(a) Subject to subsection (b), an instrument is paid to the extent payment is made (i) by or on behalf of a party obliged to pay the instrument, and (ii) to a person entitled to enforce the instrument. To the extent of the payment, the obligation of the party obliged to pay the instrument is discharged even though payment is made with knowledge of a claim to the instrument under Section 3-306 by another person.

(b) The obligation of a party to pay the instrument is not discharged under subsection (a) if:

(1) a claim to the instrument under Section 3-306 is enforceable against the party receiving payment and (i) payment is made with knowledge by the payor that payment is prohibited by injunction or similar process of a court of competent jurisdiction, or (ii) in the case of an instrument other than a cashier's check, teller's check, or certified check, the party making payment accepted, from the person having a claim to the instrument, indemnity against loss resulting from refusal to pay the person entitled to enforce the instrument; or

(2) the person making payment knows that the instrument is a stolen instrument and pays a person it knows is in wrongful possession of the instrument.

§ 3-603. Tender of Payment.

(a) If tender of payment of an obligation to pay an instrument is made to a person entitled to enforce the instrument, the effect of tender is governed by principles of law applicable to tender of payment under a simple contract.

(b) If tender of payment of an obligation to pay an instrument is made to a person entitled to enforce the instrument and the tender is refused, there is discharge, to the extent of the amount of the tender, of the obligation of an indorser or accommodation party having a right of recourse with respect to the obligation to which the tender relates.

(c) If tender of payment of an amount due on an instrument is made to a person entitled to enforce the instrument, the obligation of the obligor to pay interest after the due date on the amount tendered is discharged. If presentment is required with respect to an instrument and the obligor is able and ready to pay on the due date at every place of payment stated in the instrument, the obligor is deemed to have made tender of payment on the due date to the person entitled to enforce the instrument.

§ 3-604. Discharge by Cancellation or Renunciation.

(a) A person entitled to enforce an instrument, with or without consideration, may discharge the obligation of a party to pay the instrument (i) by an intentional voluntary act, such as surrender of the instrument to the party, destruction, mutilation, or cancellation of the instrument, cancellation or striking out of the party's signature, or the addition of words to the instrument indicating discharge, or (ii) by agreeing not to sue or otherwise renouncing rights against the party by a signed writing.

(b) Cancellation or striking out of an indorsement pursuant to subsection (a) does not affect the status and rights of a party derived from the indorsement.

§ 3-605. Discharge of Indorsers and Accommodation Parties.

(a) In this section, the term "indorser" includes a drawer having the obligation described in Section 3-414(d).

(b) Discharge, under Section 3-604, of the obligation of a party to pay an instrument does not discharge the obligation of an indorser or accommodation party having a right of recourse against the discharged party.

(c) If a person entitled to enforce an instrument agrees, with or without consideration, to an extension of the due date of the obligation of a party to pay the instrument, the extension discharges an indorser or accommodation party having a right of recourse against the party whose obligation is extended to the extent the indorser or accommodation party proves that the extension caused loss to the indorser or accommodation party with respect to the right of recourse.

(d) If a person entitled to enforce an instrument agrees, with or without consideration, to a material modification of the obligation of a party other than an extension of the due date, the modification discharges the obligation of an indorser or accommodation party having a right of recourse against the person whose obligation is modified to the extent the modification causes loss to the indorser or accommodation party with respect to the right of recourse. The loss suffered by the indorser or accommodation party as a result of the modification is equal to the amount of the right of recourse unless the person enforcing the instrument proves that no loss was caused by the modification or that the loss caused by the modification was an amount less than the amount of the right of recourse.

(e) If the obligation of a party to pay an instrument is secured by an interest in collateral and a person entitled to enforce the instrument impairs the value of the interest in collateral, the obligation of an indorser or accommodation party having a right of recourse against the obligor is discharged to the extent of the impairment. The value of an interest in collateral is impaired to the extent (i) the value of the interest is reduced to an amount less than the amount of the right of recourse of the party asserting discharge, or (ii) the reduction in value of the interest causes an increase in the amount by which the amount of the right of recourse exceeds the value of the interest. The burden of proving impairment is on the party asserting discharge.

(f) If the obligation of a party is secured by an interest in collateral not provided by an accommodation party and a person entitled to enforce the instrument impairs the value of the interest in collateral, the obligation of any party who is jointly and severally liable with respect to the secured obligation is discharged to the extent the impairment causes the party asserting discharge to pay more than that party would have been obliged to pay, taking into account rights of contribution, if impairment had not occurred. If the party asserting discharge is an accommodation party not entitled to discharge under subsection (e), the party is deemed to have a right to contribution based on joint and several liability rather than a right to reimbursement. The burden of proving impairment is on the party asserting discharge.

(g) Under subsection (e) or (f), impairing value of an interest in collateral includes (i) failure to obtain or maintain perfection or recordation of the interest in collateral, (ii) release of collateral without substitution of collateral of equal value, (iii) failure to perform a duty to preserve the value of collateral owed, under Article 9 or other law, to a debtor or surety or other person secondarily liable, or (iv) failure to comply with applicable law in disposing of collateral.

(h) An accommodation party is not discharged under subsection (c), (d), or (e) unless the person entitled to enforce the instrument knows of the accommodation or has notice under Section 3-419(c) that the instrument was signed for accommodation.

(i) A party is not discharged under this section if (i) the party asserting discharge consents to the event or conduct that is the basis of the discharge, or (ii) the instrument or a separate agreement of the party provides for waiver of discharge under this section either specifically or by general language indicating that parties waive defenses based on suretyship or impairment of collateral.

REVISED ARTICLE 4 / Bank Deposits and Collections

Part 1 General Provisions and Definitions

§ 4-101. Short Title.

This Article may be cited as Uniform Commercial Code—Bank Deposits and Collections.

§ 4-102. Applicability.

(a) To the extent that items within this Article are also within Articles 3 and 8, they are subject to those Articles. If there is conflict, this Article governs Article 3, but Article 8 governs this Article.

(b) The liability of a bank for action or non-action with respect to an item handled by it for purposes of presentment, payment, or collection is governed by the law of the place where the bank is located. In the case of action or non-action by or at a branch or separate office of a bank, its liability is governed by the law of the place where the branch or separate office is located.

§ 4-103. Variation by Agreement; Measure of Damages; Action Constituting Ordinary Care.

(a) The effect of the provisions of this Article may be varied by agreement, but the parties to the agreement cannot disclaim a bank's responsibility for its lack of good faith or failure to exercise ordinary care or limit the measure of damages for the lack or failure. However, the parties may determine by agreement the standards by which the bank's responsibility is to be measured if those standards are not manifestly unreasonable.

(b) Federal Reserve regulations and operating circulars, clearing-house rules, and the like have the effect of agreements under subsection (a), whether or not specifically assented to by all parties interested in items handled.

(c) Action or non-action approved by this Article or pursuant to Federal Reserve regulations or operating circulars is the exercise of ordinary care and, in the absence of special instructions, action or non-action consistent with clearing-house rules and the like or with a general banking usage not disapproved by this Article, is prima facie the exercise of ordinary care.

(d) The specification or approval of certain procedures by this Article is not disapproval of other procedures that may be reasonable under the circumstances.

(e) The measure of damages for failure to exercise ordinary care in handling an item is the amount of the item reduced by an amount that could not have been realized by the exercise of ordinary care. If there is also bad faith it includes any other damages the party suffered as a proximate consequence.

§ 4-104. Definitions and Index of Definitions.

(a) In this Article, unless the context otherwise requires:

(1) "Account" means any deposit or credit account with a bank, including a demand, time, savings, passbook, share draft, or like account, other than an account evidenced by a certificate of deposit;

(2) "Afternoon" means the period of a day between noon and midnight;

(3) "Banking day" means the part of a day on which a bank is open to the public for carrying on substantially all of its banking functions;

(4) "Clearing house" means an association of banks or other payors regularly clearing items;

(5) "Customer" means a person having an account with a bank or for whom a bank has agreed to collect items, including a bank that maintains an account at another bank;

(6) "Documentary draft" means a draft to be presented for acceptance or payment if specified documents, certificated securities (Section 8-102) or instructions for uncertificated securities (Section 8-308), or other certificates, statements, or the like are to be received by the drawee or other payor before acceptance or payment of the draft;

(7) "Draft" means a draft as defined in Section 3-104 or an item, other than an instrument, that is an order;

(8) "Drawee" means a person ordered in a draft to make payment;

(9) "Item" means an instrument or a promise or order to pay money handled by a bank for collection or payment. The term does not include a payment order governed by Article 4A or a credit or debit card slip;

(10) "Midnight deadline" with respect to a bank is midnight on its next banking day following the banking day on which it receives the relevant item or notice or from which the time for taking action commences to run, whichever is later;

(11) "Settle" means to pay in cash, by clearing-house settlement, in a charge or credit or by remittance, or otherwise as agreed. A settlement may be either provisional or final;

(12) "Suspends payments" with respect to a bank means that it has been closed by order of the supervisory authorities, that a public officer has been appointed to take it over, or that it ceases or refuses to make payments in the ordinary course of business.

(b) Other definitions applying to this Article and the sections in which they appear are:

"Agreement for electronic presentment"   Section 4-110.
"Bank"   Section 4-105.
"Collecting bank"   Section 4-105.
"Depositary bank"   Section 4-105.
"Intermediary bank"   Section 4-105.
"Payor bank"   Section 4-105.
"Presenting bank"   Section 4-105.
"Presentment notice"   Section 4-110.

(c) The following definitions in other Articles apply to this Article:

"Acceptance"   Section 3-409.
"Alteration"   Section 3-407.
"Cashier's check"   Section 3-104.
"Certificate of deposit"   Section 3-104.
"Certified check"   Section 3-409.
"Check"   Section 3-104.
"Good faith"   Section 3-103.
"Holder in due course"   Section 3-302.
"Instrument"   Section 3-104.
"Notice of dishonor"   Section 3-503.
"Order"   Section 3-103.
"Ordinary care"   Section 3-103.
"Person entitled to enforce"   Section 3-301.
"Presentment"   Section 3-501.
"Promise"   Section 3-103.
"Prove"   Section 3-103.
"Teller's check"   Section 3-104.
"Unauthorized signature"   Section 3-403.

(d) In addition, Article 1 contains general definitions and principles of construction and interpretation applicable throughout this Article.

§ 4-105.   "Bank"; "Depositary Bank"; "Payor Bank"; "Intermediary Bank"; "Collecting Bank"; "Presenting Bank".

In this Article:

(1) "Bank" means a person engaged in the business of banking, including a savings bank, savings and loan association, credit union, or trust company;

(2) "Depositary bank" means the first bank to take an item even though it is also the payor bank, unless the item is presented for immediate payment over the counter;

(3) "Payor bank" means a bank that is the drawee of a draft;

(4) "Intermediary bank" means a bank to which an item is transferred in course of collection except the depositary or payor bank;

(5) "Collecting bank" means a bank handling an item for collection except the payor bank;

(6) "Presenting bank" means a bank presenting an item except a payor bank.

§ 4-106.   Payable Through or Payable at Bank: Collecting Bank.

(a) If an item states that it is "payable through" a bank identified in the item, (i) the item designates the bank as a collecting bank and does not by itself authorize the bank to pay the item, and (ii) the item may be presented for payment only by or through the bank.

(b) If an item states that it is "payable at" a bank identified in the item, the item is equivalent to a draft drawn on the bank.

Alternative B

(b) If an item states that it is "payable at" a bank identified in the item, (i) the item designates the bank as a collecting bank and does not by itself authorize the bank to pay the item, and (ii) the item may be presented for payment only by or through the bank.

(c) If a draft names a nonbank drawee and it is unclear whether a bank named in the draft is a co-drawee or a collecting bank, the bank is a collecting bank.

§ 4-107.   Separate Office of Bank.

A branch or separate office of a bank is a separate bank for the purpose of computing the time within which and determining the place at or to which action may be taken or notices or orders shall be given under this Article and under Article 3.

§ 4-108.   Time of Receipt of Items.

(a) For the purpose of allowing time to process items, prove balances, and make the necessary entries on its books to determine its position for the day, a bank may fix an afternoon hour of 2 P.M. or later as a cutoff hour for the handling of money and items and the making of entries on its books.

(b) An item or deposit of money received on any day after a cutoff hour so fixed or after the close of the banking day may be treated as being received at the opening of the next banking day.

§ 4-109. Delays.

(a) Unless otherwise instructed, a collecting bank in a good faith effort to secure payment of a specific item drawn on a payor other than a bank, and with or without the approval of any person involved, may waive, modify, or extend time limits imposed or permitted by this |Act| for a period not exceeding two additional banking days without discharge of drawers or indorsers or liability to its transferor or a prior party.

(b) Delay by a collecting bank or payor bank beyond time limits prescribed or permitted by this |Act| or by instructions is excused if (i) the delay is caused by interruption of communication or computer facilities, suspension of payments by another bank, war, emergency conditions, failure of equipment, or other circumstances beyond the control of the bank, and (ii) the bank exercises such diligence as the circumstances require.

§ 4-110. Electronic Presentment.

(a) "Agreement for electronic presentment" means an agreement, clearing-house rule, or Federal Reserve regulation or operating circular, providing that presentment of an item may be made by transmission of an image of an item or information describing the item ("presentment notice") rather than delivery of the item itself. The agreement may provide for procedures governing retention, presentment, payment, dishonor, and other matters concerning items subject to the agreement.

(b) Presentment of an item pursuant to an agreement for presentment is made when the presentment notice is received.

(c) If presentment is made by presentment notice, a reference to "item" or "check" in this Article means the presentment notice unless the context otherwise indicates.

§ 4-111. Statute of Limitations.

An action to enforce an obligation, duty, or right arising under this Article must be commenced within three years after the |cause of action| accrues.

Part 2 Collection of Items: Depositary and Collecting Banks

§ 4-201. Status of Collecting Bank as Agent and Provisional Status of Credits; Applicability of Article; Item Indorsed "Pay Any Bank".

(a) Unless a contrary intent clearly appears and before the time that a settlement given by a collecting bank for an item is or becomes final, the bank, with respect to an item, is an agent or sub-agent of the owner of the item and any settlement given for the item is provisional. This provision applies regardless of the form of indorsement or lack of indorsement and even though credit given for the item is subject to immediate withdrawal as of right or is in fact withdrawn; but the continuance of ownership of an item by its owner and any rights of the owner to proceeds of the item are subject to rights of a collecting bank, such as those resulting from outstanding advances on the item and rights of recoupment or

setoff. If an item is handled by banks for purposes of presentment, payment, collection, or return, the relevant provisions of this Article apply even though action of the parties clearly establishes that a particular bank has purchased the item and is the owner of it.

(b) After an item has been indorsed with the words "pay any bank" or the like, only a bank may acquire the rights of a holder until the item has been:

(1) returned to the customer initiating collection; or
(2) specially indorsed by a bank to a person who is not a bank.

§ 4-202. Responsibility for Collection or Return; When Action Timely.

(a) A collecting bank must exercise ordinary care in:

(1) presenting an item or sending it for presentment;
(2) sending notice of dishonor or nonpayment or returning an item other than a documentary draft to the bank's transferor after learning that the item has not been paid or accepted, as the case may be;
(3) settling for an item when the bank receives final settlement; and
(4) notifying its transferor of any loss or delay in transit within a reasonable time after discovery thereof.

(b) A collecting bank exercises ordinary care under subsection (a) by taking proper action before its midnight deadline following receipt of an item, notice, or settlement. Taking proper action within a reasonably longer time may constitute the exercise of ordinary care, but the bank has the burden of establishing timeliness.

(c) Subject to subsection (a)(1), a bank is not liable for the insolvency, neglect, misconduct, mistake, or default of another bank or person or for loss or destruction of an item in the possession of others or in transit.

§ 4-203. Effect of Instructions.

Subject to Article 3 concerning conversion of instruments (Section 3-420) and restrictive indorsements (Section 3-206), only a collecting bank's transferor can give instructions that affect the bank or constitute notice to it, and a collecting bank is not liable to prior parties for any action taken pursuant to the instructions or in accordance with any agreement with its transferor.

§ 4-204. Methods of Sending and Presenting; Sending Directly to Payor Bank.

(a) A collecting bank shall send items by a reasonably prompt method, taking into consideration relevant instructions, the nature of the item, the number of those items on hand, the cost of collection involved, and the method generally used by it or others to present those items.

(b) A collecting bank may send:

(1) an item directly to the payor bank;
(2) an item to a nonbank payor if authorized by its transferor; and
(3) an item other than documentary drafts to a nonbank payor, if authorized by Federal Reserve regulation or operating circular, clearing-house rule, or the like.

(c) Presentment may be made by a presenting bank at a place where the payor bank or other payor has requested that presentment be made. As amended in 1962 and 1990.

§ 4-205. Depositary Bank Holder of Unindorsed Item.

If a customer delivers an item to a depositary bank for collection:

(1) the depositary bank becomes a holder of the item at the time it receives the item for collection if the customer at the time of delivery was a holder of the item, whether or not the customer indorses the item, and, if the bank satisfies the other requirements of Section 3-302, it is a holder in due course; and

(2) the depositary bank warrants to collecting banks, the payor bank or other payor, and the drawer that the amount of the item was paid to the customer or deposited to the customer's account.

§ 4-206. Transfer Between Banks.

Any agreed method that identifies the transferor bank is sufficient for the item's further transfer to another bank.

§ 4-207. Transfer Warranties.

(a) A customer or collecting bank that transfers an item and receives a settlement or other consideration warrants to the transferee and to any subsequent collecting bank that:

(1) the warrantor is a person entitled to enforce the item;

(2) all signatures on the item are authentic and authorized;

(3) the item has not been altered;

(4) the item is not subject to a defense or claim in recoupment (Section 3-305(a)) of any party that can be asserted against the warrantor; and

(5) the warrantor has no knowledge of any insolvency proceeding commenced with respect to the maker or acceptor or, in the case of an unaccepted draft, the drawer.

(b) If an item is dishonored, a customer or collecting bank transferring the item and receiving settlement or other consideration is obliged to pay the amount due on the item (i) according to the terms of the item at the time it was transferred, or (ii) if the transfer was of an incomplete item, according to its terms when completed as stated in Sections 3-115 and 3-407. The obligation of a transferor is owed to the transferee and to any subsequent collecting bank that takes the item in good faith. A transferor cannot disclaim its obligation under this subsection by an indorsement stating that it is made "without recourse" or otherwise disclaiming liability.

(c) A person to whom the warranties under subsection (a) are made and who took the item in good faith may recover from the warrantor as damages for breach of warranty an amount equal to the loss suffered as a result of the breach, but not more than the amount of the item plus expenses and loss of interest incurred as a result of the breach.

(d) The warranties stated in subsection (a) cannot be disclaimed with respect to checks. Unless notice of a claim for breach of warranty is given to the warrantor within 30 days after the claimant has reason to know of the breach and the identity of the warrantor, the warrantor is discharged to the extent of any loss caused by the delay in giving notice of the claim.

(e) A cause of action for breach of warranty under this section accrues when the claimant has reason to know of the breach.

§ 4-208. Presentment Warranties.

(a) If an unaccepted draft is presented to the drawee for payment or acceptance and the drawee pays or accepts the draft, (i) the person obtaining payment or acceptance, at the time of presentment, and (ii) a previous transferor of the draft, at the time of transfer, warrant to the drawee that pays or accepts the draft in good faith that:

(1) the warrantor is, or was, at the time the warrantor transferred the draft, a person entitled to enforce the draft or authorized to obtain payment or acceptance of the draft on behalf of a person entitled to enforce the draft;

(2) the draft has not been altered; and

(3) the warrantor has no knowledge that the signature of the purported drawer of the draft is unauthorized.

(b) A drawee making payment may recover from a warrantor damages for breach of warranty equal to the amount paid by the drawee less the amount the drawee received or is entitled to receive from the drawer because of the payment. In addition, the drawee is entitled to compensation for expenses and loss of interest resulting from the breach. The right of the drawee to recover damages under this subsection is not affected by any failure of the drawee to exercise ordinary care in making payment. If the drawee accepts the draft (i) breach of warranty is a defense to the obligation of the acceptor, and (ii) if the acceptor makes payment with respect to the draft, the acceptor is entitled to recover from a warrantor for breach of warranty the amounts stated in this subsection.

(c) If a drawee asserts a claim for breach of warranty under subsection (a) based on an unauthorized indorsement of the draft or an alteration of the draft, the warrantor may defend by proving that the indorsement is effective under Section 3-404 or 3-405 or the drawer is precluded under Section 3-406 or 4-406 from asserting against the drawee the unauthorized indorsement or alteration.

(d) If (i) a dishonored draft is presented for payment to the drawer or an indorser or (ii) any other item is presented for payment to a party obliged to pay the item, and the item is paid, the person obtaining payment and a prior transferor of the item warrant to the person making payment in good faith that the warrantor is, or was, at the time the warrantor transferred the item, a person entitled to enforce the item or authorized to obtain payment on behalf of a person entitled to enforce the item. The person making payment may recover from any warrantor for breach of warranty an amount equal to the amount paid plus expenses and loss of interest resulting from the breach.

(e) The warranties stated in subsections (a) and (d) cannot be disclaimed with respect to checks. Unless notice of a claim for breach of warranty is given to the warrantor within 30 days after the claimant has reason to know of the breach and the identity of the warrantor, the warrantor is discharged to the extent of any loss caused by the delay in giving notice of the claim.

(f) A cause of action for breach of warranty under this section accrues when the claimant has reason to know of the breach.

§ 4-209. Encoding and Retention Warranties.

(a) A person who encodes information on or with respect to an item after issue warrants to any subsequent collecting bank and to the payor bank or other payor that the information is correctly encoded. If the customer of a depositary bank encodes, that bank also makes the warranty.

(b) A person who undertakes to retain an item pursuant to an agreement for electronic presentment warrants to any subsequent collecting bank and to the payor bank or other payor that retention and presentment of the item comply with the agreement. If a customer of a depositary bank undertakes to retain an item, that bank also makes this warranty.

(c) A person to whom warranties are made under this section and who took the item in good faith may recover from the warrantor as damages for breach of warranty an amount equal to the loss suffered as a result of the breach, plus expenses and loss of interest incurred as a result of the breach.

§ 4-210. Security Interest of Collecting Bank in Items, Accompanying Documents and Proceeds.

(a) A collecting bank has a security interest in an item and any accompanying documents or the proceeds of either:

(1) in case of an item deposited in an account, to the extent to which credit given for the item has been withdrawn or applied;

(2) in case of an item for which it has given credit available for withdrawal as of right, to the extent of the credit given, whether or not the credit is drawn upon or there is a right of chargeback; or

(3) if it makes an advance on or against the item.

(b) If credit given for several items received at one time or pursuant to a single agreement is withdrawn or applied in part, the security interest remains upon all the items, any accompanying documents or the proceeds of either. For the purpose of this section, credits first given are first withdrawn.

(c) Receipt by a collecting bank of a final settlement for an item is a realization on its security interest in the item, accompanying documents, and proceeds. So long as the bank does not receive final settlement for the item or give up possession of the item or accompanying documents for purposes other than collection, the security interest continues to that extent and is subject to Article 9, but:

(1) no security agreement is necessary to make the security interest enforceable (Section 9-203(1)(a));

(2) no filing is required to perfect the security interest; and

(3) the security interest has priority over conflicting perfected security interests in the item, accompanying documents, or proceeds.

§ 4-211. When Bank Gives Value for Purposes of Holder in Due Course.

For purposes of determining its status as a holder in due course, a bank has given value to the extent it has a security interest in an item, if the bank otherwise complies with the requirements of Section 3-302 on what constitutes a holder in due course.

§ 4-212. Presentment by Notice of Item Not Payable by, Through, or at Bank; Liability of Drawer or Indorser.

(a) Unless otherwise instructed, a collecting bank may present an item not payable by, through, or at a bank by sending to the party to accept or pay a written notice that the bank holds the item for acceptance or payment. The notice must be sent in time to be received on or before the day when presentment is due and the bank must meet any requirement of the party to accept or pay under Section 3-501 by the close of the bank's next banking day after it knows of the requirement.

(b) If presentment is made by notice and payment, acceptance, or request for compliance with a requirement under Section 3-501 is not received by the close of business on the day after maturity or, in the case of demand items, by the close of business on the third banking day after notice was sent, the presenting bank may treat the item as dishonored and charge any drawer or indorser by sending it notice of the facts.

As amended in 1990.

§ 4-213. Medium and Time of Settlement by Bank.

(a) With respect to settlement by a bank, the medium and time of settlement may be prescribed by Federal Reserve regulations or circulars, clearing-house rules, and the like, or agreement. In the absence of such prescription:

(1) the medium of settlement is cash or credit to an account in a Federal Reserve bank of or specified by the person to receive settlement; and

(2) the time of settlement, is:

(i) with respect to tender of settlement by cash, a cashier's check, or teller's check, when the cash or check is sent or delivered;

(ii) with respect to tender of settlement by credit in an account in a Federal Reserve Bank, when the credit is made;

(iii) with respect to tender of settlement by a credit or debit to an account in a bank, when the credit or debit is made or, in the case of tender of settlement by authority to charge an account, when the authority is sent or delivered; or

(iv) with respect to tender of settlement by a funds transfer, when payment is made pursuant to Section 4A-406(a) to the person receiving settlement.

(b) If the tender of settlement is not by a medium authorized by subsection (a) or the time of settlement is not fixed by subsection (a), no settlement occurs until the tender of settlement is accepted by the person receiving settlement.

(c) If settlement for an item is made by cashier's check or teller's check and the person receiving settlement, before its midnight deadline:

(1) presents or forwards the check for collection, settlement is final when the check is finally paid; or

(2) fails to present or forward the check for collection, settlement is final at the midnight deadline of the person receiving settlement.

(d) If settlement for an item is made by giving authority to charge the account of the bank giving settlement in the bank receiving settlement, settlement is final when the charge is made by the bank receiving settlement if there are funds available in the account for the amount of the item.

§ 4-214. Right of Charge-Back or Refund; Liability of Collecting Bank: Return of Item.

(a) If a collecting bank has made provisional settlement with its customer for an item and fails by reason of dishonor, suspension of payments by a bank, or otherwise to receive settlement for the item which is or becomes final, the bank may revoke the settlement given by it, charge back the amount of any credit given for the item to its customer's account, or obtain refund from its customer, whether or not it is able to return the item, if by its midnight deadline or within a longer reasonable time after it learns the facts it returns the item or sends notification of the facts. If the return or notice is delayed beyond the bank's midnight deadline or a longer reasonable time after it learns the facts, the bank may revoke the settlement, charge back the credit, or obtain refund from its customer, but it is liable for any loss resulting from the delay. These rights to revoke, charge back, and obtain refund terminate if and when a settlement for the item received by the bank is or becomes final.

(b) A collecting bank returns an item when it is sent or delivered to the bank's customer or transferor or pursuant to its instructions.

(c) A depositary bank that is also the payor may charge back the amount of an item to its customer's account or obtain refund in accordance with the section governing return of an item received by a payor bank for credit on its books (Section 4-301).

(d) The right to charge back is not affected by:

(1) previous use of a credit given for the item; or

(2) failure by any bank to exercise ordinary care with respect to the item, but a bank so failing remains liable.

(e) A failure to charge back or claim refund does not affect other rights of the bank against the customer or any other party.

(f) If credit is given in dollars as the equivalent of the value of an item payable in foreign money, the dollar amount of any charge-back or refund must be calculated on the basis of the bank-offered spot rate for the foreign money prevailing on the day when the person entitled to the charge-back or refund learns that it will not receive payment in ordinary course.

§ 4-215. Final Payment of Item by Payor Bank; When Provisional Debits and Credits Become Final; When Certain Credits Become Available for Withdrawal.

(a) An item is finally paid by a payor bank when the bank has first done any of the following:

(1) paid the item in cash;

(2) settled for the item without having a right to revoke the settlement under statute, clearing-house rule, or agreement; or

(3) made a provisional settlement for the item and failed to revoke the settlement in the time and manner permitted by statute, clearing-house rule, or agreement.

(b) If provisional settlement for an item does not become final, the item is not finally paid.

(c) If provisional settlement for an item between the presenting and payor banks is made through a clearing house or by debits or credits in an account between them, then to the extent that provisional debits or credits for the item are entered in accounts between the presenting and payor banks or between the presenting and successive prior collecting banks seriatim, they become final upon final payment of the item by the payor bank.

(d) If a collecting bank receives a settlement for an item which is or becomes final, the bank is accountable to its customer for the amount of the item and any provisional credit given for the item in an account with its customer becomes final.

(e) Subject to (i) applicable law stating a time for availability of funds and (ii) any right of the bank to apply the credit to an obligation of the customer, credit given by a bank for an item in a customer's account becomes available for withdrawal as of right:

(1) if the bank has received a provisional settlement for the item, when the settlement becomes final and the bank has had a reasonable time to receive return of the item and the item has not been received within that time;

(2) if the bank is both the depositary bank and the payor bank, and the item is finally paid, at the opening of the bank's second banking day following receipt of the item.

(f) Subject to applicable law stating a time for availability of funds and any right of a bank to apply a deposit to an obligation of the depositor, a deposit of money becomes available for withdrawal as of right at the opening of the bank's next banking day after receipt of the deposit.

§ 4-216. Insolvency and Preference.

(a) If an item is in or comes into the possession of a payor or collecting bank that suspends payment and the item has not been finally paid, the item must be returned by the receiver, trustee, or agent in charge of the closed bank to the presenting bank or the closed bank's customer.

(b) If a payor bank finally pays an item and suspends payments without making a settlement for the item with its customer or the presenting bank which settlement is or becomes final, the owner of the item has a preferred claim against the payor bank.

(c) If a payor bank gives or a collecting bank gives or receives a provisional settlement for an item and thereafter suspends payments, the suspension does not prevent or interfere with the settlement's becoming final if the finality occurs automatically upon the lapse of certain time or the happening of certain events.

(d) If a collecting bank receives from subsequent parties settlement for an item, which settlement is or becomes final and the bank suspends payments without making a settlement for the item with its customer which settlement is or becomes final, the owner of the item has a preferred claim against the collecting bank.

§ 4-301.   Deferred Posting; Recovery of Payment by Return of Items; Time of Dishonor; Return of Items by Payor Bank.

(a) If a payor bank settles for a demand item other than a documentary draft presented otherwise than for immediate payment over the counter before midnight of the banking day of receipt, the payor bank may revoke the settlement and recover the settlement if, before it has made final payment and before its midnight deadline, it

(1) returns the item; or
(2) sends written notice of dishonor or nonpayment if the item is unavailable for return.

(b) If a demand item is received by a payor bank for credit on its books, it may return the item or send notice of dishonor and may revoke any credit given or recover the amount thereof withdrawn by its customer, if it acts within the time limit and in the manner specified in subsection (a).

(c) Unless previous notice of dishonor has been sent, an item is dishonored at the time when for purposes of dishonor it is returned or notice sent in accordance with this section.

(d) An item is returned:

(1) as to an item presented through a clearing house, when it is delivered to the presenting or last collecting bank or to the clearing house or is sent or delivered in accordance with clearing-house rules; or
(2) in all other cases, when it is sent or delivered to the bank's customer or transferor or pursuant to instructions.

§ 4-302.   Payor Bank's Responsibility for Late Return of Item.

(a) If an item is presented to and received by a payor bank, the bank is accountable for the amount of:

(1) a demand item, other than a documentary draft, whether properly payable or not, if the bank, in any case in which it is not also the depositary bank, retains the item beyond midnight of the banking day of receipt without settling for it or, whether or not it is also the depositary bank, does not pay or return the item or send notice of dishonor until after its midnight deadline; or
(2) any other properly payable item unless, within the time allowed for acceptance or payment of that item, the bank either accepts or pays the item or returns it and accompanying documents.

(b) The liability of a payor bank to pay an item pursuant to subsection (a) is subject to defenses based on breach of a presentment warranty (Section 4-208) or proof that the person seeking enforcement of the liability presented or transferred the item for the purpose of defrauding the payor bank.

§ 4-303.   When Items Subject to Notice, Stop-Payment Order, Legal Process, or Setoff; Order in Which Items May Be Charged or Certified.

(a) Any knowledge, notice, or stop-payment order received by, legal process served upon, or setoff exercised by a payor bank comes too late to terminate, suspend, or modify the bank's right or duty to pay an item or to charge its customer's account for the item if the knowledge, notice, stop-payment order, or legal process is received or served and a reasonable time for the bank to act thereon expires or the setoff is exercised after the earliest of the following:

(1) the bank accepts or certifies the item;
(2) the bank pays the item in cash;
(3) the bank settles for the item without having a right to revoke the settlement under statute, clearing-house rule, or agreement;
(4) the bank becomes accountable for the amount of the item under Section 4-302 dealing with the payor bank's responsibility for late return of items; or
(5) with respect to checks, a cutoff hour no earlier than one hour after the opening of the next banking day after the banking day on which the bank received the check and no later than the close of that next banking day or, if no cutoff hour is fixed, the close of the next banking day after the banking day on which the bank received the check.

(b) Subject to subsection (a), items may be accepted, paid, certified, or charged to the indicated account of its customer in any order.

Part 4   Relationship Between Payor Bank and its Customer

§ 4-401.   When Bank May Charge Customer's Account.

(a) A bank may charge against the account of a customer an item that is properly payable from the account even though the charge creates an overdraft. An item is properly payable if it is authorized by the customer and is in accordance with any agreement between the customer and bank.

(b) A customer is not liable for the amount of an overdraft if the customer neither signed the item nor benefited from the proceeds of the item.

(c) A bank may charge against the account of a customer a check that is otherwise properly payable from the account, even though payment was made before the date of the check, unless the customer has given notice to the bank of the postdating describing the check with reasonable certainty. The notice is effective for the period stated in Section 4-403(b) for stop-payment orders, and must be received at such time and in such manner as to afford the bank a reasonable opportunity to act on it before the bank takes any action with respect to the check described in Section 4-303. If a bank charges against the account of a customer a check before the date stated in the notice of postdating, the bank is liable for damages for the loss resulting from its act. The loss may include damages for dishonor of subsequent items under Section 4-402.

(d) A bank that in good faith makes payment to a holder may charge the indicated account of its customer according to:

(1) the original terms of the altered item; or
(2) the terms of the completed item, even though the bank knows the item has been completed unless the bank has notice that the completion was improper.

§ 4-402. Bank's Liability to Customer for Wrongful Dishonor; Time of Determining Insufficiency of Account.

(a) Except as otherwise provided in this Article, a payor bank wrongfully dishonors an item if it dishonors an item that is properly payable, but a bank may dishonor an item that would create an overdraft unless it has agreed to pay the overdraft.

(b) A payor bank is liable to its customer for damages proximately caused by the wrongful dishonor of an item. Liability is limited to actual damages proved and may include damages for an arrest or prosecution of the customer or other consequential damages. Whether any consequential damages are proximately caused by the wrongful dishonor is a question of fact to be determined in each case.

(c) A payor bank's determination of the customer's account balance on which a decision to dishonor for insufficiency of available funds is based may be made at any time between the time the item is received by the payor bank and the time that the payor bank returns the item or gives notice in lieu of return, and no more than one determination need be made. If, at the election of the payor bank, a subsequent balance determination is made for the purpose of reevaluating the bank's decision to dishonor the item, the account balance at that time is determinative of whether a dishonor for insufficiency of available funds is wrongful.

§ 4-403. Customer's Right to Stop Payment; Burden of Proof of Loss.

(a) A customer or any person authorized to draw on the account if there is more than one person may stop payment of any item drawn on the customer's account or close the account by an order to the bank describing the item or account with reasonable certainty received at a time and in a manner that affords the bank a reasonable opportunity to act on it before any action by the bank with respect to the item described in Section 4-303. If the signature of more than one person is required to draw on an account, any of these persons may stop payment or close the account.

(b) A stop-payment order is effective for six months, but it lapses after 14 calendar days if the original order was oral and was not confirmed in writing within that period. A stop-payment order may be renewed for additional six-month periods by a writing given to the bank within a period during which the stop-payment order is effective.

(c) The burden of establishing the fact and amount of loss resulting from the payment of an item contrary to a stop-payment order or order to close an account is on the customer. The loss from payment of an item contrary to a stop-payment order may include damages for dishonor of subsequent items under Section 4-402.

§ 4-404. Bank Not Obliged to Pay Check More Than Six Months Old.

A bank is under no obligation to a customer having a checking account to pay a check, other than a certified check, which is presented more than six months after its date, but it may charge its customer's account for a payment made thereafter in good faith.

§ 4-405. Death or Incompetence of Customer.

(a) A payor or collecting bank's authority to accept, pay, or collect an item or to account for proceeds of its collection, if otherwise effective, is not rendered ineffective by incompetence of a customer of either bank existing at the time the item is issued or its collection is undertaken if the bank does not know of an adjudication of incompetence. Neither death nor incompetence of a customer revokes the authority to accept, pay, collect, or account until the bank knows of the fact of death or of an adjudication of incompetence and has reasonable opportunity to act on it.

(b) Even with knowledge, a bank may for 10 days after the date of death pay or certify checks drawn on or before that date unless ordered to stop payment by a person claiming an interest in the account.

§ 4-406. Customer's Duty to Discover and Report Unauthorized Signature or Alteration.

(a) A bank that sends or makes available to a customer a statement of account showing payment of items for the account shall either return or make available to the customer the items paid or provide information in the statement of account sufficient to allow the customer reasonably to identify the items paid. The statement of account provides sufficient information if the item is described by item number, amount, and date of payment.

(b) If the items are not returned to the customer, the person retaining the items shall either retain the items or, if the items are destroyed, maintain the capacity to furnish legible copies of the items until the expiration of seven years after receipt of the items. A customer may request an item from the bank that paid the item, and that bank must provide in a reasonable time either the item or, if the item has been destroyed or is not otherwise obtainable, a legible copy of the item.

(c) If a bank sends or makes available a statement of account or items pursuant to subsection (a), the customer must exercise reasonable promptness in examining the statement or the items to determine whether any payment was not authorized because of an alteration of an item or because a purported signature by or on behalf of the customer was not authorized. If, based on the statement or items provided, the customer should reasonably have discovered the unauthorized payment, the customer must promptly notify the bank of the relevant facts.

(d) If the bank proves that the customer failed, with respect to an item, to comply with the duties imposed on the customer by subsection (c), the customer is precluded from asserting against the bank:

(1) the customer's unauthorized signature or any alteration on the item, if the bank also proves that it suffered a loss by reason of the failure; and

(2) the customer's unauthorized signature or alteration by the same wrongdoer on any other item paid in good faith by the bank if the payment was made before the bank received notice from the customer of the unauthorized signature or alteration and after the customer had been afforded a reasonable period of time, not exceeding 30 days, in which to examine the item or statement of account and notify the bank.

(e) If subsection (d) applies and the customer proves that the bank failed to exercise ordinary care in paying the item and that the failure substantially contributed to loss, the loss is allocated between the customer precluded and the bank asserting the preclusion according to the extent to which the failure of the customer to comply with subsection (c) and the failure of the bank to exercise ordinary care contributed to the loss. If the customer proves that the bank did not pay the item in good faith, the preclusion under subsection (d) does not apply.

(f) Without regard to care or lack of care of either the customer or the bank, a customer who does not within one year after the statement or items are made available to the customer (subsection (a)) discover and report the customer's unauthorized signature on or any alteration on the item is precluded from asserting against the bank the unauthorized signature or alteration. If there is a preclusion under this subsection, the payor bank may not recover for breach or warranty under Section 4-208 with respect to the unauthorized signature or alteration to which the preclusion applies.

§ 4-407. Payor Bank's Right to Subrogation on Improper Payment.

If a payor bank has paid an item over the order of the drawer or maker to stop payment, or after an account has been closed, or otherwise under circumstances giving a basis for objection by the drawer or maker, to prevent unjust enrichment and only to the extent necessary to prevent loss to the bank by reason of its payment of the item, the payor bank is subrogated to the rights

(1) of any holder in due course on the item against the drawer or maker;

(2) of the payee or any other holder of the item against the drawer or maker either on the item or under the transaction out of which the item arose; and

(3) of the drawer or maker against the payee or any other holder of the item with respect to the transaction out of which the item arose.

Part 5 Collection of Documentary Drafts

§ 4-501. Handling of Documentary Drafts; Duty to Send for Presentment and to Notify Customer of Dishonor.

A bank that takes a documentary draft for collection shall present or send the draft and accompanying documents for presentment and, upon learning that the draft has not been paid or accepted in due course, shall seasonably notify its customer of the fact even though it may have discounted or bought the draft or extended credit available for withdrawal as of right.

§ 4-502. Presentment of "On Arrival" Drafts.

If a draft or the relevant instructions require presentment "on arrival", "when goods arrive" or the like, the collecting bank need not present until in its judgment a reasonable time for arrival of the goods has expired. Refusal to pay or accept because the goods have not arrived is not dishonor; the bank must notify its transferor of the refusal but need not present

the draft again until it is instructed to do so or learns of the arrival of the goods.

§ 4-503. Responsibility of Presenting Bank for Documents and Goods; Report of Reasons for Dishonor; Referee in Case of Need.

Unless otherwise instructed and except as provided in Article 5, a bank presenting a documentary draft:

(1) must deliver the documents to the drawee on acceptance of the draft if it is payable more than three days after presentment; otherwise, only on payment; and

(2) upon dishonor, either in the case of presentment for acceptance of presentment for payment, may seek and follow instructions from any referee in case of need designated in the draft or, if the presenting bank does not choose to utilize the referee's services, it must use diligence and good faith to ascertain the reason for dishonor, must notify its transferor of the dishonor and of the results of its effort to ascertain the reasons therefor, and must request instructions.

However the presenting bank is under no obligation with respect to goods represented by the documents except to follow any reasonable instructions seasonably received; it has a right to reimbursement for any expense incurred in following instructions and to prepayment of or indemnity for those expenses.

§ 4-504. Privilege of Presenting Bank to Deal With Goods; Security Interest for Expenses.

(a) A presenting bank that, following the dishonor of a documentary draft, has seasonably requested instructions but does not receive them within a reasonable time may store, sell, or otherwise deal with the goods in any reasonable manner.

(b) For its reasonable expenses incurred by action under subsection (a) the presenting bank has a lien upon the goods or their proceeds, which may be foreclosed in the same manner as an unpaid seller's lien.

ARTICLE 4A / Funds Transfers

Prefatory Note

The National Conference of Commissioners on Uniform State laws and The American Law Institute have approved a new Article 4A to the Uniform Commercial Code. Comments that follow each of the sections of the statute are intended as official comments. They explain in detail the purpose and meaning of the various sections and the policy considerations on which they are based.

Description of transaction covered by Article 4A.

There are a number of mechanisms for making payments through the banking system. Most of these mechanisms are covered in whole or part by state or federal statutes. In terms of number of transactions, payments made by check or credit card are the most common payment methods. Payment by check is covered by Articles 3 and 4 of the UCC and some aspects of payment by credit card are covered by federal law. In recent years electronic funds transfers have been increasingly common in consumer transactions. For example, in some cases a retail customer can pay for purchases by use of an access or debit card inserted in a terminal at the retail store that allows the bank account of the customer to be instantly debited. Some aspects of these point-of-sale transactions and other consumer payments that are effected electronically are covered by a federal statute, the Electronic Fund Transfer Act (EFTA). If any part of a funds transfer is covered by EFTA, the entire funds transfer is excluded from Article 4A.

Another type of payment, commonly referred to as a wholesale wire transfer, is the primary focus of Article 4A. Payments that are covered by Article 4A are overwhelmingly between business or financial institutions. The dollar volume of payments made by wire transfer far exceeds the dollar volume of payments made by other means. The volume of payments by wire transfer over the two principal wire payment systems—the Federal Reserve wire transfer network (Fedwire) and the New York Clearing House Interbank Payments Systems (CHIPS)—exceeds one trillion dollars per day. Most payments carried out by use of automated clearing houses are consumer payments covered by EFTA and therefore not covered by Article 4A. There is, however, a significant volume of nonconsumer ACH payments that closely resemble wholesale wire transfers. These payments are also covered by Article 4A.

There is some resemblance between payments made by wire transfer and payments made by other means such as paper-based checks and credit cards or electronically-based consumer payments, but there are also many differences. Article 4A excludes from its coverage these other payment mechanisms. Article 4A follows a policy of treating the transaction that it covers—a "funds transfer"—as a unique method of payment that is governed by unique principles of law that address the operational and policy issues presented by this kind of payment.

The funds transfer that is covered by Article 4A is not a complex transaction and can be illustrated by the following example which is used throughout the Prefatory Note as a basis for discussion. X, a debtor, wants to pay an obligation owed to Y. Instead of delivering to Y a negotiable instrument such as a check or some other writing such as a credit card slip that enables Y to obtain payment from a bank, X transmits an instruction to X's bank to credit a sum of money to the bank account of Y. In most cases X's bank and Y's bank are different banks. X's bank may carry out X's instruction by instructing Y's bank to credit Y's account in the amount that X requested. The instruction that X issues to its bank is a "payment order." X is the "sender" of the payment order and X's bank is the "receiving bank" with respect to X's order. Y is the "beneficiary" of X's order. When X's bank issues an instruction to Y's bank to carry out X's payment order, X's bank "executes" X's order. The instruction of X's bank to Y's bank is also a payment order. With respect to that order, X's bank is the sender, Y's bank is the receiving bank, and Y is the beneficiary. The entire series of transactions by which X pays Y is knows as the "funds transfer." With respect to the funds transfer, X is the "originator," X's bank is the "originator's

bank," Y is the "beneficiary" and Y's bank is the "beneficiary's bank." In more complex transactions there are one or more additional banks known as "intermediary banks" between X's bank and Y's bank. In the funds transfer the instruction contained in the payment order of X to its bank is carried out by a series of payment orders by each bank in the transmission chain to the next bank in the chain until Y's bank receives a payment order to make the credit to Y's account. In most cases, the payment order of each bank to the next bank in the chain is transmitted electronically, and often the payment order of X to its bank is also transmitted electronically, but the means of transmission does not have any legal significance. A payment order may be transmitted by any means, and in some cases the payment order is transmitted by a slow means such as first class mail. To reflect this fact, the broader term "funds transfer" rather than the narrower term "wire transfer" is used in Article 4A to describe the overall payment transaction.

Funds transfers are divided into two categories determined by whether the instruction to pay is given by the person making payment or the person receiving payment. If the instruction is given by the person making the payment, the transfer is commonly referred to as a "credit transfer." If the instruction is given by the person receiving payment, the transfer is commonly referred to as a "debit transfer." Article 4A governs credit transfers and excludes debit transfers.

Why is Article 4A needed?

There is no comprehensive body of law that defines the rights and obligations that arise from wire transfers. Some aspects of wire transfers are governed by rules of the principal transfer systems. Transfers made by Fedwire are governed by Federal Reserve Regulation J and transfers over CHIPS are governed by the CHIPS rules. Transfers made by means of automated clearing houses are governed by uniform rules adopted by various associations of banks in various parts of the nation or by Federal Reserve rules or operating circulars. But the various funds transfer system rules apply to only limited aspects of wire transfer transactions. The resolution of the many issues that are not covered by funds transfer system rules depends on contracts of the parties, to the extent that they exist, or principles of law applicable to other payment mechanisms that might be applied by analogy. The result is a great deal of uncertainty. There is no consensus about the juridical nature of a wire transfer and consequently of the rights and obligations that are created. Article 4A is intended to provide the comprehensive body of law that we do not have today.

Characteristics of a funds transfer.

There are a number of characteristics of funds transfers covered by Article 4A that have influenced the drafting of the statute. The typical funds transfer involves a large amount of money. Multimillion dollar transactions are commonplace. The originator of the transfer and the beneficiary are typically sophisticated business or financial organizations. High speed is another predominant characteristic. Most funds transfers are completed on the same day, even in complex transactions in which there are several intermediary banks in the transmission chain. A funds transfer is a highly efficient substitute for payments made by the delivery of paper instruments. Another characteristic is extremely low cost. A transfer that involves many millions of dollars can be made for a price of a few dollars. Price does not normally vary very much or at all with the amount of the transfer. This system of pricing may not be feasible if the bank is exposed to very large liabilities in connection with the transaction. The pricing system assumes that the price reflects primarily the cost of the mechanical operation performed by the bank, but in fact, a bank may have more or less potential liability with respect to a funds transfer depending upon the amount of the transfer. Risk of loss to banks carrying out a funds transfer may arise from a variety of causes. In some funds transfers, there may be extensions of very large amounts of credit for short periods of time by the banks that carry out a funds transfer. If a payment order is issued to the beneficiary's bank, it is normal for the bank to release funds to the beneficiary immediately. Sometimes, payment to the beneficiary's bank by the bank that issued the order to the beneficiary's bank is delayed until the end of the day. If that payment is not received because of the insolvency of the bank that is obliged to pay, the beneficiary's bank may suffer a loss. There is also risk of loss if a bank fails to execute the payment order of a customer, or if the order is executed late. There also may be an error in the payment order issued by a bank that is executing the payment order of its customer. For example, the error might relate to the amount to be paid or to the identity of the person to be paid. Because the dollar amounts involved in funds transfers are so large, the risk of loss if something goes wrong in a transaction may also be very large. A major policy issue in the drafting of Article 4A is that of determining how risk of loss is to be allocated given the price structure in the industry.

Concept of acceptance and effect of acceptance by the beneficiary's bank.

Rights and obligations under Article 4A arise as the result of "acceptance" of a payment order by the bank to which the order is addressed. Section 4A-209. The effect of acceptance varies depending upon whether the payment order is issued to the beneficiary's bank or to a bank other than the beneficiary's bank. Acceptance by the beneficiary's bank is particularly important because it defines when the beneficiary's bank becomes obligated to the beneficiary to pay the amount of the payment order. Although Article 4A follows convention in using the term "funds transfer" to identify the payment from X to Y that is described above, no money or property right of X is actually transferred to Y. X pays Y by causing Y's bank to become indebted to Y in the amount of the payment. This debt arises when Y's bank accepts the payment order that X's bank issued to Y's bank to execute X's order. If the funds transfer was carried out by use of one or more intermediary banks between X's bank and Y's bank, Y's bank becomes indebted to Y when Y's bank accepts the payment order issued to it by an intermediary bank. The funds transfer is completed when this debt is incurred. Acceptance, the event that determines when the debt of Y's bank to Y arises, occurs (i) when Y's bank pays Y or notifies Y of receipt of the payment order, or (ii) when Y's bank receives payment from the bank that issued a payment order to Y's bank.

The only obligation of the beneficiary's bank that results from acceptance of a payment order is to pay the amount of the order to the beneficiary. No obligation is owed to either the sender of the payment order accepted by the beneficiary's bank or to the originator of the funds transfer. The obligation created by acceptance by the beneficiary's bank is for the benefit of the beneficiary. The purpose of the sender's payment order is to effect payment by the originator to the beneficiary and that purpose is achieved when the beneficiary's bank accepts the payment order. Section 4A-405 states rules for determining when the obligation of the beneficiary's bank to the beneficiary has been paid.

Acceptance by a bank other than the beneficiary's bank.

In the funds transfer described above, what is the obligation of X's bank when it receives X's payment order? Funds transfers by a bank on behalf of its customer are made pursuant to an agreement or arrangement that may or may not be reduced to a formal document signed by the parties. It is probably true that in most cases there is either no express agreement or the agreement addresses only some aspects of the transaction. Substantial risk is involved in funds transfers and a bank may not be willing to give this service to all customers, and may not be willing to offer it to any customer unless certain safeguards against loss such as security procedures are in effect. Funds transfers often involve the giving of credit by the receiving bank to the customer, and that also may involve an agreement. These considerations are reflected in Article 4A by the principle that, in the absence of a contrary agreement, a receiving bank does not incur liability with respect to a payment order until it accepts it. If X and X's bank in the hypothetical case had an agreement that obliged the bank to act on X's payment orders and the bank failed to comply with the agreement, the bank can be held liable for breach of the agreement. But apart from any obligation arising by agreement, the bank does not incur any liability with respect to X's payment order until the bank accepts the order. X's payment order is treated by Article 4A as a request by X to the bank to take action that will cause X's payment order to be carried out. That request can be accepted by X's bank by "executing" X's payment order. Execution occurs when X's bank sends a payment order to Y's bank intended by X's bank to carry out the payment order of X. X's bank could also execute X's payment order by issuing a payment order to an intermediary bank instructing the intermediary bank to instruct Y's bank to make the credit to Y's account. In that case execution and acceptance of X's order occur when the payment order of X's bank is sent to the intermediary bank. When X's bank executes X's payment order the bank is entitled to receive payment from X and may debit an authorized account of X. If X's bank does not execute X's order and the amount of the order is covered by a withdrawable credit balance in X's authorized account, the bank must pay X interest on the money represented by X's order unless X is given prompt notice of rejection of the order. Section 4A-210(b).

Bank error in funds transfers.

If a bank, other than the beneficiary's bank, accepts a payment order, the obligations and liabilities are owed to the originator of the funds transfer. Assume in the example stated above, that X's bank executes X's payment order by issuing a payment order to an intermediary bank that executes the order of X's bank by issuing a payment order to Y's bank. The obligations of X's bank with respect to execution are owed to X. The obligations of the intermediary bank with respect to execution are also owed to X. Section 4A-302 states standards with respect to the time and manner of execution of payment orders. Section 4A-305 states the measure of damages for improper execution. It also states that a receiving bank is liable for damages if it fails to execute a payment order that it was obliged by express agreement to execute. In each case consequential damages are not recoverable unless an express agreement of the receiving bank provides for them. The policy basis for this limitation is discussed in Comment 2 to Section 4A-305.

Error in the consummation of a funds transfer is not uncommon. There may be a discrepancy in the amount that the originator orders to be paid to the beneficiary and the amount that the beneficiary's bank is ordered to pay. For example, if the originator's payment order instructs payment of $100,000 and the payment order of the originator's bank instructs payment of $1,000,000, the originator's bank is entitled to receive only $100,000 from the originator and has the burden of recovering the additional $900,000 paid to the beneficiary by mistake. In some cases the originator's bank or an intermediary bank instructs payment to a beneficiary other than the beneficiary stated in the originator's payment order. If the wrong beneficiary is paid the bank that issued the erroneous payment order is not entitled to receive payment of the payment order that it executed and has the burden of recovering the mistaken payment. The originator is not obliged to pay its payment order. Section 4A-303 and Section 4A-207 state rules for determining the rights and obligations of the various parties to the funds transfer in these cases and in other typical cases in which error is made.

Pursuant to Section 4A-402(c) the originator is excused from the obligation to pay the originator's bank if the funds transfer is not completed, i.e. payment by the originator to the beneficiary is not made. Payment by the originator to the beneficiary occurs when the beneficiary's bank accepts a payment order for the benefit of the beneficiary of the originator's payment order. Section 4A-406. If for any reason that acceptance does not occur, the originator is not required to pay the payment order that it issued or, if it already paid, is entitled to refund of the payment with interest. This "money-back guarantee" is an important protection of the originator of a funds transfer. The same rule applies to any other sender in the funds transfer. Each sender's obligation to pay is excused if the beneficiary's bank does not accept a payment order for the benefit of the beneficiary of that sender's order. There is an important exception to this rule. It is common practice for the originator of a funds transfer to designate the intermediary bank or banks through which the funds transfer is to be routed. The originator's bank is required by Section 4A-302 to follow the instruction of the originator with respect to intermediary banks. If the originator's bank sends a payment order to the intermediary bank designated in the originator's order and the intermediary bank causes the funds transfer to miscarry by failing to execute the payment order or by instructing payment to the wrong beneficiary, the originator's bank is not required to pay its payment order and if it has already paid it is entitled to recover payment from the

intermediary bank. This remedy is normally adequate, but if the originator's bank already paid its order and the intermediary bank has suspended payments or is not permitted by law to refund payment, the originator's bank will suffer a loss. Since the originator required the originator's bank to use the failed intermediary bank, Section 4A-402(e) provides that in this case the originator is obliged to pay its payment order and has a claim against the intermediary bank for the amount of the order. The same principle applies to any other sender that designates a subsequent intermediary bank.

Unauthorized payment orders.

An important issue addressed in Section 4A-202 and Section 4A-203 is how the risk of loss from unauthorized payment orders is to be allocated. In a large percentage of cases, the payment order of the originator of the funds transfer is transmitted electronically to the originator's bank. In these cases it may not be possible for the bank to know whether the electronic message has been authorized by its customer. To ensure that no unauthorized person is transmitting messages to the bank, the normal practice is to establish security procedures that usually involve the use of codes or identifying numbers or words. If the bank accepts a payment order that purports to be that of its customer after verifying its authenticity by complying with a security procedure agreed to by the customer and the bank, the customer is bound to pay the order even if it was not authorized. But there is an important limitation on this rule. The bank is entitled to payment in the case of an unauthorized order only if the court finds that the security procedure was a commercially reasonable method of providing security against unauthorized payment orders. The customer can also avoid liability if it can prove that the unauthorized order was not initiated by an employee or other agent of the customer having access to confidential security information or by a person who obtained that information from a source controlled by the customer. The policy issues are discussed in the comments following Section 4A-203. If the bank accepts an unauthorized payment order without verifying it in compliance with a security procedure, the loss falls on the bank.

Security procedures are also important in cases of error in the transmission of payment orders. There may be an error by the sender in the amount of the order, or a sender may transmit a payment order and then erroneously transmit a duplicate of the order. Normally, the sender is bound by the payment order even if it is issued by mistake. But in some cases an error of this kind can be detected by a security procedure. Although the receiving bank is not obliged to provide a security procedure for the detection of error, if such a procedure is agreed to by the bank Section 4A-205 provides that if the error is not detected because the receiving bank does not comply with the procedure, any resulting loss is borne by the bank failing to comply with the security procedure.

Insolvency losses.

Some payment orders do not involve the granting of credit to the sender by the receiving bank. In those cases, the receiving bank accepts the sender's order at the same time the bank receives payment of the order. This is true of a transfer of funds by Fedwire or of cases in which the receiving bank can debit a funded account of the sender. But in some cases the granting of credit is the norm. This is true of a payment order over CHIPS. In a CHIPS transaction the receiving bank usually will accept the order before receiving payment from the sending bank. Payment is delayed until the end of the day when settlement is made through the Federal Reserve System. If the receiving bank is an intermediary bank, it will accept by issuing a payment order to another bank and the intermediary bank is obliged to pay that payment order. If the receiving bank is the beneficiary's bank, the bank usually will accept by releasing funds to the beneficiary before the bank has received payment. If a sending bank suspends payments before settling its liabilities at the end of the day, the financial stability of banks that are net creditors of the insolvent bank may also be put into jeopardy, because the dollar volume of funds transfers between the banks may be extremely large. With respect to two banks that are dealing with each other in a series of transactions in which each bank is sometimes a receiving bank and sometimes a sender, the risk of insolvency can be managed if amounts payable as a sender and amounts receivable as a receiving bank are roughly equal. But if these amounts are significantly out of balance, a net creditor bank may have a very significant credit risk during the day before settlement occurs. The Federal Reserve System and the banking community are greatly concerned with this risk, and various measures have been instituted to reduce this credit exposure. Article 4A also addresses this problem. A receiving bank can always avoid this risk by delaying acceptance of a payment order until after the bank has received payment. For example, if the beneficiary's bank credits the beneficiary's account it can avoid acceptance by not notifying the beneficiary of the receipt of the order or by notifying the beneficiary that the credit may not be withdrawn until the beneficiary's bank receives payment. But if the beneficiary's bank releases funds to the beneficiary before receiving settlement, the result in a funds transfer other than a transfer by means of an automated clearing house or similar provisional settlement system is that the beneficiary's bank may not recover the funds if it fails to receive settlement. This rule encourages the banking system to impose credit limitations on banks that issue payment orders. These limitations are already in effect. CHIPS has also proposed a loss-sharing plan to be adopted for implementation in the second half of 1990 under which CHIPS participants will be required to provide funds necessary to complete settlement of the obligations of one or more participants that are unable to meet settlement obligations. Under this plan, it will be a virtual certainty that there will be settlement on CHIPS in the event of failure by a single bank. Section 4A-403(b) and (c) are also addressed to reducing risks of insolvency. Under these provisions the amount owed by a failed bank with respect to payment orders it issued is the net amount owing after setting off amounts owed to the failed bank with respect to payment orders it received. This rule allows credit exposure to be managed by limitations on the net debit position of a bank.

Part 1   Subject Matter and Definitions

§ 4A-101.   Short Title.

This Article may be cited as Uniform Commercial Code— Funds Transfers.

§ 4A-102.   Subject Matter.

Except as otherwise provided in Section 4A-108, this Article applies to funds transfers defined in Section 4A-104.

§ 4A-103.   Payment Order—Definitions.

(a) In this Article:

(1) "Payment order" means an instruction of a sender to a receiving bank, transmitted orally, electronically, or in writing, to pay, or to cause another bank to pay, a fixed or determinable amount of money to a beneficiary if:

(i) the instruction does not state a condition to payment to the beneficiary other than time of payment,
(ii) the receiving bank is to be reimbursed by debiting an account of, or otherwise receiving payment from, the sender, and
(iii) the instruction is transmitted by the sender directly to the receiving bank or to an agent, funds-transfer system, or communication system for transmittal to the receiving bank.

(2) "Beneficiary" means the person to be paid by the beneficiary's bank.
(3) "Beneficiary's bank" means the bank identified in a payment order in which an account of the beneficiary is to be credited pursuant to the order or which otherwise is to make payment to the beneficiary if the order does not provide for payment to an account.
(4) "Receiving bank" means the bank to which the sender's instruction is addressed.
(5) "Sender" means the person giving the instruction to the receiving bank.

(b) If an instruction complying with subsection (a)(1) is to make more than one payment to a beneficiary, the instruction is a separate payment order with respect to each payment.
(c) A payment order is issued when it is sent to the receiving bank.

§ 4A-104.   Funds Transfer—Definitions.

In this Article:

(a) "Funds transfer" means the series of transactions, beginning with the originator's payment order, made for the purpose of making payment to the beneficiary of the order. The term includes any payment order issued by the originator's bank or an intermediary bank intended to carry out the originator's payment order. A funds transfer is completed by acceptance by the beneficiary's bank of a payment order for the benefit of the beneficiary of the originator's payment order.
(b) "Intermediary bank" means a receiving bank other than the originator's bank or the beneficiary's bank.
(c) "Originator" means the sender of the first payment order in a funds transfer.
(d) "Originator's bank" means (i) the receiving bank to which the payment order of the originator is issued if the originator is not a bank, or (ii) the originator if the originator is a bank.

§ 4A-105.   Other Definitions.

(a) In this Article:

(1) "Authorized account" means a deposit account of a customer in a bank designated by the customer as a source

of payment of payment orders issued by the customer to the bank. If a customer does not so designate an account, any account of the customer is an authorized account if payment of a payment order from that account is not inconsistent with a restriction on the use of that account.

(2) "Bank" means a person engaged in the business of banking and includes a savings bank, savings and loan association, credit union, and trust company. A branch or separate office of a bank is a separate bank for purposes of this Article.

(3) "Customer" means a person, including a bank, having an account with a bank or from whom a bank has agreed to receive payment orders.

(4) "Funds-transfer business day" of a receiving bank means the part of a day during which the receiving bank is open for the receipt, processing, and transmittal of payment orders and cancellations and amendments of payment orders.

(5) "Funds-transfer system" means a wire transfer network, automated clearing house, or other communication system of a clearing house or other association of banks through which a payment order by a bank may be transmitted to the bank to which the order is addressed.

(6) "Good faith" means honesty in fact and the observance of reasonable commercial standards of fair dealing.

(7) "Prove" with respect to a fact means to meet the burden of establishing the fact (Section 1-201(8)).

(b) Other definitions applying to this Article and the sections in which they appear are:

"Acceptance"   Section 4A-209
"Beneficiary"   Section 4A-103
"Beneficiary's bank"   Section 4A-103
"Executed"   Section 4A-301
"Execution date"   Section 4A-301
"Funds transfer"   Section 4A-104
"Funds-transfer system rule"   Section 4A-501
"Intermediary bank"   Section 4A-104
"Originator"   Section 4A-104
"Originator's bank"   Section 4A-104
"Payment by beneficiary's bank to beneficiary"   Section 4A-405
"Payment by originator to beneficiary"   Section 4A-406
"Payment by sender to receiving bank"   Section 4A-403
"Payment date"   Section 4A-401
"Payment order"   Section 4A-103
"Receiving bank"   Section 4A-103
"Security procedure"   Section 4A-201
"Sender"   Section 4A-103

(c) The following definitions in Article 4 apply to this Article:

"Clearing house"   Section 4-104
"Item"   Section 4-104
"Suspends payments"   Section 4-104

(d) In addition Article 1 contains general definitions and principles of construction and interpretation applicable throughout this Article.

§ 4A-106.   Time Payment Order Is Received.

(a) The time of receipt of a payment order or communication cancelling or amending a payment order is determined by the rules applicable to receipt of a notice stated in Section 1-201(27). A receiving bank may fix a cut-off time or times on a funds-transfer business day for the receipt and processing of payment orders and communications cancelling or amending payment orders. Different cut-off times may apply to payment orders, cancellations, or amendments, or to different categories of payment orders, cancellations, or amendments. A cut-off time may apply to senders generally or different cut-off times may apply to different senders or categories of payment orders. If a payment order or communication cancelling or amending a payment order is received after the close of a funds-transfer business day or after the appropriate cut-off time on a funds-transfer business day, the receiving bank may treat the payment order or communication as received at the opening of the next funds-transfer business day.

(b) If this Article refers to an execution date or payment date or states a day on which a receiving bank is required to take action, and the date or day does not fall on a funds-transfer business day, the next day that is a funds-transfer business day is treated as the date or day stated, unless the contrary is stated in this Article.

§ 4A-107.   Federal Reserve Regulations and Operating Circulars.

Regulations of the Board of Governors of the Federal Reserve System and operating circulars of the Federal Reserve Banks supersede any inconsistent provision of this Article to the extent of the inconsistency.

§ 4A-108.   Exclusion of Consumer Transactions Governed by Federal Law

This Article does not apply to a funds transfer any part of which is governed by the Electronic Fund Transfer Act of 1978 (Title XX, Public Law 95-630, 92 Stat. 3728, 15 U.S.C. § 1693 et seq.) as amended from time to time.

Part 2   Issue and Acceptance of Payment Order

§ 4A-201.   Security Procedure.

"Security procedure" means a procedure established by agreement of a customer and a receiving bank for the purpose of (i) verifying that a payment order or communication amending or cancelling a payment order is that of the customer, or (ii) detecting error in the transmission or the content of the payment order or communication. A security procedure may require the use of algorithms or other codes, identifying words or numbers, encryption, callback procedures, or similar security devices. Comparison of a signature on a payment order or communication with an authorized specimen signature of the customer is not by itself a security procedure.

§ 4A-202.   Authorized and Verified Payment Orders.

(a) A payment order received by the receiving bank is the authorized order of the person identified as sender if that person authorized the order or is otherwise bound by it under the law of agency.

(b) If a bank and its customer have agreed that the authenticity of payment orders issued to the bank in the name of the customer as sender will be verified pursuant to a security procedure, a payment order received by the receiving bank is effective as the order of the customer, whether or not authorized, if (i) the security procedure is a commercially reasonable method of providing security against unauthorized payment orders, and (ii) the bank proves that it accepted the payment order in good faith and in compliance with the security procedure and any written agreement or instruction of the customer restricting acceptance of payment orders issued in the name of the customer. The bank is not required to follow an instruction that violates a written agreement with the customer or notice of which is not received at a time and in a manner affording the bank a reasonable opportunity to act on it before the payment order is accepted.

(c) Commercial reasonableness of a security procedure is a question of law to be determined by considering the wishes of the customer expressed to the bank, the circumstances of the customer known to the bank, including the size, type, and frequency of payment orders normally issued by the customer to the bank, alternative security procedures offered to the customer, and security procedures in general use by customers and receiving banks similarly situated. A security procedure is deemed to be commercially reasonable if (i) the security procedure was chosen by the customer after the bank offered, and the customer refused, a security procedure that was commercially reasonable for that customer, and (ii) the customer expressly agreed in writing to be bound by any payment order, whether or not authorized, issued in its name and accepted by the bank in compliance with the security procedure chosen by the customer.

(d) The term "sender" in this Article includes the customer in whose name a payment order is issued if the order is the authorized order of the customer under subsection (a), or it is effective as the order of the customer under subsection (b).

(e) This section applies to amendments and cancellations of payment orders to the same extent it applies to payment orders.

(f) Except as provided in this section and in Section 4A-203(a)(1), rights and obligations arising under this section or Section 4A-203 may not be varied by agreement.

§ 4A-203. Unenforceability of Certain Verified Payment Orders.

(a) If an accepted payment order is not, under Section 4A-202(a), an authorized order of a customer identified as sender, but is effective as an order of the customer pursuant to Section 4A-202(b), the following rules apply:

(1) By express written agreement, the receiving bank may limit the extent to which it is entitled to enforce or retain payment of the payment order.

(2) The receiving bank is not entitled to enforce or retain payment of the payment order if the customer proves that the order was not caused, directly or indirectly, by a person (i) entrusted at any time with duties to act for the customer with respect to payment orders or the security procedure, or (ii) who obtained access to transmitting facilities of the customer or who obtained, from a source controlled by the customer and without authority of the receiving bank, information facilitating breach of the security procedure, regardless of how the information was obtained or whether the customer was at fault. Information includes any access device, computer software, or the like.

(b) This section applies to amendments of payment orders to the same extent it applies to payment orders.

§ 4A-204. Refund of Payment and Duty of Customer to Report With Respect to Unauthorized Payment Order.

(a) If a receiving bank accepts a payment order issued in the name of its customer as sender which is (i) not authorized and not effective as the order of the customer under Section 4A-202, or (ii) not enforceable, in whole or in part, against the customer under Section 4A-203, the bank shall refund any payment of the payment order received from the customer to the extent the bank is not entitled to enforce payment and shall pay interest on the refundable amount calculated from the date the bank received payment to the date of the refund. However, the customer is not entitled to interest from the bank on the amount to be refunded if the customer fails to exercise ordinary care to determine that the order was not authorized by the customer and to notify the bank of the relevant facts within a reasonable time not exceeding 90 days after the date the customer received notification from the bank that the order was accepted or that the customer's account was debited with respect to the order. The bank is not entitled to any recovery from the customer on account of a failure by the customer to give notification as stated in this section.

(b) Reasonable time under subsection (a) may be fixed by agreement as stated in Section 1-204(1), but the obligation of a receiving bank to refund payment as stated in subsection (a) may not otherwise be varied by agreement.

§ 4A-205. Erroneous Payment Orders.

(a) If an accepted payment order was transmitted pursuant to a security procedure for the detection of error and the payment order (i) erroneously instructed payment to a beneficiary not intended by the sender, (ii) erroneously instructed payment in an amount greater than the amount intended by the sender, or (iii) was an erroneously transmitted duplicate of a payment order previously sent by the sender, the following rules apply:

(1) If the sender proves that the sender or a person acting on behalf of the sender pursuant to Section 4A-206 complied with the security procedure and that the error would have been detected if the receiving bank had also complied, the sender is not obliged to pay the order to the extent stated in paragraphs (2) and (3).

(2) If the funds transfer is completed on the basis of an erroneous payment order described in clause (i) or (iii) of subsection (a), the sender is not obliged to pay the order and the receiving bank is entitled to recover from the beneficiary any amount paid to the beneficiary to the extent allowed by the law governing mistake and restitution.

(3) If the funds transfer is completed on the basis of a payment order described in clause (ii) of subsection (a), the sender is not obliged to pay the order to the extent the amount received by the beneficiary is greater than the amount intended by the sender. In that case, the receiving bank is entitled to recover from the beneficiary the excess amount received to the extent allowed by the law governing mistake and restitution.

(b) If (i) the sender of an erroneous payment order described in subsection (a) is not obliged to pay all or part of the order, and (ii) the sender receives notification from the receiving bank that the order was accepted by the bank or that the sender's account was debited with respect to the order, the sender has a duty to exercise ordinary care, on the basis of information available to the sender, to discover the error with respect to the order and to advise the bank of the relevant facts within a reasonable time, not exceeding 90 days, after the bank's notification was received by the sender. If the bank proves that the sender failed to perform that duty, the sender is liable to the bank for the loss the bank proves it incurred as a result of the failure, but the liability of the sender may not exceed the amount of the sender's order.

(c) This section applies to amendments to payment orders to the same extent it applies to payment orders.

§ 4A-206. Transmission of Payment Order Through Funds-Transfer or Other Communication System.

(a) If a payment order addressed to a receiving bank is transmitted to a funds-transfer system or other third-party communication system for transmittal to the bank, the system is deemed to be an agent of the sender for the purpose of transmitting the payment order to the bank. If there is a discrepancy between the terms of the payment order transmitted to the system and the terms of the payment order transmitted by the system to the bank, the terms of the payment order of the sender are those transmitted by the system. This section does not apply to a funds-transfer system of the Federal Reserve Banks.

(b) This section applies to cancellations and amendments of payment orders to the same extent it applies to payment orders.

§ 4A-207. Misdescription of Beneficiary.

(a) Subject to subsection (b), if, in a payment order received by the beneficiary's bank, the name, bank account number, or other identification of the beneficiary refers to a nonexistent or unidentifiable person or account, no person has rights as a beneficiary of the order and acceptance of the order cannot occur.

(b) If a payment order received by the beneficiary's bank identifies the beneficiary both by name and by an identifying or bank account number and the name and number identify different persons, the following rules apply:

(1) Except as otherwise provided in subsection (c), if the beneficiary's bank does not know that the name and number refer to different persons, it may rely on the number as the proper identification of the beneficiary of the order. The beneficiary's bank need not determine whether the name and number refer to the same person.

(2) If the beneficiary's bank pays the person identified by name or knows that the name and number identify different persons, no person has rights as beneficiary except the person paid by the beneficiary's bank if that person was entitled to receive payment from the originator of the funds transfer. If no person has rights as beneficiary, acceptance of the order cannot occur.

(c) If (i) a payment order described in subsection (b) is accepted, (ii) the originator's payment order described the ben-

eficiary inconsistently by name and number, and (iii) the beneficiary's bank pays the person identified by number as permitted by subsection (b)(1), the following rules apply:

(1) If the originator is a bank, the originator is obliged to pay its order.

(2) If the originator is not a bank and proves that the person identified by number was not entitled to receive payment from the originator, the originator is not obliged to pay its order unless the originator's bank proves that the originator, before acceptance of the originator's order, had notice that payment of a payment order issued by the originator might be made by the beneficiary's bank on the basis of an identifying or bank account number even if it identifies a person different from the named beneficiary. Proof of notice may be made by any admissible evidence. The originator's bank satisfies the burden of proof if it proves that the originator, before the payment order was accepted, signed a writing stating the information to which the notice relates.

(d) In a case governed by subsection (b)(1), if the beneficiary's bank rightfully pays the person identified by number and that person was not entitled to receive payment from the originator, the amount paid may be recovered from that person to the extent allowed by the law governing mistake and restitution as follows:

(1) If the originator is obliged to pay its payment order as stated in subsection (c), the originator has the right to recover.

(2) If the originator is not a bank and is not obliged to pay its payment order, the originator's bank has the right to recover.

§ 4A-208. Misdescription of Intermediary Bank or Beneficiary's Bank.

(a) This subsection applies to a payment order identifying an intermediary bank or the beneficiary's bank only by an identifying number.

(1) The receiving bank may rely on the number as the proper identification of the intermediary or beneficiary's bank and need not determine whether the number identifies a bank.

(2) The sender is obliged to compensate the receiving bank for any loss and expenses incurred by the receiving bank as a result of its reliance on the number in executing or attempting to execute the order.

(b) This subsection applies to a payment order identifying an intermediary bank or the beneficiary's bank both by name and an identifying number if the name and number identify different persons.

(1) If the sender is a bank, the receiving bank may rely on the number as the proper identification of the intermediary or beneficiary's bank if the receiving bank, when it executes the sender's order, does not know that the name and number identify different persons. The receiving bank need not determine whether the name and number refer to the same person or whether the number refers to a bank. The sender is obliged to compensate the receiving bank for any loss and expenses incurred by the receiving bank as a result of its reliance on the number in executing or attempting to execute the order.

(2) If the sender is not a bank and the receiving bank proves that the sender, before the payment order was accepted, had notice that the receiving bank might rely on the number as the proper identification of the intermediary or beneficiary's bank even if it identifies a person different from the bank identified by name, the rights and obligations of the sender and the receiving bank are governed by subsection (b)(1), as though the sender were a bank. Proof of notice may be made by any admissible evidence. The receiving bank satisfies the burden of proof if it proves that the sender, before the payment order was accepted, signed a writing stating the information to which the notice relates.

(3) Regardless of whether the sender is a bank, the receiving bank may rely on the name as the proper identification of the intermediary or beneficiary's bank if the receiving bank, at the time it executes the sender's order, does not know that the name and number identify different persons. The receiving bank need not determine whether the name and number refer to the same person.

(4) If the receiving bank knows that the name and number identify different persons, reliance on either the name or the number in executing the sender's payment order is a breach of the obligation stated in Section 4A-302(a)(1).

§ 4A-209. Acceptance of Payment Order.

(a) Subject to subsection (d), a receiving bank other than the beneficiary's bank accepts a payment order when it executes the order.

(b) Subject to subsections (c) and (d), a beneficiary's bank accepts a payment order at the earliest of the following times:

(1) when the bank (i) pays the beneficiary as stated in Section 4A-405(a) or 4A-405(b), or (ii) notifies the beneficiary of receipt of the order or that the account of the beneficiary has been credited with respect to the order unless the notice indicates that the bank is rejecting the order or that funds with respect to the order may not be withdrawn or used until receipt of payment from the sender of the order;

(2) when the bank receives payment of the entire amount of the sender's order pursuant to Section 4A-403(a)(1) or 4A-403(a)(2); or

(3) the opening of the next funds-transfer business day of the bank following the payment date of the order if, at that time, the amount of the sender's order is fully covered by a withdrawable credit balance in an authorized account of the sender or the bank has otherwise received full payment from the sender, unless the order was rejected before that time or is rejected within (i) one hour after that time, or (ii) one hour after the opening of the next business day of the sender following the payment date if that time is later. If notice of rejection is received by the sender after the payment date and the authorized account of the sender does not bear interest, the bank is obliged to pay interest to the sender on the amount of the order for the number of days elapsing after the payment date to the day the sender receives notice or learns that the order was not accepted, counting that day as an elapsed day. If the withdrawable credit balance during that period falls below the amount of the order, the amount of interest payable is reduced accordingly.

(c) Acceptance of a payment order cannot occur before the order is received by the receiving bank. Acceptance does not occur under subsection (b)(2) or (b)(3) if the beneficiary of the payment order does not have an account with the receiving bank, the account has been closed, or the receiving bank is not permitted by law to receive credits for the beneficiary's account.

(d) A payment order issued to the originator's bank cannot be accepted until the payment date if the bank is the beneficiary's bank, or the execution date if the bank is not the beneficiary's bank. If the originator's bank executes the originator's payment order before the execution date or pays the beneficiary of the originator's payment order before the payment date and the payment order is subsequently canceled pursuant to Section 4A-211(b), the bank may recover from the beneficiary any payment received to the extent allowed by the law governing mistake and restitution.

§ 4A-210. Rejection of Payment Order.

(a) A payment order is rejected by the receiving bank by a notice of rejection transmitted to the sender orally, electronically, or in writing. A notice of rejection need not use any particular words and is sufficient if it indicates that the receiving bank is rejecting the order or will not execute or pay the order. Rejection is effective when the notice is given if transmission is by a means that is reasonable in the circumstances. If notice of rejection is given by a means that is not reasonable, rejection is effective when the notice is received. If an agreement of the sender and receiving bank establishes the means to be used to reject a payment order, (i) any means complying with the agreement is reasonable and (ii) any means not complying is not reasonable unless no significant delay in receipt of the notice resulted from the use of the noncomplying means.

(b) This subsection applies if a receiving bank other than the beneficiary's bank fails to execute a payment order despite the existence on the execution date of a withdrawable credit balance in an authorized account of the sender sufficient to cover the order. If the sender does not receive notice of rejection of the order on the execution date and the authorized account of the sender does not bear interest, the bank is obliged to pay interest to the sender on the amount of the order for the number of days elapsing after the execution date to the earlier of the day the order is canceled pursuant to Section 4A-211(d) or the day the sender receives notice or learns that the order was not executed, counting the final day of the period as an elapsed day. If the withdrawable credit balance during that period falls below the amount of the order, the amount of interest is reduced accordingly.

(c) If a receiving bank suspends payments, all unaccepted payment orders issued to it are deemed rejected at the time the bank suspends payments.

(d) Acceptance of a payment order precludes a later rejection of the order. Rejection of a payment order precludes a later acceptance of the order.

§ 4A-211. Cancellation and Amendment of Payment Order.

(a) A communication of the sender of a payment order cancelling or amending the order may be transmitted to the receiving bank orally, electronically, or in writing. If a security procedure is in effect between the sender and the receiving bank, the communication is not effective to cancel or amend the order unless the communication is verified pursuant to the security procedure or the bank agrees to the cancellation or amendment.

(b) Subject to subsection (a), a communication by the sender cancelling or amending a payment order is effective to cancel or amend the order if notice of the communication is received at a time and in a manner affording the receiving bank a reasonable opportunity to act on the communication before the bank accepts the payment order.

(c) After a payment order has been accepted, cancellation or amendment of the order is not effective unless the receiving bank agrees or a funds-transfer system rule allows cancellation or amendment without agreement of the bank.

(1) With respect to a payment order accepted by a receiving bank other than the beneficiary's bank, cancellation or amendment is not effective unless a conforming cancellation or amendment of the payment order issued by the receiving bank is also made.

(2) With respect to a payment order accepted by the beneficiary's bank, cancellation or amendment is not effective unless the order was issued in execution of an unauthorized payment order, or because of a mistake by a sender in the funds transfer which resulted in the issuance of a payment order (i) that is a duplicate of a payment order previously issued by the sender, (ii) that orders payment to a beneficiary not entitled to receive payment from the originator, or (iii) that orders payment in an amount greater than the amount the beneficiary was entitled to receive from the originator. If the payment order is canceled or amended, the beneficiary's bank is entitled to recover from the beneficiary any amount paid to the beneficiary to the extent allowed by the law governing mistake and restitution.

(d) An unaccepted payment order is canceled by operation of law at the close of the fifth funds-transfer business day of the receiving bank after the execution date or payment date of the order.

(e) A canceled payment order cannot be accepted. If an accepted payment order is canceled, the acceptance is nullified and no person has any right or obligation based on the acceptance. Amendment of a payment order is deemed to be cancellation of the original order at the time of amendment and issue of a new payment order in the amended form at the same time.

(f) Unless otherwise provided in an agreement of the parties or in a funds-transfer system rule, if the receiving bank, after accepting a payment order, agrees to cancellation or amendment of the order by the sender or is bound by a funds-transfer system rule allowing cancellation or amendment without the bank's agreement, the sender, whether or not cancellation or amendment is effective, is liable to the bank for any loss and expenses, including reasonable attorney's fees, incurred by the bank as a result of the cancellation or amendment or attempted cancellation or amendment.

(g) A payment order is not revoked by the death or legal incapacity of the sender unless the receiving bank knows of the death or of an adjudication of incapacity by a court of competent jurisdiction and has reasonable opportunity to act before acceptance of the order.

(h) A funds-transfer system rule is not effective to the extent it conflicts with subsection (c)(2).

§ 4A-212. Liability and Duty of Receiving Bank Regarding Unaccepted Payment Order.

If a receiving bank fails to accept a payment order that it is obliged by express agreement to accept, the bank is liable for breach of the agreement to the extent provided in the agreement or in this Article, but does not otherwise have any duty to accept a payment order or, before acceptance, to take any action, or refrain from taking action, with respect to the order except as provided in this Article or by express agreement. Liability based on acceptance arises only when acceptance occurs as stated in Section 4A-209, and liability is limited to that provided in this Article. A receiving bank is not the agent of the sender or beneficiary of the payment order it accepts, or of any other party to the funds transfer, and the bank owes no duty to any party to the funds transfer except as provided in this Article or by express agreement.

Part 3 Execution of Sender's Payment Order by Receiving Bank

§ 4A-301. Execution and Execution Date.

(a) A payment order is "executed" by the receiving bank when it issues a payment order intended to carry out the payment order received by the bank. A payment order received by the beneficiary's bank can be accepted but cannot be executed.

(b) "Execution date" of a payment order means the day on which the receiving bank may properly issue a payment order in execution of the sender's order. The execution date may be determined by instruction of the sender but cannot be earlier than the day the order is received and, unless otherwise determined, is the day the order is received. If the sender's instruction states a payment date, the execution date is the payment date or an earlier date on which execution is reasonably necessary to allow payment to the beneficiary on the payment date.

§ 4A-302. Obligations of Receiving Bank in Execution of Payment Order.

(a) Except as provided in subsections (b) through (d), if the receiving bank accepts a payment order pursuant to Section 4A-209(a), the bank has the following obligations in executing the order:

(1) The receiving bank is obliged to issue, on the execution date, a payment order complying with the sender's order and to follow the sender's instructions concerning (i) any intermediary bank or funds-transfer system to be used in carrying out the funds transfer, or (ii) the means by which payment orders are to be transmitted in the funds transfer. If the originator's bank issues a payment order to an intermediary bank, the originator's bank is obliged to instruct the intermediary bank according to the instruction of the originator. An intermediary bank in the funds transfer is similarly bound by an instruction given to it by the sender of the payment order it accepts.

(2) If the sender's instruction states that the funds transfer is to be carried out telephonically or by wire transfer or otherwise indicates that the funds transfer is to be carried out by the most expeditious means, the receiving bank is

obliged to transmit its payment order by the most expeditious available means, and to instruct any intermediary bank accordingly. If a sender's instruction states a payment date, the receiving bank is obliged to transmit its payment order at a time and by means reasonably necessary to allow payment to the beneficiary on the payment date or as soon thereafter as is feasible.

(b) Unless otherwise instructed, a receiving bank executing a payment order may (i) use any funds-transfer system if use of that system is reasonable in the circumstances, and (ii) issue a payment order to the beneficiary's bank or to an intermediary bank through which a payment order conforming to the sender's order can expeditiously be issued to the beneficiary's bank if the receiving bank exercises ordinary care in the selection of the intermediary bank. A receiving bank is not required to follow an instruction of the sender designating a funds-transfer system to be used in carrying out the funds transfer if the receiving bank, in good faith, determines that it is not feasible to follow the instruction or that following the instruction would unduly delay completion of the funds transfer.

(c) Unless subsection (a)(2) applies or the receiving bank is otherwise instructed, the bank may execute a payment order by transmitting its payment order by first class mail or by any means reasonable in the circumstances. If the receiving bank is instructed to execute the sender's order by transmitting its payment order by a particular means, the receiving bank may issue its payment order by the means stated or by any means as expeditious as the means stated.

(d) Unless instructed by the sender, (i) the receiving bank may not obtain payment of its charges for services and expenses in connection with the execution of the sender's order by issuing a payment order in an amount equal to the amount of the sender's order less the amount of the charges, and (ii) may not instruct a subsequent receiving bank to obtain payment of its charges in the same manner.

§ 4A-303. Erroneous Execution of Payment Order.

(a) A receiving bank that (i) executes the payment order of the sender by issuing a payment order in an amount greater than the amount of the sender's order, or (ii) issues a payment order in execution of the sender's order and then issues a duplicate order, is entitled to payment of the amount of the sender's order under Section 4A-402(c) if that subsection is otherwise satisfied. The bank is entitled to recover from the beneficiary of the erroneous order the excess payment received to the extent allowed by the law governing mistake and restitution.

(b) A receiving bank that executes the payment order of the sender by issuing a payment order in an amount less than the amount of the sender's order is entitled to payment of the amount of the sender's order under Section 4A-402(c) if (i) that subsection is otherwise satisfied and (ii) the bank corrects its mistake by issuing an additional payment order for the benefit of the beneficiary of the sender's order. If the error is not corrected, the issuer of the erroneous order is entitled to receive or retain payment from the sender of the order it accepted only to the extent of the amount of the erroneous order. This subsection does not apply if the receiving bank executes the sender's payment order by issuing a payment order in an amount less than the amount of the sender's

order for the purpose of obtaining payment of its charges for services and expenses pursuant to instruction of the sender.

(c) If a receiving bank executes the payment order of the sender by issuing a payment order to a beneficiary different from the beneficiary of the sender's order and the funds transfer is completed on the basis of that error, the sender of the payment order that was erroneously executed and all previous senders in the funds transfer are not obliged to pay the payment orders they issued. The issuer of the erroneous order is entitled to recover from the beneficiary of the order the payment received to the extent allowed by the law governing mistake and restitution.

§ 4A-304. Duty of Sender to Report Erroneously Executed Payment Order.

If the sender of a payment order that is erroneously executed as stated in Section 4A-303 receives notification from the receiving bank that the order was executed or that the sender's account was debited with respect to the order, the sender has a duty to exercise ordinary care to determine, on the basis of information available to the sender, that the order was erroneously executed and to notify the bank of the relevant facts within a reasonable time not exceeding 90 days after the notification from the bank was received by the sender. If the sender fails to perform that duty, the bank is not obliged to pay interest on any amount refundable to the sender under Section 4A-402(d) for the period before the bank learns of the execution error. The bank is not entitled to any recovery from the sender on account of a failure by the sender to perform the duty stated in this section.

§ 4A-305. Liability for Late or Improper Execution or Failure to Execute Payment Order.

(a) If a funds transfer is completed but execution of a payment order by the receiving bank in breach of Section 4A-302 results in delay in payment to the beneficiary, the bank is obliged to pay interest to either the originator or the beneficiary of the funds transfer for the period of delay caused by the improper execution. Except as provided in subsection (c), additional damages are not recoverable.

(b) If execution of a payment order by a receiving bank in breach of Section 4A-302 results in (i) noncompletion of the funds transfer, (ii) failure to use an intermediary bank designated by the originator, or (iii) issuance of a payment order that does not comply with the terms of the payment order of the originator, the bank is liable to the originator for its expenses in the funds transfer and for incidental expenses and interest losses, to the extent not covered by subsection (a), resulting from the improper execution. Except as provided in subsection (c), additional damages are not recoverable.

(c) In addition to the amounts payable under subsections (a) and (b), damages, including consequential damages, are recoverable to the extent provided in an express written agreement of the receiving bank.

(d) If a receiving bank fails to execute a payment order it was obliged by express agreement to execute, the receiving bank is liable to the sender for its expenses in the transaction and for incidental expenses and interest losses resulting from the failure to execute. Additional damages, including consequential damages, are recoverable to the extent provided in an express written agreement of the receiving bank, but are not otherwise recoverable.

(e) Reasonable attorney's fees are recoverable if demand for compensation under subsection (a) or (b) is made and refused before an action is brought on the claim. If a claim is made for breach of an agreement under subsection (d) and the agreement does not provide for damages, reasonable attorney's fees are recoverable if demand for compensation under subsection (d) is made and refused before an action is brought on the claim.

(f) Except as stated in this section, the liability of a receiving bank under subsections (a) and (b) may not be varied by agreement.

Part 4 Payment

§ 4A-401. Payment Date.

"Payment date" of a payment order means the day on which the amount of the order is payable to the beneficiary by the beneficiary's bank. The payment date may be determined by instruction of the sender but cannot be earlier than the day the order is received by the beneficiary's bank and, unless otherwise determined, is the day the order is received by the beneficiary's bank.

§ 4A-402. Obligation of Sender to Pay Receiving Bank.

(a) This section is subject to Sections 4A-205 and 4A-207.

(b) With respect to a payment order issued to the beneficiary's bank, acceptance of the order by the bank obliges the sender to pay the bank the amount of the order, but payment is not due until the payment date of the order.

(c) This subsection is subject to subsection (e) and to Section 4A-303. With respect to a payment order issued to a receiving bank other than the beneficiary's bank, acceptance of the order by the receiving bank obliges the sender to pay the bank the amount of the sender's order. Payment by the sender is not due until the execution date of the sender's order. The obligation of that sender to pay its payment order is excused if the funds transfer is not completed by acceptance by the beneficiary's bank of a payment order instructing payment to the beneficiary of that sender's payment order.

(d) If the sender of a payment order pays the order and was not obliged to pay all or part of the amount paid, the bank receiving payment is obliged to refund payment to the extent the sender was not obliged to pay. Except as provided in Sections 4A-204 and 4A-304, interest is payable on the refundable amount from the date of payment.

(e) If a funds transfer is not completed as stated in subsection (c) and an intermediary bank is obliged to refund payment as stated in subsection (d) but is unable to do so because not permitted by applicable law or because the bank suspends payments, a sender in the funds transfer that executed a payment order in compliance with an instruction, as stated in Section 4A-302(a)(1), to route the funds transfer through that intermediary bank is entitled to receive or retain payment from the sender of the payment order that it accepted. The first sender in the funds transfer that issued an instruction requiring routing through that intermediary bank is subrogated to the right of the bank that paid the intermediary bank to refund as stated in subsection (d).

(f) The right of the sender of a payment order to be excused from the obligation to pay the order as stated in subsection (c) or to receive refund under subsection (d) may not be varied by agreement.

§ 4A-403. Payment by Sender to Receiving Bank.

(a) Payment of the sender's obligation under Section 4A-402 to pay the receiving bank occurs as follows:

(1) If the sender is a bank, payment occurs when the receiving bank receives final settlement of the obligation through a Federal Reserve Bank or through a funds-transfer system.

(2) If the sender is a bank and the sender (i) credited an account of the receiving bank with the sender, or (ii) caused an account of the receiving bank in another bank to be credited, payment occurs when the credit is withdrawn or, if not withdrawn, at midnight of the day on which the credit is withdrawable and the receiving bank learns of that fact.

(3) If the receiving bank debits an account of the sender with the receiving bank, payment occurs when the debit is made to the extent the debit is covered by a withdrawable credit balance in the account.

(b) If the sender and receiving bank are members of a funds-transfer system that nets obligations multilaterally among participants, the receiving bank receives final settlement when settlement is complete in accordance with the rules of the system. The obligation of the sender to pay the amount of a payment order transmitted through the funds-transfer system may be satisfied, to the extent permitted by the rules of the system, by setting off and applying against the sender's obligation the right of the sender to receive payment from the receiving bank of the amount of any other payment order transmitted to the sender by the receiving bank through the funds-transfer system. The aggregate balance of obligations owed by each sender to each receiving bank in the funds-transfer system may be satisfied, to the extent permitted by the rules of the system, by setting off and applying against that balance the aggregate balance of obligations owed to the sender by other members of the system. The aggregate balance is determined after the right of setoff stated in the second sentence of this subsection has been exercised.

(c) If two banks transmit payment orders to each other under an agreement that settlement of the obligations of each bank to the other under Section 4A-402 will be made at the end of the day or other period, the total amount owed with respect to all orders transmitted by one bank shall be set off against the total amount owed with respect to all orders transmitted by the other bank. To the extent of the setoff, each bank has made payment to the other.

(d) In a case not covered by subsection (a), the time when payment of the sender's obligation under Section 4A-402(b) or 4A-402(c) occurs is governed by applicable principles of law that determine when an obligation is satisfied.

§ 4A-404. Obligation of Beneficiary's Bank to Pay and Give Notice to Beneficiary.

(a) Subject to Sections 4A-211(e), 4A-405(d), and 4A-405(e), if a beneficiary's bank accepts a payment order, the bank is obliged to pay the amount of the order to the beneficiary of the order. Payment is due on the payment date of the order, but if acceptance occurs on the payment date after the close of the funds-transfer business day of the bank, payment is due on the next funds-transfer business day. If the bank refuses to pay after demand by the beneficiary and receipt of notice of particular circumstances that will give rise to consequential damages as a result of nonpayment, the beneficiary may recover damages resulting from the refusal to pay to the extent the bank had notice of the damages, unless the bank proves that it did not pay because of a reasonable doubt concerning the right of the beneficiary to payment.

(b) If a payment order accepted by the beneficiary's bank instructs payment to an account of the beneficiary, the bank is obliged to notify the beneficiary of receipt of the order before midnight of the next funds-transfer business day following the payment date. If the payment order does not instruct payment to an account of the beneficiary, the bank is required to notify the beneficiary only if notice is required by the order. Notice may be given by first class mail or any other means reasonable in the circumstances. If the bank fails to give the required notice, the bank is obliged to pay interest to the beneficiary on the amount of the payment order from the day notice should have been given until the day the beneficiary learned of receipt of the payment order by the bank. No other damages are recoverable. Reasonable attorney's fees are also recoverable if demand for interest is made and refused before an action is brought on the claim.

(c) The right of a beneficiary to receive payment and damages as stated in subsection (a) may not be varied by agreement or a funds-transfer system rule. The right of a beneficiary to be notified as stated in subsection (b) may be varied by agreement of the beneficiary or by a funds-transfer system rule if the beneficiary is notified of the rule before initiation of the funds transfer.

§ 4A-405. Payment by Beneficiary's Bank to Beneficiary.

(a) If the beneficiary's bank credits an account of the beneficiary of a payment order, payment of the bank's obligation under Section 4A-404(a) occurs when and to the extent (i) the beneficiary is notified of the right to withdraw the credit, (ii) the bank lawfully applies the credit to a debt of the beneficiary, or (iii) funds with respect to the order are otherwise made available to the beneficiary by the bank.

(b) If the beneficiary's bank does not credit an account of the beneficiary of a payment order, the time when payment of the bank's obligation under Section 4A-404(a) occurs is governed by principles of law that determine when an obligation is satisfied.

(c) Except as stated in subsections (d) and (e), if the beneficiary's bank pays the beneficiary of a payment order under a condition to payment or agreement of the beneficiary giving the bank the right to recover payment from the beneficiary if the bank does not receive payment of the order, the condition to payment or agreement is not enforceable.

(d) A funds-transfer system rule may provide that payments made to beneficiaries of funds transfers made through the system are provisional until receipt of payment by the beneficiary's bank of the payment order it accepted. A beneficiary's bank that makes a payment that is provisional under the rule is entitled to refund from the beneficiary if (i)

the rule requires that both the beneficiary and the originator be given notice of the provisional nature of the payment before the funds transfer is initiated, (ii) the beneficiary, the beneficiary's bank and the originator's bank agreed to be bound by the rule, and (iii) the beneficiary's bank did not receive payment of the payment order that it accepted. If the beneficiary is obliged to refund payment to the beneficiary's bank, acceptance of the payment order by the beneficiary's bank is nullified and no payment by the originator of the funds transfer to the beneficiary occurs under Section 4A-406.

(e) This subsection applies to a funds transfer that includes a payment order transmitted over a funds-transfer system that (i) nets obligations multilaterally among participants, and (ii) has in effect a loss-sharing agreement among participants for the purpose of providing funds necessary to complete settlement of the obligations of one or more participants that do not meet their settlement obligations. If the beneficiary's bank in the funds transfer accepts a payment order and the system fails to complete settlement pursuant to its rules with respect to any payment order in the funds transfer, (i) the acceptance by the beneficiary's bank is nullified and no person has any right or obligation based on the acceptance, (ii) the beneficiary's bank is entitled to recover payment from the beneficiary, (iii) no payment by the originator to the beneficiary occurs under Section 4A-406, and (iv) subject to Section 4A-402(e), each sender in the funds transfer is excused from its obligation to pay its payment order under Section 4A-402(c) because the funds transfer has not been completed.

§ 4A-406. Payment by Originator to Beneficiary; Discharge of Underlying Obligation.

(a) Subject to Sections 4A-211(e), 4A-405(d), and 4A-405(e), the originator of a funds transfer pays the beneficiary of the originator's payment order (i) at the time a payment order for the benefit of the beneficiary is accepted by the beneficiary's bank in the funds transfer and (ii) in an amount equal to the amount of the order accepted by the beneficiary's bank, but not more than the amount of the originator's order.

(b) If payment under subsection (a) is made to satisfy an obligation, the obligation is discharged to the same extent discharge would result from payment to the beneficiary of the same amount in money, unless (i) the payment under subsection (a) was made by a means prohibited by the contract of the beneficiary with respect to the obligation, (ii) the beneficiary, within a reasonable time after receiving notice of receipt of the order by the beneficiary's bank, notified the originator of the beneficiary's refusal of the payment, (iii) funds with respect to the order were not withdrawn by the beneficiary or applied to a debt of the beneficiary, and (iv) the beneficiary would suffer a loss that could reasonably have been avoided if payment had been made by a means complying with the contract. If payment by the originator does not result in discharge under this section, the originator is subrogated to the rights of the beneficiary to receive payment from the beneficiary's bank under Section 4A-404(a).

(c) For the purpose of determining whether discharge of an obligation occurs under subsection (b), if the beneficiary's bank accepts a payment order in an amount equal to the amount of the originator's payment order less charges of one or more receiving banks in the funds transfer, payment to the beneficiary is deemed to be in the amount of the originator's order unless upon demand by the beneficiary the originator does not pay the beneficiary the amount of the deducted charges.

(d) Rights of the originator or of the beneficiary of a funds transfer under this section may be varied only by agreement of the originator and the beneficiary.

Part 5   Miscellaneous Provisions

§ 4A-501.   Variation by Agreement and Effect of Funds-Transfer System Rule.

(a) Except as otherwise provided in this Article, the rights and obligations of a party to a funds transfer may be varied by agreement of the affected party.

(b) "Funds-transfer system rule" means a rule of an association of banks (i) governing transmission of payment orders by means of a funds-transfer system of the association or rights and obligations with respect to those orders, or (ii) to the extent the rule governs rights and obligations between banks that are parties to a funds transfer in which a Federal Reserve Bank, acting as an intermediary bank, sends a payment order to the beneficiary's bank. Except as otherwise provided in this Article, a funds-transfer system rule governing rights and obligations between participating banks using the system may be effective even if the rule conflicts with this Article and indirectly affects another party to the funds transfer who does not consent to the rule. A funds-transfer system rule may also govern rights and obligations of parties other than participating banks using the system to the extent stated in Sections 4A-404(c), 4A-405(d), and 4A-507(c).

§ 4A-502.   Creditor Process Served on Receiving Bank; Setoff by Beneficiary's Bank.

(a) As used in this section, "creditor process" means levy, attachment, garnishment, notice of lien, sequestration, or similar process issued by or on behalf of a creditor or other claimant with respect to an account.

(b) This subsection applies to creditor process with respect to an authorized account of the sender of a payment order if the creditor process is served on the receiving bank. For the purpose of determining rights with respect to the creditor process, if the receiving bank accepts the payment order the balance in the authorized account is deemed to be reduced by the amount of the payment order to the extent the bank did not otherwise receive payment of the order, unless the creditor process is served at a time and in a manner affording the bank a reasonable opportunity to act on it before the bank accepts the payment order.

(c) If a beneficiary's bank has received a payment order for payment to the beneficiary's account in the bank, the following rules apply:

(1) The bank may credit the beneficiary's account. The amount credited may be set off against an obligation owed by the beneficiary to the bank or may be applied to satisfy creditor process served on the bank with respect to the account.

(2) The bank may credit the beneficiary's account and allow withdrawal of the amount credited unless creditor process with respect to the account is served at a time and in a manner affording the bank a reasonable opportunity to act to prevent withdrawal.

(3) If creditor process with respect to the beneficiary's account has been served and the bank has had a reasonable opportunity to act on it, the bank may not reject the payment order except for a reason unrelated to the service of process.

(d) Creditor process with respect to a payment by the originator to the beneficiary pursuant to a funds transfer may be served only on the beneficiary's bank with respect to the debt owed by that bank to the beneficiary. Any other bank served with the creditor process is not obliged to act with respect to the process.

§ 4A-503.   Injunction or Restraining Order With Respect to Funds Transfer.

For proper cause and in compliance with applicable law, a court may restrain (i) a person from issuing a payment order to initiate a funds transfer, (ii) an originator's bank from executing the payment order of the originator, or (iii) the beneficiary's bank from releasing funds to the beneficiary or the beneficiary from withdrawing the funds. A court may not otherwise restrain a person from issuing a payment order, paying or receiving payment of a payment order, or otherwise acting with respect to a funds transfer.

§ 4A-504.   Order in Which Items and Payment Orders May Be Charged to Account; Order of Withdrawals From Account.

(a) If a receiving bank has received more than one payment order of the sender or one or more payment orders and other items that are payable from the sender's account, the bank may charge the sender's account with respect to the various orders and items in any sequence.

(b) In determining whether a credit to an account has been withdrawn by the holder of the account or applied to a debt of the holder of the account, credits first made to the account are first withdrawn or applied.

§ 4A-505.   Preclusion of Objection to Debit of Customer's Account.

If a receiving bank has received payment from its customer with respect to a payment order issued in the name of the customer as sender and accepted by the bank, and the customer received notification reasonably identifying the order, the customer is precluded from asserting that the bank is not entitled to retain the payment unless the customer notifies the bank of the customer's objection to the payment within one year after the notification was received by the customer.

§ 4A-506.   Rate of Interest.

(a) If, under this Article, a receiving bank is obliged to pay interest with respect to a payment order issued to the bank, the amount payable may be determined (i) by agreement of the sender and receiving bank, or (ii) by a funds-transfer system rule if the payment order is transmitted through a funds-transfer system.

(b) If the amount of interest is not determined by an agreement or rule as stated in subsection (a), the amount is calculated by multiplying the applicable Federal Funds rate by the amount on which interest is payable, and then multiplying the product by the number of days for which interest is payable. The applicable Federal Funds rate is the average of the Federal Funds rates published by the Federal Reserve Bank of New York for each of the days for which interest is payable divided by 360. The Federal Funds rate for any day on which a published rate is not available is the same as the published rate for the next preceding day for which there is a published rate. If a receiving bank that accepted a payment order is required to refund payment to the sender of the order because the funds transfer was not completed, but the failure to complete was not due to any fault by the bank, the interest payable is reduced by a percentage equal to the reserve requirement on deposits of the receiving bank.

§ 4A-507.   Choice of Law.

(a) The following rules apply unless the affected parties otherwise agree or subsection (c) applies:

(1) The rights and obligations between the sender of a payment order and the receiving bank are governed by the law of the jurisdiction in which the receiving bank is located.

(2) The rights and obligations between the beneficiary's bank and the beneficiary are governed by the law of the jurisdiction in which the beneficiary's bank is located.

(3) The issue of when payment is made pursuant to a funds transfer by the originator to the beneficiary is governed by the law of the jurisdiction in which the beneficiary's bank is located.

(b) If the parties described in each paragraph of subsection (a) have made an agreement selecting the law of a particular jurisdiction to govern rights and obligations between each other, the law of that jurisdiction governs those rights and obligations, whether or not the payment order or the funds transfer bears a reasonable relation to that jurisdiction.

(c) A funds-transfer system rule may select the law of a particular jurisdiction to govern (i) rights and obligations between participating banks with respect to payment orders transmitted or processed through the system, or (ii) the rights and obligations of some or all parties to a funds transfer any part of which is carried out by means of the system. A choice of law made pursuant to clause (i) is binding on participating banks. A choice of law made pursuant to clause (ii) is binding on the originator, other sender, or a receiving bank having notice that the funds-transfer system might be used in the funds transfer and of the choice of law by the system when the originator, other sender, or receiving bank issued or accepted a payment order. The beneficiary of a funds transfer is bound by the choice of law if, when the funds transfer is initiated, the beneficiary has notice that the funds-transfer system might be used in the funds transfer and of the choice of law by the system. The law of a jurisdiction selected pursuant to this subsection may govern, whether or not that law bears a reasonable relation to the matter in issue.

(d) In the event of inconsistency between an agreement under subsection (b) and a choice-of-law rule under subsection (c), the agreement under subsection (b) prevails.

(e) If a funds transfer is made by use of more than one funds-transfer system and there is inconsistency between choice-of-law rules of the systems, the matter in issue is governed by the law of the selected jurisdiction that has the most significant relationship to the matter in issue.

GLOSSARY

Abandonment   Applies to many situations. Abandonment of property is giving up dominion and control over it, with intention to relinquish all claims to it. Losing property is an involuntary act; abandonment is voluntary. When used with duty, the word *abandonment* is synonymous with *repudiation*.

Abatement of a nuisance   An action to end any act detrimental to the public; e.g., suit to enjoin a plant from permitting the escape of noxious vapors.

Acceptance   A statement by one party (called the offeree) that he is prepared to be bound to the contractual position stated in an offer. The acceptance is a second essential element to the meeting of the minds of the contracting parties. *See* Offer.

Acceptance*   Under Article 3—Commercial Paper, this is the drawee's signed engagement to honor a draft as presented. It must be written on the draft and may consist of drawee's signature alone. It becomes operative when completed by delivery or notification.

Accessions   Items of personal property that become incorporated into other items of personal property.

Accommodation party*   In the law of commercial paper, any person who signs an instrument for the purpose of lending his name and his credit.

Accord and satisfaction   An agreement between two persons—one of whom has a right of action against the other—that the latter should do or give, and the former accept, something in satisfaction of the right of action—something different from, and usually less than, what might legally be enforced.

Account*   Any right to payment for goods sold or leased or for services rendered but not evidenced by an instrument or chattel paper. Under Article 4—Bank Deposits and Collections, *account* is any account with a bank and includes a checking, time, interest, or savings account.

Account debtor   The person who is obligated on an account, chattel paper, contract right, or general intangible.

Accretion   Gradual, imperceptible accumulation of land by natural causes, usually next to a stream or river.

Action ex contractu   An action at law to recover damages for the breach of a duty arising out of contract. There are two types of causes of action: those arising out of contract, ex contractu, and those arising out of tort, ex delicto.

Action ex delicto   An action at law to recover damages for the breach of a duty existing by reason of a general law. An action to recover damages for an injury caused by the negligent use of an automobile is an ex delicto action. Tort or wrong is the basis of the action. *See* Action ex contractu.

Adjudicate   The exercise of judicial power by hearing, trying, and determining the claims of litigants before the court.

Administrative law   The branch of public law dealing with the operation of the various agency boards and commissions of government.

*Terms followed by an asterisk are defined in the Uniform Commercial Code and have significance in connection with Code materials. They are often given a particular meaning in relation to the Code, and their definitions do not necessarily conform with meanings outside the framework of the Code.

Administrator A person to whom letters of administration have been issued by a probate court, giving such person authority to administer, manage, and close the estate of a deceased person.

Adverse possession Acquisition of legal title to another's land by being in continuous possession during a period prescribed in the statute. Possession must be actual, visible, known to the world, and with intent to claim title as owner, against the rights of the true owner. Claimant usually must pay taxes and liens lawfully charged against the property. Cutting timber or grass from time to time on the land of another is not the kind of adverse possession that will confer title.

Advising bank* A bank that gives notification of the issuance of a credit by another bank.

Affidavit A voluntary statement of facts formally reduced to writing, sworn to, or affirmed before, some officer authorized to administer oaths. The officer is usually a notary public.

Affirmative action program Active recruitment and advancement of minority workers.

Affirmative defense A matter that constitutes opposition to the allegations of a complaint, which are assumed to be true.

A fortiori Latin words meaning "by a stronger reason." Often used in judicial opinions to say that since specific, proven facts lead to a certain conclusion, there are for this reason other facts that logically follow and strengthen the argument for the conclusion.

Agency coupled with an interest When an agent has possession or control over the property of his principal and has a right of action against interference by third parties, an agency with an interest has been created. An agent who advances freight for goods sent him by his principal has an interest in the goods.

Agency coupled with an obligation When an agent is owed money by his principal and the agency relationship is created to facilitate the agent collecting this money from a third party, an agency coupled with an obligation is created. This type of agency cannot be terminated by the actions of the principal, but it may be terminated by operation of law.

Agent A person authorized to act for another (principal). The term may apply to a person in the service of another; but in the strict sense, an agent is one who stands in place of his principal. A works for B as a gardener and is thus a servant, but he may be an agent. If A sells goods for B, he becomes more than a servant. He acts in the place of B.

Agreement* The bargain of the parties in fact as found in their language or by implication from other circumstances, including course of dealing or usage of trade or course of performance as provided in the Uniform Commercial Code.

Amicus curiae A friend of the court who participates in litigation, usually on appeal, though not a party to the lawsuit.

Annuity A sum of money paid yearly to a person during his lifetime. The sum arises out of a contract by which the recipient or another had previously deposited sums in whole or in part with the grantor—the grantor to return a designated portion of the principal and interest in periodic payments when the beneficiary attains a designated age.

Appellant The party who takes an appeal from one court or jurisdiction to another.

Appellee The party in a cause against whom an appeal is taken.

A priori A generalization resting on presuppositions, not upon proven facts.

Arbitration The submission for determination of disputed matter to private, unofficial persons selected in a manner provided by law or agreement.

Architect's certificate A formal statement signed by an architect that a contractor has performed under his contract and is entitled to be paid. The construction contract provides when and how such certificates shall be issued.

Artisan's lien One who has expended labor upon, or added to, another's property is entitled to possession of the property as security until reinbursed for the value of labor or material. A repairs B's watch. A may keep the watch in his possession until B pays for the repairs.

Assignee An assign or assignee is one to whom an assignment has been made.

Assignment The transfer by one person to another of a right that usually arises out of a contract. Such rights are called *choses in action*. A sells and assigns to C his contract right to purchase B's house. A is an assignor. C is an assignee. The transfer is an assignment.

Assignment* A transfer of the "contract" or of "all my rights under the contract" or an assignment in similar general terms is an assignment of rights. Unless the language or the circumstances (as in an assignment for security) indicate the contrary, it is a delegation of performance by the duties of the assignor, and its acceptance by the assignee constitutes a promise by him to perform those duties. This promise is enforceable by either the assignor or the other party to the original contract.

Assignment for the benefit of creditors A, a debtor, has many creditors. An assignment of his property to X, a third party, with directions to make distribution of his property to his creditors, is called an assignment for the benefit of creditors. *See* Composition of creditors.

Assignor One who makes an assignment.

Assumption of the risk Negligence doctrine that bars the recovery of damages by an injured party on the ground that such party acted with actual or constructive knowledge of the hazard causing the injury.

Attachment A legal proceeding accompanying an action in court by which a plaintiff may acquire a lien on a defendant's property as a security for the payment of any judgment that the plaintiff may recover. It is provisional and independent of the court action and is usually provided for by statute. A sues B. Before judgment, A attaches B's automobile, in order to make sure of the payment of any judgment that A may secure.

Attorney at law A person to whom the state grants a license to practice law.

Attorney in fact A person acting for another under a grant of special power created by an instrument in writing. B, in writing, grants special power A to execute and deliver for B a conveyance of B's land to X.

Bad faith "Actual intent" to mislead or deceive another. It does not mean misleading by an honest, inadvertent, or careless misstatement.

Bail (verb) To set at liberty an arrested or imprisoned person after that person or at least two others have given security to the state that the accused will appear at the proper time and place for trial.

Bailee A person into whose possession personal property is delivered.

Bailee* The person who, by a warehouse receipt, bill of lading, or other document of title, acknowledges possession of goods and contracts to deliver it.

Bailment Delivery of personal property to another for a special purpose. Delivery is made under a contract, either expressed or implied, that upon the completion of the special purpose, the property shall be redelivered to the bailor or placed at his disposal. A loans B his truck. A places his watch with B for re-

pair. A places his furniture in B's warehouse. A places his securities in B's bank safety deposit vault. In each case, A is a bailor and B is a bailee.

Bailor One who delivers personal property into the possession of another.

Banking day* Under Article 4—Bank Deposits and Collections, this is the part of any day on which a bank is open to the public for carrying on substantially all of its banking functions.

Bankruptcy The law which provides a process for protecting creditors and debtors when a debtor is unable to pay his obligations.

Bearer* The person in possession of an instrument, document of title, or security payable to bearer or indorsed in blank.

Bearer form* A security is in bearer form when it runs to bearer according to its terms and not by reason of any indorsement.

Beneficiary A person (not a promisee) for whose benefit a trust, an insurance policy, a will, or a contract promise is made.

Beneficiary* A person who is entitled under a letter of credit to draw or demand payment.

Bequest In a will, a gift of personal property.

Bid An offering of money in exchange for property placed for sale. At an ordinary auction sale, a bid is an offer to purchase. It may be withdrawn before acceptance is indicated by the fall of the hammer.

Bilateral contract One containing mutual promises, with each party being both a promisor and a promisee.

Bilateral mistake A situation in which parties to a contract reach a bargain on the basis of an incorrect assumption common to each party.

Bill of lading* A document evidencing the receipt of goods for shipment, issued by a person engaged in the business of transporting or forwarding goods. Includes an airbill, a document that serves air transportation as a bill of lading serves marine or rail transportation. It includes an air consignment note or air waybill.

Bill of particulars In legal practice, a written statement that one party to a lawsuit gives to another, describing in detail the elements upon which the claim of the first party is based.

Bill of sale Written evidence that the title to personal property has been transferred from one person to another. It must contain words of transfer and be more than a receipt.

Blue-sky laws Popular name for acts providing for the regulation and supervision of investment securities.

Bona fide purchaser* A purchaser of a security for value, in good faith, and without notice of any adverse claim, who takes delivery of a security in bearer form or in registered form issued to him or indorsed to him or in blank.

Bond A promise under seal to pay money. The term generally designates the promise made by a corporation, either public or private, to pay money to bearer; e.g., U.S. government bonds or Illinois Central Railroad bonds. Also, an obligation by which one person promises to answer for the debt or default of another—a surety bond.

Breach of the peace* In the law of secured transactions, this occurrence invalidates the creditor's legal right to take possession of the collateral without the assistance of a court. This event occurs whenever the possession by the creditor is accompanied by violence, deception, or an objection by the debtor.

Broker A person employed to make contracts with third persons on behalf of his principal. The contracts involve trade, commerce, buying and selling for a fee (called brokerage or commission).

Broker* A person engaged full or part time in the business of buying and selling securities, who in the transaction concerned acts for, or buys a security from, or sells a security to, a customer.

Bulk transfer* Transfer made outside the ordinary course of the transferor's business but involving a major part of the materials, supplies, merchandise, or other inventory of an enterprise subject to Article 6.

Burden of proof This term has two distinctive meanings. One meaning is used to identify the party that has the burden of coming forward with evidence of a particular fact. The second meaning is used to identify the party with the burden of persuasion. This second meaning is used in litigation to determine whether one party or another wins regarding an issue in dispute.

Business judgment rule A legal doctrine requiring the officers and directors of corporations to act in good faith as if they were dealing with their own property interests.

Buyer* A person who buys or contracts to buy goods.

Buyer in ordinary course of business* A person who, in good faith and without knowledge that the sale to him is in violation of the ownership rights or security interest of a third party in the goods, buys in ordinary course from a person in the business of selling goods of that kind. Does not include a pawnbroker. "Buying" may be for cash or by exchange of other property or on secured or unsecured credit. Includes receiving goods or documents of title under a preexisting contract for sale but does not include a transfer in bulk or as security for, or in total or partial satisfaction of, a money debt.

Bylaws Rules for government of a corporation or other organization. Adopted by members or the board of directors, these rules must not be contrary to the law of the land. They affect the rights and duties of the members of the corporation or organization, only, not third persons.

Call An assessment upon a subscriber for partial or full payment on shares of unpaid stock of a corporation. Also, the power of a corporation to make an assessment, notice of an assessment, or the time when the assessment is to be paid.

Cancellation* Either party puts an end to the contract because of breach by the other. Its effect is the same as that of "termination," except that the canceling party also retains any remedy for breach of the whole contract or any unperformed balance.

Capital The net assets of an individual enterprise, partnership, joint stock company, corporation, or business institution, including not only the original investment but also all gains and profits realized from the continued conduct of the business.

Carrier A natural person or a corporation who receives goods under a contract to transport for a consideration from one place to another. A railroad, truckline, busline, airline.

Cashier's check A bill of exchange drawn by the cashier of a bank, for the bank, upon the bank. After the check is delivered or issued to the payee or holder, the drawer bank cannot put a "stop order" against itself. By delivery of the check, the drawer bank has accepted and thus becomes the primary obligor.

Cause of action When one's legal rights have been invaded either by a breach of a contract or by a breach of a legal duty toward one's person or property, a cause of action has been created.

Caveat Literally, "let him beware." It is used generally to mean a warning.

Caveat emptor An old idea at common law—"let the buyer beware." When a vendor sells goods without an express warranty as to their quality and capacity for a particular use and purpose, the buyer must take the risk of loss due to all defects in the goods.

Caveat venditor "Let the seller beware." Unless the seller, by express language, disclaims any responsibility, he shall be liable to the buyer if the goods delivered are different in kind, quality, use, and purpose from those described in the contract of sale.

Cease and desist order An administrative agency order directing a party to refrain from doing a specified act.

Certiorari An order issuing out of an appellate court to a lower court, at the request of an appellant, directing that the record of a case pending in the lower court be transmitted to the upper court for review.

Cestui que trust A person who is the real or beneficial owner of property held in trust. The trustee holds the legal title to the property for the benefit of the cestui que trust.

Chancery Court of equity.

Charter Referring to a private corporation, *charter* includes the contract between the created corporation and the state, the act creating the corporation, and the articles of association granted to the corporation by authority of the legislative act. Referring to municipal corporations, *charter* does not mean a contract between the legislature and the city created. A city charter is a delegation of powers by a state legislature to the governing body of the city. The term includes the creative act, the powers enumerated, and the organization authorized.

Chattel A very broad term derived from the word *cattle*. Includes every kind of property that is not real property. Movable properties, such as horses, automobiles, choses in action, stock certificates, bills of lading, and all "good wares, and merchandise" are chattels personal. Chattels real concern real property such as a lease for years, in which case the lessee owns a chattel real.

Chattel paper* A writing or writings that evidence both a monetary obligation and a security interest in, or a lease of, specific goods. When a transaction is evidenced both by such a security agreement or a lease and by an instrument or a series of instruments, the group of writings taken together constitutes chattel paper.

Chose in action The "right" one person has to recover money or property from another by a judicial proceeding. The right arises out of contract, claims for money, debts, and rights against property. Notes, drafts, stock certificates, bills of lading, warehouse receipts, and insurance policies are illustrations of choses in action. They are called tangible choses. Book accounts, simple debts, and obligations not evidenced by formal writing are called intangible choses. Choses in action are transferred by assignment.

Circumstantial evidence If, from certain facts and circumstances, according to the experience of mankind, an ordinary, intelligent person may infer that other connected facts and circumstances must necessarily exist, the latter facts and circumstances are considered proven by circumstantial evidence. Proof of fact A from which fact B may be inferred is proof of fact B by circumstantial evidence.

Civil action A proceeding in a law court or a suit in equity by one person against another for the enforcement or protection of a private right or the prevention of a wrong. It includes actions on contract, ex delicto, and all suits in equity. Civil action is in contradistinction to criminal action, in which the state prosecutes a person for breach of a duty.

Civil law The area of law dealing with rights and duties of private parties as individual entities. To be distinguished from criminal law. Sometimes the phrase refers to the European system of codified law.

Claim A creditor's right to payment in a bankruptcy case.

Class-action suit A legal proceeding whereby one or more persons represent in litigation a larger group of people who might have a claim similar to the representative(s).

Clearinghouse* Under Article 4—Bank Deposits and Collections, clearinghouse is any association of banks or other payors regularly clearing items.

Cloud on title Some evidence of record that shows a third person has some prima facie interest in another's property.

Code A collection or compilation of the statutes passed by the legislative body of a state. Often annotated with citations of cases decided by the state supreme courts. These decisions construe the statutes. Examples: Oregon Compiled Laws Annotated, United States Code Annotated.

Codicil An addition to, or a change in, an executed last will and testament. It is a part of the original will and must be executed with the same formality as the original will.

Coinsurer A term in a fire insurance policy that requires the insured to bear a certain portion of the loss when he fails to carry complete coverage. For example, unless the insured carries insurance that totals 80 percent of the value of the property, the insurer shall be liable for only that portion of the loss that the total insurance carried bears to 80 percent of the value of the property.

Collateral With reference to debts or other obligations, *collateral* means security placed with a creditor to assure the performance of the obligator. If the obligator performs, the collateral is returend by the creditor. A owes B $1,000. To secure the payment, A places with B a $500 certificate of stock in X company. The $500 certificate is called collateral security.

Collateral* The property subject to a security interest. Includes accounts, contract rights, and chattel paper that have been sold.

Collecting bank* Under Article 4—Bank Deposits and Collections, any bank handling the item for collateral except the payor bank.

Collective bargaining The process of good-faith negotiation between employer's and employees' representatives, concerning issues of mutual interest.

Commerce clause Article I, Section 8, Clause 3 of the Constitution of the United States, granting Congress the authority to regulate commerce with foreign nations and among the states.

Commercial unit* A unit of goods that, by commercial usage, is a single whole for purposes of sale. Its division would materially impair its character or value on the market or in use. A commercial unit may be a single article (as a machine) or a set of articles (as a suite of furniture or an assortment of sizes) or a quantity (as a bale, gross, or carload) or any other unit treated in use or in the relevant market as a single whole.

Commission The sum of money, interest, brokerage, compensation, or allowance given to a factor or broker for carrying on the business of his principal.

Commission merchant An agent or factor employed to sell "goods, wares, and merchandise" consigned or delivered to him by his principal.

Common carrier One who is engaged in the business of transporting personal property from one place to another for compensation. Such person is bound to carry for all who tender their goods and the price for transportation. A common carrier operates as a public utility and is subject to state and federal regulations.

Common law That body of law deriving from judicial decisions, as opposed to legislatively enacted statutes and administrative regulations.

Common stock In the law of corporations, the type of ownership interest that must exist.

Community property All property acquired after marriage by husband and wife, other than separate property acquired by devise, bequest, or from the proceeds of noncommunity property. Community property is a concept of property ownership by husband and wife inherited from the civil law. The husband and wife are somewhat like partners in their ownership of property acquired during marriage.

Comparative negligence A modification to the defense of contributory negligence. Under this doctrine, a plaintiff's negligence is compared to that of a defendant. The plaintiff's right to recover against the defendant is reduced by the percentage of the plaintiff's negligence. *See* Contributory negligence.

Compensatory damages *See* Damages.

Complaint The first paper a plaintiff files in a court in a lawsuit. It is called a pleading. It is a statement of the facts upon which the plaintiff rests his cause of action.

Composition of creditors An agreement among creditors and their debtors by which the creditors will take a lesser amount in complete satisfaction of the total debt. A owes B and C $500 each. A agrees to pay B and C $250 each in complete satisfaction of the $500 due each. B and C agree to take $250 in satisfaction.

Compromise An agreement between two or more persons, usually opposing parties in a lawsuit, to settle the matters of the controversy without further resort to hostile litigation. An adjustment of issues in dispute by mutual concessions before resorting to a lawsuit.

Condemnation proceedings An action or proceeding in court authorized by legislation (federal or state) for the purpose of taking private property for public use. It is the exercise by the judiciary of the sovereign power of eminent domain.

Condition A clause in a contract, either expressed or implied, that has the effect of investing or divesting the legal rights and duties of the parties to the contract. In a deed, a condition is a qualification or restriction providing for the happening or nonhappening of events that, on occurrence, will destroy, commence, or enlarge an estate. "A grants Blackacre to B, so long as said land shall be used for church purposes." If it ceases to be used for church purposes, the title to Blackacre will revert to the grantor.

Condition precedent A clause in a contract providing that immediate rights and duties shall vest only upon the happening of some event. Securing an architect's certificate by a contractor before the contractor is entitled to payment is a condition precedent. A condition is not a promise; hence, its breach will not give rise to a cause of action for damages. A breach of a condition is the basis for a defense. If the contractor sues the owner without securing the architect's certificate, the owner has a defense.

Conditions concurrent   Conditions concurrent are mutually dependent and must be performed at the same time by the parties to the contract. Payment of money and delivery of goods in a cash sale are conditions concurrent. Failure to perform by one party permits a cause of action upon tender by the other party. If S refuses to deliver goods in a cash sale, B, upon tender but not delivery of the money, places S in default and thus may sue S. B does not part with his money without getting the goods. If S sued B, B would have a defense.

Condition subsequent   A clause in a contract providing for the happening of an event that divests legal rights and duties. A clause in a fire insurance policy providing that the policy shall be null and void if combustible material is stored within 10 feet of the building is a condition subsequent. If a fire occurs and combustible material was within 10 feet of the building, the insurance company is excused from its duty to pay for the loss.

Confirming bank   A bank that engages either that it will itself honor a credit already issued by another bank or that such a credit will be honored by the issuer or a third bank.

Conforming*   Goods or conduct, including any part of a performance, are "conforming" or conform to the contract when they are in accordance with the obligations under contract.

Conglomerate merger   Merging of companies that have neither the relationship of competitors nor that of supplier and customer.

Consequential damages   Those damages, beyond the compensatory damages, which arise from special circumstances causing special damages that are not clearly foreseeable. However, before becoming liable for these damages, the breaching party must be aware of the special circumstances that may cause consequential damages.

Consideration   An essential element in the creation of contract obligation. A detriment to the promisee and a benefit to the promisor. One promise is consideration for another promise. They create a bilateral contract. An act is consideration for a promise. This creates a unilateral contract. Performance of the act asked for by the promisee is a legal detriment to the promisee and a benefit to the promisor.

Consignee   A person to whom a shipper usually directs a carrier to deliver goods; generally the buyer of goods and called a consignee on a bill of lading.

Consignee*   The person named in a bill to whom or to whose order the bill promises delivery.

Consignment   The delivery, sending, or transferring of property, "goods, wares, and merchandise" into the possession of another, usually for the purpose of sale. Consignment may be a bailment or an agency for sale.

Consignor   The shipper who delivers freight to a carrier for shipment and who directs the bill of lading to be executed by the carrier. May be the consignor-consignee if the bill of lading is made to his own order.

Consignor*   The person named in a bill as the person from whom the goods have been received for shipment.

Consolidation   Two corporations are consolidated when both corporations are dissolved and a new one created, the new one taking over the assets of the dissolved corporations.

Conspicuous*   A term or clause is conspicuous when it is written so that a reasonable person against whom it is to operate ought to have noticed it. A printed heading in capitals (as NONNEGOTIABLE BILL OF LADING) is conspicuous. Language in the body of a form is "conspicuous" if it is in larger or other contrasting type or color. But in a telegram, any stated term is "conspicuous." Whether a term or clause is "conspicuous" or not is for decision by the court.

Conspiracy   A combination or agreement between two or more persons for the commission of a criminal act.

Constructive delivery   Although physical delivery of personal property has not occurred, the conduct of the parties may imply that possession and title has passed between them. S sells large and bulky goods to B. Title and possession may pass by the act and conduct of the parties.

Consumer   A person who does not intend to resell an item of property but rather intends to use it for a personal, noncommercial purpose.

Consumer goods*   Goods that are used or bought for use primarily for personal, family, or household purposes.

Contingent fee An arrangement whereby an attorney is compensated for services in a lawsuit according to an agreed percentage of the amount of money recovered.

Contract An agreement involving one or more promises that courts will enforce or for the breach of which courts provide a remedy.

Contract right* Under a contract, any right to payment not yet earned by performance and not evidenced by an instrument or chattel paper.

Contributory negligence In a negligence suit, failure of the plaintiff to use reasonable care.

Conversion A legal theory used to create a "sale" of property to a person who interferes with the owner's use of the property to the extent that damages must be paid to compensate the owner for the loss of property.

Conversion* Under Article 3—Commercial Paper, an instrument is converted when a drawee to whom it is delivered for acceptance refuses to return it on demand; or any person to whom it is delivered for payment refuses on demand either to pay or to return it; or it is paid on a forged indorsement.

Conveyance A formal written instrument, usually called a deed, by which the title or other interests in land (real property) are transferred from one person to another. The word expresses also the fact that the title to real property has been transferred from one person to another.

Corporation A collection of individuals created by statute as a legal person, vested with powers and capacity to contract, own, control, convey property, and transact business within the limits of the powers granted.

Corporation de facto If persons have attempted in good faith to organize a corporation under a valid law (statute) and have failed in some minor particular but have thereafter exercised corporate powers, they are a corporation de facto. Failure to notarize incorporators' signatures on applications for charter is an illustration of non-compliance with statutory requirements.

Corporation de jure A corporation that has been formed by complying with the mandatory requirements of the law authorizing such a corporation.

Corporeal Physical; perceptible by the senses. Automobiles, grain, fruit, and horses are corporeal and tangible and are called chattels. *Corporeal* is used in contradistinction to *incorporeal* or *intangible*. A chose in action (such as a check) is corporeal and

tangible, or a chose in action may be a simple debt, incorporeal and intangible.

Costs In litigation, an allowance authorized by statute to a party for expenses incurred in prosecuting or defending a lawsuit. The word *costs*, unless specifically designated by statute or contract, does not include attorney's fees.

Counterclaims By cross-action, the defendant claims that he is entitled to recover from the plaintiff. Claim must arise out of the same transaction set forth in the plaintiff's complaint and be connected with the same subject matter. S sues B for the purchase price. B counterclaims that the goods were defective and that he thereby suffered damages.

Course of dealing A sequence of previous conduct between the parties to a particular transaction. The conduct is fairly to be regarded as establishing a common basis of understanding for interpreting their expressions and other conduct.

Course of performance A term used to give meaning to a contract based on the parties having had a history of dealings or an agreement that requires repeated performances.

Covenant A promise in writing under seal. It is often used as a substitute for the word *contract*. There are covenants (promises) in deeds, leases, mortgages, and other instruments under seal. The word is used sometimes to name promises in unsealed instruments such as insurance policies.

Cover* After a breach by a seller, the buyer may "cover" by making in good faith and without unreasonable delay any reasonable purchase of, or contract to purchase, goods in substitution for those due from the seller.

Credit* ("Letter of credit") An engagement by a bank or other person made at the request of a customer and of a kind within the scope of Article 5—Letters of Credit, that the issuer will honor drafts or other demands for payment upon compliance with the conditions specified in the credit. A credit may be either revocable or irrevocable. The engagement may be either an agreement to honor or a statement that the bank or other person is authorized to honor.

Creditor* Includes a general creditor, a secured creditor, a lien creditor, and any representative of creditors, including an assignee for the benefit of creditors, a trustee in bankruptcy, a receiver in equity, and an executor or administrator of an insolvent debtor's or assignor's estate.

Creditor-beneficiary One who, for a consideration, promises to discharge another's duty to a third party. A owes C $100. B, for a consideration, promises A to pay A's debt to C. B is a creditor beneficiary.

Cumulative voting In voting for directors, a stockholder may cast as many votes as he has shares of stock multiplied by the number to be elected. His votes may be all for one candidate or distributed among as many candidates as there are offices to be filled.

Cure* An opportunity for the seller of defective goods to correct the defect and thereby not be held to have breached the sales contract.

Custodian bank* A bank or trust company that acts as custodian for a clearing corporation. It must be supervised and examined by the appropriate state or federal authority.

Custody (personal property) The words *custody* and *possession* are not synonymous. *Custody* means in charge of, to keep and care for under the direction of the true owner, without any interest therein adverse to the true owner. A servant is in custody of his master's goods. See Possession.

Customer* Under Article 4—Bank Deposits and Collections, a customer is any person having an account with a bank or for whom a bank has agreed to collect items. It includes a bank carrying an account with another bank. As used in Letters of Credit, a customer is a buyer or other person who causes an issuer to issue a credit. The term also includes a bank that procures insurance or confirmation on behalf of that bank's customer.

Damages A sum of money the court imposes upon a defendant as compensation for the plaintiff because the defendant has injured the plaintiff by breach of a legal duty.

d.b.a. "Doing business as." A person who conducts his business under an assumed name is designated "John Doe d.b.a. Excelsior Co."

Debenture A corporate obligation sold as an investment. Similar to a corporate bond but not secured by a trust deed. It is not like corporate stock.

Debtor* The person who owes payment or other performance of the obligation secured, whether or not he owns, or has rights in, the collateral. Includes the seller of accounts, contract rights, or chattel paper. When the debtor and the owner of the collateral are not the same person, *debtor* means the owner of the collateral in any provision of the Article dealing with the obligation and may include both if the context so requires.

Deceit Conduct in a business transaction by which one person, through fraudulent representations, misleads another who has a right to rely on such representations as the truth or who, by reason of an unequal station in life, has no means of detecting such fraud.

Declaratory judgment A determination by a court on a question of law, the court simply declaring the rights of the parties but not ordering anything to be done.

Decree The judgment of the chancellor (judge) in a suit in equity. Like a judgment at law, it is the determination of the rights between the parties and is in the form of an order that requires the decree to be carried out. An order that a contract be specifically enforced is an example of a decree.

Deed A written instrument in a special form, signed, sealed, delivered, and used to pass the legal title of real property from one person to another. (See Conveyance.) In order that the public may know about the title to real property, deeds are recorded in the Deed Record office of the county where the land is situated.

Deed of trust An instrument by which title to real property is conveyed to a trustee to hold as security for the holder of notes or bonds. It is like a mortgage, except the security title is held by a person other than the mortgagee-creditor. Most corporate bonds are secured by a deed of trust.

De facto Arising out of, or founded upon, fact, although merely apparent or colorable. A de facto officer is one who assumes to be an officer under some color of right, acts as an officer, but in point of law is not a real officer. See Corporation de facto.

Defendant A person who has been sued in a court of law; the person who answers the plaintiff's complaint. The word is applied to the defending party in civil actions. In criminal actions, the defending party is referred to as the accused.

Deficiency judgment If, upon the foreclosure of a mortgage, the mortgaged property does not sell for an amount sufficient to pay the mortgage indebtedness, the difference is called a deficiency and is chargeable to the mortgagor or to any person who has purchased the property and assumed and agreed to pay the mortgage. M borrows $10,000 from B and as security gives a mortgage on Blackacre. At maturity, M does not pay the debt. B forecloses, and at public sale Blackacre sells for $8,000. There is a deficiency of $2,000, chargeable against M. If M had sold Blackacre to C and C had assumed and agreed to pay the mortgage, he would also be liable for the deficiency.

Defraud To deprive one of some right by deceitful means. To cheat; to withhold wrongfully that which belongs to another. Conveying one's property for the purpose of avoiding payment of debts is a transfer to "hinder, delay, or defraud creditors."

Del credere agency When an agent, factor, or broker guarantees to his principal the payment of a debt due from a buyer of goods, that agent, factor, or broker is operating under a del credere commission or agency.

Delivery A voluntary transfer of the possession of property, actual or constructive, from one person to another, with the intention that title vests in the transferee. In the law of sales, delivery contemplates the absolute giving up of control and dominion over the property by the vendor, and the assumption of the same by the vendee.

Delivery* With respect to instruments, documents of title, chattel paper, or securities, delivery means voluntary transfer of possession.

Delivery order* A written order to deliver goods directed to a warehouseman, carrier, or other person who, in the ordinary course of business, issues warehouse receipts or bills of lading.

Demand A request by a party entitled, under a claim of right, to the performance of a particular act. In order to bind an indorser on a negotiable instrument, the holder must first make a demand on the primary party, who must dishonor the instrument. Demand notes mean "due when demanded." The word *demand* is also used to mean a claim or legal obligation.

Demurrage Demurrage is a sum provided for in a contract of shipment, to be paid for the delay or detention of vessels or railroad cars beyond the time agreed upon for loading or unloading.

Demurrer A common law procedural method by which the defendant admits all the facts alleged in the plaintiff's complaint but denies that such facts state a cause of action. It raises a question of law on the facts, which must be decided by the court.

Dependent covenants (promises) In contracts, covenants are either concurrent or mutual, dependent or independent. Dependent covenants mean the performance of one promise must occur before the performance of the other promise. In a cash sale, the buyer must pay the money before the seller is under a duty to deliver the goods.

Depositary bank* Under Article 4—Bank Deposits and Collections, this means the first bank to which an item is transferred for collection, even though it is also the payor bank.

Descent The transfer of the title of property to the heirs upon the death of the ancestor; heredity succession. If a person dies without making a will, his property will "descend" according to the Statute of Descent of the state wherein the property is located.

Devise A gift, usually of real property, by a last will and testament.

Devisee The person who receives title to real property by will.

Dictum (dicta—plural) The written opinion of a judge, expressing an idea, argument, or rule that is not essential for the determination of the issues. It lacks the force of a decision in a judgment.

Directed verdict If it is apparent to reasonable men and the court that the plaintiff, by his evidence, has not made out his case, the court may instruct the jury to bring in a verdict for the defendant. If, however, different inferences may be drawn from the evidence by reasonable men, then the court cannot direct a verdict.

Discharge The word has many meanings. An employee, upon being released from employment, is discharged. A guardian or trustee, upon termination of his trust, is discharged by the court. A debtor released from his debts is discharged in bankruptcy. A person who is released from any legal obligation is discharged.

Discovery The disclosure by one party of facts, titles, documents, and other things in his knowledge of possession and necessary to the party seeking the discovery as a part of a cause of action pending.

Dishonor A negotiable instrument is dishonored when it is presented for acceptance or payment but acceptance or payment is refused or cannot be obtained.

Dissolution In the law of partnerships, this event occurs any time there is a change in the partners, either by adding a new partner or by having a preexisting partner die, retire, or otherwise leave.

Distress for rent The taking of personal property of a tenant in payment of rent on real estate.

Divestiture The antitrust remedy that forces a company to get rid of assets acquired through illegal mergers or monopolistic practices.

Dividend A stockholder's pro rata share in the profits of a corporation. Dividends are declared by the board of directors of a corporation. They are paid in cash, script, property, and stock.

Docket A book containing a brief summary of all acts done in court in the conduct of each case.

Documentary collateral* In the law of secured transactions, this category of collateral consists of documents of title, chattel paper, and instruments.

Documentary draft* Under Article 4—Bank Deposits and Collections, this means any negotiable or nonnegotiable draft with accompanying documents, securities, or other papers to be delivered against honor of the draft. Also called a "documentary demand for payment" (Article 5—Letters of Credit). Honoring is conditioned upon the presentation of a document or documents. "Document" means any paper, including document of title, security, invoice, certificate, notice of default, and the like.

Document of title* Includes bill of lading, dock warrant, dock receipt, warehouse receipt, or order for the delivery of goods, and any other document that in the regular course of business or financing is treated as adequately evidencing that the person in possession of it is entitled to receive, hold, and dispose of the document and the goods it covers. To be a document of title, a document must purport to be issued by, or addressed to, a bailee and purport to cover goods in the bailee's possession that are either identified or are fungible portions of an identified mass.

Domicile The place a person intends as his fixed and permanent home and establishment and to which, if he is absent, he intends to return. A person can have but one domicile. The old one continues until the acquisition of a new one. One can have more than one residence at a time, but only one domicile. The word is not synonymous with *residence*.

Dominion Applied to the delivery of property by one person to another, *dominion* means all control over the possession and ownership of the property being separated from the transferor or donor and endowed upon the transferee or donee. *See* Gift.

Donee Recipient of a gift.

Donee-beneficiary If a promisee is under no duty to a third party, but for a consideration secures a promise from a promisor for the purpose of making a gift to a third party, then the third party is a donee-beneficiary. A, promisee for a premium paid, secures a promise from the insurance company, the promisor, to pay A's wife $10,000 upon A's death. A's wife is a donee-beneficiary.

Donor One that gives, donates, or presents.

Dormant partner A partner who is not known to third persons but is entitled to share in the profits and is subject to the losses. Since credit is not extended upon the strength of the dormant partner's name, he may withdraw without notice and not be subject to debts contracted after his withdrawal.

Double jeopardy A constitutional doctrine that prohibits an individual from being prosecuted twice in the same tribunal for the same criminal offense.

Due process Fundamental fairness. Applied to judicial proceedings, it includes adequate notice of a hearing and an opportunity to appear and defend in an orderly tribunal.

Duress (of person) A threat of bodily injury, criminal prosecution, or imprisonment of a contracting party or his near relative to such extent that the threatened party is unable to exercise free will at the time of entering into or discharging a legal obligation.

Duress (of property) Seizing by force or withholding goods by one not entitled, and such person's demanding something as a condition for the release of the goods.

Duty (in law) A legal obligation imposed by general law or voluntarily imposed by the creation of a binding promise. For every legal duty there is a corresponding legal right. By general law, A is under a legal duty not to injure B's person or property. B has a right that A not injure his person or property. X may voluntarily create a duty in himself to Y by a promise to sell Y a horse for $100. If Y accepts, X is under a legal duty to perform his promise. *See* Right.

Earnest money A term used to describe money that one contracting party gives to another at the time of entering into the contract in order to "bind the bargain" and which will be forfeited by the donor if he fails to carry out the contract. Generally, in real estate contracts such money is used as part payment of the purchase price.

Easement An easement is an interest in land—a right that one person has to some profit, benefit, or use in or over the land of another. Such right is created by a deed, or it may be acquired by prescription (the continued use of another's land for a statutory period).

Ejectment An action to recover the possession of real property. It is now generally defined by statute and is a statutory action. *See* Forcible entry and detainer.

Ejusdem generis "Of the same class." General words taking their meaning from specific words which precede the general words. General words have the same meaning as specific words mentioned.

Election A concept applicable in agency relationships when the principal is undisclosed. The third party may elect to hold either the agent or the previously undisclosed principal liable. By electing to hold one party liable, the third party has chosen not to seek a recovery against the other party.

Embezzlement The fraudulent appropriation by one person, acting in a fiduciary capacity, of the money or property of another. *See* Conversion.

Eminent domain The right that resides in the United States, state, county, city, school, or other public body to take private property for public use upon payment of just compensation.

Employment-at-will A doctrine stating that an employee who has no specific agreement as to the length of his employment may be discharged at any time without any reason being given by the employer. This doctrine has been modified in many states in recent years.

Encumbrance A burden on either the title to land or thing or upon the land or thing itself. A mortgage or other lien is an encumbrance upon the title. A right-of-way over the land is an encumbrance upon the land and affects its physical condition.

Enjoin To require performance or abstention from some act through issuance of an injunction.

Entity "In being" or "existing." The artificial person created when a corporation is organized is "in being" or "existing" for legal purposes, thus an entity. It is separate from the stockholders. The estate of a deceased person while in administration is an entity. A partnership for many legal purposes is an entity.

Equal protection A principle of the Fifth and Fourteenth Amendments to the Constitution, ensuring that individuals under like circumstances shall be accorded the same benefits and burdens under the law of the sovereign.

Equipment* Goods that are used or bought for use primarily in business (including farming or a profession) or by a debtor who is a nonprofit organization or a governmental subdivision or agency; or goods not included in the definitions of inventory, farm products, or consumer goods.

Equitable action In Anglo-American law, there have developed two types of courts and procedures for the administration of justice: law courts and equity courts. Law courts give as a remedy money damages only, whereas equity courts give the plaintiff what he bargains for. A suit for specific performance of a contract is an equitable action. In many states these two courts are now merged.

Equitable conversion An equitable principle that, for certain purposes, permits real property to be converted into personalty. Thus, real property owned by a partnership is, for the purpose of the partnership, personal property because to ascertain a partner's interest, the real property must be reduced to cash. This is an application of the equitable maxim, "Equity considers that done which ought to be done."

Equitable estoppel A legal theory used to prevent a party to an oral contract that has been partially performed from asserting the defense of the statute of frauds. *See* Part performance.

Equitable mortgage A written agreement to make certain property security for a debt, and upon the faith of which the parties have acted in making advances, loans, and thus creating a debt. Example: an improperly executed mortgage, one without seal where a seal is required. An absolute deed made to the mortgagee and intended for security only is an equitable mortgage.

Equity Because the law courts in early English law did not always give an adequate remedy, an aggrieved party sought redress from the king. Since this appeal was to the king's conscience, he referred the case to his spiritual adviser, the chancellor. The chancellor decided the case according to rules of fairness, honesty, right, and natural justice. From this there developed the rules in equity. The laws of trust, divorce, rescission of contracts for fraud, injunction, and specific performance are enforced in courts of equity.

Equity of redemption The right a mortgagor has to redeem or get back his property after it has been forfeited for nonpayment of the debt it secured. By statute, within a certain time before final foreclosure decree, a mortgagor has the privilege of redeeming his property by paying the amount of the debt, interest, and costs.

Escrow An agreement under which a grantor, promisor, or obligor places the instrument upon which he is bound with a third person called escrow holder, until the performance of a condition or the happening of an event stated in the agreement permits the escrow holder to make delivery or performance to the grantee, promisee, or obligee. A (grantor) places a deed to C (grantee) accompanied by the contract of conveyance with B bank, conditioned upon B bank delivering the deed to C (grantee) when C pays all moneys due under contract. The contract and deed have been placed in "escrow."

Estate All the property of a living, deceased, bankrupt, or insane person. Also applied to the property of a ward. In the law of taxation, wills, and inheritance, *estate* has a broad meaning. Historically, the word was limited to an interest in land: i.e., estate in fee simple, estate for years, estate for life, and so forth.

Estoppel When one ought to speak the truth but does not, and by one's acts, representations, or silence intentionally or through negligence induces another to believe certain facts exist, and the other person acts to his detriment on the belief that such facts are true, the first person is estopped to deny the truth of the facts. B, knowingly having kept and used defective goods delivered by S under a contract of sale, is estopped to deny the goods are defective. X holds out Y as his agent. X is estopped to deny that Y is his agent. Persons are estopped to deny the legal effect of written instruments such as deeds, contracts, bills and notes, court records, and judgments. A man's own acts speak louder than his words.

Et al. "And other persons." Used in pleadings and cases to indicate that persons other than those specifically named are parties to a lawsuit.

Ethics Conduct based on a commitment of what is right. This conduct often is at a level above that required by legal standards.

Eviction An action to expel a tenant from the estate of the landlord. Interfering with the tenant's right of possession or enjoyment amounts to an eviction. Eviction may be actual or constructive. Premises made uninhabitable because the landlord maintains a nuisance is constructive eviction.

Evidence In law, *evidence* has two meanings. (1) Testimony of witnesses and facts presented to the court and jury by way of writings and exhibits, which impress the minds of the court and jury, to the extent that an allegation has been proven. *Testimony* and *evidence* are not synonymous. Testimony is a broader word and includes all the witness says. *Proof* is distinguished from *evidence*, in that proof is the legal consequence of evidence. (2) The rules of law, called the law of evidence, that determine what evidence shall be introduced at a trial and what shall not; also, what importance shall be placed upon the evidence.

Exclusive dealing contract A contract under which a buyer agrees to purchase a certain product exclusively from the seller or in which the seller agrees to sell all his product production to the buyer.

Ex contractu *See* Action ex contractu.

Exculpatory clause A provision in a contract whereby one of the parties attempts to relieve itself of liability for breach of a legal duty.

Ex delicto *See* Action ex delicto.

Executed Applied to contracts or other written instruments, *executed* means signed, sealed, and delivered. Effective legal obligations have thus been created. The term is also used to mean that the performances of a contract have been completed. The contract is then at an end. All is done that is to be done.

Execution Execution of a judgment is the process by which the court, through the sheriff, enforces the payment of the judgment received by the successful party. The sheriff, by a "writ," levies upon the unsuccessful party's property and sells it to pay the judgment creditor.

Executor (of an estate) The person whom the testator (the one who makes the will) names or appoints to administer his estate upon his death and to dispose of it according to his intention. The terms *executor* and *administrator* are not synonyms. A person who makes a will appoints an executor to administer his estate. A court appoints an administrator to administer the estate of a person who dies without having made a will. *See* Intestate.

Executory contract Until the performance required in a contract is completed, it is said to be executory as to that part not executed. *See* Executed.

Exemplary damages A sum assessed by the jury in a tort action (over and above the compensatory damages) as punishment, in order to make an example of the wrongdoer and to deter like conduct by others. Injuries caused by willful, malicious, wanton, and reckless conduct will subject the wrongdoers to exemplary damages.

Exemption The condition of a person who is free or excused from a duty imposed by some rule of law, statutory or otherwise.

Express contract An agreement which is either spoken or written by the parties. *See* Contract.

Express warranty When a seller makes some positive representation concerning the nature, quality, character, use, and purpose of goods, which induces the buyer to buy, and the seller intends the buyer to rely thereon, the seller has made an express warranty.

Factor An agent for the sale of merchandise. He may hold possession of the goods in his own name or in the name of his principal. He is authorized to sell and to receive payment for the goods. *See* Agent.

Factor's lien A factor's right to keep goods consigned to him if he may reimburse himself for advances previously made to the consignor.

Farm products* Crops or livestock or supplies used or produced in farming operations; products of crops or livestock in their unmanufactured states (such as ginned cotton, wool-clip, maple syrup, milk, and eggs); and goods in the possession of a debtor engaged in raising, fattening, grazing, or other farming operations. If goods are farm products, they are neither equipment or inventory.

Featherbedding In labor relations, a demand for the payment of wages for a service not actually rendered.

Fee simple absolute The total interest a person may have in land. Such an estate is not qualified by any other interest, and it passes upon the death of the owners to the heirs, free from any conditions.

Fellow-servant doctrine Precludes an injured employee from recovering damages from his employer when the injury resulted from the negligent act of another employee.

Felony All criminal offenses that are punishable by death or imprisonment in a penitentiary.

Fiduciary In general, a person is a fiduciary when he occupies a position of trust or confidence in relation to another person or his property. Trustees, guardians, and executors occupy fiduciary positions.

Final decree *See* Decree.

Financing agency* A bank, finance company, or person who, in the ordinary course of business, makes advances against goods or documents of title; or who, by arrangement with either the seller or the buyer, intervenes in ordinary course to make a collect payment due or claimed under the contract for sale, as by purchasing or paying the seller's draft or making advances against it or by merely taking it for collection, whether or not documents of title accompany the draft. "Financing agency" includes a bank or person who similarly intervenes between persons who are in the position of seller and buyer in respect to the goods.

Fine A sum of money collected by a court from a person guilty of some criminal offense. The amount may be fixed by statute or left to the discretion of the court.

Firm offer* An offer by a merchant to buy or sell goods in a signed writing that, by its terms, gives assurance it will be held open.

Fixture An item of personal property that has become attached or annexed to real estate. Fixtures generally are treated as part of the real estate.

Floating lien* In the law of secured transactions, this concept allows a creditor to become secured with regards to future advances and to collateral acquired by the debtor after the perfection occurs.

Forbearance Giving up the right to enforce what one honestly believes to be a valid claim, in return for a promise. It is sufficient "consideration" to make a promise binding.

Forcible entry and detainer A remedy given to a land owner to evict persons unlawfully in possession of his land. A landlord may use such remedy to evict a tenant in default.

Foreclosure The forced sale of a defaulting debtor's property at the insistence of the creditor.

Forfeiture Money or property taken as compensation and punishment for injury or damage to the person or property of another or to the state. One may forfeit interest earnings for charging a usurious rate.

Forgery False writing or alteration of an instrument with the fraudulent intent of deceiving and injuring another. Writing another's name upon a check, without his consent, to secure money.

Franchise A right conferred or granted by a legislative body. It is a contract right and cannot be revoked without cause. A franchise is more than a license. A license is only a privilege and may be revoked. A corporation exists by virtue of a "franchise." A corporation secures a franchise from the city council to operate a waterworks within the city. *See* License.

Franchise tax A tax on the right of a corporation to do business under its corporate name.

Fraud An intentional misrepresentation of the truth for the purpose of deceiving another person. The elements of fraud are (1) intentionally false representation of fact, not opinion, (2) intent that the deceived person act thereon, (3) knowledge that such statements would naturally deceive, and (4) that the deceived person acted to his injury.

Fraudulent conveyance A conveyance of property by a debtor for the intent and purpose of defrauding his creditors. It is of no effect, and such property may be reached by the creditors through appropriate legal proceedings.

Freehold An estate in fee or for life. A freeholder is usually a person who has a property right in the title to real estate amounting to an estate of inheritance (in fee), or one who has title for life or an indeterminate period.

Full-line forcing An arrangement in which a manufacturer refuses to supply any portion of the product line unless the retailer agrees to accept the entire line.

Fungible* Goods and securities of which any unit is, by nature or usage of trade, the equivalent of any other like unit.

Fungible goods Fungible goods are those "of which any unit is from its nature of mercantile usage treated as the equivalent of any other unit." Grain, wine, and similar items are examples.

Future goods* Goods that are not both existing and identified.

Futures Contracts for the sale and delivery of commodities in the future, made with the intention that no commodity be delivered or received immediately.

Garnishee A person upon whom a garnishment is served. He is a debtor of a defendant and has money or property that the plaintiff is trying to reach in order to satisfy a debt due from the defendant. Also used as a verb: "to garnishee wages or property."

Garnishment A proceeding by which a plaintiff seeks to reach the credits of the defendant that are in the hands of a third party, the garnishee. A garnishment is distinguished from an attachment in that by an attachment, an officer of the court takes actual possession of property by virtue of his writ. In a garnishment, the property or money is left with the garnishee until final adjudication.

General agent An agent authorized to do all the acts connected with carrying on a particular trade, business, or profession.

General intangibles* Any personal property (including things in action) other than goods, accounts, contract rights, chattel paper, documents, and instruments.

General verdict *See* Verdict *in contrast to* Special verdict.

Gift A gift is made when a donor delivers the subject matter of the gift into the donee's hands or places in the donee the means of obtaining possession of the subject matter, accompanied by such acts that show clearly the donor's intentions to divest himself of all dominion and control over the property.

Gift *causa mortis* A gift made in anticipation of death. The donor must have been in sickness and have died as expected, otherwise no effective gift has been made. If the donor survives, the gift is revocable.

Gift *inter vivos* An effective gift made during the life of the donor. By a gift inter vivos, property vests immediately in the donee at the time of delivery, whereas a gift causa mortis is made in contemplation of death and is effective only upon the donor's death.

Good faith* Honesty in fact is the conduct or transaction concerned. Referring to a merchant, good faith means honesty in fact and the observance of reasonable commercial standards of fair dealing in the trade.

Goods* All things that are movable at the time of identification to the contract for sale, including specially manufactured goods but not money in which the price is to be paid, investment securities, and things in action. Includes unborn young animals, growing crops, and other identified things attached to realty as described in the section on goods to be severed from realty.

Goodwill The value, beyond its assets, of a business organization created by its customers.

Grant A term used in deeds for the transfer of the title to real property. The words *convey, transfer,* and *grant,* as operative words in a deed to pass title, are equivalent. The words *grant, bargain,* and *sell* in a deed, in absence of statute, mean the grantor promises he has good title to transfer free from incumbrances and warrants it to be such.

Grantee A person to whom a grant is made; one named in a deed to receive title.

Grantor A person who makes a grant. The grantor executes the deed by which he divests himself of title.

Gross negligence The lack of even slight or ordinary care.

Guarantor One who by contract undertakes "to answer for the debt, default, and miscarriage of another." In general, a guarantor undertakes to pay if the principal debtor does not; a surety, on the other hand, joins in the contract of the principal and becomes an original party with the principal.

Guardian A person appointed by the court to look after the property rights and person of minors, the insane, and other incompetents or legally incapacitated persons.

Guardian ad litem A special guardian appointed for the sole purpose of carrying on litigation and preserving the interests of a ward. He exercises no control or power over property.

Habeas corpus A writ issued to a sheriff, warden, or other official having allegedly unlawful custody of a person, directing the official to bring the person before a court, in order to determine the legality of the imprisonment.

Hearsay evidence   Evidence that is learned from someone else. It does not derive its value from the credit of the witness testifying but rests upon the veracity of another person. It is not good evidence, because there is no opportunity to cross-examine the person who is the source of the testimony.

Hedging contract   A contract of purchase or sale of an equal amount of commodities in the future, by which brokers, dealers, or manufacturers protect themselves against the fluctuations of the market. It is a type of insurance against changing prices. A grain dealer, to protect himself, may contract to sell for future delivery the same amount of grain he has purchased in the present market.

Heirs   Persons upon whom the statute of descent casts the title to real property upon the death of the ancestor. Consult Statute of Descent for the appropriate state. *See* Descent.

Holder*   A person who is in possession of a document of title or an instrument or an investment security drawn, issued, or indorsed to him or to his order or to bearer or in blank.

Holder in due course   One who has acquired possession of a negotiable instrument through proper negotiation for value, in good faith, and without notice of any defenses to it. Such a holder is not subject to personal defenses that would otherwise defeat the obligation embodied in the instrument.

Holding company   A corporation organized for the purpose of owning and holding the stock of other corporations. Shareholders of underlying corporations receive in exchange for their stock, upon an agreed value, the shares in the holding corporation.

Homestead   A parcel of land upon which a family dwells or resides, and which to them is home. The statute of the state or federal governments should be consulted to determine the meaning of the term as applied to debtor's exemptions, federal land grants, and so forth.

Honor*   To pay or to accept and pay or, where a creditor so engages, to purchase or discount a draft complying with the terms of the instrument.

Horizontal merger   Merger of corporations that were competitors prior to the merger.

Hot-cargo contract   An agreement between employer and union, whereby an employer agrees to refrain from handling, using, selling, transporting, or otherwise dealing in the products of another employer or agrees to cease doing business with some other person.

Illegal   Contrary to public policy and the fundamental principles of law. Illegal conduct includes not only violations of criminal statutes but also the creation of agreements that are prohibited by statute and the common law.

Illusory   That which has a false appearance. If that which appears to be a promise is not a promise, it is said to be illusory. "I promise to buy your lunch if I decide to." This equivocal statement would not justify reliance, so it is not a promise.

Immunity   Freedom from the legal duties and penalties imposed upon others. The "privileges and immunities" clause of the United States Constitution means no state can deny to the citizens of another state the same rights granted to its own citizens. This does not apply to office holding. *See* Exemption.

Implied   The finding of a legal right or duty by inference from facts or circumstances. *See* Warranty.

Implied-in-fact contract   A legally enforceable agreement inferred from the circumstances and conduct of the parties.

Imputed negligence   Negligence that is not directly attributable to the person himself but is the negligence of a person who is in privity with him and with whose fault he is chargeable.

Incidental beneficiary   If the performance of a promise would indirectly benefit a person not a party to a contract, such person is an incidental beneficiary. A promises B, for a consideration, to plant a valuable nut orchard on B's land. Such improvement would increase the value of the adjacent land. C, the owner of the adjacent land, is an incidental beneficiary. He has no remedy if A breaches his promise with B.

Indemnify   Literally, "to save harmless." Thus, one person agrees to protect another against loss.

Indenture   A deed executed by both parties, as distinguished from a deed poll that is executed only by the grantor.

Independent contractor   The following elements are essential to establish the relation of independent contractor, in contradistinction to principal and agent. An independent contractor must (1) exercise his independent judgment on the means used to accomplish the result; (2) be free from control or orders from any other person; (3) be responsible only under his contract for the result obtained.

Indictment   A finding by a grand jury that it has reason to believe the accused is guilty as charged. It informs the accused of the offense with which he is charged, so that he may prepare its defense. It is a pleading in a criminal action.

Indorsement Writing one's name upon paper for the purpose of transferring the title. When a payee of a negotiable instrument writes his name on the back of the instrument, his writing is an indorsement.

Infringement Infringement of a patent on a machine is the manufacturing of a machine that produces the same result by the same means and operation as the patented machine. Infringement of a trademark consists in reproduction of a registered trademark and its use upon goods in order to mislead the public to believe that the goods are the genuine, original product.

Inherit The word is used in contradistinction to acquiring property by will. *See* Descent.

Inheritance An estate that descends to heirs. *See* Descent.

Injunction A writ of judicial process issued by a court of equity, by which a party is required to do a particular thing or to refrain from doing a particular thing.

In personam A legal proceeding, the judgment of which binds the defeated party to a personal liability.

In rem A legal proceeding, the judgment of which binds, affects, or determines the status of property.

Insolvent* Refers to a person who either has ceased to pay his debts in the ordinary course of business or cannot pay his debts as they become due or is insolvent within the meaning of the federal bankruptcy law.

Installment contract* One which requires or authorizes the delivery of goods in separate lots to be separately accepted, even though the contract contains a clause "each delivery is a separate contract" or its equivalent.

Instrument* A negotiable instrument or a security or any other writing that evidences a right to the payment of money and is not itself a security agreement or lease and is of a type that is in ordinary course of business transferred by delivery with any necessary indorsement or assignment.

Insurable interest A person has an insurable interest in a person or property if he will be directly and financially affected by the death of the person or the loss of the property.

Insurance By an insurance contract, one party, for an agreed premium, binds himself to another, called the insured, to pay the insured a sum of money con-

ditioned upon the loss of life or property of the insured.

Intangible Something which represents value but has no intrinsic value of its own, such as a note or bond.

Intent A state of mind that exists prior to, or contemporaneous with, an act. A purpose or design to do or forbear to do an act. It cannot be directly proven but is inferred from known facts.

Interlocutory decree A decree of a court of equity that does not settle the complete issue but settles only some intervening part, awaiting a final decree.

Intermediary bank* Under Article 4—Bank Deposits and Collections, it is any bank—except the depositary or payor bank—to which an item is transferred in course of collection.

Interpleader A procedure whereby a person who has an obligation, e.g., to pay money, but does not know which of two or more claimants are entitled to performance, can bring a suit that requires the contesting parties to litigate between themselves.

Interrogatory A written question from one party to another in a lawsuit; a type of discovery procedure.

Intestate The intestate laws are the laws of descent or distribution of the estate of a deceased person. A person who has not made a will dies intestate.

Inventory* Goods that a person holds for sale or lease or to be—or which have been—furnished under contracts of service, or goods that are raw materials, work in process or materials used or consumed in a business. Inventory of a person is not to be classified as his equipment.

Irreparable damage or injury *Irreparable* does not mean injury beyond the possibility of repair, but it does mean that it is so constant and frequent in occurrence that no fair or reasonable redress can be had in a court of law. Thus, the plaintiff must seek a remedy in equity by way of an injunction.

Issue* Under Article 3—Commercial Paper, *issue* means the first delivery of an instrument to a holder or a remitter.

Issuer* A bailee who issues a document; but in relation to an unaccepted delivery order, the issuer is the person who orders the possessor of goods to deliver. Issuer includes any person for whom an agent or employee purports to act in issuing a document if the agent or employee has real or apparent authority to issue documents, notwithstanding that the issuer received no goods or that the goods were misdescribed or that in any other respect the agent or employee violated the issuer's instructions.

Item* Under Article 4—Bank Deposits and Collections, *item* means any instrument for the payment of money, even though it is not negotiable, but does not include money.

Jeopardy A person is in jeopardy when he is regularly charged with a crime before a court properly organized and competent to try him. If acquitted, he cannot be tried again for the same offense.

Joint and several Two or more persons have an obligation that binds them individually as well as jointly. The obligation can be enforced either by joint action against all of them or by separate actions against one or more.

Joint ownership The interest that two or more parties have in property.

Joint tenancy Two or more persons to whom land is deeded in such manner that they have "one and the same interest, accruing by one and the same conveyance, commencing at one and the same time, and held by one and the same undivided possession." Upon the death of one joint tenant, his property passes to the survivor or survivors.

Joint tortfeasors When two persons commit an injury with a common intent, they are joint tortfeasors.

Judgment (in law) The decision, pronouncement, or sentence rendered by a court upon an issue in which it has jurisdiction.

Judgment *in personam* A judgment against a person, directing the defendant to do or not to do something. *See In personam.*

Judgment *in rem* A judgment against a thing, as distinguished from a judgment against a person. *See In rem.*

Judicial restraint A judicial philosophy. Those following it believe that the power of judicial review should be exercised with great restraint.

Judicial review The power of courts to declare laws and executive actions unconstitutional.

Judicial sale A sale authorized by a court that has jurisdiction to grant such authority. Such sales are conducted by an officer of the court.

Jurisdiction The authority to try causes and determine cases. Conferred upon a court by the Constitution.

Jury A group of persons, usually twelve, sworn to declare the facts of a case as they are proved from the evidence presented to them and, upon instructions from the court, to find a verdict in the cause before them.

Juvenile court A court with jurisdiction to hear matters pertaining to those persons under a certain age (usually 16 or 18). This court will hear cases involving delinquent behavior.

Laches A term used in equity to name conduct that neglects to assert one's rights or to do what, by the law, a person should have done. Failure on the part of one to assert a right will give an equitable defense to another party.

Latent defect A defect in materials not discernible by examination. Used in contradistinction to patent defect, which is discernible.

Lease A contract by which one person divests himself of possession of lands or chattels and grants such possession to another for a period of time. The relationship in which land is involved is called landlord and tenant.

Leasehold The land held by a tenant under a lease.

Legacy Personal property disposed of by a will. Sometimes the term is synonymous with *bequest*. The word *devise* is used in connection with real property distributed by will. *See* Bequest; Devise.

Legal benefit An analysis used to determine if contractual consideration exists. As an inducement for a party to make a promise, that party (promisor) must receive a legal benefit, or the other party (promisee) must suffer a legal detriment, or both. *See* Consideration; Legal Detriment.

Legal detriment An analysis used to determine if contractual consideration exists. Parties suffer legal detriment when they promise to perform an act that they have no obligation to perform or promise to refrain from taking action that they have the right to take. *See* Consideration; Legal benefit.

Legatee A person to whom a legacy is given by will.

Liability In its broadest legal sense, *liability* means any obligation one may be under by reason of some rule of law. It includes debt, duty, and responsibility.

Libel Malicious publication of a defamation of a person by printing, writing, signs, or pictures, for the purposes of injuring the reputation and good name of such person. "The exposing of a person to public hatred, contempt, or ridicule."

License (governmental regulation) A license is a privilege granted by a state or city upon the payment of a fee. It confers authority upon the licensee to do some act or series of acts, which otherwise would be illegal. A license is not a contract and may be revoked for cause. It is a method of governmental regulation exercised under the police power.

License (privilege)   A mere personal privilege given by the owner to another to do designated acts upon the land of the owner. It is revocable at will and creates no estate in the land. The licensee is not in possession. "It is a mere excuse for what otherwise would be a trespass."

Lien   The right of one person, usually a creditor, to keep possession of, or control, the property of another for the purpose of satisfying a debt. There are many kinds of liens: judgment lien, attorney's lien, innkeeper's lien, logger's lien, vendor's lien. Consult statute of state for type of lien. *See* Judgment.

Lien creditor*   A creditor who has acquired a lien on property involved by attachment, levy, or the like. Includes an assignee for benefit of creditors from the time of assignment and a trustee in bankruptcy from the date of the filing of the petition or a receiver in equity from the time of appointment. Unless all the creditors represented had knowledge of the security interest, such a representative of creditors is a lien creditor without knowledge even though he personally has knowledge of the security interest.

Life estate   An interest in real property that lasts only as long as a designated person lives.

Limited partnership   A partnership in which one or more individuals are general partners and one or more individuals are limited partners. The limited partners contribute assets to the partnership without taking part in the conduct of the business. They are liable for the debts of the partnership only to the extent of their contributions.

Liquidated   A claim is liquidated when it has been made fixed and certain by the parties concerned.

Liquidated damages   A fixed sum agreed upon between the parties to a contract, to be paid as ascertained damages by the party who breaches the contract. If the sum is excessive, the courts will declare it to be a penalty and unenforceable.

Liquidation   The process of winding up the affairs of a corporation or firm for the purpose of paying its debts and disposing of its assets. May be done voluntarily or under the orders of a court.

Lis pendens   "Pending the suit nothing should be changed." The court, having control of the property involved in the suit, issues notice *lis pendens*, that persons dealing with the defendant regarding the subject matter of the suit do so subject to final determination of the action.

Long-arm statute   A law which allows courts in the state court systems to extend their personal jurisdiction beyond the state boundaries to nonresident defendants if such defendants have had sufficient minimal contacts with the state to justify the exercise of personal jurisdiction.

Lot*   A parcel or a single article that is the subject matter of a separate sale or delivery, whether or not it is sufficient to perform the contract.

Magistrate   A public officer, usually a judge, "who has power to issue a warrant for the arrest of a person charged with a public offense." The word has wide application and includes justices of the peace, notaries public, recorders, and other public officers who have power to issue executive orders.

Malice   Describes a wrongful act done intentionally without excuse. It does not necessarily mean ill will, but it indicates a state of mind that is reckless concerning the law and the rights of others. *Malice* is distinguished from *negligence*. With *malice* there is always a purpose to injure, whereas such is not true of the word *negligence*.

Malicious prosecution   The prosecution of another at law with malice and without probable cause to believe that such legal action will be successful.

Mandamus   A writ issued by a court of law, in the name of the state. Writs of mandamus are directed to inferior courts, officers, corporations, or persons, commanding them to do particular things that appertain to their offices or duties.

Mandatory injunction   An injunctive order issued by a court of equity that compels affirmative action by the defendant.

Market extension merger   A combination of two business organizations allowing one to extend its business to new products or geographical areas. *See* Product extension merger.

Marketable title   A title of such character that no apprehension as to its validity would occur to the mind of a reasonable and intelligent person. The title to goods is not marketable if it is in litigation, subject to incumbrances, in doubt as to a third party's right, or subject to lien.

Marshaling of assets   A principle in equity for a fair distribution of a debtor's assets among his creditors. For example, a creditor of A, by reason of prior right, has two funds, X and Y, belonging to A, out of which he may satisfy his debt. But another creditor of A also has a right to X fund. The first creditor will be compelled to exhaust Y fund before he will be permitted to participate in X fund.

Master In agency relationships involving torts, this party is in a position similar to that of a principal.

Master in chancery An officer appointed by the court to assist the court of equity in taking testimony, computing interest, auditing accounts, estimating damages, ascertaining liens, and doing other tasks incidental to a suit, as the court requires. The power of a master is merely advisory, and his tasks are largely fact finding.

Maxim A proposition of law that because of its universal approval needs no proof or argument; the mere statement of which gives it authority. Example: "A principal is bound by the acts of his agent when the agent is acting within the scope of his authority."

Mechanic's lien Created by statute to assist suppliers and laborers in collecting their accounts and wages. Its purpose is to subject the land of an owner to a lien for material and labor expended in the construction of buildings and other improvements.

Mediation The process by which a third party attempts to help the parties in dispute find a resolution. The mediator has no authority to bind the parties to any particular resolution.

Merchant A person who deals in goods of the kind involved in a transaction; or one who otherwise, by his occupation, holds himself out as having knowledge or skill peculiar to the practices or goods involved; or one to whom such knowledge or skill may be attributed because he employs an agent or broker or other intermediary who, by his occupation, holds himself out as having such knowledge or skill.

Merger Two corporations are merged when one corporation continues in existence and the other loses its identity by its absorption into the first. *Merger* must be distinguished from *consolidation*. In *consolidation*, both corporations are dissolved, and a new one is created, the new one taking over the assets of the dissolved corporations.

Metes and bounds The description of the boundaries of real property.

Midnight deadline* Under Article 4—Bank Deposits and Collections, this is midnight on the next banking day following the banking day on which a bank receives the relevant item or notice, or from which the time for taking action commences to run, whichever is later.

Ministerial duty A prescribed duty that requires little judgment or discretion. A sheriff performs ministerial duties.

Minutes The record of a court or the written transactions of the members or board of directors of a corporation. Under the certificate of the clerk of a court or the secretary of a corporation, the minutes are the official evidence of court or corporate action.

Misdemeanor A criminal offense, less than a felony, that is not punishable by death or imprisonment. Consult the local statute.

Misrepresentation The affirmative statement or affirmation of a fact that is not true; the term does not include concealment of true facts or nondisclosure or the mere expression of opinion.

Mistake (of fact) The unconscious ignorance or forgetfulness of the existence or nonexistence of a fact, past or present, which is material and important to the creation of a legal obligation.

Mistake (of law) An erroneous conclusion of the legal effect of known facts.

Mitigation of damages A plaintiff is entitled to recover damages caused by the defendant's breach, but the plaintiff is also under a duty to avoid increasing or enhancing such damages. This duty is called a duty to *mitigate the damages*. If a seller fails to deliver the proper goods on time, the buyer, where possible, must buy other goods, thus mitigating damages.

Monopoly Exclusive control of the supply and price of a commodity. May be acquired by a franchise or patent from the government; or the ownership of the source of a commodity or the control of its distribution.

Mortgage A conveyance or transfer of an interest in property for the purpose of creating a security for a debt. The mortgage becomes void upon payment of the debt, although the recording of a release is necessary to clear the title of the mortgaged property.

Municipal court Another name for a police court. *See* Police court.

Mutual assent In every contract, each party must agree to the same thing. Each must know what the other intends; they must mutually assent or be in agreement.

Mutual mistake *See* Bilateral mistake.

Mutuality The binding of both parties in every contract. Each party to the contract must be bound to the other party to do something by virtue of the legal duty created.

Negligence Failure to do that which an ordinary, reasonable, prudent man would do, or the doing of some act that an ordinary, prudent man would not do. Reference must always be made to the situation, the circumstances, and the knowledge of the parties.

Negotiation* Under Article 3—Commercial Paper, this is the transfer of an instrument in such form that the transferee becomes a holder. If the instrument is payable to order, it is negotiated by delivery with any necessary indorsement; if payable to bearer, it is negotiated by delivery.

Net assets Property or effects of a firm, corporation, institution, or estate, remaining after all its obligations have been paid.

Nexus Connection, tie, or link used in the law of taxation to establish a connection between a tax and the activity or person being taxed.

NLRB National Labor Relations Board

No-fault laws Laws barring tort actions by injured persons against third-party tortfeasors and requiring injured persons to obtain recovery from their own insurers.

Nolo contendere A plea by an accused in a criminal action. It does not admit guilt of the offense charged but does equal a plea of guilty for purpose of sentencing.

Nominal damages A small sum assessed as sufficient to award the case and cover the costs when no actual damages have been proven.

Nonsuit A judgment given against the plaintiff when he is unable to prove his case or fails to proceed with the trial after the case is at issue.

Noscitur a sociis The meaning of a word is or may be known from the accompanying words.

Notary public A public officer authorized to administer oaths by way of affidavits and depositions. Attests deeds and other formal papers, in order that they may be used as evidence and be qualified for recording.

Notice* A person has "notice" of a fact when (a) he has actual knowledge of it; or (b) he has received a notice or notification of it; or (c) from all the facts and circumstances known to him at the time in question, he has reason to know that it exists. A person "knows" or has "knowledge" of a fact when he has actual knowledge of it. "Discover" or "learn" or a word or phrase of similar import refers to knowledge rather than to reason to know.

Novation The substitution of one obligation for another. When debtor A is substituted for debtor B, and by agreement with the creditor C, debtor B is discharged, a novation has occurred.

Nudum pactum A naked promise—one for which no consideration has been given.

Nuisance Generally, any continuous or continued conduct that causes annoyance, inconvenience, or damage to person or property. *Nuisance* usually applies to unreasonable, wrongful use of property, causing material discomfort, hurt, and damage to the person or property of another. Example: fumes from a factory.

Obligee A creditor or promisee.

Obligor A debtor or promisor.

Offer A statement by one party (called the offeror) that he is prepared to be bound to a contractual position. The offer is the first essential element to the meeting of the minds of the contracting parties. *See* Acceptance.

Oligopoly Control of a commodity or service in a given market by a small number of companies or suppliers.

Option A right secured by a contract to accept or reject an offer to purchase property at a fixed price within a fixed time. It is an irrevocable offer sometimes called a "paid-for offer."

Order* Under Article 3—Commercial Paper, *order* is a direction to pay and must be more than an authorization or request. It must, with reasonable certainty, identify the person to pay. It may be addressed to one or more such persons jointly or in the alternative but not in succession.

Order of relief The ruling by a bankruptcy judge that a particular case is properly before the bankruptcy court.

Ordinance Generally speaking, the legislative act of a municipality. A city council is a legislative body, and it passes ordinances that are the laws of the city.

Ordinary care Care that a prudent man would take under the circumstances of the particular case.

Par value "Face value." The par value of stocks and bonds on the date of issuance is the principal. At a later date, the par value is the principal plus interest.

Pari delicto The fault or blame is shared equally.

Pari materia "Related to the same matter or subject." Statutes and covenants concerning the same subject matter are in pari materia and as a general rule, for the purpose of ascertaining their meaning, are construed together.

Parol evidence   Legal proof based on oral statements; with regard to a document, any evidence extrinsic to the document itself.

Part performance   A legal doctrine created as an exception to the requirement that contracts be in written form pursuant to the statute of frauds. If the contracting parties have partially performed an oral contract to the extent that a judge is comfortable in ruling that the contract exists, this doctrine is used to enforce the contract. *See* Equitable estoppel.

Partition   Court proceedings brought by an interested party's request that the court divide real property among respective owners as their interests appear. If the property cannot be divided in kind, then it is to be sold and the money divided as each interest appears.

Partnership   A business organization consisting of two or more owners who agree to carry on a business and to share profits and losses.

Party*   A person who has engaged in a transaction or made an agreement within the Uniform Commercial Code.

Patent ambiguity   An obvious uncertainty in a written instrument.

Payor bank*   Under Article 4—Bank Deposits and Collections, a bank by which an item is payable as drawn or accepted.

Penal bond   A bond given by an accused, or by another person in his behalf, for the payment of money if the accused fails to appear in court on a certain day.

Pendente lite   "Pending during the progress of a suit at law."

Per curiam   A decision by the full court without indicating the author of the decision.

Peremptory challenge   An objection raised by a party to a lawsuit who rejects a person serving as a juror. No reason need be given.

Perfection*   In the law of secured transactions, this process is essential to inform the public that a creditor has an interest in the debtor's personal property. Perfection may occur by attachment, by filing a financing statement, by possession, and by noting the security interest on a certificate of title.

Perjury   False swearing upon an oath properly administered in some judicial proceedings.

Per se   "By itself." Thus, a contract clause may be inherently unconscionable—unconscionable *per se*.

Personal property   The rights, powers, and privileges a person has in movable things, such as chattels and choses in actions. Personal property is used in contradistinction to real property.

Personal representative   The administrator or executor of a deceased person or the guardian of a child or the conservator of an incompetent.

Personal service   The sheriff personally delivers a service of process to the defendant.

Petitioner   The party who files a claim in a court of equity. Also the party who petitions the Supreme Court for a writ of certiorari.

Plaintiff   In an action at law, the complaining party or the one who commences the action. The person who seeks a remedy in court.

Pleading   Process by which the parties in a lawsuit arrive at an issue.

Pledge   Personal property, as security for a debt or other obligation, deposited or placed with a person called a pledgee. The pledgee has the implied power to sell the property if the debt is not paid. If the debt is paid, the right to possession returns to the pledgor.

Police court   A court with jurisdiction to hear cases involving violations of local ordinances which are punishable as misdemeanors.

Polling jury   Calling the name of each juror to inquire what his verdict is before it is made a matter of record.

Possession   The method recognized by law and used by one's self or by another to hold, detain, or control either personal or real property, thereby excluding others from holding, detaining, or controlling such property.

Power of attorney   An instrument authorizing another to act as one's agent or attorney in fact.

Precedent   A previously decided case that can serve as an authority to help decide a present controversy. Use of such case is called the doctrine of *stare decisis*, which means to adhere to decided cases and settled principles. Literally, "to stand as decided."

Preference   The term is used most generally in bankruptcy law. If an insolvent debtor pays some creditors a greater percentage of the debts than he pays other creditors in the same class, and if the payments are made within ninety days prior to his filing a bankruptcy petition, those payments constitute illegal and voidable preference. An intention to prefer such creditors must be shown.

Preferred stock   Stock that entitles the holder to dividends from earnings before the owners of common stock can receive a dividend.

Preponderance Preponderance of the evidence means that evidence, in the judgment of the jurors, is entitled to the greatest weight, appears to be more credible, has greater force, and overcomes not only the opposing presumptions but also the opposing evidence.

Presenting bank* Under Article 4—Bank Deposits and Collections, this is any bank presenting an item except a payor bank.

Presentment* Under Article 3—Commercial Paper, presentment is a demand for acceptance or payment made upon the maker, acceptor, drawee, or other payor by, or on behalf of, the holder.

Presumption (presumed)* The trier of fact must find the existence of the fact presumed unless and until evidence is introduced that would support a finding of its nonexistence.

Prima facie Literally, "at first view." Thus, that which first appears seems to be true. A prima facie case is one that stands until contrary evidence is produced.

Primary party* In the law of commercial paper, this person is the one all other parties expect to pay. The maker of a note and the drawee of a draft are the primary party to those instruments.

Principal In agency relationships, this party employs the services of an agent to accomplish those goals that he cannot accomplish on his own.

Privilege A legal idea or concept of lesser significance than a right. An invitee has only a privilege to walk on another's land, because such privilege may be revoked at will; whereas a person who has an easement to go on another's land has a right created by a grant, which is an interest in land and cannot be revoked at will. To be exempt from jury service is a privilege.

Privity Mutual and successive relationship to the same interest. Offeror and offeree, assignor and assignee, grantor and grantee are in privity. Privity of estate means that one takes title from another. In contract law, privity denotes parties in mutual legal relationship to each other by virtue of being promisees and promisors. At early common law, third-party beneficiaries and assignees were said to be not in "privity."

Probate court Handles the settlement of estates.

Procedural law The laws which establish the process by which a lawsuit is filed, a trial is conducted, an appeal is perfected, and a judgment is enforced. In essence, these laws can be called the rules of litigation.

Proceeds* Whatever is received when collateral or proceeds are sold, exchanged, collected, or otherwise disposed of. Includes the account arising when the right to payment is earned under a contract right. Money, checks, and the like are "cash proceeds." All other proceeds are "noncash proceeds."

Process In a court proceeding, before or during the progress of the trial, an instrument issued by the court in the name of the state and under the seal of the court, directing an officer of the court to do, act, or cause some act to be done incidental to the trial.

Product extension merger A merger that extends the products of the acquiring company into a similar or related product but one which is not directly in competition with existing products.

Promise* Under Article 3—Commercial Paper, it is an undertaking to pay, and it must be more than an acknowledgment of an obligation.

Promissory note The legal writing that evidences a debtor's promise to repay an amount of money borrowed.

Property All rights, powers, privileges, and immunities that one has concerning tangibles and intangibles. The term includes everything of value subject to ownership.

Protest* In the law of commercial paper, this event signifies that a proper presentment has been made, that dishonor has occurred, and that notice of dishonor was given in a timely fashion. Protest is required in international commercial paper transactions, but it is optional in domestic transactions.

Proximate cause The cause that sets other causes in operation. The responsible cause of an injury.

Proxy Authority to act for another, used by absent stockholders or members of legislative bodies to have their votes cast by others.

Punitive damages Damages by way of punishment. Allowed for an injury caused by a wrong that is willful and malicious.

Purchase* Includes taking by sale, discount, negotiation, mortgage, pledge, lien, issue or re-issue, gift, or any other voluntary transaction creating an interest in property.

Purchase-money security interest* A security interest that is taken or retained by the seller of the collateral to secure all or part of its price; or taken by a person who, by making advances or incurring an obligation, gives value to enable the debtor to acquire rights in, or the use of, collateral if such value is in fact so used.

Quantum meruit   "As much as he deserves." This remedy is used to avoid the unjust enrichment of one party at the expenses of another. This remedy usually is in association with quasi-contracts.

Quasi-contract   A situation in which there arises a legal duty that does not rest upon a promise but does involve the payment of money. In order to do justice by a legal fiction, the court enforces the duty as if a promise in fact exists. Thus, if A gives B money by mistake, A can compel B to return the money by an action in quasi-contract.

Quasi-judicial   Administrative actions involving factual determinations and the discretionary application of rules and regulations.

Quasi-legislative   The function of administrative agencies whereby rules and regulations are promulgated. This authority permits agencies to make enforceable "laws."

Quid pro quo   The exchange of one thing of value for another.

Quiet title   A suit brought by the owner of real property for the purpose of bringing into court any person who claims an adverse interest in the property, requiring him either to establish his claim or be barred from asserting it thereafter. It may be said that the purpose is to remove "clouds" from the title.

Quitclaim   A deed that releases a right or interest in land but does not include any covenants of warranty. The grantor transfers only that which he has.

Quo warranto   A proceeding in court by which a governmental body tests or inquires into the authority or legality of the claim of any person to a public office, franchise, or privilege.

Ratification   The confirmation of one's own previous act or act of another: e.g., a principal may ratify the previous unauthorized act of his agent. B's agent, without authority, buys goods. B, by keeping the goods and receiving the benefits of the agent's act, ratifies the agency.

Ratio decidendi   Logical basis of judicial decision.

Real property   Land with all its buildings, appurtenances, equitable and legal interests therein. In contradistinction to personal property, which refers to movables or chattels.

Reasonable care   The care that prudent persons would exercise under the same circumstances.

Receiver   An officer of the court appointed on behalf of all parties to the litigation to take possession of, hold, and control the property involved in the suit, for the benefit of the party who will be determined to be entitled thereto.

Recoupment   "A cutting back." A right to deduct from the plaintiff's claim any payment or loss that the defendant has suffered by reason of the plaintiff's wrongful act.

Redemption   To buy back. A debtor buys back or redeems his mortgaged property when he pays the debt.

Referee   A person to whom a cause pending in a court is referred by the court, to take testimony, hear the parties, and report thereon to the court.

Registered form*   A security is in registered form when it specifies a person entitled to the security or to the rights it evidences and when its transfer may be registered upon books maintained for that purpose by, or on behalf of, an issuer, as security states.

Reinsurance   In a contract of reinsurance, one insurance company agrees to indemnify another insurance company in whole or in part against risks that the first company has assumed. The original contract of insurance and the reinsurance contract are distinct contracts. There is no privity between the original insured and the reinsurer.

Release   The voluntary relinquishing of a right, lien, or any other obligation. A release need not be under seal, nor does it necessarily require consideration. The words *release, remise,* and *discharge* are often used together to mean the same thing.

Remand   To send back a case from the appellate court to the lower court, in order that the lower court may comply with the instructions of the appellate court. Also to return a prisoner to jail.

Remedy   The word is used to signify the judicial means or court procedures by which legal and equitable rights are enforced.

Remitting bank*   Under Article 4—Bank Deposits and Collections, any payor or intermediary bank remitting for an item.

Replevin   A remedy given by statute for the recovery of the possession of a chattel. Only the right to possession can be tried in such action.

Res   "Thing."

Res judicata   A controversy once having been decided or adjudged upon its merits is forever settled so far as the particular parties involved are concerned. Such a doctrine avoids vexatious lawsuits. 限以後可再行起诉

Rescind   To cancel or annul a contract and return the parties to their original positions.

Rescission   An apparently valid act may conceal a defect that will make it null and void if any of the parties demand that it be rescinded.

Respondeat superior "The master is liable for the acts of his agent."

Respondent One who answers another's bill or pleading, particularly in an equity case. Quite similar, in many instances, to a defendant in a law case.

Responsible bidder In the phrase "lowest responsible bidder," *responsible,* as used by most statutes concerning public works, means that such bidder has the requisite skill, judgment, and integrity necessary to perform the contract involved and has the financial resources and ability to carry the task to completion.

Restitution When a contract is rescinded, all parties must return that which they have received. This remedy attempts to place the parties in the same positions they were in prior to making the contract.

Restraining order Issued by a court of equity in aid of a suit, to hold matters in abeyance until parties may be heard. A temporary injunction.

Restraint of trade Monopolies, combinations, and contracts that impede free competition.

Right The phrase "legal right" is a correlative of the phrase "legal duty." One has a legal right if, upon the breach of the correlative legal duty, he can secure a remedy in a court of law.

Right of action Synonymous with *cause of action:* a right to enforce a claim in a court.

Right-to-work law A state statute that outlaws a union shop contract; one by which an employer agrees to require membership in the union sometime after an employee has been hired, as a condition of continued employment.

Riparian A person is a riparian owner if his land is situated beside a stream of water, either flowing over or along the border of the land.

Sale* The agreement to exchange title to goods for a price.

Satisfaction In legal phraseology, the release and discharge of a legal obligation. Satisfaction may be partial or full performance of the obligation. The word is used with *accord,* a promise to give a substituted performance for a contract obligation; *satisfaction* means the acceptance by the obligee of such performance.

Scienter Knowledge by a defrauding party of the falsity of a representation. In a tort action of deceit, knowledge that a representation is false must be proved.

Seal A seal shows that an instrument was executed in a formal manner. At early common law, sealing legal documents was of great legal significance. A promise under seal was binding by virtue of the seal. Today under most statutes, any stamp, wafer, mark, scroll, or impression made, adopted and affixed, is adequate. The printed word *seal* or the letters *L.S. (locus sigilli,* "the place of the seal") are sufficient.

Seasonably* An action is taken "seasonably" when it is taken at, or within, the time agreed; or if no time is agreed, at or within a reasonable time.

Secondary boycott Conspiracy or combination to cause the customers or suppliers of an employer to cease doing business with that employer.

Secondary party* Under Article 3—Commercial Paper, a drawer or indorser.

Secret partner A partner whose existence is not known to the public.

Secured party* A lender, seller, or other person in whose favor there is a security interest, including a person to whom accounts, contract rights, or chattel paper have been sold. When the holders of obligations issued under an indenture of trust, equipment trust agreement, or the like are represented by a trustee or other person, the representative is the secured party.

Security May be bonds, stocks, and other property that a debtor places with a creditor, who may sell them if the debt is not paid. The plural, *securities,* is used broadly to mean tangible choses in action, such as promissory notes, bonds, stocks, and other vendible obligations.

Security* An instrument issued in bearer form or registered form; commonly dealt in on securities exchanges or markets or commonly recognized in any area in which it is issued or dealt in as a medium for investment; one of a class or series of instruments; evidences a share, a participation or other interest in property or in an enterprise or evidences an obligation of the issuer.

Security agreement* Creates or provides for a security interest.

Security interest* An interest in personal property or fixtures that secures payment or performance of an obligation.

Self-help* In the law of secured transactions, this term describes the creditor's attempt to take possession of collateral without the court's assistance.

Sell To negotiate or make arrangement for a sale. A sale is an executed contract, a result of the process of selling.

Separation of powers The doctrine that the legislative, executive, and judicial branches of government function independently of one another and that each branch serves as a check on the others.

Servant   A person employed by another and subject to the direction and control of the employer in performance of his duties.

Setoff   A matter of defense, called a cross-complaint, used by the defendant for the purpose of making a demand on the plaintiff. It arises out of contract but is independent and unconnected with the cause of action set out in the complaint. *See* Counterclaims and Recoupment.

Settle*   Under Article 4—Bank Deposits and Collections, *settle* means to pay in cash, by clearinghouse settlement, in a charge or credit or by remittance or otherwise as instructed. A settlement may be either provisional or final.

Settlement   A concept applicable in agency relationships when the principal is undisclosed. By paying (or settling with) the agent, the principal is relieved of liability to the third party. This third party will look to the agent for performance of their agreement.

Severable contract   A contract in which the performance is divisible. Two or more parts may be set over against each other. Items and prices may be apportioned to each other without relation to the full performance of all of its parts.

Shareholders (stockholders)   Persons whose names appear on the books of a corporation as owners of shares of stock and who are entitled to participate in the management and control of the corporation.

Share of stock   A proportional part of the rights in the management and assets of a corporation. It is a chose in action. The certificate is the evidence of the share.

Silent partner   A partner who has no voice in the management of the partnership.

Situs   "Place, situation." The place where a thing is located. The situs of personal property is the domicile of the owner. The situs of land is the state or county where it is located.

Slander   An oral utterance that tends to injure the reputation of another. *See* Libel.

Small claims court   A court with jurisdiction to hear cases involving a limited amount of money. The jurisdictional amount varies among the states and local communities.

Special agent   In agency relationships, an agent with a limited amount of specific authority. This agent usually has instructions to accomplish one specific task.

Special appearance   The appearance in court of a person through his attorney for a limited purpose only. A court does not get jurisdiction over a person by special appearance.

Special verdict   The jury finds the facts only, leaving it to the court to apply the law and draw the conclusion as to the proper disposition of the case.

Specific performance   A remedy in personam in equity that compels performance of a contract to be substantial enough to do justice among the parties. A person who fails to obey a writ for specific performance may be put in jail by the equity judge for contempt of court. The remedy applies to contracts involving real property. In the absence of unique goods or peculiar circumstances, damages generally are an adequate remedy for breach of contracts involving personal property.

Standing to sue   The doctrine that requires the plaintiff in a lawsuit to have a sufficient legal interest in the subject matter of the case.

Stare decisis   "Stand by the decision." The law should adhere to decided cases. *See* Precedent.

Statute   A law passed by the legislative body of a state.

Statutes of limitations   Laws that exist for the purpose of bringing to an end old claims. Because witnesses die, memory fails, papers are lost, and the evidence becomes inadequate, stale claims are barred. Such statutes are called statutes of repose. Within a certain period of time, action on claims must be brought; otherwise, they are barred. The period varies from six months to twenty years.

Status quo   The conditions or state of affairs at a given time.

Stay   In the bankruptcy law, this occurs upon the entry of an order of relief. This order prevents all creditors from taking any action to collect debts owed by the protected debtor.

Stock dividend   New shares of its own stock issued as a dividend by a corporation to its shareholders, in order to transfer retained earnings to capital stock.

Stock split   A readjustment of the financial plan of a corporation, whereby each existing share of stock is split into new shares, usually with a lowering of par value.

Stock warrant   A certificate that gives the holder the right to subscribe for and purchase, at a stated price, a given number of shares of stock in a corporation.

Stoppage in transit   Upon learning of the insolvency of a buyer of goods, the seller has the right to stop the goods in transit and hold them as security for the purchase price. The right is an extension of the unpaid seller's lien.

Unfair competition   The imitation, by design, of the goods of another, for the purpose of palming them off on the public, misleading it, and inducing it to buy goods made by the imitator. Includes misrepresentation and deceit; thus, such conduct is fraudulent not only to competitors but to the public.

Unilateral contract   A promise for an act or an act for a promise, a single enforceable promise. C promises B $10 if B will mow C's lawn. B mows the lawn. C's promise, now binding, is a unilateral contract. *See* Bilateral contract.

Usage of trade*   Any practice or method of dealing so regularly observed in a place, vocation, or trade that observance may justly be expected in the transaction in question. The existence and scope of such usage are to be proved as facts. If it is established that such a usage is embodied in a written trade code or similar writing, the interpretation of the writing is for the court.

Usurious   A contract is usurious if made for a loan of money at a rate of interest in excess of that permitted by statute.

Utter   "Put out" or "pass off." To utter a check is to offer it to another in payment of a debt. To "utter a forged writing" means to put such writing in circulation, knowing of the falsity of the instrument, with the intent to injure another.

Value*   Except as otherwise provided with respect to negotiable instruments and bank collections, a person gives "value" for rights if he acquires them (a) in return for a binding commitment to extend credit or for the extension of immediately available credit, whether or not drawn upon and whether or not a chargeback is provided for in the event of difficulties in collection; or (b) as security for, or in, total or partial satisfaction of a preexisting claim; or (c) by accepting delivery pursuant to a preexisting contract for purchase; or (d) generally, in return for any consideration sufficient to support a simple contract.

Vendee   A purchaser of property. Generally, the purchaser of real property. A *buyer* is usually a purchaser of chattels.

Vendor   The seller of property, usually real property. The word *seller* is used with personal property.

Vendor's lien   An unpaid seller's right to hold possession of property until he has recovered the purchase price.

Venire   To come into court, a writ used to summon potential jurors.

Venue   The geographical area over which a court presides. Venue designates the county in which the action is tried. Change of venue means to move to another county.

Verdict   The decision of a jury, reported to the court, on matters properly submitted to the jury for consideration.

Vertical merger   A merger of corporations, one corporation being the supplier of the other.

Void   Has no legal effect. A contract that is void is a nullity and confers no rights or duties.

Voidable   That which is valid until one party, who has the power of avoidance, exercises such power. An infant has the power of avoidance of his contract. A defrauded party has the power to avoid his contract. Such contract is voidable.

Voir dire   Preliminary examination of a prospective juror.

Voting trust   Two or more persons owning stock with voting powers divorce those voting rights from ownership but retain to all intents and purposes the ownership in themselves and transfer the voting rights to trustees in whom voting rights of all depositors in the trust are pooled.

Wager   A relationship between persons by which they agree that a certain sum of money or thing owned by one of them will be paid or delivered to the other upon the happening of an uncertain event, which event is not within the control of the parties and rests upon chance.

Waive   (verb)   To "waive" at law is to relinquish or give up intentionally a known right or to do an act that is inconsistent with the claiming of a known right.

Waiver   (noun)   The intentional relinquishment or giving up of a known right. It may be done by express words or conduct that involves any acts inconsistent with an intention to claim the right. Such conduct creates an estoppel on the part of the claimant. *See* Estoppel.

Warehouseman*   A person engaged in the business of storing goods for hire.

Warehouse receipt*   Issued by a person engaged in the business of storing goods for hire.

Warehouse receipt   An instrument showing that the signer has in his possession certain described goods for storage. It obligates the signer, the warehouseman, to deliver the goods to a specified person or to his order or bearer upon the return of the instrument. Consult Uniform Warehouse Receipts Act.

Warrant (noun) An order in writing in the name of the state, signed by a magistrate, directed to an officer, commanding him to arrest a person. (verb) To guarantee, to answer for, to assure that a state of facts exists.

Warranty An undertaking, either expressed or implied, that a certain fact regarding the subject matter of a contract is presently true or will be true. The word has particular application in the law of sales of chattels. It relates to title and quality. *Warranty* should be distinguished from *guaranty,* which means a contract or promise by one person to answer for the performance of another.

Warranty of fitness for a particular purpose* An implied promise by a seller of goods that arises when a buyer explains the special needs and relies on the seller's advice.

Warranty of merchantability* A promise implied in a sale of goods by merchants: that the goods are reasonably fit for the general purpose for which they are sold.

Waste Damage to the real property, so that its value as security is impaired.

Watered stock Corporate stock issued by a corporation for property at an overvaluation, or stock issued for which the corporation receives nothing in payment.

Will (testament) The formal instrument by which a person makes disposition of his property, to take effect upon his death.

Winding up The process of liquidating a business organization.

Working capital The amount of cash necessary for the convenient and safe transaction of present business.

Workers' compensation A plan for compensating employees for occupational disease, accidental injury, and death suffered in connection with employment.

Writ An instrument in writing, under seal in the name of the state, issued out of a court of justice at the commencement of, or during, a legal proceeding; directed to an officer of the court, commanding him to do some act or requiring some person to refrain from doing some act pertinent or relative to the cause being tried.

Writ of certiorari A discretionary proceeding by which an appellate court may review the ruling of an inferior tribunal.

Writ of *habeas corpus* A court order to one holding custody of another, to produce that individual before the court for the purpose of determining whether such custody is proper.

Yellow-dog contract A worker agrees not to join a union and to be discharged if he breaches the contract.

Zoning ordinance Passed by a city council by virtue of police power. Regulates and prescribes the kind of buildings, residences, or businesses that shall be built and used in different parts of a city.

INDEX

E

E.S.P., Inc. v. Midway National Bank, 749–50

Earnings, disposable, 884

Easement, 940, 942–44, 950

Easley v. Sky, Inc., 263–64

East Side Prescription v. E.P. Fournier, 382–83

Economic relations, interference with, 84, 89–90, 498

Edmonson v. Leesville Concrete Company, Inc., 41–42

Edwards v. Mesch, 712

Eighth Amendment, 122

Elderly, and undue influence, 248

Election (agency), 469–70

Electronic Fund Transfer Act, 681

Elkins Manor Assoc. v. Eleanor Concrete, 300–301

Embezzlement, 106

Eminent domain, 950–53

Employer-employee relationships. *See also* Agency
 and agent's duties, 443–49
 Boeing guidelines on, 453
 and compensation, 449–52
 and employer liability, 448, 494–98
 rights of wronged employee, 512–13
 termination of, 505–13
 third-party interference in, 90, 498

Employment-at-will, 506–10

Encumbrances, 940, 971

End-user's certification, 160

Entrapment, 115

Equal Credit Opportunity Act, 868–70

Equipment, as collateral, 763, 764

Equitable actions, 25

Equitable conversion, 936

Equitable estoppel, 282–84

Equitable mortgage, 825

Equitable remedies, 177, 184–85

Equitable theory of mortgage, 817–18

Equity, 25–27
 and corporation, 598, 622–23, 624
 and foreclosure, 825
 and partnership, 540–41, 556, 565
 and quasi-contracts, 175
 and unconscionability, 266

Equity of redemption, 829

Erie Railroad v. Tompkins, 22–23

Ernst & Ernst v. Hochfelder et al., 652–54

Erskine Florida Properties, Inc. v. First American Title Insurance Co., 981–82

Escrow, 825, 890

Escrow agent, 970

Estate, 940–41

bankruptcy, 902
 and negotiability, 692
 trustee and, 916

Estate in remainder, 942

Estate planning, 976

Estoppel, 462
 equitable, 282–84
 partnership by, 525–26
 promissory, 229–30, 284

Ethan Dairy Products v. Austin, 129–30

Ethics, 72, 73–76

European Community, 147, 157, 158

Eviction, 990–91

Evidence, 43–44
 preponderance of, 44

Exclusionary rule, 117–18

Exclusionary techniques, 156

Exculpatory clause, 267–69, 648–49, 1002

Excuses for nonperformance, 313–21

Ex-dividend date, 602

Executed contract, 171, 176

Execution, 50

Executor (of estate), 976

Executory contract, 171, 176, 918

Exemplary damages, 82, 180–82

Exhaustion of remedies, 69

Expedited Funds Availability Act, 671

Expert testimony, 640

Export Administration Act of 1979, 160, 164

Export/import operation, 149–50

Express agreement, 358

Express authority, 459

Express conditions, 300–303

Express contract, 171, 172

Express partnerships, 521–23

Express warranty, 395–96, 402, 885

Expropriation, 157
 creeping, 158

Extension clause, 695

Extraterritoriality, 162

F

F.A.S., 357

F.O.B., 357

Factor, 438

Fair average quality, 399

Fair comment, 93

Fair Credit Billing Act (FCBA), 879–80

Fair Credit Reporting Act (FCRA), 870–73

Fair Debt Collection Practices Act (FDCPA), 881–83

Fairness, and contracts of adhesion, 266–67. *See also* Equity

False imprisonment, 84, 85

False representation, 245

"Family car doctrine," 486

"Family-purpose" doctrine, 83

Farmers, 284, 355, 901–2, 912–13

Farm products, as collateral, 763, 764

FDIC (Federal Deposit Insurance Corporation), 108, 632

Federal Arbitration Act, 60

Federal court system, 20–24

Federal Employers' Liability Act (FELA), 496

Federal questions, 22

Federal Reserve Board, 632, 866, 875

Federal system, 6, 8

Federal Trade Commission, 340, 405, 723–24, 866, 884, 888

Fee simple estates, 940–41

Fellow-servant doctrine, 494

Fellows v. Martin, 992

Felony, 105

Fictitious payees, 736–38, 753

Fidelity bonds, 849

Fiduciary relationship, 245
 agency as, 436, 443–53
 in corporations, 602–6, 610, 623–24, 627
 partnership as, 543
 promoters-corporations, 582
 surety relationship as, 850–52
 and undue influence on will, 978

Fifth Amendment, 43, 118–21, 573, 950, 952

Filing, 770–76, 793, 797
 of artisan's lien, 843–44
 of mechanic's lien, 830, 834–35

Finance charge, and TILA, 876

Finance lease, 1010

Financial Institutions Reform, Recovery and Enforcement Act of 1989, 107

Financial powers, 473, 548

Financial statements, corporate, 613

Financing agency, 766

Financing statement, 771–75
 for fixture filing, 797
 importance of filing, 793

Firm offers, 201, 230

First Florida Bank v. Max Mitchell & Co., 646–47

First-in-time rule, 793, 800

First Investment Company v. Andersen, 696

First Nat. Bank & Trust v. Ohio Cas. Ins. Co., 363–64

First National Bank in Lenox v. Creston Livestock Auction, Inc., 716–17

First National Bank v. First Interstate Bank, 772–73

First State Bank v. Producers Livestock